visualize

INORGANIC CHEMISTRY

A COMPLETE BLUEPRINT FOR

JEE Main & Advanced

Gaurav Shrivastava
B.Tech
Ex. Faculty Allen Kota

arihant
SUCCESS AND NOTHING LESS

SUCCESS AND NOTHING LESS

Arihant Prakashan (Series), Meerut

卐 **Administrative & Production Offices**

Regd. Office

'Ramchhaya' 4577/15, Agarwal Road, Darya Ganj, New Delhi -110002
Tele: 011- 47630600, 43518550

Head Office

Kalindi, TP Nagar, Meerut (UP) - 250002
Tel: 0121-7156203, 7156204

卐 **Sales & Support Offices**

Agra, Ahmedabad, Bengaluru, Bareilly, Chennai, Delhi, Guwahati, Hyderabad, Jaipur, Jhansi, Kolkata, Lucknow, Nagpur & Pune.

卐 **PO No :** TXT-XX-XXXXXXX-X-XX

Published by Arihant Publications (India) Ltd.

For further information about the books published by Arihant, log on to www.arihantbooks.com or e-mail at info@arihantbooks.com

Follow us on

Preface

Inorganic Chemistry is one of the most dynamic and fascinating branches of chemistry, playing a pivotal role in the preparation for competitive exams like JEE Main and Advanced.

This book is meticulously crafted for students preparing for JEE Main and Advanced. With its clear explanations, systematic approach and extensive problem sets, it aims to provide a solid conceptual foundation while, also honing the problem-solving skills necessary for success in these high-stakes exams. The content is carefully curated to match the depth and difficulty required for both exams, with an emphasis on building a deep understanding of core principles that are critical to mastering Inorganic Chemistry.

Special Features of this First Edition are

- Modular theory and Practice as **Elements** and **Elemental Practice.**
- JEE Main & Advanced Analysis on the first page of every chapter as **Trend Insight** with **Insightful Advice.**
- Important JEE specific info as **JEE Spotlite** and **JEE Alert.**
- Theory and PYQs syncing through **JEE Mapper** and **JEE Quicker.**
- Figure Enhancement by merging text with figure as **Concept Visualizer** for better visualization and concept clarity.
- **Advanced Exclusive Different Strokes** as JEE Advanced targeted special tip/fact elaboration / important info.
- **Separate exercises for JEE Main and Advanced** with selected PYQs as **Check through PYQs.**

The book also incorporates the latest patterns of the JEE exams, ensuring that students are well-prepared for the types of questions they are likely to encounter. Furthermore, the inclusion of previous years' questions from both JEE Main and Advanced will help students understand the nature of the exam and gauge their progress.

As you embark on your journey to mastering **Inorganic Chemistry,** remember that success lies not only in memorizing formulas but in understanding the concepts and applying them in different contexts. With dedication, practice, and the right approach, you will not only excel in your exams but also develop an enduring interest in the world of chemistry.

We wish you all the best in your preparation and encourage you to make the most of this resource. Stay focused, stay curious, and keep pushing your limits!

Gaurav Shrivastava

Key Features

Trend Insight

JEE Main & Advanced Analysis on the First Page of Every Chapter with Insightfull Advice

Trend Insights

JEE Main

	2024				2023				2022			
Topics	**E**	**M**	**T**	**O**	**E**	**M**	**T**	**O**	**E**	**M**	**T**	**O**
Historical Development, Classification of Elements and Modern Periodic Table	1	1	2	4	–	1	–	1	3	–	1	4
Periodic Properties	2	8	3	13	2	5	1	8	9	5	–	14

JEE Advanced

Typology	Years				
	2024	**2023**	**2022**	**2021**	**2020**
1. One option correct	–	–	–	–	–
2. One or More than one correct	–	–	–	–	1
3. Numerical/Integer Type)	–	–	–	–	–
4. Matching Type	–	–	–	–	–
5. Paragraph Based	–	–	–	–	–

Elements

Learning and Practice Modules of the Chapter as Elements and Practice Elements respectively.

Element 1 Historical Development, Classification of Elements and Modern Periodic Table

In the beginning of 18th century, only 31 elements known but by 1865 the number of elements had more than double, i.e. 63. Till now 118 elements been discovered and efforts to discover new still in progress. With such a large number of is difficult to study the chemistry or properties element and their compounds. Therefore, to properties of each element, scientists felt the

Newland's Law of Octaves

In 1865, John Alexander Newland's suggested that elements are arranged in increasing order of their masses then every eighth element, resembles in its with the first one just like the eighth note of a musical. Due to similarity in pattern with musical octaves this generalisation is kno wn as **Newland›s law of octaves.**

JEE Mapper

Concept Enhancement tool, helpful in syncing PYQs with theory and provide additional practice with competency enhancer.

JEE MAPPER

Example Similar to PYQ Asked in JEE Main 2022

The IUPAC name of the element which is placed after Db_{105} in the periodic table, will be

(a) Unnilpentium (b) Ununnilium

(c) Unnilhexium (d) Unnilquadium

Sol. (c) IUPAC nomenclature is

1 0 6

↓ ↓ ↓

un nil hex + ium

= Unnilhexium

Competency Enhancer 1.1

An element which is recently discovered is placed in 7th period and 10th group. IUPAC name of the element will be

(a) Unnilseptium (b) Ununnilium

(c) Ununbium (d) Ununpentium

JEE Spotlite

General steps to write the Lewis structure for charged species

- Calculate the total number of valence electrons of atom(s) involved in a molecule.
- Addition of charge on anion and subtraction of charge on cation is done.
- Select the central atom which is generally the least electronegative atom and draw the skeletal structure w.r.t. valence electrons and charges involved in it.

JEE Spotlite

Box Matter Having Pointers / Important info from JEE Perspective

Key Features

JEE Alert

In case of Noble gases (as in Ne) there is no covalent bond fomation, hence only van der Waals' radius is considered. Thus, there is a high jump in the value of radius from F to Ne.

JEE Alert

JEE Related Caution Points Helpful in Providing Usual Error Insights. Thus, helpful in Performance Enhancement.

JEE Quicker

Unique feature having PYQ facts and their elaborations as syncing of selected PYQs with theory.

JEE Quicker

The metal that has very low melting point and its periodic position is closer to a metalloid is Gallium. *JEE Main 2022*

↘ In long form of periodic table, gallium is placed in group 13 which is closer to a metalloid germanium (Group 14). The bonds between gallium atoms is weaker due to which it has very low melting point.

Concept Visualizer

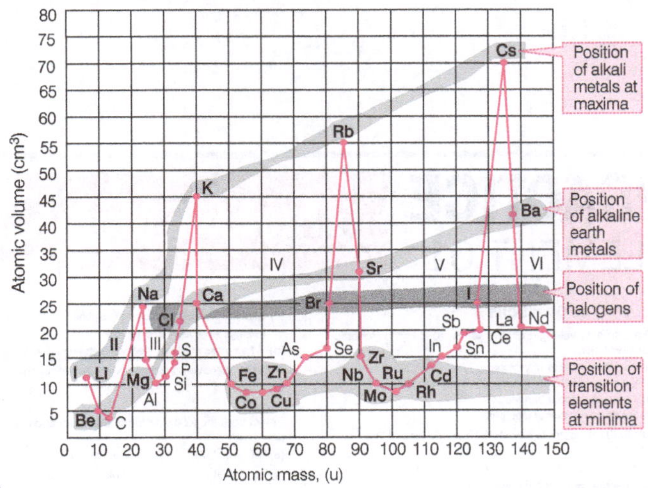

Concept Visualizer

Figure enhancement merged with text for better visualisation and concept clarity

Key Features

Advanced Exclusive Different Strokes

JEE Advanced Targeted Content as Problem Solving Tips/Fact Elaborations/Important Info

Advanced Exclusive Different Strokes

Determination of Period and Group of an Element

- The **period number** can be predicted from the principal quantum number (n) of the valence shell.
  e.g. Electronic configuration of chlorine is $1s^2 2s^2 2p^6 3s^2 3p^5$. Therefore, the period number is 3 as the $3s^2 3p^5$.
- The **block number** can be predicted from the orbital which receives the last electron.
  e.g. An element having electronic configuration '$1s^2 2s^2 2p^6 3s^2 3p^6 3d^{10} 4s^2 4p^5$' is a p-block element p-orbital.
- **Group number** can be predicted from the number of electrons in the valence shell and penultimate
  (i) s-block : The group number is equal to number of valence electron.
  (ii) p-block : The group number is equal to the 10 + number of valence shell electrons.

Elemental Practice

Scientifically designed first Practice Exercise to check Modular Learning.

Elemental Practice 1.2

Type I MCQs with Only One Correct Option

1. Consider the isoelectronic ions K^+, S^{2-}, Cl^- and Ca^{2+}
   The radii of these ionic species follow the order
   (a) $Ca^{2+} > K^+ > Cl^- > S^{2-}$ (b) $Cl^- > S^{2-} > K^+ > Ca^{2+}$
   (c) $S^{2-} > Cl^- > K^+ > Ca^{2+}$ (d) $K^+ > Ca^{2+} > S^{2-} > Cl^-$
2. For the element (X), student (A) measured its radius 102 nm, student (B) as 103 nm and (C) as 100 nm same apparatus. Their teacher explained that measurements were correct by saying that recorded values by (A), (B) and (C) are
   (a) crystal, van der Waals' and covalent radii
   (b) covalent, crystal and van der Waals' radii
   (c) van der Waals', ionic and covalent
   (d) crystal, covalent and vander Waals' radii
3. Select the incorrect order of the properties.
   (a) $Ni^{2+} > Cr^{2+} > Fe^{2+} > Mn^{2+}$ (size)
   (b) Sc > Ti > Cr > Mn (size)
   (c) $Ni^{2+} < Co^{2+} < Fe^{2+} < Mn^{2+}$ (unpaired electron)
   (d) $Fe^{2+} > Co^{2+} > Ni^{2+} > Cu^{2+}$ (unpaired electron)

10. The factors that influence the ionisation energies
    (a) the size of the atom
    (b) the charge on the nucleus
    (c) how effectively the inner electron shell screen the charge
    (d) all of the above
11. Select the match that represents alkali metals $(IE)_1$ and $(IE)_2$ values.

		$(IE)_1$	$(IE)_2$
(a)	X	100	110
(b)	Y	95	120
(c)	Z	195	500
(d)	M	200	250

12. The correct order of non-metallic character of elements are
    B, C, Si, N, F
    (a) F > N > C > B > Si
    (b) F > N > C > Si > B
    (c) Si > C > N > B > F
    (d) B > C > N > F > Si

Practice Element 1

JEE Main targeted practice with single choice correct MCQs and Integer/Numerical type questions.

PRACTICE ELEMENT 01 — Target JEE Main

Objective Type Questions

1. The elements belonging to the same group of the Periodic Table will have
   (a) the same number of protons
   (b) the same number of electrons in the valence-shell
   (c) the same number of neutrons
   (d) the same number of isotopes
2. If Aufbau rule is not followed, K-19 will be placed in .... block.
   (a) s (b) p (c) d (d) f
3. Representative elements belong to
   (a) s-and p-block (b) d-block
   (c) d- and f-block (d) f-block

   (c) Element with electronic configuration $(n-1)d^5 ns^1$ belongs to group 7 and s-block
   (d) S has more negative electron gain enthalpy than 0.
10. Recently discovered element with atomic number 115 is
    (a) Uun (b) Uub
    (c) Uup (d) Uus
11. Select from the following triads that have approximately equal size
    (a) Na^+, Mg^{2+}, Al^{3+} (b) F^-, Ne, O^{2-}
    (c) Fe, Co, Ni (d) Mn^+, Fe^{2+}, Cr
12. Choose the correct order of ionic radii.
    (a) $Mn^{+4} < Mn^{+2}$ (b) $O^- < O^+$
    (c) $N^{-3} < Na^+$ (d) $P^{3+} > P^{5+}$

Key Features

PRACTICE ELEMENT 02

Target JEE Advanced

Single Correct Choice MCQs

1. The statement that is not correct for the periodic classification of elements is
   (a) the properties of elements are the periodic functions of their atomic numbers
   (b) non-metallic elements are lesser in number than metallic elements
   (c) the first ionisation energies of elements along a period do not vary in a regular manner with increase in atomic number
   (d) for transition elements the *d*-subshells are filled with electrons monotonically with increase in atomic number
2. The statement is not true for the long form of the Periodic Table
   (a) It reflects the sequence of filling the electrons in the order of the sub-energy shells *s*, *p*, *d* and *f*
   (b) It helps to predict the stable valency states of the elements
   (c) It reflects trends in physical and chemical properties of the elements
   (d) It helps to predict the relative ionicity of the bond between any two elements
3. Select the incorrect statement from the following.
   (a) Elements of IB and IIB groups are transition elements
   (b) Elements of VB group do not contain metalloids
   (c) Elements of IA and IIA groups are normal elements
   (d) Elements of IVB group are neither strongly electronegative nor strongly electropositive.
4. Match list-I (atomic number of elements) with list-II (position of elements in Periodic Table) and select the
6. *AB* is predominantly ionic as A^+B^- if
   (a) $(IP)_A < (IP)_B$ (b) $(EA)_A < (EA)_B$
   (c) $(EN)_A < (EN)_B$ (d) $(IP)_B < (IP)_A$
   (IP stands for ionisation potential, EA for electron affinity and EN for electronegativity).
7. Following graph shows variation of ionisation potential (IP) with atomic number in second period (Li—Ne). Value of ionisation potential (IP) of Na (11) will be

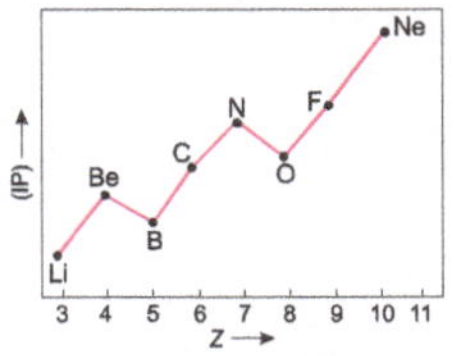

   (a) above Ne (b) below Ne but above O
   (c) below Li (d) between N and O
8. Select the incorrect statements from the following.
   (a) Boron has the smallest atomic volume.
   (b) The correct order of atomic radii is W < C < P < Si.
   (c) Electron gain enthalpy is the property of a bonded atom.
   (d) The correct order for non-metallic character is F > N > C > B > Si.

Practice Element 2

JEE Advanced targeted practice with all formats covered as asked in Exam

Check Through PYQs

Element 1 Historical Development, Classification of Elements Modern Periodic Table

1. Given below are two statements :
   Statement I According to the Law of Octaves, elements were arranged in the increasing order atomic number.
   Statement II Meyer observed a periodically pattern upon plotting physical properties of elements against their respective atomic.
   In the light of the above statements, answer from the options given below. *2024, 28 Jan Shift-II*
   (a) Statement I is true but Statement II is false.
   (b) Both Statement I and Statement II are true.
   (c) Statement I is false but Statement II is true.
   (d) Both Statement I and Statement II are false.
2. If IUPAC name of an element is "Unununium" element belongs to *n*th group of periodic table. of *n* is .... *2024, 30 Jan Shift-I*
4. Given below are two statements: *2024, 27 Jan Shift-I*
   Statement I The 4*f* and 5*f*-series of elements are separately in the periodic table to preserve the classification.
   Statement II *s*-block elements can be found in in nature.
   In the light of the above statements, choose **appropriate** answer from the options given
   (a) Statement I is true but Statement II is false.
   (b) Both Statement I and Statement II are false.
   (c) Both Statement I and Statement II are true.
   (d) Statement I is false but Statement II is true.
5. Henry Moseley studied characteristic X-ray elements. The graph which represents his correctly is
   Given v = frequency of X-ray emitted
   Z = atomic number *2023, 8 April Shift-II*

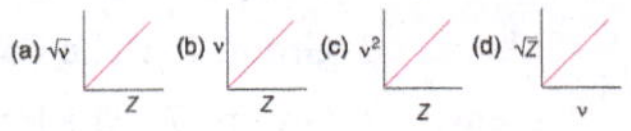

Check through PYQs

PYQ segment Present in Practice Elements 1 & 2 with selected Past year Questions of JEE Main and Advanced respectively.

Content

1. Classification of Elements & Periodicity in Properties **1-44**

Element 1 Historical Development, Classification of Elements, Modern Periodic Table 2-9

Element 2 Periodic Properties 10-25

Practice Element 1 Target JEE Main 26-29

Practice Element 2 Target JEE Advanced 30-34

Hints & Solutions **35-44**

2. Chemical Bonding and Molecular Structure **45-104**

Element 1 Ionic and Covalent Bonds, Fajan's Rule 46-55

Element 2 Bond Parameters, Valence Bond Theory and VSEPR Theory 56-66

Element 3 Molecular Orbital Theory (MOT) and Hydrogen Bonding 67-75

Practice Element 1 Target JEE Main 76-80

Practice Element 2 Target JEE Advanced 81-85

Hints & Solutions **86-104**

3. Hydrogen **105-127**

Element Hydrogen and Their Compounds 106-118

Practice Element Target JEE Advanced 119-122

Hints & Solutions **123-127**

4. s-Block Elements **128-161**

Element 1 Group 1 Elements and Their Compounds : Alkali Metals 129-142

Element 2 Group 2 Elements and Their Compounds : Alkaline Earth Metals 143-152

Practice Element Target JEE Advanced 153-156

Hints & Solutions **157-161**

5. *p*-Block Elements-I **162-207**

Element 1 Group-13 Elements and Compounds (The Boron Family) 163-174

Element 2 Group-14 Elements and Compounds (The Carbon Family) 175-188

Practice Element 1 Target JEE Main 189-193

Practice Element 2 Target JEE Advanced 194-197

Hints & Solutions **198-207**

6. *p*-Block Elements-II **208-295**

Element 1 Group 15 : The Nitrogen Family and their Compounds 209-227

Element 2 Group 16 : The Oxygen Family and their Compounds 228-240

Element 3 Group 17 : The Halogen Family and their Compounds 241-257

Element 4 Group 18 : The Noble Gases and their Compounds 258-264
Practice Element 1 Target JEE Main 265-270
Practice Element 2 Target JEE Advanced 271-275
Hints & Solutions **276-295**

7. General Principles and Processes of Isolation of Elements **296-325**

Element 1 Metallurgy: General Principles 297-306
Element 2 Thermodynamics of Metallurgy and Extraction of Metal 307-314
Practice Element Target JEE Advanced 315-319
Hints & Solutions **320-325**

8. *d*- and *f*-Block Elements **326-374**

Element 1 Transition Elements and Their Properties 327-337
Element 2 Some Important Compounds of *d*-Block Elements; *f*-Block Elements 338-351
Practice Element 1 Target JEE Main 352-357
Practice Element 2 Target JEE Advanced 358-361
Hints & Solutions **362-374**

9. Coordination Compounds **375-441**

Element 1 Basic Terms Used in Coordination Compounds and IUPAC Nomenclature 376-385
Element 2 Isomerism in Coordination Compounds 386-393
Element 3 Bonding in Coordination Compounds 394-408
Practice Element 1 Target JEE Main 409-414
Practice Element 2 Target JEE Advanced 415-420
Hints & Solutions **421-441**

10. Salt Analysis **442-485**

Element 1 Preliminary Tests and Qualitative Analysis of Acidic Radicals 443-453
Element 2 Qualitative Analysis of Basic Radicals 454-468
Practice Element 1 Target JEE Main 469-471
Practice Element 2 Target JEE Advanced 472-476
Hints & Solutions **477-485**

CHAPTER 1

Classification of Elements & Periodicity in Properties

Learning Elements

Element 1 **Historical Development, Classification of Elements, Modern Periodic Table**

Earlier Attempts to Classify the Elements, Modern Periodic Table, Long form of Periodic Table and Their Characteristics, Electronic Configuration in Periodic Table, Nomenclature of Elements with Atomic Number > 100

Element 2 **Periodic Properties**

Trend in Physical Properties, Atomic Radius, Ionic Radius, Electron Affinity (EA), Electronegativity (EN), Metallic Nature, Melting Points and Boiling Points, Atomic Volume, Trends in Chemical Properties, Anomalous Properties of Second Period Elements

Practice Elements

Practice Element 1 Target JEE Main
Practice Element 2 Target JEE Advanced

Trend Insights

JEE Main

	2024				2023				2022			
Topics	**E**	**M**	**T**	**O**	**E**	**M**	**T**	**O**	**E**	**M**	**T**	**O**
Historical Development, Classification of Elements and Modern Periodic Table	1	1	2	4	–	1	–	1	3	–	1	4
Periodic Properties	2	8	3	13	2	5	1	8	9	5	–	14

E = Easy, **M** = Medium, **T** = Tough, **O** = Overall

Current Dynamics

- Overall weightage and difficulty level of questions had been increased in 2024.
- More number of questions involving ionisation energy, electron gain enthalpy atomic and ionic size were asked in recent years.
- Some new typology questions i.e. Matching type, Statement I and II, A/R type were also been asked in 2024.

JEE Advanced

Typology	Years				
	2024	**2023**	**2022**	**2021**	**2020**
1. One option correct	–	–	–	–	–
2. One or More than one correct	–	–	–	–	1
3. Numerical/Integer Type	–	–	–	–	–
4. Matching Type	–	–	–	–	–
5. Paragraph Based	–	–	–	–	–

Current Dynamics

- The weightage of this chapter is less i.e. 0-1 question were asked in previous years.
- Direct questions are rarely visible, instead concept based question is visible regarding properties and compounds.

Insightful Advice

- This chapter is important from JEE Main perspective as questions were asked in JEE Main exam.
- At JEE Advanced level students are advised to understand and memorise the exceptions in Periodic trends like ionisation energy, electron affinity and atomic size.

Element 1 Historical Development, Classification of Elements and Modern Periodic Table

In the beginning of 18th century, only 31 elements were known but by 1865 the number of elements had became more than double, i.e. 63. Till now 118 elements have been discovered and efforts to discover new elements are still in progress. With such a large number of elements, it is difficult to study the chemistry or properties of each element and their compounds. Therefore, to study the properties of each element, scientists felt the need to classify the elements into various groups or family.

The properties of elements can be predicted based on their position in the periodic table. We will discuss about these properties one by one in detail.

Earlier Attempts to Classify the Elements

For development of classification of the elements. Some important attempts in chronological order are given below.

Dobereiner's Triad

In 1829, Dobereiner classified the elements on the basis of their properties. He made groups of three elements having similar chemical properties called **TRIAD**. In Dobereiner triad, atomic weight of middle element is equal to the average atomic weight of first and third element.

Element	Atomic mass	
Li	7	
Na	23	$\rightarrow \frac{7+39}{2} = 23$
K	39	
Ca	40	
Sr	88	$\rightarrow \frac{40+137}{2} = 88.5$
Ba	137	
P	31	
As	75	$\rightarrow \frac{31+122}{2} = 76.5$
Sb	122	
S	32	
Se	78	$\rightarrow \frac{32+128}{2} = 80$
Te	128	
Cl	35.5	
Br	80	$\rightarrow \frac{35.5+127}{2} = 81.25$
I	127	

Law of triads was rejected as some triads have nearly same atomic masses, e.g. (Fe, Co, Ni).

Newland's Law of Octaves

In 1865, John Alexander Newland's suggested that "if elements are arranged in increasing order of their atomic masses then every eighth element, resembles in its properties with the first one just like the eighth note of a musical octave". Due to similarity in pattern with musical octaves this generalisation is known as **Newland's law of octaves.**

Newland octaves with musical octave

Musical scale	Sa	Re	Ga	Ma	Pa	Dha	Ni
Element	Li	Be	B	C	N	O	F
Atomic weight	7	9	11	12	14	16	19
Element	Na	Mg	Al	Si	P	S	Cl
Atomic weight	23	24	27	29	31	32	35.5
Element	K	Ca					
Atomic weight	39	40					

Law of octaves worked quite well for lighter elements, i.e. up to calcium but failed in the case of heavier elements.

Lothar Meyer's Atomic Volume Curve

The German chemist Lothar Meyer in 1870, independently introduced the idea of periodicity in properties of the elements from study of their atomic volumes [gram atomic mass/density] . A periodic variation is obtained when the atomic volumes of elements are plotted against their atomic mass. It is shown as below

Concept Visualizer

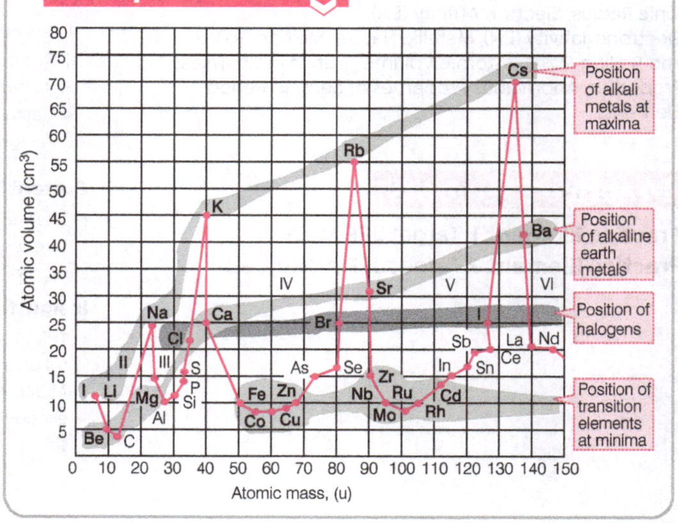

From the above curve, it can be concluded that elements having similar properties occupy similar position on the curve. On the basis of this, Lothar Meyer proposed that the physical properties of the elements are periodic function of their atomic weights.

JEE Quicker

According to law of octaves, the elements were arranged in increasing atomic number order. While Lother Meyer plotted the physical properties of elements against their respective atomic number. *JEE Main 2025*

Both statements are incorrect. In law of octaves elements were arranged in increasing atomic mass. While Lother Meyer plotted $\sqrt{v}$ graph against their respective atomic mass.

Mendeleev's Periodic Table

This periodic table was given by Demitri Mendeleev in 1869. He proposed that when elements are arranged in increasing order of their atomic masses then elements having similar properties are repeated at regular intervals.

This repetition of properties of elements after certain regular intervals is called the periodicity of properties.

On this basis, he gave a law, called the Mendeleev's periodic law, according to which the **physical and chemical properties of the elements are the periodic function of their atomic masses.**

He arranged 63 known elements in horizontal rows and vertical columns of a table in order of their increasing atomic masses.

Periodic system of the elements in groups and series

Series	Group of Elements								
	0	I	II	III	IV	V	VI	VII	VIII
1	—	Hydrogen H 1.008	—		—				
2	Helium He 4.0	Lithium Li 7.03	Beryllium Be 9.1	Boron B 11.0	Carbon C 12.0	Nitrogen N 14.04	Oxygen O 16.00	Fluorine F 19.0	
3	Neon Ne 19.9	Sodium Na 23.5	Magnesium Mg 24.3	Aluminium Al 27.0	Silicon Si 28.4	Phosphorus P 31.0	Sulphur S 32.06	Chlorine Cl 35.45	
4	Argon Ar 38	Potassium K 39.1	Calcium Ca 40.1	Scandium Sc 44.1	Titanium Ti 48.1	Vanadium V 51.4	Chromium Cr 52.1	Manganese Mn 55.0	Iron Fe 55.9, Cobalt Co 59, Nickel Ni 59 (Cu)
5		Copper Cu 63.6	Zinc Zn 65.4	Gallium Ga 70.0	Germanium Ge 72.3	Arsenic As 75	Selenium Se 79	Bromine Br 79.95	
6	Krypton Kr 81.8	Rubidium Rb 85.4	Strontium Sr 87.6	Yttrium Y 89.0	Zirconium Zr 90.6	Niobium Nb 94.0	Molybdenum Mo 96.0		Ruthenium Ru 101.7, Rhodium Rh 103.0, Palladium Pd 106.5 (Ag)
7		Silver Ag 107.9	Cadmium Cd 112.4	Indium In 114.0	Tin Sn 119.0	Antimony Sb 120.0	Tellurium Te 127.6	Iodine I 126.9	
8	Xenon Xe 128	Caesium Cs 132.9	Barium Ba 137.4	Lanthanum La 139	Cerium Ce 140	—	—	—	
9	—	—	—	—	—	—	—	—	
10	—	—	—	Ytterbium Yb 173	—	Tantalum Ta 183	Tungsten W 184	—	Osmium Os 191, Iridium Ir 193, Platinum Pt 194.9 (Au)
11	—	Gold Au 197.2	Mercury Hg 200.0	Thallium Tl 204.0	Lead Pb 206.9	Bismuth Bi 208	—	—	
12	—	—	Radium Ra 224	—	Thorium Th 232	—	Uranium U 239		
HIGHER SALINE OXIDES	R	R_2O	RO	R_2O_3	RO_2	R_2O_5	RO_3	R_2O_7	RO_4
HIGHER GASEOUS HYDROGEN COMPOUNDS					RH_4	RH_3	RH_2	RH	

Characteristic of Mendeleev's Periodic Table

(i) It is based on atomic weight.
(ii) Only 63 elements were known, noble gases were not discovered.
(iii) Each group upto VIIth is divided into A and B subgroups. 'A' sub groups elements are called **normal elements** and 'B' sub groups elements are called **transition elements.**
(iv) The VIIIth group was consists of 9 elements in three rows (Transitional metals group).
(v) The elements belonging to same group exhibit similar properties.

Merits or Advantages of Mendeleev's Periodic Table

(i) **Study of Elements** First time all known elements were classified in groups according to their similar properties. So, study of the properties of elements become easier.

(ii) **Prediction of New Elements** It gave encouragement to the discovery of new elements as some gaps were left in it.

Sc (Scandium), Ga (Gallium), Ge (Germanium), Tc (Technetium) were the elements for which position and properties were defined by Mendeleev even before their discoveries and he left the blank spaces for them in his table for e.g. Blank space at atomic weight 72 in silicon group was called Eka silicon (means properties like silicon) and element discovered later was named Germanium.
Similarly other elements discovered after Mendeleev periodic table were

- Eka aluminium — Gallium (Ga)
- Eka Boron — Scandium (Sc)
- Eka Mangense — Technetium (Tc)

Demerits of Mendeleev's Periodic Table

(i) **Position of Hydrogen** Hydrogen resembles both, the alkali metals and the halogens in properties. So, the placing of hydrogen was not fixed in Mendeleev's periodic table.

(ii) **Position of Isotopes** As atomic weight of isotopes differs, they should have placed in different position in Mendeleev's periodic table. But there were no such places for isotopes in Mendeleev's table.

(iii) **Anomalous Pairs of Elements** There were some pair of elements which did not follow the increasing order of atomic weights. e.g. Ar and Co were placed before K and Ni respectively in the periodic table, but having higher atomic weights.

Ar	K	Te	I
39.95	39.10	127.60	126.90
Co	Ni	Th	Pa
58.95	58.71	232.04	231.04

(iv) **Like Elements were Placed in Different Groups** There were some elements like Platinum (Pt) and Gold (Au) which have similar properties but were placed in different groups in Mendeleev's table.

Pt	Au
VIII	IB

(v) **Unlike Elements were Placed in Same Group** — Cu, Ag and Au placed in Ist group along with Na, K, etc. While they differ in their properties (Only similar in having ns^1 electronic configuration).

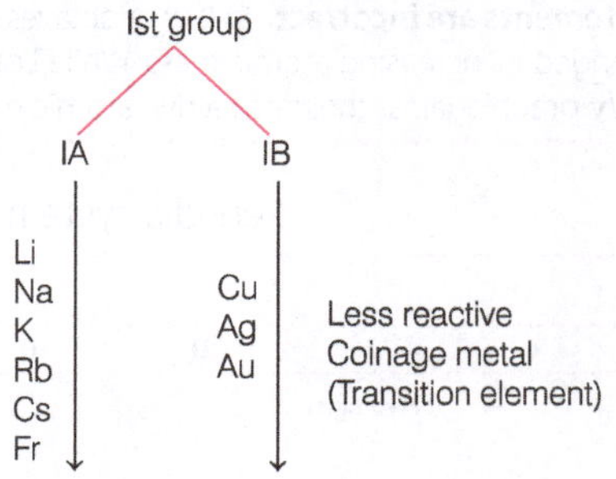

Moseley's Experiment and Modern Periodic Law

Moseley, working in Rutherford's team, in 1913 studied the wavelength of the characteristics X-rays, using different metals as anti-cathode. He postulated that the frequency of the X-rays produced in this manner was related to the charge present on the nucleus of an atom of the element used as anti-cathode. He gave an equation called **Moseley's law.**

$$\sqrt{\nu} = a\,(Z - b)$$

where, ν is frequency and b is screening constant and a is also a constant. He plotted a graph between $\sqrt{\nu}$ and Z, which gives a straight line.

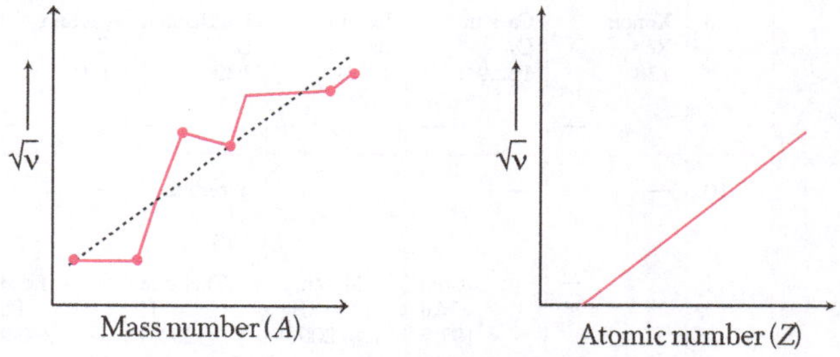

(a) Plot between $\sqrt{\nu}$ and mass number (A)
(b) Plot between $\sqrt{\nu}$ and atomic number (Z)

You can see that the graph relating frequency to atomic number is a straight line. While that relating frequency to atomic mass is not straight line.

Based upon his studies, Moseley proposed the **modern periodic law** which states that: **"the physical and chemical properties of the elements are periodic functions of their atomic numbers."** i.e. when elements are arranged in increasing order of their atomic numbers, the elements having similar properties are repeated after certain regular intervals.

Modern Periodic Table

On the basis of modern periodic law, a new form of periodic table was formulated known as **modern periodic table.**

Characteristics

(i) The comparative studies of elements were made easier.
(ii) It shows the relationship in properties of elements in a group.
(iii) The study of sub-groups explains the properties of elements of that group.
(iv) Atomic mass of some elements i.e. atomic mass of Au, Pt, U etc. were corrected.
(v) Valency of many elements were corrected, for e.g. Be was assumed to be trivalent but it was later reported to be bivalent.

Long Form of Periodic Table

It is an extension of modern periodic table. It is based upon the electronic configuration of elements as it was concluded that electronic configuration of element is also a periodic function. **Rang, Werner, Bohr** and **Burry** were responsible for this extension. The long form of periodic table sometimes also called as **Bohr's periodic table** as the concept of electronic configuration was given by Bohr.

1 ← Atomic number
H ← Symbol
1.00794 ← Atomic weight

s-Block **Representative elements** | *d*-Block **Transition elements** | *p*-Block **Representative elements**

	s^1	s^2	d^1s^2	d^2s^2	d^3s^2	d^5s^1	d^5s^2	d^6s^2	d^7s^2	d^8s^2	$d^{10}s^1$	$d^{10}s^2$	s^2p^1	s^2p^2	s^2p^3	s^2p^4	s^2p^5	s^2p^6
*n = 1																		$2s^2$ He
n = 2	3 Li	4 Be											5 B	6 C	7 N	8 O	9 F	10 Ne
n = 3	11 Na	12 Mg											13 Al	14 Si	15 P	16 S	17 Cl	18 Ar
n = 4	19 K	20 Ca	21 Sc	22 Ti	23 V	24 Cr	25 Mn	26 Fe	27 Co	28 Ni	29 Cu	30 Zn	31 Ga	32 Ge	33 As	34 Se	35 Br	36 Kr
n = 5	37 Rb	38 Sr	39 Y	40 Zr	41 Nb d^4s^1	42 Mo	43 Tc	44 Ru d^7s^1	45 Rh d^8s^1	46 Pd	47 Ag	48 Cd	49 In	50 Sn	51 Sb	52 Te	53 I	54 Xe
n = 6	55 Cs	56 Ba	57 La	72 Hf	73 Ta	74 W d^4s^2	75 Re	76 Os	77 Ir	78 Pt d^9s^1	79 Au	80 Hg	81 Tl	82 Pb	83 Bi	84 Po	85 At	86 Rn
n = 7	87 Fr	88 Ra	89 Ac	104 Rf	105 Db	106 Sg	107 Bh	108 Hs	109 Mt	110 Ds	111 Rg	112 Cn	113 Nh	114 Fl	115 Mc	116 Lv	117 Ts	118 Og

f-Block
Inner-transition elements

n = 6 *Lanthanide series $4f^n5d^{0-1}6s^2$	58 Ce	59 Pr	60 Nd	61 Pm	62 Sm	63 Eu	64 Gd	65 Tb	66 Dy	67 Ho	68 Er	69 Tm	70 Yb	71 Lu	$4f$-subshell being filled
n = 7 **Actinide series $5f^n6d^{0-2}7s^2$	90 Th	91 Pa	92 U	93 Np	94 Pu	95 Am	96 Cm	97 Bk	98 Cf	99 Es	100 Fm	101 Md	102 No	103 Lr	$5f$-subshell being filled

*n is the principal quantum number. The d^1s^2, d^2s^2... designations represent electronic configurations. They refer to (n−1) d and ns-orbital.

Characteristic of long form of peirodic table are

- This table consists of 18 vertical columns called **groups** and 7 horizontal rows called **periods**. The groups are numbered from 1 to 18.
- The co-relation between the groups in long form of periodic table and in modern form of periodic table are given below.

Modern form →	IA	IIA	IIIB	IVB	VB	VIB	VIIB	VIII			IB	IIB	IIIA	IVA	VA	VIA	VIIA	0
Long form →	1	2	3	4	5	6	7	8	9	10	11	12	13	14	15	16	17	18

Description of Groups

The salient features of groups are as follows

(i) There are 18 vertical columns in the periodic table which constitute 18 group. The groups are numbered as 1, 2, 3, ... upto 18. All the members of a particular group have similar outer shell electronic configuration.

(ii) The elements of groups 1, 2, 13, 14, 15, 16, 17 and 18 are known as **representative elements.**

(iii) Except group 18 elements, elements from each group have their outermost energy level (valence shell) incomplete while the inner energy level (core shell) are partially filled (*d*-block) or completely filled.

(iv) The elements belonging to same group have same number of electrons in the outermost shell so their properties are similar.

Description of Periods

The salient features of periods are as follows

(i) Each period begins with the outermost electron entering into a new principal quantum number and completes after the outermost shell is complete.

(ii) The number of period denotes the number of outermost shell of that element.

(iii) The first element of each period (except I period) is an alkali metal and the last element is an inert gas.

Period	*n*	Subshell	No. of elements	Element	Name of Period
1	1	1*s*	2	$_1H$-$_2He$	Shortest
2	2	2*s*, 2*p*	8	$_3Li$-$_{10}Ne$	Short
3	3	3*s*, 3*p*	8	$_{11}Na$-$_{18}Ar$	Short
4	4	4*s*, 3*d*, 4*p*	18	$_{19}K$-$_{36}Kr$	Long
5	5	5*s*, 4*d*, 5*p*	18	$_{37}Rb$-$_{54}Xe$	Long
6	6	6*s*, 4*f*, 5*d*, 6*p*	32	$_{55}Cs$-$_{86}Rn$	Longest
7	7	7*s*,5*f*,6*d*,7*p*	32	$_{87}Fr$-$_{118}Uuo$	Longest

(iv) Oganesson (Og) is recently discovered radioactive element which has electronic configuration as inert gas so it can be considered as inert gas.

Position of Metals and Non-metals in Periodic Table

All the elements on the left side and in the middle of the periodic table (except hydrogen) are **metals**.

The majority of elements are metals which posses a variety of "metallic" character like shiny, good conductor of heat and electricity, ductility and malleable.

- Hydrogen although on the left side of the periodic table is non-metals.
- Non-metals posses characteristics that are generally quite different from those of metals. Non-metals are generally gas, some are liquids and rest are solids at room temperature.
- These are poor conductor of electricity.
- Between the metals and non-metals in the periodic table we find elements known as metalloids or semimetals. For example boron, silicon, germanium, arsenic, antimony, tellurium and astatine make up the list of elements called **metalloids**.

JEE Quicker

The metal that has very low melting point and its periodic position is closer to a metalloid is Gallium. *JEE Main 2022*

↘ In long form of periodic table, gallium is placed in group 13 which is closer to a metalloid germanium (Group 14). The bonds between gallium atoms is weaker due to which it has very low melting point.

Electronic Configuration and Periodic Table

The elements present in a group exhibit similar properties, as these have same number of valence electrons and same electronic configuration. So, on the basis of type of subshell in which the differentiating or last electron enters, the elements are grouped into *s*-block, *p*-block, *d*-block and *f*-block elements.

s-Block Elements

In these elements, the differentiating (i.e. last) electron enters the *s*-orbital of their respective outermost shell.

(i) First two groups of periodic table (i.e. 1 and 2) constitute this block and comprises of only metals.

(ii) Their general outermost electronic configuration is [inert gas]ns^x (where, $x = 1, 2$)

- If $x = 1$, elements constitute a group of alkali metals, placed in first group.
- If $x = 2$, elements constitute a group of alkaline earth metals, placed in second group.

(iii) General valencies of the elements of this block are either 1 or 2.

(iv) These elements are good reducing agents as they have tendency to loose electrons.

(v) These are good conductors of heat and electricity.

p-Block Elements

In these elements, the differentiating electron enters in the *p*-orbital of their respective outermost shell.

(i) Their general outermost electronic configuration is

$$ns^2 \cdot np^x \qquad \text{(where, } x = 1 \text{ to } 6)$$

(ii) The six groups in this block are groups 13, 14, 15, 16, 17 and 18. Every *p*-subshell consists of 3 degenerate orbitals which can accommodate a maximum of six electrons.

(iii) Group number for an element of p-block with an outermost electronic configuration ns^2np^x is given as $(12+x)$, where 'x' ranges from 1 to 6.

(iv) General valencies of elements belonging to groups 13, 14, 15, 16, 17 and 18 are 3, 4, 3, 2, 1 and 0 respectively.

(v) The p-block elements include metals, non-metals and metalloids. The group 15 members are called **pnicogens**, group 16 members are called **chalcogens** (ore forming) and group 17 members are called **halogens** (salt forming).

(vi) The oxidising power of these elements increases along the period but decreases down the group.

(vii) The s-block and p-block elements together are called **representative elements** or **main group elements.**

d-Block Elements

In these elements, the differentiating electron enters in one of the inner d-orbitals.

(i) The d-block elements are placed between s-block and p-block elements and thus are also called **transition elements.**

(ii) The general outermost electronic configuration is $(n-1)d^x\ ns^y$

where, $x = 1$ to 10 (except 4 and 9)

y = number of electrons in ns-orbital either 1 or 2

(iii) The elements of d-block are all metals and shows variable valency.

(iv) As per the IUPAC recommendation a group of d-block is numbered according to their electronic configuration. For a group with general outermost electronic configuration $(n-1)d^x ns^y$, the group number will be $(x+y)$.

(v) This block consists of ten groups (3 to 12).

f-Block Elements

In these elements, differentiating electron enters in f-orbital of anti-penultimate shell.

(i) Their general electronic configuration is $(n-2)\ f^{1\text{-}14}\ (n-1)\ d^{0\text{-}1}\ ns^2$.

If $n = 6$, then elements belong to lanthanide series with electronic configuration $4f^{2-14}\ 5d^{0-1}\ 6s^2$.

(ii) These elements have atomic number from 58 to 71, i.e. Ce to Lu

$Ce_{58} = [Xe]4f^1\ 5d^1\ 6s^2$

$Gd_{64} = [Xe]4f^7\ 5d^1\ 6s^2$

$Lu_{71} = [Xe]4f^{14}\ 5d^1\ 6s^2$

(iii) The name lanthanide is assigned to them because these follow lanthanum, La (57) in their properties.

(iv) If $n = 7$, then elements belong to actinide series with electronic configuration $5f^{1\text{-}14} 6d^{0-1} 7s^2$. These elements have atomic number from 90 to 103, i.e Th to Lr.

$Th_{90} = [Rn]6d^2\ 7s^2$

$Cm_{96} = [Rn]5f^7\ 6d^1\ 7s^2$

$Lr_{103} = [Rn]5f^{14}\ 6d^1\ 7s^2$

(v) The name actinide is assigned to them as these follow actinium, Ac (89) in their properties.

(vi) All the elements of f-block ($4f$ series- lanthanides and $5f$ series-actinides) are placed in 3rd group and are also called **inner transition elements.**

(vii) These were also called rare-earth elements.

Nomenclature of Elements with Atomic Numbers > 100

IUPAC appointed a Commission on Nomenclature of Inorganic Chemistry (CNIC) in 1994 to give a rational system of nomenclature for elements having atomic number greater than 100.

The basic rules to write the name of an element in accordance with the system of nomenclature are as follows

(i) The elements name are derived directly from their atomic numbers by using the numerical roots for required numbers from 0 to 9. These root names are listed below

Digit	0	1	2	3	4	5	6	7	8	9
Root name	nil	un	bi	tri	quad	pent	hex	sept	oct	enn
Abbreviation	n	u	b	t	q	p	h	s	o	e

(ii) The roots are put together in order of digits which make the atomic number and at the end suffix-ium is added. If there is already an 'i' present in root name (like bi, tri) then 'i' is ignored while fixing the 'ium' suffix.

(iii) The symbol of these elements constitute abbreviation for each root names, with the first one being capital.

Elements with $Z > 100$ and their names and symbols are listed below

Atomic number	IUPAC name	Symbol	Elemental name	IUPAC symbol
101	Unnilunium	Unu	Mendelevium	Md
102	Unnilbium	Unb	Nobelium	No
103	Unniltrium	Unt	Lawrencium	Lr
104	Unnilquadium	Unq	Rutherfordium	Rf
105	Unnilpentium	Unp	Dubnium	Db

Atomic number	IUPAC name	Symbol	Elemental name	IUPAC symbol
106	Unnilhexium	Unh	Seaborgium	Sg
107	Unnilseptium	Uns	Bohrium	Bh
108	Unniloctium	Uno	Hassium	Hs
109	Unnilennium	Une	Meitnerium	Mt
110	Ununnilium	Uun	Darmstadtium	Ds
111	Unununium	Uuu	Rontgenium	Rg
112	Ununbium	Uub	Copernicium	Cn
113	Ununtrium	Uut	Nihonium	Nh
114	Ununquadium	Uuq	Flerovium	Fl
115	Ununpentium	Uup	Mosovium	Mc
116	Ununhexium	Uuh	Livermorium	Lv
117	Ununseptium	Uus	Tennessine	Ts
118	Ununoctium	Uuo	Oganesson	Og

JEE MAPPER

Example Similar to PYQ Asked in JEE Main 2022

The IUPAC name of the element which is placed after Db_{105} in the periodic table, will be

(a) Unnilpentium (b) Ununnilium
(c) Unnilhexium (d) Unnilquadium

Sol. (c) IUPAC nomenclature is

1 0 6
↓ ↓ ↓
un nil hex + ium
= Unnilhexium

Competency Enhancer 1.1

An element which is recently discovered is placed in 7th period and 10th group. IUPAC name of the element will be

(a) Unnilseptium (b) Ununnilium
(c) Ununbium (d) Ununpentium

Elemental Practice 1.1

Type I » MCQs with Only One Correct Option

1. Newland's law of octave applies to which of the following set of elements?
(a) Be, Mg, Ca (b) As, K, Ca (c) B, N, C (d) H, Li, Na

2. The limitation that is correct regarding limitation of Mendeleev's periodic table
(a) many elements have several isotopes
(b) noble gases do not form compounds
(c) some groups are divided into two sub groups *A* and *B*
(d) atomic weights of elements are not always whole numbers

3. The IUPAC name of the element which is placed after Bh_{107} in the periodic table, will be —
(a) Unnilquadium (b) Unniloctium
(c) Unnilheptium (d) Unnilhexium

4. Which of the following statements related to the modern periodic table is incorrect?
(a) The *p*-block has 6 columns, because a maximum of 6 electrons can occupy all the orbitals in a *p*-shell
(b) The *d*-block has 8 columns because a maximum of 8 electrons can occupy all the orbitals in a *d*-subshell
(c) Each block contains a number of columns equal to the number of electrons that can occupy that subshell
(d) The block indicates value of azimuthal quantum number (l) for the last subshell that received electrons in building up the electronic configuration

5. Choose the incorrect match for the given electronic configuration with its placing in periodic table.
(a) $[Ar]\ 4s^1 \rightarrow$ 4th period, 1st group
(b) $[Kr]\ 4d^1 5s^2 \rightarrow$ 5th period, 3rd group
(c) $[Rn]\ 6d^1 7s^2 \rightarrow$ 7th period, 3rd group
(d) $[Xe]\ 4f^{14} 5d^2 6s^2 \rightarrow$ 6th period, 5th group

6. If the atomic number of an element is 34, it will be placed in the periodic table in the
(a) first group (b) sixteenth group
(c) fifth group (d) seventh group

7. Consider the following pairs :
I. Mg and Sb II. Ca and Zn III. Ca and Cl IV. Na and Ca
V. Sr and Rh
The total number of pair of elements that belongs to the same period is
(a) 3 (b) 4 (c) 2 (d) 1

8. Elements in the same group have similar physical and chemical properties. It is because of the same
(a) electronic configuration (b) number of electrons
(c) number of protons (d) number of valence electrons

9. Consider the following statements :
I. The number of elements presents in fifth period is 18.
II. Transition metals are not characterised by fixed valency.
III. Tantalum is a representative element.
IV. Cesium is most electropositive in nature.
V. The element with atomic number 118 is transition metal.
Choose the option containing incorrect statement?
(a) III and V (b) I and II (c) II and IV (d) II and III

10. The period number in the long form of the periodic table is equal to
(a) magnetic quantum number of any element of the period
(b) atomic number of any element of the period
(c) maximum principal quantum number of any element of the period
(d) maximum azimuthal quantum number of any element of the period

11. Choose the element having outer electronic configuration $(n-1)d^2ns^2$ for $n=4$.
(a) Scandium (b) Vanadium (c) Titanium (d) Tungsten

12. Consider the following statements :
Statement I The element with outershell electronic configuration $(n-2)f^7(n-1)d^1ns^2$ for $n=6$ is gadolinium.
Statement II The IUPAC nomenclature of an element with electronic configuration $[Rn]5f^{14}6d^17s^2$ is unnilunium.
In the light of the above statements choose the most appropriate answer from the options given below
(a) Statement I is correct but statement II is incorrect.
(b) Both statement I and statement II are correct.
(c) Statement I is incorrect but statement II is correct.
(d) Both statement I and statement II are incorrect.

13. The position of the element having outer shell electronic configuration, ns^2np^4 for $n=3$ is
(a) II period, fourth group (b) III period, fourth group
(c) II period, 16 group (d) III period, 16 group

14. Which one of the following belongs to representative group of elements in the periodic table?
(a) Aluminium (b) Chromium (c) Zinc (d) Lanthanum

15. The characteristics of elements X, Y and Z atomic numbers, respectively, 33, 53 and 83 are
(a) X and Y are metalloids and Z is a metal.
(b) X is a metalloid, Y is a non-metal and Z is a metal.
(c) X, Y and Z are metals.
(d) X and Z are non-metals and Y is a metalloid.

16. Consider the following elements
Mo, Ge, Cd, Os, W
(I) (II) (III) (IV) (V)
Which of the following is the correct decreasing order of atomic number?
(a) IV > III > I > II > V (b) II > IV > III > V > I
(c) IV > V > III > I > II (d) II > V > I > III > IV

17. According to IUPAC nomenclature, a newly discovered element has a symbol of Uun. The atomic number of this element is
(a) 111 (b) 112 (c) 109 (d) 110

Type II 》 MCQs with One or More than One Correct Option

18. Select the correct statement(s) from the following?
(a) An element with three electrons in the outer most subshell belongs to nitrogen family.
(b) An element that would tend to lose two electrons belongs to alkaline earth metal group.
(c) An element that would tend to gain two electrons belongs to chalcogen family.
(d) 17th group have only non-metals which may exist as solid, liquid as well as gas at room temperature.

19. Choose the correct statement(s) from the following.
(a) In the long form of periodic table, the number of period indicates the value of principal quantum number.
(b) There are four d-block series comprising of total 10 elements in the long form of periodic table.
(c) s-block, d-block and f-block elements are metals.
(d) All p-block elements are non-metal.

20. An element X belongs to fourth period and fifteenth group of the periodic table. Which one of the following is/are false regarding the outer shell electronic configuration of X? It has :
(a) partially filled d-orbital and completely filled s-orbital
(b) completely filled s-orbital and completely filled p-orbital
(c) completely filled s-orbital and half filled p-orbital
(d) completely filled d-orbital and completely filled s-orbital

21. Which prediction(s) is/are incorrect according to the Lother Meyer's curve?
(a) Each peak of the curve is occupied by the alkali metals
(b) Alkaline earth metals occupy ascending positions of curve
(c) Atomic volume increases first and then decreases in a period in Lother Meyer's curve
(d) The transition elements occupy at the middle part of the curve.

Type III 》 Numerical/Integer Answer Type Questions

22. The element having the electronic configuration $1s^2, 2s^2, 2p^6, 3s^2, 3p^6, 3d^6, 4s^2$ belong to ……… group number.

23. The number of elements from the following that are not transition element is. (Zr, Co, Cd, Hg, Au, Cu)

24. Among the given elements the number of elements that have metallic nature is …… .
As, Fe, Xe, Li, B, Cl, Ba, P, I, Si

25. The atomic number of unnilunium is …… .

26. If there were 8 periods in the periodic table and each orbital could have maximum 5 electrons then the maximum number of elements that would be present in period 8 are

Elemental Practice 1.1 | Chapter 01

Connect with **Answers**

1. (a)	2. (a)	3. (b)	4. (b)	5. (d)	6. (b)
7. (c)	8. (d)	9. (a)	10. (c)	11. (c)	12. (a)
13. (d)	14. (a)	15. (b)	16. (c)	17. (d)	18. (a,b,c)
19. (a,b,c)	20. (c,d)	21. (b,c,d)	22. (8)	23. (2)	24. (3)
25. (101)	26. (125)				

Element 2 Periodic Properties

The repetition of the properties of elements after certain interval when the elements are arranged in order of increasing atomic number is known as periodicity. The cause of periodicity in properties is due to the same outermost shell electronic configuration occuring at regular intervals of 2, 8, 18 or 32 elements. The properties which show periodicity are called **periodic properties.**

So, in this module, we will consider how the periodic table can be used to correlate properties on an atomic scale.

Trends in Physical Properties

It is important to understand the shielding effect and effective nuclear charge before studying the concept of atomic and ionic radii.

Shielding (Screening) Effect and Effective Nuclear Charge

A valence-electron in a multi-electron atom is attracted by the nucleus and repelled by the electrons of inner-shells. The combined effect of this attractive and repulsive force acting on the valence-electron is that the valence-electron experiences less attraction from the nucleus. This is called **shielding** or **screening effect.**

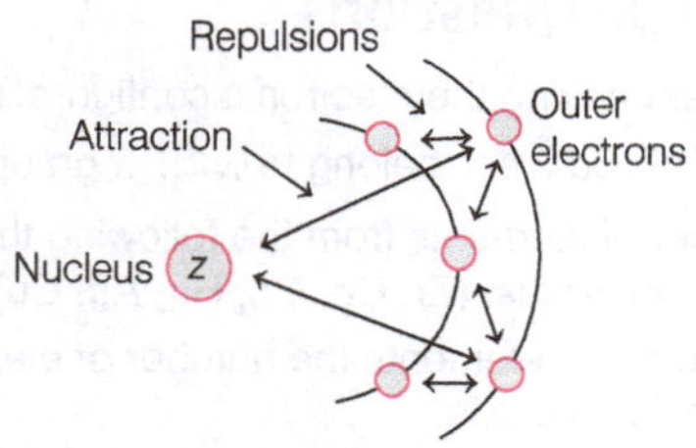

Some important points related to Screening are given below:

- According to **J.C. Slater,** effective nuclear charge Z^* due to screening is not the actual charge Z of the nucleus of the atom, it actually depends on the type of orbital in which the electron is present and on the ability of the other electrons in more penetrating orbitals to screen (or shield) the electron
- The relative extent to which the various orbitals penetrate the electron clouds of other orbitals is $s > p > d > f$. Thus, for any given principal quantum number n, an electron will experience the greatest effective nuclear charge when it is present in a s-orbital, than a p-orbital and so on.
- The electron is more stable in the more penetrating orbital.

Effective nuclear charge Z^* due to screening is given by

$$Z^* = Z - \sigma$$

where Z is the atomic number and σ-is Slater's screening constant. Values of σ are given below for various types of orbitals. In all cases $0 < \sigma < Z$.

σ (sigma) can be calculated by using the formula given below

$\sigma = 0.35 \times$ no.of e^- in nth orbit $+ 0.85 \times$ no. of e^- in $(n-1)$th orbit $+ 1 \times$ rest of the e^-.

Electrons in orbitals ↓ (of shell) →	σ per electron of orbit n	$(n-1)$	$(n-2), (n-3)\ldots$
s-or p-orbital	0.35	0.85	1.00
d-or f-orbital	0.35	1.00*	1.00

*For all groups on left, including s or p-electrons of the same n.

For H-atom $(Z = 1)$, there is no screening, being one-electron system. Thus

$$\sigma = 0 \quad \text{and} \quad Z^* = Z = 1$$

For He-atom $(Z = 2)$, $1s^2$, there is screening by one electron on the other electron.

$$\sigma = 0.30 \text{ (of } 1s \text{ electron)}$$

$$\therefore \quad Z^* = 2 - 0.30 = 1.70$$

For Li-atom, there is screening on outermost electron by 2 electrons in 1st orbit, $(n-1)$.

Thus σ for two electrons in $(n-1) = 2 \times 0.85 = 1.70$

$$\therefore \quad Z^* = 3 - 1.70 = 1.3$$

JEE Alert

- One electron system will have $\sigma = 0$ and thus $Z^* = Z$. Thus in case of H, He^+, Li^{2+}, Be^{3+} ... with one electron Z^* = atomic number.
- For second period with n valence electron
$$Z^* = 0.65[1+n]$$
- For third period with n valence electron
$$Z^* = 1.55 + 0.65n$$
- For higher periods with d- and f-orbitals, variation may differ.
- Except for Li (2nd period) all other elements have constant value of Z^* (2.2 in case of alkali metals). Thus while studying variation of any property in a group, not Z but principal quantum number, n will be the deciding factor.
Variation of radius in a group is given by
$$r_n = \frac{n^2 a_0}{Z}, \qquad (a_0 = \text{Bohr's radius})$$
will be decided by n and not by Z (that will be actually Z^* and which we have seen is constant).

Z_{eff} for different ions of an element

$$Z_{eff} \propto \frac{\text{positive charge}}{\text{negative charge}}$$

e.g. $N^+ > N > N^-$

Z_{eff} for isoelectronic species

e.g. $H^- < Li^+ < Be^{2+} < B^{3+}$ ($2e^-$ species)

$N^{3-} < O^{2-} < F^- < Na^+ < Mg^{2+}$ (10 electron species)

Atomic Radius

- It may be defined as the average distance of valence shell electron from the centre of nucleus to the outermost shell containing electrons.
- Atomic radii can be determined by X-ray diffraction, electron diffraction method and nuclear magnetic resonance (NMR) spectrum methods.
- However, due to uncertainity in the position of the electron in atom, this definition is hypothetical in practical. It is referred to both **covalent** and **metallic radius** depending upon whether the element is a non-metal or a metal respectively.

  In general, atomic radius decreases across a period from left to right and increases down the group in the periodic table.

Types of Atomic Radius

Depending on the chemical bonds, atomic radius is divided into following three categories.

1. Covalent Radius

(SBCR = Single Bonded Covalent Radius) Covalent radius is the half of the internuclear distance between two singly bonded homo atoms e.g. internuclear distance of $A-A,(A_2)$ molecule is (d_{A-A}) and covalent radius is r_A then

$$d_{A-A} = r_A + r_A \text{ or } 2r_A$$

$$r_A = \frac{d_{A-A}}{2}$$

- For atoms known to form single bonds in their elemental state, the experimental bond length may be halved to obtain the respective covalent radius. e.g.,

Element	Bond length (pm)	Atomic radius (pm)
H_2	74	37*
F_2	144	72*
Cl_2	199	99.5
C (diamond)	154	77

- Covalent bonds are formed by overlapping of atomic orbitals.
- Internuclear distance is minimum in this case.
- SBCR of O, N and C etc. elements can be determined by taking H_2O_2, N_2H_4, C_2H_6 respectively.

Calculation of covalent radius for heteroatomic molecule can be discussed by the following cases

Case I For Heteroatomic molecule with non-zero E.N. difference.

For A –B molecule–electronegativities of A and B are approximately equal e.g. C–I, E.N. of C and I are almost equal (2.5) internuclear distance of C–I is 2.13 Å.

$$d_{C\text{-}I} = r_C + r_I \quad (r_C \text{ is } 0.77 \text{ Å})$$

$$\therefore \quad r_I = 2.13 - 0.77 = 1.36 \text{ Å}$$

Case II Heteroatomic molecule with E.N. difference more :

Shoemaker and Stevenson Law

If in a diatomic molecule electronegativities of $A-B$ have more difference. Then actual bond length will be reduced.

As per shoemaker and Stevenson — The reduction in bond length depends on the difference in electronegativities of atoms by following manner

$$d_{A-B} = r_A + r_B - 0.09\,|X_A - X_B|$$

Here, X_A is E.N. of A and X_B is E.N. of B.

2. Metallic Radius (Crystal Radius)

- It may be defined as half of the nuclear distance between two adjacent metallic atoms in crystalline, lattice structure. There is no overlapping of atomic orbitals.
- In a metallic lattice, the valence electrons are mobile, therefore, they are only weakly attracted by metal ions.
- In contrast in a covalent bond a pair of electrons are strongly attracted by the nuclei of two atoms. Thus, metallic radius is greater than its covalent radius. So, metallic radius > covalent radius.
- Metallic radius $\propto \dfrac{1}{\text{Metallic bond strength}}$
- More metallic radius → loose crystal packing → less bond strength (body centred packing)
- Less metallic radius → Tight crystal packing FCC → High bond strength (Hexagonal close packing)

3. van der Waals' Radius

It is one-half of the internucleus distance between two adjacent atoms in two nearest neighbouring molecules of the substance in **gaseous state.**

This is obtained from the shortest distance to which two non-bonded atoms can approach before repulsion between their electron clouds come into play.

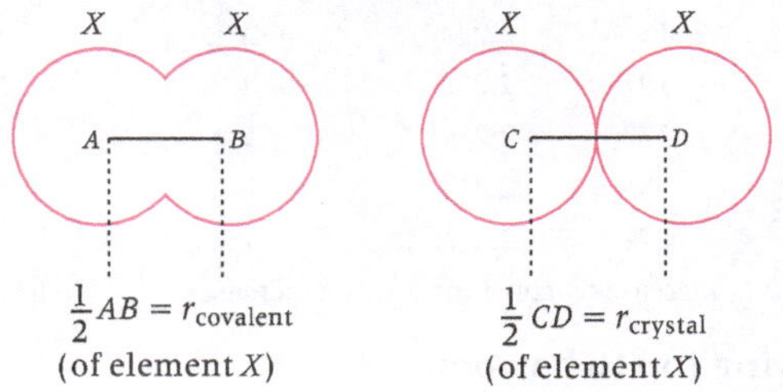

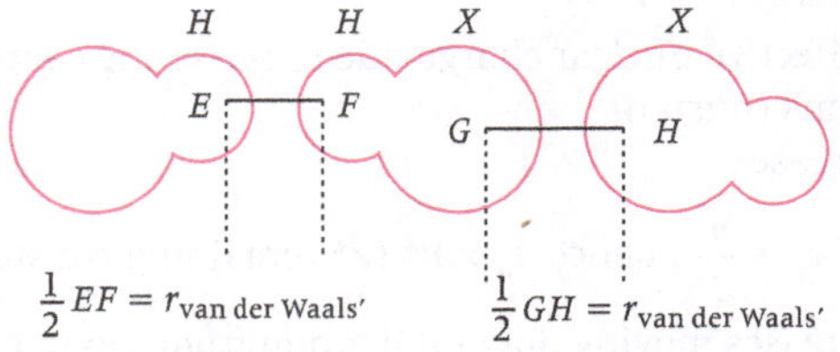

- $\frac{1}{2}EF = r_{\text{van der Waals'}}$ of hydrogen in HX molecule
- $\frac{1}{2}GH = r_{\text{van der Waals'}}$ of X in HX molecule.

$$r_{\text{covalent}} < r_{\text{crystal}} < r_{\text{van der Waals'}}$$

Variation in a Period

	Li	Be	B	C	N	O	F	Ne
Z	3	4	5	6	7	8	9	10
Z^*	1.30	1.95	2.60	3.25	3.90	4.55	5.20	5.85
n	2	2	2	2	2	2	2	2
r_n (pm)	152	111	88	77	74	66	64	160
Atomic radii								

In a Period Left to Right

- As Z (atomic number) increases (by one unit) then Z^* (effective nuclear charge due to screening) also increases (but by 0.65 unit).
- As n (number of shells) remains constant. Electrons are pulled close to the nucleus by the increased Z^*.

Thus, $r_n \propto \frac{1}{Z^*}$

On moving from left to right in a period, Z^* increases due to which size of atom decreases (except noble gas).

JEE Alert

In case of Noble gases (as in Ne) there is no covalent bond fomation, hence only van der Waals' radius is considered. Thus, there is a high jump in the value of radius from F to Ne.

Variation in a Group

We consider 1st group (alkali metals) elements :

Element	Z	Z*	n Principal Quantum number	Radius (pm)
Li	3	1.3	2	152
Na	11	2.2	3	186
K	19	2.2	4	231
Rb	37	2.2	5	244
Cs	55	2.2	6	262
Fr	87	2.2	7	—
	increases	constant	increases	increases

On moving top to bottom,

- Z increases
- Z^* (effective nuclear charge due to screening) almost remains constant
- n increases

Since $r_n \propto \frac{n^2}{Z^*}$, hence $r_n \propto n^2$ (Z* remaining constant) thus r_n increases moving down the group from top to bottom.

Exceptions Transition elements

Sc Ti V Cr Mn	Fe Co Ni	Cu Zn
$Z_{\text{eff}} >$ Screening effect	$Z_{\text{eff}} \approx$ Screening effect	$Z_{\text{eff}} <$ Screening effect

Order of covalent radius :

$$\text{Sc} > \text{Ti} > \text{V} > \text{Cr} > \text{Mn} > \text{Fe} \approx \text{Co} \approx \text{Ni} < \text{Cu} < \text{Zn}$$

Ionic Radius

The effective distance from the nucleus of the ion up to which it has an influence in the ionic bond is called ionic radius.

- **Metal ions (positive ions) are smaller than the atoms from which they were formed** due to two factors :

(i) Positive ion (cation) results from the loss of one or more electrons from the outer shell. This causes, the removal of the whole of the outer shell of electrons.

(ii) With the removal of one or more outer electron decreases while the nuclear charge remains the same.

(iii) In other words, the effective nuclear charge per electron increases and the electrons are therefore pulled more towards the nucleus than before.

Thus, $Mg > Mg^+ > Mg^{2+}$

$$Fe > Fe^{2+} > Fe^{3+}$$

(Greater the charge on the ion, smaller the ion becomes.)

- **The negative ion is always larger than that of the corresponding atom.** This is due to :

(i) negative ion is formed by gain of one or more electrons in the neutral atom and thus number of electrons increases but magnitude of nuclear charge remains the same.

(ii) nuclear charge per electron is thus reduced and the electron cloud is held less tightly by the nucleus resulting in the expansion of the outer-shell. Thus size of negative ion is increased.

$$O^{2-} > O^- > O, \quad F^- > F, \quad I^- > I > I^+$$

- *Iso*-electronic species (containing equal number of electrons) will have different size due to different values of Z. Thus, N^{3-}, O^{2-}, F^-, Na^+, Mg^{2+}, Al^{3+}, Si^{4+} (each having 10 e^-) are *iso*-electronic but their radii differ and varies inversely with atomic number.

	Z	Electron	e/Z
N^{3-}	7	10	1.43
O^{2-}	8	10	1.25
F^-	9	10	1.11
Na^+	11	10	0.91
Mg^{2+}	12	10	0.83
Al^{3+}	13	10	0.77
Si^{4+}	14	10	0.71

Thus, greater the value of (e/Z), greater the size of iso-electronic species.

- In the main groups, radii increase on descending the group because extra shell is added.

Li^+	Na^+	K^+
76 pm	102 pm	138 pm

- The ionic radii decrease on moving from left to right across any period in the Periodic Table.

Na^+	Mg^{2+}	Al^{3+}
102 pm	72 pm	53.5 pm

JEE MAPPER

Example Similar to PYQ Asked in JEE Main 2020

Consider the isoelectronic species, Na^+, Mg^{2+}, F^- and N^{3-}. The correct order of increasing radii is

(a) $F^- < N^{3-} < Mg^{2+} < Na^+$
(b) $Mg^{2+} < Na^+ < F^- < N^{3-}$
(c) $N^{3-} < F^- < Na^+ < Mg^{2+}$
(d) $N^{3-} < F^- < Mg^{2+} < Na^+$

Sol. (b) In case of isoelectronic species

$$\text{Ionic radii} \propto \frac{1}{\text{atomic number}}$$

Ion	$Mg^{2+} < Na^+ < F^- < N^{3-}$
Atomic number	(12) (11) (9) (7)

Thus, ionic radii have the following order

$$Mg^{2+} < Na^+ < F^- < N^{3-}$$

Competency Enhancer 2.1

The correct order of the ionic radii of $Mn^{2+}, Mn^{3+}, Mn^{5+}$ and Mn^{+7} is.

(a) $Mn^{7+} < Mn^{5+} < Mn^{3+} < Mn^{2+}$
(b) $Mn^{7+} > Mn^{5+} > Mn^{3+} > Mn^{2+}$
(c) $Mn^{7+} > Mn^{3+} > Mn^{5+} > Mn^{2+}$
(d) $Mn^{7+} < Mn^{2+} > Mn^{3+} > Mn^{5+}$

Ionisation Potential or Ionisation Energy or Ionisation Enthalpy

- Ionisation energy (IE), sometimes also called ionisation potential (IP), of an element is defined as the amount of energy required to remove an electron from an isolated gaseous atom of that element resulting in the formation of positive ion.

$$M(g) \xrightarrow{(\text{IE})} M^+(g) + e^-$$

- IE is thus a direct measure of the ease with which an atom can change into cation. The smaller the ionisation energy, the easier for the neutral atom to change into a positive ion.

- $(\text{IE})_1$, $(\text{IE})_2$ and $(\text{IE})_3$ are respectively first, second and third, ionisation energies required to remove first, second and third electron from the isolated gaseous atoms.

$$M(g) \xrightarrow{(\text{IE})_1} M^+(g) + e^-$$
$$M^+(g) \xrightarrow{(\text{IE})_2} M^{2+}(g) + e^-$$
$$M^{2+}(g) \xrightarrow{(\text{IE})_3} M^{3+}(g) + e^-$$

Thus, second ionisation energy, $(\text{IE})_2$, causes ionisation of $M^+(g)$ to form $M^{2+}(g)$ and third ionisation energy, $(\text{IE})_3$ causes ionisation of $M^{2+}(g)$ to form $M^{3+}(g)$ and so on

- $(\text{IE})_3$ is also called first ionisation energy of $M^{2+}(g)$ and second ionisation energy of $M^+(g)$. $(\text{IE})_2$, is also called first **ionisation energy of $M^+(g)$.**

- If an electron has been removed from an atom, it becomes increasingly difficult to remove the second and subsequent electrons from the resulting positively charged ions on account of electrostatic attraction. This is due to the fact that after the removal of an electron, the number of electrons decreases while the nuclear charge remains the same.

  Consequently, the remaining electrons are held more tightly by the nucleus and it becomes difficult to remove second electron. Similarly it is further difficult to remove electron from $M^{2+}(g)$. Thus

$$(\text{IE})_1 < (\text{IE})_2 < (\text{IE})_3 < \ldots$$

Note : 1 eV = 1.602×10^{-19} J, 1 J = 6.242×10^{18} eV

Successive ionisation energies (kJ mol^{-1}) of some elements are given below :

Element	Electronic configuration	$(\text{IE})_1$	$(\text{IE})_2$	$(\text{IE})_3$
Li	$1s^2 2s^1$	520	7297	11810
Be	$1s^2 2s^2$	899.3	1758	14810
B	$1s^2 2s^2 2p^1$	800.1	2428	3660
C	$1s^2 2s^2 2p^2$	1086.1	2353	4618
N	$1s^2 2s^2 2p^3$	1402.1	2855	4577
O	$1s^2 2s^2 2p^4$	1313.7	3388	5297
F	$1s^2 2s^2 2p^5$	1680.8	3375	6045
Ne	$1s^2 2s^2 2p^6$	2080.4	3963	6130

Factors Influencing Ionisation Energy

(IE) variation in a period and group may or may not be regular and can be influenced by :

1. Size of the Atom

In a small atom, the electrons are tightly held, while in a larger atom, the electrons are less strongly held, the larger the atomic size the smaller is the ionisation energy. The reason for this is that, as the size of the atom increases, the outer electrons lie farther away from the nucleus. Hence, according to Coulombic force of attraction F

$$F = k\frac{Ze^2}{r^2}$$

where, Z is charge on nucleus, e is the electronic charge, r is the atomic size and k the constant.

2. Nuclear Charge

The force of attraction between the nucleus and the outermost electron increases with increase in nuclear charge. Greater the nuclear charge, greater the energy required to pull the electron from the atom. Hence, (IE) increases with increase in nuclear charge.

3. Shielding Effect

The larger the number of electrons in the inner-shells, greater is the screening effect and smaller the force of attraction and thus (IE) decreases.

Shielding is most effective whenever there is a fully filled electrons between the outermost electron and the nucleus, as in case of noble gases (group 18). Hence, there is a sharp decrease in (IE) on going from noble gas to alkali metals as given below:

	He	→	Li	Ne	→	Na	Ar	→	K
I.E (kJ mol^{-1})	2372.1		520	2080		496	1521		419

4. Penetration Power of Subshells

- Order of attraction of subshell electrons towards nucleus. (Penetration power) is — $s > p > d > f$
- As s-subshell is more closer to nucleus so more energy will be required to remove e^- in comparison to p, d and f.
- Order of decreasing IP is $s > p > d > f$

e.g. IP_1 of Be > IP_1 of B
($1s^2 2s^2$) ($1s^2 2s^2 2p^1$)

After loosing one e^-, B attains electronic configuration of Be, so second IP of B is more than that to first IP of Be.

IP_2 of B > IP_1 of Be

5. Stability of Half-Filled and Fully Filled Orbitals

- Half filled p^3, d^5, f^7 or fully filled s^2, p^6, d^{10}, f^{14} are more stable than others so it requires more energy.
  e.g. In C, N, O, F
  IP_1 order is C < O < N < F
- Because of half filled p-orbitals in N, its ionisation energy (stability) is higher than O.
  IP_1 order Na < Al < Mg
- As s-orbital in Mg is completely filled and its penetration power is also higher than p-orbital (Al).
  IP_2 order $Mg^+ < Al^+ < Na^+$
  (2,8,1) (2,8,2) (2,8)

6. Oxidation State

I.P. ∝ oxidation state of an atom. Ion with high oxidation state will have high ionisation potential.

e.g. $Fe^{3+} > Fe^{2+} > Fe$

The stability of a particular oxidation state for the metal is determined by the difference in their ionisation enthalpies.

- If the difference between two successive IP ≥ 16 eV atom^{-1} then lower oxidation state is stable.

  e.g. $$\left.\begin{array}{ll} Na \longrightarrow Na^+ & IE_1 \\ Na^+ \longrightarrow Na^{2+} & IE_2 \end{array}\right\} 42.7\ \text{eV atom}^{-1}$$

  So, Na^+ is stable.
- If the difference between two successive IP ≤ 16 eV then higher oxidation state is stable.

  e.g. $$\left.\begin{array}{ll} Mg \longrightarrow Mg^+ & IE_1 \\ Mg^+ \longrightarrow Mg^{2+} & IE_2 \end{array}\right\} 7.4\ \text{eV atom}^{-1}$$

  So, Mg^{2+} is stable.

Variation of Ionisation Energy in a Group

On moving down the group :

(i) nuclear charge increases
(ii) number of shells increases, hence atomic size increases.
(iii) there is increase in the number of inner electrons which shield the valence electrons from the nucleus.

The combined effect of the increase in the atomic size and the screening effect is much more than overall effect of increase in nuclear charge. Thus, force of attraction between electrons and nucleus decreases and tendency to remove the valence electron increases.

Hence (IE) decreases on moving down the group. Variations of $(IE)_1$ of alkali metals (group I) and boron family (group 13) are given in

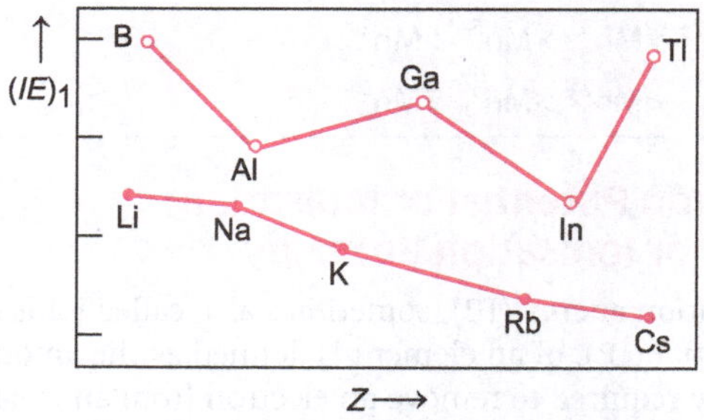

Variation of $(IE)_1$ of groups 1 (•) and 13 (o)

In general the first ionisation energy decreases in a regular way on descending the main groups. A variation from this trend occurs in group 13 (boron family), where the expected decrease occurs between B and Al, but the values for the remaining elements Ga, In and Tl do not continue the trend and are irregular. Ga with completely filled $3d$-orbitals (no e^- in $3d$ of Al) decreases screening thus Ga is smaller in size than it would otherwise be.

$(IE)_1$ Group 1	in kJ mol^{-1}		$(IE)_1$ Group 13	
Li	520	B	801 ↑	
Na	496	Al	577 ↓	decrease
K	419	Ga	579 ↑	decrease
Rb	403	In	558 ↓	decrease
Cs	374 ↓ decrease	Tl	589 ↓	increase

As expected the first ionisation energies decrease down the groups in case of the main group elements in the Periodic Table. But in case of transition elements opposite trends are observed.

Thus, $(IE)_1$ of the corresponding elements of $3d$ and $4d$-series are almost similar but these are smaller than the $(IE)_1$ of the $5d$- series elements. Certainly, the higher values of ionisation energies of the $5d$-transition elements are consistent with the relatively small size of the atoms.

Variation of Ionisation Energy in a Period

On moving across a period, the atomic size decreases and nuclear charge increases and therefore the force of attraction exerted by the nucleus on the electron in outermost shell increases. Hence (IE) increases along a period from left to right.

JEE MAPPER

Example Similar to PYQ Asked in JEE Main 2022

The first ionisation energy (in kJ/mol) of Na, Mg, Al and Si respectively are

(a) 496, 577, 737, 786 (b) 786, 737, 577, 496
(c) 496, 577, 786, 737 (d) 496, 737, 577, 786

Sol. (d) Follow the following steps to solve such problems.

	Steps	Apply
Step I	Write the electronic configuration to find position in the periodic table.	$Na_{11}=[Ne]3s^1$ $Mg_{12}=[Ne]3s^2$ $Al_{13}=[Ne]3s^23p^1$ $Si_{14}=[Ne]3s^23p^2$
Step II	Arrange them in the order as they are in the periodic table.	$\overset{11}{Na}\ \overset{12}{Mg}\ \overset{13}{Al}\ \overset{14}{Si}$
Step III	Follow the general trend and also keep in mind the exception.	The IP increases along a period from left to right but IP of Mg is higher than that of Al due to completely filled $3s$ orbital in Mg.
Step IV	On the above basis find the order.	The order of IP is Na < Mg > Al < Si. Thus, (d) is the correct option.

Competency Enhancer 2.2

The element having greatest difference between its first and second ionisation energy, is

(a) Ca (b) Se (c) Ba (d) K

Electron Affinity (EA)

- It is the amount of energy associated with the gain of electrons by the gaseous atom.

$$F(g)+e^- \longrightarrow F^-(g), \qquad EA=328\ kJ\ mol^{-1}$$

JEE Alert

Electron gain enthalpy is related to electron affinity with the relation, $\Delta_{eg}H^{\ominus}=-EA-\frac{5}{2}RT$. The contribution of $\frac{5}{2}RT$ is commonly ignored. So, $\Delta_{eg}H^{\ominus}=-EA$

In this topic we will use the term electron affinity instead of electron gain enthalpy.

(i) The electron affinity of an element is equal to the negative of the electron gain enthalpy change at temperature $T=0$.

(ii) A large positive electron affinity indicates that an atom has a strong tendency to accept an electron. However, the stability of the resulting negative ion depends upon energetically favourable the electron configuration is, as well as factors such as electron-electron repulsion.

- The greater the energy released in the process of taking up the extra electron, the greater is the electron affinity.
- In terms of orbital diagram:

$$F + e^- \rightarrow F^-$$

F: 1s [↑↓] 2s [↑↓] 2p [↑↓ | ↑↓ | ↑] → F$^-$: 1s [↑↓] 2s [↑↓] 2p [↑↓ | ↑↓ | ↑↓] EA = 328 kJ mol^{-1}

In becoming F^-, fluorine acquires the electronic configuration of noble gas (Ne).

- By the line of reasoning outlined above, we might expect that even metal atoms can form negative ions in the gaseous state, and this happens too.

$$Li + e^- \longrightarrow Li^-$$

Li: 1s [↑↓] 2s [↑] → Li$^-$: 1s [↑↓] 2s [↑↓] EA = 57 kJ mol^{-1}

- There are also cases when addition of electron experiences repulsion; in such cases (EA) is a negative quantity. This is the case for the noble gases [group 18 (VIII A)], where the added electron goes into $(n+1)s$ orbital of higher energy.

Ne: 1s [↑↓] 2s [↑↓] 2p [↑↓ | ↑↓ | ↑↓] + e^- ⟶

Ne$^-$: 1s [↑↓] 2s [↑↓] 2p [↑↓ | ↑↓ | ↑↓] 3s [↑] EA = –116 kJ mol^{-1}

The group 2 (IIA) elements with filled *s*-subshell (ns^2), have pairly small EA.

Even better examples of nagative electron affinities are those associated with gaining a second electron. Here the electron to be added is approaching not a neutral atom but a negative ion. A strong repulsion is felt and the energy of the system increases.

$$O^- + e^- \longrightarrow O^{2-}; EA = -780 \text{ kJ mol}^{-1}$$

$$S^- + e^- \longrightarrow S^{2-}; EA = -492 \text{ kJ mol}^{-1}$$

This process [$O^-(g) + e^- \longrightarrow O^{2-}(g)$] is unfavourable in the gas phase because the resulting increase in electron-electron repulsion overweighs the stability gained by achieving the noble gas configuration. However, note that O^{2-} is common in ionic compounds; in solids, O^{2-} is stabilised by neighbouring cations.

Factors Affecting Electron Affinity

(i) **Atomic size**

$$EA \propto \frac{1}{\text{Atomic size}}$$

(ii) **Screening effect**

$$EA \propto \frac{1}{\text{Screening effect}}$$

(iii) **Effective nuclear charge (Z_{eff})** $EA \propto Z_{eff}$

(iv) **Stability of completely filled or half-filled orbitals**

Electron affinity of fully filled or half filled orbital is very less or zero or energy has to be given to introduce any electron. It is because of its stability.

Variation of (EA) in a Period

(i) Electron affinity increases along the period due to increase in Z_{eff} and decrease in atomic size.

(ii) Halogens possess maximum electron affinity due to small size and maximum Z_{eff} and after gaining one electron. They attain a stable inert gas configuration.

(iii) In IInd period from $_6C$ to $_7N$ value of electron affinity decreases, because of half filled orbitals present in $_7N$ which is more stable.

(iv) In IIIrd period value of electron affinity of Si is higher than P, because of half-filled *p*-orbitals present in P.

(v) The value of electron affinity of inert gases is negaive due to fully-filled valence shell, making them extremely stable.

Li	Be	B	C	N	O	F	Ne
Na	Mg	Al	Si	P	S	Cl	Ar
	Zero			Less			Zero

1st EA order of period elements

$$F > O > C > B > Be > N > Ne$$

$$Cl > S > Si > P > Al > Mg > Ar$$

Variation of (EA) in a Group

- On moving down a group, the atomic size increases and, therefore, the effective nuclear attraction decreases and thus, electron affinity decreases.
- Fluorine has a less electron affinity than chlorine. It seems to be due to the relatively greater effectiveness of 2*p*-electrons in the small F atom to repel the additional electron entering the atom than 3*p*-electrons in the larger Cl atom.

  Order of electron affinity

  $$Cl > F > Br > I$$

  $$S > O > P > N$$

  $$Si > C > P > N$$

  N and P have low electron affinity due to stable half-filled electronic configuration.
- The small negative value of (EA) of Be, Mg and N are also interesting. The stability of the filled *s*-shell (in Be and Mg) and half-filled *p*-shell (in N) and the resulting reluctance of these atoms to add any extra electron is indicated.

Some Electron Affinity (–EA) Values (kJ mol^{-1})

		$H \rightarrow H^-$	−72				
		$He \rightarrow He^-$	54				
$Li \rightarrow Li^-$	−57	$Na \rightarrow Na^-$	−21				
$Be \rightarrow Be^-$	66	$Mg \rightarrow Mg^-$	67				
$B \rightarrow B^-$	−15	$Al \rightarrow Al^-$	−26				
$C \rightarrow C^-$	−121	$Si \rightarrow Si^-$	−135				
$N \rightarrow N^-$	31	$P \rightarrow P^-$	−60				
$O \rightarrow O^-$	−142	$S \rightarrow S^-$	−200				
$O^- \rightarrow O^{2-}$	780	$S^- \rightarrow S^{2-}$	492				
$F \rightarrow F^-$	−333	$Cl \rightarrow Cl^-$	−348	$Br \rightarrow Br^{-1}$	−324	$I \rightarrow I^-$	−295
$Ne \rightarrow Ne^-$	99						

Application of Electron Affinity

(i) Electron affinity ∝ Oxidising nature

But F has more oxidising power than Cl because F has more standard reduction potential.

(ii) Electron affinity ∝ Reactivity

- They form anions by gaining electron
- Their bond nature is ionic.

(iii) Electron affinity ∝ electronegativity

(iv) Elements of high electron affinity form oxide and hydroxides, which are acidic in nature. This trend is found mainly among **non-metals**, particularly in groups 15, 16 and 17 of the periodic table.

JEE MAPPER

Example Similar to PYQ Asked in JEE Main 2020

The electron gain enthalpy (in kJ/mol) of fluorine, chlorine, bromine and astatine, respectively, are

(a) –328, –325, –349 and –270
(b) –270, –325, –328 and –349
(c) –328, –349, –325 and –270
(d) –349, –328, –325 and –270

Sol. (*c*)

- Chlorine has most negative electron gain enthalpy due to its optimal size and attraction of electron.
- Fluorine despite being smaller has more electron-electron repulsion making its electron gain enthalpy less negative than chlorine.
- Bromine and astatine have less negative value due to their large size and lower effective nuclear charge as compare to chlorine and flourine. So, correct order is Cl > F > Br > At.

Thus, option (c) is correct.

Competency Enhancer 2.3

Within each pair of elements F and Cl, S and Se and Li and Na, respectively, the elements that release more energy upon an electron gain are

(a) F, Se and Na
(b) F, S and Li
(c) Cl, S and Li
(d) Cl, Se and Na

Electronegativity (EN)

It is the measure of the tendency of an element to attract electrons to itself.

$$HCl \longrightarrow H^+ + Cl^-$$

In the above molecule, Cl is said to be more electronegative than H if it pulls bonding pair towards itself.

The absolute magnitude of the electronegativity value (EN) of an element is however not fixed. Different values may be assigned to the same element from different theoretical approaches.

Variation of Electronegativity in a Group

On moving down the group

- Z increases but Z^* almost remains constant,
- number of shells (n) increases,
- r_n (atomic radius) increases,
- force of attraction $\left(F = \dfrac{k\,Ze^2}{r_n^2}\right)$ between added electron and nucleus decreases,

Hence, (EN) decreases down the group.

Variation of Electronegativity in a Period

- On moving across the period from left to right
  - Z, Z^* increases,
  - n (number of shells) remains constant,
  - r_n decreases,
  - $F\left(=k\dfrac{Ze^2}{r_n^2}\right)$ increases.

  Hence, (EN) increases along a period.
- **Fluorine is the most electronegative element in the periodic table.**
- Graph represents variation of electronegativity of elements with atomic number. In this :

The strongest non-metals, the halogens, appear at the peaks; the alkali metals mark the troughs. This is largely a result of new shell of electrons starting with noble gases which have zero values of electronegativities.

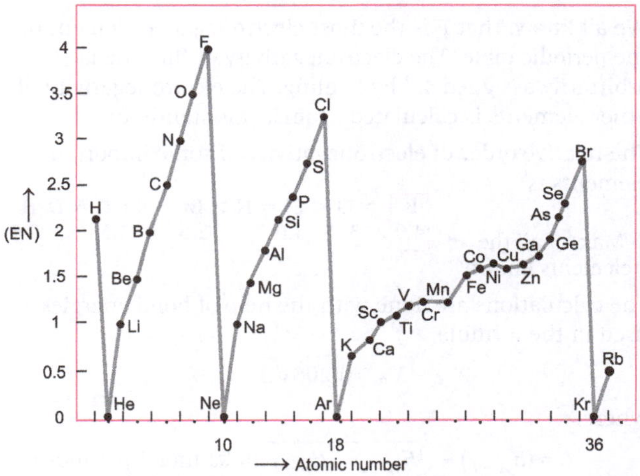

Electronegativities of the elements H(1) to Rb (37). The (EN) of the noble gases have been set at zero.

- The group 1 (IA) metals have their nuclei shielded quite strongly. Hence, they show little tendency to gain new electron the electronegativities of transition metals like their (IE), do not change greatly from one another.

Diagonal Relationship and Electronegativity

- Moving one place to the right across period, the increased nuclear charge holds the electrons more tightly to the atom.

  Moving down one place in a group, the extra shell of electrons decreases the attraction of the nucleus for the outer electrons. A **diagonal** move means that these effects tend to compensate one another.
- The electronegativity increases as we go from Li to Be but it decreases as we move from Be to Mg. As we move diagonally, these two effects partly cancel each other and

there is no marked change in electronegativity and thus Li and Mg have close values of electronegativities.
Because of this, Li and Mg show similarity in properties—a diagonal relationship (between elements lying diagonally in Periodic Table).

- Elements' pairs showing this relationship are :

Li—Mg, Be—Al, B—Si

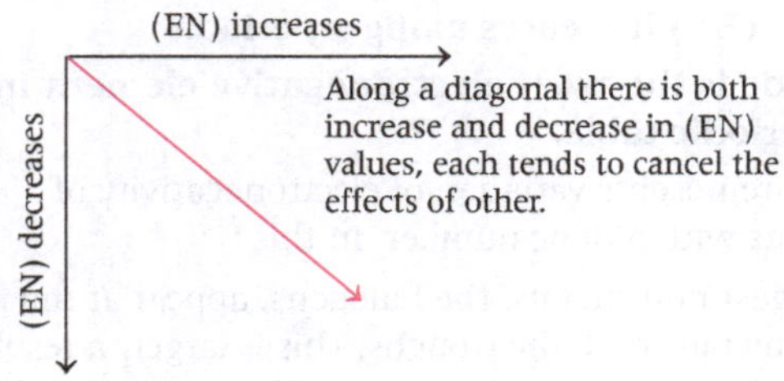

Pauling's Electronegativity

We all know, that F is the most electronegative element of the periodic table. The electronegativity of fluorine is arbitrarily assigned 4.0 by Pauling. The electronegativity of other elements is calculated against this standard.

The relative order of electronegativity of some important elements is

F	> O	< Cl	= N	> Br	> S	= C	= I	> H
4.0	3.5	3.0		2.8	2.5			2.1

Max. of all the elements known (F, 4.0)

The calculations are done with the help of bond energies used in the formula,

$$X_A - X_B = 0.208\sqrt{\Delta}$$

where,

$$\Delta = (E_{A-B}) - \sqrt{E_{A-A} \times E_{B-B}} \text{ in kJ mol}^{-1} \text{ per molecule}$$

$X_A - X_B$ = electronegativity difference between two atom A and B.

E_{A-B}, E_{A-A} and E_{B-B} are the bond energies in kJ mol^{-1} of the molecules AB, A_2 and B_2 respectively.

Mulliken-Jaffe Electronegativity

Electronegativity (EN) can be regarded as the average of the ionisation energy (IE) and the electron affinity (EA) of an atom.

$$(\text{EN}) = \frac{\text{IE} + \text{EA}}{2}$$

If both (EA) and (IE) are determined in eV units then Pauling's electronegativity $(\text{EN})_P$ is related to Mulliken's electronegativity $(\text{EN})_M$ by the equation :

$$(\text{EN})_P = 0.336\,[(\text{EN})_M - 0.615]$$

- If (EA) and (IE) are in eV, then (EN) in eV is given by

$$0.187\,(\text{IE} + \text{EA}) + 0.17$$

- Mulliken's values are about 2.8 times larger than the Pauling's values.

Factors Affecting Electronegativity

(i) **Atomic size** It decreases with increase in atomic size.

$$\text{Electronegativity} \propto \frac{1}{\text{Atomic size}}$$

(ii) **Effective Nuclear Charge (Z_{eff})**

$$\text{Electronegativity} \propto Z_{eff}$$

(iii) **Hybridisation State of an Atom**

Electronegativity ∝ % of s character in hybridised atom

	sp	>	sp^2	>	sp^3
s-character	50%		33%		25%
Electronegativity	3.25		2.75		2.5

As s-orbital is nearer to nucleus so by increasing s-character in hybridisation state, EN also increases.

(iv) **Oxidation state**

- Electronegativity ∝ oxidation state

$$Mn^{2+} < Mn^{4+} < Mn^{7+}$$

$$O^- < O < O^+$$

$$Fe < Fe^{2+} < Fe^{3+}$$

- As atomic radius decreases by increasing oxidation state of cation species, EN increases.
- In anionic species, the order of electronegativity is $O^{2-} < O^- < O$.

(v) Electronegativity does not depend on filled or half filled orbitals, because it is tendency to attract bonded electron, not to gain electron from outside.

Application of Electronegativity

It is useful to determine the properties of element which is discussed below.

(i) **Metallic and Non-metallic Nature**

Low electronegativity ⟶ Metals

High electronegativity ⟶ Non metals

Metallic character increases down the group but decreases along a period.

(ii) **Bond Length**

$$\Delta\text{EN} \propto \frac{1}{\text{Bond length}}$$

Here ΔEN = difference in electronegativity of bonded atoms

$$HF < HCl < HBr < HI$$

- HF has minimum bond length because of much difference in the electronegativities of H and F.

(iii) **Bond Energy** By increasing ΔEN bond length decreases and hence bond energy increases.

Bond energy ∝ Electronegativity difference

$$HF > HCl > HBr > HI$$

(iv) **Acidic Strength of Hydrides**

Bond energy (Strength) ∝ stability of molecules.

Order of stability of hydrohalides is

HF > HCl > HBr > HI and so order of their acidic strength will be HF < HCl < HBr < HI

In group 15

NH_3 * Thermal stability decreases
PH_3 * Basic character decreases
AsH_3 ↓ * Acidic character increases

In PH_3 and AsH_3 there is less difference in the electronegativities of X_A and X_B, so their bond energy decreases and hence acidic character (losing H^+ ion) increases.

Metallic Nature

Metals have the tendency to form cations by loss of electrons and this property makes the elements as **electropositive** elements or metals.

$$M(g) \longrightarrow M^+(g) + e$$

- The tendency of an element to lose electron is closely connected to the (IE) of the element. **The smaller the (IE) of an element, the greater will be its tendency to lose electrons** and **thus greater will be its metallic character.**
- Tendency to oxidise itself provides reducing property to the elements thus, smaller the (IE), greater is the metallic character, hence greater is the reducing nature :
(IE) increases moving along a period left to right and decreases down the group, hence metallic and reducing nature decrease along the period and increase down the group.
- The most reactive metals (the top of the activity series) are present on the left side of the Periodic Table, whereas the least reactive metals (the bottom of the activity series) are in the transition metal groups closer to the right side of the table.

(i) The reactivity of metals increases with decrease in IE, electronegativity and increase in atomic radii and electropositive character.

(ii) The reactivity of non-metals increases with increase in electronegativity and electron gain enthalpy (or electron affinity) and decrease with increase in atomic radii.

(iii) In metals on moving down in a group, chemical reactivity increases while for non-metals it decreases.

(iv) Across a period, the reactivity of metals decreases while those of non-metals increases.

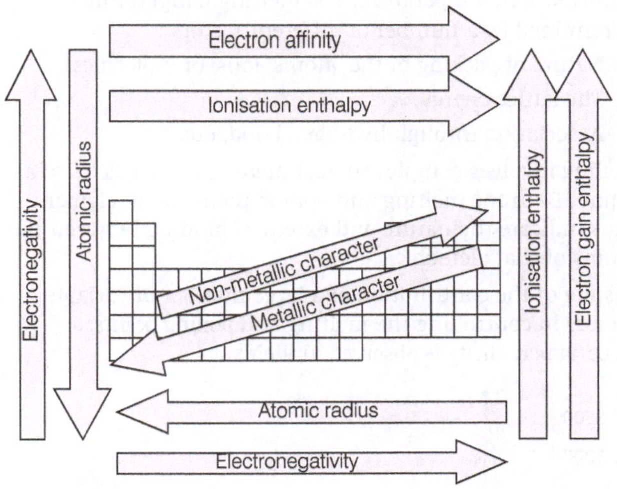

Hydration and Hydration Energy

Hydration energy is the enthalpy change that accompanies by dissolving of one mole of gaseous ions in water.

$$Li^+(g) + H_2O \longrightarrow [Li(H_2O)]^+, \quad \Delta H = -806 \text{ kJ mol}^{-1}$$

Size of the ion and its charge determines extent of hydration. Greater the charge, smaller the size of the ion, greater the attraction for the lone pair of O of H_2O, hence greater the extent of hydration and hence greater the hydration energy. Also size of the hydrated ions increases as a result ionic mobility decreases [heavier (hydrated) ions moves slower].

Hydration and Ionic Mobilities

Ion	Ionic radius (Å)	Ionic mobilities*	Radius of hydrated ion (Å)	Hydration energy** $\Delta H°_{hyd.}$	Oxidation energy** $\Delta H°_{ox.}$	$E°_{redn.}$ (V)
Li^+	0.60	33.5	3.40	–544	169	– 3.045
Na^+	0.98	43.5	2.76	–435	208	– 2.714
K^+	1.33	64.5	2.32	–352	191	– 2.925
Rb^+	1.48	67.5	2.28	–326	200	– 2.925
Cs^+	1.67	68.0	2.28	–293	196	– 2.923

* Values in 10^{-8} m^2 V^{-1} s^{-1}

** Values in kJ mol^{-1}

Melting Points and Boiling Points

A solid melts when the forces holding its constituent units in position is overcome by thermal energy as a consequence of increase in temperature. The melting temperature is determined by a number of different factors :

- Nature of packing of the atoms, ions, or molecules,
- The lattice energy,
- Association through hydrogen bond, etc.

Boiling involves complete detachment of the particles of a liquid. Both the melting and boiling points of an element thus indicate the nature and extent of binding between the atoms of that element.

Inspite of the contribution of a large number of variable factors in controlling the melting and boiling points, a striking periodicity is observed in their values.

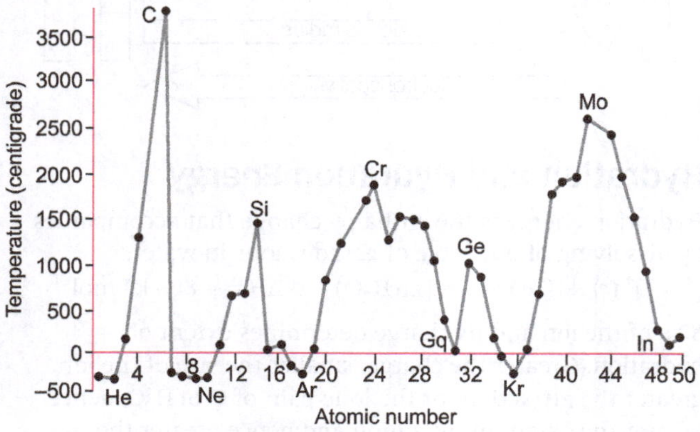

Periodic variation of melting point of elements

The above graph represents a plot of melting points of some elements against their respective atomic numbers. The shape of the curve indicates periodic variation. It may be further observed that :

(i) The noble gases have very low melting points.

(ii) The melting point of the elements in any period increases gradually upto group 14 where it becomes maximum afterwards to the next noble gas.

(iii) The melting points of elements occurring in a group usually decrease downwards, *i.e.*, as the elements have higher atomic numbers.

Density

The densities of the elements in the solid state also exhibit periodic variation when plotted against their atomic numbers. It may be observed from figure given below that the densities of the alkali metals occupy the minima in the curve; the density first rises and then decreases along a period, the elements in the middle having the highest density values.

Here again the underlying reason is largely complicated by the nature of packing of the atoms. A simple interpretation may be provided by remembering that **stronger and compact binding leads to high density. The binding force is again dependent on the number of valence electrons provided by each atom.** This is why the density of the central elements in any period is highest.

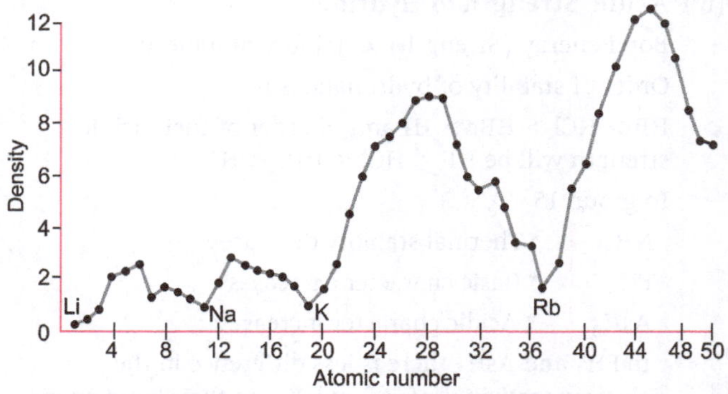

Periodic variation of density with atomic number

The increase of density down any group in the Periodic Table is similarly explained from the increasing number of neutrons and protons in the nuclei.

JEE Spotlite

- The noble gas atoms contain a completed electron shell. So there exists little tendency for these atoms to combine between themselves. This is why they occupy the lowest range of melting points.
- The alkali metals have only one electron in their outermost shells. Their contribution to metallic bonding is therefore weak resulting in low melting points.
- As the number of electrons participating in metallic bonding increases, the melting point also increases : Be > Li; Mg > Na.
- Boron, carbon and silicon form giant three-dimensional structures; breaking of these arrangements require large amount of energy. Hence, they have very high melting points.
- Nitrogen, oxygen, fluorine—all form stable diatomic molecules containing triple, double and single bonds (between their atoms) respectively. They do not form giant three-dimensional lattices. It may be due to greater repulsion between the non-bonding electrons and the greater stabilities of these multiple bonds. At the same time, very poor binding exists among the molecules. Consequently they have very low melting points.

Atomic Volume

Lothar Meyer, in 1870, independently introduced the idea of periodicity in properties of the elements from study of their atomic volumes.

The atomic volume is the volume of one mole of atoms of an element; it was obtained as atomic volume (cc mol^{-1}) = atomic weight/density.

This is only a rough indication of atomic size since the density of an element is determined by several factors like physical state, allotropic form, number of atoms per molecule, nature of packing and so on.

Concept Visualizer

The periodic trends of the elements in a periodic table can be visualised as follows —

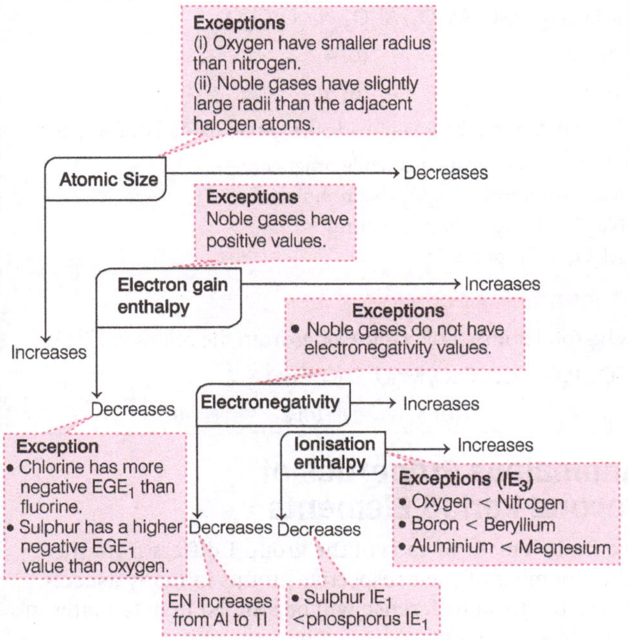

Trends in Chemical Properties

The elements of the periodic table show chemical properties. Some of the properties which show periodic variation are explained below :

Valency or Oxidation States

The valency of an element is directly related to the electronic configuration of its atom and is usually determined by the number of electrons in the outermost shell. This is because the outer electrons are majorly responsible for the chemical behaviour as the electrons in these orbitals usually participate in chemical bonding.

The number of valence electrons of any representative element is the same as the group number of the element in periodic table. In some cases, it is either equal to 8 minus group number or 18 minus group number.

Now-a-days, the term **oxidation state** is frequently used for valency. The oxidation state of an element in a particular compound can be defined as "the charge acquired by its atom on the basis of electronegative consideration from other atoms in the molecule".

Periodicity of Valency or Oxidation State

Variation of valency or oxidation state in groups and period is discussed below

1. Variation of Valency in a Period

On moving left to right in a period, the number of valence electrons increases from 1 to 7. Consequently, the valency of the elements with respect to hydrogen increases from 1 to 4 upto group IV and then decreases to 1 as shown in table.

	Li	Be	B	C	N	O	F
Compounds with hydrogen	LiH	BeH_2	BH_3	CH_4	NH_3	H_2O	HF
Valency	1	2	3	4	3	2	1

- However, valency with respect to oxygen increases from one to seven along the period.

	Na	Mg	Al	Si	P	S	Cl
Compounds with oxygen	Na_2O	MgO	Al_2O_3	SiO_2	P_2O_5	SO_3	Cl_2O_7
Valency	1	2	3	4	5	6	7

- Inert gases, i.e., group 18 elements have zero valency.

2. Variation of Valency in Groups

On moving down the group, the number of valence electrons remains the same. Therefore, all the elements in a group have the same valency. For example, elements of group I have valency 1 and elements of group II have valency 2.

Transition metals show variable valency of 1, 2 or 3 as they can use electrons from their outermost as well as penultimate shell, during chemical reactions as energy difference between them is small. It may also be pointed out that there are some exceptions to this rule in *p*-block elements which too show variable valency on account of inert pair effect.

Reducing and Oxidising Properties

- Metals acts as good reducing agents as they provide electrons. Non-metals are good oxidising agents as they accept electrons easily.
- The reducing power of elements in the periodic table decreases across the period (left to right) and increases down the group (up to down).
- The oxidising power of elements increases across the period and decreases down the group.

So, we can conclude that alkali metals are powerful reducing agents while halogens are powerful oxidising agents in the periodic table.

Nature of Oxides

On moving across a period, the basic character of the oxides gradually changes first into amphoteric and finally into acidic character. On moving down the group, reverse behaviour is observed, i.e., from more acidic to more basic.

Oxides of the element M in H_2O produce MOH. Nature of MOH can be explain by the following cases.

Case I If electronegativities difference of M and O is greater than that of H and O in H_2O then MOH is acidic due to formation of H_3O^+

$$M\text{—O—H} + H_2O \longrightarrow H_3O^+ + MO^-$$

Case II If electronegativities difference of M and O is less than that of H and O in H_2O then MOH is basic due to formation of OH^-

$$M—O—H + H—O—H \longrightarrow [MOH_2]^+ + OH^-$$

- Stability of oxides decreases across a period.
- Behaviour of the elements is shown in figure below.

Increasing acidic character ⟶

↓ Increasing basic character

(1)	(2)	(13)	(14)	(15)	(16)	(17)
Li_2O	BeO	B_2O_3	CO_2	N_2O_5		
Na_2O	MgO	Al_2O_3	SiO_2	P_4O_{10}	SO_3	Cl_2O_7
K_2O	CaO	Ga_2O_3	GeO_2	As_2O_5	SeO_3	
Rb_2O	SrO	In_2O_3	SnO_2	Sb_2O_5	TeO_3	
Cs_2O	BaO		PbO_2	Bi_2O_3	PoO_3	

- Oxides of the following elements are **amphoteric**
  H, Be, Al, Ga, In, Tl, Sn, Pb, Sb, Bi, Po

  H_2O is amphoteric (also called amphiprotic)

$$H_2O + H_2O \longrightarrow H_3O^+ + OH^-$$

since it is H^+ **acceptor** (base) as well as H^+ donor (acid). BeO, Al_2O_3, SnO_2, PbO_2, ... are **amphoteric** since they form salts with acid as well as with base

$$\underset{\text{base}}{Al_2O_3} + \underset{\text{acid}}{6HCl} \longrightarrow 2AlCl_3 + 3H_2O$$

$$\underset{\text{acid}}{Al_2O_3} + \underset{\text{base}}{2NaOH} + 3H_2O \longrightarrow 2Na[Al(OH)_4]$$

– Oxide is acidic if it reacts with a base.

– Oxide is basic if it reacts with an acid.

Nature of Hydride

- Hydrogen combines with a number of other elements including metals and non-metals to form compounds called hydrides (with H^-).
- Covalent nature of hydrides increases across a period and decreases down the group.
- Ionic hydride are better reducing agents than covalent hydride and reducing nature of hydride decreases across a period and increases down the group.
- The variation in acidic and basic character of hydrides is an exceptional behaviour among chemical properties which have similar trends across the period or down the group.

JEE MAPPER

Example Similar to PYQ Asked in JEE Main 2022

The total number of acidic oxides from the following list is —
$B_2O_3, N_2O, NO, As_2O_3, Al_2O_3, Na_2O, Cl_2O_7$

(a) 2 (b) 4

(c) 5 (d) 3

Sol. (a) Among the given oxides only two oxide i.e., B_2O_3 and Cl_2O_7 are acidic oxides while others are —

$N_2O \rightarrow$ neutral $As_2O_3 \rightarrow$ amphoteric

$Na_2O \rightarrow$ basic NO $\rightarrow$ neutral

$Al_2O_3 \rightarrow$ amphoteric

Competency Enhancer 2.4

The total number of acidic oxides from the following list is
$SO_3, P_4O_{10}, CO, CaO, MgO, ZnO, CuO$

(a) 4 (b) 3 (c) 2 (d) 1

Anomalous Properties of Second Period Elements

The first element of each of the group 1 differs from the other member of their respective groups in many aspects. (These points of difference will be studied in detail later in *s* and *p*-block elements.)

Some anomalous properties of II period elements are given below with their explanation.

1. Covalency

The maximum covalency of II period elements is four while other members may shown higher covalency also. *e.g.*, BF_4^- and $[AlF_6]^{3-}$ exist but $[BF_6]^{3-}$ does not.

Similarly, OF_2 is known but OF_4, OF_6 are not while SF_4 and SF_6 are known, N is never pentavalent etc.

Explanation These elements have only two shells in their atom and valence shell contain 4 orbitals only (one 2*s* and three 2*p*) so a maximum of four bonds can be formed. In element of period III and onwards, valence shell contain empty *d*-orbitals also. So covalency may be more than four.

2. $p\pi$ - $p\pi$ Multiple Bonding

Bonds like C=C, C≡C, N≡N, C=O etc. exist due to $p\pi$ - $p\pi$ multiple bonding. These elements are smaller in size and most electronegative in their respective group so they form multiple bonds.

Elemental Practice 1.2

Type I MCQs with Only One Correct Option

1. Consider the isoelectronic ions K^+, S^{2-}, Cl^- and Ca^{2+}
The radii of these ionic species follow the order
(a) $Ca^{2+} > K^+ > Cl^- > S^{2-}$ (b) $Cl^- > S^{2-} > K^+ > Ca^{2+}$
(c) $S^{2-} > Cl^- > K^+ > Ca^{2+}$ (d) $K^+ > Ca^{2+} > S^{2-} > Cl^-$

2. For the element (X), student (A) measured its radius as 102 nm, student (B) as 103 nm and (C) as 100 nm using same apparatus. Their teacher explained that measurements were correct by saying that recorded values by (A), (B) and (C) are
(a) crystal, van der Waals' and covalent radii
(b) covalent, crystal and van der Waals' radii
(c) van der Waals', ionic and covalent
(d) crystal, covalent and vander Waals' radii

3. Select the incorrect order of the properties indicated.
(a) $Ni^{2+} > Cr^{2+} > Fe^{2+} > Mn^{2+}$ (size)
(b) Sc > Ti > Cr > Mn (size)
(c) $Ni^{2+} < Co^{2+} < Fe^{2+} < Mn^{2+}$ (unpaired electron)
(d) $Fe^{2+} > Co^{2+} > Ni^{2+} > Cu^{2+}$ (unpaired electron)

4. The ions $O^{2-}, F^-, Na^+, Mg^{2+}$ and Al^{3+} are isoelectronic. Their ionic radii show
(a) an increase from O^{2-} to F^- and then decrease from Na^+ to Al^{3+}
(b) a decrease from O^{2-} to F^- and then increase from Na^+ to Al^{3+}
(c) a significant increase from O^{2-} to Al^{3+}
(d) a significant decrease from O^{2-} to Al^{3+}

5. The correct decreasing order of ionic radius is
(a) $C^{4-} > N^{3-} > O^{2-} > F^-$ (b) $F^- > O^{2-} > N^{3-} > C^{4-}$
(c) $O^{2-} > F^- > C^{4-} > N^{3-}$ (d) $N^{3-} > O^{2-} > F^- > C^{4-}$

6. For Be, $Z_{eff} = 1.95$ and for Be^{z+}, $Z_{eff} = 2.30$. Hence, ion is
(a) Be^+ (b) Be^{2+}
(c) Be^{3+} (d) Both (b) and (c)

7. Select the incorrect order for the property mentioned in brackets.
(a) F < Cl < Br < I (atomic radius)
(b) K < Rb < Li < Cs (Ionisation enthalpy)
(c) $Be^{2+} < Mg^{2+} < Li^+ < Na^+$ (Ionic radius)
(d) Li < Be < N < Ne (Ionisation enthalpy)

8. Sodium forms Na^+ ion but it does not form Na^{2+} because
(a) very low value of $(IE)_1$ and $(IE)_2$
(b) very high value of $(IE)_1$ and $(IE)_2$
(c) low value of $(IE)_1$ and low value of $(IE)_2$
(d) low value of $(IE)_1$ and high value of $(IE)_2$

9. Select the element with highest first ionisation energy
(a) Cs (b) Cl
(c) I (d) Li

10. The factors that influence the ionisation energies are
(a) the size of the atom
(b) the charge on the nucleus
(c) how effectively the inner electron shell screen the nuclear charge
(d) all of the above

11. Select the match that represents alkali metals based on $(IE)_1$ and $(IE)_2$ values.

		$(IE)_1$	$(IE)_2$
(a)	X	100	110
(b)	Y	95	120
(c)	Z	195	500
(d)	M	200	250

12. The correct order of non-metallic character of given elements are
B, C, Si, N, F
(a) F > N > C > B > Si
(b) F > N > C > Si > B
(c) Si > C > N > B > F
(d) B > C > N > F > Si

13. The second ionisation energy is always higher than the first ionisation energy because the
(a) ion becomes more stable attaining an octet or duplet configurations
(b) electron is more tightly bound to the nucleus in an ion
(c) electron is attracted more by the core electrons
(d) second electron is easier to remove due to less shielding.

14. Select the oxide that is basic in nature.
(a) SO_2 (b) CaO
(c) SiO_2 (d) Al_2O_3

15. For the process
$X(g) + e^- \longrightarrow X^-(g)$, $\Delta H = x$
and $X^-(g) \longrightarrow X(g) + e^-$, $\Delta H = y$
Select correct alternate
(a) Ionisation energy of $X^-(g)$ is y
(b) Electron affinity of $X(g)$ is x
(c) Electron affinity of $X(g)$ is $-y$
(d) All the above are correct statements

16. Ionisation energy of the element $X(g)$ is I and the electron affinity of $X^+(g)$ is E then
(a) $I = E$ (b) $I = -E$
(c) $I = \frac{E}{2}$ (d) $I = -\frac{E}{2}$

17. EN of the element (A) is E_1 and IP is E_2. Hence, EA will be
(a) $2E_1 - E_2$
(b) $E_1 - E_2$
(c) $E_1 - 2E_2$
(d) $(E_1 + E_2)/2$

18. The correct decreasing order of the basic nature of the given oxides is
(a) $K_2O > Na_2O > MgO > Al_2O_3$
(b) $Na_2O > Al_2O_3 > K_2O > MgO$
(c) $Al_2O_3 > MgO > K_2O > Na_2O$
(d) $MgO > Al_2O_3 > Na_2O > K_2O$

19. The electron gain enthalpy (in kJ/mol) of Tellurium, selenium, polonium and sulphur respectively, are
(a) –195, –186, –174 and –270
(b) –190, –186, –270 and –200
(c) –190, –195, –174 and –200
(d) –195, –190, –174 and –200

20. Select the correct statement from the following.
(a) Across a transition series, there is only a small decrease in atomic radius from one element to another due to very small increase in effective nuclear charge.
(b) The rate of decrease in the size across the lanthanide series is less than the across the first transition series.
(c) Both (a) & (b) are correct statements.
(d) Electron affinity of F is greater than Cl.

Type II 》 MCQs with One or More than One Correct Option

21. The order Al ≤ Ga is true for
(a) ionisation energy
(b) atomic radius
(c) electronegativity
(d) electron affinity

22. Select the correct statements from the following.
(a) Ionic radii of N^{3-} is greater than O^{2-}.
(b) Increasing order of ionic radii is $F^- < O^{2-} < N^{3-} < S^{2-}$
(c) Due to lower effective nuclear charge, ionic radius of Na^+ is higher than that of Mg^{2+}.
(d) K^+ has higher atomic size than K.

23. The size of hydride ion is less than or equal to
(a) Br^-
(b) Cl^-
(c) F^-
(d) O^{2-}

24. The incorrect statement/s among the following is/are
(a) The aqueous solution of LiCl will be more conducting than that of NaCl.
(b) The extent of hydration varies $Na^+ < Mg^{2+} < Al^{3+}$.
(c) Nitrogen has a zero electron gain enthalpy value.
(d) The ionisation energy order is C > Si > Ge > Pb > Sn.

25. Choose the oxides that show acidic nature in their aqueous solution.
(a) NO_2
(b) SiO_2
(c) CO_2
(d) SnO_2

26. The neutral oxides among the following is/are
(a) NO
(b) N_2O
(c) CO
(d) N_2O_3

27. On moving down the group in nitrogen family
(a) Ionisation energy decreases regularly.
(b) Atomic radius increases regularly.
(c) Electron affinity decreases.
(d) Metallic character decreases.

Type III 》 Numerical/Integer Answer Type Questions

28. Given below are oxides
SnO_2, Na_2O, As_2O_3, N_2O, NO and Cl_2O_7
The total number of amphoteric oxides is

29. The first ionisation potential of Na is 5.1 eV. The value of electron gain enthalpy of Na^+ will be $-x$. The value of x is ....

30. $X(g) \longrightarrow X^-(g) + e^-, \Delta H = +720 \text{ kJ mol}^{-1}$
The amount of energy required to convert 120 mg of 'X' atom in gaseous state into X^+ ion.
(Atomic weight, for $X = 7$ g mol)

31. Total number of acidic oxides among N_2O_3, NO_2, N_2O, Cl_2O_7, SO_2, CO, CaO, Na_2O and NO is ....

Elemental Practice 1.2 | Chapter 01

Connect with **Answers**

1. (c)	2. (a)	3. (a)	4. (d)	5. (a)	6. (a)
7. (b)	8. (d)	9. (b)	10. (d)	11. (c)	12. (a)
13. (b)	14. (b)	15. (d)	16. (b)	17. (a)	18. (a)
19. (c)	20. (c)	21. (a,c)	22. (a,b,c)	23. (a,b,d)	24. (a,c)
25. (a,b,c,d)	26. (a,b,c)	27. (a,b)	28. (2)	29. (5.1)	30. (12.24)
31. (4)					

Advanced Exclusive Different Strokes

Determination of Period and Group of an Element

- The **period number** can be predicted from the principal quantum number (n) of the valence shell.
  e.g. Electronic configuration of chlorine is $1s^2 2s^2 2p^6 3s^2 3p^5$. Therefore, the period number is 3 as the valence shell configuration is $3s^2 3p^5$.
- The **block number** can be predicted from the orbital which receives the last electron.
  e.g. An element having electronic configuration '$1s^2 2s^2 2p^6 3s^2 3p^6 3d^{10} 4s^2 4p^5$' is a p-block element as its last electron enters in the p-orbital.
- **Group number** can be predicted from the number of electrons in the valence shell and penultimate shell as follows.
  (i) s-block : The group number is equal to number of valence electron.
  (ii) p-block : The group number is equal to the 10 + number of valence shell electrons.
  (iii) d-block : Group number is equal to the number of electrons in the $(n-1)\,d$ subshell + number of electrons in the ns subshell.
  (iv) f-block : The group number is always 3.

Thus, with the help of above key points, one can easily solve the problems related to placing of elements in periodic table.

PRACTICE
ELEMENT 01

Target JEE Main

Objective Type Questions

1. The elements belonging to the same group of the Periodic Table will have
(a) the same number of protons
(b) the same number of electrons in the valence-shell
(c) the same number of neutrons
(d) the same number of isotopes

2. If Aufbau rule is not followed, K-19 will be placed in .... block.
(a) *s* (b) *p* (c) *d* (d) *f*

3. Representative elements belong to
(a) *s*-and *p*-block (b) *d*-block
(c) *d*- and *f*-block (d) *f*-block

4. Select the correct order of size of O^-, O^{2-}, F^- and F.
(a) $O^{2-} > O^- > F^- > F$ (b) $O^- > O^{2-} > F^- > F$
(c) $O^{2-} > F^- > F > O^-$ (d) $O^{2-} > F^- > O^- > F$

5. The sizes of the second and third row of transition elements being almost the same. This is due to
(a) *d*-and *f*-orbitals do not shield the nuclear charge very effectively
(b) lanthanide contraction
(c) both (a) and (b)
(d) Actinide contraction

6. Valence electrons in the element *A* are 3 and that in element *B* are 6. Most probable compound formed from *A* and *B* is
(a) A_2B (b) AB_2 (c) A_6B_3 (d) A_2B_3

7. Choose the element/ion that has the electronic configuration [Ar] $3d^5$.
(a) Cr (b) Fe^{3+} (c) Mn (d) V

8. Fluorine does not form any polyhalide as other halogens because
(a) it has maximum ionic character
(b) it has low F—F bond energy (38.5 kcal mol^{-1})
(c) of the absence of *d*-orbitals in the valence shell of fluorine
(d) it brings about maximum coordination number in other elements

9. Select the incorrect statement from the following.
(a) Due to lanthanide contraction Zr and Hf have almost equal size.
(b) Due to completion of 3*d*-subshell, the electronic charge density in this subshell becomes very high which increases the inter-electronic repulsion hence, size increases.
(c) Element with electronic configuration $(n-1)\,d^5\,ns^1$ belongs to group 7 and *s*-block
(d) S has more negative electron gain enthalpy than O.

10. Recently discovered element with atomic number 115 is
(a) Uun (b) Uub
(c) Uup (d) Uus

11. Select from the following triads that have approximately equal size
(a) Na^+, Mg^{2+}, Al^{3+} (b) F^-, Ne, O^{2-}
(c) Fe, Co, Ni (d) Mn^+, Fe^{2+}, Cr

12. Choose the correct order of ionic radii.
(a) $Mn^{+4} < Mn^{+2}$ (b) $O^- < O^+$
(c) $N^{-3} < Na^+$ (d) $P^{3+} > P^{5+}$

13. Choose the ions that has the smallest radius.
(a) Mn^{+2} (b) Mn^{+3} (c) Mn^{+5} (d) Mn^{+7}

14. When the following five anions are arranged in order of decreasing ionic radius, the correct sequence is
(a) $Se^{2-}, I^-, Br^-, O^{2-}, F^-$ (b) $I^-, Se^{2-}, O^{2-}, Br^-, F^-$
(c) $Se^{2-}, I^-, Br^-, F^-, O^{2-}$ (d) $I^-, Se^{2-}, Br^-, O^{2-}, F^-$

15. First, second and third IP values are 100 eV, 150 eV and 1500 eV. Element can be
(a) Be (b) B (c) F (d) Na

16. Which has maximum ionisation potential?
(a) N (b) O (c) O^+ (d) Na

17. Stability of ions of Ge, Sn and Pb will be in the order
(a) $Ge^{2+} > Sn^{2+} > Pb^{2+}$ (b) $Ge^{4+} > Sn^{4+} > Pb^{4+}$
(c) $Sn^{4+} > Sn^{2+}$ (d) $Pb^{4+} > Pb^{2+}$

18. (*A*), (*B*), (*C*) are elements in the third short period. Oxide of (*A*) is ionic, that of (*B*) is amphoteric and of (*C*) a giant molecule. (*A*), (*B*) and (*C*) will have atomic number in the order
(a) (*A*) < (*B*) < (*C*) (b) (*C*) < (*B*) < (*A*)
(c) (*A*) < (*C*) < (*B*) (d) (*B*) < (*A*) < (*C*)

19. Going down in a group from F to I, which of the following properties increases?
(a) Ionic radius (b) Ionisation energy
(c) Oxidising power (d) Electronegativity

20. Which of the following will have maximum electron affinity?
(a) $1s^2 2s^2 2p^5$ (b) $1s^2 2s^2 2p^6$
(c) $1s^2 2s^2 2p^6 3s^2 3p^5$ (d) $1s^2 2s^2 2p^6 3s^2 3p^6$

21. Size of cation is smaller than that of the atom because of
(a) outer electrons is removed
(b) effective nuclear charge increases
(c) due to gain of electrons
(d) effective nuclear charge decreases

22. The first ionisation potential (in eV) of N, O atoms are
(a) 14.6, 13.6 (b) 13.6, 14.6 (c) 13.6, 13.6 (d) 14.6, 14.6

23. Which of the following is the correct order of electronegativity of C. N, P and Si?
(a) P < Si < C < N (b) Si < P < N < C
(c) Si < P < C < N (d) P < Si < N < C

24. The correct order of electron affinity of N, O, S and Cl is
(a) N < O < S < Cl (b) O < N < Cl < S
(c) O ≈ Cl < N ≈ S (d) O < S < Cl < N

25. Electron affinity is positive when
(a) O^- is formed from O
(b) O^{2-} is formed from O^-
(c) O^+ is formed from O
(d) electron affinity is always a negative value

Numerical Type Questions

26. The number of oxides that will react with aq. HCl solution among the following are :
P_4H_{10}, CaO, ZnO, SiO_2, CO_2, BeO, SO_2, Al_2O_3, SrO, SO_3, N_2O_5 and CdO.

27. Calculate the effective nuclear charge for a 3*d* electron of nickel atom. (Nearest integer)

28. Calculate the difference in the number of protons of the largest element of the fourth period and the smallest element of the third period.

29. If the number of elements in 3rd period is *x*, then the value of $\frac{(x+8)}{2}$ is

30. The number of elements having ionisation energy less than Hg among the following are :
Zn, He, Cs, Fe, Ir, Ar, Tl, N, Cr, Os, O, Pd and Cl.

31. From the data given, calculate the energy in the formation of $BeCl_2$ (it is a stable molecule).
$I.E._1$ for Be = 899 kJ/mol
$I.E._2$ for Be = 1757 kJ/mol
EA. for Cl = −348 kJ/mol

32. The first four ionisation energy values of an element are 120, 240, 520 and 6420 kcal. The number of valence electrons in the element is ....

33. The number of elements among the following having an electronegativity values less than that of hydrogen are :
Li, B, C, N, O, Si, S, Be, Zn and Fe.

34. How many of the following elements have a negative value of first electron gain enthalpy?
N, P, O, Be, Mg, Ca, Li, Na and H.

Check Through PYQs

Element 1 Historical Development, Classification of Elements Modern Periodic Table

1. Given below are two statements :
Statement I According to the law of octaves, the elements were arranged in the increasing order of their atomic number.
Statement II Meyer observed a periodically repeated pattern upon plotting physical properties of certain elements against their respective atomic number.
In the light of the above statements, choose the correct answer from the options given below. *2025, 28 Jan Shift-II*
(a) Statement I is true but Statement II is false.
(b) Both Statement I and Statement II are true.
(c) Statement I is false but Statement II is true.
(d) Both Statement I and Statement II are false.

2. If IUPAC name of an element is "Unununium" then the element belongs to *n*th group of periodic table. The value of *n* is .... *2024, 30 Jan Shift-I*

3. Total number of ions from the following with noble gas configuration is ....
$Sr^{2+}(Z=38)$, $Cs^+(Z=55)$, $La^{2+}(Z=57)$, $Pb^{2+}(Z=82)$, $Yb^{2+}(Z=70)$ and $Fe^{2+}(Z=26)$ *2024, 27 Jan Shift-II*

4. Given below are two statements: *2024, 27 Jan Shift-I*
Statement I The 4*f* and 5*f*-series of elements are placed separately in the periodic table to preserve the principle of classification.
Statement II *s*-block elements can be found in pure form in nature.
In the light of the above statements, choose the **most appropriate** answer from the options given below
(a) Statement I is true but Statement II is false.
(b) Both Statement I and Statement II are false.
(c) Both Statement I and Statement II are true.
(d) Statement I is false but Statement II is true.

5. Henry Moseley studied characteristic X-ray spectra of elements. The graph which represents his observation correctly is
Given v = frequency of X-ray emitted
Z = atomic number *2023, 8 April Shift-II*

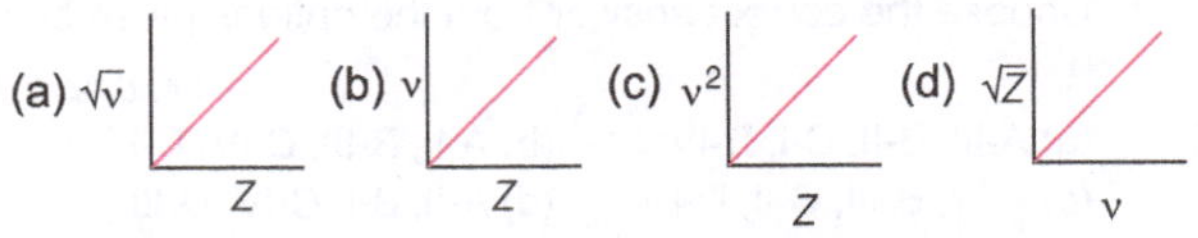

6. The metal that has very low melting point and its periodic position is closer to a metalloid is *2022, 26 July Shift-II*
(a) Al (b) Ga (c) Se (d) In

7. The IUPAC nomenclature of an element with electronic configuration $[Rn]\,5f^{14}6d^{1}7s^{2}$ is *2022, 25 July Shift-I*
(a) unnilbium (b) unnilunium (c) unnilquadium (d) unniltrium

8. Element "E" belongs to the period 4 and group 16 of the periodic table. The valence shell electronic configuration of the element, which is just above "E" in the group is *2022, 28 June Shift-I*
(a) $3s^2, 3p^4$ (b) $3d^{10}, 4s^2, 4p^4$
(c) $4d^{10}, 5s^2, 5p^4$ (d) $2s^2, 2p^4$

9. The set of elements that differ in mutual relationship from those of the other sets is *2021, 17 March Shift-II*
(a) Li-Mg (b) B-Si (c) Be-Al (d) Li-Na

Element 2 Periodic Properties

10. **Statement I** Correct order of ionic radius for Mg^{2+}, Na^+, O^{2-} and F^- is $F^- > O^{2-} > Na^+ > Mg^{2+}$.
Statement II Correct order of electron gain enthalpy for 17th group elements follows order Cl > F > Br > I (Magnitude only). *2025, 29 Jan Shift-I*
(a) Statement I and Statement II are correct.
(b) Statement I is correct Statement II is incorrect.
(c) Statement I and Statement II are incorrect.
(d) Statement I is incorrect and Statement II is correct.

11. Match the column and choose the correct option. *2025, 22 Jan Shift-I*

Column-I (Properties)		Column-II (Order)
A. Electronegativity	I.	B < C < N < O
B. Cationic size	II.	$Li^+ > Mg^{2+} > Be^{2+}$
C. Metallic character	III.	K > Mg > Al
D. Electron affinity	IV.	Cl > F > Br > I

(a) A-I, B-II, C-III, D-IV (b) A-IV, B-III, C-II, D-I
(c) A-II, B-III, C-IV, D-I (d) A-III, B-II, C-IV, D-I

12. Match List-I with List-II.

List-I (Elements)		List-II (Properties in their respective groups)
A. Cl, S	I.	Elements with highest electronegativity
B. Ge, As	II.	Elements with largest atomic size
C. Fr, Ra	III.	Elements which show properties of both metals and non-metal
D. F, O	IV.	Elements with highest negative electron gain enthalpy

Choose the correct answer from the options given below. *2024, 8 April Shift-I*
(a) A-III, B-II, C-I, D-IV (b) A-II, B-III, C-IV, D-I
(c) A-IV, B-III, C-II, D-I (d) A-II, B-I, C-IV, D-III

13. The correct order of first ionisation enthalpy values of the following elements is *2024, 4 April Shift-I*
A. O B. N
C. Be D. F E. B
Choose the correct answer from the options given below :
(a) A < B < D < C < E (b) B < D < C < E < A
(c) C < E < A < B < D (d) E < C < A < B < D

14. Consider the following elements. *2024, 31 Jan Shift-II*

Group ↓ A′B′ ⟶ Period
C′D′

Which of the following is are true about A', B', C' and D'?
A. Order of atomic radii : $B' < A' < D' < C'$
B. Order of metallic character : $B' < A' < D' < C'$
C. Size of the element : $D' < C' < B' < A'$
D. Order of ionic radii : $B'^{+} < A'^{+} < D'^{+} < C'^{+}$
Choose the correct answer from the options given below :
(a) B, C and D (b) A only (c) A, B and D (d) A and B

15. The element having the highest first ionisation enthalpy is *2024, 29 Jan Shift-II*
(a) Al (b) N
(c) Si (d) C

16. The total number of isoelectronic species from the given set is .... *2023, 15 April Shift-I*
O^{2-}, F^-, Al, Mg^{2+}, Na^+, O^+, Mg, Al^{3+}, F

17. For elements B, C, N, Li, Be, O and F, the correct order of first ionisation enthalpy is *2023, 11 April Shift-I*
(a) B > Li > Be > C > N > O > F
(b) Li < B < Be < C < O < N < F
(c) Li < Be < B < C < O < N < F
(d) Li < Be < B < C < N < O < F

18. The correct order of metallic character is *2023, 10 April Shift-II*
(a) K > Be > Ca (b) K > Ca > Be
(c) Be > Ca > K (d) Ca > K > Be

19. The correct order of electronegativity for given elements is *2023, 8 April Shift-I*
(a) P > Br > C > At (b) C > P > At > Br
(c) Br > P > At > C (d) Br > C > At > P

20. The correct order of hydration enthalpies is
(A) K^+ (B) Rb^+ (C) Mg^{2+} (D) Cs^+ (E) Ca^{2+}
Choose the correct answer from the options given below. *2023, 29 Jan Shift-I*
(a) C > E > A > B > D (b) C > A > E > B > D
(c) E > C > A > B > D (d) C > E > A > D > B

21. In which of the following pairs, electron gain enthalpies of constituent elements are nearly the same or identical?
(A) Rb and Cs (B) Na and K (C) Ar and Kr (D) I and At
Choose the correct answer from the options given below : *2022, 28 July Shift-I*
(a) (A) and (B) (b) (B) and (C)
(c) (A) and (C) (d) (C) and (D)

22. The first ionisation enthalpies of Be, B, N and O follow the order *2022, 25 July Shift-II*
(a) O < N < B < Be (b) Be < B < N < O
(c) B < Be < N < O (d) B < Be < O < N

23. The total number of acidic oxides from the following list is
NO, N_2O, B_2O_3, N_2O_5, CO, SO_3, P_4O_{10} *2022, 25 July Shift-II*
(a) 3 (b) 4
(c) 5 (d) 6

24. Given below are two statements. One is labelled as Assertion A and the other is labelled as Reason R.
Assertion (A) The first ionisation enthalpy for oxygen is lower than that of nitrogen.
Reason (R) The four electrons in 2*p*-orbitals of oxygen experience more electron-electron repulsion.
In the light of the above statements, choose the correct answer from the options given below. *2022, 29 June Shift-II*
(a) Both A and R are correct and R is the correct explanation of A.
(b) Both A and R are correct but R is not the correct explanation of A.
(c) A is correct but R is not correct.
(d) A is not correct but R is correct.

25. Match List-I with List-II.

List-I (Oxide)		List-II (Nature)
A. Cl_2O_7	(I)	Amphoteric
B. Na_2O	(II)	Basic
C. Al_2O_3	(III)	Neutral
D. N_2O	(IV)	Acidic

Choose the correct answer from the option given below *2022, 28 June Shift-II*
(a) (A)–(IV), (B)–(III), (C)–(I), (D)–(II)
(b) (A)–(IV), (B)–(II), (C)–(I), (D)–(III)
(c) (A)–(II), (B)–(IV), (C)–(III), (D)–(I)
(d) (A)–(I), (B)–(II), (C)–(III), (D)–(IV)

26. The pair, in which ions are isoelectronic with Al^{3+} is *2022, 25 June Shift-I*
(a) Br^- and Be^{2+} (b) Cl^- and Li^+
(c) S^{2-} and K^+ (d) O^{2-} and Mg^{2+}

27. Metals generally melt at very high temperature. Amongst the following, the metal with the highest melting point will be *2022, 24 June Shift-II*
(a) Hg (b) Ag (c) Ga (d) Cs

28. Match list-I with list-II.

List-I		List-II
(A) NaOH	(i)	Acidic
(B) $Be(OH)_2$	(ii)	Basic
(C) $Ca(OH)_2$	(iii)	Amphoteric
(D) $B(OH)_3$		
(E) $Al(OH)_3$		

Choose the most appropriate answer from the options given below. *2021, 27 July Shift-I*
(a) (A)-(ii), (B)-(ii), (C)-(iii), (D)-(i), (E)-(iii)
(b) (A)-(ii), (B)-(iii), (C)-(ii), (D)-(i), (E)-(iii)
(c) (A)-(ii), (B)-(ii), (C)-(iii), (D)-(ii), (E)-(iii)
(d) (A)-(ii), (B)-(i), (C)-(ii), (D)-(iii), (E)-(iii)

29. The ionic radii of F^- and O^{2-} respectively are 1.33 Å and 1.4 Å while the covalent radius of N is 0.74Å. The correct statement for the ionic radius of N^{3-} from the following is *2021, 25 July Shift-II*
(a) it is smaller than F^- and N
(b) it is bigger than O^{2-} and F^-
(c) it is bigger than F^- and N, but smaller than of O^{2-}
(d) it is smaller than O^{2-} and F^-, but bigger than of N

30. The set in which compounds have different nature is *2021, 20 July Shift-I*
(a) $Be(OH)_2$ and $Al(OH)_3$ (b) $B(OH)_3$ and $Al(OH)_3$
(c) $B(OH)_3$ and H_3PO_3 (d) NaOH and $Ca(OH)_2$

31. The first ionisation energy of magnesium is smaller as compared to that of elements *X* and *Y*, but higher than that of *Z*. The elements *X*, *Y* and *Z*, respectively, are
(a) chlorine, lithium and sodium *2021, 18 March Shift-II*
(b) argon, lithium and sodium
(c) argon, chlorine and sodium (d) neon, sodium and chlorine

32. Identify the elements *X* and *Y* using the ionisation energy values given below. *2021, 16 March Shift-II*

	Ionisation energy (Ist)	kJ/mol (IInd)
X	495	4563
Y	731	1450

(a) X = Na, Y = Mg (b) X = Mg, Y = F
(c) X = Mg, Y = Na (d) X = F, Y = Mg

33. Match List-I with List-II.

List-I (Electronic configuration of elements)		List-II ($\Delta_i H$ in kJ mol^{-1})
A. $1s^2 2s^2$	(i)	801
B. $1s^2 2s^2 2p^4$	(ii)	899
C. $1s^2 2s^2 2p^3$	(iii)	1314
D. $1s^2 2s^2 2p^1$	(iv)	1402

Choose the most appropriate answer from the options given below. *2021, 26 Feb Shift-I*

	A	B	C	D		A	B	C	D
(a)	(ii)	(iii)	(iv)	(i)	(b)	(i)	(iv)	(iii)	(ii)
(c)	(i)	(iii)	(iv)	(ii)	(d)	(iv)	(i)	(ii)	(iii)

34. The process that is not endothermic in nature is *2020, 4 Sep Shift-II*
(a) $O^-(g) + e^- \longrightarrow O^{2-}(g)$ (b) $Na(g) \longrightarrow Na^+(g) + e^-$
(c) $H(g) + e^- \longrightarrow H^-(g)$ (d) $Ar(g) + e^- \longrightarrow Ar^-(g)$

35. Among the statements (I-IV), *2020, 3 Sept Shift-II*
(I) Be has smaller atomic radius compared to Mg.
(II) Be has higher ionisation enthalpy than Al.
(III) Charge/radius ratio of Be is greater than that of Al.
(IV) Both Be and Al form mainly covalent compounds.
Choose the option containing correct statement.
(a) (I), (II) and (IV) (b) (I), (III) and (IV)
(c) (II), (III) and (IV) (d) (I), (II) and (III)

36. Three elements *X*, *Y* and *Z* are in the 3rd period of the periodic table. The oxides of *X*, *Y* and *Z*, respectively, are basic, amphoteric and acidic. The correct order of the atomic number of *X*, *Y* and *Z* is *2020, 2 Sep Shift-II*
(a) $Z < Y < X$ (b) $X < Y < Z$ (c) $X < Z < Y$ (d) $Y < X < Z$

37. The electron gain enthalpy (in kJ/mol) of fluorine, chlorine, bromine and iodine, respectively, are *2020, 7 Jan Shift-I*
(a) –333, –325, –349 and –296
(b) –296, –325, –333 and –349
(c) –333, –349, –325 and –296
(d) –349, –333, –325 and –296

PRACTICE ELEMENT 02

Target JEE Advanced

Single Correct Choice MCQs

1. The statement that is not correct for the periodic classification of elements is
   (a) the properties of elements are the periodic functions of their atomic numbers
   (b) non-metallic elements are lesser in number than metallic elements
   (c) the first ionisation energies of elements along a period do not vary in a regular manner with increase in atomic number
   (d) for transition elements the *d*-subshells are filled with electrons monotonically with increase in atomic number

2. The statement is not true for the long form of the Periodic Table
   (a) It reflects the sequence of filling the electrons in the order of the sub-energy shells *s, p, d* and *f*
   (b) It helps to predict the stable valency states of the elements
   (c) It reflects trends in physical and chemical properties of the elements
   (d) It helps to predict the relative ionicity of the bond between any two elements

3. Select the incorrect statement from the following.
   (a) Elements of IB and IIB groups are transition elements
   (b) Elements of VB group do not contain metalloids
   (c) Elements of IA and IIA groups are normal elements
   (d) Elements of IVB group are neither strongly electronegative nor strongly electropositive.

4. Match list-I (atomic number of elements) with list-II (position of elements in Periodic Table) and select the correct answer using the codes given below the lists

List-I (Oxide)		List-II (Nature)	
A.	19	1.	*p*-block
B.	22	2.	*f-block*
C.	32	3.	*d*-block
D.	64	4.	*s*-block

Codes

	A	B	C	D		A	B	C	D
(a)	1	2	3	4	(b)	4	3	1	2
(c)	4	1	3	2	(d)	2	1	3	4

5. $M(g) \longrightarrow M^+(g) + e^-, \Delta H = 100$ eV
   $M(g) \longrightarrow M^{2+}(g) + 2e^-, \Delta H = 250$ eV
   which is incorrect statement?
   (a) I_1 of $M(g)$ is 100 eV (b) I_1 of $M^+(g)$ is 150 eV
   (c) I_2 of $M(g)$ is 250 eV (d) I_2 of $M(g)$ is 150 eV

6. AB is predominantly ionic as A^+B^- if
   (a) $(IP)_A < (IP)_B$ (b) $(EA)_A < (EA)_B$
   (c) $(EN)_A < (EN)_B$ (d) $(IP)_B < (IP)_A$
   (IP stands for ionisation potential, EA for electron affinity and EN for electronegativity).

7. Following graph shows variation of ionisation potential (IP) with atomic number in second period (Li—Ne). Value of ionisation potential (IP) of Na (11) will be

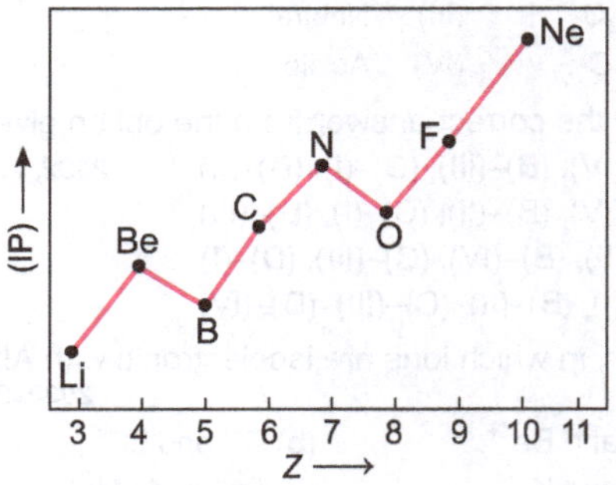

   (a) above Ne (b) below Ne but above O
   (c) below Li (d) between N and O

8. Select the incorrect statements from the following.
   (a) Boron has the smallest atomic volume.
   (b) The correct order of atomic radii is W < C < P < Si.
   (c) Electron gain enthalpy is the property of a bonded atom.
   (d) The correct order for non-metallic character is F > N > C > B > Si.

9. $N_0/2$ atoms of $X(g)$ are converted into $X^+(g)$ by energy E_1. $N_0/2$ atoms of $X(g)$ are converted into $X^-(g)$ by energy E_2. Hence, ionisation potential and electron affinity of $X(g)$ are
   (a) $\dfrac{2E_1}{N_0}, \dfrac{2(E_1 - E_2)}{N_0}$ (b) $\dfrac{2E_1}{N_0}, \dfrac{2E_2}{N_0}$
   (c) $\dfrac{(E_1 - E_2)}{N_0}, \dfrac{2E_2}{N_0}$ (d) $\dfrac{E_1}{N_0}, \dfrac{E_1}{N_0}$

One or More than One Correct MCQs

10. Stability of ions of Ge, Sn and Pb will be in order
    (a) $Ge^{2+} < Sn^{2+} < Pb^{2+}$
    (b) $Pb^{4+} < Sn^{4+} < Ge^{4+}$
    (c) $Sn^{2+} < Sn^{4+}$
    (d) $Pb^{4+} < Pb^{2+}$

11. The first element of a group in many ways differs from the other heavier members of the group. This is due to
(a) the smaller size
(b) the high electronegativity and high ionisation potential
(c) the unavailability of *d*-orbitals
(d) the higher shielding effect

12. The factors that influence the ionisation energies are
(a) the size of the atom
(b) the charge on the nucleus
(c) how effectively the inner electrons screen the nuclear charge
(d) the atomic mass

13. An increase in both atomic and ionic radii with atomic number occurs in any group of the Periodic Table and in accordance with this the ionic radii of Ti(IV) and Zr(IV) ions are 0.68 Å and 0.74 Å respectively; but for Hf(IV) ion the ionic radius is 0.75 Å which is almost the same as that for Zr(IV) ion. The incorrect reason for the statement is/are.
(a) greater degree of covalency in compound of Hf^{4+}
(b) lanthanide contraction
(c) difference in the coordination number of Zr^{4+} and Hf^{4+} in their compounds
(d) actinide contraction

14. The melting point of RbBr is 682°C while that of NaF is 988°C. The incorrect reason that the melting point of NaF is much higher than that of RbBr is that
(a) the molar mass of NaF is smaller than that of RbBr
(b) the bond in RbBr has more covalent character than the bond in NaF
(c) the difference in electronegativity between Rb and Br is smaller than the difference between Na and F.
(d) the internuclear distance, $r_c + r_a$ is greater for RbBr than for NaF

15. Select incorrect statement(s).
(a) Cs^+ is more highly hydrated than the other alkali metal ions
(b) Among the alkali metals Li, Na, K and Rb, lithium has the highest melting point
(c) Ionic mobility of Li^+ is maximum among Li^+, Na^+ and K^+ ions
(d) Ionisation potential of Li is smaller than that of Na

16. Choose the correct statements from the following.
(a) Ce, Pr and Nd are *f*-block elements
(b) Cu, Pd and Ni are *d*-block elements
(c) Cu($[Ar]3d^{10}4s^1$) and K($[Ar]4s^1$) have been placed in *s*-block
(d) Si, Ge and As are metalloids

17. In which of the following arrangements is/are the order correct according to the property indicated against it?
(a) Increasing size : $Al^{3+} < Mg^{2+} < Na^+ < F^-$
(b) Increasing $I.E._1$: B < C < O < N
(c) Increasing $E.A._1$: I < Br < F < Cl
(d) Increasing metallic radius : Li < Na < K < Rb

18. Select the incorrect ionisation energy order :
(a) Li < B < Be < C < N < O < F
(b) Na < Mg < Al < Si < S < P < Cl
(c) K < Ga < Ca < Ge < As < Se < Br
(d) Rb < Sr < In < Sn < Sb < Te < I

19. Select the incorrect statements from the following.
(a) *d*-orbital can accomodate $6e^-$
(b) $Na \xrightarrow{I.E._1} Na^+ \xrightarrow{I.E._2} Na^{2+} \xrightarrow{I.E._3} Na^{+3}$; the correct order of ionisation energy is $I.E._2 > I.E._3 > I.E._1$
(c) Xe is a noble gas
(d) B is a non-metal

20. The correct statement(s) among the following is/are :
(a) The first ionisation potential of Al is less than the first ionisation potential of Mg
(b) The second ionisation potential of Mg is greater than the second ionisation potential of Na
(c) The first ionisation potential of Na is less than the first ionization potential of Mg
(d) The third ionisation potential of Mg is greater than the third ionisation potential of Al

Numerical/Integer Type Questions

21. $x \times 10^y$ number of chlorine atoms that can be ionised in the process $Cl \longrightarrow Cl^+ + e^-Cl$, by the energy liberated for the process $Cl + e^- \longrightarrow Cl^-$ for one Avogadro number of atoms is [IE = 13.0 eV, $\Delta H = 3.60$ eV]. The value of $x + y$ will be ....

22. The amount of energy when million atoms of iodine are completely converted into I^- ions in the vapour state according to the equation
$I(g) + e^- \longrightarrow I^-(g)$ is 4.9×10^{-13} J. The electron gain enthalpy of iodine (in eV per atom) is ....

23. The Ist IE of Li is 5.4 eV and the electron gain enthalpy of Cl is 3.6 eV. If the following reaction,
$$Li(g) + Cl(g) \longrightarrow Li^+ + Cl^-,$$
is carried out at such a low pressure that resulting ions do not combine with each other, the ΔH of the reaction (in kcal mol^{-1}) is .... kcal mol^{-1}.

24. The effective nuclear charge for 4*s* electrons of Zn will be ....

25. The ionisation energy of Li is 520 kJ mol^{-1}. The amount of energy required to convert 140 mg of Li atoms into gaseous Li^+ ion, is .... kJ.

26. The electron gain enthalpy of chlorine is 3.7 eV. How much energy in kJ is released when 1 g of chlorine is converted completely to $Cl^{\ominus}$ ion in the gaseous state ....

27. The ionisation potential of hydrogen is 13.60 eV. If *x* kJ energy required to produce one mole of H^+ ion. Then the value of *x* ....

28. Total number of elements which are belong to same period (II). Li, Na, Mg, F, Ne, Sc, P, Ar

Matching Type Questions

29. Match atomic number of elements (in List-I) with position of elements in the Periodic Table (in List-II).

	List-I		List-II
A.	11	1.	*p*-block
B.	24	2.	*f*-block
C.	15	3.	*d*-block
D.	59	4.	*s*-block

Choose the correct answer from the options given below.
(a) A-4, B-3, C-1, D-2 (b) A-1, B-2, C-3, D-4
(c) A-3, B-4, C-2, D-1 (d) A-2, B-3, C-1, D-4

30. Match the type of elements (in List-I) with the corresponding electronic configuration (in List-II).

	List-I		List-II
A.	Inert gas elements	1.	ns^1 to ns^2np^5
B.	Main group elements	2.	$1s^2$ to ns^2np^6
C.	Transition elements	3.	$(n-2)f^{1-14}$ $(n-1)d^{-1}ns^2$
D.	Inner transition elements	4.	$(n-1)d^{1-10}ns^{1-2}$

Choose the correct answer from the options given below.
(a) A-1, B-2, C-3, D-4 (b) A-2, B-1, C-4, D-3
(c) A-4, B-2, C-3, D-1 (d) A-3, B-4, C-2, D-1

31. Electronic configuration of some elements is given in Column-I and their electron gain enthalpies are given in Column-II. Match the electronic configuration with electron gain enthalpy.

	Column-I (Electronic configuration)		Column-II (Electron gain enthalpy/kJ mol^{-1})
A.	$1s^22s^22p^6$	1.	–53
B.	$1s^22s^22p^63s^1$	2.	–328
C.	$1s^22s^22p^5$	3.	–141
D.	$1s^22s^22p^4$	4.	+48

Choose the correct answer from the options given below.
(a) A-3, B-1, C-2, D-4 (b) A-2, B-3, C-4, D-1
(c) A-4, B-1, C-2, D-3 (d) A-1, B-2, C-3, D-4

32. Match the atomic number (in List-I) with its IUPAC nomenclature (in List-II).

	List-I		List-II
A.	105	1.	Uuh
B.	107	2.	Uun
C.	109	3.	Uns
D.	110	4.	Unp
E.	116	5.	Une

Choose the correct answer from the options given below.
(a) A-1, B-4, C-2, D-5, E-3 (b) A-3, B-5, C-2, D-1, E-4
(c) A-1, B-2, C-3, D-4, E-5 (d) A-4, B-3, C-5, D-2, E-1

33. Match the elements given i in Column-I with their characteristics in Column-II.

Column-I		Column-II	
(A)	F	1.	Highest negative electron gain enthalpy
(B)	He	2.	Largest size
(C)	Cl	3.	Highest ionization energy
(D)	Cs	4.	Highest electronegativity

Choose the correct answer from the options given below.
(a) A-4, B-3, C-1, D-2 (b) A-1, B-2, C-3, D-4
(c) A-2, B-3, C-1, D-4 (d) A-2, B-4, C-3, D-1

34. Match the oxides given i in Column-I with their characteristics in Column-II.

Column-I		Column-II	
(A)	ZnO	1.	Acidic oxide
(B)	Na_2O	2.	Neutral oxide
(C)	N_2O	3.	Basic oxide
(D)	Cl_2O_7	4.	Amphoteric oxide

Choose the correct answer from the options given below.
(a) A-1, B-2, C-3, D-4 (b) A-4, B-3, C-2, D-1
(c) A-3, B-1, C-2, D-4 (d) A-2, B-3, C-1, D-1

35. Match the variation of properties given in Column-I with the order of elements in Column-II.

Column-I		Column-II	
(A)	Ionisation energy increases	1.	O to S
(B)	Electron affinity increases	2.	Sn to Pb
(C)	Atomic radius decreases	3.	O to F
(D)	Electronegativity increases	4.	Al to Ga

Choose the correct answer from the options given below.
(a) A-4, B-3, C-1, D-2 (b) A-3, B-2, C-4, D-1
(c) A-1, B-2, C-3, D-4 (d) A-2, B-3, C-4, D-1

Paragraph Based Questions

Paragraph 1

Consider following table comparing ionic radius

Ion →	N^{3-}	O^{2-}	F^-	Na^+	Mg^{2+}
Number of electron	10	10	10	10	10
Number of nuclear protons	7	8	9	11	12
Ionic radius (pm)	146	140	133	98	79

Answer the following questions.

36. How many are correct in terms of size?
(a) $Na > Na^+$ (b) $Mg > Mg^+ > Mg^{+2}$
(c) $F^{\ominus} > F$ (d) $O^{-2} > O^- > O$
(e) $Mg^{+2} > Mg^+ > Mg$ (f) $O^{-2} > O > O^-$

37. Number of isoelectronic species are:
Na^+, Mg^{+2}, O^{-2}, F^-, O^-, Na, Mg

Paragraph 2

Following rule in general, classifies *p*-block elements into metals, non-metals and metalloids (where *P* is the period and *N* the valence electrons)

$(P+1) > N$, the element would be metal

$(P+1) < N$, the element would be non-metal

$(P+1) = N$, the element would be metalloid

Answer the following questions

38. Metalloids will be out of elements with atomic no.
13, 14, 15, 16, 17, 18

39. Select the atomic number of elements which behaves as metals. 13, 31, 35, 54, 30, 24, 29

Paragraph 3

In the following table I_1, I_2 and I_3 of the main group elements in 2nd period have been given.

	Li	Be	B	C	N	O	F	Ne
IE_1	513	899	801	1086	1402	1314	1681	2080
IE_2	7298	1757	2427	2352	2856	3388	3374	3952
IE_3	11815	14848	3660	4620	4578	5300	6050	6122

Answer the following question based on the above table.

40. There is increase in ionisation energy along a period going Li to Ne, but IE_1 of B is less than that of Be. This is due to
(a) valence electron in B is in 2*p*-orbital of higher energy than that of Be in 2*s*-orbital of lower energy
(b) removal of paired electron in Be requires higher energy than that of removal of unpaired electron in B.
(c) both (a) and (b)
(d) Be is metal while B is non metal.

41. We observe that IE_1 of Be > IE_1 of B but IE_2 of Be < IE_2 of B. Select correct explanation(s).
(a) Electron in Be in paired while in B, electron is unpaired, hence IE_1 of Be > IE_1 of B
(b) Electron in Be^+ is unpaired while in B^+, electron is paired, hence IE_2 of Be < IE_2 of B.
(c) Both (a) and (b)
(d) Be is electropositive and B is electronegative.

Paragraph 4

The heats of formation (ΔH_f°) of the oxides of the third period, sodium to chlorine, are in kJ mol^{-1}

Na_2O	MgO	Al_2O_3	SiO_2	P_4O_{10}	SO_3	Cl_2O_7
– 416	– 602	– 1676	– 911	– 2984	– 395	+250

Based on these data, answer the following questions

42. Which oxide has maximum negative heat of formation per oxygen atom?
(a) P_4O_{10} (b) Al_2O_3 (c) Na_2O (d) MgO

43. Most stable and least stable oxides are
(a) P_4O_{10}, Cl_2O_7 (b) Na_2O, Cl_2O_7
(c) MgO, Cl_2O_7 (d) Cl_2O_7, MgO

Paragraph 5

Four elements *P*, *Q*, *R* and *S* have ground state electronic configuration as :

$$P \rightarrow 1s^2 2s^2 2p^6 3s^2 3p^3$$
$$Q \rightarrow 1s^2 2s^2 2p^6 3s^2 3p^1$$
$$R \rightarrow 1s^2 2s^2 2p^6 3s^2 3p^6 3d^{10} 4s^2 4p^3$$
$$S \rightarrow 1s^2 2s^2 2p^6 3s^2 3p^6 3d^{10} 4s^2 4p^1$$

44. Comment how many of the following statement is/are correct?
(a) Size of *P* < Size of *Q* (b) Size of *R* < Size of *S*
(c) Size of *P* < Size of *R* (d) Size of *Q* < Size of *S*

45. Count the element that has IE_1 less than *P* in above paragraph.

Species Selection (With 5 Species)

46. Consider the following set of elements
(i) Be, Mg, Ca (ii) As, K, Ca
(iii) B, N, C (iv) Li, Na, K
(v) Si, P, S
Newland's law octave applies to which of the following sets of elements —
(a) 4 (b) 2 (c) 1 (d) 3

47. Among, $BeCO_3$, $CaCO_3$, $SrCO_3$, $BaCO_3$, how many number of these compounds are thermally more stable than $MgCO_3$?
(a) 1 (b) 4
(c) 2 (d) 3

48. Consider the following elements,
(i) Th (ii) Pa
(iii) Pu (iv) Cm
(v) Es
The total number of transuranium elements are
(a) 2 (b) 3
(c) 1 (d) 4

Species Selection (with 7 Species)

49. The total number of acidic oxides from the following list is
PbO, ZnO, MnO_2, MoO_3, ZnO_2, B_2O_3, N_2O_5
(a) 5 (b) 2
(c) 4 (d) 3

50. Consider the following pairs,
(i) Cs^+, Na^+, N^{3-} (ii) Li^+, Be^{2+}, Rb^+
(iii) K^+, Ar, O^{2-} (iv) O^{2-}, F^-, Na^+
(v) Ne, Mg^{2+}, F^- (vi) Sc^{3+}, Cl^-, Ca^{2+}
(vii) Mg^{2+}, Be^{2+}, Sr^{2+}
The total number of pairs which are isoelectric with Al^{3+} are
(a) 4 (b) 2 (c) 5 (d) 3

51. Consider the following pairs,
(i) Be and B (ii) P and S
(iii) O and S (iv) Br and Kr
(v) N and O (vi) $Li^{\oplus}$ and Li
(vii) Sr and Ba
The total number of pairs, in which 2nd species has lower ionisation energy than first species are —
(a) 4 (b) 3 (c) 4 (d) 5

52. Consider the IUPAC official name with their IUPAC nomenclature,
(i) Oganesson (Og); (Ununoctium)
(ii) Nihonium (Nh); (Ununtrium)
(iii) Hassium (Hs); Unnilseptium
(iv) Rutherfordium (Rf); Unnilquadium
(v) Dubnium (Db); Unnilhexium
(vi) Nobelium (No); Unnilbium
(vii) Rontgenium (Rg); Unununnium
The total number of correct representation are —
(a) 3 (b) 6 (c) 4 (d) 5

53. The total number of elements which have only single oxidation state (other than zero) in their corresponding stable compound is ………
Cs, Zn, Ba, Ga, Pb, Sr, Al
(a) 4 (b) 5
(c) 2 (d) 6

54. Consider the following elements,
(i) Cd (ii) Nb
(iii) Ta (iv) Te
(v) Ra (vi) Mo
(vii) Po
The total number of representative elements are —
(a) 3 (b) 5 (c) 4 (d) 6

Check Through PYQs

Element 2 Periodic Properties

1. The 1st, 2nd and 3rd ionisation enthalpies, I_1, I_2, and I_3, of four atoms with atomic numbers $n, n+1, n+2$, and $n+3$, where $n < 10$, are tabulated below. What is the value of n? **2020 Adv.**

Atomic number	Ionisation enthalpy (kJ/mol)		
	I_1	I_2	I_3
n	1681	3374	6050
$n+1$	2081	3952	6122
$n+2$	496	4562	6910
$n+3$	738	1451	7733

2. The option(s) with only amphoteric oxides is(are) **2017 Adv.**
(a) NO, B_2O_3, PbO, SnO_2
(b) Cr_2O_3, CrO, SnO, PbO
(c) Cr_2O_3, BeO, SnO, SnO_2
(d) ZnO, Al_2O_3, PbO, PbO_2

HINTS & Solutions

Solutions : Competency Enhancer

1.1. ***(b)*** The element with placement in 7th period and 10th group has 110 atomic number. Thus, its IUPAC name will be ununnilium.

2.1. ***(a)*** Ionic radius $\propto \frac{(-\text{ve})\text{ ion}}{(+\text{ve})\text{ ion}}$

Thus $Mn^{+7} < Mn^{+5} < Mn^{+3} < Mn^{+2}$ option (a) is correct.

2.2. ***(d)*** Potassium has one electron in its outermost shell. So. Ist ionisation energy is low but IInd ionisation energy is high because K^+ has an inert gas Ar like configuration.

2.3. ***(c)*** In case of F addition of e^- becomes little tough than Cl. So, e^- affinity is less than Cl. It is due to more e^- density and smaller size of F-atom, which causes more e^- repulsion.

S > Se and Li > Na (as on moving down the group size increases and effective nuclear charge decreases). So electron affinity decreases.

2.4. ***(c)*** Among the given oxides, only two i.e., SO_3 and P_4O_{10} are acidic, others CaO, MgO and CuO are basic, ZnO is an amphoteric oxide and CO is a neutral oxide.

Elemental Practice 1.1

1. ***(a)*** Newland's law of octaves states that when elements are arranged in order of increasing atomic weight then every eighth element has similar properties. Thus, Be, Mg, Ca have the similar properties and follows the Newland is law of octave.

2. ***(a)*** Mendeleev failed to assign positions of the isotopes on the basis of atomic mass, according to his periodic law.

3. ***(b)*** IUPAC nomenclature of the element which is placed after Bh_{107} is unniloctium, i.e., Hs_{108}.

4. ***(b)*** Statement (b) is incorrect. The correct statement of (b) is, the *d*-block has 10 columns, because a maximum of 10 electrons can occupy all the orbitals in a *d*-subshell.
All other given statements are correct.

5. ***(d)*** Among the given options the incorrect match is (d). Its correct form is

$[Xe]\ 4f^{14} 5d^2 6s^2 \rightarrow$ 6th period, 4th group

The element is $_{72}Hf$.

6. ***(b)*** The electronic configuration of element having atomic number of 34 is $[Ar]\ 3d^{10} 4s^2 4p^4$. So, it belongs to sixteen group in long form of periodic table.

7. ***(c)*** Among the given pair of elements only two i.e., II and V belong to same period.

Ca and Zn —— 4th period

Sr and Rh —— 5th period

8. ***(d)*** Same group elements have same number of valence electrons therefore, have similar physical and chemical properties.

9. ***(a)*** Among the given statements only statement III and V are incorrect. Their corrected form are as follows :

III. Tantalum is not a representative element. It is a transition element ($Z = 73$).

V. The element with atomic number 118 is noble gas.

10. ***(c)*** Period number = Maximum principal quantum number (n) of any element of the respective period.

11. ***(c)*** $(n-1)d^2ns^2$ for $n = 4$

$n = 4$ means the element belongs to fourth period.

So, the outer electronic configuration will become $3d^2 4s^2$.

The complete electronic configuration of the element is as follows,

$$1s^2, 2s^2, 2p^6, 3s^2, 3p^6, 3d^2, 4s^2$$

Thus, the element is titanium.

12. ***(a)*** Statement I is correct but statement II is incorrect. The correct form of statement II is —

The IUPAC nomenclature of an element with electronic configuration $[Rn]\ 5f^{14} 6d^1 7s^2$ is unniltrium.

$[Rn]\ 5f^{14} 6d^1 7s^2 = 86 + 14 + 1 + 2 = 103$

13. ***(d)*** ns^2np^4 for $n = 3$

$n = 3$ means elements belongs to third period. Since, last electron enters in the *p*-orbital, it belongs to *p*-block.

For *p*-block elements, the group number = 10 + valence shell electrons = 10 + (2 + 4) = 16

Hence, the given element belongs to 16th group.

The complete electronic configuration of the element is:
$1s^2, 2s^2, 2p^6, 3s^2, 3p^4$

Thus, the given element is sulphur.

14. ***(a)*** Aluminium is a representative element whereas chromium and zinc are transition elements and lanthanum belongs to lanthanoid series.

15. ***(b)*** $X = {}_{33}As \rightarrow$ Metalloid, $Y = {}_{53}I \rightarrow$ Non-metal

$Z = {}_{83}Bi \rightarrow$ Metal

16. ***(c)*** The correct decreasing order of atomic number is

IV > V > III > I > II

i.e., $_{76}Os > {}_{74}W > {}_{48}Cd > {}_{42}Mo > {}_{32}Ge$

17. ***(d)*** The atomic number of the element is 110.

18. ***(a,b,c)*** Among the given statements only (d) is incorrect while all are incorrect. The correct form (d) is

In halogen family all our non-metals except astatine which is a metalliod.

19. ***(a,b,c)*** Statement (a), (b) and (c) are correct whereas (d) is incorrect. The correct form of (d) is

In *p*-block alongwith non-metals, metals and metalloid are also present.

e.g. Al is a metal; Ge — Metalloid

20. ***(c,d)*** An element X belong to 4th period and 15th group is As and its electronic configuration is As_{33} : [Ar] $4s^2 3d^{10} 4p^3$

21. ***(b,c,d)*** Statement (a) is correct about Lother Meyer's curve rest all are incorrect. Their correct forms are

(a) Alkaline earth metals occupy the descending portion of Lother Meyer's curve.

(c) Atomic volume first decreases and then increases in a period in Lother Meyer's curve.

(d) The transition elements occupy at the bottom part of the curve.

22. ***(8)*** As last electron enters in *d* subshell therefore this belong to *d*-block. For *d*-block the group number. is equal to the number of valence shell electron + No. of electron in $(n-1)d$ subshell. So, group number = 6 + 2 = 8

23. ***(2)*** Cd and Hg are *d*-block elements but not transition elements.

24. ***(3)*** Li, Fe and Ba are metals.

25. ***(101)*** Unnilunium IUPAC symbol = Unu

Atomic number = 101

26. ***(125)*** Possible subshells are present in the 8th period —

8*s*, 7*d*, 6*f*, 5*g*, 8*p*

Total number of electrons = 5 + 25 + 35 + 45 + 15 = 125

Elemental Practice 1.2

1. ***(c)***

	Z	Electron
K^+	19	18
S^{2-}	16	18
Cl^-	17	18
Ca^{2+}	20	18

For isoelectronic species, size $\propto \frac{1}{Z}$

Thus, $S^{2-} > Cl^- > K^+ > Ca^{2+}$

So, option (c) is the correct answer.

2. ***(a)*** ∴ Value of 102 nm is for metallic (crystal) radii, 100 nm is for covalent and 103 nm is for van der Waals' radii.

Thus, (a) is the correct answer.

3. ***(a)*** In a period on moving from left to right ionic radii decreases.

So, order of cationic radii is

$$Cr^{2+} > Mn^{2+} > Fe^{2+} > Ni^{2+}$$

4. ***(d)*** Size $\propto \frac{1}{Z}$ for isoelectronic ion.

Thus, the correct order is

$O^{2-} > F^- > Na^+ > Mg^{2+} > Al^{3+}$

(*Z*) 8 9 11 12 13

5. ***(a)*** Size $\propto \frac{1}{Z}$ for isoelectronic ion

Size : $C^{4-} > N^{3-} > O^{2-} > F^-$

Z: 6 7 8 9

6. ***(a)*** Effective nuclear charge $Z_{eff} = Z - S$

For $Be^+ = 1s^2 2s^1$

$S = 2 \times 0.85 = 1.70$

∴ $Z_{eff} = 4 - 1.70 = 2.30$

$Be^{2+} : 1s^2$

$S = 0.30$

∴ $Z_{eff} = 4 - 0.30 = 3.70$

$Be^{3+} : 1s^1$ no-screening

$Z_{eff} = 4$

7. ***(b)*** The correct order of ionisation enthalpy are as —

Cs < Rb < K < Li

8. ***(d)*** Sodium has one valence electron. Sodium form Na^+ ion by losing its valence electron and attains the stable electronic configuration of Ne with completed octet. This requires less amount of energy. The removal of 2nd electron will break this stable electronic configuration and requires high amount of energy.

9. ***(b)*** The first ionisation energy of non-metals is very high. On moving down the group ionisation energy value decreases. Thus, Cl has the highest first ionisation energy.

10. ***(d)***

11. ***(c)*** For alkali metals

$$(IE)_1 << (IE)_2$$

Z has $IE_1 << IE_2$

Thus, (c) is the correct option.

12. ***(a)*** In a period, the non-metallic character increases from left to right.

Thus, among B, C, N and F, non-metallic character decreases in the order F > N > C > B. However, within a group, non-metallic character decreases from top to bottom. Thus, C is more non-metallic than Si.

Thus, the correct order of non-metallic character is

$$F > N > C > B > Si$$

13. ***(b)*** In 1st IE, electron is removed from a neutral atom but for 2nd-ionisation electron is removed from a positive atom, where electrons are more tightly bounded to increased attractive force.

14. ***(b)*** Aluminium form amphoteric oxides. Non-metals such as sulphur forms acidic oxides. Metals (group 1 and 2) form basic oxides. So, Al_2O_3 is amphoteric. SO_2 and SiO_2 is acidic and CaO is basic oxide.

15. ***(d)*** $X(g) + e^- \longrightarrow X^-(g); \quad \Delta H = x = \text{EA of } X(g)$

$X^-(g) \longrightarrow X(g) + e^-; \quad \Delta H = y = (\text{IE}) \text{ of } X^-(g)$

$= -(\text{EA}) \text{ of } X(g)$

Thus, (a), (b), (c) are true

Thus, (d) is the correct option.

16. ***(b)*** $X(g) \longrightarrow X^+(g) + e^-; \quad \Delta H = I$

$X^+(g) + e^- \longrightarrow X(g); \quad \Delta H = E = -I$

Thus, (b) is the correct option.

17. ***(a)*** $(EN) = \frac{(IP) + (EA)}{2}$

$(EA) = 2(EN) - (IP) = 2E_1 - E_2$

Thus, (a) is the correct option.

18. ***(a)*** On moving from left to right in a period, the basic character of oxides of element decreases. So, the order will be $Na_2O > MgO > Al_2O_3$.

While on moving down the group, basic character of oxides increases. So, the order will be $K_2O > Na_2O$.

Hence, the overall order will be

$K_2O > Na_2O > MgO > Al_2O_3$

19. ***(c)*** The electron gain enthalpy (in kJ/mol) for element of group-16 decrease down the group except sulphur.

The correct order is

O	S	Se	Te	Po
–141	–200	–195	–190	–174
(kJ/mol)	(kJ/mol)	(kJ/mol)	(kJ/mol)	(kJ/mol)

20. ***(c)*** Both statements (a) and (b) are correct.

21. ***(a, c)*** **Ionisation Energy** Ga has more ionisation energy than Al due to uneffective screening effect.

Atomic radii Effective nuclear charge of Ga is greater than that of aluminium due to which atomic radii of Al is greater than Ga.

Electronegativity Electronegativity value of Ga = 1.6 and Al = 1.5. As the size increases, the effective nuclear charge also increases due to presence of fully filled lesser shielding *d*/*f*-orbital present between valence shell electrons and noble gas core. As a result, force of attraction of the nucleus for the valence shell electrons increases and the electronegativity increases from Al to Tl.

Electron Affinity Electron affinity decreases from Al to Tl due to increase in nuclear charge.

22. ***(a, b, c)*** Statements (a, b, c) are correct whereas (d) is incorrect. The correct form of (d) is

K^+ has lower atomic size than K due to higher effective nuclear charge.

23. ***(a,b,d)*** The ionic radii of the species given are $H^- = 140$ pm, $O^{2-} = 145$ pm, $F^- = 133$ pm, $Cl^- = 181$ pm and $Br^- = 196$ pm.

24. ***(a, c)*** The order of conductance in aqueous solution is $Li^+ < Na^+ < K^+ < Rb^+ < Cs^+$ and also nitrogen has a positive electron gain enthalpy.

25. ***(a, b, c, d)*** In aqueous solution these oxides will exist as acids e.g. NO_2 will form $HNO_2 + HNO_3$, SiO_2 will form H_4SiO_4 (silicic acid), CO_2 will form H_2CO_3 (carbonic acid) and SnO_2 will form H_2SnO_3 (metastannic acid).

26. ***(a, b, c)*** Oxides of non-metals are acidic in nature except NO, CO, N_2O, N_2O_3 is acidic.

27. ***(a, b)*** The atomic radii increases down the group. This is due to successive use of orbitals with principal quantum number (*n*) one higher than the last.

The Z_{eff} decreases in a group, hence IE decreases.

28. ***(2)*** Among the given oxides only two i.e., SnO_2 and As_2O_3 are amphoteric oxides.

29. ***(5.1)*** $Na \longrightarrow Na^+ + e^-$

$Na^+ + e^- \longrightarrow Na$

Electron gain enthalpy of Na^+ is reverse of IE_1 of Na.

Because reaction is reverse so, $\Delta_{eg}H = -5.1$ eV

30. ***(12.24)*** $\Delta H = +720$ kJ / mol

1 mole of X to $X^+ = 720 \times 10^3$ J

$$\text{Mole} = \frac{\text{Given mass}}{\text{Molecular mass}}$$

$$= \frac{120 \times 10^{-3}\text{ g}}{7\text{ g / mol}} = 17.14 \times 10^{-3}\text{ mol}$$

$$= 0.017\text{ mol}$$

Energy required = (moles of X) $\times \Delta H$

$$= 0.017\text{ mol} \times 720\text{ kJ/mol} = 12.24$$

31. ***(4)*** The oxides of non-metal are acidic in nature. Hence, N_2O_3, NO_2, Cl_2O_7 and SO_2 are acidic except N_2O, NO, CO which are neutral oxides. CaO and Na_2O are basic oxides.

Practice Element 01 : Target JEE Main

1. ***(b)*** The elements belonging to the same group of the periodic table will have the same number of electrons in valence shell.

2. ***(c)*** K-19 (in absence of Aufbau rule) :

$$1s^2 2s^2 2p^6 3s^2 3p^6 \underset{\uparrow}{\underline{3d^1}}$$

Last-filled electron goes into *d*-orbital. Thus, it belongs to *d*-block element.

3. ***(a)*** *s* and *p* block elements are called representative elements.

d block elements ar called transition elements. *f* block elements are called inner transition elements.

4. ***(a)*** Atomic size decreases from left to right. So, atomic size of $O^- > F^-$

Also, O^{2-} and F^- are isoelectronic and O^- and F are isoelectronic.

For isoelectronic species, the element with higher atomic number is smaller. Also, for ions of same element more negative ions are bigger

$$\text{Size} \propto \frac{(-ve)}{(+ve)}$$

Thus, $O^{2-} > O^- > F^- > F$

5. ***(c)*** The sizes of 2nd and 3rd row of transition elements are almost same due to lesser shielding effect of *d* and *f* orbitals and also due to lanthanide contraction.

6. ***(d)*** Valence electrons in $A = 3$

Valence electrons in $B = 6$

Thus A is electropositive and B is electronegative; A can lose three electrons and B can gain two electrons to attain stable configuration.

A exists as A^{3+} and B as B^{2-}

Thus, compound is A_2B_3

7. ***(b)*** Fe : [Ar] $3d^6 4s^2$

Fe^{+3} : [Ar] $3d^5$

8. ***(c)*** Fluorine does not form any polyhalide as other halogens due to the absence of d orbital, F cannot expand its valency.

9. ***(c)*** Group No $= (n-1)d + ns$ electrons $= 6$

So, the element with electronic configuration $(n-1)d^5\, ns^1$ belongs to group 6 and d-block.

10. ***(c)*** IUPAC name of element (115) is Ununpentium so it can be represented as Uup.

11. ***(c)*** Na^+, Mg^{2+}, Al^{3+} contains 10 electrons. So, they are isoelectronic species.

F^-, Ne, O^{2-} contains 10 electrons. So, they are isoelectronic species.

Mn^+, Fe^{2+}, Cr contains 24 electrons. So, they are isoelectronic species.

Isoelectronic species does not have equal size.

∴ Fe, Co, Ni (group 8) elements shows similar properties and have same size.

12. ***(d)*** Lesser the charge on the cation, more is the ionic radii.

More the charge on the anion, more is the ionic radii.

Thus, ionic radii of $P^{3+} > P^{5+}$.

13. ***(d)*** The ionic radius of a cation decreases when oxidation number increases. This decrease occurs because the ion is losing electrons which causes the ion to have a stronger pull on the remaining electrons, decreasing the ion's size.

Thus, the order of radii is

$$Mn^{2+} > Mn^{3+} > Mn^{4+} > Mn^{7+}$$

14. ***(d)***

O	F	F < O	I > Br > F
S	Cl	Thus, $F^- < O^{2-}$	$I^- > Br^- > F^-$
Se	Br	Se > O	
	I	$Se^{2-} > O^{2-}$	

I > Se

∴ $I^- > Se^{2-}$

Thus, $I^- > Se^{2-} > Br^- > O^{2-} > F^-$

15. ***(a)*** IE_3 is very high indicating +2 oxidation state is most stable. Thus, element is Be.

16. ***(c)*** $\left.\begin{array}{l} N(7) \\ \text{and } O^+(8) \end{array}\right]$ $1s^2 2s^2\ \underbrace{2p_x^1 2p_y^1 2p_z^1}_{\text{Maximum multiplicity most stable}}$

[O] $1s^2 2s^2 2p_x^2 2p_y^1 2p_z^1$

(IP) is dependent on the value of Z.

Z of $O^+(8) > Z$ of N(7)

Thus, (IP) of $O^+ > N$

Na with one valence electron has least IP

17. ***(b)*** On moving down the group higher oxidation state becomes less stable due to inert pair effect.

18. ***(a)*** Oxides of C is a giant molecule indicating covalent nature

Oxide of B is amphoteric

Oxide of A is ionic

Thus, A is largest in size.

Thus, atomic number of A is least

$$A < B < C$$

19. ***(a)***

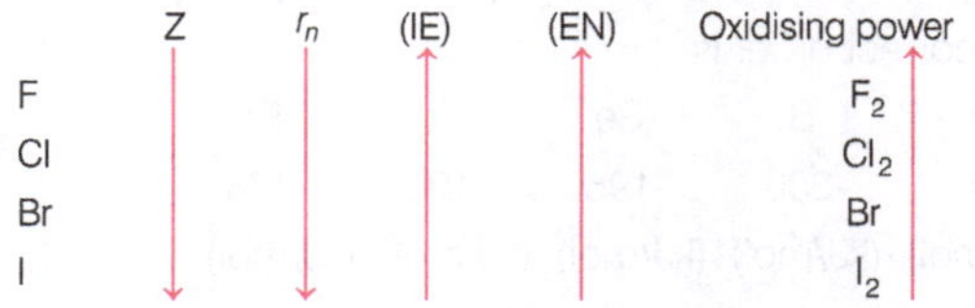

20. ***(c)*** $1s^2 2s^2 2p^5$—F

$1s^2 2s^2 2p^6$ —Ne

$1s^2 2s^2 2p^6 3s^2 3p^5$ — Cl

$1s^2 2s^2 2p^6 3s^2 3p^6$ —Ar

EA of Cl > EA of F due to empty d-orbital in Cl

21. ***(b)***

22. ***(a)*** (IP) of N > O because of half filled configuration of N.

23. ***(c)*** Electronegativity values of N = 3.0

P = 2.19

C = 2.5

Si = 1.8

Thus, the correct order is

$$N > C > P > Si$$

24. ***(a)*** Electron affinity increases in a period and decreases in a group.

But in case of O and S, S has more electron affinity due to smaller size of O there is a interelectronic repulsion between the $2p$ electrons and the incoming electrons.

Thus, the correct order is

$$N < O < S < Cl$$

25. ***(b)*** Electron affinity is positive for noble gases. When O^{2-} is formed from O^-, it carries 10 electrons which means similar electronic configuration as that of Ne. Thus, electron affinity is positive when O^{2-} is formed from O^-.

26. ***(6)*** Basic and amphoteric oxides will react with aq. HCl i.e., CaO, ZnO, BeO, Al_2O_3, SrO and CdO.

27. ***(8)*** Ni = [Ar] $3d^8 4s^2$

$$Z_{eff} = Z - S$$

For $3d$ electron, $S = 7 \times 0.35 + 18 \times 1$
$= 20.45$

$$Z_{eff} = 28 - 20.45$$
$$= 7.55 \simeq 8$$

28. ***(8)***

3rd → Na	Mg	Al	Si	PS		Cl	Ar (Smallest)
4th → K (largest)	Ca	Ga	Ge	As	Se	Br	Kr

Total protons = 19 − 17 = 2

29. ***(8)*** There are 8 elements 3rd period.

Thus, value of $\frac{x+8}{2}$ is equal to 8.

30. ***(8)*** All d-block elements will have lower ionisation energy than that of Hg, Cs has the lowest ionisation energy in the periodic table and Tl has lower ionisation energy than Hg due to poor penetration effect of singly occupied p-subshell.

31. ***(1960)*** Be ⟶ Be^+ energy required = 889
$Be^+ \longrightarrow Be^{2+}$ energy required = 1757
Be ⟶ Be^{2+} energy required = 2656
Cl ⟶ Cl^- energy released = − 348
For $2Cl^-$, energy released = − 696

Therefore, the energy required for the formation

$Be + 2Cl \longrightarrow BeCl_2$ is

2656 − 696 = 1960 kJ/mol

32. ***(3)*** As there is very high difference between $I.E._3$ and $I.E_4$, thus it has three electrons in its valence shell.

33. ***(6)*** Li, B, Si, Be, Zn and Fe have an electronegativity values lower than that of hydrogen.

34. ***(6)*** P, O, Ca, Li, Na and H all have negative values of first electron gain enthalpy.

Check Through PYQs : JEE Main

1. ***(d)*** Both Statement I and Statement II are false.
   - Law of octaves was arranged in the increasing order of their atomic weight.
   - Lother Mayer plotted the physical properties against atomic weight.

2. ***(11)*** Unununium is the IUPAC name of Roentgenium

Atomic number → 111

Group belong → 11th group.

Hence, it belongs to group 11.

3. ***(2)*** Configuration of given ions are as follows.

$[Sr^{2+}]$ = [Kr]
$[Cs^+]$ = [Xe]
$[Yb^{2+}]$ = [Xe] $4f^{14}$
$[La^{2+}]$ = [Xe] $5d^1$
$[Pb^{2+}]$ = [Xe] $4f^{14} 5d^{10} 6s^2$
$[Fe^{2+}]$ = [Ar] $3d^6$

Thus, only 2 ions i.e., $[Sr^{2+}]$, $[Cs^+]$ has noble gas configuration.

4. ***(a)*** Statement I is true but Statement II is false.

The correct form of Statement II is as follows, s-block element never occurs in pure form in nature. As, they are highly reactive. Thus, they are found as ore or minerals.

5. ***(a)*** Moseley's observation on characteristic X-ray spectra of elements relates frequency (ν) of X-rays emitted to the atomic number by the following relation : $\sqrt{\nu} = a(Z - b)$

The plot of $\sqrt{\nu}$ *vs* Z was found as linear straight line.

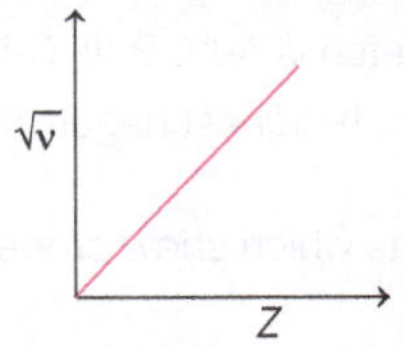

6. ***(b)*** Aluminium (Al), gallium (Ga) and indium (In) are members of group 13 whereas selenium (Se) is the element of group 16. Gallium (Ga) is closer to a metalloid germanium (Ge) and has low melting point. Aluminium has high melting point. Selenium is a metalloid, whereas indium is not closer to a metalloid.

7. ***(d)*** The given electronic configuration of an element is
$= [Rn]\, 5f^{14} 6d^1 7s^2$

Atomic number of Rn = 86

Atomic number of given element will be

86 + 14 + 1 + 2 = 103

IUPAC nomenclature is

1 0 3
↓ ↓ ↓
un nil tri +ium
= Unniltrium

8. ***(a)*** Period number 4 and group 16 of the periodic table indicate that the element 'E' is selenium (Se). The element present just above 'E' is sulphur.
The general outermost electronic configuration of group 16 is $ns^2 np^4$. Thus, the electronic configuration of sulphur is [Ne] $3s^2 3p^4$.

So, option (a) is correct.

9. ***(d)*** Li-Na pair is different from remaining three options as it do not shows diagonal relationship. Both Li-Na belong to same group and are not placed diagonally.

Li-Mg, B-Si and Be-Al show diagonal relationship with each other.

Li ↘ Mg, Be ↘ Al, B ↘ Si (Diagonal relationship)
Li Be B
Na Mg Al Si

10. ***(d)*** Correct order of ionic radius $O^{2-} > F^- > Na^+ > Mg^{2+}$.
Correct order for electron gain enthalpy (Magnitude) $Cl > F > Br > I$.

11. ***(1)***
- $\underset{(2.0)}{B} < \underset{(2.6)}{C} < \underset{(3.0)}{N} < \underset{(3.4)}{O}$ – Electronegativity – Pauling scale
- $\underset{76\,pm}{Li^+} < \underset{72\,pm}{Mg^{2+}} < \underset{31\,pm}{Be^{2+}}$
- Metallic character increases down group and decreases from left to right across a period
So, K > Mg > Al.
- Electron affinity :
$\underset{349}{Cl} < \underset{328}{F} < \underset{325}{Br} < \underset{295}{I}$ $(kJ\ mol^{-1})$

12. ***(c)*** The correct match is A-IV, B-III, C-II, D-I
Cl, S ⇒ Element with highest negative electron gain enthalpy.
Ge, As ⇒ Elements which show property of both metal and non-metal.
Fr, Ra ⇒ Elements with largest atomic size.
F, O ⇒ Element with highest electronegativity.

13. ***(d)*** Generally, ionisation enthalpy increases along the period, due to decrease in size of atoms across a period. Moreover, elements with half filled or fully-filled electronic configuration will have higher ionisation enthalpy. Thus the correct order of 1st ionisation enthalpy across the period is
Li < B < Be < C < O < N < F < Ne
i.e. E < C < A < B < D

14. ***(c)*** Statement given in option (c) is correct, and remaining statements are incorrect.
In general along the period from left to right, atomic and ionic size decreases and metallic character decreases. While on moving down the group, atomic and ionic size increases and metallic character increases.

15. ***(b)*** Among the given elements, nitrogen has highest first ionisation enthalpy. The sequence of ionisation enthalpy among the given elements is
Al < Si < C < N

16. ***(5)*** The number of electrons in the given species are as follows:
$O^{2-} = 10$, $O^+ = 7$, $Al^{3+} = 10$, $Al = 13$
$F = 9$, $F^- = 10$, $Mg^{2+} = 10$, $Mg = 12$
$Na^+ = 10$

17. ***(b)*** The correct order of first ionisation energy is
Li < B < Be < C < O < N < F.
On moving from left to right in a period, atomic size decreases, Z_{eff} increases, so ionisation enthalpy increases. The IE of N is more than O because of presence of half-filled and fully filled configuration which will make an atom more stable thus more will be the ionisation enthalpy.

18. ***(b)*** On moving from top to bottom in group metallic character increases while on moving from left to right in a period it decreases.
Hence, the correct order of metallic character is
K > Ca > Be.

19. ***(d)*** The correct order of electronegativity is
Br > C > At > P

Element	Br	C	At	P
EN	2.8	2.5	2.2	2.1

20. ***(a)*** Smaller the size of cation, higher will be its hydration enthalpy.
$$\left[\text{Hydration enthalpy} \propto \frac{1}{\text{Size}}\right]$$
Hence, group 2 (alkaline earth metal) cations will be having higher hydration enthalpy than group 1 (alkali metals) cations.
Hence correct answer is
$Mg^{2+} > Ca^{2+} > K^+ > Rb^+ > Cs^+$
i.e. C > E > A > B > D.

21. ***(c)*** Rb and Cs will have nearly same electron gain enthalpy i.e., –47 kJ/mol and – 46 kJ/mol respectively.
Ar and Kr will also have identical electron gain enthalpy as noble gases are inert and they are not found in combined state.

22. ***(d)*** The electronic configuration of given elements are as follows.
$Be = 1s^2 2s^2 \rightarrow$ Fully-filled
$B = 1s^2 2s^2 2p^1$
$N = 1s^2 2s^2 2p^3 \rightarrow$ Half-filled
$O = 1s^2 2s^2 2p^4$
The ionisation enthalpy increases from left to right in a period. It is due to increase in Z_{eff}, so order should be Be < B < N < O.
But, due to greater stablility nature of fully-filled and half-filled orbitals, the $2p^3$ is more stable configuration than $2p^4$. Also $2s^2$ is more stable than $2s^2 2p^1$.
So, the correct order of first ionisation energy is
B < Be < O < N.

23. ***(b)*** Acidic oxides are B_2O_3, N_2O_5, SO_3, P_4O_{10}.

24. ***(a)*** Both A and R are correct and R is the correct explanation of A.
1st ionisation enthalpy of oxygen is lower than nitrogen as N has half-filled electronic configuration.
Oxygen atom on the other hand has four electrons in the *p*-subshell causing greater electron-electron repulsion and lesser stability.
N (7) : $1s^2 2s^2 2p^3$
O (8) : $1s^2 2s^2 2p^4$

25. ***(b)*** The correct matching is A-IV, B-II, C-I, D-III.

26. ***(d)*** Atomic number of Al = 13

Number of electrons in Al^{3+} = 10

Number of electrons in Br^- = 36

Number of electrons in Be^{2+} = 2

Number of electrons in Cl^- = 18

Number of electrons in Li^+ = 2

Number of electrons in S^{2-} = 18

Number of electrons in K^+ = 18

Number of electrons in O^{2-} = 10

Number of electrons in Mg^{2+} = 10

The ions that are isoelectronic with Al^{3+} are O^{2-} and Mg^{2+}.

27. ***(b)*** Mercury is a liquid at room temperature, so it has lowest melting point and Ga and Cs are liquid at slightly above room temperature and hence have melting points around 30°C. So, being solid, Ag has highest melting point among the given elements.

28. ***(b)*** The most appropriate answer is A-(ii), B-(iii), C-(ii), D-(i), E-(iii)

29. ***(b)*** Ionic radii of N^{3-} is greater than F^- and O^{2-}, due to higher negative charge. Size of anion increases with increase in magnitude of negative charge.

30. ***(b)*** From the given sets amphoteric oxides are $Be(OH)_2$, $Al(OH)_3$

Acidic oxides are $B(OH)_3$

Basic oxides are NaOH, $Ca(OH)_2$

Among the given sets option (b) has different nature of oxides.

31. ***(c)*** The order of first ionisation energy of 3rd period is as follows

Na < Al < Mg < Si < S < P < Cl < Ar

On moving along a period from left to right, ionisation enthalpy increases.

Ionisation enthalpy of group 2 is greater than group 13 and that of group 15 is greater than group 16. This is due to fully filled and half-filled orbital.

∴ *X*, *Y* and *Z* are argon, chlorine and sodium respectively.

32. ***(a)*** *X* is Na ($3s^1$) as it has very high second ionisation energy due to removal of electron from highly stable noble gas configuration.

$$\text{Na} \xrightarrow{IE_1} \text{Na}^+ + e^-;$$

$$1s^2 2s^2 2p^6 3s^1 \quad 1s^2 2s^2 2p^6 \text{ or [Ne] } IE_1 = 495 \text{ kJ/mol}$$

$$\text{Na}^+ \xrightarrow{IE_2} \text{Na}^{2+} + e^-;$$

$$1s^2 2s^2 2p^6 \quad 1s^2 2s^2 2p^5 \quad IE_2 = 4563 \text{ kJ/mol}$$

(Stable noble gas configuration).

In case of Mg, noble gas configuration is achieved after removal of second electron. So, IE_2 is comparatively less.

$$\underset{[\text{Ne}]3s^2}{\text{Mg}} \longrightarrow \underset{[\text{Ne}]3s^1}{\text{Mg}^+} + e^-; \quad IE_1 = 731 \text{ kJ/mol}$$

$$\underset{[\text{Ne}]\,3s^1}{\text{Mg}^+} \longrightarrow \underset{[\text{Ne}]}{\text{Mg}^{2+}} + e^-; \quad IE_2 = 1450 \text{ kJ/mol}$$

33. ***(a)*** The correct matching is

(A)-(ii), (B)-(iii), (C)-(iv), (D)-(i)

34. ***(c)*** (a) $O^-(g) + e^- \longrightarrow O^{2-}(g)$ (endothermic)

(b) $Na(g) \longrightarrow Na^+(g) + e^-$ (endothermic)

(c) $H(g) + e^- \longrightarrow H^-(g)$ (exothermic)

(d) $Ar(g) + e^- \longrightarrow Ar^-(g)$ (endothermic)

Reaction (c) is not endothermic. It is exothermic. Electron gain enthalpy of H(*g*) is negative, due to '1*s*' configuration.

35. ***(a)*** Statements I, II and IV are correct while Statements III is incorrect. It is because the ratio of charge/radius of Be and Al are same due to diagonal relationship.

36. ***(b)*** While moving across a period, metallic property of elements changes first into metalloids than into non-metallic nature therefore.

⇒ Metal gives basic oxides.

Metalloid produces amphoteric oxides.

Non-metal gives acidic oxides.

So, $X \rightarrow$ metal, $Y \rightarrow$ metalloid and $Z \rightarrow$ non-metal

Thus, the order of atomic number is

$$X < Y < Z$$

37. ***(c)*** Generally, $\Delta_{eg}H$ becomes less negative when comparing elements of the same group from top to bottom. But among fluorine and chlorine there is an anomaly because inter-electron- electron repulsion is stronger in fluorine due to its extra small size.

∴ $\Delta_{eg}H$ is less exothermic than expected for F-atom.

Thus, the correct values of electron gain enthalpies

$$\underset{(-333)}{\text{F}} < \underset{(-349)}{\text{Cl}} > \underset{(-325)}{\text{Br}} > \underset{(-296)}{\text{I}} \quad \text{kJ mol}^{-1}$$

Practice Element 02 : Target JEE Advanced

1. ***(d)*** The *d*-subshell are not filled with electrons monotonically with increase in atomic number. There are some exceptions like Cr, Cu in which *d* electrons are not fully filled.

2. ***(b)***

3. ***(d)*** (IV) A contains C, Si, Ge, Sn, Pb

Ge, Sn, Pb are strongly electropositive.

Thus, option (d) is correct.

4. ***(b)*** A-19 *s*-block

B-22 *d*-block

C-32 *p*-block

D-64 *f*-block

Thus, option (b) is correct.

5. ***(c)*** $M(s) \xrightarrow{IE_1} M^+(g) + e^- \quad 100 \text{ eV}$

$M(g) \xrightarrow{IE_1 + IE_2} M^{2+}(g) + 2e^- \quad 250 \text{ eV}$

Thus, $M^+(g) \xrightarrow{IE_2} M^{2+}(g) + e^- \quad 150 \text{ eV}$

Thus, (a) is true, (b) is also true (IE_1 of $M^+(g)$ is IE_2 of $M(g)$)

Thus, option (c) is correct

6. ***(c)*** $A \longrightarrow A^+ + e^-$ if $(IP)_A < (IP)_B$

$B + e^- \longrightarrow B^-$ if $(EA)_B > (EA)_A$

$$(EN) = \frac{(IP) + (EA)}{2}$$

A^+B^- is formed

if $(EN)_A < (EA)_B$

Thus, option (c) is correct.

7. ***(c)*** I.P. of Li > Na

Thus, Na falls below Li.

Thus, option (c) is correct.

8. ***(c)*** Electron gain enthalpy is the property of an isolated atom whereas electronegativity is the property of a bonded atom.

9. ***(b)*** Let IP = I

EA = E

$$X(g) \longrightarrow X^+(g) + e^-$$

$$\frac{N_0}{2} I = E_1$$

$$\therefore \quad I = \frac{2E_1}{N_0}$$

$$X(g) + e^- \longrightarrow X^-(g)$$

$$\frac{N_0 E}{2} = E_2$$

$$\therefore \quad E = \frac{2E_2}{N_0}$$

Thus, option (b) is correct.

10. ***(a, b, c, d)*** Down the group stability of lower oxidation state increases and higher oxidation state decreases due to inert pair effect.

$\therefore$ Stability orders are

$$Ge^{2+} < Sn^{2+} < Pb^{2+}$$

$$Ge^{4+} > Sn^{4+} > Pb^{4+}$$

$$Pb^{2+} > Pb^{4+}$$

$$Sn^{2+} < Sn^{4+}$$

11. ***(a, b, c)***

12. ***(a,b,c)*** Atomic mass do not influences the ionisation potential. Because ionisation potential is the energy required to remove an electron from outermost orbit not from entire atom.

13. ***(a, c, d)***

14. ***(a, b, c)*** In ionic compounds as internuclear distance increases, melting point decreases on moving down the group, melting point decreases. So, $r_c + r_a$ is greater for RbBr than NaF.

15. ***(a, c, d)*** With the increase in the size of metal atom, the repulsion of the non-bonding increases and therefore MP and BP decreases from Li to Cs. Also, ionic mobility in aqueous solution increases from Li to Cs.

On moving down the group, ionisation potential decreases.

$\therefore$ Ionization potential of Li is higher than Na.

16. ***(a, b, d)*** Statements a, b and d are correct whereas c is incorrect. The correct form of c is:

Cu has correct electronic configuration of [Ar] $4s^2 3d^9$ and it belongs to d block element whereas K[Ar]$4s^1$ is placed in s-block.

17. ***(a, c, d)***

IE_1 of N > IE_1 of O, due to half filled nature in N.

18. ***(b, c)***

(i) I.E. order : $s > p > d > f$

for a particular principal quantum number.

(ii) I.E. depends upon half filled and fully filled configuration.

Factors (i) and (ii) disappear in the 5th and 6th periods because Z_{eff} dominates over all others.

19. ***(a, b)***

(a) $\rightarrow$ d-orbital can accomodate a maximum of 10 electrons.

(b) $\rightarrow$ Na : $1s^2 2s^2 2p^6 3s^1$

Na^{3+} : $1s^2 2s^2 2p^4$

Na^+ : $1s^2 2s^2 2p^6$

Na^{2+} : $1s^2 2s^2 2p^5$

$IE_3 > IE_2 > IE_1$

IE_3 is greater than I.E.$_2$ because to convert $Na^{2+} \longrightarrow Na^{3+}$, electron is removed from a cation having more positive charge.

20. ***(a, b, c, d)*** Statements (a, c, d) are correct whereas (b) is incorrect. The correct form of (b) is:

The 2nd ionisation potential of Mg is lesser than that of Na.

The removal of 2nd electron from Mg takes place from 3s orbital whereas the removal of 2nd electron from Na takes place from 2p-orbitals. More closer are shells to the nucleus, difficult is the removal of electron.

21. ***(24.667)*** Let n Cl-atoms are ionised.

Thus, $6.02 \times 10^{23} \times \Delta H = n \times IE$

$$n = \frac{6.02 \times 10^{23} \times 3.6}{13.0}$$

$$= 1.667 \times 10^{23}$$

The value of $x = 1.667$ and $y = 23$. Thus, $x + y = 24.667$

22. ***(– 3.06)*** Electron gain enthalpy per mol

$$= -\frac{4.9 \times 10^{-13} \times 6.023 \times 10^{23}}{10^6}$$

$$= -29.5 \times 10^4 \text{ J} = -295 \text{ kJ}$$

$$= -\frac{295}{96.49} = -3.06$$

23. ***(41.508)*** Given, $Li(g) \longrightarrow Li^+(g) + e^-; \Delta E_1 = 5.4$ eV

$Cl(g) + e^- \longrightarrow Cl^-(g); \Delta E_2 = -3.6$ eV

$\Delta H = 5.4 - 3.6 = 1.8$ eV

$= 1.8 \times 23.06$ kcal mol^{-1} $= 41.508$ kcal mol^{-1}

24. ***(4.35)*** The electronic configuration of Zn is

$1s^2 2s^2 2p^6 3s^2 3p^6 3d^{10} 4s^2$

$Z_{eff} = Z - \sigma$

$\sigma = 0.35 \times 1 + 18 \times 0.85 + 10 \times 1 = 25.65$

$Z_{eff} = 30 - 25.65 = 4.35$

25. ***(10.4)*** Number of moles of Li $= \frac{\text{Mass}}{\text{Atomic mass}}$

$= \frac{140 \times 10^{-3}}{7} = 2 \times 10^{-2}$ mol

$\because$ For the conversion of 1 mole atoms of Li into Li^+, the energy required = 520 kJ mol^{-1}

$\therefore$ For the conversion 2×10^{-2} mole atoms of Li into Li^+ ions, the energy required will be $520 \times 2 \times 10^{-2}$

= 10.4 kJ

26. ***(10.04)*** The electron gain enthalpy in kJ is represented as

$Cl(g) + e^- \longrightarrow Cl^-(g) + 3.7$ eV

Now, 1 eV atom^{-1} = 96.3 kJ mol^{-1}

$\therefore$ 3.7 eV = 3.7 eV × 96.3 kJ mol^{-1}

Energy released when 35.5 g of chlorine is completely converted to Cl^- ion = 3.7 × 96.3 kJ

Energy released when 1 g of chlorine is completely converted to $Cl^-(g)$ ion $= \frac{3.7 \times 96.3}{35.5} = 10.04$ kJ

27. ***(1309.68 kJ)*** The ionisation potential may be represented as

$H(g) + 13.60\text{eV} \longrightarrow H^{\oplus}(g) + e^-$

We know 1 eV = 96.3 kJ mol^{-1}

13.60 eV = 96.3 × 13.60 = 1309.68 kJ

Thus, energy per mol = 1309.68 kJ

28. ***(3)*** Li, F, Ne are belong from 2nd period.

29. ***(a)*** (A)—(4); (B)—(3); (C)—(1); (D)—(2)

30. ***(b)***(A)—(2); (B)—(1); (C)—(4); (D)—(3)

31. ***(c)***(A) → (4); (B) → (1); (C) → (2); (D) → (3)

32. ***(d)***(A)—(4); (B)—(3); (C)—(5); (D)—(2); (E)—(1)

33. ***(a)***(A) →(4); (B) → (3); (C) → (1); (D) → (2)

34. ***(b)***(A) → (4); (B) → (3); (C) → (2) and (D) → (1)

Zn, Be, Sn, Pb, Sb and Al form amphoteric oxides. Oxides of non metals are acidic in nature and form acids on hydrolysis. However, N_2O, NO, CO and H_2O are neutral oxides.

35. ***(a)***(A) → (4); (B) →(3); (C) → (1) and (D) → (2)

36. ***(4)*** Atomic Size $\propto \frac{\text{(–ve) Charge}}{\text{(+ve) Charge}}$

37. ***(4)*** Na^+, Mg^{+2}, O^{-2}, F^- has $10e^-$ while O^- has $9e^-$, Na has $11e^-$, Mg. has $12e^-$.

38. ***(14)*** Atomic no. 13 (Al) is metal, Atomic no. 14 (Si) is metalloid while 15, 16, 17, 18 are non metals.

39. ***(5)*** Atomic no. 13, 31, 30, 24, 29 are metals.

40. ***(c)*** $B = 1s^2\ 2s^2\ 2p^1$

$Be = 1s^2\ 2s^2$

Valence electron in B is in $2p$ orbital which are of higher energy than 2s orbital of Be and it is different to remove electrons from Be due to its stable electronic configuration. This is the reason that IE_1, of B is less than of Be.

41. ***(c)*** $Be^+ = 1s^2 2s^1$

$B^+ = 1s^2\ 2s^2$

Be^+ has 1 unpaired electron. So, it require more energy to remove an electron.

That is why IE_2 of B > Be.

42. ***(a)***

43. ***(a)*** Compounds with more negative heat of formation values are most stable than compounds with more positive values.

44. ***(b)*** The elements P, Q, R, S are phosphorus, aluminium, arsenic and gallium respectively.

Atomic size of P = 180 pm

Al = 143 pm

As = 114 pm

Ga = 135 pm

$\therefore$ Atomic size of R < S

As < Ga

45. ***(3)*** On moving left to right, ionisation energy increases as Z_{eff} increases and on moving top to bottom ionisation energy decreases as the size increases.

$\therefore$ Al, Ga, As has lesser IE_1 than P.

46. ***(b)*** Among the given sets of elements, only two i.e., (i) and (iv) on which Newland's law of octave can be apply that of according to this law, when elements are arranged according to their increasing atomic weights then every eight elements have similar properties as that of first element.

47. ***(d)*** Among the given compounds, only three i.e., $CaCO_3$, $SrCO_3$ and $BaCO_3$ are thermally more stable than $MgCO_3$ because stability of the carbonates of group 2 increases down the group.

48. ***(b)*** Among the given elements, only three i.e., Pu, Cm and Es are transuranium elements because these elements lie after uranium (U) in actinide series.

49. ***(d)*** Among the given oxides, only three i.e., MoO_3, B_2O_3 and N_2O_5 are acidic oxides while others are —

PbO → Amphoteric

ZnO → Amphoteric

MnO_2 → Amphoteric

MoO_3 → Acidic

$ZnO_2 \rightarrow$ Amphoteric

$B_2O_3 \rightarrow$ Acidic

$N_2O_5 \rightarrow$ Acidic

50. ***(b)*** Among the given pairs, only two i.e., (iv) and (v) are isoelectronic with Al^{3+}.

51. ***(b)*** Among the given pairs, only three i.e., (ii), (vi) and (vii) in which 2nd species has lower ionisation energy than first species.

As, ionisation energy increase along a period and decreases down the group in the periodic table.

52. ***(d)*** Among the given names, only five i.e., (i), (ii), (iv), (vi) and (vii) has correct representation.
    - Hassium ($_{108}Hs$); Unniloctium
    - Dubnium ($_{105}Db$); Unnilpentium

53. ***(b)*** Among the given elements, only five i.e, Cs, Zn, Ba, Sr and Al have only single oxidation state (other than zero) in their corresponding stable compounds.

Cs $\rightarrow (+1)$

Zn $\rightarrow (+2)$

Ba $\rightarrow (+2)$

Ga $\rightarrow (+1, +3)$

Pb $\rightarrow (+2, +4)$

Sr $\rightarrow (+2)$

Al $\rightarrow (+3)$

54. ***(a)*** Among the given elements, only three i.e., Te, Po and Ra are representative elements.

Check Through PYQs : JEE Advanced

1. ***(9)*** By observing the values of different ionisation energies, I_1, I_2 and I_3 for atomic number $(n + 2) \rightarrow$ there is a very large difference between 2nd and 1st. It $(I_2 >> I_1)$

This indicates that number of valences shell electron is 1 and atomic number $(n + 2)$ should be an alkali metal. Also for $(n + 3)$, $I_3 >> I_2$. This alkali earth metal which suggests atomic number $(n + 1)$ is a noble gas.

Since $n < 10$; then $n = 9$ (factor)

2. ***(c,d)*** ZnO, Al_2O_3, PbO, PbO_2, BeO, SnO, SnO_2, Cr_2O_3 are amphoteric oxides.

NO is neutral oxide.

CrO is basic oxide.

B_2O_3 is an acidic oxide.

CHAPTER 2

Chemical Bonding and Molecular Structure

Learning Elements

Element 1 Ionic and Covalent Bonds, Fajan's Rule

Chemical Bond, Kossel-Lewis Approach to Chemical Bonding : Octet Rule, Lewis Symbols, Ionic Bonds, Covalent Character in Ionic Bonds : Fajan Rule, Covalent Bond, Coordinate Bond, Formal Charge, Polarity of Covalent Bonds, Dipole Moment.

Element 2 Bond Parameters, Valence Bond Theory and VSEPR Theory

Bond Parameter, Resonance, VBT, Types of Overlapping and Nature of Covalent Bonds, Hybridisation, VSEPR Theory

Element 3 Molecular Orbital Theory (MOT) and Hydrogen Bonding

Postulates of MOT, Linear Combination of Atomic Orbitals (LCAO), Hydrogen Bonding

Practice Elements

Practice Element 1 Target JEE Main
Practice Element 2 Target JEE Advanced

Trend Insights

JEE Main

	2024				2023				2022			
Topics	**E**	**M**	**T**	**O**	**E**	**M**	**T**	**O**	**E**	**M**	**T**	**O**
Ionic and Covalent Bonds, Fajan's Rule	2	3	2	7	2	1	1	4	1	1	2	4
Bond Parameter, VBT Theory and VSEPR	3	7	9	19	3	4	6	13	3	5	5	13
MOT, Hydrogen Bonding	1	1	8	10	0	0	2	2	1	2	3	6

E = Easy, **M** = Medium, **T** = Tough, **O** = Overall

Current Dynamics

- Overall weightage and difficulty level of questions had been increased in 2024.
- Standard and scoring questions were asked from the topics VBT, VSEPR and MOT.
- Frequent number of questions involving Fajan's rule and bond parameter were also asked in past years.
- The trend is changing now-a-days, less number of questions from dipole moment, molecular polarity, bond angle, resonance and formal charge had been asked.

JEE Advanced

S.No.	Typology	Years				
		2024	2023	2022	2021	2020
1.	One Option Correct	–	1	–	–	–
2.	One or More than One Correct	1	–	1	–	–
3.	Numerical/Integer Type	1	1	1	–	1
4.	Matching Type	1	–	–	–	–
5.	Paragraph Based	–	–	–	–	–

Current Dynamics

- In present scenario more number of Numerical/Integer type questions are expected from this chapter.

Insightful Advice

- Focus on exceptions and special cases and practice on predicting molecular shapes and bond angles.
- Practice the filling of molecular orbitals systematically and then analyse bond order, paramagnetism and diamagnetism behaviour of a molecule/ions.
- Understand distortion in bond angles caused by lone pairs, multiple bonds or back bonding.

Element 1 Ionic and Covalent Bonds, Fajan's Rule

It is a well known fact that except for inert gases, no other element exists as independent atoms under ordinary condition. Most of the elements exist as molecules which are cluster of atoms. How do atoms combine to form molecules and why do atoms form bonds ? Such doubts will be discussed in the given modules. A molecule will only be formed if it is more stable and has a lower energy, than the individual atoms.

Chemical Bond

It is a kind of attraction which holds two or more constituents (atoms, molecules or ions) together as a stable molecule. The process of their combination is called **chemical bonding.**

For an element, bond formation is valency dependent phenomenon.

- The valency is defined as the combining capacity of an element. In simpler words, the number of bonds formed by an element with the other similar species is called the valency of that element.
- The formation of a chemical bond is always accompanied by release of energy.

  So, decrease in energy $\propto$ Strength of the bond
- All the attractive forces constituting a chemical bond are electrostatic in nature.
- Ionic, covalent, coordinate are such types of chemical bonds which are present in a molecule.

Cause of Chemical Combination

It is described by the following factors

(i) **Tendency to Acquire Minimum Energy** When two atoms approaches each other then nucleus of one atom attracts the electron of another atom.Two nuclei and electron of both the atoms repel each other. If net result is attraction, the total energy of the system (molecule) decreases and a chemical bond forms.

So, Attraction $\propto$ 1/energy $\propto$ Stability.

(ii) **Tendency to Acquire Noble Gas Configuration** Atom combines to acquire noble gas configuration. Only outermost electron i.e. *ns*, *np* and $(n-1)d$-electrons participate in bond formation. Inert gas elements do not participate, as they have stable electronic configuration $1s^2$ or ns^2np^6 and hence minimum energy.

Kossel-Lewis Approach to Chemical Bonding: Octet Rule

In 1916, Kossel and Lewis theory was the first explanation of a chemical bond in terms of electrons that was accepted.

According to this theory,

(i) Outer most electrons (valence electrons) play a fundamental role in chemical bonding.

(ii) Ionic bonding involves the transfer of one or more electrons from one atom to another.

(iii) Covalent bonding involves sharing of electrons between two atoms.

(iv) Electrons are transferred or shared such that each atom attains electronic configuration of a noble gas (ns^2np^6), i.e. having 8 outer shell (valence) electrons. This arrangement is called **octet rule.**

Lewis Symbols

In the formation of a molecule, only the outer shell electrons take part in a chemical combination. These electrons are known as **valence electrons**. The inner shell electrons are well protected and are generally not involved in the combination process.

Lewis introduced simple notations to represent valence electrons of an atom. These notations are called Lewis symbols.

e.g.

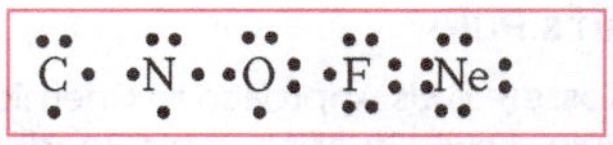

All the valence (outer-shell) electrons of the atoms in a Lewis structure are represented by the dots surrounding the symbol.

JEE Spotlite

General steps to write the Lewis structure for charged species

- Calculate the total number of valence electrons of atom(s) involved in a molecule.
- Addition of charge on anion and subtraction of charge on cation is done.
- Select the central atom which is generally the least electronegative atom and draw the skeletal structure w.r.t. valence electrons and charges involved in it.

Significance of Lewis Symbols

The common valency of the element is either equal to the number of dots in Lewis symbols or 8 minus the number of dots. e.g. Li, Be, B have 1, 2, 3 valency respectively while N, O, F have 8 minus number of dots, i.e. 3, 2 and 1 valency respectively.

Limitations of Octet Rule

The octet rule, though useful in explaining the formation of a large number of compounds but there are some limitations which are discussed below

(i) **Incomplete Octet Molecules** (or electron deficient molecules) Some stable molecules exist in nature in which central atom has less than 8 electrons in their outer most or valence shell.

e.g. BeF_2, BF_3, $AlCl_3$, LiCl, BeH_2, etc.

Due to their electron deficient character these have higher tendency to accept electron pair. That's why these molecules are also called **'Lewis acids'.**

(ii) **Odd Electron Molecules** Some molecules or ions possesses odd number of electrons in their outermost shell. These are paramagnetic in nature, e.g. NO, NO_2.

Unpaired electron →•N̈=Ö:⟷ 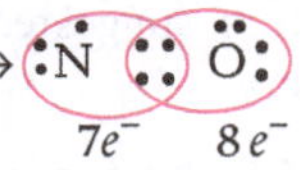

(iii) **Electron Rich Molecules** Some molecules have more than 8 electrons in the valence shell of central atom. This is called super octet or expanded octet. e.g. In SF_6, there are six S—F bonds having all 12 electrons in the valence shell of sulphur.

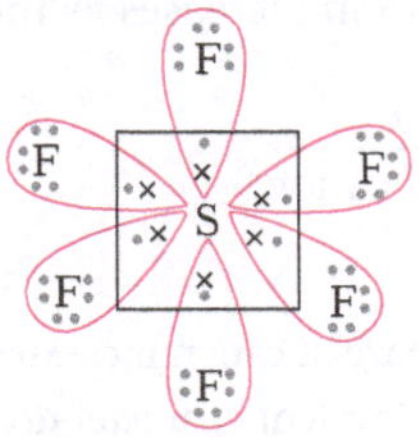

Other e.g. are PCl_5, IF_7, PF_5, H_2SO_4.

(iv) **Formation of Compounds of Noble Gases** Octet rule suggested that noble gases are inert but Xe and Kr take part in bonding to form compounds with elements like fluorine and oxygen XeF_2, XeF_4, $XeOF_4$, $XeOF_2$, KrF_2.

(v) It also does not explain the formation of 3 centre two electron bonds as found in B_2H_6.

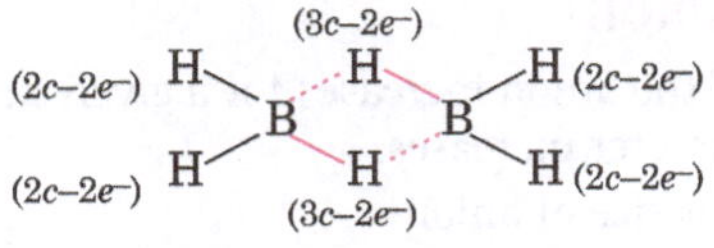

It does not explain the relative stability of the molecules.

Ionic Bond (Electrovalent Bond)

The electrostatic force of attraction that holds the oppositely charged ions together is known as ionic bond or electrovalent bond. This type of bond is formed when a metal atom (electropositive element) transfers one or more electrons to a non-metal atom (highly electronegative element). i.e.,

Group 1 and 17 elements forms maximum ionic compound.

$$\underset{2,\,8,\,1}{Na} + \underset{2,\,8,\,7}{Cl} \xrightarrow{1e^-} \underset{\substack{2,\,8\\(\text{Ne configuration})}}{Na^+} + \underset{\substack{2,\,8,\,8\\(\text{Ar configuration})}}{Cl^-}$$

More the distance between two elements in periodic table more will be the ionic character of bond. Total number of electron lose or gained is called electrovalency.

JEE Alert

- Electronegativity difference ∝ polarity of ionic bond.
- The force of attraction is equal in all directions so ionic bond is non-directional.
- Ionic compound do not have molecular formula. It has only empirical formula. e.g. NaCl is empirical formula of sodium chloride.

Factors Affecting the Formation of Ionic Bond

It depends upon following factors

1. Ionisation Energy

Amount of energy required to remove an electron from the outermost orbit of an isolated gaseous atom to form the positive ion or cation (energy absorbed).

Lesser is the ionisation energy greater is the tendency to form cation. For e.g.,

$$\left.\begin{array}{l} Na^+ > Mg^{2+} > Al^{3+} \\ Cs^+ > Rb^+ > K^+ > Na^+ > Li^+ \end{array}\right\} \text{Cation formation tendency}$$

2. Electron Affinity

Amount of energy released when an electron is added to an isolated gaseous ion to form negative ion i.e. anion.

Higher is the electron affinity greater is the tendency to form anion

e.g. $Cl^- > F^- > Br^- > I^-$; $F^- > O^{2-} > N^{3-}$

3. Lattice Energy

Amount of energy released when one mole of crystal lattice is formed.

Higher lattice energy → Greater will be the stability or strength of ionic compound.

Factors Affecting Lattice Energy

(i) **Magnitude of Charge** → $U \propto z^+z^-$ (Ionic charge)

Lattice energy ∝ Magnitude of charge

$$NaCl < MgCl_2 < AlCl_3$$
$$Na^+ < Mg^{2+} < Al^{3+}$$

The higher the charges on the ions and smaller the distance between them, greater is the lattice energy.

(ii) **Size of Cation** As the size of cation increases, lattice energy decreases. Thus, the order of lattice energies is

$$LiCl > NaCl > KCl > RbCl > CsCl$$

JEE Spotlite

- If the anion and the cation are of comparable size, the cationic radius will influence the lattice energy. Since lattice energy generally decreases more rapidly than the hydration energy with increasing ionic size, solubility of most ionic compounds tends to increase as we go down the group provided that hydration energy does not decrease at a faster rate than lattice energy.

$$Be(OH)_2 < Mg(OH)_2 < Ca(OH)_2 < Sr(OH)_2 < Ba(OH)_2$$

- If the anion is significantly large compared to the cation, the lattice energy will remain almost constant within a particular group. Since the hydration energies decreases on moving down the group, solubility in general will decrease as found for alkaline earth metal carbonates and sulphates.

Characteristics of Ionic Compounds

Some important characteristics of ionic compounds are as follows

- These are generally crystalline in nature. The constituent ions are arranged in a regular way in their crystal lattices.
- These possess high melting and boiling points as they, are held by strong electrostatic forces of attraction.
- These are hard and brittle in nature.
- In solid state, they do not conduct electricity. In molten state or in solution they conduct electricity due to the presence of free ions in aqueous state.
- These are soluble in polar solvent and insoluble in non-polar solvent.
- The electrovalent bonds are non-rigid and non-directional. Thus, these compounds do not show configurational isomerism,i.e. geometrical and optical isomerism.
- Electrovalent compounds show isomorphism (compounds with a similar number of valence e^-, i.e similar configuration of their cation and anion, e.g. NaF and MgO, both have the same number of valence electrons in Na^+, F^-, Mg^{2+} and O^{2-}).

Covalent Character in Ionic Bonds: Fajan's Rule

According to this rule, all the covalent bonds possess some partial ionic character. Similarly, the ionic bonds also have partial covalent character. When a cation approaches an anion, the positive ion tends to distort the electron cloud of the negative ion towards itself.

This effect is called **polarisation.** Hence, no bond is 100% ionic as it has some covalent character also.

Polarisation Power

The ability of cation to polarise a nearby anion is called Polarisation power of cation.

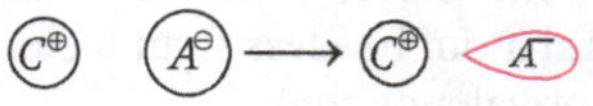

Polarisability

(i) It is the ability of anion to get polarised by the cation.

(ii) Polarisation of anion causes some sharing of electron between the ions so ionic bond acquires certain covalent character.

(iii) Polarisation ∝ Covalent character

(iv) Magnitude of polarisation depends upon a number of factors, suggested by Fajan and are known as Fajan's rule.

Following Factors Affect Polarisation

Fajan gave the following rules to decide the magnitude of polarisation or covalent character in an ionic bond.

1. Size of Cation

- Polarisation of the anion increases as the size of cation decreases.
- Polarisation $\propto \dfrac{1}{\text{size of cation}}$

In a Group

$BeCl_2$, $MgCl_2$, $CaCl_2$, $SrCl_2$, $BaCl_2$ (↓)
Size of cation increases
Covalent character decreases
Ionic character increases

Greatest polarising power of Be^{2+}, shows its maximum covalent character

In a Period

Na^+, Mg^{2+}, Al^{3+}, Si^{4+} (→)
Size of cation decreases
Covalent character increases

2. Size of Anion

- If the size of the anion increases for a given cation, the covalent character increases.
- Polarisation ∝ size of anion

CaF_2, $CaCl_2$, $CaBr_2$, CaI_2 (↓)
Size of anion increases
Covalent character increases
Ionic character decreases

3. Charge on Cation and Anion

- Polarisation ∝ charge on cation or anion
- Charge on cation ∝ Polarisation (covalent character)

e.g. $\xrightarrow[\text{Na}^+ \quad \text{Mg}^{2+} \quad \text{Al}^{3+} \quad \text{Si}^{4+}]{\text{NaCl} \quad \text{MgCl}_2 \quad \text{AlCl}_3 \quad \text{SiCl}_4}$

Charge on cation increases
Covalent character increases
Ionic character decreases

Charge on anion ∝ Polarisation ∝ Covalent nature $\propto \frac{1}{\text{M.P.}}$

4. Non-Inert Gas Configuration

The polarising power of those cations which do not have inert gas configuration will be more in comparision to cations having inert gas configuration.

Solved Booster 1.1

Compound with maximum ionic character is formed from

(a) Na and Cl (b) Cs and F (c) Cs and I (d) Na and F

Solution *(b)*

Using Fajan's rule, larger cation and smaller anion will have maximum ionic character. Thus Cs and F have maximum ionic characters.

Solved Booster 1.2

Out of the following which one has the highest values of covalent character.

(a) $ZnCl_2$ (b) $CaCl_2$ (c) $CdCl_2$ (d) CuCl

Solution *(a)*

As Zn^{2+} has smallest size among all the given options, thus $ZnCl_2$ has highest value of covalent character.

Covalent Bond

The concept of covalent bond was first proposed by Lewis in 1916. The bond formed between the two atoms by mutual sharing of electrons so as to complete their octets or duplets (in case of elements having only one shell) is called covalent bond or covalent linkage.

A covalent bond between two similar atoms is non-polar covalent bond while it is polar between two different atom having different electronegativities. Covalent bond may be single, double or a triple bond.

1. Formation of Cl_2 Molecule

Chlorine atom has seven electrons in its valence shell. In the formation of chlorine molecule, each chlorine atom contributes one electron and the pair of electrons is shared between two atoms. Both the atoms acquire stable configuration of argon.

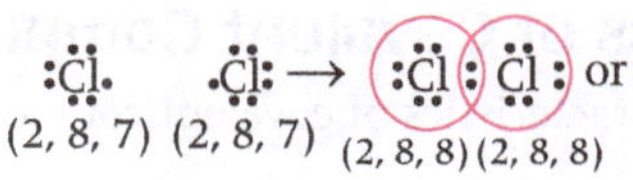

2. Formation of HCl Molecule

Both hydrogen and chlorine contribute one electron each and then the pair of electrons is equally shared. Hydrogen acquires the configuration of helium and chlorine acquires the configuration of argon.

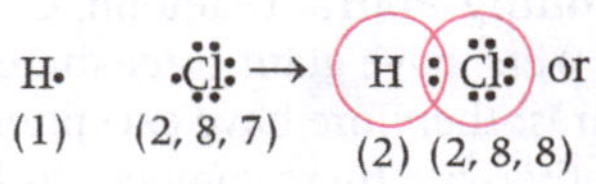

3. Formation of H_2O Molecule

Oxygen atom has 6 valence electrons. It can achieve configuration of neon by sharing two electrons, one with each hydrogen atom.

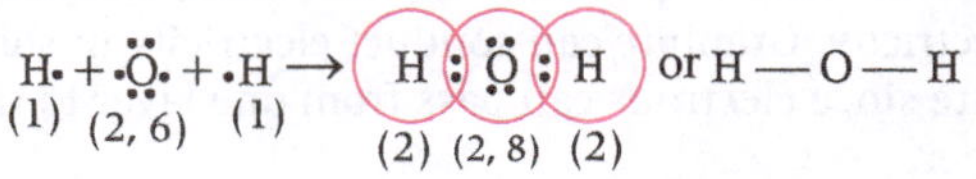

4. Formation of O_2 Molecule

Each oxygen atom contributes two electrons and two pairs of electrons are shared equally. Both the atoms acquire configuration of neon.

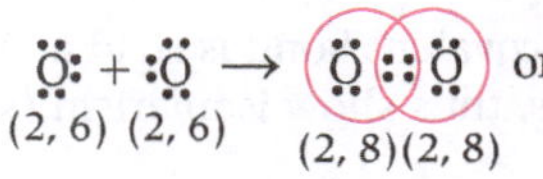

5. Formation of N_2 Molecule

Nitrogen atom has five valence electrons. Both nitrogen atoms achieve configuration of neon by sharing 3 pairs of electrons, i.e., each atom contributes 3 electrons.

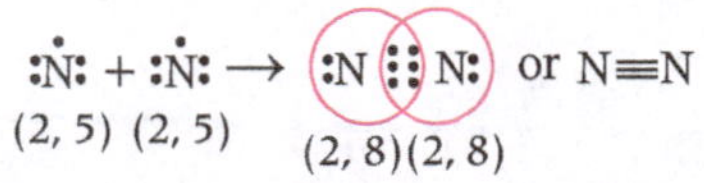

Conditions for Formation of Covalent Bonds

Some important condition for formation of covalent bonds are as follows.

(i) **Number of Valence Electrons** The combining atoms should be short by 1, 2 or 3 electrons in the valence shell in comparison to stable noble gas configuration.

(ii) **Electronegativity Difference** Difference between the electronegativity of two atoms should be zero or very small.

(iii) **Small Decrease in Energy** The approach of the atoms towards one another should be accompanied by decrease of energy.

Characteristics of Covalent Compounds

Some important characteristics of covalent compounds are as follows

(i) **Physical State** These exist as gases or liquids under the normal conditions of temperature and pressure. This is because very weak forces of attraction exist between discrete molecules. Some covalent compounds exist as soft solids. e.g., S_8, P_4 and I_2.

(ii) **Melting and Boiling Points** Diamond, Carborundum (SiC), Silica (SiO_2) etc. have giant three dimensional network structures; therefore have exceptionally high melting points otherwise these compounds have relatively low melting and boiling points. This is due to weak forces of attraction between the molecules.

(iii) **Electrical Conductivity** In general covalent substances are bad conductor of electricity. Polar covalent compounds like HCl in solution conduct electricity. Graphite can conduct electricity in solid state since electrons can pass from one layer to the other.

(iv) **Solubility** These compounds are generally insoluble in polar solvent like water but soluble in non-polar solvents like benzene etc. Some covalent compounds like alcohol, dissolve in water due to hydrogen bonding.

(v) **Isomerism** The covalent bond is rigid and directional. These compounds, thus show isomerism (structural and space).

(vi) **Molecular Reactions** Covalent substances show molecular reactions. The reaction rates are usually low because it involves two steps (i) breaking of covalent bonds of the reactants and (ii) formation of new bonds while the ionic reactions involved only regrouping of ions.

JEE Alert

The number of electrons contributed by an atom of the element for sharing with other atoms is called covalency of the element. The variable covalency of an element is equal to the total number of unpaired electrons in *s*, *p* and *d*-orbitals of its valency shell.

Extended Covalent Bond

Banana bond is an extended covalent bond found in diboranes in which a hydrogen atom is shared by two boron atoms and form a three centre two electron bond.

e.g., - B_2H_6

Structure of B_2H_6

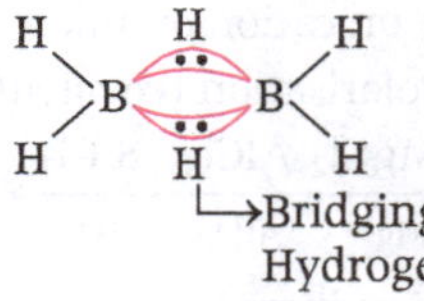

Coordinate Bond

A covalent bond results from the sharing of pair of electrons between two atoms where each atom contributes one electron to the bond. It is also possible to have an electron pair bond where both electrons originate from one atom and none from the other. Such bonds are called **coordinate bonds** or **dative bonds.**

Since in coordinate bonds, two electrons are shared by two atoms, they differ from normal covalent bonds only in the way they are formed, and once formed they are identical to normal covalent bonds.

It is represented as

- Atom/ion/molecule donating electron pair is called **Donor** or **Lewis Base**
- Atom/ion/molecule accepting electron pair is called **Acceptor** or **Lewis Acid;** (→) points donor to acceptor.
- **NH_4^+** NH_3 has three (N—H) bonds and one lone pair on N-atom. In NH_4^+ formation this lone pair is donated to H^+ (having no electron)

$$\underset{\text{Lewis base}}{NH_3} + \underset{\text{Lewis acid}}{H^+} \longrightarrow NH_4^+$$

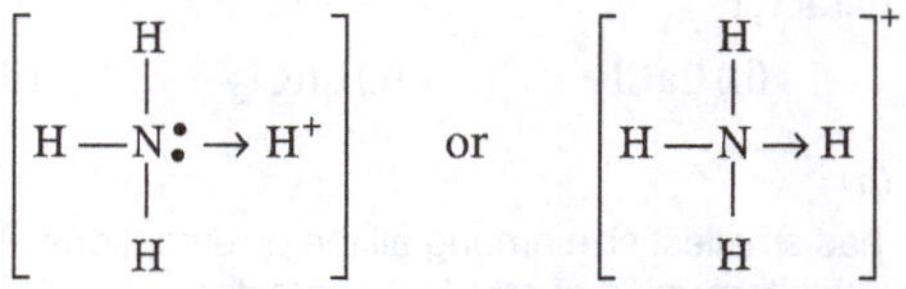

- **BF_4^-** In BF_3, B has incomplete octet. F^- can donate its one of the lone pairs to B forming BF_4^-

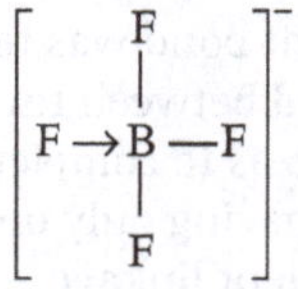

- **SO_3**

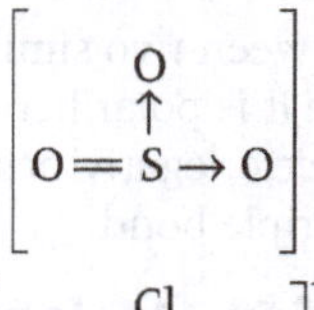

- **PCl_6^-**

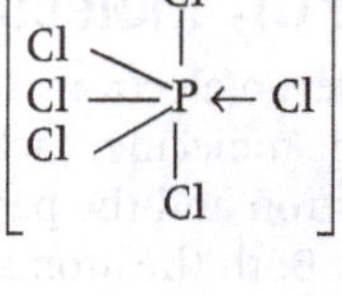

- **SbF_6^-** 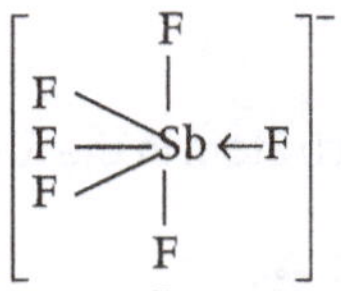
- **NH_3 and BF_3** 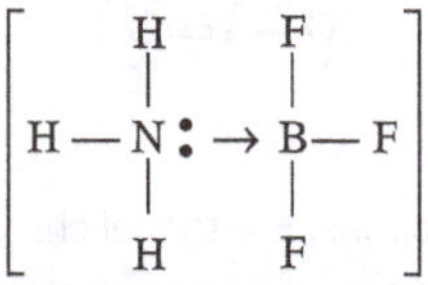
- **$[Fe(H_2O)_6]^{2+}$** 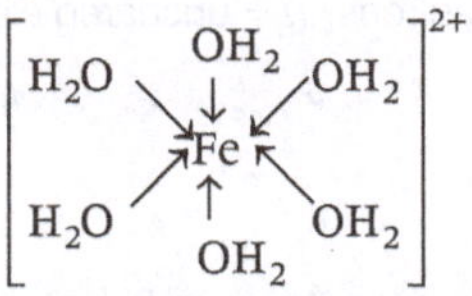

Properties of the coordinate compounds are intermediates of ionic and covalent compounds.

JEE Spotlite

Comparison of Ionic, Covalent and Coordinate Compounds

Characteristic	Ionic	Covalent	Coordinate
(i) Binding force	between ions (strong coulombic attraction)	between molecules (van der Waals' force)	coordinate covalent bond
(ii) m.p./b.p.	high	less than ionic	higher than covalent, lower than ionic
(iii) Conduction	conductor of electricity in fused state and in aqueous solution.	bad conductor	conductor if ionic in nature
(iv) Solubility in polar solvent (H_2O)	high	less	in between
(v) Solubility in non-polar solvents (ether)	low	high	in between
(vi) Physical state	generally solid	solid, liquid and gas	solid, liquid, gas

Characteristics of Dative Bond or Coordinate Bond

The important characteristics of dative compounds are as follows

- These compounds exist in all the three states, under ordinary conditions, i.e. solids, liquids and gases.
- The melting and boiling points of these compounds are higher as compared to covalent compounds but lower than those of ionic compounds.
- Like covalent compounds these are also poor conductors of electricity in solid as well as in fused state.
- These compounds are sparingly soluble in polar solvents like water, however, these are readily soluble in organic solvents.
- These compounds are generally as stable as covalent compounds.
- Coordinate linkage is rigid and directional, thus they exhibit space isomerism.
- Dative compounds show molecular reactions just like covalent compounds.
- The dielectric constants for these compounds are higher.

Solved Booster 1.3

Classify the following bonds as ionic, polar covalent or covalent and give your reasons :

(a) SiSi bond in $Cl_3SiSiCl_3$ (b) SiCl bond in $Cl_3SiSiCl_3$

(c) CaF bond in CaF_2 (d) NH bond in NH_3

Solution

(a) Covalent due to identical electronegativity.

(b) One electron pair is shared between Si and Cl and thus, covalent bond is expected but electronegativity of Cl is greater than that of Si and some polarity develops giving polar-covalent nature.

(c) Ionic since Ca completes its octet by transfer of two outer-shell electrons and two F atoms gain these two electrons thus, completing their octets

Ca : [Ar] $4s^2$, F : [He] $2s^2\,2p^5$

(d) Polar covalent, (explanation as in (b).)

Solved Booster 1.4

The type of bond present in N_2O_5 is/are

(a) Only covalent (b) Only ionic

(c) Ionic and covalent (d) Covalent and coordinate

Solution

(d) The structure of N_2O_5 is as follows

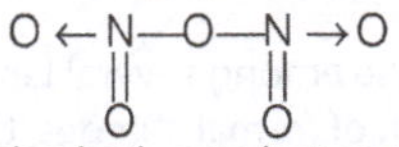

Thus, it contains both covalent and coordinate bond.

Formal Charge

The formal charge of an atom in a molecule is the hypothetical charge used to determine the distribution of electrons in a molecule or ion. Formal charge (F) is determined by using

Formal charge (F.C.) on an atom in a Lewis structure

$$= \begin{bmatrix}\text{Total number of valence} \\ \text{electrons in the free} \\ \text{atom.}\end{bmatrix} - \begin{bmatrix}\text{Total number of} \\ \text{non-bonding (lone} \\ \text{pair) electrons.}\end{bmatrix} - \frac{1}{2}\begin{bmatrix}\text{Total number of} \\ \text{bonding (shared)} \\ \text{electrons.}\end{bmatrix}$$

or $$\text{F.C.} = v - u - \frac{1}{2}(s)$$

- In $BrCl_3$, 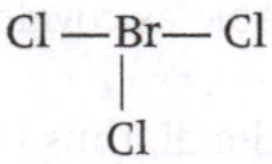

	v	s	u	Formal charge
Br	7	6	4	0
Cl	7	2	6	0

- In ICl_4^-

	v	s	u	Formal charge
I	7	8	4 (one extra)	–1
Cl	7	2	6	0

- In NH_4^+

	v	s	u	Formal charge
N	5	8	0	+1
H	1	2	0	0

In many cases, we can draw more than one structure for a molecule, with different arrangement of atoms.

JEE Spotlite

We can use the following guidelines involving formal charge to decide between two or more possible structures for a molecule or ion.

- A molecular structure that gives a Lewis structure in which all formal charges are zero is preferable to the one in which some formal charges are not zero.
- If the Lewis structure have non-zero formal charges, the structure with the lowest number of non-zero formal charge is preferable.
- When we have to choose among several Lewis structures with similar distribution of formal charges, then the structure in which formal charge is present on the more electronegative atom is preferable.

Thiocyanate ion can be assigned three structures

	Formal charges			Total charge
	N	C	S	
$[:\ddot{N}=C=\ddot{S}:]^-$	–1	0	0	–1
$[:\ddot{C}=N=\ddot{S}:]^-$	+1	–2	0	–1
$[:\ddot{C}=S=\ddot{N}:]^-$	–1	–2	+2	–1

In all these cases total formal charge is –1. But we prefer structure I because it has the lowest number of atoms with non-zero formal charge [guideline (b)].

Solved Booster 1.5

Calculate the formal charge on each atom in the following electron-dot structure for SO_2

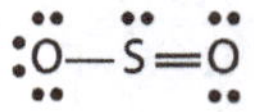

Solution

Let v = valence electrons, F = formal charge,
s = shared electrons, u = unshared electrons.

Atom	v	s	u	$F = v - \frac{s}{2} - u$
Sulphur	6	6	2	+1
Single-bonded oxygen	6	2	6	–1
Double-bonded oxygen	6	4	4	0

SO_2 may be written as 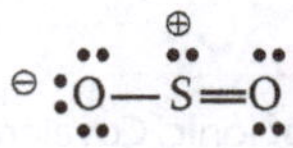

Polarity of Covalent Bonds

Difference between electronegativities of participating atoms, results in polarisability of the covalent bond. Thus, on the basis of polarity, covalent bonds are of two types

(i) **Non-polar Covalent Bond** The covalent bond formed between two atoms having zero or almost zero difference in their electronegativities is called non-polar covalent bond, e.g. H_2, Cl_2, F_2, Br_2, etc. In such molecules, the shared pair of electrons is equally attracted by the two atoms.

(ii) **Polar Covalent Bond** The covalent bond formed between two atoms having significance difference in their electronegativities, is called polar covalent bond.

In such molecules, the shared pair of electrons get attracted towards the more electronegative atom, therefore, more electronegative atom acquires a partial negative charge (δ^-) and less electronegative atom acquires a partial positive charge (δ^+).

e.g. $\overset{\delta+}{H}—\overset{\delta-}{Cl}$; $\overset{\delta+}{H}—\overset{\delta-}{O}—\overset{\delta+}{H}$

Hence, a covalent bond develops a partial ionic character as a result of the difference of electronegativities of the atoms forming a polar covalent bond.

Dipole Moment

- The magnitude of ionic character in a polar covalent bond is measured through a quantity called **dipole moment.** It is usually represented by a *Greek* letter μ.
- Dipole moment is defined as the product of the magnitude of the charge and the distance between the centres of positive and negative charges.
- Mathematically, it is expressed as
  Dipole moment (μ) = charge (q) × distance of separation (d)

- It is expressed in Debye (D).
  If $q = 4.8\times 10^{-10}$ esu and $d = 1$ Å $= 1\times 10^{-8}$ cm
  then $\mu = 4.8\times 10^{-10}\times 1\times 10^{-8} = 4.8\times 10^{-18}$ esu cm
- A molecule will have a dipole moment of 1 Debye (1D) if charges of 1.0×10^{-10} esu are separated by a distance of 1 Å.
  Thus, 1.0×10^{-18} esu cm = 1.0 D
  In SI unit, 1 D = 3.336×10^{-30} Cm

JEE MAPPER

Example Similar to PYQ Asked in JEE Main 2024 & 2025

Number of compound from the following with zero dipole moment is ....

$CO_2, H_2, H_2S, HBr, CHCl_3, H_2O, BeF_2, CH_4, CCl_4, NH_3$, 1, 4-dichlorobenzene.

Sol. (6) Among the given compounds only six compounds i.e., $CO_2, H_2, BeF_2, CH_4, CCl_4$ and 1,4-dichlorobenzene has zero dipole moment.

Competency Enhancer 1.1

Number of compounds / species from the following with non-zero dipole moment is ....

$HF, SO_2, CO_2, NF_3, NH_3, H_2, CH_4, BF_3, HCl, SiF_4$

- Dipole moment is a vector quantity as it has direction as well as magnitude. The direction of the dipole moment is represented by a small arrow with tail on the positive centre and head pointing towards the negative centre. e.g. The dipole moment of HCl may be represented as

$$\overset{\delta+}{H} \longrightarrow \overset{\delta-}{Cl}$$

- The shift in electron density is symbolised by crossed arrow ($\longrightarrow$) in a Lewis structure is used to indicate the direction of the shift.
- In diatomic molecule, $\mu = q\times d$
- In polyatomic molecule with angle θ, resultant dipole moment is the vector summation of the vector moments.

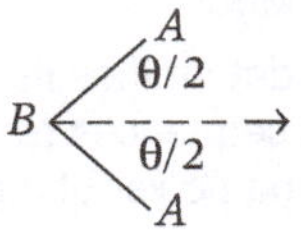

$$\mu_{resultant} = 2\mu_{AB}\cos\left(\frac{\theta}{2}\right)$$

where, μ_{AB} is the vector moment of the side AB.

Also, $\mu_{resultant} \propto \cos\left(\frac{\theta}{2}\right)$

Thus, greater the value of θ, smaller the value of μ. Symmetrical molecules without lone pair of electrons will have $\mu = 0$, e.g. BH_3, CO_2.

- Unsymmetrical molecules with lone pair of electrons have some dipole moment as lone pair of electron also possesses some dipole moment.

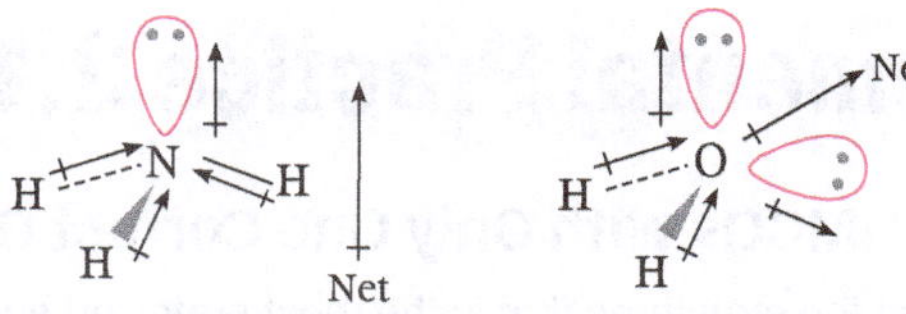

Ammonia (μ = 1.47 D) Water (μ = 1.85 D)

$$\mu_{H_2O}(\theta = 104.5°) > \mu_{NH_3}(\theta = 107°) > \mu_{SO_2}(\theta = 120°)$$

- Dipole moment of NH_3 is greater than that of NF_3. This is because, in case of NH_3, the orbital dipole of lone pair is in the same direction as the resultant dipole moment of the N—H bonds whereas in NF_3, the orbital dipole is in the direction opposite to the resultant dipole moment of the three N—F bonds.

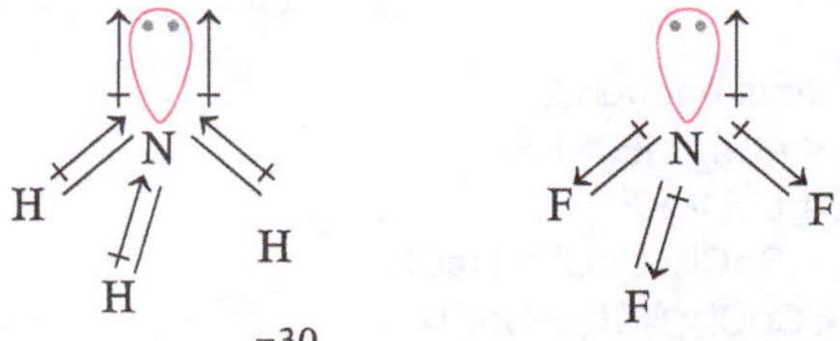

$\mu_{net} = 4.90\times 10^{-30}$ Cm $\mu_{net} = 0.80\times 10^{-30}$ Cm

By using dipole moment, the percentage ionic character of a polar bond (A—B) can be calculated as

$$\%\text{ ionic character in a molecule} = \frac{\text{observed value of } \mu}{\text{theoretical value of } \mu}\times 100$$

% ionic character of $\underset{39.4\%}{HF} > \underset{16.0\%}{HCl} > \underset{10.8\%}{HBr} > \underset{4.7\%}{HI}$

Solved Booster 1.6

The dipole moment of HBr is 2.60×10^{-30} Cm and the interatomic spacing is 1.41 Å. Then the per cent ionic character of HBr is

(a) 11.5 (b) 19.5 (c) 21.5 (d) 14.5

Solution (a)

Theoretical value of dipole moment of a 100% ionic character

$= q\times d$

$= (1.60\times 10^{-19}\text{ C})(1.41\times 10^{-10}\text{ m}) = 2.26\times 10^{-29}$ Cm

Observed value of dipole moment = 2.60×10^{-30} Cm

$$\text{percent ionic character} = \frac{\text{observed value}}{\text{theoretical value}}\times 100$$

$$= \frac{2.60\times 10^{-30}}{2.26\times 10^{-29}}\times 100 = 11.5\%$$

Solved Booster 1.7

The dipole moment of the ammonia molecule is 1.48D. The length of the dipole is

(a) 3.08×10^{-11} m (b) 5×10^{2} m (c) 308 m (d) 5.91×10^{-4} m

Solution (a)

$\mu = 1.48\times 3.33\times 10^{-30}$ Cm $= 4.93\times 10^{-30}$ Cm.

$q = 1.6\times 10^{-19}$C

$$d = \frac{\mu}{q} = \frac{4.93\times 10^{-30}}{1.6\times 10^{-19}} = 3.08\times 10^{-11}\text{m}$$

Elemental Practice 2.1

Type I MCQs with Only One Correct Option

1. Select the structures that is the most preferred and have lowest energy for SO_3.

(a) 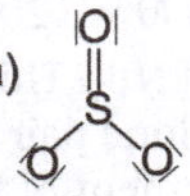 (b) 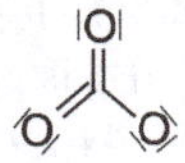

(c) 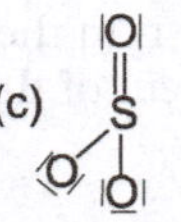 (d) 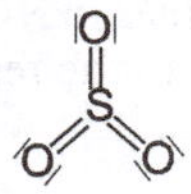

2. Order of covalent bond;
A. $SnCl_4 < AlCl_3$; $LiF > KF$
B. $KF < KI$; $LiF > KF$
C. $SnCl_4 > SnCl_2$; $CuCl > NaCl$
D. $AgCl < CoCl_2$; $BCl_3 < BeCl_2$
E. $KF < KI$; $CuCl > NaCl$
Choose the correct answer from the options given below.
(a) Only B, C (b) Only A, B
(c) Only C, E (d) Only B, C, E

3. The total number of species not having eight electrons around central atom in its outer most shell, is
NH_3, $AlCl_3$, $BeCl_2$, CCl_4, PCl_5
(a) 2 (b) 4 (c) 1 (d) 3

4. Given below are two statements.
Statement (I) According to Fajan's rule, MgF_2 is more ionic than $MgCl_2$ hence, MgF_2 is less soluble in H_2O than $MgCl_2$.
Statement (II) Among the compounds, P_4O_{10}, MnO, CrO_3 and Mn_2O_7 the compound MnO is most ionic.
In the light of the above statement choose the correct answer from the options given below.
(a) Both statement I and statement II are true.
(b) Statement I is true but statement II is false.
(c) Statement I is false but statement II is true.
(d) Both statement I and statement II are false.

5. The correct sequence of increasing covalent character is represented by
(a) $LiCl < NaCl < BeCl_2$
(b) $BeCl_2 < LiCl < NaCl$
(c) $NaCl < LiCl < BeCl_2$
(d) $BeCl_2 < NaCl < LiCl$

6. In PO_4^{3-} ion, the formal charge on each oxygen atom is
(a) + 0.75 (b) 1.0
(c) – 0.75 (d) – 3

7. For two ionic solids CaO and KI, choose the incorrect statement from the following.
(a) Lattice energy of CaO is much larger than that of KI
(b) KI is soluble in benzene
(c) KI has lower melting point
(d) CaO has higher melting point

8. The dielectric constant of H_2O is 80. The electrostatic force of attraction between Na^+ and Cl^- will be
(a) reduced to $\frac{1}{40}$ in water than in air
(b) reduced to $\frac{1}{80}$ in water than in air
(c) will be increased to 80 in water than in air
(d) will remain unchanged

9. Select the pairs that will form the most stable ionic bond.
(a) Na and Cl (b) Mg and F
(c) Li and F (d) Na and F

10. Select the formulae that does not correctly represent the bonding capacities of the atoms involved.

(a) 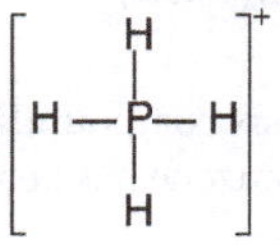 (b) 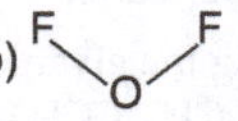

(c) 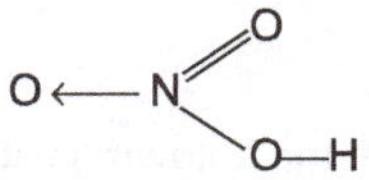 (d) 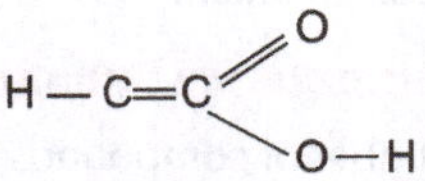

11. Number of covalent and coordinate bond in pyrosulphuric acid are
(a) 6, 4 (b) 6, 6 (c) 4, 4 (d) 4, 6

12. Among the following which compound will show the highest lattice energy?
(a) KF (b) NaF (c) CsF (d) RbF

13. Consider the compounds given below
A. *trans*-pent-2-ene
B. *cis*-hex-3-ene
C. 2, 2-dimethyl propane
D. 2, 2, 3, 3-tetramethyl butane
Choose the pair of compound that possess dipole moment
(a) A, B (b) B, C (c) A, C (d) A, D

14. The maximum covalent character is shown by which of the following compound
(a) $FeCl_2$ (b) $SnCl_2$
(c) $AlCl_3$ (d) $MgCl_2$

15. The charge / size ratio of a cation determines its polarising power. Which one of the following sequences represents the increasing order of the polarising power of the cationic species,
$K^+, Ca^{2+}, Mg^{2+}, Be^{2+}$?
(a) $Mg^{2+} < Be^{2+} < K^+ < Ca^{2+}$ (b) $Be^{2+} < K^+ < Ca^{2+} < Mg^{2+}$
(c) $K^+ < Ca^{2+} < Mg^{2+} < Be^{2+}$ (d) $Ca^{2+} < Mg^{2+} < Be^{2+} < K^+$

16. Among the following mixtures, dipole-dipole as the major interaction, is present in
(a) benzene and ethanol
(b) acetonitrile and acetone
(c) KCl and hexane
(d) Benzene and carbon tetrachloride

Type II 》 MCQs with One or More than One Correct Option

17. Which of the following statements is incorrect regarding Lewis dot structure?
    (a) The total no. of electrons required for writing the structures are obtained by adding the valence electrons of the combining atoms.
    (b) Each combining atom contributes at least two electrons to the shared pair.
    (c) For anions, each negative charge would mean subtraction of one electron from the total no. of valence electrons.
    (d) The least electronegative atom occupies the central position in the molecule/ion.
18. Select the correct statements about ionic and covalent bonds.
    (a) Ionic compounds conduct electricity in solid form .
    (b) Covalent compounds are usually non-electrolytes.
    (c) Ionic compounds generally have low melting points.
    (d) Covalent bonds are formed by the sharing of electrons between atoms.
19. Select the correct order of polarising powers of cations when their sizes are almost same
    (a) $Cd^{2+} > Ca^{2+}$ (b) $Ca^{2+} > Cd^{2+}$
    (c) $Au^{+} < Rb^{+}$ (d) $Au^{+} > Rb^{+}$
20. Which of the following statements are correct regarding octet theory/rule?
    (a) It does not explain the relative stability of the molecules being totally silent about the energy of molecule.
    (b) Among the compound PF_5, SF_6, H_2SO_4 only PF_5 and SF_6 show exception to the octet rule.
    (c) This theory tells about the shape of molecules.
    (d) In molecule with an odd number of electrons like nitric oxide and nitrogen dioxide, the octet rule is not satisfied for all the atoms.
21. Select the correct order from the following.
    (a) $LiCl < BeCl_2 < BCl_3 < CCl_4$ (Covalent bond character)
    (b) $SnCl_4 > AlCl_3 > CaCl_2 > KCl$ (Covalent bond character)
    (c) $CHCl_3 < CH_4 = CCl_4$ (Dipole moment)
    (d) $K^{+} < Ca^{2+} < Mg^{2+} < Be^{2+}$ (Polarising power)
22. Select the correct order for the given properties
    (a) Thermal stability : $NaNO_3 < KNO_3 < RbNO_3$
    (b) Solubility in water : $NaNO_3 > KNO_3 > RbNO_3$
    (c) Melting point : NaF > KF > RbF
    (d) Covalent character : NaF > KF > RbF

Type III 》 Numerical/Integer Type Answer Questions

23. Number of compounds from the following with zero dipole moment is ....
    1, 4 dichlorobenzene, 1-4, dicyanobenzene, trans-1,2-dichloroethene, trans-2,3-dichloro-2-butene, cis-1,2 dichloroethane,
24. Consider the following sets.
    Set I $\rightarrow$ KCl, PH_3, O_2, B_2H_6, H_2SO_4
    Set II $\rightarrow$ CBr_4, H_2SO_4, ClO_2, NO_2, C_2H_6
    [Using : X = no. of compounds that have covalent nature in set-I Y = no. of molecules which are exceptions to octet rule.]
    The sum of $X + Y$ is ________ .
25. A. In PO_4^{3-} the formal charge on each O—atom is x.
    B. The formal charge of the O—atom in the ion $[\ddot{:N} \equiv \ddot{O}:]$ is y.
    The value of $x + y + 38$ is ....
26. The value of EN of atoms A and B are 1.80 and 4.0 respectively. The percentage of ionic character of A—B bond is _________ %.
27. Molecule AB has a bond length of 1.617Å and a dipole moment of 0.38 D. The fractional charge on each atom (absolute magnitude) is __________
    ($E_0 = 4.802 \times 10^{-10}$ esu)

Connect with Answers
Elemental Practice 2.1 | Chapter 02

1. (d)	2. (d)	3. (d)	4. (c)	5. (c)	6. (c)
7. (b)	8. (b)	9. (b)	10. (d)	11. (a)	12. (b)
13. (a)	14. (c)	15. (c)	16. (b)	17. (b,c)	18. (b,c,d)
19. (a,d)	20. (a,d)	21. (a,b,d)	22. (a,b,c,d)	23. (4)	24. (7)
25. (37.25)	26. (65)	27. (0.05)			

Element 2 Bond Parameters, Valence Bond Theory and VSEPR Theory

Bond Parameters

These are the set of characteristics that describes the nature and strength of a bond between two atoms. These are as follows.

1. Bond Length

"The average distance between the centre of the nuclei of the two bonded atoms is called bond length."

It is expressed in terms of Angstrom ($1\ \text{Å} = 10^{-10}$m) or picometer ($1\ \text{pm} = 10^{-12}$ m). It is determined experimentally by X-ray diffraction methods or spectroscopic method.

In an ionic compound, the bond length is the sum of their ionic radii ($d = r_+ + r_-$) and in a covalent compound, it is the sum of their covalent radii.

Factors Affecting Bond Length

(i) **Size of the Atoms** The bond length increases with increase in the size of the atoms. For example, bond length of H—X are in the order, HI > HBr > HCl > HF

(ii) **Multiplicity of Bond** The bond length decreases as the multiplicity of the bond increases. Thus, bond length of carbon - carbon bonds are in the order,

$$C\equiv C < C=C < C—C$$

(iii) **Type of Hybridisation** Greater the s-character shorter is the hybrid orbital and hence shorter is the bond length. e.g., $sp^3 > sp^2 > sp$

(iv) **Resonance** Bond length is also affected by resonance as in benzene and CO_2. In benzene bond length is 1.39 Å which is in between C—C bond length 1.54 Å and C=C bond length 1.34Å.

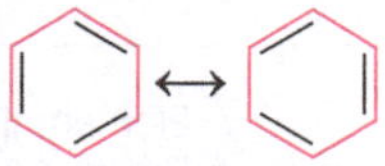

In CO_2 the C—O bond length is 1.15 Å.
(In between C≡O and C=O)

$$O=C=O \leftrightarrow \bar{O}—C\equiv \overset{+}{O} \leftrightarrow \overset{+}{O}\equiv C—\bar{O}$$

(vi) **Polarity of Bond** Polar bond length is usually smaller than the theoretical non-polar bond length.

2. Bond Energy

"The amount of energy required to break one mole of bonds of a particular type so as to separate them into gaseous atoms is called bond dissociation energy or simple bond energy". Greater is the bond energy, stronger is the bond length.

Bond energy is usually expressed in kJ mol^{-1}.

Factors Affecting Bond Energy

(i) **Size of the Atoms** Bond energy $\propto \dfrac{1}{\text{atomic size}}$ Greater the size of the atom, greater is the bond length and less is the bond dissociation energy i.e., lesser is the bond strength.

(ii) **Multiplicity of Bonds** For the bond between the two similar atoms, greater is the multiplicity of the bond, greater is the bond dissociation energy. This is because atoms come closer and the number of bonds to be broken is more,

$$C—C < C=C < C\equiv C,$$
$$C\equiv C < C\equiv N < N\equiv N$$

(iii) **Number of Lone Pairs of Electrons Present** Greater the number of lone pairs of electrons present on the bonded atoms, greater is the repulsion between the atoms and hence less is the bond dissociation energy.

(iv) **Percentage s-character** The bond energy increases as the hybrid orbitals have greater amount of s orbital contribution. Thus, bond energy decreases in the following order, $sp > sp^2 > sp^3$

(v) **Bond Polarity** Greater the electronegativity difference greater is the bond polarity and hence greater will be the bond strength i.e, bond energy,

H—F > H—Cl > H—Br > H—I

3. Bond Angle

In case of molecules made up of three or more atoms, the average angle between the bonded orbitals (i.e., between the two covalent bonds) is known as bond angle θ. It gives an idea about the distribution of orbitals around the central atom in a molecules or the shape of a molecule.

Factors Affecting of Bond Angle

(i) **Repulsion between Atoms or Groups Attached to the Central Atom** The positive charge, developed due to high electronegativity of oxygen, on the two hydrogen atoms in water causes repulsion among themselves which increases the bond angle, H—O—H from 90° to 104.5°.

(ii) **Hybridisation of Bonding Orbitals** In hybridisation as the s character of the s hybrid bond increases, the bond angle increases.

Bond type	sp^3	sp^2	sp
Bond angle	109°28′	120°	180°

(iii) **Repulsion due to Non-bonded Electrons**

Bond angle $\propto \dfrac{1}{\text{No. of lone pair of electrons}}$. By increasing lone pair of electron, bond angle decreases approximately by 2.5%.

	CH_4	NH_3	H_2O
Bond angle	109.5°	107°	104.5°

(iv) **Electronegativity of the Atoms** If the electronegativity of the central atom decreases, bond angle decreases.

	H_2O >	H_2S >	H_2Se >	H_2Te
Bond angle	104.5°	92.2°	91.2°	89.5°

In case the central atom remains the same, bond angle increases with the decrease in electronegativity of the surrounding atom, e.g.,

	PCl_3	PBr_3	PI_3	$AsCl_3$	$AsBr_3$	AsI_3
Bond angle	100°	101.5°	102°	98.4°	100.5°	101°

4. Bond Order

It is defined as the number of covalent bonds present between the two atoms in a molecule.

Solved Booster 2.1

Chlorine reacts with hot and concentrated NaOH and produces compounds (*X*) and (*Y*). Compound (*X*) gives white precipitate with silver nitrate solution. The average bond order between Cl and O atoms in (*Y*) is

Solution *(1.67)*

The reaction is,

$$\underset{\text{(Hot and conc.)}}{3Cl_2 + 6\,NaOH} \longrightarrow \underset{(X)}{5\,NaCl} + \underset{(Y)}{NaClO_3} + 3H_2O$$

$$NaCl \xrightarrow{+\,AgNO_3} \underset{\text{(White ppt.)}}{AgCl}$$

Y = $NaClO_3$ (Na^+ and ClO_3^-)

The structure of ClO_3^- (chlorate ion) is,

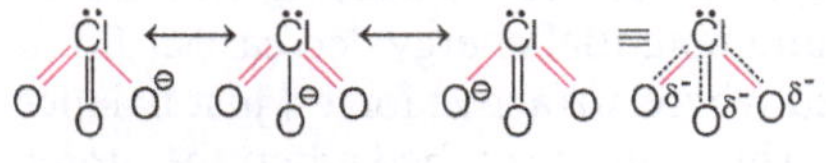

'Cl—O' bond order in the hybrid

$$= \frac{\text{Number of bonds between Cl and O}}{\text{Total number of O (surrounding atoms)}}$$

$$= \frac{5}{3} = 1.66 \text{ or } 1.67$$

JEE Spotlite

- Isoelectronic molecules have identical bond orders.
- The hybrid orbitals with more *p*-character are more directional in nature. More directional the bond, greater is the bond strength and vice versa. For example.
  $sp^3 - sp^3 > sp^2 - sp^2 > sp - sp > p - p > s - p > s - s$
- The terms 'bond energy' and 'bond dissociation energy' are same only for di-atomic molecules.
- The order of O—O bond length in O_2, H_2O_2 and O_3 is $H_2O_2 > O_3 > O_2$.
- The bond length increases as the bond order decreases.
- Isovolent resonance occurs when different resonating structure have same number of bonds.

Resonance

The concept of resonance was put forward by Heisenberg (1920) to explain the properties of certain molecules. It has been found that the experimentally observed properties of certain compounds like benzene, CO_3^{2-} etc cannot be satisfactorily explained by a single Lewis structure.

Then many structures with similar energy, position of nuclei, bonding and non-bonding pair of electrons are drawn with the conditions that each of these will explain the properties of a compound. These structures are called resonating structure or canonical forms.

This can be explained by the following resonance structures of CO_3^{2-}

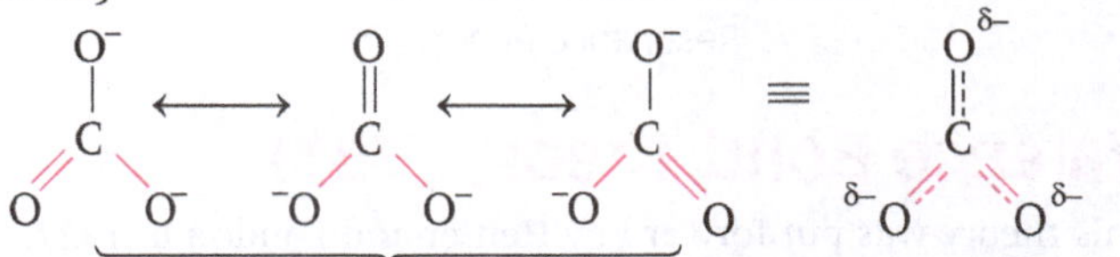

Resonance structures or canonical forms   Resonance hybrid

It should be noted that

- the various resonating structures differ in the position of electrons and not in the relative position of atoms.
- all the contributing structures should have same number of unpaired electrons.

The stability of a resonance structure can be decided by considering the following points

(i) A non-polar canonical form is more stable.

(ii) More the number of covalent bonds, more is the stability.

(iii) Resonance structure in which negative charge resides on more electronegative atom and positive charge on electropositive atom is more stable as compared to the other structures (containing charge).

(iv) Larger the number of the contributing structures, greater is the stability of the molecule.

(v) Bond lengths in hybrid structures are intermediate of the bond lengths in various resonating structures., e.g. The C—C bond length in benzene is 139 pm. Which is intermediate of C—C (154 pm) and C=C (134 pm)

(vi) Structure with bond order (BO) more than one are more stable than those having BO less than one.

Resonance Energy

The difference in the energy of the resonance hybrid and the most stable contributing structure (having least energy) is called resonance energy, e.g. benzene has resonance energy 150.3 kJ mol^{-1} or 36 kcal mol^{-1}.

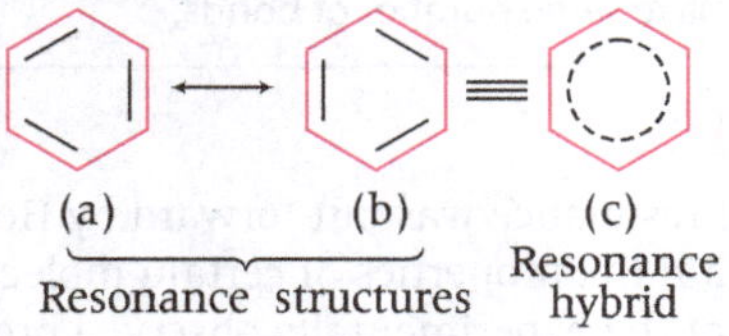

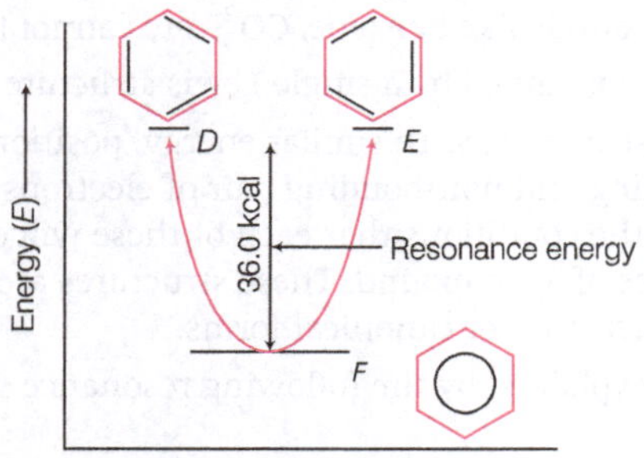

Resonance energy

Valence Bond Theory (VBT)

This theory was put forward by Heitler and London in 1927. It was based on quantum mechanical model and concept of atomic orbital overlapping. It was further extended by Pauling and Slater in 1931.

Postulates

(i) Overlapping of two distinct atomic orbital, each having an unpaired electron, results in formation of covalent bond.

(ii) This process of overlapping completes with release in energy. This make the resulting bond stable. Hence, overlapping results decrease in energy.

(iii) The overlapping of two atomic orbitals form a single merged orbital. This newly formed orbital is called bonding orbital or a localised molecular orbital.

(iv) The electrostatic attraction between the electron cloud and the nuclei of atoms acts as the major binding force of the covalent bond.

(v) Opposite spin of the two electrons, neutralises their spin magnetic moments. This further contributes to the covalent bonding.

The extension suggested by Pauling and Slater are

(i) The strength of chemical bond formed depends on the extent of atomic overlapping. Greater is the extent of overlapping, stronger is the bond formed and larger is the bond energy.

(ii) For overlapping to take place, the participating atomic orbital must have valence electrons.

(iii) Overlapping of orbitals with directional electron cloud (like *p*-orbitals) results in stronger bond.

Structure of H_2 Molecule as per VBT

Consider two hydrogen atoms H_A and H_B are approaching each other. Their nuclei are N_A and N_B and electrons present in them are represented by e_A and e_B. Different kinds of new forces act during this approach.

1. Attractive forces are between

Nucleus of one atom and its own electrons, i.e. $N_A - e_A$ and $N_B - e_B$.

Nucleus of one atom and electron of other atom, i.e. $N_A - e_B$ and $N_B - e_A$.

2. Repulsive forces are between

Electron e_A and electron e_B.

Nucleus N_A and nucleus N_B.

Attractive forces tend to bring the combining atoms close to each other. On the other hand repulsive forces tend to push them apart.

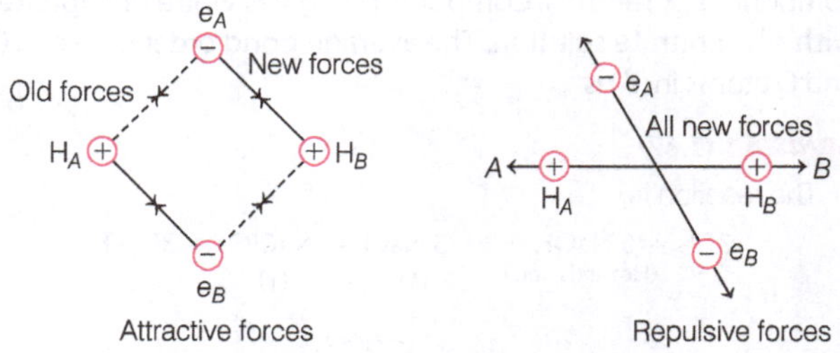

Forces of attraction and repulsion during the formation of H_2 molecule

The magnitude of new attractive forces is more than the new repulsive forces. As a result, two atoms approach each other and potential energy decreases. Ultimately, a state is reached where attractive forces, just balance the repulsive forces. This state is reached when the atoms are at critical distance r_0.

At a distance greater than r_0, the attractive forces are dominant whereas at a distance smaller than r_0, the repulsive forces dominant over the attractive forces which leads to increase of potential energy. Maximum lowering of energy takes place at critical distance r_0.

The lowering of PE as a function of inter-nuclear distance has been shown in figure below

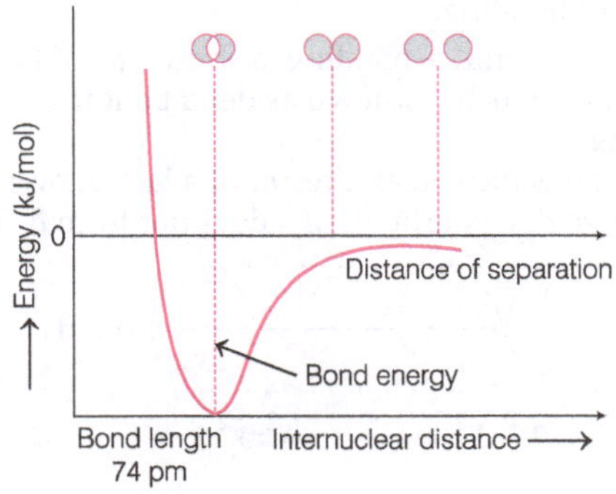

Potential energy (PE) curve for the formation of H_2 molecule as a function of internuclear distance of the H-atoms

It is clear from the curve that, the energy of two H-atoms when they are held at a distance r_0 is smaller than the energy of individual H-atoms. Therefore, the H-atoms constitute a stable grouping called hydrogen molecule. The critical distance r_0 corresponding to minimum energy is called **bond length**. Experiments have shown that the value of r_0 is 74 pm.

The energy corresponding to the minimum in the curve is called **bond energy/enthalpy**. If this much energy is supplied from outside, the bond will break and the molecule will dissociate into atoms.

$$H_2(g) + 435.8 \text{ kJ mol}^{-1} \longrightarrow H(g) + H(g)$$

Directional Properties of Bonds

When two atoms approach each other to form bonds, their atomic orbitals overlap. The overlap between the atomic orbitals can be positive, negative or zero depending upon the characteristics of the orbitals participating to overlap. Positive overlap involves the overlap of the lobes of same signs. It leads to attractive interactions.

Negative overlap involves the overlap of the lobes of opposite signs. It leads to repulsive interactions. Zero overlap implies inability of any kind of interactions. The various arrangements of *s* and *p*-orbitals resulting in positive, negative and zero overlap are depicted in figure below

Positive or in phase overlap Negative or out of phase overlap

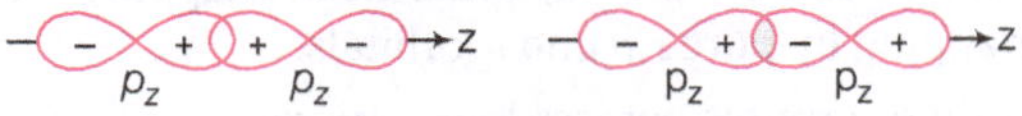

Combination of $2p_z$ atomic orbitals

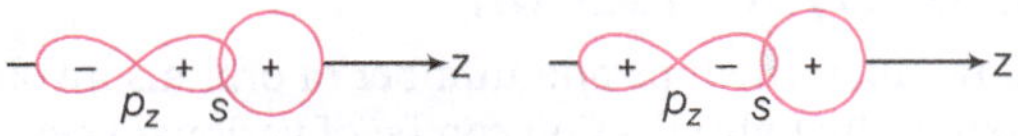

Combination of $2p_z$ and 2s atomic orbitals

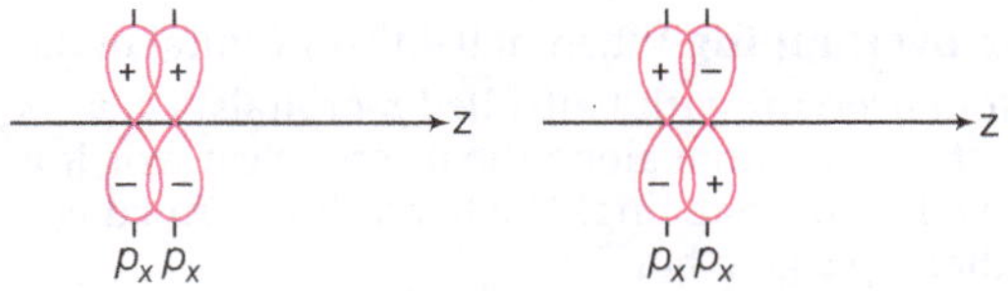

Combination of $2p_x$ atomic orbitals

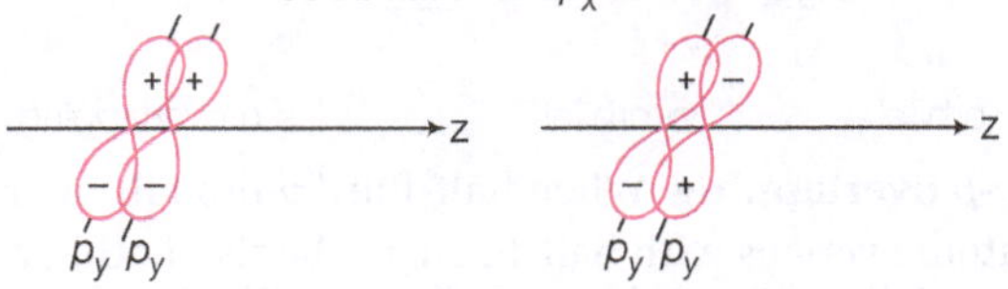

Combination of $2p_y$ atomic orbitals

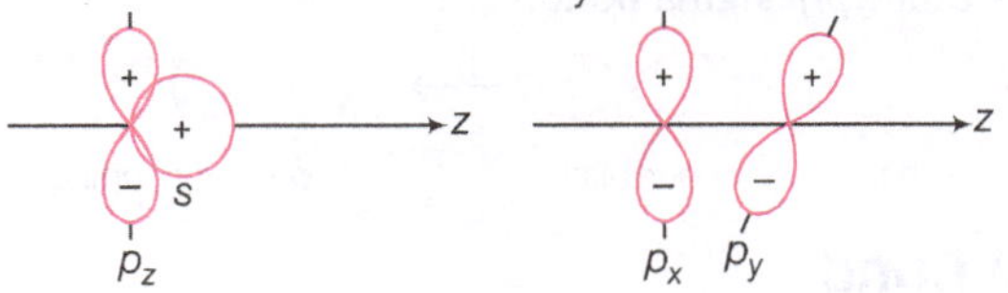

Zero overlap

(Zero overlap out of phase due to different orientation, direction of approach)

Positive, negative and zero overlaps of s and p atomic orbitals

The criterion of overlap of atomic orbitals of combining atoms is the main factor for the formation of covalent bonds both in homonuclear as well as in heteronuclear diatomic molecules and polyatomic molecules. In case of polyatomic molecules like CH_4, NH_3 and H_2O, the VBT should be taken into consideration for their characteristics shapes.

As we know the shapes of CH_4, NH_3 and H_2O molecules are tetrahedral, pyramidal and bent respectively. Their shapes can be described in terms of the orbital overlaps.

Types of Overlapping and Nature of Covalent Bonds

Based on types of overlapping, covalent bond of two distinct natures are formed, as discussed below

Sigma (σ) Bond

This type of covalent bond is formed by head-on overlap, i.e. end-to-end overlap along the internuclear axis. The electron density of a sigma bond is concentrated between the nuclei of the bonding atoms (along the inter-nuclear axis).

The electrons constituting sigma bond are called **sigma electrons.** Sigma bond can be formed by any one of the following types of combinations of atomic orbitals.

(i) ***s-s* overlapping** When two half-filled *s*-orbitals overlap along the inter-nuclear axis, it is called *s-s* overlapping.

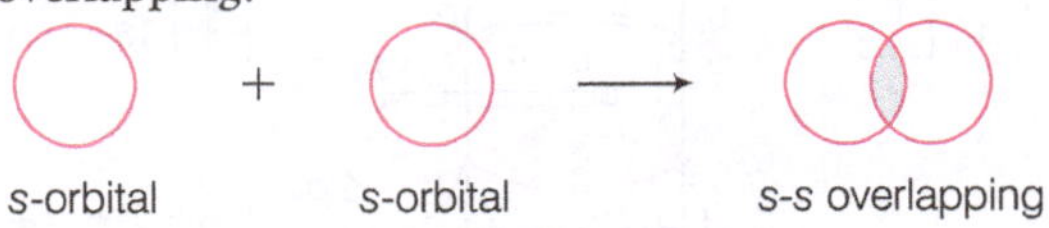

(ii) ***s-p* overlapping** When half-filled *s*-orbital of one atom overlaps with half-filled *p*-orbitals, i.e. p_x, p_y or p_z of the other atom along the internuclear axis it is called *s-p* overlapping. The bond thus formed is called *s-p* sigma bond.

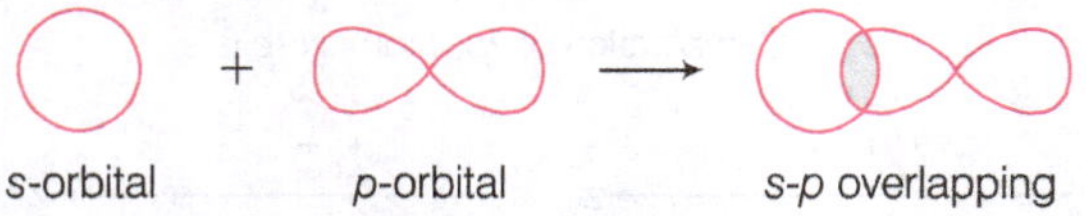

(iii) ***p-p* overlapping** When half-filled *p*-orbitals of one atom overlaps with half-filled *p*-orbitals of other atom coaxially it is called *p-p* overlapping. The bond formed is called *p-p* sigma bond.

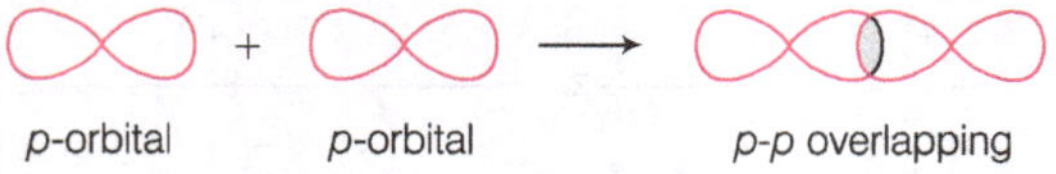

Pi (π) Bond

This type of covalent bond is formed by sidewise overlap (or lateral overlap) of bonding orbitals. Their axes remain parallel to each other and perpendicular to the inter-nuclear axis.

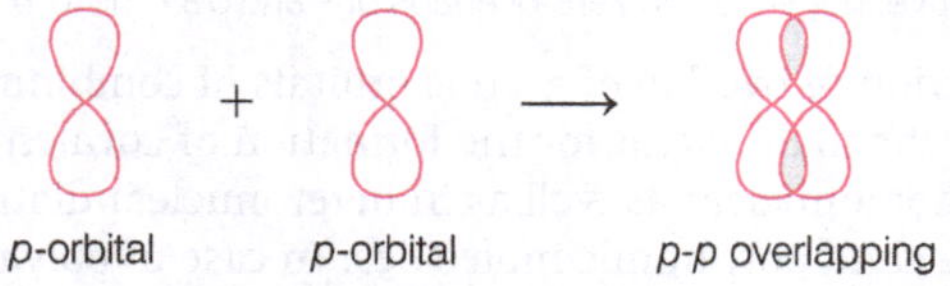

Double or triple bonds formed by sidewise overlap of orbitals like $(p_y - p_y)$ and $(p_z - p_z)$ orbitals giving pi (π) bonds in which electron density also concentrates between the atoms. It is on either side of the line joining the atoms. A π-bond always follows a σ-bond and thus a double bond always contains one π and one σ-bond.

e.g. $\underset{\sigma}{\text{H—H}}$ $\quad \overset{\pi}{\underset{\sigma}{\text{O=O}}}$ $\quad \overset{2\pi}{\underset{\sigma}{\text{N≡N}}}$

In the π-bond formation, overlapping takes place on both sides of the inter-nuclear axis, free rotation of atoms around a π-bond is not possible.

Concept Visualizer

Let us visualise different types of bonding (σ & π) with the help of N_2 molecule.

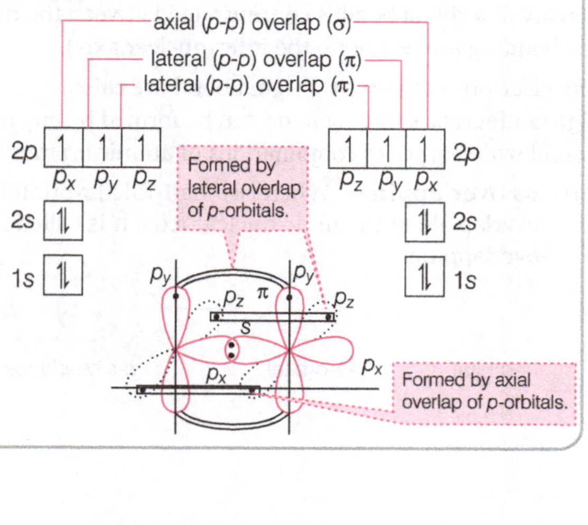

- π-bonds are more reactive than sigma-bonds. This is due to the fact that electron cloud in π-bond lies below and above the plane of bonding.
- In addition to σ and π-bonding, a third type of bonding is also possible, which is known as delta bonding (δ-bonding).
  A delta bond is formed as a result of a lateral overlapping between two $d_{x^2-y^2}$ orbitals. d_{z^2} does not form δ –bond.

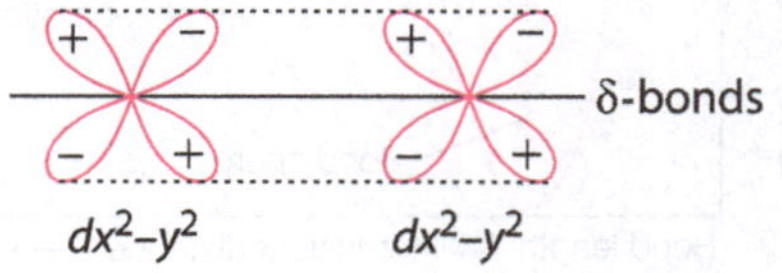

Hybridisation

The concept of hybridisation was introduced by Pauling and Slater. It is defined as the intermixing of dissimilar orbitals of the same atom but having slightly different energies to form same number of new orbitals of equal energies and identical shapes. The new orbitals so formed are known as hybrid orbitals.

Characteristics of Hybridisation

(i) Only orbital of almost similar energies and belonging to the same atom or ion undergoes hybridisation.

(ii) Hybridisation takes place only in orbitals, electrons are not involved in it.

(iii) The number of hybrid orbitals produced is equal to the number of pure orbitals, mixed during hybridisation.

(iv) In the excited state, the number of unpaired electrons must correspond to the oxidation state of the central atom in the molecule.

(v) Both half filled orbitals or fully filled orbitals of equivalent energy can involve in hybridisation.

(vi) Hybrid orbitals form only sigma bonds.

(vii) Orbitals involved in π- bond formation do not participate in hybridisation.

(viii) Hybridisation never takes place in an isolated atom but it occurs only at the time of bond formation.

(ix) The hybrid orbitals are distributed in space as apart as possible resulting in a definite geometry of molecule.

(x) Hybridised orbitals provide efficient overlapping than overlapping by pure *s*,*p* and *d*-orbitals.

(xi) Hybridised orbitals possess lower energy.

Types of Hybridisation

Depending upon the type and number of orbitals involved in intermixing, the hybridisation can be of various types namely $sp, sp^2, sp^3, sp^3d, dsp^2, sp^3d^2, sp^3d^3$. The nature and number of orbitals involved in the above mentioned types of hybridisation.

sp-Hybridisation

In this type, one *s* and one *p*-orbital hybridise to produce two equivalent *sp*-hybrid orbitals. The two *sp*-hybrid orbitals are oriented in a straight line making an angle of 180° and thus, molecule possesses linear geometry. Each of hybrid orbitals has 50% *s*-character and 50% *p*-character.

e.g.

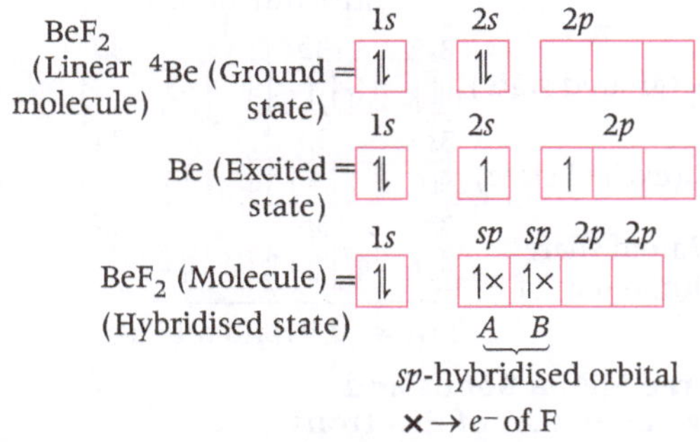

The two half-filled *A* and *B* *sp*-hybrid orbitals form σ-bonds with half-filled *p*-orbitals of two F-atoms by (*sp*-*p*) overlap thus, forming two Be — F bonds.

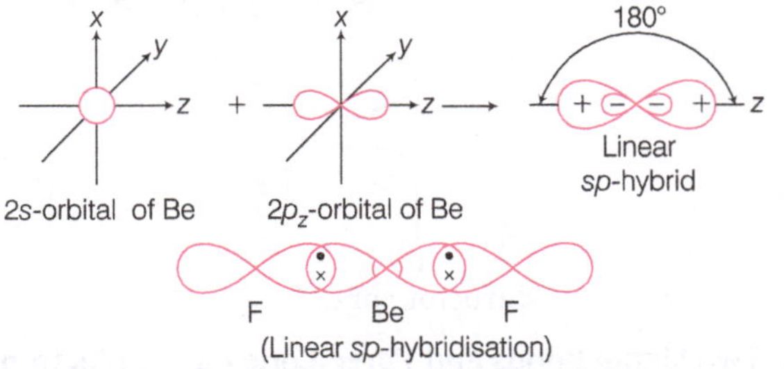

Various other examples are $BeH_2, CO_2, CO, NO_2^+, N_2O, N_3^-$ etc.

sp^2-Hybridisation

In this type, one *s* and two *p* (p_x and p_y) orbitals of an atom hybridise to give three equivalent sp^2-hybrid orbitals. These three sp^2-hybrid orbitals are directed towards the three corners of an equilateral triangle with an angle of 120°. This gives a triangular geometry to the molecule. Each sp^2-hybrid orbitals has 1/3rd (or 33.33%) *s*-character and 2/3rd (or 66.7%) *p*-character.

e.g. BF_3, BCl_3, BH_3, $AlCl_3$, carbon containing double bond, like $CH_2{=}CH_2$, SO_2, SO_3, CO_3^{2-} etc.,

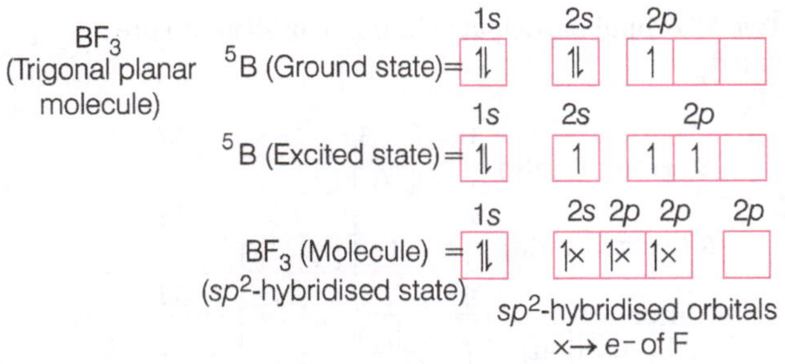

The three half-filled *A*, *B* and *C* sp^2-hybrid orbitals form σ-bonds with half-filled *p*-orbitals of three F-atoms by (sp^2-*p*) overlap and give trigonal planar geometry.

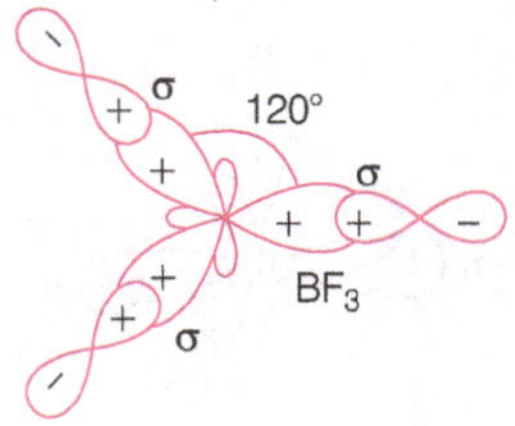

JEE MAPPER

Example Similar to PYQ Asked in JEE Main 2024

In which one of the following pairs the central atom exhibit sp^2 hybridisation?

(a) NH_2^- and H_2O (b) I_3^- and SF_4

(c) ClO_3 and NO_3^- (d) BCl_3 and NO_2^-

Sol. (d) The hybridisation of central atom of given species in different options are

NH_2^- and $H_2O \rightarrow sp^3$-hybridisation

I_3^- and $SF_4 \rightarrow sp^3d$-hybridisation

ClO_3 and $NO_3^- \rightarrow sp^3$ and sp^2 hybridisation

BCl_3 and $NO_2^- \rightarrow sp^2$ hybridisation

So, the pair of central atoms that exhibit sp^2 -hybridisation is BCl_3 and NO_2^-.

Competency Enhancer 2.1

In which one of the following pairs the central atom exhibit sp^3 hybridisation?

(a) NO_2^+ and NH_4^+ (b) SF_2 and $[FeCl_4]^{2-}$

(c) SF_4 and NH_3 (d) BCl_3 and CO_2

sp^3-Hybridisation

In this type, one *s* and three *p*-orbitals intermix to form four sp^3-hybrid orbitals of equivalent energy. These four sp^3-hybrid orbitals are directed towards the four corners of a tetrahedron separated by an angle of 109° 28′. sp^3-hybrid orbitals have 1/4th (or 25%) *s*-character and 3/4th (or 75%) *p*-character.

e.g.

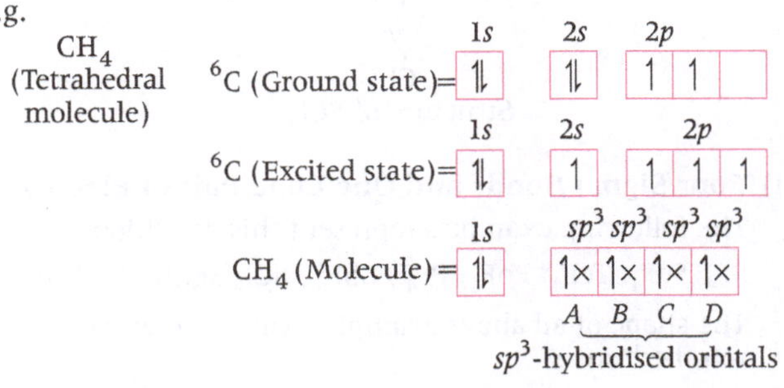

The four half-filled A, B, C and D sp^3-hybrid orbitals form σ-bonds with half-filled s-orbitals of four H-atoms by $(sp^3\text{-}s)$ overlap and gives tetrahedral geometry.

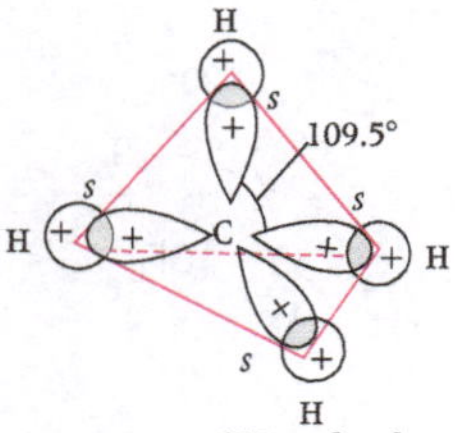

CH_4 molecule

Tetrahedral sp^3-hybridisation

sp^3d-Hybridisation

In this hybridisation there are four conditions

(i) **Five sigma bonds and zero lone pair electron**

The following examples represent this condition.

PF_5, PCl_5, PBr_5, PI_5, AsF_5, $AsCl_5$, $SbCl_5$ SbF_5 etc.

The shape of all above molecules is trigonal bipyramidal

	3s	3p	3d
P (ground state)	↑↓	↑ ↑ ↑	(empty)
P* (excited state)	↑	↑ ↑ ↑	↑
P atom share with five e^- of F	↑↓	↑↓ ↑↓ ↑↓	↑↓

sp^3d hybridisation

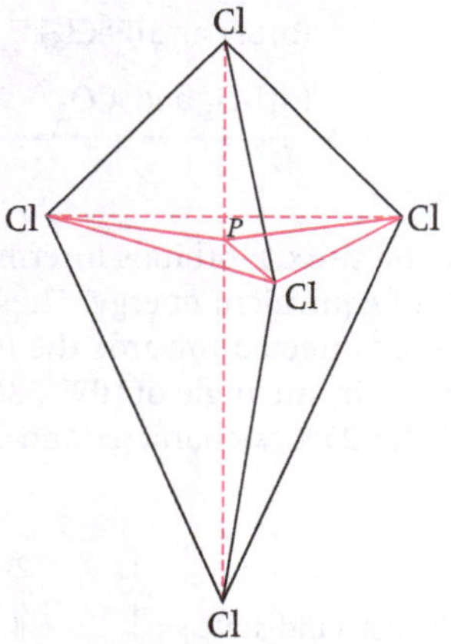

Structure of PCl_5

(ii) **Four Sigma Bonds and One Lone Pair of Electron**

The following examples represent this condition.

SF_4, SeF_4, TeF_4, PoF_4, PF_4^-, SbF_4^-, SCl_4 $SeCl_4$, $TeCl_4$ etc.

The shape of all above examples will be irregular tetrahedron.

Example SF_4

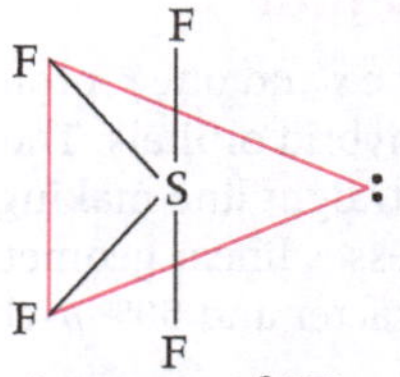

Structure of SF_4

	3s	3p	3d
S (ground state)	↑↓	↑↓ ↑ ↑	(empty)
S (excited state)	↑↓	↑ ↑ ↑	↑
S (atom share with four e^- of F	↑↓	↑↓ ↑↓ ↑↓	↑↓

Five-sp^3d hybrid orbitals

(iii) **Three Sigma Bonds and Two Lone Pair of Electrons**

The following examples represent this condition.

ClF_3, BrF_3, IF_3, $BrCl_3$, ICl_3 etc.

The shape of all above compounds is 'T' shape.

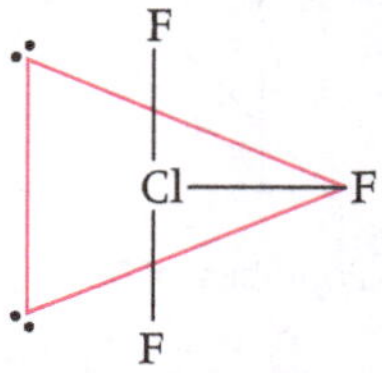

Structure of ClF_3

(iv) **Two Sigma Bonds and Three Lone Pair of Electrons**

The following examples represent this condition

ICl_2^-, IBr_2^-, ClF_2^-, IF_2^-, BrF_2^-, XeF_2^-, I_3^-, Br_3^-

The geometry of above examples will be linear

sp^3d^2-Hybridisation

- In this hybridisation, one s-orbitals, three p-orbitals and two d-orbitals are mixed to give six new hybrid orbitals known as sp^3d^2 hybrid orbitals.
- The shape of molecule obtained from above six hybrid orbitals will be symmetrical octahedral.
- The angle between all hybrid orbitals will be 90°.

  Example : SF_6, AlF_6^{2-}, PF_6^-, ICl_5, XeF_4, $XeOF_4$, ICl_4^-,
- Two 'd' orbital participates in the hybridisation are $d_{x^2-y^2}$ and d_{z^2}

SF_6

	3s	3p	3d
S (ground state)	↑↓	↑↓ ↑ ↑	(empty)
S (excited state)	↑	↑ ↑ ↑	↑ ↑
S (after hybridisation)	↑↓	↑↓ ↑↓ ↑↓	↑↓ ↑↓

sp^3d^2 hybridisation

sp^3d^3-Hybridisation

- In this hybridisation, one *s*-orbitals, three *p*-orbitals and three *d*-orbitals are mixed to give seven new hybrid orbitals known as sp^3d^3 hybrid orbitals.
- In this hybridisation *d*-orbitals used are $d_{xy}d_{xz}$ and d_{yz} orbitals.
- These seven sp^3d^3 orbitals are configurated in pentagonal bipyramidal shape.
- Five bond angles are of 72° & two bond angles of 90°.
- The following examples showing sp^3d^3 hybridisation —IF_7 and XeF_6

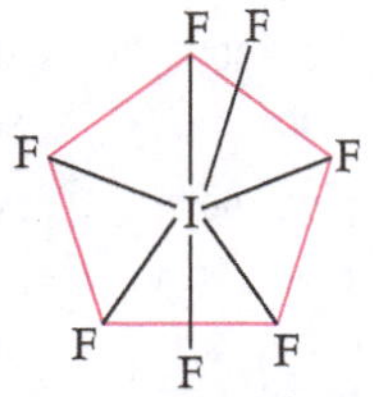

Structure of IF_7

Hybridisation of Elements Involving *d*-orbitals

The involvement of *d*-orbitals in hybridisation takes place when *d*-orbitals are lying vacant or partially filled. Electrons in *s* and *p*-orbitals of the outermost shell can use *d*-orbitals of the outer shell as well as *d*-orbitals of the inner shell for hybridisation depending upon the nature of molecule, e.g. 3*d*-orbitals are involved in hybridisation with 3*s* and 3*p* and also with 4*s* and 4*p*.

This is because the energy of the 3*d*-orbitals are comparable to the energy of the 3*s* and 3*p*-orbitals and also with 4*s* and 4*p*-orbitals.

JEE Spotlite

Bent rule states that a more electronegative substituent prefer to form bond with that hybrid which has more *p*-character.
- The lone pairs prefers to occupy orbitals having higher % of *s*-character around a central atom and *vice versa*.

Valence Shell Electron Pair Repulsion Theory (VSEPR) (Gillespie Theory)

Lewis concept is unable to explain the shape of molecules but VSEPR theory provides a simple method to predict the shapes of covalent molecules. This theory, was proposed by **Sidgwick** and **Powell** in 1940. It was further developed by **Gillespie** and **Nyholm** in 1957. This theory provides a simple procedure to predict the shapes of covalent molecules.

The main postulates of VSEPR theory are as follows

- The shape of a molecule depends upon the number of valence shell electron pairs (bonded as well as non-bonded) around the central atom.
- The electron pairs surrounding the central atom repel each other because of similar charge.
- Pairs of electrons tend to occupy such positions in space where there is a minimum repulsion. This results in maximum possible distance between them.

The repulsive interaction between the electron pairs decrease in the order

Lone pair (*lp*)-lone pair (*lp*) > lone pair (*lp*)-bond pair (*bp*) > bond pair (*bp*)-bond pair (*bp*)

These repulsive effects results in deviations from idealised shapes and alterations in bond angles in molecules.

Geometrical shapes of molecules can be identified with the help of VSEPR theory. It is convenient to divide the molecule into two categories as

- Molecule in which the central atom has no lone pair.
- Molecule in which the central atom has one or more lone pairs.

The geometries of molecules based on the number of bond pairs of electrons and the shape and hybridisation is determined by the following table

The effect of bonding and lone pair on geometry and bond angle are given in the table below.

Compounds	Orbitals on central atom	Theoretical shape	Number of: Bond pairs	Number of: Lone pairs	Number of: VSEPR notation (*E* stands for lone pair)	Bond angle	Distorted geometry due to repulsion
$BeCl_2$	2	Linear	2	0	AX_2	180°	Linear
BF_3	3	Plane triangle	3	0	AX_3	120°	Plane Triangle/ trigonal planar
SO_2	3	Plane triangle	2	1	AX_2E	119°	Angular
CH_4, SiH_4	4	Tetrahedral	4	0	AX_4	109° 28′	Tetrahedral
NH_3	4	Tetrahedral	3	1	AX_3E	107° 48′	Trigonal pyramidal
NF_3	4	Tetrahedral	3	1	AX_3E	102° 35′	Pyramidal
H_2O	4	Tetrahedral	2	2	AX_2E_2	104° 27′	Angular
F_2O	4	Tetrahedral	2	2	AX_2E_2	102°	Angular

Compounds	Orbitals on central atom	Theoretical shape	Number of			Bond angle	Distorted geometry due to repulsion
			Bond pairs	Lone pairs	VSEPR notation (*E* stands for lone pair)		
H_2S	4	Tetrahedral	2	2	AX_2E_2	90°	Angular
PCl_5	5	Trigonal bipyramidal	5	0	AX_5	120° and 90°	Trigonal bipyramidal
XeO_2F_2, SF_4, IF_4^+	5	Trigonal bipyramidal	4	1	AX_4E	101° 36′ and 86° 33′	Irregular tetrahedral (*see-saw*)
$XeOF_2$	5	Trigonal bipyramidal	3	2	AX_3E_2		T-shaped
ClF_3	5	Trigonal bipyramidal	3	2	AX_3E_2	87° 40′	T-shaped
I_3^-, XeF_2	5	Trigonal bipyramidal	2	3	AX_2E_3	180°	Linear
SF_6	6	Octahedral	6	0	AX_6	90°	Octahedral
$XeOF_4$, BrF_5	6	Octahedral	5	1	AX_5E	84° 30′	Square pyramidal
ICl_4^-, XeF_4	6	Octahedral	4	2	AX_4E_2	90°	Square planar
IF_7	7	Pentagonal bipyramidal	7	0	AX_7	72°, 90°	Pentagonal bipyramidal

Solved Booster 2.2

Explain abnormal behaviour in the following structures based on VSEPR mode.

(i) ClF_3 (ii) SF_4 (iii) I_3^-

Solution

(i) **Chlorine trifluoride (ClF_3)** There are three bond pairs and two lone pairs. As a general rule, if lone pairs occur in a trigonal bipyramidal they will be located in the equatorial positions (round the middle) rather than the axial (top and bottom), since this arrangement minimises the repulsive forces.

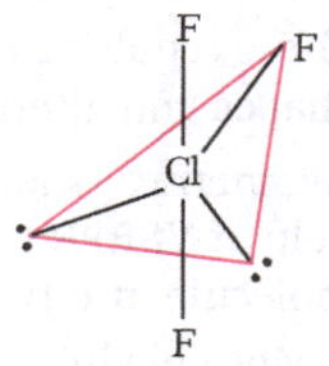

(ii) **Sulphur tetrafluoride (SF_4)** There are four bond pairs and one lone pair. To minimise the repulsive forces the lone pair occupies an equatorial position, and F atoms are located at the other four corners.

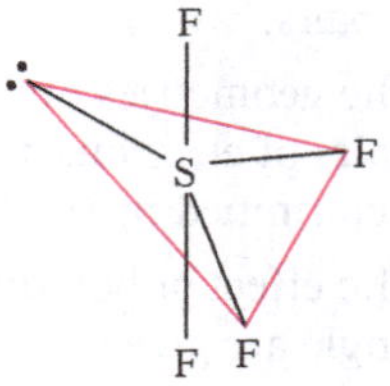

(iii) **Triiodide ion (I_3^-)** I_3^- ion is made up of an I_2 molecule with an I^- bonded to it by means of a coordinate bond in which I_2 is **lone pair acceptor (Lewis acid) and I^- the lone pair donor (Lewis base).** There are two bond pairs and three lone pairs in the outer-shell of central atom. To minimise the repulsive forces the three lone pairs occupy the equatorial position. The ion is therefore linear in shape with a bond angle of exactly 180°.

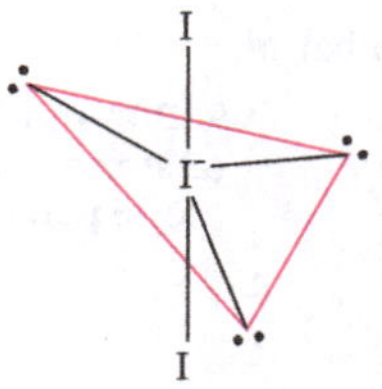

$$\underset{\text{Lewis base}}{I_2} + \underset{\text{Lewis base}}{I^-} \longrightarrow [I—I \leftarrow I]^-$$

Solved Booster 2.3

Which of the following statement is incorrect.

(a) Non-bonding pairs occupy more space than bonding pairs.

(b) The bonding orbitals in a trigonal bipyramidal molecule are described as sp^3d hybrid

(c) $SnCl_2$ has linear shape

(d) PCl_4^+ and $AlCl_4^-$ are isoelectronic

Solution *(c)*

$SnCl_2$ is a bent shape molecule due to presence of lone pair of electron while other options are correct.

JEE MAPPER

Example Similar to PYQ Asked in JEE Main 2024

Which of the following are isostructural pairs?

A. H_3O^+ and BrO_3^- B. $XeOF_2$ and XeF_3^+

C. SO_3^{2-} and PCl_3 D. NH_3 and NO_3^-

(a) only A and B (b) only A and C

(c) only B and C (d) only C and D

Sol. *(b)* If number of sigma bond (σ). coordinate bond and lone pair are same for given pairs, they are isostructural. Hence, H_3O^+, BrO_3^-, SO_3^{2-} and PCl_3 have pyramidal shape and are isostructural.

Competency Enhancer 2.2

Which of the following are isostructural pairs?

A. XeF_2 and BrF_3 B. ClF_3 and XeF_3^+

C. PCl_5 and XeO_2F_2 D. BCl_3 and $BrCl_3$

(a) only A and B (b) only A and C

(c) only B and C (d) only C and D

Elemental Practice 2.2

Type I MCQs with Only One Correct Option

1. The BCl_3 is a planar molecule whereas NCl_3 is pyramidal because
(a) B — Cl bond is more polar than N — Cl bond
(b) N — Cl bond is more covalent than B — Cl bond
(c) nitrogen atom is smaller than boron atom
(d) BCl_3 has no lone pair but NCl_3 has a lone pair of electrons

2. In an octahedral structure, the pair of d orbitals involved in d^2sp^3-hybridisation is
(a) $d_{x^2-y^2}, d_{z^2}$ (b) $d_{xz}, d_{x^2-y^2}$
(c) d_{z^2}, d_{xz} (d) d_{xy}, d_{yz}

3. The correct order of bond angle of given ions/molecule is NO_2, NO_2^+, NO_2^-
(a) $NO_2^+ > NO_2 > NO_2^-$ (b) $NO_2^- > NO_2^+ > NO_2$
(c) $NO_2 > NO_2^- > NO_2^+$ (d) $NO_2^- > NO_2 > NO_2^+$

4. Which of the following species has a linear shape?
(a) NO_2^- (b) SO_2
(c) NO_2^+ (d) O_3

5. H_2O is dipolar, whereas BeF_2 is not. It is because
(a) the electronegativity of F is greater than that of O
(b) H_2O involves hydrogen bonding whereas BeF_2 is a discrete molecule
(c) H_2O is linear and BeF_2 is angular
(d) H_2O is angular and BeF_2 is linear

6. Match list-I with list-II.

	List-I		List-II
A.	PCl_5	I.	Square pyramidal
B.	SF_6	II.	Trigonal planar
C.	BrF_5	III.	Octahedral
D.	BF_3	IV.	Trigonal bipyramidal

Choose the correct answer from the options given below

	A	B	C	D
(a)	IV	III	I	II
(b)	II	III	IV	I
(c)	III	I	IV	II
(d)	IV	III	II	I

7. Select the species that shows $p\pi$ - $d\pi$ bonding?
(a) NO_3^- (b) SO_3^{2-} (c) BO_3^{3-} (d) CO_3^{2-}

8. Choose the planar molecule from the following.
(a) XeF_4 (b) XeO_4
(c) XeO_3F (d) XeO_3F_2

9. The type of hybridisation of boron in diborane is
(a) sp hybridisation (b) sp^2 hybridisation
(c) sp^3 hybridisation (d) sp^3d^2 hybridisation

10. PF_5 molecule is trigonal bipyramidal. The hybrid orbitals used by P-atoms for bonding are
(a) $d_{x^2-y^2}, d_{z^2}, s, p_x, p_y$ (b) d_{xy}, s, p_x, p_y, p_z
(c) $s, p_x, p_y, p_z, d_{z^2}$ (d) $d_{x^2-y^2}, s, p_x, p_y, p_z$

11. From the following orbital bonds, the angle is minimum between
(a) sp^3 bonds (b) p_x and p_y-orbitals
(c) H — O — H in water (d) sp bonds

12. Select the correct statement.
(a) SF_4, CH_4, $SiCl_4$ and CCl_4 have tetrahedral structures.
(b) BF_3, ClF_3 and ICl_3 have trigonal planar structure
(c) XeF_2, $BeCl_2$ and ICl_2^- have linear structures.
(d) SF_4, ClF_3 and XeF_2 have distorted geometries.

13. Select the molecule that has same geometry as that of CO_2.
(i) $HgCl_2$ (ii) NO_2
(iii) $SnCl_4$ (iv) C_2H_2
(a) (i) and (iii) (b) (ii) and (iv)
(c) (i) and (iv) (d) (iii) and (iv)

14. Which of the following species have undistorted octahedral structures?
1. SF_6 2. PF_6^-
3. SiF_6^{2-} 4. XeF_6
Select the correct answer using the codes given below.
(a) 2, 3 and 4 (b) 1, 3 and 4
(c) 2 and 3 (d) 1, 2 and 3

15. Select the reaction that involves a change in the electron pair geometry for the underlined atom.
(a) $BF_3 + F^- \longrightarrow BF_4^-$ (b) $NH_3 + H^+ \longrightarrow NH_4^+$
(c) $2SO_2 + O_2 \longrightarrow 2SO_3$ (d) $H_2O + H^+ \longrightarrow H_3O^+$

Type II MCQs with One or More than One Correct Option

16. The nitrogen oxide(s) that contain(s) N—N bonds is (are)
(a) N_2O (b) N_2O_3 (c) N_2O_4 (d) N_2O_5

17. The species that have same bond orders are
(a) CO_3^{-2} (b) NO_3^- (c) NO_2^- (d) NO

18. Select the incorrect statement about hybridisation.
(a) It involves the mixing of atomic orbitals of the atom at the time of their participation in bonding.
(b) sp^3d^2 hybridisation orbital point out towards the corners of regular hexagon.
(c) Hybrid orbitals form weaker bonds than pure atomic orbitals.
(d) For hybridisation to occur, the atom must have vacant orbitals in the valence shell.

19. Which of the following statements is/are correct?
(a) O—hydroxybenzaldehyde is a liquid at room temperature due to intramolecular H—bonding.
(b) Order of boiling point is $H_2O > H_2Te > H_2Se > H_2S$
(c) Order of boiling point is HF > HI > HBr > HCl
(d) Order of boiling point is $SbH_3 > NH_3 > AsH_3 > PH_3$

20. Select correct statement(s) regarding σ and π-bonds.
(a) σ-bond lies on the line joining the nuclei of bonded atoms.
(b) π-electron cloud lies on either side to the line joining the nuclei of bonded atoms.
(c) $(2p\pi - 3d\pi)$ pi-bond is stronger than $(2p\pi - 3p\pi)$ pi-bond
(d) σ-bond has primary effect to decide direction of covalent bond, while π-bond has no primary effect in direction of bond.

21. Select the correct order of bond angle
(a) $NH_3 > PH_3 > AsH_3 > SbH_3 > BiH_3$
(b) $H_2O > H_2S > H_2Se > H_2Te$
(c) $BF_3 = BCl_3 = BBr_3 = BI_3$
(d) $BF_3 < BCl_3 < BBr_3 < BI_3$

Type III 》Numerical / Integer Answer Type Questions

22. The number of species having unequal bond length are PCl_5, SF_4, ClF_3, XeF_2, $[ClF_4]^+$, $[XeF_3]^+$ O_3, P_4 (white).

23. The number of molecules having sp^3 hybridisation are $SnCl_4$, $[Ni(CN)_4]^{2-}$, PCl_5, NH_4^+, $HgCl_2$, CO_3^{2-}

24. The number of possible resonance structures of HN_3 are

25. If the total number of $\angle FSF$ angles equal to 90° in the molecule of SF_6 is 'x'. Then the value of $(x+3)/5$ will be

26. The number of molecules that are planar from the following are
I_3^-, H_2O, ICl_2^-, C_2H_4, C_2H_2, H_3O^+

27. The number of molecules having the same type of shape from the following are
H_3O^+, NH_3, ClO_3^+, PH_3, H_2O, CH_3^-

Elemental Practice 2.2 | Chapter 02

Connect with **Answers**

1. (d)	2. (a)	3. (a)	4. (c)	5. (d)	6. (a)
7. (b)	8. (a)	9. (c)	10. (c)	11. (b)	12. (c)
13. (c)	14. (d)	15. (a)	16. (a,b,c)	17. (a,b)	18. (c,d)
19. (b,c,d)	20. (a,b,c,d)	21. (a,b,c)	22. (5)	23. (2)	24. (3)
25. (3)	26. (4)	27. (5)			

Element 3 Molecular Orbital Theory and Hydrogen Bonding

In 1932 F **Hund** and **R.S. Mulliken** put forward a theory, known as Molecular Orbital Theory. The theory was forwarded to explain the limitation of VBT on the basis of **Schrodinger** wave equation and its solutions for electrons.

Postulates of MOT

- A molecule is supposed to have orbitals of varying energy levels in the same way as an isolated atom. These orbitals of molecule are called **molecular orbitals** (MO).
- Molecular orbitals are formed by the combination of atomic orbitals of comparable energy and proportional symmetry.
- In atomic orbitals, one electron is influenced by one nucleus. Whereas, in a molecular orbital, it is influenced by two or more nuclei depending upon the number of atoms in the molecule. Thus, orbitals of atoms loose their individual identity. Hence, an atomic orbital is monocentric while a molecular orbital is polycentric.
- Just as the electron probability distribution around a nucleus in an atom is given by an atomic orbital, the electron probability distribution in molecule is given by the molecular orbital.
- The number of molecular orbitals formed is equal to the number of combining atomic orbitals.
- Two atomic orbitals combine to give, two types of molecular orbitals. One of these is known as **bonding molecular orbital** (BMO), whereas other is known as **anti-bonding molecular orbital** (ABMO).
- BMO has lower energy and hence, greater stability than the corresponding ABMO.

JEE Spotlite

- At the time of electron filling in the molecule BMOs are preferred and filled first due to their lower energy or more stability. Hence, the highest filled BMO's are also called HOMOs, i.e. **Highest Occupied Molecular Orbitals.**
- ABMOs, on the other hand are less preferred during electron filling due to their higher energy and lower stability. Hence, the lowest empty ABMO's also called **LUMOs**, i.e. **Lowest Unoccupied Molecular Orbitals.**

- The shapes of molecular orbitals formed depends upon the type of combining atomic orbitals.
- The filling of molecular orbital obey Aufbau principle, Pauli's exclusion principle and Hund's rule of maximum multiplicity.

Linear Combination of Atomic Orbitals (LCAO)

The Schrodinger wave equation is very difficult to apply on the system containing more than one electron. It is because in these system one electron moves in the field of several nuclei. So, some approximation method is used in the formation of molecular orbitals. This can be explained on the basis of LCAO. It is a very convenient method of approximation.

According to LCAO, the wave function (ψ) of individual atomic orbitals linearly combines and form molecular orbitals, i.e. during the formation of AB molecule ψ of A i.e., ψ_A and ψ of B i.e., ψ_B will linearly combine as

$$\psi_{MO} = \psi_A + \psi_B$$

Following two cases may be possible in such a linear combination.

Case I When two waves are in phase, the waves adds up and constructive interference occurs. The amplitude of new wave is, $\Psi_{MO} = \Psi_A + \Psi_B$ (Bonding MO). Here, Ψ_{MO} is also called Ψ_g, i.e. GERADE MO corresponding to increased electron density between the two nuclei due to in phase overlap.

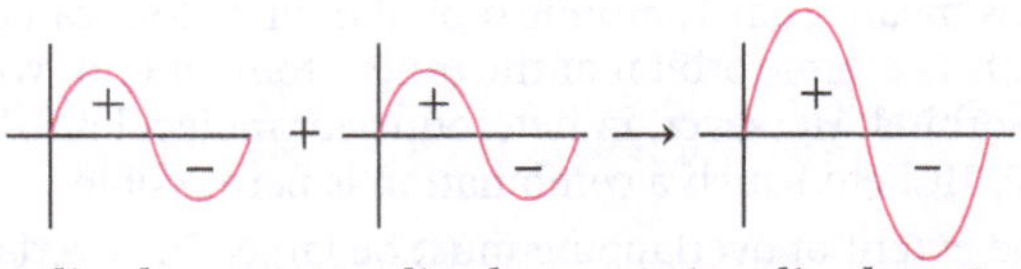

Amplitude = a Amplitude = a Amplitude = $2a$

Constructive interference

Case II When two waves are out of phase, the wave are subtracted from each others and destructive interference occurs. The amplitude of new wave is

$\Psi^*_{MO} = \Psi_A - \Psi_B$ (Anti-bonding MO)

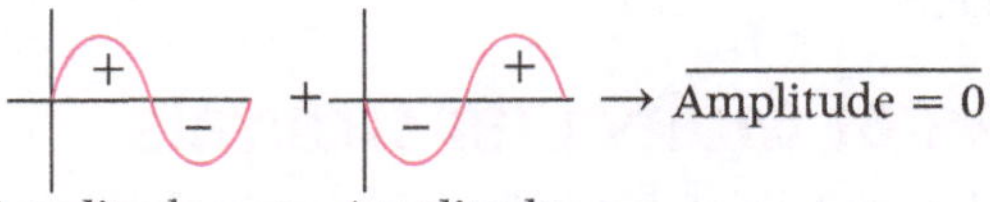

Amplitude = a Amplitude = a

Destructive interference

The condition of lower energy (bonding molecular orbital) is also called **attractive state** for electrons while condition of higher energy (antibonding molecular orbital) is also called **repulsive state for electrons**.

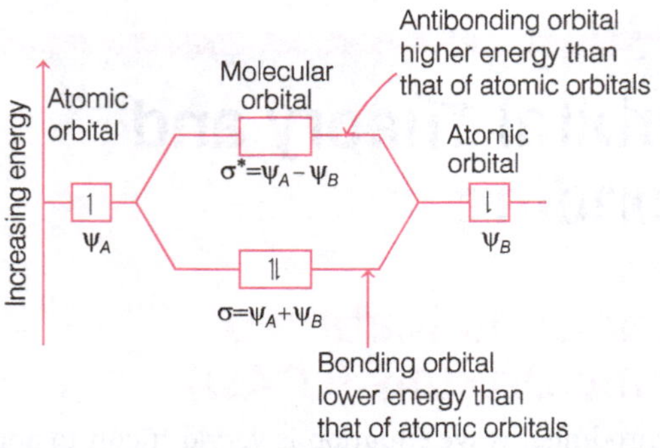

Formation of bonding (σ) and antibonding (σ^*) molecular orbitals by LCAO ψ_A and ψ_B.

JEE Quicker

When Ψ_A and Ψ_B are the wave functions of atomic orbitals, then σ* is represented by $\Psi_A - \Psi_B$. *JEE Main 2024*

$\Psi_A - \Psi_B$ represents the destructive interference, where the two wave function are subtracted which leads to the formation of a node. It is a region where the electron density is zero between the two nuclei. This is the characteristics of an anti-bonding molecular orbital σ *.

Conditions for Combination of Atomic Orbitals

- The combining atomic orbitals must have comparable energies. It may be noted that in the homonuclear diatomic molecules of the type A_2 (e.g. H_2, O_2, N_2, F_2 etc.), the participating atomic orbitals must have comparable energies.
- This means that 1*s* atomic orbital of one atom can combine with 1*s* atomic orbital of the other atom and not with its 2*s*-orbital. However, in heteronuclear molecules *AB* (e.g. HF, HCl etc.) such a combination is permissible.
- The extent of overlapping must be large. The overlapping of the atomic orbitals results in decrease in energy and increase in stability. Thus, greater the extent of the overlapping, more will be the stability of the molecular orbital formed.
- The combining atomic orbitals must have same symmetry about internuclear axis. The atomic orbitals taking part in the overlap must have same orientation or same sign of symmetry.

Types of Molecular Orbitals

Molecular orbital's of diatomic molecule are designated as σ (sigma) π (pi) or δ (delta). Sigma (σ) molecular orbitals are symmetrical around the bond axis while pi (π) molecular orbitals are not symmetrical. The bonding molecular orbitals are shown as σ or π *ns* or *np* while antibonding molecular orbitals are shown as σ^* or π^* *ns* or *np* accordingly.

The total energy of two molecular orbitals, however, remains the same as that of two original atomic orbitals.

Formation of σ- and π-HOMOs and LUMOs

(i) Combination of *s*-orbitals

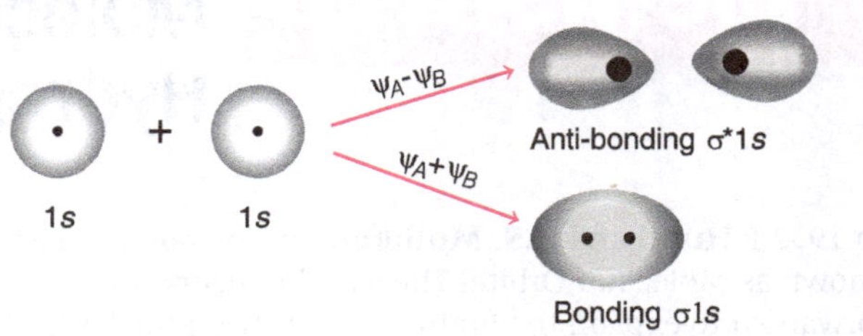

(ii) Head on combination of two *p*-orbitals

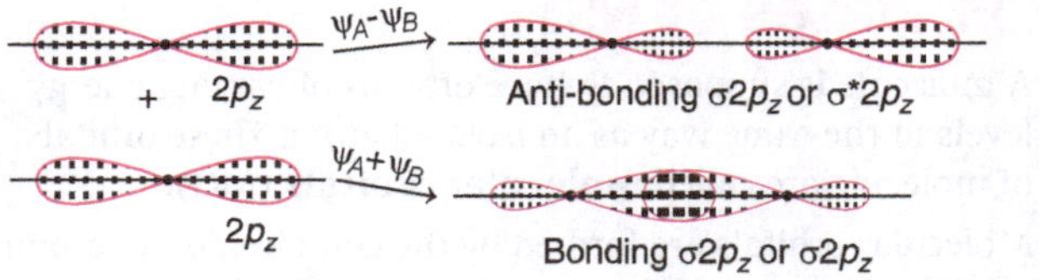

(iii) Sidewise combination of two *p*-orbitals

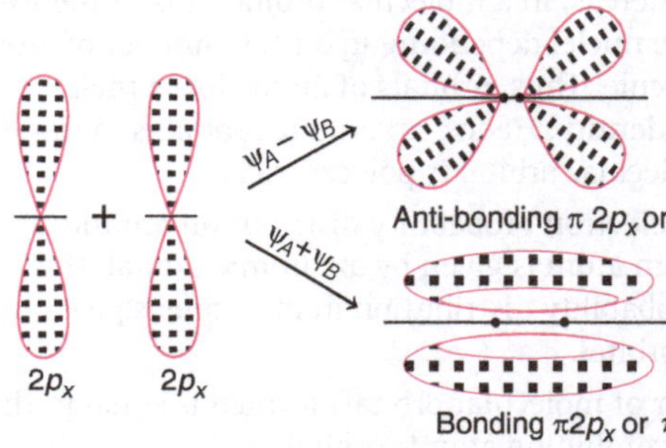

[Here, *z* axis is considered as internuclear axis]

Differences between bonding and anti-bonding molecular orbitals

S. No.	Bonding MO (BMO)	Anti-bonding MO (ABMO)
1.	Bonding molecular orbital is formed by the addition overlap of atomic orbitals.	Anti-bonding molecular orbital is formed by the subtraction overlap of atomic orbitals.
2.	It may or may not have a node.	It always has a node in between the nuclei of bonded atoms.
3.	In this orbital electron density is more in between the nuclei. Electrons in this orbital lead to attraction between atoms.	In this orbital electron density is less in between the nuclei. Electrons in this orbital lead to repulsion between atoms.
4.	Its energy is less than the energy of the atomic orbitals.	Its energy is more than the energy of the atomic orbitals.

Electronic Configuration of Molecules

It is the key to get informations like bond order, bond length, bond strength and magnetic nature of a molecule. Just like electronic configuration of atoms this electronic configuration is also aligned with the energy of orbitals.

For homonuclear diatomic molecules of the 2nd period elements of periodic table the energy levels of molecular orbitals have been determined experimentally from spectroscopic data.

The increasing order of energies of molecular orbitals for O_2 and F_2 molecules are given as

$$\sigma 1s < \overset{*}{\sigma} 1s < \sigma 2s < \overset{*}{\sigma} 2s < \sigma 2p_z < \pi 2p_x = \pi 2p_y < \overset{*}{\pi} 2p_x = \overset{*}{\pi} 2p_y < \overset{*}{\sigma} 2p_z$$

However, for remaining molecules, i.e. $Li_2, Be_2, B_2, C_2, N_2$ the order is $\sigma 1s < \overset{*}{\sigma} 1s < \sigma 2s < \overset{*}{\sigma} 2s < \pi 2p_x = \pi 2p_y$

$$< \sigma 2p_z < \overset{*}{\pi} 2p_x = \overset{*}{\pi} 2p_y < \overset{*}{\sigma} 2p_z$$

i.e. Here the energy of $\pi 2p_x = \pi 2p_y$ is less than the energy of $\sigma 2p_z$ molecular orbital.

It is so because except O_2 and F_2 the energy difference between 2*s* and 2*p* atomic energy level is small.

Stability of the Molecules

If N_b is the number of electrons occupying bonding orbitals and N_a is the number of electrons occupying the antibonding orbitals, then

(i) The molecule is stable if $N_b > N_a$.

(ii) The molecule is unstable if $N_b < N_a$.

(iii) The molecule is unstable if $N_b = N_a$.

Bond Order

(i) It can be defined as number of covalent bonds present between two atoms in a molecule.

(ii) It is given by one half of the differences between the number of electrons in bonding molecular orbitals and those in anti-bonding molecular orbitals.

(iii) Bond order = 1/2 [No. of electrons in bonding molecular orbitals − No. of electrons in anti bonding molecular orbitals].

(iv) The bond order of 1, 2 and 3 corresponds to single, double and triple bonds respectively. It may be mentioned that according to M.O theory, even a fractional bond order is possible, but cannot be negative.

(v) Bond order ∝ Stability of molecule ∝ Dissociation energy $\propto \dfrac{1}{\text{Bond length}}$

(vi) If all the electrons in a molecule are paired then the substance is a diamagnetic on the other hand if there are unpaired electrons in the molecule, then the substance is paramagnetic. More the number of unpaired electron in the molecule greater is the paramagnetism of the substance.

Bonding in Some Homonuclear Diatomic Molecules

(i) **H_2 Molecule**

Electronic configuration : $\sigma 1s^2$

$$\text{Bond order} = \frac{2-0}{2} = 1$$

Conclusion Stable molecule, with single bond between 2H atoms, **diamagnetic**.

(ii) **He_2 Molecule**

Electronic configuration : $\sigma 1s^2, \overset{*}{\sigma} 1s^2$

$$\text{Bond order} = \frac{2-2}{2} = 0$$

Conclusion Unstable molecule, does not exist. Similarly, Be_2 molecule with possible electronic configuration $\sigma 1s^2 \overset{*}{\sigma} 1s^2 \sigma 2s^2 \overset{*}{\sigma} 2s^2$ does not exist.

(iii) **Li_2 Molecule**

Electronic configuration : $\sigma 1s^2, \sigma^* 1s^2, \sigma 2s^2$

$$\text{Bond order} = \frac{4-2}{2} = 1$$

Conclusion Stable (known in vapour phase) with single bond between 2 Li atoms, **diamagnetic.**

(iv) **C_2 Molecule**

Electronic configuration

$$\sigma 1s^2, \sigma^* 1s^2, \sigma 2s^2, \overset{*}{\sigma} 2s^2, \pi 2p_x^2 \approx \pi 2p_y^2$$

$$\text{Bond order} = \frac{8-4}{2} = 2$$

Conclusion Stable (detected in vapour phase), with **2π-bonds between two C-atoms** instead of 1σ and 1π, **diamagnetic**.

(v) **O_2 Molecule**

Electronic configuration

$$\sigma 1s^2, \overset{*}{\sigma} 1s^2, \sigma 2s^2, \overset{*}{\sigma} 2s^2, \sigma 2p_z^2, \pi 2p_x^2 \approx \pi 2p_y^2, \overset{*}{\pi} 2p_x^1 \approx \overset{*}{\pi} 2p_y^1$$

$$\text{Bond order} = \frac{10-6}{2} = 2$$

Conclusion Stable, with double bond between two oxygen atoms, **paramagnetic**.

(vi) **F_2 Molecule**

Electronic configuration : $\sigma 1s^2, \overset{*}{\sigma} 1s^2, \sigma 2s^2, \overset{*}{\sigma} 2s^2$

$$\sigma 2p_z^2, \pi 2p_x^2 \approx \pi 2p_y^2, \overset{*}{\pi} 2p_x^2 \approx \overset{*}{\pi} 2p_y^2$$

$$\text{Bond order} = \frac{10-8}{2} = 1$$

Conclusion Stable, with one σ bond between two F-atoms, **diamagnetic**.

A brief summary to our discussion can be visualised as following table.

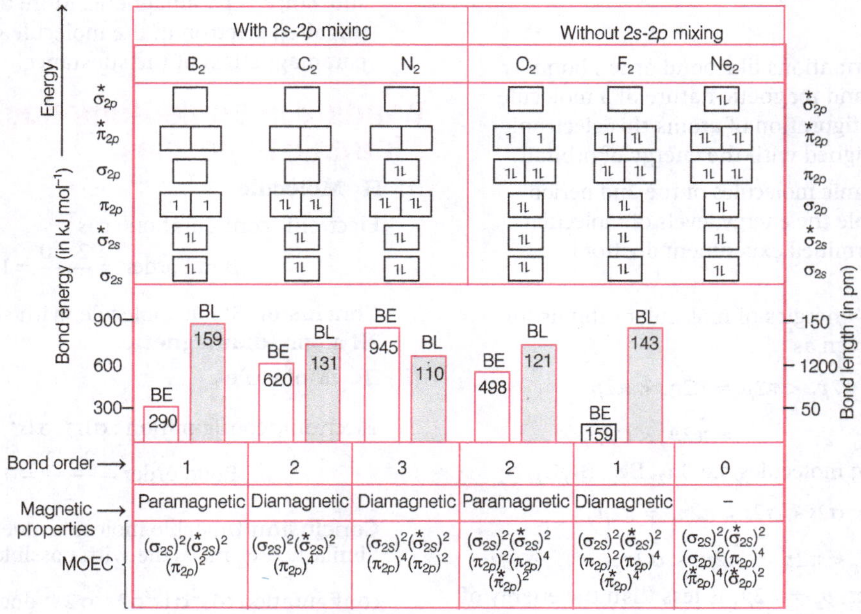

MOEC = Molecular Orbital Electronic Configuration

Tabular depiction of homonuclear molecules

JEE MAPPER

Example Similar to PYQ Asked in JEE Advanced 2023

The correct molecular orbital diagram for Ne_2 molecule is

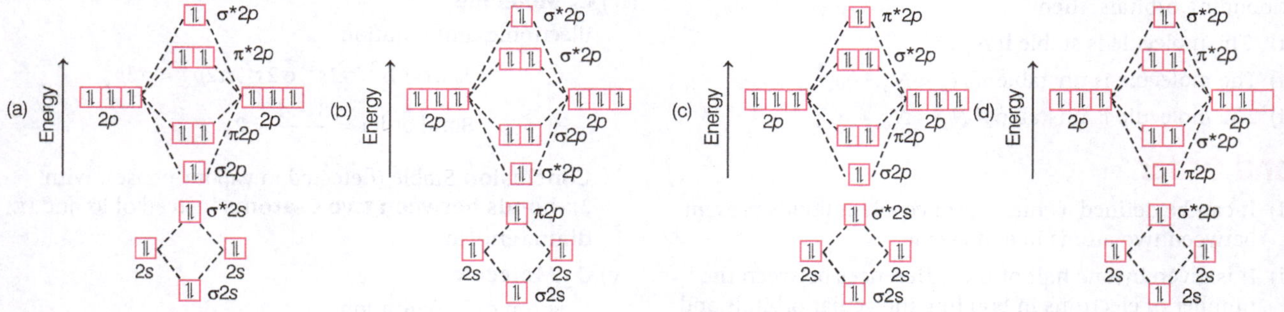

Sol. (*a*) Ne_2 contains 20 electrons and its molecular orbital configuration is $Ne_2 : \sigma 1s^2\, \sigma^*1s^2\, \sigma 2s^2\, \sigma^*2s^2\, \sigma 2p_z^2\, \pi 2p_x^2\, \pi 2p_y^2\, \pi^*2p_x^2\, \pi^*2p_y^2\, \sigma^*2p_z^2$

Competency Enhancer 2.3

The correct molecular orbital diagram for F_2 molecule in ground state is

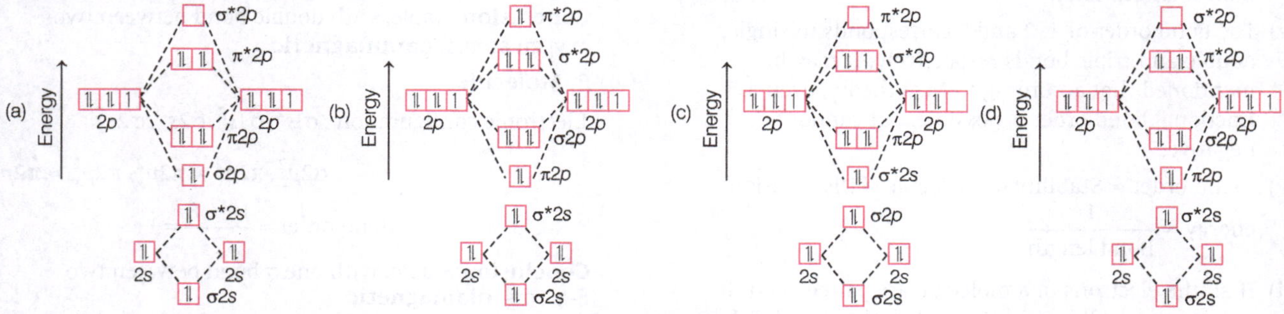

Hydrogen Bonding

The concept of the hydrogen bonding was introduced by **Latimer** and **Rodebush** (1920).

Hydrogen bonding is said to be formed when slightly acidic hydrogen attached to a strongly electronegative atom such as F, N and O, is held with weak electrostatic forces by the non-bonded pair of electrons of another atom.

The coordination number of hydrogen in such cases is two. It acts as a bridge between two atoms, to one of which it is covalently bonded, and to the other attached through electrostatic forces, also called **Hydrogen Bond.**

Of all the electronegative donor atoms, only F, N and O atoms enter into stable hydrogen bond formation.

The weak electrostatic interaction leading to the hydrogen bond formation is shown by dotted (....) lines. Thus *X*—H....*Y* represents hydrogen bonding between hydrogen and *Y* atom.

Nature of Hydrogen-Bonding

Since the hydrogen bond is formed by the most electronegative elements only, it is considered that its nature is ion-dipole, dipole-induced dipole or dipole-dipole interaction of the type :

$$\overset{\delta-}{A}—\overset{\delta+}{H}...\overset{\delta-}{B} \quad \text{or} \quad \overset{\delta-}{A}—\overset{\delta+}{H}..\overset{\delta-}{B}—\overset{\delta+}{R}$$

(*R* is the part of the molecule *B*—*R*)

Bond energy of H—bonding in $(\overset{\delta+}{H}...\overset{\delta-}{F}—\overset{\delta+}{H})$ is 113.4 kJ mol^{-1} due to dipole-dipole interactions.

Types of Hydrogen Bonding

Following two types of H-bonding are usually found.

Intramolecular H-Bonding

This type of H-bonding occurs when polar H and electronegative atom are present in the same molecule.

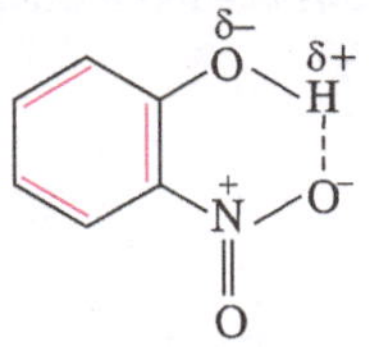

o-nitro phenol

The necessary conditions for the formation of intramolecular hydrogen-bonding are :

- the ring formed as a result of hydrogen bonding should be planar.
- a 5- or 6- membered ring should be formed.
- interacting atoms should be placed in such a way that there is minimum strain during the ring closure.

In case of *anti*-form of pyridine-2-carboxaldoxime there is intramolecular hydrogen bonding but it is not shown in *syn*-form

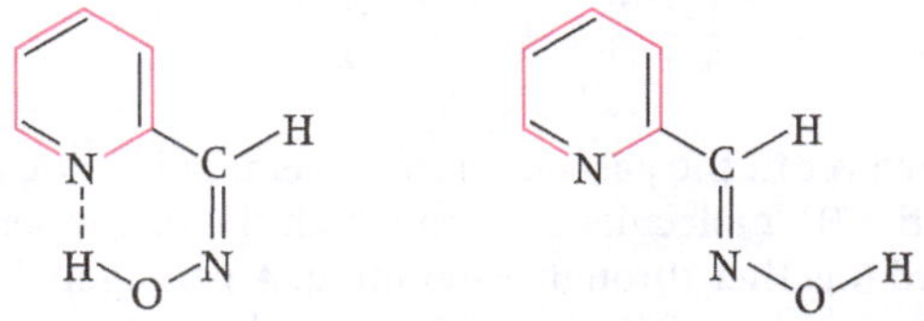

anti *syn*

Intermolecular H-Bonding

This type of H-bonding takes place between H and electronegative element present in the different molecules of the same substance (as in between H_2O and H_2O) or different substances (as in between H_2O and NH_3)

(i) **In Water Molecules** Due to polar nature of H_2O, there is association of water molecules giving a liquid state of abnormally high boiling point.

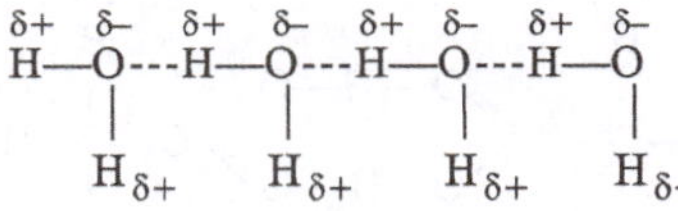

When one water molecule is joined to four water molecules — two with H-atoms and other two with O-atoms. Then coordination number of water molecule in water is **four.**

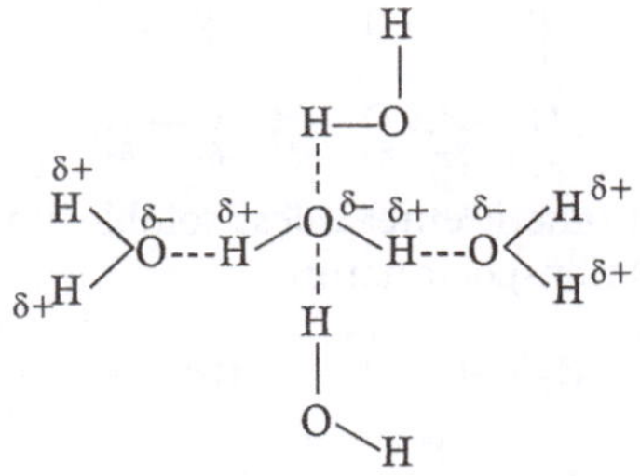

> **JEE Alert**
>
> - When ice is formed from liquid water, some air gap is formed (in tetrahedral packing of water molecules). **Due to this volume of ice is greater than liquid water and thus ice is lighter than water.** We can say that density decreases when ice is formed.
> - Conversely when ice melts, density increases but only up to 4°C, after this intermolecular H-bonding between water molecules breaks hence volume increases and hence density decreases. **Thus, water has maximum density at 4°C.**

(ii) **In Hydrofluoric Acid (HF),** there is again association by H-bonding.

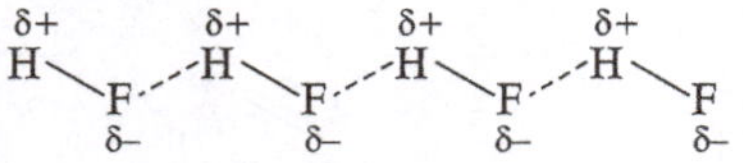

However in the gaseous state, several polymeric forms of the HF molecules exist in which the monomers are held together through H-bonding. A pentagonal arrangement of H—F molecules is shown below :

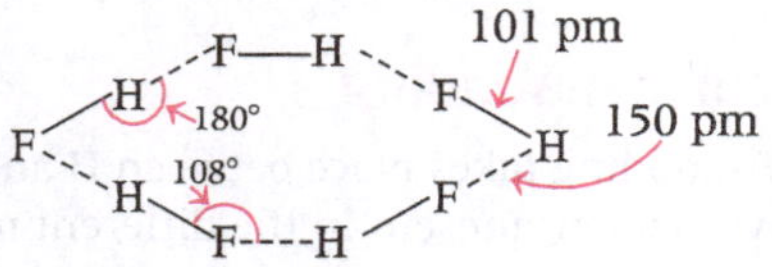

(iii) There is also similar H-bonding in alcohol (*R*—OH) ammonia (NH_3) and phenol (C_6H_5OH) molecules.

(iv) Carboxylic acid dimerises in gaseous state due to H-bonding

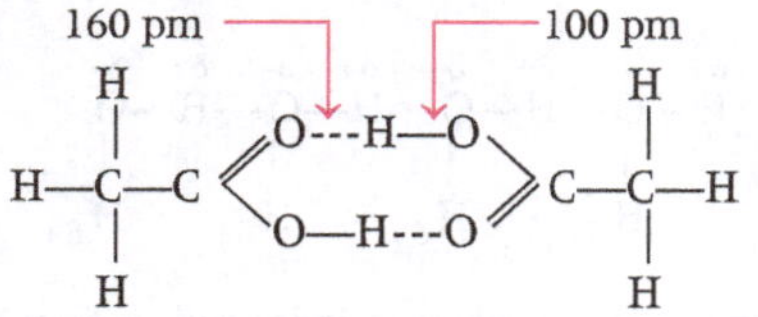

(v) Alcohol is said to be highly soluble in water due to *crossed* intermolecular H-bonding (between H_2O and *R*—OH molecules).

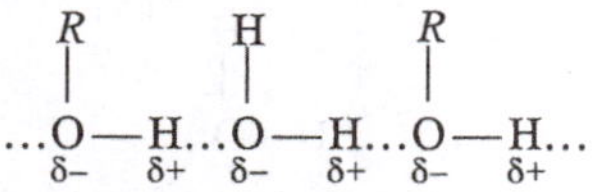

However isomeric ether is less soluble in water due to its (ether) non-polar nature.

$CH_3 — CH_2 — \underbrace{\overset{\delta-}{O} — \overset{\delta+}{H}}_{\text{polar}}$ $\quad$ $\underbrace{CH_3 — \overset{\delta-}{O} — \overset{\delta+}{CH_3}}_{\text{less polar}}$

(vi) Though the hydrogen atoms in a methyl groups are not polarised, if an electronegative group like chloro, carbonyl, nitro or cyano is attached to it, the C—H bond gets polarised due to the inductive effect and the hydrogen atom becomes slightly acidic resulting in the formation of weak hydrogen bonds.

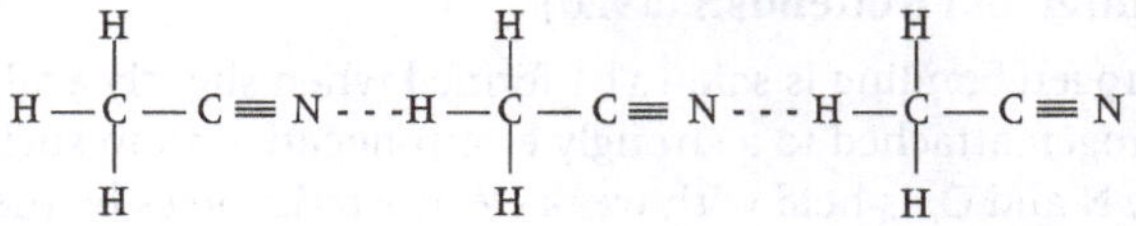

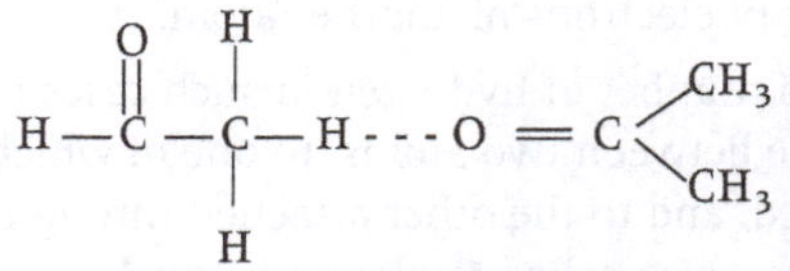

Consequences of the Hydrogen-Bonding

- Due to H-bonding boiling points of water, ammonia, hydrofluoric acid are abnormally high.
- B.P. : $H_2O > HF > NH_3 > CH_4$
- M.P. : $H_2O > NH_3 > HF > CH_4$
- Solubility of the organic compounds in water is due to H-bond formation.
- Due to hydrogen-bonding, viscosity (η) of the liquid increases.

Solved Booster 3.1

Which one of the following does not have intermolecular H—bonding.

(a) H_2O (b) *o*-Nitrophenol (c) HF (d) NH_3

Solution *(b)*

Nitrophenol has intramolecular H-bonding as shown below.

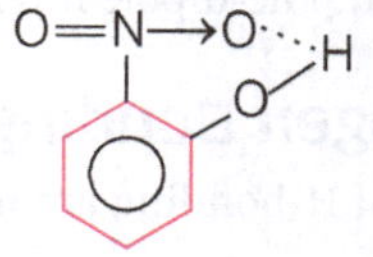

Hydrogen bonding depends on the electronegative difference between the hydrogen and the electronegative atom. More the electronegativity difference stronger is the hydrogen bond. Thus, H_2O, NH_3 and HF shows intermolecular H-bonding and *o*-nitrophenol does not.

Elemental Practice 2.3

Type I MCQs with Only One Correct Option

1. The correct order of energies of molecular orbitals of N_2 molecule, is
   (a) $\sigma 1s < \sigma^* 1s < \sigma 2s < \sigma^* 2s < \sigma 2p_z < (\pi 2p_x = \pi 2p_y) < (\pi^* 2p_x = \pi^* 2p_y) < \sigma^* 2p_z$
   (b) $\sigma 1s < \sigma^* 1s < \sigma 2s < \sigma^* 2s < \sigma 2p_z < \sigma^* 2p_z < (\pi 2p_x = \pi 2p_y) < (\pi^* 2p_x = \pi^* 2p_y)$
   (c) $\sigma 1s < \sigma^* 1s < \sigma 2s < \sigma^* 2s < (\pi 2p_x = \pi 2p_y) < (\pi^* 2p_x = \pi^* 2p_y) < \sigma 2p_z < \sigma^* 2p_z$
   (d) $\sigma 1s < \sigma^* 1s < \sigma 2s < \sigma^* 2s < (\pi 2p_x = \pi 2p_y) < \sigma 2p_z < (\pi^* 2p_x = \pi^* 2p_y) < \sigma^* 2p_z$
2. The incorrect statement from the following is
   (a) C_2 molecule has four electrons in its two degenerate π-molecular orbitals.
   (b) H_2^+ ion has one electron.
   (c) O_2^+ ion is diamagnetic.
   (d) The bond orders of O_2^+, O_2, O_2^- and O_2^{2-} are 2.5, 2, 1.5 and 1 respectively.
3. Identify a molecule which does not exist.
   (a) Li_2 (b) C_2
   (c) O_2 (d) He_2
4. Select the diatomic molecular species that has only π-bonds according to molecular orbital theory.
   (a) N_2 (b) C_2
   (c) Be_2 (d) O_2
5. Select the paramagnetic species.
   (a) N_2 (b) H_2
   (c) Li_2 (d) O_2
6. Select the molecule/ions which has bond order 1
   (a) Ne_2 (b) F_2
   (c) NO (d) CN^+
7. The species that does not exist under normal conditions is
   (a) Be_2^+ (b) Be_2
   (c) B_2 (d) Li_2
8. Choose the incorrect statement according to molecular orbital theory
   (a) C_2^{2-} is expected to be diamagnetic
   (b) O_2^{2+} is expected to have a longer bond length than O_2.
   (c) N_2^+ and N_2^- have the same bond order
   (d) He_2^+ is paramagnetic
9. Choose the correct statement from the following.
   (a) Both CN and NC groups are highly polar.
   (b) Amines have lesser boiling points than hydrocarbons of comparable molecular mass.
   (c) Carboxylic acid does not dimerises in solvent.
   (d) Ethers are more soluble in water.
10. The species having bond order is same as in C_2^{2+}.
    (a) N_2^- (b) B_2
    (c) NO^+ (d) O_2^-
11. Choose the species from the following that are diamagnetic in nature.
    (a) NO^- (b) CO^+
    (c) CN (d) BN
12. The bond order and magnetic property of NO is same as that of
    (a) O_2^- (b) BN
    (c) CN (d) CO
13. Which of the following statement about the molecular orbitals is incorrect?
    (a) ψ^2 represents the wave density.
    (b) Each ψ is associated with a definite energy.
    (c) Each electron in a molecular orbital belongs to all nuclei present in the molecule.
    (d) Atomic orbitals of the atoms in a molecule completely lose their identity after formation of molecular orbitals.
14. According to molecular orbital theory, which of the following statement is incorrect?
    (a) MOT explains the existence of H_2^+ ion.
    (b) N_2^+ and N_2^- have the same bond order.
    (c) C_2^{2-} is expected to be diamagnetic.
    (d) Resonance play an important role.
15. The difference between the bond order of CN^- and NO^- is $3x$. The value of x is
    (a) 2/3 (b) 1/3
    (c) 2 (d) 1

Type II MCQs with One or More than One Correct Option

16. Which of the following species will undergo on increase in bond order on ionisation ?
    (a) NO (b) CO
    (c) O_2^+ (d) Li_2^+
17. On ionisation, which of the following will show a change in its magnetic behavior?
    (a) O_2 (b) O_2^+
    (c) O_2^{2+} (d) O_2^{2-}
18. The species involving an decrease in magnetic moment on ionisation is
    (a) N_2^- (b) N_2
    (c) N_2^+ (d) N_2^{2-}

19. Select the correct statements from the following.
(a) In NH_2OH, N is sp^3 hybridised but pyramidal in shape
(b) CH_2^{2+} is linear molecule
(c) N_2^- has bond order = 1.5
(d) $CH_2=NH$ is a planar molecule.

20. Select the molecule that will not have a higher boiling point than *meta*-nitrophenol.
(a) *ortho*-nitrophenol (b) *para*-nitrophenol
(c) Benzene (d) Nitrobenzene

Type III 》 Numerical/Integer Answer Type Questions

21. The number of unpaired electrons in a paramagnetic diatomic molecule of an element with atomic number 16 is

22. Total number of species which has/have symmetrical electronic distribution in their HOMO also paramagnetic $N_2^+, O_2^{2-}, C_2, O_2, B_2, C_2^{-2}, N_2^{2-}$

23. There are some species given below.
(i) O_2^+ (ii) CO
(iii) B_2 (iv) O_2^-
(v) NO^+ (vi) He_2^+
(vii) C_2^{2+} (viii) CN^-
(ix) N_2^-
The number of species with bond order 3 are …… .

24. The number of antibonding electron pairs in O_2^{2-} molecular ion on the basis of molecular orbital theory is (at. number of O is 8)

25. The total number of diamagnetic species is from the following are …… .
H atom
NO_2 monomer
O_2^- (superoxide)
Dimeric sulphur in vapour phase (S_2)
K_2MnO_4
K_2CrO_4

26. The maximum number of hydrogen bonds in which H_2O_2 molecule can participate are …… .

Elemental Practice 2.3 | Chapter 02

Connect with Answers

1. (d)	2. (c)	3. (d)	4. (b)	5. (d)	6. (b)
7. (b)	8. (b)	9. (a)	10. (b)	11. (d)	12. (c)
13. (a)	14. (d)	15. (b)	16. (a,b,c)	17. (b,c,d)	18. (a,c,d)
19. (a,b,d)	20. (a,c,d)	21. (2)	22. (4)	23. (3)	24. (8)
25. (1)	26. (4)				

Advanced Exclusive Different Strokes

A short trick to identify the hybridisation of any molecule.

The structure of any molecule can be predicted on the basis of hybridisation which in turn can be known by the following general formulation.

$$H = \frac{1}{2}(V + M - C + A)$$

Where H = Number of orbitals involved in hybridisation viz. 2, 3, 4, 5, 6 and 7, hence nature of hybridisation will be $sp, sp^2, sp^3, sp^3d, sp^3d^2, sp^3d^3$ respectively.

V = Number electrons in valence shell of the central atom.

M = Number of monovalent atom

C = Charge on cation,

A = Charge on anion

Few examples are given below to illustrate this :

Type (A) When the central atom is surrounded by monovalent atoms only, e.g, $BeF_2, BCl_3, CCl_4, NCl_3, PCl_5, NH_3, H_2O, OF_2, TeCl_4, SCl_2, IF_7, ClF_3$ SF_4, SF_6, XeF_2, XeF_4 etc. Let us take the case of PCl_5.

$H = \frac{1}{2}(5 + 5 - 0 + 0) = 5$. Thus, the type of hybridisation is sp^3d.

Type (B) When the central atom is surrounded by divalent atoms only; e.g, $CO_2, CS_2, SO_2, SO_3, XeO_3$ etc. Let us take the case of SO_3.

$H = \frac{1}{2}(6 + 0 - 0 + 0) = 3$. Thus, the type of hybridisation in SO_3 is sp^2.

Type (C) When the central atom is surrounded by monovalent as well as divalent atoms, e.g., $COCl_2$, $POCl_3$, XeO_2F_2 etc. Let us take the case of $POCl_3$.

$H = \frac{1}{2}(5 + 3 - 0 + 0) = 4$. Thus, the nature of hybridisation in $POCl_3$ is sp^3.

Type (D) When the species is a cation, e.g., NH_4^+, CH_3^+, H_3O^+ etc. Let us take the case of CH_3^+.

$H = \frac{1}{2}(4 + 3 - 1 + 0) = 3$. Thus, the hybridisation in CH_3^+ is sp^2.

Type (E) When the species is an anion, e.g, $SO_4^{2-}, CO_3^{2-}, PO_4^{3-}, NO_2^-, NO_3^-$, etc. Let us take the case of SO_4^{2-}.

$$H = \frac{1}{2}(6 + 0 - 0 + 2) = 4.$$

Thus, hybridisation in SO_4^{2-} is sp^3.

Type (F) When the species is a complex ion of the type ICl_4^-, I_3^-, ClF_2^-, etc. Let us take the case of ClF_2^-.

$H = \frac{1}{2}(7 + 2 - 0 + 1) = 5$. Thus in ClF_2^-, Cl is sp^3d hybridized.

Thus, this formula will help to tackle the problems related to hybridisation. As almost every year questions related to hybridisation have been asked in JEE Main and Advanced Exam.

PRACTICE
ELEMENT 01

Target JEE Main

Objective Type Questions 》

1. Which of the following would result in the formation of strongest π-bond if the molecular axis is x-axis?
   (a) $2p_x + 2p_x$ (b) $2p_y + 2p_y$
   (c) $2p_y + 3d_{xy}$ (d) $2p_x + 4p_z$
2. Select the incorrect statement from the following.
   (a) d-orbital taking part in dsp^2 is $d_{x^2-y^2}$
   (b) d –orbital taking part in sp^3d is d_{xy}
   (c) d – orbital taking part in sp^3d^2 are $d_{x^2-y^2}$ and d_z^2
   (d) d-orbital taking part in sp^3d^3 are d_{xy}, d_{z^2} and $d_{x^2-y^2}$
3. Choose the incorrect set from the following options
   (a) N_2O, O_3, NH_4^+ all have co-ordinate bonds.
   (b) H_2O, NO_2, ClO_2 all are 'V' shape molecules.
   (c) I_3^-, ICl_2^-, NO_2^+ all are linear molecules.
   (d) SF_4, SiF_4, XeF_4 all are tetrahedral in shape.
4. The incorrect order of bond dissociation energy will be
   (a) H—H > Cl—Cl > Br—Br (b) Si—Si > P—P > Cl—Cl
   (c) C—C > N—N > O—O (d) H—Cl > H—Br > H—I
5. In which of the following d-orbital's are not used by central atom in hybridisation ?
   (a) $PF_5(s)$ (b) $PCl_5(s)$
   (c) $PBr_5(s)$ (d) $XeF_6(s)$
6. Dipole moment of 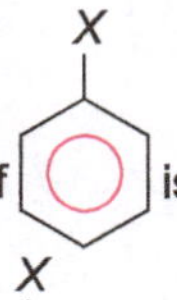 is 1.5 D. Calculate Dipole moment of 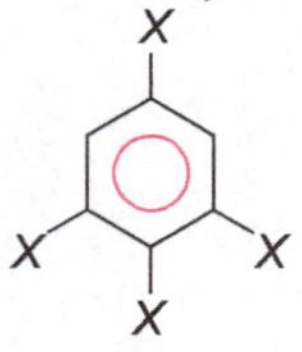
   (a) 1.5 D (b) 1 D
   (c) 2.35 D (d) 3 D
7. Which of the following pair of compounds are polar, planar and sp^2 hybridised?
   (a) H_2CO_3, SO_2 (b) $HClO_2$, H_2CO_3
   (c) BFClBr, ClF_3 (d) SO_3, O_3
8. Select the incorrect order from the following.
   (a) $NH_3 > SbH_3 > PH_3 > AsH_3$ (Melting point)
   (b) $NH_3 > PH_3 > AsH_3 > SbH_3$ (Proton affinity)
   (c) $CH_4 > SiH_4 > GeH_4 > SnH_4$ (Thermal stability)
   (d) $H_2O > H_2Te > H_2Se > H_2S$ (Boiling point)
9. The correct order of Cl—O bond order is
   (a) $ClO_3^- < ClO_4^- < ClO^- < ClO_2^-$
   (b) $ClO^- < ClO_4^- < ClO_3^- < ClO_2^-$
   (c) $ClO^- < ClO_2^- < ClO_3^- < ClO_4^-$
   (d) $ClO_4^- < ClO_3^- < ClO_2^- < ClO^-$
10. Choose the pair of species that have identical shapes.
    (a) NO_2^+ and NO_2^- (b) PCl_5 and BrF_5
    (c) XeF_4 and ICl_4^- (d) $TeCl_4$ and XeO_4
11. The bond having the highest bond energy is
    (a) C═C (b) C═S
    (c) C═O (d) P═N
12. Identify the isostructural pairs from the following species
    (a) [NF_3 and BF_3] (b) [BF_4^- and NH_4^+]
    (c) [BCl_3 and $BrCl_3$] (d) [NH_3 and NO_3^-]
13. The molecules exhibiting maximum number of non-bonding electron pairs (lp) around the central atom is
    (a) $XeOF_4$ (b) XeO_2F_2 (c) XeF_3^- (d) XeO_3
14. The shapes of XeF_4, XeF_5^- and $SnCl_2$ are
    (a) Octahedral, trigonalbipyramidal and bent
    (b) Square pyramidal, pentagonal planar and linear
    (c) Square planar, pentagonal planar and angular
    (d) See-saw, T-shaped and linear
15. Choose the incorrectly matched pair
    (a) XeO_3- Trigonal bipyramidal
    (b) ClF_3 - bent T-shape
    (c) $XeOF_4$ - Square pyramidal
    (d) XeF_2 - Linear shape
16. Given below are few statements
    I. The order of repulsion between different pair of electrons is
    $$lp - lp > lp - bp > bp - bp$$
    II. In general, as the number of lone pair of electrons on central atom increases, value of bond angle from normal bond angle also increases
    III. The number of lone pair on O in H_2O is 2 while on N in NH_3 is 1.
    IV. The structures of xenon fluorides and xenon oxofluorides could not be explained on the basis of VSEPR theory

Choose the correct statements from the option given below

(a) I, II, III (b) I, III
(c) I, III, IV (d) III, IV

17. Select the incorrect overlap from the following (assuming Z-axis is internuclear axis)?

I. $2p_y + 2p_y \rightarrow \pi$–Bond formation
II. $2p_x + 2p_x \rightarrow \sigma$– Bond formation
III. $3d_{xy} + 3d_{xy} \rightarrow \pi$–bond formation
IV. $2s + 2p_y \rightarrow \pi$–bond formation
V. $2p_z + 2p_z \rightarrow \sigma$–bond formation

Choose the correct answer from the options given below

(a) I, II, III (b) III, IV
(c) II, V (d) II, III, IV

18. Assuming the bond direction to the z-axis, which of the overlapping of atomic orbitals of two atom (A) and (B) will result in bonding?

I. s-orbital of A and p_x-orbital of B
II. s-orbital of A and p_z-orbital of B
III. p_y-orbital of A and p_z-orbital of B
IV. s- orbital of both (A) and (B)

Choose the correct answer from the options given below

(a) I and IV (b) I and II
(c) III and IV (d) II and IV

19. The type of bonds, between two C-atoms in SrC_2 are :

(a) $1\pi, 1\sigma$ (b) $2\pi, 1\sigma$
(c) 1π (d) $1\pi, 2\sigma$

20. Choose the correct decreasing order of dipole moments in the options given below

(a) $NH_3 > BF_3 > NF_3$ (b) $NH_3 > NF_3 > BF_3$
(c) $BF_3 > NH_3 > NF_3$ (d) $NF_3 > NH_3 > BF_3$

21. The maximum number of 90° angles between bp - bp of electrons is observed in

(a) sp^3d hybridisation (b) dsp^3 hybridisation
(c) dsp^2 hybridisation (d) sp^3d^2 hybridisation

22. The bond angles of SO_3, SO_2 and SO_3^{2-} are in the order

(a) $SO_3 > SO_2 > SO_3^{2-}$ (b) $SO_3^{2-} > SO_3 > SO_2$
(c) $SO_2 > SO_3 > SO_3^{2-}$ (d) $SO_3 > SO_3^{2-} > SO_2$

Numerical Type Questions

23. The number of Cl = O bonds in perchloric acid is "..........".

24. The bond angle between two hybrid orbital is 105°. The percentage of s-character of hybrid orbital is between x–23%. The value of x will be....... (nearest integer)

25. H_2^-, H_2^+, H_2 and He_2^+ are given species. The number of species that are paramagnetic in nature are

26. Bond order of N—O bonds in nitrate ion is y. If y is added with 8.67 the value obtained is

27. The molecule ML_x is planar with six pairs of electrons around M in the valence shell. The value of x is … .

28. A σ-bonded molecule MX_3 is T-shaped. The number of non-bonding pairs of electron in any MX_3 molecule is … .

29. In a polar molecule, the ionic charge is 4.8×10^{-10} esu. If the interionic distance is 1 Å unit, then the dipole moment is .... debye (nearest integer).

The value of 'x' is

30. Consider two elements with atomic no. 37 and 53. Suppose their valencies are x and y. Then the product $x \times y$ is … .

31. Consider the following molecule/ion O_2^{2-}, B_2, N_2^+ and O_2 i.e. Number of molecule/ion contain unpaired electrons are.

32. Number of hybrid orbital of carbon in carbon suboxide is … .

Check Through PYQs

Element 1 Ionic & Covalent Bonding, Fajan's Rule

1. Match the Column I with Column II and choose the correct option. *2025, 23 Jan Shift-I*

	Column I		Column II
A.	BF_3	(i)	Odd e^- species
B.	CCl_4, CO_2	(ii)	Expanded octet
C.	PCl_5, BrF_5	(iii)	Complete octet
D.	NO	(iv)	Electron deficient

(a) A-(iii), B-(iv), C-(i), D-(ii)
(b) A-(iv), B-(ii), C-(iii), D-(i)
(c) A-(iv), B-(iii), C-(ii), D-(i)
(d) A-(i), B-(ii), C-(iii), D-(iv)

2. Number of molecules from the following which are exceptions to octet rule is ....
CO_2, NO_2, H_2SO_4, BF_3, CH_4, SiF_4, ClO_2, PCl_5, BeF_2, C_2H_6, $CHCl_3$, CBr_4 *2024, 8 April Shift-II*

3. In the Lewis dot structure for NO_2^-, total number of valence electrons around nitrogen is .... *2024, 5 April Shift-I*

4. Arrange the bonds in order of increasing ionic character in the molecules, LiF, K_2O, N_2, SO_2 and ClF_3 : *2024, 1st Feb Shift-I*

(a) $N_2 < SO_2 < ClF_3 < K_2O < LiF$
(b) $LiF < K_2O < ClF_3 < SO_2 < N_2$
(c) $ClF_3 < N_2 < SO_2 < K_2O < LiF$
(d) $N_2 < ClF_3 < SO_2 < K_2O < LiF$

5. Order of covalent bond;
A. KF > KI; LiF > KF
B. KF < KI; LiF > KF
C. $SnCl_4 > SnCl_2$; CuCl > NaCl
D. LiF > KF; CuCl < NaCl
E. KF < KI; CuCl > NaCl
Choose the correct answer from the options given below.
2023, 24 Jan Shift-I
(a) B and C (b) A and B
(c) C and E (d) B, C and E

Element 2 Bond Parameter, VBT and VSEPR Theory

6. How many of the following molecules are polar?
CH_4, CCl_4, CH_2Cl_2, H_2O, NH_3, H_2O_2, O_2F_2 *2025, 28 Jan Shift-II*

7. In which one of the following pairs the central atoms exhibit sp^2 hybridisation? *2024, 9 April Shift-I*
(a) H_2O and NO_2 (b) NH_2^- and H_2O
(c) BF_3 and NO_2^- (d) NH_2^- and BF_3

8. Match List I with List II.

List-I (Molecule)	List-II (Shape)
A. NH_3	I. Square pyramid
B. BrF_5	II. Tetrahedral
C. PCl_5	III. Trigonal pyramidal
D. CH_4	IV. Trigonal bipyramidal

Choose the correct answer from the options given below:
2024, 8 April Shift-I
(a) A-IV, B-III, C-I, D-II (b) A-II, B-IV, C-I, D-III
(c) A-III, B-I, C-IV, D-II (d) A-III, B-IV, C-I, D-II

9. Total number of species from the following with central atom utilising sp^2 hybrid orbitals for bonding is............
NH_3, SO_2, SiO_2, $BeCl_2$, C_2H_2, C_2H_4, BCl_3, HCHO, C_6H_6, BF_3, $C_2H_4Cl_2$.
2024, 6 April Shift-II

10. Match list I with list II.

List-I (Molecule/species)	List-II (Property/shape)
A. SO_2Cl_2	I. Paramagnetic
B. NO	II. Diamagnetic
C. NO_2^-	III. Tetrahedral
D. I_3^-	IV. Linear

Choose the correct answer from the options given below.
2024, 6 April Shift-I
(a) A-II, B-III, C-I, D-IV
(b) A-IV. B-I. C-III, D-II
(c) A-III, B-I, C-II, D-IV
(d) A-III, B-IV, C-II, D-I

11. Match List I with List II.

List I (Compound/species)	List II (Shape/Geometry)
A. SF_4	I. Tetrahedral
B. BrF_3	II. Pyramidal
C. BrO_3^-	III. See-saw
D. NH_4^+	IV. Bent T-Shape

Choose the correct answer from the options given below.
2024, 6 April Shift-I
(a) A-III, B-IV, C-II, D-I (b) A-II, B-IV, C-III, D-I
(c) A-III, B-II, C-IV, D-I (d) A-II, B-III, C-I, D-IV

12. Given below are two statements : one is labelled as Assertion (A) and the other is labelled as Reason (R).
2024, 5 April Shift-II
Assertion (A) NH_3 and NF_3 molecule have pyramidal shape with a lone pair of electrons on nitrogen atom. The resultant dipole moment of NH_3 is greater than that of NF_3.
Reason (R) In NH_3, the orbital dipole due to lone pair is in the same direction as the resultant dipole moment of the N—H bond. F is the most electronegative element.
In the light of the above statements, choose the correct answer from the options given below :
(a) (A) is true but (R) is false
(b) (A) is false but (R) is true
(c) Both (A) and (R) are true and (R) is the correct explanation of (A)
(d) Both (A) and (R) are true but (R) is not the correct explanation of (A)

13. Number of compounds from the following with zero dipole moment is ....
HF, H_2, H_2S, CO_2, NH_3, BF_3, CH_4, $CHCl_3$, SiF_4, H_2O, BeF_2
2024, 5 April Shift-II

14. Given below are two statements : one is labelled as Assertion (A) and the other is labelled as Reason (R).
Assertion (A) *cis*-form of alkene is found to be more polar than the *trans*-form.
Reason (R) Dipole moment of *trans*-isomer of 2-butene is zero. *2024, 5 April Shift-I*
In the light of the above statements, choose the correct answer from the options given below.
(a) Both A and R are true but R is not the correct explanation of A.
(b) A is false but R is true.
(c) Both A and R are true and R is the correct explanation of A.
(d) A is true but R is false.

15. Number of compounds/ species from the following with non-zero dipole moment is...... .
$BeCl_2$, BCl_3, NF_3, XeF_4, CCl_4, H_2O, H_2S, HBr, CO_2, H_2, HCl
2024, 4 April Shift-II

16. The number of species from the following that have pyramidal geometry around the central atom is......
$S_2O_3^{2-}, SO_4^{2-}, SO_3^{2-}, S_2O_7^{2-}$ *2024, 4 April Shift-II*
(a) 3 (b) 4 (c) 1 (d) 2

17. The number of species from the following in which the central atom uses sp^3 hybrid orbitals in its bonding is ....
NH_3, SO_2, SiO_2, $BeCl_2$, CO_2, H_2O, CH_4, BF_3 *2024, 31 Jan Shift-I*

18. Choose the polar molecule from the following *2024, 27 Jan Shift-I*
(a) $CH_2 = CH_2$ (b) CCl_4 (c) CO_2 (d) $CHCl_3$

19. Given below are two statements.
Statement I SO_2 and H_2O both possess V-shaped structure.
Statement II The bond angle of SO_2 is less than that of H_2O.
In the light of the above statements, choose the most appropriate answer from the options given below. *2023, 13 April Shift-II*
(a) Both Statement I and Statement II are incorrect.
(b) Statement I is correct but Statement II is incorrect.
(c) Both Statement I and Statement II are correct.
(d) Statement I is incorrect but Statement II is correct.

20. The number of molecules from the following which contain only two lone pair of electrons is ....
H_2O, N_2, CO, XeF_4, NH_3, NO, CO_2, F_2 *2023, 10 April Shift-II*

21. Given below are two statements.
Statement I Dipole moment is a vector quantity and by convention it is depicted by a small arrow with tail on the negative centre and head pointing towards the positive centre.
Statement II The crossed arrow of the dipole moment symbolises the direction of the shift of charges in the molecules.
In the light of the above statements, choose the most appropriate answer from the options given below. *2023, 25 Jan Shift-II*
(a) Both Statement I and Statement II are incorrect.
(b) Statement I is correct but Statement II is incorrect.
(c) Statement I is incorrect but Statement II is correct.
(d) Both Statement I and Statement II are correct.

22. The number of molecule(s) or ion(s) from the following having non-planar structure is ....
NO_3^-, H_2O_2, BF_3, PCl_3, XeF_4, SF_4, XeO_3, PH_4^+, SO_3, $[Al(OH)_4]^-$ *2022, 27 July Shift-II*

23. Consider the species CH_4, NH_4^+ and BH_4^-. Choose the correct option with respect to these species. *2022, 29 June Shift-II*
(a) They are isoelectronic and only two have tetrahedral structures.
(b) They are isoelectronic and all have tetrahedral structures.
(c) Only two are isoelectronic and all have tetrahedral structures.
(d) Only two are isoelectronic and only two have tetrahedral structures.

24. In the structure of SF_4, the lone pair of electrons on S is in *2022, 28 June Shift-II*
(a) equatorial position and there are two lone pair-bond pair repulsions at 90°.
(b) equatorial position and there are three lone pair-bond pair repulsions at 90°.
(c) axial position and there are three lone pair-bond pair repulsion at 90°.
(d) axial position and there are two lone pair-bond pair repulsion at 90°.

25. For increasing bond order the correct option is *2022, 26 June Shift-I*
(a) $O_2^{2-} < O_2^- < O_2 < O_2^+$ (b) $O_2^- < O_2^{2-} < O_2 < O_2^+$
(c) $O_2^- < O_2^{2-} < O_2^+ < O_2$ (d) $O_2^- < O_2^+ < O_2^{2-} < O_2$

26. The total number of molecules with zero dipole moment among CH_4, BF_3, H_2O, HF, NH_3, CO_2 and SO_2 is .... *2022, 29 Jan Shift-II*

27. The Born-Haber cycle for KCl is evaluated with the following data

$$\Delta_f H^\circ \text{ for KCl} = -436.7 \text{ kJ mol}^{-1}$$
$$\Delta_{sub} H^\circ \text{ for K} = 89.2 \text{ kJ mol}^{-1}$$
$$\Delta_{ionisation} H^\circ \text{ for K} = 419.0 \text{ kJ mol}^{-1}$$
$$\Delta_{electron\ gain} H^\circ \text{ for Cl}(g) = -348.6 \text{ kJ mol}^{-1}$$
$$\Delta_{bond} H^\circ \text{ for } Cl_2 = 243.0 \text{ kJ mol}^{-1}$$

The magnitude of lattice enthalpy of KCl (in kJ mol^{-1}) is .... *2021, 26 Aug Shift-I*

28. The hybridisations of the atomic orbitals of nitrogen in NO_2^-, NO_2^+ and NH_4^+ respectively are *2021, 20 July Shift-II*
(a) sp^3, sp^2 and sp (b) sp, sp^2 and sp^3
(c) sp^3, sp and sp^2 (d) sp^2, sp and sp^3

29. A central atom in a molecule has two lone pairs of electrons and forms three single bonds. The shape of this molecule is *2021, 17 March Shift-I*
(a) *see-saw* (b) planar triangular
(c) T-shaped (d) trigonal pyramidal

30. Given below are two statements : one is labelled as Assertion (A) and the other is labelled as Reason (R).
Assertion (A) The H—O—H bond angle in water molecule is 104.5°.
Reason (R) The lone pair - lone pair repulsion of electrons is higher than the bond pair - bond pair repulsion. *2021, 16 March Shift-I*
(a) A is false but R is true.
(b) Both A and R are true, but R is not the correct explanation of A.
(c) A is true but R is false.
(d) Both A and R are true, and R is the correct explanation of A.

31. Which among the following species has unequal bond lengths ? *2021, 25 Feb Shift-II*
(a) XeF_4 (b) SiF_4
(c) SF_4 (d) BF_4^-

32. Which of the following are isostructural pairs ?
A. SO_4^{2-} and CrO_4^{2-} B. $SiCl_4$ and $TiCl_4$
C. NH_3 and NO_3^- D. BCl_3 and $BrCl_3$ **2021, 24 Feb Shift-I**
(a) Only A and B (b) Only A and C
(c) Only B and C (d) Only C and D

33. The compound that has the largest H—*M*—H bond angle (M = N, O, S, C) is **2020, 5 Sep Shift-II**
(a) H_2O (b) NH_3 (c) H_2S (d) CH_4

34. Arrange the following bonds according to their average bond energies in descending order
C—Cl, C—Br, C—F, C—I **2020, 8 Jan Shift-II**
(a) C—F > C—Cl > C—Br > C—I
(b) C—Br > C—I > C—Cl > C—F
(c) C—I > C—Br > C—Cl > C—F
(d) C—Cl > C—Br > C—I > C—F

35. Complexes (ML_5) of metals Ni and Fe have ideal square pyramidal and trigonal bipyramidal geometrics, respectively. The sum of the 90°, 120° and 180° *L-M-L* angles in the two complexes is .... **2020, 8 Jan Shift-II**

Element 3 MOT and Hydrogen Bonding

36. Number of paramagnetic species among the following is
$O_2, O_2^+, O_2^-, NO_2, NO, CO$ **2025, 28 Jan Shift-II**

37. The total number of molecular orbitals formed from 2*s* and 2*p* atomic orbitals of a diatomic molecule is .... **2024, 30 Jan Shift-I**

38. The total number of anti-bonding molecular orbitals, formed from 2*s* and 2*p* atomic orbitals in a diatomic molecule is .... **2024, 29 Jan Shift-II**

39. The number of species from the following which are paramagnetic and with bond order equal to one is ....
$H_2, He_2^+, O_2^+, N_2^{2-}, O_2^{2-}, F_2, Ne_2^+, B_2$ **2024, 29 Jan Shift-I**

40. What is the number of unpaired electrons in the highest occupied molecular orbital of the following species N_2; N_2^+; O_2; O_2^+? **2023, 24 Jan Shift-II**
(a) 2, 1, 2, 1 (b) 0, 1, 0, 1
(c) 2, 1, 0, 1 (d) 0, 1, 2, 1

41. According to MO theory, the bond orders for O_2^{2-}, CO and NO^+ respectively, are **2023, 29 Jan Shift-II**
(a) 2, 3 and 3 (b) 1, 2 and 3
(c) 1, 3 and 3 (d) 1, 3 and 2

42. Match List I with List II.

List-I		List-II	
(A)	$\psi_{MO} = \psi_A - \psi_B$	(I)	Dipole moment
(B)	$\mu = Q \times r$	(II)	Bonding molecular orbital
(C)	$\frac{N_b - N_a}{2}$	(III)	Anti-bonding molecular orbital
(D)	$\psi_{MO} = \psi_A + \psi_B$	(IV)	Bond order

Choose the correct answer from options given below: **2022, 27 July Shift-II**
(a) (A)-(II), (B)-(I), (C)-(IV), (D)-(III)
(b) (A)-(III), (B)-(IV), (C)-(I), (D)-(II)
(c) (A)-(III), (B)-(I), (C)-(IV), (D)-(II)
(d) (A)-(III), (B)-(IV), (C)-(II), (D)-(I)

43. Among the following species
$N_2, N_2^+, N_2^-, N_2^{2-}, O_2, O_2^+, O_2^-, O_2^{2-}$
the number of species showing diamagnetism is .... **2022, 25 July Shift-I**

44. Bonding in which of the following diatomic molecule(s) become(s) stronger, on the basis of MO theory, by removal of an electron?
(A) NO (B) N_2 (C) O_2 (D) C_2 (E) B_2
Choose the most appropriate answer from the options given below. **[2022, 25 June Shift-I]**
(a) (A), (B) and (C) (b) (B), (C) and (E)
(c) (A) and (C) (d) (D) only

45. The compound/s which will show significant intermolecular H–bonding is/are

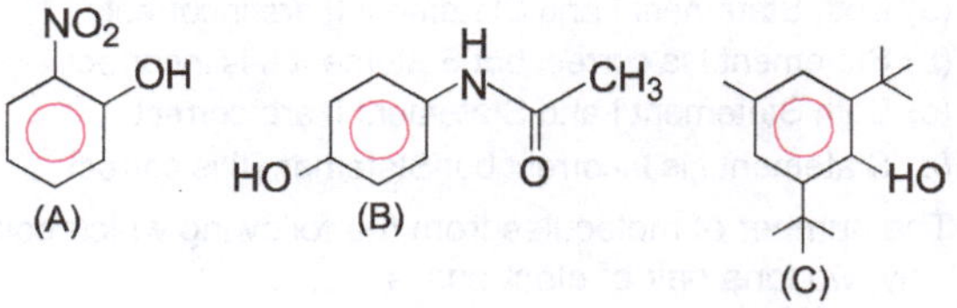

(A) (B) (C)

2021, 27 Aug Shift-II
(a) Only (B) (b) Only (C)
(c) (A) and (B) (d) (A), (B) and (C)

46. The bond order and magnetic behaviour of O_2^- ion are, respectively **2021, 26 Aug Shift-II**
(a) 1.5 and paramagnetic (b) 1.5 and diamagnetic
(c) 2 and diamagnetic (d) 1 and paramagnetic

47. The total number of electrons in all bonding molecular orbitals of O_2^{2-} is ....
(Round off to the nearest integer) **2021, 27 July Shift-II**

48. Given below are two statements: One is labelled as Assertion (A) and the other is labelled as Reason (R).
Assertion (A) Dipole-dipole interactions are the only non-covalent interactions, resulting in hydrogen bond formation.
Reason (R) Fluorine is the most electronegative element and hydrogen bonds in HF are symmetrical.
In the light of the above statements, choose the most appropriate answer from the options given below.
(a) A is false but R is true. **2021, 26 Feb Shift-I**
(b) Both A and R are true and R is the correct explanation of A.
(c) A is true R is false.
(d) Both A and R are true but R is not the correct explanation of A.

49. The correct order of increasing intermolecular hydrogen bond strength is **[2020, 27 June Shift-II]**
(a) HCN < H_2O < NH_3 (b) HCN < CH_4 < NH_3
(c) CH_4 < HCN < NH_3 (d) CH_4 < NH_3 < HCN

PRACTICE ELEMENT 02

Target JEE Advanced

Single Correct Choice MCQs

1. Which of the following order is incorrect?
   (a) Ionic character : $MCl < MCl_2 < MCl_3$
   (b) Polarisibility : $F^- < Cl^- < Br^- < I^-$
   (c) Polarising power : $Na^+ < Ca^{+2} < Mg^{+2} < Al^{+3}$
   (d) Covalent character : LiF < LiCl < LiBr < LiI

2. In which one of the following pairs the central atoms exhibit sp^3d^2 hybridisation?
   (a) IF_5 and ICl_4^- (b) PF_5 and $XeOF_4$
   (c) ClO_2^- and SF_4 (d) SO_2Cl_2 and BrO_3^-

3. Select the option containing species which are paramagnetic in nature.
   (a) He_2^+, B_2 (b) He_2, H_2
   (c) N_2^{2-}, Li_2 (d) Be_2, C_2

4. Select the isostructural pairs from the following.
   (A) NH_4^+ and SF_4 (B) BrF_5 and $XeOF_4$
   (C) ClF_5 and IF_5 (D) NO_3^- and CrO_4^{2-}
   (a) A and B (b) A and C
   (c) B and C (d) C and D

5. Which of the following molecule has $2p\pi - 3p\pi$ back bonding?
   (a) OCl_2 (b) BF_3
   (c) $:CCl_2$ (d) CCl_3^-

6. The correct order of the increasing bond strength of the given ions is
   $$C_2^+, O_2^{2+}, C_2^-, O_2^{2-}$$
   (a) $O_2^{2+} < C_2^- < C_2^+ < O_2^{2-}$ (b) $C_2^- < C_2^+ < O_2^{2+} < O_2^{2-}$
   (c) $O_2^{2-} < C_2^+ < C_2^- < O_2^{2+}$ (d) $C_2^+ < O_2^{2-} < C_2^- < O_2^{2+}$

7. Choose the incorrect statements regarding molecular orbital theory.
   (a) The atomic orbitals of the combining atoms retain a large amount of their individual character.
   (b) Resonance plays no role in this theory.
   (c) It explains the existence of H_2^+ ion.
   (d) The shapes of the molecular orbitals formed depend upon the type of the combining atomic orbital.

8. In the molecule of N_2 which of the following set of orbitals represents HOMO and LUMO ?
   (a) $\pi 2p_x$ and $\sigma 2p_z$ (b) $\sigma 2p_z$ and $\pi^* 2p_x$
   (c) $\pi^* 2p_x$ and $\sigma 2p_z$ (d) $\sigma 2p_z$ and $\sigma 2p_x$

9. Which of the following represents correct order of bond lengths?
   (a) $H_2O_2 < O_2F_2$ (O—O bond length)
   (b) $S_2Cl_2 > S_2F_2$ (S—S bond length)
   (c) $N_2H_2 < N_2H_2F_2 < N_2H_4$ (N—N bond length)
   (d) $P_2H_4 < P_2F_4$

10. Select from each set the molecule or ion having the smallest bond angle
    (i) NH_3, PH_3, AsH_3
    (ii) O_3^+, O_3
    (iii) NO_2^-, O_3
    (iv) X—S—X angle in $SOCl_2$ and SOF_2
    (a) $NH_3, O_3^+, O_3, SOCl_2$ (b) $PH_3, O_3^+, NO_2^-, SOF_2$
    (c) $AsH_3, O_3, NO_2^-, SOF_2$ (d) $AsH_3, O_3^+, O_3 SOF_2$

One or More than One Correct MCQs

11. Which of the following compounds has linear shape?
    (a) NO_2^+ (b) XeF_2
    (c) I_3^- (d) I_3^+

12. Select the correct statements from the following.
    (a) In F_2O, the bond pair of electrons lie closer to fluorine atom.
    (b) In H_2O, the bond pair of electrons lie closer to oxygen atom.
    (c) Force of repulsion between the bonded pairs of electrons decreases from H_2O to H_2Te.
    (d) The position of the bond pairs of electrons shifts more and more away from central atom in moving from H_2O to H_2Te.

13. Select correct statement(s) regarding σ and π-bonds.
    (a) σ-bond lies on the line joining the nuclei of bonded atoms.
    (b) π-electron cloud lies on either side to the line joining the nuclei of bonded atoms
    (c) $(2p\pi - 3d\pi)$ pi-bond is stronger than $(2p\pi - 3p\pi)$ pi-bond.
    (d) π-bond has primary effect to decide direction of covalent bond, while π-bond has no primary effect in direction of bond.

14. Which of the following statements are correct about sulphur hexafluoride?
    (a) All S—F bonds are equivalent
    (b) SF_6 is a planar molecule
    (c) Oxidation number of sulphur is the same as number of electrons of sulphur involved in bonding
    (d) Sulphur has acquired the electronic structure of the gas argon.

15. Correct order of decreasing boiling points is
(a) HF > HI > HBr > HCl (b) $H_2O > H_2Te > H_2Se > H_2S$
(c) $Br_2 > Cl_2 > F_2$ (d) $CH_4 > GeH_4 > SiH_4$

16. The option(s) in which at least three molecules follows octet rule is (are)
(a) NO_2, BeF_2, BF_3 and N_2O
(b) $O_3, H_2SO_4, CHCl_3$ and SiF_4
(c) BF_3, SiF_4, CO_2 and C_2H_6
(d) ClO_2, PCl_5, $BeCl_2$ and NO_2

17. Which of the following pairs contain non-polar as well as non-planar species?
(a) PF_3Cl_2 and XeO_4 (b) XeO_4 and PF_2Cl_3
(c) PCl_5 and CCl_4 (d) XeO_2F_4 and PF_2Cl_3

18. Select the correct statement(s) for bond distance :
(a) The bond distance decreases with the increase of bond order.
(b) $\equiv C-H < \; >C-H < \; -\!\!>C-H$ (order of C—H bond distance)
(c) $\equiv C-C\equiv \; < \; >C-C\equiv \; < \; >C-C< \; < \; -\!\!>C-C<$
(order of C—C bond distance)
(d) The S—F length is longer in SF_6 compared to that in SF_2.

Numerical/Integer Type Questions 》

19. The ratio of the total number of bonds to the total number of lone pairs in $C_3N_3Cl_3$ is ....

20. The dipole moment of LiH is 1.964×10^{-29} Cm and the inter atomic distance between Li and H in this molecule is 1.596 Å. Then per cent ionic character in LiH is ....

21. The number of species that exhibits square pyramidal geometry are
$IF_5, PF_5, SF_4, ClF_5, (SbF_5)^{2-}, ICl_4$

22. How many of the following have $p\pi - d\pi$ bonding?
(a) CO_3^{-2} (b) NO_3^-
(c) SO_3^{-2} (d) SO_4^{-2}
(e) PO_4^{-3} (f) NO_2^-
(g) $S_2O_8^{-2}$ (h) $R_3PO_3^{2-}$
(i) $S_2O_3^{-2}$ (j) ClO_4^-
(k) ClO_3^- (l) SO_2

23. Find the number of species having fractional bond order.
$N_2^+, N_2^-, O_2, O_2^+, F_2, B_2, C_2^+, CN^-, NO^+$

24. Select the number of species that will show hydrogen bonding.
NH_3, CH_4, H_2O, HI, HF, HCOOH, $B(OH)_3$
CH_3COOH, HCO_2^- ion

25. Select the number of species that are V-shaped.
$H_2O, SeCl_2, NH_2^-, NH_3, BCl_3, BH_3$

26. Find the sum of axial d-orbital which are used in hybridisation of species XeF_5^- and XeF_5^+.

27. The compound MX_6 is octahedral. Find the number of X—M—X angles in the compound.

28. Consider the following six changes.
(i) $NO \longrightarrow NO^+$ (ii) $O_2^- \longrightarrow O_2^{2-}$
(iii) $O_2 \longrightarrow O_2^+$ (iv) $NO^+ \longrightarrow NO^-$
(v) $CO \longrightarrow CO^+$
Then calculate value of "$c^3 - b^2 - a$", where a, b and c are total number of transformations in which magnetic property will be changed, bond order increases and bond order decreases respectively.

Paragraph Based Questions 》

Paragraph 1

According to MOT, two atomic orbitals overlap resulting in the formation of molecular orbitals. Number of atomic orbitals overlapping together is equal to the molecular orbital formed. The two atomic orbital thus formed by LCAO (linear combination of atomic orbital) in the same phase or in the different phase are known as bonding and anti-bonding molecular orbitals respectively. The energy of bonding molecular orbital is lower than that of the pure atomic orbital by an amount Δ. This known as the stabilisation energy. The energy of anti-bonding molecular orbital is increased by Δ' (destabilisation energy)

29. Total nodal plane is present in $\sigma_{(s \text{ and } p)}$ bonding molecular orbital are

30. The total number of angular nodes present in $4f$-orbital is.

Paragraph 2

The concept of hybridisation is used to explain the structure of various covalent molecules along with the VSEPR theory. The geometry of a molecule is the theoretical arrangement of the hybrid orbitals henceforth minimising the repulsion between them according to the rules of vector addition. The structure or shape of a molecule is the appearance of the molecule to the human eye.

31. % of s character in $CH \equiv CH$ molecule.

32. No. of planar and polar molecule among the following.
$IF_4^+, SeF_3^-, IClBr^-, SO_2, IF_4^-, PCl_3F_2$

Paragraph 3

The molecule in which an atom is associated with more than 8 electrons is known as hypervalent molecule and less than 8 electrons is known as hypovalent molecule. All hypervalent molecules must have $p\pi - d\pi$ bonding but the molecules having back bonding need vacant d-orbitals. All hypervalent molecules must have $p\pi - d\pi$ bonding but the molecules having back bonding need not to have always $p\pi - d\pi$ bonding.

33. The total no. of molecules having $p\pi - p\pi$ bond from the molecules given below are
$CO_3^{-2}, SO_3^{-2}, NO_3^-, SO_4^{-2}, PO_4^{-3}, NO_2^-, S_2O_8^{-2}$,
$S_2O_3^{-2}, ClO_4^-, ClO_3^-, SO_2$

34. The total no. of hypovalent species present in the given molecules are :
$H_2SO_4, SO_3, BCl_3, BF_3, BeCl_2, AlBr_3, H_3PO_4$

Matching Type Questions

35. Match the following.

Column I		Column II	
A.	C—H bond in ethyne	I.	*sp-s* overlap
B.	P—Cl bond in $POCl_3$	II.	sp^3d-p overlap
C.	Br—Br bond in $Br_3^{\ominus}$	III.	sp^3-p overlap
D.	C—C bond in ethane	IV.	sp^3-sp^3 overlap

Choose the correct answer from the given options
(a) A-I, B-II, C-III, D-IV (b) A-I, B-III, C-II, D-IV
(c) A-I, B-IV, C-II, D-III (d) A-I, B-III, C-IV, D-II

36. Match the following.

Column I		Column II	
A.	σ-bonding MO's and π antibonding MO's e.g., σ2s and $\pi^* 2p_y$	I.	Gerade
B.	σ^* antibonding MO's and π bonding MO's e.g.,$\sigma^* 2s$, $\pi\ 2p_y$	II.	Ungerade
C.	$\pi\ (2p_x)$	III.	One nodal plane
D.	$\pi^*\ (2p_x)$	IV.	Two nodal plane

Choose the correct answer from the given options
(a) A-I, B-II, C-III, D-IV (b) A-I, B-II, C-IV, D-III
(c) A-II, B-III, C-IV, D-I (d) A-IV, B-III, C-II, D-I

37. Match the following.

Column I		Column II	
A.	$H_2O < H_2S < H_2Se < H_2Te$	I.	Bond angle
B.	$H_2O > H_2S > H_2Se > H_2Te$	II.	Melting and boiling points
C.	$H_2O >> H_2S < H_2Se < H_2Te$	III.	Acidic strength
D.	$SbH_3 > NH_3 > AsH_3 > PH_3$	IV.	Order of boiling point

Choose the correct answer from the given options
(a) A-III, B-I, C-II, D-IV (b) A-IV, B-I, C-II, D-III
(c) A-III, B-II, C-I, D-IV (d) A-III, B-II, C-IV, D-I

38. The process of combination of atomic orbital are listed in column I. Match them with column II.

Column I		Column II Consider only the orientation of orbitals	
A.	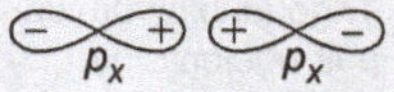	I.	σ-overlapping
B.	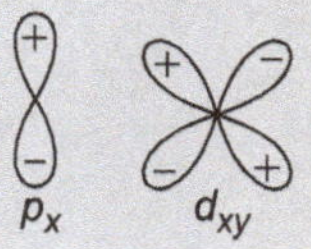	II.	π-overlapping
C.	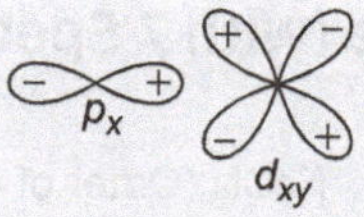	III.	Non-bonding
D.	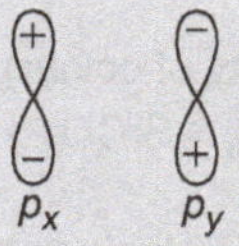	IV.	Anti-bonding

Choose the correct answer from the given options.
(a) A-I, B-II, C-IV, D-III (b) A-IV, B-II, C-I, D-III
(c) A-IV, B-II, C-IV, D-III (d) A-I, B-II, C-III, D-IV

39. Match the type of compound given in column I with the possible shapes in column II. Also, X = monovalent atoms, Y = lone pair and M = central atom.

Column I		Column II	
A.	MX_3Y_2	I.	Square planar
B.	MX_5Y	II.	Octahedral
C.	MX_6Y	III.	T-shape
D.	MX_4Y_2	IV.	Distorted square pyramidal

Choose the correct answer from the given options.
(a) A-III, B-IV, C-II, D-I (b) A-IV, B-III, C-II, D-I
(c) A-II, B-IV, C-III, D-I (d) A-I, B-II, C-III, D-IV

Species Selection Type (with 5 Species)

40. Consider the following species
1. CH_3^+ 2. HCHO 3. CH_4 4. $TiCl_4$
5. CO_2
Then find out total number of species which can act as Lewis acid from given options
(a) 3 (b) 2 (c) 5 (d) 4

41. Number of species having bond angle 120° or greater than 120° from given species are
$H_2O, H_2S, NH_3, SO_3, BF_3$
Select the correct answer from the given options
(a) 1 (b) 3 (c) 5 (d) 2

42. Among the following.
A. Maleic acid > fumeric acid (order of K_{a_2})
B. $H_2O > H_2Te$ and $NH_3 > SbH_3$(order of boiling point)
C. $H_3PO_4 > H_2SO_4 > HNO_3$ (Order of valatility)
D. $CH_3NH_2 > CH_3OH$ and $C_2H_5NH_2 > C_2H_5OH$ (order of solubility in water)
E. Methanol > acetone (order of viscocity)
F. $C_2H_5OH > O(C_2H_5)$ (order of vapour pressure)
G. HF > HCl (extent of H-bonding)
Hydrogen bonding is responsible for how many of following observation?
(a) 3 (b) 4
(c) 5 (d) 6

Species Selection Type (with 7 Species)

43. Among the following.
A. $Al^{+3} > Be^{+2}$ and $FeCl_3 > FeCl_2$ (Order of case of Hydrolysis)
B. $HgI_2 > AgI > AgBr$ (Intensity of colour)
C. $BeCO_3 > MgCO_3 > CaCO_3 > SrCO_3 > BaCO_3$ (Thermal stability.)
D. $K_2O > Na_2O > Cu_2O > Ag_2O$ (Basic nature)
E. $PbI_4 > PbBr_4 > PbCl_4$ (Order of stability)
F. $Li^+ > Na^+ > K^+$ and $Be^{+2} > Mg^{+2} > Ca^{+2}$ (complex forming tendency)
G. $CuBr > AgBr > AuBr$ (Solubility in organic solvent.)
Choose the number of correct order from the given options.
(a) 3 (b) 4 (c) 5 (d) 6

44. Among the following.
(i) PCl_3 (ii) $NH_2^{\ominus}$
(iii) BrF_3 (iv) XeO_2F_2
(v) XeF_4 (vi) SiO_2
(vii) CO_2
Number of polar species from the given species are
(a) 3 (b) 4 (c) 5 (d) 6

45. Consider the following ions/molecules.
(i) N_2 (ii) N_2^{+2}
(iii) O_2 (iv) O_2^+
(v) C_2 (vi) C_2^{+2}
(vii) B_2
The number of species, which will show a change in their magnetic behaviour if *sp* mixing of the atomic orbitals is considered obsolete are
(a) 3 (b) 4
(c) 5 (d) 6

46. Among the following.
(i) B_2H_6 (ii) $(AlH_3)_x$
(iii) Ga_2H_6 (iv) Al_2Cl_6
(v) Be_2Cl_4 (vi) Be_2H_4
(vii) $(BeH_2)_x$
The total number of molecules having equal bond length are
(a) 3 (b) 4
(c) 5 (d) 6

47. Among the species given below some are planar while the others are non-planar. Find the ratio of number of the non-planar species to the number of planar species.
$B_2H_6, (AlH_3)_x, Ga_2H_6, Al_2Cl_6, (BeCl_2)_x, Be_2Cl_4, (BeH_2)_x, Be_2H_4$.
Choose the correct option from the given options
(a) 1 : 7 (b) 1 : 3
(c) 3 : 1 (d) 7 : 1

Check Through PYQs

Element 1 Ionic and Covalent Bonding, Fajan's Rule

1. The option(s) in which at least three molecules follows octet rule is (are) *2024 Adv.*
(a) CO_2, C_2H_4, NO and HCl
(b) NO_2, O_3, HCl and H_2SO_4
(c) BCl_3, NO, NO_2 and H_2SO_4
(d) CO_2, BCl_3, O_3 and C_2H_4

2. Each of the following options contains a set of four molecules. Identify the option(s) where all four molecules posses permanent dipole moment at room temperature. *2019 Adv.*
(a) SO_2, C_6H_5Cl, H_2Se, BrF_5 (b) $BeCl_2$, CO_2, BCl_3, $CHCl_3$
(c) NO_2, NH_3, $POCl_3$, CH_3Cl (d) BF_3, O_3, SF_6, XeF_6

Element 2 Bond Parameter, VBT and VSEPR Theory

3. Among $[I_3]^+$, $[SiO_4]^{4-}$, SO_2Cl_2, XeF_2, SF_4, ClF_3, $Ni(CO)_4$, XeO_2F_2, $[PtCl_4]^{2-}$, XeF_4 and $SOCl_2$, the total number of species having sp^3-hybridised central atom is ...... *2023 Adv.*

4. Based on VSEPR model, match the xenon compounds given in List-I with the corresponding geometries and the number of lone pairs on xenon given in List-II and choose the correct option. *2024 Adv.*

List-I		List-II	
(P)	XeF_2	(1)	Trigonal bipyramidal and two lone pair of electrons
(Q)	XeF_4	(2)	Tetrahedral and one lone pair of electrons
(R)	XeO_3	(3)	Octahedral and two lone pair of electrons
(S)	XeO_3F_2	(4)	Trigonal bipyramidal and no lone pair of electrons
		(5)	Trigonal bipyramidal and three lone pair of electrons.

(a) P - 5, Q - 2, R - 3, S - 1
(b) P - 5, Q - 3, R - 2, S - 4
(c) P - 4, Q - 3, R - 2, S - 1
(d) P - 4, Q - 2, R - 5, S - 3

Element 3 MOT and Hydrogen Bonding

5. The correct molecular orbital diagram for F_2 molecule in the ground state is *2023 Adv.*

(a)
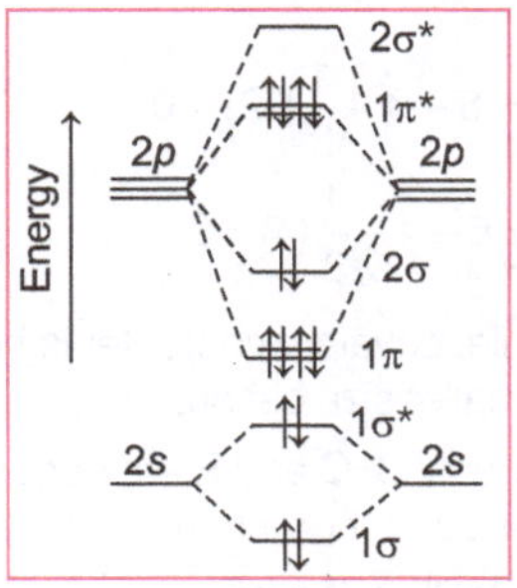

(b)
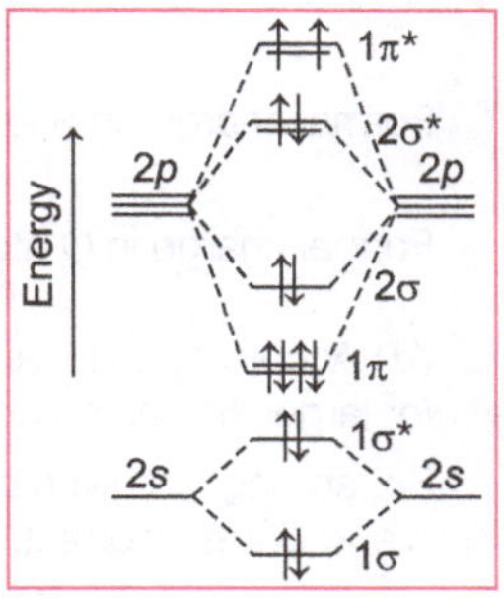

(c)
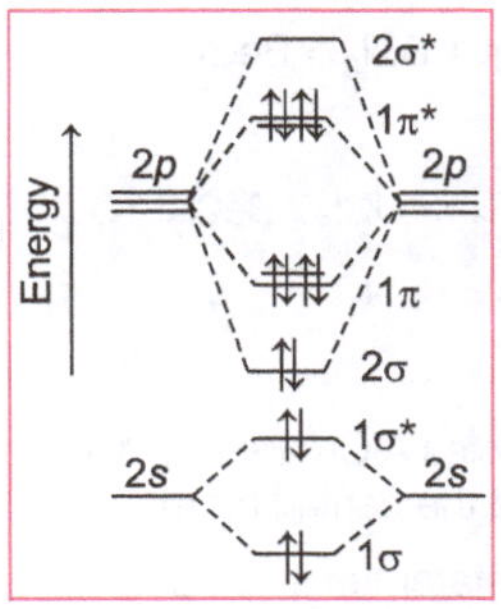

(d)
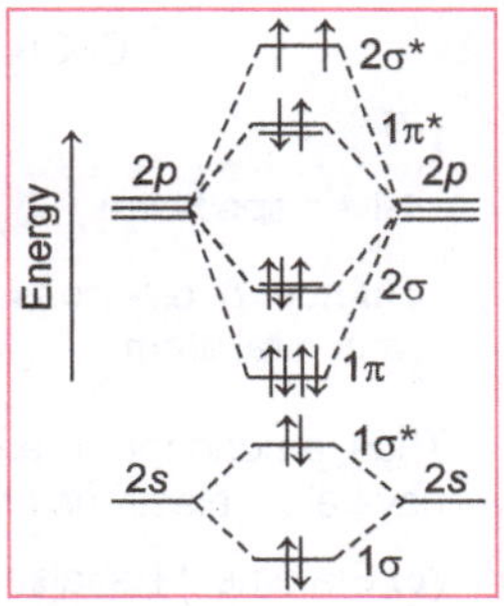

6. For diatomic molecules, the correct statement(s) about the molecular orbitals formed by the overlap of two $2p_z$ orbitals is (are) *2022 Adv.*
   (a) σ orbital has a total of two nodal planes.
   (b) σ^* orbital has one node in the *xz*-plane containing the molecular axis.
   (c) π orbital has one node in the plane which is perpendicular to the molecular axis and goes through the centre of the molecule.
   (d) π^* orbital has one node in the *xy*-plane containing the molecular axis.

7. According to molecular orbital theory, which of the following statements is (are) correct? *2016 adv.*
   (a) C_2^{2-} is expected to be diamagnetic
   (b) O_2^{2+} is expected to have a longer bond length than O_2
   (c) N_2^+ and N_2^- have the same bond order
   (d) He_2^+ has the same energy as two isolated He atoms

8. Among $[Co(CN)_4]^{4-}$, $[Co(CO)_3(NO)]$, XeF_4, $[PCl_4]^+$ $[PdCl_4]^{2-}$, $[ICl_4]^-$, $[Cu(CN)_4]^{3-}$ and P_4 the total number of species with tetrahedral geometry is __________.

9. Thermal decompositon of $AgNO_3$ produces two paramagnetic gases. The total number of electrons present in the antibonding molecular orbitals of the gas that has the higher number of unpaired electrons is .... *2022 Adv.*

10. Consider the following compounds in the liquid form $O_2, HF, H_2O, NH_3, H_2O_2, CCl_4, CHCl_3, C_6H_6, C_6H_5Cl$ When a charged comb is brought near their flowing stream, how many of them show deflection as per the following figure? *2020 Adv.*

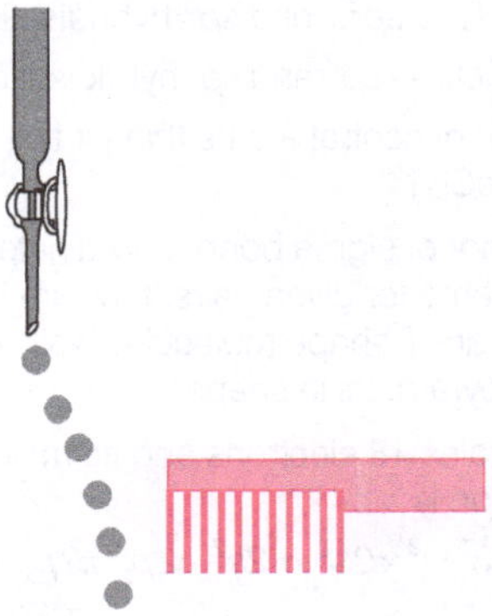

11. The sum of the number of lone pairs of electrons on each central atom in the following species is $[TeBr_6]^{2-}$, $[BrF_2]^+$, SNF_3 and $[XeF_3]^-$
    (Atomic numbers : N = 7, F = 9, S = 16, Br = 35, Te = 52, Xe = 54) *2017 Adv.*

12. Among $H_2, He_2^+, Li_2, Be_2, B_2, C_2, N_2, O_2^-$ and F_2, the number of diamagnetic species is
    (Atomic numbers : H = 1, He = 2, Li = 3, Be = 4, B = 5, C = 6, N = 7, O = 8, F = 9) *2017 Adv.*

13. Among the triatomic molecules/ions $BeCl_2$, N_3^-, N_2O, NO_2^+, O_3, SCl_2, ICl_2^-, I_3^- and XeF_2, the total number of linear molecules(s)/ion(s) where the hybridisation of the central atom does not have contribution from the *d*-orbital(s) is [atomic number of S = 16, Cl = 17, I = 53 and Xe = 54] *2015 Adv.*

HINTS & Solutions

Solutions : Competency Enhancer

1.1 ***(5)*** Among the given compoounds/species only five i-e, HF, SO_2, NF_3, NH_3 and HCl will show non-zero dipole moment.

2.1 ***(b)*** The hybridisation of central atom of given species in different options are

NO_2^+ and $NH_4^+ \rightarrow sp$ and sp^3 hybridisation

SF_2 and $[FeCl_4]^{2-} \rightarrow sp^3$ hybridisation

SF_4 and $NH_3 \rightarrow sp^3d$ and sp^3 hybridisation

BCl_3 and $CO_2 \rightarrow sp^2$ and sp- hybridisation

So, the pair of central atoms that exhibit sp^3-hybridisation is SF_2 and $[FeCl_4]^{2-}$.

2.2 ***(c)*** When no. of sigma bond, coordinate bond and lone pairs are same for given pairs, they are isostructural. ClF_3, XeF_3^+ are T-shape molecules while PCl_5, XeO_2F_2 ae trigonal bipyramidal in shape.

3.1 ***(a)*** F_2 contains 18 electrons and its molecular orbital configuration is

$$F_2 : \sigma 1s^2\ \sigma^* 1s^2\ \sigma 2s^2\ \sigma^* 2s^2\ \sigma 2p_z^2\ \pi 2p_x^2\ \pi 2p_y^2\ \pi^* 2p_x^2\ \pi^* 2p_y^2$$

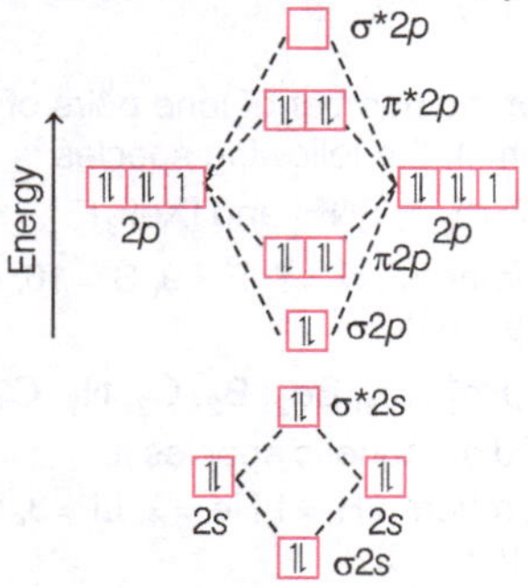

Elemental Practice 2.1

1. ***(d)*** The lowest energy structure is the one with the smallest formal charges on the atoms and is most stable. Option (b) and (c) are not the possible structures of SO_3.

Option (a)

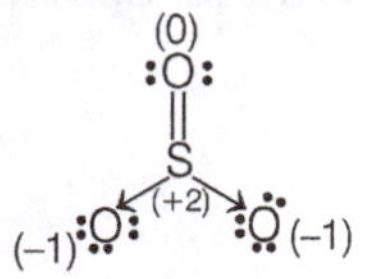

Formal charge on S atom $= 6 - 0 - \frac{1}{2}(8) = +2$

Similarly, formal charges on coordinated bonded oxygen atom and covalently bonded oxygen atom are −1 and 0 respectively.

Option (d)

Formal charge on S atom $= 6 - 0 - \frac{1}{2}(12) = 0$

Formal charge in O atom $= 6 - 4 - \frac{1}{2}(4) = 0$

2. ***(d)*** According to Fajan's rule, covalent character is higher for larger size anion and smaller size cation.

So, among the given order only B, C and E are correct while A and D are incorrect. Their correct order are

$$AlCl_3 < SnCl_4;\ LiF > KF$$
$$CoCl_2 < AgCl;\ BCl_3 > BeCl_2$$

3. ***(d)***

Given species	NH_3	$AlCl_3$	$BeCl_2$	CCl_4	PCl_5
Number of electrons in central atom	8	6	4	8	10

Thus, among the given species $AlCl_3$, $BeCl_2$, PCl_5 does not have eight electrons around the central atom.

4. ***(c)*** Statement I is false but statement II is true.

Its correct form is

According to Fajan's rule, MgF_2 is more ionic than $MgCl_2$ hence MgF_2 is more soluble in H_2O than $MgCl_2$.

In MnO, the oxidation state of Mn is +2 which is lowest hence it is most ionic.

$$\overset{+5}{P_4O_{10}},\quad \overset{+6}{CrO_3},\quad \overset{+7}{Mn_2O_7}$$

5. ***(c)*** According to Fajan's rule covalent character is directly propotional to charge on cation and inversely propotional to size of cation. Be^{2+} has more charge. So, it has more covalent character. Now Li^+ is smaller in size. So, it has more covalent character as compared to Na^+. Thus, the correct order of covalent character is $NaCl < LiCl < BeCl_2$.

6. ***(c)*** Resonating structures are of PO_4^{3-}

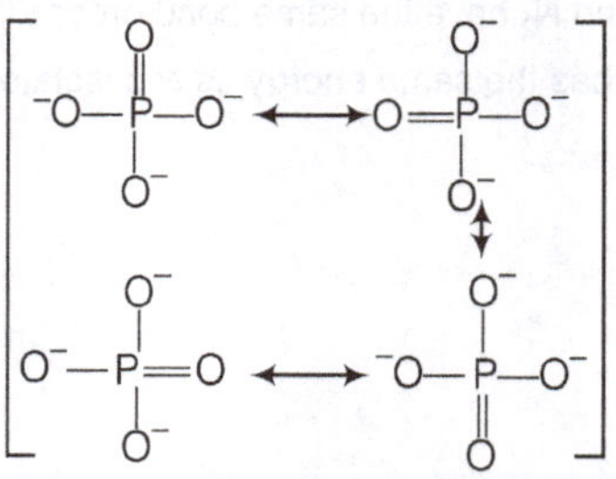

Total charge on PO_4^{3-} ion is $-3 = \dfrac{\text{Total charge}}{\text{Total entity of O -atom}}$

So, the average formal charge on each O-atom is

$$= -\frac{3}{4} = -0.75$$

7. ***(b)*** KI is ionic compound, so it is not soluble in non-polar solvent (i.e. dipole moment (μ) for benzene = 0).

8. ***(b)*** Water is a polar solvent and have dielectric constant 80. As NaCl is a polar compound and like dissolves like so, forces of attraction between Na^+ and Cl^- ion will reduce to $\frac{1}{80}$ in water.

9. ***(b)*** The ionic bond between Mg and F is most stable because in these the electrostatic force of attraction is maximum. As Mg has high electropositive character and F has high electronegative character among all other options that are given in question.

10. ***(d)*** In 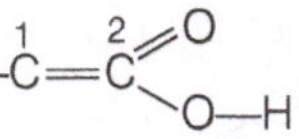

Carbon number 2 have five valency which is not possible, so it does not correctly represent the bonding capacities of C atom.

11. ***(a)*** Structure of $H_2S_2O_7$ is as follows

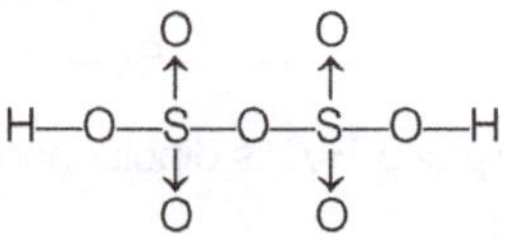

Hence, the total number of covalent and coordinate bond are 6 and 4 respectively.

12. ***(b)*** NaF has high lattice energy because Na^+ is smallest in size and lattice energy increases as the size of cation decreases. (In the given question anion is common in all compound).

13. ***(a)*** Among the given molecules only A and B have dipole moment while the molecule C and D do not have dipole moment.

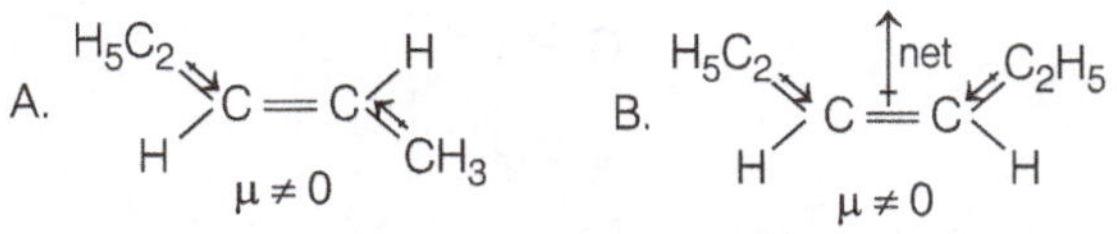

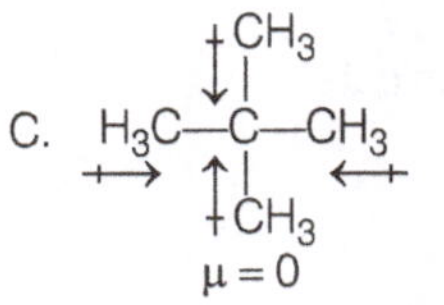

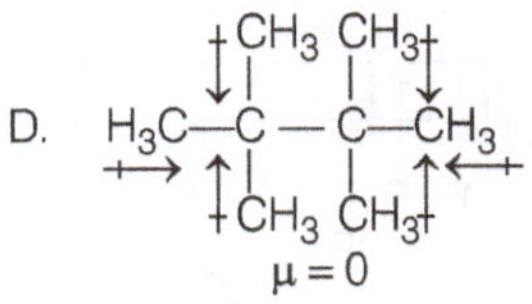

(All vectors cancel out)

14. ***(c)*** In all the given compounds, anion is same (Cl^-), hence, polarising power is decided by size and charge of cation.

Al^{3+} with maximum charge and smallest size has maximum polarising power hence, $AlCl_3$ has is maximum covalent character.

15. ***(c)*** Higher the charge / size ratio, larger is the polarising power. Thus, the correct order is

$\therefore \qquad K^+ < Ca^{2+} < Mg^{2+} < Be^{2+}$

16. ***(b)*** Dipole-dipole interactions occur in the polar molecules, as polar molecules have permanent dipole moment.

17. ***(b,c)*** Among the given statements (b) and (c) are incorrect. while (a) and (d) are correct.

The correct form of (b) and (c) are —

Each combining atom contributes at least one electron to the shared pair.

For anions each negative charge would mean addition of one electron.

18. ***(b,c,d)*** Among the given statement (b), (c) and (d) are correct while statement a is incorrect. Its correct form is Ionic compounds conduct electricity only in molten or dissolved form, not in solid form.

19. ***(a,d)*** Among the given order only (a) and (d) are correct regarding polarising power of cation.

20. ***(a,d)*** Among the given statements (a) and (d) are correct while (b) and (c) is incorrect . Its correct form is

(b) All the given compound PF_5, SF_6 and H_2SO_4 show exception to the octet rule.

(c) This theory does not account for the shape of molecules.

21. ***(a,b,d)*** Among the given order (a), (b) and (d) are correct while (c) is incorrect.

It correct order is $\rightarrow CH_4 = CCl_4 < CHCl_3$

22. ***(a,b,c,d)*** All the given orders are correct.

23. ***(4)*** Among the given species only four i.e,

1, 4 dichlorobenzene, 1-4-dicyanobenzene, trans-1, -2-dichloroethene and trans-2, 3-dichloro-2-butene will show zero dipole moment.

24. ***(7)*** In Set (I) $\rightarrow$The total no. of compounds which have covalent nature are PH_3, O_2, B_2H_6 and H_2SO_4 only KCl is ionic compound.

In Set (II) $\rightarrow$ The total no. of molecules which are exceptions to octet rule are H_2SO_4, ClO_2 and NO_2.

So, $\qquad X = 4$ and $Y = 3$

Hence, $\qquad X + Y = 7$

25. ***(37.25)*** A. The structure of PO_4^{3-} is ......

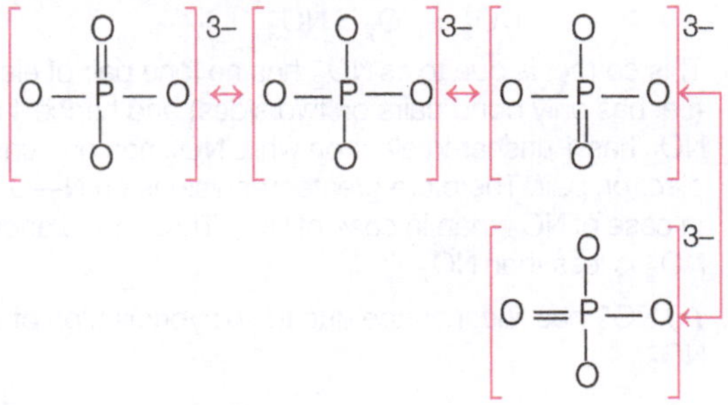

[Formal charge on each O-atom]

$$= \frac{\text{Total charge}}{\text{No. of O-atoms}}$$

$$= \frac{-3}{4} = -0.75$$

B. Formal change on O-atom

$$= \frac{\text{Total charge}}{\text{No. of O-atoms}} = 0$$

Hence, the value of $x + y + 38$

$$= -0.75 + 0 + 38$$

$$= 37.25$$

26. ***(65)*** When EN difference = 1.7, the bond is 50% ionic and 50% covalent . If EN difference < 1.7, the covalent character is more than 50%.

If EN difference > 1.7 the ionic character is more than 50%. The EN difference between A and B is $(4.0 - 1.8) = 2.2$.
Therefore, % ionic character is ≈ 65%

27. ***(0.05)*** By using

$$\mu = q \times d$$

$$d = 1.617\ \text{Å} = 1.617 \times 10^{-8}\ \text{cm}$$

$$\mu = 0.38\ \text{D} = 0.38 \times 10^{-18}\ \text{esu cm}$$

$$q = \frac{\mu}{d} = \frac{0.38 \times 10^{-18}}{1.617 \times 10^{-8}}$$

Therefore, fractional charge

$$= \frac{\text{Particle charge}}{\text{Total charge}} = \frac{q}{Q}$$

$$= \frac{0.38 \times 10^{-18}}{1.617 \times 10^{-8} \times 4.802 \times 10^{-10}}$$

$$= 0.0489 \approx 0.05$$

Elemental Practice 2.2

1. ***(d)*** BCl_3 has sp^2 hybridisation and no lone pair of electron on central atom i.e boron but NCl_3 has sp^3 hybridisation and also contains one lone pair of electron on central atom i.e. nitrogen, so BCl_3 is planar.

2. ***(a)*** In the formation of d^2sp^3 hybrid orbitals, two $(n-1)d$-orbitals of e_g set, i.e. $(n-1)\ d_{z^2}$ and $(n-1)\ d_{x^2-y^2}$ orbitals, one ns and three np (np_x, np_y and np_z.) orbitals combine together.

3. ***(a)*** The correct order is :

$$NO_2^+ > NO_2 > NO_2^-$$

This correct is due to as NO_2^+ has no lone pair of electron (i.e. has only bond pairs on two sides) and hence it is linear. NO_2 has 1 unshared electron while NO_2^- has one unshared electron pair. There are greater repulsions on N—O bonds in case of NO_2^- than in case of NO_2. Thus, bond angle of NO_2^- is less than NO_2.

4. ***(c)*** NO_2^+ has linear shape due to sp hybridisation of N in NO_2^+

$$O{=}\overset{+}{N}{=}O$$

While SO_2, NO_2^- and O_3 have angular shape

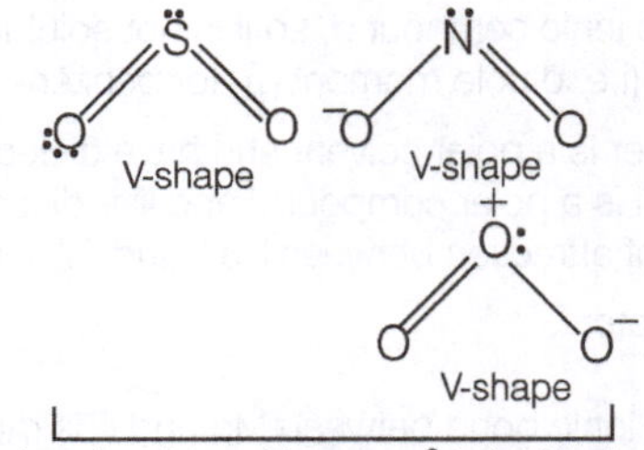

Angular shape (due to sp^2 hybridisation of central atom or ion)

5. ***(d)*** The structure of H_2O is angular or V-shape and has sp^3-hybridisation and 104.5° bond angle. Thus, its dipole moment is positive or more than zero.

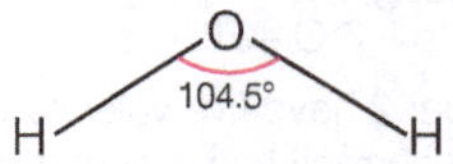

But in BeF_2, structure is linear due to sp hybridisation ($\mu = 0$)

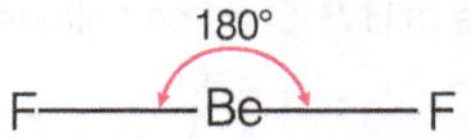

Thus, due to $\mu > 0$, H_2O is dipolar and due to $\mu = 0$, BeF_2 is non-polar.

6. ***(a)*** (A) **PCl_5**

P (Ground state) = $3s^2 3p^3$

P* (excited state)

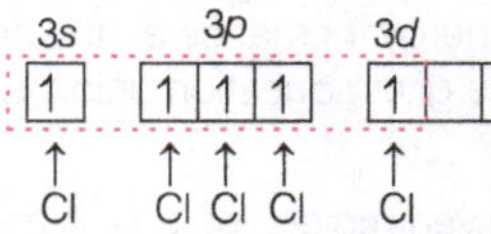

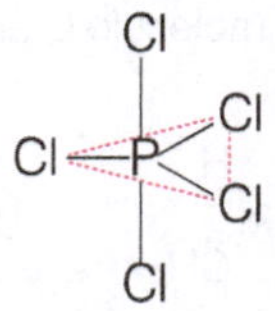

Hybridisation of P → sp^3d

Shape of PCl_5 → Trigonal bipyramidal

(B) **SF_6**

S (Ground state) = $3s^2 3p^4$

S* (excited state)

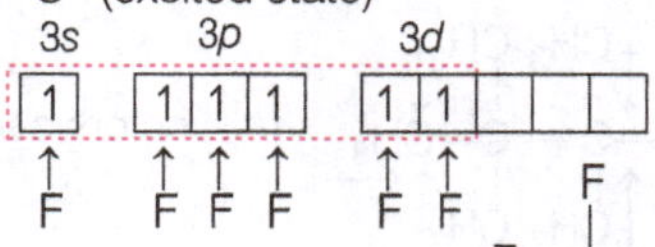

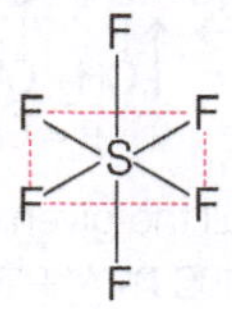

Hybridisation of S → sp^3d^2

Shape of SF_6 → Octahedral

(C) **BrF_5** Br (Ground state) $= 4s^2 4p^5$

Br* (excited state)

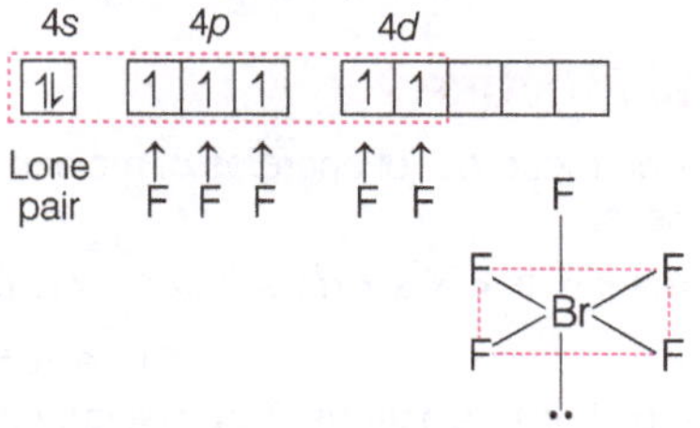

Hybridisation of Br $\rightarrow sp^3d^2$

Shape of $BrF_5 \rightarrow$ Square pyramidal

(D) **BF_3**

B (Ground state) $= 2s^2 2p^1$

B* (excited state)

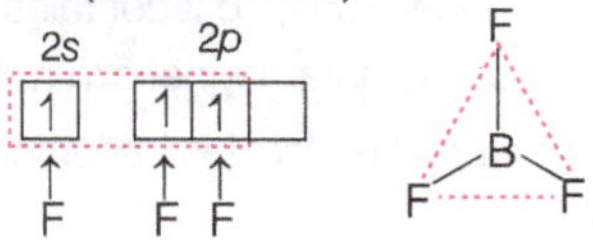

Hybridisation of B $\rightarrow sp^2$

Shape of $BF_3 \rightarrow$ Trigonal planar

$\therefore$ Correct match is

(A)-(IV); (B)-(III); (C)-(I); (D)-(II)

7. ***(b)*** In SO_3^{2-}, S is sp^3hybridised, so

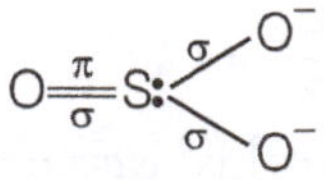

$_{16}S = 1s^2, 2s^2 2p^6, \underbrace{3s^2 3p_x^1\ 3p_y^1 3p_z^1}_{sp^3 \text{ hybridisation}}\quad 3d_{xy}^1$ Unhybridised

(Sulphur atom in excited state)

In 'S' the three p-orbitals forms σ-bonds with three oxygen atoms and unhybridised d-orbital is involved in π-bond formation.

$$O_8 = 1s^2, 2s^2 2p_x^2\ 2p_y^1 2p_z^1$$

In oxygen two unpaired p-orbitals are present, one is involved in σ-bond formation while other is used in π-bond formation.

Thus in SO_3^{2-}, p and d-orbitals are involved for $p\pi$-$d\pi$ bonding.

8. ***(a)*** Structure of XeF_4 is as follows

It involves sp^3d^2 hybridisation in Xe-atom. The molecules has square planar structure. Xe and four F-atoms are coplanar. The lone pairs are present on axial positions, minimise electron pair repulsion.

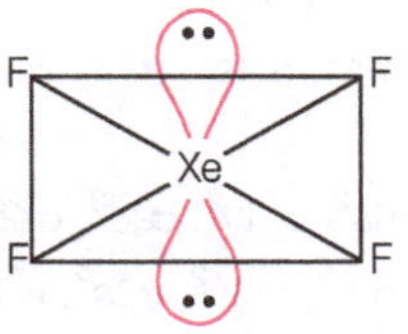

9. ***(c)*** Each boron atom in diborane (B_2H_6) is sp^3 hybridised. In the structure of diborane four H-atoms, two on the left and two on the right, known as **terminal hydrogens,** are in different environments from the other two hydrogen atoms which are known as **bridging hydrogen.** The two boron atoms and the four terminal hydrogen atoms lie in the same plane while the two boron atoms and the two bridging hydrogen atoms, one above and the other below, lie in a plane perpendicular to this plane.

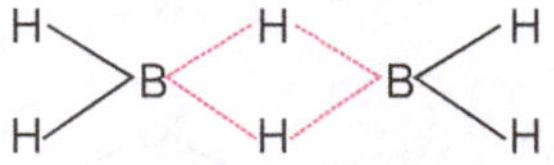

Structure of diborane molecule

10. ***(c)*** $P = 1s^2, 2s^2, 2p^6, \underbrace{3s^1 3p_x^1\ 3p_y^1\ 3p_z^1\ 3d_{z^2}^1}_{sp^3d \text{ hybridisation}}$

Due to this hybridisation, geometry of the PF_5 molecule is trigonal bipyramidal and the hybrid orbitals used by P-atom are s, p_x, p_y, p_z and d_z^2.

11. ***(b)*** When p_x and p_y form bond, then the bond angle is minimum and it is only 90°.

12. ***(c)*** Statement (c) is correct, while others are incorrect, explanation is

SF_4 is not tetrahedral (it has a see-saw shape due to lone pairs).

ClF_3 and ICl_3 are T-shaped, not trigonal planar.

XeF_2 is linear, not distorted (it has a well-defined geometry).

13. ***(c)***

Molecule	Geometry	Matches CO_2 ?
$HgCl_2$	Linear	Yes
NO_2	Bent	No
$SnCl_4$	Tetrahedral	No
C_2H_2	Linear	Yes

14. ***(d)*** Species with undistorted octahedral structures : SF_6, PF_6^-, SiF_6^{2-} while XeF_6 has distorted octahedral.

15. ***(a)*** Only reaction in option (a) involves a change in the electron pair geometry from trigonal planar to tetrahedral.

16. ***(a,b,c)*** $N{\equiv}N \rightarrow O$ (N_2O)

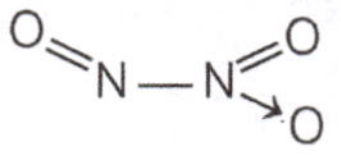

(N_2O_3)

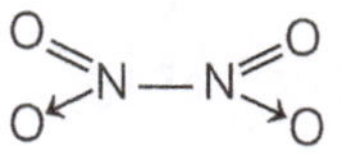

(N_2O_4)

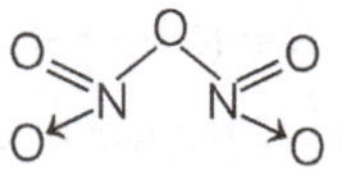

(N_2O_5)

17. ***(a,b)***

Species	Structure	Bond order
CO_3^{2-}	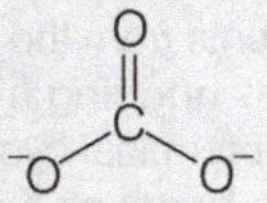	1.33
NO_3^-	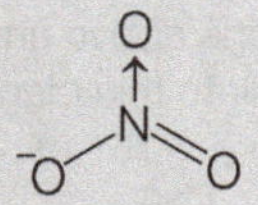	1.33
NO_2^-	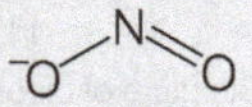	1.5
NO	$:N\equiv O^+:$	2.5

18. ***(c,d)*** Hybridisation involves the mixing of atomic orbitals of the atom at the time of their participation in bonding.

Among the given statements only (c) and (d) are incorrect.

Their corrected from are as —

Hybrid orbitals form stronger bonds than pure atomic orbital.

For hybridisation, vacant orbitals in the valence shell are not required.

19. ***(b,c,d)*** The corrected form of statement (a) is

Cause of a particular physical state of a molecular compound is strength of intermolecular bonding not intramolecular bonding.

20. ***(a,b,c,d)*** e^- density of σ-bond lies on the internuclear axis e^- density of π-bond lies on the either side on internuclear axis. Direction of a covalent bond is decided by σ-bond.

Order of strength of π-bond.

$$2p\pi - 2p\pi > 2p\pi - 3d\pi > 2p\pi - 3p\pi$$

21. ***(a,b,c)*** are correct while (d) is incorrect because the bond angles decrease as the size of the halogens increases because larger halogens create less electron pair repulsion. Hence, this order is incorrect.

22. ***(5)*** $PCl_5, SF_4, ClF_3, [ClF_4]^+, [XeF_3]^- \rightarrow$ all bond lengths are not equal

$XeF_2, O_3, P_4 \rightarrow$ all bond lengths are equal.

23. ***(2)*** $SnCl_4$ and NH_4^+ are sp^3 hybridised molecule.

$[Ni(CN)_4]^{2-}$ is dsp^2 hybridised.

PCl_5 is sp^3d hybridised.

$HgCl_2$ is sp hybridised.

CO_3^{2-} is sp^2 hybridised.

24. ***(3)***

$$H-\overset{-}{\ddot{N}}=\overset{+}{N}=\overset{-}{\underset{..}{N}}: \leftrightarrow H-\overset{..}{\underset{..}{N}}-\overset{+}{N}\equiv N: \leftrightarrow H-\overset{+}{N}\equiv\overset{+}{N}-\overset{..}{\underset{..}{N}}^{2-}$$

25. ***(3)*** In SF_6 molecules, there are 12 number of $\angle$LFSF angle.

The value of $\frac{x+3}{5}$ will $= \frac{12+3}{5} = \frac{15}{5} = 3$

26. ***(4)*** $I_3^-, C_2H_4, C_2H_2, ICl_2^-$

27. ***(5)*** Molecules with the same shape (trigonal pyramidal)

$$H_3O^+, NH_3, ClO_3^+, PH_3, CH_3^-$$

Elemental Practice 2.3

1. ***(d)*** The correct order of energies of molecular orbitals of N_2 molecule is,

$$\sigma 1s < \sigma^* 1s < \sigma 2s < \sigma^* 2s < (\pi 2p_x = \pi 2p_y) < \sigma 2p_z < (\pi^* 2p_x = \pi^* 2p_y) < \sigma^* 2p_z$$

N_2 has total of 14 electrons. Thus, electrons can be filled as

$$\sigma 1s^2 < \sigma^* 1s^2 < \sigma 2s^2 < \sigma^* 2s^2 < (\pi 2p_x^2 = \pi 2p_y^2) < \sigma 2p_z^2$$

2. ***(c)*** Among the given options, the incorrect statement is option (c).

$$O_2^+ = \sigma 1s^2 \sigma^* 1s^2 \sigma 2s^2 \sigma^* 2s^2 \sigma 2p_z^2\, \pi 2p_x^2\, \pi 2p_y^2\, \pi^* 2p_x^1$$

O_2^+ ions have 15 electrons, so it contains one unpaired electron. Hence, it is paramagnetic in nature.

3. ***(d)*** If bond order of a molecules becomes zero, the molecule will not exist.

$$\text{Bond order} = \frac{\text{Number of bonding electrons} - \text{Number of antibonding electrons}}{2} = \frac{N_b - N_a}{2}$$

$Li_2(6e^-) \Rightarrow \sigma 1s^2\, \sigma^* 1s^2\, \sigma 2s^2$;

$$BO = \frac{4-2}{2} = 1$$

$C_2\ (12e^-) \Rightarrow \sigma^*\, \sigma 1s^2\ 1s^2\ \sigma 2s^2\ \sigma^* 2s^2\ \pi 2p_x^2 = \pi^* 2p_y^2$;

$$BO = \frac{8-4}{2} = 2\sigma^* 2s^2$$

$O_2\ (16e^-) \Rightarrow \sigma 1s^2\ \sigma^* 1s^1\ \sigma 2s^2\ \sigma^* 2s^2\ \sigma 2p_z^2 \pi 2p_x^2 = \pi 2p_y^2 \pi^* 2p_x^1 = \pi^* 2p_y^1$;

$$BO = \frac{10-6}{2} = 2$$

$He_2(4e^-) = \sigma 1s^2\ \sigma 1s^{*2}$

$$BO = \frac{2-2}{2} = 0$$

So, He_2 does not exist.

4. ***(b)*** The molecular orbital configuration of C_2 is

$$C_2(Z=12) = \sigma 1s^2, \sigma^* 1s^2, \sigma 2s^2, \sigma^* 2s^2, \pi 2p_x^2 = \pi 2p_y^2.$$

Double bond in C_2 consists of both π-bonds because of the presence of last (valence) four electrons in two π-molecular orbitals.

The configuration of N_2, Be_2 and O_2 are as follows :

$N_2(Z=14) = \sigma 1s^2, \sigma^* 1s^2, \sigma 2s^2, \sigma^* 2s^2, \pi 2p_x^2 = \pi 2p_y^2, \sigma 2p_z^2$ (1 σ and 2π-bonds)

$Be_2(Z=8) = \sigma 1s^2, \sigma^* 1s^2, \sigma 2s^2, \sigma^* 2s^2$ (σ bonds only)

$O_2(Z=16) = \sigma 1s^2, \sigma^* 1s^2, \sigma 2s^2, \sigma^* 2\,s^2, \sigma^* 2p_z^2$,

$\pi 2p_x^2 = \pi 2p_y^2, \pi^* 2p_x^1 = \pi^* 2p_z^1$ (σ, π and 1π^* bond)

Hence, option (b) is correct.

5. ***(d)*** Molecular orbital configuration of given molecules are as follows :

(a) $N_2 (Z = 14) = \sigma 1s^2, \sigma^* 1s^2, \sigma 2s^2,$

$$\sigma^* 2s^2, \pi 2p_x^2 = \pi 2p_y^2, \sigma 2p_z^2$$

It is a diamagnetic molecule due to absence of unpaired electron.

(b) $H_2 (Z = 2) - 1s^2$

It is a diamagnetic molecule.

(c) $Li_2 (Z = 6) - \sigma 1s^2, \sigma^* 1s^2, \sigma 2s^2$

It is a diamagnetic molecule.

(d) $O_2 (Z = 16) - \sigma 1s^2, \sigma^* 1s^2, \sigma 2s^2,$

$$\sigma^* 2s^2, \sigma 2p_z^2, \pi 2p_x^2 = \pi 2p_y^2, \pi^* 2p_x^1 = \pi^* 2p_y^1$$

It is a paramagnetic molecule due to presence of unpaired electrons in each orbital of degenerate levels.

Thus, option (d) is correct.

6. ***(b)*** $Ne_2 = \sigma 1s^2\ \sigma^* 1s^2\ \sigma 2s^2\ \sigma^* 2s^2\ \sigma 2pz^2\ \pi 2px^2 = \pi 2py^2$

$$\pi^* 2px^2 = \pi^* 2py^2\ \sigma 2pz^2$$

$$\text{B.O.} = \frac{N_b - N_a}{2} = \frac{10 - 10}{2} = 0$$

$$F_2 = \sigma 1s^2\ \sigma^* 1s^2\ \sigma 2s^2\ \sigma^* 2s^2\ \sigma 2pz^2\ \pi 2px^2\ \pi 2py^2$$

$$\pi^* 2px^2\ \pi^* 2py^2$$

$$\text{BO} = \frac{10 - 8}{2} = 1$$

$$NO = \sigma 1s^2 \sigma^* 1s^2\ \sigma 2s^2\ \sigma^* 2s^2\ \sigma 2pz^2\ \pi 2px^2\ \pi 2py^2$$

$$\pi^* 2px^1$$

$$\text{BO} = \frac{10 - 5}{2} = 2.5$$

$$CN^+ = \sigma 1s^2\ \sigma^* 1s^2\ \sigma 2s^2 \sigma^* 2s^2\ \pi 2px^2 = \pi 2py^2$$

$$\text{BO} = \frac{8 - 4}{2} = 2$$

Thus, F_2 has one bond order.

7. ***(b)*** According to molecular orbital theory,

(a) $Be_2^+ (4 + 4 - 1 = 7) = \sigma 1s^2, \overset{*}{\sigma} 1s^2, \sigma 2s^2, \overset{*}{\sigma} 2s^1$

$$\text{Bond order (BO)} = \frac{4 - 3}{2} = 0.5$$

(b) $Be_2\ (4 + 4 = 8) = \sigma 1s^2, \overset{*}{\sigma} 1s^2, \sigma 2s^2, \overset{*}{\sigma} 2s^2$

$$\text{BO} = \frac{4 - 4}{2} = 0$$

(c) $B_2 (5 + 5 = 10) = \sigma 1s^2, \overset{*}{\sigma} 1s^2, \sigma 2s^2, \overset{*}{\sigma} 2s^2, \pi 2p_x^1 \approx \pi 2p_y^1$

$$\text{Bond order (B.O.)} = \frac{6 - 4}{2} = 1$$

(d) $Li_2\ (3 + 3 = 6) = \sigma 1s^2, \overset{*}{\sigma} 1s^2, \sigma 2s^2$

$$\text{B.O.} = \frac{4 - 2}{2} = 1$$

Thus, Be_2 does not exist under normal conditions.

8. ***(b)*** Correct form of (b) will

O_2^{2+} has a bond order of 3, while O_2 has a bond order of 2.

A higher bond order means a shorter bond length.

While rest statements are correct.

9. ***(a)*** (a) is the correct statement whereas (b), (c) and (d) are incorrect. Their correct forms are

(b) Amines have higher boiling points than hydrocarbons due to amines being polar form intermolecular H-bonds (except 3° amines).

(c) Carboxylic acid dimerises in gaseous state or in solvent of low dielectric constant.

(d) Ether is less soluble in water due to ether's non-polar nature.

10. ***(b)*** The bond order of C_2^{2+} is 1. B_2 is isoelectronic with C_2^{2+} and have same bond order as C_2^{2+}. $B_2\ (10\, e^-)$ has bond order of 1.

11. ***(d)*** Electronic configuration of BN

$$= kk^* (\sigma 2s)^2 < (\sigma^* 2s)^2 < (\pi 2px)^2 \equiv (\pi 2py)^2$$

It is diamagnetic in nature, $\mu_{mm} = 0$

12. ***(c)*** The bond order of NO is 2.5 and is paramagnetic in nature.

$$\text{Bond order of } O_2^- = \frac{10 - 7}{2} = 1.5, \text{ paramagnetic}$$

$$\text{Bond order of BN} = \frac{1}{2}(4 - 0) = 2, \text{ diamagnetic}$$

$$\text{Bond order of CN} = \frac{1}{2}(5 - 0) = 2.5 \text{ paramagnetic}$$

$$\text{Bond order of CO} = \frac{1}{2}(6 - 0) = 3 \text{ diamagnetic.}$$

Thus, bond order and magnetic property of NO is same as that of CN.

13. ***(a)*** Statements (a) is incorrect whereas (b), (c), (d) all are correct. The correct form of (a) is

The molecular wave function ψ is such that ψ^2 represents the probability density or electron charge density.

14. ***(d)*** Resonance has no role in molecular orbital theory

15. ***(b)*** Bond order of $CN^- = 3$

Bond order of $NO^- = 2$

$$\text{Difference} = 3 - 2 = 1 = 3x$$

$$x = 1/3$$

16. ***(a,b,c)*** Electron will be removed from highest occupied molecular orbital (HOMO) which is an anti-bonding molecular orbital in all the three given cases. (Also, in CO molecule, electron will be removed from a non-bonding molecular orbital (NBMO) having anti-bonding character).

17. ***(b,c,d)*** $O_2^+ : \sigma 1s^2, \sigma^* 1s^2, \sigma 2s^2, \sigma^* 2s^2, \sigma 2p_z^2, \pi 2p_x^2, \pi 2p_y^2,$ $\pi^* 2p_x^1$ has one unpaired electron in which on ionisation will result in the absence of unpaired electron thus change of nature from paramagnetic to diamagnetic. Similarly O_2^{2+} ($\pi 2p_y^2 \to \pi 2p_y^1$, i.e., diamagnetic to paramagnetic) and O_2^{2-} ($\pi^* 2p_x^2 \to \pi^* 2p_x^1$, diamagnetic to paramagnetic).

18. ***(a,c,d)*** On ionisation of N_2, the configuration changes from $N_2 = \sigma 1s^2 \sigma^* 1s^2, \sigma 2s^2, \sigma^* 2s^2\ \pi 2p_x^2 = \pi 2p_y^2\ \sigma 2p_z^2$ to $N_2^+ = \sigma 1s^2 \sigma^* 1s^2, \sigma 2s^2, \sigma^* 2s^2 \pi 2p_x^2 = \pi 2p_y^2\ \sigma 2p_z^1$; thus number of unpaired electron increases from 0 to 1 and magnetic moment increase from 0 to $\sqrt{3}$ BM.

19. ***(a,b,d)*** Statements (a, b and d) are correct whereas (c) is incorrect. The correct form of (c) is

In N_2^-, total number of electrons = 15

It's molecular orbital electronic configuration is 6

$$\sigma 1s^2 \sigma^* 1s^2 \sigma 2s^2 \sigma^* 2s^2 \pi 2p_x^2 = \pi 2p_y^2\ \sigma 2p_z^2 \pi^* 2p_x^1$$

$$\text{Bond order} = \frac{1}{2}\text{(Bonding orbitals – Antibonding orbitals)}$$

$$= \frac{10-5}{2} = 2.5$$

So, N_2^- has bond order = 2.5

20. ***(a,c,d)*** Ortho-nitrophenol has a lower boiling point than meta-nitrophenol due to intramolecular hydrogen bonding in the former.

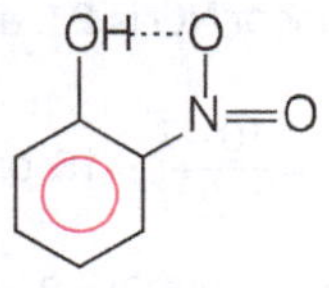

Also, benzene and nitrobenzene do not show hydrogen bonding, thus will have lower boiling point.

21. ***(2)*** Suppose the diatomic molecule is *X*.

It has 162 $e^{\ominus}$ and in diatomic it will behave same as O_2. Then, molecular orbital electronic configuration of O_2 which will be similar to X_2.

Due to presence of two unpaired electrons, it shows paramagnetic character.

22. ***(4)*** $N_2^+, O_2, B_2, N_2^{2-}$ have symmetrical electronic distribution in their HOMO and are also paramagnetic.

whereas O_2^{2-}, C_2, C_2^{2-} is diamagnetic and have symmetrical electronic distribution in their HOMO.

23. ***(3)*** Bond order = $\frac{1}{2}$ number or electrons in [Bonding M.O. – Anti-bonding M.O.]

		Bonding MO	Anti-bonding MO	BOMO⁻ AMO₂	Bond order
(i)	O_2^+	15	10	5	2.5
(ii)	CO	14	10	4	3
(iii)	B_2	10	6	4	1.0
(iv)	O_2^-	17	10	7	1.5
(v)	NO^+	14	10	4	3
(vi)	He_2^+	3	2	1	0.5
(vii)	C_2^{++}	10	6	4	1.0
(viii)	CN^-	14	10	4	3.0
(ix)	N_2	15	10	5	2.5

24. ***(8)*** Total number of electrons in $O_2^{2-} = 16 + 2 = 18$

According to MOT, the configuration of O_2^{2-} is

$$\sigma 1s^2, \overset{*}{\sigma} 1s^2, \sigma 2s^2, \overset{*}{\sigma} 2s^2, \sigma 2p_z^2, \pi 2p_y^2 \approx \sigma 2p_z^2, \overset{*}{\pi} 2p_y^2 \approx \overset{*}{\pi} 2p_z^2$$

So, the number of antibonding electron pairs = 4

25. ***(1)*** K_2CrO_4 : Diamagnetic (Cr^{6+} with no unpaired electrons). While rest species are paramagnetic. .

26. ***(4)*** H_2O_2 has two O—H groups, where each H can act as a hydrogen bond donor, and each O can act as a hydrogen bond acceptor. This allows H_2O_2 to from a total of 4 hydrogen bonds (2 as donors and 2 as acceptors).

Practice Element 01 : Target JEE Main

1. ***(b)*** $2p_x + 2p_x$ will form σ-bond

$2p_y + 2p_y$ and $2p_x + 3d_{xy}$ will form π-bond but $2p\pi + 2p\pi$ bond is stronger than $2p\pi + 2d\pi$

2. ***(b)*** dsp^2 $(s + p_x + p_y + d_{x^2-y^2})$

$sp^3d (s + p_x + p_y)(p_z + d_{z^2})$

$sp^3d^2 (s + p_x + p_y + d_{x^2-y^2})(p_z + d_{z^2})$

$sp^3d^3 (s + p_x + p_y + d_{xy} + p_{xy} + d_{x^2+y^2})(p_z + d_{z^2})$

3. ***(d)*** $N \equiv N \rightarrow O$ (Forms coordinate bond)

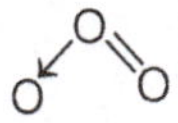 $NH_3 \rightarrow H^+$ (all have co-ordinate bond)

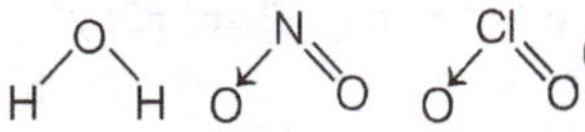 (*V* shape)

I_3^-, ICl_2^-, NO_2^+ (all are linear)

SF_4 (see-saw shape) SiF_4 (Tetrahedral) XeF_4 (square planar shape)

4. ***(b)*** Triple bond has more bond dissociaton energy compared to double and single bond

$$P \equiv P > Si = Si > Cl—Cl$$

∴ The correct bond dissociation energy order :

$$P—P > Si—Si > Cl—Cl$$

5. ***(c)*** Solid form of PF_5 is PF_4^+ PF_6^-
sp^3 sp^3d^2

Solid form of PCl_5 is PCl_4^+ PCl_6^-
sp^3 sp^3d^2

Solid form of PBr_5 is PBr_4^+ Br^-
sp^3

Solid form of XeF_6 is XeF_5^+ XeF_7^-
sp^3d^2 sp^3d^4

6. ***(a)***

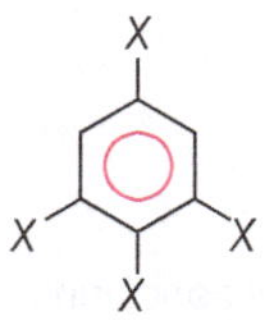

Three bond moments are equal in magnitude and they are 120° apart hence, their result is zero. Net dipole moment of this molecule equals to the that of 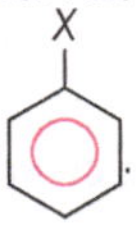.

7. ***(a)*** H_2CO_3 and SO_2

(Both are polar, planar and have sp^2 hybridised)

In $HClO_2$, hybridisation of Cl is sp^3

In ClF_3, hybridisation of Cl is sp^3d

SO_3 is non-polar

8. ***(a)*** The correct order of melting point is

$$NH_3 > SbH_3 > AsH_3 > PH_3$$

The order depends on strength of intermolecular bonding. In solid state, intermolecular bonding in NH_3 is much stronger than in liquid state.

9. ***(c)*** Bond order = Valency of peripheral atom

$$+\frac{\text{Charge on acid radical}}{\text{Total number of peripheral atoms}}$$

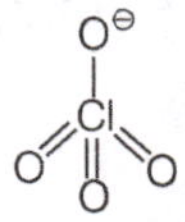

$BO = 2 + \left(-\frac{1}{4}\right)$

BO = 1.75

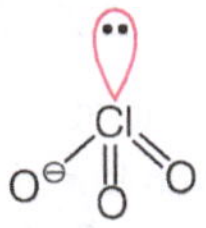

$BO = 2 + \left(-\frac{1}{3}\right)$

BO = 1.66

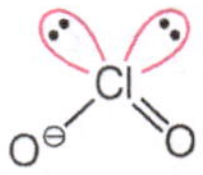

$BO = 2 + \left(-\frac{1}{2}\right)$

BO = 1.5

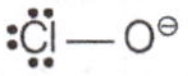

$BO = 2 + \left(-\frac{1}{1}\right)$

BO = 1

10. ***(c)***

Species	Shape
NO_2^+	linear
NO_2^-	'V'-shape
PCl_5	Trigonal bipyramidal
BrF_5	Square pyramidal
XeF_4, ICl_4	Square planar
$TeCl_4$	See-saw
XeO_4	Tetrahedral

11. ***(c)*** $>C=O$ has highest energy.

Electronegativity is directly related to bond energy.

12. ***(b)***

Species	Shape
NH_3, NF_3	Pyramidal
BF_3, BCl_3, NO_3^-	Trigonal planar
BF_4^-, NH_4^+	Tetrahedral
$BrCl_3$	'T'-shape

13. ***(c)***

Species	*lp* on central atom
$XeOF_4$	1
XeO_2F_2	1
XeF_3^-	3
XeO_3	1

14. ***(c)***

Species	Shape
XeF_4	Square planar
XeF_5^-	Pentagonal planar
$SnCl_2$	Angular or 'V'-shape

15. ***(a)*** XeO_3 (Pyramidal shape)

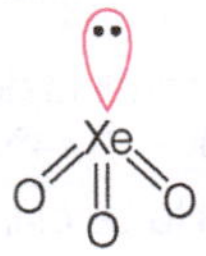

16. ***(b)*** Order of repulsion is

$$lp-lp > lp-bp > bp-bp$$

As number of *lp* on central atom increases, bond angle decreases.

The number of *lp* on O in H_2O is 2 while on N in NH_3 is 1. The structures of xenon fluorides and xenon oxofluorides could be explained on the basis of VSEPR theory.

17. ***(d)*** $2p_x + 2p_x \rightarrow \pi$-bond

$3d_{xy} + 3d_{xy} \rightarrow \delta$ - bond

$2s + 2p_y \rightarrow$ no bond

18. ***(d)*** $s + p_x \rightarrow$ no bond

$p_y + p_z \rightarrow$ no bond

19. ***(b)*** $SrC_2(Sr^{+2}—C\equiv C)$

There is $C\equiv C$ which contains 2π bonds and 1σ bond.

20. ***(b)*** Due to regular geometry, BF_3 has zero dipole moment. NH_3 has higher dipole moment than NF_3 because in NH_3 *lp* supports dipole moment while in NF_3 *lp* opposes dipole moment.

21. ***(d)*** In sp^3d^2 hybridisation (octahedral geometry), 90° angles are observed between *bp* – *bp* of electron.

22. ***(a)*** Order of bond angle

$$\underset{(120^\circ)}{SO_3} > \underset{(\approx 119^\circ)}{SO_2} > \underset{(109.5^\circ)}{SO_3^{2-}}$$

23. ***(3)*** Perchloric acid is $HClO_4$. Its structure is as follows

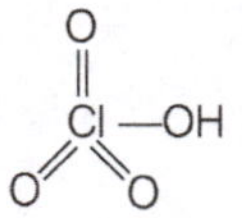

Thus, $Cl{=}O$ bond is 3. Hence, the correct answer is 3.

24. ***(21)*** s-character $\propto$ bond angle.

For 25% s-character (as in sp^3-hybrid orbital), bond angle is 109.5°, for 33.3%, s-character (as in sp^2-hybrid orbital), bond angle is 120° and for 50%, s-character (as in sp-hybrid orbital), bond angle is 180°.

Similarly, when the bond angle decreases below 109.5°, the s-character will decrease accordingly.

Decrease in bond angle $= 120^\circ - 109.5^\circ = 10.5^\circ$

$\therefore$ Decrease in s-character $= 33.3 - 25 = 8.3$

Actual decrease in bond angle $= 109.5^\circ - 105^\circ = 4.5^\circ$

$\therefore$ Expected decrease in s-character $= \dfrac{8.3}{10.5} \times 4.5 = 3.56\%$

Thus, the s-character should decrease by about 3.56%, i.e. s-character $= 25 - 3.56 = 21.44\%$

25. ***(3)*** A species is said to be diamagnetic, if it has all paired electrons.

Species	Electrons	M.O electronic configuration	Magnetic behaviour
H_2^-	3	$\sigma 1s^2, \overset{*}{\sigma} 1s^1$	Paramagnetic
H_2^+	1	$\sigma 1s^1$	Paramagnetic
H_2	2	$\sigma 1s^2$	Diamagnetic
He_2^+	3	$\sigma 1s^2, \overset{*}{\sigma} 1s^1$	Paramagnetic

26. ***(10)*** Nitrate ion has the following three resonating structure.

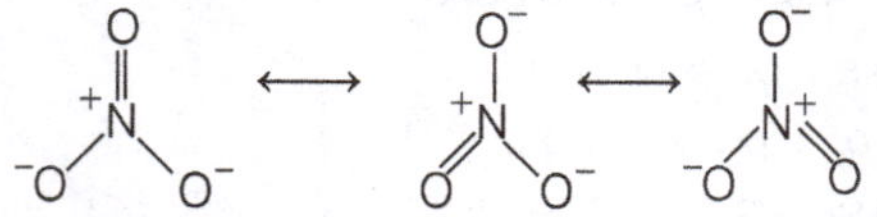

As it evident, three O-atoms are attached to the N atom by four bonds, therefore, bond order of N—O bond is $\dfrac{4}{3} = 1.33$. So, the value of y is 1.33. If 1.33 is added with 8.67 we get the value 10.

27. ***(4)*** Since, the molecule has six pairs, it should have octahedral geometry. But the structure is planar, therefore, it should have two lone pairs and four bond pairs. Therefore, value of x in ML_x is 4.

28. ***(2)*** The formula of MX_3 shows the presence of 3σ-bonds. Since, it has T-shape geometry, it must contain 2 lone pair as

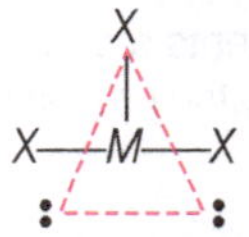

29. ***(5)*** Given, ionic charge $= 4.8 \times 10^{-10}$ esu

and ionic distance $= 1\ \text{Å} = 10^{-8}$ cm

We know that,

Dipole moment = ionic charge × ionic distance

$= 4.8 \times 10^{-10} \times 10^{-8}$

$= 4.8 \times 10^{-18}$ esu cm^{-1} $= 4.8$ debye $\simeq 5$

30. ***(1)*** $37 = 1s^2, 2s^2, 2p^6, 3s^2, 3p^6, 4s^2, 3d^{10}, 4p^6, 5s^1$

Thus, the element belongs to group 1 and has valency +1.

$53 = 1s^2, 2s^2, 2p^6, 3s^2, 3p^6, 4s^2, 3d^{10}, 4p^6, 5s^2, 4d^{10}, 5p^5$

There are 7 electrons in the valence shell of this element, it belong to group 17. Its valency is − 1.

The magnitude of product of x and y is = 1

31. ***(3)*** O_2^{2-} (Total numbers of electron = 18)

$\sigma 1s^2, \sigma^* 1s^2, \sigma 2s^2, \sigma^* 2s^2, \sigma 2p_z^2, \pi 2p_x^2 \approx \pi 2p_y^2, \overset{*}{\pi} 2p_x^2 \approx \overset{*}{\pi} 2p_y^2$

Unpaired electron = 0

B_2 (Total number of electron = 10)

$\sigma 1s^2, \sigma^* 1s^2, \sigma 2s^2, \sigma^* 2s^2, \pi 2p_x^1 \approx \pi 2p_y^1$

Unpaired electron = 2

N_2^+ (Total number of electron = 13)

$\sigma 1s^2, \sigma^* 1s^2, \sigma 2s^2, \sigma^* 2s^2, \pi 2p_x^2 \approx \pi 2py^2, \sigma 2p_z^1$

Unpaired electron = 1

O_2 (Total number of electron = 16)

$\sigma 1s^2, \sigma^* 1s^2, \sigma 2s^2, \sigma^* 2s^2, \sigma 2p_z^2, \pi 2p_x^2 \approx \pi 2p_y^2, \overset{*}{\pi} 2p_x^1 \approx \overset{*}{\pi} 2p_y^1$

Unpaired electron = 2

And hence, there are 3 ion/molecule which contain unpaired electron.

32. ***(2)*** The structure of carbon suboxide is

$$:\ddot{O} \underset{1\pi}{\overset{1\sigma}{=}} C \underset{1\pi}{\overset{1\sigma}{=}} C \underset{1\pi}{\overset{1\sigma}{=}} C \underset{1\pi}{\overset{1\sigma}{=}} \ddot{O}:$$

In C_3O_2, each carbon forms 2 pi bond and 2 sigma bond, so, each carbon is sp-hybridised thus, number of hybrid orbital is 2.

Check Through PYQs : JEE Main

1. ***(3)*** $BF_3 \Rightarrow 6e^-$ in central atom, octet incomplete, e^- difficient

- $CCl_4, CO_2 \Rightarrow 8e^-$ in central atom $\Rightarrow$ Complete octet.
- $PCl_5 \Rightarrow 10e^-$ in central atom, $BrF_5 \Rightarrow 12e^-$ in central atom

$\therefore PCl_5, BrF_5$ = Expanded octet

- NO $\Rightarrow$ It is an odd electron species [$\cdot\ddot{N}{=}O$]

$\Rightarrow$ 1 odd e^- is present

2. ***(6)*** NO_2, H_2SO_4, BF_3, ClO_2, PCl_5, BeF_2. These are exception to octet rule.

   Hence, among the given molecules total 6 molecule are exception to octet rule.

3. ***(8)*** The bond structure of NO_2^- is,

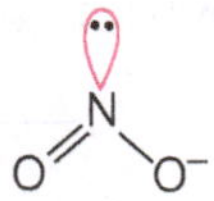

   Number of valence e^- around N-atom = 8.

4. ***(a)*** The ionic character in a molecule is dependent upon electronegativity difference between the constituting atoms.

   Greater the electronegativity difference, greater will be the ionic character of molecules.

   Therefore, the correct sequence of increasing order of ionic character.

$$N_2 < SO_2 < ClF_3 < K_2O < LiF.$$

   Hence, option (a) is correct.

5. ***(d)*** Greater the difference of electronegativity between the cation and anion, greater will be the ionic character and lesser will be the covalent character.

   Hence, correct order is

$$KI > KF, LiF > KF; CuCl > NaCl$$

   Smaller the size of the cation higher will be its polarising capacity. Since, Sn^{4+} is smaller in size hence it will have more covalent character. So, $SnCl_4 > SnCl_2$.

6. ***(5)*** Compounds having permanent dipole moment ($\mu \neq 0$) are polar.

   $CH_4, CCl_4 \Rightarrow \mu = 0$

   $CH_2Cl_2, H_2O, NH_3, H_2O_2, O_2F_2 \Rightarrow \mu \neq 0$

   Number of polar molecules = 5

7. ***(c)*** The hybridisation of central atom of given species in different options are

   BF_3, NO_2^-, $NO_2 \Rightarrow sp^2$-hybridisation

   H_2O and $NH_2^- \Rightarrow sp^3$-hybridisation

   So, the pair of central atoms that exhibit sp^2-hybridisation is BF_3 and NO_2^-.

8. ***(c)*** The correct match is

   A-III, B-I, C-IV, D-II

   NH_3 = Trigonal pyramidal

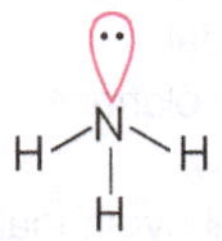

   BrF_5 = Square pyramidal

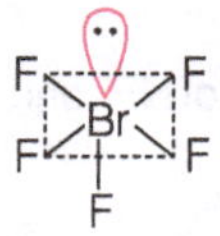

   PCl_5 = Trigonal bipyramidal

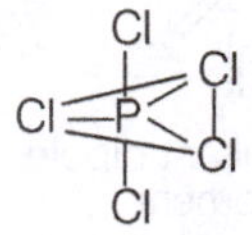

   CH_4 = Tetrahedral

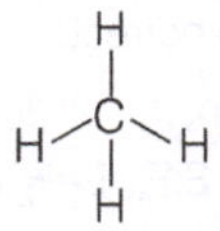

9. ***(6)*** Among the given species, total 6 species have sp^2 hybrid orbital for bonding with central atoms.

   These are SO_2, C_2H_4, BCl_3, HCHO, C_6H_6, BF_3

10. ***(c)*** The correct match is A-III, B-I, C-II, D-IV.

    SO_2Cl_2 has sp^3-hybridisation and has tetrahedral geometry.

    NO is paramagnetic in nature.

    NO_2^- is diamagnetic in nature.

    I_3^- has sp^3d-hybridisation and has linear geometry.

11. ***(a)***

Molecules	Hybridisation	Shape/geometry
A. SF_4	sp^3d	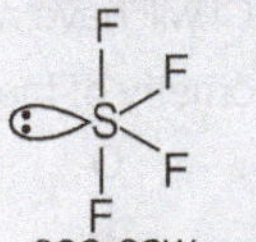 *see-saw*
B. BrF_3	sp^3d	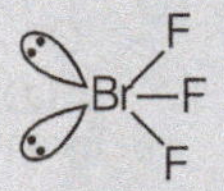 Bent T-shape
C. BrO_3^-	sp^3	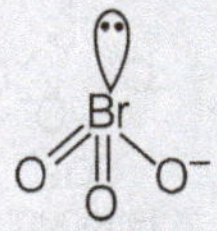 Pyramidal
D. NH_4^+	sp^3	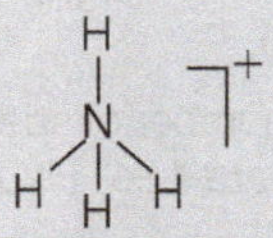 Tetrahedral

Hence, correct match is A-III, B-IV, C-II, D-I.

12. ***(c)*** Both A and R are true and R is the correct explanation of A.

The bond structure of NF_3 and NH_3 with dipole moment direction are

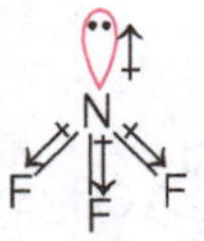

Resultant dipole moment $= 0.80 \times 10^{-30}$ Cm

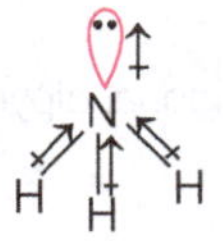

Resultant dipole moment $= 4.9 \times 10^{-30}$ Cm

Hence, option (c) is correct.

13. ***(6)*** Among the given,

H_2, CO_2, BF_3, CH_4, SiF_4, BeF_2 are symmetrical molecules.

Hence, total 6 molecules will show zero dipole moment.

14. ***(c)*** Both A and R are true and R is correct explanation of A.

Dipole moment is a vector quantity and for compound net dipole moment is the vector sum of all dipoles. Hence dipole moment of *cis*-form is greater than *trans*-form.

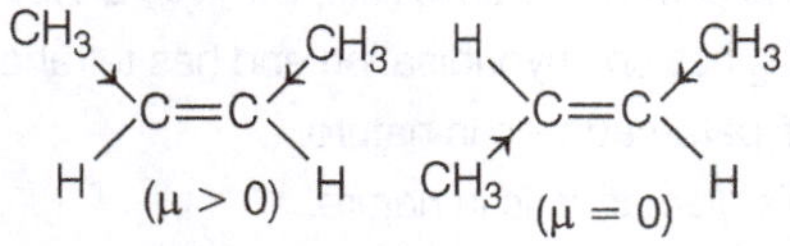

15. ***(5)*** Polar molecules will have non-zero dipole moments while non-polar molecules will have zero dipole moments.

Thus, among the given species/ compounds NF_3, H_2O, H_2S, HBr and HCl will have non-zero dipole moment

16. ***(c)*** The geometry of the given species are as follows

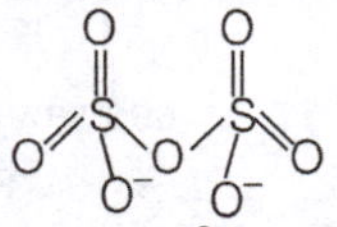

$S_2O_7^{2-}$ Tetrahedral

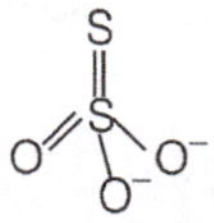

$S_2O_3^{2-}$ Tetrahedral

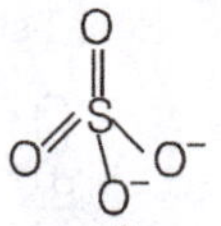

SO_4^{2-} Tetrahedral

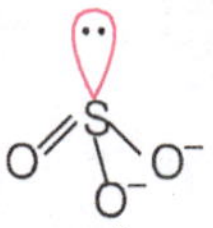

SO_3^{2-} Pyramidal

Thus, among the given species only SO_3^{2-} has pyramidal geometry.

17. ***(4)*** The number of species that uses sp^3 hybrid orbitals in bonding are 4 i.e., H_2O, NH_3, SiO_2, CH_4.

While other species uses sp^2 and *sp*-hybrid orbitals which are as follows.

sp^2 — SO_2, BCl_3

sp — $BeCl_2$, CO_2

18. ***(d)*** Polar molecules are those molecules in which there exists an electronegativity difference between the bonded atom. They have non-zero dipole moment.

Hence, $CHCl_3$ is a polar molecule.

Non-polar molecules are those molecules in which electrons are shared equally. They have zero dipole moment.

$CH_2 = CH_2$, CCl_4, CO_2 are non-polar molecules.

Hence, option (d) is correct.

19. ***(b)*** Shape of SO_2 and H_2O are given as

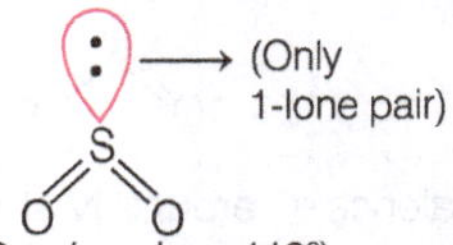

(Bond angle = 119°)

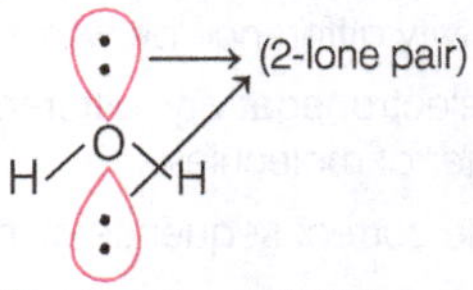

(Bond angle = 104.5°)

Hence, both has V-shape, but bond angle in SO_2 is greater than H_2O, due to repulsion between lone pairs at oxygen. So, statement I is correct but statement II is incorrect.

20. ***(3)*** In water (H_2O) molecule, oxygen is bonded to two hydrogen atoms. Total number of valence electrons present in oxygen atom is 6. It share one electron with each hydrogen atom to form two single bonds.

Since, four valence electrons do not participate in any bond formation, there are two lone pair in water molecule.

In CO each carbon and oxygen atom contains one lone pair of electrons. Hence total number of lone pair is 2.

In N_2 the nitrogen atoms are bonded with triple bonds. So, each of them have a lone pair of electron. Hence, total number of lone pair is 2.

21. ***(b)*** Statement I is correct but Statement II is incorrect.

Dipole moment is a vector quantity i.e., it has magnitude as well as definite directions.

In chemistry, the dipole moment is represented by cross on the positive centre and arrowhead on the negative centre. This arrow symbolises the shift of electron density in the molecules.

22. ***(6)*** General planar structures are linear, bent, T-shaped, trigonal planar and square planar.

$NO_3^- \rightarrow$ Trigonal planar

$H_2O_2 \rightarrow$ Open book like (3D) (non-planar)

$BF_3 \rightarrow$ Trigonal planar

$PCl_3 \rightarrow$ Pyramidal

$XeF_4 \rightarrow$ Square planar

$SF_4 \rightarrow$ *See-saw*

$XeO_3 \rightarrow$ Trigonal pyramidal

$PH_4^+ \rightarrow$ Tetrahedral

$SO_3 \rightarrow$ Trigonal planar

$[Al(OH)_4]^- \rightarrow$ Tetrahedral

Hence, only 6 have non-polar geometry.

23. ***(b)*** Number of electron in given species

$CH_4 = 6 + 4 = 10$

$NH_4^+ = 7 + 3 = 10$

$BH_4^- = 5 + 4 + 1 = 10$

They all have same number of electron, i.e. are isoelectronic (species with same number of electron) and also have same structure, i.e. tetrahedral.

24. ***(a)*** The hybridisation of SF_4 is sp^3d and geometry is trigonal bipyramidal. At axial position, there are 3 *lp-bp* at 90°. But at equatorial position, there are only two lone pair-bond pair repulsions at 90°.

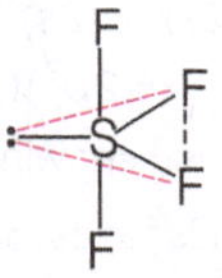

So, shape of SF_4 molecule is *see-saw*.

25. ***(a)***

Species	O_2^+	O_2	O_2^-	O_2^{2-}
No. of e^-	15	16	17	18
Bond order	2.5	2	1.5	1

Increasing bond order is $O_2^{2-} < O_2^- < O_2 < O_2^+$.

26. ***(3)*** Molecule with net zero dipole moment are CO_2, CH_4 and BF_3 i.e. 3

Remaining all molecules have non-zero dipole moment.

27. ***(718)*** $\Delta H_{formation}$ is given as

$$\Delta_f H°_{(KCl)} = \Delta_{sub}H°_{(K)} + \Delta_{ion}H°_{(K)} + \frac{1}{2}\Delta_{bond}H°_{(Cl_2)} + \Delta_{e.g.}H°_{(Cl)} + \Delta_{lattice}H°_{(KCl)}$$

$$\Delta_{lattice}H°_{(KCl)} = \Delta_f H°_{(KCl)} - \Delta_{sub}H°_{(K)} - \Delta_{ion}H°_{(K)} - \frac{1}{2}\Delta_{bond}H°_{(Cl_2)} - \Delta_{e.g.}H°_{(Cl)}$$

$$= -436.7 - 89.2 - 419.0 - \frac{1}{2}(243) - (-348.6)$$

$$= -717.8 \approx 718 \text{ kJ/mol}$$

28. ***(d)*** In NO_2^-

In N is sp^2-hybridised.

NO_2^- 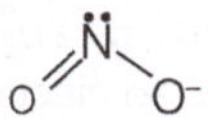

In NO_2^+, N *sp*-hybridised.

NO_2^+ 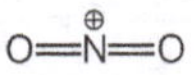

In NH_4^+, N is sp^3-hybridised.

NH_4^+ 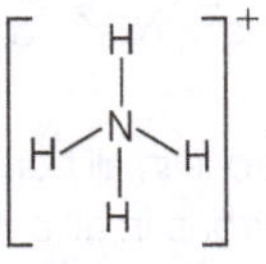

Therefore, hybridisation of N in NO_2^-, NO_2^+, NH_4^+ are sp^2, *sp*, sp^3 respectively.

29. ***(c)*** 2 lone pair + 3 bond pair

Steric number = 5

Hybridisation = sp^3d.

So, the shape is T- shape.

Concept Enhancer

Geometry of the compound having sp^3d hybridisation have tetragonal bipyramidal TBP geometry according to VSEPR theory.

In TBP lone pair occupy equatorial position.

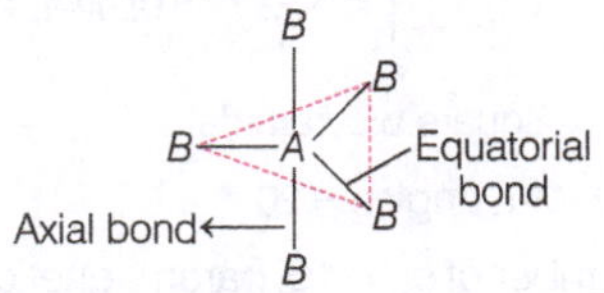

30. ***(d)*** Bond angle of sp^3-hybridised compound should be 109.5°.

But in case of water, it is only 104.5° due to repulsion between the lone pairs. Lone pair-lone pair repulsion is higher than bond pair-bond pair repulsion.

(VSEPR Theory)

So, both A and R are true and R is the correct explanation of A.

31. ***(c)*** $SF_4 \Rightarrow$

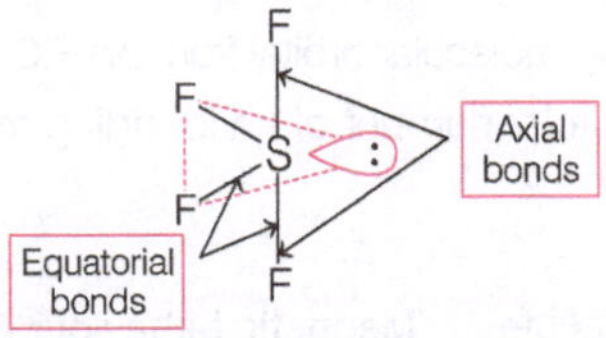

S (sp^3d-hybridised)

Geometry : Trigonal bipyramidal

Shape : *see-saw*

Axial S—F bonds are longer than equatorial bonds.

Hence, among given species only SF_4 has unequal bond lengths.

32. ***(a)*** If number of sigma bond (σ), co-ordinate bond and lone pair are same for given pairs, they are isostructural. Hence, SO_4^{2-}, CrO_4^{2-}, $SiCl_4$ and $TiCl_4$ have tetrahedral shape and are isostructural.

33. ***(d)***

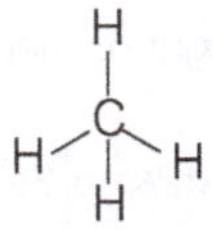

[CH_4 = hybridisation is sp^3, lone pair of electrons is 0, so that bond angle is maximum i.e., = 109°28′]

34. ***(a)*** The correct descending order of bonds according to their average bond energies is as follows :

C—F > C—Cl > C—Br > C—I

Bond length is inversely proportional to bond energy. So, bond length decreases as bond energy increases.

35. ***(20)***

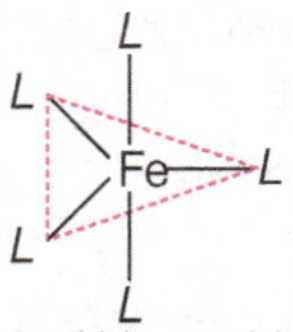

$1L\text{-}M\text{-}L = 180°$
$6L\text{-}M\text{-}L = 90°$
$3L\text{-}M\text{-}L = 120°$
$10L\text{-}M\text{-}L$ angles

Trigonal bipyramidal

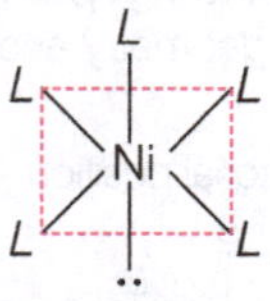

$8L\text{-}M\text{-}L = 90°$
$2L\text{-}M\text{-}L = 180°$
$10L\text{-}M\text{-}L$ angles

Square bipyramidal

$\therefore$ Sum of $L\text{-}M\text{-}L$ angles = 20

36. ***(5)*** O_2, Number of $e^- = 16$, paramagnetic
O_2^+, Number of $e^- = 15$, paramagnetic
O_2^-, Number of $e^- = 17$, paramagnetic
NO_2, odd e^- specie, paramagnetic
NO, Number of $e^- = 15$, paramagnetic
CO, Number of $e^- = 14$, diamagnetic

37. ***(8)*** Molecular orbital formed by 2s atomic orbital = 2 ($\sigma 2s$ and $\sigma^* 2s$)
Molecular orbital formed by $2p$ atomic orbital
$= 6(\sigma 2p_z$ and $\sigma^* 2p_z, \pi 2p_x\ \pi 2p_y$ and $\pi^* 2p_x, \pi^* 2p_y)$
So, total molecular orbitals = 2 + 6 = 8

38. ***(4)*** Antibonding molecular orbital from 2s = 1
Antibonding molecular orbital from $2p = 3$
Therefore, total number of antibonding molecular orbitals are = 1 + 3 = 4

39. ***(1)***

Ion/molecule	Magnetic behaviour	Bond order
H_2	Diamagnetic	1
He_2^+	Paramagnetic	0.5
N_2^{2-}	Paramagnetic	2
O_2^{2-}	Diamagnetic	1
O_2^+	Paramagnetic	2.5
F_2	Diamagnetic	1
Ne_2^+	Paramagnetic	0.5
B_2	Paramagnetic	1

Only B_2 has paramagnetic magnetic behaviour and bond order of 1.

40. ***(d)*** $N_2 = \sigma 1s^2\ \sigma^* 1s^2\ \sigma 2s^2\ \sigma^* 2s^2 \pi 2p_x^2 = \pi 2p_y^2, \sigma 2p_z^2$
Number of unpaired electron present in HOMO = 0
$$N_2^+ = \sigma 1s^2, \sigma^* 1s^2, \sigma 2s^2, \sigma^* 2s^2, \pi 2p_x^2 = \pi 2p_y^2, \sigma 2p_z^1$$
Number of unpaired electron present in HOMO = 1
$$O_2 = \sigma 1s^2, \sigma^* 1s^2, \sigma 2s^2, \sigma^* 2s^2, \sigma 2p_z^2, \pi 2p_x^2 \approx \pi 2p_y^2, \pi^* 2p_x^1 \approx \pi^* 2p_y^1$$
Number of unpaired electron present in HOMO = 2
$$O_2^+ = \sigma 1s^2, \sigma^* 1s^2, \sigma 2s^2, \sigma^* 2s^2, \sigma 2p_z^2, \pi 2p_x^2 = \pi 2p_y^2, \pi^* 2p_x^1 = \pi^* 2p_y^0$$
Number of unpaired electron present in HOMO = 1
Thus, the number of unpaired electrons are 0, 1, 2, 1.

41. ***(c)*** According to MO theory, the bond orders for O_2^{2-}, CO and NO^+ are 1, 3 and 3.

42. ***(c)*** So, the correct match is
(A) → (III), B → (I), (C) → (IV), D → (II).

43. ***(2)*** $N_2 : (\sigma 1s)^2(\sigma^* 1s)^2(\sigma 2s)^2(\sigma^* 2s)^2 (\pi 2p_x^2 = \pi 2p_y^2)(\sigma 2p_z)^2$; Diamagnetic
O_2^{2-}: $(\sigma 1s)^2(\sigma^* 1s)^2(\sigma 2s)^2(\sigma^* 2s)^2(\sigma 2p_z)^2 (\pi 2p_x^2 = \pi 2p_y^2)(\pi^* 2p_x^2 = \pi^* 2p_y^2)$; Diamagnetic
The number of species showing diamagnetism are 2.

44. ***(c)*** NO : $\sigma 1s^2 \sigma^* 1s^2 \sigma 2s^2 \sigma^* 2s^2 \sigma 2p_z^2 \pi 2p_x^2 = \pi 2p_y^2 \pi^* 2p_x^1$
Bond order $= \dfrac{10-5}{2} = 2.5$
$O_2 : \sigma 1s^2 \sigma^* 1s^2 \sigma 2s^2 \sigma^* 2s^2 \sigma 2p_z^2 \pi 2p_x^2 = \pi 2p_y^2 \pi^* 2p_x^1 = \pi^* 2p_y^1$
Bond order $= \dfrac{10-6}{2} = 2$
$C_2 : \sigma 1s^2 \sigma^* 1s^2 \sigma 2s^2 \sigma^* 2s^2 \pi 2p_x^2 = \pi 2p_y^2$
Bond order $= \dfrac{1}{2}(8-4) = \dfrac{4}{2} = 2$
Removal of electron from antibonding MO increases BO.
$N_2 : \sigma 1s^2 \sigma^* 1s^2 \sigma 2s^2 \sigma^* 2s^2 \pi 2p_x^2 = \pi 2p_y^2 \sigma 2p_z^2$
Bond order $= \dfrac{1}{2}(10-4) = \dfrac{6}{2} = 3$
$B_2 : \sigma 1s^2 \sigma^* 1s^2 \sigma 2s^2 \sigma^* 2s^2 \pi 2p_x^1 = \pi 2p_y^1$
Bond order $= \dfrac{1}{2}(6-4) = 1$
Increase in bond order indicates increased strength of bond. Hence, correct answer is option c.

45. ***(a)*** Extensive H-bonding is observed in this case as two H-atoms bonded to strongly electronegative atoms (nitrogen, oxygen) are present. H-bonding occurs when H-bonded to strongly electronegative atoms exists in the vicinity of other electronegative atoms possessing lone pairs of electron.

46. ***(a)*** O_2^- (Total electrons = 17)
$$= \sigma 1s^2, \sigma^* 1s^2\ \sigma 2s^2\ \sigma^* 2s^2\ \sigma 2p_z^2, \pi 2p_x^2 = \pi 2p_y^2, \pi^* 2p_x^2 = \pi^* 2p_y^1, \sigma^* 2p_z^0$$
Number of unpaired electron = 1
So, it is paramagnetic.
Bond order $= \dfrac{n_b - n_a}{2} = \dfrac{10-7}{2} = 1.5$

47. ***(10)*** Configuration of O_2^{2-} is
$$(O_2^{2-}) = \sigma 1s^2, \sigma^* 1s^2, \sigma 2s^2, \sigma^* 2s^2, \sigma 2p_z^2, \pi 2p_x^2 = \pi 2p_y^2, \pi^* 2p_x^2 = \pi^* 2p_y^2$$
Number of electrons in all bonding molecular orbitals = 10
Number of electrons in all anti-bonding molecular orbitals = 8

48. ***(a)*** A is false but R is true.
Corrected form of A is diple-dipole interactions are purely covalent interactions of dipolar covalent bonds. Ends of dipoles of a polar covalent bonds possess partial charges (δ^+ and δ^-) which are less than unit electronic charge, $e = 1.6 \times 10^{-19}$ C.

49. ***(c)*** CH_4 doesn't show intermolecular hydrogen bonding while out of HCN and NH_3, extent of hydrogen bonding is more in NH_3 as ammonia could form 'three' hydrogen bond per molecule while HCN could form only one hydrogen bond per molecule.

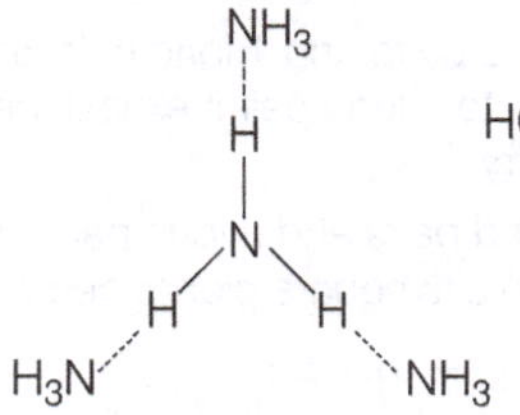

HCN ······ HCN

H_2O have even more stronger hydrogen bonding due to the presence of highly electronegative oxygen atom.

Hence, the correct order of increasing intermolecular H-bond strength is : $CH_4 < HCN < NH_3$.

Practice Element 02 : Target JEE Advanced

1. ***(a)*** Ionic character $\propto \dfrac{1}{\text{Polarising power of cation}}$

As positive oxidation state increases or, size of cation decreases, polarising power of cation increases hence, the correct order of ionic character is : $MCl > MCl_2 > MCl_3$

2. ***(a)*** The hybridisation of central atom of given species in different options are

IF_5 and $ICl_4^- \longrightarrow sp^3d^2$ hybridisation

PF_5 and $XeOF_4 \longrightarrow sp^3d$ and sp^3d^2 hybridisation

ClO_2^- and $SF_4 \longrightarrow sp^3$ and sp^3d hybridisation

SO_2Cl_2 and $BrO_3^- \longrightarrow sp^3$hybridisation

So, the pair of central atom that exhibits sp^3d^2 hybridisation is IF_5 and ICl_4^-.

3. ***(a)*** (a) $He_2^+ : \sigma 1s^2\ \sigma^* 1s^1$

1 unpaired electron. So, it is paramagnetic.

$B_2 : \sigma 1s^2\ \sigma^* 1s^2\ \sigma 2s^2\ \sigma^* 2s^2\ \pi 2p_x^1\ \pi 2p_y^1$

1 unpaired electron. So, it is paramagnetic.

(b) $He_2 : \sigma 1s^2\ \sigma^* 1s^2$

He_2 does not exist.

$H_2\ \sigma 1s^2$

No unpaired electron. So, it is diamagnetic.

(c) $N_2^{2-} : \sigma 1s^2\ \sigma^* 1s^2\ \sigma 2s^2\ \sigma^* 2s^2\ \pi 2p_x^2\ \pi 2p_y^2\ \sigma 2p_z^2$
$\pi^* 2p_x^1\ \pi^* 2p_y^1$

Contains unpaired electron, so it is paramagnetic.

$Li_2 : \sigma 1s^2\ \sigma^* 1s^1\ \sigma 2s^2\ \sigma^* 2s^2$

No unpaired electron. So it diamagnetic.

(d) $Be_2 : \sigma 1s^2\ \sigma^* 1s^2\ \sigma 2s^2\ \sigma^* 2s^2$

No unpaired electron so it is diamagnetic.

$C_2 : \sigma 1s^2\ \sigma^* 1s^2\ \sigma 2s^2\ \sigma^* 2s^2\ \pi 2p_x^2\ \pi 2p_y^2$

Contains no unpaired electron. So, it is diamagnetic.

4. ***(c)*** If number of sigma bond (σ), coordinate bond and lone pair are same for given pairs, they are isostructural. Hence BrF_5, $XeOF_4$, ClF_5 and IF_5 have square pyramidal and are isostructural.

5. ***(c)***

Molecule	Type of back bonding
OCl_2	$2p\pi - 3d\pi$
BF_3	$2p\pi - 2p\pi$
CCl_3^-	$2p\pi - 3d\pi$
$:CCl_2$	$2p\pi - 3p\pi$

In : $:CCl_2$ vacant $2p$-orbital of 'C' and paired $3p$-orbital of 'Cl' form back bonding.

6. ***(c)*** $C_2^+ : \sigma 1s^2\ \sigma^* 1s^2\ \sigma 2s^2\ \sigma^* 2s^2\ \pi 2p_x^2 = \pi 2p_y^1$

Bond order $= \dfrac{1}{2}(N_b - N_a) = \dfrac{1}{2}(7 - 4) = 1.5$

$O_2^{2+} : \sigma 1s^2\ \sigma^* 1s^2\ \sigma 2s^2\ \sigma^* 2s^2\ \sigma 2p_z^2\ \pi 2p_x^2 = \pi 2p_y^2$

Bond order $= \dfrac{1}{2}(10 - 4) = 3$

$C_2^- : \sigma 1s^2\ \sigma^* 1s^2\ \sigma 2s^2\ \sigma^* 2s^2\ \pi 2p_x^2 = \pi 2p_y^2\ \sigma 2p_z^1$

Bond order $= \dfrac{1}{2}(9 - 4) = 2.5$

$O_2^{2-} : \sigma 1s^2\ \sigma^* 1s^2\ \sigma 2s^2\ \sigma^* 2s^2\ \sigma 2p_z^2\ \pi 2p_x^2$
$= \pi 2py^2\ \pi^* 2p_x^2 = \pi^* 2p_y^2$

Bond order $= \dfrac{1}{2}(10 - 8) = 1$

Greater the bond order, greater is the bond strength

$O_2^{2-} < C_2^+ < C_2^- < O_2^{2+}$

7. ***(a)*** Statement (a) is incorrect about the MOT rest all the correct.

Statement (a) is related to valence bond theory. It's correct form is.

Atomic orbitals of the combining atoms lose their individual identity in the resulting molecular orbital.

8. ***(b)*** The electronic configuration of N_2 is $\sigma 1s^2\ \sigma^* 1s^2 \sigma 2s^2$ $\sigma^* 2s^2 \pi 2p_x^2 = \pi 2p_y^2 \sigma 2p_z^2$. Therefore, $\sigma 2p_z^2$ represents HOMO while $\pi^* 2p_x$ and $\pi^* 2p_y$ represents LUMO.

9. ***(b)*** In S_2F_2; presence of highly electronegative F-atom increases the % of s-character of S—S bond and thus decreasing the S—S bond length.

10. ***(c)*** (i) Bond angle decreases down the group due to less electronegativity and larger size, smallest bond angle in AsH_3.

(ii) O_3^+ has largest bond angle due to positive charge.

(iii) NO_2^- has small bond angle.

(iv) chlorine atom in $SOCl_2$ reduce repulsion compared to smaller fluorine atoms in SOF_2.

Thus, option (c) is the correct answer.

11. ***(a,b,c)***

Species	Molecular shape
NO_2^+	Linear
XeF_2	Linear
I_3^-	Linear
I_3^+	'V'-shape

12. ***(a,b,c,d)*** All the given statemens are correct.

13. ***(a,b,c,d)*** e^-density of σ-bond lies on the internuclear axis. e^-density of π-bond lies on the either side of internuclear axis. Direction of a covalent bond is decided by σ-bond.

Order of strength of π-bond.

$$2p\pi - 2p\pi > 2p\pi - 3d\pi > 2p\pi - 3p\pi$$

14. ***(a,c)*** SF_6 has octahedral geometry (Non-planar)

In SF_6 'S' has $12e^-$ in outermost shell after sharing hence, it does not acquire e^- configuration of Ar gas.

15. ***(a,b,c)*** The correct of boiling point is

$$CH_4 > SiH_4 > GeH_4$$

16. ***(b,c)*** Among the given molecules only $O_3, CHCl_3, SiF_4, CO_2$ and C_2H_6 follows octet rule while $NO_2, BeF_2, BF_3, N_2O, H_2SO_4$, $BeCl_2$, ClO_2, PCl_5 and NO_2 do not follow octet rule. Thus, option with at least three molecules that follows octet rule are b and c.

17. ***(b,c,d)*** PCl_5, PF_3Cl_2 and PF_2Cl_3 have a trigonal bipyramidal shape, XeO_4 and CCl_4 have a tetrahedral shape and XeO_2F_4 has an octahedral shape and thus all are non-planar. XeO_4, PCl_5 and CCl_4 have symmetrical structures and thus are non-polar as $\mu_{net} = 0$. PF_3Cl_2 is polar since $\mu_{net} \neq 0$ whereas PF_2Cl_3 has $\mu_{net} = 0$ due to cancellation of individual bond pair moments thus is non-polar.

18. ***(a,b,c)*** (a), (b), (c) are correct, while correct form of (d) will be SF_2 bond are longer than SF_6 bonds.

19. ***(1)*** $\frac{12}{12} = 1$

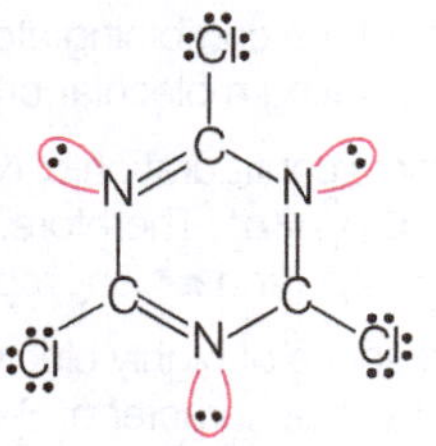

20. ***(76.8)*** The dipole moment of 100% ionic molecule (Li^+H)

$= (1 \text{ electronic charge}) (\text{inter atomic distance})$

$= (1.602 \times 10^{-19} \text{ C}) (1.596 \times 10^{-10} \text{ m})$

$= 2.557 \times 10^{-29} \text{ Cm}$

Fractional ionic character

$$= \frac{\text{Experimental dipole moment}}{\text{Theoretical value of dipole moment}}$$

$$= \frac{1.94 \times 10^{-29}}{2.557 \times 10^{-29}} = 0.768$$

The bond in LiH is 76.8% ionic.

21. ***(3)*** IF_5, ClF_5, $[SbF_5]^{2-}$ contains 5 bond pair of electrons and 1 lone pair. So, it is sp^3d^2 hybridised and exhibits square pyramidal geometry.

PF_5 contains 5 bond pairs. So, it is sp^3d hybridised and exhibits trigonal bipyramidal geometry.

SF_4 contains 4 bond pairs and 1 lone pair. So, it is sp^3d hybridised but due to 1 lone pair it exhibit irregular tetrahedal geometry.

ICl_4 contains 4 bond pairs and 2 lone pair. So, it is sp^3d^2 hybridised and exhibits square planar geometry.

22. ***(9)*** $CO_3^{-2}, NO_3^-, NO_2^- \rightarrow p\pi - p\pi$

$SO_3^{-2}, SO_4^{-2}, PO_4^{-3}, S_2O_8^{-2}, R_3PO_3^{-2}, S_2O_3^{-2}, ClO_4^-, ClO_3, SO_2^- \rightarrow p\pi - d\pi$

23. ***(4)***

Species	Bond order
N_2^+	2.5
N_2^-	2.5
O_2	2
O_2^+	2.5
F_2	1
B_2	1
C_2^+	1.5
CN^-	3
NO^+	3

24. ***(6)*** NH_3, H_2O, HF, HCOOH, $B(OH)_3$ and CH_3COOH shows hydrogen bonding.

25. ***(3)*** H_2O, $SeCl_2$, NH_2^- are sp^3 hybridised and exhibit V-shaped molecular geometry NH_3 is sp^3 hybridised and have trigonal pyramidal geometry BCl_3 and BH_3 are sp^2 hybridised and have trigonal planar geometry.

26. ***(4)*** In both species two $d_{x^2-y^2}$ and d_z^2 are participating in hybridisation.

27. ***(12)***

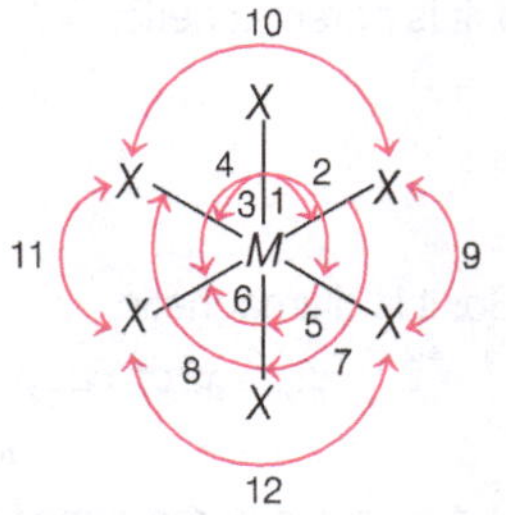

28. ***(20)*** (i) $NO \rightarrow NO^+$

2.5 3.0

Paramagnetic Diamagnetic

(ii) $O_2^- \rightarrow O_2^{2-}$

(1.5) (1)

Paramagnetic Diamagnetic

(iii) $O_2 \rightarrow O_2^+$

(2) (2.5)

Paramagnetic Paramagnetic

(iv) $NO^+ \rightarrow NO^-$

(3) (2.5)

Diamagnetic Diamagnetic

(v) $CO \rightarrow CO^+$

(3) (2.5)

Diamagnetic Paramagnetic

$c^3 - b^2 - a = 3^3 - 2^2 - 3 = 27 - 4 - 3 = 20$

29. ***(0)***

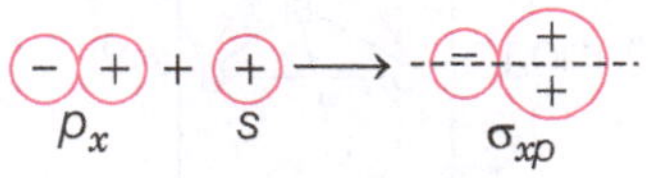

30. ***(3)*** The number of angular nodes is equal to the value of azimuthal quantum number (l).

For $4f$ orbital, $l = 3$

$\therefore$ Total number of angular nodes in $4f$ orbital = 3.

31. ***(50)*** Hybridisation of C in $CH \equiv CH$ is sp so % of S is 50%.

32. ***(2)*** Among the given species IF_4^-, $ICIBr^-$, SeF_3^-, (linear, sp^3d hybrid, three bond pairs and two lone pairs each) and SO_2 (V-shaped, sp^2 hybrid, two bond pairs and one lone pair) are planar whereas IF_4^+ (*see-saw*, sp^3d hybrid, four bond pairs and one lone pair) and PCl_3F_2 (trigonal bipyramidal, sp^3d, five bond pairs) are non-planar. Also, among the planar species only $ICIBr^-$ and SO_2 are polar, all others are non-polar.

33. ***(3)*** $CO_3^{-2}, NO_3^-, NO_2^- \rightarrow p\pi - p\pi$

34. ***(4)*** $BCl_3, BF_3, AlBr_3, BeCl_2$ contains less than 8 valence electrons. So, they are hypovalent species whereas H_2SO_3, SO_3, H_3PO_4 contains more than 8 valence electrons. So, they are hypervalent species.

35. ***(b)*** The correct match is : A-I, B-III, C-II, D-IV.

(A) (I) H—C≡C—H (sp – $1s$) overlap

(B) (III)

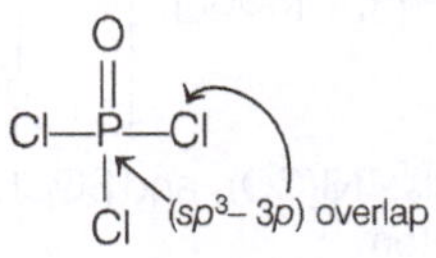

(C) (II)

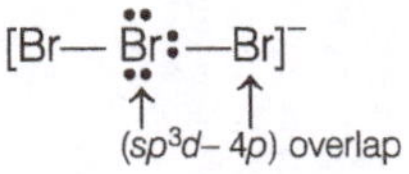

(D) (IV) $H_3C—CH_3$ (sp^3 – sp^3) overlap

36. ***(a)*** The correct match is : A-I, B-II, C-III, D-IV

37. ***(a)*** The correct match is : A-III, B-I, C-II, D-IV.

(A) (III) Acidic strength of hydrides of group 16 increases down the group, due to increases in size of central atom.

(B) (I) Bond angle of hydrides of group 16 decreases down the group.

(C) (II) H_2O has the highest melting and boiling points due to the intermolecular H-bonding.

(D) (IV) SbH_3 has highest mass so highest boiling point then NH_3 is due to H-bonding, PH_3 has lowest boiling point.

38. ***(d)*** A-I, B-II, C-III, D-IV

39. ***(a)*** A-III, B-IV, C-II, D-I

MX_6Y e.g., $TeCl_6^{2-}$, $SbCl_6^{3-}$ etc. are perfectly octahedral.

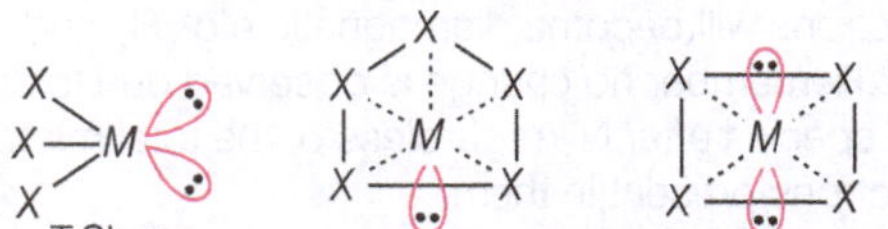

T-Shape Distorted square pyramidal Square planar

40. ***(d)*** CH_3^+, HCHO, $TiCl_4$, CO_2 act as Lewis acid.

41. ***(d)*** BF_3 and SO_2 have bond angle 120°, rest species have less than 120°.

(H_2O - 105°, H_2S - 90°, NH_3 – 107°)

42. ***(c)*** A. The removal of the second H^+ ion from the maleic acid is more difficult than fumaric acid due intramolecular hydrogen bond formation.

B. Boiling points increase due to molecular association (intermolecular hydrogen bonding) and thus $H_2O > H_2Te$ and $NH_3 < SbH_3$

E. Viscosity increases due to increase in intermolecular association e.g., methanol (0.59 cP) > acetone (0.36 cP)

F. Vapour pressure decreases as boiling point increases due to intermolecular hydrogen bonding e.g,

$$C_2H_5OH < O(C_2H_5)$$

G. HF has greater extent of H—bonding.

43. ***(b)*** A. Ease of hydrolysis increases as $Al^{3+} > Be^{2+}$ and $FeCl_3 > FeCl_2$.

B. Intensity of colour increases as $HgI_2 > AgI > AgBr$.

C. Thermal stability of carbonates decreases as

$$BeCO_3 < MgCO_3 < CaCO_3 < SrCO_3 < BaCO_3$$

D. Basic nature of oxides decreases as

$$K_2O > Na_2O > Cu_2O > Ag_2O$$

E. Stability of higher halides decreases as

$$PbI_4 < PbBr_4 < PbCl_4$$

F. Complex forming tendency increases as

$$Li^+ > Na^+ > K^+ \text{ and } Be^{2+} > Mg^{2+} > Ca^{2+}$$

G. Solubility in organic solvent increases as

$$CuBr < AgBr < AuBr.$$

44. ***(c)*** CO_2 and XeF_4 are non-polar rest all are polar.

45. ***(b)*** In the molecular species from B_2 to N_2, *sp* mixing is observed due to which the order of the energies of the molecular orbitals is:

$$\sigma 1s^2, \sigma^* 1s^2, \sigma 2s^2, \sigma^* 2s^2, \pi 2p_x^2, \pi 2p_y^2, \sigma 2p_z$$

$\pi^* 2p_x \pi^* 2p_y, \sigma 2p_z$ thus the species having a total of 12 electrons are diamagnetic e.g., C_2 and B_2^{2-} and the species with a total of 10 electrons are paramagnetic with two unpaired electrons e.g., B_2 and C_2^{2+}. If the *sp* mixing is discarded, then the order of the energies of the molecular orbital will change to:

$$\sigma 1s^2, \sigma^* 1s^2, \sigma 2s^2, \sigma^* 2s^2, \pi 2p_z^2, \pi 2p_x^1, \sigma 2p_y^1$$

$\pi^* 2p_x, \pi^* 2p_y, \sigma 2p_z$ and the species with a total of 12 electrons will become paramagnetic with two unpaired electrons e.g., C_2 and B_2^{2-} and the species with a total of 10 electrons will become diamagnetic e.g., B_2 and C_2^{2+}. Remember no change is observed due to *sp* mixing in the species after N_2 regardless of the total number of electrons present in them.

46. ***(a)*** The polymeric species $(AlH_3)_x$, $(BeCl_2)_x$ and $(BeH_2)_x$ will have all bond lengths equal. All the bonds are bridge bonds whereas in other species two types of bonds are present i.e., the bridge bonds and the terminal bonds.

47. ***(b)*** The species in which the central atom is *sp* or sp^2 hybridised will be planar e.g, Be_2Cl_4, Be_2H_4 whereas the species having a central atom in any other hybridisation state will be non-planar since no lone pair is present on the central atom e.g., B_2H_6, $(AlH_3)_x$, Ga_2H_6 Al_2Cl_6 $(BeCl_2)_x$, $(BeH_2)_x$.

Check Through PYQs : JEE Advanced

1. ***(a, d)*** Among the given molecules only CO_2, C_2H_4, HCl and O_3 follows octet rule while NO, NO_2, BCl_3, H_2SO_4 do not follow octet rule. Thus, option with at three molecule that follow octet rule are a and *d*.

2. ***(a,c)***

(a)

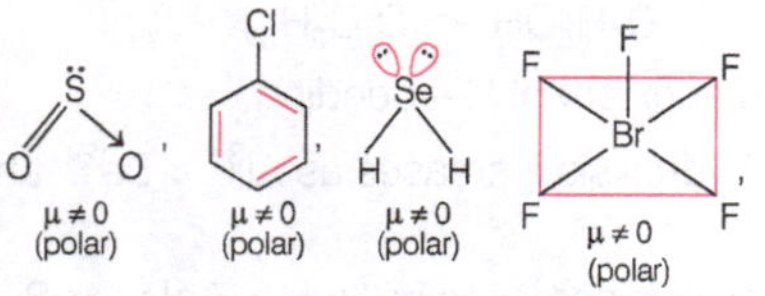

(b)

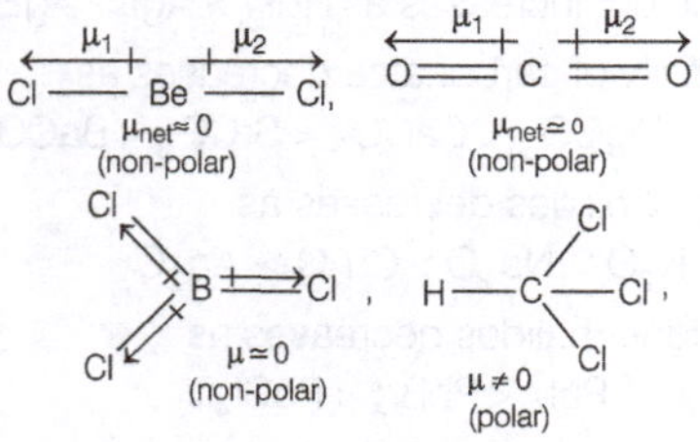

(c)

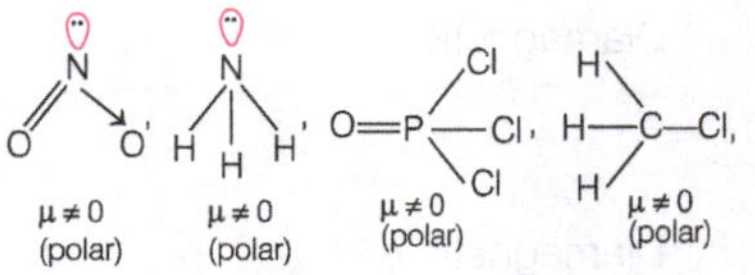

(d)

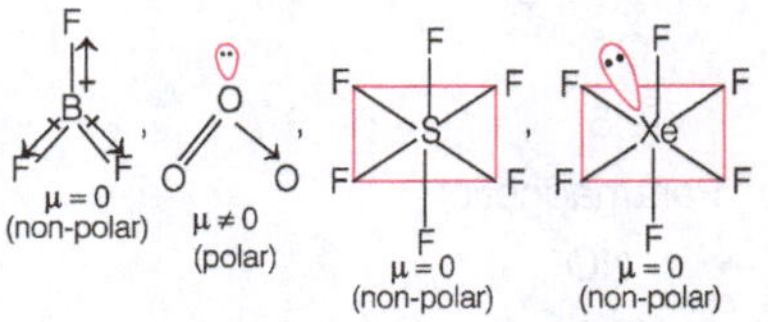

Thus, options (a, c) are correct.

3. ***(5)*** The structures of given species along with their hybridisation is given below

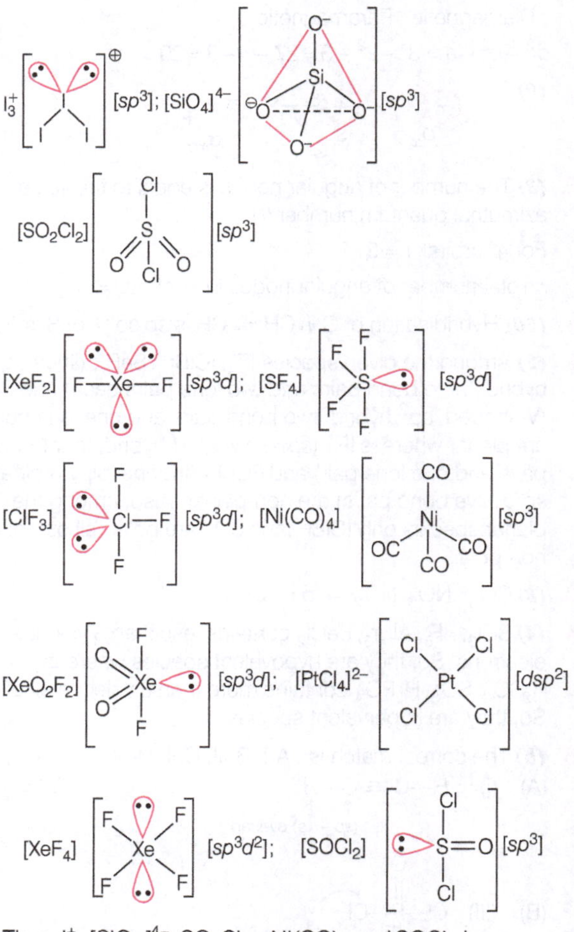

Thus, I_3^+, $[SiO_4]^{4-}$, SO_2Cl_2, $Ni(CO)_4$ and $SOCl_2$ have sp^3-hybridised central atom.

4. ***(b)*** The correct match is P—5, Q—3, R—2, S—4

XeF_2

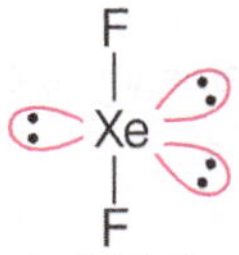

Trigonal bipyramidal and 3 *lp* of electrons

XeF_4

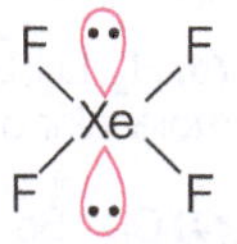

Octahedral and 2 *lp* of electrons

XeO_3

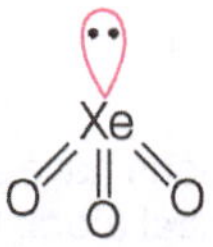

Tetrahedral and 1 *lp* of electrons

XeO_3F_2

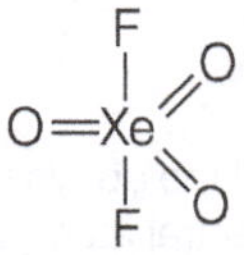

Trigonal bipyramidal and no lone pair of electrons

5. ***(c)*** Molecular orbital electronic configuration of F_2 molecule is given by $(\sigma 1s)^2(\sigma^* 1s^2)(\sigma 2s)^2(\sigma^* 2s^2)(\sigma 2p_z)^2$ $(\pi 2p_x)^2 = (\pi 2p_y)^2\ (\pi^* 2p_x^2) = (\pi^* 2p_y^2)$

Its molecular orbital diagram is given below

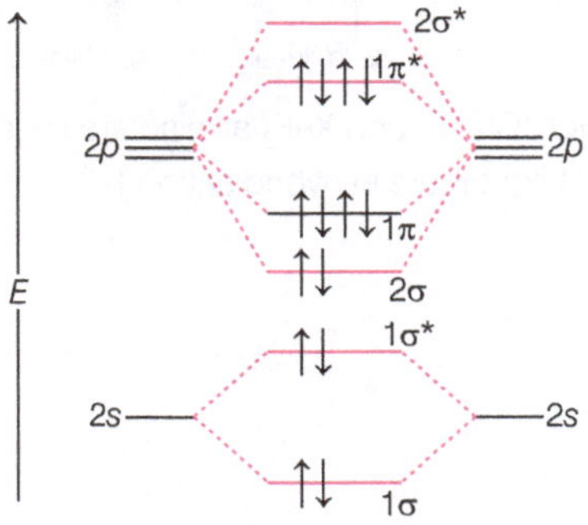

6. ***(a, d)*** Considering *Z* is molecular axis

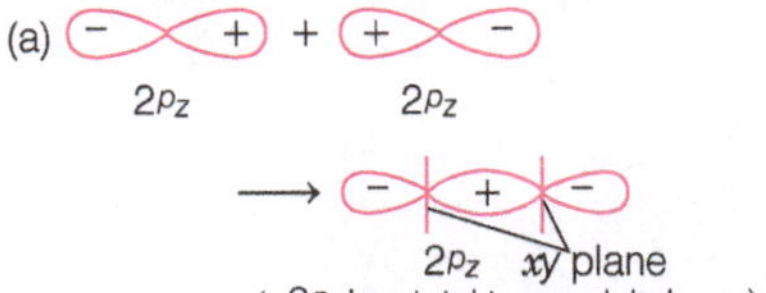

(σ2pz has total two nodal planes)

So, statement (a) is correct.

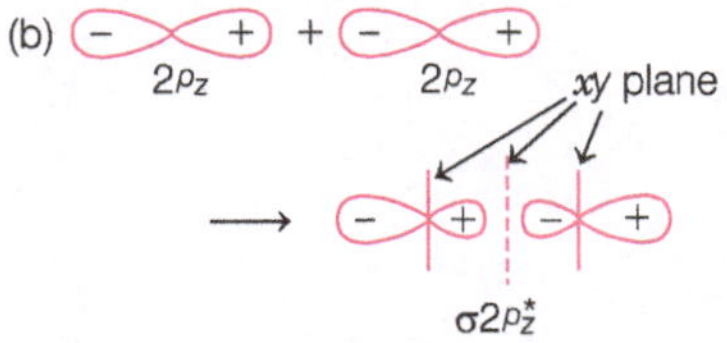

(Total 3 nodal planes.
The nodal plane between two orbitals is *xy* not *xz*.)
Since, the orbitals are along *z*-axis.

So, statement (b) is incorrect.

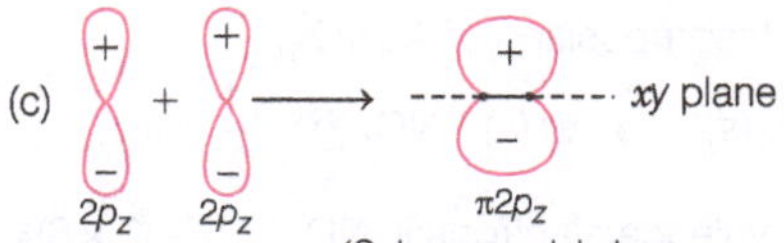

(Only one nodal plane passing through the internuclear axis and is parallel to molecular axis and not perpendicular.)

So, statement (c) is also incorrect.

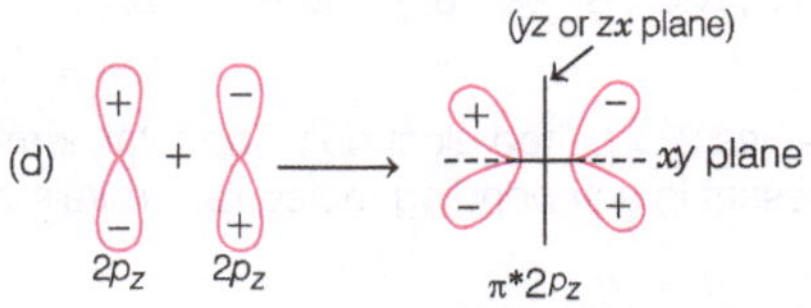

(Two nodal planes are present, one is present in the *xy*-plane.)

So, statement (d) is correct.

7. ***(a, c)***

Species	Electrons	N_B	N_A	BO	Magnetic character
C_2^{2-}	14	10	4	3	Diamagnetic
O_2^{2+}	14	10	4	3	Diamagnetic
O_2	16	10	6	2	Paramagnetic
N_2^+	13	9	4	2.5	Paramagnetic
N_2^-	15	10	5	2.5	Paramagnetic
He_2^+	3	2	1	0.5	Paramagnetic

Thus, (a, c) is correct.

(b) Bond order $O_2^{2+} > O_2$ thus,

Bond length of $O_2^{2+} < O_2$ thus, incorrect.

(c) N_2^+ and N_2^- have same bond order thus correct.

(d) He_2^+ with bond order = 0.5 is more stable thus, less energy than isolated He atoms. Thus, (d) is incorrect.

8. ***(5)*** The geometry of the given species are as follows

$[Co(CN)_4]^{4-} \rightarrow$ Tetrahedral

$[Co(CO)_3(NO)] \rightarrow$ Tetrahedral

$[XeF_4] \rightarrow$ Square planar

$[PCl_4]^+ \rightarrow$ Tetrahedral

$[PdCl_4]^{2-} \rightarrow$ Square planar

$[ICl_4]^- \rightarrow$ Square planar

$[Cu(CN)_4]^{3-} \rightarrow$ Tetrahedral

$P_4 \rightarrow$ Tetrahedral

Thus, among the given species only 5 species have tetrahedral geometry.

9. ***(6)*** On thermal decomposition of $AgNO_3$.

$$AgNO_3(s) \longrightarrow Ag(s) + NO_2(g) + \frac{1}{2}O_2(g)$$

Total number of valence electrons in $NO_2 = 5 + (2 \times 6) = 17$ electrons

Number of unpaired electrons in $NO_2 = 1$

Writing electronic configuration of O_2

$$O_2 = \sigma 1s^2, \sigma^* 1s^2, \sigma 2s^2, \sigma^* 2s^2, \sigma 2p_z^2, \pi 2p_x^2 = \pi 2p_y^2, \pi^* 2p_x^1 = \pi^* 2p_y^1.$$

So oxygen gas has 2 unpaired electrons. The total number of electrons present in anti-bonding molecular orbitals of the gas is 6.

10. ***(6)*** Only polar liquid will be attracted towards charged comb due to the formation of electrically charged droplets in the polar liquid stream, induced by a nearby charged object. Hence, liquid showing deflection are $HF, H_2O, NH_3, H_2O_2, CHCl_3, C_6H_5Cl$.

11. ***(6)***

S.N.	Species	No. of σ-bonds with central atom	No. of L.P at central atom
(i)	$[TeBr_6]^{2-}$	6	1
(ii)	$[BrF_2]^+$	2	2
(iii)	SNF_3	4	0
(iv)	$[XeF_3]^-$	3	3

Hence, the sum of the lone pairs of electrons on each central atom is 6.

12. ***(6)*** $H_2, Li_2, Be_2, C_2, N_2$ and F_2 are diamagnetic according to molecular orbital theory.

13. ***(4)***

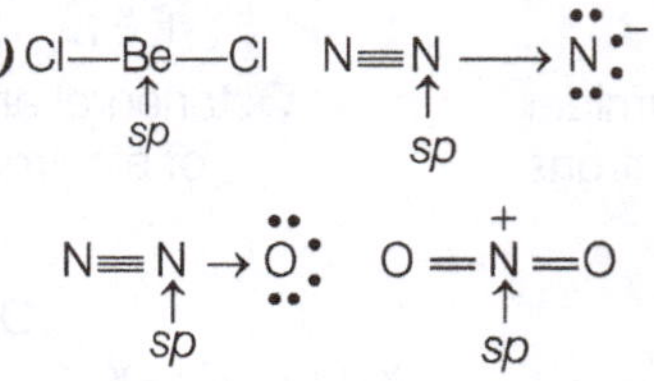

All the above mentioned molecules/ions have *sp*-hybridised central atom and no lone pair at central atom, hence linear Others are :

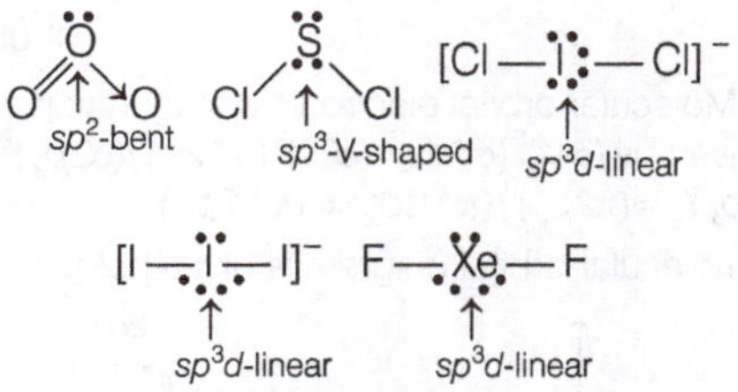

[Although ICl_2^-, I_3^- and XeF_2 all also are linear but in them *d*-orbital contribute in hybridisation.]

CHAPTER 3

Hydrogen

Trend Insights

JEE Advanced

Typology	Years				
	2024	2023	2022	2021	2020
1. One option correct	–	–	–	–	–
2. One or More than one correct	–	–	–	–	–
3. Numerical/Integer Type	–	–	–	–	–
4. Matching Type	–	–	–	–	–
5. Paragraph Based	–	–	–	–	–

E = Easy, **M** = Medium, **T** = Tough, **O** = Overall

Current Dynamics

- This chapter is present only in the syllabus of JEE Advanced.
- No direct question was visible from this chapter but the application of this chapter had been asked indirectly in question based on redox reactions that involved the properties of hydrogen.

Insightful Advice

- Students are advised to focus on the properties and preparation methods of hydrogen and hydrogen peroxide.
- Practice more on application based question of hydrogen as no direct questions are visible in recent years.

Learning Elements

Element Hydrogen and Their Compounds

Hydrogen, Dihydrogen, Different forms of Hydrogen, Isotopes of Hydrogen, Hydrides, Water, Hard and Soft Water, Heavy Water, Hydrogen Peroxide

Practice Element

Practice Element Target JEE Advanced

Element

Hydrogen and Their Compounds

Hydrogen is the lightest element and also the lightest gas in the periodic table. It is the most abundant element in the universe.

It is found in atomic form while on earth it is generally found in molecular form. It is most reactive element in atomic form but it is less reactive in molecular form.

Electronic Configuration

Hydrogen has the simplest atomic structure of all the elements. It consists of a nucleus containing one proton with a charge +1 and one orbital electron.

Its general electronic configuration is $1s^1$. Atoms of hydrogen may attain stability in three different ways :

- by forming an electron pair (covalent bond) with another atom as in H_2, H_2O, NH_3, HCl, CH_4.
- by losing an electron to form as in H_3O^+, $H_9O_4^+$ or $[H(H_2O)_n]^+$ ions.

$$H_2O + H^+ \longrightarrow H_3O^+$$

$$(H_2O)_n + H^+ \longrightarrow [H(H_2O)_n]^+$$

Free protons do not exist under normal conditions though they are found in low pressure gaseous beams (as in spectrometer).

- by gaining an electron to form H^-; crystalline solid such as LiH contains the H^- ion and are formed by highly electropositive metals.

Position of Hydrogen in the Periodic Table

Hydrogen is the first element in the periodic table. It cannot be placed in any specific group due to its property of accepting one electron (When H^- is formed) and also by losing one electron (When H^+ is formed).

Analogy of Hydrogen with Group 1 (Alkali Metal)

(i) It has one electron in its (Outer) shell- $1s^1$ like other alkali metals which have (inert gas) ns^1 configuration.

(ii) It forms monovalent H^+ ion like Li^+, Na^+ ...

(iii) Its valency is also 1.

(iv) Its oxide (H_2O) is stable as Li_2O, Na_2O.

(v) Its a good reducing agent (in atomic as well as molecular state) like Na, Li etc.

Analogy with Group 17 (Halogens)

(i) H is one electron short of duplet (stable configuration) like F, Cl, etc. which are also one electron deficient of octet, F = [He] $2s^2 2p^5$; Cl = [Ne] $3s^2 3p^5$.

(ii) It also forms anion H^- like F^-, Cl^- etc by gaining of one electron.

(iii) H^- has stable inert gas (He) configuration like halogens.

(iv) It also forms diatomic molecule (H_2) like F_2, Cl_2 etc.

(v) IE of H (1312 kJ mol^{-1}) is of the same order as that of halogens.

(vi) IE of H is very high in comparison with alkali metals. Also size of H^+ is very small compared to that of alkali metal ion. H forms stable hydride only with strongly electropositive metals due to smaller value of its electron affinity (72.8 kJ mol^{-1}).

In view of the anomalous behaviour of hydrogen, it is difficult to assign any definite position to it in the periodic table. Hence, it is customary to place it in group 1 (Along with alkali metals) as well as in group 17 (Along with halogens).

JEE Spotlite

- At very high pressure, hydrogen may behave as metal, thus it resembles more to alkali metals.
- Hydrogen forms both cation and anion, whereas alkali metals predominantly form cations and halogens primarily form anions.
- Oxides of hydrogen is amphoteric in nature whereas oxide of alkali metals are basic and oxides of halogens are acidic in nature.

Dihydrogen (H_2)

It is also known as **diprotium**. The molecules of hydrogen gas contain two hydrogen atom. This gas is highly inflammable.

Preparation of Dihydrogen

- Water is the natural abundant source for the manufacture of hydrogen.
- Reduction of water for hydrogen can be carried out chemically and electrolytically by using common reducing agents such as coke, carbon monoxide, hydrocarbons, etc.

(i) Hydrogen is manufactured by allowing steam to react with red hot coke at about 1270 K.

$$C(s) + H_2O(g) \xrightarrow{1270\text{ K}} CO(g) + H_2(g)$$

This mixture of **CO and H_2** is also known as **water gas** and the reaction is referred to as water gas shift reaction. As this mixture ($CO + H_2$) is used for the synthesis of methanol and a number of hydrocarbons., thus it is also called **synthesis gas** or ***syn* gas**.

(ii) Hydrogen is now produced by the reaction of natural gas (chiefly methane) with steam in presence of a nickel catalyst.

$$CH_4(g) + H_2O(g) \xrightarrow[1270\text{ K}]{\text{Ni catalyst}} CO(g) + 3H_2(g)$$

The production of dihydrogen can be increased by reacting carbon monoxide of syngas mixture with steam in presence of iron chromate as catalyst.

$$CO(g) + H_2O(g) \xrightarrow[673\text{ K}]{\text{Catalyst}} CO_2 + 2H_2$$

This reaction is called water gas **shift reaction.**

JEE Alert

Hydrogen and carbon dioxide can be easily separated from each other by bubbling the gas mixture through water in which CO_2 is fairly soluble and H_2 is virtually insoluble.

$$H_2O + CO_2 \longrightarrow H_2CO_3$$

(iii) At higher temperature, in the presence of catalysts (silica, alumina) hydrocarbons decompose and rearrange. These reactions are called **cracking reactions.** They are used in refining of petroleum and produce hydrogen as a by-product.

$$\underset{\text{Propane}}{2CH_3{-}CH_2{-}CH_3} \xrightarrow[\text{Catalyst}]{875\text{ K}} CH_4 + CH_2{=}CH_2 + CH_3{-}CH{=}CH_2 + H_2\uparrow$$

(iv) **Electrolysis of acidified water** using platinum electrodes. On a large scale, very pure hydrogen (> 99.95%) can be obtained from the electrolysis of aqueous solutions of barium hydroxide between nickel electrodes.

$$2H_2O \xrightarrow{\text{Current}} \underset{\text{At cathode}}{2H_2(g)} + \underset{\text{At anode}}{O_2(g)}$$

Hydrogen is economically obtained as a by-product in the electrolysis of brine solution in the manufacture of sodium hydroxide.

At Anode

During electrolysis there is a competition at the anode between the oxidation of chloride ion and the oxidation of water.

$$2Cl^-(aq) \longrightarrow Cl_2(g) + 2e^-$$

$$2H_2O(l) \longrightarrow O_2(g) + 4H^+(aq) + 4e^-$$

When a concentrated salt solution (brine) is used, the first reaction is the one that is observed.

At Cathode

Here, the reaction is the reduction of water because it is more easily reduced than Na^+

$$2H_2O(l) + 2e^- \longrightarrow H_2(g) + 2OH^-(aq)$$

Overall Reaction

$$2Cl^- + 2H_2O \longrightarrow Cl_2(g) + H_2(g) + 2OH^-$$

Water is very stable to thermal decomposition, it does not decompose to hydrogen and oxygen to any appreciable extent at practically viable temperatures.

(v) **Non-electrolytic methods of preparation of hydrogen,** e.g., thermochemical and photochemical. In thermochemical hydrogen generation, water is heated with certain chemicals to liberate hydrogen at much lower temperatures. Two potentially useful cycles are given below :

Cycle 1

I. $3FeCl_2 + 4H_2O \xrightarrow{775\text{ K}} Fe_3O_4 + 6HCl + H_2$

II. $Fe_3O_4 + \frac{3}{2}Cl_2 + 6HCl \xrightarrow{375\text{ K}} 3FeCl_3 + 3H_2O + \frac{1}{2}O_2$

III. $3FeCl_3 \xrightarrow{575\text{ K}} 3FeCl_2 + \frac{3}{2}Cl_2$

Cycle 2

I. $CaBr_2 + H_2O \xrightarrow{1025\text{ K}} CaO + 2HBr$

II. $Hg + 2HBr \xrightarrow{375\text{ K}} HgBr_2 + H_2$

III. $HgBr_2 + CaO \xrightarrow{280\text{ K}} HgO + CaBr_2$

IV. $HgO \xrightarrow{775\text{ K}} Hg + \frac{1}{2}O_2$

Thus, by repeating reactions I—III in cycle 1 or reactions I—IV in cycle 2, water can be splitting to H_2 and O_2.

Net reaction is : $H_2O \longrightarrow H_2 + \frac{1}{2}O_2$

Decomposition of water by solar energy in presence of catalyst is known as **photochemical decomposition** of water.

Physical Properties of Dihydrogen

- Some of the physical properties of hydrogen atoms are summarised below.

Relative atomic mass	1.008 g/mol
(IE), $H(g) \longrightarrow H^+(g) + e^-$	1312 kJ mol^{-1}
Electronegativity (Pauling scale)	2.20
Electron gain enthalpy	–73 kJ mol^{-1}
Melting point	13.96 K
Boiling point	20.39 K
Density	0.09 g L^{-1}
B.E. (H—H) at 298.2 K	~436 kJ mol^{-1}
Covalent radius	37 pm
van der Waals' radius	120 pm
Ionic radius (H^-)	208 pm

- At ordinary temperatures and pressures, hydrogen is a colourless, odourless and tasteless gas composed of diatomic H_2 molecules. In H_2, intermolecular forces are very weak because H_2 is a non-polar molecule that contains only two electrons.

  That's why in the solid form it has hexagonal close-packed structure. The bonding forces within the H_2 molecule are exceptionally strong and thus, it is thermally stable. Even at 2000 K, only 1 of every 2500 H_2 molecules is dissociated into H-atoms.

Chemical Properties of Dihydrogen

Dihydrogen is quite stable and dissociates into hydrogen atoms only when heated above 2000 K, due to which

$$H_2 \xrightarrow{>2000\text{ K}} H + H; \qquad \Delta H = 435.9 \text{ kJ mol}^{-1}$$

Its bonds dissociation energy is very high, due to which, it is not very reactive. However, it combines with many elements or compounds.

1. Action with Metals

To form corresponding hydrides with transition metals such as Pd, Ni, Pt etc. dihydrogen forms interstitial hydrides in which the small molecules of dihydrogen occupy the interstitial sites in the crystal lattices of these hydrides.

As a result of formation of interstitial hydrides, these metals adsorb large volume of hydrogen on their surface. This property of adsorption of a gas by a metal is called **occlusion.** The occluded hydrogen can be liberated from the metals by strong heating.

2. Reaction with Non-metals

$$2H_2 + O_2 \xrightarrow{970\text{ K}} 2H_2O; N_2 + 3H_2 \xrightarrow[750\text{ K, Pressure}]{\text{Fe, Mo}} 2NH_3$$

$$H_2 + F_2 \xrightarrow{\text{Dark}} 2HF; H_2 + Cl_2 \xrightarrow[673\text{ K, Pressure}]{\text{Sunlight}} 2HCl$$

$$H_2 + Br_2 \longrightarrow 2HBr; H_2 + I_2 \xrightarrow[\text{Pt}]{673\text{ K}} 2HI$$

The reactivity of halogen towards dihydrogen decreases as, $F_2 > Cl_2 > Br_2 > I_2$.

As a result, F_2 reacts in dark, Cl_2 in the presence of sunlight, Br_2 reacts only upon heating while the reaction with I_2 occurs in the presence of a catalyst.

3. Reaction with Unsaturated Hydrocarbons

H_2 reacts with unsaturated hydrocarbons such as ethylene and acetylene to give saturated hydrocarbons.

$$\underset{\text{Ethylene}}{H_2C{=}CH_2} + H_2 \xrightarrow[473\text{ K}]{\text{Ni or Pt or Pd}} \underset{\text{Ethane}}{CH_3{-}CH_3};$$

$$\underset{\text{Acetylene}}{HC{\equiv}CH} + 2H_2 \xrightarrow[473\text{ K}]{\text{Ni or Pt or Pd}} \underset{\text{Ethane}}{CH_3{-}CH_3}$$

This reaction is used in the hydrogenation of oils. The vegetable oils such as groundnut oil or cottonseed oil are unsaturated in nature due to presence of one double bond in their molecules.

Dihydrogen is passed through the oil at about 473 K in the presence of catalyst to form solid fats. The vegetable ghee such as Dalda are usually prepared by this process.

$$\underset{\text{(Liquid)}}{\text{Vegetable oil}} + H_2 \xrightarrow[473\text{ K}]{\text{Ni}} \underset{\text{(Solid)}}{\text{Fat}}$$

Uses

Hydrogen is used

(i) as a reducing agent.

(ii) in the hydrogenation of vegetable oils.

(iii) as a rocket fuel in the form of liquid H_2.

(iv) in the manufacture of synthetic petrol.

(v) in the preparation of many compounds such as NH_3, CH_3OH, urea etc.

(vi) it is used in the oxy-hydrogen torch for welding and works at the temperature around 2500°C. It is also used in atomic hydrogen torch for welding purposes in which temperature of the order of 4000°C is required.

Different forms of Hydrogen

Following are the different forms of hydrogen.

Atomic Hydrogen

- It is obtained by the dissociation of hydrogen molecules. The atomic hydrogen is stable only for the fraction of a second and is extremely reactive.
- It is obtained by passing dihydrogen gas at atmospheric pressure through an electric arc between two tungsten rods.

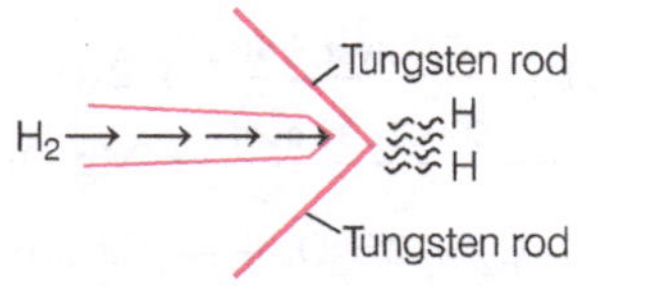

Atomic hydrogen torch

- The electric arc maintains a temperature around 4000-4500°C. As the molecules of dihydrogen gas pass through the electric arc, these absorb energy and get dissociated into atoms as

$$H_2(g) \xrightarrow[\text{arc}]{\text{Electric}} 2H(g)$$

$$\Delta H = 435.90 \text{ kJ mol}^{-1}$$

This arrangement is also called **atomic hydrogen torch.**

Nascent Hydrogen

- The hydrogen prepared in the reaction mixture is in contact with the substance with which it has to react, is called nascent hydrogen.
- It is more reactive than ordinary hydrogen. For example, if ordinary hydrogen is passed through acidified $KMnO_4$ (pink in colour), its colour is not discharged.

$$KMnO_4 + \underset{\text{Molecular}}{H_2} + H_2SO_4 \longrightarrow \text{No reaction;}$$

- On the other hand, if zinc pieces are added to the same solution, bubbles of hydrogen rise through the solution and the colour is discharged due to the reduction of $KMnO_4$ by nascent hydrogen.

$$Zn + H_2SO_4 \longrightarrow ZnSO_4 + \underset{\text{Nascent hydrogen}}{2[H]}$$

$$2KMnO_4 + 3H_2SO_4 + 10[H] \longrightarrow K_2SO_4 + 2MnSO_4 + 8H_2O$$

ortho and *para* Hydrogen

A molecule of dihydrogen contains two atoms. The nuclei of both the atoms in each molecule of dihydrogen are spinning. Depending upon the direction of the spin of the nuclei, the hydrogen is of two types,

i.e., *ortho* hydrogen and *para* hydrogen. So let us visualise this with the help of concept visualiser.

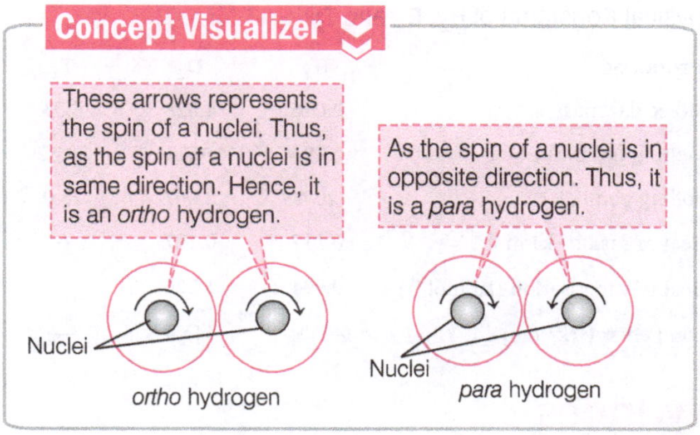

Ordinary dihydrogen is an equilibrium mixture of *ortho* and *para* hydrogen. The amount of *ortho* and *para* hydrogen varies with temperature as,

(i) At 0 K, only *para* hydrogen is present which is more stable.

(ii) At the temperature of liquefaction of air, the ratio of *ortho* and *para* hydrogen is 1 : 1.

(iii) At the room temperature, the ratio of *ortho* to *para* hydrogen is 3 : 1.

(iv) Even at very high temperature, the ratio of *ortho* to *para* hydrogen can never be more than 3 : 1.

Thus, it is possible to get pure *para* hydrogen by cooling ordinary hydrogen gas to a very low temperature (close to 20 K) but it is never possible to get a sample of hydrogen containing more than 75% of *ortho* hydrogen. i.e., Pure *ortho* hydrogen cannot be obtained.

Isotopes of Hydrogen

Isotopes are the different forms of the same element which have the same atomic number but different mass numbers.

Isotopes of Hydrogen

Name	Protium	Deuterium	Tritium
Symbol	${}_1^1H$ or H	${}_1^2H$ or D	${}_1^3H$ or T
Atomic number	1	1	1
Mass number	1	2	3
Relative abundance	99.985%	0.015%	10^{-15} %
Nature (radioactive or non-radioactive)	Non-radioactive	Non-radioactive	Radioactive

- Protium and deuterium are stable isotopes of hydrogen but tritium is radioactive isotope.
- Tritium can be easily incorporated into biological molecules because it behaves chemically, just like ordinary hydrogen, The radiation that tritium gives off within an organism, as a result of its decay, can cause many diseases such as cancer.
- Tritium is non-toxic, except when inhaled in large quantities.
- Tritium is also known as **β-emitter**. Its half-life is 12.4 years.

Physical Constants of H_2, D_2 and T_2

Property	H_2	D_2	T_2
Molecular mass	2.016	4.028	6.03
Melting point (K)	13.96	18.73	20.62
Boiling point (K)	20.4	23.67	25.0
Heat of fusion (kJ mol^{-1})	0.117	0.197	—
Heat of vaporisation (kJ mol^{-1})	0.904	1.226	—
Bond energy (kJ mol^{-1})	435.9	443.4	—

Hydrides

Binary compounds of the elements (metal or non-metal) with hydrogen are called hydrides. The type of hydride which an element forms depends on its electronegativity and hence the type of bond formed. They are classified into following hydrides

- ionic or salt like hydride
- covalent or molecular hydride
- metallic or interstitial hydride

Ionic or Saline Hydrides

- They are formed when molecular hydrogen combines directly with any alkali metal or with the alkaline earth metals Ca, Sr or Ba (electropositive metal).

$$2Li(s) + H_2(g) \xrightarrow{973\ K} 2LiH(s)$$

$$Ca(s) + H_2(g) \xrightarrow{973\ K} CaH_2(s)$$

- **Ionic hydrides** are solids and they have the high melting point also conduct electricity in fused state liberating H_2 at the anode. Anion of these hydrides is H^- which is a very strong **Bronsted base.**
- Due to their high reactivity with water, ionic hydrides are used to remove traces of water from organic solvents.
- They are powerful reducing agent specially at higher temperature, e.g.,

$$2CO + NaH \longrightarrow HCOONa + C$$

$$SiCl_4 + 4NaH \longrightarrow SiH_4 + 4NaCl$$

$$PbSO_4 + 2CaH_2 \longrightarrow PbS + 2Ca(OH)_2$$

JEE Spotlite

Li^+H^- and Na^+H^- are used in making valuable reducing agents like lithium aluminium hydride ($LiAlH_4$) and sodium borohydride ($NaBH_4$). These complex hydrides are frequently used in the reduction of aldehydes, ketones, organic acids and their derivatives to give alcohols.

$$\underset{\text{Organic acid}}{R—COOH} \xrightarrow{LiAlH_4/NaBH_4} \underset{\text{Primary alcohol}}{R—CH_2OH}$$

$$\underset{\text{Ketone/Aldehyde}}{>C=O} \xrightarrow{LiAlH_4/NaBH_4} \underset{\text{Secondary alcohol}}{>CH—OH}$$

Covalent or Molecular Hydride

- These are formed by elements of comparatively higher electronegativity. The bonds in this class of hydrides are mostly covalent in character but in some cases, for example, in HF, the bond may be partially ionic.
- The covalent hydrides can be prepared either by direct reaction of non-metals with hydrogen under suitable conditions or by the reaction of H_2O or acids on nitrides, carbides, borides, silicides, stannides of alkali and alkaline earth metals or by the reduction of halides. These are illustrated by the following reactions :

$$N_2 + 3H_2 \xrightarrow[600–1000\ atm]{Catalyst,\ 750\ K} 2NH_3$$

$$Mg_3N_2 + 6H_2O \longrightarrow Mg(OH)_2 + 2NH_3$$

$$CaC_2 + 2H_2O \longrightarrow Ca(OH)_2 + C_2H_2$$

$$AsCl_3 + 6H \xrightarrow{Zn + HCl} 4AsH_3 + 3HCl$$

$$4PCl_3 + 3LiAlH_4 \xrightarrow{Ether} 4PH_3 + 3LiCl + 3AlCl_3$$

- These hydrides have a molecular lattice made up of individual saturated covalent molecules, with only weak van der Waals' forces and in some cases hydrogen bonds holding the molecules together. This accounts for their softness, low melting and boiling points, their volatility and lack of conductivity. Some covalent hydrides are unstable in the presence of air, e.g., stannane, SnH_4.

These hydrides are further classified according to the relative number of electrons.

- **Electron Deficient Hydrides** These have few electrons in their conventional Lewis structure. Thus, they acts as Lewis acids i.e. electron acceptors. Elements of group-13 form such compounds e.g. B_2H_6
- **Electron Precise Hydrides** These have required number of electrons in their conventional Lewis strucures. Elements of group-14 elements such compounds e.g. CH_4.
- **Electron Rich Hydrides** These have excess of electrons which are present as lone pairs. These hydrides are usually formed by group. 15-17 element e.g. NH_3, H_2O. They behaves as Lewis bases i.e. electron donors.

Metallic or Non-stoichiometric or Interstitial Hydrides

- On heating, hydrogen reacts with many transition metals, lanthanides and actinides to form metallic hydrides.
- Most of these have metallic appearance and are less dense than the parent metal. These hydrides generally have properties similar to those of the parent metals, they are hard, have a metallic luster, conduct electricity.
- Unlike the saline hydrides, they are almost always non-stoichiometric, being deficient in hydrogen.
- For example, $TiH_{1.5-1.8}$, $VH_{1.6}$, $CH_{1.7}$, $NiH_{0.6-0.7}$, $PdH_{0.6-0.8}$, $TaH_{2.76}$, $LaH_{2.87}$, $YbH_{2.55}$, etc., approach the stoichiometric formulae given in following Table.

Stoichiometric Formulae of Some Metallic Hydrides

MH	MH (M = V, Cr, Ni, Cu, Pd)
MH_2	(M = Ti, Zr, Hf, V, Nb, Cr, Zn, Y; La-Lu except Pm; Th, Np, Pu, Am, Cm)
MH_3	(M = Y, La, La-Lu except Pm and Eu; Pa, U, Np, Pu, Am)

- Most of these hydrides are stable to water up to 375 K but are quantitatively decomposed by acids and show reducing properties. Formerly, these hydrides were termed as interstitial compounds in which hydrogen was thought to be accommodated in the interstices of the metal lattice producing distortion but no change in its type.

  But recent studies have shown that except for the hydrides of nickel, palladium, cerium and actinium, other hydrides of this class have lattice of a type different from that of the parent metal.

JEE Alert

Hydrides of Eu and Yb are ionic in nature.

Properties of Hydrides

- The physical and chemical properties of these compounds change from ionic to covalent across a given period (on moving from left to right).

LiH — Ionic high m.p. (950 K)
BeH_2 — Covalent polymeric in solid state
B_2H_6 CH_4 — Non-polar
NH_3 H_2O HF — Polar with H atom as positive end of the polar bond
HF — Acidic in nature

- As we move down any group, the compounds change from covalent to ionic.
- The ΔH_f° values shows that the energetic stability of the covalent hydrides tends to increase on passing from left to right across a period, and it decreases on moving down any group.

BeH_2, MgH_2, CaH_2, SrH_2, BaH_2 (Covalent ↑, Ionic ↓)

- The main reason for this is the change in the strength of the X—H bond.
- The attraction of an atom for a shared pair of electrons increases across a period as nuclear charge increases and atomic radius falls, but decreases down the group as both atomic size and the number of inner screening electrons increases.
- Although all CH_4, NH_3, H_2O and HF are described as covalent, the bonds are polar to some extent. **The degree of this polarity depends upon the electronegativity difference between the two elements concerned.**
- In the case of the Group 14 hydrides, this bond polarity does not result in a polar molecule. In the tetrahedral XH_4 molecule, there is no overall dipole moment as the centre of the δ^+ charges coincides with the centre of the δ^- charge, for example methane.
- As they have no overall dipole, **the only forces of attraction between XH_4 molecules are relatively weak van der Waals' forces due to temporary dipoles.** Since, these forces result from mutual repulsion of the electron clouds of neighbouring molecules, they increase as the size of the molecule increases, thus, accounting for the steady increase in the boiling point of the hydrides on passing down the group 14.

Water

It is a crucial compound for the survival of all life forms.

Structure

- Due to the presence of lone pairs, the geometry of water is distorted and the H—O—H bond angle is 104.5°, which is less than the normal tetrahedral angle (109.5°).
- The geometry of the molecule is regarded as angular or bent.
- In water, each O—H bond is polar because of the high electronegativity of oxygen (3.5) in comparison to that of hydrogen (2.1).
- The resultant dipole moment of water molecule is 1.84D.
- **In ice,** each oxygen atom is tetrahedrally surrounded by four hydrogen atoms; **two by covalent bonds and two by hydrogen bonds.**

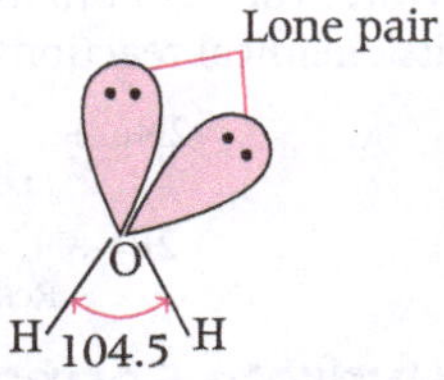

- The resulting structure of ice is open structure having a number of vacant spaces.
- Therefore, the density of ice is less than that of water and ice floats over water. It may be noted that water has maximum density (1 g cm^{-3}) at 4°C.

Physical Properties of Water

It is colourless, odourless and tasteless liquid at ordinary temperature.

Some physical constant of H_2O and D_2O at 298 K

Constant	Ordinary Water H_2O	Heavy water D_2O
Molecular mass (g/mol^{-1})	18.0151	20.0276
Density 298 K (g cm^{-3})	0.997	1.106
Melting point (K)	273.0	276.8
Boiling point (K)	373.0	374.4
Heat of fusion (kJ mol^{-1}) at 273 K	6.01	—
Heat of vaporisation (kJ mol^{-1}) at 373 K	40.66	41.61
Heat of formation (kJ mol^{-1})	−285.9	−294.6

Chemical Properties

Water shows a versatile chemical behaviour. It behaves as an acid, a base, an oxidant, a reductant and as ligand.

1. Dissociation of Water

Water is quite stable and does not dissociate into its elements even at high temperatures. Pure water has a small but measurable electrical conductivity and it dissociates as,

$$H_2O + H_2O \rightleftharpoons \underset{\text{Hydronium ion}}{H_3O^+} + OH^-$$

2. Amphoteric Nature

Water can act both as an acid and as a base and is said to be amphoteric. However, water is neutral towards litmus and its pH is 7. In the Bronsted sense, it acts as an acid with NH_3 and a base with H_2S.

$$H_2O(l) + NH_3(aq) \rightleftharpoons OH^-(aq) + NH_4^+(aq)$$

$$H_2O(l) + H_2S(aq) \rightleftharpoons H_3O^+(aq) + HS^-(aq)$$

The self ionisation of water occurs as follows

$$\underset{\text{Acid}}{H_2O(l)} + \underset{\text{Base}}{H_2O^+(l)} \longrightarrow \underset{\text{Conjugate base}}{H_3O(aq)} + \underset{\text{Conjugate base}}{OH^-(aq)}$$

3. Oxidising and Reducing Nature

Water can act both as an oxidising and a reducing agent in its chemical reactions. e.g.

$$2Na + \underset{\text{Oxidising agent}}{2H_2O} \longrightarrow 2NaOH + H_2;$$

$$2F_2 + \underset{\text{Reducing agent}}{2H_2O} \longrightarrow 4HF + O_2$$

Hydrate Formation

Reaction of water, with salts during the process of crystallisation leds to formation of hydrates. Such as association of water can be classified into different types. For example,

- Coordinated water, example $[Fe(OH_2)_6]^{3+}3Cl^-$
- Interstial water, example $BaCl_2 \cdot 2H_2O$
- Hydrogen bonded water, example $[Cu(H_2O)_4]^{2+}SO_4^{2-} \cdot H_2O$ in $CuSO_4 \cdot 5H_2O$

Hydrolysis Reaction

Water with a high dielectric constant has a very strong hydrating tendency. Hydrolysis of ionic and covalent both compound occurs in water due to high affinity for oxygen.

- $CaO(s) + H_2O(l) \longrightarrow Ca(OH)_2(aq)$
- $P_4O_{10}(s) + 6H_2O\ (l) \longrightarrow 4H_3PO_4(aq)$

Hard and Soft Water

Water which produces lather with soap solution readily is called **soft water**. e.g. distilled water, rain water and demineralised water.

Water which does not produce lather with soap solution readily is called **hard water**. e.g. sea water, river water, well water and tap water.

Cause of Hardness of Water

The hardness of water is due to the presence of bicarbonates, chlorides and sulphates of calcium and magnesium.

Hard water does not produce lather because the cations (Ca^{2+} and Mg^{2+}) present in hard water react with soap to form insoluble precipitates,

$$\underset{\text{From hard water}}{M^{2+}} + \underset{\text{Sodium stearate (Soap)}}{2C_{17}H_{35}COONa} \longrightarrow \underset{\text{Metal stearate (ppt.)}}{(C_{17}H_{35}COO)_2M} + 2Na^+,$$

Where $M = Ca$ or Mg

Therefore, no lather is produced until all the calcium and magnesium ions are precipitated. This also results into wastage a lot of soap.

Type of Hardness of Water

It is of two types,

(i) **Temporary Hardness** This is due to the presence of bicarbonates of calcium and magnesium. It is also called carbonate hardness.

(ii) **Permanent Hardness** This is due to the presence of chlorides and sulphates of calcium and magnesium. It is also called non-carbonate hardness.

Softening of Water

The process of the removal of hardness from water is called softening of water.

- **Removal of Temporary Hardness** It can be removed by the following methods,

(i) **By Boiling** During boiling, the bicarbonates of Ca decompose to give $CaCO_3$. While bicarbonate of Mg gives $Mg(OH)_2$. It is because of the high solubility product of $Mg(OH)_2$ as compared of $MgCO_3$, that $Mg(OH)_2$ is precipitated. This insoluble precipitates can be removed by filtration.

$$\underset{\text{Calcium bicarbonate}}{Ca(HCO_3)_2} \xrightarrow{\text{Heat}} \underset{\text{ppt.}}{CaCO_3} + CO_2\uparrow + H_2O;$$

$$\underset{\text{Magnesium bicarbonate}}{Mg(HCO_3)_2} \xrightarrow{\text{Heat}} Mg(OH)_2\downarrow + 2CO_2\uparrow + H_2O$$

(ii) **Clark's Method** This process is used on a commercial scale. In this process, calculated amount of lime $[Ca(OH)_2]$ is added to temporary hard water.

It precipitates out calcium carbonate and magnesium hydroxide which can be filtered off.

$$\underset{\text{Soluble}}{Ca(HCO_3)_2} + \underset{\text{Lime}}{Ca(OH)_2} \longrightarrow \underset{\text{Insoluble}}{2CaCO_3\downarrow} + 2H_2O$$

$$\underset{\text{Soluble}}{Mg(HCO_3)_2} + \underset{\text{Lime}}{2Ca(OH_2)} \longrightarrow \underset{\text{Insoluble}}{Mg(OH)_2\downarrow + 2CaCO_3\downarrow} + 2H_2O$$

- **Removal of Permanent Hardness** Permanent hardness can be removed by the following methods,

(i) **By Washing Soda Method** In this method, water is treated with a calculated amount of washing soda (Na_2CO_3) which converts the chlorides and sulphates of Ca and Mg into their respective carbonates which get precipitated.

$$CaCl_2 + Na_2CO_3 \longrightarrow \underset{\text{ppt.}}{CaCO_3\downarrow} + 2NaCl;$$

$$MgCl_2 + Na_2CO_3 \longrightarrow MgCO_3\downarrow + 2NaCl$$

$$CaSO_4 + Na_2CO_3 \longrightarrow CaCO_3\downarrow + Na_2SO_4$$

$$MgSO_4 + Na_2CO_3 \longrightarrow \underset{\text{ppt.}}{MgCO_3\downarrow} + Na_2SO_4$$

(ii) **Ion-exchange Method** This is a modern method employed for the softening of hard water by using hydrated sodium aluminium silicate ($Na_2Al_2Si_2O_8 \cdot xH_2O$) which is also called permutit or zeolites.

The permutit is loosely packed in a big tank over a layer of coarse sand. Hard water is introduced into the tank from the top. Water reaches the bottom of the tank and then slowly rises through the permutit layer in the tank. The cations present in hard water are exchanged for sodium ions. Therefore, this method is also called ion exchange method.

$$2NaZ(s) + M^{2+}(aq) \longrightarrow MZ_2(s) + 2Na^+(aq)$$

(where, $Z = Al_2Si_2O_8 \cdot xH_2O$ and $M = Mg, Ca$)

Concept Visualizer

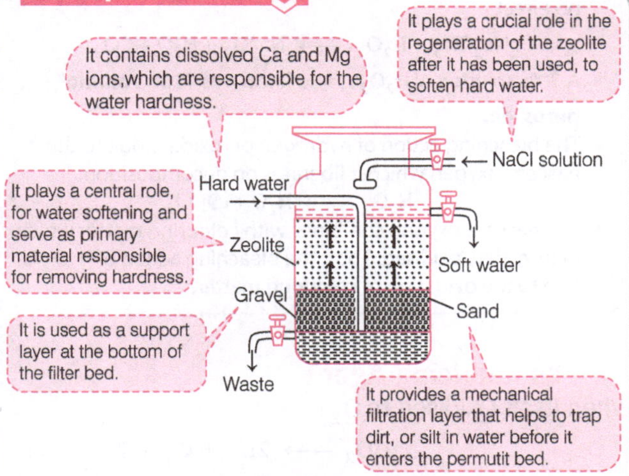

Ion-Exchange Method : used for softening of hard water

Heavy Water

Chemically heavy water is deuterium oxide (D_2O). It was discovered by Urey. It is used in nuclear reactors as a moderator because it slows down the fast moving neutrons and therefore, helps in controlling the nuclear fission process.

Preparation

Heavy water (D_2O) is obtained mainly by the multistage electrolysis of ordinary water as shown by Washburn and Urey. It is also obtained by fractional distillation of ordinary water or by fractional freezing.

Physical Properties

Heavy water is a colourless, odourless and tasteless mobile liquid. Nearly all the physical constants are higher for heavy water than the corresponding values for ordinary water see table given under physical properties of H_2O comparing H_2O abd D_2O physical properties

Chemical Properties

It gives all the reactions that are given by ordinary water but with a slower rate. This is called **isotopic effect.** e.g.

$$2Na + 2D_2O \longrightarrow 2NaOD + D_2\uparrow$$

$$SO_2 + D_2O \longrightarrow D_2SO_3$$

$$CaC_2 + 2D_2O \longrightarrow Ca(OD)_2 + C_2D_2$$

It also reacts with a number of compounds containing labile hydrogen atoms, where H-atom is partially or completely replaced by D-atom as,

$$NaOH + D_2O \rightleftharpoons NaOD + HOD$$

$$HCl(aq) + D_2O \rightleftharpoons DCl + HOD$$

$$NH_4Cl + 4D_2O \rightleftharpoons ND_4Cl + 4HOD$$

$$Na_2O + D_2O \longrightarrow 2NaOD$$

$$P_4O_{10} + 6\,D_2O \longrightarrow 4D_3PO_4$$

Electrolysis

On electrolysis, D_2O+ gives following reaction,

$$2D_2O \xrightarrow{\text{Electrolysis}} \underset{\text{(At cathode)}}{2D_2} + \underset{\text{(At anode)}}{O_2}$$

Deuterolysis

As water does hydrolysis, heavy water undergoes deuterolysis.

$$AlCl_3 + 3D_2O \longrightarrow Al(OD)_3 + 3DCl$$

$$SiCl_4 + 4D_2O \longrightarrow D_4SiO_4 + 4DCl$$

(If the compound contains ionic (polar) hydrogen atoms, the exchange reactions take place more readily in comparison to compounds containing non-ionic hydrogen).

Deutero-hydrate

Heavy water like ordinary water may be associated with salts as water of crystallisation, giving deutero-hydrate, e.g. $Na_2SO_4 \cdot 10D_2O, CuSO_4 \cdot 5D_2O, MgSO_4 \cdot 7H_2O$, etc.

Biological and Physiological Effects

- Heavy water of high concentration retards the growth of plants and animals.
- Pure heavy water kills small fishes, tadpoles and mice, when fed on with H_2O.
- Heavy water has germicide and bactericide properties.

- Water containing small quantity of D_2O acts as a tonic and stimulates vegetable growth.

Uses

It is used

- as a moderator in nuclear reactors, in the study of mechanisms of chemical reactions involving hydrogen and its compounds etc.
- for the preparation of deuterium.

Hydrogen Peroxide

It is the simplest compound containing an oxygen-oxygen single bond. It is considered as highly reactive oxygen species due to its strong oxidising properties.

Preparation

(i) Hydrogen peroxide is prepared by acidifying barium peroxide and removing excess water by evaporation under reduced pressure.

$$\underset{\text{Barium peroxide}}{BaO_2 \cdot 8H_2O(s)} + H_2SO_4(aq) \longrightarrow BaSO_4(s) + H_2O_2(aq) + 8H_2O(l)$$

(ii) Electrolytic oxidation of acidified sulphate solution at high current density yields peroxodisulphate which on hydrolysis yields hydrogen peroxide.

$$2HSO_4^-(aq) \xrightarrow{\text{Electrolysis}} HO_3SOO\,SO_3H(aq)$$

$$\downarrow \text{Hydrolysis}$$

$$2HSO_4^-(aq) + 2H^+(aq) + H_2O_2(aq)$$

(iii) Industrially it is obtained by a **cyclic process**. 2-ethyl anthraquinol (A) is oxidised by air to 2-ethyl anthraquinone (B) and H_2O_2: (B) is reduced back to (A) with H_2 at a moderate temperature using Pt, Pd or Raney Ni as a catalyst. The cycle is repeated.

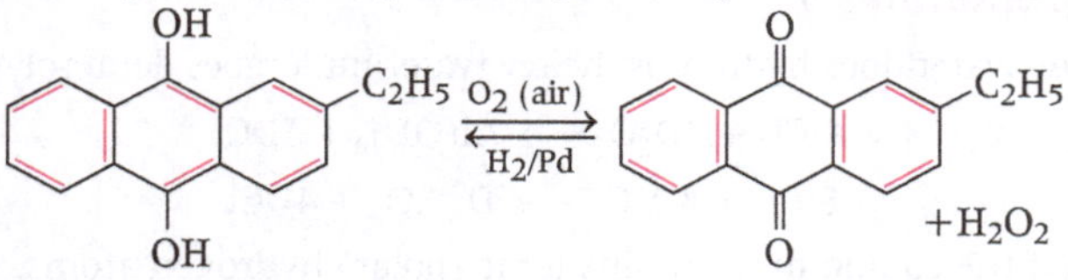

- The reaction is carried out in a mixture of organic solvents which must
  - dissolve both (A) and (B).
  - resist oxidation.
  - be immiscible with water.
- Solvent is generally a mixture of ester and hydrocarbon or octanol and methyl naphthalene.
- In this case, H_2O_2 is extracted with water as a 1% solution. This is concentrated under reduced pressure.

Storage

It is decomposes on the exposure of light to give H_2O and O_2. Thus, H_2O_2 solutions are stored in plastic or wax coated glass vessels, often with negative catalysts **such as urea or sodium stannate added as stabilisers.**

Physical Properties

Pure H_2O_2 is a colourless liquid which resembles water quite closely. It is more hydrogen bonded than water so has a higher boiling point and is more denser than H_2O.

Property	H_2O_2	H_2O
Boiling point	423 K	373 K
Melting point	272.4 K	273 K
Density	1.44 g cm^{-3}	1.0 g cm^{-3}

Chemical Properties

Following are the chemical properties of H_2O_2.

Acidic Nature

Pure H_2O_2 is a weak dibasic acid. The ionisation constant of hydrogen peroxide in aqueous solution at 20°C for the acid equilibrium is

$$H_2O_2 \rightleftharpoons H^+ + HO_2^-$$

$$K_a = \frac{[H^+][HO_2^-]}{[H_2O_2]} = 2 \times 10^{-12}$$

In alkaline medium, therefore, it is present as the HO_2^- ion.

JEE Spotlite

- H_2O_2 decomposes carbonates to give CO_2 and thus behaves as an acid. It turns blue litmus red but aqueous solutions has no effect.

$$Na_2CO_3 + H_2O_2 \longrightarrow Na_2O_2 + H_2O + CO_2$$

- A 30% solution of H_2O_2 is also known as **"100 volume" peroxide.**
- The bleaching action of hydrogen peroxide is due to the nascent oxygen which it liberates on decomposition.

$$H_2O_2 \longrightarrow H_2O + [O]$$

- The nascent oxygen combines with colouring matter which in turn, gets oxidised. Thus, the bleaching action of H_2O_2 is due to the oxidation of colouring matter.

H_2O_2 as Reducing Agent

(When Itself Oxidised to O_2)

$$H_2O_2 \longrightarrow 2H^+ + O_2 + 2e^-$$

$$2MnO_4^- + 5H_2O_2 + 6H^+ \longrightarrow 2Mn^{2+} + 5O_2 + 8H_2O$$

$$IO_4^- + H_2O_2 \longrightarrow IO_3^- + O_2 + H_2O$$

$$2Ce^{4+} + H_2O_2 \longrightarrow 2Ce^{3+} + O_2 + 2H^+$$

$$Ag_2O + H_2O_2 \longrightarrow 2Ag + H_2O + O_2$$

$$PbO_2 + H_2O_2 \longrightarrow PbO + H_2O + O_2$$

$$O_3 + H_2O_2 \longrightarrow 2O_2 + H_2O$$

$$Au_2O + H_2O_2 \longrightarrow 2Au + H_2O + O_2$$

$$MnO_2 + H_2O_2 + 2H^+ \longrightarrow Mn^{2+} + O_2 + 2H_2O$$

$$[Fe^{III}(CN)_6]^{3-} + H_2O_2 + 2OH^- \longrightarrow [Fe^{II}(CN)_6]^{4-} + 2H_2O + O_2$$

$$2MnO_4^- + 3H_2O_2 \longrightarrow 2MnO_2\downarrow + 3O_2 + 2H_2O + 2OH^-$$

H_2O_2 as an Oxidising Agent

(When Itself Reduced to H_2O)

$$H_2O_2 \longrightarrow H_2O + O$$

$$H_2O_2 + 2H^+ + 2e^- \longrightarrow 2H_2O$$

and at $[H^+] = 1$ M, $E° = +1.77$ V

hence, it is a strong oxidising agent.

- Its bleaching action is also due to its oxidising property. Oil paintings contain Pb^{2+} salts which are blackened by atmospheric H_2S (due to PbS). PbS (black), on reaction with H_2O_2, changes to $PbSO_4$ (white). Hence H_2O_2 is used to clean oil paintings.

JEE MAPPER

Example Similar to PYQ Asked in JEE Advanced 2014

Hydrogen peroxide on reaction with acidified $FeSO_4$ and $KMnO_4$ act as a

(a) oxidising agent, reducing agent
(b) oxidising agent, oxidising agent
(c) reducing agent, oxidising agent
(d) reducing agent, reducing agent

Sol. (a) Reaction of H_2O_2 with $FeSO_4$

$$2\overset{+2}{Fe}SO_4 + H_2SO_4 + H_2O_2 \longrightarrow Fe_2^{+3}(SO_4)_3 + 2H_2O$$

H_2O_2 oxidises acidified ferrous sulphate to ferric sulphate. So, it acts as an oxidising agent.

Reaction of H_2O_2 with $KMnO_4$

$$2K\overset{+7}{Mn}O_4 + 3H_2SO_4 + 5H_2O_2 \longrightarrow K_2SO_4 + 2\overset{+2}{Mn}SO_4 + 8H_2O + 5O_2$$

H_2O_2 reduces acidified potassium permanganate solution. As a result of this reaction, the pink of $KMnO_4$ solution is discharged. So, here H_2O_2 act as a reducing agent.

Competency Enhancer 1.1

Hydrogen peroxide in its reaction with $MnSO_4$ and NaOBr in alkaline medium behaves as a

(a) reducing agent, reducing agent
(b) oxidising agent, oxidising agent
(c) oxidising agent, reducing agent
(d) reducing agent, oxidising agent

Reaction with Caro's Acid

H_2SO_5 when warmed with H_2O_2, loses O_2 and is converted to H_2SO_4.

$$H_2SO_5 + H_2O_2 \xrightarrow{\Delta} H_2SO_4 + H_2O + O_2\uparrow$$

Reaction with Sulphur Trioxide (SO_3)

SO_3 on rection with anhydrous H_2O_2 gives Caro's acid.

$$H_2O_2 + SO_3 \longrightarrow H_2SO_5$$

Reaction with Alkenes

H_2O_2 reacts with alkenes to form glycols.

$$H_2C{=}CH_2 + H_2O_2 \longrightarrow \underset{OH}{H_2C}{-}\underset{OH}{CH_2}$$

Stability

- H_2O_2 is unstable and the rate at which it disproportionates, depends on the temperature and concentration. Many impurities catalyse the decomposition, which may become very violent, especially with concentrated solutions.

$$2H_2O_2 \longrightarrow 2H_2O + O_2$$

(Reduction: $H_2O_2 \rightarrow H_2O$; Oxidation: $H_2O_2 \rightarrow O_2$)

Catalysts include metal ions Fe^{2+}, Fe^{3+}, Cu^{2+}, Ni^{2+}, metal surfaces such as Pt or Ag, MnO_2, charcoal or alkali. They are best stored in polythene bottles in a refrigerator. Traces of complexing agents (e.g., 8-hydroquinoline)or adsorbing material (e.g., sodium stannate) are often added as stabilisers.

Structure

It has a non-planar and non-linear structure. In gas phase structure the dihedral angle is 111.5° and in solid phase it is 90.2° (at 110 K).

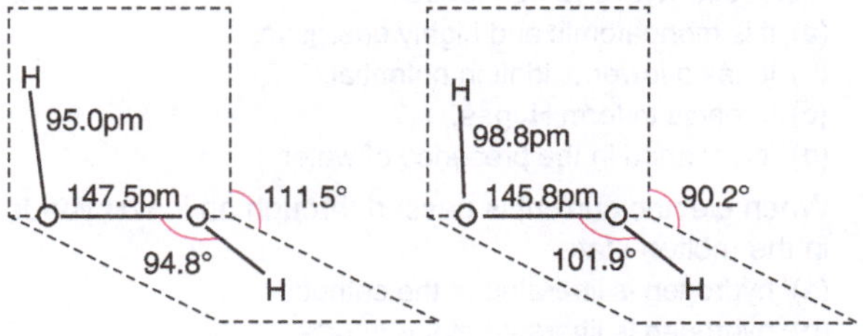

(a) Gas phase (b) Solid phase

Uses

- It is used in the industries as a bleaching agent.
- In laboratory it is used as an oxidising agent.
- As a propellent fuel in submarines and rockets.
- It is used in the production of epoxides, propylene oxide and polyurethanes.
- Domestically, used as a hair bleach and as a mild disinfectant.

Elemental Practice

Type I MCQs with Only One Correct Option

1. In which of the properties listed below hydrogen does not show similarity with halogens ?
   I. Nature of the oxide
   II. Electropositive character
   III. Combination with alkali metals
   IV. Atomicity
   (a) I and II (b) III and IV
   (c) II only (d) I and III

2. If same mass of liquid water and a piece of ice is taken, then the reason for less density of ice than that of liquid water is
   (a) ice is a solid
   (b) molecules of ice are closely packed
   (c) vacant spaces are present in the crystal lattice
   (d) ice has disordered three dimensional hydrogen bonded structure

3. Hydrogen acts as an oxidising agent in its reaction with
   (a) bromine (b) calcium
   (c) nitrogen (d) sulphur

4. Non-stoichiometric hydrides are
   (a) hydrides of all *d*-block elements
   (b) deficient in hydrogen
   (c) the hydrides having hydrogen atom in interstitial sites
   (d) Both (b) and (c)

5. Choose the correct statements about hydrides?
   (a) Metallic hydrides exhibit high electrical conductivity at room temperature
   (b) Ionic hydrides are formed by highly electropositive elements of group 1 and 2.
   (c) Covalent hydrides are always volatile and non-polar.
   (d) Metallic hydrides are formed by non-metals like S and P.

6. Nascent hydrogen is a stronger reducing agent than molecular hydrogen because
   (a) it is monoatomic and highly energetic.
   (b) it has a lower oxidation potential.
   (c) it reacts to form H_2 gas.
   (d) it is formed in the presence of water.

7. When electric current is passed through an ionic hydride in the molten state,
   (a) hydrogen is liberated at the cathode
   (b) hydrogen is liberated at the anode
   (c) hydride ion migrates towards cathode
   (d) no reaction takes place

8. H_2 gas is liberated at cathode and anode both by electrolysis of the following aqueous solutions except in
   (a) NaH (b) HCOONa
   (c) NaCl (d) LiH

9. Which one of the following statement about water is false ?
   (a) Water can act as an acid and as a base
   (b) There is an extensive intramolecular hydrogen bonding in the condensed phase
   (c) Ice formed by heavy water sinks in normal
   (d) Water is oxidised to oxygen during photosynthesis

10. In laboratory, H_2O_2 is prepared by which of the following method
    (a) cold $H_2SO_4 + BaO_2 \cdot 8H_2O$
    (b) $HCl + BaO_2$
    (c) conc. $H_2SO_4 + Na_2O_2$
    (d) $H_2 + O_2$

11. The atomic hydrogen torch is used for high temperature welding because
    (a) atomic hydrogen combines to form molecular hydrogen, releasing energy.
    (b) hydrogen gas has a very high calorific value.
    (c) it burns with a hot blue flame.
    (d) it involves catalytic decomposition of water.

12. The strength of 20 volume solution of hydrogen peroxide is
    (a) 73.21 g/L (b) 43.21 g/L
    (c) 30.36 g/L (d) 60.71 g/L

13. Select the incorrect statement from the following.
    (a) D_2O freezes at lower temperature than H_2O
    (b) Reaction between H_2 and Cl_2 is much faster than D_2 and Cl_2
    (c) Ordinary water electrolysed more rapidly than D_2O
    (d) Bond dissociation energy of D_2 is greater than H_2

14. The reagent commonly used to determine hardness of water titrimetrically is
    (a) oxalic acid
    (b) sodium thiosulphate
    (c) sodium citrate
    (d) disodium salt of EDTA

15. Polyphosphates are used as water softening agents because they
    (a) form soluble complexes with anionic species
    (b) precipitate anionic species
    (c) precipitate cationic species
    (d) form soluble complexes with cationic species

16. Which of the following equations depict the oxidising nature of H_2O_2?
    (a) $2MnO_4^- + 6H^+ + 5H_2O_2 \longrightarrow 2Mn^{2+} + 8H_2O + 5O_2$
    (b) $2Fe^{3+} + 2H^+ + H_2O_2 \longrightarrow 2Fe^{2+} + 2H_2O + O_2$
    (c) $2I^- + 2H^+ + H_2O_2 \longrightarrow I_2 + 2H_2O$
    (d) $KIO_4 + H_2O_2 \longrightarrow KIO_3 + H_2O + O_2$

17. Out of the following metals which will give H_2 on reaction with NaOH
    I. Zn II. Mg III. Al IV. Sn
    (a) I, II, III, IV (b) I, III, IV
    (c) II, IV (d) I, III only

Type II 》 MCQs with One or More than One Correct Option

18. Select the species that are not covalent hydrides?
(a) BeH_2 (b) MgH_2 (c) LiH (d) $LaH_{2.87}$

19. The more reactive species than nascent hydrogen is/are
(a) molecular hydrogen (b) atomic hydrogen
(c) active hydrogen (d) occluded hydrogen

20. Choose the correct statement about hydrides
(a) Metallic hydrides are non-stoichiometric compounds.
(b) Element of group 6, 7 and 8 do not form metallic hydrides.
(c) Metallic hydrides have metallic lustre and conduct electricity.
(d) All hydrides have a similar lattice as the parent.

21. H_2O_2 is obtained by
(a) $Na_2O_2 + H_2SO_4 \xrightarrow{\text{cold}}$
(b) $H_2S_2O_8 + H_2O \xrightarrow{\text{cold}}$
(c) $BaO_2 + H_2O + CO_2 \xrightarrow{\text{cold}}$
(d) $PbO_2 + H_2O + CO_2 \xrightarrow{\text{cold}}$

22. Which of the following can be used to remove hardness caused by $MgCl_2$?
(a) Hydrated sodium aluminium silicate
(b) Sodium hexametaphosphate
(c) Na_2CO_3
(d) Na_3PO_4

23. Choose the incorrest statement from the following
(a) A 20 Vol labelled sample of H_2O_2 will produce lesser O_2 gas at STP than a 500 mL sample of 2*M* CH_2O_2.
(b) Urea and acetanilide accelerate the decomposition of H_2O_2.
(c) D_2O_2 is prepared in laboratory as
$K_2S_2O_8(aq) + 2D_2O(l) \longrightarrow 2KDSO_4(aq) + D_2O_2(l)$
(d) Pure anhydrous H_2O_2 is a colorless syrupy liquid but it gives a bluish tinge in thick layers.

Type III 》 Numerical/Integer Type Questions

24. A bottle of H_2O_2 is labelled as 10 vol H_2O_2. 112 mL of this solution of H_2O_2 is titrated against 0.04 M acidified solution of $KMnO_4$. The volume of $KMnO_4$ in terms of litre will be …… .

25. Given that a sample of water has degree of hardness equal to 40 ppm. If the entire hardness is due to $MgSO_4$, the amount of $MgSO_4$ present per kg of water is ……… mg.

26. The volume strength of perhydrol is …… .

27. H_2O_2 is "5.6 volume", then it is …… % by volume.

28. If the mass of hydrogen peroxide present in 1L of 2M solution is 68 g, then the volume of oxygen at STP liberated upon complete decomposition of 100 cm^3 of this solution (2M) is …… (L).

Elemental Practice | Chapter 03

Connect with **Answers**

1. (a)	2. (c)	3. (b)	4. (d)	5. (b)	6. (a)
7. (b)	8. (c)	9. (b)	10. (a)	11. (a)	12. (d)
13. (a)	14. (d)	15. (d)	16. (c)	17. (b)	18. (c,d)
19. (b,c)	20. (a,c)	21. (a,b,c)	22. (a,b,c,d)	23. (a,b,c)	24. (1)
25. (48)	26. (100)	27. (1.7)	28. (2.24)		

Advanced Exclusive Different Strokes

Tips to Solve the Problems Related to Hardness of Water

The quantitative determination of temporary and permanent hardness of water separately can be done by the following way. If a water sample is boiled for some time, the bicarbonate Ca and Mg are preciptated as white insoluble carbonates and are removed by filtration and weighed.

The filtered water sample may now be titrated with EDTA salt which gives only permanent hardness. The temporary hardness can be manipulated by subtracting the permanent hardness from the total hardness of water sample.

Temporary hardness = Total hardness – Permanent hardness

$$= \frac{M(Ca^{2+} \text{ and } Mg^{2+}) \times MW\ CaCO_3 \times 10^6}{10^3}$$

$= \ldots$ ppm of $CaCO_3$

Permanent hardness of the given water sample

$$= \frac{M(Ca^{2+} \text{ and } Mg^{2+}) \text{ after heating } \times MW\ (CaCO_3) \times 10^6}{10^3}$$

$= \ldots$ ppm of $CaCO_3$

Let us understand this with the help of an example,

A 100 mL sample of hard water is titrated with 300 mL of 0.002 M EDTA solution at pH = 10, using eriochrome black-T indicator to reach equivalence point.

An equal amount of hard water sample is boiled for 30 min. After filtration and cooling, the same sample is titrated with 500 mL of 0.001 M EDTA solution at pH = 10 using Mg-EDTA complex solution and erichrome black-T indicator to reach equivalence point.

(a) *Calculate the total hardness of water sample (temporary + permanent) in ppm in* $CaCO_3$.

(b) *Calculate the permanent hardness of water sample in ppm of* $CaCO_3$.

(c) *Calculate the temporary hardness of water sample in ppm of* $CaCO_3$.

Sol. (a) Total hardness (first titration) :

$M_1V_1(\text{EDTA}) = M_2V_2$ (Total Ca^{2+} and Mg^{2+} in temporary and permanent hardness)

$300 \times 0.002 = M_2 \times 100$

$M_2 = 0.006$ (Total Ca^{2+} and Mg^{2+})

$$\text{Total hardness in ppm of } CaCO_3 = \frac{0.006 \times 100 \times 10^6}{10^3} = 600 \text{ ppm}$$

(b) Permanent hardness (second titration) :

$M_1V_1(\text{EDTA}) = M_2V_2$ (Total Ca^{2+} and Mg^{2+} due to permanent hardness)

$500 \times 0.001 = M_2 \times 100$

$M_2 = 0.005$ (Total Ca^{2+} and Mg^{2+} in permanent hardness)

Permanent hardness in ppm of $CaCO_3$

$$= \frac{0.005 \times 100 \times 10^6}{10^3} = 500 \text{ ppm}$$

(c) Temporary hardness in ppm of $CaCO_3 = 600 - 500$

$= 100$ ppm

Thus, with the help of this formula, we can approach the questions related to calculation of hardness of water, which is important from Advanced perspective.

PRACTICE ELEMENT

Target JEE Advanced

Single Correct Answer MCQs

1. Which of the following is correct statement?
   (a) $Fe_2O_3 + Cr_2O_3$ catalyst is used in manufacturing of H_2 from water gas.
   (b) The most abundant isotope of hydrogen is *para* hydrogen.
   (c) Ratio of *ortho* hydrogen to *para*-hydrogen is 1 : 3.
   (d) Hydrogen economy refers to economical use of hydrogen.

2. Tritium, a radioactive isotope of hydrogen, emits which of the following particles?
   (a) Beta (β^-) (b) Alpha (α)
   (c) Gamma (γ) (d) Neutron (n)

3. Which of the following is incorrect statement?
   (a) H_2O_2 is prepared in the laboratory by adding Na_2O_2 in boiling water.
   (b) H_2O_2 is stored in plastic container after addition of stabiliser.
   (c) The bleaching properties of H_2O_2 is due to its oxidising properties.
   (d) Decomposition of H_2O_2 is retarded by acetanilide.

4. Choose the incorrect match from the following.

(a)	LaHn	Covalent hydride
(b)	GeH_4	Electron precise hydride
(c)	B_2H_6	Electron deficient hydride
(d)	HF	Electron rich hydride

5. Calgon used as a water softener is
   (a) $Na_2[Na_4(PO_3)_6]$ (b) $Na_4[Na_2(PO_3)_6]$
   (c) $Na_4[Na_4(PO_4)_5]$ (d) $Na_4[Na_2(PO_4)_6]$

6. At its melting point, ice is lighter than water because
   (a) H_2O molecules are more closely packed in solid state
   (b) Ice crystals have hollow hexagonal arrangement of H_2O molecules
   (c) On melting of ice the H_2O molecule shrinks in size
   (d) Ice forms mostly heavy water on first melting.

7. Permutit is the technical name given to
   (a) aluminates of calcium and sodium
   (b) hydrated silicate of aluminium and sodium
   (c) silicates of calcium and magnesium
   (d) silicates of calcium and sodium

8. Hydrogen peroxide molecules are
   (a) monoatomic and form X_2^{2-} ions
   (b) diatomic and form X^- ions
   (c) diatomic and form X_2 ions
   (d) monoatomic and form X^- ions

One or More than One Correct MCQs

9. Which one of the following statements is/are correct ?
   (a) Atomic hydrogen is produced when H_2 molecules at a high temperature are irradiated with UV radiation.
   (b) At around 2000 K, the dissociation of dihydrogen into its atoms is nearly 8.1%.
   (c) Bond dissociation enthalpy of H_2 is highest among diatomic gaseous molecules which contain a single bond.
   (d) Dihydrogen is produced on reacting zinc with HCl as well as NaOH(*aq*).

10. The correct statement(s) about heavy water is (are)
    (a) used as a moderator in nuclear reactor.
    (b) obtained as a by-product in fertiliser industry.
    (c) used for the study of reaction mechanism.
    (d) has a higher dielectric constant than water.

11. Calgon is used for water treatment. Which of the following statement is true about Calgon?
    (a) Calgon contains the 2nd most abundant element by weight in the Earth's crust.
    (b) It is polymeric compound and is water soluble.
    (c) It is also known as Graham's salt.
    (d) It does not remove Ca^{2+} ion by precipitation

12. Identify the correct statement regarding heavy water.
    (a) It reacts with SO_3 to form deuterated sulphuric acid D_2SO_4.
    (b) It is used as a coolant in nuclear reactors.
    (c) It reacts with CaC_2 to produce C_2D_2 and $Ca(OD)_2$.
    (d) It reacts with Al_4C_3 to produce CD_4 and $Al(OD)_3$.

13. Select the correct statements from the following.
    (a) decomposition of hydrogen peroxide gives dioxygen.
    (b) like hydrogen peroxide, compounds, such as $KClO_3$, $Pb(NO_3)_2$ and $NaNO_3$ when heated liberate dioxygen.
    (c) 2-ethylanthraquinone is useful for the industrial preparation of hydrogen peroxide.
    (d) hydrogen peroxide is used for the manufacture of sodium perborate.

14. From the following statements regarding H_2O_2, choose the correct statement.
    (a) It can act only as an oxidising agent.
    (b) It decomposed on exposure to light.
    (c) It has to be stored in plastic or wax lined glass bottles in dark.
    (d) It has to be kept away from dust.

15. Which of the following statement(s) is/are correct?
    (a) Hardness of water is due to dissolved impurities of calcium and magnesium salts.
    (b) Hydrogen peroxide is manufactured by the auto-oxidation of 2-ethylanthra quinol.

(c) Temporary hardness is caused due to the presence of $CaCl_2$.
(d) Electrolysis of molten saline hydrides produces hydrogen gas at cathode.

Numerical/Integer Type Questions

16. The hardness of a water sample containing 10^{-3} M $MgSO_4$ expressed as $CaCO_3$ equivalents (in ppm) is .... (Molar mass of $MgSO_4$ is 120.37 g/mol)
17. The volume strength of 8.9 M H_2O_2 solution calculated at 273 K and 1 atm is .... ($R = 0.0821$ L atm K^{-1} mol^{-1}) (rounded off to the nearest integer)
18. In an ice crystal, each water molecule is hydrogen bonded to .... neighbouring water molecules.
19. The number of hydrogen bonded water molecules associated with stoichiometry $CuSO_4 \cdot 5H_2O$ is ....
20. A 20.0 mL solution containing 0.2 g impure H_2O_2 reacts completely with 0.316 g of $KMnO_4$ in acid solution. The purity of H_2O_2 (in %) is .... (mol weight of H_2O_2 = 34 ; mol wt. of $KMnO_4$ = 158)

Matching Type Questions

21. Match the compounds in Column in I with their characteristics in Column II.

	Column I (Hyderides)		Column II (Boiling Point °C)
(A)	HF	(P)	+ 19.4
(B)	HCl	(Q)	– 85.0
(C)	HBr	(R)	– 35.5
(D)	HI	(S)	– 67.1
		(T)	– 42.0

Choose the correct answer from the options given below
(a) A → (P); B → (Q); C → (S); D → (R)
(b) A → (T); B → (P); C → (S); D → (Q)
(c) A → (R); B → (T); C → (S); D → (P)
(d) A → (Q); B → (R); S → (T); D → (P)

22. Match the compounds given in Column-I with their chemical formula in Column-II.

	Column-I		Column-II
(A)	Permutit	(P)	CaH_2
(B)	Calgon	(Q)	$LiBH_4$
(C)	Hydrolith	(R)	$Na_2[Na_4(PO_3)_6]$
(D)	Alanate	(S)	$Na_2Al_2Si_2O_8 \cdot xH_2O$

Choose the correct answer from the options given below
(a) A → (P); B → (Q); C → (S); D → (R)
(b) A → (Q); B → (P); C → (R); D → (S)
(c) A → (R); B → (S); C → (Q); D → (P)
(d) A → (S); B → (R); C → (P); D → (Q)

23. Match the compounds in List-I with their hydrides List-II

	List-I		List-II
(A)	LiH	(P)	Complex hydride
(B)	BeH_2	(Q)	Interstitial hydride
(C)	CuH	(R)	Molecular hydride
(D)	CaH_3	(S)	Ionic hydride

Choose the correct answer from the options given below.
(a) A → (S); B → (R); C → (Q); D → (P)
(b) A → (P); B → (S); C → (R); D → (Q)
(c) A → (Q); B → (R); C → (S); D → (P)
(d) A → (P); B → (Q); C → (R); D → (S)

24. Match the Column I with Column II.

	Column-I		Column-II
(A)	H_2	(P)	Used in hydroformylation of olefin.
(B)	H_2O_2	(Q)	Only act as oxidising agent.
(C)	$LiAlH_4$	(R)	Only act as reducing agent.
(D)	H	(S)	Used in cutting and welding.
		(T)	Oxidising as well as reducing agent.

Choose the correct answer from the options given below.
(a) A → (P); B → (T); C → (R); D → (S)
(b) A → (P); B → (Q); C → (R); D → (S)
(c) A → (Q); B → (R); C → (P); D → (T)
(d) A → (Q); B → (T); C → (S); D → (P)

25. Match List-I with List-II

	List-I		List-II
(A)	Metallic hydride	(I)	Rhenium hydride
(B)	Molecular hydride	(II)	Insoluble in non-aqueous solvent
(C)	Saline hydride	(III)	Phosphine
(D)	Hydrogen storage medium for full cell	(IV)	Magnesium hydride

Choose the correct answer from the options given below
(a) A → IV, B → III, C → II, D → I
(b) A → II, B → III, C → I, D → IV
(c) A → I, B → III, C → II, D → IV
(d) A → IV, B → I, C → II, D → III

Paragraph of Two Questions Each

Paragraph 1

Hydrogen peroxide is a powerful oxidising agent, both in the acidic and alkaline medium.

In acidic medium : $H_2O_2 + 2H^+ + 2e^- \longrightarrow 2H_2O$

In alkaline medium : $H_2O_2 + 2e^- \longrightarrow 2OH$

Hydrogen peroxide acts a a reducing agent towards powerful oxidising agents.

In acidic medium : $H_2O_2 \longrightarrow 2H^+ + O_2 + 2e^-$

In alkaline medium, however, its reducing nature is more effective.

$$H_2O_2 + 2OH^- \longrightarrow 2H_2O + O_2 + 2e^-$$

26. On addition of H_2O_2 to acidified $KMnO_4$, $KMnO_4$ gets decolourised due to :
(a) oxidation of $KMnO_4$
(b) reduction of $KMnO_4$
(c) Both oxidation and reduction
(d) $KMnO_4$ does not react with H_2O_2

27. H_2O_2 behaves as a bleaching agent due to
(a) oxidising nature (b) reducing nature
(c) acidic nature (d) unstable nature

Paragraph 2

Red hot coke + Steam $\xrightarrow{1000°C} (X) \xrightarrow[500°C \text{ catalyst } (y)]{\text{Steam}} (Z) + H_2$

28. Catalyst '*Y*' is
(a) V_2O_5 (b) Cr_2O_3
(c) Fe_2O_3 (d) $Fe_2O_3 + Cr_2O_3$

29. '*Z*' is removed by passing the gaseous mixture through
(a) acidic solution
(b) alkaline solution
(c) water under high pressure of 25 atm
(d) an organic solvent

Paragraph 3

H_2O_2 is reduced rapidly by Sn^{2+} to give H_2O and Sn^{4+}, H_2O_2 is decomposed slowly at room temperature to yield O_2 and H_2O. 125 g of 10% by mass of H_2O_2 in water is treated with 100 ml of 4 M Sn^{2+} and then a mixture is allowed to stand until no further reaction occurs.

30. The equivalent of H_2O_2 reacted with Sn^{2+} is ....

31. The volume of O_2 produced at 37°C and 1 atm after H_2O_2 is reacted with Sn^{2+} and the mixture is allowed to stand is ....

Species Selection Type (with 5 Species)

32. Consider the following reagents :
A. $Ca_3(PO_4)_2$ E. Borax
B. $Ca(OH)_2$ F. $NaAlO_2$
C. Na_2CO_3 G. NH_3
D. NaOCl

The total number of reagents used for softening the temporary hardness of water is
(a) 3 (b) 6
(c) 2 (d) 4

33. Consider the following ions
I. H^+ II. Ca^{2+} III. SO_4^{2-} IV. Mg^{2+} V. Si^{4+}

When zeolite, which is hydrated sodium aluminium silicate, is treated with hard water then the total number of ions that will be exchange with sodium ions is
(a) 2 (b) 3
(c) 4 (d) 1

34. Consider the following oxides
A. PbO_2 B. MnO_2 C. Na_2O_2 D. BaO_2 E. KO_2

The total number of oxides that will give H_2O_2 on treatment with dil. H_2SO_4 is
(a) 2 (b) 3
(c) 4 (d) 1

35. Consider the following reactions
A. $2[Fe(CN)_6]^{4-} + H_2O_2 + 2H^+ \longrightarrow 2[Fe(CN)_6]^{3-} + 2H_2O$
B. $3N_2H_4 + 2H_2O_2 \xrightarrow[\text{catalyst}]{Cu^{2+}} N_2 + 4H_2O$
C. $Hg + H_2O_2 \xrightarrow{H_2SO_4} HgO + H_2O$
D. $AsO_3^{3-} + H_2O_2 \longrightarrow AsO_4^{3-} + H_2O$
E. $H_2O_2 + NH_2OH \longrightarrow O_2 + NH_3 + H_2O$

The total number of equations that will show the oxidising nature of H_2O_2 is
(a) 5 (b) 3
(c) 4 (d) 2

Species Selection Type (with 7 Species)

36. Consider the following metals
1. Zn 2. Sn 3. Mg
4. Al 5. Fe 6. Pb
7. Ga

The total number of metals that on treatment with NaOH will liberate H_2 gas ....
(a) 3 (b) 5
(c) 6 (d) 4

37. Consider the following species
I. $FeSO_4$ II. I^- III. PbS IV. $KMnO_4$/acid
V. Na_3AsO_3 VI. H_2S VII. C_6H_6

The total number of species that with H_2O_2 acts as reductant ....
(a) 4 (b) 2
(c) 5 (d) 3

38. Consider the following reagents

I. Zn + dilute HCl II. $NH_3 + H_2O$

III. $K_2Cr_2O_7/H^+ + H_2O_2$ IV. $BaO_2 + H_2SO_4$

V. $Al + KOH + H_2O$ VI. $NaH + H_2O$

VII. Zn + dil.H_2SO_4

The total number of combinations that produce H_2 gas will be ?

(a) 5 (b) 3

(c) 4 (d) 2

39. Consider the following reactions

I. $2KI + H_2O_2 \longrightarrow 2KOH + I_2$

II. $KNO_2 + H_2O_2 \longrightarrow KNO_3 + H_2O$

III. $Na_2SO_3 + H_2O_2 \longrightarrow Na_2SO_4 + H_2O$

IV. $PbO_2 + H_2O_2 \longrightarrow PbO + H_2O + O_2$

V. $IO_4^- + H_2O_2 \longrightarrow IO_3^- + H_2O + O_2$

VI. $Ag_2O + H_2O_2 \longrightarrow 2Ag + H_2O + O_2$

VII. $2MnO_4^- + 6H^+ + 5H_2O_2 \longrightarrow 2Mn^{2+} + 8H_2O + 5O_2$

The total number of reactions in which H_2O_2 acts as reducing agent …… .

(a) 3 (b) 4

(c) 2 (d) 5

40. Consider the following reactions

A. MnO_2 + dil.$HCl \longrightarrow$

B. BaO_2 + cold $H_3PO_4 \longrightarrow$

C. BaO_2 + cold $H_2SO_4 \longrightarrow$

D. MgO_2 + cold $H_2SO_4 \longrightarrow$

E. $KO_2 + H_2O \longrightarrow$

F. $Na_2O_2 + H_2O \longrightarrow$

G. $Al + NaOH + H_2O \longrightarrow$

The total number of reactions in which H_2O_2 can be prepared …… .

(a) 4 (b) 3

(c) 5 (d) 2

Check Through PYQs

1. Hydrogen peroxide in its reaction with KIO_4 and NH_2OH respectively, is acting as a *Adv. 2014*

(a) reducing agent, oxidising agent

(b) reducing agent, reducing agent

(c) oxidising agent, oxidising agent

(d) oxidising agent, reducing agent

HINTS & Solutions

Solutions : Competency Enhancer

1.1. ***(c)*** Reaction of H_2O_2 with $MnSO_4$ in alkaline medium is :

$$\overset{+2}{Mn}SO_4 + H_2O_2 + 2NaOH \longrightarrow Na_2SO_4 + \overset{+4}{Mn}O_2 + 2H_2O$$

Here, H_2O_2 oxidises manganese salts to manganese dioxide.

Reaction of H_2O_2 with NaOBr

$$NaOBr + H_2O_2 \longrightarrow NaBr + H_2O + O_2$$

H_2O_2 reduces sodium hypobromite to sodium bromide.

Elemental Practice

1. ***(a)*** Hydrogen forms a neutral oxide, i.e. H_2O (water) while the oxide of halogens. i.e. HCl,HI, HBr, are acidic. Hydrogen atom is electropositive in nature while halogens are mostly electronegative in nature.

2. ***(c)*** In ice, molecules of H_2O are not packed so closely as in liquid water. There exists vacant spaces in the crystal lattice. This results in larger volume and lower density.

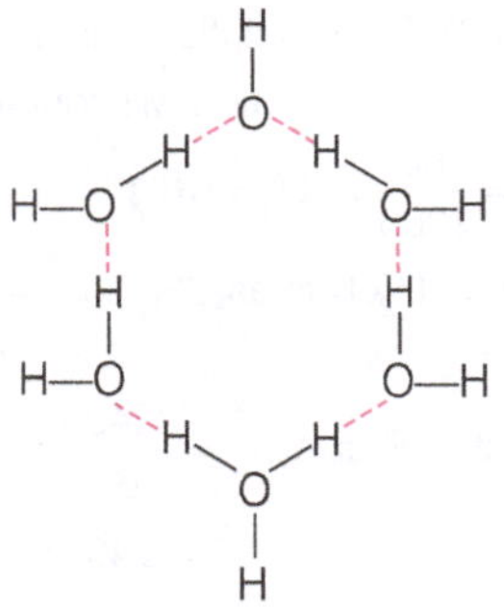

3. ***(b)*** Ca is more electropositive than hydrogen and hence here hydrogen acts as an oxidising agent for Ca.

$$Ca + H_2 \longrightarrow CaH_2$$

Oxidation state of Ca changes from 0 to +2.

4. ***(d)*** Non-stoichiometric hydride are formed by many *d*-block (except metals of 7, 8 and 9 group) and *f*-block elements.

These hydrides are always non-stoichiometric, i.e. deficient in hydrogen. In these hydrides hydrogen atom occupies interstitial sites, e.g. $LaH_{2.87}$, $YbH_{2.55}$, $TiH_{1.5-1.2}$, $PdH_{0.6-0.8}$, etc.

5. ***(b)*** (a) Metallic hydrides are poor electrical conductors at room temperature.

(c) Many covalent hydrides (like H_2O, NH_3) are polar.

(d) Metallic hydrides are formed by metals not from non-metals.

6. ***(a)*** Nascent hydrogen is atomic hydrogen (H) rather than molecular hydrogen (H_2). Being monoatomic, it has higher energy and greater reducing power since it does not need to break the H—H bond before reacting.

7. ***(b)*** $M^+H^- \longrightarrow M^+ + \underset{\text{Hydride ion}}{H^-}$

$$H^- \longrightarrow \frac{1}{2}H_2 + e^- \text{ (at anode)}$$

8. ***(c)*** $NaH \rightleftharpoons Na^+ + H^-$

At cathode

$$Na^+ + e^- \longrightarrow Na$$

$$Na + H_2O \longrightarrow NaOH + \frac{1}{2}H_2$$

At anode

$$H^- \longrightarrow \frac{1}{2}H_2 + e^-$$

(b) $HCOONa \rightleftharpoons HCOO^- + Na^+$

At cathode same as above

At anode

$$HCOO^- \longrightarrow \frac{1}{2}H_2 + CO_2 + e^-$$

(c) $NaCl \rightleftharpoons Na^+ + Cl^-$

At cathode $2H^+ + 2e^- \longrightarrow H_2\uparrow$

At anode $Cl^- \longrightarrow \frac{1}{2}Cl_2 + e^-$

(d) $LiH \rightleftharpoons Li^+ + H^-$

At cathode

$$Li^+ + e^- \longrightarrow Li$$

$$Li + H_2O \longrightarrow LiOH + \frac{1}{2}H_2$$

At anode $H^- \longrightarrow \frac{1}{2}H_2 + e^-$

9. ***(b)*** Actually, there is extensive intermolecular (instead of intramolecular) hydrogen bonding.

10. ***(a)*** In laboratory, acidifying barium peroxide and removing excess water by evaporation under reduced pressure gives hydrogen peroxide.

$$BaO_2 \cdot 8H_2O(s) + H_2SO_4(aq) \longrightarrow BaSO_4(s)\downarrow + H_2O_2(aq) + 8H_2O(l)$$

11. ***(a)*** The extreme heat in atomic hydrogen welding comes from the recombination of atomic hydrogen [H] into molecular hydrogen (H_2), which releases significant energy (– 436 kJ/mol).

12. ***(d)*** 20 volume solution of H_2O_2 means that 1 L of this H_2O_2 will give 20 L of oxygen at STP

$$\underset{\substack{2\times 34\,g\\68\,g}}{2H_2O_2(l)} \longrightarrow \underset{22.4\text{ L at STP}}{O_2(g)} + 2H_2O(l)$$

22.4 L of O_2 at STP is produced from $H_2O_2 = 68\,g$

20 L of O_2 at STP is produced from H_2O_2

$$= \frac{68 \times 20}{22.4} = 60.71\,g/L$$

So, the strength of H_2O_2 in 20 volume $H_2O_2 = 60.714\,g/L$

13. ***(a)*** D_2O actually has higher freezing point (3.8°C) than water $H_2O(0°C)$.

14. ***(d)*** Disodium salt of EDTA is commonly used to determine the hardness of water.

15. ***(d)*** Polyphosphates being negatively charged form soluble complexes with cationic species.

16. ***(c)*** The reaction in which H_2O_2 is reduced, i.e. oxidation state of oxygen decreases from –1 to –2 depicts the oxidising nature of, H_2O_2 e.g.

Reduction

$$2I^- + 2H^+ + H_2\overset{-1}{O_2} \longrightarrow \overset{0}{I_2} + 2H_2\overset{-2}{O}$$

Oxidising agent

Increase in O.S. (Oxidation)

17. ***(b)*** $Zn + 2NaOH \longrightarrow Na_2ZnO_2 + H_2\uparrow$

$2Al + 2NaOH + 2H_2O \longrightarrow NaAlO_2 + 3H_2\uparrow$

$Sn + 2NaOH + H_2O \longrightarrow Na_2SnO_3 + 2H_2\uparrow$

18. ***(c,d)*** LiH is an ionic hydride whereas $LaH_{2.87}$ is an interstitial hydride.

19. ***(b,c)*** The order of reactivity is atomic > active > nascent > molecular. Thus, atomic and active hydrogens are more reactive than nascent hydrogen.

20. ***(a,c)*** Hydride gap is observed in group 7, 8 and 9. Also except for hydrides of Ni, Pd, Ce and Ac, other metallic hydrides have different lattice than the parent metal.

21. ***(a,b,c)*** $Na_2O_2 + H_2SO_4 \longrightarrow Na_2SO_4 + H_2O_2$

$H_2S_2O_8 + 2H_2O \longrightarrow 2H_2SO_4 + H_2O_2$

$BaO_2 + CO_2 + H_2O \longrightarrow BaCO_3 + H_2O_2$

22. ***(a,b,c,d)***

(a) $Na_2Al_2Si_2O_8 \cdot xH_2O + MgCl_2 \longrightarrow MgAl_2Si_2O_8 \cdot xH_2O + 2NaCl$

(b) $Mg^{2+} + Na_4P_6O_{18}^{2-} \longrightarrow Na_2[Mg_2)PO_3)_6] + 2Na^+$

(c) $MgCl_2 + Na_2CO_3 \longrightarrow MgCO_3\downarrow + 2NaCl$

(d) $3MgCl_2 + 2Na_3PO_4 \longrightarrow Mg_3(PO_4)_2\downarrow + 6NaCl$

23. ***(a,b,c)*** Urea and acetanilide act as stabilisers or retard the decomposition of H_2O_2.

24. ***(1)*** 5.6 vol of $H_2O_2 = 1\,N$

10 vol of $H_2O_2 = \frac{10}{5.6}\,N$

M. eq. of H_2O_2 = M. eq. of MnO_4^-

$$\frac{10}{5.6} \times 112 = 0.04 \times 5 \times V$$

or $V = 1000\,mL = 1\,L$

25. ***(48)*** Degree of hardness of H_2O is 40 ppm.

i.e. 10^6 g of water contains $CaCO_3 = 40\,g$

Since, 1 mole of $CaCO_3$ = 1 mole of $MgSO_4$

$\therefore$ 100 g of $CaCO_3$ = 120 g of $MgSO_4$

$\therefore 10^6$ g of water contains $MgSO_4 = \frac{40 \times 120}{100} = 48\,g$

10^3 g water contain $= \frac{48 \times 10^3}{106} \times 10^3$ mg of $MgSO_4$

$= 48\,mg$

26. ***(100)*** Perhydrol is 30% H_2O_2.

$\because$ 10 vol $H_2O_2 = 3\%$

$\therefore$ 30% H_2O_2 has volume $= \frac{10}{3} \times 30 = 100$ volume

27. ***(1.7)*** For H_2O_2

Molarity = Volume × strength/11.2 = 5.6/11.2 = 0.5 M

Assuming 1 L solution

mass of solution = 1000 mL × 1g mL = 1000 g

mass of solute = mass × molar mass

= 0.5 mole × 34 g /mol = 17 gm

$$\text{mass } \% = \frac{17}{1000} = 1.7\%$$

28. ***(2.24)*** 1 litre of 2M H_2O_2 solution contains $H_2O_2 = 68\,g$

$\therefore 100\,cm^3$ of 2M H_2O_2 solution will contain H_2O_2

$$= \frac{68}{1000} \times 100 = 6.8\,g$$

Decomposition of H_2O_2 is as, $2H_2O_2 \longrightarrow 2H_2O + O_2$
(22400 cm^3 at STP)

6.8 g of H_2O_2 at STP give $O_2 = \frac{22400}{68} \times 6.8$

$= 2240\,cm^3 = 2.24\,L$

Practice Element : Target JEE Advanced

1. ***(a)***
   - The most abundant isotope of hydrogen in protium.
   - Ratio of *ortho*-hydrogen and *para*-hydrogen at room temperature is 3 : 1.
   - Hydrogen economy refers to use of hydrogen as fuel.

2. ***(a)*** Tritium (^3_1H) is an isotope of hydrogen. It is a radioactive isotope and decays by emitting beta-particle (β^-) to form $^3_2He^+$.

$$\underset{\text{Tritium}}{^3_1H} \longrightarrow {}^3_2He^+ + \underset{\beta\text{-particle }(\beta^-)}{e^-} + 18.6\text{ keV}$$

3. ***(a)*** BaO_2 is added to CO_2 and bubbling through cold water, gives H_2O_2

$BaO_2 + CO_2 + H_2O \longrightarrow BaCO_3\downarrow + H_2O$

4. ***(d)*** The incorrect match is given in option (a). It is because LaHn is an interestial hydride.
   - Electron deficient hydride contains less than 8 electrons.

- Electron precise hydride contains 8 electrons without lone pair.
- Electron rich hydride contains 8 electrons along with lone pair(s).

5. ***(a)*** Calgon used as a water softener is $Na_2[Na_4(PO_3)_6]$, it is the complex salt of metaphosphoric acid, sodium hexametaphosphate $(NaPO_3)_6$.

6. ***(b)*** Ice is lighter than water because when water freezes at atmospheric pressure it crystalises in normal hexagonal form. In it, each oxygen atom is surrounded by 4 hydrogen atoms, two by strong covalent bonds and two by weak hydrogen bonds. As we know, hydrogen bonds are longer than covalent bonds. The molecules of water are not closely packed in crystal lattice. There exists a number of hollow space in the crystal lattice, which decreases the density of ice.

7. ***(b)*** Permutit is the technical name given to hydrated silicate of aluminium and sodium.

   i.e $\quad Na_2Al_2Si_2O_8 \cdot xH_2O$

8. ***(b)*** Hydrogen peroxide is diatomic and forms $H^+ + HO_2^-(X^-)$ ions.

9. ***(a,c,d)*** Statement (b) is incorrect. The corrected statement is :

   At around 2000 K, the dissociation of dihydrogen into its atoms is only ~0.081%.

   Bond dissociation enthalpy of H_2 molecule is highest due to very strong attraction between the atoms.

   $$Zn + 2HCl \longrightarrow H_2 + ZnCl_2$$
   $$Zn + NaOH \longrightarrow Na_2ZnO_2 + H_2$$

   H_2 can be dissociated into atomic hydrogen when subjected to UV radiation at high temperatures.

10. ***(a, b, c)*** Dielectric constant of water is greater than heavy water (D_2O).

    (a) It is widely used as moderator in nuclear reactors.

    (b) It can be prepared as a by-product in some fertiliser industries.

    (c) It is used in exchange reactions for the study of the reaction mechanism.

    (d)

Species	**Dielectric constant** (C^2 / Nm^2)
D_2O	78.06
H_2O	78.39

11. ***(b,c,d)*** Calgon is not an element, it is a compound. The 2nd most abundant element by weight in the Earth's crust is silicon (Si). So, the statement in option (a) is not true.

    Calgon is sodium hexametaphosphate $(NaPO_3)_6$ or $Na_2[Na_4(PO_3)_6]$. It is a polymeric water soluble compound. It is also named as Graham's salt.

    Mg^{2+} in hard water is removed as

    $$\underset{\text{Calgon}}{Na_2[Na_4(PO_3)_6]} + 2Mg^{2+}(aq) \longrightarrow Na_2[Mg_2(PO_3)_6](s) + 4Na^+(aq)$$

    Ca^{2+} ion cannot be removed by calgon as Ca^{2+} is larger in size than Mg^{2+}.

    So, the statement of option (b), (c) and (d) are true.

12. ***(a,b,c,d)*** Heavy water is used as a moderator in nuclear reactors as it slows down the fast moving neutrons and helps in controlling the nuclear fission process.

13. ***(a, b, c, d)*** The complete chemical equations for the given reactions are as follows

    (A) $H_2O_2 \xrightarrow{\Delta} H_2O + \frac{1}{2}O_2$

    Thus, statement (a) is correct

    (B) $KClO_3 \xrightarrow{\Delta} KCl + \frac{3}{2}O_2$

    $Pb(NO_3)_2 \xrightarrow{\Delta} PbO + 2NO_2 + \frac{1}{2}O_2$

    $NaNO_3 \xrightarrow{\Delta} NaNO_2 + \frac{1}{2}O_2$

    Thus, statement (b) is correct.

    (C)

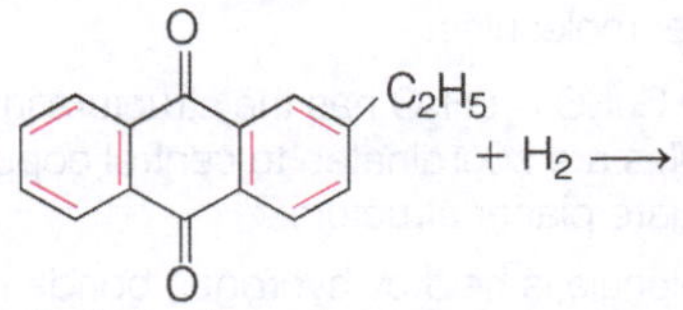

2-ethyl anthraquinone

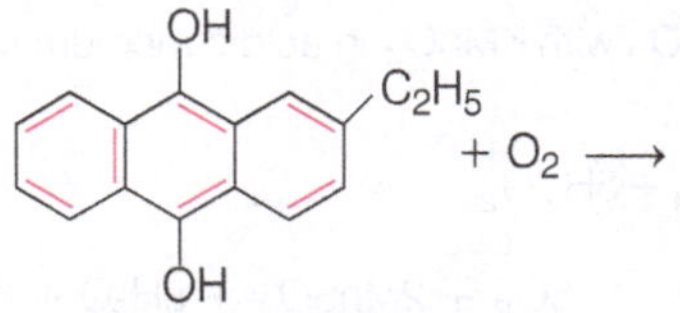

2-ethyl anthraquinol

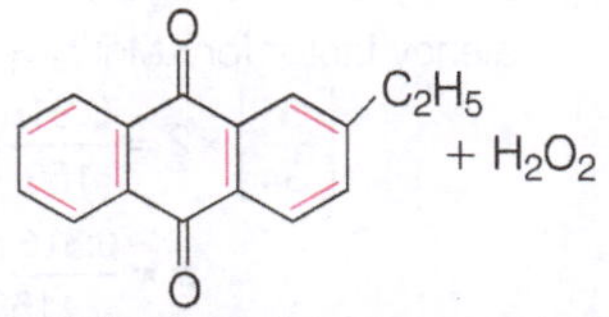

2-ethyl anthraquinone regenerated

    Thus, statement (c) is also correct.

    (D) $2NaBO_2 + 2H_2O_2 \longrightarrow \underset{\text{(sodium perborate)}}{Na_2B_2O_4(OH)_4 \text{ or } Na_2H_4B_2O_8}$

    Statement (d) is also correct.

14. ***(b, c, d)*** H_2O_2 acts as an oxidising agent as well as reducing agent, because oxidation number of oxygen in H_2O_2 is –1.

    So, it can be oxidised to oxidation state 0 or reduced to oxidation state –2.

    H_2O_2 decomposes on exposure to light. So, it has to be stored in plastic or wax lined glass bottles in dark for the prevention of exposure. It also has to be kept away from dust.

15. ***(a,b)*** Among the given statements only *a* and *b* are correct. The corrected form of incorrect statement is

- Temporary hardness is caused due to the presence of $Ca(HCO_3)_2$.
- Electrolysis of molten saline hydrides produces hydrogen gas at anode.

16. ***(100)*** $\text{ppm} = \frac{\text{Mass of component}}{\text{Total mass of solution}} \times 10^6$

MM of $CaCO_3 = 40 + 12 + 48 = 100$

10^{-3} moles of $MgSO_4 = 10^{-3}$ moles of $CaCO_3$ in 1L solution

Hence, ppm

$$(CaCO_3) = \frac{10^{-3} \times 100}{1000} \times 10^6 = 100 \text{ ppm}$$

17. ***(100)*** Volume strength of H_2O_2 at 273 K and one atm pressure

$= 11.2 \times \text{molarity}$

$= 11.2 \times 8.9 \text{ M (Given)}$

$= 99.68 \approx 100$

18. ***(4)*** In ice, each water molecule is H-bonded to 4 other neighbouring water molecules.

19. ***(1)*** The crystalline $CuSO_4 \cdot 5H_2O$ has the structure in which four water molecules are coordinated to central copper cation Cu^{2+} in square planar structure.

The fifth water molecule is held by hydrogen bonds between a sulphate anion and a co-ordinated water molecule.

20. ***(85)*** Reaction of H_2O_2 with $KMnO_4$ in acidic medium is given as

$$3H_2SO_4 + K\overset{+7}{M}nO_4 + 5H_2\overset{-1}{O_2} \longrightarrow 5\overset{0}{O_2} + 2MnSO_4 + 8H_2O + K_2SO_4$$

Valency factor for $H_2O_2 = 2$;

Valency factor for $KMnO_4 = 5$

$$\left[\frac{x}{34}\right] \times 2 = \frac{0.316}{158} \times 5$$

$$x = \frac{0.316 \times 5 \times 34}{158 \times 2}$$

$$= 0.17 \text{ g}$$

$$\text{Percentage purity} = \frac{\text{Weight of pure substance}}{\text{Weight of given sample}} \times 100$$

$$= \frac{0.17}{0.2} \times 100 = 85\%$$

21. ***(a)*** (A) → (P); (B) → (Q); (C) → (S); (D) → (R)

22. ***(d)*** (A) → (S); (B) → (R); (C) → (P); (D) → (Q)

23. ***(a)*** (A) → (S); (B) → (R); (C) → (Q); (D) → (P)

24. ***(a)*** (A) → (P); (B) → (T); (C) → (R); (D) → (S)

25. ***(c)*** The correct match is

A-I, B-III, C-II, D-IV

26. ***(b)*** With H_2O_2, $KMnO_4$ behaves as oxidising agent. Thus, reduction of $KMnO_4$ takes place.

27. ***(a)*** H_2O_2 behaves as a bleaching agent due to its oxidising nature.

28. ***(d)*** Catalyst 'Y' is $Fe_2O_3 + Cr_2O_3$

29. ***(c)*** CO_2 is removed by passing the gaseous mixture through water under high pressure of 25 atm.

$$CO_2 + H_2O \longrightarrow H_2CO_3$$

30. ***(0.8)*** $\underset{}{2H^+} + \underset{1\text{ mol}}{H_2O_2} + \underset{1\text{ mol}}{Sn^{2+}} \longrightarrow Sn^{4+} + 2H_2O$

m mol of H_2O_2 = m mol of Sn^{2+}

$100 \text{ mL} \times 4\text{M} = 400 \text{ m mol}$

$= 400$ m mol of H_2O_2

$= 400 \times 2$ (n factor) m Eq. of H_2O_2

$= 800 \text{ m Eq} = 0.8 \text{ Eq}$

31. ***(1.27)*** $\underset{2\text{ mol}}{2H_2O_2} \longrightarrow \underset{2\text{ mol}}{2H_2O} + \underset{1\text{ mol}}{O_2}$

2 mol of H_2O_2 gives 1 mol of O_2

0.1 mol of H_2O_2 gives $\frac{0.1}{2}$ mole of O_2 = 0.05 mole of O_2

$$V = \frac{nRT}{p} = \frac{0.05 \times 0.082 \times 310}{1}$$

$$= 1.27 \text{ L}$$

32. ***(b)*** Temporary hardness is due to the bicarbonates of calcium and magnesium salt.

It can be removed by $Ca(OH)_2$, Na_2CO_3, NaOCl, borax, $NaAlO_2$ and NH_3.

33. ***(a)*** Among the given ions only two i.e. Ca^{2+} and Mg^{2+} will exchange with sodium when zeolite is treated with hard water.

$$Na_2Al_2Si_2O_8 \cdot xH_2O + Ca^{2+} \longrightarrow CaAl_2Si_2O_8 \cdot xH_2O + 2Na^+$$

$$Na_2Al_2Si_2O_8 \cdot xH_2O + Mg^{2+} \longrightarrow MgAl_2Si_2O_8 \cdot xH_2O + 2Na^+$$

34. ***(a)*** Among the given oxides only two i.e. (c), (d) will give H_2O_2 on treatment with dil. H_2SO_4.

$$PbO_2 + H_2SO_4 \longrightarrow PbSO_4 + H_2O + \frac{1}{2}O_2$$

$$MnO_2 + H_2SO_4 \longrightarrow MnSO_4 + H_2O + \frac{1}{2}O_2$$

$$Na_2O_2 + H_2SO_4 \longrightarrow Na_2SO_4 + H_2O_2$$

$$BaO_2 + H_2SO_4 \longrightarrow BaSO_4 + H_2O_2$$

$$4KO_2 + 2H_2SO_4 \longrightarrow 2K_2SO_4 + 2H_2O + 3O_2$$

35. ***(c)*** Among the given reaction except (E), all will show the oxidising nature of H_2O_2.

36. ***(c)*** Amphoteric metals react with NaOH will liberate H_2 gas.

$$Zn + 2NaOH \longrightarrow Na_2ZnO_2 + H_2$$

$$Sn + 2NaOH + H_2O \longrightarrow Na_2SnO_3 + 2H_2$$

$$2Al + 2NaOH + 2H_2O \longrightarrow 2NaAlO_2 + 3H_2$$

$$2Fe + 2NaOH + 2H_2O \xrightarrow{\Delta} Na_2[Fe(OH)_4] + H_2$$

$$Pb + 2NaOH + 2H_2O \longrightarrow Na_2[Pb(OH)_4] + H_2$$
$$2Ga + 2NaOH + 6H_2O \longrightarrow 2Na[Ga(OH)_4] + 3H_2$$

37. ***(d)*** Among the given species only three i.e. $FeSO_4$, Na_3AsO_3 and H_2S with H_2O_2 acts as reductant.

$$2FeSO_4 + H_2O_2 + H_2SO_4 \longrightarrow Fe_2(SO_4)_3 + 2H_2O$$
$$Na_3AsO_3 + H_2O_2 \longrightarrow Na_3AsO_4 + H_2O$$
$$H_2S + H_2O_2 \longrightarrow S\downarrow + 2H_2O$$

38. ***(c)*** Among the given reagents only four i.e. Zn + dil. HCl, Al + KOH + H_2O, NaH + H_2O and Zn + dil. H_2SO_4 will produce H_2 gas.

39. ***(b)*** Among the given reactions there are only four i.e. IV, V, VI and VII reactions in which H_2O_2 acts as reducing agents.

40. ***(a)*** Among the given reactions only four reactions will produce H_2O_2.

$$3BaO_2 + \text{cold.}H_3PO_4 \longrightarrow Ba_3(PO_4)_2 + 3H_2O_2$$
$$BaO_2 + \text{cold.}H_2SO_4 \longrightarrow BaSO_4 + H_2O_2$$
$$2KO_2 + 2H_2O \longrightarrow 2KOH + H_2O_2 + O_2$$
$$Na_2O_2 + 2H_2O \longrightarrow 2NaOH + H_2O_2$$

Check Through PYQs : JEE Advanced

1. ***(a)*** H_2O_2 reacts with KIO_4 in the following manner:

$$\overset{+7}{KIO_4} + H_2O_2 \longrightarrow \overset{+5}{KIO_3} + H_2O + O_2$$

On reaction of KIO_4 with H_2O_2, oxidation state of I varies from +7 to +5, i.e. decreases. Thus, KIO_4 gets reduced hence, H_2O_2 is a reducing agent here.

With NH_2OH, it is given in the following reaction:

$$\overset{-1}{N}H_2OH + H_2O_2 \longrightarrow \overset{+3}{N_2O_3} + H_2O$$

In the above reaction, oxidation state of N varies from −1 to +3. Here, oxidation number increases, hence H_2O_2 is acting as an oxidising agent here.

Hence, (a) is the correct choice.

CHAPTER 4

S-Block Elements

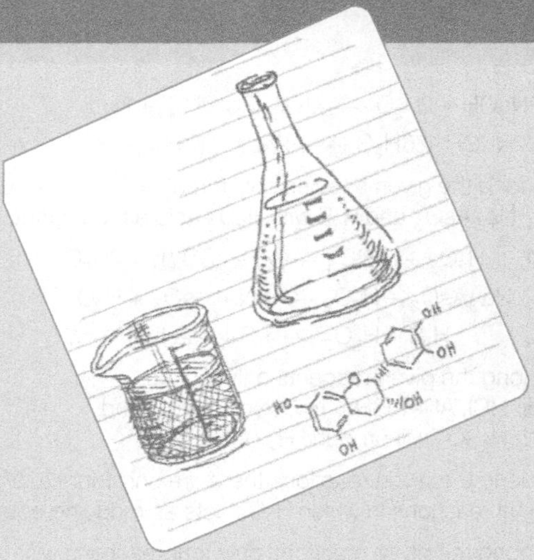

Learning Elements

Element 1 : Group 1 Elements and Their Compounds : Alkali Metals

Electronic Configuration, General Trends in Physical Properties, Trends in Chemical Properties, Anomalous Behaviour of Lithium, Diagonal Relationship of Li with Mg, Compounds of Group 1 Elements

Element 2 : Group 2 Elements and Their Compounds : Alkaline Earth Metals

Electronic Configuration, General Trends in Physical Properties, Trends in Chemical Properties, Anomalous, Behaviour of Beryllium, Diagnoal Relationship of Be with Al, Important Facts of Alkaline Earth Metals

Practice Element

Practice Element Target JEE Advanced

Trend Insights

JEE Advanced

Typology	Years				
	2024	2023	2022	2021	2020
1. One option correct	–	–	–	–	1
2. One or More than one correct	–	–	–	–	–
3. Numerical/Integer Type	–	–	–	–	–
4. Matching Type	–	–	1	–	–
5. Paragraph Based	–	–	–	–	–

Current Dynamics

- This chapter holds its importance from JEE Advance perspective only as it is not present in JEE Main syllabus.
- Direct questions were rarely asked, but its applications based questions had been asked in previous years.

Insightful Advice

- Focus on trends of properties, anomalous behaviour, and application-based questions from group 1 and 2.
- Understand the anomalous behaviour of lithium and beryllium and the reasons behind them.
- Memorise the preparation, properties and uses of important compounds like Na_2CO_3, NaOH, $CaCO_3$ and $Ca(OH)_2$.

Element 1

Group 1 Elements and Their Compounds : Alkali Metals

The elements in which the last (valence) electron enters in the outermost *s*-orbital are called ***s*-block elements**. The maximum capacity of this shell is of two electrons, thus, this block includes two groups : IA or group1, having ns^1 configuration and IIA or group 2 with ns^2 configuration.

This block lies on the extreme left of the periodic table. Due to the presence of 1 or 2 electron in the outermost shell, these elements generally form ionic compounds (with the exception of Li and Be).

Group 1 Elements : Alkali Metals

Lithium ($Z=3$), sodium ($Z=11$), potassium ($Z=19$), rubidium ($Z=37$), caesium ($Z=55$) and francium ($Z=87$) are the elements of group 1 of the periodic table. These elements because of the highly alkaline nature of their water soluble hydroxides are known as **alkali metals.**

Abundance

- The alkali metals occur in nature only in the form of their compounds, i.e. they are never found in free state as they are highly reactive.
- Among alkali metals, the less electropositive metal, i.e. lithium is found in the form of silicate while the more electropositive elements are found in the form of their chlorides.
- Compounds of sodium and potassium are the most abundant, while those of remaining alkali metals occur in nature rarely.
- Francium is a radioactive element and short lived.

Electronic Configuration

General outer electronic configuration of alkali metals is ns^1 (where, $n=2,3,4,5,6$ and 7). They are paramagnetic in nature due to the presence of single unpaired valence electron in valence shell.

These metals form unipositive cation M^+ (where, M is an alkali metal) and show +1 oxidation state. All these cations have stable s^2p^6 noble gas configuration [For Li^+ is $1s^2$].

Alkali metals				EC of M^+ (of IA) M^{2+} (of IIA)
I(IA)	Z	EC	Ion	
Li	3	[He] $2s^1$	Li^+	[He]
Na	11	[Ne] $3s^1$	Na^+	[Ne]
K	19	[Ar] $4s^1$	K^+	[Ar]
Rb	37	[Kr] $5s^1$	Rb^+	[Kr]
Cs	55	[Xe] $6s^1$	Cs^+	[Xe]
Fr	87	[Rn] $7s^1$	Fr^+	[Rn]

The relatively simple chemistry of alkali metals is probably due to the ease with which their valence electron can be lost in order to achieve stable noble gas electronic configuration.

General Trends in Physical Properties

The various physical properties are given below.

Physical Properties of Alkali Metals

Property	Lithium	Sodium	Potassium	Rubidium	Caesium
Aomic mass ($g\ mol^{-1}$)	6.94	22.99	39.10	85.48	132.91
Density at ($g\ cm^{-3}$)	0.53	0.97	0.86	1.53	1.90
Molar volume ($cm^3\ mol^{-1}$)	12.97	23.68	45.36	55.80	69.95
Melting point (°C)	179	98	63.0	39	29
Boiling point (°C)	1342	883	759	688	671
Atomic radius (Å)	1.52	1.86	2.27	2.48	2.65
Ionic radius (Å)	0.76	1.02	1.38	1.52	1.67
Heat of atomisation ($kJ\ mol^{-1}$)	159.0	108.1	90.2	82.1	78.2
Ionisation energy ($kJ\ mol^{-1}$)	520.1	495.2	418.7	403.0	375.7
Electronegativity	1.0	0.9	0.8	0.8	0.7
Flame colouration	Crimson red	Golden yellow	Violet	Red-violet	Blue

These properties are briefly discuss below

1. Physical Appearance

They all are silvery white, soft and malleable metals. They are so soft that they can easily be cut with a knife. This softness is due to the presence of weak metallic bonds because of the presence of only one valence electron in them.

On moving down the group softness increases, as increase in number of non-bonding electrons, down the group repulsion increases which results in decrease in cohesive force and energy.

2. Atomic and Ionic Radii

Their atomic and ionic radii are largest in the respective period and increases as we move down the group.

The size of an atom or ion is based on the relation

$$r_n = \frac{n^2 a_0}{Z^*}$$

where r_n = radius of an atom or ion

n = number of shells; a_0 = Bohr's radius

Z^* = Effective nuclear charge due to screening

($Z^* = 1.3$ for Li and 2.2 for Na—Fr)

Thus, atomic or ionic size is mainly dependent on n.

3. Density

All these elements are light metals with low density. Li, Na and K are even lighter than water. Density generally increases on moving down the group but K has slightly lower density as compared to Na due to increase in its atomic volume. Li is the lightest metal known.

4. Melting and Boiling Points

Due to the presence of weak intermetallic bonds these metals have very low melting and boiling points which decreases on moving down the group with increase in size of metal.

5. Ionisation Energy

The first ionisation energy of these elements is the lowest among corresponding period, however their second ionisation energy is very high. On moving down the group, ionisation energy decreases progressively.

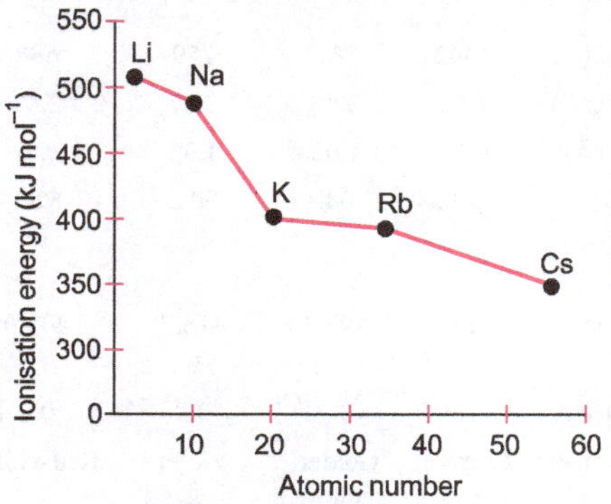

Trend in first ionisation energy of alkali metals

JEE Spotlite

The ionisation energies of K, Rb and Cs are so less that these elements shows photoelectric effect, i.e. these can emit electrons even with the fall of light on them.

6. Electropositive or Metallic Character

Alkali metals are the most electropositive elements in the Periodic Table and their metallic character increases on moving down the group. All of these are metals and thus, are good conductors of heat and electricity. They exhibit metallic lusture which is due to the oscillation of free electrons.

7. Electronegativity

Alkali metals have very low tendency to attract the electrons, i.e. their electronegativity is low because of their electropositive nature. The electronegativity decreases from Li to Cs whereas the electropositive character increases.

8. Flame or Colouration

The vapours of alkali metals impart characteristic colours to the flame. The reason for this is that, the loosely bound electron gets excited on heating and jumps to higher energy level. When this excited electron returns to its ground state, energy is emitted in the form of radiations. This extra energy, in visible region give characteristic colour to the flame. Different alkali metals give different colour to the flame as they have different ionisation energies.

9. Lattice Energy and Solubility

- The lattice energy is defined as the energy released when cation and anion in gaseous state combine to form one mole of ionic crystal or is the driving force for the formation of an ionic compound and its stability.
- For fluorides the value of lattice energy is greater than the variation in lattice energy for chlorides, bromides and iodides.
- This is because lattice energy is proportional to $\left(\dfrac{1}{r_+ + r_-}\right)$ and charge on the ions. Hence, the variation in lattice energy is the greatest when r_- is smallest and least when r_- is largest.
- The solubility of most of the salts of group 1 (alkali metals) elements in water **decreases on descending the group.**
- For a substance to dissolve, the energy evolved when the ions are hydrated (hydration energy) must be larger than the energy required to break the crystal lattice (Lattice energy). We can say that if the solid is insoluble then

  Hydration energy < Lattice energy
- In case of alkali metals, lattice energy only changes slightly, but the free energy of hydration changes rather more.

	Free energy of hydration, $\Delta G^\circ_{\text{hydration}}$ (kJ mol^{-1})	Lattice energy (U) (kJ mol^{-1})
Li^+	–485	–845
Na^+	–379	–770
K^+	–308	–703
Rb^+	–285	–674
Cs^+	–362	–644

- Difference in lattice energy between NaCl and KCl is 67 kJ mol^{-1}, and yet the difference in $\Delta G_{(\text{hydration})}$ for Na^+ and K^+ is 71 kJ mol^{-1}. Thus, KCl is less soluble than NaCl.

Lattice Energies of Alkali Metal Halides

M	*U (MX)*/kJ mol^{-1}			
	MF	*MCl*	*MBr*	*MI*
Li	–1035	–845	–800	–740
Na	–908	–770	–736	–690
K	–803	–703	–674	–636
Rb	–770	–674	–653	–615
Cs	–720	–644	–623	–590

- We observe that for the common halogen (anion) the lattice energy decreases regularly from Li to Cs and for the same alkali metal it decreases from F^- to I^-.
- The higher the charge and smaller the size of the ion, the more is the hydration energy. In a group, lattice energy and hydration energy decreases as we go down. While the decrease in lattice energy favours the solubility, the decrease in hydration energy makes the compound insoluble.

JEE Spotlite

- Whenever cation is small and anion is large or *vice-versa*, the solubility will be larger. Thus, solubility order is CsF > CsCl > CsBr > CsI and solubility of LiF < LiCl < LiBr < LiI.
- LiCl, LiBr, LiI, and NaI are readily soluble in some oxygen-containing organic solvents such as ether.
- NaI and LiI both are very soluble and form complexes in NH_3. The unstable complex $[Na(NH_3)_4]^+$ has been isolated and shown to contain a tetrahedrally coordinated sodium ion.
- In the vapour phase, alkali metal halides are present as ion-pairs, but measurement of bond length and dipole moment suggests that under these conditions electron-sharing is also involved to a considerable extent, especially for the lithium halides.
- For the salts of small anions (like F^-, OH^-, O^{2-}, CO_3^{2-} etc.), lattice energy which is inversely proportional to $(r_+ + r_-)$ is very sensitive to the change in the size of the cation. Anion being very small in size has little contribution in the total and decreases sharply along the group.
- Decrease in lattice energy is greater than decrease in hydration energy and thus solubility of these salts increases as we go down the group. Solubility of the alkali fluorides is thus in order:

$$LiF < NaF < KF < RbF < CsF$$
$$Li_2CO_3 < Na_2CO_3 < K_2CO_3 < Rb_2CO_3 < Cs_2CO_3$$

10. Thermal Stability of Salts

- The stability of the compounds can also be explained by using the concept of polarising power.
- As **the charge density of the metal ions increases, the thermal stability of the salts of large polarisable anions, relative to some decomposition product decreases.**
- In general, the least polarising metal ions are those of the most electropositive metal ions and these form the most stable salts with large anions.
- In other words, **small cations form stable salts with small anions and large cations form stable salts with large anions.** Let us take the example of carbonates of Group I metals. The carbonates of sodium, potassium, rubidium and caesium are resistant to the heat of a bunsen burner flame, however, lithium carbonate decomposes to its oxide and carbon dioxide under the same conditions :

$$Li_2CO_3 \xrightarrow{\Delta} Li_2O + CO_2$$
$$Na_2CO_3 \xrightarrow{\Delta} \text{No effect}$$

- The tendency of Li_2CO_3 to undergo thermal decomposition may be explained in terms of the gain in electrostatic attraction that occurs when extremely small Li^+ ion combines with the smaller oxide ion rather than the much larger carbonate ion.
- The other carbonates of Group I (Na–Cs) are more stable because the cations have a lower charge density and conside.rably larger in size and thus decomposition in less favourable energetically.
- All the metals except lithium form stable bicarbonates.
- Lithium bicarbonate is formed only when aqueous solutions has not been isolated. It is due to strong polarising power of Li^+ on the HCO_3^- ion of larger size.
- When we heat the alkali metal bicarbonates, they are decomposed to carbonates and simultaneously, carbon dioxide and water are liberated.

$$2NaHCO_3 \xrightarrow{\Delta} Na_2CO_3 + CO_2 + H_2O$$

This reaction forms the basis for the use of $NaHCO_3$ in baking powder.

- As the electropositive character increases down the group the stability of carbonates and bicarbonates increases. (Na < K < Rb < Cs)
- The crystal structures of $NaHCO_3$ and $KHCO_3$ both show hydrogen bonding, but are different. In $NaHCO_3$ the HCO_3^- ions are linked into **infinite chain,** while in $KHCO_3$ a dimeric anion is formed.

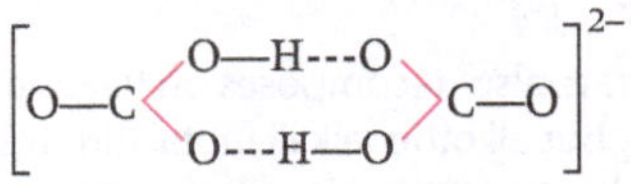

H-bonding in $KHCO_3$ (a-dimer)

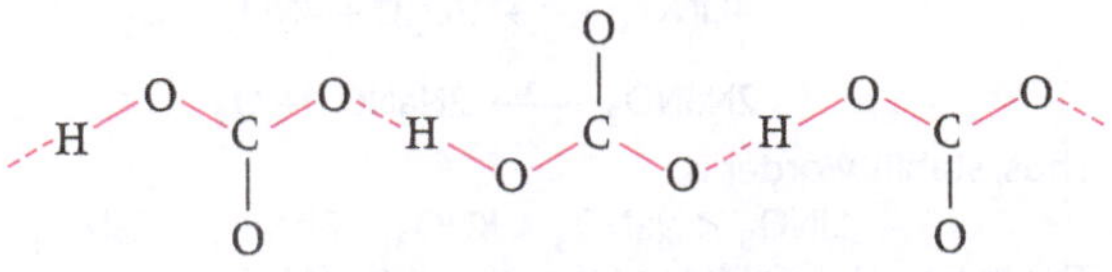

H-bonding in $NaHCO_3$ an infinite chain

- The thermal stability of Group I hydroxides also follows a similar trend as that of carbonates. Thus, except LiOH, which on heating decomposes to Li_2O, all other Group I hydroxides are stable.

$$2LiOH \xrightarrow{\Delta} Li_2O + H_2O$$

$$\left.\begin{array}{l} 2NaOH \xrightarrow{\Delta} \\ KOH \xrightarrow{\Delta} \end{array}\right] \text{no effect, thermally stable.}$$

- The ease of thermal decomposition of a salt is related to the **enthalpy of formation** of the salt. The **enthalpy of formation,** ΔH_f°, of a salt *MA* (*M* is the metal, *A* is anion) is given by

$$\Delta H_f^\circ = (\Delta H_{\text{atom}} + I)_{\text{metal}} + (\Delta H_{\text{atom}} - E_A)_{\text{anion}} - \Delta H_{\text{lattice}}$$

where ΔH_{atom} is the **enthalpy of atomisation,** I is the ionisation energy and E_A is the electron affinity.

- For any salt in a particular group the terms involving the anion alone remain constant, the value of ΔH_f° for such compounds is dependent upon the sum of the enthalpy terms of the particular metal, $(\Delta H_{atom} + I)_{metal}$ and the lattice energy, $\Delta H_{lattice}$.
- The larger the lattice energy, the more negative the enthalpy of formation and so, more stable is the compound. All these terms become smaller on descending the group from lithium to caesium.
- The relative stabilities of the salts, therefore, decided by the parameter which decreases more rapidly—the lattice energy or the sum of the metal enthalpies.
- In the salts having **small anions of high charge density,** e.g., $F^-, N^{3-}, OH^-, O^{2-}$ etc., the change in lattice energy is much dependent on the size of the cation and decreases rapidly on descending the group.
- Thus, as the size of the cation increases, lattice energy decreases more than the change in the sum of the metal enthalpies.
- Therefore, as we go down the group, the stability of these salts having small anions decreases. Thus, in alkali metal fluorides, the stability decreases in the order LiF > NaF > KF > RbF > CsF.

JEE Spotlite

- Lithium nitrate also decomposes on heating to give Li_2O, NO_2 and O_2 but all other alkali metal nitrates decompose on strong heating to nitrites liberating oxygen :

$$4LiNO_3 \xrightarrow{\Delta} 2Li_2O + 4NO_2 + O_2$$

$$2NaNO_3 \xrightarrow{\Delta} 2NaNO_2 + O_2$$

Thus, stability order is

$$LiNO_3 < NaNO_3 < KNO_3 < RbNO_3 < CsNO_3$$

- The increasing stability of the peroxides (M_2O_2) or superoxides (MO_2), as the size of the metal ion increases is due to the stabilisation of large anions by larger cations through lattice energy effects.
- The melting point and boiling pont of alkali halides always follow trend $MF > MCl > MBr > MI$.

11. Reducing Character

- Due to of their strong tendency to lose the *s*-electron, **the alkali metals are powerful reducing agents.**
- The reducing character or reactivity in the gaseous state increases from Li to Cs, i.e. Li < Na < K < Rb < Cs.
- In aqueous solution, lithium is strong reducing agent as compared to Cs. This is probably due to its low E° value (standard electrode potential), i.e. −3.04 V.
- E° value depends upon, (i) sublimation enthalpy (ii) ionisation enthalpy and (iii) hydration enthalpy.
- Sublimation enthalpy of all alkali metals are almost similar.
- Ionisation enthalpy of lithium is the highest among all alkali metals.

Hydration enthalpy of small lithium ion is very high as compared to other alkali metals which compensates its high ionisation energy.

Thus, most powerful reducing agent in solution is lithium.

Solved Booster 1.1

The alkali metals have low melting. Which of the following alkali metal is expected to melt if the room temperature rises above 30°C?

(a) Na (b) K (c) Rb (d) Cs

Solution *(d)*

The melting point of caesium, (Cs) is 28.7°C which is below 30°C. Thus, as the temperature rises above 30°C, it will melt.

Trends in Chemical Properties

The chemical properties of alkali metals are as follows

1. Reactivity

Due to the presence of only one electron in their outermost shell, alkali metals are highly reactive and their reactivity towards all reagents (except nitrogen) increases down the group from lithium to caesium.

- To prevent the reactivity, these elements are usually stored in airtight containers filled with mineral oil or kerosene. Lithium is the lightest among all metals, hence, it is kept wrapped in paraffin wax.

2. Nature of Compounds

The metals form ionic compounds because they readily give up the *s*-electron of their valence shell. Highly polarising ion such as Li^+ tend to form covalent compounds. Most other cations of IA group elements are large and have low charge densities. Hence, they form stable compounds even with polarising ions such as carbonates, peroxides, tri-iodide etc. **LiCl is soluble in pyridine because of its partly covalent nature** due to the polarising power of lithium ion.

3. Reaction with Air (Nature of Oxides and Hydroxides)

- Alkali metals when exposed to air, react readily with O_2, H_2O and CO_2 and get tarnished. That's why these metals must be protected from exposure to air.
- When burnt in air, lithium forms monoxide (Li_2O) only, sodium forms monoxide (Na_2O) in limited O_2 and peroxide (Na_2O_2) in excess O_2.
- Other alkali metals form largely the superoxides. In the presence of atmospheric oxygen, we get a mixture of oxides in the case of rest of the metals.

$$2Li + \frac{1}{2}O_2 \longrightarrow Li_2O; \quad 2Na + O_2 \longrightarrow Na_2O_2$$

$$2Na + \frac{1}{2}O_2 \longrightarrow Na_2O; Rb + O_2 \longrightarrow \underset{\text{(Superoxide, containing } O_2^- \text{ ion)}}{RbO_2}$$

Stability of Oxides

- The formation and stability of these oxides can be explained on the basis of lattice energy effects. Li^+ ion being a small ion has a strong positive field around it and can stabilise only a small anion, O^{2-} whereas Na^+ being a large cation can stabilise a large ion and so on.

$$\underset{\text{Oxide ion}}{O^{2-}} \qquad \underset{\text{Peroxide ion}}{[-O-O-]^{2-}} \qquad \underset{\text{Superoxide ion}}{[:\ddot{O}\cdots\ddot{O}:]^{-}}$$

- In order to prepare any particular oxide, peroxide or superoxide for K, Rb and Cs with the help of atmospheric oxygen, the metal is dissolved in liquid NH_3 and then, treated with required quantity of oxygen to get requisite product.

Nature of Higher Oxides

The higher oxides, *viz.*, peroxides and superoxides are strong oxidising agents. They react with dilute acid to form hydrogen peroxide and oxygen respectively.

$$\underset{\text{Sodium peroxide}}{Na_2O_2} + H_2SO_4 \longrightarrow Na_2SO_4 + H_2O_2$$

$$\underset{\text{Potassium superoxide}}{4KO_2} + 2H_2SO_4 \longrightarrow 2K_2SO_4 + 2H_2O + 3O_2$$

The peroxides are diamagnetic in nature (all the electrons are paired) and regarded as the salts of the dibasic acid, H_2O_2. The superoxides are paramagnetic and have colour as odd electron bond is present between two oxygen atoms.

Yellow colour of Na_2O_2 is probably due to the presence of small amount of superoxide. Superoxides are even stronger oxidising agents than peroxides.

The normal oxide 'M_2O' react with water to form hydroxides with evolution of heat.

$$M_2O + H_2O \longrightarrow 2MOH + \text{heat}$$

$$\underset{\text{Potassium superoxide}}{2KO_2} + 2H_2O \longrightarrow 2KOH + H_2O_2 + O_2$$

The basic nature of the oxides (M_2O) increases gradually on moving down in the group. The hydroxides (MOH) are hygroscopic, readily absorb CO_2 from air and destroy glass. These are colourless, strong alkaline and corrosive compounds. These are soluble in water and dissolve with the evolution of heat.

$$Na + O_2 \longrightarrow Na_2O \xrightarrow{H_2O,\ \text{air}} NaOH \xrightarrow{CO_2,\ \text{air}} Na_2CO_3$$

4. Reaction with Water

All alkali metals are more reactive than hydrogen. Thus, these are easily and readily oxidised by water liberating hydrogen and forming hydroxide.

This reaction is so exothermic that the heat generated often ignites the $H_2(g)$ produced, if air is present.

$$2M + 2H_2O \longrightarrow 2MOH + H_2$$

[M = Li, Na, K, Rb, Cs]

The vigorous nature of the reaction increases from Li to Cs. The fact that lithium reacts with water less vigorously, probably due to its higher melting point. Other alkali metals have low melting points (below 373 K) and melt due to the heat liberated in their initial reaction with water, thus exposing more metal surface to attack.

The reaction, therefore, proceeds much more rapidly than with lithium which remains in solid state.

The hydroxides are thermally stable except LiOH. The relative strength of the hydroxide decreases from CsOH to LiOH.

$$CsOH > RbOH > KOH > NaOH > LiOH$$

JEE Quicker

Hydrolysis of KO_2 gives oxygen gas, hydrogen peroxide and potassium hydroxide

$$KO_2 + 2H_2O \longrightarrow KOH + H_2O_2 + \frac{1}{2}O_2$$

JEE Adv. 2020

- Hydrolysis is a chemical reaction where a water molecule breaks one or more chemical bonds. KO_2 is a strong oxidant that convert oxides into peroxides and liberates molecular oxygen upon hydrolysis.

5. Reaction with Oxidising and Non-oxidising Acids

The alkali metals replace hydrogen from non-oxidising acids (e.g. HCl, dil. H_2SO_4). While reacting with oxidising acids such as conc. H_2SO_4, conc. HNO_3 and dil. HNO_3, these metals do not replace hydrogen but H_2S, N_2O and NH_3 are formed respectively as,

$$5H_2SO_4 + 8M \longrightarrow 4M_2SO_4 + H_2S + 4H_2O$$

$$10HNO_3(\text{conc.}) + 8M \longrightarrow 8MNO_3 + N_2O + 5H_2O$$

$$9HNO_3(\text{dil.}) + 8M \longrightarrow 8MNO_3 + NH_3 + 3H_2O$$

(Here, M = alkali metals)

6. Reaction with Ammonia

The alkali metals dissolve in pure liquid ammonia without evolution of hydrogen; the metals can be recovered from such solution by evaporation.

(i) **Colour** Dilute solution of alkali metals in liquid NH_3 is blue due to solvated electrons and the solvated metal ions. But in the concentration of NH_3 above 3M, metal ion cluster are formed, the solutions are copper-coloured with metallic lustre.

The electron is trapped in the resultant polarisation field, and repulsion between the electron and the electrons of the solvent molecules leads to the formation of cavity within which the electron has the highest probability of being found.

In ammonia this is estimated to be approximately 3.0-3.4 Å in diameter, this cavity concept is based on the fact that solutions are of much lower density than the pure solvent, that is, they occupy far greater volume than that expected from the sum of the volumes of metal and solvent.

(ii) **Conductance and magnetic properties** The solutions are good conductors of electricity as these are paramagnetic in nature, which decreases as concentration increases.

Explanation

When alkali metal is dissolved in liquid NH_3, there is

Step I Ionisation of alkali metal

$$M(s) \longrightarrow M^+(g) + e^-$$

Step II Cation M^+ and e^- both are solvated by NH_3 forming $[M(NH_3)_x]^+$ and $[e(NH_3)_y]^-$.

$$M + (x+y)\,NH_3 \longrightarrow [M(NH_3)_x]^+ + [e(NH_3)_y]^-$$

- It is the ammoniated electron which is responsible for the blue colour of the solution, and the electrical conductivity is due to the ammoniated cation, $[M(NH_3)_x]^+$ as well as the ammoniated electron, $[e(NH_3)_y]^-$, values of x and y depend on the extent of solvation (by NH_3).
- Dilute solutions are paramagnetic due to free electrons. In concentrated solutions, ammoniated electrons associate to form electron-pairs and their paramagnetic character decreases.
- The solutions of alkali metals in liquid NH_3 are extremely good conductors of electricity, they have higher conductivity than that of completely ionised salt in any known solvent.
- The equivalence conductance decreases as the solution become more concentrated and reaches a minimum around 0.05 M. Beyond this concentration the conductivity increases dramatically and sharply and the saturated solutions practically conduct electricity like liquid metals

Conductance of Hg $\approx 10^4$ ohm^{-1} while Na in liquid NH_3 $\approx 0.5 \times 10^4$ ohm^{-1}

$$[e(NH_3)_y]^- + [e(NH_3)_y]^- \longrightarrow [e(NH_3)_y]_2^{2-}$$

- The solutions are themselves unstable with respect to amide formation.

$$Na^+(NH_3) + e^-(NH_3) \longrightarrow NaNH_2 + H_2$$

However, under anhydrous conditions and in the absence of catalytic impurities such as transition metal ions, solutions can be stored for several days.

7. Nature of Sulphates

These form sulphates of the type M_2SO_4. Except Li_2SO_4, other sulphates are soluble in water. The sulphates when fused with carbon form sulphides.

$$M_2SO_4 + 4C \longrightarrow M_2S + 4CO$$

The sulphates of alkali metals form double salts with the sulphates of the trivalent metals like Fe, Al, Cr, etc. The double sulphates crystallise with large number of water molecules as potash alum, $K_2SO_4 \cdot Al_2(SO_4)_3 \cdot 24H_2O$ consists of 24 water molecules. Sulphates of lithium are not known to form alum.

8. Reaction with Nitrogen and Carbon

Despite its high ionisation energy, lithium is the only alkali metal, which reacts directly with nitrogen and carbon to form the nitride and carbide respectively.

Other alkali metals do not react directly with either nitrogen or carbon. This is probably due to the fact that small size of the nitride and carbide ions coupled with the small size of Li^+ ions results in high lattice energies for these compounds. Thus, heats of formation of these compounds are also high results in more stability.

9. Solvation

- When a metal ion is surrounded by the solvent molecules, the phenomenon is called **solvation** of the metal ion. When the solvent is water, it is called **hydration.**
- The alkali metal ions are highly hydrated. The smaller the size of the ion, the greater is its degree of hydration. This is because the smaller the size, the more will be its charge density and the more will be its attraction for the polar solvent molecules.
- Thus, Li^+ ion, which is the smallest gets more hydrated than the Na^+ ion and so on. The degree of hydration decreases on moving down the group. As a result of differences in their degree of hydration, the hydrated ionic radii of the alkali metal ions decreases as we go down the group from lithium to caesium.
- Li^+ ion has the largest hydrated radius while Cs^+ has the smallest hydrated radius in the first group.
- The smaller the size of the ion and the lighter it is, the more will be its mobility and thus conductance.

  In this regard we should expect the highest conductance for Li^+ which is the smallest of the alkali metals but this is not so. The hydrated radius of Li^+ is the largest of all the alkali metal ions, in solution. Therefore, Li^+ ion is the least conducting in solution. The ionic conductance in solution actually decreases in the order

  $Cs^+ > Rb^+ > K^+ > Na^+ > Li^+$.

10. Alkali Metal Hydrides

Hydrides of the type MH have been prepared for all alkali metals on reaction with H_2 except francium. They are colourless, crystalline and ionic solids.

The hydrides are largely ionic with the negative hydride ion H^- present in the lattice. The alkali metal hydrides possess NaCl type structure. The ionic character of the bonds in these hydrides increases as the atomic number of metal increases. Their stability decreases in the same order, i.e. from LiH to CsH.

The alkali metal hydrides are strong reducing agents and their reducing property increases with decrease in stability. Lithium also forms some complex simple hydrides, i.e. $LiAlH_4$ and $LiBH_4$, which are also good reducing agents.

11. Complex Formation

Alkali metals have a very little tendency to form complexes. Lithium being small in size forms certain complexes but this tendency decreases as the size increases.

> **JEE Alert**
> The alkali metals cannot be prepared by the reduction of their oxides, as these metals themselves are strong reducing agents.

Electrolysis of the aqueous solutions of their salts produces the metal hydroxide, as the metals are very reactive towards water. For these reasons, the isolation of alkali metals is usually carried out by the electrolysis of their molten salts.

Anomalous Behaviour of Lithium

Lithium, due to its small size and high charge density, differs from rest of the elements of this group.

It shows the following anomalous properties

- Li is the hardest metal. Its boiling and melting points are highest among the group.
- It is the only alkali metal which reacts directly with N_2 to give **nitride** (Li_3N).
- LiH is much more stable,

$$Li + H_2 \xrightarrow{700\text{-}800^\circ C} \text{hydrides}$$

(other alkali metals hydrides are formed at 350-430°C.)

- With air or O_2, it only gives Li_2O, i.e. monoxide while other akali metals give M_2O_2 (peroxide) and MO_2 (superoxide) also.
- Lithium hydroxide decomposes at red hot to form Li_2O while hydroxides of other alkali metals do not decompose.

$$2LiOH \xrightarrow{\text{Red hot}} Li_2O + H_2O$$

- LiOH shows lowest solubility.
- $LiHCO_3$ exists in solution form while the bicarbonates of other alkali metals exists in solid state.
- Li_2O is least basic.
- Fluoride, phosphates, oxalate and carbonates of Li are sparingly soluble in water while that of other alkali metals are feebly soluble.
- Carbonates and hydroxide of Li are least stable (thermally) while that of other alkali metals are highly stable (thermally).
- $LiNO_3$, on heating gives a mixture of NO_2 and O_2 while nitrates of rest of alkali metals yield only oxygen.

$$4LiNO_3 \xrightarrow{\Delta} 2Li_2O + 4NO_2\uparrow + O_2\uparrow$$

$$2NaNO_3 \xrightarrow{\Delta} 2NaNO_2 + O_2\uparrow$$

(Nitrates of other alkali metals also give same reactions as that of $NaNO_3$).

- Li_2SO_4 is the only alkali metal sulphate which does not form double salts, e.g. alum.
- Lithium reacts with bromine very slowly. Other alkali metals react violently.
- LiCl is highly deliquescent and soluble in alcohol and pyridine. LiCl separates out from aqueous solution as hydrated crystals $LiCl\cdot 2H_2O$ whereas chlorides of other alkali metals are insoluble in organic solvents and do not form hydrated crystals under ordinary temperature.

Diagonal Relationship of Li with Mg

Lithium shows resemblance with magnesium, (Mg) an element of group IIA placed diagonally opposite. This resemblance is termed as diagonal relationship.

Group I	Group II
Li ↘	Be
Na	↘ Mg

Reasons for the diagonal relationship are

(i) Comparable electronegativity of Li and Mg (Li = 1.00 and Mg = 1.20)

(ii) Small difference in radii of Li and Mg

Atomic radii (pm)	Li	152	Mg	160
Ionic radii (pm)	Li^+	76	Mg^{2+}	72

(iii) Both have high polarising power (ionic potential)

$$\text{Polarising power } (\phi) = \frac{\text{Ionic charge}}{(\text{Ionic radius})^2}$$

Lithium resembles magnesium in the following respects :

- Both Li and Mg are harder and have higher melting points than the other metals in their respective groups.
- Li like Mg decomposes water slowly to liberate hydrogen gas.

$$2Li + 2H_2O \xrightarrow{\Delta} 2LiOH + H_2\uparrow$$

$$Mg + 2H_2O \xrightarrow{\Delta} Mg(OH)_2 + H_2\uparrow$$

- Lithium forms only monoxide when heated in oxygen. Mg also forms the monoxide.

$$4Li + O_2 \xrightarrow{\Delta} 2Li_2O$$

$$2Mg + O_2 \xrightarrow{\Delta} 2MgO$$

Both the oxides are less soluble in water.

- Both the elements combine with nitrogen on heating to give nitrides.

$$6Li + N_2 \xrightarrow{\Delta} 2Li_3N$$

$$3Mg + N_2 \xrightarrow{\Delta} Mg_3N_2$$

Both the nitrides get decomposed by water to give ammonia (NH_3).

$$Li_3N + 3H_2O \longrightarrow 3LiOH + NH_3$$

$$Mg_3N_2 + 6H_2O \longrightarrow 3Mg(OH)_2 + 2NH_3$$

- Carbonates of Li and Mg decompose on heating.

$$Li_2CO_3 \xrightarrow{\Delta} Li_2O + CO_2$$
$$MgCO_3 \xrightarrow{\Delta} MgO + CO_2$$

- Hydroxides of Li and Mg are weak bases and are slightly soluble in water. Both decompose on heating.

$$2LiOH \xrightarrow{\Delta} Li_2O + H_2O$$
$$Mg(OH)_2 \xrightarrow{\Delta} MgO + H_2O$$

- Nitrates of Li and Mg decompose on heating giving mixture of nitrogen dioxide and oxygen.

$$4LiNO_3 \xrightarrow{\Delta} 2Li_2O + 4NO_2 + O_2$$
$$2Mg(NO_3)_2 \xrightarrow{\Delta} 2MgO + 4NO_2 + O_2$$

- Lithium fluoride, phosphate, oxalate and carbonate, like the corresponding salts of Mg, are sparingly soluble in water.
- Chlorides of both Li and Mg are deliquescent and soluble in alcohol and pyridine. Lithium chloride like magnesium chloride, ($MgCl_2 \cdot 6H_2O$) separates out from solutions as hydrated crystals, ($LiCl \cdot 2H_2O$).
- Li_2SO_4 like $MgSO_4$ does not form double salts, i.e. alums.
- Lithium salts like magnesium salts undergo hydrolysis.

Solved Booster 1.2

Consider the statements given below

A. lithium has the highest hydration enthalpy among alkali metals.

B. lithium chloride is insoluble in pyridine.

C. lithium cannot form ethynide upon its reactions with ethyne.

D. Both lithium and magnesium react slowly with H_2O.

Choose the options containing correct statements.

(a) (A) and (D) (b) (B) and (C)

(c) (A), (C) and (D) (d) (A), (B) and (D)

Solution

(c) Statements (A), (C) and (D) are correct whereas statement (B) is incorrect. It's corrected form is, lithium chloride is soluble in pyridine.

Compounds of Group 1 Elements

Being highly reactive, all the elements of group 1 form compounds. Here, we will discuss only some important compounds of them.

Sodium Chloride or Common Salt or Table Salt (NaCl)

Sodium chloride (NaCl) is responsible for the salinity of the ocean and of the extracellular fluid of many multicellular organisms.

Preparation

Now-a-days, salt is produced by evaporation of sea water or brine from other sources, such as brine wells and salt lakes, and by mining **rock salt,** called halite.

Properties and Uses

It is commonly used as a flavour enhancer and preservative for food. A large number of chemicals like NaOH, Na_2CO_3, Cl_2, HCl, bleaching powder etc., are synthesised from sodium chloride. 0.9% NaCl in water is called a physiological solution as it is iso-osmotic with blood plasma.

It is used in manufacturing pulp and paper to setting dyes in textiles and fabric, to produce soaps and detergents. It is also used in clearing highways of ice during winter.

Sodium Hydroxide or Caustic Soda (NaOH)

It is an inorganic compound, also known as **lye.** Its method of preparation, properties and uses are as follows

Preparation

It is prepared by the electrolysis of NaCl [brine] in **Nelson cell** or **Castner-Kellner cell** or in **Kellner Solvay cell.**

(i) Reactions occurring in **Nelson cell** are as follow

$$NaCl \rightleftharpoons Na^+ + Cl^- \text{ (in solution)}$$

At cathode $2H_2O + 2e^- \rightleftharpoons H_2 + 2OH^-$

$$Na^+ + OH^- \rightleftharpoons NaOH$$

At anode $2Cl^- \longrightarrow Cl_2 + 2e^-$

The solution containing NaOH and NaCl as impurity is taken out and evaporated to dryness. This process is also called **porous diaphragm process.**

(ii) **Castner-Kellner cell** is the common cell in which mercury is used as cathode. The advantage of using Hg as a cathode is that the discharge potential of Na^+ ions is less than that of H^+ ions.

Na^+ ions get discharged on mercury and sodium so deposited combines with mercury to form sodium amalgam.

Reactions occurring in this cell are

$$NaCl \rightleftharpoons Na^+ + Cl^-$$

At anode $2Cl^- \longrightarrow Cl_2 + 2e^-$

At cathode $Na^+ + e^- \longrightarrow Na$

$$Na + Hg \longrightarrow Na\text{–Amalgam}$$

The sodium amalgam, thus formed, comes in the inner compartment due to rocking. Here, the sodium amalgam acts as the anode and iron rods act as cathode.

At anode $\text{Na-amalgam} \longrightarrow Na^+ + Hg + e^-$

At cathode $2H_2O + 2e^- \longrightarrow H_2\uparrow + 2OH^-$

The concentrated solution of sodium hydroxide (about 20%) is taken out from inner compartment and evaporated to dryness to get solid NaOH.

(iii) A modified cell is **Kellner-Solvay cell.** It has no compartments. The flowing mercury as shown in figure below acts as cathode.

A number of graphite rods dipping in sodium chloride solution act as anode. A constant level of sodium chloride solution is maintained in the cell.

On electrolysis chlorine gas is liberated and Na^+ ions are discharged at cathode (mercury).

Discharged sodium dissolves in Hg and forms amalgam. This amalgam flows out in a vessel containing water. Sodium hydroxide is formed with the evolution of hydrogen.

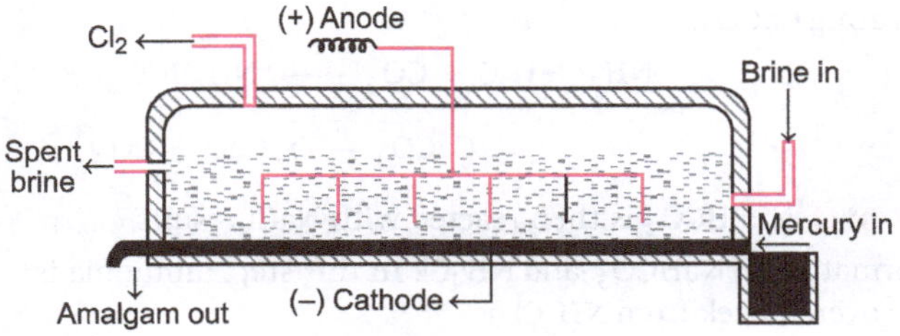

Kellner-Solvay cell

Purification of Sodium Hydroxide

Commercial sodium hydroxide is purified with the help of alcohol. Sodium hydroxide dissolves in alcohol while impurities like NaCl, Na_2CO_3, Na_2SO_4, etc., remain insoluble.

The alcoholic filtrate is distilled. The alcohol distills off while pure solid sodium hydroxide is left behind.

Properties

- It is white solid with melting point 318°C. It is hygroscopic, highly soluble in water and gives strongly alkaline solution. However, it is sparingly soluble in alcohol but less soluble than KOH.
- It decomposes at 1300°C as,

$$2NaOH \xrightarrow{\Delta} 2Na + H_2 + O_2$$

- It combines with acidic oxides to form salts, e.g.

$$2NaOH + CO_2 \longrightarrow \underset{\text{Sodium carbonate}}{Na_2CO_3} + H_2O$$

$$2NaOH + SO_2 \longrightarrow \underset{\text{Sodium sulphite}}{Na_2SO_3} + H_2O$$

$$2NaOH + 2NO_2 \longrightarrow \underset{\text{Sodium nitrate}}{NaNO_3} + \underset{\text{Sodium nitrite}}{NaNO_2} + H_2O$$

- It dissolves amphoteric oxides of aluminium, zinc, tin and lead to give corresponding salts.

$$Al_2O_3 + 2NaOH \longrightarrow \underset{\text{Sodium meta-aluminate}}{2NaAlO_2} + H_2O$$

$$ZnO + 2NaOH \longrightarrow \underset{\text{Sodium zincate}}{Na_2ZnO_2} + H_2O$$

$$PbO + 2NaOH \longrightarrow \underset{\text{Sodium plumbite}}{Na_2PbO_2} + H_2O$$

$$PbO_2 + 2NaOH \longrightarrow \underset{\text{Sodium plumbate}}{Na_2PbO_3} + H_2O$$

$$SnO + 2NaOH \longrightarrow \underset{\text{Sodium stannite}}{Na_2SnO_2} + H_2O$$

$$SnO_2 + 2NaOH \longrightarrow \underset{\text{Sodium stannate}}{Na_2SnO_3} + H_2O$$

- With non-metals (e.g. B, Si, white P, S and halogens) sodium salt of oxyacid of non-metal are obtained, e.g.

(i) **Halogens** give hypohalites and halides with cold and dilute solution of NaOH.

e.g.

$$\underset{(X=\text{Cl, Br, I})}{X_2} + \underset{\text{Cold and dilute}}{2NaOH} \longrightarrow NaX + \underset{\text{Sodium hypohalite}}{NaXO} + H_2O$$

Halogens form halates and halides with hot and concentrated solution of NaOH.

$$\underset{(X=\text{Halogen})}{2X_2} + \underset{\text{Hot and conc.}}{6NaOH} \longrightarrow \underset{\text{Sodium halide}}{5NaX_3} + \underset{\text{Sodium halate}}{NaXO_3} + 3H_2O$$

(ii) Yellow phosphorus (white) when heated with NaOH solution evolves phosphine gas (PH_3) along with the formation of sodium hypophosphite.

$$P_4 + 3NaOH + 3H_2O \xrightarrow{\Delta} \underset{\text{Sodium hypophosphite}}{3NaH_2PO_2} + \underset{\text{Phosphine}}{PH_3}$$

(iii) Sulphur on heating with sodium hydroxide solution forms sodium thiosulphate.

$$4S + 6NaOH \xrightarrow{\Delta} \underset{\text{Sodium thiosulphate}}{Na_2S_2O_3} + \underset{\text{Sodium sulphide}}{2Na_2S} + 3H_2O$$

(iv) Silicon evolves hydrogen when heated with NaOH solution.

$$2NaOH + Si + H_2O \xrightarrow{\Delta} \underset{\text{Sodium silicate}}{Na_2SiO_3} + 2H_2$$

(v) Boron also evolves hydrogen when fused with NaOH.

$$2B + 6NaOH \longrightarrow \underset{\text{Sodium borate}}{2Na_3BO_3} + 3H_2$$

- Weakly electropositive metals like Zn, Al, Sn etc., dissolve in NaOH and evolve H_2, after forming complexes like sodium zincate (Na_2ZnO_2), sodium meta-aluminate ($NaAlO_2$), sodium stannate (Na_2SnO_3) respectively.
- It precipitates hydroxide from many salt solutions, e.g. it precipitates $Fe(OH)_2$ from $FeSO_4$ solution. However, hydroxides of amphoteric elements like Al, Zn, etc., are initially precipitated by NaOH followed by re-dissolution

due to complex formation like sodium zincate, sodium meta-aluminate as,

$$ZnSO_4 + 2NaOH \longrightarrow Na_2SO_4 + Zn(OH)_2 \text{(ppt.)}$$

$$Zn(OH)_2 \xrightarrow[\text{re-dissolution}]{NaOH} Na_2ZnO_2 \text{ (soluble)}$$

- With CO under pressure, it gives sodium formate.

$$NaOH + CO \xrightarrow[\text{5-10 atm}]{150\text{-}200°C} \underset{\text{Sodium formate}}{HCOO^-Na^+}$$

- Ammonium salts are decomposed on heating with sodium hydroxide solution with the evolution of ammonia gas.

$$NH_4Cl + NaOH \xrightarrow{\Delta} NH_3\uparrow + NaCl + H_2O$$

$$(NH_4)_2SO_4 + 2NaOH \xrightarrow{\Delta} Na_2SO_4 + 2NH_3\uparrow + 2H_2O$$

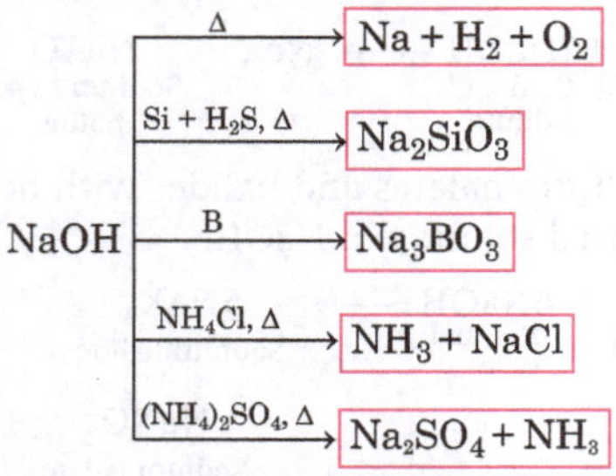

Flow chart showing chemistry of NaOH

Uses

NaOH is used

- as a reagent in the laboratory.
- in the manufacture of soap.
- in the manufacture of paper and rayon.
- in the manufacture of dyes and drugs.
- as an absorber of gases.
- in the manufacture of sodium hypochlorite, sodium chlorate and sodium nitrite.

Sodium Carbonate or Washing Soda ($Na_2CO_3 \cdot 10H_2O$)

Since, pre-historic times a natural deposit called Trona, $Na_2CO_3 \cdot NaHCO_3 \cdot 2H_2O$ (sodium sesquicarbonate) has been obtained from dried-up lake beds in Egypt. On heating it, Na_2CO_3 is obtained.

$$2(Na_2CO_3 \cdot NaHCO_3 \cdot 2H_2O) \xrightarrow{\Delta} 3Na_2CO_3 + CO_2 + 5H_2O$$

Preparation

It is manufactured by **Solvay ammonia process.**

The process involves following three steps :

Step I CO_2 is passed through a solution of NH_3, NH_4HCO_3 is produced. The CO_2 used in this process, is obtained by heating $CaCO_3$.

$$NH_3 + H_2O + CO_2 \longrightarrow NH_4HCO_3$$

$$CaCO_3 \xrightarrow{\Delta} CaO + CO_2$$

Step II NH_4HCO_3 is then reacted with NaCl results formation of $NaHCO_3$ and NH_4Cl. In this step, ammonia is recovered back from NH_4Cl as

$$NaCl + NH_4HCO_3 \longrightarrow NaHCO_3 + NH_4Cl$$

$$CaO + H_2O \longrightarrow Ca(OH)_2$$

$$2NH_4Cl + Ca(OH)_2 \longrightarrow CaCl_2 + 2NH_3 + 2H_2O$$

Step III The bicarbonate formed, on heating gives Na_2CO_3, H_2O and CO_2.

$$2NaHCO_3 \xrightarrow{\Delta} Na_2CO_3 + H_2O + CO_2$$

Raw materials used in this process are NaCl, NH_3 and limestone (for CO_2). Most of the NH_3 can be recovered in the process. $CaCl_2$ is the only by-product formed.

Concept Visualizer

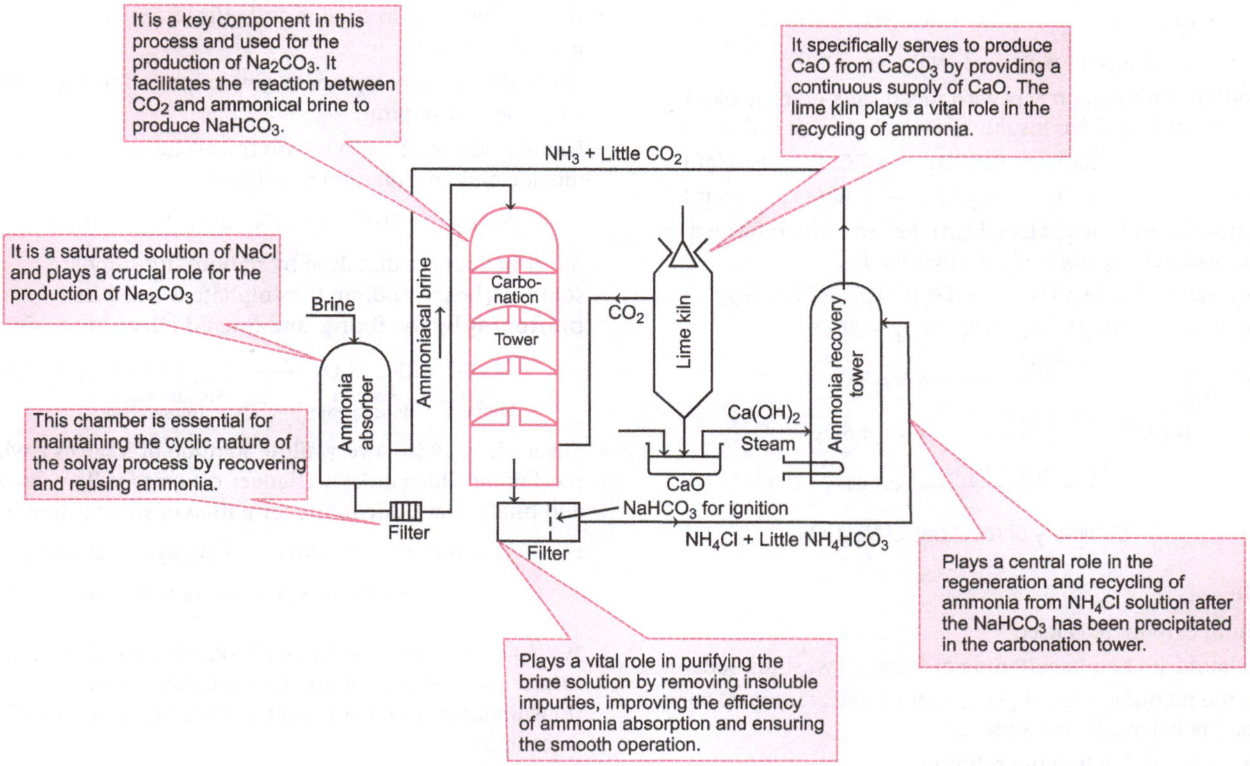

Solvay's ammonia soda process for the manufacture of sodium carbonate

Properties

- $Na_2CO_3 \cdot 10H_2O$, is also known as washing soda. It crystallises as sodium carbonate decahydrate. The formed decahydrate on standing in air lose moisture and turn to a fine powder of monohydrated form, $Na_2CO_3 \cdot H_2O$. It also forms a heptahydrate, $Na_2CO_3 \cdot 7H_2O$.

  On heating, the monohydrate changes to the anhydrous form which does not decompose further on heating even to redness. It is the amorphous powder and called **soda ash**. It melts at 852°C.

$$Na_2CO_3 \cdot 10H_2O \xrightarrow[\text{to air}]{\text{On exposure}} \underset{\substack{\text{Soluble in water;}\\ \text{solution alkaline}}}{Na_2CO_3 \cdot H_2O} + 9H_2O$$

$$\downarrow \Delta$$

$$\underset{\text{decomposition}}{\text{No}} \longleftarrow \underset{\substack{\text{Thermally}\\ \text{stable}}}{Na_2CO_3}$$

- It is soluble in water with the evolution of considerable amount of heat. The solution is alkaline in nature due to hydrolysis.

$$Na_2CO_3 + 2H_2O \rightleftharpoons 2NaOH + H_2CO_3$$

When the hot solution of sodium carbonate is concentrated and cooled, crystals of its decahydrate form are obtained.

- On passing CO_2 through the concentrated solution of sodium carbonate, sodium bicarbonate gets precipitated.

$$Na_2CO_3 + H_2O + CO_2 \longrightarrow \underset{\substack{\text{Sodium}\\ \text{bicarbonate}}}{2NaHCO_3}$$

- It is readily decomposed by acids. The reaction occurs in two steps.

$$Na_2CO_3 + HCl \longrightarrow NaHCO_3 + NaCl$$
$$NaHCO_3 + HCl \longrightarrow NaCl + H_2O + CO_2$$

- When the mixture of sodium carbonate and silica is fused, sodium silicate (soft glass) is formed.

$$Na_2CO_3 + SiO_2 \longrightarrow Na_2SiO_3 + CO_2\uparrow$$

  Sodium silicate is called **soluble glass** or **water glass** as it is soluble in water.

- When the solution of sodium carbonate and slaked lime is heated, sodium hydroxide is formed.

$$Na_2CO_3 + Ca(OH)_2 \xrightarrow{\Delta} 2NaOH + CaCO_3$$

- When aqueous solution of sodium carbonate is treated with sulphur dioxide, sodium sulfite is formed which on further reacting with sulphur gives sodium thiosulphate ($Na_2S_2O_3$).

$$Na_2CO_3 + SO_2 \xrightarrow{H_2O} Na_2SO_3 + CO_2\uparrow$$

$$Na_2SO_3 + S \longrightarrow Na_2S_2O_3$$

- Sodium carbonate reacts with metal salts (except alkali metal salts) to form insoluble normal or basic carbonates.

$$CaCl_2 + Na_2CO_3 \longrightarrow CaCO_3 + 2NaCl$$

$$BaCl_2 + Na_2CO_3 \longrightarrow BaCO_3 + 2NaCl$$

- Carbonates of metals like Fe, Al, Sn, etc., when formed are immediately hydrolysed into hydroxides.

$$Fe_2(SO_4)_3 + 3Na_2CO_3 \longrightarrow Fe_2(CO_3)_3 + 3Na_2SO_4$$

$$Fe_2(CO_3)_3 + 3H_2O \longrightarrow 2Fe(OH)_3 + 3CO_2$$

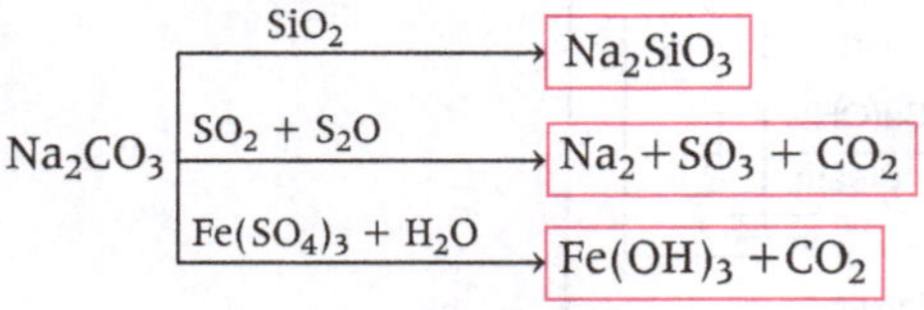

Summary of reactions of Na_2CO_3

Uses

Sodium carbonate is used

- in laundries and in softening of water as washing soda.
- in the manufactures of glass, sodium silicate, paper, borax, soap powders, caustic soda, etc.
- in textile and petroleum refining.
- for the preparation of various carbonates of metals.
- the mixture of Na_2CO_3 and K_2CO_3, called the **fusion mixture,** is used in quantitative analysis to standardise acid solutions. In qualitative analysis, it is used in the detection of acidic radicals especially of insoluble salts.

Sodium Thiosulphate or Hyposulphite ($Na_2S_2O_3 \cdot 5H_2O$)

It is an inorganic compound, typically available as the white or colourless pentahydrate. Its methods of preparation, properties and uses are as follows:

Methods of Preparation

- It is prepared by boiling sodium sulphite solution with flowers of sulphur and stirring till the alkaline reaction has disappeared.

$$Na_2SO_3 + S \longrightarrow Na_2S_2O_3$$

The excess of sulphur is filtered off and the filtrate evaporated to undergo crystallisation and crystals of sodium thiosulphate is obtained.

- It is also formed when sulphur is boiled with sodium hydroxide solution.

$$6NaOH + 4S \xrightarrow{Boil} Na_2S_2O_3 + 2Na_2S + 3H_2O$$

Properties

Properties of sodium thiosulphate are as follows:

- It is a colourless, crystalline and efflorescent substance. It is soluble in water.
- On heating, it decomposes to give sulphur dioxide, sodium sulphide and sulphur.
- Dilute acids decompose it with the evolution of sulphur dioxide and precipitation of sulphur.

$$Na_2S_2O_3 + 2HCl \longrightarrow 2NaCl + SO_2 + S + H_2O$$

- Silver halides are dissolved by sodium thiosulphate solution (hence, sodium thiosulphate is **used in photography for fixing unexposed silver bromide**).

$$\underset{\text{Silver bromide}}{AgBr} + \underset{\text{Sodium thiosulphate}}{2Na_2S_2O_3} \longrightarrow \underset{\text{Sodium argento thiosulphate}}{Na_3[Ag(S_2O_3)_2]} + NaBr$$

- Silver nitrate with a very dilute solution of it, gives a white precipitate which quickly changes colour to yellow, brown and finally black due to the formation of silver sulphide.

$$Na_2S_2O_3 + 2AgNO_3 \longrightarrow Ag_2S_2O_3 + 2NaNO_3$$

$$Ag_2S_2O_3 + H_2O \longrightarrow \underset{\text{(Black)}}{Ag_2S} + H_2SO_4$$

With a concentrated solution of sodium thiosulphate, silver nitrate gives no precipitate. This is because silver thiosulphate formed, is readily soluble in excess of sodium thiosulphate.

$$Ag_2S_2O_3 + 3Na_2S_2O_3 \longrightarrow \underset{\text{(Soluble)}}{2Na_3[Ag(S_2O_3)_2]}$$

- Chlorine oxidises hypo to sodium sulphate while iodine is decolourised due to the formation of tetrathionate.

$$Na_2S_2O_3 + Cl_2 + H_2O \longrightarrow Na_2SO_4 + 2HCl + S$$

$$2Na_2S_2O_3 + I_2 \longrightarrow \underset{\text{Sodium tetrathionate}}{Na_2S_4O_6} + 2NaI$$

- A moderately concentrated solution of sodium thiosulphate gives a white precipitate of barium thiosulphate with barium chloride. No precipitate is obtained with calcium chloride. Since, calcium thiosulphate is fairly soluble in water.

$$Na_2S_2O_3 + BaCl_2 \longrightarrow \underset{\text{(White)}}{BaS_2O_3} + 2NaCl$$

- On addition of a few drops of ferric chloride to thiosulphate solution, a violet colouration is obtained due to the formation of ferric thiosulphate.

$$3Na_2S_2O_3 + 2FeCl_3 \rightleftharpoons \underset{\text{(Violet)}}{Fe_2(S_2O_3)_3} + 6NaCl$$

The violet colour disappears quickly due to the reduction of ferric chloride by sodium thiosulphate. This shifts the above equilibrium to the left.

$$2FeCl_3 + 2Na_2S_2O_3 \longrightarrow 2FeCl_2 + Na_2S_4O_6 + 2NaCl$$

Uses

Sodium thiosulphate is used

- in photography for fixing, under the name of hypo.
- in textile industry as antichlor.
- in the laboratory for the volume estimation of iodine and as a reagent.
- in medicine to reduce side effects of chemotherapy cyanide poisoning and to treat tinea versicolor.

Potassium Superoxide (KO_2)

- **Preparation** It is formed by burning potassium in excess of moisture free oxygen or air. It is a better oxidising agent than K_2O_2, since it produces O_2 and H_2O_2 both in aqueous or acidic solution.
- **Uses** KO_2 thus, finds applications in **space capsules, submarines** and **breathing masks,** because it both produces O_2 and removes CO_2 and CO.

Elemental Practice 4.1

Type I MCQs with Only One Correct Option

1. Which one of the following is the most basic in character?
(a) NaOH (b) KOH
(c) RbOH (d) LiOH

2. The products obtained on heating $LiNO_3$ will be
(a) $LiNO_2 + O_2$ (b) $Li_2O + NO_2 + O_2$
(c) $Li_3N + O_2$ (d) $Li_2O + OH^- + O_2$

3. Sodium is less reactive than potassium because
(a) of its higher ionisation enthalpy
(b) of its less negative $E°$
(c) of its lower ionisation enthalpy
(d) of its larger atomic radius

4. LiF is almost insoluble in water whereas LiCl is soluble not only in water but also in acetone. This is due to
(a) high hydration enthalpy of Li^+
(b) low hydration enthalpy of Li^+
(c) more ionic character in LiCl
(d) more covalent character LiF

5. The metallic sodium dissolves in liquid ammonia to form a deep blue coloured solution. The deep blue colour is due to the formation of
(a) solvated electron $e^-(NH_3)_y$
(b) solvated atomic sodium, $Na(NH_3)_y$
(c) Na^+ ions
(d) $NaNH_2 + H_2$

6. Both lithium and magnesium shows several similar properties due to the diagonal relationship, then which statement is incorrect among the following?
(a) both form basic carbonates
(b) both form soluble bicarbonates
(c) both form nitrides
(d) nitrates of both Li and Mg yield NO_2 and O_2 on heating

7. On combustion of Li, Na and K in excess of air, the major oxides formed respectively are
(a) Li_2O, Na_2O and K_2O_2
(b) Li_2O, Na_2O_2 and K_2O
(c) Li_2O, Na_2O_2 and KO_2
(d) Li_2O_2, Na_2O_2 and K_2O_2

8. When washing soda is heated
(a) CO_2 is released
(b) $CO + CO_2$ is released
(c) CO is released
(d) water vapour is released

9. When sodium chloride solution is electrolysed, the gas that is liberated at the anode is
(a) oxygen (b) chlorine
(c) hydrogen (d) air

10. KO_2 is used in space and submarines because it
(a) absorbs CO_2 and increases O_2 concentration
(b) absorbs moisture
(c) absorbs CO
(d) produces ozone

11. Several sodium compounds find use in industries. Which of the following compounds is/are used for textile industry?
(a) Na_2CO_3 (b) $NaHCO_3$
(c) NaCl (d) Both (a) and (b)

12. In the synthesis of sodium carbonate, the recovery of ammonia is done by treating NH_4Cl with $Ca(OH)_2$. The by product obtained in this process is
(a) $CaCl_2$ (b) NaCl
(c) NaOH (d) $NaHCO_3$

13. Ions of an element of group 1 participate in the transmission of nerve signals and transport of sugars and amino acids into cells. This element imparts yellow colour to the flame in flame test and forms an oxide and a peroxide with oxygen. Identify the element.
(a) Sodium (b) Potassium
(c) Francium (d) Caesium

14. The solubility of metal halides depends on their nature, lattice enthalpy and hydration enthalpy of the individual ions. Amongst fluorides of alkali metals, the lowest solubility of LiF in water is due to
(a) ionic nature of lithium fluoride
(b) high lattice enthalpy
(c) high hydration enthalpy for lithium ion
(d) low ionisation enthalpy of lithium atom

15. Sodium metal on dissolution in liquid ammonia gives a deep blue solution due to the formation of
(a) sodium ammonia complex
(b) sodium ion-ammonia complex
(c) sodamide
(d) ammoniated electrons

Type II 》 One or More than One Correct Option

16. Which of the following metals float on water?
(a) Li (b) Na (c) K (d) Rb

17. Sparingly soluble salts of lithium are
(a) Li_3PO_4 (b) Li_2CO_3
(c) $LiHCO_3$ (d) $Li_2C_2O_4$

18. Which of the following alkali metal compounds decompose on heating?
(a) Li_2CO_3 (b) $LiNO_3$
(c) LiOH (d) $NaNO_3$

19. Sodium hydroxide is obtained by
(a) Lowing's process
(b) Kellner Solvay process
(c) Castner's process
(d) Gossage process

20. Select the incorrect statements
(a) Sodium can be prepared by the electrolysis of aqueous NaCl.
(b) Magnesium carbide and nitride form acetylene and ammonia respectively on hydrolysis.
(c) The order of ionic mobility in gaseous phase is $Li^+ < Na^+ < K^+ < Rb^+$.
(d) Lithium nitrate decomposes to lithium nitrite and liberates oxygen gas on heating.

Type III 》 Numerical/Integer Answer Type Questions

21. Copper sulphate reacts with NaCN to form a cyanide complex. Find the number of NaCN molecules involved in the equation for one mole of $CuSO_4$.

22. On heating 8 moles of Li_2CO_3. 8 moles of CO_x is evolved. Then value of x is.

23. Trona a natural hydrated mixed compound of sodium found in nature. In one molecule of Trona, x molecules of sodium bicarbonate and y molecules of water are present. Then what will be the sum of $x + y$.

24. Washing soda on standing in air efflorescences. The number of water molecules lost by washing soda on standing in air efflorescences are:

25. *A* is an important constituent of cement which is responsible for slowing the setting of cement. The number of water of crystallisation present in *A* is ....

26. What will be the heat of solution in kJ mol^{-1} of NaCl from the following data:

Hydration energy of $Na^+ = -389$ kJ mol^{-1}

Hydration energy of $Cl^- = -382$ kJ mol^{-1}

Lattice energy of NaCl $= -776$ kJ mol^{-1}

Elemental Practice 4.1 | Chapter 04

Connect with **Answers**

1. (c)	2. (b)	3. (a)	4. (a)	5. (a)	6. (a)
7. (c)	8. (d)	9. (b)	10. (a)	11. (a)	12. (a)
13. (a)	14. (b)	15. (d)	16. (a,b,c)	17. (a,b,d)	18. (a,b,c,d)
19. (a,b,d)	20. (a,b,c,d)	21. (5)	22. (2)	23. (3)	24. (9)
25. (2)	26. (5)				

Element 2

Group 2 Elements and their Compounds : Alkaline Earth Metals

Groups 2 elements consists of beryllium (Be), magnesium (Mg), calcium (Ca), strontium (Sr), barium (Ba) and radium (Ra). These are known as alkaline earth metals except beryllium.

Alkaline earth metals form compounds with +2 oxidation state ions, having nearest stable noble gas configuration.

Element	Atomic number	Electronic configuration
Beryllium (Be)	($Z = 4$)	[He]$2s^2$
Magnesium (Mg)	($Z = 12$)	[Ne]$3s^2$
Calcium (Ca)	($Z = 20$)	[Ar]$4s^2$
Strontium (Sr)	($Z = 38$)	[Kr]$5s^2$
Barium (Ba)	($Z = 56$)	[Xe]$6s^2$
Radium (Ra)	($Z = 88$)	[Rn]$7s^2$

Abundance

These metals are highly reactive and hence do not occur in the free state but found in combined states as silicates, carbonates, phosphates and sulphates.

Electronic Configuration

The general electronic configuration of alkaline earth metals is ns^2 (where $n = 2$ to 7)

General Trends in Physical Properties

All these metals exhibit resemblance in their physical and chemical properties on going down the group.

Some important physical properties of alkaline earth metals are given below

Properties of the Alkaline Earth Metals

Properties	Be	Mg	Ca	Sr	Ba	Ra
Atomic number	4	12	20	38	56	88
Atomic mass	9.01	24.31	40.08	87.62	137.33	226.03
Effective nuclear charge	1.95	2.85	2.85	2.85	2.85	2.85
Metallic radius, (pm)	90	136	174	192	198	—
Ionic radius, (pm)	31	65	100	113	135	—
Ionic charge density (ionic charge/ionic radius (Å))	6	3.07	2.00	1.76	1.48	—
$(IE)_1$, kJ mol^{-1}	899	737	590	549	503	508
$(IE)_2$, kJ mol^{-1}	1757	1450	1145	1064	965	975
$[(IE)_1 + (IE)_2]$ kJ mol^{-1}	2656	2187	1735	1613	1468	1483
$(IE)_3$, (kJ mol^{-1})	14850	7730	4940	4150	3440	—
Pauling's electronegativity	1.5	1.2	1.0	1.0	0.9	—
$\Delta S^\circ_{\text{hydration ratio}}$ of M^{2+} /JK^{-1} mol^{-1}	−300	−320	−230	−220	−200	—
$\Delta H^\circ_{\text{atomis}}$ / kJ mol^{-1}	326	149	177	164	178	130
Density at 25°C (g cm^{-3})	1.84	1.74	1.55	2.63	3.59	5.5
Colour	Grey	Silver	Silver	Silver	Silver-yellow	Silver
Enthalpy of fusion $\Delta H^\circ_{\text{fusion}}$ / kJ mol^{-1}	7.95	8.70	8.54	7.50	8.00	20.5
Electrode potential, E°, (V) $M^{2+}(aq) + 2e^- \longrightarrow M(s)$	−1.85	−2.37	−2.87	−2.89	−2.90	−2.92
Melting point/°C	1287	649	839	768	727	700
Boiling point/°C	2700	1105	1494	1381	1640	1140
Abundance on earth %	2.8×10^{-3}	2.33	4.15	0.038	0.042	trace

These properties are briefly discussed below.

1. Atomic and Ionic Radii

- The atoms of the alkaline earth metals are smaller than those of the corresponding group 1 elements. This is because of the increase in effective nuclear charge with increase in atomic number.
- Due to increase in effective nuclear charge, valence shell electrons are pulled in more firmly by the nucleus, thereby reducing the size of the atoms.
- Similarly, the ionic radii of group 2 elements are also smaller than those of group 1 elements, because the removal of two valence electrons increase the effective nuclear charge even further.
- The atomic and ionic radii increase from Be to Ra due to the effect of extra shells of electrons being added. This outweighs the effect of increased nuclear charge.

2. Density

- These elements are denser than group 1 metals because they have two valence electrons per atom for bonding the atoms into a metallic lattice and as a result more mass can be packed into a smaller volume.
- The density decreases slightly on moving down the group from Be to Ca but increases considerably thereafter upto Ra.

3. Melting Point

- Group 2 elements have higher melting points when compared to the group 1 elements.
- The reason being +2 charge on the cations in the metallic lattice, causing them to be more strongly attracted to the 'sea of electrons' and making it difficult to pull them apart.

4. Ionisation Energy

- The first ionisation energy of alkaline earth metals is more than that of corresponding alkali metals. This is because the alkaline earth metals have higher effective nuclear charge and are smaller in size, thereby the electrons are more tightly held to the nucleus.
- The second ionisation energy of these elements is almost twice first ionisation energy. This is because once one electron has been removed, the effective nuclear charge felt by orbital electrons is increased, so that the remaining electrons are more tightly held and hence, much more energy is needed to remove the second electron.
- However, their second ionisation energy is less than that of the corresponding alkali metals because of stability of a closed shell configuration of the univalent cations that are formed in the latter cases.
- The ionisation energy of alkaline earth metals also decreases on moving down the group.
- Lower second ionisation energies of the alkaline earth metals as compared to those of alkali metals can be examplified below :

$$\underset{(2,\,8,\,2)}{Mg} \longrightarrow \underset{(2,\,8,\,1)}{Mg^+} + e^-$$

$$\underset{(2,\,8,\,1)}{Mg^+} \longrightarrow \underset{\substack{(2,\,8)\\ \text{stable closed}\\ \text{shell}}}{Mg^{2+}} + e^-$$

$$\underset{(2,\,8,\,1)}{Na} \longrightarrow \underset{\substack{(2,\,8)\\ \text{stable}}}{Na^+} + e^-$$

$$\underset{\substack{(2,\,8)\\ \text{stable closed}\\ \text{shell}}}{Na^+} \longrightarrow \underset{(2,\,7)}{Na^{2+}} + e^-$$

Electropositive character and the reducing property (tendency to lose electrons) increases on moving down the group.

5. Flame Colouration

As the alkaline earth metals may lose electrons quite easily, they form divalent cations which have a noble gas structure with no unpaired electrons. Therefore, their compounds are diamagnetic and colourless, unless the anion is coloured. Ca, Sr and Ba compounds give characteristic flame colourations which are used to identify them

Ion	Colour
Ca^{2+}	Brick-red
Sr^{2+}	Crimson
Ba^{2+}	Apple-green
Ra^{2+}	Crimson-red

JEE Alert

Beryllium and Magnesium do not impart colour to the bunsen flame.

6. Solubility, Lattice Energy and Hydration Energy

- The metal ions are easily hydrated, e.g., $MgCl_2 \cdot 6H_2O$, $CaCl_2 \cdot 6H_2O, BaCl_2 \cdot 2H_2O$.
  The hydration energies of these ions are much greater than those of alkali metal ions, because of their smaller size and increased cationic charge.
- The lattice energies of alkaline earth metal salts are also much higher than those of alkali metal salts.
- For most of the salt of this group (except fluoride and hydroxides) the hydration energy decreases more rapidly than the lattice energy on moving down the group. Thus, the compound becomes less soluble.
- In case of fluorides and hydroxides, the lattice energy decreases more rapidly than their hydration energy. This causes a reverse trend, i.e., the solubility of fluorides and hydroxides increases on moving down the group.
- Enthalpies of hydration, (ΔH_{hyd}), of alkaline earth metal ions, M^{2+} and lattice energies, $(\Delta H_{\text{lattice}})$ of their oxides, carbonates, fluorides and iodides in kJ mol^{-1} is given as

Element	ΔH_{hyd}			$\Delta H_{lattice}$	
	M^{2+}	MO	MCO_3	MF_2	MI_2
Be	–2494	—	—	—	—
Mg	–1921	–3923	–3178	–2906	–2292
Ca	–1577	–3517	–2986	–2610	–2058
Sr	–1443	–3312	–2718	–2459	—
Ba	–1305	–3120	–2614	–2367	—

Reactions of Alkaline Earth Metals

Table given below summarises reactions of group 2 (IIA). From this, it is evident that as we go down the group, reactivity increases.

Reaction	Comment
$M + 2H_2O \longrightarrow M(OH)_2 + H_2\uparrow$	Beryllium probably reacts with steam, Mg with hot water, and Ca, Sr and Ba react rapidly with cold water.
$M + 2HCl \longrightarrow MCl_2 + H_2\uparrow$	All the metals react with acids liberating H_2. With HNO_3, Be becomes passive due to formation of oxide layer.
$3M + N_2 \xrightarrow{\text{High. temp}} M_3N_2$	All form nitrides at high temperatures.
$M_3N_2 + 6H_2O \longrightarrow 2NH_3 + 3M(OH)_2$	Stability order Be > Mg > Ca (hydrolysis to NH_3).
$M + X_2 \longrightarrow MX_2$ ($X_2 = F_2, Cr_2, Br_2, I_2$)	All the alkaline earth metals form MX_2. No polyhalides are formed. (except BeX_2)
$M + 2NH_3 \longrightarrow M(NH_2)_2 + H_2\uparrow$	All the metals dissolve in liquid NH_3 to give deep blue black solutions which further ammoniates $[M(NH_3)_6]^{2+}$ and form amides at high temperatures.
$2M + O_2 \longrightarrow 2MO$ $Ba + O_2 \longrightarrow BaO_2$	All the metals form normal oxide. Ba also forms peroxide (BaO_2).
$M + H_2 \longrightarrow MH_2$	Ionic salt like hydrides formed at high temperatures by Ca, Sr and Ba. Be forms electron-deficient hydrides.
$Be + 2H_2O + 2OH^- \longrightarrow [Be(OH)_4]^{2-} + H_2(g)$	Not occur with other alkaline earth metals.
$M(s) + 2C(s) \longrightarrow MC_2(s)$	At high temperature Be forms Be_2C, ionic compounds.
$M + S \longrightarrow MS(s)$	The sulphides are soluble in water, but hydrolyse if heated in water.

With Water

- Ca, Sr and Ba have reduction potentials ($E°$) similar to those of the corresponding alkali metal and are quite high in the electrochemical series. They react with cold water quite readily.

$$Ca + 2H_2O \longrightarrow Ca(OH)_2 + H_2\uparrow$$

- Mg has an intermediate value and it does not react with cold water but it decomposes in hot water.

$$Mg + 2H_2O \longrightarrow Mg(OH)_2 + H_2\uparrow$$

or $$Mg + H_2O \longrightarrow MgO + H_2\uparrow$$

Mg forms a protective layer of oxide, so despite its favourable reduction potential, it does not react readily unless the oxide layer is removed by amalgamating with mercury. In the formation of the oxide film, it resembles aluminium.

- Be is amphoteric, as it reacts with acid as well as with base while Mg, Ca, Sr and Ba are purely basic.

With Ammonia

- All the alkaline earth metals dissolve in liquid ammonia as do the alkali metals. Dilute solutions are **bright blue** in colour due to the spectrum from the solvated electrons. These solutions decompose very slowly, forming amide and H_2, but the reaction is accelerated by many transition metals and their compounds.

$$2NH_3 + 2e^- \longrightarrow 2NH_2^- + H_2\uparrow$$

Evaporation of the ammonia from solutions of alkali metals yields the metal, but in case of alkaline earth metals, evaporation of ammonia gives hexammoniates of the metals, which slowly decompose to give amides:

$$M(NH_3)_6 \longrightarrow M(NH_2)_2 + 4NH_3 + H_2\uparrow$$

Concentrated solutions of the metals in ammonia are bronze coloured, due to the formation of metal clusters.

Formation of Hydrides

All the group 2 elements except beryllium form hydrides, MH_2, by direct combination with hydrogen. Beryllium hydride can be formed by reducing beryllium chloride with lithium aluminium hydride, $LiAlH_4$.

$$2BeCl_2 + Li[AlH_4] \longrightarrow 2BeH_2 + LiCl + AlCl_3$$

All these hydrides are reducing agents which react with water and liberate hydrogen. Calcium, strontium and barium hydrides are ionic and contain the hydride ion, H^-.

- Beryllium and magnesium hydrides are covalent.

Formation of Carbides

All the oxide of metals from Mg to Ba react directly with carbon to give the carbides (acetylides), MC_2. These carbides are ionic in nature. Beryllium oxide forms **methanide, Be_2C,** with carbon and acetylide, BeC_2, with acetylene.

Magnesium on heating with carbon forms Mg_2C_3 also, which is an allylide since with water it liberates **allylene (methylacetylene).**

The carbides are named depending upon the hydrocarbon they liberate on reaction with water. If it liberates acetylene, it will be named **acetylide**, and if methane is liberated, it will be called as **'methanide'**, etc.

$$\underset{\text{Carbide}}{CaC_2} + 2H_2O \longrightarrow Ca(OH)_2 + \underset{\text{Acetylene}}{C_2H_2}$$

$$\underset{\text{Methanide}}{Be_2C} + 4H_2O \longrightarrow 2Be(OH)_2 + \underset{\text{Methane}}{CH_4}$$

$$\underset{\text{Allylide}}{Mg_2C_3} + 4H_2O \longrightarrow 2Mg(OH)_2 + \underset{\text{Allylene}}{CH_3-C\equiv CH}$$

Formation of Nitrides

The alkaline earth metals burn in nitrogen to form nitrides, M_3N_2. It requires a lot of energy to convert the stable N_2 molecule into nitride ion, N^{3-}, and this is recovered from the very high lattice energies of the alkaline earth metal nitrides. The beryllium compound is rather volatile while others are not. They are all colourless crystalline solids which decompose on heating and react with water to liberate ammonia and form either the metal oxide or hydroxide, *e.g.*,

$$3Mg(s) + N_2(g) \longrightarrow Mg_3N_2(s)$$

$$Mg_3N_2(s) + 6H_2O(l) \longrightarrow 3Mg(OH)_2 + 2NH_3(g)$$

Complex Formation

This is favoured by small, highly charged cations with suitable empty orbitals of approximately the right energy with which the ligand orbitals can combine. Alkaline earth metals form more complexes as compared to alkali metals. The tendency to form complexes (mostly with O and N donors) decreases with increasing atomic number. Thus, of the heavier ions only Ca^{2+} forms a complex with ethanol. Beryllium having the smallest ion in the group tends to form complexes most readily. It mostly form complexes with tetrahedral arrangement because of the available orbitals as shown below :

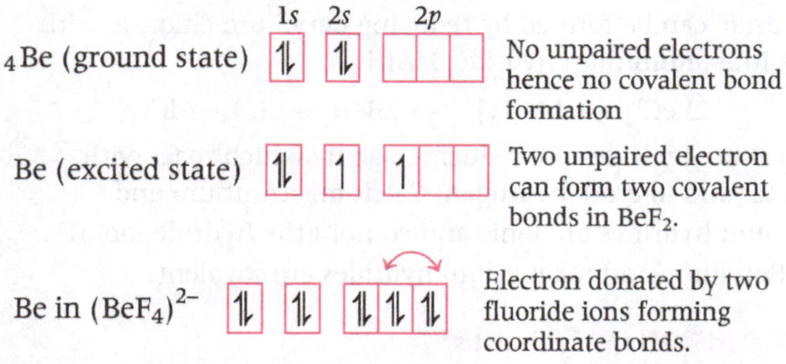

However, once these are formed, all the Be—F bonds tend to become similar.

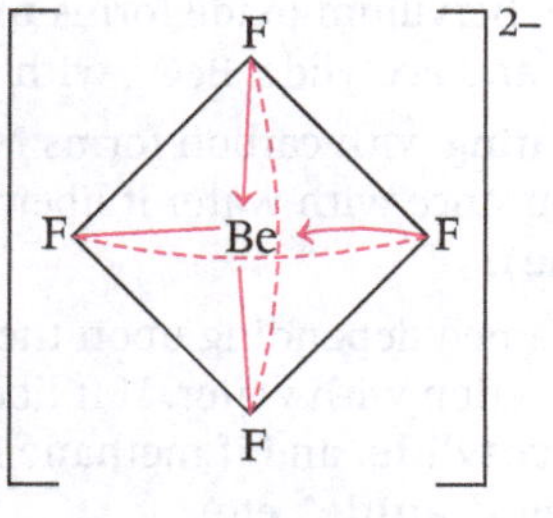

In the hydrated salts, e.g., $BeCO_3 \cdot 4H_2O$ and $BeSO_4 \cdot 4H_2O$, beryllium ions exist in the form $[Be(H_2O)_4]^{2+}$, where they show a coordination number of four.

Magnesium is known to form a very important complex occurring in nature, *viz*; chlorophyll; a green pigment of the plants which produces sugar for the plants in presence of sunlight, CO_2 and H_2O in a process called photosynthesis.

$$6CO_2 + 6H_2O \xrightarrow[\text{Sunlight}]{\text{Chlorophyll}} \underset{\text{Glucose}}{C_6H_{12}O_6} + 6O_2$$

Uses

- Magnesium is an important constituent of chlorophyll which initiates the process of photosynthesis in green plants.
- Magnesium ion are concentrated more in intracellular than in extracellular fluids in animal bodies. Their presence is also necessary for the activation of phosphate-transfer enzymes. These enzymes take part in the biochemical process (exothermic) occurring in animal body. Mg^{2+} ions are also involved in carbohydrate metabolism.
- Ca^{2+} ions are essential for the formation of bones and teeth. The main component of tooth enamel is calcium phosphate.
- Mg^{2+} and Ca^{2+} ions are also involved in the transmission of electrical impulses along the nerve fibre and for the contraction of muscles.

Compounds of Alkaline Earth Metals

The general characteristics of compounds of alkaline earth metals are given below

Oxides and Hydroxides

- The monoxides of alkaline earth metals are more stable than those of alkali metals.
- Oxides are formed either by heating the metals in oxygen:

$$2Be + O_2 \xrightarrow{\Delta} 2BeO$$

$$2Ca + O_2 \xrightarrow{\Delta} 2CaO$$

or by heating their carbonates at high temperatures:

$$CaCO_3 \xrightarrow{\Delta} CaO + CO_2$$

$$MgCO_3 \xrightarrow{\Delta} MgO + CO_2$$

- The oxides are highly stable due to large ionic crystal lattice energies. The values are so high in the case of oxides of Be and Mg that these compounds are almost insoluble in water. BeO is amphoteric and other oxides are basic and yield hydroxides in aqueous solution.

$$MgO + H_2O \longrightarrow Mg(OH)_2$$

$$CaO + H_2O \longrightarrow Ca(OH)_2$$

- Basic strength of the hydroxides increases on going down the group

$$Be(OH)_2 < Mg(OH)_2 < Ca(OH)_2 < Sr(OH)_2 < Ba(OH)_2$$

BeO is insoluble in H_2O but dissolves in acid and alkali and is thus amphoteric

$$BeO + 2HCl \longrightarrow BeCl_2 + H_2O$$

$$BeO + 2NaOH \longrightarrow \underset{\text{(sodium beryllate)}}{Na_2BeO_2} + H_2O$$

- CaO combines with solid acidic oxides at high temperatures

$$CaO + SiO_2 \xrightarrow{\text{High temp.}} CaSiO_3$$

$$6CaO + P_4O_{10} \longrightarrow 2Ca_3(PO_4)_2$$

- MgO is not very reactive, especially if it has been ignited at high temperature and for this reason it is used as a refractory material. BeO is also used as a refractory material.
- Solubility of group 2 metal hydroxides increases while going down the group

$$Be(OH)_2 < Mg(OH)_2 < Ca(OH)_2 < Sr(OH)_2 < Ba(OH)_2$$

- $Ca(OH)_2$ is called **lime water** or **slaked lime** and $Ba(OH)_2$ is called **baryta water**; lime water and baryta turns milky by CO_2

$$Ca(OH)_2 + CO_2 \longrightarrow \underset{\text{Milky}}{CaCO_3} + H_2O$$

$$Ba(OH)_2 + CO_2 \longrightarrow \underset{\text{Milky}}{BaCO_3} + H_2O$$

$Ba(OH)_2$ gives turbidity (milkyness) even on exhaling breath on it.

Milkyness of $CaCO_3$ disappears when excess of CO_2 is passed, due to formation of soluble bicarbonates.

$$CaCO_3 + H_2O + \underset{\text{excess}}{CO_2} \longrightarrow \underset{\text{soluble}}{Ca(HCO_3)_2}$$

- $Ca(OH)_2 + Na_2CO_3 \longrightarrow CaCO_3\downarrow + 2NaOH$

This reaction was used in earlier days to manufacture NaOH from $Ca(OH)_2$.

- $2Ca(OH)_2 + 2Cl_2 \longrightarrow CaCl_2 + \underset{\text{calcium hypochlorite}}{Ca(ClO)_2} + 2H_2O$

- Solutions of beryllium salts are acidic and dissolve appreciable quantities of $Be(OH)_2$. In alkali solution $[Be(OH)_4]^{2-}$ is formed

$$[Be(H_2O)_4]^{2+} \rightleftharpoons [Be(H_2O)_3(OH)]^+ + H^+$$

$$[Be(H_2O)_3(OH)]^+ \rightleftharpoons [Be(H_2O)_2(OH)_2] + H^+$$

$$[Be(H_2O)_2(OH)_2] \rightleftharpoons [Be(H_2O)(OH)_3]^- + H^+$$

$$[Be(H_2O)(OH)_3]^- \rightleftharpoons [Be(OH)_4]^{2-} + H^+$$

- Beryllium forms only monoxide and not peroxide or superoxide
- Down the group the stalbility of peroxides formed also increases $MgO_2 < CaO_2 < SrO_2 < BaO_2$.
- BaO cannot be prepared by heating with oxygen.

Bicarbonates and Carbonates

- The alkaline earth metal carbonates are all ionic hence stable, but due to excessive hydration of Be^{2+}, $BeCO_3$ is unusual and less stable because it contains the hydrated ion $[Be(H_2O)_4]^{2+}$. This unstability is attributed due to strong polarising effect of Be^{2+} ion.
- The carbonates decompose to give MO and CO_2, the temperature of decomposition increase from Mg to Ba.

$$MCO_3 \longrightarrow CO_2 + MO$$

- $BeCO_3$ decomposes at low temperature and is placed in the atmosphere of CO_2

$$BeCO_3 \longrightarrow BeO + CO_2$$

Thermal stability increases with increase in atomic weight down the group or with increasing cationic size.

$BeCO_3 < MgCO_3 < CaCO_3 < SrCO_3 < BaCO_3$

- $Ca(HCO_3)_2$ and $Mg(HCO_3)_2$ exist in water causing temporary hardness which can be removed as insoluble carbonates by boiling:

$$Ca(HCO_3)_2 \xrightarrow{\Delta} CaCO_3\downarrow + H_2O + CO_2$$

$$Mg(HCO_3)_2 \xrightarrow{\Delta} MgCO_3\downarrow + H_2O + CO_2$$

- $Ca(HCO_3)_2$ and $Mg(HCO_3)_2$ are amphoteric thus neutralised by acid as well as base:

$$Ca(HCO_3)_2 + H_2SO_4 \longrightarrow CaSO_4 + 2H_2O + 2CO_2$$

$$Ca(HCO_3)_2 + Ca(OH)_2 \longrightarrow 2CaCO_3\downarrow + 2H_2O$$

- All of these carbonates are much soluble in a solution of CO_2 than in water due to formation of bicarbonates

$$CaCO_3 + H_2O + CO_2 \longrightarrow Ca(HCO_3)_2$$

- $SrCO_3$ is used in the manufacture of glass for colour TV picture tube.
- Calcium and barium bicarbonates are stable only in solution and decompose on removal of water to give carbonates. This property of bicarbonates is the reason for **stalactite** and **stalagmite** formation.

JEE MAPPER

Example Similar to PYQ Asked in JEE Advanced 2022

Match List-I with List-II.

	Lits-I (Compounds)		List-II (Reaction)
A.	Mg_3N_2	I.	$MgCl_2 + 2NaHCO_3 \longrightarrow$
B.	$CaCO_3$	II.	$3Mg + 2NH_3 \xrightarrow{700°C}$
C.	$Mg(OH)_2$	III.	$Ca(HCO_3)_2 + Ca(OH)_2 \longrightarrow$
D.	$Mg(HCO_3)_2$	IV.	$Ca(OH)_2 + CO_2 \longrightarrow$
		V.	$Mg_3N_2 + 6H_2O \xrightarrow{Boiling}$

Match each compound in List-I with its formation reaction(s) in List-II and choose the correct option.

(a) A $\rightarrow$ II, B $\rightarrow$ I, C $\rightarrow$ IV, D $\rightarrow$ III
(b) A $\rightarrow$ II, B $\rightarrow$ IV, C $\rightarrow$ V, D $\rightarrow$ I
(c) A $\rightarrow$ I, B $\rightarrow$ III, C $\rightarrow$ V, D $\rightarrow$ II
(d) A $\rightarrow$ V, B $\rightarrow$ II, C $\rightarrow$ IV, D $\rightarrow$ I

Sol. (b) The correct match is A-II, B-IV, C-V, D-I

Competency Enhancer 2.1

Match List-I with List-II.

	Lits-I (Reactions)		List-II (Compounds)
A.	$2NaOH + SO_2 \longrightarrow$	I.	Na_2SO_4
B.	$(NH_4)_2SO_4 + 2NaOH \longrightarrow$	II.	$Ag_2S_2O_3$
C.	$Na_2S_2O_3 + 2AgNO_3 \longrightarrow$	III.	$Na_3[Ag(S_2O_3)_2]$
D.	$AgBr + 2Na_2S_2O_3$	IV.	Na_2SO_3
		V.	Ag_2S

Match each reaction in List-I with compounds formula in List-II and choose the correct option.

(a) A $\rightarrow$ II, B $\rightarrow$ IV, C $\rightarrow$ V, D $\rightarrow$ I
(b) A $\rightarrow$ IV, B $\rightarrow$ I, C $\rightarrow$ IV, D $\rightarrow$ II
(c) A $\rightarrow$ IV, B $\rightarrow$ I, C $\rightarrow$ II, D $\rightarrow$ III
(d) A $\rightarrow$ III, B $\rightarrow$ I, C $\rightarrow$ V, D $\rightarrow$ II

Sulphates

- The solubility of the sulphates in water decreases down the group.

$$\underbrace{BeSO_4 > MgSO_4}_{\text{soluble}} > \underbrace{CaSO_4}_{\text{sparingly soluble}} > \underbrace{SrSO_4 > BaSO_4}_{\text{insoluble}}$$

High solubilities of $BeSO_4$ and $MgSO_4$ are due to the high enthalpy of hydration of the smaller Be^{2+} and Mg^{2+} ions, which overcomes the lattice energy factor.

- The sulphates decompose into oxides and SO_3.

$$MSO_4 \xrightarrow{\Delta} MO + SO_3$$

Thermal stability of the sulphates increases on going down the group as shown by decomposition temperatures :

$BeSO_4$	$MgSO_4$	$CaSO_4$	$SrSO_4$
500°C	845°C	1149°C	1374°C

- $MgSO_4 \cdot 7H_2O$ is called **Epsom salt** and is used as mild laxative. Correct formulation is $[Mg(H_2O)_6]\,SO_4 \cdot H_2O$ and is isomorphous with zinc sulphate $ZnSO_4 \cdot 7H_2O \cdot MgSO_4$. It is deliquescent and readily soluble in water. It forms double salts with alkali metal sulphates. $K_2SO_4 \cdot MgSO_4 \cdot 6H_2O$ is sold as a fertilizer in the name of **'potash magnesia'**.
- $CaSO_4 \cdot 2H_2O$ is called **gypsum**. Heating converts it into variety of compounds depending on the temperature.

$$\underset{\text{Gypsum}}{CaSO_4 \cdot 2H_2O} \xrightarrow{150°C} \underset{\text{Plaster of Paris}}{CaSO_4 \cdot \frac{1}{2}H_2O} \xrightarrow{200°C} \underset{\text{Anhydrite}}{CaSO_4}$$

$$\xrightarrow{1100°C} CaO + SO_3$$

when powdered Plaster of Paris, $CaSO_4 \cdot \frac{1}{2}\,H_2O$ ($2CaSO_4 \cdot H_2O$ or $(CaSO_4)_2 \cdot H_2O$) is mixed with stoichiometric amount of water, it sets into a solid mass $CaSO_4 \cdot 2H_2O$ — gypsum. Plaster of Paris finds use in plastering walls in making plaster casts (moulds as industrial material as sculptural material and for encasing limbs so that broken bones are set straight).

- $CaSO_4 \cdot H_2O$ is called **Alabaster** — a shiny-like marble is used to make ornaments.
- $MSO_4 + 4C \xrightarrow{\Delta} MS + 4CO\uparrow$

Nitrates

- Alkaline earth metal nitrates can be prepared in solution and are crystallised as hydrated salt by the action of nitric acid (HNO_3) on oxides, hydroxides and carbonates.

$$MO + 2HNO_3 \longrightarrow M(NO_3)_2 + H_2\uparrow$$
$$M(OH)_2 + 2HNO_3 \longrightarrow M(NO_3)_2 + 2H_2O$$
$$MCO_3 + 2HNO_3 \longrightarrow M(NO_3)_2 + CO_2 + H_2O$$

- The nitrate of magnesium crystallises as $Mg(NO_3)_2 \cdot 6H_2O$, whereas barium nitrate crystallises as $Ba(NO_3)_2$, an anhydrous salt.
- The tendency for hydration decreases down the group. It is due to the decreasing hydration enthalpy with increasing size of the cation, from Be^{2+} to Ba^{2+}.

Alkali metal nitrates decompose into nitrites on heating whereas alkaline earth metal nitrates decompose on heating to metal oxide, nitrogen dioxide and oxygen.

$$2Ca(NO_3)_2 \longrightarrow 2CaO + 4NO_2 + O_2$$

Halides

The tendency for the smaller cations to get hydrated is so strong that it is not possible to prepare anhydrous salts by simply heating the hydrated ones. Thus, anhydrous $BaCl_2$ may be prepared by heating the hydrated salts beyond 127°C.

$$BaCl_2 \cdot 2H_2O \xrightarrow{\text{heat}} BaCl_2 + 2H_2O$$

However analogous reaction cannot be carried out for magnesium chloride.

$$MgCl_2 \cdot 6H_2O \xrightarrow{\text{heat}} MgCl(OH) + HCl + 5H_2O$$
$$MgCl(OH) \longrightarrow MgO + HCl$$

If anhydrous $MgCl_2$ is required, it may be obtained by mixing the hydrated salt with thionyl chloride $SOCl_2$.

$$MgCl_2 \cdot 6H_2O + 6SOCl_2 \longrightarrow MgCl_2 + 6SO_2 + 12HCl$$

- Halides MX_2 of alkaline earth metals can be prepared by heating the metals with the halogen acid on either metal or its carbonate :

$$M + 2HCl \longrightarrow MCl_2 + H_2\uparrow$$
$$MCO_3 + 2HCl \longrightarrow MCl_2 + H_2O + CO_2$$

- **The beryllium halides are covalent, hygroscopic and form fumes in air due to hydrolysis:**

$$BeCl_2 + 2H_2O \longrightarrow Be(OH)_2 + 2HCl \text{ (fumes)}$$

- BeX_2 sublimes on heating and are bad conductor of electricity. In aqueous solution it is difficult to crystallise anhydrous BeX_2 since dehydration results in hydrolysis:

$$[Be(H_2O)_4]Cl_2 \xrightarrow{\Delta} Be(OH)_2 + 2HCl + 2H_2O$$

- Anhydrous BeX_2 can be obtained by :

$$BeO + C + Cl_2 \xrightarrow{700°C} BeCl_2 + CO$$
$$2BeO + CCl_4 \xrightarrow{800°C} 2BeCl_2 + CO_2$$
$$BeO \xrightarrow[\Delta]{NH_4F} (NH_4)_2BeF_4 \xrightarrow{\Delta} BeF_2 + 2NH_4F$$

- In solid phase $BeCl_2$ has polymeric structure with chloro bridges in which a halogen atom bonded to one beryllium atom uses a lone pair of electron to form a coordinate bond to another beryllium atom.

Polymer $(BeCl_2)_n$

- In the vapour phase it form a chloro bridged diomer which dissociates into linear triatomic monomer at high temperature.

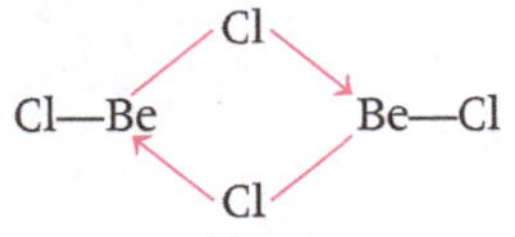

dimer

- BeF_2 is very soluble in water. The other fluorides $MF_2(M^{2+} = Mg^{2+}, Ca^{2+}, Sr^{2+}, Ba^{2+})$ are all almost insoluble.
- The chlorides, bromides and iodides of Mg, Ca, Sr and Ba are ionic and are readily soluble in water.
- The group 2 metal halides form hydrates by absorbing moisture from air. These hydrates can be dehydrated by heating them.
- $CaCl_2$ is widely used for treating ice on roads, particularly in very cold countries when it prevents ice formation even upto −55°C.
- Mixed chloride hydrides of formula MClH which have layer lattices (the different anions occupying different layers) are formed when the hydrides and chlorides of alkaline earth metals are heated together:

$$CaH_2 + CaCl_2 \xrightarrow{\Delta} 2CaHCl$$

Anomalous Behaviour of Beryllium

The beryllium, show an anomalous behaviour from the rest of the family. The main reasons for this difference are as follows.

(a) exceptionally small atomic and ionic size

(b) high ionisation energy

(c) absence of d-orbitals in its valence shell.

Some of its anomalous properties are as follows,

- It forms compounds which are largely covalent and its salts are easily hydrolysed.
- BeO and $Be(OH)_2$ are amphoteric while other oxides are basic.
- The cohesive properties of beryllium are much greater than those of magnesium and other elements in the group. As a result, it is much harder and has higher melting and boiling points.
- Its higher polarising power leads to all of its compounds being largely covalent, with lower melting and boiling points. (MP of BeF_2 is 800°C that of other alkaline earth metal fluorides about 1300°C). All the compounds of Be are more soluble in organic solvents than the corresponding magnesium compounds. They hydrolyse in water, and in this respect they rather resemble aluminium (diagonal relationship)
- Beryllium carbide reacts with water to give methane gas while carbides of other alkaline metals give acetylene gas.
- Beryllium does not react with water even at high temperatures while other metals of this group.

Diagonal Relationship of Beryllium with Aluminium

- Beryllium shows a diagonal relationship with aluminium : The chlorides of both Be and Al have bridged structures in vapour phase

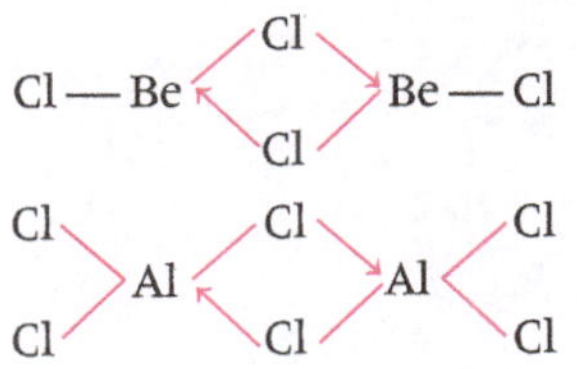

- Both metals have similar standard electrode potential:

$$Be^{2+}(aq) + 2e^- \longrightarrow Be(s), \quad E° = -1.85 \text{ V}$$
$$Al^{3+}(aq) + 3e^- \longrightarrow Al(s), \quad E° = -1.66 \text{ V}$$

- Both are rendered passive by nitric oxide due to formation of oxide layer

$$2HNO_3 \longrightarrow H_2O + 2NO_2 + O$$
$$Be + O \longrightarrow \underset{\text{passive}}{BeO} \xrightarrow{HNO_3} \text{no reaction}$$
$$Al + O \longrightarrow \underset{\text{passive}}{Al_2O_3} \xrightarrow{HNO_3} \text{no reaction}$$

Thus, HNO_3 can be stored in a vessel made of Al or Be.

- Both form electron-deficient hydrides and volatile chlorides. BeH_2, AlH_3, etc, are some electron-deficient hydrides.
- Both form carbides which on hydrolysis give methane.

$$Al_4C_3 + 12H_2O \longrightarrow 3CH_4 + 4Al(OH)_3$$
$$Be_2C + 2H_2O \longrightarrow 2BeO + CH_4$$
$$BeO + H_2O \longrightarrow Be(OH)_2$$

- Both metals dissolve in aqueous alkali evolving H_2

$$Be + 2NaOH \longrightarrow \underset{\text{Sodium beryllate}}{Na_2BeO_2} + H_2$$
$$2Al + 2NaOH + 2H_2O \longrightarrow \underset{\text{Sodium aluminate}}{2NaAlO_2} + 3H_2$$

- Oxides and hydroxides are amphoteric

In dil acid (showing basic nature of oxide or hydroxide)	In alkali solution (showing acidic nature of oxide or hydroxide)
$BeO + 2HCl \longrightarrow BeCl_2 + H_2O$	$BeO + 2NaOH \longrightarrow Na_2BeO_2 + H_2O$
$Be(OH)_2 + 2HCl \longrightarrow BeCl_2 + 2H_2O$	$Be(OH)_2 + 2NaOH \longrightarrow \underset{\text{sodium beryllate}}{Na_2BeO_2} + 2H_2O$
$\underset{\text{Alumina}}{Al_2O_3} + 6HCl \longrightarrow 2AlCl_3 + 3H_2O$	$Al_2O_3 + 2NaOH \longrightarrow \underset{\text{sodium meta-aluminate}}{2NaAlO_2} + H_2O$
$Al(OH)_3 + 3HCl \longrightarrow AlCl_3 + 3H_2O$	

- The two elements have almost same electronegativity (Be = 1.5 and Al = 1.5) and their charge/radius ratios (0.064 and 0.060 respectively) are very similar indicating similar field strengths.
- They also have strong tendency to form complexes: Be forms tetrahedral complexes as BeF_4^{2-} and $[Be(C_2O_4)_2]^{2-}$. Al forms octahedral complexes like AlF_6^{3-} and $[Al(C_2O_4)_3]^{3-}$.

Important Facts of Alkaline Earth Metals

- Be and Mg are kinetically inert to oxygen and water because of the formation of a surface film of oxide.
- Be and Mg burn in air forming oxides and nitrides (BeO, MgO, Be_3N_2, Mg_3N_2). Ca, Sr and Ba are readily attacked by air forming oxides and nitrides.
- Alkaline earth metals dissolve in liquid NH_3 to give deep blue black solutions from which ammoniated $[M(NH_3)_6]^{2+}$ can be recovered.
- Metals are electropositive and strong reducing agents. The particular less negative value for Be arises from the large hydration energy associated with the small size of Be^{2+} and the relatively large value of heat of sublimation.
- The solubility, thermal stability and the basic character of hydroxides increases with atomic number from $Mg(OH)_2$ to $Ba(OH)_2$.
- $Be(OH)_2$ and BeO are amphoteric.
- Except BeX_2 (X = F, Cl, Br, I), all other hallides MX_2 are ionic. BeX_2 exists in gas phase only but in condensed phase it exists as polymer. Solubility of halides in water increases with increase in size of cation.
- Carbonates and bicarbonates decompose on heating. $BeCO_3$ is least stable and is kept in the atmosphere of CO_2.
- Sulphates are stable to heat. $BeSO_4$ and $MgSO_4$ are soluble in water but solubility decreases from $CaSO_4$ to $BaSO_4$. The greater hydration energies of Be^{2+} and Mg^{2+} ions overcome the lattice energy factor, and hence sulphates are soluble.
- Oxalates of Ca, Sr, and Ba are sparingly soluble and solubility increases from CaC_2O_4 to BaC_2O_4.
- Nitrates decompose to form oxide, O_2 and NO_2

$$2M(NO_3)_2 \xrightarrow{\Delta} 2MO + 4NO_2 + O_2$$

Elemental Practice 4.2

Type I MCQs with Only One Correct Option

1. Among the following alkaline earth metal halides, one which is covalent and soluble in organic solvents is
(a) calcium chloride (b) strontium chloride
(c) magnesium chloride (d) beryllium chloride

2. Which of the following is an amphoteric hydroxide?
(a) $Ca(OH)_2$ (b) $Mg(OH)_2$ (c) $Be(OH)_2$ (d) $Sr(OH)_2$

3. Magnesium reacts with an element (X) to form an ionic compound. If the ground state electronic configuration of (X) is $1s^2 2s^2 2p^3$, the simplest formula for this compound is
(a) Mg_2X_3 (b) MgX_2
(c) Mg_2X (d) Mg_3X_2

4. Among CaH_2, BeH_2, BaH_2, the order of ionic character is
(a) $BeH_2 < CaH_2 < BaH_2$ (b) $CaH_2 < BeH_2 < BaH_2$
(c) $BeH_2 < BaH_2 < CaH_2$ (d) $BaH_2 < BeH_2 < CaH_2$

5. The product obtained as a result of a reaction of nitrogen with CaC_2 is
(a) CaCN (b) $CaCN_2$ (c) Ca_2CN (d) $Ca(CN)_2$

6. In which of the following the hydration energy is higher than the lattice energy?
(a) $BaSO_4$ (b) $MgSO_4$ (c) $RaSO_4$ (d) $SrSO_4$

7. A nuclide of an alkaline earth metal undergoes radioactive decay by emission of three α-particles in succession. The group of the periodic table to which the resulting daughter element would belong is
(a) Group 4 (b) Group 6 (c) Group 14 (d) Group 16

8. For two ionic solids CaO and KI, identify the wrong statement amongst the following.
(a) The lattice energy of CaO is much larger than that of KI.
(b) KI is more soluble in water.
(c) KI has higher melting point.
(d) CaO has higher melting point.

9. Which one is the correct statement with reference to the solubility of $MgSO_4$ in water?
(a) SO_4^{2-} ions mainly contributes towards hydration energy
(b) Sizes of Mg^{2+} and SO_4^{2-} are similar
(c) Hydration energy of $MgSO_4$ is higher in comparison to its lattice energy
(d) Ionic potential (charge/radius ratio) of Mg^{2+} is very low

10. The solubility of sulphates in water down the Be group is Be > Mg > Ca > Sr > Ba. This is due to
(a) decreasing lattice energy
(b) high heat of solvation for smaller ions like Be^{2+}
(c) increase in melting points
(d) increasing molecular weight

11. All the following substances react with water. The pair that gives the same gaseous product is
(a) K and CO_2 (b) Na and Na_2O_2
(c) Ca and CaH_2 (d) Ba and BaO_2

12. Which one of the following has minimum value of size of cation/anion ratio?
(a) NaCl (b) KCl (c) $MgCl_2$ (d) CaF_2

13. HCl was passed through a solution of $CaCl_2$, $MgCl_2$ and NaCl. Which of the following compound(s) crystallise(s)?
(a) Only NaCl (b) Only $MgCl_2$
(c) NaCl, $MgCl_2$ and $CaCl_2$ (d) Both $MgCl_2$ and $CaCl_2$

14. Which one of the following is present as an active ingredient in bleaching powder for bleaching action?
(a) $Ca(OCl)_2$ (b) CaO_2Cl_2
(c) $CaCl_2$ (d) $CaOCl_2$

15. The correct solubility order of the given carbonates are
$BeCO_3, BaCO_3, MgCO_3, CrCO_3, SaCO_3$
(a) $BeCO_3 > MgCO_3 > CaCO_3 > SrCO_3 > BaCO_3$
(b) $BeCO_3 > CaCO_3 > SrCO_3 > BaCO_3 > MgCO_3$
(c) $MgCO_3 > BaCO_3 > CaCO_3 > BeCO_3 > SrCO_3$
(d) $BaCO_3 > SrCO_3 > MgCO_3 > BeCO_3 > CaCO_3$

16. The compound A on heating gives a colourless gas and a residue that is dissolved in water to obtain B. Excess of CO_2 is bubbled through aqueous solution of B, C is formed which is recovered in the solid form. Solid C on gentle heating gives back A. The compound is
(a) $CaCO_3$ (b) Na_2CO_3
(c) K_2CO_3 (d) $CaSO_4 \cdot 2H_2O$

17. Calcium is obtained by the
(a) electrolysis of solution of calcium chloride in water
(b) electrolysis of molten anhydrous calcium chloride or fused calcium chloride
(c) roasting of limestone
(d) reduction of calcium chloride with carbon

18. Bleaching powder is obtained by the action of chlorine gas and
(a) dilute solution of $Ca(OH)_2$
(b) concentrated solution of $Ca(OH)_2$
(c) dry CaO
(d) dry slaked lime

Type II One or More than One Correct Option

19. In context with beryllium, which one of the following statements is incorrect?
(a) It is rendered passive by nitric acid
(b) It forms Be_2C
(c) Its salts rarely hydrolyse
(d) Its hydride is electron-deficient and polymeric

20. Which of the following statement is true?
(a) Strontium decomposes water readily than beryllium
(b) $BaCO_3$ melts at a higher temperature than $CaCO_3$
(c) Barium hydroxide is more soluble in water than $Mg(OH)_2$
(d) Beryllium hydroxide is more basic than barium hydroxide

21. In solvay ammonia process, mixture of NH_3 and CO_2 removes the impurities of ions of
(a) Ca (b) Mg (c) Fe (d) Ni

22. An alkaline earth metal '*X*' produces carbide '*Y*' on direct reaction with carbon. '*Y*' on hydrolysis produces an unsaturated hydrocarbon. Then *X* can be
(a) Mg (b) Be (c) Ca (d) Ba

23. Magnesium powder burns in air to give
(a) MgO (b) Mg_3N_2
(c) $Mg(NO_3)_2$ (d) $Mg(OH)_2$

Type III 》 Numerical/Integer Answer Type Questions

24. $Ca_XAl_YO_Z$ represents formula of the ingredient present in portland cement and $Na_2CO_3 \cdot wH_2O$ is manufactured in solvay process sum of *x*, *y*, *z* and *w* is ....

25. Consider the following reactions

I. $(NH_4)_2BeF_4 \xrightarrow{\Delta} BeF_2$
II. $2BeCl_2 + LiAlH_4 \longrightarrow 2BeH_2 + LiCl + AlCl_3$
III. $Be(OH)_2 + Sr(OH)_2 \longrightarrow Sr^{2+}[Be(OH)_4]^{2-}$
IV. $Be(OH)_2 + 2NaOH \longrightarrow Na_2[Be(OH)_4]$
V. $NH_3 + CaOCl_2 \longrightarrow NH_4Cl + CaO + HCl$
VI. $6CaO \cdot Al_2O_3 + 3CaSO_4 + 2H_2O \longrightarrow 2CaO \cdot Al_2O_6 \cdot 3CaSO_4 \cdot 2H_2O$
VII. $Mg_3N_2(s) + 6H_2O(l) \longrightarrow 3Mg(OH)_2 + 2NH_3(g)$

The number of incorrect reaction are ......

26. Consider the following reaction.

$$2Ca + N_2 \xrightarrow{\Delta} P$$

$$P + 6H_2O \xrightarrow{\Delta} M + NH_3$$

$$M + \underset{\text{From air}}{CO_2} \longrightarrow W + H_2O$$

The total number of incorrect statement(s) among the following is/are
(a) The product *M* is used in mortar production and as disinfectant.
(b) The colour of product *W* is blue
(c) The oxidation number of product *P* is zero.
(d) *W* is unstable in air and is decomposed in CO_2 of atmosphere.

27. Consider the following metal carbonates
$Na_2CO_3, MgCO_3, K_2CO_3, Rb_2CO_3, CaCO_3, BaCO_3, Li_2CO_3$
The total number of metal carbonates that decomposes upon heating is

28. Consider the following substances
A. $(NH_4)_2SO_4$ B. $Ca_3(PO_4)_2$
C. $Ca(H_2PO_4)_2$ D. $CaCN_2 + C$
E. $CaSO_4$ F. $CaCO_3 \cdot MgCO_3$
G. $MgNO_3$
The total number of substances that can be used directly as fertilizer

Elemental Practice 4.2 | Chapter 04

Connect with Answers

1. (d)	2. (c)	3. (d)	4. (a)	5. (b)	6. (b)
7. (c)	8. (c)	9. (c)	10. (b)	11. (c)	12. (c)
13. (a)	14. (a)	15. (a)	16. (a)	17. (b)	18. (d)
19. (a,b,d)	20. (a,b,c)	21. (a,b,c)	22. (a,c,d)	23. (a,b)	24. (21)
25. (2)	26. (2)	27. (5)	28. (6)		

Advanced Exclusive Different Strokes

- At normal temperatures all the group 1 metals adopt a body-centred cubic type of lattice with coordination number of 8.
- At very low temperatures lithium forms a hexagonal close-packed structure with coordination number of 12.
- The cohesive energies of group 1 metals are about half of those for group 2 and one third of those for group 13 elements.
- The magnitude of cohesive energy determines the hardness, and it depends on the number of electrons that can participate in bonding and on the strength of the bonds formed.

Thus, with the help of above key points we can approach problems related to blend concept of solid state and *s*-block elements or surface chemistry and *s*-block elements.

PRACTICE ELEMENT

Target JEE Advanced

Single Correct Choice MCQs

1. Which of the following statement is incorrect?
   (a) Mg_2C_3 reacts with water to form propyne gas.
   (b) Plaster of paris when mixed with the correct amount of water sets into $CaSO_4 \cdot 2H_2O$.
   (c) Lithium and magnesium do not form superoxide.
   (d) Beryllium has high negative value of reduction potential compared to other alkaline earth metals.

2. In the case of alkali metals, the covalent character decreases in the order
   (a) $MF > MCl > MBr > MI$
   (b) $MF > MCl > MI > MBr$
   (c) $MI > MBr > MCl > MF$
   (d) $MCl > MI > MBr > MF$

3. Which of the following statements is incorrect?
   (a) Pure sodium metal dissolves in liquid ammonia to given blue solution.
   (b) NaOH reacts with glass to give sodium silicate.
   (c) Aluminium reacts with excess NaOH to give $Al(OH)_3$.
   (d) $NaHCO_3$ on heating gives Na_2CO_3.

4. When a substance (A) reacts with water it produces a combustible gas (B) and a solution of substance (C) in water. When another substance (D) reacts with this solution of (C), it also produces the same gas (B) on warming, but (D) can produce gas (B) on reaction with dilute sulphuric acid at room temperature. Substance (A) imparts a deep golden yellow colour to a smokeless flame of Bunsen burner. Then (A), (B), (C) and (D) respectively are
   (a) Ca, H_2, $Ca(OH)_2$, Sn
   (b) K, H_2, KOH, Al
   (c) Na, H_2, NaOH, Zn
   (d) CaC_2, C_2H_2, $Ca(OH)_2$, Fe

5. Which of the following statements regarding lithium is incorrect?
   (a) It forms ethynide on reaction with ethyne.
   (b) It is least reactive and strongest reducing agent among all the alkali metals.
   (c) It is much harder and have high boiling point.
   (d) The chlorides of lithium are insoluble in ethanol.

6. Choose the incorrect order from the following.
   (a) $BeCO_3 < MgCO_3 < CaCO_3$ (Thermal stability)
   (b) $Ca(OH)_2 < Sr(OH)_2 < Ba(OH)_2$ (Solubility in water)
   (c) Sr > Be > Mg (Density)
   (d) Be < Ca < Sr (Melting point)

7. The alkali metals and their salts show characteristic colour to
   (a) an oxidising flame
   (b) a reducing flame
   (c) they do not show any colour to any flame
   (d) Both (a) and (b)

8. Select the correct statement from the following.
   (a) $BeCl_2 < MgCl_2 < CaCl_2 < BaCl_2$ is the correct order of ionic character.
   (b) Sodium is the strongest reducing agent in aqueous solution.
   (c) $Mg(ClO_4)_2$ is used as a drying agent.
   (d) LiCl has the lowest melting point.

9. Which one of the following statements is correct?
   (a) All enzymes that utilise ATP in phosphate transfer require Ca as the co-factor.
   (b) The bone in human body is an inert and unchanging substance.
   (c) Mg plays roles in neuromuscular function and interneuronal transmission.
   (d) The daily requirement of Mg and Ca in the human body is estimated to be 0.2-0.3 g.

10. Consider the following statements.
    A. Lithium nitrate when heated separately give Li_2O.
    B. CsI is less soluble in water due to less hydration enthalpy of its ions.
    C. Highly pure dilute solution of sodium in liquid ammonia shows blue colour.
    D. NaO_2 and NaOH are formed upon combustion of sodium metal in excess air.
    E. Lithium is least reactive with water among the alkali metals.

    Choose the option containing correct statements.
    (a) A, B and D (b) B, C and D
    (c) A, B, C and E (d) D and E

One or More than One Correct MCQs

11. Which of the following reaction(s) is/are correct?
    (a) $Cl_2 + NaOH \longrightarrow NaCl + NaClO_3 + H_2O$
    (b) $P_4 + NaOH + H_2O \longrightarrow NaH_2PO_2 + PH_3$
    (c) $S + NaOH \xrightarrow{\Delta} Na_2S_2O_3 + Na_2S + H_2O$
    (d) $Si + NaOH + H_2O \xrightarrow{\Delta} Na_2SiO_3 + H_2$

12. Nitrogen dioxide cannot be obtained by heating
    (a) KNO_3 (b) $NaNO_3$
    (c) $AgNO_3$ (d) $Cu(NO_3)_2$

13. In which of the following, hydration enthalpy is greater than the lattice enthalpy?
(a) $BaSO_4$ (b) $BaCO_3$
(c) Na_2SO_4 (d) Na_2CO_3

14. Select the incorrect statement(s)
(a) Cs^+ is more hydrated than the other alkali metal ions
(b) Among the alkali metals Li, Na, K and Rb, lithium has the highest melting point
(c) Ionic mobility of Li^+ is maximum among alkali metal cations
(d) Ionisation potential of Li is lower than that of Na

15. Which of the following alkaline earth metal sulphate have hydration enthalpy lesser than its lattice enthalpy?
(a) $CaSO_4$ (b) $BeSO_4$
(c) $BaSO_4$ (d) $SrSO_4$

16. Which of the following reactions is/are correct?
(a) $Al_2O_3 + 2NaOH \longrightarrow 2NaAlO_2 + H_2O$
(b) $BeO + 2NaOH \longrightarrow Na_2BeO_2 + H_2O$
(c) $CaCN_2 + 3H_2O \longrightarrow CaCO_3 + 2NH_3$
(d) $CaC_2 + N_2 \longrightarrow CaCN_2 + C$

17. Which of the following statements is/are correct about magnesium ion?
(a) Magnesium is an important constituent of chlorophyll.
(b) Magnesium ions are concentrated more in extracellular fluids in animal bodies.
(c) Mg^{2+} ions is a necessary requirement for the activation of phosphate transfer enzymes.
(d) Mg^{2+} ions are responsible for the transmission of electrical impulses along the nerve fibre.

18. Which of the following statements about Lithium is/are incorrect?
(a) Lithium is much softer than the rest of the alkali metals.
(b) Lithium is the only alkali metal which reacts with nitrogen to give lithium nitride, Li_3N.
(c) Lithium reacts with bromine very fast.
(d) The carbonate of lithium is thermally less stable and decomposes into oxide on moderate heating.

Numerical/Integer Type Questions

19. On heating, $LiNO_3$ gives how many compounds among the following?

$$Li_2O, N_2, O_2, LiNO_2, NO_2$$

20. Number of amphoteric compounds among the following is ....
(a) BeO (b) BaO
(c) $Be(OH)_2$ (d) $Sr(OH)_2$

21. $Mg(NO_3)_2 \cdot xH_2O$ and $Ba(NO_3)_2 \cdot yH_2O$, represent formula of the crystalline forms of nitrate salts. Sum of x and y is ....

22. BeO reacts with HF in presence of ammonia to give [*A*] which on thermal decomposition produces [*B*] and ammonium fluoride. Oxidation state of Be in [*A*] is ....

23. The number of sulphates that will dissolve in water are:
$SrSO_4, K_2SO_4, BeSO_4, Li_2SO_4, MgSO_4, CaSO_4, Rb_2SO_4$

Matching Type Questions

24. Match List-I with List-II.

	List-I		List-II
A.	$NaOH + NO_2 \longrightarrow$	(P)	Evolution of hydrogen
B.	$NaOH + Sn \xrightarrow{H_2O}$	(Q)	Rotten fish smell
C.	$NaOH + Br_2 \xrightarrow{Cold}$	(R)	More than one salt is formed
D.	$NaOH + P_4 \longrightarrow$	(S)	Salt with highest oxidation state of central atom

Choose the correct answer from the options given below.
(a) A-S, B-P, C-R, D-Q (b) A-P, B-Q, C-R, D-S
(c) A-S, B-R, C-Q, D-P (d) A-S, B-R, C-P, D-Q

25. Match List-I with List-II.

	List-I (Element)		List-II (Colour to flame)
A.	Cs	I.	Violet
B.	Na	II.	Brick red
C.	K	III.	Crimson red
D.	Ca	IV.	Blue
		V.	Yellow

Choose the correct answer from the options given below.
(a) A-II, B-III, C-IV, D-I
(b) A-IV, B-V, C-I, D-II
(c) A-IV, B-I, C-V, D-II
(d) A-II, B-IV, C-III, D-I

26. Match List-I with List-II.

	List-I		List-II
A.	Mg	I.	Blood clotting
B.	Ca	II.	Cancer treatment
C.	Be	III.	Chlorophyll
D.	Ra	IV.	Windows of *X*-ray tubes
		V.	Special glasses

Choose the most appropriate answer from the options given below
(a) A-V, B-I, C-II, D-IV
(b) A-III, B-I, C-IV, D-II
(c) A-III, B-II, C-IV, D-I
(d) A-IV, B-V, C-II, D-III

27. Match List-I with List-II for the composition of substances and select the correct answer using the code given.

	List-I (Substances)		List-II (Composition)
(A)	Plaster of Paris	(i)	$CaSO_4 \cdot 2H_2O$
(B)	Epsomite	(ii)	$CaSO_4 \cdot \frac{1}{2}H_2O$
(C)	Kieserite	(iii)	$MgSO_4 \cdot 7H_2O$
(D)	Gypsum	(iv)	$MgSO_4 \cdot H_2O$
		(v)	$CaSO_4$

(a) (A)-(iii), (B)-(iv), (C)-(i), (D)-(ii)
(b) (A)-(ii), (B)-(iii), (C)-(iv), (D)-(i)
(c) (A)-(i), (B)-(ii), (C)-(iii), (D)-(v)
(d) (A)-(iv), (B)-(iii), (C)-(ii), (D)-(i)

28. Match List-I with List-II.

	List-I		List-II
A.	Potassium	I.	Soft soap
B.	Potassium chloride	II.	Fertiliser
C.	Potassium hydroxide	III.	Photoelectric cells
D.	Caesium	IV.	Biological nerve impulse

Choose the correct answer from the options given below.
(a) A → III; B → IV; C → I; D → II;
(b) A → IV; B → III; C → II; D → I;
(c) A → III; B → I; C → IV; D → II;
(d) A → IV; B → II; C → I; D → III;

Paragraph Based Questions

Paragraph 1

Hydrides of the type *M*H have been prepared for all alkali metals on reaction with H_2 except francium. They are colourless, crystalline, ionic solids. The alkali metal hydrides are strong reducing agents and their reducing property increases with decrease in stability.

29. The total number of factors that make Li as strongest reducing agent is
(a) high ionisation enthalpy
(b) high electron gain enthalpy
(c) low sublimation enthalpy
(d) high hydration enthalpy
(e) small size
(f) lowest reduction potential

30. The total number of elements that does not form hydride by direct heating with dihydrogen are
Be, Sr, Mg, Ba, Ca

Paragraph 2

Alkali metals when exposed to air, react readily with O_2, H_2O and CO_2 and get tarnished. That's why these metals must be protected from exposure to air.

Most metal oxides are thermally stable at temperature upto 1000°C but the oxide of metals below hydrogen in the electrochemical series decompose fairly easily. Thus, HgO and Ag_2O decompose on heating.

31. The total number of salt that does not give NO_2 gas on heating is ....
$Pb(NO_3)_2$, $Zn(NO_3)_2$, $AgNO_3$, KNO_3, $NaNO_3$

32. Consider the following metal carbonates
$CsHCO_3$, Rb_2CO_3, Li_2CO_3, $(NH_4)_2CO_3$, $CaCO_3$
The total number of compounds that can not be thermally decomposed even at high temperature.

Species Selection (with 5 Species)

33. Consider the following reactions.
I. $BeCO_3 \xrightarrow{\Delta}$ II. $FeSO_4 \xrightarrow{300\,°C}$
III. $ZnSO_4 \xrightarrow[T\,<\,800\,°C]{\Delta}$ IV. $(NH_4)_2Cr_2O_7 \xrightarrow{\Delta}$
V. $Pb(NO_3)_2 \xrightarrow{\Delta}$
The total number of thermal decomposition reaction that evolve different gases which have equal number of σ-and π-bond
(a) 3 (b) 4 (c) 2 (d) 1

34. Consider the following compounds.
I. $CaCl_2$ II. $CuSO_4$ III. $ZnCl_2$ IV. $HgCl_2$
V. $AgNO_3$
How many of the above compounds will form a coloured precipitate with Na_2CO_3?
(a) 2 (b) 3 (c) 4 (d) 5

35. Consider the following compounds.
I. KOH + HI II. K_2CO_3 + HI
III. KIO_3+C IV. $Fe_3I_8 + H_2O + K_2CO_3$
V. I_2 + KOH
The number of combination of reactants can form KI is
(a) 2 (b) 4 (c) 5 (d) 6

Species Selection (with 7 Species)

36. Consider the following compounds.
I. SiO_2 II. ClO_2 III. SO_2 IV. SO_3
V. $Ca(OH)_2$ VI. MgO VII. $CaCl_2$
How many of the following compound will react with Na_2CO_3?
(a) 3 (b) 4
(c) 5 (d) 7

37. Consider the following compounds.
I. $CaCl_2$ II. $BaCl_2$ III. $MgCl_2$ IV. $AgNO_3$
V. $CuSO_4$ VI. $ZnCl_2$ VII. $HgCl_2$
The species that will form basic carbonate with Na_2CO_3 are
(a) 2 (b) 3 (c) 4 (d) 5

38. Consider the following compounds.
I. MgO II. $MgCO_3$ III. $MgCl_2$
IV. Fe_2O_3 V. CaO VI. SiO_2
VII. $CaSO_4$
The number of compounds that are present in portland cement is
(a) 2 (b) 3
(c) 4 (d) 5

39. Consider the following compounds.
I. $CuSO_4$ II. $Pb(CH_3COO)_2$ III. H_2O_2
IV. $K_2Cr_2O_7$ V. HNO_3 VI. $KMnO_4$
VII. $AgNO_3$
Select the compounds that will react with, KI to liberate iodine.
(a) 2 (b) 3
(c) 4 (d) 5

40. On heating, $NaNO_3$ gives how many compounds among the following?
I. Na_2O II. Na_2O_2 III. $NaNO_2$ IV. O_2
V. N_2 VI. NO_2 VII. O_3
(a) 5 (b) 4
(c) 2 (d) O_3

Check Through PYQs

Element 1 Group 1 Elements (Alkali Metals)

1. Which of the following liberates O_2 upon hydrolysis? *2020 Adv.*
(a) Pb_3O_4 (b) KO_2
(c) Na_2O_2 (d) Li_2O_2

Element 2 Group 2 Elements (Alkaline Earth Metal)

2. List-I contains compounds and List-II contains reactions.

List-I		List-II	
(I)	H_2O_2	(P)	$Mg(HCO_3)_2 + Ca(OH)_2 \longrightarrow$
(II)	$Mg(OH)_2$	(Q)	$BaO_2 + H_2SO_4 \longrightarrow$
(III)	$BaCl_2$	(R)	$Ca(OH)_2 + MgCl_2 \longrightarrow$
(IV)	$CaCO_3$	(S)	$BaO_2 + HCl \longrightarrow$
		(T)	$Ca(HCO_3)_2 + Ca(OH)_2 \longrightarrow$

Match each compound in List-I with its formation reaction(s) in List-II, and choose the correct option. *2022 Adv.*
(a) I → Q; II → P; III → S; IV → R
(b) I → T; II → P; III → Q; IV → R
(c) I → T; II → R; III → Q; IV → P
(d) I → Q; II → R; III → S; IV → P

HINTS & Solutions

Solutions : Competency Enhancer

2.1 *(c)* The correct match is A-IV, B-I, C-II, D-III.

Elemental Practice 4.1

1. *(c)* $LiOH < NaOH < KOH < RbOH$

   On moving down the group basic character increases, thus RbOH is most basic in character.

2. *(b)* The products obtained on heating $LiNO_3$ will be $Li_2O + NO_2 + O_2$. The reaction involved is as follows.

$$2LiNO_3 \xrightarrow{\Delta} Li_2O + 2NO_2 + \frac{1}{2}O_2$$

3. *(a)* Sodium is less reactive than potassium because it has higher ionisation enthalpy and is smaller in atomic size than potassium. Potassium has higher reduction potential (Negative) than sodium means it can more easily lose electrons than sodium.

4. *(a)* LiF is almost insoluble in water due to its high lattice energy. But LiCl is soluble in water due to high hydration energy of Li^+ ion.

   LiCl is also soluble in acetone due to its predominantly covalent nature. (Because covalent character increases with increase in the size of anion). $LiF < LiCl < LiBr < LiI$

5. *(a)* All alkali metals dissolve in liquid ammonia.

$$M + (x+y)NH_3 \longrightarrow M^+(NH_3)_x + [e(NH_3)_y]^-$$

   These electrons are excited to higher energy levels and the absorption of photons occurs in the red region of the spectrum. Thus, solution appears as blue.

6. *(a)* Mg can form basic carbonate while Li can not.

$$5Mg^{2+} + 6CO_3^{2-} + 7H_2O \longrightarrow 4MgCO_3 \cdot Mg(OH)_2 \cdot 5H_2O + 2HCO_3^-$$

7. *(c)* Reactions are as follows

$$4Li + \underset{\text{Excess}}{O_2} \xrightarrow{\Delta} \underset{\text{Oxide}}{2Li_2O}$$

$$Na + \underset{\text{Excess}}{O_2} \longrightarrow \underset{\text{Peroxide}}{Na_2O_2}$$

$$K + \underset{\text{Excess}}{O_2} \longrightarrow \underset{\text{Superoxide}}{KO_2}$$

8. *(d)* $Na_2CO_3 \cdot 10H_2O \xrightarrow{\Delta} Na_2CO_3 \cdot H_2O \xrightarrow{\Delta} Na_2CO_3 + H_2O\uparrow$

9. *(b)* During the electrolysis of NaCl, sodium is liberated at the cathode and Cl_2 is evolved at anode.

$$NaCl \xrightarrow{\text{Dissociation}} Na^+ + Cl^-$$

   At cathode: $Na^- + e^- \longrightarrow Na$

   At anode $Cl^- \longrightarrow Cl + e^-$

$$Cl + Cl \longrightarrow Cl_2$$

$$2NaCl + 2H_2O \xrightarrow{\text{Electrolysis}} 2NaOH + \underset{\text{Anode}}{Cl_2} + \underset{\text{Cathode}}{H_2\uparrow}$$

10. *(a)* $4KO_2 + 2CO_2 \longrightarrow 2K_2CO_3 + 3O_2$

    Hence, KO_2 absorbs CO_2 and increases O_2 concentration.

11. *(a)* Among the given compounds sodium carbonate (Na_2CO_3) is used in textile industry. It is used in dying scouring, bleaching, rayon production etc.

12. *(a)* $2NH_4Cl + Ca(OH)_2 \longrightarrow CaCl_2 + 2NH_3 + 2H_2O$

13. *(a)* Sodium ions participate in the transmission of nerve signals through Na-K pump. This pump triggers an electrical impulse which goes between the nerve cells and transmitting messages between the spinal cord, brain and rest of the body.

14. *(b)* The lattice energy of LiF is much higher due to their high lattice energy, hence it is less soluble in water.

15. *(d)* When sodium metal is dissolved in liquid ammonia, sodium donates its valence electron to ammonium molecule. This electron is surrounded by a number of ammonia molecules.

    Thus, the deep blue colour of solution is due to the ammoniated electrons.

16. *(a, b, c)* Li, Na and K have lower density than water.

17. *(a, b, d)* Due to high polarizing power of Li^+, the lithium salts are generally sparingly soluble.

18. *(a, b, c, d)* Among alkali metal carbonates and hydroxides only Li_2CO_3 and LiOH decompose on heating.

$$Li_2CO_3 \xrightarrow{\Delta} LiO_2 + CO_2\uparrow$$

$$2LiNO_3 \xrightarrow{\Delta} Li_2O + 2NO_2 + \frac{1}{2}O_2$$

$$LiOH \xrightarrow{\Delta} Li_2O + H_2O$$

$$NaNO_3 \xrightarrow{\Delta} NaNO_2 + \frac{1}{2}O_2$$

19. *(a, b, d)* Castner's process is used to obtain sodium by electrolysing fused NaOH at 330°C.

20. *(a, b, c, d)* Option (a) The electrolysis of aqueous NaCl leads to the formation of products like NaOH and Cl_2.

    Option (b) $Mg_2C_3 + H_2O \longrightarrow Mg(OH)_2 + \underset{\text{Propyne}}{C_3H_4}$

$$Mg_3N_2 + H_2O \longrightarrow Mg(OH)_2 + NH_3$$

    Option (c) The correct order of ionic mobility will be $Li^+(aq) < Na^+(aq) < K^+(aq) < Rb^+(aq)$ but in gaseous phase the order is reverse.

    Option (d) $2LiNO_3 \xrightarrow{\Delta} Li_2O + NO_2 + O_2$

21. ***(5)*** $[CuSO_4 + 2NaCN \longrightarrow Cu(CN)_2 + Na_2SO_4] \times 2$

$$Cu(CN)_2 \longrightarrow 2CuCN + (CN)_2$$

$$[CuCN + 3NaCN \longrightarrow Na_3[Cu(CN)_4]] \times 2$$

$$2CuSO_4 + 10NaCN \longrightarrow 2Na_3[Cu(CN)_4] + (CN)_2 + 2Na_2SO_4$$

1 mole of $CuSO_4$ = 5 mole of NaCN

22. ***(2)*** On heating, Li_2CO_3 decomposes as

$$5Li_2CO_3 \longrightarrow 8Li_2O + 8CO_2$$

8 moles of CO_2 will be evolved on heating 8 mole of Li_2CO_3. Hence, here x signify 2.

23. ***(3)*** Formula of Trona is,

$$Na_2CO_3 \cdot NaHCO_3 \cdot 2H_2O$$

only one sodium bicarbonate molecules is present and two water molecules is present so the value of $\underset{(1)}{x} + \underset{(2)}{y}$ is 3.

24. ***(9)*** $\underset{\text{Washing soda}}{Na_2CO_3 \cdot 10H_2O} \longrightarrow \underset{\text{Monohydrate}}{Na_2CO_3 \cdot H_2O} + 9H_2O$

25. ***(2)*** The constituent of cement '*A*' responsible for reducing its increase setting time is gypsum. Molecular formula of gypsum = $CaSO_4 \cdot 2H_2O$ and number of water of crystallisation of gypsum is 2.

26. ***(5)*** Hydration energy of NaCl = Hydration energy of Na^+ + Hydration energy of Cl^-

$$= -389 \text{ kJ mol}^{-1} - 382 \text{ kJ mol}^{-1}$$

$$= -771 \text{ kJ mol}^{-1}$$

Heat solution $(\Delta_{sol}H^-)$ = Hydration energy − Lattice energy

$$= [-771 - (-776)] \text{ kJ mol}^{-1}$$

$$= 5 \text{ kJ mol}^{-1}$$

Elemental Practice 4.2

1. ***(d)*** On moving down the group, the ionic size of alkaline earth metals increases. So, due to small size of Be^{2+} ion, Be has highest polarising power [ability to attract the electron cloud of anion (Cl^-)].

So, $BeCl_2$ is more covalent than other alkaline earth metal halides.

Organic molecules are covalent in nature. Rule for solubility is "like dissolves like". So, $BeCl_2$ is soluble in organic solvents as both are covalent in nature.

2. ***(c)*** $Be(OH)_2$ is amphoteric in nature as it reacts with acid and base both.:

$$Be(OH)_2 + 2HCl \longrightarrow BeCl_2 + 2H_2O$$

$$Be(OH)_2 + 2NaOH \longrightarrow Na_2[Be(OH)_4]$$

This amphoteric nature of Be is due to small size of Be. The other hydroxides of alkaline earth metals are basic in nature.

3. ***(d)*** Electronic configuration of X is $1s^2, 2s^2, 2p^3$.

So, valency of X will be 3.

Magnesium ion = Mg^{2+}

Formula : Mg_3X_2

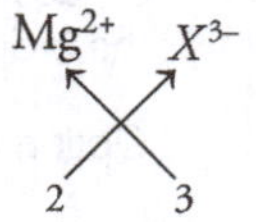

4. ***(a)*** The correct option is $BeH_2 < CaH_2 < BaH_2$. On moving down the group metallic character of metals increases. So, ionic character of metal hydrides increases. Hence, BeH_2 will be least ionic.

5. ***(b)*** When calcium carbide (CaC_2) reacts with nitrogen (N_2) under high temperature, it forms calcium cyanamide which is also called **nitrolim.**

$$CaC_2 + N_2 \xrightarrow[\text{temperature}]{\text{High}} \underset{\substack{\text{Calcium} \\ \text{cyanamide}}}{CaCN_2} + C$$

Hence, option (b) is correct.

6. ***(b)*** Hydration energy of sulphate decreases from top to bottom in II group. Mg^{2+} is smaller than other given ions of group II, so Mg^{2+} is readily hydrated. Thus, $MgSO_4$ has higher hydration energy than lattice energy.

7. ***(c)*** After alpha decay atomic number decreases by 2. Since, three α-particles decay,atomic number will be decreased by 6. Parent atom i.e. (Ra) was in the 2nd group so the daughter element will belong to the 14th group since the atomic number decreases by 6.

8. ***(c)*** Since there will be more delocalised electrons per atom throughout calcium than potassium, the bond strength is stronger in calcium than potassium. Since more energy is required to break the bonds, the melting point of CaO will be higher than that of KI. Hence, statement (c) is false.

9. ***(c)*** With reference to $MgSO_4$, statement given in option (c) is correct while all other options are incorrect. Its is because in $MgSO_4$, Mg^{2+} ions mainly contributes towards hydration enthalpy.
   - Size of Mg^{2+} is smaller than SO_4^{2-}.
   - Ionic potential of Mg^{2+} is high.

10. ***(b)*** The hydration energy decreases from Be^{2+} to Ba^{2+} due to decrease in charge density. This causes the decrease in the solubilities of the sulphates in this order. In other words the solubilities decreases with increase in the ionic size.

11. ***(c)*** Ca and CaH_2 gives H_2 and calcium hydroxide when reacted with water.

$$Ca + H_2O \longrightarrow Ca(OH)_2 + H_2 \uparrow$$

$$CaH_2 + 2H_2O \longrightarrow Ca(OH)_2 + 2H_2 \uparrow$$

12. ***(c)*** The size of Mg^{2+} is minimum among Na^+, Ca^{2+}, K^+ and Mg^{2+} and size of Cl^- is more than F^-, so the ratio of size of cation and anion are minimum in $MgCl_2$.

13. ***(a)*** When HCl is passed through a solution of $CaCl_2$, $MgCl_2$ and NaCl, only NaCl crystallises.

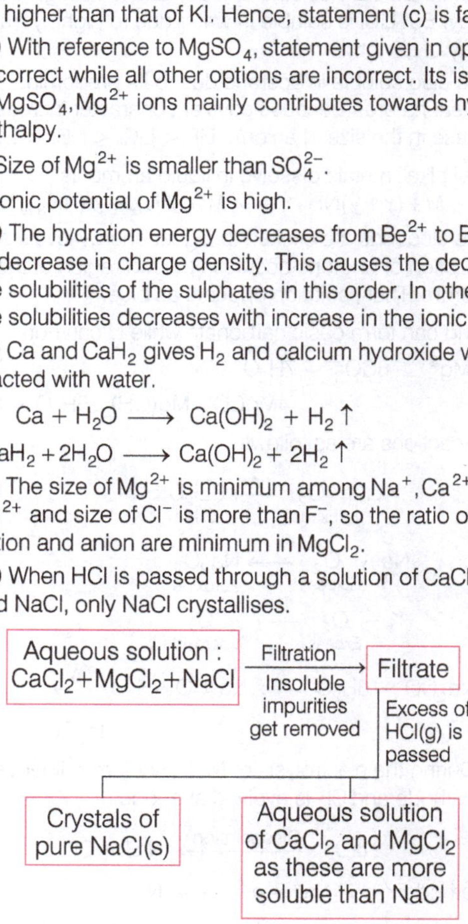

14. ***(a)*** $Ca(OCl)_2$, calcium hypochlorite is the active ingredient in bleaching powder which releases chlorine.

15. ***(a)*** The solubilities of the carbonates decreases on moving down the group-due to the reason that as the size of the cation increases, the lattice enthalpies of their carbonates remains almost unchanged but the enthalpies of hydration of the cations decreases.

$\therefore$The correct order :

$$BeCO_3 > MgCO_3 > CaCO_3 > SrCO_3 > BaCO_3$$

16. ***(a)*** The reaction can be summarised as follows,

$$A \xrightarrow{\Delta} \text{colourless gas} + \text{residue}$$

$$\text{Residue} + H_2O \longrightarrow B \xrightarrow{\text{Excess } CO_2} C \xrightarrow{\Delta} A$$

This is possible only when A is $CaCO_3$. The reactions are as follows,

$$\underset{(A)}{CaCO_3} \xrightarrow{\Delta} \underset{\text{(Colourless gas)}}{CO_2} + \underset{\text{(Residue)}}{CaO}$$

$$CaO + H_2O \longrightarrow \underset{(B)}{Ca(OH)_2} \xrightarrow[\text{(Excess)}]{CO_2}$$

$$\underset{(C)}{Ca(HCO_3)_2} \xrightarrow{\Delta} \underset{(A)}{CaCO_3} + H_2O + CO_2$$

Hence, the compound is $CaCO_3$ (calcium carbonate).

17. ***(b)*** Calcium is formed by electrolysis of fused mass having 6 calcium chloride and one calcium fluoride in electrolytic cell at 700°C.

Calcium is obtained at cathode and chlorine is obtained at anode.

$$Ca^{2+} + 2e^- \longrightarrow Ca \qquad \text{At Cathode}$$
$$2Cl^- \longrightarrow Cl_2 + 2e^- \qquad \text{At Anode}$$

18. ***(d)*** Bleaching powder is prepared by passing chlorine gas over dry slaked lime $Ca(OH)_2$ by Hasenclever method (involves fedding dry slaked line into the top cylinder of a series of cast iron cylinders, while chlorine gas is fed into the bottom cylinder) or by Bachmann method (involves passing chlorine gas over dry slaked lime in a vertical cast-iron tower).

$$Ca(OH)_2 + Cl_2 \longrightarrow Ca(OCl)_2 + H_2O$$

19. ***(a, b, d)*** Beryllium salts are covalent in nature because of very small size of Be^{2+} ion and its high polarising power, so easily get hydrolysed.

e.g. $BeCl_2 + 2H_2O \longrightarrow Be(OH)_2 + 2HCl$

20. ***(a, b, c)*** The size of beryllium is very small and the hydroxide formed by it, is amphoteric in nature, so its hydroxide is less basic than barium hydroxide.

21. ***(a, b, c)*** Impurities of calcium, magnesium and iron ions present in sodium chloride are removed as insoluble carbonates or insoluble hydroxides by a mixture of NH_3 and CO_2.

$$MgCl_2 + 2NH_3 \longrightarrow Mg(OH)_2 \downarrow + 2NH_2Cl$$

22. ***(a, c, d)*** Mg Forms (Mg_2C_3) on reaction with carbon which on hydrolysis produces propyne. Ca forms CaC_2 which on hydrolysis produces acetylene Ba forms BaC_2 which on hydrolysis produces acetylene whereas Be form Be_2C which produces methane on hydrolysis.

23. ***(a, b)*** Magnesium powder burns in air to give MgO and Mg_3N_2.

$$Mg + O_2 \longrightarrow MgO$$
$$3Mg + N_2 \longrightarrow Mg_3N_2$$

24. ***(21)*** $Ca_3Al_2O_6$ is an ingredient present in portland cement and $Na_2CO_3 \cdot 10H_2O$ is manufactured in solvay process.

Thus, the sum of $x + y + z + w$ is $3 + 2 + 6 + 10 = 21$

25. ***(2)*** Among the given reactions only two i.e. (V and VI) are incorrect. Their corrected form is as

$$2NH_3 + 3CaOCl_2 \longrightarrow N_2(g) + 3CaCl_2 + 3H_2O$$
$$3CaO \cdot Al_2O_3 + 3CaSO_4 + 2H_2O \longrightarrow 3CaO \cdot Al_2O_3 \cdot 3CaSO_4 \cdot 2H_2O$$

26. ***(2)*** Among the given statements only b and d are incorrect. Their corrected form are as

$$3Ca + N_2 \xrightarrow{\text{Heat}} \underset{(P)}{Ca_3N_2}$$

$$Ca_3N_2 + 6H_2O \xrightarrow{\Delta} \underset{(M)}{3Ca(OH)_2} + 2NH_3$$

$$Ca(OH)_2 + \underset{\text{From air}}{CO_2} \longrightarrow \underset{\substack{(W)\\ \text{White ppt.}}}{CaCO_3} + H_2O$$

The colour of product W is white.

W is stable in air at room temperature but decomposes when heated at high temperature.

27. ***(5)*** Among the given metal carbonates only five i.e. Na_2CO_3, $MgCO_3$, $CaCO_3$, $BaCO_3$ and Li_2CO_3 get decomposed upon heating.

$$MgCO_3 \xrightarrow{\Delta} MgO + CO_2$$
$$Li_2CO_3 \xrightarrow{\Delta} Li_2O + CO_2$$
$$CaCO_3 \xrightarrow{\Delta} CaO + CO_2$$
$$Na_2CO_3 \xrightarrow{\Delta} Na_2O + CO_2$$
$$BaCO_3 \xrightarrow{\Delta} BaO + CO_2$$

28. ***(6)*** Among the given compounds except $Ca_3(H_2PO_4)_2$, all can be used directly as fertilizer.

Practice Element : Target JEE Advanced

1. ***(d)*** Beryllium has less negative value of reduction potential compared to other alkaline earth metals.

2. ***(c)*** In the case of alkali metals, the covalent character decreases in the order: $MI > MBr > MCl > MF$. With an increase in the electronegativity of halogen, the electron pair of M—X bond is more attracted towards halogen atom. Hence, ionic character increases and the covalent character decreases.

3. ***(c)*** Sodium aluminate is formed when aluminium (Al) reacts with sodium hydroxide (NaOH).

$$Al + 3NaOH \longrightarrow \underset{\text{White ppt.}}{Al(OH)_3 \downarrow} + 3Na^+$$

$$Al(OH)_3 + \underset{\text{(Excess)}}{NaOH} \longrightarrow \underset{\text{sodium}}{2Na^+} \underset{\text{tetrahydroxoaluminate (III)}}{[Al(OH)_4]}$$

4. ***(c)*** Substance *A* is sodium metal. It reacts with water to produce hydrogen (gas *B*) and sodium hydroxide (compound *C*).

$$\underset{(A)}{2Na} + 2H_2O \longrightarrow \underset{(C)}{2NaOH} + \underset{(B)}{H_2\uparrow}$$

Another substance *D* is zinc.
It reacts with solution of sodium hydroxide, it produces hydrogen gas on warming.

$$\underset{(D)}{Zn} + 2NaOH \longrightarrow Na_2ZnO_2 + H_2\uparrow$$

Zinc also reacts with sulphuric acid at room temperature to produce hydrogen gas.

$$Zn + H_2SO_4 \xrightarrow{\text{Room temperature}} ZnSO_4 + H_2\uparrow$$

Thus, substance *A, B, C* and *D*, respectively are Na, H_2, NaOH, Zn.

5. ***(d)*** The chlorides of lithium are soluble in ethanol.

6. ***(d)*** Melting point decreases down the group. So, the order given in option (d) is incorrect.

Elements	Melting point
Be	1560 K
Ca	1124 K
Sr	1062 K

7. ***(a)*** Alkali metals and their salts impart characteristic colour to an oxidising flame. This is because, heat from the flame excites the outermost electron to a higher energy level, which comes back to the ground state with the emission of radiation in the visible region of spectrum.

8. ***(b)*** Statements (a), (c) and (d) are correct whereas statement (b) is incorrect. The correct form of (b) is :
Lithium is the strongest reducing agent in the aqueous solution.

9. ***(d)*** Among the given options. Only option (d) is correct while other options are incorrect. The correct form of other statements are as follows.
   (a) All enzymes that utilise ATP in phosphate transfer require Mg as the co-factor.
   (b) The bone in human body is not an inert and unchanging substance. Infact it changes throughout the life.
   (c) Ca plays an important roles in neuromuscular function and interneuronal transmission.

10. ***(c)*** Among the given statements all are correct except statement (D). Its corrected form is
The compounds formed upon combustion of sodium metal in excess air are Na_2O_2 and Na_2O.

11. ***(a,b,c,d)*** All reactions are correct.

12. ***(a,b)*** Nitrates of Na^+, K^+, Rb^+Cs^+ do not release NO_2 gas on heating.

13. ***(c,d)*** For salts, which are soluble in water, hydration enthalpy is greater than the lattice enthalpy. Na_2SO_4 and Na_2CO_3 are soluble in water.

14. ***(a,c,d)*** Hydration enthalpy decreases as on moving down the alkali metals group. Thus, lithium have the highest hydration enthalpy. Since Li^+, has the smallest size among group 1 element. It have maximum charge density, so surrounded by more water molecules. Thus, Li^+ have minimum ionic mobility as compare to others.

15. ***(a,c,d)*** Down the group, solubility of sulphates of group 2 metal in water decreases. $BeSO_4$ is more in magnitude than its lattice energy. All other alkaline earth metal sulphate have lesser hydration enthalpy than lattice enthalpy.

16. ***(a,b,c,d)*** All given reactions are correct.

17. ***(a,c,d)*** Magnesium ions are concentrated more in intracellular fluids in animal bodies.

18. ***(a,c)*** Lithium is much harder than the rest of the alkali metals because of its smaller size. Lithium reacts with bromine very slowly while other alkali metals react violently.

19. ***(3)*** When lithium nitrate ($LiNO_3$) is heated, it undergoes decomposition reaction and gives lithium oxide, oxygen and nitrogen dioxide according to the following equation,

$$4LiNO_3(s) \xrightarrow{\Delta} 2Li_2O(s) + 4NO_2(g) + O_2(g)$$

Unlike other alkali metal nitrate, which on decomposition forms nitrite and oxygen. Lithium nitrate behave differently due to its small size.
Hence, Li_2O, NO_2, O_2.

20. ***(2)*** An amphoteric compound is a molecule or ion that can react with both acid and base.

$$BeO = \text{Amphoteric}$$
$$BaO = \text{Basic}$$
$$Be(OH)_2 = \text{Amphoteric}$$
$$Sr(OH)_2 = \text{Basic}$$

Both beryllium compounds BeO and $Be(OH)_2$ are amphoteric in nature while compound BaO and $Sr(OH)_2$ are basic in nature, they form alkaline solution in H_2O.

21. ***(6)*** $Mg(NO_3)_2 \cdot 6H_2O$ is a hydrated salt while $Ba(NO_3)_2$ is an anhydrous salt.
Thus, $x = 6$ and $y = 0 \Rightarrow x + y = 6$

22. ***(2)*** BeO reacts with HF in presence of ammonia to give ammonium beryllium fluoride (*A*) which on thermal decomposition produces ammonium fluoride along with beryllium fluoride (*B*).

$$BeO + HF + NH_3 \longrightarrow \underset{(A)}{(NH_4)_2[BeF_4]} \xrightarrow{\Delta} NH_4F + \underset{(B)}{BeF_2}$$

Oxidation state of Be in BeF_2

$$\Rightarrow x + (-1) \times 2 = 0 \Rightarrow x = +2$$

23. ***(5)*** K_2SO_4, $BeSO_4$, Li_2SO_4, $MgSO_4$, Rb_2SO_4 are the sulphates that are soluble in water.

24. ***(a)*** (A) → (R), (S); (B) → (P), (S); (C) → (R); (D) → (Q)

$$2NaOH + 2NO_2 \longrightarrow NaNO_3 + NaNO_2 + H_2O$$

$2NaOH + Sn \xrightarrow{H_2O} Na_2SnO_3 + H_2\uparrow$

$NaOH + Br_2 \xrightarrow{Cold} NaBr + NaBrO_3 + H_2O$

$2NaOH + P_4 + 3H_2O \longrightarrow 3NaH_2PO_2 + \underset{\text{rotten fish smell}}{PH_3\uparrow}$

So, the most appropriate match from the given option is A-S, B-P, C-R, D-Q.

25. ***(b)*** The correct match is

$A \to IV;\ B \to V;\ C \to I;\ D \to II$

26. ***(b)*** The correct match is A-III, B-I, C-IV, D-II.

27. ***(b)*** The correct match is A-(ii), B-(iii), C-(iv), D-(i)

Plaster of Paris — $CaSO_4 \cdot \frac{1}{2} H_2O$

Epsomite — $MgSO_4 \cdot 7H_2O$

Kieserite — $MgSO_4 \cdot H_2O$

Gypsum — $CaSO_4 \cdot 2H_2O$

28. ***(a)*** $A \to IV;\ B \to II;\ C \to I;\ D \to III.$

29. ***(4)*** Hydration energy of Li is high due to its small size, which compensates for its high ionisation energy. Consequently, its reduction potential is lowest amongst alkali metal and hence it is strongest reducing agent.

30. ***(1)*** Because of the small size of Be, it does not form hydride directly by heating with dihydrogen.

31. ***(2)*** Among the following metal nitrates only two i.e. KNO_3 and $NaNO_3$ upon heating does not give NO_2 gas.

$$KNO_3 \xrightarrow{\Delta} KNO_2 + O_2$$

$$NaNO_3 \xrightarrow{\Delta} NaNO_2 + O_2$$

32. ***(1)*** Rb_2CO_3 does not decompose at high temperature Group I carbonates (i.e. $Na_2CO_3, K_2CO_3, Rb_2CO_3$ and Cs_2CO_3) are thermally stable.

33. ***(c)***

I. $BeCO_3 \xrightarrow{\Delta} BeO + CO_2$

II. $2FeSO_4 \xrightarrow{\Delta} Fe_2O_3 + SO_2 + SO_3$

III. $3ZnSO_4 \longrightarrow 3ZnO + 2SO_3$

IV. $(NH_4)_2Cr_2O_7 \longrightarrow Cr_2O_3(s) + 4H_2O + N_2$

V. $2Pb(NO_3)_2 \longrightarrow 2PbO + 4NO_2 + O_2$

In the above reactions, different gases evolve are $CO_2, SO_2, SO_3, N_2, O_2$ and NO_2 respectively.

The structures of these gases are as follows :

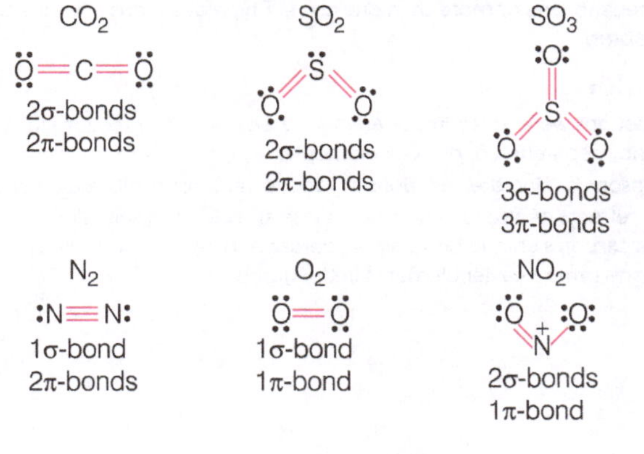

Thus, CO_2 and SO_2 have same number of σ and π bonds. So. total number of thermal decomposition reactions will be 2.

34. ***(b)*** $CuSO_4$, $HgCl_2$ and $AgNO_3$ will form coloured carbonate.

35. ***(c)*** All of these methods of preparation can form KI.

36. ***(d)*** It reacts with acids and acidic oxides (SiO_2, ClO_2, SO_2 and SO_3) to form corresponding salts sodium carbonate reacts with basic oxides, basic hydroxides and various non alkali metals salts ($Ca(OH)_2$, MgO, $CaCl_2$, $BaCl_2$) to form corresponding insoluble carbonates.

37. ***(c)*** Insoluble basic carbonates are formed when polarising power of the cation is high resulting in the hydrolysis of carbonate to form basic carbonates. For example $MgCl_2$, $ZnCl_2$, $CuSO_4$, $HgCl_2$.

38. ***(c)*** Portland cement contains MgO, CaO, SiO_2, Fe_2O_3.

39. ***(c)*** KI acts as reducing agent and reacts with oxidising agents such as $K_2Cr_2O_7$, HNO_3, H_2O_2, $CuSO_4$ etc and liberates iodine.

40. ***(c)*** Sodium nitrate upon heating gives $NaNO_2$ and O_2 gas.

$$2NaNO_3 \xrightarrow{\Delta} 2NaNO_2 + O_2\uparrow$$

Check Through PYQs : JEE Advanced

1. ***(b)***

(a) $Pb_3O_4 + H_2O \longrightarrow$ No reaction

Pb_3O_4 is insoluble in water or do not react with water.

(b) $KO_2 + 2H_2O \longrightarrow KOH + H_2O_2 + 1/2\ O_2$

Hydrolysis of KO_2 gives oxygen gas, hydrogen peroxide and potassium hydroxide.

(c) $Na_2O_2 + 2H_2O \longrightarrow 2NaOH + H_2O_2$

When sodium peroxide dissolves in water, it is hydrolysed and formed sodium hydroxide and hydrogen peroxide. The reaction is highly exothermic.

(d) $Li_2O_2 + 2H_2O \longrightarrow 2LiOH + H_2O_2$

The reactivity of Li_2O_2 towards water differs from LiO_2, Li_2O_2 results in H_2O_2 as a product.

Hence, the correct option is (b).

2. ***(d)*** Formation reactions given in List-II are

(P) $Mg(HCO_3)_2 + 2Ca(OH)_2 \longrightarrow \underset{(IV)}{2CaCO_3} + \underset{(II)}{Mg(OH)_2} + 2H_2O$

(Q) $BaO_2 + H_2SO_4 \longrightarrow BaSO_4 + \underset{(I)}{H_2O_2}$

(R) $Ca(OH)_2 + MgCl_2 \longrightarrow \underset{(II)}{Mg(OH)_2} + CaCl_2$

(S) $BaO_2 + 2HCl \longrightarrow \underset{(III)}{BaCl_2} + \underset{(I)}{H_2O_2}$

(T) $Ca(HCO_3)_2 + Ca(OH)_2 \longrightarrow \underset{(IV)}{2CaCO_3} + 2H_2O$

Thus, the correct matches are

$(I) \to Q \qquad (II) \to R$

$(III) \to S \qquad (IV) \to P$

Hence, option (d) is correct.

CHAPTER 5

p-Block Elements-I

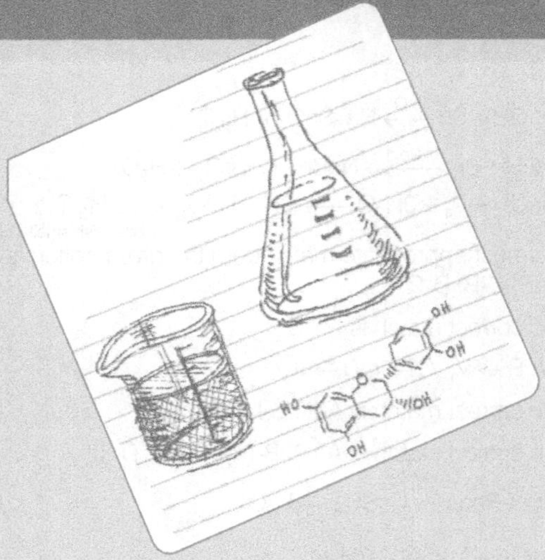

Learning Elements

Element 1 Group-13 Elements and Their Compounds (The Boron Family)

General and Physical Properties, Chemical Properties, Anomalous Behaviour of Boron, Compounds of Boron and Aluminium

Element 2 Group-14 Elements and Their Compounds (The Carbon Family)

General and Physical Properties, Chemical Properties, Anomalous Behaviour of Carbon, Compounds of Carbon and Silicon

Practice Elements

Practice Element 1 Target JEE Main
Practice Element 2 Target JEE Advanced

Trend Insights

JEE Main

	2024				2023				2022			
Topics	**E**	**M**	**T**	**O**	**E**	**M**	**T**	**O**	**E**	**M**	**T**	**O**
Group 13 Elements and Compounds (The Boron Family)	1	5	2	8	4	2	–	6	5	3	1	9
Group 14 Elements and Compounds (The Carbon Family)	1	4	1	6	–	1	–	1	–	1	2	3

E = Easy, **M** = Medium, **T** = Tough, **O** = Overall

Current Dynamics

- Questions based on trends of properties of p-block elements, their applications and compounds had been asked in previous years.
- More number of questions had been asked from group 13 elements as compared to that of Group 14.

JEE Advanced

Typology	Years				
	2024	2023	2022	2021	2020
1. Simple MCQs	–	–	–	–	–
2. One or More than one correct	–	–	1	–	1
3. Numerical/Integer Type	–	–	–	–	–
4. Matching Type	–	–	–	–	–
5. Paragraph Based	–	–	–	–	–

Current Dynamics

- 0-1 question was asked in recent years PYQ's of JEE Advanced
- In present scenario, one or more than one correct type questions are expected from this chapter.

Insightful Advice

- As direct questions were asked in JEE Advanced. So, focus on reactions involving properties and preparation of p-block elements.
- Grasp the reasons behind the variations in various trends of p-block elements including the effects of effective nuclear charge and electron shielding.
- Memorise on carbon's unique bonding properties and behaviour of silicon, germanium and other heavier elements in the group.

Element 1 Group-13 Elements and Their Compounds (The Boron Family)

Group 13 marks the beginning of the *p*-block elements. It contains six elements **Boron** (B), **Aluminium** (Al), **Gallium** (Ga), **Indium** (In), **Thallium** (Tl) and **Ununtrium** (Uut) or **Nihonium** (Nh).

Abundance

Boron is less abundant element in earth's crust and is found mainly in the form of borax. It occurs in two isotopic forms viz., $_5B^{10}$(18%) and $_5B^{11}$(82%). Aluminium is the third most abundant element in the earth's crust. Rest other member of this family are very less abundant.

General and Physical Properties

Important general and physical properties of Group-13 are as follows

1. Electronic Configuration

The general electronic configuration of these elements is ns^2np^1 (where $n = 2,3,4..$). These elements have three electrons in their valence shell.

In ground state, the single electron present in the $2p$ orbital is the only unpaired electron, allowing to form only one bond. While in the excited state they can form three bonds.

2. Atomic and Ionic Radii

The elements of group 13 have smaller atomic radii as compared to *s*-block elements of the same period. Since, the size of atoms depends on effective nuclear charge of the atom, insertion of transition elements results in higher effective nuclear charge of the fourth row elements Ga, Ge, etc., than expected from the second and third row elements. In other words, the nuclei of these fourth row elements attract electrons more strongly than expected and this affects their properties.

The order of atomic radii of the group members is

$$B < Ga < Al < In < Tl$$

3. Density

It increases gradually on moving down the group with exceptionally low increase density of Al. The low density of Al is attributed to its unexpected large molar density.

4. Melting and Boiling Point

The melting point generally decreases from boron to gallium then increases again for indium and thallium, with boron having the highest melting point and gallium having the lowest.

The boiling point decreases regularly on moving down the group as the interatomic distance decreases down the group.

Melting Point Order Boron > Aluminium > Thallium > Indium > Gallium

Boiling Point Order Boron > Aluminium > Gallium > Indium > Thallium

Gallium has an unusal electronic configuration that weakens metallic bond, resulting in a exceptional low melting point, making it suitable for thermometer.

JEE Quicker

A Thermometer containing gallium is useful for measuring the freezing point (256 K) of brine solution. *JEE Main 2024*

The given statement is incorrect. Among the group 13 elements, Gallium has lowest melting point (302.9 K) It is typically used to measure high temperature in thermometer. It is not used to measure freezing point of brine solution.

5. Ionisation Energy

The ionisation energy changes in oscillating manner. It first decreases from B to Al then increases from Al to Ga, again decreases from Ga to Tl and again increases from In to Tl.

The order of first ionisation energy is

Boron (B) > Thallium (Tl) > Gallium (Ga) > Aluminium (Al) > Indium (In)

The decrease from B to Al is due to increase in size while Al to Tl is due to inability of *d* and *f* electrons which have low screening effect.

Boron always forms covalent compounds and does not form B^{3+} ions because of its very high ionisation energy.

Many simple compounds of Al and Ga like $AlCl_3$ and $GaCl_3$ are covalent when present in anhydrous form while ionic when present in aqueous solution.

6. Metallic Character

This group shows a wide variation in properties. Boron is the only non-metal in the group 13 among all the members. Aluminium is a metal but shows many chemical similarities with boron and gallium.

Indiun and thallium are almost exclusively metallic in character.

7. Oxidation States

Boron and aluminium show an oxidation state of +3 in their compounds while gallium, indium and thallium shows both +1 and +3 oxidation states. On moving down the group +1 oxidation state is more stable than +3, it is due to the inert pair effect.

$$Ga^{3+} > In^{3+} > Tl^{3+}$$

$$Ga^{+} < In^{+} < Tl^{+}$$

Inert Pair Effect is defined as the tendency of *s*-electrons to remain together or the reluctance of *s*-electrons to participate in bond formation.

The decrease is stability of the higher oxidation state (+3) with increasing atomic number arises because of the decrease in bond energy with size from Al to Tl. As a result, the energy required to unpair ns^2 electrons is not compensated by the energy released in forming the two additional bonds.

This effect is more pronounced in Tl. The effect of inert pair can be seen in following cases.

- Ga^{3+} is more stable than Ga^{+}, hence Ga^{+} salts act as strong reducing agent.
- Tl^{+} is more stable than Tl^{3+}, hence Tl^{3+} compounds behave as strong oxidising agent.

8. Electronegativity

The electronegativity of group 13 elements follows an unusal trend. Boron (B) being the smallest atom in the group exhibits the highest electronegativity due to its strong nuclear pull on the valence electrons.

As we move down the group to Aluminium (Al) the atomic size increases leading to decrease in electronegativity.

However from Gallium onwards, the trend reverses.

Therefore the order of electronegativity for group 13 elements is B >Tl > In > Ga > Al.

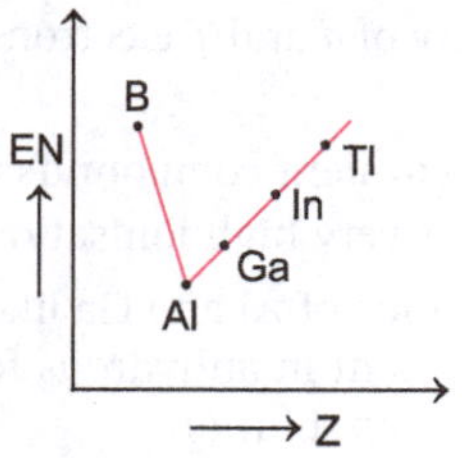

Physical Properties of the Elements of Group 13

Property	B	Al	Ga	In	Tl
Electronic Configuration	[He] $2s^2 2p^1$	[Ne] $3s^2 3p^1$	[Ar] $3d^{10} 4s^2 4p^1$	[Kr]$4d^{10} 5s^2 5p^1$	[Xe]$4f^{14} 5d^{10} 6s^2 6p^1$
Electronegativity (Pauling)	2.0	1.5	1.6	1.7	1.8
$\Delta_i H_1$ kJ mol^{-1}	801	577	579	558	589
$\Delta_i H_2$ kJ mol^{-1}	2427	1816	1979	1820	1971
$\Delta_i H_3$ kJ mol^{-1}	3659	2744	2962	2704	2877
m.p./°C	2180	660	30	157	303
b.p./°C	3650	2467	2403	2080	1457
Density/gcm^{-3} at 298 K	2.35	2.70	5.90	7.31	11.85
Metallic radius/pm	88.5	143	141	166	170
Ionic radius/pm M^{3+}	27.0	53.5	62	80	88.5
$E^{\circ}_{M^{3+}/M}$ / V *	—	−1.66	−0.56	−0.34	+1. 26
$E^{\circ}_{M^{+}/M}$ / V	—	+0.55	−0.79 (acid) −1. 39 (alkali)	−0.18	−0.34

Chemical Properties

- Pure **Boron** is unreactive to air at room temperature. It reacts when heated with air.
- It does not react with water. It is attacked only by hot concentrated acids like H_2SO_4 etc.
- **Aluminium** reacts with air even at room temperature forming a protective layer of oxide (Al_2O_3).
- **Gallium** and **Indium** are attacked neither by cold water nor by hot water unless oxygen is present. **Thallium** is a little more reactive than Gallium and forms an oxide layer on its surface.

Boron

Brief study of occurrence, structure, important properties and important compounds of boron are as follows

Occurrence

Boron is not found in free state in nature. In the combined state, it is found as the salts of boric acid. It is also present to some extent in plants and sometimes in coal ash. The important minerals of boron are as follows

(i)	Borax (Tincal)	$Na_2B_4O_7 \cdot 10H_2O$ - It is found in Tibet, Ceylon, California and Kashmir.
(ii)	Colemanite	$Ca_2B_6O_{11} \cdot 5H_2O$ - It is found in Asia (Turkey) and America.
	Panderinite	$Ca_2B_6O_{11} \cdot 3H_2O$
(iii)	Boracite	$Mg_3B_7O_{13}Cl$ - It is found in stassfurt, Germany.
(iv)	Boronatrocalcite	$CaB_4O_2 \cdot NaBO_2 \cdot 8H_2O$ It is found in Chile.
(v)	Kernite (Rasorite)	$Na_2B_4O_7 \cdot 4H_2O$ - It is found in Mojave dessert in America.
(vi)	Boric acid	H_3BO_3- It occurs in the jets of steam called soffioni escaping from ground in the volcanic regions of Tuscany.

Structure

Elemental boron exists as B_{12}, icosahedral, units which is shown as

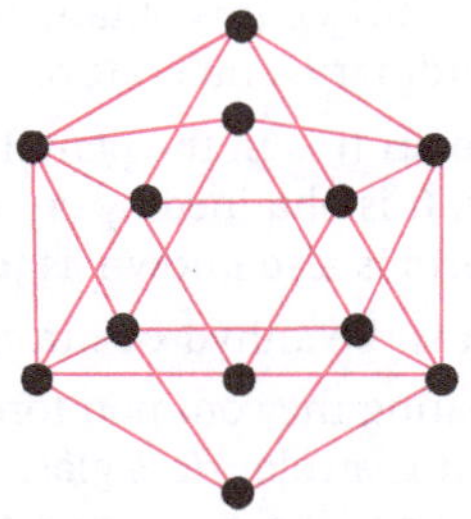

Preparation

Amorphous boron (called Moissan boron) is obtained by reduction of B_2O_3 with Na or Mg at a high temperature. B_2O_3 in turn is obtained by decomposing borax with acid and subsequent heating.

$$Na_2B_4O_7 \cdot 10H_2O \xrightarrow{\text{Acid}} \underset{\text{Orthoboric acid}}{2H_3BO_3} \xrightarrow{\Delta} 3H_2O + B_2O_3$$

$$B_2O_3 + 6Na \xrightarrow{\Delta} 2B + 3Na_2O$$

$$B_2O_3 + 3Mg \xrightarrow{\Delta} 2B + 3MgO$$

Boron obtained is 95–98% pure and black in colour. Pure crystalline boron is obtained by

- Reducing BCl_3 with H_2

$$2BCl_3 + 3H_2 \xrightarrow[\text{filament}]{\text{Red hot W or Ta}} 2B + 6HCl$$

- Pyrolysis of BI_3

$$2BI_3 \xrightarrow[\text{(van Arkel method)}]{\text{Red hot W or Ta filament}} 2B + 3I_2$$

- Thermal decomposition of B_2H_6

$$B_2H_6 \xrightarrow{\Delta} 2B + 3H_2$$

Physical Properties

- Boron exists in two allotropic forms, (a) crystalline and (b) amorphous.
- Crystalline boron is black, hard and chemically inert in nature.
- Amorphous boron is brown and chemically active. It melts at 2300°C and boils at 2550°C. It is difficult to fuse.
- Amorphous boron is bad conductor of heat and electricity.

Chemical Properties

(i) **Action of Air and Oxygen** Amorphous boron when heated in air or oxygen at 700°C, burns with a reddish flame forming a mixture of oxide and nitride.

$$4B + 3O_2 \xrightarrow{\Delta} 2B_2O_3$$

$$2B + \underset{\text{(From air)}}{N_2} \xrightarrow{\Delta} 2BN$$

(ii) **Action of Water** Boron is not affected by water under ordinary conditions, however, when steam is passed over red hot boron, hydrogen is liberated.

$$2B + \underset{\text{(Steam)}}{3H_2O} \longrightarrow B_2O_3 + 3H_2\uparrow$$

(iii) **Action of Acids** Boron is not affected by non-oxidising acids. It is attacked by oxidising acids like conc. H_2SO_4 and HNO_3.

$$B + \underset{\text{(conc.)}}{3HNO_3} \longrightarrow H_3BO_3 + 3NO_2\uparrow$$

$$2B + \underset{\text{(conc.)}}{3H_2SO_4} \longrightarrow 2H_3BO_3 + 3SO_2\uparrow$$

(iv) **Action of Alkalies** Boron dissolves in fused alkalies, liberating hydrogen.

$$2B + 6NaOH \longrightarrow 2Na_3BO_3 + 3H_2\uparrow$$

(v) **Action of Metals** Boron combines with strongly electropositive metals at high temperatures to form borides.

$$3Mg + B_2 \xrightarrow{\text{High temp.}} Mg_3B_2$$

(vi) **Action of Non-metals** Boron forms B_2S_3 when heated with sulphur. It forms extremely hard substance boron carbide (B_4C), when heated with carbon in an electric furnace. Boron combines directly with chlorine and bromine at higher temperatures.

(vii) **Reducing Nature** It is a powerful reducing agent.

e.g.

$$3CO_2 + 4B \longrightarrow 2B_2O_3 + 3C$$

$$3SiO_2 + 4B \longrightarrow 2B_2O_3 + 3Si$$

Uses

(i) It is used as a deoxidiser in the casting of copper.

(ii) It is used for making boron steels which are very hard and are used as control rods in atomic reactors.

(iii) It is used as a catalytic agent.

(iv) Boron steel or boron carbide rods are used to control the nuclear reactions. It has a very high cross-section to capture the neutrons. According to another concept boron absorbs neutron to make the boron having even number of neutrons.

$$_5B^{10} + {_0n^1} \longrightarrow {_5B^{11}}$$

Anomalous Behaviour of Boron

Due to small size, high electron density high electronegativity and non-availability of *d*-electrons, boron exhibits the following anomalous properties.

- It is the only non-metal among group-13 elements.
- It has higher melting and boiling points than the other members of group.

- It forms only covalent compound.
- Only boron exhibits allotropy and exists in crystalline as well as amorphous forms.
- Its hydrides are comparatively more stable than that of other members.
- Dilute acids have no action on boron.

Compounds of Boron

Boron forms a number of compounds, some of them are given below.

Boron Trioxide, B_2O_3

It is also called **sesquioxide**. It is an anhydride of orthoboric acid.

It is prepared by burning boron in oxygen.

$$4B + 3O_2 \longrightarrow 2B_2O_3$$

or heating *ortho*boric acid to redness.

$$2H_3BO_3 \xrightarrow{\Delta} B_2O_3 + 3H_2O$$

It is a white hygroscopic solid thus, absorbs moisture (becoming opaque from transparent glassy mass) and finally converted into boric acid.

$$B_2O_3 + H_2O \longrightarrow 2HBO_2 \text{ (metaboric acid)}$$

$$HBO_2 + H_2O \longrightarrow H_3BO_3 \text{ (orthoboric acid)}$$

(B_2O_3 is, thus, the anhydride of *ortho*boric acid)

It is an acidic oxide. It combines with metal oxides when fused and forms metaborates.

Borax $Na_2B_4O_7 \cdot 10H_2O$ or $Na_2[B_4O_5(OH)_4 \cdot 8H_2O]$

Its chemical name is sodium tetraborate and commonly known as Tincal or Suhaga.

Method of Preparation

(i) **From Colemanite** When colemanite powder is heated with Na_2CO_3 solution, the following reaction occurs with the precipitation of $CaCO_3$.

$$Ca_2B_6O_{11} + 2Na_2CO_3 \xrightarrow{\Delta} + 2CaCO_3\downarrow + Na_2B_4O_7 + 2NaBO_2$$

The filtrate is cooled when white crystals of borax are precipitated.

The mother liquor on treatment with CO_2 converts $NaBO_2$ to $Na_2B_4O_7$ which precipitates out on crystallisation.

$$4NaBO_2 + CO_2 \longrightarrow Na_2B_4O_7 + Na_2CO_3$$

(ii) **From Orthoboric Acid** Borax is obtained by the action of Na_2CO_3 on *ortho*boric acid.

$$4H_3BO_3 + Na_2CO_3 \longrightarrow Na_2B_4O_7 + 6H_2O + CO_2\uparrow$$

Physical Properties

Borax is known in following three forms

(i) **Prismatic Borax** It is the common decahydrated form, $Na_2B_4H_7 \cdot 10H_2O$. It is obtained by crystallisation of solution at ordinary temperature.

(ii) **Octahedral Form** It is in the pentahydrate form i.e. $Na_2B_4O_7 \cdot 5H_2O$. It is obtained by crystallising solution at 60°C. This form is also known as **jeweller's borax**.

(iii) **Borax Glass** It is the anhydrous from, $Na_2B_4O_7$. It is obtained by heating the common form above its melting point. It is a colourless glassy mass and is not stable in moist air as it absorbs moisture and is gradually converted into decahydrated form.

Chemical Properties

- **Basic Nature** The solution of borax is alkaline in nature. As it is a salt of strong alkali and weak acid.

$$Na_2B_4O_7 + 7H_2O \rightleftharpoons \underset{\text{Stong alkali}}{2NaOH} + \underset{\text{weak acid}}{4H_3BO_3}$$

- **Action of Heat** On heating, borax first swells up due to elimination of water molecules. On further heating, it melts into a liquid which then solidifies into a transparent glassy bead.

$$Na_2B_4O_7 \cdot 10H_2O \xrightarrow[-10H_2O]{\text{Heat}} \underset{\text{Anhydrous}}{Na_2B_4O_7} \xrightarrow{740°C} \underbrace{\underset{\text{Sodium metaborate}}{2NaBO_2} + \underset{\text{Boric anhydride}}{B_2O_3}}_{\text{Transparent glassy beads or Borax beads}}$$

The metaborates of many transition metals have characteristics colours. Thus, borax bead test can be used to identify them qualitatively in laboratory.

When hot glassy bead is brought in contact with a coloured salt and heated again in the flame, B_2O_3 displaces the volatile oxides and combines with basic oxides to form metaborates.

e.g. $CuO + B_2O_3 \longrightarrow \underset{\text{Blue bead}}{Cu(BO_2)_2}$

- Aqueous solution of borax acts as a **buffer** because it contains weak acid and its salt with strong base.

$$Na_2B_4O_7 + 7H_2O \longrightarrow 2Na[B(OH)_4] + 2H_3BO_3$$

JEE Spotlite

- Borax is used as a primary standard in titrations against acids.
  $Na_2B_4O_7 \cdot 10H_2O + 2HCl \longrightarrow 2NaCl + 4H_3BO_3 + 5H_2O$
  One of the products H_3BO_3 is itself a weak acid. Thus, the indicator used to detect end point of this reaction must be the one that is unaffected by H_3BO_3. **Methyl orange (pH range 3.1–4.4) is normally used.**

Structure

Borax ($Na_2[B_4O_5(OH)_4]\cdot 8H_2O$) is actually made of two tetrahedra and two triangular units joined as shown below

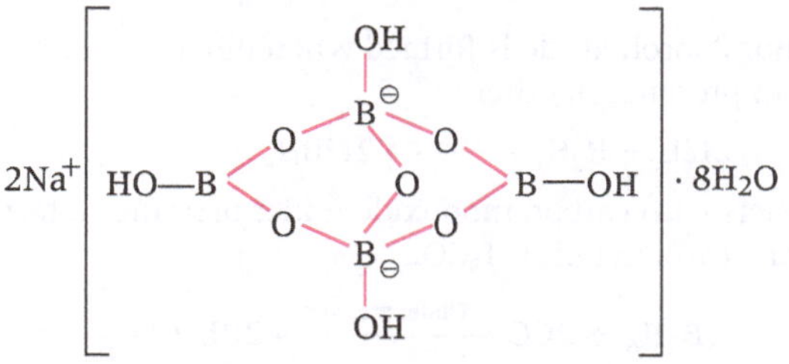

Uses

Borax is used

(i) for the borax bead test in qualitative analysis.

(ii) as a flux. [This is based on its property to dissolve many metal oxides to form borates of low melting points.]

(iii) as an antiseptic.

(iv) in water softening as it forms insoluble calcium and magnesium borates (CaB_4O_7, MgB_4O_7).

(v) in the manufacture of enamels and glazes for pottery and tiles.

(vi) in making optical glasses and also borosilicate glass which is very resistant to heat and shock.

(vii) in leather industry for cleaning hides and skins.

(viii) for impregnating match-sticks to prevent after glow.

(ix) for stiffening of candles.

Boric Acids, H_3BO_3

It is the trivial name for orthoboric acid. In aqueous solution meta (HBO_2) and pyroboric acid ($H_2B_4O_7$) are changed into orthoboric acid.

Method of Preparation

- It can be prepared by acidifying an aqueous solution of $Na_2B_4O_7$.

  $$Na_2B_4O_7 + H_2SO_4 + 5H_2O \longrightarrow Na_2SO_4 + 4H_3BO_3$$

- On a commercial scale, boric acid is prepared from colemanite mineral, $Ca_2B_6O_{11}\cdot 5H_2O$. In this method the finely powdered from of colemanites is dissolved in boiling water and SO_2 is passed into hot aqueous suspension.

  On cooling crystals of boric acid crystallises out

  $$Ca_2B_6O_{11} + \underset{\text{(Boiled)}}{9H_2O} + 2SO_2 \longrightarrow 2CaSO_3 + 6H_3BO_3$$

  Excess of SO_2 dissolves $CaSO_3$ as $Ca(HSO_3)_2$

  $$\underset{\text{Insoluble}}{CaSO_3} + H_2O + SO_2 \longrightarrow \underset{\text{Calcium bisulphite (Soluble)}}{Ca(HSO_3)_2}$$

Physical Properties

Orthoboric acid is seen as pearly white needle like crystals with greasy feel. It is moderately soluble in water.
Its solubility increases with increase in temperature.

Chemical Properties

- On heating above 100°C, orthoboric acid forms metaboric acid (HBO_2) which on heating at 140°C gives pyroboric acid ($H_2B_4O_7$), which on further heating to red hot gives boron trioxides as the product.

  $$H_3BO_3 \xrightarrow{100°C} HBO_2 \xrightarrow{140°C} H_2B_4O_7 \xrightarrow{\text{red hot}} B_2O_3$$

- Orthoboric acid, H_3BO_3 is soluble in water and behaves as a weak monobasic acid. It does not donate protons like most acids, but rather it accepts OH^-. It is therefore a Lewis acid, and is better written as $B(OH)_3$.

  $$B(OH)_3 + 2H_2O \rightleftharpoons H_3O^+ + [B(OH)_4]^-;\ pK_a = 9.25$$

  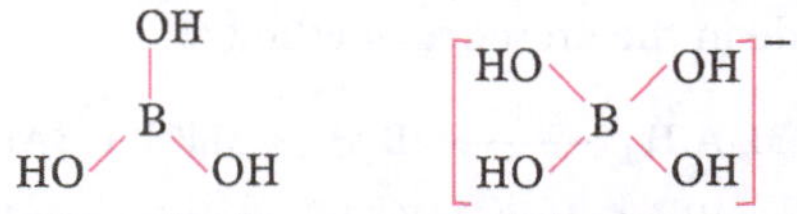

  plane triangle tetrahedral metaborate ion

- Polymeric metaborate species are formed at higher concentration,

  $$3B(OH)_3 \rightleftharpoons H_3O^+ + [B_3O_3(OH)_4]^- + H_2O\quad pK_a = 6.84$$

  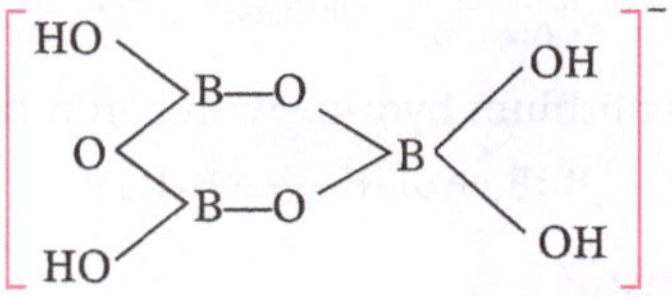

Structure

- Orthoboric acid contains triangular BO_3^{3-} units. In the solid state, $B(OH)_3$ units are hydrogen bonded together into two-dimensional sheets with almost hexagonal symmetry. The layers are quite a larger distance apart (3.18Å) and thus the crystal breaks quite easily into very fine particles.

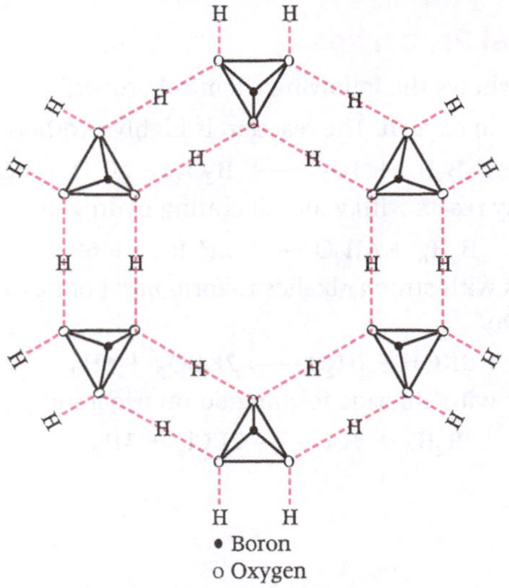

Hydrogen bonded structure of orthoboric acid

Uses

Orthoboric acid is used

- as an antiseptic and eye wash under the name 'boric lotion'.
- in the manufacture of enamels and glazes for pottery.
- as food preservative.
- in glass industry.

Diborane, B_2H_6

It is the first member of B_nH_{n+4} series of boron hydrides. It is a dimer of BH_3.

Methods of Preparation

It is prepared by the following methods.

(i) By the action of lithium aluminium hydride on boron trichloride in the presence of ether.

$$4BCl_3 + 3LiAlH_4 \xrightarrow{\text{Ether}} 2B_2H_6 + 3LiCl + 3AlCl_3$$

(ii) By passing silent electric discharge at low pressure through a mixture of boron trichloride or tribromide and excess of hydrogen.

$$2BCl_3 + \underset{\text{(Excess)}}{6H_2} \xrightarrow[\text{discharge}]{\text{Silent electric}} B_2H_6 + 6HCl$$

(iii) By reacting lithium hydride with boron trifluoride

$$8BF_3 + 6LiH \longrightarrow B_2H_6 + 6LiBF_4$$

Physical Properties

(i) It is a colourless gas which is stable at low temperature in the absence of moisture and greases .

(ii) At higher temperatures it changes to higher boranes and on further heating at very high temperature it decomposes to boron and hydrogen.

(iii) It has disagreeable odour and causes headache.

Chemical Properties

Diborane shows the following chemical properties.

- It burns in oxygen. The reaction is highly exothermic.

$$B_2H_6 + 3O_2 \longrightarrow B_2O_3 + 3H_2O + \text{heat}$$

- It readily reacts with water liberating hydrogen.

$$B_2H_6 + 6H_2O \longrightarrow 2H_3BO_3 + 6H_2$$

- It reacts with strong alkalies to form *meta*borates and hydrogen.

$$B_2H_6 + 2KOH + 2H_2O \longrightarrow 2KBO_2 + 6H_2$$

- It reacts with chlorine forming boron trichloride.

$$B_2H_6 + 3Cl_2 \longrightarrow 2BCl_3 + 3H_2$$

- In presence of anhydrous aluminium chloride, it reacts with dry HCl to give chlorodiborane.

$$B_2H_6 + \underset{\text{Dry}}{HCl} \xrightarrow{\text{Anhy. AlCl}_3} \underset{\text{Chlorodiborane}}{B_2H_5Cl} + H_2$$

- Lithium borohydride is formed when diborane reacts with LiH in presence of ether.

$$2LiH + B_2H_6 \xrightarrow{\text{Ether}} 2LiBH_4$$

- It reacts with carbon monoxide under pressure to form borane carbonyl i.e. BH_3CO.

$$B_2H_6 + 2CO \xrightarrow{\text{Under pressure}} 2BH_3CO$$

- Complex borohydrides are formed by the raction of B_2H_6 with alkali metals and their hydrides

$$2B_2H_6 + 2Na \xrightarrow{\text{Slow}} Na^+[BH_4]^- + Na^+[B_3H_8]^-$$

$$B_2H_6 + 2NaH \longrightarrow 2Na^+[BH_4]^-$$

These complex borohydrides are used as reducing agents in organic synthesis.

JEE Alert

Remember that, B_2H_6 selectively changes alkenes to alcohol with alkaline H_2O_2 against Markovnikov's rule :

$$CH_3CH{=}CH_2 \xrightarrow[\text{(ii) } H_2O_2,\, OH^-]{\text{(i) } B_2H_6} CH_3CH_2CH_2OH$$

Diborane reacts with NH_3 and the product formed depends upon the conditions of reaction. The different conditions are as follow

(i) **At low temperature** and in excess of a ammonia, an addition product $B_2H_6 \cdot 2NH_3$ is obtained.

$$B_2H_6 + \underset{\text{(Excess)}}{2NH_3} \xrightarrow{\text{Low temp }(-120°C)} B_2H_6 \cdot 2NH_3$$

$$\text{or } [H_2B(NH_3)_2]^+ [BH_4]^\ominus$$

(ii) **At high temperature** and in excess ammonia boron nitride is formed.

$$nB_2H_6 \xrightarrow[\text{High temp.}]{\text{Excess NH}_3} \underset{\text{Boron nitride}}{(BN)_x}$$

(iii) At 200°C, borazine is formed

$$3B_2H_6 + 3NH_3 \xrightarrow{200°C} \underset{\text{Borazine}}{2B_3N_3H_6} + 12H_2$$

- Borazine, $B_3N_3H_6$ is also called 'inorganic benzene' because its structure shows some formal similarity with benzene, with delocalised electrons and aromatic character.

- Boron nitride is a white slippery solid. One B atom and one N atom together have the same number of valence electrons as two C atoms.

  Thus boron nitride has almost the same structure as graphite, with sheets made up of hexagonal rings of alternate B and N atoms joined together. Thus, it's also known as **inorganic graphite**.

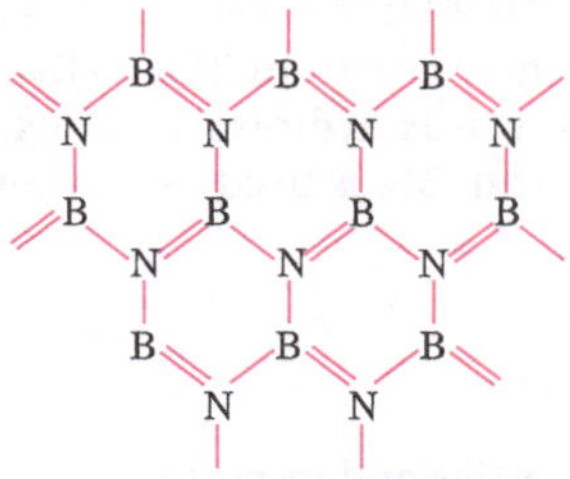
Boron-nitride

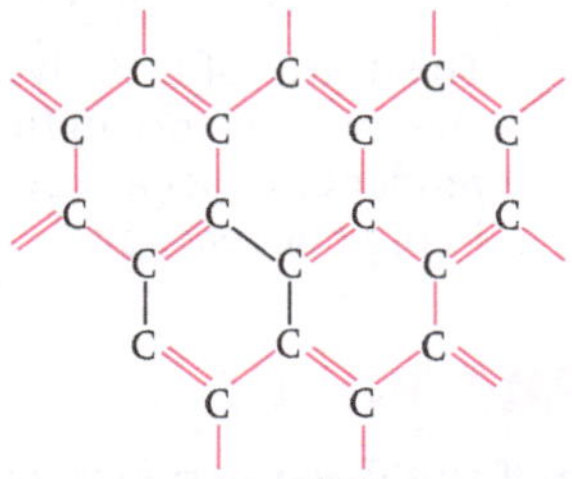
Graphite

Structure

- Diborane is an example of electron deficient compound.

  Dilthey in 1921 proposed a bridge structure for diborane. Four hydrogen atoms, two on the left and two on the right, known as terminal hydrogens and two boron atoms lie in the same plane.

  Two hydrogen atoms forms bridges, one above and other below, lie in a plane perpendicular to the rest of molecule.

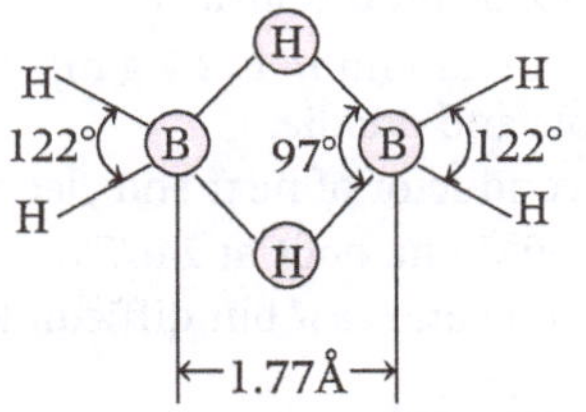

The above structure shows that there are two types of hydrogen atoms-Terminal and bridging. 4-terminal hydrogen atoms can easily be replaced by methyl groups but when two bridging hydrogen atoms are attacked, the molecule is ruptured.

- According to molecular orbital theory, each of the two boron atoms is in sp^3 hybrid state. Of the four hybrid orbitals, three have one electron each, while the fourth is empty. Two of the four orbitals of each of the boron atom overlap with two terminal hydrogen atoms forming two normal B—H, σ -bonds.

  One of the remaining hybrid orbital (either filled or empty) of one of the boron atoms, 1*s* orbital of hydrogen atom (bridge atom and one of the hybrid orbitals of the other boron atom) overlap to form a delocalised orbital covering the three nuclei with a pair of electrons. Such a bond is known as **three centre two electron bonds.**

- Similar overlapping occurs in one hydrogen atom (bridging) and fourth hybrid orbital of each boron atom.

Thus, the formation of diborane molecule can be depicted in the following structure.

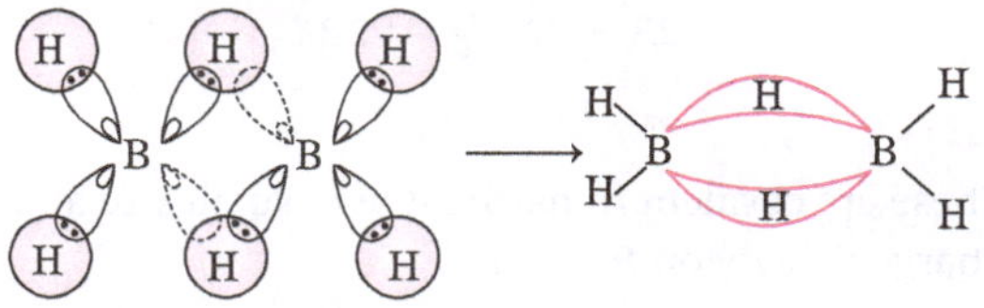

- On account of repulsion between the two hydrogen nuclei, the delocalised orbitals of bridges are drifted away from each other giving the shape of a banana. The three centre two electron bonds are also known as **banana bonds.**

Uses

Diborane can be used

(i) as a catalyst in polymerisation reactions.
(ii) as a reducing agent in organic reactions
(iii) for making high energy fuels and propellants
(iv) for preparing hydrocarbons, alcohols, ketones and acids through hydroboration method.

JEE MAPPER

Example Similar to PYQ Asked in JEE Advanced 2022

The compound(*P*) which reacts with B_2H_6 to give $[BH_2P_2]^+[BH_4]^-$ is (are)

(a) $CH_3CH_2NH_2$ (b) NH_3 (c) $(CH_3CH_2)_2NH$ (d) $(CH_3CH_2)_3N$

Sol. (a,b,c) Diborane (B_2H_6) undergoes unsymmetric cleavage with NH_3, primary and secondary amine while tertiary amine bring about symmetrical cleavage of B_2H_6 as

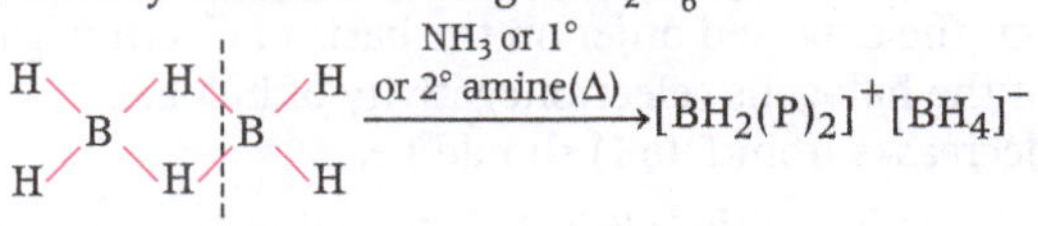

Unsymmetrical Cleavage

Competency Enhancer 1.1

The compound which reacts with BF_3 to give diborane is (are)

(a) NaH (b) $NaBH_4$ (c) LiH (d) $LiAlH_4$

Halides of Boron

Boron combines with halogens and forms the halides of type BX_3, $(X = F, Cl, Br, I)$.

Except BF_3, the other trihalides can be prepared by the treatment of halogens on a mixture of B_2O_3 and carbon at high temperature.

$$B_2O_3 + 3C + 3X_2 \xrightarrow{\text{High temp.}} 2BX_3 + 3CO$$
$$(X_2 = Cl_2, Br_2, I_2)$$

BF_3 may be obtained by reacting concentrated sulphuric acid, CaF_2 and boric anhydride

$$3CaF_2 + B_2O_3 + \underset{\text{(conc.)}}{3H_2SO_4} \longrightarrow 2BF_3 + 3CaSO_4 + 3H_2O$$

Boron trihalides are also obtained by direct combination of boron and halogens under suitable conditions.

$$2B + 3X_2 \longrightarrow 2BX_3$$

Properties

(i) These are covalent in nature due to small size and high charge density on B^{3+} ion.

(ii) These are non-electrolytes, as in liquid state do not conduct electricity.

(iii) The boiling points are very low. The boiling points increase as the atomic number of halogens increases. BF_3 a colourless gas, BCl_3, is a colourless fuming liquid (b. pt = 13° C), BBr_3 is also a colourless fuming liquid (b.pt=90°C) while BI_3 a white fusible solid (b.pt. 210°C)

(iv) The trihalides are electron deficient compounds. Boron atom acquires six electrons on account of three B—*X* bonds, i.e., 2 electrons short of an octet. Thus, the boron atom in BX_3, molecule can accept two more electrons, i.e., an electron pair from the donor atoms like N, P, O, S, F etc., in NH_3, PH_3, H_2O, H_2S, HF etc., respectively to form addition compounds (donor-acceptor compound).

$$\underset{\substack{\text{Donor}\\\text{(Lewis base)}}}{H_3N:} + \underset{\substack{\text{Acceptor}\\\text{(Lewis acid)}}}{BF_3} \longrightarrow [H_3N \rightarrow BF_3]$$

The relative Lewis acid character of boron trihalides is found to follow the following order.

$$BI_3 > BBr_3 > BCl_3 > BF_3$$

but the expected order on the basis of electronegativity of the halogens (electronegativity of halogens decreases from F to I) should be,

$$BF_3 > BCl_3 > BBr_3 > BI_3$$

This anomaly is explained on the basis of the relative tendency of the halogen atom to back donate its unutilised electrons to vacant *p*-orbital of boron atom. In BF_3 boron has a vacant 2*p* orbital and each fluorine has fully filled unutilised 2*p*-orbitals. Fluorine transfers two electrons to vacant 2*p*- orbital of boron, thus forming $p\pi - p\pi$ bond.

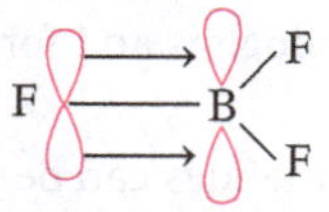

This type of bond has some double bond character and is known as **dative or back bonding.** All the three bond lengths are same. It is possible when double bond is delocalised. The delocalisation may be represented as

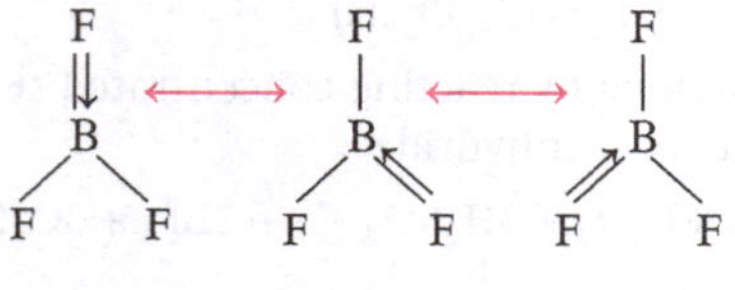

This bond reduces the electron deficieny of boron atom hence its Lewis acid character decreases. The tendency to form back bonding its maximum in BF_3 and decreases from BF_3 to BI_3 Thus, BCl_3, BBr_3 and BI_3 are stronger Lewis acids than BF_3.'

(v) All boron trihalides, except boron trifluoride, are hydrolysed to give boric acid.

$$BCl_3 + 3H_2O \longrightarrow H_3BO_3 + 3HCl$$

The degree of hydrolysis increases from BCl_3 to BI_3. Due to resistance of BF_3 towards hydrolysis and its tendency to act as Lewis acid, BF_3 is used as a catalyst in organic reaction.

Aluminium

Brief study of occurrence, properties and important compounds are as follows.

Occurrence

Aluminium is a third most abundant element forming 8.3% of earth's crust. It is a constituent of clay, slate and many types of silicate rocks. It is found only in the combined state.

Physical Properties

(i) Aluminium is a bluish white lustre metal. The lustre is destroyed on long exposure to air due to formation of a thin film of oxide on the surface.

(ii) The density of aluminium is 2.7 g mL^{-1} (light metal). It is malleable and ductile.

(iii) It is a good conductor of heat and electricity.

(iv) It melts at 660°C and boils at 2467°C.

(v) It can be welded and cast but difficult to solder.

Chemical Properties

(i) **Action of Air** Aluminium is far more reactive than boron but in air however, in water it is stable. It is due to the formation of aluminium oxide, Al_2O_3, layer that makes it passive for further attack.

The layer is so useful that in industry it is purposely increased by an electrolytic process called **anodising.** This is done by electrolysing dilute H_2SO_4 with Al as anode. This produces much thicker layer of oxide on the surface (0.01 mm). Aluminium burns in oxygen producing brilliant light.

The reaction is highly exothermic and the heat evolved is used in the thermite process for the reduction of oxides of Cr, Fe, Mn, etc.

(ii) **Action of Water** Pure aluminium is not affected by pure water. The impure aluminium is readily corroded by water containing salts (sea water). Aluminium decomposes boiling water evolving hydrogen gas.

$$2Al + \underset{\text{(Boiled)}}{6H_2O} \longrightarrow 2Al(OH)_3 + 3H_2\uparrow$$

(iii) **Action of Acids** The oxidation potential of aluminium is 1.66 volts thus, it is strongly electropositive, very reactive and a powerful reducing agent. It dissolves in HCl (dil. and conc.) and dilute sulphuric acid, evolving hydrogen.

$$2Al + \underset{\text{(dil. or conc.)}}{6HCl} \longrightarrow 2AlCl_3 + 3H_2\uparrow$$

$$2Al + \underset{\text{(dil.)}}{3H_2SO_4} \longrightarrow Al_2(SO_4)_3 + 3H_2\uparrow$$

The reaction with dil. H_2SO_4 is very slow probably on account of the insolubility of the oxide film in this acid. Hot concentrated sulphuric acid dissolves Al with evolution of SO_2.

$$2Al + \underset{\text{(Hot and conc.)}}{6H_2SO_4} \longrightarrow Al_2(SO_4)_3 + 3SO_2 + 6H_2O$$

Dilute and concentrated HNO_3 has no effect on Al, i.e., Al is rendered passive by nitric acid. This is due to surface oxidation and formation of a thin film of oxide on its surface.

Organic acids have little action on Al at ordinary temperatures.

(iv) **Action of Alkalies** Aluminium is attacked by caustic alkalies with the evolution of hydrogen gas.

$$2Al + \underbrace{2NaOH + 2H_2O}_{\text{solution}} \longrightarrow \underset{\substack{\text{Sodium} \\ \textit{meta}\text{-aluminate} \\ \text{(soluble)}}}{2NaAlO_2} + 3H_2\uparrow$$

$$2Al + 6NaOH \xrightarrow{\text{Fused}} \underset{\text{Sodium aluminate}}{2Na_3AlO_3} + 3H_2$$

(v) **Action of Non-metals** Besides oxygen, aluminium reacts with non-metals directly to form corresponding compounds. Aluminium when heated in the atmosphere of nitrogen, forms aluminium nitride.

$$2Al + N_2 \xrightarrow{\Delta} 2AlN$$

Aluminium powder when fused with sulphur forms aluminium sulphide.

$$2Al + 3S \longrightarrow Al_2S_3$$

Finely powdered heated aluminium combines with halogens to form corresponding halides.

$$2Al + 3X_2 \longrightarrow 2AlX_3;\ (X_2 = F_2, Cl_2, Br_2, I_2)$$

All these above compounds are hydrolysed with water.

$$AlN + 3H_2O \longrightarrow Al(OH)_3 + NH_3$$

$$Al_2S_3 + 6H_2O \longrightarrow 2Al(OH)_3 + 3H_2S$$

$$AlX_3 + 3H_2O \longrightarrow Al(OH)_3 + 3HX$$

(vi) **Reducing Agent** It is a good reducing agent and reduces oxides of metals like Cr, Fe, Mn etc

$$Cr_2O_3 + 2Al \longrightarrow 2Cr + Al_2O_3 + \text{heat}$$

$$Fe_2O_3 + 2Al \longrightarrow 2Fe + Al_2O_3 + \text{heat}$$

$$3Mn_3O_4 + 8Al \longrightarrow 9Mn + 4Al_2O_3 + \text{heat}$$

It reduces oxides of non-metals also,

$$3CO_2 + 4Al \longrightarrow 2Al_2O_3 + 3C$$

$$3SiO_2 + 4Al \longrightarrow 2Al_2O_3 + 3Si$$

(vii) **Displacement of Other Metals** Being more electropositive it displaces metals like copper, zinc lead etc. from the solution of their salts.

$$3ZnSO_4 + 2Al \longrightarrow Al_2(SO_4)_3 + 3Zn$$

$$3CuSO_4 + 2Al \longrightarrow Al_2(SO_4)_3 + 3Cu$$

Uses

(i) Aluminium being cheap and light metal is largely used for making household utensils, trays, frames, etc. Bodies of automobiles, aircraft and roofing are made of aluminium sheet.

(ii) Thin foils of Al are used in wrapping soaps, cigarettes and confectionary.

(iii) Al wire is used in transmission lines and coils for dynamos and motors.

(iv) It is used for making silvery paints for covering iron and other materials.

(v) It is used in thermic process for the extraction of Cr, Mn, etc.

Important Compounds of Aluminium

Some of the important compounds of aluminium are discussed below

1. Aluminium Chloride ($AlCl_3$)

It is also called as **aluminium trichloride**.

Concept Visualizer

Preparation of Anhydrous $AlCl_3$

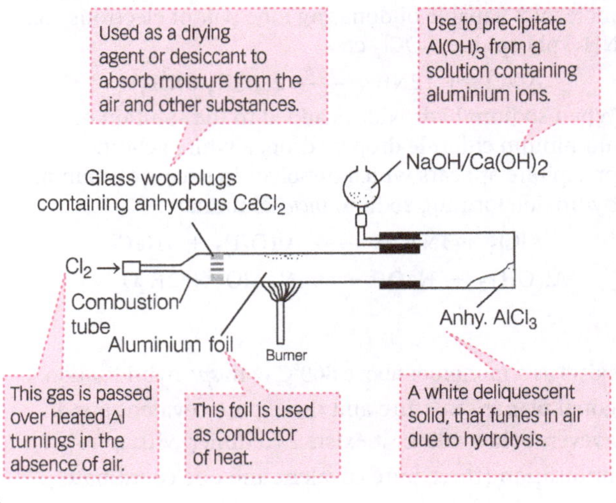

Methods of preparation and properties of $AlCl_3$ are as follows

Methods of Preparation

(i) $AlCl_3$ is prepared by dissolving Al in excess of HCl. It is deposited as the crystals of $Al_2Cl_6 \cdot 12H_2O$. This hydrate on heating decomposes to give alumina as,

$$2Al + 6HCl \longrightarrow 2AlCl_3 + 3H_2\uparrow$$

$$Al_2Cl_6 \cdot 12H_2O \xrightarrow{\Delta} Al_2O_3 + 6HCl + 9H_2O$$

(ii) For preparing anhydrous $AlCl_3$, Al is heated in a steam of dry chlorine or hydrogen chloride gas as,

$$2Al + \underset{(Dry)}{3Cl_2} \xrightarrow{\Delta} 2AlCl_3$$

(iii) **Other Important Methods**

- A mixture of Al_2O_3 and C is strongly heated in dry chlorine gas as,

$$Al_2O_3 + \underset{(Dry)}{3Cl_2} + 3C \xrightarrow{\Delta} 2AlCl_3 + 3CO$$

- A mixture of CO and Cl_2 is passed over heated Al_2O_3 as,

$$\underset{Heated}{Al_2O_3} + 3CO + 3Cl_2 \longrightarrow 2AlCl_3 + 3CO_2$$

- AlI_3 reacts with CCl_4, also gives $AlCl_3$.

$$4AlI_3 + 3CCl_4 \longrightarrow 4AlCl_3 + 3CI_4$$

Properties

- $AlCl_3$ is white in its pure form and sublimes at 183°C. It is extremely hygroscopic and fumes strongly in moist air due to the formation of HCl as,

$$2AlCl_3 + 6H_2O \longrightarrow 2Al(OH)_3 + 6HCl$$

- When dissolved in water, it changes into hydrated aluminium chloride which is ionic in nature.

$$Al_2Cl_6 + 12H_2O \longrightarrow 2AlCl_3 \cdot 6H_2O$$

- Aluminium chloride forms addition compounds with the molecules capable of donating lone pair of electrons e.g. NH_3, phosphine, $COCl_2$ etc.

$$Al_2Cl_6 + 12NH_3 \longrightarrow 2(AlCl_3 \cdot 6NH_3)$$

- When sodium hydroxide is added to the solution of aluminium chloride drop by drop, a white gelatinous precipitate appears which dissolves in excess of sodium hydroxide forming sodium *meta*-aluminate.

$$AlCl_3 + 3NaOH \longrightarrow Al(OH)_3 + 3NaCl$$

$$Al(OH)_3 + NaOH \longrightarrow NaAlO_2 + 2H_2O$$

Structure

It exists as a monomer above 800°C with sp^2 hybridisation, trigonal planar structure and three pure covalent bond. However, below 400°C, it exists as a dimer with sp^3 hybridisation (three pure covalent and one coordinate bond). In solid state also, $AlCl_3$ exists as a dimer and is non-conducting.

- The structure of Al_2Cl_6 can be represented as,

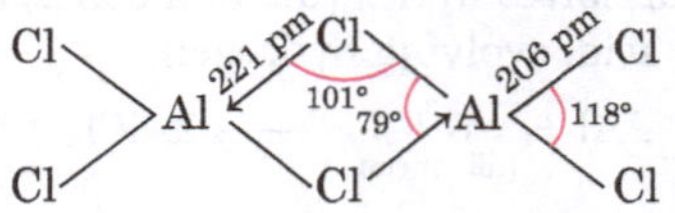

Dimer form of $AlCl_3$

JEE Alert

The dimeric form of $AlCl_3$ exists in non-polar solvents such as benzene but due to higher heat of hydration, it changes into $[Al(H_2O)_6]^{3+}$ and $3Cl^-$ ions in aqueous solution.

Uses

(i) $AlCl_3$ is a strong Lewis acid and readily forms adducts with Lewis base. These adducts have many uses.

(ii) It is use as a catalyst in 'organic chemistry' and also used in the manufacture of dyes and many pharmaceuticals drugs etc.

2. Alums

The name *alum*, is given to all double salts with the formula, $(M')_2SO_4 \cdot (M'')_2(SO_4)_3 \cdot 24H_2O$.

where, M' = univalent basic radicals like Na^+, K^+, NH_4^+, Ag^+ etc.

M'' = trivalent metal like Al^{3+}, Cr^{3+}, Fe^{3+}, Co^{3+} etc.

Some common examples include

$K_2SO_4 \cdot Al_2(SO_4)_3 \cdot 24H_2O$, potash alum or common alum;

$Na_2SO_4 \cdot Al_2(SO_4)_3 \cdot 24H_2O$, sodium alum,

$(NH_4)_2SO_4 \cdot Al_2(SO_4)_3 \cdot 24H_2O$, ammonium alum,

$K_2SO_4 \cdot Cr_2(SO_4)_3 \cdot 24H_2O$, chrome alum.

Methods of Preparation

Common alum is potash alum, Being an ionic compound, it does not contain discrete molecules and is usually represented as, $[KAl(SO_4)_2 \cdot 12H_2O]$. It is prepared by following methods

(i) **From Alunite or Alum Stone** Alunite is boiled with dilute sulphuric acid and filtered. The filtrate is mixed with a requisite amount of potassium sulphate and crystallised.

$$K_2SO_4 \cdot Al_2(SO_4)_3 \cdot 4Al(OH)_3 + 6H_2SO_4 \longrightarrow K_2SO_4 + 3Al_2(SO_4)_3 + 12H_2O$$

$$K_2SO_4 + Al_2(SO_4)_3 + 24H_2O \longrightarrow 2[KAl(SO_4)_2 \cdot 12H_2O]$$

(ii) **From Bauxite** Bauxite is dissolved in sulphuric acid, treated with calculated amount of potassium sulphate and crystallised.

(iii) **From Pyrites Shale with $Al_2O_3 \cdot xSiO_2$ and FeS_2**

It is also known as alum shale which is aluminium silicate mixed with iron sulphide.

It is roasted in excess of air when ferrous sulphide gives ferrous sulphate and sulphuric acid and the latter then reacts with alumina to form aluminium sulphate.

$$2FeS_2 + 2H_2O + 7O_2 \longrightarrow 2FeSO_4 + 2H_2SO_4$$

$$Al_2O_3 \cdot xSiO_2 + 3H_2SO_4 \longrightarrow Al_2(SO_4)_3 + xSiO_2 + 3H_2O$$

Ferrous sulphate is removed by **fractional crystallisation.** Also potassium sulphate is added to the mother liquor and potash alum crystallises out.

Properties

All the alums are isomorphous, form mixed crystals in all proportions.

- Each alum has different melting point. These are usually much more soluble in hot water than in cold water.
- On heating, alum loses its water of crystallisation and swells up leaving behind a porous mass, called the **burnt alum**.

Uses

(i) It is used in purification of water, water proofing of textiles, in dyeing and paper industry.

(ii) It is also employed as a styptic to arrest bleeding.

Elemental Practice 5.1

Type I MCQs with Only One Correct Option

1. Choose the correct option from the following statement.
   (a) In borane, each boron atom is sp^2 hybridised.
   (b) Each boron atom in borane contributes one electron to form the 3*c*-2*e* B—H—B bond with bridged H-atom.
   (c) Tetrahydridoborates cannot be prepared by the action of sodium hydride and methyl borates in THF.
   (d) B atom in BH_4^- is dsp^2 hybridised and the structure of BH_4^- is square planar.
2. Choose the incorrect option from the following.
   (a) Tendency to form ionic compound increases from B to Tl.
   (b) Boron forms only covalent compound.
   (c) Thallium forms only ionic compounds.
   (d) Group 13 elements have less tendency to form complexes than the *s*-block elements.
3. Consider the reaction below
   $BF_3 + D \longrightarrow [D-BF_3]$ adduct
   D in the reaction cannot be
   (a) H_2O (b) Et_2O (c) F^- (d) CCl_4
4. On small scale, boron is best isolated by reducing boron trioxide with
   (a) metallic zinc (b) metallic aluminium
   (c) metallic copper (d) metallic magnesium
5. Select the hydroxide that is most basic in nature
   (a) $B(OH)_3$ (b) $Al(OH)_3$ (c) $Ga(OH)_3$ (d) $Tl(OH)_3$
6. The shape of jeweller's borax is
   (a) prismatic (b) octahedral
   (c) triangular (d) tetrahedral
7. H_3BO_3 on neutralization with which of the following compound gives borax.
   (a) B_2O_3 (b) $CaCO_3$
   (c) Na_2CO_3 (d) NaOH
8. The correct order of thermal stability for group 13 hydrides is:
   (a) $B_2H_6 > AlH_3 > GaH_3 > TlH_3$
   (b) $TlH_3 > GaH_3 > AlH_3 > B_2H_6$
   (c) $AlH_3 > B_2H_6 > GaH_3 > TlH_3$
   (d) $B_2H_6 > GaH_3 > AlH_3 > TlH_3$
9. The power of halides of boron to act as Lewis acids decreases in the order
   (a) $BF_3 > BCl_3 > BBr_3$ (b) $BBr_3 > BCl_3 > BF_3$
   (c) $BCl_3 > BF_3 > BBr_3$ (d) $BCl_3 > BBr_3 > BF_3$
10. In diborane
    (a) 2 bridged hydrogen and four terminal hydrogen are present.
    (b) 3 bridged and three terminal hydrogen are present.
    (c) 4 bridged hydrogen and two terminal hydrogen are present.
    (d) 1 bridged hydrogen and 1 terminal hydrogen are present.
11. Aluminium is obtained by
    (a) reduction of Al_2O_3 with coke
    (b) electrolysis of Al_2O_3 dissolved in Na_3AlF_6
    (c) reduction of Al_2O_3 with chromium
    (d) heating cryolite and alumina
12. The reaction taking place at the cathode in the aluminium extraction is
    (a) $Al^{3+} + 3e^- \longrightarrow Al$
    (b) $6F^- \longrightarrow 3F_2 + 6e^-$
    (c) $Al_2O_3 + 3F_2 \longrightarrow 2Al^{3+} + \frac{3}{2}O_2$
    (d) $C(s) + 2O_2^{2-} \longrightarrow CO_2(g) + 4e^-$
13. In alums, each metal ion is surrounded by
    (a) two water molecules
    (b) four water molecules
    (c) six water molecules
    (d) eight water molecules
14. Select the method that is used to prepare borax crystals.
    (a) A hot conc. solution of B_2O_3 is made to react with calculated quantity of conc. H_2SO_4.
    (b) Tincal is dried up and heated to red heat.
    (c) Tincal is powdered, treated with water and evaporated.
    (d) An alcoholic solution of boric acid is evaporated and cooled.

15. BCl_3 does not exist as dimer but BH_3 exists as dimer (B_2H_6). It is because
(a) chlorine is more electronegative than hydrogen.
(b) there is $p\pi - p\pi$ back bonding in BCl_3 but BH_3 does not contain such multiple bonding.
(c) large sized chlorine atoms do not fit in between the small boron atoms whereas small sized hydrogen atoms get fitted in between boron atoms.
(d) BH_3 is not an electron deficient species.

Type II 》 MCQs with One or More than One Correct Option

16. Select the correct statement(s) about boron carbide.
(a) Its molecular formula is B_4C_3.
(b) It is also called Norbia.
(c) It is the extremely hard substance.
(d) It is used for cutting glasses.

17. Select the correct statement(s) about Al_2Cl_6.
(a) Four Al—Cl bonds are of same length and four of different length.
(b) Six Al—Cl bonds are of same length and two of different length.
(c) There two in Cl—Al—Cl are 118° and 79°.
(d) The angle Al—Cl—Al is 101°.

18. Select the correct statement(s) from the following
(a) aluminium hydroxide is a white gelatinous precipitate formed by the addition of sodium hydroxide to the solution of aluminium nitrate.
(b) The precipitate, $Al(OH)_3$, dissolves in excess of base to give aluminates while excess of acid gives corresponding salts.
(c) $AlCl_3$ exits or a close packed structure of chloride ions with octahedral holes occupied by Al^{3+} ions.
(d) Gallium hydroxides unlike aluminium hydroxide does not form gallates with caustic alkalis.

19. Orthoboric acid (H_3BO_3) and *meta*boric acid (HBO_2) differ from each other with respect to
(a) basicity (b) structure
(c) melting point (d) oxidation number

20. Select the correct statement(s) from the following
(a) boron trioxide is a colourless, hygroscopic substance which slowly reacts with water to give boric anhydride.
(b) boron sesquioxide forms glassy beads of metaborates when heated with metal oxides.
(c) borax is used as a primary standard for titrating acids.
(d) due to acidic character, $B(OH)_3$ can be titrated with NaOH and a sharp end point is attained.

Type III 》 Numerical/Integer Answer Type Questions

21. The number of aluminates or *meta*-aluminates formed by aluminium on reaction with strong bases is /are

22. The number of trichlorides, MCl_3 (where M = B, Al, Ga and In) which exists as dimer are ....

23. The number of reactions that gives diborane as a product are:
(a) $BF_3 \cdot Et_2O + LiAlH_4 \xrightarrow{\text{Diethyl ether}}$
(b) $NaBH_4 + I_2 \xrightarrow{\text{Diglyme}}$
(c) $BF_3 + NaH \xrightarrow{450\,K}$
(d) $H_3BO_3 \xrightarrow{370\,K}$

24. The number of compounds that exhibit acidic behaviour when dissolved in water is/are.
B_2O_3, Al_2O_3, Ga_2O_3, Tl_2O_3, In_2O_3

25. The total number of statement that is correct regarding crystalline form of borax is
(a) equal number of sp^2 and sp^3 hybridised B-atom.
(b) tetranuclear $[B_4O_5(OH)_4]^{2-}$ unit
(c) all boron atoms in the same plane
(d) It has fixed melting point.
(e) One terminal hydroxide per boron atom.

Elemental Practice 5.1 | Chapter 05

Connect with **Answers**

1. (b)	2. (d)	3. (d)	4. (d)	5. (d)	6. (b)
7. (c)	8. (a)	9. (b)	10. (a)	11. (b)	12. (a)
13. (c)	14. (c)	15. (c)	16. (b,c,d)	17. (a,c,d)	18. (a,b,c)
19. (a,b,c)	20. (a,b,c)	21. (2)	22. (3)	23. (3)	24. (1)
25. (4)					

Element 2

Group-14 Elements and Their Compounds (The Carbon Family)

Carbon is the first member of group 14 of the periodic table. This group consists of five elements i.e., **carbon** (C), **silicon** (Si), **germanium** (Ge), **tin** (Sn) and **lead** (Pb).

Carbon is non-metals, silicon and germanium are metalloid while tin and lead are metals.

Abundance

Carbon and silicon are most abundant elements in earth's crust whereas germanium occurs only as traces. Tin and lead also occur in small amounts. Only carbon occurs in free state as coal, diamond and graphite, in combined state as carbonates, CO_2 petroleum and natural gas.

Silicon is the second most abundant element after oxygen in Earth's crust in form of silicates and silica. Germanium found in traces in coal and in certain deposits. It is an important constituent for making conductors and transistors.

The important ore of tin is tin stone (SnO_2), or cassiterite. Lead is found is form of galena (PbS) anglesite ($PbSO_4$) and cerussite ($PbCO_3$). The approximated abundance ratio of these elements in Earth's crust is given below,

Element	C	Si	Ge	Sn	Pb
Abundance in Earth's crust (ppm)	200	277200	1.6	2.2	16

General and Physical Properties

The variation of general and physical properties of group 14 elements are given below.

1. Electronic Configuration

The general electronic configuration of group 14 elements is ns^2np^2, where $n = 2$ to 6.

Elements	Electronic configuration (ns^2np^2)
$_6C$	[He] $2s^2\ 2p^2$
$_{14}Si$	[Ne] $3s^2\ 3p^2$
$_{32}Ge$	[Ar] $3d^{10}\ 4s^2\ 4p^2$
$_{50}Sn$	[Kr] $4d^{10}\ 5s^2\ 5p^2$
$_{82}Pb$	[Xe] $4f^{14}\ 5d^{10}\ 6s^2\ 6p^2$

2. Non-metallic Nature

The non-metallic nature decreases down the group.

C	Si	Ge	Sn	Pb
Non-metal	Metalloid	Metalloid	Metal	Metal

3. Density

The density of these elements increases down the group. This is due to large increase in atomic mass as compared to increase in the atomic size. However, diamond has higher density than silicon.

Element	C	Si	Ge	Sn	Pb
Density (g/mL)	3.51 (for diamond) 2.22 (for graphite)	2.34	5.32	7.26	11.34

4. Melting Point and Boiling Point

The melting point and boiling point of group 14 elements are higher than their corresponding group 13 elements. This is due to the formation of four covalent bonds on account of four electrons in their valence shells which results in strong binding forces in between their atoms in solid as well as in liquid state.

The melting point and boiling point of this group members decrease down the group.

Element	C	Si	Ge	Sn	Pb
Melting point (K)	4373	1693	1218	505	600
Boiling point (K)	—	3550	3123	2896	2024

5. Atomic Radii and Atomic Volume

- Both atomic radii and atomic volume increases gradually on moving down the group due to the effect of extra shell being added from member to member.
- The atomic radii of group 14 elements are smaller than their corresponding group 13 elements due to increase in nuclear charge in the same period.

6. Electronegativity

The electronegativity decreases from C to Si and then almost becomes constant.

Elements	C	Si	Ge	Sn	Pb
Electronegativity on pauling scale	2.5	1.8	1.8	1.8	1.9

7. Ionisation Energy

(i) The ionisation energy decreases regularly down the group. However, Pb shows a higher value than Sn. It is because Pb has poor shielding of inner f-orbitals as a result of which effective nuclear charge experienced by outer shell electrons becomes more.

Ionisation energy (kJ mol^{-1})	C	Si	Ge	Sn	Pb
$\Delta_i H_1$	1086	786	761	708	715
$\Delta_i H_2$	2352	1577	1537	1411	1450
$\Delta_i H_3$	4620	3228	3300	2942	3081
$\Delta_i H_4$	6220	4354	4409	3929	4082

(ii) The first ionisation energies of group 14 elements are higher than their corresponding group 13 elements because of smaller size.

(iii) The electropositive character of these elements increases down the group because of decrease in ionisation energy.

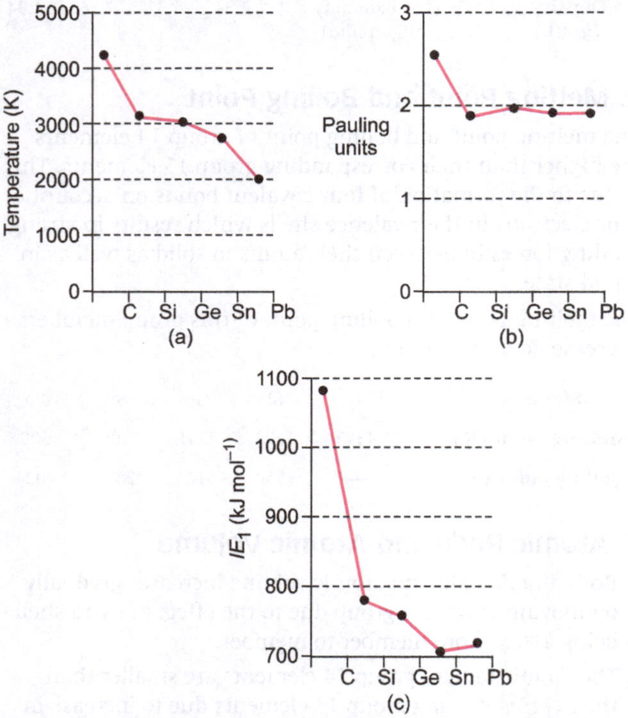

Graphical representation of trends of the group 14 elements; (a) Boiling point, (b) Pauling electronegativity and (c) First ionisation energy (IE_1).

8. Oxidation State

(i) Presence of four electrons in outermost shell of these elements reveals that the members of this family can gain or loss four electrons forming M^{4+} or M^{4-} ions respectively to show ionic nature or exhibit tetravalent covalent nature by sharing of four electron pairs in order to attain stable configuration.

(ii) The formation of M^{4+} or M^{4-} ions require huge amount of energy which is normally not available during normal course of reactions. Therefore, these elements usually do not form M^{4+} or M^{4-} ions, but they usually form compounds with covalency of four.

(iii) Carbon and silicon have tetravalent nature in most of the compounds when ns^2 pair is also involved in bonding.

(iv) Germanium, tin and lead show +2 and +4 oxidation states depending on whether ns^2 pair is inert (and is not involved in bonding) or involved in bonding—a case of **inert pair effect.**

As we go down the group, inertness of ns^2 pair increases hence tendency to exhibit +2 oxidation state increases and that of +4 oxidation state decreases. Thus, stability of ions with different oxidation number follows the order :

$$Ge^{4+} > Sn^{4+} > Pb^{4+} \quad \text{and} \quad Ge^{2+} < Sn^{2+} < Pb^{2+}$$

Also $Sn^{2+} < Sn^{4+}$ and $Pb^{2+} > Pb^{4+}$

Thus, $\Delta G^\circ < 0$ for the reactions :

$$Sn^{2+} \longrightarrow Sn^{4+} + 2e^-$$

$$Pb^{4+} + 2e^- \longrightarrow Pb^{2+}$$

$$Ge^{2+} \longrightarrow Ge^{4+} + 2e^-$$

Thus, Sn^{2+} salts are better reducing agents and Pb^{4+} salts are better oxidising agents.

(v) The +2 oxidation state occurs for tin and lead and is the most stable oxidation state for lead. Both $Sn^{2+}(aq)$ and $Pb^{2+}(aq)$ are common solution species, but there are no simple $M^{4+}(aq)$ ions solution for any of the group 14 (IVA) elements. Instead M^{4+} species exist in solution as covalently bonded complex ions, e.g., SiF_6^{2-}, $GeCl_6^{2-}$, $Sn(OH)_6^{2-}$ and $Pb(OH)_6^{2-}$.

In general, the +4 oxidation state compounds are covalent, and the compounds with the Sn and Pb in the +2 oxidation state are largely ionic.

9. Catenation

The tendency of formation of long open or closed atom chains by the combination of same atoms in themselves is known as catenation.

The catenation is maximum in carbon and decreases down the group due to an increase in atomic size. Larger atoms forms longer and weaker bonds, making them less stable for catenation. The tendency of catenation is as follows

C>> Si > Ge = Sn.

Bond	Bond Energy in kJ mol^{-1}
C—C	348
Si—Si	180
Ge—Ge	167
Sn—Sn	155
Pb—Pb	No catenation

The other characteristics are

- Only carbon atoms among group-14 elements form double or triple bonds involving $p\pi - p\pi$ multiple bond with carbon atom and also with other elements particularly nitrogen, oxygen and sulphur e.g. $C=O, C=N, C\equiv N$ etc.
  $>C=C<; C\equiv C-$
- Carbon also possesses the tendency to form closed chain compounds with O, S and N atoms.
- Carbon can form chain containing any number of carbon atoms. Si and Ge cannot extend the chain beyond 6 atoms, while Sn and Pb do not form chains containing more than one or two atoms.
- The reason for greater tendency of carbon for catenation than other elements in the group may further be explained by the fact that the C—C bond energy is approximately of the same magnitude as the energies of the bond between C and other elements. On the other hand, the Si—Si bond is weaker than the bond between silicon and other elements.

Bond	Bond energy (kJ/mol)	Bond	Bond energy (kJ/mol)
C—C	348	Si—Si	180
C—O	315	Si—O	372
C—H	414	Si—H	339
C—Cl	326	Si—Cl	360
C—F	439	Si—F	536

10. Allotropy

All the elements of the carbon family with the exception of lead exhibit allotropy. It decreases from C to Pb.

Chemical Properties

Important chemical properties of group-14 are as follows.

1. Hydrides

All the elements of group 14 combine with hydrogen directly or indirectly to form the covalent hydrides, MH_4 (M = C, Si, Ge, Sn or Pb). The number of hydrides and the ease of preparation decreases on going form carbon to lead.

The hydrides of silicon are called **silanes** having the general formula Si_nH_{2n+2}. The hydrides of germanium are called **germanes** while those of tin are called the **stannanes**. Only lead forms an unstable hydride of the formula, PbH_4 called the **plumbane**.

Three hydrides of germanium, i.e., GeH_4, Ge_2H_6 and Ge_3H_8 and only two hydrides of tin i.e., SnH_4 and Sn_2H_6 are well known.

2. Halides

Elements of group 14 react with halogens directly to form tetrahedral and covalent halides except C where its halide is produced by the action of halogens on hydrocarbons. $PbBr_4$ and PbI_4 do not exist because Pb^{4+} is a strong oxidant and Br^- and I^- are strong reductants.

- The stability of halides of different elements with same halogen decreases with increasing atomic number
  $CX_4 > SiX_4 > GeX_4 > SnX_4 > PbX_4$
- The tetrahalides of Ge, Sn and Pb behave as oxidising agent. So, GeX_2 is less stable than GeX_4 whereas, PbX_2 is more stable than PbX_4.
- Heavier members of of this family also form dihalides, MX_2. The stability of these halides increases down the group. Dihalides are generally ionic in nature and behave as reducing agents.

JEE Spotlite

The tetrahalides of carbon cannot be hydrolysed by water due to absence of *d*-orbital while other elements tetrachlorides can be hydrolysed to their respective oxides.

3. Oxides

Carbon forms five oxides i.e., CO, CO_2, C_3O_2 (carbon suboxide), $C_{10}O_8$ (tetra-carboxylic dianhydride) and $C_{12}O_9$ (metallic trianhydride). C_3O_2 is the anhydride of malonic acid $CH_2(COOH)_2$ and CO_2 is the anhydride of H_2CO_3 (carbonic acid).

Si forms SiO_2 while Pb forms a number of oxides. One of the oxide of Pb is PbO which can be obtained by heating $Pb(NO_3)_2$,

$$2Pb(NO_3)_2 \xrightarrow{\text{Heat}} 2PbO + 4NO_2 + O_2$$

The red form of PbO is called litharge and the yellow form is massicot. Pb_3O_4 (Red lead, or Sindur) is prepared by heating litharge in air at 470°C,

$$6PbO + O_2 \xrightarrow{470°C} 2Pb_3O_4,$$

Pb_3O_4 is a mixed oxide of $PbO_2 \cdot 2PbO \cdot Pb_2O_3$ is called lead sesquioxide.

- GeO_2, SnO_2 etc are also network solids.
- As we descend the group, acidic nature of the oxides decreases and basic nature of the oxides increases.

Oxides	Nature	Oxides	Nature
CO, CO_2	acidic	SnO, SnO_2	amphoteric
SiO_2	acidic	PbO, PbO_2	basic
GeO, GeO_2	amphoteric	Pb_3O_4	amphoteric

Si, Ge, Sn and Pb form MO_2 type of oxide. In SiO_2, each Si atom is bonded to four oxygen atoms which are arranged tetrahedrally around Si and each O atom is covalently bonded to two Si atoms.

GeO_2, SnO_2 and PbO_2 are all solids and exist in several modifications.

4. Reaction with Water

C, Si and Ge are unaffected by H_2O. Sn reacts with steam forming SnO_2 and H_2 :

$$\underset{}{Sn} + \underset{\text{(Steam)}}{2H_2O} \longrightarrow SnO_2 + 2H_2$$

Pb is unaffected by H_2O probably because of protective oxide film.

5. Reaction with Acid

C, Si and Ge are unaffected by dilute acid. Sn dissolves in dilute HNO_3 forming $Sn(NO_3)_2$.

- Pb dissolves slowly in dilute HCl forming $PbCl_2$ (sparingly soluble) and quite readily in dilute HNO_3 forming $Pb(NO_3)_2$ and oxides of nitrogen.
- Pb does not dissolve in dilute H_2SO_4 due to formation of $PbSO_4$ coating.
- Diamond is unaffected by concentrated acids, but graphite changes into mellitic acid ($C_{12}H_6O_{12}$) also called benzene hexa-carboxylic acid (A).

A :

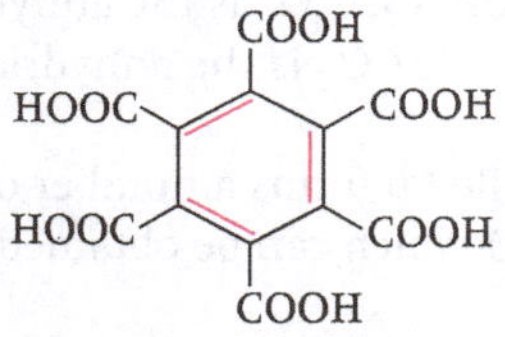

- Si is oxidised and changes to SiF_4 by hot concentrated HNO_3/HF.
- Ge dissolves slowly in hot concentrated H_2SO_4 and HNO_3.
- Sn also dissolves in concentrated acids.
- Pb does not dissolve in concentrated HCl due to formation of $PbCl_2$ coating.

Anomalous Behaviour of Carbon

Carbon is found to differ in many properties from the rest of the members of group 14. This is because of the following reason : (i) Its smaller size (ii) Its high electronegativity (iii) Its property to catenate (iv) Absence of d-orbitals in it.

Some of the properties in which it differs from other members are as follows,

- The melting and boiling points of carbon are very high as compared to the rest of the members of the family.
- Carbon in its diamond form is one of the hardest substance known.
- It has maximum tendency to show catenation.
- Carbon has high tendency to form $p\pi - p\pi$ multiple bonds with other elements like nitrogen, oxygen, sulphur etc. Other members of the family form $p\pi - d\pi$ bonds and that also to a lesser extent.
- CO_2 is a gas while the dioxides of all other members are solids.
- Carbon shows a maximum covalency of four while other members of the family may expand their covalency upto six e.g., $[SiCl_6]^{2-}$, $[PbCl_6]^{2-}$ etc.
- Carbon is not affected by alkalies whereas other members react on fusion. For example, silicon form silicates,

$$Si + 2NaOH + \frac{1}{2}O_2 \longrightarrow \underset{\text{Sodium silicate}}{Na_2SiO_3} + H_2$$

JEE MAPPER

Example Similar to PYQ Asked in JEE Main 2024

Evaluate the following statements related to group 14 elements for their incorrectness.

A. Electronegativity decreases from C to Si down the group and then becomes almost constant.
B. GeX_4 is more stable than GeX_2, whereas PbX_2 is more than PbX_4.
C. GeO is distinctly acidic whereas SnO and PbO are amphoteric in nature.
D. Bond enthalpy between Ge—Ge is greater than Si—Si.
E. $SiCl_4$ on hydrolysis gives silica.

Select the incorrect statements and choose the correct answer from the options given below.

(a) B and C (b) D and E (c) A, B and C (d) B, D and E

Sol. (b) Among the given statements only D and E are incorrect. Their corrected form are given as

D. Bond enthalpy between Ge-Ge (260 kJ/mol) is less than Si-Si (297 kJ mol^{-1})

E. $SiCl_4$ on hydrolysis gives silicic acid.

Competency Enhancer 2.1

Consider the following statements.

I. Carborundum is an amorphous solid.
II. Silicon dissolves in excess of HF due to formation of SiH_4.
III. For a good quality cement, the ratio of silica to alumina is 3 : 1.
IV. C—C bond length is maximum in diamond than C_{70}.
V. Quartz is an amorphous form of silica.

Which of the following statements are correct?

(a) I and III (b) II, III and IV
(c) III and IV (d) I, III and V

Allotropes of Carbon

Different form of allotropes of carbon are as follows.

Diamond

It is the purest form of carbon and one of the hardest substances with very high density as well as high refractive index. It has a three dimensional structure in which sp^3-hybridised C-atoms are arranged tetrahedrally.

The C—C bond distance in diamond molecule is 1.54Å. Each C-atom lies at the centre of a regular tetrahedron and is linked to four C-atoms lying at the corners of the tetrahedron as shown in the figure. It is therefore hard and non-conducting.

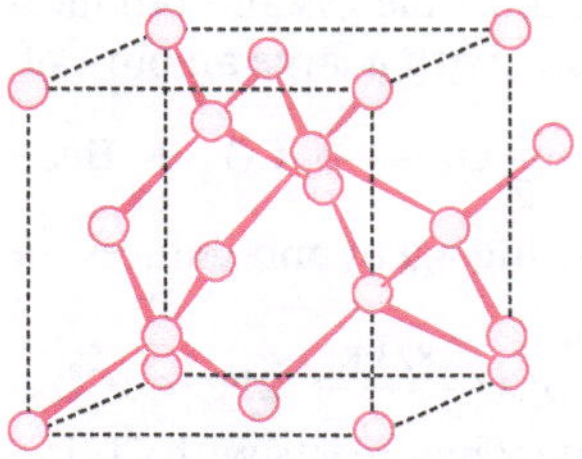

The crystal structure of diamond

Graphite

It consists of planar hexagonal layers of carbon atoms held together by relatively weak van der Waals' forces. Within each layer, a carbon atom is bonded to three other carbon atoms by sp^2 hybrid bonds and the additional *p* electron from each carbon forms an extended delocalised π-bonding system encompassing the entire layer.

This makes graphite a good conductor of electricity in directions along the planes of carbon atoms. The covalent bonds in graphite account for its hardness; however, because the layers can slide over one another, graphite is slippery to touch and is effective as a lubricant.

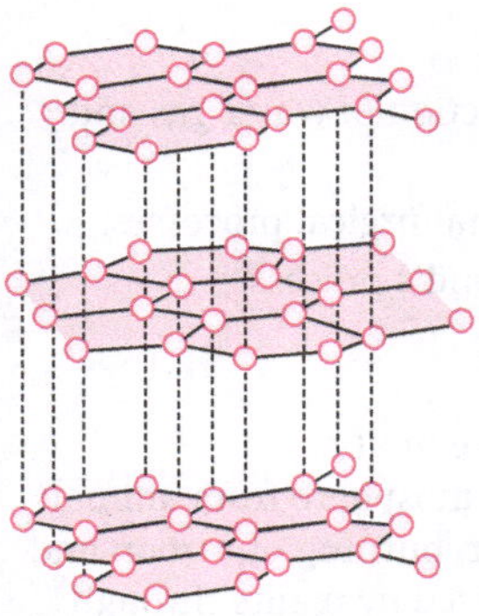

Structure of α-graphite

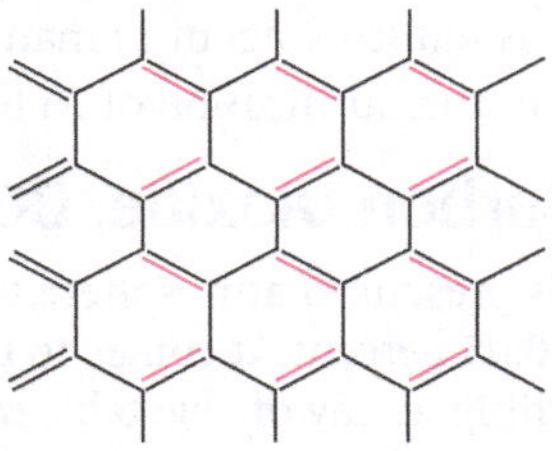

The structure of a graphite sheet

JEE Alert

Graphite is thermodynamically more stable than diamond.

Difference Between Diamond and Graphite

Diamond	Graphite
Crystalline, transparent with extra brilliance.	Crystalline, opaque and shiny substance
Hardest form	Soft having soapy touch
Bad conductor of electricity	Good conductor of electricity
High density (3.51 g/cm^3) heavy	Low density (2.25 g/cm^3), lighter than diamond
Colourless	Greyish white
Tetrahedral shaped	Two dimensional layer structure having regular hexagonal sheets.
sp^3 hybridisation	sp^2 hybridisation
Less stable, more energy	More stable, less energy
$C_D \rightarrow C_G; \Delta H = -0.5\,\text{kcal}$	$C_G \rightarrow C_D$ at high temperature and high pressure
Used in cutting glass and jewellery; an abrasive etc.	Used as lubricating agent, electrodes, in pencils, crucibles (due to high m.pt) etc.

Fullerene

It is a carbon allotrope which was discovered in 1990 as a constituent of soot, consists of spherical C_{60} molecules with the extraordinary shape of a soccer ball. The C_{60}. ball has 12 pentagonal and 20 hexagonal faces with each atom sp^2-hybridised and bonded to three other atoms.

C_{60} was first prepared in 1985, by laser vaporisation of graphite (at about 10000°C) followed by sweeping of the carbon atoms by a blast of high pressure helium gas and rapid cooling in a vacuum chamber.

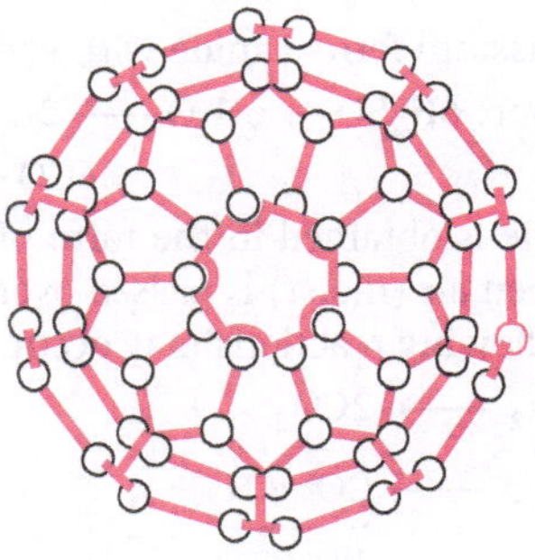

Structure of Buckminster fullerene

Uses

Following table summarises uses of elements of group 14 (IVA):

Elements	Uses
Carbon	Diamond in jewellery and glass cutter; graphite as lubricant and electrode
Silicon	As a semiconductor, in silicone waxes and polymers, as silicates in the ceramic and glass industries.
Germanium	As a semiconductor.
Tin	In alloys, as a protective coating for iron and steel.
Lead	In alloys, in car batteries etc.

Compounds of Carbon

Carbon forms several compounds. Some of them are given below.

Oxides of Carbon

Two main oxides of carbon are carbon monoxide and carbon dioxide. Their preparation methods, properties, structure and uses are described below.

1. Carbon Monoxide, CO

It is mainly found in small amounts in volcanic gases, chimney gases, exhaust gases of internal combustion engines and coal gas.

Methods of Preparation

- Carbon monoxide is obtained by burning C in limited supply of oxygen.
  Pure CO can be obtained by heating HCOOH with H_2SO_4 where, H_2SO_4 acts as, dehydrating agent.
- It is also prepared by, heating carbonates of Ca, Ba or Mg with Zn

  e.g. $$MgCO_3 + Zn \xrightarrow{\Delta} MgO + ZnO + CO$$

  - Heating potassium ferrocyanide with conc. H_2SO_4.

  $$K_4Fe(CN)_6 + \text{conc. } 6H_2SO_4 + 6H_2O \longrightarrow 2K_2SO_4 + FeSO_4 + 6CO + 3(NH_4)_2SO_4$$
- Carbon monoxide is obtained in the form of water gas and producer gas when air (moist) is passed over a bed of white hot coke. The following reactions may occur.

  $$2C + O_2 \longrightarrow 2CO_2;$$

  $$C + H_2O \longrightarrow \underbrace{CO + H_2}_{\text{Water gas}}$$

  Carbon dioxide is reduced by passing the mixture over heated charcoal.

  $$CO_2 + \underset{\text{(Charcoal)}}{C} \longrightarrow 2CO$$

  The CO produced, always consists of N_2, H_2, CO_2, etc.

Properties

- It is a colourless and odourless gas.
- It is slightly soluble in water.
- Its density is nearly equal to the density of air.
- It is highly poisonous in nature. One part in 100 parts of air causes death in few minutes.
  The poisonous nature of CO is due to the fact that it combines with haemoglobin (a red colouring matter of blood which is carrier of oxygen) to form carboxy-haemoglobin which is not capable to absorb oxygen and as a result of this, suffocation takes place.
- It is an essential constituent of gaseous fuels like water gas, producer gas etc.
- CO is highly combustible gas and produces CO_2 on combustion, along with a large amount of heat.

  $$CO + \frac{1}{2}O_2 \longrightarrow CO_2 + \text{Heat}$$
- It is a good reducing agent and reduces metal oxides to metals as

  $$Fe_2O_3 + 3CO \xrightarrow{823\text{ K}} 2Fe + 3CO_2$$
- It gives phosgene when reacts with Cl_2 in sunlight.
- It forms metal carbonyls with transition metals like Ni, Fe, Co, etc.

Structure

The structure of CO can be represented as,

$$:C \overset{\leftarrow}{=} O:$$

Two pairs of electrons are considered to be shared between carbon and oxygen. Oxygen also donates a lone pair to carbon resulting a coordinate bond. The properties of CO can be explained satisfactorily if we consider CO as the resonance hybrid of following three structures.

$$:C{=}\ddot{\underset{..}{O}} \longleftrightarrow \overset{-}{C}{\equiv}\overset{+}{O}: \longleftrightarrow :\overset{+}{C}{-}\ddot{\underset{..}{O}}:^{-}$$

Uses

CO is used

(i) as industrial fuels, as in production of water gas and producer gas.

(ii) as reducing agent in many metallurgical processes.

(iii) in the purification of Ni by Mond's process.

2. Carbon Dioxide, CO_2

CO_2 is present in atmosphere to the extent of 0.03-0.05 percent. It comes to the atmosphere from animal breathing, decay of vegetable matter, burning of carbon and carbonous matter, etc. It is also utilised by plants through photosynthesis process.

Methods of Preparation

CO_2 is obtained by burning C in air (excess). In laboratory, it can be prepared by the action of cold dilute HCl on $CaCO_3$ (marble).

Properties

- CO_2 is colourless gas with a faint pungent smell and slight acidic taste. It dissolves in water forming H_2CO_3 as,

$$CO_2 + H_2O \rightleftharpoons H_2CO_3$$

H_2CO_3 is a weak acid and dissolves in alkalies to form salts as,

$$H_2CO_3 + 2NaOH \longrightarrow Na_2CO_3 + 2H_2O$$

- It turns lime water milky which disappears, if CO_2 is passed for a long time due to the formation of soluble calcium bicarbonate.
- It reacts with liquid NH_3 at 473 K and 220 atm, and gives ammonium carbonate which subsequently decomposes to give urea.
- Solid CO_2 is commonly called **"dry ice"**. It is a soft white snow like compound with specific gravity 1.53 and m.p. –56.6°C at 5.2 atm pressure. It is produced by evaporating liquid CO_2 at 20°C and 70 atm pressure to a pressure less than 5.2 atm.

Structure

The electron dot structure for CO_2 may be represented by either $:\ddot{O}::C::\ddot{O}:$ or $:\ddot{O}{=}C{=}\ddot{O}:$. However, the properties of CO_2 can be explained satisfactorily by the resonance hybrid of following three structures.

$$O{=}C{=}O \longleftrightarrow \overset{-}{O}{-}C{\equiv}\overset{+}{O} \longleftrightarrow \overset{+}{O}{\equiv}C{-}\overset{-}{O}$$

(linear structure of CO_2)

The formation of the molecule can be explained on the basis of hybridisation. Carbon is *sp*-hybridised. The hybrid orbitals form sigma bonds with *p*-orbitals of each oxygen atoms. The unhybridised two *p*-orbitals of carbon atom form two π-bonds with two oxygen atoms.

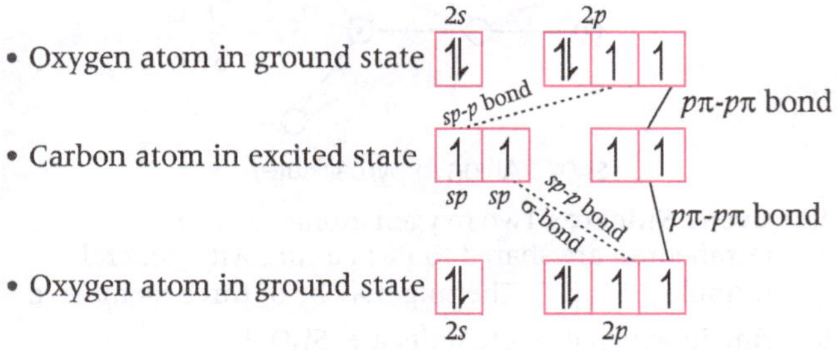

Uses

CO_2 is used

(i) in a refrigerant under the commercial name **Drikold.**

(ii) as a substitute of ice in cold drinks and in ice cream preparation.

(iii) in hospitals, it is used for surgical operations of sores.

(iv) as important constituent of carbogen (a mixture of 95% O_2 and 5% CO_2) which is used for artifical respiration.

(v) as a fire extinguisher.

Solved Booster 2.1

The C—C bond length is maximum in

(a) graphite (b) C_{70} (c) C_{60} (d) diamond

Solution. *(d)*

The C—C bond length is maximum in diamond having value 154 pm. Here, each carbon atom undergoes sp^3 hybridisation and linked to four other carbon atoms by using hybridised orbitals in tetrahedral fashion. It has a rigid three dimensional network of carbon atoms.

C—C bond length within the layers of graphite is 141.5 pm.

In C_{60}, C—C distances between single and double bonds are 143.5 pm and 138.3 pm respectively.

Compounds of Silicon

Silicon forms several compounds, some important of them are as follows.

1. Silicon Tetrachloride, $SiCl_4$

It is also called as tetrachlorosilane. Its preparation methods and properties are as follows

Methods of Preparation

$SiCl_4$ is prepared by heating Si or SiC with Cl_2.

$$Si(s) + 2Cl_2(g) \xrightarrow{\Delta} SiCl_4(l)$$

$$SiC(s) + 4Cl_2(g) \xrightarrow{\Delta} SiCl_4(l) + CCl_4(l)$$

Properties and Uses

- It is a volatile liquid with boiling point 330.57 K.
- On hydrolysis, it gives silicic acid $Si(OH)_4$ which on further heating form silica gel.

$$SiCl_4 + 2H_2O \xrightarrow{\Delta} \underset{\text{Silicic acid}}{Si(OH)_4} \xrightarrow{\Delta} \underset{\text{Silica gel}}{SiO_2 \cdot xH_2O}$$

(Silica gel being very porous is used as a catalyst in petroleum industry and as an adsorbent in column chromatography).

- On reduction, it gets converted into Si. The silicon obtained is ultrapure and is used for making transistors, computer chips and solar cells.

2. Silica

SiO_2 is commonly called as silica. It occurs in Earth's crust as crystalline quartz, tridymite and cristobalite. The amorphous form of silica is **Kieselguhr**.

Methods of Preparation

- It is obtained by heating silicon in oxygen as,

$$Si + O_2 \xrightarrow{\Delta} SiO_2$$

- Pure SiO_2 is prepared in its amorphous form as a white powder by reacting $SiCl_4$ or SiF_4 with water as

$$SiCl_4 + 2H_2O \longrightarrow SiO_2 + 4HCl$$
$$SiF_4 + 2H_2O \longrightarrow SiO_2 + 4HF$$

The latter method is normally less used as SiO_2 further reacts with HF to form H_2SiF_6 (fluorosilicic acid).

Properties

- SiO_2 is insoluble in water and in all acids except HF with which it reacts to form SiF_4 as,

$$SiO_2 + 4HF \longrightarrow SiF_4 + 2H_2O$$

If we take HF in excess, SiF_4 further reacts with it to form fluorosilicic acid as

$$SiF_4 + \underset{(Excess)}{2HF} \longrightarrow H_2SiF_6$$

- SiO_2 melts in oxyhydrogen flame above 1875 K to colourless glass, called **quartz glass**. It has remarkably low coefficient of expansion. Red hot quartz when plunged into water does not shatter to pieces.
- SiO_2 is acidic and dissolves in hot conc. alkalies to form sodium silicate as,

$$SiO_2 + \underset{(Hot\ conc.)}{2NaOH} \longrightarrow Na_2SiO_3 + H_2O$$

- It acts as a powerful acid anhydride and combines with bases and many metallic oxides to form silicates.

e.g. $$SiO_2 + Na_2O \longrightarrow Na_2SiO_3 \uparrow$$
$$SiO_2 + CaO \longrightarrow CaSiO_3 \uparrow$$

- It also reacts with carbonates of many metals at high temperatures forming silicates with liberation of CO_2.

e.g. $$SiO_2 + Na_2CO_3 \xrightarrow{High\ temp.} Na_2SiO_3 + CO_2 \uparrow$$
$$SiO_2 + CaCO_3 \xrightarrow{High\ temp.} CaSiO_3 + CO_2 \uparrow$$

- When heated with carbon in an electric furnace, it is reduced to **carborundum or silicon carbide** as,

$$SiO_2 + 3C \xrightarrow[Electric\ fumare]{\Delta} SiC + 2CO$$

Uses

Silica is used

(i) as an adsorbent in column chromatography.

(ii) as a catalyst in petroleum industry.

(iii) as a humidity detector.

(iv) as Kieselguhr, in filtration plants and as an inert support or filler.

3. Silicates

Silicon, mica, asbestos, cement, bricks, tiles, porcelains, glass, pottery, etc., are made from silicates. The basic building unit of all silicates is the tetrahedral SiO_4^{4-} ion.

The three dimensional tetrahedral structure i.e. (a) is represented by a planar structure i.e. (b) for convenience

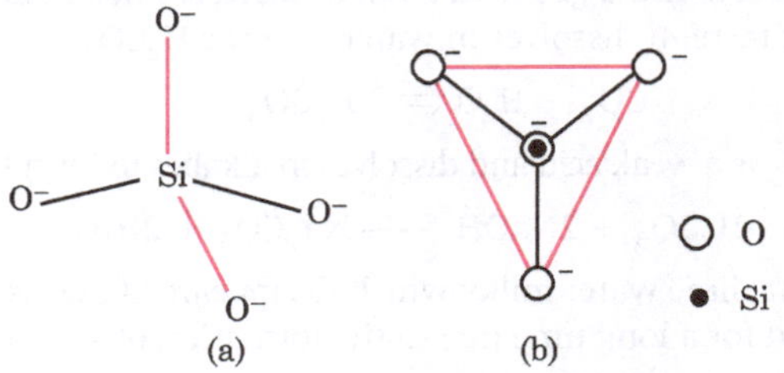

Structure of SiO_4^{4-} ion

All silicates involve Si—O bonds of following two types

- Terminal Si—O bonds in which oxygen is bonded to a silicon and not other atom.
- Bridging Si— O—Si bonds in which oxygen is bonded to two silicon atoms.

On the basis of the way, the SiO_4^{4-} tetrahedral units are linked together, the silicates minerals are classified into following types

(i) **Orthosilicates** These contains discrete SiO_4^{4-} units in which oxygen atoms are found to associate only with metal ions and are not associated with one another e.g. **zircon** ($ZrSiO_4$), **willemite** (Zn_2SiO_4) and **phenakite** (Be_2SiO_4) etc.

(ii) **Pyrosilicates or Islands** Two SiO_4^{4-} tetrahedrons share a corner oxygen atom. They contain $[Si_2O_7]^{6-}$ ions as discrete units. This ion is formed when two SiO_4^{4-} tetrahedrons share one O-atom (bridging O-atom). These silicates are not very common. e.g. **thortveitite** ($Sc_2Si_2O_7$) and **hemimorphite** $[Zn_4(OH)_2Si_2O_7 \cdot H_2O]$.

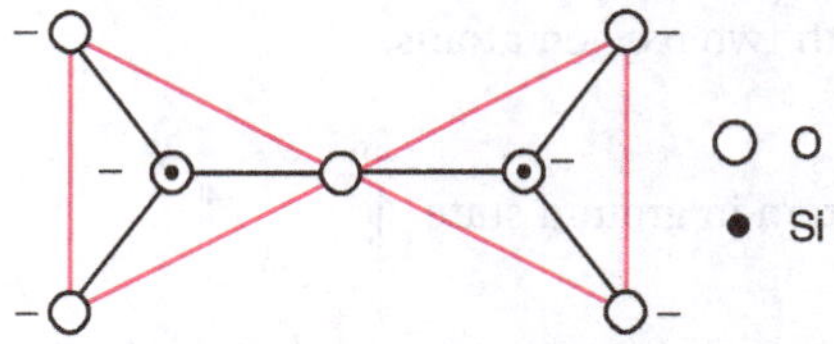

$Si_2O_7^{6-}$ (Anion of pyrosilicate)

(iii) **Cyclic Silicates** Two oxygen atoms of each tetrahedron are shared to form a ring with general formula $[SiO_3]_n^{2n-}$. The ring may be of three membered ring in which discrete units are $[Si_3O_9]^{6-}$, e.g. **wollastonite** ($Ca_3Si_3O_9$), **benitoite** ($BaTi[Si_3O_9]$) etc.

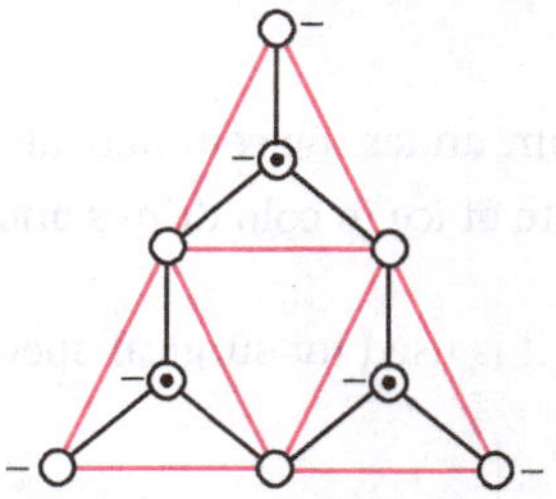

$Si_3O_9^{6-}$ ion (Anion of three membered cyclic silicate)

If the ring is six membered ring then discrete units are $[Si_6O_{18}]^{12-}$, e.g. **beryl** $(Be_3Al_2Si_6O_{18})$

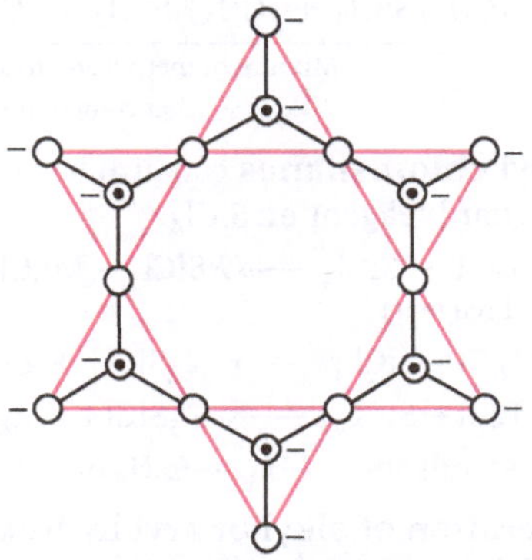

$Si_6O_{18}^{12-}$ ion (Anion of six membered cyclic silicates)

(iv) **Chain Silicates** Two oxygen atoms per tetrahedron are shared to form an extensively long chain. The primary units is $[SiO_3]^{2-}$ and the general formula is $[SiO_3]_n^{2n-}$. There are two following type of chain silicates.

- **Single Chain Silicates,** in which $[SiO_3]_2^{4-}$ combines to form a chain like polymer, these are also called pyroxenes, e.g. **diopside** $[CaMg(SiO_3)_2]$.

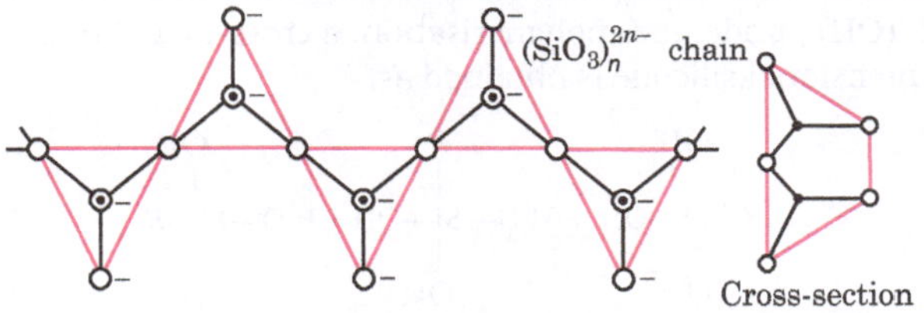

Single chain silicates

- **Double Chain Silicates,** in which $[Si_4O_{11}]^{6-}$ are primary units. Two simple chains are joined together through one of the four oxygen atoms of SiO_4^{4-} tetrahedra. These structures are known as **amphiboles.**
  Some tetrahedra share three oxygen. e.g. **termolite** $Ca_2Mg_5(Si_4O_{11})_2(OH)_2$, **asbestos** $CaMg_3O(Si_4O_{11})$.

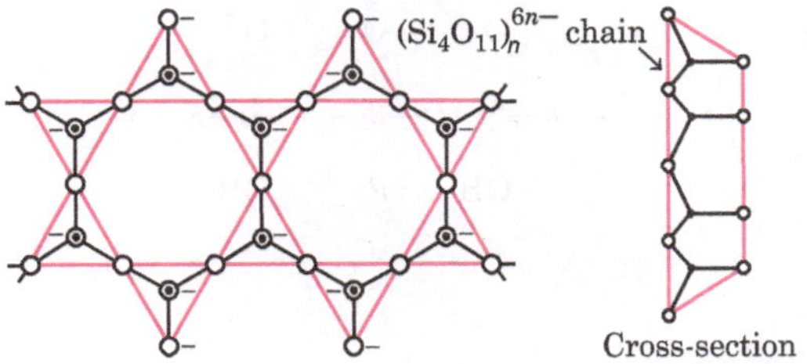

Double chain silicates

(v) **Sheet Silicates** Three oxygen atoms per tetrahedron are shared to form an infinite plane sheet, containing $[Si_2O_5]_n^{2n-}$. e.g. **kaolinite** $[Al_2(OH)_4Si_2O_5]$, talc $[Mg_3(OH)_2(Si_2O_5)_2]$, mica minerals, etc.

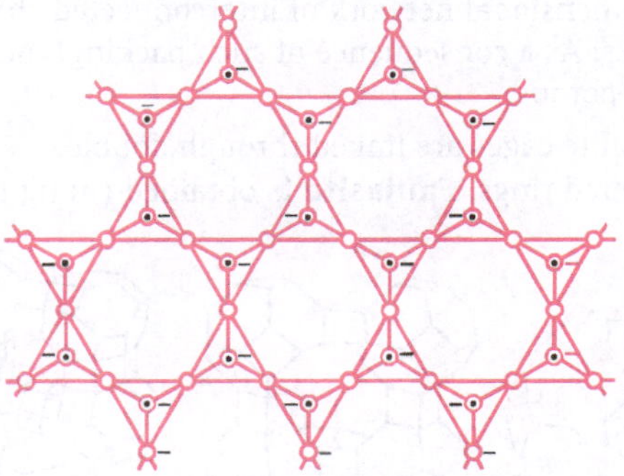

$(Si_2O_5)_n^{2n-}$ sheet silicates

(vi) **Three Dimensional Silicates** All the four oxygen atoms are shared in each tetrahedron to form an infinite three dimensional structure. Each silicon atom (sp^3-hybridised) is surrounded tetrahedrally by four oxygen atoms and each oxygen atom is linked covalently to two silicon atoms. These silicates are neutral.

Various forms of silica occur in three dimensional silicate structure, have general formula $(SiO_3)_n^{2n-}$.

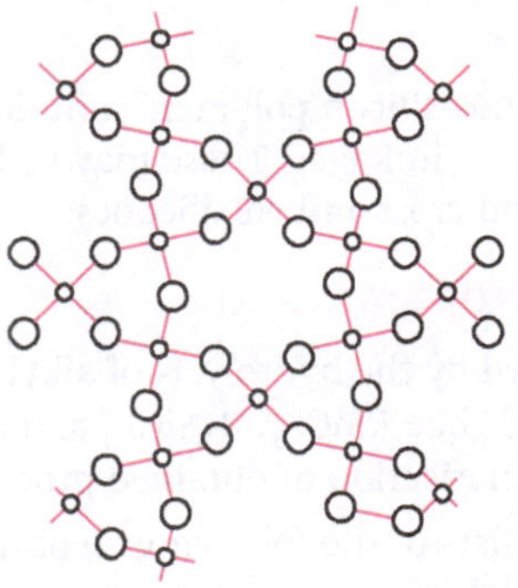

Three dimensional structure of silica

4. Zeolites

These are microporous aluminosilicate having general formula $M_{x/n}[AlO_2]_x[SiO_2]_y \cdot mH_2O$.

Preparation

Aluminosilicates are obtained by substituting some of the silicon atoms in a three dimensional network silicate by Al^{3+} ions. The negative charge carried by aluminosilicate framework is neutralised by exchangeable cations of valence *n*, while *m* water molecules fill the voids.

Structure

The **cubo** octahedron shown in figure (a) is the building block of zeolites. The **sodalite cages** in figure (b) are linked to each other through four membered rings to produce two or three dimensional network of interconnected channels and cavities. As a consequence of such packing, the zeolites are highly porous.

When sodalite cages are linked through double six-membered rings, **Faujasite is** obtained (in figure (c).

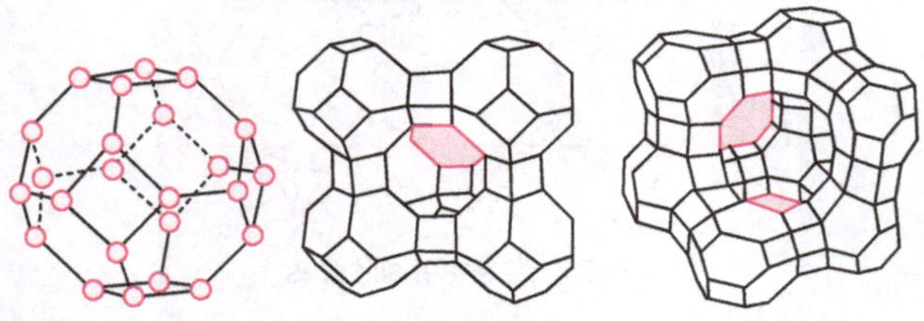

(a) Cubo octahedron (b) Sodalite cages (c) Faujasite

The three dimensional structure of zeolites

Uses

Zeolites are used as

(i) molecular sieves and can separate molecules of different sizes.

(ii) as catalyst due to their porous structure.

5. Silicones

Silicones are organo-silicon polymers containing ...... O—Si—O ...... linkages. These may be linear silicones, cyclic silicones and cross-linked silicones.

Methods of Preparation

These are prepared by the hydrolysis of alkyl or aryl derivatives of $SiCl_4$ like $RSiCl_3$, R_2SiCl_2 and R_3SiCl followed by polymerisation of obtained product.

This method consists of the following steps as,

Step I Preparation of alkyl or aryl derivatives of silicon tetrachloride. Examples of such derivatives are $RSiCl_3$, R_2SiCl_2 and R_3SiCl where R is an alkyl (e.g. CH_3, C_2H_5 etc.,) or aryl (e.g. C_6H_5) group.

Preparation of some of the above derivatives are as follows

- **Methyl chlorosilanes** [like $(CH_3)SiCl_3$, $(CH_3)_2SiCl_2$ and $(CH_3)_3SiCl$] are prepared by heating methyl chloride, CH_3Cl with Si, catalysed by Cu, at 300°C. This reaction gives a mixture of methyl chlorosilanes.

$$2CH_3Cl + Si \xrightarrow[300°C]{Cu} \underbrace{(CH_3)SiCl_3 + (CH_3)_2SiCl_2 + (CH_3)_3SiCl}_{\substack{\text{Mixture of methyl chlorosilanes}\\ \text{+ other compounds}}}$$

- **Alkyl or aryl chlorosilanes** can also be obtained by the action of Grignard reagent on $SiCl_4$.

$$\underset{\text{(Grignard reagent)}}{RMgCl} + SiCl_4 \longrightarrow RSiCl_3 + MgCl_2$$

$$2RMgCl + SiCl_4 \longrightarrow R_2SiCl_2 + 2MgCl_2$$

$$3RMgCl + SiCl_4 \longrightarrow R_3SiCl + 3MgCl_2$$

['R' stands for —CH_3, —C_2H_5 or —C_6H_5 groups].

Step II Preparation of alkyl or aryl hydroxy derivatives of silicone tetrachloride (called silanols or silandiols) These silanols are obtained by the hydrolysis of $RSiCl_3$, R_2SiCl_2 and R_3SiCl e.g.

$$R_2SiCl_2 + 2H\cdot OH \xrightarrow{\text{Hydrolysis}} R_2Si(OH)_2 + 2HCl$$

Step III Polymerisation of alkyl or aryl hydroxy derivatives. The type of silicon obtained depends on the nature of alkyl or aryl hydroxy derivative and the way in which the hydroxy derivative undergoes polymerisation. e.g.

Case I When many molecules of alkyl trihydroxy silane, $RSi(OH)_3$ undergoes polymerisation, a cross-linked two dimensional silicone is obtained as,

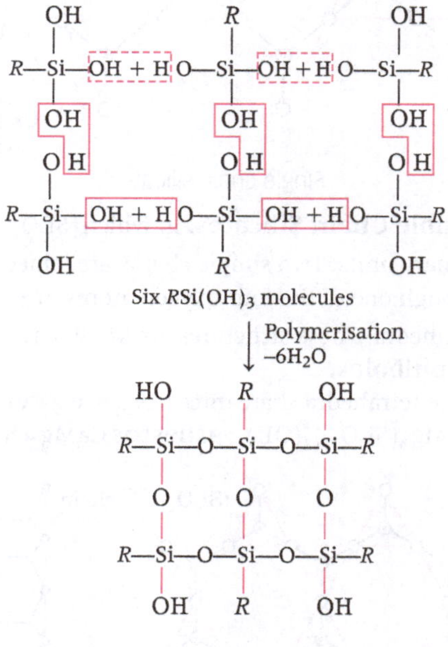

Since, an active OH group is present at each end of the chain, polymerisation continues on both the ends and hence, the length of the chain increases. The increase in the length of the chain produces cross-linked silicone as shown below

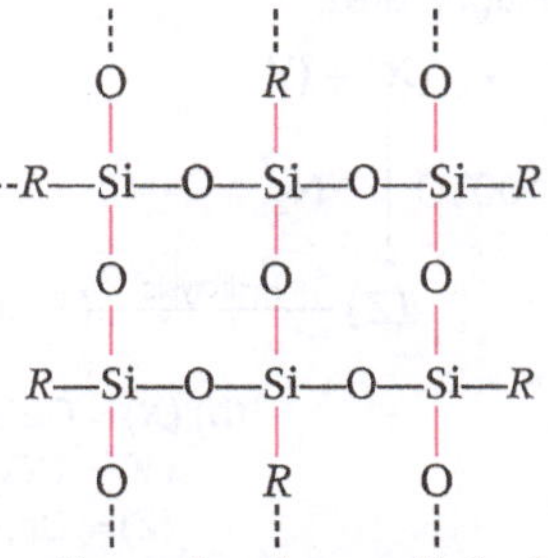

Two dimensional cross-linked silicon

Case II When many molecules of dialkyl dihydroxysilane, $R_2Si(OH)_2$ undergo polymerisation, a straight chain (linear) or cyclic (ring) silicone is obtained as,

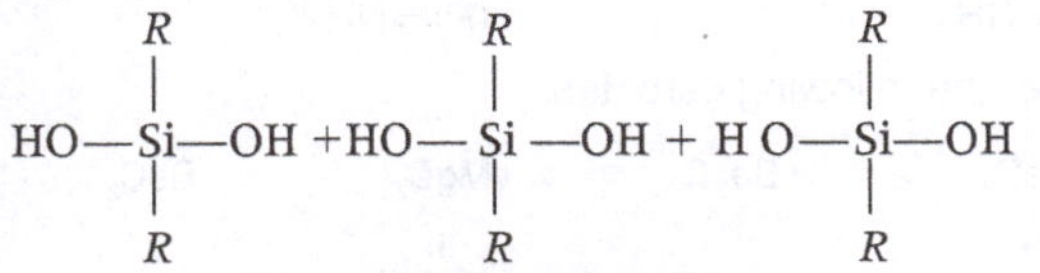

Three molecules of $R_2Si(OH)_2$

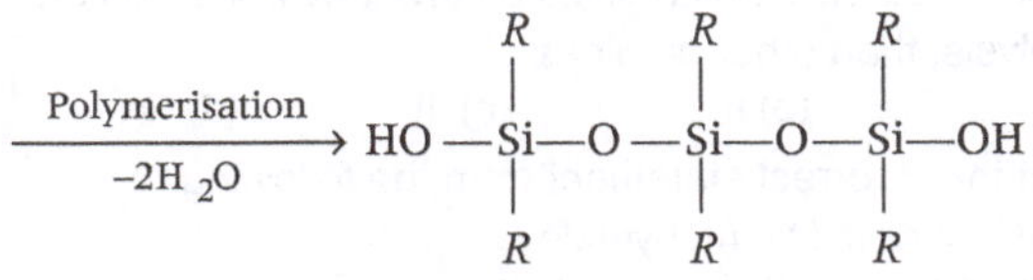

(Straight chain)

Since, an active OH group is present at each end of the chain, polymerisation continues and hence, the length of the chain increases and gives rise to the formation of long chain silicon, as shown below

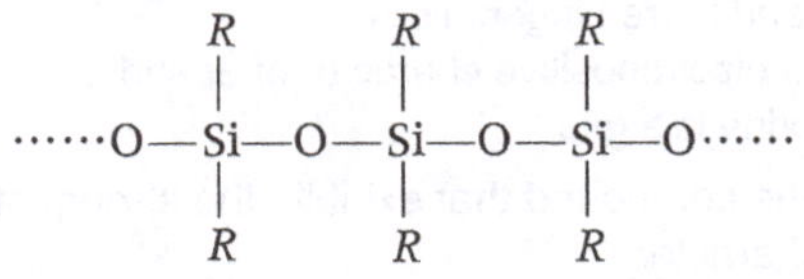

Cyclic trimer silicon (thermoplastic polymer)

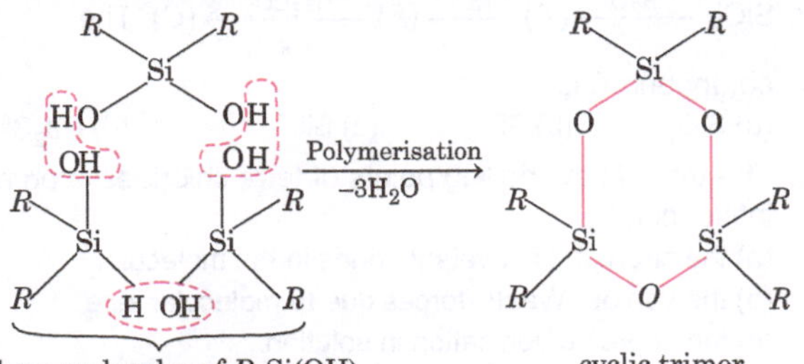

Three molecules of $R_2Si(OH)_2$ cyclic trimer

Case III When two molecules of trialkyl monohydroxysilane, $R_3Si(OH)$ undergo polymerisation, a straight chain silicone (dimer) is obtained as,

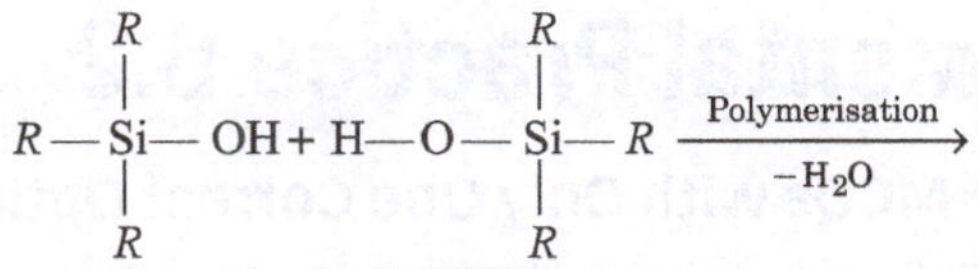

Two molecule of $R_3Si(OH)$

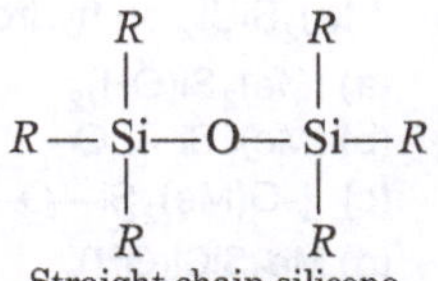

Straight chain silicone, $R_3Si—O—SiR_3$ (dimer) (It is a siloxane)

This chain length of the polymer can be controlled by R_3SiCl. Which block the further polymerisation

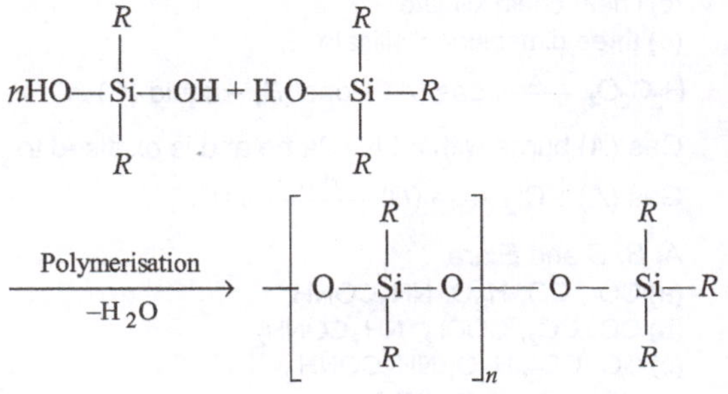

Straight chain

Properties and Uses

Important properties and uses of silicones are as follows

- They have high **thermal stability** in the absence of air and withstand temperature up to 250-300°C.
- They remain unaffected by most of the chemical reagents, such as weak acids, alkalies and salt solution. Thus, **silicones are chemically inert.**
- Many of low molecular weight silicones dissolve in solvents like C_6H_6, ether and CCl_4.
- They become less viscous on cooling and are, therefore, used for low temperature lubrication.

Solved Booster 2.2

The basic structural unit of feldspar, zeolites, mica and asbestos is

(a) $(SiO_3)^{2-}$ (b) SiO_2

(c) $(SiO_4)^{4-}$ (d) $-(Si(R)_2—O)_n-$ (R = Me)

Solution. *(c)*

The basic structural unit of feldspar, zeolites, mica and asbestos is $(SiO_4)^{4-}$. These all are silicates.

Elemental Practice 5.2

Type I MCQs with Only One Correct Option

1. $(Me)_2SiCl_2$ on hydrolysis will produce
   (a) $(Me)_2Si(OH)_2$
   (b) $(Me)_2Si{=}O$
   (c) $\left[O(Me)_2Si{-}O{-}Si(Me)_2O\right]_n$
   (d) $Me_2SiCl(OH)$

2. The silicates in which three oxygen atoms of $[SiO_4]^{4-}$ are shared is called
   (a) pyrosilicate
   (b) sheet silicate
   (c) linear chain silicate
   (d) three dimensional silicate

3. $H_2C_2O_4 \xrightarrow{\Delta}$ gas (*A*) + gas (*B*) + liquid (*C*)

   Gas (*A*) burns with a blue flame and is oxidised to gas (*B*)

   Gas $(A) + Cl_2 \longrightarrow (D) \xrightarrow{NH_3, \Delta} (E)$

   A, *B*, *C* and *E* are
   (a) CO_2, CO, H_2O, NH_2CONH_2
   (b) CO, CO_2, $COCl_2$, NH_2CONH_2
   (c) CO, CO_2, H_2O, NH_2CONH_2
   (d) CO, CO_2, H_2O, $COCl_2$

4. The melting point of AlF_3 is 104°C and that of SiF_4 is −77°C (it sublimes) because
   (a) there is a very large difference in the ionic character of the Al—F and Si—F bonds.
   (b) in AlF_3, Al^{3+} interacts very strongly with the neighbouring F^- ions to give three dimensional structure but in SiF_4 no such interaction is possible.
   (c) the silicon ion in tetrahedral SiF_4 molecule is not shielded effectively from the fluoride ions whereas in AlF_3, Al^{3+} ion is shielded on all sides.
   (d) the attractive forces between the SiF_4 molecules are strong whereas those between the AlF_3 molecules are weak.

5. A scarlet red compound (*X*) on treatment with conc. HNO_3 give compounds (*Y*) and (*Z*). (*Z*) with HCl produces a chloride compound (*A*) which can also be produced by treating (*X*) with conc. HCl. Compounds (*X*), (*Z*) and (*A*) will be
   (a) Mn_3O_4, MnO_2, $MnCl_2$
   (b) Pb_3O_4, $Pb(NO_3)_2$, $PbCl_2$
   (c) Fe_3O_4, Fe_2O_3, $FeCl_2$
   (d) Fe_3O_4, Fe_2O_3, $FeCl_3$

6. Identify (*X*), (*Y*) and (*Z*) in the following sequence of reactions

   $BeO + C \xrightarrow{2000°C} (X) \xrightarrow{\text{dil. acid}} (Y) + (Z)$

   (a) $(X) = Be_2C$, $(Y) = Be(OH)_2$, $(Z) = C_2H_4$
   (b) $(X) = BeC_2$, $(Y) = Be(OH)_2$, $(Z) = CH_4$
   (c) $(X) = Be_2C$, $(Y) = Be(OH)_2$, $(Z) = CH_4$
   (d) $(X) = BeC_2$, $(Y) = Be(OH)_2$, $(Z) = C_2H_4$

7. The compounds (*X*), (*Y*), (*Z*) and (*P*) in the following sequence of reactions are

   $CaO + C \xrightarrow{2000°C} (X) + (Y)$

   $(X) \xrightarrow[1100°C]{+N_2} (Z) \xrightarrow{\text{Hydrolysis}} (P)$ gas

   (a) $(X) = CaCO_3$, $(Y) = CO$, $(Z) = Ca_3N_2$, $(P) = NH_3$
   (b) $(X) = CaCO_3$, $(Y) = CO_2$, $(Z) = Ca(NH_3)_2$, $(P) = NH_3$
   (c) $(X) = CaC_2$, $(Y) = CO_2$, $(Z) = Ca(NH_3)_2$, $(P) = NH_3$
   (d) $(X) = CaC_2$, $(Y) = CO$, $(Z) = CaCN_2$, $(P) = NH_3$

8. Consider the following carbides.

CaC_2	Be_2C	MgC_2	BeC_2
I	II	III	IV

   Select the carbide which gives different hydrocarbon on hydrolysis, than other carbides
   (a) I (b) II (c) III (d) IV

9. Select the incorrect statement from the following.
   (a) SnH_4 is called tin (II) hydride.
   (b) CH_4, CS_2 and CI_4 are covalent compounds.
   (c) Mg_2C_3 on hydrolysis gives allylene.
   (d) SiC is thermally stable, hard and chemically inert.

10. $PbCl_4$ exists but $PbBr_4$ and PbI_4 do not because of
    (a) Inability of bromine and iodine to oxidise Pb^{2+} to Pb^{4+}
    (b) Br^- and I^- are bigger in size
    (c) More electropositive character of Br and I.
    (d) Chlorine is a gas

11. Select the compound that exhibits the strongest Lewis acidic character.
    (a) $SnCl_4$ (b) $GeCl_4$ (c) $SiCl_4$ (d) $PbCl_4$

12. $SiCl_4 \xrightarrow{H_2O} (A) \xrightarrow{\Delta} (B) \xrightarrow[\text{heat}]{Na_2CO_3} (C)$. The compound *C* is
    (a) SiO_2 (b) Si (c) SiC (d) Na_2SiO_3

13. The trend in the boiling points of tetra chlorides is primarily influenced by
    (a) the strength of covalent bonds in the molecule.
    (b) the van der Waals' forces due to molecular size.
    (c) the degree of ionisation in solution.
    (d) the dipole moment of the molecule.

14. $[SiO_4]^{4-}$ units of silicates
    (a) each silicon atom is surrounded by four oxygen atoms and each oxygen atom is bonded to two silicon atoms
    (b) each silicon atoms in a crystal lattice are bonded by metallic bonds

(c) silicon atom is bonded to two oxygen atoms
(d) there are double bonds between silicon and oxygen atoms

15. Among the following substituted silanes the one which will give rise to cross linked silicons polymer on hydrolysis is
(a) R_4Si (b) $RSiCl_3$ (c) R_2SiCl_2 (d) R_3SiCl

16. Butter of tin is
(a) $SnCl_2 \cdot 5H_2O$ (b) $SnCl_4 \cdot 5H_2O$
(c) $SnBr_2 \cdot 2H_2O$ (d) $SnBr_4 \cdot 5H_2O$

17. The product formed when steam is passed over red hot carbon
(a) $CO_2 + 2H_2$ (b) $CO + H_2$
(c) Water vapour dissociates into H_2 and O_2
(d) $CO + H_2O$

18. Ge(II) compounds are powerful reducing agents, whereas Pb(IV) compounds are strong oxidants. It can be due to
(a) lead is more electropositive than germanium
(b) the ionisation potential of lead is less than that of germanium
(c) the ionic radii of Pb^{2+} and Pb^{4+} are larger than those of Ge^{2+} and Ge^{4+}
(d) more pronounced inert pair effect in lead than in germanium

19. The correct order of stability of hydrides of carbon family is
(a) $CH_4 > SiH_4 > GeH_4 > SnH_4 > PbH_4$
(b) $CH_4 < SiH_4 < GeH_4 < SnH_4 < PbH_4$
(c) $CH_4 > SiH_4 > GeH_4 > SnH_4 < PbH_4$
(d) $CH_4 < SiH_4 < GeH_4 > SnH_4 < PbH_4$

20. The tendency for ionic compound formation
(a) decreases from carbon to lead
(b) increases from carbon to lead
(c) remains unchanged
(d) is highest in germanium

Type II 》MCQs with One or More than One Correct Option

21. Select the incorrect statements from the following.
(a) $SnCl_4$ is ionic and is strong reducing agent.
(b) $SnCl_4$ is covalent.
(c) $PbCl_4$ is reducing agent .
(d) Lower valencies are more ionic because of the greater radius of M^{2+} than of M^{4+}.

22. $SnCl_2$ was dissolved in sodium hydroxide to give a compound (*P*) which dissolves in excess NaOH to give (*Q*). (*Q*) then reacts with $Bi(OH)_3$ to form black substance (*R*). Then,
(a) Compound $P = Sn(OH)_2$ (b) Compound $Q = Na_2SnO_2$
(c) Substance $R = Na_2SnO_3$ (d) Substance $(R) = Bi$

23. Select the correct statement regarding fullerene (C_{60}).
(a) All carbon atoms are sp^2 hybridised.
(b) In fullerence the five membered and six membered rings are in the ratio 1 : 2.
(c) A six membered ring may be fused with another five membered ring or with a six membered ring.
(d) It is aromatic.

24. Choose the correct statements about silicones.
(a) They are formed by the hydrolysis of R_2SiCl_2.
(b) They are polymer made by R_2SiO_2 units.
(c) They are toxic.
(d) The are macromolecules.

25. The non-existence of PbI_4 is due to
(a) highly oxidising nature of Pb^{4+}
(b) low charge density of Pb^{4+}
(c) sufficiently large covalent character
(d) highly reducing power of I^-

Type III 》Numerical/Integer Answer Type Questions

26. The number of correct statements from the following are:
(i) garnets is the ortho silicate with formula $[M_3^{II} M_2^{III}(SiO_4)_3]$
(ii) in pyrosilicates $(Si_2O_7)^{6-}$ units are formed by joining 1 tetrahedral (SiO_4^{4-}) unit.
(iii) cyclic silicates are formed by sharing of 2 oxygen atoms per Si atom.
(iv) sheet silicates are formed by sharing 3 bridging oxygens per Si atom.
(v) biotite is a type of sheet silicates

27. The coordination number of Sn in crystalline structure of solid SnF_4 is ....

28. The number of oxygen atoms shared in cyclic silicate ion $Si_6O_{18}^{12-}$ is ....

29. The total number of correct statements among the following is
(a) In conc.HCl, $PbCl_2$ exists as chloroplumbous acid.
(b) $SnCl_2 \cdot 2H_2O$ is a reducing agent.
(c) SnO_2 reacts with KOH to form $K_2[Sn(OH)_6]$.
(d) In graphite, only three valence electrons are involved in bonding.
(e) The reaction of Pb_3O_4 with hot dilute nitric acid to give PbO_2 is a redox reaction.

30. The number of elements that shows greater ability to form $p\pi - p\pi$ multiple bonds is are
Ge, Si, Sn, C, Pb

Elemental Practice 5.2 | Chapter 05

Connect with **Answers**

1. (c)	**2.** (b)	**3.** (c)	**4.** (b)	**5.** (b)	**6.** (b)
7. (d)	**8.** (b)	**9.** (a)	**10.** (a)	**11.** (c)	**12.** (d)
13. (b)	**14.** (a)	**15.** (b)	**16.** (b)	**17.** (b)	**18.** (d)
19. (a)	**20.** (b)	**21.** (a,c)	**22.** (a,b,d)	**23.** (a,c,d)	**24.** (a,d)
25. (a,d)	**26.** (4)	**27.** (6)	**28.** (6)	**29.** (4)	**30.** (1)

Advanced Exclusive Different Strokes

Important Points to solve problems related to compounds of lead

- Lead reacts with dil. HCl producing insoluble $PbCl_2$ which protects the metal from further attack. But due to the formation of the soluble complex ion $[PbCl_3]^-$, $PbCl_2$ dissolves in conc. HCl. Thus lead dissolves in conc. HCl.

$$Pb + 3HCl\,(conc.) \longrightarrow [PbCl_3]^- + H^+ + H_2(g)$$

- Pb can also be converted into $PbCl_2$ on reaction with Cl_2:

$$Pb + Cl_2 \longrightarrow PbCl_2$$

- $PbCl_2$ is partially hydrolysed by H_2O:

$$PbCl_2 + H_2O \longrightarrow Pb(OH)Cl + HCl$$

or
$$Pb^{2+} + 2H_2O \longrightarrow [Pb(OH)]^+ + H_3O^+$$

- Aqueous hot solution of $PbCl_2$ gives black ppt of PbS on passing H_2S gas:

$$PbCl_2 + \underset{\text{Gas}}{H_2S} \longrightarrow \underset{\text{black ppt}}{PbS\downarrow} + 2HCl$$

- $PbCl_4$ decomposes very readily into $PbCl_2$ and Cl_2 due to greater stability of Pb^{2+} than Pb^{4+} (inert-pair effect)

$$PbCl_4(s) \longrightarrow PbCl_2(s) + Cl_2(g)$$

$$Pb^{4+} + 2e^- \longrightarrow Pb^{2+}$$

$$2Cl^- \longrightarrow Cl_2 + 2e^-$$

Thus, Pb^{4+} salts are better oxidising agents.

- Lead shows the ability to make a complex with chloride ions. If ice cold conc. HCl is added to lead dioxide [lead (IV) oxide], PbO_2, yellow hexachloroplumbate (IV) ions, $PbCl_6^{2-}$ are formed. While $PbCl_4^{2-}$ are formed from PbO

$$PbO_2(s) + 6Cl^-(aq) + 4H^+(aq) \longrightarrow PbCl_6^{2-}(aq) + 2H_2O(l)$$

$$PbO(s) + 4Cl^-(aq) + 2H^+(aq) \longrightarrow PbCl_4^{2-}(aq) + H_2O(l)$$

- Three oxides of lead are known :

(a) PbO — lead (II) oxide called **litharge** (a yellow- orange solid)

(b) PbO_2 — lead (IV) oxide also called **lead dioxide** (a dark brown solid)

(c) Pb_3O_4 — dilead (II) lead (IV) oxide.

It can be written as $2(2PbO \cdot PbO_2)$.

It is also called **red lead.**

Some properties of these lead oxides are as follows :

(a) PbO is obtained by roasting of PbS (galena):

$$2PbS + 3O_2 \xrightarrow{\Delta} 2PbO + 2SO_2$$

- PbO is reduced to Pb by heating with carbon or by CO :

$$PbO + C \xrightarrow{\Delta} Pb + CO$$

$$PbO + CO \xrightarrow{\Delta} Pb + CO_2$$

- PbO is amphoteric, being soluble both in acid and alkali:

$$PbO + 2H^+ \longrightarrow Pb^{2+} + H_2O$$

$$PbO + 2OH^- + H_2O \longrightarrow [Pb(OH)_4]^{2-}$$

- Crystal structure shows that it has predominantly covalent character.

(b) PbO_2 is an oxidising agent and reduced to PbO since stability of Pb (II) > Pb (IV) based on 'inert pair' effect:

$$Pb^{4+} + 2e^- \longrightarrow Pb^{2+}$$

$$PbO_2 + 4HCl \longrightarrow PbCl_2 + 2H_2O + Cl_2$$

$$PbO_2 + SO_2 \longrightarrow PbSO_4$$

$$PbO_2 + 2H_2SO_4 \longrightarrow 2PbSO_4 + 2H_2O + O_2$$

$$2PbO_2 \xrightarrow{\Delta} 2PbO + O_2$$

It is insoluble in an acid but soluble in concentrated alkali thus indicating its acidic nature:

$$PbO_2 + 2OH^- + 2H_2O \longrightarrow [Pb(OH)_6]^{2-}$$

(c) Pb_3O_4, a double oxide, is obtained by heating lead (II) oxide in air:

$$3PbO + \frac{1}{2}O_2 \xrightarrow{\Delta} Pb_3O_4$$

Its crystal structure shows that it is predominantly covalent and composed of a combination **of two types of lead atom. One type is bonded to six oxygen atoms, the other to three oxygen atoms. But in the reactions, it behaves like a mixture of PbO and PbO_2 :**

$$2Pb_3O_4 \xrightarrow{\Delta} 6PbO + O_2$$

When it reacts with H_2SO_4, $PbSO_4$ is formed along with O_2 only :

$$Pb_3O_4 + 3H_2SO_4 \longrightarrow 3PbSO_4 + 3H_2O + \frac{1}{2}O_2$$

Thus, with the help of above key points, we can approach the problems related to compounds of lead in JEE Advanced Exam.

PRACTICE

ELEMENT 01

Target JEE Main

Objective Type Questions

1. Select the silicate that have only one monovalent corner oxygen atom in each tetrahedron unit.
(a) Cyclic silicate (b) Sheet silicate
(c) Double chain silicate (d) Single chain silicate

2. The incorrect statement regarding silicates is
(a) Feldspar and zeolites are example of silicates.
(b) The basic structural unit of silicates is SiO_4^{4-}.
(c) Silicates can link together to form chain, ring or sheet structures.
(d) Four oxygen atom of $[SiO_4]^{4-}$ are shared in pyrosilicate.

3. Select the correct statement from the following.
(a) Borazine is aromatic and non-polar.
(b) Borazine has sp^3 hybridised boron atoms.
(c) Borazine is more reactive towards addition reactions than benzene.
(d) In B_2H_6 the banana bonds are stronger and shorter than the normal $2c-2e$ B—H bonds.

4. Choose the incorrect statement about boron?
(a) Boron has non-metallic character and its oxide is acidic in nature.
(b) Boron and silicon have nearly equal densities.
(c) Boron forms weak acidic oxy-acid similar to silicon.
(d) Boron forms a tri-basic weak acid on reaction with concentrated HNO_3.

5. Select the incorrect statement about boron trihalides.
(a) All boron trihalides are covalent with low boiling points.
(b) The order of ease of hydrolysis of trihalides of boron is $BF_3 < BCl_3 < BBr_3 < BI_3$ due to strength of $p\pi - p\pi$ bonding.
(c) All boron trihalides can be prepared by the treatment of halogens with a mixture of B_2O_3 and carbon at high temperature.
(d) Boron trifluoride can be obtained by heating CaF_2 with concentrated sulphuric acid and boric anhydride.

6. Consider the following reaction

$$Pb(NO_3)_2 \xrightarrow{673\text{ K}} A + PbO + O_2$$

$$A \xrightarrow{\text{Dimerise}} B$$

Oxidation number of N in product B is
(a) 4 (b) 0 (c) 2 (d) 3

7. Anhydrous $AlCl_3$ can be obtained from Al_2O_3 by heating
(a) Al_2O_3 with Cl_2 gas
(b) Al_2O_3 with HCl gas
(c) Al_2O_3 with NaCl in solid state
(d) A mixture of Al_2O_3 and carbon in dry Cl_2 gas

8. Choose the incorrect match from the following
(a) $Ga^+ < In^+ < Tl^+ \longrightarrow$ stability
(b) B < Al < Ga $\longrightarrow$ second ionisation enthalpy
(c) Ga < In < Tl $\longrightarrow$ Density
(d) In < Al < B $\longrightarrow$ melting point

9. A compound of boron X reacts with NH_3 at 200°C to form an aromatic compound Y. Y is colourless and highly light sensitive. Also compound X reacts with excess of NH_3 at high temperature to form a compound Z having graphite like crystalline structure, then
(a) $X = B_2H_6, Y = (BN)_x$ and $Z = B_3N_3H_6$
(b) $X = B_2H_6, Y = B_3N_3H_6$ and $Z = (BN)_x$
(c) $X = B_2O_3, Y = B_3N_3H_6$ and $Z = (BN)_x$
(d) $X = H_3BO_3, Y = B_3N_3H_6$ and $Z = (BN)_x$

10. Select the pair of oxide that is amphoteric in nature?
(a) SiO_2, GeO_2
(b) SnO_2, PbO_2
(c) CO, GeO
(d) SnO_2, GeO_2

11. Choose the statement that is not a use of SiO_2.
(a) Acidic flux in metallurgy
(b) A drying agent as silica gel.
(c) Removal of sulphur compounds from petroleum.
(d) in the production of porcelain

12. Carbon forms carbide on reaction with
(a) $CaSO_4$ (b) CaO (c) $CaCl_2$ (d) $CaCO_3$

13. Select the reagent that will oxidise carbon?
(a) Hot conc. HCl (b) Hot conc. H_3PO_4
(c) Hot conc. H_2SO_4 (d) Hot conc. CH_3COOH

14. Carbon dioxide gas cannot be prepared by
(a) $ZnCO_3 \xrightarrow{\Delta}$ (b) $Na_2CO_3 \xrightarrow{\Delta}$
(c) $Li_2CO_3 \xrightarrow{\Delta}$ (d) $NaHCO_3 \xrightarrow{\Delta}$

15. $X + Ca(OH)_2 \longrightarrow$ white ppt.
White ppt. + X + $H_2O \longrightarrow$ Soluble compound (Y)
$X + K_2Cr_2O_7 + H^+ \longrightarrow$ No reaction
Then (X) and the soluble compound (Y) are
(a) SO_2 and $Ca(HSO_3)_2$
(b) CO_2 and $Ca(HCO_3)_2$
(c) SO_3 and $Ca(HSO_4)_2$
(d) CO and $Ca(HCO_3)_2$

16. Pyrosilicate ion is
(a) SiO_4^{4-} (b) SiO_3^{2-}
(c) $SiO_{2.5}^{-}$ (d) $SiO_{3.5}^{3-}$

17. The compound $(SiH_3)_3N$ is
(a) pyramidal and more basic than $(CH_3)_3N$
(b) planar and less basic than $(CH_3)_3N$
(c) pyramidal and less basic than $(CH_3)_3N$
(d) planar and more basic than $(CH_3)_3N$

18. A compound (*A*) of boron reacts with NMe_3 to give an adduct (*B*) which on hydrolysis gives a compound (*C*) and hydrogen gas. Compound (*C*) is an acid. The adduct (*B*) is
(a) $B_3N_3H_6$ (b) $2BH_3 \cdot NMe_3$
(c) $BH_3 \cdot 2NMe_3$ (d) $BH_3 \cdot 3NMe_3$

19. The product formed when Sn is heated with alkali solution is
(a) stannous oxide (b) stannic oxide
(c) sodium stannate (d) stannane

20. Identify the compound *Z* in the following reaction sequence.

$$A + 2HCl + 5H_2O \longrightarrow 2NaCl + X$$

$$X \xrightarrow[370\text{ K}]{\Delta} Y \xrightarrow[>370\text{ K}]{\Delta} Z$$

(a) Borax (b) *Ortho*boric acid
(c) *Meta*boric acid (d) Boron trioxide

21. The bond dissociation energy of B—F in BF_3 is 646 kJ mol^{-1} whereas that of C—F in CF_4 is 515 kJ mol^{-1}. The correct reason for higher B—F bond dissociation energy as compared to that of C—F is
(a) smaller size of B-atom as compared to that of C-atom
(b) stronger σ-bond between B and F in BF_3 as compared to that between C and F in CF_4
(c) significant $p\pi$ - $p\pi$ interaction between B and F in BF_3 whereas there is no possibility of such interaction between C and F in CF_4
(d) lower degree of $p\pi$ - $p\pi$ interaction between B and F in BF_3 than that between C and F in CF_4

22. When aqueous solution of borax is acidified with hydrochloric acid, a white crystalline solid is formed which is soapy to touch. The nature of the solid is
(a) acidic
(b) basic
(c) neutral
(d) depends upon the nature of solvent

23. When BCl_3 is treated with water, it hydrolysis and forms $[B(OH)_4]^-$ only whereas $AlCl_3$ in acidified aqueous solution forms $[Al(H_2O)_6]^{3+}$ ion. The hybridisation of boron and aluminium in these species is respectively.
(a) sp^3, sp^3d (b) sp^3, sp^3d^2
(c) sp^3d, sp^3d^2 (d) sp^2, sp^3d^2

Numerical Type Questions

24. The value obtained when we add the oxidation number of boron and number of H_2O molecule present in the compound $Na_2[B_4O_5(OH)_4 \cdot xH_2O]$ is ....

25. In B_2H_6, the sum of total number of 2-centre 2-electron and 3-centre-2-electron bonds is ....

26. C_{60}, an allotrope of carbon contains *x* hexagonal and *y* pentagons rings of carbon atoms. The product of *x* and *y* will be ....

27. The number of B—O—B bonds present in structure of borax is/are ....

28. A certain salt (*X*) gives the following tests:
(i) Its aqueous solution is alkaline to litmus.
(ii) On strong heating, it swells to give a glassy bead.
(iii) When conc. H_2SO_4 is added to a hot conc. solution of (*X*), white crystal of (*Z*) separate out. (*Z*) is a boron containing compound and contain *x* number of *B* atoms in its formula unit.
The value of *x* will be ....

29. A compound *X* of boron reacts with NH_3 on heating to give another compound *Y*, which is called inorganic benzene. The compound *X* can be prepared by treating BF_3 with lithium hydride. The sum of the number of B atoms present in the molecular formulae of compounds *X* and *Y* are ....

30. Consider the following information regarding compounds *X* and *Y*
(i) Compound (*X*) on reduction with $LiAlH_4$ gives a hydride (*Y*) along with other products.
(ii) The compound (*Y*) reacts with air explosively resulting in boron trioxide.
The mass percentage of hydrogen present in compound *X* is ...... (nearest integer).

31. The sum of covalency and oxidation state of B in $[BF_4]^-$ is

32. The total number of ions from the following that are expected to behave as reducing agent is
Ge^{4+}, Tl^+, Pb^{4+}, Tl^{3+}, Pb^{2+}, Sn^{2+}, Sn^{4+}, Si^{2+}

33. The number of skeletal electrons present in B_4H_{10} are

Check Through PYQs

Element 1 Group 13 Elements and Their Compounds

1. Match List-I with List-II. *2024, 9 April Shift-II*

	List-I		List-II
A.	Melting point [K]	I.	Tl > In > Ga > Al > B
B.	Ionic radius [M^{3+}/pm]	II.	B > Tl > Al ≈ Ga > In
C.	$\Delta_{IE}H_1$ [kJ mol^{-1}]	III.	Tl > In > Al > Ga > B
D.	Atomic radius [pm]	IV.	B > Al > Tl > In > Ga

Choose the correct answer from the options given below.
(a) A-II, B-III, C-IV, D-I
(b) A-III, B-IV, C-I, D-II
(c) A-I, B-II, C-III, D-IV
(d) A-IV, B-I, C-II, D-III

2. Given below are two statements : One is labelled as **Assertion (A)** and other is labelled as **Reason (R)**.
Assertion (A) The stability order of +1 oxidation state of Ga, In and Tl is Ga < In < Tl.
Reason (R) The inert pair effect stabilises the lower oxidation state down the group. *2024, 8 April Shift-I*
In the light of the above statements, choose the correct answer from the options given below.
(a) A is false, but R is true.
(b) Both A and R are true but R is not the correct explanation of A.
(c) Both A and R are true and R is the correct explanation of A.
(d) A is true, but R is false.

3. Given below are two statements : *2024, 6 April Shift-I*
Statement I Gallium is used in the manufacturing of thermometers.
Statement II A thermometer containing gallium is useful for measuring the freezing point (256 K) of brine solution.
In the light of the above statements. choose the correct answer from the options given below
(a) Statement I is true but Statement II is false
(b) Statement I is false but Statement II is true
(c) Both Statement I and Statement II are true
(d) Both Statement I and Statement II are false

4. The correct order of the first ionisation enthalpy is *2024, 4 April Shift-II*
(a) B > Al > Ga
(b) Ga > Al > B
(c) Al > Ga > Tl
(d) Tl > Ga > Al

5. Given below are two statements : one is labelled as **Assertion (A)** and the other is labelled as **Reason (R)**. *2024, 1 Feb Shift-I*
Assertion (A) Melting point of boron (2453 K) is unusually high in group 13 elements.
Reason (R) Solid boron has very strong crystalline lattice.
In the light of the above statements, choose the **most appropriate** answer from the options given below
(a) Both (A) and (R) are correct and (R) is the correct explanation of (A).
(b) (A) is true but (R) is false.
(c) Both (A) and (R) are correct and (R) is not the correct explanation of (A).
(d) (A) is false but (R) is true.

6. The incorrect statement from the following for borazine is *2023, 13 April Shift-I*
(a) it is a cyclic compound.
(b) it contains banana bonds.
(c) it has electronic delocalisation.
(d) it can react with water.

7. Given below are two statements.
Statement I Boron is extremely hard indicating its high lattice energy.
Statement II Boron has highest melting and boiling point compared to its other group members.
In the light of the above statements, choose the most appropriate answer from the options given below. *2023, 12 April Shift-I*
(a) Both Statement I and Statement II are correct.
(b) Statement I is incorrect but Statement II is correct.
(c) Statement I is correct but Statement II is incorrect.
(d) Both Statement I and Statement II are incorrect.

8. For compound having the formula $GaAlCl_4$, the correct option from the following is *2023, 11 April Shift-I*
(a) Ga is more electronegative than Al and is present as a cationic part of the salt $GaAlCl_4$.
(b) Ga is coordinated with Cl in $GaAlCl_4$.
(c) Cl forms bond with both Al and Ga in $GaAlCl_4$.
(d) Oxidation state of Ga in the salt $GaAlCl_4$ is + 3.

9. Which one of the following elements will remain as liquid inside pure boiling water? *2023, 6 April Shift-I*
(a) Ga (b) Li
(c) Cs (d) Br

10. The Lewis acid character of boron trihalides follows the order *2023, 31 Jan Shift-II*
(a) $BBr_3 > BI_3 > BCl_3 > BF_3$
(b) $BF_3 > BCl_3 > BBr_3 > BI_3$
(c) $BI_3 > BBr_3 > BCl_3 > BF_3$
(d) $BCl_3 > BF_3 > BBr_3 > BI_3$

11. Given below are two statements, one is labelled as Assertion A and the other is labelled as Reason R.

Assertion (A) Boron is unable to form BF_6^{3-}.

Reason (R) Size of B is very small.

In the light of the above statements, choose the correct answer from the options given below. *2022, 27 July Shift-II*

(a) Both A and R are true and R is the correct explanation of A.
(b) Both A and R are true but R is not the correct explanation of A.
(c) A is true but R is false.
(d) A is false but R is true.

12. Borazine, also known as inorganic benzene, can be prepared by the reaction of 3-equivalents of "*X*" with 6-equivalents of "*Y*". "*X*" and "*Y*", respectively are *2022, 26 July Shift-I*

(a) $B(OH)_3$ and NH_3 (b) B_2H_6 and NH_3
(c) BH_3 and NH_3 (d) NH_3 and B_2O_3

13. The metal that has very low melting point and its periodic position is closer to a metalloid is *2022, 26 July Shift-II*

(a) Al (b) Ga
(c) Se (d) In

14. The geometry around boron in the product '*B*' formed from the following reaction is *2022, 25 July Shift-I*

$$BF_3 + NaH \xrightarrow{450\text{ K}} A + NaF$$
$$A + NMe_3 \longrightarrow B$$

(a) trigonal planar (b) tetrahedral
(c) pyramidal (d) square planar

15. Choose the correct stability order of group 13 elements in their + 1 oxidation state. *2022, 26 June Shift-I*

(a) Al < Ga < In < Tl (b) Tl < In < Ga < Al
(c) Al < Ga < Tl < In (d) Al < Tl < Ga < In

16. Identify the correct statement for B_2H_6 from those given below :

(A) In B_2H_6, all B — H bonds are equivalent.
(B) In B_2H_6 there are four 3-centre-2-electron bonds.
(C) B_2H_6 is a lewis acid.
(D) B_2H_6 can be synthesised from both BF_3 and $NaBH_4$.
(E) B_2H_6 is a planar molecule.

Choose the most appropriate answer from the options given below : *2022, 24 June Shift-I*

(a) (A) and (E) only
(b) (B), (C) and (E) only
(c) (C) and (D) only
(d) (C) and (E) only

17. In which one of the following molecules strongest back donation of an electron pair from halide to boron is expected? *2021, 27 Aug Shift-I*

(a) BCl_3 (b) BF_3
(c) BBr_3 (d) BI_3

18. Given below are the statements about diborane.

(A) Diborane is prepared by the oxidation of $NaBH_4$ and I_2.
(B) Each boron atom is in sp^2-hybridised state.
(C) Diborane has one bridged 3-centre -2-electron bond.
(D) Diborane is a planar molecule.

The option with correct statement(s) is *2021, 22 July Shift-II*

(a) (C) and (D) only (b) (A) only
(c) (C) only (d) (A) and (B) only

19. Given below are two statements: one is labelled as Assertion (A) and the other is labelled as Reason (R). *2021, 26 Feb Shift-II*

Asertion (A) In TlI_3, isomorphous to CsI_3, the metal is present in +1 oxidation state.

Reason (R) Tl metal has fourteen *f* electrons in its electronic configuration.

In the light of the above statements, choose the most appropriate answer from the options given below:

(a) Both A and R are correct but R is not the correct explanation of A.
(b) Both A and R are correct and R is the correct explanation of A.
(c) A is correct but R is not correct.
(d) A is not correct but R is correct.

20. The reaction of $H_3N_3B_3Cl_3$(*A*) with $LiBH_4$ in tetrahydrofuran gives inorganic benzene (*B*). Further, the reaction of (*A*) with (*C*) leads to $H_3N_3B_3(Me)_3$. Compounds (*B*) and (*C*) respectively, are *2020, 9 Jan Shift-II*

(a) borazine and MeBr
(b) diborane and MeMgBr
(c) boron nitride and MeBr
(d) borazine and MeMgBr

21. The correct statements among I to III regarding group 13 element oxides are : *2019, 9 April Shift-II*

I. Boron trioxide is acidic.
II. Oxides of aluminium and gallium are amphoteric.
III. Oxides of indium and thallium are basic.

(a) I, II and III (b) I and III only
(c) I and II only (d) II and III only

Element 2 Group 14 Elements and Their Compounds

22. Which of the following material is not a semiconductor? *2024, 6 April Shift-I*

(a) Silicon (b) Graphite
(c) Germanium (d) Copper oxide

23. The number of ions from the following that are expected to behave as oxidising agent is

Sn^{4+}, Sn^{2+}, Pb^{2+}, Tl^{3+}, Pb^{4+}, Tl^{+} *2024, 6 April Shift-II*

(a) 1 (b) 3 (c) 4 (d) 2

24. Evaluate the following statements related to group 14 elements for their correctness. *2024, 6 April Shift-II*

A. Covalent radius decreases down the group from C to Pb in a regular manner.
B. Eletronegativity decreases from C to Pb down the group gradually.
C. Maximum covalance of C is 4 whereas other elements can expand their covalence due to presence of *d*-orbitals.
D. Heavier elements do not from $p\pi$-$p\pi$ bonds.
E. Carbon can exhibit negative oxidation states.

Choose the correct answer from the options given below.
(a) C and D only
(b) C, D and E only
(c) A and B only
(d) A, B and C only

25. Given below are two statements. *2024, 1 Feb Shift-II*

Statement I SiO_2 and GeO_2 are acidic while SnO and PbO are amphoteric in nature.

Statement II Allotropic forms of carbon are due to property of catenation and $p\pi$ - $d\pi$ bond formation.

In the light of the above statements, choose the **most appropriate** answer from the options given below
(a) Both Statement I and Statement II are false
(b) Statement I is true but Statement II is false
(c) Statement I is false but Statement II is true
(d) Both Statement I and Statement II are true

26. Consider the oxides of group 14 elements.

SiO_2, GeO_2, SnO_2, PbO_2, CO and GeO. The amphoteric oxides are *2024, 31 Jan Shift-I*
(a) SnO_2, CO (b) SnO_2, PbO_2
(c) SiO_2, GeO_2 (d) GeO, GeO_2

27. Given below are two statements.

Statement I The electronegativity of group 14 elements from Si to Pb, gradually decreases.

Statement II Group 14 contains non-metallic, metallic, as well as metalloid elements. *2024, 29 Jan Shift-I*

In the light of the above statements, choose the **most appropriate** from the options given below.
(a) Statement I is false but Statement II is true.
(b) Both Statement I and Statement II are false.
(c) Statement I is true but Statement II is false.
(d) Both Statement I and Statement II are true.

28. Given below are two statements, one is labelled as Assertion (A) and the other is labelled as Reason (R).

Assertion (A) Carbon forms two important oxides —CO and CO_2, CO is neutral whereas CO_2 is acidic in nature.

Reason (R) CO_2 can combine with water in a limited way to form carbonic acid, while CO is sparingly soluble in water.

In the light of the above statements, choose the most appropriate answer from the options given below. *2023, 25 Jan Shift-II*
(a) Both A and R are correct but R is not the correct explanation of A.
(b) Both A and R are correct and R is the correct explanation of A.
(c) A is correct but R is not correct.
(d) A is not correct but R is correct.

29. Match List-I with List-II.

List-I (Metal)		List-II (Application)	
(A)	Cs	(I)	High temperature thermometer
(B)	Ga	(II)	Water repellent sprays
(C)	B	(III)	Photoelectric cells
(D)	Si	(IV)	Bullet proof vest

Choose the most appropriate answer from the options given below *2022, 29 June Shift-I*
(a) (A)-(III), (B)-(I), (C)-(IV), (D)-(II)
(b) (A)-(IV), (B)-(III), (C)-(II), (D)-(I)
(c) (A)-(II), (B)-(III), (C)-(IV), (D)-(I)
(d) (A)-(I), (B)-(IV), (C)-(II), (D)-(III)

30. Match List-I with List-II. *2022, 27 June Shift-I*

List-I (Si-compounds)		List-II (Si-polymeric/ Other products)	
A.	$(CH_3)_4Si$	I.	Chain silicone
B.	$(CH_3)Si(OH)_3$	II.	Dimeric silicone
C.	$(CH_3)_2Si(OH)_2$	III.	Silane
D.	$(CH_3)_3Si(OH)$	IV.	2D–silicone

Choose the correct answer from the options given below

	A	B	C	D
(a)	III	II	I	IV
(b)	IV	I	II	III
(c)	II	I	IV	III
(d)	III	IV	I	II

PRACTICE ELEMENT 02

Target JEE Advanced

Single Correct Choice MCQs

1. The correct order of reducing character of alkali metals in aqueous solution is:
(a) Li < Na < K < Rb < Cs (b) Na < K < Rb < Cs < Li
(c) Cs < Rb < K < Na < Li (d) Li < Cs < Rb < K < Na

2. $Si_2O_7^{6-}$ anion is obtained when
(a) no oxygen of a SiO_4^{4-} tetrahedron is shared with another SiO_{44}^{4-} tetrahedron
(b) one oxygen of a SiO_4^{4-} tetrahedron is shared with another SiO_4^{4-} tetrahedron
(c) two oxygen of a SiO_4^{4-} tetrahedron are shared with another SiO_4^{4-} tetrahedron
(d) three or all four oxygen of a tetrahedron are shared with other SiO_4^{4-} tetrahedron.

3. The amphoteric nature of Ga_2O_3 is less pronounced than Al_2O_3 due to:
(a) Ga has larger ionic radius and lower charge density.
(b) Ga has fewer electrons in its valence shell.
(c) Ga exhibits a lower ionisation energy than Al
(d) Gallium oxide is more stable and less reactive than aluminium oxide.

4. Select the incorrect statements from the following.
(a) Talc is an example of sheet silicate.
(b) Phenacite is an example of *ortho*silicates
(c) Carbides react with tertiary amines to give dithiocarbamates.
(d) Magnesium carbide on hydrolysis yields allylene.

5. Choose the correct statement about silicones.
(a) They contain alternate Si—C bonds.
(b) They are hydrophilic due to presence of Si—O bonds.
(c) They are thermally stable polymers.
(d) They are linear polymers with only Si—C bonds.

6. Select the correctly matched pair.
(a) BF_3: Catalyst in Friedel Craft reaction.
(b) $PbCl_2$: Oxidising agent in redox reactions.
(c) SiO_2: Basic oxide used in metallurgy
(d) B_2H_6: Does not undergo hydrolysis

7. Select the incorrect statement about group 14 elements.
(a) Graphite is a black substance and possesses metallic luster.
(b) Graphite is used for making crucibles
(c) Diamond can be attacked by dilute acids.
(d) Carbon black is used as black pigment in black ink.

8. Select the correct reaction from the following.
(a) $SiO_2 + C \xrightarrow[\text{Electric furnace}]{2273-2773\text{ K}} SiC + CO$
(b) $Si + C \xrightarrow[\text{Electric furnace}]{2273-2773\text{ K}} SiC$
(c) $Na_2SiO_3 + HCl + H_2O \longrightarrow SiO_2 + NaCl$
(d) $SiC + NaOH + O_2 \longrightarrow Na_2SiO_3 + Na_2CO_3 + H_2O$

One or More than One Correct MCQs

9. Select the correct statement(s)
(a) Graphite is diamagnetic and diamond is paramagnetic in nature.
(b) Graphite acts as a metallic conductor along the layers of carbon atoms.
(c) Graphite is less denser than diamond.
(d) C_{60} is called as Buckminster fullerene.

10. Borax bead test is given by
(a) An aluminium salt
(b) A cobalt salt
(c) A copper (II) salt
(d) A nickel salt

11. Select the species that exists
(a) $[BF_6]^{3-}$ (b) $[AlF_6]^{3-}$
(c) $[GaF_6]^{3-}$ (d) $[InF_6]^{3-}$

12. A complex cross-lined polymer (silicone) not formed by :
(a) Hydrolysis of $(CH_3)_3SiCl$
(b) Hydrolysis of a mixture of $(CH_3)_3SiCl$ and $(CH_3)_2SiCl_2$
(c) Hydrolysis of CH_3SiCl_3
(d) Hydrolysis of $SiCl_4$

13. Which of the following statements is/are correct?
(a) Allotropic forms of carbon are due to property of catenation and $p\pi$ - $d\pi$ bond formation.
(b) Group 14 contains non-metallic, metallic, as well as metalloid elements.
(c) The electronegativity of group 14 elements from Si to Pb gradually decreases.
(d) Stannane is an example of a molecular hydride.

14. Select the incorrect statements from the following.
(a) Stannane is a planar molecule.
(b) Pb^{4+} compounds are stronger oxidising agents than Sn^{2+} compounds.
(c) Between $SiCl_4$ and CCl_4, only $SiCl_4$ reacts with water.
(d) Carbon tetrachloride burns in air when lighted to give phosgene gas.

15. Concentrated H_2SO_4 is used to produce CO in the laboratory on reacting with
(a) $K_4[Fe(CN)_6]$ (b) $CaCO_3$
(c) HCOOH (d) C

16. The melting point of boron is much higher than that of aluminium due to:
(a) boron's larger atomic radius.
(b) the strong covalent network structure in boron.
(c) boron's low electronegativity and low density.
(d) boron's ability to form metallic bonds.

Numerical/Integer Type Questions

17. The difference between total number of lone pairs and total number of σ-bonds in $[B_3O_3(OH)_6]^{3-}$ molecular ion is.

18. Calculate value of $|x + y - z|$ for the following silicate $[Si_xO_{y+z}]^{z-}$ anion.

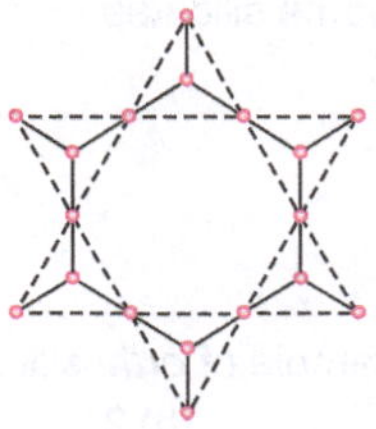

19. The general formula of polythionate ion is $S_{n+2}O_6^{2-}$. If average oxidation state of 'S' atom in any polythionate ion is equal to bond order of 'S—O' bond. Then calculate the value of '*n*' for the corresponding polythionate ion.

20. Consider $Al_2(OH)_6$ compound and calculate the value of $(X+Y) \div Z$
Where X = Total number of $(2c - 2e^-)$ bond.
Y = Total number of $(3c - 2e^-)$ bond.
Z = Total number of $(3c - 4e^-)$ bond.

21. Consider the structure of Al_2Me_6 compound and find the value of $\frac{x-y}{z}$.
Where x = maximum number of atoms that can lie in plane having terminal (Al—Me) bonds.
y = Total number of $3c-2e^-$ bonds.
z = Total number of atoms that are sp^3 hybridised.

22. The value of *x* in the tremolite asbestos is $Ca_2Mg_x(Si_2O_{11})_2(OH)_2$

23. Consider the following silicates
(a) $BaTi(Si_3O_9)$ (b) $ZnCa_2Si_2O_7$
Then calculate $X \div Y$, where X and Y are total number of monovalent and divalent oxygen atoms in both silicates respectively.

24. B_2H_6 is allowed to react with following lewis bases, then the number of given lewis bases that form adduct through symmetrical cleavage of B_2H_6 are
NH_3, $MeNH_2$, Pyridine, CO, THF, PH_3, PF_3, Me_3N, Me_2NH

Matching Type Questions

25. Match the List I with List II.

	List I		List II
A.	Biotite	I.	3D silicate
B.	Kaolin	II.	Chain silicate
C.	Crocidolite	III.	Cyclic silicate
D.	Wollastonite	IV.	Sheet silicate

Choose the correct answer from the options given below.
(a) A-IV, B-I, C-II, D-III
(b) A-I, B-II, C-III, D-IV
(c) A-II, B-III, C-IV, D-I
(d) A-IV, B-II, C-III, D-I

26. Match the List I with List II.

	List I		List II
A.	$HgCl_2 + SnCl_2 \longrightarrow$	I.	$Hg_2Cl_2 + SnCl_4$
B.	$Hg_2Cl_2 + SnCl_2 \longrightarrow$	II.	$Hg + SnCl_4$
C.	$Sn + H_2O \longrightarrow$	III.	$SnO_2 + H_2$
D.	$SnCl_4 + H_2O \longrightarrow$	IV.	$SnO_2 + HCl$

Choose the correct answer from the options given below.
(a) A-III, B-IV, C-I, D-II (b) A-IV, B-II, C-III, D-I
(c) A-II, B-III, C-IV, D-I (d) A-I, B-II, C-III, D-IV

27.

	Column I (Reaction)		Column II (One of the product)
A.	Borax $\xrightarrow{\Delta}$	P.	BN
B.	$B_2H_6 + H_2O \longrightarrow$	Q.	B_2H_6
C.	$B_2H_6 + NH_3$ (excess)	R.	H_3BO_3
D.	$BCl_3 + LiAlH_4 \longrightarrow$	S.	B_2O_3

Choose the correct answer from the options given below.
(a) A-S, B-R, C-P, D-Q
(b) A-Q, B-S, C-P, D-R
(c) A-R, B-S, C-P, D-Q
(d) A-S, B-R, C-Q, D-P

28. Match the List I with List II.

	List I		List II
A.	$B_2O_3 + NaOH \longrightarrow$	I.	$H_2B_4O_7$
B.	$B + HNO_3 \longrightarrow$	II.	HBO_2
C.	$H_3BO_3 \xrightarrow{370\text{ K}}$	III.	H_3BO_3
D.	$HBO_2 \xrightarrow{410\text{ K}}$	IV.	$2NaBO_2$

Choose the correct answer from the options given below.
(a) A-IV, B-I, C-II, D-III
(b) A-III, B-I, C-IV, D-II
(c) A-IV, B-III, C-I, D-II
(d) A-IV, B-III, C-II, D-I

29. Match the List I with List II.

	List I		List II
A.	Aluminium bronze	I.	Used in paints
B.	Magnalium	II.	Making aeroplanes
C.	Duralumin	III.	Used in coins, utensils
D.	Cerussite	IV.	Used in light instruments, pressure cookers

Choose the correct answer from the options given below.
(a) A-I, B-II, C-III, D-IV
(b) A-III, B-IV, C-II, D-I
(c) A-IV, B-II, C-III, D-I
(d) A-II, B-I, C-III, D-IV

30. Match the List I with List II.

	List I		List II
A.	$AlCl_3$ acts as Lewis acid	I.	Formation of covalent bonds in vapour phase
B.	Aluminium dissolves in alkali	II.	Reacts with acids and bases
C.	Tl (III)	III.	Unstable due inert pair effect
D.	Tl (I)	IV.	Stable in its Oxidation state

Choose the correct answer from the options given below.
(a) A-I, B-II, C-III, D-IV (b) A-II, B-III, C-IV, D-I
(c) A-IV, B-II, C-III, D-I (d) A-III, B-I, C-II, D-IV

Paragraph Based Questions

Paragraph 1

Zeolites are hydrated 3-dimensional aluminosilicates obtained by replacing some of the silicon atom in three dimensional network silicate by Al^{3+}. Zeolites have SiO_4 and AlO_4 tetrahedrons linked together in three dimensional open structure. It can be used as ion exchange material since cation can move freely in the cavities.

31. A zeolite with formula $Na_{12}[Al_{12}Si_{12}O_{48}]\cdot 27H_2O$ is used for ion exchange. If this zeolite is completely exchanged with Ca^{2+} ions, then the moles of Ca^{2+} required is

32. A zeolite has the formula $Na_8[Al_8Si_{40}O_{96}]\cdot 20H_2O$. If the framework contains 40 Si—atoms. Then the percentage of aluminium in the framework is (nearest integer)

Paragraph 2

Diborane is an electron deficient compound. Stoichiometrically, it is analogous to ethane, C_2H_6. However, the total number of electrons involved in bonding are less in diborane.

33. The sum of total number of bonding electrons involved in B_2H_6 and C_2H_6 is

34. A x-membered ring is formed in $(BN)_n$ where the value of x is

Paragraph 3

The name silica covers an entire group of minerals, which have the general formula SiO_2, the most common of which is quartz. Quartz is a frame work silicate with SiO_4 tetraheral arranged in spirals.

Silicates can be called as metal derivatives of silicic acid. The silicate minerals contain some metal cations such as Li^+, Na^+, K^+, Ca^{2+} and Al^{3+} which provide ionic interaction to hold the solid silicate together.

35. Total number of oxygen atoms present in *ortho*silicate is

36. Total number of oxygen atom present in *pyro*silicate is

Species Selection (with 5 Species)

37. Given below are some silicates
(i) Zircon ($ZrSiO_4$)
(ii) Willemite
(iii) Phenacite
(iv) Thortveitite
(v) Hemimorphite
The number of example of *ortho*silicate.
(a) 1 (b) 2
(c) 3 (d) 4

38. Given below are few oxides
(i) B_2O_3 (ii) Al_2O_3
(iii) Ga_2O_3 (iv) In_2O_3
(v) Tl_2O_3
The number amphoteric oxides in nature are
(a) 1 (b) 2
(c) 3 (d) 4

39. Given below are few oxides
(i) CO_2 (ii) SiO_2
(iii) GeO_2 (iv) SnO_2
(v) PbO_2
The number of oxide that are acidic in nature are
(a) 1 (b) 2
(c) 3 (d) 4

Species Selection (with 7 Species)

40. Gelow below are few reactions.
(a) $BCl_3 + 3H_2O \longrightarrow B(OH)_3 + 3HCl$
(b) $SiCl_4 + 4H_2O \longrightarrow Si(OH)_4 + 4HCl$
(c) $Na_2B_4O_7 + 2HCl \longrightarrow 2NaCl + H_2B_4O_7$
(d) $4B + 3SiO_2 \longrightarrow 2B_2O_3 + 3Si$
(e) $B_2H_6 + 2NH_3 \xrightarrow[\text{Temp}]{\text{low}} B_2H_6 \cdot 2NH_3$
(f) $B_2H_6 + \underset{(\text{excess})}{NH_3} \xrightarrow[\text{Temp}]{\text{at high}} (BN)_x$
(g) $3B_2H_6 + 6NH_3 \longrightarrow \underset{\text{Borazine}}{2B_3N_3H_6} + 12H_2$

The number of correct reactions are

(a) 2 (b) 4 (c) 5 (d) 7

41. Given below are few species

(i) B_2H_6 (ii) B_2Cl_6

(iii) Al_2Cl_6 (iv) Fe_2Cl_6

(v) $B_2(CH_3)_6$ (vi) I_2Cl_6

(vii) $Al_2(CH_3)_6$

The number of species are that will have $3c—2e^-$ bond.

(a) 1 (b) 2

(c) 3 (d) 4

42. Given below are some statements

(i) CO is neutral oxide.

(ii) CO is π acceptor ligand in complex compound.

(iii) $Ni(CO)_4$ is sp^3 hybridised.

(iv) C—C bond length is max in diamond among all allotropes.

(v) The stability order of dihalide is $SiX_2 < GeX_2 < SnX_2 < PbX_2$

(vi) Diamond is sp^3 hybridised.

(vii) Graphite is sp^2 hybridised and used as a lubricant in machinery.

The number of correct statements are

(a) 4 (b) 5 (c) 6 (d) 7

43. Given below are some reactions

(i) $Li_2CO_3 \xrightarrow{\Delta}$ (ii) $Na_2CO_3 \xrightarrow{\Delta}$

(iii) $PbCO_3 \xrightarrow{\Delta}$ (iv) $NaHCO_3 \xrightarrow{\Delta}$

(v) $ZnCO_3 \xrightarrow{\Delta}$ (vi) 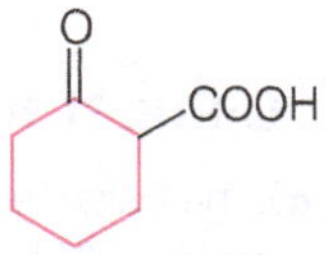

(vii) $BaCO_3 \xrightarrow{\Delta}$

The number of reactions that produce CO_2 on strong heating are

(a) 3 (b) 4 (c) 5 (d) 6

44. Given below are few statements

(i) The general formula of sheet silicates is $(Si_2O_5)_n^{2n-}$.

(ii) Al_2O_3 is amphoteric in nature.

(iii) B_2O_3 reacts with acidic oxides such as P_4O_{10}.

(iv) The case of hydrolysis of trihalides of boron is $BF_3 > BCl_3 > BBr_3 > BI_3$

(v) B_2H_6 forms bridge bonding.

(vi) B_2H_6 reacts with excess of NH_3 at high temperature to form inorganic benzene.

(vii) B_2H_6 is electron deficient.

The number of correct statement are

(a) 3 (b) 4 (c) 5 (d) 7

Check Through PYQs

Element 1 Group 13 Elements and Compounds

1. The green colour produced in the borax bead test of a chromium (III) salt is due to *2019 Adv.*

(a) Cr_2O_3 (b) CrB

(c) $Cr(BO_2)_3$ (d) $Cr_2(B_4O_7)_3$

2. The increasing order of atomic radii of the following group 13 elements is *2016 Adv.*

(a) Al < Ga < In < Tl (b) Ga < Al < In < Tl

(c) Al < In < Ga < Tl (d) Al < Ga < Tl < In

3. The compound(s) which react(s) with NH_3 to give boron nitride (BN) is(are) *2022 Adv.*

(a) B (b) B_2H_6

(c) B_2O_3 (d) HBF_4

4. Among the following, the correct statement(s) is(are) *2017 Adv.*

(a) $Al(CH_3)_3$ has the three-centre two-electron bonds in its dimeric structure

(b) The Lewis acidity of BCl_3 is greater than that of $AlCl_3$

(c) $AlCl_3$ has the three-centre two-electron bonds in its dimeric structure

(d) BH_3 has the three-centre two-electron bonds in its dimeric structure

5. The crystalline form of borax has *2016 Adv.*

(a) tetranuclear $[B_4O_5(OH)_4]^{2-}$ unit

(b) all boron atoms in the same plane

(c) equal number of sp^2 and sp^3 hybridised boron atoms

(d) one terminal hydroxide per boron atom

6. Three moles of B_2H_6 are completely reacted with methanol. The number of moles of boron containing product formed is

Element 2 Group 14 Elements and Compounds

7. Choose the correct statement(s) among the following: *2020 Adv.*

(a) $SnCl_2 \cdot 2H_2O$ is a reducing agent.

(b) SnO_2 reacts with KOH to form $K_2[Sn(OH)_6]$.

(c) A solution of $PbCl_2$ in HCl contains Pb^{2+} and Cl^- ions.

(d) The reaction of Pb_3O_4 with hot dilute nitric acid to give PbO_2 is a redox reaction.

HINTS & Solutions

Solutions : Competency Enhancer

1.1 ***(a, b, c, d)*** The balanced reaction is

(a) $2BF_3 + 6NaH \xrightarrow{450\ K} \underset{\text{(Diborane)}}{B_2H_6} + 6NaF$

(b) $4BF_3 + 3NaBH_4 \longrightarrow 3NaBF_4 + 2B_2H_6$

(c) $8BF_3 + 6LiH \xrightarrow{Et_2O} B_2H_6 + 6LiBF_4$

(d) $4BF_3 + 3LiAlH_4 \longrightarrow 2B_2H_6 + 3LiF + 3AlF_3$

2.1 ***(c)*** Among the given statements only III and IV are correct. The corrected form of incorrect statement are as

I. Carborundum is a covalent solid consisting of alternate C and Si atoms.

II. Silicon dissolves in excess of HF due to formation of H_2SiF_6.

V. Amorphous form of silica is kieselguhr.

Elemental Practice 5.1

1. ***(b)*** Statement given in option (b) is correct. While a, c and d are incorrect. The correct form of (a), (c) and (d) are
   - In borane, each boron atom is sp^3 hybridised.
   - Tetrahydridoborates can be prepared by the action of sodium hydrides and methyl borates in THF

     $B(OCH_3)_3 + 4NaH \xrightarrow[\text{250°C, high pressure}]{THF} NaBH_4 + 3Na[(OCH_3)]$
   - B atom in BH_4^- is sp^3-hybridised and is tetrahedral in structure.

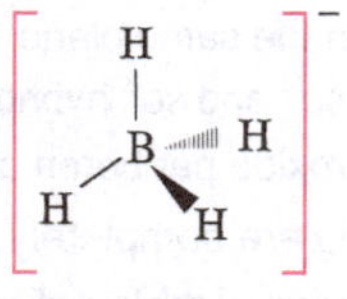

2. ***(d)*** Statement given in option (d) is incorrect. Its correct form is Group 13 elements have more tendency to form complexes than *s*-block elements. It is due to their small size, more effective nuclear charge as well as vacant orbitals to accept electrons.
3. ***(d)*** Boron trifluoride can act as a Lewis acid by accepting a pair of electrons from donor molecules such as $H_2O, Et_2O, NH_3, (CH_3)_3N$ and F^- etc. Since CCl_4 has no lone pair of electrons. It does not form adduct with CCl_4.
4. ***(d)*** $B_2O_3 + 3Mg \xrightarrow{1100°C} 2B + 3MgO$
5. ***(d)*** The basicity of hydroxides increases down the group as metallic character increases.

   Thus, the order of basicity is:

   $$Tl(OH)_3 > Ga(OH)_3 > Al(OH)_3 > B(OH)_3$$
6. ***(b)*** $Na_2B_4O_7 \cdot 5H_2O$ = Jeweller's borax

   It is pentahydrate form and its shape is octahedral
7. ***(c)*** $4H_3BO_3 + Na_2CO_3 \longrightarrow \underset{\text{Borax}}{Na_2B_4O_7} + 6H_2O + CO_2$
8. ***(a)*** The thermal stability decreases down the group due to weaker metal-hydrogen bonds for heavier elements.
9. ***(b)*** Order of Lewis acid strength of boron halides is

   $$BI_3 > BBr_3 > BCl_3 > BF_3$$

   This order is explained on the basis of $p\pi - p\pi$ back bonding opposite to expected order due to electronegativity.
10. ***(a)***

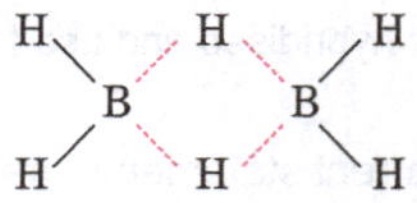

   Two bridged hydrogen and four terminal hydrogen are present.
11. ***(b)*** Aluminium is obtained by electrolysis of Al_2O_3 dissolved is Na_3AlF_6. Al_2O_3 is infusible, so it cannot be electrolysed. So, pure alumina dissolved in molten cryolite (Na_3AlF_6) containing some CaF_2 or NaF is electrolysed at about 800 – 1000° C.
12. ***(a)*** At cathode, $Al^{3+} + 3e^- \longrightarrow Al$
13. ***(c)*** Potash alum : $K_2SO_4 \cdot Al_2(SO_4)_3 \cdot 24H_2O$

    There are 2K and 2Al, means 4 metals containing $24H_2O$. So, 1 metal contains $6H_2O$ molecule.
14. ***(c)*** It is prepared by natural tincal which is highly soluble in hot water.

    The insoluble impurities filtered off and solution is concentrated and cooled, the crystal borax is obtained.
15. ***(c)*** Small size of hydrogen atom.
16. ***(b,c, d)*** Statements given in (b), (c) and (d) are correct while (a) is incorrect. Its correct form is boron carbide molecular formula is B_4C (extremely hard substance).
17. ***(a,c, d)***

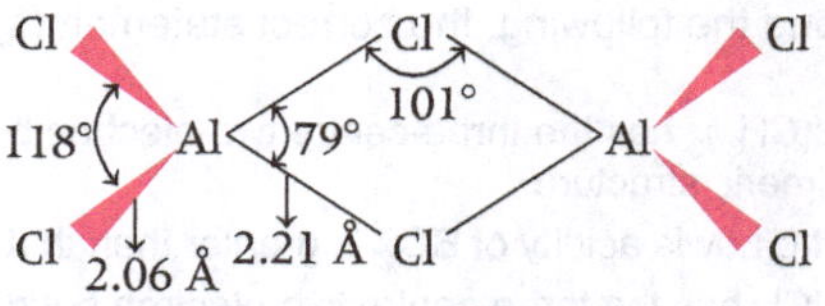

18. ***(a,b,c)*** Statements (a),(b) and (c) are correct. Statement (d) is incorrect. The correct form of statement (d) is

    Gallium hydroxide forms gallates with caustic alkalis.

    $NaOH + Ga(OH)_3 \longrightarrow NaGaO_2 + 2H_2O$ or $NaGa(OH)_4$.

19. ***(a, b, c)*** *Ortho*boric acid and *meta*boric acid differ in terms of basicity, melting point and structure. However they show same oxidation number of boron i.e, 3.

*Ortho*boric acid *Meta*boric acid

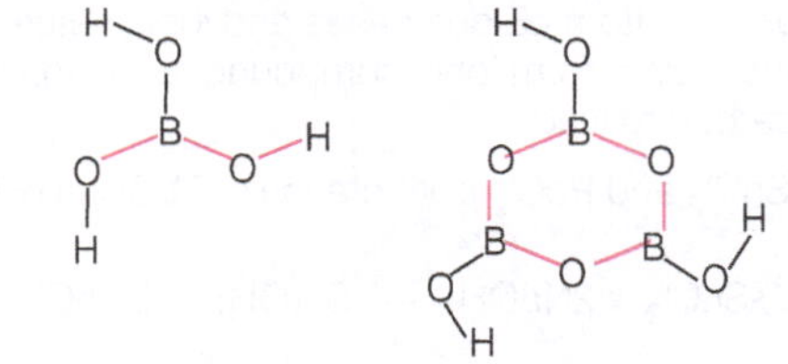

20. ***(a,b,c)*** Statements (a), (b), (c) are correct. Statement (d) is incorrect. The correct form of statement (d) is

Due to its weak acidic character, $B(OH)_3$ cannot be titrated completely with NaOH and no sharp end point is attained

$$B(OH)_3 + NaOH \rightleftharpoons Na^+[B(OH)_4]^- \longrightarrow \underset{\text{Sodium metaborate}}{NaBO_2} + 2H_2O$$

However, if a cis-dial is added it behaves as a stronger acid and titration with NaOH can be carried out in the presence of phenolphthalein.

21. ***(2)*** Aluminium forms *meta*-aluminate or aluminates with strong bases and liberate hydrogen gas.

$$2Al + 2NaOH + 6H_2O \longrightarrow 2Na[Al(OH)_4] + 3H_2\uparrow$$

$$2Al + 6NaOH + 6H_2O \longrightarrow 2Na_3[Al(OH)_6] + 3H_2\uparrow$$

22. ***(3)*** Except BCl_3, all the other chlorides of group 13 elements exists as dimer. This is due to the reason that boron cannot expand its octet. The other elements can expand their octet due to the presence of vacant *d* orbitals and can accept more than one electron pair, and form bridged structure. Chlorides of Al, Ga and In dimerises in vapour state.

So, the number of trichlorides which exists as dimer is 3.

23. ***(3)*** $4BF_3 \cdot Et_2O + 3LiAlH_4 \xrightarrow{\text{Diethyl ether}} 2B_2H_6 + 3LiF + 3AlF_3 + 4Et_2O$

$$2NaBH_4 + I_2 \xrightarrow{\text{Diglyme}} B_2H_6 + 2NaI + H_2$$

$$2BF_3 + 6NaH \xrightarrow{450\,K} B_2H_6 + 6NaF$$

$$H_3BO_3 \xrightarrow{370\,K} HBO_2 + H_2O$$

24. ***(1)*** Among the given compounds, only B_2O_3 is acidic whereas Al_2O_3 and Ga_2O_3 are amphoteric while Tl_2O_3 and In_2O_3 are basic in nature.

25. ***(4)*** Among the given statements only four statements about crystalline form of borax is correct except (c). Its corrected form is as, all B-atoms are not in same plane.

Elemental Practice 5.2

1. ***(c)*** Hydrolysis of $(Me)_2SiCl_2$ takes place as follows

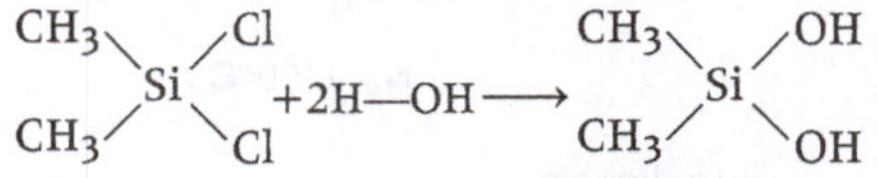

Dialkylsilandiol

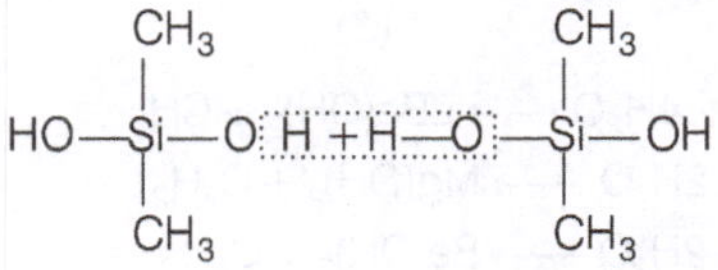

Where, $R = CH_3$

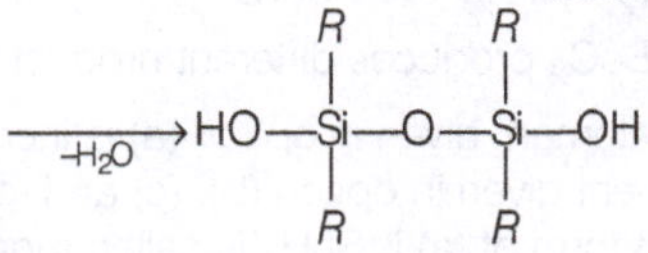

For *n* molecules of $(Me)_2SiCl_2$ product will be $-[O(Me)_2Si—O—Si(Me)_2O]_n-$

2. ***(b)*** In sheet silicates three oxygen atoms each tetrahedron are shared with adjacent, SiO_4^{4-} tetrahedron.

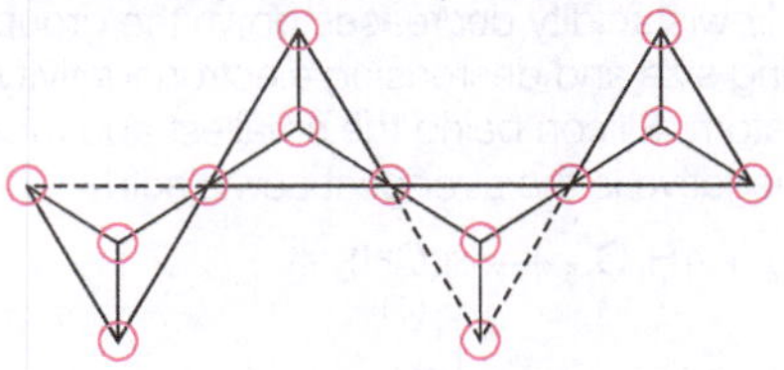

3. ***(c)*** $\underset{(C)}{H_2C_2O_4} \xrightarrow{\Delta} H_2O + \underset{(A)}{CO} + \underset{(B)}{CO_2}$

$$2CO + O_2 \longrightarrow 2CO_2$$

$$\underset{(A)}{CO} + Cl_2 \longrightarrow \underset{(D)}{COCl_2} \xrightarrow{NH_3,\ \Delta} \underset{(E)}{NH_2CONH_2} + 2HCl$$

4. ***(b)*** AlF_3 is ionic compound and between Al^{3+} ion and F^- ion, strong electrostatic attractive forces exists. So, (b) is the correct option.

5. ***(b)*** *X* is Pb_3O_4.

$$\underset{(X)}{Pb_3O_4} + 4HNO_3 \longrightarrow \underset{(Z)}{Pb(NO_3)_2} + \underset{(Y)}{PbO_2} + 2H_2O$$

$$\underset{(Z)}{Pb(NO_3)_2} + 2HCl \longrightarrow \underset{(A)}{PbCl_2} + 2HNO_3$$

$$\underset{(X)}{Pb_3O_4} + 8HCl \longrightarrow \underset{(A)}{3PbCl_2} + 4H_2O + Cl_2$$

6. ***(b)*** $2BeO + 3C \xrightarrow{2000°C} BeC_2(X) + 2CO$

$$\downarrow \text{dil. Acid}$$

$$\underset{(Y)}{Be(OH)_2} + \underset{(Z)}{CH_4}$$

7. ***(d)*** $CaO + 3C \xrightarrow{2000^\circ C} \underset{(X)}{CaC_2} + \underset{(Y)}{CO}$

$\underset{(X)}{CaC_2} \xrightarrow{N_2,\ 1100^\circ C} \underset{(Z)}{CaCN_2} \xrightarrow{\text{Hydrolysis}} \underset{(P)}{NH_3}$

8. ***(b)*** $Be_2C + 4H_2O \longrightarrow 2Be(OH)_2 + CH_4$

$MgC_2 + 2H_2O \longrightarrow Mg(OH)_2 + C_2H_2$

$BeC_2 + 2H_2O \longrightarrow Be(OH)_2 + C_2H_2$

$CaC_2 + 2H_2O \longrightarrow Ca(OH)_2 + C_2H_2$

Thus, BeC_2 produces different product on hydrolysis.

9. ***(a)*** Statement given in option (a) is incorrect whereas statement given in option (b), (c) and (d) are correct. The correct form of (a) is SnH_4 is called monostannane.

10. ***(a)*** Due to inability of bromine and iodine to oxidise Pb^{2+} to Pb^{4+}. $PbBr_4$ and PbI_4 does not exist. However Cl_2 can oxidise Pb^{2+} to Pb^{4+}. Thus $PbCl_4$ exists.

11. ***(c)*** The Lewis acidity decreases down the group due to the increasing size and decreasing electronegativity of the central atom. Silicon being the smallest and most electronegative is the strongest Lewis acid.

12. ***(d)*** $SiCl_4 + 4H_2O \longrightarrow \underset{(A)}{Si(OH)_4}$

$\underset{(A)}{Si(OH)_4} \xrightarrow{\Delta} \underset{(B)}{SiO_2} + 2H_2O$

$\underset{(B)}{SiO_2} \xrightarrow[\Delta]{Na_2CO_3} \underset{(C)}{Na_2SiO_3}$

13. ***(b)*** In group 14 as the molecular size increases down the group; boiling points increases due to stronger van der Waals' interactions.

14. ***(a)*** $[SiO_4]^{4-}$ units are in silicates.

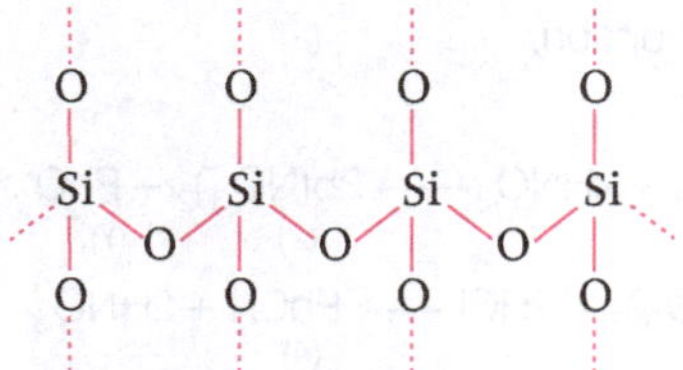

15. ***(b)*** $RSiCl_3$ gives cross linked polymer.

16. ***(b)*** Butter of tin $SnCl_4 \cdot 5H_2O$

17. ***(b)*** $C + H_2O \xrightarrow[\text{Steam}]{\text{Red hot carbon}} CO + H_2$

18. ***(d)*** Due to inert pair effect, Pb^{2+} oxidation state is more stable over Pb^{4+} oxidation state.

$Ge^{2+} \xrightarrow{-2e^-} Ge^{4+}$ (possible) reducing agent

$Pb^{4+} \xrightarrow{+2e^-} Pb^{2+}$ (Possible) oxidising agent

$Pb^{2+} > Pb^{+4}$ due to inert pair effect.

More pronounced inert pair effect in lead than Ge.

19. ***(a)*** Stability of hydride of carbon family carbon is near to nucleus thus it's attraction is more towards valence shell electron so, it is more stable

$CH_4 > SiH_4 > GeH_4 > SnH_4 > PbH_4$

20. ***(b)*** Top to bottom I.E decreases and ionic nature increases. So, tendency to form ionic compound formation increases from carbon to lead.

21. ***(a,c)*** $SnCl_2$ and $PbCl_2$ both are ionic. $PbCl_4$ is oxidising agent.

22. ***(a,b,d)*** $SnCl_2 + 2NaOH \longrightarrow \underset{(P)}{Sn(OH)_2} + 2NaCl$

$Sn(OH)_2 + 2NaOH \longrightarrow \underset{(Q)}{Na_2SnO_2} + H_2O$

$3Na_2SnO_2 + 2Bi(OH)_3 \longrightarrow 3Na_2SnO_3 + \underset{(R)}{2Bi} + 3H_2O$

23. ***(a,c,d)*** Statements (a),(c) and (d) are correct. Statement (b) is incorrect. The correct form of statement (b) is

A Buckminster fullerene C_{60} contains 20 six-membered rings and 12 five membered rings.

24. ***(a,d)*** Correct statement about silicones are given in option (a) and (d) while (b) and (c) are incorrect.

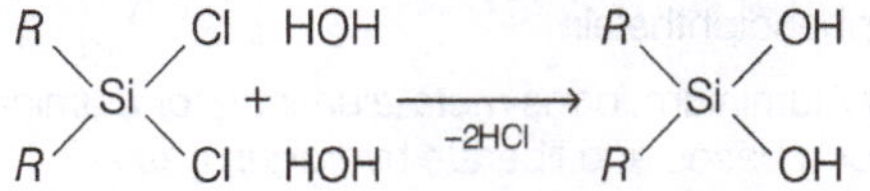

Dialkyl silane diol

25. ***(a,d)*** The non-existence of PbI_4 is due to the fact that Pb^{4+} is a strong oxidising agent and I^- is a reducing agent. When these species come into contact, a redox reaction occurs with Pb^{4+} reduced to Pb^{2+} and I^- being oxidised to I_2. This reaction prevents the stable formation of PbI_4, leading instead to the formation of PbI_2, where Pb exists in the more stable +2 oxidation state.

26. ***(4)*** Statement (i), (iii), (iv) and (v) are correct whereas (ii) is incorrect.

The correct form of (ii) is:

In pyrosilicates $(Si_2O_7)^{6-}$ units are formed by joining 2 tetrahedral units through one oxygen atom.

27. ***(6)*** In the crystalline structure of solid SnF_4, tin (Sn) is coordinated by six fluorine atoms, giving it a co-ordination number 6.

28. ***(6)*** In $Si_6O_{18}^{12-}$, six oxygen atoms are shared in the formation of cyclic silicate.

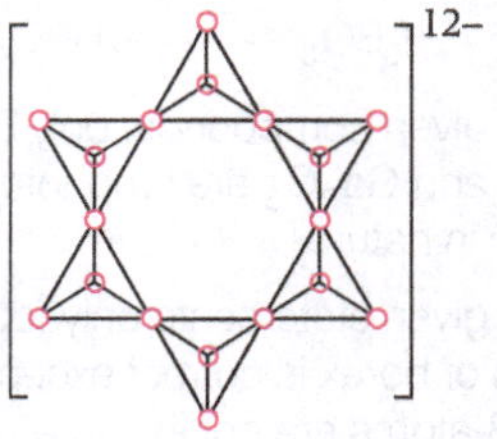

29. ***(4)*** Among the given statements four statements are correct. The corrected form of incorrect statement (e) is

The reaction of Pb_3O_4 with hot dil. HNO_3 is as follows:

$Pb_3O_4 + 4HNO_3 \rightarrow 2\overset{+2}{Pb}(NO_3)_2 + \overset{+4}{Pb}O_2 + 2H_2O$

It is not a redox reaction.

30. ***(1)*** Among the given elements only one i.e., carbon forms $p\pi - p\pi$ multiple bonds. 2*p*-orbitals of this element participate in the process. The smaller size of *C* plays a significant role in the process.

Practice Element 01 : Target JEE Main

1. ***(b)*** Sheet silicates have only one monovalent corner oxygen atom in each tetrahedron unit.
2. ***(d)*** In sheet silicate, three out of four oxygen atoms of SiO_4^{4-} unit are shared while in pyrosilicate only one oxygen is shared.
3. ***(c)*** Borazine $B_3N_3H_6$ is also called inorganic benzene because its structure shows some similarity with benzene with delocalised electrons and aromatic character. It is considerably more reactive than benzene due to low aromaticity and addition reactions occur quite readily.
4. ***(d)*** Statement given in option (d) is incorrect. It is because boron forms a monobasic weak acid on reaction with concentrated HNO_3.

$$B + \text{Conc.}HNO_3 \longrightarrow \underset{\text{(Weak, monobasic and non-protic acid)}}{H_3BO_3}$$

5. ***(c)*** BF_3 cannot be prepared by treatment of halogens with a mixture of B_2O_3 and carbon at high temperature.

It is instead prepared by

$$B_2O_3 + 3CaF_2 + \text{conc.}3H_2SO_4 \xrightarrow{\text{heat}} 2BF_3 + 3CaSO_4 + 3H_2O$$

$$B_2O_3 + 6NH_4BF_4 \xrightarrow{\text{Heat}} 8BF_3 + 6NH_3 + 3H_2O$$

6. ***(a)*** $Pb(NO_3)_2 \xrightarrow[673K]{\Delta} PbO + \underset{(A)}{NO_2} + O_2$

$$2NO_2 \xrightarrow{\text{Dimerise}} N_2O_4 :$$

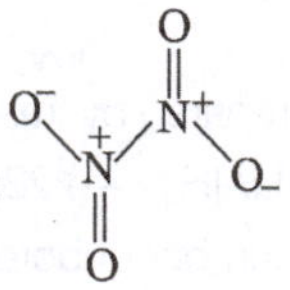

The oxidation number of N in (*B*) is +4.

N_2O_4

$2x + (-8) = 0 \Rightarrow x = +4$

7. ***(d)*** $Al_2O_3 + 3C + 3Cl_2(\text{dry}) \xrightarrow[1500°C]{\Delta} 2AlCl_3(\text{vap}) + 3CO$

$\downarrow$ Cooled

$AlCl_3$ (anhy.)

8. ***(b)*** Incorrect match is given in option (b). It is because the correct order of second ionisation enthalpy is

$$Al < Ga < B$$

9. ***(b)*** $\underset{(X)}{B_2H_6} + NH_3 \xrightarrow{200°C} \underset{\text{(Inorganic benzene)}}{\underset{(Y)}{B_3N_3H_6}}$

$$\underset{(X)}{B_2H_6} + NH_3(\text{excess}) \xrightarrow{\Delta} \underset{\text{(Boron nitride)}}{\underset{(Z)}{(BN)_x}}$$

10. ***(b)*** Among the given oxides option (b) consists pair of amphoteric oxide while SiO_2, GeO_2 and GeO are acidic oxide and CO is a neutral oxide.
11. ***(c)*** Removal of sulphur compounds from petroleum is not a use of silicon dioxide.
12. ***(b)*** Carbon forms carbides when reacted with elements like Be or oxides of elements like Ca, Si, Al etc., at high temperatures.

$$CaO + 3C \longrightarrow CaC_2 + CO$$

13. ***(c)*** Carbon is oxidised only by oxidising acids such as conc. HNO_3 and conc. H_2SO_4. Carbon reacts with hot and concentrated sulphuric acid to produce carbon dioxide and sulphur dioxide gas along with water.
14. ***(b)*** Carbonates of alkali metals except that of lithium do not decompose to produce carbon dioxide.
15. ***(b)*** CO_2 does not react with acidified $K_2Cr_2O_7$ or any other oxidising agent whereas SO_2 reacts with it. CO_2 and SO_2 both turn lime water milky.

$$\underset{(X)}{CO_2} + Ca(OH)_2 \longrightarrow \underset{\text{(White ppt.)}}{CaCO_3}$$

$$CaCO_3 + \underset{(X)}{CO_2} + H_2O \rightarrow \underset{\text{(Soluble) }(Y)}{Ca(HCO_3)_2}$$

$$\underset{(X)}{CO_2} + K_2Cr_2O_7 + H^+ \longrightarrow \text{No reaction}$$

16. ***(d)*** Pyrosilicates involve sharing of only one oxygen atom thus decreasing the number of oxygen atoms by 0.5 and charge from −4 to −3 in the general formula, SiO_4^{4-}.
17. ***(b)*** In trisilylamine, three sp^2 orbitals are used for σ bonding, giving a plane triangular structure. The lone pair of electrons occupy a *p*-orbital at right angles to the plane triangle. This overlaps with empty *d* – orbitals on each of the three silicon atoms, and results in π bonding, more accurately described as $p\pi - p\pi$ bonding, because it forms by donating electrons from a full *p*-orbital to an empty *d*-orbital.

This shortens the bond length N—Si. Since the nitrogen no longer has a lone pair of electrons, the molecule has no donor properties, so it is less basic. Similar $p\pi - d\pi$ bonding is impossible in $(CH_3)_3N$ because C does not possess *d*-orbitals and hence this molecule is pyramidal.

18. ***(b)*** Since, compound '*A*' of boron reacts with NMe_3 to form an adduct '*B*'.

Thus, compound '*A*' is a lewis acid. Since, adduct '*B*' on hydrolysis gives an acid '*C*' and hydrogen gas, therefore, '*A*' is B_2H_6 and '*C*' is boric acid.

$$\underset{\text{Diborane }(A)}{B_2H_6} + 2NMe_3 \longrightarrow \underset{\text{Adduct }(B)}{2BH_3 \cdot NMe_3}$$

$$BH_3 \cdot NMe_3 + 3H_2O \longrightarrow \underset{\text{Boric acid }(C)}{H_3BO_3} + NMe_3 + 3H_2 \uparrow$$

19. ***(c)*** Following reaction takes place when Sn is heated with alkali solution.

$$Sn + 2NaOH + H_2O \longrightarrow \underset{\text{Sodium Stannate}}{Na_2SnO_3} + 2H_2$$

20. ***(d)***

(i) $Na_2B_4O_7 + 2HCl + 5H_2O \longrightarrow 2NaCl + 4H_3BO_3$
Borax (*A*) — Orthoboric acid (*X*)

(ii) $H_3BO_3 \xrightarrow{\Delta,\ 370\ K} HBO_2 + H_2O$
(*X*) — Metaboric acid

$4HBO_2 \xrightarrow[-H_2O]{\Delta,\ >370\ K} [H_2B_4O_7]$
Tetraboric acid

$\xrightarrow{\text{Red heat}} 2B_2O_3 + H_2O$
Boron trioxide (*Z*)

21. ***(c)*** In BF_3 there is significant $p\pi$-$p\pi$ interaction between unshared p-orbital (having no electron) over boron and the lone pair of electron over fluorine in $2p$ orbital.

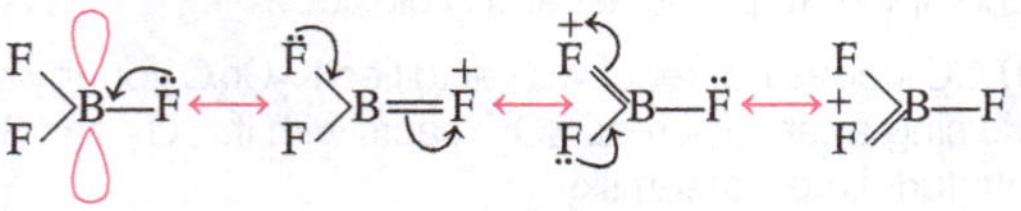

22. ***(a)*** When an aqueous solution of borax is acidified with HCl, boric acid is formed.

$Na_2B_4O_7 + 2HCl + 5H_2O \longrightarrow 2NaCl + 4H_3BO_3$
Borax — Boric acid

Boric acid is a white crystalline solid. It is soapy to touch because of its planar layered structure. Boric acid is a weak monobasic acid. It is not a protonic acid but acts as a lewis acid by accepting electrons from a hydroxyl ion.

$$B(OH)_3 + 2HOH \longrightarrow [B(OH)_4]^- + H_3O^+$$

23. ***(b)*** BCl_3 on hydrolysis in water forms tetrahedral $[B(OH)_4]^-$ species; in which the hybridisation state of B is sp^3.

$$BCl_3 + 3H_2O \longrightarrow B(OH)_3 + 3HCl$$
$$B(OH)_3 + H_2O \longrightarrow [B(OH)_4]^- + H^+$$

$AlCl_3$ in acidified aqueous solution forms octahedral $[Al(H_2O)_6]^{3+}$ ion.

$$AlCl_3 + \text{water} \xrightarrow{HCl} [Al(H_2O)_6]^{3+} + 3Cl^-(aq)$$

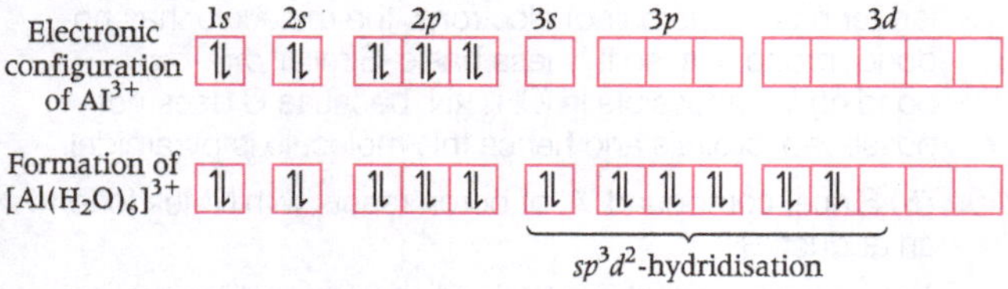

In this complex, the $3d$ orbitals of Al are involved and the hybridisation state of Al is sp^3d^2.

24. ***(9)*** The more representative formula of $NaBO_3$ is $Na_2[B_2(O_2)_2(OH)_4]\cdot 6H_2O$ with O_2 signifying peroxide linkage and with a +3 oxidation number of boron.

Thus, oxidation number of boron + Number of H_2O molecules = 3 + 6 = 9

25. ***(6)*** In B_2H_6, four 2-centre-2-electron bond and two 3-centre-2-electron bonds are present.

Thus, 4 + 2 = 6

26. ***(240)*** C_{60} an allotrope of carbon contains 20 hexagonal and 12 pentagonal rings of carbon atoms. Thus, the product of x and y is 240.

27. ***(4)*** Borax contains the tetrahedral unit, i.e. $[B_4O_5(OH)_4]^{2-}$ and its structure can be shown as

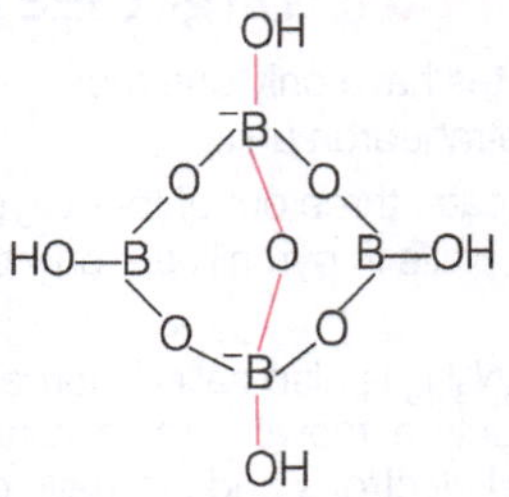

28. ***(4)*** (*X*) is borax, $Na_2B_4O_7\cdot 10H_2O$ as its aqueous solution is weakly alkaline, it gives a glassy bead on strong heating. The reactions are as follows

(i) $Na_2B_4O_7 + 7H_2O \rightleftharpoons 2NaOH + 4H_3BO_3$
(*X*) — Strong — Weak

Due to the presence of a strong base (NaOH), the aqueous solution is alkaline to litmus.

(ii) $Na_2B_4O_7 \xrightarrow[\text{Swells}]{\Delta} 2NaBO_2 + B_2O_3$
(*X*) — Glassy bead

(iii) $Na_2B_4O_7\cdot 10H_2O + \text{Conc. } H_2SO_4 \longrightarrow Na_2SO_4 + 4H_3BO_3 + 5H_2$
White crystal (*Z*)

Thus, the value of x is 1.

29. ***(5)*** $B_3N_3H_6$ or borazine is called inorganic benzene. It is obtained by heating diborane with NH_3.

$$3B_2H_6 + 6NH_3 \longrightarrow 2B_3N_3H_6 + 12H_2\uparrow$$
(*X*) — (*Y*) Inorganic benzene

Diborane is also prepared by treating BF_3 with $LiAlH_4$.

$$4BF_3 + 3LiAlH_4 \longrightarrow 2B_2H_6 + 3LiF + 3AlF_3$$

Thus, the sum of number of boron present in B_2H_6 and $B_3N_3H_6$ is 5.

30. ***(22)*** $4BCl_3 + 3LiAlH_4 \longrightarrow 2B_2H_6 + 3AlCl_3 + 3LiCl$
(*X*) — (*Y*)

Mass percentage of hydrogen in $B_2H_6 = \frac{6}{27.62}\times 100 = 21.72 \approx 22\%$

$$B_2H_6 + 3O_2 \xrightarrow{\text{Explosion}} B_2O_3 + 3H_2O$$
Boron trioxide

31. ***(7)*** As four F-atoms are bonded, hence,

Covalency = 4

Let oxidation number of B = x

$$x + 4(-1) = -1 \Rightarrow x = 3$$

thus, covalency + oxidation number = 4 + 3 = 7

32. ***(4)*** The number of ions from the following which are expected to behave as reducing agent are namely Tl^+, Pb^{2+}, Sn^{2+} and Si^{2+}.

33. ***(14)*** Four BH units contribute 4 × 2 = 8 electrons and the six additional H-atoms contribute a further six electrons giving 14 in all.

Check Through PYQs : JEE Main

1. ***(d)*** The correct match is

A-IV, B-I, C-II, D-III

Melting point (K)

$\Rightarrow$ B > Al > Tl > In > Ga

Ionic radius (M^{3+} / pm)

$\Rightarrow$ Tl > In > Ga > Al > B

$(\Delta_{IE}H)_1 \left[\frac{\text{kJ}}{\text{mol}}\right]$

$\Rightarrow$ B > Tl > Al $\approx$ Ga > In

Atomic radius (in pm)

$\Rightarrow$ Tl > In > Al > Ga > B

2. ***(c)*** Both A and R are true and R is the correct explanation of A.

3. ***(a)*** Statement I is true but statement II is false.

The correct form of statement II is,

Thermometer containing gallium is not used to measure freezing point of brine solution instead gallium is used to measure high temperature.

4. ***(d)*** The values of Ist ionisaion enthalpy of Tl, Ga and Al are 589 kJ/mol, 579 kJ/mol and 577 kJ/mol respectively. Thus, the correct order of first ionisation enthalpy is

Tl > Ga > Al

5. ***(a)*** Both (A) and (R) are correct and (R) is the correct explanation of A.

6. ***(b)*** Borazine is $B_3N_3H_6$.

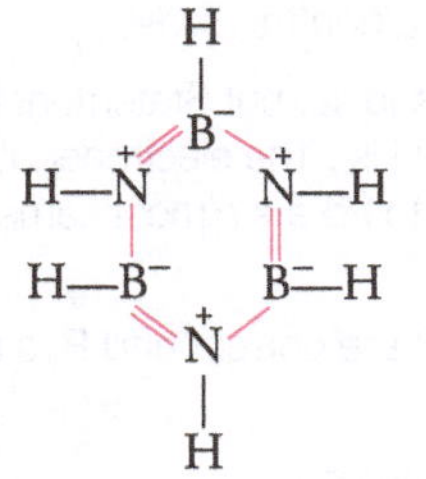

Due to $(p\pi - p\pi)$ back bonding, nitrogen donates its lone pair to empty *p*-orbital of boron and hence forming double bond, leads to its resemblance with benzene.

It slowly reacts with water and gives H_3BO_3.

$$B_3N_3H_6 + H_2O\text{ (excess)} \longrightarrow NH_3 + H_3BO_3 + H_2\uparrow$$

But it does not contain banana bond. Hence option (b) is an incorrect statement.

7. ***(a)*** Both statement I and statement II are correct.

Boron is non-metallic in nature. It is extremely hard and black coloured solid. Due to its small atomic size has very strong crystalline lattice. Thus it has high melting and boiling point.

8. ***(a)*** Structure of $Ga^+ AlCl_4^-$ is

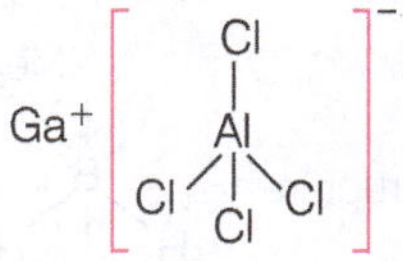

Thus, Ga is cationic part in the given salt. Also it is more electronegative than Al.

According to Pauling scale, Al has an electronegativity of 1.61 and Ga has an electronegativity of 1.81.

So, option (a) is correct.

9. ***(a)*** Gallium (Ga) will remain as liquid inside pure boiling water. It has large liquid range, melting at 29.78°C and boiling at 2400°C, at atmospheric pressure.

10. ***(c)*** Extent of back bonding decreases down the group leading to more lewis acidic strength. The order of extent of back bonding is

$$\underset{(2p\text{-}2p)}{BF_3} > \underset{(2p\text{-}3p)}{BCl_3} > \underset{(2p\text{-}4p)}{BBr_3} > \underset{(2p\text{-}5p)}{BI_3}$$

Thus, the order of lewis acidic character is

$$BF_3 < BCl_3 < BBr_3 < BI_3$$

11. ***(b)*** Since boron is 2nd period element and cannot expand its octet due to unavailability of *d*-orbitals, it cannot form $[BF_6]^{3-}$. Also the size of boron is very small.

Hence, both A and R are correct but R is not the correct explanation of A.

12. ***(b)*** Borazine or inorganic benzene is $B_3N_3H_6$. Its structure is as follows

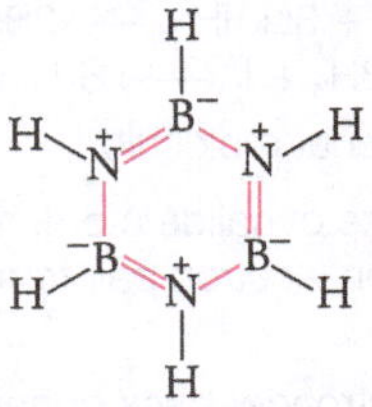

It is prepared by heating diborane (B_2H_6) with ammonia at temperature of 250-300°C.

$$3B_2H_6 + 6NH_3 \xrightarrow[250-300^\circ C]{\Delta} 2B_3H_6N_3 + 12H_2$$

13. ***(b)***

Metal		Melting point
Al	$\rightarrow$	933 K
Ga	$\rightarrow$	303 K
In	$\rightarrow$	430 K
Se	$\rightarrow$	490 K

Gallium has low melting point and its periodic position is closer to metalloids.

14. ***(b)*** Complete and balanced reaction is

$$2BF_3 + 6NaH \xrightarrow{450\text{ K}} \underset{\substack{\text{(Diborane)} \\ (A)}}{B_2H_6} + 6NaF$$

$$B_2H_6 + \underset{(C)}{2NMe_3} \longrightarrow \underset{(B)}{2BH_3 \cdot NMe_3}$$

BH_3 is electron deficient, so NMe_3 forms a coordinate bond with it.

Structure = 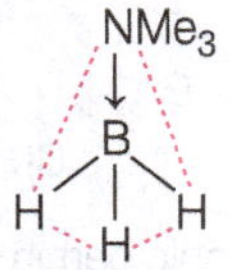

The geometry around boron in the product is tetrahedral.

15. ***(a)*** On moving down the 13th group from B to Tl, stability of elements showing +1 oxidation state increases. This is due to inert pair effect. This inert pair effect increases down the group due to increase in atomic size.
Hence, stability order of group 13 elements in their +1 oxidation state is

$$Al < Ga < In < Tl.$$

16. ***(c)*** The structure of B_2H_6 is given below

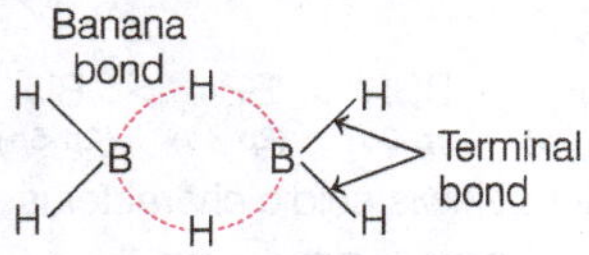

(A) In B_2H_6, not all B—H bonds are equivalent.
(B) There are two types of bonds present in B_2H_6, four normal covalent bonds and two 3-centre-2-electrons bonds.
(C) B_2H_6 is electron deficient and able to accept a pair of electron. Hence, acts as lewis acid.
(D) B_2H_6 can be synthesised from both BF_3 and $NaBH_4$ as follows :

$$4BF_3 + 3LiAlH_4 \longrightarrow 2B_2H_6 + 3LiF + 3AlF_3$$
$$NaBH_4 + I_2 \longrightarrow B_2H_6 + 2NaI + H_2$$

(E) B_2H_6 is a non-planar molecule.

17. ***(b)*** Smaller the size of halide atom, more effective is the back donation of an electron pair from halide atom to Boron.
So, BF_3 will show stronger back donation from halide to B.

18. ***(b)*** Statement (A) is correct whereas all other statements are incorrect.
(A) The oxidation of sodium borohydride with iodine in diglyme gives diborane.

$$I_2 + 2NaBH_4 \xrightarrow{\text{Diglyme}} 2NaI + \underset{\text{(Diborane)}}{B_2H_6} + H_2$$

(B) 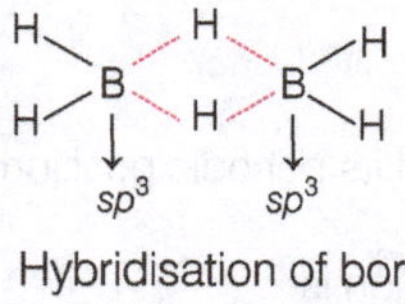

Hybridisation of boron in B_2H_6 is sp^3.
(C) B_2H_6 has two bridged, 3-centre-2-electron bond.
(D) B_2H_6 is a non-planar molecule.

19. ***(a)*** Due to inert pair effect, Thallium is more stable in +1 oxidation state due to inert pair effect.
So, TlI_3 and CsI_3 are isomorphous. Electronic configuration of thallium = [Xe] $4f^{14}5d^{10}6s^26p^1$. Hence, both A and R are correct but R is not the correct explanation of A.

20. ***(d)*** $\underset{(A)}{H_3N_3B_3Cl_3} + 3LiBH_4 \xrightarrow{\text{THF}} \underset{(B)}{B_3N_3H_6} + 3LiCl + 3BH_3$

$$\underset{(A)}{H_3N_3B_3Cl_3} + \underset{(C)}{3MeMgBr} \longrightarrow H_3N_3B_3(Me)_3 + 3MgBrCl$$

So, B = $B_3N_3H_6$; C = MeMgBr

21. ***(a)*** All the given statements are correct. For group 13 elements, the acidic nature of oxides decreases down the group and the basic nature of oxides increases on moving from B to Tl. While, Al_2O_3 and Ga_2O_3 are amphoteric oxides.

22. ***(b)*** In semiconductor energy band gap falls between conductor and insulator (around 1eV).
Silicon, germanium and copper oxide falls into semiconductor category, while graphite is a conductor

23. ***(d)*** The number of ions from the following which are expected to behave as oxidising agent are two, namely Tl^{3+} and Pb^{4+}. Due to inert pair effect; Tl^{3+} and Pb^{4+} can behave as oxidising agent.

24. ***(b)*** Statement given in *C, D* and *E* are correct, while statement *A* and *B* are incorrect. Their correct forms are down the group covalent radius increases.
Electronegativity does not decreases gradually from C to Pb.

25. ***(b)*** Statement I is true but Statement II is false.
The correct form of Statement II is :
Due to property of catenation and $p\pi - p\pi$ bond formation carbon shows allotropic forms.

26. ***(b)*** Among the given options only SnO_2, PbO_2 are amphoteric oxides while SiO_2, GeO_2 and GeO are acidic oxide and CO is a neutral oxide.

27. ***(a)*** Statement I is false, but Statement II is true. The correct form of Statement I is : The electronegativity value of group 14 elements from Si to Pb are almost same. Hence, option (a) is correct.

28. ***(b)*** Both A and R are correct and R is the correct explanation of A.

29. ***(a)*** The correct match is
A-III, B-I, C-IV, D-II.

30. ***(d)*** Correct match is
A—(III), B—(IV), C—(I), D—(II)

	List-I (Si-compound)		List-II (Si-polymer/ other products)	Explanation
(A)	$(CH_3)_4Si$	(III)	Silane	Tetramethyl silane is an organosilicon compound.
(B)	$(CH_3)Si(OH)_3$	(IV)	2D-silicone	Methylsilanol when polymerise, a cross-linked 2D silicone is obtained.

	List-I (Si-compound)		List-II (Si-polymer/ other products)	Explanation
(C)	$(CH_3)_2Si(OH)_2$	(I)	Chain silicone	Dimethylsilanediol is an example of chain silicon.
(D)	$(CH_3)_3Si(OH)$	(II)	Dimeric silicone	Trimethylsilanol exists as dimer.

Practice Element 02 : Target JEE Advanced

1. ***(b)*** More negative is the electrode reduction potential, higher is the tendency of the element to lose electrons and hence stronger is the reducing agent.

   Thus, the correct order is: Na < K < Rb < Cs < Li

2. ***(b)*** When one oxygen of a SiO_4^{4-} tetrahedron is shared with another SiO_4^{4-} tetrahedron, it results in the formation of $Si_2O_7^{6-}$ (pyrosilicates).

3. ***(a)*** The larger ionic radius and lower charge density of Ga^{3+} compared to Al^{3+} reduce its ability to polarise the oxide ion, making its amphoteric behaviour less pronounced.

4. ***(c)*** Carbon disulphide reacts with ammonia, primary and secondary amines to give dithiocarbamate

   $2NH_3 + CS_2 \longrightarrow NH_4(H_2NCS_2)$

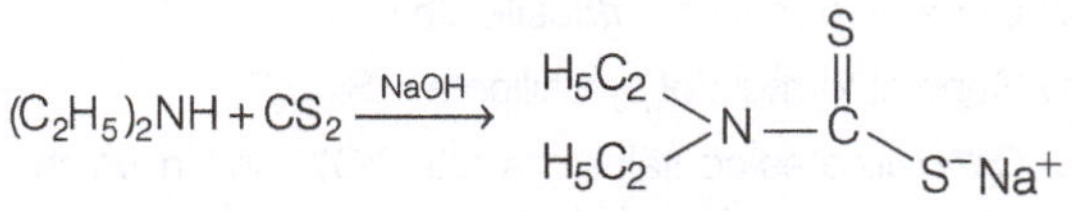

5. ***(c)*** Silicones have a Si—O—Si back bone, which makes them thermally stable and hydrophobic in nature.

6. ***(a)*** BF_3 acts a Lewis acid catalyst.

   $PbCl_2$ is not an oxidising agent.

   SiO_2 is acidic not basic

   B_2H_6 hydrolyses to form H_3BO_3

7. ***(c)*** Diamond cannot be attacked by dilute acids. It can be slowly oxidised by chromic acid.

8. ***(d)*** (a) $SiO_2 + 2C \xrightarrow[\text{Electric furnace}]{2273-2773\,K} Si + 2CO$

   (c) $Na_2SiO_3 + 2HCl + H_2O \longrightarrow Si(OH)_2 + 2NaCl$

   (d) $SiC + 4NaOH + 2O_2 \xrightarrow{\text{Fuse}} Na_2CO_3 + Na_2SiO_3 + 2H_2O$

9. ***(b,c,d)*** Both graphite and diamond are diamagnetic in nature.

10. ***(b,c,d)*** Co^{3+}, Cu^{2+} and Ni^{2+} give borax bead test.

11. ***(b,c,d)*** $[BF_6]^{3-}$ does not exist due to unavailability of *d*-orbital B can not form more than 3 bonds.

12. ***(a,b,d)***

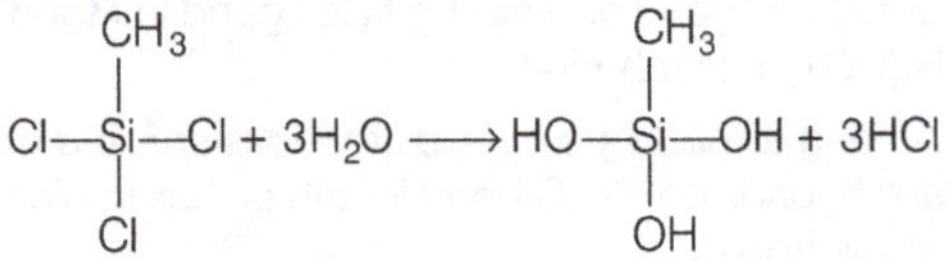

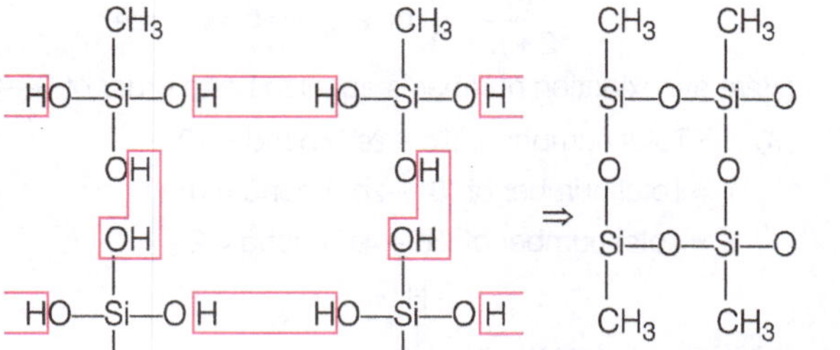

Cross linked silicones

13. ***(b, d)*** Among the given statements only (b) and (d) are correct. The corrected form of incorrect statements are
    - Due to property of catenation and $p\pi - p\pi$ bond formation carbon shows allotropic forms.
    - The electronegativity value of group 14 elements from Si to Pb are almost same.

14. ***(a,d)*** Among the given statements only (a) and (d) are incorrect. Their corrected form are as
    - Stannane is a non-planar molecular hydride. It has tetrahedral shape.
    - Phosgene gas is obtained by treatment of CCl_4 with superheated steam:

   $$CCl_4 + H_2O(\text{vapour}) \longrightarrow COCl_2 + 2HCl$$

15. ***(a,c)*** There are the two laboratory methods of preparation of carbon monoxide

   $K_4[Fe(CN)_6] + 6H_2SO_4 \text{ (conc.)} + 6H_2O \longrightarrow 2K_2SO_4 + FeSO_4 + 3(NH_4)_2SO_4 + 6CO$

   $HCOOH \xrightarrow{H_2SO_4 \text{ (conc.)}} CO + H_2O$

16. ***(b)*** Boron exists as a covalent network solid with strong B—B bonds, leading to its high melting point.

17. ***(0)***

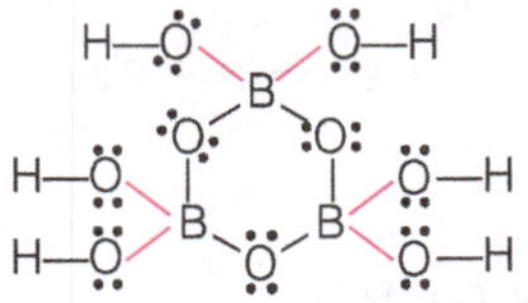

   Total number of σ-bonds = 18

   Total number of lone pairs = 18

   So difference is zero.

18. ***(0)*** $x = 6$

   $y = 6$

   $z = 12$

   So $(x + y - z) = (6 + 6 - 12) = 0$

19. ***(4)***

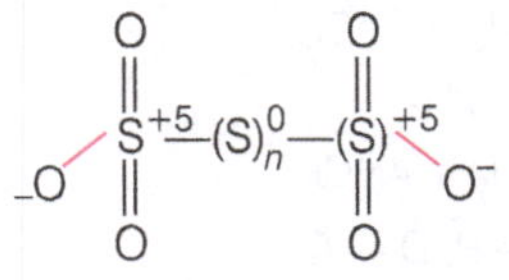

   Bond order of 'S—O' bond is 1.66. Average oxidation state of 'S' atom is

$$\frac{10}{2+n}=\frac{5}{3} \text{ or } 2+n=6 \Rightarrow n=4$$

(Here av. oxidation number is equal to bond order of S—O.)

20. ***(5)*** X = Total number of ($2c-2e^-$) bond = 10

Y = Total number of ($3c-2e^-$) bond = 0

Z = Total number of ($3c-4e^-$) bond = 2

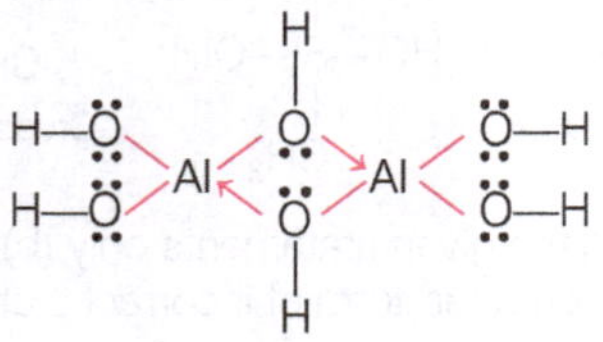

$(10+0)\div 2=5$

21. ***(1)*** $x=10, y=2, z=8$

$$=\frac{10-2}{8}=1$$

22. ***(5)*** The charge on $Si_4O_{11}^{6-}$ anion is −6. Ca and Mg have +2 charge each. OH has −1 charge.

$$2(+2)+x(+2)+2(-1)+2(-6)=0$$
$$x=5$$

23. ***(3)*** For $BaTi(Si_3O_9)$, the number of monovalent oxygen atom (X) is 6 and the number of divalent O atom is (Y) is 3.

For $ZnCa_2Si_2O_7$ the number of monovalent oxygen atom (X) is 6 and the number of divalent O-atom (Y) is 1.

Hence, total $X=6+6=12$ and total $Y=3+1=4$

Thus, $\frac{X}{Y}=\frac{12}{4}=3$

24. ***(6)*** Upon symmetrical cleavage of B_2H_6. With large sized strong lewis or weaker lewis base like :
PH_3, PF_3, CO, T.H.F., Me_3N and pyridine.

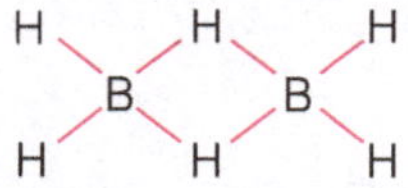 $+ 2L \longrightarrow 2BH_3L$

25. ***(a)*** The correct match is:

A-IV, B-I, C-II, D-III

Biotite - $K(Mg,Fe)_3(OH)_2(AlSi_3O_{10})$ (Sheet silicate)

Kaolin - $Al_2O_3\cdot 2SiO_2\cdot 2H_2O$ (3D silicate)

Crocidolite -$Na_2Fe_3^{II}\cdot Fe_2^{III}Si_8O_{22}(OH)_2$ (Chain silicates)

Wollastonite - $Ca_3Si_3O_9$ (Cyclic silicates)

26. ***(d)*** The correct match is:

A-I, B-II, C-III, D-IV

$$2HgCl_2 + SnCl_2 \longrightarrow Hg_2Cl_2 + SnCl_4$$
$$Hg_2Cl_2 + SnCl_2 \longrightarrow 2Hg + SnCl_4$$
$$Sn + 2H_2O \longrightarrow SnO_2 + 2H_2$$
$$SnCl_2 + 2H_2O \longrightarrow SnO_2 + 4HCl$$

27. ***(a)*** A → S, B → R, C → P, D → Q.

28. ***(d)*** The correct match is: A-IV, B-III, C-II, D-I.

$$B_2O_3 + 2NaOH \longrightarrow 2NaBO_2 + H_2O$$
$$B + 3HNO_3 \longrightarrow H_3BO_3 + 3NO_2$$
$$H_3BO_3 \xrightarrow{370\,K} HBO_2 + H_2O$$
$$HBO_2 \xrightarrow{410\,K} H_2B_4O_7$$

29. ***(b)*** The correct match is
A-III, B-IV, C-II, D-I.

30. ***(a)*** The correct match is A-I, B-II, C-III, C-IV.

31. ***(6)*** Each mole of zeolite contains 12 moles of Na^+ ions

$$\text{Moles of } Ca^{2+} \text{ ions required} = \frac{\text{moles of } Na^+}{2}$$
$$=\frac{12}{2}=6 \text{ moles}$$

32. ***(17)*** Total number of framework atoms = Al + Si

$= 8 + 40 = 48$

$$\text{Percentage of Al in the framework} = \frac{8}{48}\times 100$$
$$=16.67\%$$

33. ***(26)*** Bonding electrons involved in B_2H_6 is 12 and in C_2H_6 is 14. Thus, their sum = 12 + 14

$= 26$

34. ***(6)*** A six membered ring is formed in $(BN)_n$ where x is 6.

35. ***(4)*** General formula of *ortho*silicate is SiO_4^{4-}.

36. ***(7)*** General formula of *pyro*silicate is $Si_2O_7^{6-}$.

37. ***(c)*** *Ortho*silicates contains discrete SiO_4^{4-} unit in which oxygen atoms are found to associate only with metal ion.
e.g. Zircon, willemite, phenacite.

$(ZrSiO_4)$ (Zn_2SiO_4) (Be_2SiO_4)

Thortveitite and Hemimorphite are pyrosilicates
Asbestos is double chain silicate.

38. ***(b)*** The basic character of oxide and hydroxide of boron family are increase down the group so

$$\underbrace{B_2O_3}_{\text{Acidic}}\ \underbrace{Al_2O_3,\ Ga_2O_3}_{\text{Amphoteric}}\ \underbrace{In_2O_3,\ Tl_2O_3}_{\text{Basic in nature}}$$

39. ***(b)*** Acidic character decrease down the goup so

$$\underbrace{CO_2, SiO_2}_{\text{Acidic}}\ \underbrace{GeO_2,\ SnO_2}_{\text{Amphoteric}}\ \underbrace{PbO_2}_{\text{Weakly basic}}$$

40. ***(d)*** All the given reaction are correct refer theory.

41. ***(c)*** In hypovalent molecule when the surrounding atoms or groups do not have any lone pair (e.g, —H, —CH_3, —C_2H_5 etc) $3c-2e^-$ bridge bond always formed on dimerisation or polymerisation.

42. ***(d)*** CO is mono oxide of C it is neutral oxide and has vacant *p*-orbital when it attach with *d*-block element it behaves as π acceptor ligand and strong field ligand in Mond's process $Ni(CO)_4$ is tetrahedral.

Among all allotrope of C, diamond is sp^3 and graphite is sp^2 hybridised C—C bond length is max in diamond among all allotropes.

43. ***(d)*** In alkali metal carbonates only Li_2CO_3 gives CO_2 other metal carbonates do not produce CO_2 on heating. Alkaline metal with divalent cation always produce CO_2 on heat. β –keto acid also give $CO_2\uparrow$ on strong heating.

Bicarbonate on strong heating give $CO_2\uparrow$ and metal carbonate.

44. ***(d)*** All the statements are correct.

Check Through PYQs : JEE Advanced

1. ***(c)*** Borax bead test is performed only for coloured salt. Borax (sodium tetraborate decahydrate), $Na_2B_4O_7\cdot10H_2O$ on heating gets fused and loses water of crystallisation. It swells up into fluffy white porous mass which melts into a colourless liquid which later form a clear transparent glassy bead consisting of boric anhydride and sodium *meta*borate.

$$Na_2B_4O_7\cdot10H_2O \xrightarrow{\Delta} Na_2B_4O_7 + 10H_2O\uparrow$$

$$Na_2B_4O_7 \xrightarrow{\Delta} \underbrace{\underset{\text{Boric anhydride}}{B_2O_3} + \underset{\text{Sodium } metaborate}{2NaBO_2}}_{\text{glassy bead}}$$

Boric anhydride is non-volalite. When it react with Cr(III) salt then deep green complex is formed.

$$2Cr^{3+} + 3B_2O_3 \longrightarrow \underset{\text{Deep green}}{2Cr(BO_2)_3}$$

Hence, option (c) is correct.

2. ***(b)*** On moving down the group atomic radii increases but due to poor shielding of *d*-orbital in Ga, atomic radius of Ga is smaller than that of Al.

Thus, Ga < Al < In < Tl.

3. ***(b,c)***

(a) Boron metal reacts with NH_3 to form various compounds. But boron is an element not a compound

$$B + NH_3 \longrightarrow BN + H_2$$

(b) Hydrides of boron react with hydride of N to give boron nitrides and hydrogen gas is released.

$$B_2H_6 + 2NH_3 \longrightarrow 2BN + 6H_2\uparrow$$

(c) Oxides of boron react with hydride of nitrogen to form boron nitride and eliminate water.

$$B_2O_3 + 2NH_3 \longrightarrow 2BN + 3H_2O$$

(d) HBF_4 is fluoroboric acid. It reacts with basic ammonia to form ammonium fluoroborate salt.

$$HBF_4 + NH_3 \longrightarrow NH_4BF_4$$

Ammonium fluoroborate

So, options (b) and (c) are correct.

4. ***(a,b,d)***

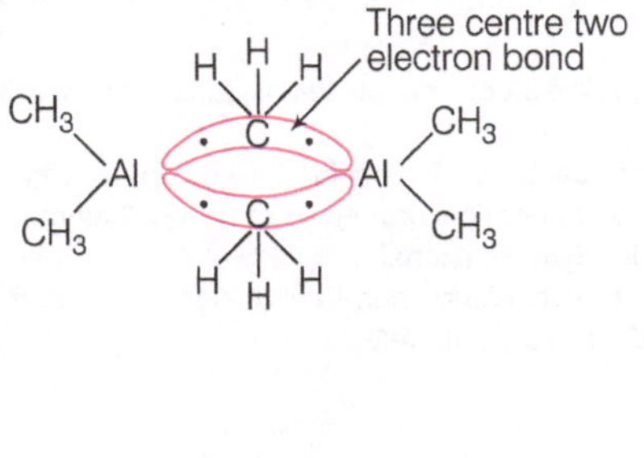

(b) BCl_3 is stronger Lewis acid than $AlCl_3$ due to greater extent of $p\pi - p\pi$ back bonding in $AlCl_3$.

(c)

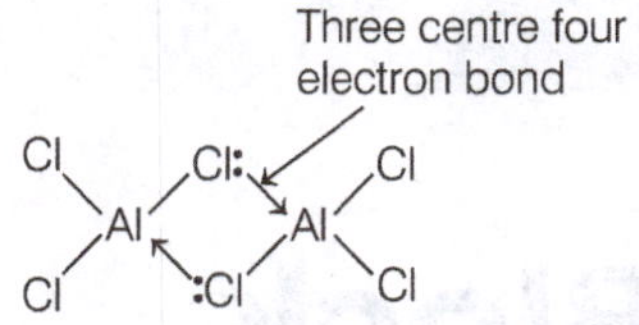

(d)

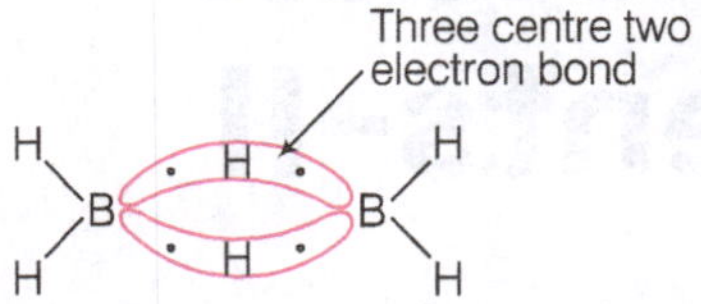

5. ***(a,c,d)*** $Na_2B_4O_7\cdot10H_2O$ (borax) is actually made of two tetrahedral and two triangular units, and is actually written as $Na_2[B_4O_5(OH)_4]\cdot5H_2O$.

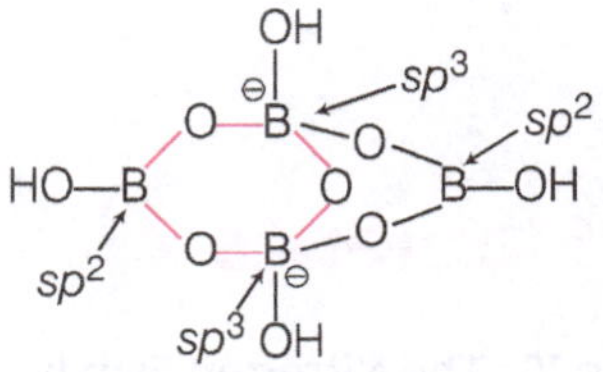

Thus, statement (a) is correct.

Boron atoms are in different planes thus, (b) is incorrect.

Two sp^2 and two sp^3-hybridised B atoms thus, (c) is correct.

Each boron has one — OH group thus, (d) is correct.

6. ***(6)*** $B_2H_6 + 6CH_3OH \longrightarrow 2[B(OCH_3)_3] + 6H_2$

Therefore, from 3 moles of B_2H_6, 6 moles of $B(OCH_3)_3$ will be formed.

7. ***(a,b)***

(a) Sn^{2+} of stannous chloride dihydrate ($SnCl_2\cdot2H_2O$) tends to convert into Sn^{4+}.

Hence, statement (a) is correct.

(b) SnO_2 reacts with KOH and gives $K_2SnO_3\cdot3H_2O$ or $K_2[Sn(OH)_6]$ because it is amphoteric in nature.

$$SnO_2 + 2KOH \longrightarrow K_2SnO_3 + H_2O$$

or $K_2[Sn(OH)_6]$

Hence, statement (b) is correct.

(c) In conc. HCl, $PbCl_2$ exists as chloroplumbic acid, $H_2[PbCl_6]$

$$\overset{II}{Pb}Cl_2 + 2HCl \longrightarrow H_2[\overset{IV}{Pb}Cl_6]$$

Hence, statement (c) is incorrect.

(d) The reaction of Pb_3O_4 with hot dil. HNO_3 is as follows

$$Pb_3O_4 + 4HNO_3 \longrightarrow 2\overset{+2}{Pb}(NO_3)_2 + \overset{+4}{Pb}O_2 + 2H_2O$$

It is not a redox reaction. Thus, the statement (d) is incorrect.

CHAPTER 6

p-Block Elements-II

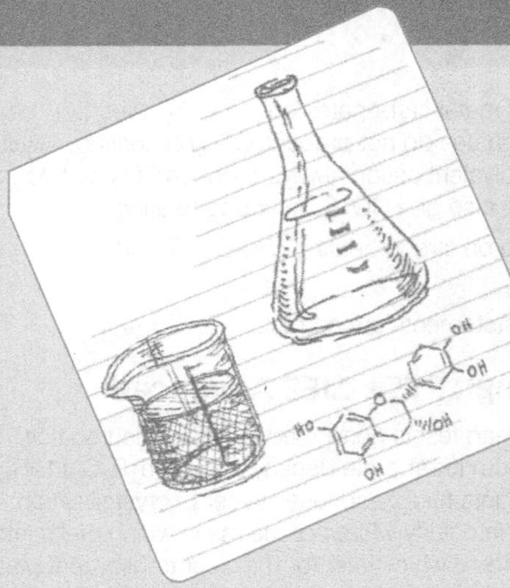

Learning Elements

Element 1 Group 15 : The Nitrogen Family and their Compounds

General and Physical Properties, Chemical Properties, Anomalous Behaviour of Nitrogen, Nitrogen (N_2), Oxides of Nitrogen, Phosphorus, Allotropic forms of Phosphorus, Compounds of Phosphorus, Oxoacids of Phosphorus

Element 2 Group 16 : The Oxygen Family and their Compounds

General and Physical Properties, Chemical Properties, Anomalous Behaviour of Oxygen, Dioxygen/Oxygen (O_2), Ozone (O_3), Sulphur, Oxides of Sulphur, Oxoacids

Element 3 Group 17 : The Halogen Family and their Compounds

General and Physical Properties, Chemical Properties, Anomalus Behaviour of Fluorine, Study of Halogens (X_2), Compounds of Group 17 Elements, Oxides of Chlorine, Oxo-Acids of Chlorine, Interhalogen Compounds, Polyhalides and Polyhalonium Ions, Pseudohalogens and Pseudohalides

Element 4 Group 18 : The Noble Gases and their Compounds

Occurrence, General and Physical Properties, Study of Compounds of Group 18, Xenon Oxides, Uses of Noble Gases

Practice Elements

Practice Element 1 Target JEE Main
Practice Element 2 Target JEE Advanced

Trend Insights

JEE Main

	2024				2023				2022			
Topics	**E**	**M**	**T**	**O**	**E**	**M**	**T**	**O**	**E**	**M**	**T**	**O**
Group 15 : The Nitrogen Family and their Compounds	0	5	2	7	0	2	2	4	4	8	6	18
Group 16 : The Oxygen Family and their Compounds	1	2	0	3	0	1	0	1	1	2	1	4
Group 17 : The Halogen Family and their Compounds	0	4	1	5	4	2	1	7	0	3	3	6
Group 18 : The Noble Gases and their Compounds	0	1	0	1	0	2	1	3	0	1	1	2

E = Easy, **M** = Medium, **T** = Tough, **O** = Overall

Current Dynamics

- Questions from acidic strength, thermal stability and oxidation numbers of HClO, $HClO_2$, $HClO_3$ and $HClO_4$ had been asked in past years.
- Recent exams had asked questions on the synthesis, structure and bonding of interhalogen compounds.
- Questions based on properties, preparation of group 15, 16 ,17 and 18 had been asked majorly.

JEE Advanced

Typology	Years				
	2024	**2023**	**2022**	**2021**	**2020**
1. Simple MCQs	2	–	1	–	–
2. One or More than one correct	1	–	1	1	1
3. Numerical/Integer Value	–	1	–	1	–
4. Matching Type	–	1	–	–	–
5. Paragraph Based	–	–	–	–	–

Current Dynamics

- Question based on chemical reactions of group 15 elements were asked in previous years.
- Questions based on structure of compounds of group 16 elements were also asked.
- In present scenario 1-2 questions have been asked from this chapter.

Insightful Advice

- Focus on periodic trends like electronegativity, oxidation states and atomic/ionic sizes.
- Practice the preparation reactions of oxoacids, interhalogen compounds and noble gas compounds and chemical properties of group 15 elements as more questions were asked in JEE Main exams.
- Pay attention on calculating oxidation numbers of elements in complex compounds like $H_2S_2O_8$, $HClO_4$, and XeO_3.

Element 1

Group-15 : The Nitrogen Family and Their Compounds

Group 15 contains six elements namely **nitrogen** (N), **phosphorus** (P), **arsenic** (As), **antimony** (Sb), **bismuth** (Bi) and **moscovium** (Mc). These elements in the periodic table are collectively known as pnictogens.

General and Physical Properties

The trends of general and physical properties of group 15 elements are given below

Electronic Configuration

The general electronic configuration is ns^2np^3 where n represents principal quantum number whose value varies from to 2 to 7. Electronic configuration of each element of group 15 elements are given below.

Electronic Configurations of Group 15 Elements

Element	Atomic number	Electronic configuration
Nitrogen (N)	7	[He] $2s^2 2p^3$
Phosphorus (P)	15	[Ne] $3s^2 3p^3$
Arsenic (As)	33	[Ar] $3d^{10} 4s^2 4p^3$
Antimony (Sb)	51	[Kr] $4d^{10} 5s^2 5p^3$
Bismuth (Bi)	83	[Xe] $4f^{14} 5d^{10} 6s^2 6p^3$
Moscovium (Mc)	115	[Rn] $5f^{14} 6d^{10} 7s^2 7p^3$

Atomic and Ionic Radii

It increases on moving down the group due to addition of new electron shells in each successive element.

The atomic radii of elements of group 15 are less than that of corresponding elements of group 14 due to increase in effective nuclear charge on moving from left to right in a period.

Ionisation Enthalpy

The ionisation enthalpies of the elements of group 15 are much higher than the corresponding elements of group 14 because of half-filled stability of np^3 subshell of respective group 15 elements. The ionisation values of elements decreases down the group due to gradual increase in atomic size.

The order of ionisation energy is N > P > As > Sb > Bi

Electronegativity

The elements of this group are more electronegative than group 14 elements. Down the group, the electronegativity decreases.

Elements	N	P	As	Sb	Bi
Electronegativity	3.0	2.1	2.0	1.9	1.9

Metallic Character

The metallic character of elements increases down the group. First two elements nitrogen (N) and phosphorus (P) are non-metals, arsenic (As) and antimony (Sb) are metalloid bismuth (Bi) and moscovium (Mc) are metals.

Melting and Boiling Points

The melting points of group 15 elements first increase from nitrogen to arsenic and then decrease to antimony and bismuth. The boiling point however increases regularly from nitrogen to bismuth.

JEE Spotlite

- The unexpected decrease in the melting points of antimony and bismuth is because of their tendency to form three covalent bonds instead of five covalent bonds due to inert pair effect. This results in weakening the attraction among their atoms thus lowering their melting points.
- Except Bismuth, all the members show catenation property. Phosphorus has maximum tendency to form cyclic as well as open chain compounds.
- Nitrogen because of its small size and high electronegativity forms $p\pi$ - $p\pi$ orbital multiple bonds with itself and with other elements.

Oxidation State

The elements of group 15 have five valence electrons. Thus, the element of this group exhibits +3 and +5 oxidation states. Down the group, the stability of +3 oxidation state increases while that of +5 decreases due to **inert pair effect**.

N and P also show oxidation states of –2 and –3 in hydrazine (NH_2NH_2), NH_3 and diphosphine (PH_2PH_2), PH_3 respectively. Nitrogen also shows an oxidation state –1 in hydroxylamine (NH_2OH) but phosphorous does not. All the oxidation state of nitrogen from +1 to +4 tend to disproportionate in acid solution.

Chemical Properties

The trend of chemical properties of group 15 elements are given below.

Reactivity Towards Hydrogen

Elements of group 15 reacts to form volatile trihydrides of the formula MH_3 where M = N, P, As, Sb and Bi.

All the hydrides of this group have pyramidal shape.

These hydrides are prepared from binary metal compounds like Mg_3N_2, Ca_3P_2, Zn_3As_2 etc. by the action of not water or dilute acids.

$$Mg_3N_2 + 6H_2O \longrightarrow 3Mg(OH)_2 + 2NH_3$$
$$Zn_3As_2 + 6HCl \longrightarrow 3ZnCl_2 + 2AsH_3$$

1. Melting and Boiling Points

The melting point of the trihydrides follows the trend as

$$PH_3 < AsH_3 < SbH_3 < BiH_3 < NH_3$$

As molecular mass increases, melting point also increases. So, melting point of BiH_3, should be maximum, as it has maximum molecular mass. The melting point of NH_3 is maximum although it has minimum molecular mass. The reason of this abonormality is strong hydrogen bonding between NH_3 molecules while other group 15 halides primarily experience weak van der waals forces. Thus, ammonia shows maximum melting point while, the other group 15 hydrides show melting point according to their molecular masses.

The boiling point of these trihydrides follow the trend as

$$PH_3 < AsH_3 < NH_3 < SbH_3 < BiH_3$$

The boiling point of NH_3 is slightly lower than those of BiH_3 and SbH_3 due to their high molecular mass as compared to that of NH_3. The increased molecular masses of BiH_3 and SbH_3 increases the **van der Waals** forces of attraction in liquid state.

2. Thermal Stability

The thermal stability of trihydrides decreases on moving from NH_3 to BiH_3. The decrease in thermal stability can be explained by increase in size of central atom which leads to decrease the strength of M—H bond. Thus, the order of thermal stability is

$$NH_3 > PH_3 > AsH_3 > SbH_3 > BiH_3.$$

3. Reducing Behaviour

The reducing behaviour depends on the stability of the hydrides. The lower the stability, greater is its reducing property.

Except NH_3, all the hydrides are strong reducing agents.

4. Bond Angles

The variation in bond angles may be explained on the basis of size and electronegativity of central atom.

On moving down the group, the size of central atom increases and electronegativity decreases. So, the location of bond pairs of electrons shifts more and more away from the central atom as we go from NH_3 to SbH_3.

Due to such a shifting, the repulsion between bond pair of electrons decreases owing to which bond angle also decreases.

Thus, the order will be,

$$\underset{107.8^\circ}{NH_3} > \underset{93.6^\circ}{PH_3} > \underset{91.8^\circ}{AsH_3} > \underset{91.3^\circ}{SbH_3}$$

5. Basic Nature

All these hydrides behave as Lewis bases because the central atom possess a lone pair of electrons.

As the size of central atom increases, the electron density on central atom decreases and consequently its tendency to donate a pair of electrons decreases. Hence, the basic character decreases in order as

$$NH_3 > PH_3 > AsH_3 > SbH_3 > BiH_3$$

6. Solubility

Because of tendency towards hydrogen bonding with water molecules, ammonia is soluble in water while PH_3 and other hydrides are insoluble in water.

Solved Booster 6.1

Consider the following reactions

$$NCl_3 + LiAlH_4 \longrightarrow X + LiCl + AlH_3$$
$$Zn_3As_2 + HCl \longrightarrow Y + ZnCl_2$$
$$Ca_3P_2 + H_2O \longrightarrow Z + Ca(OH)_2$$

The correct statements regarding these reactions are

(a) Y has higher boiling point than X.
(b) The correct order of reducing behaviour of products X, Y and Z is $X < Z < Y$.
(c) Bond angle of Z is greater than Y.
(d) Order of thermal stability is $Y > Z > X$.

Solution *(b, c)*

Among the given statements only (b) and (c) are correct. The corrected forms of incorrect statements are

$$NCl_3 + 3LiAlH_4 \longrightarrow \underset{(X)}{NH_3} + 3LiCl + 3AlH_3$$

$$Zn_3As_2 + 6HCl \longrightarrow 3ZnCl_2 + \underset{(Y)}{2AsH_3}$$

$$Ca_3P_2 + 6H_2O \longrightarrow 3Ca(OH)_2 + \underset{(Z)}{2PH_3}$$

(a) Boiling point of *X* i.e., NH_3 is higher than *Y* i.e., AsH_3.
The abnormally high boiling point of NH_3 is due to the presence of intermolecular H-bonding in NH_3.

(d) The correct order of thermal stability is $X > Z > Y$
The decrease in thermal stability is explained by increase in size of central atom. Due to such increase, the tendency to form stable covalent bond with comparatively small H-atom decreases.

Reactivity Towards Oxygen (Oxide Formation)

Nitrogen due to its small size has a strong tendency to form $p\pi$-$p\pi$ multiple bonds between N and O atoms, while other elements of group do not. Consequently, N forms a number of oxides which have no P, As, Sb or Bi analogues.

Oxides of Group 15 Elements

Nitrogen forms a number of oxides, phosphorus forms P_4O_6, P_4O_8 and P_4O_{10} while other members form oxides of type R_2O_3 and R_2O_5.

Different Oxides of Group 15 Elements

Oxidation state	N	P	As	Sb	Bi
+1	N_2O	—	—	—	—
+2	NO	—	—	—	—
+3	N_2O_3	P_4O_6	As_2O_3	Sb_2O_3	Bi_2O_3
+4	N_2O_4	P_4O_8	—	—	—
+5	N_2O_5	P_4O_{10}	As_2O_5	Sb_2O_5	Bi_2O_5

Properties of Oxides

- The trioxides of nitrogen and phosphorus are acidic; the trioxides of As and Sb are **amphoteric** while that of Bi is **basic** in nature. This is because on moving down the group, metallic character increases, and metal oxides are more basic than the non-metal oxides.
- However, the pentoxides are acidic in all the cases. Their acidic nature decreases down the group. All the pentoxides (except P_2O_5) can readily lose oxygen to form lower oxides.
- Thus, they act as **strong oxidising agents**. The stability of pentaoxides follows the order

$$P_2O_5 > As_2O_5 > Sb_2O_5 > N_2O_5 > Bi_2O_5$$

Reactivity Towards Halogens

Group 15 elements react to form two series of halides, RX_3 and RX_5.

Trihalides

Some important characteristics of these trihalides are as follows

(i) **Structure** These have pyramidal structure in which the central atom is sp^3 hybridised.

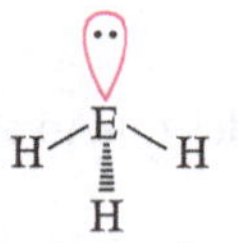
(E=N, P, As, Sb)

JEE Spotlite

- The bond angle of the trihalides of an element increases with the decrease in electronegativity of the halogen atom and increase in the size of the halogen atom.

$$PF_3 < PCl_3 < PBr_3 < PI_3$$

- Bond angle 98.5° 100° 101.5° 102°
With the decrease in the electronegativity of the halogen atom, bond pairs remain more close to the central atom and hence *bp-bp* repulsion increases and bond angle increases.

(ii) **Ionic character** These trihalides are mostly covalent and their ionic character increases on moving down the group, (i.e. trihalides of Bi are ionic in nature).

(iii) **Hydrolysis** The trihalides, particularly the chlorides, are readily hydrolysed. However, the products of hydrolysis differ in different cases. e.g.

If trihalides are completely hydrolysed

$$PCl_3 + 3H_2O \longrightarrow H_3PO_3 + 3HCl$$
$$NCl_3 + 3H_2O \longrightarrow NH_3 + 3HClO$$
$$2AsCl_3 + 3H_2O \longrightarrow 2H_3AsO_3 + 6HCl$$

If partially hydrolysed,

$$SbCl_3 + H_2O \rightleftharpoons SbOCl + 2HCl$$
$$BiCl_3 + H_2O \rightleftharpoons BiOCl + 2HCl$$

The ease of hydrolysis of trihalides (for same halogens) decreases in the order as

$$NCl_3 > PCl_3 > AsCl_3 > SbCl_3 > BiCl_3$$

NF_3 and PF_3 do not undergo hydrolysis.

(iv) **Stability** Trihalides of N are least stable as compared to trihalide of other elements of this group. This is because their is a large difference in the size of N and *X* atoms. This results in the weakening of N—*X* bond. However, NF_3 is stable because size difference in N and F is small.

(v) **Acidic character** The trihalides of P, As and Sb, especially fluorides and chlorides, are Lewis acids. Thus, the order will be

$$NX_3 < PX_3 < AsX_3 < SbX_3$$
$$PF_3 + F_2 \longrightarrow PF_5$$
$$SbF_3 + 2F^- \longrightarrow [SbF_5]^{2-}$$
$$SbCl_3 + 2Cl^- \longrightarrow [SbCl_5]^{2-}$$

(vi) **Basic character** The order of basic character of trihalides of nitrogen is

$$NI_3 > NBr_3 > NCl_3 > NF_3$$

Except NF_3, all other trihalides of nitrogen are unstable. They decompose with explosive sound.

Pentahalides

Nitrogen does not form pentahalides due to absence of vacant *d* orbitals while other form.

The pentahalides of P (except PCl_5) are not stable. Pentahalides are thermally less stable than corresponding trihalides. Therefore, PCl_5 decomposes to give PCl_3 and Cl_2.

Structure In gaseous phase, PX_5 are covalent and have trigonal bipyramidal structure with sp^3d hybridisation of P.

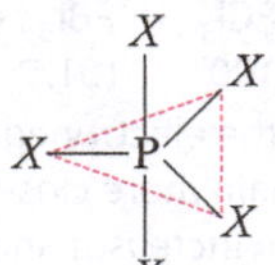

Anomalous Behaviour of Nitrogen

Nitrogen, shows many properties that are quite different from other members of the group due to :

- small size
- high electronegativity
- high ionisation energy
- non-availability of *d*-orbitals
- capacity of $p\pi$-$p\pi$ multiple bond formation.

These properties are as follows,

(i) It is found in a gas while other members are found in solid state.

(ii) It exists in diatomic form (N_2) while other elements like phosphorus, arsenic and antimony exist as tetra-atomic molecules (P_4, As_4, Sb_4).

(iii) It forms trinegative ion, i.e. N^{3-}, while other members do not form, except P (P^{3-}).

(iv) It is chemically inert under ordinary conditions due to high bond dissociation energy. While other members are quite reactive because of the presence of single bonds in their molecules.

(v) It does not show pentacovalency due to non-availability of *d*-orbitals while it is shown by all other elements.

(vi) The hydride of nitrogen (NH_3) is highly basic in nature while the hydrides of other elements are slightly basic. Moreover, only hydrides of nitrogen show H-bonding while other members do not.

(vii) It forms oxides of five types (i.e. N_2O, NO, N_2O_3, N_2O_4 and N_2O_5) while other members of this family form oxides of only two types (i.e. tri and pentaoxides).

(viii) Except NF_3, other halides of nitrogen i.e. NCl_3, NBr_3 and NI_3 are unstable while the halides of other elements are fairly stable with anions.

(ix) It does not form complexes with anions due to the non- availability of *d*-orbitals while other members have a tendency of complex formation, e.g. $[PCl_6]^-$, $[AsCl_6]^-$ etc.

Nitrogen (N)

Nitrogen is widely distributed in nature both in free as well as in the combined state. Air is the most abundant source of free nitrogen. It forms 75% by mass and 78% by volume of the air. In combined state, it is found as nitrates such as Chile saltpetre ($NaNO_3$), Indian saltpetre (KNO_3) and ammonium compounds.

1. Dinitrogen (N_2)

Nitrogen exists as a diatomic gas, N_2 in the elemental state.

Preparation

Nitrogen can be obtained from the following two sources :

(i) **Nitrogen Compounds**

- Nitrogen in the laboratory can be obtained by heating ammonium nitrite or ammonium dichromate.

$$NH_4Cl(aq) + NaNO_2(aq) \longrightarrow N_2(g) + 2H_2O(l) + NaCl(aq)$$

$$(NH_4)_2Cr_2O_7 \longrightarrow N_2 + Cr_2O_3 + 4H_2O$$

Nitrogen is collected by downward displacement of water.

- Pure nitrogen can be obtained by passing the ammonia vapours over heated CuO.

$$2NH_3 + 3CuO \longrightarrow N_2 + 3Cu + 3H_2O$$

- It can be obtained by the action of nitrous acid (or $NaNO_2$ and dil. H_2SO_4) on urea.

$$\underset{\text{Urea}}{NH_2CONH_2} + 2HNO_2 \longrightarrow 2N_2 + CO_2 + 3H_2O$$

- Pure nitrogen is obtained in small amounts by heating sodium or barium azides in vacuum.

$$\underset{\text{Barium azide}}{Ba(N_3)_2} \longrightarrow 3N_2 + Ba$$

(ii) **From Air**

- Dinitrogen is commercially prepared by the liquification and fractional distillation of air.
- Liquid dinitrogen (b.p. 77.2 K) distills out first leaving behind liquid oxygen (b.p. 90 K).

Physical Properties

(i) It is a colourless. tasteless and odourless gas. It is slightly lighter than air as its vapour density is 14.0. It is sparingly soluble in water.

(ii) It can be liquefied to a colourless liquid (b.pt. –195.8°C).

(iii) It does not help in combustion. Nitrogen itself is non-combustible.

(iv) It is chemically inert under ordinary conditions. However, it shows chemical activity under high temperature.

Chemical Properties

(i) Nitrogen combines with oxygen under the influence of very high temperature like electric spark.

$$N_2(g) + O_2(g) \xrightleftharpoons{2000\text{ K}} 2NO(g) \text{ (Nitric oxide)}$$

(ii) Nitrogen combines with hydrogen in the presence of a catalyst (finely divided iron) at 200 atmospheres and 400-500°C temperature.

$$N_2(g) + 3H_2(g) \rightleftharpoons 2NH_3(g) \text{ (Ammonia)}$$

(ii) Nitrogen combines with metals at red heat to form nitrides.

$$6Li + N_2 \xrightarrow{450°C} 2Li_3N \text{ (Lithium nitride)}$$

$$3Mg + N_2 \xrightarrow{450°C} Mg_3N_2 \text{ (Magnesium nitride)}$$

$$2Al + N_2 \xrightarrow{800°C} 2AlN \text{ (Aluminium nitride)}$$

Non-metals like boron, silicon at bright red heat also combine with nitrogen.

$$2B + N_2 \longrightarrow 2BN \text{ (Boron nitride)}$$

$$3Si + 2N_2 \longrightarrow Si_3N_4 \text{ (Silicon nitride)}$$

(iv) Nitrogen combines with calcium carbide to form calcium cyanamide at 1000°C.

$$CaC_2 + N_2 \longrightarrow CaCN_2 + C$$

The mixture of calcium cyanamide and carbon is known as nitrolim, a fertilizer.

2. Active Nitrogen (N)

When an electric discharge is allowed to pass through nitrogen under very low pressure (about 2 mm), a brilliant luminescence is observed which persists for sometime after the stoppage of the discharge.

It is observed that nitrogen after the discharge is more active. This nitrogen is termed active nitrogen. It decomposes many organic compounds.

$$HC \equiv CH + \underset{\text{Active nitrogen}}{2N} \longrightarrow \underset{\text{Cyanogen gas}}{N \equiv C—C \equiv N} + H_2$$

Uses

Nitrogen is used

(i) for filling electric lamps.

(ii) to dilute the action of oxygen in air.

(iii) to provide inert atmosphere in certain metallurgical operations

(vi) in the packets of foodstuffs.

(v) for the manufacture of certain chemicals like NH_3, HNO_3, calcium cyanamide and other nitrogen containing compound.

3. Ammonia (NH_3)

It the most important hydride of nitrogen.

Occurrence

NH_3 is found in traces in atmopshere, Ammonium salts such as ammonium chloride and ammonium sulphate that are found in small amounts in the soil.

Preparation

(i) Ammonia is obtained on a small scale from ammonium salts which evolve it when heated with caustic soda or lime.

$$NH_4Cl + NaOH \longrightarrow NH_3 + NaCl + H_2O$$

(Laboratory Preparation)

$$2NH_4Cl + \underset{\text{(slaked lime)}}{Ca(OH)_2} \longrightarrow 2NH_3 + CaCl_2 + 2H_2O$$

(ii) Ammonia is formed when ammonium chloride is heated with litharge.

$$2NH_4Cl + PbO \longrightarrow 2NH_3 + PbCl_2 + H_2O$$

(iii) By reacting nitrides with water, ammonia is obtained.

$$AlN + 3H_2O \longrightarrow Al(OH)_3 + NH_3$$

$$Mg_3N_2 + 6H_2O \longrightarrow 3Mg(OH)_2 + 2NH_3$$

(iv) Ammonia can also be formed by doing reduction of nitrates and nitrites with zinc and caustic soda. Zinc and caustic soda produce nascent hydrogen which reacts with nitrates and nitrites to form ammonia.

$$NaNO_3 + 8H \xrightarrow{Zn/NaOH} NaOH + NH_3 + 2H_2O$$

$$NaNO_2 + 6H \xrightarrow{Zn/NaOH} NaOH + NH_3 + H_2O$$

(v) Ammonia is also obtained by heating ammonium compounds.

$$\underset{\text{Ammonium sulphate}}{(NH_4)_2SO_4} \xrightarrow{\text{Heat}} NH_3 + \underset{\text{Ammonium hydrogen sulphate}}{NH_4HSO_4}$$

$$\underset{\text{Ammonium dihydrogen phosphate}}{NH_4H_2/PO_4} \xrightarrow{\text{Heat}} NH_3 + \underset{\text{Metaphosphoric acid}}{HPO_3} + H_2O$$

(vi) Urea on treatment with caustic soda forms ammonia.

$$\underset{\text{Urea}}{NH_2CONH_2} + 2NaOH \longrightarrow Na_2CO_3 + 2NH_3$$

> **JEE Alert**
>
> The common dehydrating agents like conc. sulphuric acid or anhyd. $CaCl_2$ or P_2O_5 cannot be used to prepare ammonia. As these react with ammonia to give another compounds. Quick lime (CaO) is the suitable dehydrating agent.

(vii) **Haber's process** The method involves the direct combination of nitrogen and hydrogen according to the following reaction:

$$N_2(g) + 3H_2(g) \xrightleftharpoons{\text{Fe, 200 atm, 700 K}} 2NH_3(g);$$

$$\Delta_f H° = -46.1 \text{ kJ mol}^{-1}$$

(viii) Raw materials, H_2 is obtained by Bosch process and N_2 is obtained fractional distillation of liquid air.

(ix) **Cyanamide process**

$$CaCN_2 + \underset{(steam)}{3H_2O} \xrightarrow[3\text{-}4\ atm]{180°C} CaCO_3 + 2NH_3$$

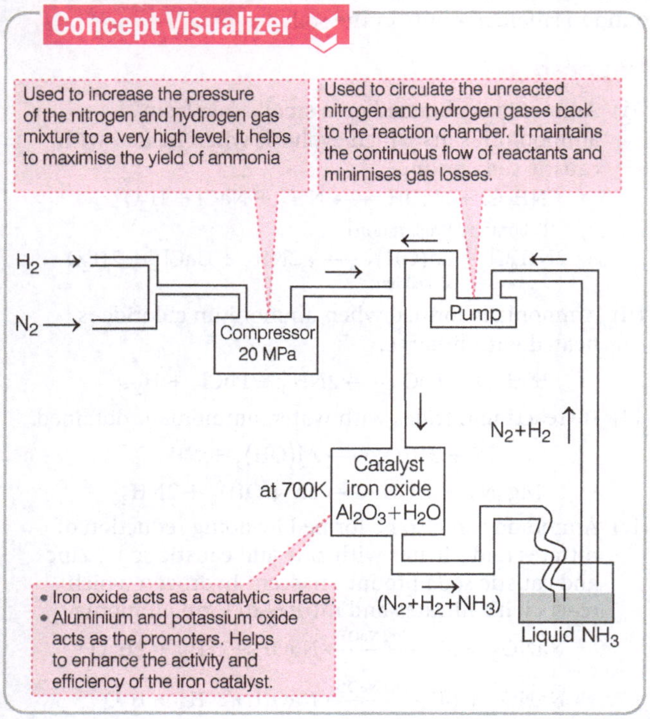

Physical Properties

(i) Ammonia is a colourless gas with a characterstic pungent odour. It brings tears to the eyes.

(ii) It is highly soluble in water. This high solubility is due to the hydrogen bonding. The solubility of ammonia increases with increase with solvent H_2O molecules of pressure and decreases of temperature.

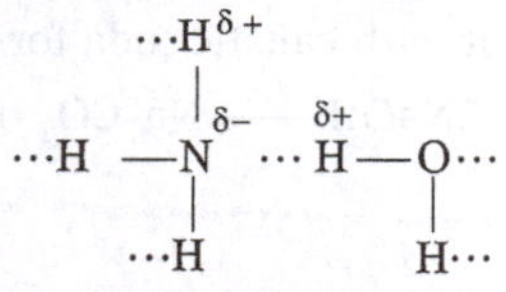

(iii) It can be easily liquefied at room temperature by the application of pressure.

(iv) Ammonia molecules link together to form associated molecules through hydrogen bonding.

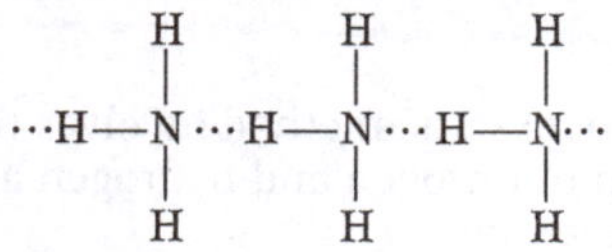

Higher melting point and boiling point of NH_3 in comparison to other hydrides of group are due to hydrogen bonding.

Chemical Properties

(i) **Stability** It is highly stable. It decomposes into nitrogen and hydrogen at red heat or when electric sparks are passed through it.

$$2NH_3 \rightleftharpoons N_2 + 3H_2$$

(ii) **Combustion** Ordinary ammonia is neither combustible nor a supporter of combustion. However, it burns in tbe presence of oxygen to form nitrogen and water.

$$4NH_3 + 3O_2 \longrightarrow 2N_2 + 6H_2O$$

The restricted oxidation of NH_3 can be done with air, when the mixture is passed over heated platinum gauze at 700-800°C.

$$4NH_3 + 5O_2 \xrightarrow{Pt/Rh} 4NO + 6H_2O$$

This is the Ostwald's process and used for the manufacturing of HNO_3.

(iii) **Basic Nature** Ammonia is a Lewis base, accepting proton to form ammonium ion as it has tendency to donate an electron pair.

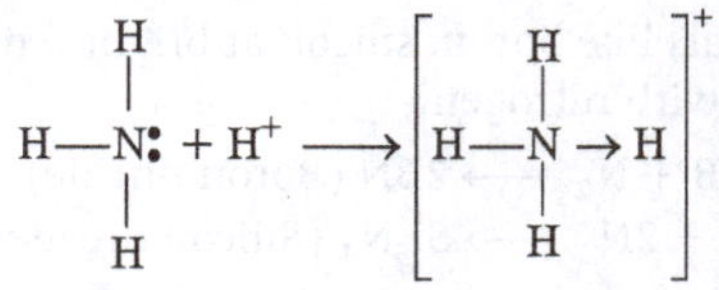

It forms salts with acids.

$$NH_3 + HCl \longrightarrow \underset{\text{Thick white fumes}}{NH_4Cl} \quad \text{(Ammonium chloride)}$$

$$2NH_3 + H_2SO_4 \longrightarrow (NH_4)_2SO_4 \text{ (Ammonium sulphate)}$$

Its aqueous solution is weakly basic due to the formation of OH^- ions.

$$NH_3 + H_2O \longrightarrow NH_4OH \rightleftharpoons NH_4^+ + OH^-$$

The solution turns red litmus to blue and phenolphthalein pink.

(iv) **Oxidation** It is oxidised to nitrogen when passed over heated CuO or PbO.

$$3CuO + 2NH_3 \longrightarrow 3Cu + N_2 + 3H_2O$$

$$3PbO + 2NH_3 \longrightarrow 3Pb + N_2 + 3H_2O$$

Both chlorine and bromine oxidise ammonia.

$$\underset{(excess)}{9NH_3} + 3Cl_2 \longrightarrow N_2 + 6NH_4Cl$$

When chlorine is in excess an explosive substance nitrogen trichloride is formed.

$$NH_3 + \underset{(excess)}{3Cl_2} \longrightarrow NCl_3 + 3HCl$$

Iodine flakes when rubbed with liquor ammonia form a dark brown precipitate of ammoniated nitrogen tri iodide which explodes readily on drying.

$$2NH_3 + 3I_2 \longrightarrow NH_3 \cdot NI_3 + 3HI$$

Hypochlorites and hypobromites oxidise ammonia to nitrogen.

$$2NH_3 + 3NaClO \longrightarrow N_2 + 3NaCl + 3H_2O$$

The oxidation of ammonia with bleaching powder occurs on warming.

$$3Ca(OCl)_2 + 2NH_3 \longrightarrow 3CaCl_2 + N_2 + 3H_2O$$

Thus, ammonia acts as a reducing agent.

(v) **Formation of Amides** When dry ammonia is passed over heated sodium or potassium, amides are formed with evolution of hydrogen.

$$2Na + 2NH_3 \longrightarrow \underset{\text{Sodamide}}{2NaNH_2} + H_2$$

(vi) **Reactions with Heavy Metal Salt Solutions** Many metal hydroxides are formed which may be precipitated or remain dissolved in the form of complex compound in excess of NH_4OH.

$$FeCl_3 + 3NH_4OH \longrightarrow \underset{\text{Brown ppt.}}{Fe(OH)_3} + 3NH_4Cl$$

$$AlCl_3 + 3NH_4OH \longrightarrow \underset{\text{White ppt.}}{Al(OH)_3} + 3NH_4Cl$$

$$CrCl_3 + 3NH_4OH \longrightarrow \underset{\text{Green ppt.}}{Cr(OH)_3} + 3NH_4Cl$$

(vii) **Reaction with Nessler's Reagent** Alkaline solution of K_2HgI_4 is called Nessler's reagent.

This gives brown ppt. with NH_3 called iodide of Million's base.

$$2K_2HgI_4 + NH_3 + 3KOH \longrightarrow$$

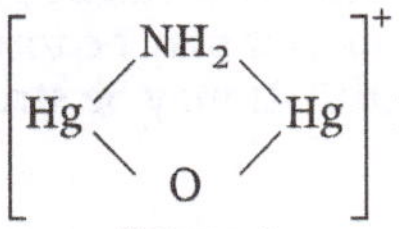

$I^- + 7KI + 2H_2O$

Brown ppt.

JEE Quicker

Oxygen is not present in Nessler's reagent

JEE Main 2023

- The chemical name of Nessler's reagent is potassium tetraiodidomercurate (II), $[K_2(HgI_4)]$. It is prepared by combining potassium iodide and mercuric chloride. It is used for confirmation test of NH_4^+ ion.

Uses

(i) Ammonia can be easily liquefied and transported safely in cylinders. Ammonia can be decomposed into hydrogen and nitrogen by passing over heated metallic catalyst. Thus, ammonia is the source for the production of hydrogen at any destination.

(ii) Ammonia is also used in the manufacture of urea which is an excellent fertilizer of nitrogen.

4. Nitric Acid, HNO_3

It was named aqua fortis (means strong water) by all chemists.

Preparation

(i) **Laboratory Method**

$$KNO_3 + \text{conc.}\, H_2SO_4 \longrightarrow KHSO_4 + HNO_3(\text{vap})$$

The vapours of nitric acid evolved are condensed in a glass receiver.

(ii) **On Commercial Scale**

Birkeland Eyde Process or Arc Process

Step 1 $N_2 + O_2 \xrightarrow[\text{Electric Arc}]{3000°C} 2NO$ - heat

Step 2 $2NO + O_2 \longrightarrow 2NO_2$

Step 3 $2NO_2 + H_2O + O_2 \longrightarrow HNO_3$

Ostwald's Process

Step 1 $4NH_3 + 5O_2 \xrightarrow[\text{500 K, 9 bar}]{\text{Pt. gauze}} 4NO + 6H_2O + \text{Heat}$

Step 2 $2NO + O_2 \longrightarrow 2NO_2$

Step 3 $3NO_2(g) + H_2O(l) \longrightarrow 2HNO_3(aq) + NO(g)$

Physical Properties

Nitric acid usually acquires yellow colour due to its decomposition by sunlight into NO_2.

$$4HNO_3 \xrightarrow{\text{Sunlight}} 4NO_2 + 2H_2O + O_2$$

The yellow colour of the acid can be removed by warming it to 60-80°C and bubbling dry air through it. It has extremely corrosive action on the skin and causes painful sores.

Chemical Properties

(i) **Acidic Nature** It is very strong acid. It exhibits usual properties of acids. It reacts with basic oxides, carbonates, bicarbonates and hydroxides forming corresponding salts.

$$CaO + 2HNO_3 \longrightarrow Ca(NO_3)_2 + H_2O$$

$$Na_2CO_3 + 2HNO_3 \longrightarrow 2NaNO_3 + H_2O + CO_2$$

$$NaOH + HNO_3 \longrightarrow NaNO_3 + H_2O$$

(ii) **Oxidising Nature** Concentration nitric acid acts as a strong oxidising agent as it decomposes to give nascent oxygen easily.

$$2HNO_3 \longrightarrow H_2O + 2NO_2 + [O]$$

or $$2HNO_3 \longrightarrow H_2O + 2NO + 3[O]$$

(iii) **Oxidation of Non-metals** HNO_3 oxidises various non-metals to their corresponding highest oxyacids.

- Sulphur is oxidised to sulphuric acid

$$S + \underset{\text{conc. and hot}}{6HNO_3} \longrightarrow H_2SO_4 + 6NO_2 + 2H_2O$$

- Carbon is oxidised to carbonic acid

$$C + \underset{\text{conc. and hot}}{4HNO_3} \longrightarrow CO_2 + 4NO_2 + 2H_2O$$

- Phosphorus is oxidised to orthophosphoric acid.

$$2P + \underset{\text{conc. and hot}}{10HNO_3} \longrightarrow 2H_3PO_4 + 10NO_2 + 2H_2O$$

- Iodine is oxidised to iodic acid.

$$I_2 + \underset{\text{Conc. and hot}}{10HNO_3} \longrightarrow 2HIO_3 + 10NO_2 + 4H_2O$$

(iv) **Oxidation of Metalloids** Metalloids (like non-metals) also form highest oxyacids.

- Arsenic is oxidised to arsenic acid.

$$As + \underset{\text{conc. and hot}}{5HNO_3} \longrightarrow H_3AsO_4 + 5NO_2 + H_2O$$

- Antimony is oxidised to antimonic acid.

$$Sb + \underset{\text{conc. and hot}}{5HNO_3} \longrightarrow H_3SbO_4 + 5NO_2 + H_2O$$

- Tin is oxidised to *meta*-stannic acid.

$$Sn + \underset{\text{conc. and hot}}{4HNO_3} \longrightarrow H_2SnO_3 + 4NO_2 + H_2O$$

(v) **Oxidation of Compounds**

- Sulphur dioxide is oxidised to sulphuric acid.

$$SO_2 + \text{conc. } 2HNO_3 \longrightarrow H_2SO_4 + 2NO_2$$

- Hydrogen sulphide is oxidised to sulphur.

$$H_2S + \text{conc. } 2HNO_3 \longrightarrow 2NO_2 + 2H_2O + S$$

- Ferrous sulphate is oxidised to ferric sulphate in presence of H_2SO_4.

$$6FeSO_4 + 3H_2SO_4 + \text{dil. } 2HNO_3 \longrightarrow 3Fe_2(SO_4)_3 + 2NO + 4H_2O$$

- Iodine is liberated from KI.

$$6KI + \text{dil. } 8HNO_3 \longrightarrow 6KNO_3 + 2NO + 3I_2 + 4H_2O$$

- HBr, HI are oxidised to Br_2 and I_2, respectively.

$$2HBr + 2HNO_3 \longrightarrow Br_2 + 2NO_2 + 2H_2O$$

Similarly,

$$2HI + 2HNO_3 \longrightarrow I_2 + 2NO_2 + 2H_2O$$

- Ferrous sulphide is oxidised to ferrous sulphate

$$FeS + 8HNO_3 \longrightarrow FeSO_4 + 8NO_2 + 4H_2O$$

- Stannous chloride is oxidised to stannic chloride is presence of HCl.

$$7SnCl_2 + 14HCl + 3HNO_3 \longrightarrow 7SnCl_4 + NH_2OH + NH_4NO_3 + 5H_2O$$

- Cane sugar is oxidised to oxalic acid.

$$C_{12}H_{22}O_{11} + 36HNO_3 \longrightarrow 6(COOH)_2 + 36NO_2 + 23H_2O$$

(vi) **Action on Metals** Most of the metals except noble metals like gold and platinum are attacked by nitric acid. Nitric acid plays a double role in the action with metals, i.e, it acts as an acid as well as an oxidising agent.

The progress of the reaction is controlled by a number of factors:

- the nature of the metal.
- the concentration of the acid.
- the temperature of the reaction.
- the presence of other impurities.

Concentration of nitric acid	Metal	Main Products
Very dilute HNO_3 (6%), Cold	Mg, Mn	H_2 + Metal nitrate
	Fe, Zn, Sn	NH_4NO_3 + metal nitrate + H_2O
Dilute HNO_3 (50%), Cold	Pb, Cu, Ag, Hg	NO + metal nitrate + H_2O
	Fe, Zn	N_2O + metal nitrate + H_2O
	Sn	$NH_4NO_3 + Sn(NO_3)_2$
Conc. HNO_3 (70%), Hot	Zn, Fe, Pb, Cu, Ag	NO_2 + metal nitrate + H_2O
	Sn	$NO_2 + H_2SnO_3$ *metas*tannic acid

(viii) **Brown ring Test** The brown ring test for nitrates depends upon the ability of Fe^{2+} ions to reduce nitrate ions to nitric oxide which then reacts with Fe^{2+} ions to form brown coloured compounds.

$$NO_3^-(aq) + 3Fe^{2+} + 4H^+ \longrightarrow NO + 3Fe^2 + 2H_2O$$

$$[Fe(H_2O)_6]^{2+} + NO \longrightarrow [Fe(H_2O)_5(NO)]^{2+} + H_2O$$

(Finally, Fe as Fe (I) and NO as NO^+)

Structure

Nitric acid is a monobasic acid, i.e., the molecule consist of one hydroxyl group as it may be formed by the hydrolysis of nitryl chloride, NO_2Cl. It may be structurally represented as below

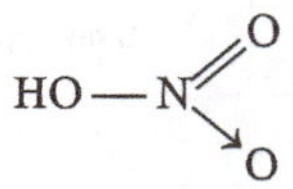

Gaseous nitric acid is a planar molecule. The bond lengths and bond angles as present in the molecule are represented in the figure:

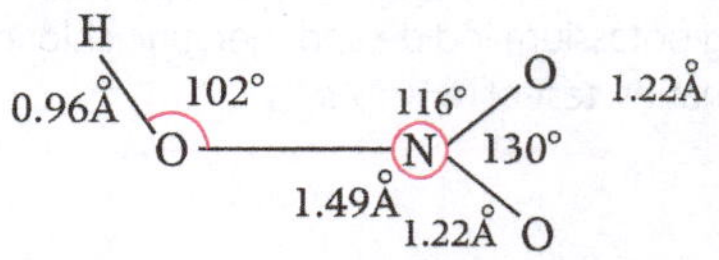

It is supposed to exist in two resonating forms,

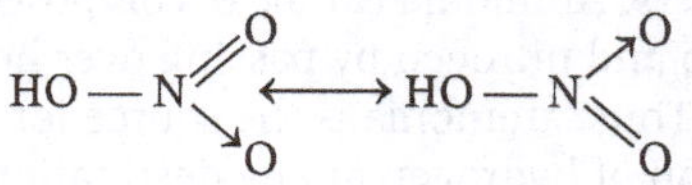

Uses

(i) Used in the manufacturing of ammonium nitrate for fertilizers and other nitrates for use in explosives and pyrotechnics.

(ii) Used in the preparation of explosives like niroglycerin, trinitrotoluene.

Oxides of Nitrogen

(N_2O_3 and N_2O_5 are Monomeric While other are Dimeric)

Nitrogen forms a number of oxides. The well known oxides of nitrogen are:

- Nitrous or Dinitrogen oxide, N_2O
- Nitric oxide or Nitrogen monoxide, NO
- Dinitrogen trioxide, N_2O_3
- Nitrogen dioxide or Dinitrogen tetroxide, NO_2 or N_2O_4
- Dinitrogen pentoxide, N_2O_5

1. Dinitrogen Oxide, N_2O

Structure N_2O is a linear molecule and has lower dipole moment. It is a colorless and neutral gas.

$$:N \equiv N \longrightarrow \ddot{\underset{\cdot\cdot}{O}}: \longleftrightarrow :\overset{-}{\ddot{N}} = \overset{+}{N} = \ddot{O}:$$

Preparation

It can be prepared by heating ammonium nitrate or a mixture of sodium nitrate and ammonium sulphate.

$$NH_4NO_3 \longrightarrow N_2O + 2H_2O$$

$$2NaNO_3 + (NH_4)_2SO_4 \longrightarrow 2NH_4NO_3 + Na_2SO_4$$

$$\downarrow$$

$$2N_2O + 4H_2O$$

The following reactions can also be used to prepare nitrous oxide.

- By the action of cold and dilute nitric acid on zinc metal.

$$4Zn + 10HNO_3 \longrightarrow 4Zn(NO_3)_2 + N_2O + 5H_2O$$

- By reducing nitric acid with stannous chloride and hydrochloric acid.

$$4SnCl_2 + 8HCl + 2HNO_3 \longrightarrow 4SnCl_4 + N_2O + 5H_2O$$

- By reducing nitric oxide with sulphur dioxide.

$$2NO + SO_2 + H_2O \longrightarrow H_2SO_4 + N_2O$$

- By heating the mixture of hydroxylamine hydrochloride and sodium nitrite (1 : 1).

$$NH_2OH \cdot HCl + NaNO_2 \longrightarrow N_2O + NaCl + 2H_2O$$

2. Nitric Oxide, NO

Structure

The molecule NO contains an odd electron which makes the gaseous nitric oxide as paramagnetic.

$$:\dot{N} = \ddot{\underset{\cdot\cdot}{O}}:$$

The structure is represented as a resonance hybrid.

$$:\dot{N} = \underset{\cdot\cdot}{O}: \longleftrightarrow :\overset{+}{N} = \dot{\underset{\cdot\cdot}{O}}\overset{-}{:}$$

In the liquid and solid states NO is known to form a dimer, N_2O_2 (diamagnetic).

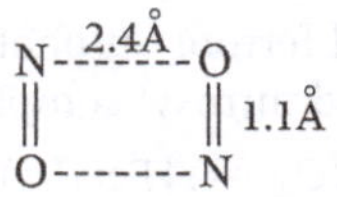

Preparation

- The most common laboratory method is reaction of small pieces of copper with dilute HNO_3 (1 : 1)

$$3Cu + 8HNO_3 \longrightarrow 3Cu(NO_3)_2 + 4H_2O + 2NO$$

- The liberated gas may contain NO_2 obtained by the action of O from air and NO. These are separated by passing the mixture through cold ferrous sulphate solution. NO forms a dark nitroso-ferrous sulphate. When this solution is heated, pure nitric oxide is liberated.

$$FeSO_4 + \underset{\text{Impure gas}}{NO} \longrightarrow \underset{\text{Dark Brown}}{FeSO_4 \cdot NO} \xrightarrow{\text{Heat}} FeSO_4 + \underset{\text{Pure gas}}{NO}$$

- A pure sample of nitric oxide is obtained when a mixture of KNO_3, $FeSO_4$ and dilute H_2SO_4 is heated. This is also a laboratory method.

$$2KNO_3 + 2FeSO_4 + 4H_2SO_4 \longrightarrow$$
$$2KHSO_4 + 3Fe_2(SO_4)_3 + 2NO + 2H_2O$$

- Nitric oxide is the first product obtained from the following two processes during the manufacture of nitric acid.
  (i) **Electric Arc Process** By passing air through an electric arc, nitrogen and oxygen of the air combine together to form nitric oxide.

$$N_2 + O_2 \overset{\text{Electric arc}}{\rightleftharpoons} 2NO$$

  (ii) **Ostwald's Process** By restricted oxidation of ammonia with air in presence of platinum gauze catalyst at 750°C, nitric oxide is formed.

$$4NH_3 + 5O_2 \xrightarrow[750°C,\ 6\ atm]{\text{Pt. gauze}} 4NO + 6H_2O$$

Properties

(i) It is a colourless gas, slightly heavier than air.

(ii) It is sparingly soluble in water.

(iii) It is paramagnetic indicating the presence of unpaired electron in the molecule.

(iv) It is neutral to litmus.

(v) It reacts with oxygen to give brown fumes of nitrogen dioxide.

$$2NO + O_2 \longrightarrow 2NO_2$$

(vi) It is a stable oxide. It decomposes into nitrogen and oxygen when heated at 800°C.

$$2NO \xrightarrow{800°C} N_2 + O_2$$

(vii) It is combustible and supports combustion of boiling sulphur and burning phosphorus.

$$S + 2NO \longrightarrow SO_2 + N_2$$

$$4P + 10NO \longrightarrow \underset{\text{Phosphorus pentoxide}}{2P_2O_5} + 5N_2$$

(viii) It dissolves in cold ferrous sulphate solution by forming a hydrated nitrosyl complex.

$$\underset{\text{Ferrous sulphate}}{[Fe(H_2O)_6]SO_4} + NO \longrightarrow \underset{\text{Hydrated nitrosyl complex (Brown colour)}}{[Fe(H_2O)_5NO]SO_4} + H_2O$$

$$\downarrow \text{Heat}$$

$$FeSO_4 + NO + 5H_2O$$

(ix) It is oxidised to nitric acid by oxidising agents like acidified $KMnO_4$ or hypochlorous acid. Thus, it acts as a reducing agent.

$$6KMnO_4 + 9H_2SO_4 + 10NO \longrightarrow 3K_2SO_4 + 6MnSO_4 + 10HNO_3 + 4H_2O$$

$$3HClO + 2NO + H_2O \longrightarrow 2HNO_3 + 3HCl$$

HNO_3 oxidises nitric oxide into NO_2.

$$2HNO_3 + NO \longrightarrow H_2O + 3NO_2$$

(x) It acts as an oxidising agent. It oxidises SO_2 to H_2SO_4 and H_2S to S.

$$SO_2 + 2NO + H_2O \longrightarrow H_2SO_4 + N_2O$$

$$H_2S + 2NO \longrightarrow H_2O + S + N_2O$$

When exploded with hydrogen it liberates nitrogen.

$$2H_2 + 2NO \longrightarrow 2H_2O + N_2$$

However, when a mixture of hydrogen and nitric oxide is passed over platinum black, ammonia is formed.

$$2NO + 5H_2 \xrightarrow{\text{Pt, Black}} 2NH_3 + 2H_2O$$

Stannous chloride reduces nitric oxide to hydroxylamine.

$$[SnCl_2 + 2HCl \longrightarrow SnCl_4 + 2H] \times 3$$

$$2NO + 6H \longrightarrow 2NH_2OH$$

$$3SnCl_2 + 6HCl + 2NO \longrightarrow 3SnCl_2 + 2NH_2OH$$

(xi) Nitric oxide directly combines with halogen (fluorine, chlorine, bromine) to form corresponding nitrosyl halides.

$$2NO + \underset{(F_2,\, Cl_2 \text{ or } Br_2)}{X_2} \longrightarrow \underset{\text{Nitrosyl halide}}{2NOX}$$

Uses

(i) In the manufacture of nitric acid.

(ii) As a catalyst in lead chamber process for the manufacture of sulphuric acid.

(iii) In the detection of oxygen to distinguish it from nitrous oxide.

3. Dinitrogen Trioxide, N_2O_3

This oxide is also called nitrogen sesquioxide or nitrous anhydride.

Structure

The oxide is unstable in liquid and gaseous states, it decomposes into NO and NO_2, it may be assumed that it has the following electronic structure:

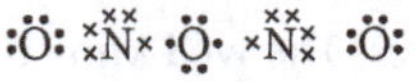 or O=N—O—N=O

The structure is supported by its diamagnetic behaviour. Structure of N_2O_3 is of two forms

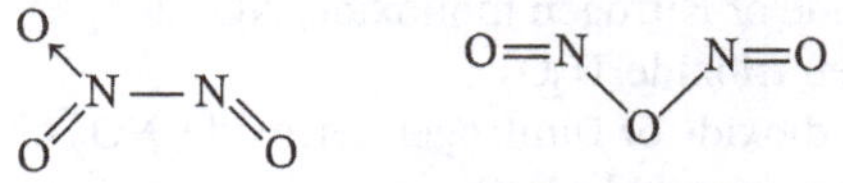

Unsymmetrical Form   Symmetrical Form

Preparation

(i) It is prepared by the reaction of NO with N_2O_4.

$$N_2O_4 + 2NO \xrightarrow{250\text{ K}} 2N_2O_3$$

(ii) It is obtained by the reduction of nitric acid with arsenic oxide.

$$2HNO_3 \longrightarrow H_2O + N_2O_3 + 2O$$

$$As_2O_3 + 2O \longrightarrow As_2O_5$$

$$As_2O_5 + 3H_2O \longrightarrow 2H_3AsO_4$$

$$As_2O_3 + 2HNO_3 + 2H_2O \longrightarrow 2H_3AsO_4 + N_2O_3$$

It is known in solid form at very low temperature. In the vapour state. it is present as an equimolar mixture of NO and NO_2. The mixture of NO and NO_2 may be obtained by the action of 6N nitric acid on copper.

$$2Cu + 6HNO_3 \longrightarrow 2Cu(NO_3)_2 + \underbrace{NO + NO_2}_{N_2O_3} + 3H_2O$$

Properties

(i) It condenses to a blue coloured liquid at –30°C. The liquid when warmed at room temperature, decomposes to a mixture of NO and NO_2 (Brown coloured).

$$\underset{\text{Blue coloured liquid}}{N_2O_3} \xrightarrow{\text{Room temperature}} \underbrace{NO + NO_2}_{\text{Brown coloured gas}}$$

(ii) It is an acidic oxide. If forms nitrous acid in water and hence the name nitrous anhydride.

$$N_2O_3 + H_2O \longrightarrow 2HNO_2$$

The oxide combines with caustic alkali forming corresponding nitrite.

$$2NaOH + N_2O_3 \longrightarrow 2NaNO_2 + H_2O$$

4. Nitrogen Dioxide, NO_2 or Dinitrogen Tetroxide, N_2O_4

This oxide exists as NO_2 in gaseous state while at low temperature, it exists as a dimer N_2O_4 (Solid state).

$$\underset{\text{Brown gas}}{2NO_2} \underset{}{\overset{-11°C}{\rightleftharpoons}} \underset{\text{Colourless solid}}{N_2O_4}$$

Structure

NO_2 molecule has V-shaped structure with O—N—O bond angle 134° and N—O bond length of about 120 pm. Which is intermediate between a single and a double bond. Hence, NO_2 is regarded as a resonance hybrid of the following two structures.

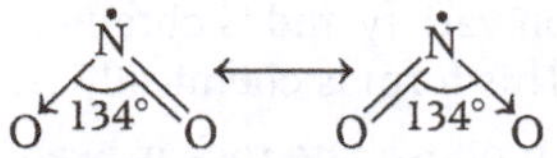

The molecule is an odd electron molecule. The paramagnetic behaviour of NO_2 confirms this view. Due to possession of odd electron, it is coloured and has a tendency to polymerise to form a colourless dimer, N_2O_4 the dimer is planar in structure with N—N bond length 1.75 Å.

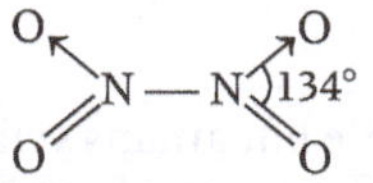

Preparation

It is prepared in the laboratory either by heating nitrates of heavy metal or by the action of concentrated nitric acid on metals like copper, silver, lead etc.

$$2Pb(NO_3)_2 \longrightarrow 2PbO + 4NO_2 + O_2$$

When the mixture of nitrogen dioxide and oxygen is passed through a U-tube and cooled by freezing mixture, nitrogen dioxide condenses to a pale yellow liquid while oxygen escapes.

$$Zn(NO_3)_2 \longrightarrow ZnO + NO_2 + O_2$$
$$AgNO_3 \longrightarrow Ag + NO_2 + O_2$$
$$Cu + 4HNO_3 \longrightarrow Cu(NO_3)_2 + 2NO_2 + 2H_2O$$

It is also obtained by air oxidation of nitric oxide.

$$2NO + O_2 \longrightarrow 2NO_2$$

Properties

(i) It is brown coloured gas with pungent odour. Above 140°C, it is 100% NO_2. In liquid as well as solid, it is entirely N_2O_4 (dimer) at low temperature. The liquid boils at 22°C and solid melts at –11°C.

(ii) It decomposes completely into nitric oxide and oxygen at 620°C.

$$2NO_2 \underset{}{\overset{620°C}{\rightleftharpoons}} \underbrace{2NO + O_2}_{\text{Gaseous mixture colourless}}$$

(iii) When reacted with cold water, it forms mixture of nitrous acid and nitric acid.

$$2NO_2 + H_2O \longrightarrow HNO_2 + HNO_3$$

On account of this, it is known as mixed anhydride of these two acids. However, with an excess of warm water it forms nitric acid and nitric oxide.

$$3NO_2 + H_2O \longrightarrow 2HNO_3 + NO$$

(iv) When absorbed by alkalies, nitrites and nitrates are formed.

$$2NO_2 + 2NaOH \longrightarrow 2NaNO_2 + NaNO_3 + H_2O$$

(v) It acts as an oxidising agent. It oxidises metals like sodium, potassium, mercury, tin, copper, etc.

$$NO_2 + 2Na \longrightarrow Na_2O + NO$$
$$NO_2 + 2Cu \longrightarrow Cu_2O + NO$$

Non metals like carbon, sulphur, phosphorus when burnt in its atmosphere, are converted into corresponding oxides.

$$5NO_2 + 2P \longrightarrow P_2O_5 + 5NO$$
$$2NO_2 + S \longrightarrow SO_2 + 2NO$$
$$2NO_2 + C \longrightarrow CO_2 + 2NO$$

It liberates iodine from KI. This iodine turns starch-iodide paper blue.

$$2KI + 2NO_2 \longrightarrow 2KNO_2 + I_2$$

In aqueous solution, it oxidises SO_2 to sulphuric acid.

$$SO_2 + H_2O + NO_2 \longrightarrow H_2SO_4 + NO$$

This reaction is used for the manufacture of H_2SO_4 by lead chamber process.

H_2S is oxidised to S and CO to CO_2.

$$H_2S + NO_2 \longrightarrow H_2O + S + NO$$
$$CO + NO_2 \longrightarrow CO_2 + NO$$

(vi) It behaves also as a reducing agent. It reduces ozone to oxygen.

$$2NO_2 + O_3 \longrightarrow N_2O_5 + O_2$$

It decolourises acidified $KMnO_4$ solution.

$$2KMnO_4 + 3H_2SO_4 + 10NO_2 + 2H_2O \longrightarrow K_2SO_4 + 2MnSO_4 + 10HNO_3$$

Uses

(i) It is used for the manufacture of nitric acid.

(ii) It is employed as a catalyst in the lead chamber process for the manufacture of sulphuric acid.

5. Dinitrogen Pentoxide, N_2O_5

This oxide is also known as nitric anhydride.

Preparation

It is prepared by distilling (dehydration by P_2O_5) concentrated nitric acid with phosphorus pentoxide in a glass apparatus.

$$P_2O_5 + 2HNO_3 \longrightarrow 2HPO_3 + N_2O_5$$

It is also prepared by the action of dry chlorine on solid silver nitrate at 95°C.

$$4AgNO_3 + 2Cl_2 \longrightarrow 4AgCl + 2N_2O_5 + O_2$$

Properties

(i) It is a white crystalline solid. The crystals melt at 30°C giving a yellow liquid which decomposes at 40°C to give brown NO_2. The decompostion occurs with explosion.

$$2N_2O_5 \longrightarrow 4NO_2 + O_2$$

(ii) It is an acidic oxide. It reacts with water with hissing sound forming nitric acid.

$$N_2O_5 + H_2O \longrightarrow 2HNO_3$$

On account of this, it is known as nitric anhydride. With alkalies if forms nitrates.

$$2NaOH + N_2O_5 \longrightarrow 2NaNO_3 + H_2O$$

(iii) It acts as a strong oxidising agent. It affects organic substances such as cork, rubber, etc. It oxidises iodine readily into iodine pentaxide.

$$I_2 + 5N_2O_5 \longrightarrow I_2O_5 + 10NO_2$$

(iv) With aqueous NaCl, the ionic reaction takes place.

$$N_2O_5 + NaCl \longrightarrow NaNO_3 + NO_2Cl$$

The reaction proves that N_2O_5 exists as ionic nitronium nitrate ($\overset{+}{N}O_2, \overset{-}{N}O_3$).

(v) N_2O_5 is decomposed by alkali metals.

$$N_2O_5 + Na \longrightarrow NaNO_3 + NO_2$$

Structure

In the gaseous state, it exists as a symmetrical molecule having the structure $O_2N—O—NO_2$, It may be represented as:

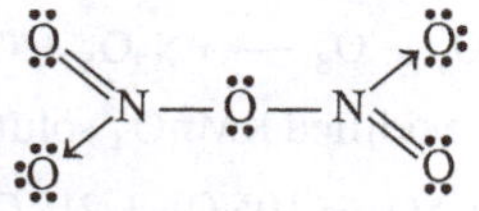

X-ray studies suggest that solid N_2O_5 is ionic in nature, i.e., nitronium nitrate ($\overset{+}{N}O_2, \overset{-}{N}O_3$).

Phosphorus

It is an active element and not found in free state in nature. It is widely distributed in nature in the combined state. It occurs as phosphates in the rocks and in the soil and as phosphoproteins in all living beings.

Bone ash contains about 80% calcium phosphate. it is present in milk, eggs and guano (excreta of seabirds). The principal minerals of phosphorous are

(i) Phosphorite	$Ca_3(PO_4)_2$
(ii) Fluorapatite	$3Ca_3(PO_4)_2 \cdot CaF_2$
(iii) Chlorapatite	$3Ca_3(PO_4)_2 \cdot CaCl_2$

Allotropic forms of Phosphorus

Phosphorus exists in a number of allotropic forms. These forms are:

(i) Yellow or white phosphorus (ii) Red phosphorus
(iii) Scarlet phosphorus
(iv) black phosphorus
(v) violet phosphorus

The main allotropic forms, however, are white and red.

White or Yellow phosphorus

This is the common variety and is obtained by the methods described below. This form is chemically very active.

It is obtained when phosphate rock is heated with coke and sand in an electric furnace at 1773 K.

$$2Ca_3(PO_4)_2 + 6SiO_2 \xrightarrow{1773\ K} 6CaSiO_3 + P_4O_{10}$$

$$P_4O_{10} + 10C \xrightarrow{1773\ K} P_4 + 10\ CO$$

Properties

- The pure form is white but attains yellow colour on long standing due to the formation of a thin film of the red variety on the surface.
- It is a transparent waxy solid (specitic gravity 1.8) and can be easily cut with knife.
- It has characteristic garlic smell and is poisonous in nature (0.15 g is the fatal dose). Vapours are also injurious. Persons working with phosphorus develops a disease in which the jaw bones decay. This disease is known as **phossy jaw**.
- It is insoluble in water but readily soluble in carbon disulphide.
- It melts at 44°C into a yellow liquid. It boils at 280°C.
- In contact with air, it undergoes slow combustion and glows in the dark. This property is called **phosphorescence.**
- Its ignition temperature is low (about 30°C). It readily catches fire giving dense fumes of phosphorus pentoxide. It is therefore, kept in water.

$$P_4 + 5O_2 \longrightarrow P_4O_{10} \text{ or } 2P_2O_5$$

- It dissolves in caustic alkalies and on boiling it in an inert atmosphere, it produces phosphine.

$$P_4 + 3\underset{\text{Caustic soda}}{NaOH} + 3H_2O \longrightarrow 3\underset{\text{Sodium hypophosphite}}{NaH_2PO_2} + PH_3\uparrow$$

- It directly combines with halogens forming first trihalides and then pentahalides.

$$P_4 + 6Cl_2 \longrightarrow 4PCl_3 \ ; \ P_4 + 10Cl_2 \longrightarrow 4PCl_5$$

- It combines with a number of metals forming phosphides.

$$6Mg + P_4 \longrightarrow 2Mg_3P_2 \quad \text{(Magnesium phosphide)}$$

$$6Ca + P_4 \rightarrow 2Ca_3P_2 \quad \text{(Calcium phosphide)}$$

- It combines with sulphur with explosive violence forming a number of sulphides such as P_2S_3, P_2S_5, P_4S_3 and P_4S_7.
- It acts as a strong reducing agent. It reduces nitric acid and sulphuric acid.

$$P_4 + 20HNO_3 \longrightarrow 4H_3PO_4 + 20NO_2 + 4H_2O$$

$$P_4 + 10H_2SO_4 \longrightarrow 4H_3PO_4 + 10SO_2 + 4H_2O$$

It reduces solutions of copper, silver and gold salts to corresponding metals,

$$P_4 + 10CuSO_4 + 16H_2O \rightarrow 10Cu + 4H_3PO_4 + 10H_2SO_4$$

When the solution is heated, cuprous phosphide (black ppt) is formed.

$$3P_4 + 12CuSO_4 + 24H_2O \xrightarrow{\text{Heat}} 4Cu_3P + 8H_3PO_3 + 12H_2SO_4$$

$$P_4 + 20AgNO_3 + 16H_2O \longrightarrow 20Ag + 4H_3PO_4 + 20HNO_3$$

- When heated in inert atmosphere at 240°C, it changes into red variety.

$$\text{Yellow P} \xrightarrow[\text{Inert atm.}]{240\text{-}250°C} \text{Red P}$$

JEE Quicker

Reaction of thionyl chloride with white phosphorus forms a compound PCl_3, which on hydrolysis gives H_3PO_3, a dibasic acid. ***JEE Main 2023***

The reaction between white phosphorus and thionyl chloride is an example of a chlorination process. Thionyl chloride is an effective chlorinating agent because it donates chlorine atoms leaving behind a stable product SO_2.

$$P_4 + 8SOCl_2 \longrightarrow 4PCl_3 + 4SO_2 + 2S_2Cl_2$$
$$PCl_3(l) + 3H_2O(l) \longrightarrow H_3PO_3(s) + 3HCl(g)$$

Structure

The vapour density of white phosphorus between 500-700°C, is 62 which corresponds to the molecular formula P_4.

The four phosphorus atoms lie at the corners of a regular tetrahedron. Each phosphorus atom is linked to each of the other three atoms by covalent bonds. The P—P bond length is equal to 2.21 Å.

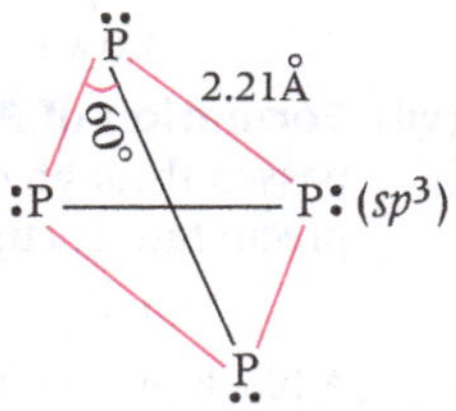

The bond angle is equal to 60° which suggests that the molecule is under angle strain and hence active in nature.

Red Phosphorus

This is also an allotropic form of phosphorus.

Preparation

It is formed by heating yellow phosphorus, between 240-250°C, in presence of an inert gas. The heating is done in an egg shaped iron vessel provided with an upright tube closed by a safety valve, the thermometers placed in iron tubes help to regulate the temperature.

$$\underset{\text{White phosphorus}}{P_4(s)} \xrightarrow[\text{Coal gas or } CO_2]{573\text{ K}} \underset{\text{Red phosphorus}}{P_4(s)}$$

Structure

The exact structure of red phosphorus is not yet known. It is regarded as a polymer consisting of chains of P_4 units linked together as shown in the figure.

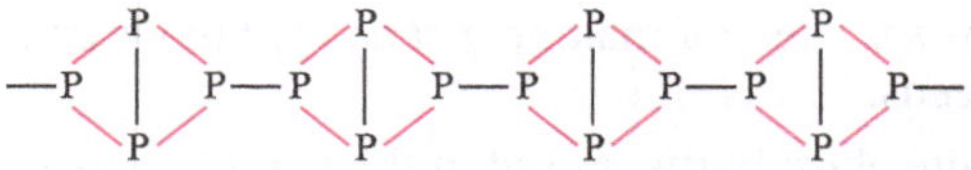

Structure of red phosphorus

Comparison between White and Red Phosphorus

S. No.	Property	White Phosphorus	Red Phosphorus
1.	Physical State	Soft waxy solid	Hard crystalline solid
2.	Colour	White when pure. Attains yellow colour on standing	Red
3.	Odour	Garlic	Odourless
4.	Specific gravity	1.8 g cm^{-3}	2.1 g cm^{-3}
5.	Melting point	44°C	Sublimes in absence of air at 290°C
6.	Ignition temperature	Low,30°C	High, 260°C
7.	Solubility in water	Insoluble	Insoluble
8.	Solubility in CS_2	Soluble	Insoluble
9.	Physiological action	Poisonous	Non-poisonous
10.	Chemical activity	Very active	Less active
11.	Stability	Unstable	Stable
12.	Phosphorescence	Glows in dark	Does not glow in dark
13.	Burning in air	Forms P_4O_{10}	Forms P_4O_{10}
14.	Reaction with NaOH	Evolves phosphine	No action
15.	Action of Cl_2	Combines spontaneously to form PCl_3 and PCl_5	Reacts on heating to form PCl_3 and PCl_5
16.	Reaction with hot HNO_3	Forms H_3PO_4	Forms H_3PO_4
17.	Molecular formula	P_4	Polymeric, $(P_4)_n$

Uses of Red and White Phosphorus

(i) Red phosphorus is largely used in the match industry. Red phosphorus or scarlet phosphorus is preferred to yellow variety.

(ii) Yellow phosphorus is used as a rat poison..

(iii) Red phosphorus is used for the preparation of HBr and HI.

(iv) Radioactive phosphorus (P^{32}) is used in the treatment of leukemia and other blood disorders.

(v) White is used for making incendiary bombs and smoke screens.

(vi) White phosphorus is used in the manufacture of phosphor bronze, an alloy of phosphorus, copper and tin.

(vii) White phosphorus is used in the manufacture of compounds like hypophosphites (medicine), phosphorus chlorides in industry, calcium phosphide used in making Holme's signals and *ortho*phosphoric acid.

Compounds of Phosphorus

1. Phosphine, PH_3

It is analogous to ammonia.

Structure of Phosphine

Phosphine is a covalent molecule. It has pyramidal structure like ammonia.

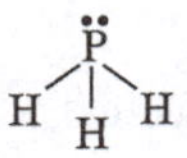

The bond angle H—P—H is 93°.

Preparation

Laboratory Preparation

(i) It is prepared by boiling yellow phosphorus with a concentrated solution of sodium hydroxide in an inert atmosphere.

$$P_4 + 3NaOH + 3H_2O \longrightarrow \underset{\text{Sodium hypophosphite}}{3NaH_2PO_2} + PH_3$$

(ii) It is also prepared by passing the gas through HI. PH_3 is absorbed forming phosphonium iodide. This on treatment with caustic potash gives pure phosphine.

$$PH_3 + HI \longrightarrow PH_4I$$

$$PH_4I + KOH \longrightarrow KI + H_2O + PH_3$$

Physical Properties

(i) Unlike NH_3 it is only slightly soluble in water; the aqueous solution is neutral. However it is more soluble in CS_2 and other organic solvents.

(ii) Its vapour density is 17, i.e. little heavier than air.

Chemical Properties

(i) **Decomposition** When heated without contact of air to 440°C or when electric sparks are passed through it, phosphine decomposes into red phosphorus and hydrogen.

$$4PH_3 \longrightarrow P_4 + 6H_2$$

(ii) **Combustibility** A pure sample of phosphine is not spontaneously inflammable. It burns in air or oxygen when heated at 150°C.

$$PH_3 + 2O_2 \longrightarrow H_3PO_4$$

(iii) **Action of Chlorine** Phosphine burns in the atmosphere of chlorine and forms phosphorus pentachloride.

$$PH_3 + 4Cl_2 \longrightarrow PCl_5 + 3HCl$$

(iv) **Basic Nature** Phosphine is neutral to litmus. However, it is a weak base, even weaker than ammonia. It reacts with HCl, HBr or HI to form phosphonium compounds.

$$PH_3 + HCl \longrightarrow PH_4Cl \quad \text{(Phosphonium chloride)}$$

$$PH_3 + HBr \longrightarrow PH_4Br \quad \text{(Phosphonium bromide)}$$

$$PH_3 + HI \longrightarrow PH_4I \quad \text{(Phosphonium iodide)}$$

(v) **Action of nitric acid** In contact with nitric acid phosphine begins to burn.

$$2PH_3 + 16HNO_3 \longrightarrow P_2O_5 + 16NO_2 + 11H_2O$$

(vi) **Addition Compounds** It forms addition compounds with anhydrous $AlCl_3$ and $SnCl_4$

$$AlCl_3 + 2PH_3 \longrightarrow AlCl_3 \cdot 2PH_3$$

$$SnCl_4 + 2PH_3 \longrightarrow SnCl_4 \cdot 2PH_3$$

When PH_3 is passed through cuprous chloride solution in HCl, it forms an addition compoun.

$$Cu_2Cl_2 + 2PH_3 \longrightarrow 2CuCl \cdot PH_3$$

(vii) **Formation of Phosphides** (i) When phosphine is passed through copper sulphate solution, a black precipitate of cupric phosphide is formed.

$$3CuSO_4 + 2PH_3 \longrightarrow Cu_3P_2 + 3H_2SO_4$$

A black precipitate of silver phosphide is formed when phosphine is circulated through silver nitrate solution.

$$3AgNO_3 + PH_3 \longrightarrow Ag_3P + 3HNO_3$$

(viii) Action with nitric and nitrous oxide.

The mixture of PH_3 and N_2O or PH_3 and NO explodes in presence of electric spark.

$$PH_3 + 4N_2O \longrightarrow H_3PO_4 + 4N_2$$

$$PH_3 + 4NO \longrightarrow H_3PO_4 + 2N_2$$

Uses

(i) For making Holme's signals.

(ii) For making smoke screens.

(iii) For making metallic phosphides.

2. Phosphorus Trichloride, PCl_3

Structure

Its structure is similar to ammonia, i.e. it has pyramidal structure.

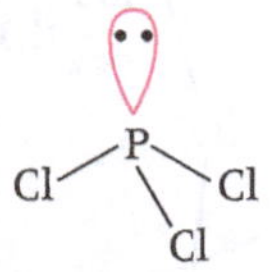

Preparation

It is obtained when dry Cl_2 is passed over red or white phosphorus and heated gently in a retort over a water bath.

$$P_4 + \underset{(Dry)}{6Cl_2} \xrightarrow{\text{Heated-water bath}} 4PCl_3$$

Physical and Chemical Properties

Some important properties of PCl_3 are as follows

- It is a low boiling liquid (b.p. 74°C) with a pungent odour and fumes in moist air.
- It violently hydrolysed by water as,

$$PCl_3 + 3H_2O \longrightarrow 3HCl + H_3PO_3$$

- It reacts with chlorine and sulphur as,

$$PCl_3 + Cl_2 \longrightarrow PCl_5$$
$$PCl_3 + S_2 \longrightarrow PSCl_3$$

- It reacts with oxygen and SO_3 as,

$$2PCl_3 + O_2 \longrightarrow 2POCl_3$$
$$3PCl_3 + SO_3 \longrightarrow POCl_3 + SO_2$$

- It gives many substitution reactions as,

$$PCl_3 + 3AgCN \longrightarrow P(CN)_3 + 3AgCl$$
$$PCl_3 \xrightarrow{PF_3} PCl_2F + PClF_2$$

- It forms adduct with BBr_3 as,

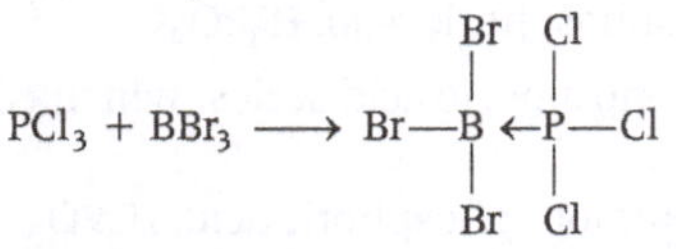

- It acts as reducing agent and reduces SO_2Cl_2 and $SOCl_2$ to SO_2 and itself gets oxidised to PCl_5 or $POCl_3$.

$$PCl_3 + SO_2Cl_2 \longrightarrow PCl_5 + SO_2\uparrow$$
$$3PCl_3 + SOCl_2 \longrightarrow POCl_3 + PSCl_3 + PCl_5$$

- It reacts with finely divided metals when hot as

$$12Ag + 4PCl_3 \longrightarrow 12AgCl + P_4$$

- It reacts with concentrated H_2SO_4 forming chloro-sulphonic acid as,

$$\underset{\text{Conc.}}{4H_2SO_4} + 2PCl_3 \longrightarrow \underset{\text{Chloro-sulphonic acid}}{2HSO_3Cl} + P_2O_5 + 2SO_2 + 4HCl + H_2O$$

- It reacts with organic compounds containing hydroxyl group to give H_3PO_3.

$$\underset{\text{Ethyl alcohol}}{3C_2H_5OH} + PCl_3 \longrightarrow \underset{\text{Ethyl chloride}}{3C_2H_5Cl} + H_3PO_3$$
$$\underset{\text{Acetic acid}}{3CH_3COOH} + PCl_3 \longrightarrow \underset{\text{Acetyl chloride}}{3CH_3COCl} + H_3PO_3$$

3. Phosphorus Pentachloride, PCl_5

Structure

X-ray studies have revealed that solid PCl_5 consists of ionic lattices, i.e. tetrahedral $[PCl_4]^+$ cations and octahedral $[PCl_6]^-$ anions. In vapour state, it has trigonal bipyramidal shape in which P has sp^3d-hybridisation.

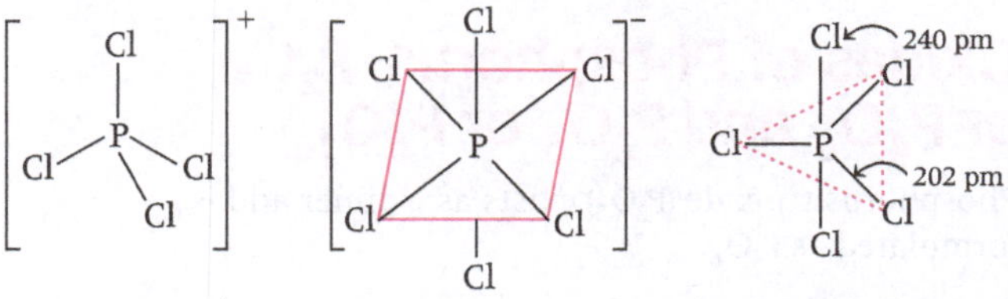

(a) $[PCl_4]^+$ (b) $[PCl_6]^-$ (c) PCl_5 in vapour state

Structure of PCl_5 in solid (a, b) and vapour phases

Preparation

It is prepared either by passing dry Cl_2 gas (in excess) over PCl_3 or by the action of SO_2Cl_2 on P_4 or PCl_3.

$$PCl_3 + \underset{(Dry)}{Cl_2} \longrightarrow PCl_5$$
$$P_4 + 10SO_2Cl_2 \longrightarrow 4PCl_5 + 10SO_2$$

Physical and Chemical Properties

Some important properties of PCl_5 are as follows

- It is yellowish white crystalline compound with a sharp odour. Its m.p. is – 45°C (under pressure) and sublimation temperature is 160°C.
- It have the ability to dissociate as

$$PCl_5 \rightleftharpoons PCl_3 + Cl_2\uparrow$$

- It is violently hydrolysed by water as

$$PCl_5 + H_2O \xrightarrow{\text{Insufficient water}} POCl_3 + 2HCl$$
$$PCl_5 + 4H_2O \xrightarrow{\text{Excess of water}} H_3PO_4 + 5HCl$$

- It reacts with compounds containing —OH group as

$$CH_3COOH + PCl_5 \longrightarrow CH_3COCl + POCl_3 + HCl$$
$$H_2SO_4 + PCl_5 \longrightarrow \underset{\text{Sulphuryl chloride}}{SO_2Cl_2} + 2POCl_3 + HCl$$

- It reacts with P_4O_{10} as

$$6PCl_5 + P_4O_{10} \longrightarrow 10POCl_3$$

- It reacts with ammonium chloride as

$$nPCl_5 + nNH_4Cl \xrightarrow{150°C} (NPCl_2)_n + 4nHCl$$

- It reacts with Cl^- acceptors as

$$PCl_5 + BCl_3 \longrightarrow [PCl_4]^+[BCl_4]^-$$

- With hydrogen it forms PCl_3 as

$$PCl_5 + H_2 \longrightarrow PCl_3 + 2HCl$$

- It reacts with KF as, $PCl_5 + 6KF \longrightarrow KPF_6 + 5KCl$

Uses

PCl_5 is used

(i) as chlorinating agent in organic chemistry.

(ii) in parmaceutical industry for manufacturing penicillin.

(iii) to produce acid chloride.

(iv) as catalyst in many reactions.

Oxides of Phosphorus, P_2O_3 or P_4O_6 and P_2O_5 or P_4O_{10}

Phosphorus trioxide (P_2O_5) exists as a dimer and is formulated as P_4O_6.

Preparation

- When white phosphorus is burnt in the limited supply of air, both P_4O_6. and P_4O_{10} are formed. The vapour of the mixture of oxides are passed through a condensor in which water at 50-60°C is circulated, P_4O_{10} being solid at 60°C separates out easily.
- P_4O_{10} is obtained by burning phosphorus in a free supply of air or oxygen. The pentoxide formed is purified further by sublimation at 360°C.

Properties and Uses

Among the various pentoxides, P_2O_5 has the strongest affinity for water. It can extract water from several inorganic and organic compounds, hence it acts as a strong **dehydrating agent**. It dehydrates H_2SO_4 to SO_3, HNO_3 to N_2O_5, **cellulose** to **carbon** and **amides** to **nitriles.**

The tetrahedral structure of P_4O_6 is

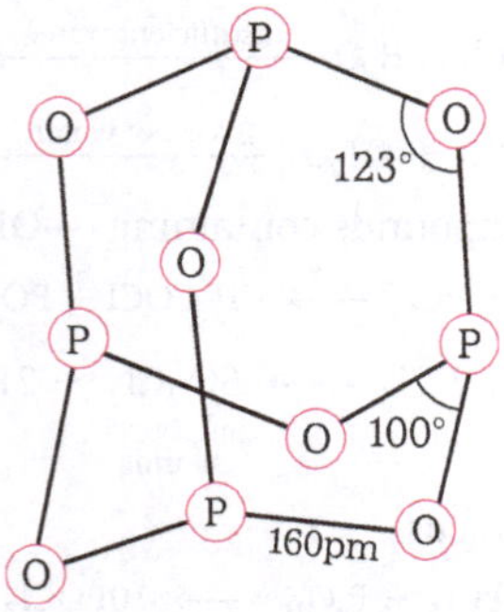

Structure of P_4O_6

This structure has been confirmed by X-ray diffraction data. The oxides As_4O_6, Sb_4O_6 also have tetrahedral structures.

The structure assigned to P_4O_{10} molecule is

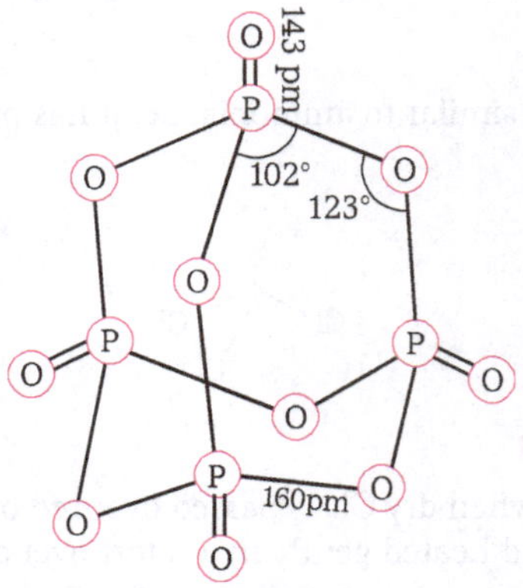

Structure of P_4O_{10}

Oxoacids of Phosphorus

The oxyocids of phosphorus can be grouped into following series are given below

(i) Phosphorous acid series which contains following acids
- Hypophosphorus acid, H_3PO_2
- Phosphorus acid, or orthophosphorus acid, H_3PO_3
- Pyrophosphorus acid, $H_4P_2O_5$
- Metaphosphorus acid, HPO_3

(ii) Phosphoric acid series, which contains following acids
- Hypophosphoric acid, $H_4P_2O_6$
- Pyrophosphoric acid, $H_4P_2O_7$

(iii) Polyphosphoric acid series with general formula $H_{n+2}P_nO_{3n+1}$
- Diphosphoric acid or pyrophosphoric acid, $H_4P_2O_7$
- Triphosphoric acid, $H_5P_3O_{10}$
- Tetraphosphoric acid, $H_6P_4O_{13}$
- Metaphosphoric acid, HPO_3 ($H_3PO_4 - H_2O \longrightarrow HPO_3$)
- Orthophosphoric acid, H_3PO_4

(iv) Peroxyphosphoric acid series, which contains following acids
- Peroxomonophosphoric acid, H_3PO_5
- Peroxodiphosphoric acid, $H_4P_2O_8$

The strength and solubility of the oxyacids follow the order,

$$HNO_3 > H_3PO_4 > H_3AsO_4 > H_3SbO_4$$

Some important facts related to oxyacids of phosphorus are

(i) H_3PO_2 is a strong reducing agent and acid as well compared to H_3PO_3.

(ii) $$4H_3PO_3 \xrightarrow[-PH_3]{475\text{ K}} 3H_3PO_4 \xrightarrow[\substack{-H_3PO_4 \\ -H_2O}]{520\text{ K}} H_4P_2O_7 \xrightarrow[-H_2O]{>520\text{ K}} HPO_3 \xrightarrow[-H_2O]{700\text{ K}} P_2O_5$$

(iii) Aqueous solutions of both pyrophosphoric acid, $H_4P_2O_7$ as well as metaphosphoric acid (HPO_3) on heating give orthophosphoric acid.

Structures

The structures of some oxoacids of phosphorus are given below

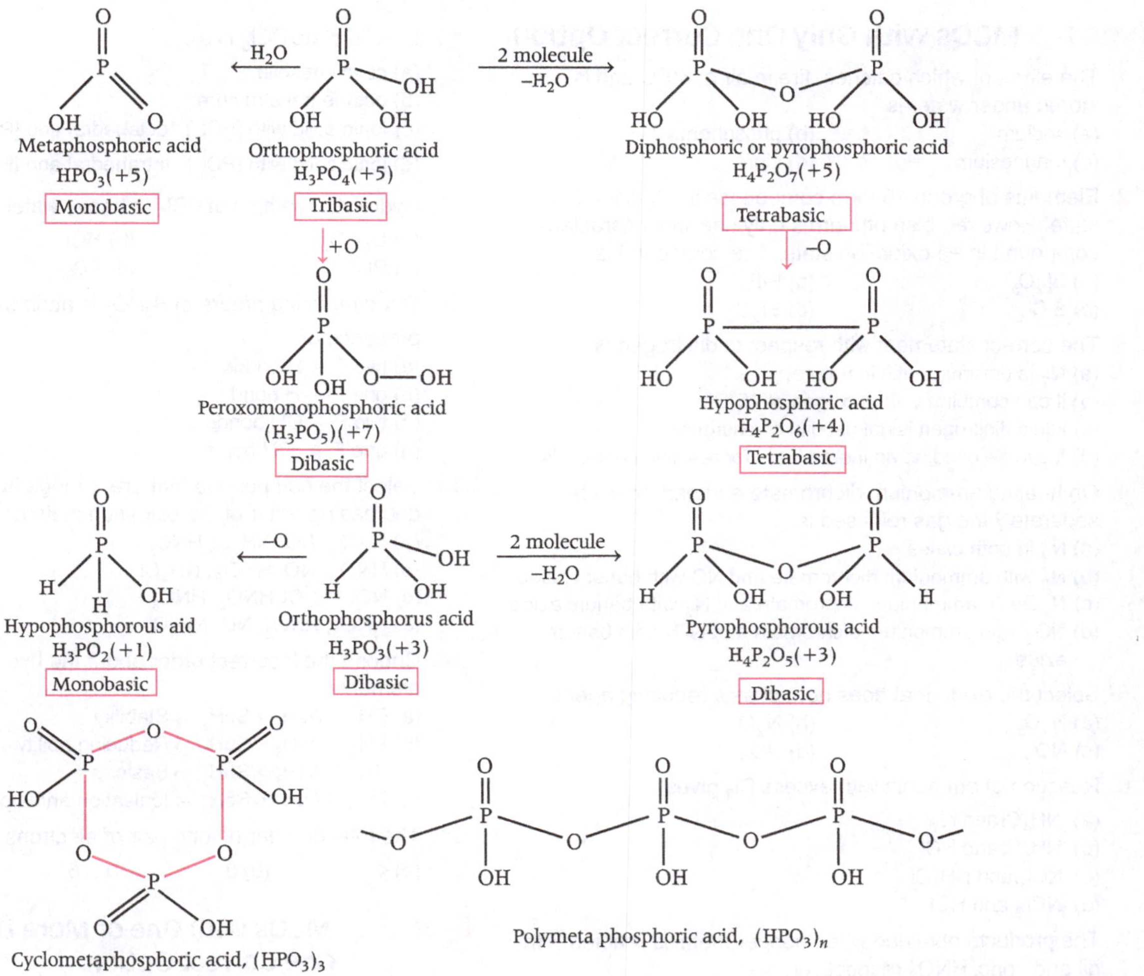

JEE MAPPER

Example Similar to PYQ Asked in JEE Advanced 2021

The correct statement(s) related to hydrated form of N_2O_5 is(are)

(a) It is colourless fuming liquid and soluble in water in all proportions.

(b) It oxidises As and Sb to H_3AsO_4 and Sb_2O_5.

(c) It produces nascent chlorine along with nitrosyl chloride by reaction with conc. HCl.

(d) Iodine reacts with its concentrated form to yield periodic acid alongwith NO_2 and H_2O.

Sol. *(a,b,c)* Among the given statements all are correct except (d). Its corrected form is as

Iodine reacts with conc. HNO_3 (hydrated form of N_2O_5) to yield HIO_3 (iodic acid) along with NO_2 and H_2O.

The reaction involved is as follows $I_2 + 10HNO_3 \longrightarrow 2HIO_3 + 10NO_2 + 4H_2O$

Competency Enhancer 1.1

Which of the following statement is/are correct?

(a) P_2O_5 has the strongest affinity for water. It dehydrates HNO_3 to N_2O_5.

(b) Phosphorous trioxide exists as a dimer.

(c) As_4O_6 and Sb_4O_6 have square pyramidal structure.

(d) Polyphosphoric acid have general formula $H_{n-2}P_{n+2}O_{2n+1}$.

Elemental Practice 6.1

Type I » MCQs with Only One Correct Option

1. The element which catches fire in air at 30°C and is stored under water is
(a) sodium (b) phosphorus
(c) magnesium (d) zinc

2. Elements of group 15 form compounds in +5 oxidation state. However, bismuth forms only one well characterised compound in +5 oxidation state. The compound is
(a) Bi_2O_5 (b) BiF_5
(c) $BiCl_5$ (d) Bi_2S_5

3. The correct statement with respect to dinitrogen is
(a) N_2 is paramagnetic in nature.
(b) it can combine with dioxygen at 25°C.
(c) liquid dinitrogen is not used in cryosurgery.
(d) it can be used as an inert diluent for reactive chemicals.

4. On heating ammonium dichromate and barium azide separately the gas released is
(a) N_2 in both cases
(b) N_2 with ammonium dichromate and NO with barium azide
(c) N_2O with ammonium dichromate and N_2 with barium azide
(d) NO_2 with ammonium dichromate and NO_2 with barium azide

5. Select the oxide that does not act as a reducing agent.
(a) N_2O_5 (b) N_2O
(c) NO_2 (d) NO_2

6. Reaction of ammonia with excess Cl_2 gives
(a) NH_4Cl and N_2
(b) NH_4Cl and HCl
(c) NCl_3 and NH_4Cl
(d) NCl_3 and HCl

7. The products obtained when copper metal is reacted with dil and conc. HNO_3 respectively are
(a) NO and N_2O_5 (b) NO_2 and N_2O_5
(c) NO and NO_2 (d) HNO_2 and N_2

8. On heating with concentrated NaOH solution in an inert atmosphere of CO_2, white phosphorus gives a gas. Which of the following statement is incorrect about the gas?
(a) It is highly poisonous and has smell like rotten fish.
(b) Its solution in water decomposes in the presence of light.
(c) It is more basic than NH_3.
(d) It is less basic than NH_3.

9. The substance used in Holme's signals of the ship is a mixture of
(a) $CaC_2 + Ca_3P_2$
(b) $Ca_3(PO_4)_2 + Pb_3O_4$
(c) $H_3PO_4 + CaCl_2$
(d) $NH_3 + HOCl$

10. In solid state PCl_5 is a
(a) covalent solid
(b) octahedral structure
(c) ionic solid with $[PCl_6]^+$ octahedral and $[PCl_4]^-$ tetrahedral
(d) ionic solid with $[PCl_4]^+$ tetrahedral and $[PCl_6]^-$ octahedral

11. Hydrolytic reaction of PCl_5 in heavy water produces.
(a) D_3PO_4 (b) HCl
(c) PCl_3 (d) PD_5

12. Good reducing nature of H_3PO_2 is attributed to the presence of
(a) two P—H bonds
(b) one P—H bond
(c) two P—OH bonds
(d) one P—OH bond

13. Select the compounds that are arrange is according to the decreasing order of the oxidation state of nitrogen.
(a) HNO_2, NO, NH_4Cl, HNO_3
(b) HNO_3, NO, HNO_2, NH_4Cl
(c) NO, NH_4Cl, HNO_2, HNO_3
(d) HNO_3, HNO_2, NO, NH_4Cl

14. Choose the incorrect order about the hydrides of group 15 elements?
(a) $PH_3 > AsH_3 > SbH_3 \rightarrow$ Stability
(b) $PH_3 < AsH_3 < SbH_3 \rightarrow$ Reducing ability
(c) $PH_3 > AsH_3 > SbH_3 \rightarrow$ Basicity
(d) $PH_3 < AsH_3 < SbH_3 \rightarrow$ Ionisation enthalpy

15. The total number of lone pair of electrons in N_2O_3 is
(a) 4 (b) 0 (c) 6 (d) 8

Type II » MCQs with One or More than One Correct Option

16. Select the correct statement from the following
(a) Hydrolysis of NCl_3 gives NH_3 and HClO.
(b) NH_3 is less stable than PH_3.
(c) NH_3 is a weak reducing agent compared to PH_3.
(d) Nitric oxide is paramagnetic.

17. Ammonia on reaction with hypochlorite anion forms
(a) NO (b) NH_4Cl (c) N_2H_4 (d) HNO_2

18. The nitrogen oxide(s) that contain(s) N—N bond(s) is(are)
(a) N_2O (b) N_2O_3
(c) N_2O_4 (d) N_2O_5

19. White phosphorus has
(a) Six P—P single bonds
(b) Four P—P single bonds
(c) Four lone pairs of electrons
(d) P—P—P angle of 60°

20. Choose the species that produce(s) ammonia on heating.
    (a) NH_4Cl
    (b) NH_4NO_3
    (c) $(NH_4)_2SO_4$
    (d) $(NH_4)_2PO_4$

21. Choose the correct statement from the following.
    (a) A clear solution is obtained by adding $CrCl_3$ to excess of NH_4OH solution.
    (b) Ammonia forms a brown coloured compound on reacting with alkaline solution of K_2HgI_4.
    (c) $NiCl_2$ gives a clear solution with excess of NH_4OH due to the formation of an octahedral complex.
    (d) $NiCl_2$ gives a clear solution with excess of NH_4OH due to the formation of a tetrahedral complex.

Type III » Numerical/Integer Answer Type Questions

22. In NO_3^- ion, the sum of number of bond pair and lone pair of electrons on nitrogen atoms are
23. The number of P—O—P bonds in cyclic *meta*phosphoric acid are.
24. The total number of lone pairs present in N_2O_5 is
25. The sum of the number of P=O, P—O—P linkages in $P_5O_{16}^{-7}$ ion.
26. PCl_3 reacts with water, to give an acid of phosphorus. Then the basicity of acid of phosphorus that is formed in the reaction is ....
27. The sum of number of P—O bonds and lone pairs present in P_4O_6 molecule is/are ....

Elemental Practice 6.1 | Chapter 06

Connect with **Answers**

1. (b)	2. (b)	3. (d)	4. (a)	5. (a)	6. (d)
7. (c)	8. (c)	9. (a)	10. (d)	11. (a)	12. (a)
13. (d)	14. (d)	15. (d)	16. (a,c,d)	17. (b,c)	18. (a,b,c)
19. (a,c,d)	20. (a,c,d)	21. (b,c)	22. (4)	23. (3)	24. (12)
25. (9)	26. (2)	27. (28)			

Element 2 Group-16 : The Oxygen Family and Their Compounds

Group 16 contains six elements namely, oxygen (O), sulphur (S), selenium (Se), tellurium (Te), polonium (Po) and livermorium (Lv).

The first four elements are non-metals while the last two are radioactive elements.

General and Physical Properties

Elements of group 16 shows following trends in their general and physical properties.

Electronic Configuration

The general electronic configuration of all the elements of this group is ns^2np^4 where $n = 2$ to 7.

Element	Atomic number	Electronic configuration
Oxygen (O)	8	$[He]2s^2 2p^4$
Sulphur (S)	16	$[Ne]3s^2 3p^4$
Selenium (Se)	34	$[Ar]3d^{10} 4s^2 4p^4$
Tellurium (Te)	52	$[Kr]4d^{10} 5s^2 5p^4$
Polonium (Po)	84	$[Xe]4f^{14} 5d^{10} 6s^2 6p^4$
Livermonium (Lv)	116	$[Rn]5f^{14} 6d^{10} 7s^2 7p^4$

Atomic and Ionic Radii

The atomic radii of group 16 elements are smaller than those the corresponding group 15 elements. This is due to increase in effective nuclear charge which results in greater attraction of the electrons by nucleus. Down the group, the atomic radii increases gradually due to an increase in the number of electronic shells.

Ionisation Enthalpy

Down the group ionisation enthalpy decreases.

This is due to increasing atomic radii, increasing shielding effect of the inner electrons or decreasing effective nuclear charge on moving down the group.

$$O > S > Se > Te > Po$$

Ionisation enthalpy of elements of this group is lower as compared to those of group 15 elements in the corresponding periods. Because of the fact that group 15 elements have extra stable half-filled *p*-orbital configurations.

The first ionisation enthalpies of the group 16 element are unexpectedly lower while their second ionisation enthalpies are higher than those of the corresponding group 15 element.

Electronegativity

The electronegativity values of group 16 elements are higher than the corresponding group 15 elements. This is due to smaller atomic radii or group 16 elements as compared to group 15 elements.

Down the group, electronegativity decreases as the atomic size increases.

$$O > S > Se > Te > Po$$

Due to high electronegativity, the elements of oxygen family (except Po) form ionic compounds with metals and covalent compounds with non-metals.

JEE Alert

Oxygen is the second most electronegative element after fluorine.

Electron Affinity

The electron affinity of these elements decreases as the atomic size increases. However, electron affinity of O is lowest in group 16. This is because of the small size and high negative charge density of O-atom.

Along the period these element have large electron affinity next only to the halogens. Thus, the order is :

$$S > Se > Te > Po > O$$

Metallic and Non-Metallic Character

The first four elements are non-metals. This non-metallic character is stronger in oxygen and sulphur. Po is distinctly a metal but it is radioactive and only short lived.

Melting and Boiling Points

Down the group, melting and boiling points increases regularly from oxygen to tellurium. However, melting and boiling points of polonium are lower than those of tellurium.

This is due to the fact that down the group (↓), with the increase in atomic size or atomic mass, van der Waals' forces of attraction also increase and hence melting and boiling points increase regularly from oxygen to tellurium. However, at polonium due to maximum number of intervening *d*- and *f*-electrons, the inert pair effect exists in Po. Hence, melting and boiling points of Po will be less than that of Te.

Molecular Structure

Oxygen exists as O_2 (diatomic gaseous molecule). S and Se occur as S_8 and Se_8 with Puckered ring structure as shown below

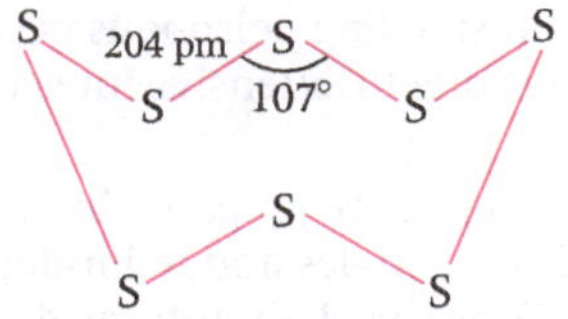

The reason for such a difference is the tendency of O-atom to form multiple bonds ($p\pi$-$p\pi$ bonds) which is missing in the case of sulphur and selenium.

Oxidation State

Elements of group 16 exhibit a number of oxidation states. Oxygen being highly electronegative exhibit +2, –2, –1, +1 oxidation states while other elements show +2, +4 and +6.

Element	Oxidation State
O	–2, –1, +1, +2
S	–2, +2, +4, +6
Se	–2, +2, +4, +6
Te	–2, +2, +4, +6
Po	+2, +4

JEE Alert

Oxygen mainly exhibits –2 oxidation state (as oxide) except in OF_2 where it shows +2 and in peroxides and superoixdes where it shows –1.

Allotropy

Oxygen exist in two allotropic forms, i.e. O_2 and O_3. Sulphur exists as–**rhombic** or **α-form, monoclinic** or **β-form, plastic** or **γ-form, colloidal** or **δ-form, λ-sulphur** and **μ-sulphur**.

- Selenium exists in two forms, i.e. **red form** and **grey form**.
- The grey form of selenium (metallic) and tellurium consists of parallel chains held together by weak metallic bonds. In the presence of light, the weak metallic bonds are excited and as a result, the number of free electrons increases and so does the conductivity.
- Tellurium has only one crystalline form, which is silvery white and semi-metallic. It is similar to grey Se but has stronger metallic interaction.
- Polonium exists in two forms namely α which is cube and β-forms which is rhombohedral. Both of them are metallic.

Chemical Properties

Some of the important chemical properties of element of group 16 are discussed below

Reactivity Towards Oxygen or Formation of Oxides

- In general, the oxides of metals are basic, that of non-metals are acidic and that of semi-metals are amphoteric in nature.
- The acidic character of oxides increases across a period from left to right and basic character of oxides increases down a group.
- The oxides are mainly **monoxides** (*A*O type)**, dioxides** (AO_2) type and trioxides (AO_3 type). However sulphur forms heptoxide with formula S_2O_7.
- Oxygen forms $p\pi$-$p\pi$ double bonds but other elements form $p\pi$-$p\pi$ and $d\pi - p\pi$ multiple bonds in their compounds.

1. Monoxides (*M*O)

All elements of this group (except Se) forms **monoxides** but all of them are not so stable. Out of these, SO is formed by passing electric discharge through SO_2 while TeO and PoO are formed by heating corresponding trioxides.

2. Dioxides (MO_2)

- Dioxides (MO_2) are formed by all the members of this group by burning them in air (except oxygen). These dioxides differ from each other considerably. For example SO_2 and SeO_2 are acidic oxides with good solubility in water while TeO_2 and PoO_2 are amphoteric in nature and have poor solubility in water.
- SO_2 has angular structure. It exists as discrete molecule even in solid state. It is held together by weak van der Waals' forces of attraction. (It exist as gas at room temperature). SeO_2 in gaseous phase has angular structure but in solid state (white volatile solid) it has polymeric structure comprising of infinite chains as

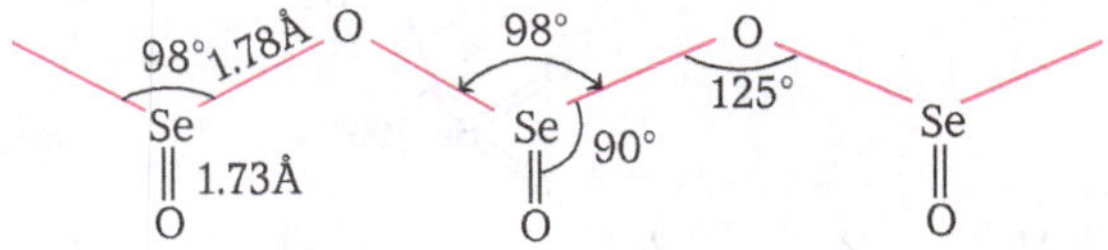

Polymeric structure of SeO_2 in solid state

Dioxides of Te and Po are also non-volatile crystalline ionic solids, out of which TeO_2 has a layer structure consisting of TeO_4 units.

JEE Spotlite

Dioxides of different element of group 16 show differences in their reaction with water as

- SO_2 dissolves in water giving H_2SO_3 (known in solution only).
- SeO_2 gives selenious acid with water which can be isolated in crystalline state.
- TeO_2 is almost insoluble in water. It however dissolves in alkalies (to form tellurites) and in acids (to form basic salts) showing its amphoteric nature.
- PoO_2 is also amphoteric though more basic in character than TeO_2.

3. Trioxides (MO_3)

- Generally, these oxides are acidic in nature, i.e. form acids with water. This acidic nature decreases on moving down the group.
- In gaseous phase, it exists as planar triangular geometry while in solid state, has linear cyclic trimer or a polymeric chain structure.
- SeO_3 on the other hand, exists as a cyclic tetramer (Se_4O_{12}) in the solid state TeO_2 exists in polymeric form.

Structure of

(i) Gaseous SO_3,
(ii) Cyclic trimer of solid SO_3,
(iii) Linear chain of solid SO_3,
(iv) Cyclic tetramer of solid SeO_3 are given as

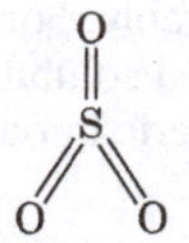

(a) Planar triangular structure of $SO_3(g)$

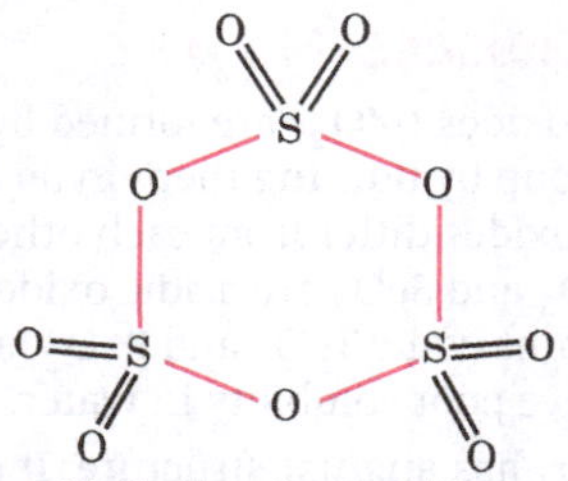

(b) Cyclic trimer of SO_3

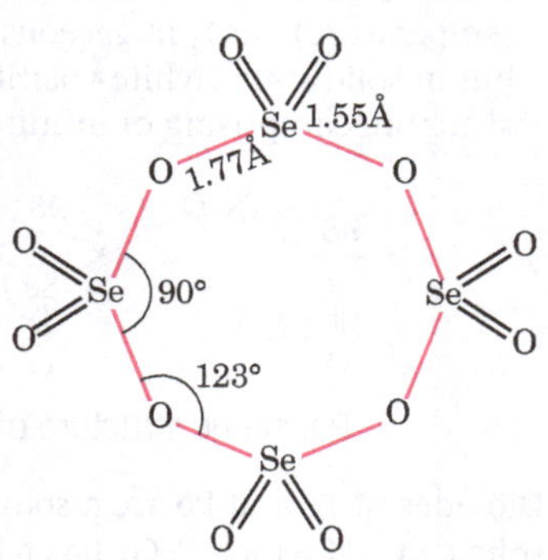

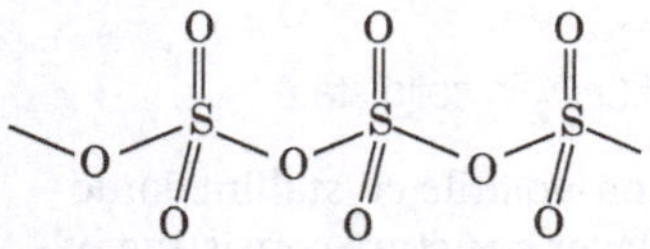

(c) Linear chain of $SO_3(g)$

(d) The cycle structure of tetrameric $Se_4O_{12}(s)$

Reactivity Towards Hydrogen or Formation of Hydrides

- Group 16 elements form binary hydrides of type M_2A (where, A = O, S, Se, Te or Po). Unlike H_2O, other hydrides are unpleasant foul smelling poisonous gases. The unique behaviour of H_2O is due to extensive intermolecular H-bonding.
- Hydrides of S, Se and Te are prepared by the action of acids on metal sulphides, selenides and tellurides respectively. H_2S, H_2Se and H_2Te are weak diprotic acids in aqueous solutions.

Structure

Hydrides of these group have angular shape involving sp^3 hybridisation of central atom.

Their bond angle decreases in order as,

$$\underset{104.5°}{H_2O} > \underset{92.5°}{H_2S} > \underset{900°}{H_2Se} > \underset{89°}{H_2Te}$$

On moving down the group, the size of the central atom increases and electronegativity decreases. Due to this the position of the two bond pair of electrons shift away from the central atom.

As a result of this repulsion between the bond pair of electrons decreases as we move down the group. Therefore, bond angle decrease in this order.

Volatility

Water has low volatility (high boiling points) as H-bonding brings associated. Volatility decreases from H_2S to H_2Te due to increase in the molecular masses of hydrides.

Thus, the order of volatility will be $H_2S > H_2Se > H_2Te > H_2O$

Boiling Point

- Due to strong intermolecular H-bonding H_2O has very high boiling point. The electronegativity of other element, (i.e. S, Se, Te) is much lower therefore, they do not show H-bonding. Thus, their boiling point is less.
- Now on moving down the group, size of central atom increases, therefore van der Waals' forces of attraction increases.

Thus the order of boiling point will be

$$H_2O > H_2Te > H_2Se > H_2S.$$

Acidic Strength

The acidity increases in the series as $H_2O < H_2S < H_2Se < H_2Te < H_2Po$. H_2O is neutral in nature. Increase in acidic strength of hydrides can be easily explained on the basis of increase in the size of central atom from oxygen to tellurium.

As result of such an increase, the length of A—H (A : central atom) bond also increases gradually which is always inversely proportional to bond strength. Thus, bond strength decreases.

JEE Spotlite

Thermal Stability

As the size of central atom increases, the A—H (A = O to Po) bond becomes longer and weaker. Consequently, the thermal stability decreases.

Thus, order of thermal stability is

$$H_2O > H_2S > H_2Se > H_2Te$$

Reducing Power

Hydrides of group 16 elements except H_2O acts as reducing agent. Their reducing character increases from H_2S to H_2Te due to decrease in thermal stability. Thus, order of reducing power is

$$H_2S < H_2Se < H_2Te$$

The properties of these hydrides are summarised given below

Properties of Hydrides of Group 16 Elements

Property	H_2O	H_2S	H_2Se	H_2Te
Melting point (°C)	0	– 85.5	– 65.7	–51.1
Boiling point (°C)	100.0	– 60.75	– 41.5	–1.8
Bond angle H—A—H	104.5°	92.5°	90°	89°
Bond length H—X (Å)	0.95	1.30	1.45	1.72
Dissociation constant as an acid at 25°C	1.0×10^{-14}	1.0×10^{-7}	1.7×10^{-4}	2.3×10^{-3}

First two members of the family also form hydrides of the formula H_2A_2 (i.e. H_2O_2 and H_2S_2). However, these two hydrides differ considerably from each other.

e.g. H_2O_2 is fairly stable but H_2S_2 is unstable. It decomposes readily to give S and H_2S as,

$$H_2S_2 \xrightarrow{OH^-} H_2S + S$$

Similarly, H_2O_2 on account of hydrogen bonding is highly associated while, H_2S_2 forms discrete molecules.

Reactivity Towards Halogens or Formation of Halides

Oxygen forms halides only with fluorine (OF_2-oxygen difluoride) and its compounds with rest of the halogens are called **oxides** (not halides) as its electronegativity is more than any other halogen. S and other chalcogens form a number of halides.

The general preparation routes for chalcogen halides involve the direct reaction of chalcogens with respective halogen, i.e.

$$\frac{1}{8}S_8(s) + 3F_2(g) \longrightarrow SF_6(g)$$

$$Te(s) + 2Cl_2(g) \longrightarrow TeCl_4(s)$$

Direct fluorination of elemental sulphur yields mainly SF_6 along with traces of SF_4 · SF_4 is also prepared by the fluorination of SCl_2 with NaF in acetonitrile at 350 K as,

$$3SCl_2 + 4NaF \xrightarrow{\text{MeCN, 350 K}} S_2Cl_2 + SF_4 + 4NaCl$$

All the halides of these elements can be tabulated as,

Halides of Oxygen Family

Elements	F	Cl	Br	I
O	OF_2, F_2O_2	Cl_2O_6, Cl_2O_7, Cl_2O, ClO_2 etc	Br_2O, BrO_2, BrO_3	I_2O, I_2O_4, I_2O_5
S	S_2F_2, SF_4, SF_6, S_2F_{10}	S_2Cl_2, SCl_2, SCl_4	SBr_2	—
Se	SeF_2, SeF_4, SeF_6	Se_2Cl_2, $SeCl_4$	Se_2Br_2, $SeBr_4$	—
Te	TeF_4, Te_2F_{10}, TeF_6	$TeCl_2$, $TeCl_4$	$TeBr_2$, $TeBr_4$	TeI_4
Po	—	$PoCl_2$, $PoCl_4$	$PoBr_2$, $PoBr_4$	PoI_4

Some important facts related to halides of 16 group elements are as follows

- The stability of halides decreases in the order F > Cl > Br > I. The highest oxidation state is found only with fluorides.
- SF_6 is an inert non-toxic gas at room temperature. It is inert due to sterically protected S-atom. In contrast, less sterically hindered SF_6 and SF_4 undergo hydrolysis readily.
- Compared to sulphur halides, the halides of Se and especially Te adopt oligomeric or polymeric structures. In +4 oxidation state, $SeCl_4$, $SeBr_4$, $TeCl_4$, $TeBr_4$ and TeI_4 exist as tetramer while, TeF_4 has polymeric structure.
- All hexafluorides have a high degree of covalency and low boiling points.
- The tetrahalides act as Lewis bases (electron pair donor) due to the presence of lone pair of electrons and also as Lewis acids (electron pair acceptors) due to the ability to extend their coordination number.
- All the member of this group form dihalides. They show sp^3 hybridisation with bent structure.
- Known monohalides are dimer in nature which disproportionate.

e.g. $$2\overset{+1}{Se_2}Cl_2 \longrightarrow \overset{+4}{Se}Cl_4 + \overset{0}{Se}$$

Anomalous Behaviour of Oxygen

Oxygen the first member of group 16 differs from the rest of members due to (a) small size, (b) high EN and (c) non-availability of *d*-orbitals in the valence shell.

The main points of difference between oxygen and the rest of the members of group 16 are as follows :

- Oxygen is a gas at room temperature while other members are solids.
- Oxygen molecule is diatomic (O_2) while the molecules of the other elements are more complex, e.g., sulphur and selenium have octa-atomic molecules (i.e., S_8 and Se_8) with puckered ring structures.
- Being most electronegative element of the group, oxygen usually shows an oxidation state of –2 in most of its compounds (except in peroxides, superoxides O_2F_2 and OF_2). Sulphur also shows an oxidation state of –2 to some extent. Other elements of this group, however, do not show negative oxidation states.
- Compounds of oxygen are ionic as well as covalent while those of sulphur and other members of this group are mostly covalent.
- Due to small size and high electronegativity, oxygen forms $p\pi$-$p\pi$ multiple bonds with elements having similar size, i.e., carbon, nitrogen (C=O, C=N, C≡N), etc. This tendency of forming multiple bonds is not shown by other elements of this group mainly due to larger size and lower electronegativity.
- Due to high electronegativity, oxygen forms H-bonds. For example, the hydride of oxygen (H_2O) forms intermolecular H-bonds while hydrides of other elements of this group (H_2S, H_2Se etc.) do not. As a result, H_2O is a liquid at room temperature while hydrides of other elements are gases.
- Due to the presence of two unpaired electrons, O_2 is paramagnetic in gaseous, liquid and solid states. The other elements of this group are however, diamagnetic, in their elemental states.

Dioxygen/Oxygen (O_2)

Preparation, properties, structure and uses of oxygen are as follows

Preparation

Oxygen can be obtained in the laboratory by following methods:

- **From Oxides** (i) By thermal decomposition of the oxides of metals which are placed in e.g. the lower part of electrochemical series.

$$2HgO \xrightarrow{450°C} 2Hg + O_2$$
$$2Ag_2O \xrightarrow{350°C} 4Ag + O_2$$

(ii) By the thermal decomposition of higher oxides.

$$3MnO_2 \xrightarrow{\text{Heat}} Mn_3O_4 + O_2$$
$$2Pb_3O_4 \xrightarrow{\text{Heat}} 6PbO + O_2$$
$$2BaO_2 \xrightarrow{\text{Heat}} 2BaO + O_2$$

(iii) By action of conc. H_2SO_4 on MnO_2.

$$2MnO_2 + 2H_2SO_4 \longrightarrow 2MnSO_4 + 2H_2O + O_2$$

(iv) By action of water on sodium peroxide

$$2Na_2O_2 + 2H_2O \longrightarrow 4NaOH + O_2$$

- **From Salts** (i) Alkali nitrates on heating evolve oxygen.

$$2NaNO_3 \longrightarrow 2NaNO_2 + O_2 ;$$
$$2KNO_3 \longrightarrow 2KNO_2 + O_2$$

(ii) $K_2Cr_2O_7$, $KMnO_4$ and $KClO_3$ decompose at high temperatures evolving oxygen.

$$4K_2Cr_2O_7 \xrightarrow{400°C} 4K_2CrO_4 + 2Cr_2O_3 + 3O_2$$
$$2KMnO_4 \xrightarrow{250°C} K_2MnO_4 + MnO_2 + O_2$$
$$2KClO_3 \xrightarrow{400°C} 2KCl + 3O_2$$

(ii) By heating $KMnO_4$ or $K_2Cr_2O_7$ with concentrated H_2SO_4.

$$4KMnO_4 + 6H_2SO_4 \longrightarrow 2K_2SO_4 + 4MnSO_4 + 6H_2O + 3O_2$$
$$2K_2Cr_2O_7 + 8H_2SO_4 \longrightarrow 2K_2SO_4 + 2Cr_2(SO_4)_3 + 8H_2O + 3O_2$$

(iv) By adding H_2O_2 to acidified $KMnO_4$ solution.

$$2KMnO_4 + 3H_2SO_4 + 5H_2O_2 \longrightarrow K_2SO_4 + 2MnSO_4 + 8H_2O + 5O_2$$

Physical Properties

Oxygen is a colourless, odourless and tasteless gas. It is little heavier than air and is slightly soluble in water. This small amount of dissolved oxygen in water supports the respiration of fish and other aquatic animals.

- It is soluble in alkaline pyrogallol.
- It exhibits allotropy. Its allotropic form is ozone (O_3).
- There are three isotopes of oxygen with mass numbers 16, 17 and 18 isotopes among the three.
- O^{16} is the main isotopes among the three with an abundance of nearly 99.8%.
- Oxygen is not a combustible gas, but it is a strong supporter of combustion. It is very active element.

Chemical Properties

- The bond dissociation energy of O_2 is high and hence the reactions of O_2 requires initiation by external heating.
- **Oxides May be Prepared** by burning of elements such as C, P, S, Na, K, Mg, etc. in air or oxygen atmosphere.

$$C + O_2 \longrightarrow CO_2 \text{ (Carbon burns with flush light)}$$
$$4K + O_2 \longrightarrow 2K_2O \text{ (Potassium burns with violet light)}$$
$$2Mg + O_2 \longrightarrow 2MgO \text{ (Magnesium burns with white light)}$$

Structure

Oxygen is a linear molecule with a bond angle of 180°.

$$:\ddot{O}=\ddot{O}:$$

The MOT configuration of O_2 molecule is as follows:

$$KK\sigma(2s)^2\sigma^*(2s)^2\sigma(2p_z)^2\pi(2p_x)^2\pi(2p_y)^2\pi^*(2p_x)^1\pi^*(2p_y)^1$$

Bond order in this case is, $\frac{1}{2}(8-4)=2$

Uses

- Liquid oxygen is an important constituent of fuels used in rockets.
- It is used as an oxidising agent in several reactions.
- It is used in the manufacturing large number of compounds such as phenol, chlorine etc.

Ozone (O_3)

Preparation, properties, structure and uses of ozone are as follows

Preparation

(i) Ozone is obtained by passing silent electric discharge through dry oxygen. It is believed that some of the oxygen molecules dissociate and then atomic oxygen combines with oxygen molecules to form ozone.

$$O_2 \xrightarrow{\text{Energy}} O + O$$

$$O_2 + O \longrightarrow O_3$$

$$3O_2 \rightleftharpoons 2O_3 - \text{energy} + 1425 \text{ kJ mol}^{-1}$$

(ii) The electrolysis of acidified water with high current density and platinum anode yields ozone on the anode.

Physical Properties

(i) It is a pale blue gas with a characteristic strong smell.

(ii) It is slightly soluble in water but more soluble in turpentine oil, glacial acetic acid or carbon tetrachloride.

Chemical Properties

(i) **Decomposition** It is unstable and decomposes completely into oxygen at 473 K.

$$2O_3 \xrightarrow{\text{Heat}} 3O_2 - 142 \text{ kJ mol}^{-1}$$

MnO_2, platinum black, silver, lead dioxide etc., decompose ozone at ordinary temperature, i.e., they catalyse its decomposition.

(ii) **Oxidising Nature** Due to the ease with which it can liberate nascent oxygen, it acts as a powerful oxidising agent. The potential equation is

$$O_3 \longrightarrow O_2 + O$$

The reduction potential in acid medium is +2.07 V.

$$O_3 + 2H^+ + 2e^- \longrightarrow O_2 + H_2O \qquad E^\circ = +2.07 \text{ V}$$

$$2HCl + O_3 \longrightarrow H_2O + Cl_2 + O_2$$

It oxidises as,

$$2FeSO_4 + H_2SO_4 + O_3 \longrightarrow Fe_2(SO_4)_3 + H_2O + O_2$$

$$2KI + H_2O + O_3 \longrightarrow 2KOH + I_2 + O_2$$

$$PbS + 4O_3 \longrightarrow PbSO_4 + 4O_2$$

$$NaNO_2 + O_3 \longrightarrow NaNO_3 + O_2$$

$$Na_2SO_3 + O_3 \longrightarrow Na_2SO_4 + O_2$$

$$\underset{\text{Sodium arsenite}}{Na_3AsO_3} + O_3 \longrightarrow \underset{\text{Sodium arsenate}}{Na_3AsO_4} + O_2$$

$$\underset{\text{Potassium manganate}}{2K_2MnO_4} + H_2O + O_3 \longrightarrow \underset{\text{Potassium permanganate}}{2KMnO_4} + 2KOH + O_2$$

$$\underset{\text{Potassium ferrocyanide}}{2K_4Fe(CN)_6} + H_2O + O_3 \longrightarrow \underset{\text{Potassium ferricyanide}}{2K_3Fe(CN)_6} + 2KOH + O_2$$

$$I_2 + H_2O + 5O_3 \longrightarrow \underset{\text{Iodic acid}}{2HIO_3} + 5O_2$$

$$S + 8H_2O + 24O_3 \longrightarrow 8H_2SO_4 + 3O_2$$

$$P_4 + 6H_2O + 10O_3 \longrightarrow 4H_3PO_4 + 10O_2$$

$$2As + 3H_2O + 5O_3 \longrightarrow 2H_3AsO_4 + 5O_2$$

$$H_2S + O_3 \longrightarrow H_2O + S + O_2$$

$$KI + 3O_3 \longrightarrow KIO_3 + 3O_2$$

(iii) **Formation of Ozonides** Ozone reacts with unsaturated organic compounds containing double bonds. The products formed are known as ozonides. The ozonides breakup when treated with Zn and water to form carbonyl compounds. The process is called ozonolysis. H_2O_2 is evolved in most of the cases.

(iv) **Reaction with Peroxide** Reaction of ozone with peroxide results in their mutual reduction with the liberation of oxygen.

$$BaO_2 + O_3 \longrightarrow BaO + 2O_2$$

$$H_2O_2 + O_3 \longrightarrow H_2O + 2O_2$$

Structure

The two O—O bond length in the ozone molecule are identical (128 pm) and the molecule is angular and have a expected bond angle of about 117°.

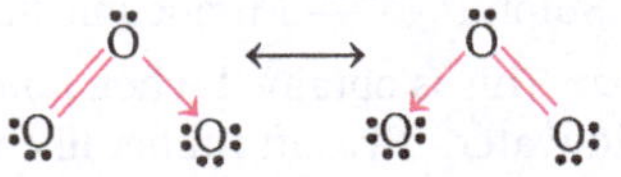

Uses

(i) As a germicide and disinfectant for sterilising water and improving the atmosphere of crowded places like tube railways mines and cinema halls.

(ii) It is a good bleaching agent. The bleaching action is due to its oxidising action on the organic matter.

coloured substance + O $\longrightarrow$ Colourless

It bleaches oil, ivory, flour, starch, waxes, wood pulp, etc.

Sulphur

Occurrence It occurs in abundance in the combined state as zine blende (ZnS), galena (PbS), cinnabar (HgS), copper pyrites ($CuFeS_2$), H_2S, SO_2, gypsum ($CaSO_4 \cdot 2H_2O$) etc.

Action of Heat on Sulphur

Ordinary sulphur melts at 114°C to a pale yellow mobile liquid. On heating further instead of becoming more mobile, it grows thicker. The colour changes to reddish brown and then to almost black. At about 180°C, the viscosity increases so much that it cannot be poured out by inverting the container. At about 200°C the viscosity begins to decrease and at its boiling point of 444°C, the liquid is again mobile.

Allotropic forms of Sulphur

Sulphur exists in several allotropic forms, the important ones are described below:

- **Rhombic or Octahedral or α-Sulphur** This is the common form of thermodynamically most stable allotrope. It is pale yellow in colour. It melts at 114.5°C. Its specific gravity is 2.06. It is insoluble in water but readily soluble in carbon disulphide.

  It is a crystalline variety and consists of S_8 structural units packed together into octahedral shape. This is the stable variety at ordinary temperature and all other forms gradually change into this form.

- **Monoclinic or Prismatic or β-Sulphur** This form is formed by melting sulphur in a dish and cooling till crust is formed. Two holes are made in the crust and liquid is poured out. On removing the crust, needle shaped crystals of monoclinic sulphur are obtained.

  This form of sulphur is stable above 95.6°C. The crystals are amber yellow in colour and have specific gravity of 1.96. Crystals melt at 119°C. It is also soluble in carbon disulphide. Below 95.6°C, it changes into rhombic form. Thus, 95.6°C is the transition temperature.

$$\text{Rhombic Sulphur} \xrightleftharpoons{95.6°C} \text{Monoclinic Sulphur}$$

- **Plastic Sulphur** This is obtained when boiling sulphur is poured into cold water. It is soft rubber like mass which hardens on standing and gradually changes into rhombic sulphur. It is amber-brown in colour and has specific gravity of 1.95. It is insoluble in CS_2 and has no sharp melting point. It consists of a completely random arrangement of chains of sulphur atoms.

Uses

Sulphur is used

(i) in the manufacture of SO_2, H_2SO_4, CS_2, matches gun powder, fire works. etc.

(ii) for vulcanising rubber and in the manufacture of sulphur dyes.

JEE MAPPER

Example Similar to PYQ Asked in JEE Main 2020

The number of bonds between sulphur and oxygen atoms in $S_2O_8^{2-}$ is 8 and the number of bonds between sulphur and sulphur atoms in rhombic sulphur is.

Sol. (8) The two important allotropes of sulphur are yellow rhombic (α-sulphur) and monoclinic (β-sulphur). Both the allotropes have S_8 molecules but the temperature at which these are stable are different.

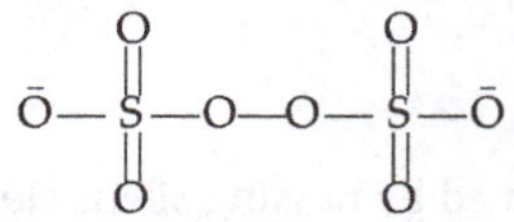

Total number of S—O = 4 and S=O bond = 4

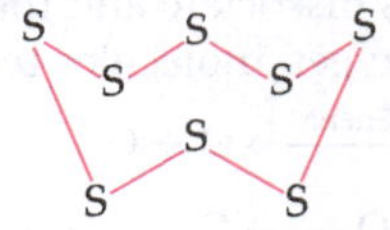

Total number of S—S bond = 8

Competency Enhancer 2.1

The number of peroxy linkage present in chemical formula of peroxodisulphuric acid is …… .

Oxides of Sulphur

Sulphur forms a number of oxides. These are:

- Sulphur suboxide, S_2O (colourless gas)
- Sulphur monoxide, SO (colourless gas)
- Sulphur sesquioxide, S_2O_3 (green crystalline solid)
- Sulphur dioxide, SO_2 (colourless gas)
- Sulphur trioxide, SO_3 (volatile liquid)
- Sulphur heptoxide, S_2O_7 (liquid)
- Sulphur tetroxide, SO_4 (white solid)

Brief explanation of some of the oxides of sulphur are as follows.

1. Sulphur Dioxide, SO_2

It is an important oxide of sulphur.

Preparation

By burning of S in air. In laboratory SO_2 can be prepared by

$$S + O_2 \longrightarrow SO_2$$

(a) $S + 2H_2SO_4 \xrightarrow{\text{Heat}} 2H_2O + 3SO_2$

(b) $Cu + 2H_2SO_4 \longrightarrow CuSO_4 + 2H_2O + SO_2$

(c) $Na_2SO_3 + 2HCl \longrightarrow 2NaCl + H_2O + SO_2$

(d) $4FeS_2 + HO_2 \longrightarrow 2Fe_2O_3 + 8SO_2$

Physical Properties

(i) It is a colourless gas, with a pungent, suffocating odour.

(ii) It is highly soluble in water.

(iii) It is heavier than air.

Chemical Properties

(i) **Non-supporter of Combustion** It is neither combustible nor a supporter of combustion. However, certain substances like magnesium, potassium etc continue to burn on heating in pressure of SO_2

$$2Mg + SO_2 \xrightarrow{\Delta} 2MgO + S$$

$$4K + 3SO_2 \xrightarrow{\Delta} K_2SO_3 + K_2S_2O_3$$

(ii) **Thermal Decomposition** It decomposes at 1200°C producing sulphur trioxide and sulphur.

$$3SO_2 \longrightarrow 2SO_3 + S$$

(iii) **Acidic Nature** It is an acidic oxide. It dissolves in water forming sulphurous acid.

$$SO_2 + H_2O \longrightarrow H_2SO_3 \text{ (Sulphurous acid)}$$

The gas is, therefore, known as sulphurous anhydride. It combines with basic oxides and forms sulphites.

$$BaO + SO_2 \longrightarrow BaSO_3$$

(iv) **Addition Reactions**

- It combines directly with halogens to form sulphuryl halides.

$$SO_2 + Cl_2 \longrightarrow SO_2Cl_2 \text{ (sulphuryl chloride)}$$

- It directly combines with lead dioxide to form lead sulphate

$$PbO_2 + SO_2 \longrightarrow PbSO_4$$

(v) **Reducing Nature** The aqueous solution of SO_2 acts as a reducing agent as sulphurous acid changes into sulphuric acid giving nascent hydrogen.

$$H_2O + SO_2 \longrightarrow H_2SO_3$$

$$H_2SO_3 + H_2O \longrightarrow H_2SO_4 + 2[H]$$

It reduces as

$$SO_2 + 2H_2O + Cl_2 \longrightarrow H_2SO_4 + 2HCl$$

$$2KMnO_4 + 5SO_2 + 2H_2O \longrightarrow K_2SO_4 + 2MnSO_4 + 2H_2SO_4$$

$$K_2Cr_2O_7 + 3SO_2 + 2H_2SO_4 \longrightarrow K_2SO_4 + \underset{\text{(Green)}}{Cr_2(SO_4)_3} + H_2O$$

$$Fe_2(SO_4)_3 + SO_2 + 2H_2O \longrightarrow 2FeSO_4 + 2H_2SO_4$$

(vi) **Oxidising Nature** It also acts as an oxidising agent particularly when treated with stronger reducing agents.

It oxidises as

$$2H_2S + SO_2 \longrightarrow 2H_2O + 3S$$

$$3Mg + SO_2 \longrightarrow 2MgO + MgS$$

$$3Fe + SO_2 \longrightarrow 2FeO + FeS$$

JEE Quicker

SO_2 acts as an oxidising agent but not as a reducing agent.
JEE Main 2025

The given statement is incorrect As central atom 'S' in SO_2 has an intermediate oxidation state of +4. So, it allows sulphur to either gain or lose electrons, depending on the reaction type. So, SO_2 can act as both oxidising and reducing agent.

(vii) **Bleaching action** SO_2 in presence of moisture acts as a bleaching agent. This is due to the reducing nature of SO_2.

$$SO_2 + 2H_2O \longrightarrow H_2SO_4 + 2H$$

$$\text{Coloured matter} + H \longrightarrow \text{Colourless matter}$$

The bleaching is temporary. The bleached matter when exposed to air regains its colour due to oxidation.

Uses

(i) As a refrigerant in the form of liquid SO_2.

(ii) It is used as an antichlor for removing, chlorine from a fabric after bleaching.

2. Sulphuric Acid (Oil of vitriol) H_2SO_4

H_2SO_4 is important oxide of sulphur.

Preparation

Old Method

In ancient days, it was called oil of vitriol as it was prepared by distilling ferrous sulphate (Green Vitriol).

$$\underset{\text{Green vitriol}}{2FeSO_4 \cdot 7H_2O} \xrightarrow{\text{Heat}} Fe_2O_3 + \underset{\text{Oil of vitriol}}{H_2SO_4} + SO_2 + 13H_2O$$

Native sulphur is the starting material for the preparation of sulphuric acid. Sulphur is burnt and easily converted into sulphur dioxide. The conversion of sulphur dioxide into sulphur trioxide is a matter of difficulty. It requires either a catalyst or a strong oxidising agent. The trioxide dissolves carefully in water to form sulphuric acid. The whole process may be summarised as:

$$S \longrightarrow SO_2 \longrightarrow SO_3 \longrightarrow H_2SO_4$$

For the oxidation of sulphur dioxide into sulphur trioxide, the following reactions may be used:

(i) By atmospheric oxygen in presence of a catalyst, V_2O_5, at 400°C.

$$2SO_2 + O_2 \xrightarrow[400°C]{V_2O_5} 2SO_3$$

$$SO_3 + H_2O \longrightarrow H_2SO_4$$

(ii) By Cl_2 or Br_2 in presence of moisture.

$$SO_2 + 2H_2O + Cl_2 \longrightarrow H_2SO_4 + 2HCl$$

$$SO_2 + 2H_2O + Br_2 \longrightarrow H_2SO_4 + 2HBr + H_2O$$

(iii) By ozone (O_3)

$$SO_2 + O_3 \longrightarrow H_2SO_4 + O_2$$

(iv) By conc. HNO_3

$$SO_2 + 2HNO_3 \longrightarrow H_2SO_4 + 2NO_2$$

Industrial Method of Preparations

Sulphuric acid is manufactured these days by the following two processes:

(a) Lead chamber process (b) Contact process

Lead Chamber Process

Principle The mixture containing sulphur dioxide, air and nitric oxide when treated with steam, sulphuric acid is formed.

$$\underset{(Air)}{2SO_2 + O_2} + 2H_2O + \underset{Catalyst}{[NO]} \longrightarrow 2H_2SO_4 + \underset{Catalyst}{[NO]}$$

Nitric oxide acts as a catalyst in this reaction.

Contact Process

Principle This process involves the oxidation of sulphur dioxide by air in the presence of a catalyst.

$$2SO_2 + O_2 \xrightleftharpoons{Catalyst} 2SO_3$$

Sulphur trioxide is dissolved in 98% sulphuric acid when oleum is formed.

$$H_2SO_4 + SO_3 \longrightarrow H_2S_2O_7 \text{ (Oleum)}$$

Sulphuric acid of any desired concentration can be obtained from oleum by dilution with water.

$$H_2S_2O_7 + H_2O \longrightarrow 2H_2SO_4$$

The oxidation of sulphur dioxide is reversible and exothermic.

$$2SO_2 + O_2 \rightleftharpoons 2SO_3 - 196.6 \text{ kJ mol}^{-1}$$

Concept Visualizer

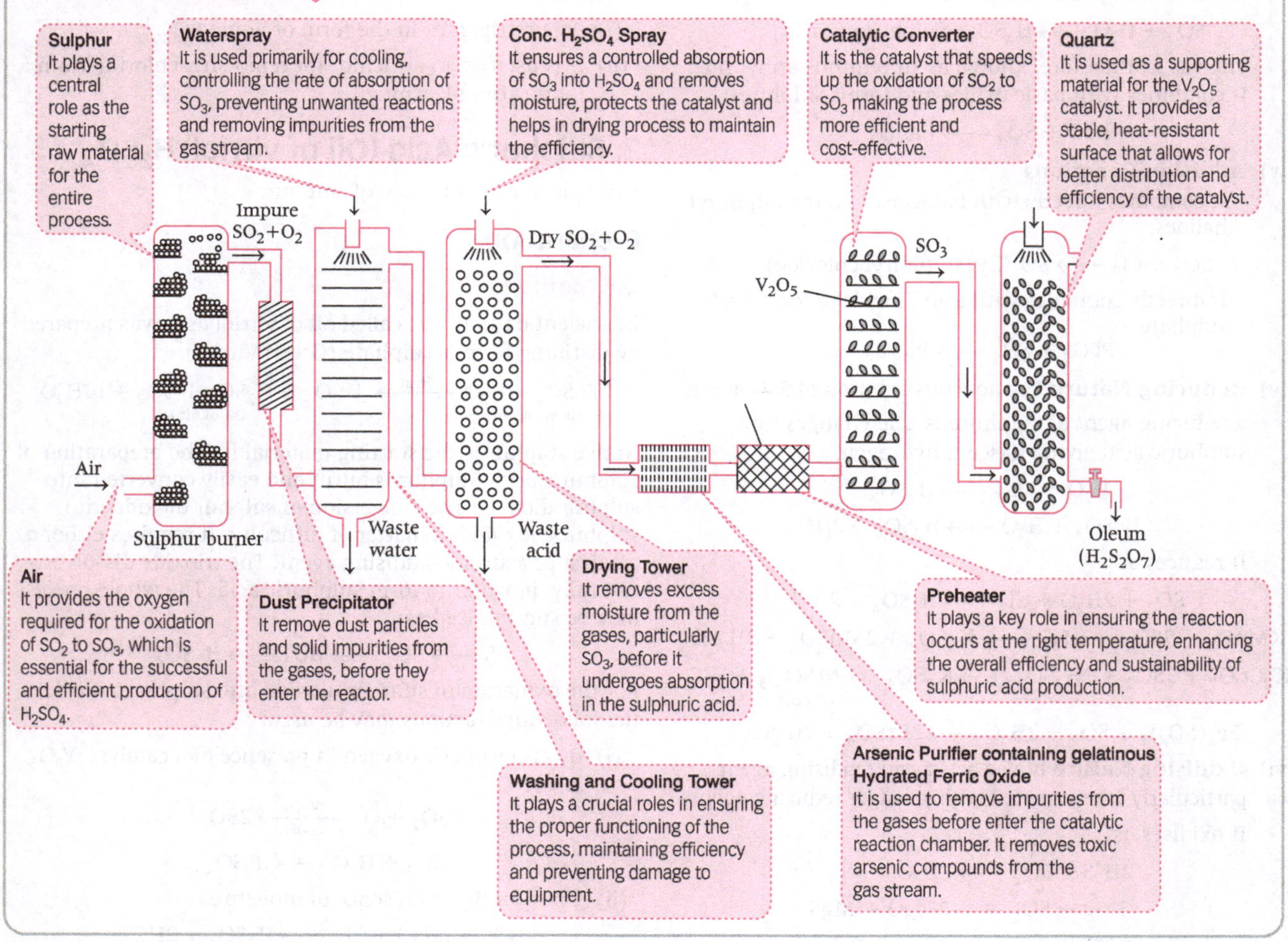

Comparison between the Lead Chamber and Contact Process

	Lead chamber process	Contact process
1.	Catalyst used is a gas-nitric oxide	Catalyst used is a solid vanadium pentoxide or platinum asbestos.
2.	Acid obtained is impure	Acid obtained is pure.
3.	Methods of concentration of the acid are troublesome.	Further concentration is not necessary.
4.	It is not necessary to purify the gases	It is absolutely necessary to purify the gases as impurities and acts as poison to catalyst.
5.	It is a cheaper method.	It is a costlier method. The cost had been reduced by the use of V_2O_5 in place of platinum.

Physical Properties

(i) It is a colourless syrupy liquid. It contains 98.3% sulphuric acid. Its specific gravity is 1.84 at 15°C.

(ii) It fumes strongly in moist air and is highly corrosive in nature.

(iii) It is highly soluble in water.

(iv) Due to its great affinity for water, it is used as a dehydrating substance.

(v) It is a conductor of heat and electricity.

(vi) Water should not be added to concentrated sulphuric acid for dilution but concentrated sulphuric acid should be added slowly to cold water with constant stirring.

Chemical Properties

(i) **Dissociation** At 444°C, the vapours of sulphuric acid dissociate into steam and sulphur trioxide.

$$H_2SO_4 \xrightleftharpoons{444°C} H_2O + SO_3$$

(ii) **Acidic Nature** Dilute sulphuric acid is a strong dibasic acid. It ionises as:

$$H_2SO_4 \rightleftharpoons H^+ + HSO_4^- \rightleftharpoons 2H^+ + SO_4^{2-}$$

- It forms two series of salts with bases.

$$NaOH + H_2SO_4 \longrightarrow \underset{\text{Sodium bisulphate}}{NaHSO_4} + H_2O$$

$$2NaOH + H_2SO_4 \longrightarrow \underset{\text{Sodium sulphate}}{Na_2SO_4} + H_2O$$

- It decomposes carbonates and bicarbonates into carbon dioxide.

$$Na_2CO_3 + H_2SO_4 \longrightarrow Na_2SO_4 + H_2O + CO_2$$

$$\underset{\text{(Dilute)}}{NaHCO_3} + H_2SO_4 \longrightarrow NaHSO_4 + H_2O + CO_2$$

- It reacts with electropositive metals evolving hydrogen.

$$Zn + H_2SO_4 \longrightarrow ZnSO_4 + H_2$$

$$Fe + H_2SO_4 \longrightarrow FeSO_4 + H_2$$

- It displaces more volatile acids from their metal salts.

$$2NaCl + H_2SO_4 \longrightarrow Na_2SO_4 + 2HCl$$

$$Ca_3(PO_4)_2 + 3H_2SO_4 \longrightarrow 3CaSO_4 + 2H_3PO_4$$

$$FeS + H_2SO_4 \longrightarrow FeSO_4 + H_2S$$

$$CaF_2 + H_2SO_4 \longrightarrow CaSO_4 + 2HF$$

(iii) **Oxidising Nature** It acts as a strong oxidising agent. The potential equation is:

$$\underset{\text{(Hot conc.)}}{H_2SO_4} \longrightarrow H_2O + SO_2 + [O]$$

- Non-metals such as carbon and sulphur are oxidised to their oxides.

$$C + 2H_2SO_4 \longrightarrow CO_2 + 2SO_2 + 2H_2O$$

$$S + 2H_2SO_4 \longrightarrow 2SO_2 + 2H_2O$$

- Metals like copper, silver, mercury, etc., are first oxidised by conc. H_2SO_4 and then the oxides combine with acid to form corresponding sulphates.

$$Cu + 2H_2SO_4 \longrightarrow CuSO_4 + SO_2 + 2H_2O$$

$$2Ag + 2H_2SO_4 \longrightarrow Ag_2SO_4 + SO_2 + 2H_2O$$

$$Hg + 2H_2SO_4 \longrightarrow HgSO_4 + SO_2 + 2H_2O$$

- Iodine is liberated from KI (HI is oxidised to I_2)

$$2KI + 2H_2SO_4 \longrightarrow K_2SO_4 + SO_2 + I_2 + 2H_2O$$

Similarly, bromine is liberated from KBr (HBr is oxidised to Br_2).

$$2KBr + 2H_2SO_4 \longrightarrow K_2SO_4 + SO_2 + Br_2 + 2H_2O$$

In presence of Hg as a catalyst, naphthalene is oxidised to phthalic acid.

$$C_{10}H_8 + 9H_2SO_4 \xrightarrow{Hg} \underset{\text{Phthalic acid}}{C_8H_6O_4} + 10H_2O + 9SO_2 + 2CO_2$$

(iv) **Dehydrating Nature** As concentrated sulphuric acid has great affinity for water, it acts as a powerful dehydrating agent. Its corrosive action on skin is also due to dehydration of skin. It absorbs water from organic compounds.

e.g.

$$\underset{\text{Cane sugar}}{C_{12}H_{22}O_{11}} \xrightarrow[(-11\,H_2O)]{H_2SO_4} 12C$$

$$\underset{\text{Glucose}}{C_6H_{12}O_6} \xrightarrow[(-6\,H_2O)]{H_2SO_4} 6C$$

$$\underset{\text{Oxalic Acid}}{(COOH)_2} \xrightarrow[(-H_2O)]{H_2SO_4} CO + CO_2$$

$$\underset{\text{Formic acid}}{HCOOH} \xrightarrow[(-H_2O)]{H_2SO_4} CO$$

$$\underset{\text{Ethyl alcohol}}{2C_2H_5OH} \xrightarrow[(-H_2O)]{H_2SO_4} \underset{\text{Ether}}{C_2H_5OC_2H_5}$$

Cloth, wood, starch, paper, etc., are all charred in concentrated sulphuric acid.

- **Sulphonation** Aromatic compounds react with sulphuric acid forming sulphonic acid.

$$\underset{\text{Benzene}}{C_6H_6} + H_2SO_4 \longrightarrow \underset{\text{Benzene Sulphonic acid}}{C_6H_5SO_3H} + H_2O$$

- **Action of PCl_5** The molecule of sulphuric acid contains two hydroxyl groups. One or both the hydroxyl groups can be replaced by chlorine when treated with PCl_5.

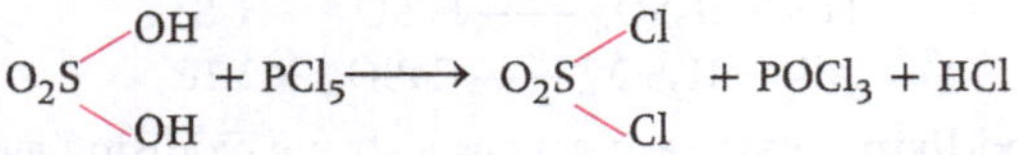

Sulphuryl chloride

Oxoacids

Among the group members members only **oxo acids** of S, Se and Te are known. S forms many **oxo acids** while Se and Te form two oxo acids each. Some of these oxoacids are given in the following table below

Oxyacids of S, Se and Te

S	Se	Te
H_2SO_3 (sulphurous acid)	H_2SeO_3 (selenous acid)	H_2TeO_3 (tellurous acid)
H_2SO_4 (sulphuric acid or oil of vitriol)	H_2SeO_4 (selenic acid)	H_6TeO_6 (telluric acid)
H_2SO_5 (permono sulphuric acid or Caro's acid)		
$H_2S_2O_8$ (perdisulphuric acid or Marshall's acid)		

Oxo acids of Sulphur

Sulphur forms a number of oxo acids which are given below.

1. Sulphurous Acid (H_2SO_3)

In H_2SO_3 S is in +4 oxidation state and sp^3 hybridised. It will acts as an oxidising and reducing agent.

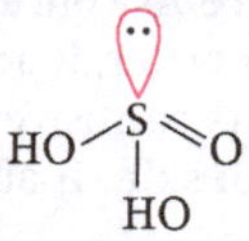

2. Thiosulphurous Acid ($H_2S_2O_2$)

In $H_2S_2O_2$ oxidation state of two sulphur atoms are −2 and +4 and sp^3 hybridised.

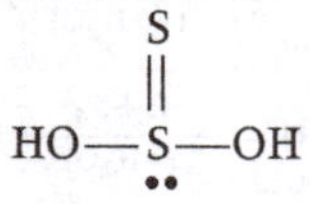

3. Hyposulphurous Acid ($H_2S_2O_4$)

In $H_2S_2O_4$ S is present in +3 oxidation state and sp^3 hybridized. It is also termed as hydrosulphurous acid and dithionous acid.

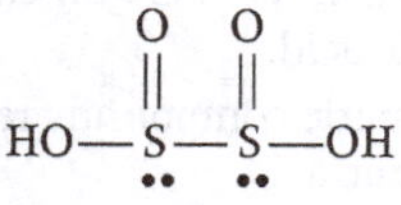

4. Di or Pyrosulphuric Acid ($H_2S_2O_5$)

In $H_2S_2O_5$, S is in +5 and +3 oxidation state and sp^3 hybridised.

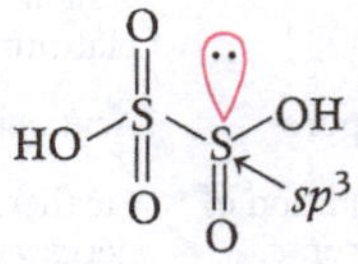

5. Sulphuric Acid (H_2SO_4)

In H_2SO_4, S is present in +6 oxidation state and sp^3 hybridised. It acts as dehydrating, oxidising and pickling agent.

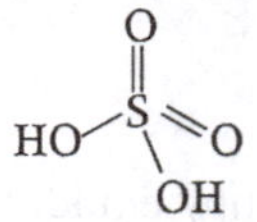

6. Thiosulphuric Acid ($H_2S_2O_3$)

In $H_2S_2O_3$, S is in +6 oxidation state and sp^3 hybridised.

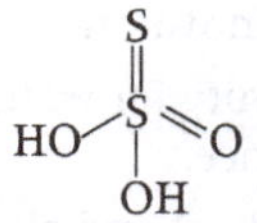

7. Pyrosulphuric Acid ($H_2S_2O_7$)

In $H_2S_2O_7$, S is present in +6 oxidation state and sp^3 hybridised. It is known as fuming sulphuric acid or anhydride of sulphuric acid or oleum.

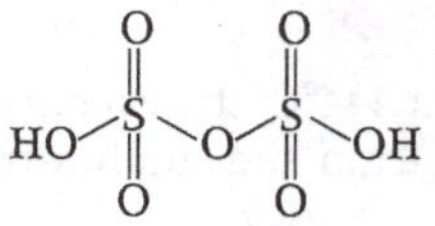

8. Dithonic Acid ($H_2S_2O_6$)

In $H_2S_2O_6$, S is present in +5 oxidation state and sp^3 hybridised.

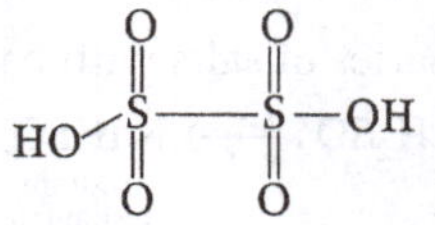

9. Polythionic Acid ($H_2S_nO_6$)

In $H_2S_nO_6$, S is in +5 oxidation state and sp^3 hybridised. Here n varies from $n = 1$ to 6.

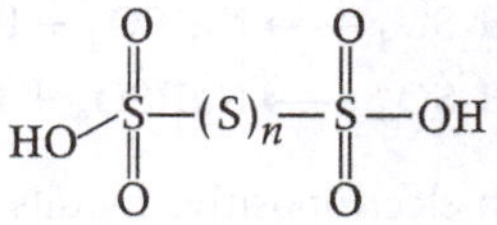

10. Peroxy Monosulphuric Acid (Caro's Acid) (H_2SO_5)

In H_2SO_5, S is in +6 oxidation state and sp^3 hybridised. There is a O—O linkage in the structure.

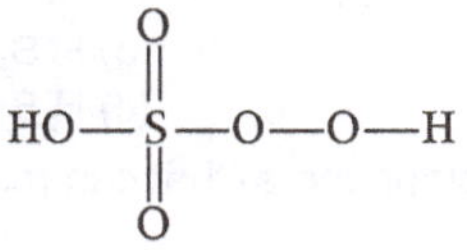

11. Peroxy Disulphuric Acid (Marshall's Acid) ($H_2S_2O_8$)

In $H_2S_2O_8$, S is in +6 oxidation state here both the S-atom are sp^3 hybridised.

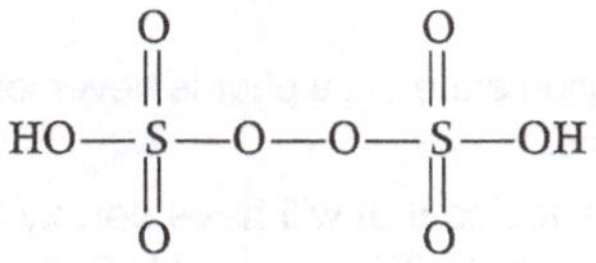

JEE MAPPER

Example Similar to PYQ Asked in JEE Advanced 2024

The compound(s) having S—S single bond is(are)

(a) $H_2S_2O_7$ (b) $H_2S_2O_6$ (c) $H_2S_2O_5$ (d) $H_2S_2O_3$

Sol. (*b*, *c*) The structure of the given compounds are as follows

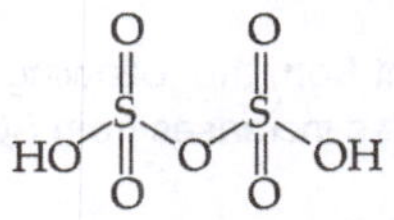

($H_2S_2O_7$)

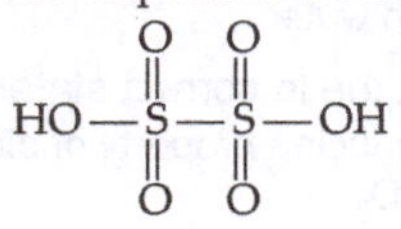

($H_2S_2O_6$)

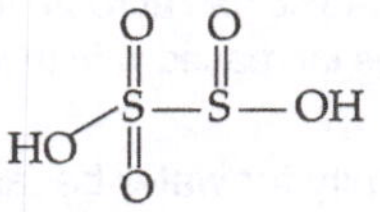

($H_2S_2O_5$)

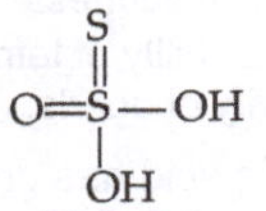

($H_2S_2O_3$)

Competency Enhancer 2.2

Among the following sulphur based oxoacids, the compound(s) having peroxide linkage is(are)

(a) H_2SO_3 (b) $H_2S_2O_5$ (c) $H_2S_2O_8$ (d) H_2SO_4

Elemental Practice 6.2

Type I MCQs with Only One Correct Option

1. Sulphur in +3 oxidation state is present in
   (a) dithionous acid
   (b) sulphurous acid
   (c) dithionic acid
   (d) pyrosulphuric acid

2. When the first electron gain enthalpy ($\Delta_{eg}H$) of oxygen is -141 kJ/mol, its second electron gain enthalpy is
   (a) a positive value
   (b) a more negative value than the first
   (c) almost the same as that of the first
   (d) negative, but less negative than the first

3. $SO_2 + H_2S \longrightarrow x + y$, the final products are
   (a) H_2SO_3 (b) H_2SO_4
   (c) $H_2S_2O_3$ (d) $H_2O + S$

4. The correct order of thermal stability of the hydrides of group 16 elements is
   (a) $H_2Po > H_2Te > H_2Se > H_2S > H_2O$
   (b) $H_2O < H_2S > H_2Se > H_2Te > H_2Po$
   (c) $H_2O > H_2S > H_2Se > H_2Te > H_2Po$
   (d) $H_2O > H_2S > H_2Po > H_2Te > H_2Se$

5. Sulphur on boiling with NaOH solution gives
   (a) $Na_2SO_3 + H_2S$
   (b) $Na_2S_2O_3 + Na_2S$
   (c) $Na_2S_2O_3 + NaHSO_3$
   (d) $Na_2SO_3 + SO_2$

6. Reaction of an inorganic sulphite *X* with dilute H_2SO_4 generates compound *Y*. Reaction of *Y* with NaOH gives *X*. Further, the reaction of *X* with *Y* and water affords compound *Z*. *Y* and *Z* respectively, are
   (a) SO_2 and Na_2SO_3 (b) SO_3 and $NaHSO_3$
   (c) SO_2 and $NaHSO_3$ (d) S and Na_2SO_3

7. $P_4 + O_3 \xrightarrow{H_2O} X$. Then *X* is
   (a) orthophosphoric acid (b) phosphorous acid
   (c) hypophosphoric acid (d) hypophosphorous acid

8. Ozone oxidizes dry iodine to
   (a) HIO (b) HIO_3 (c) I_4O_9 (d) HIO_2

9. Hydrogen sulphide forms precipitate with which of the following Compound(s)
   (a) $Cu(NO_3)_2$ (b) $AgNO_3$
   (c) $Hg(NO_3)_2$ (d) All of these

10. $H_2SO_4 + P_4O_{10} \longrightarrow A + B$, then *A* and *B* are
   (a) H_3PO_3 and SO_3 (b) H_3PO_4 and SO_3
   (c) H_3PO_4 and SO_2 (d) H_3PO_3 and SO_2

11. The incorrect statement about SO_2 is
   (a) It turns lime water milky and the milkiness disappears if it is passed for a long time.
   (b) It is obtained by heating copper with conc. H_2SO_4.
   (c) Its aqueous solution has a pH < 7 and it reacts with basic oxides such as CaO, BaO, etc.
   (d) It can act as a reducing agent but not as an oxidizing agent.

12. An aqueous solution of SO_2 acts as
(a) reducing agent as it can produce nascent oxygen on reaction with water.
(b) reducing agent as it can absorb nascent oxygen.
(c) oxidising agent as it can absorb nascent oxygen.
(d) oxidising agent as it can form nascent oxygen on reaction with water.

13. Select the in correct statement from the following
(a) Reducing property of dioxides increases from SO_2 to TeO_2.
(b) H_2S is less acidic than H_2Te.
(c) SF_6 is colourless and non-toxic gas at room temperature.
(d) The stability of tetrahalides increases with increase in polarity of bonds.

14. Sulphuric acid has great affinity for water because
(a) acid decomposes water
(b) water hydrolyses the acid
(c) water decomposes the acid
(d) acid forms hydrates with water

15. Choose the peroxoacids of sulphur from the following
(a) H_2SO_5 and $H_2S_2O_8$
(b) H_2SO_5 and $H_2S_2O_7$
(c) $H_2S_2O_7$ and $H_2S_2O_8$
(d) $H_2S_2O_6$ and $H_2S_2O_5$

Type II 》 MCQs with One or More than One Correct option

16. Select the correct statements from the following.
(a) S—S bond is present in $H_2S_2O_6$
(b) In peroxosulphuric acid (H_2SO_5) sulphur is in +6 oxidation state.
(c) Iron powder along with Al_2O_3 and K_2O is used as a catalyst in the preparation of NH_3 by Haber's process.
(d) Change in enthalpy is positive for the preparation of SO_3 by catalytic oxidation of SO_2.

17. The correct statement(s) among the following about ozone is
(a) it is a pale blue gas when pure and has a characteristic strong smell.
(b) it is more soluble in turpentine oil than in water
(c) it has an angular structure and it decomposes to form oxygen which is an exothermic reaction.
(d) it oxidizes moist I_2 to I_4O_9.

18. The compound(s) having both S-atom in +6 oxidation states is(are)
(a) $H_2S_2O_7$ (b) $H_2S_2O_3$
(c) $H_2S_2O_6$ (d) $H_2S_2O_8$

19. Select the compound(s) that can react with PCl_5 to give $POCl_3$.
(a) CO_2 (b) SO_2
(c) H_2SO_4 (d) P_4O_{10}

20. Select the correct statements regarding sulphur
(a) S_2 molecule is paramagnetic.
(b) The vapor at 200°C consists mostly by S_8 rings.
(c) Sulphuric acid is used in petroleum refining and in making fertilizers.
(d) The oxidation state of sulphur is never less than +4 in its compounds.

21. Choose the species that will have peroxy linkage.
(a) $H_2S_2O_7$ (b) H_2SO_5 (c) $H_2S_2O_8$ (d) CrO_5

22. Select the compounds that gives (+6) oxidation number on hydrolysis.
(a) SO_2 (b) SO_3 (c) $H_2S_2O_8$ (d) $H_2S_2O_7$

Type III 》 Numerical/Integer Answer Type Questions

23. The number of S—O—S bonds in sulphur trioxide trimer (S_3O_9) is
24. The sum of number of σ and π-bonds in peroxy disulphuric acid is
25. $SO_2 + H_2S \longrightarrow X + H_2O$, X belongs to which group of the periodic table?
26. The number of S—S linkage present in the product formed when thiosulphate ion is oxidised by iodine are
27. The number of ions having S—S bond from following are $S_2O_4^{2-}$, $S_2O_6^{2-}$, $S_2O_3^{2-}$, $S_2O_5^{2-}$, $S_2O_7^{2-}$

Elemental Practice 6.2 | Chapter 06
Connect with **Answers**

1. (a)	2. (a)	3. (d)	4. (c)	5. (b)	6. (c)
7. (a)	8. (c)	9. (d)	10. (b)	11. (d)	12. (b)
13. (a)	14. (d)	15. (a)	16. (a,b)	17. (a,b,c)	18. (a,d)
19. (b,c,d)	20. (a,b,c)	21. (b,c,d)	22. (b,c,d)	23. (3)	24. (15)
25. (16)	26. (3)	27. (4)			

Element 3

Group-17 : The Halogen Family and Their Compounds

This group consists of six elements namely **fluorine** (F), **chlorine** (Cl), **bromine** (Br), **iodine** (I), **astatine** (At) and **tennessine** (Ts). These elements are also called halogen (*means sea salts*), i.e., their salts are abundantly present in sea water.

General and Physical Properties

Trends of general and physical properties exhibited by these elements are as follows.

1. Electronic Configuration

The general electronic configuration of halogens is ns^2np^5 (where, $n = 2, 3, 4, 5, 6, 7$). Due to the presence of 7 electrons in their valence shell, these elements have a high tendency to gain one electron and achieve nearest noble gas configuration.

2. Atomic and Ionic Radii

Halogens have small atomic radii than the elements of group 16 due to high effective nuclear charge. On moving down the group it increases as the number of shells increases by one.

3. Physical State

On moving down the group, the tendency to form condensed molecules increases. Thus, fluorine and chlorine are gases at ordinary temperature, bromine is a highly fuming liquid while iodine is a volatile solid.

4. Melting and Boiling Points

On moving down the group from F to At, there is increase in melting and boiling points. This is because van der Waals' forces increase as the size increases.

5. Ionisation Energy

On moving down the group the ionisation energy decreases. Iodine because of the lowest IE, has some tendency to form I^+ ion as it forms compounds like ICl, ICN, etc, which in molten state conduct electricity showing the existence of I^+ cation.

6. Electron Gain Enthalpy

On moving down the group the magnitude of electron gain enthalpy (i.e., electron affinity) usually decreases. But electron affinity of fluorine is unexpectedly lower than Cl. This is because of the smaller size of F. Thus, the correct order will be Cl > F > Br > I.

7. Electronegativity

Halogens have the high values of electronegativities and it decreases on moving downward from F to I. As a result of the decrease of electronegativity, the non-metallic character decreases from F to I.

8. Oxidation State

When a halogen atom combines with an element, F being most electronegative atom shows –1 oxidation state. Other elements of this group also show +3, +5 and +7 oxidation states due to the presence of vacant *d*-orbitals in their valence shell.

9. Oxidising Power

Standard reduction potentials of halogens are positive and decrease on going down the group. Thus, halogens act as **strong oxidising agents** and their oxidising power decreases from fluorine to iodine.

JEE Spotlite

- The strength of an oxidising agent depends on several energy terms as

$$E = \frac{1}{2}H_f + \frac{1}{2}H_{ev} + \frac{1}{2}H_{diss.} - EA - H_{hyd}$$

where, H_f = enthalpy of fusion
H_{ev} = enthalpy of evaporation
H_{diss} = enthalpy of dissociation
H_{hyd} = enthalpy of hydration
EA = electron affinity

- The value of electronegativity decreases from fluorine to iodine. Hence, fluorine is the **strongest oxidising agent.**
- All the halogens are coloured and as the atomic number increases, the colour gets deepen.

F	Cl	Br	I
Light yellow	Yellow green	Reddish brown	Deep violet

- The colour is due to absorption of energy from visible light by the halogen molecules for excitation of outer electrons to higher energy levels.
- Fluorine absorbs violet portion of the light and thus, appears yellow. Iodine absorbs yellow and green portions of the light and thus, appears violet.
  Thus, it is clear that on moving down the group the colour changes. This is called **blue shift** or **bathochromic shift.**
- Fluorine reacts with water readily and forms a mixture of oxygen and ozone.
- Cl_2, Br_2 and I_2 are more soluble in non-polar solvents like $CHCl_3$, paraffins etc.
- In non-polar solvents, halogens exist as free molecules while in nucleophilic solvents like alcohols, liquid SO_2 etc halogens produce brown solution due to the formation of complex.

10. Bond Dissociation Energy

As the size increases, the bond length increases from fluorine to iodine. Since, the bond length of fluorine is minimum, its bond dissociation energy should be highest. However, the bond dissociation energy of fluorine is less than Cl—Cl and Br—Br.

It is due to the high interelectronic repulsions between non-bonding electrons in the 2*p*-orbitals of fluorine. Consequently, F—F bond becomes weaker in comparison to Cl—Cl and Br—Br bonds.

11. Nature of Bonds

Halogens due to the presence of seven electrons in their valence shell, are highly reactive. They form ionic compounds with highly electropositive metals readily. However, with weakly electropositive metals and non-metals, they form covalent bonds.

The general and physical properties described above can be summarised as :

Element	F	Cl	Br	I	At
Atomic Number	9	17	35	53	85
Atomic Mass	19	35.45	79.90	126.90	210
Electronic configuration	[He] $2s^2 2p^5$	[Ne] $3s^2 3p^5$	[Ar] $3d^{10} 4s^2 4p^5$	[Kr] $4d^{10} 5s^2 5p^5$	[Xe] $4f^{14} 5d^{10} 6s^2 6p^5$
Covalent Radius/pm	64	99	114	133	—
Ionic Radius X^-/pm	133	184	196	220	—
Ionisation enthalpy (kJ mol^{-1})	1680	1256	1142	1008	—
Electron gain enthalpy/ (kJ mol^{-1})	–333	–349	–325	–296	—
Distance *X-X*/pm	143	199	228	266	—
Enthalpy of dissociation (X_2)/kJ mol^{-1}	158.8	242.6	192.8	151.1	—
Electronegativiy	4	3.2	3.0	2.7	2.2
Melting point/K	54.4	172	265.8	386.6	—
Boiling point/K	84.9	239.0	332.5	458.2	—

Chemical Properties

Following are the chemical properties of halogens

1. Reaction with Water

Fluorine decomposes water very readily even at low temperature and in dark forming mixture of O_2 and O_3.

$$2F_2 + 2H_2O \longrightarrow 4HF + O_2\uparrow$$

$$3F_2 + 3H_2O \longrightarrow 6HF + O_3$$

Chlorine (Cl_2) decomposes water in the presence of sunlight while bromine decomposes water very slowly in presence of sunlight. Iodine, however, does not decompose water.

2. Formation of Halogen Acids

All the halogens react with hydrogen to form volatile covalent hydrides, of formula H*X* called hydrogen halides.

Since, these compounds ionise in aqueous solution to produce H^+ (or H_3O^+) these are also called **'halogen acids'.**

$$HX + H_2O \longrightarrow H_3O^+ + X^-$$

These compounds are also known by other names like **hydroacids** or **hydrohalic acid** etc. The reactivity of halogens towards hydrogen decreases from fluorine to iodine.

3. Reaction with Oxygen

Halogens form binary compounds with oxygen but most of them are unstable. Fluorine forms only two binary compounds, i.e. OF_2 and O_2F_2 (called **oxygen fluorides).** Chlorine, bromine and iodine form oxides in which the oxidation state of halogen varies from +1 to +7.

e.g. $Cl_2O(+1)$, $ClO_2(+4)$, $Cl_2O_6(+6)$, $ClO_3(+6)$, $Cl_2O_7(+7)$; $Br_2O(+1)$, $BrO_2(+4)$; $I_2O_4(+4)$, $I_2O_5(+5)$ etc.

4. Reaction with Metals and Non-metals

Halogens combine with metals and non-metals to form halides such as $MgBr_2$, XeF_6, PCl_3, PCl_5, SF_6 etc. The ionic character of *M*—*X* bond decreases as the size of halogen atom increases.

$$M\text{—F} > M\text{—Cl} > M\text{—Br} > M\text{—I}$$

Anomalous Behaviour of Fluorine

(i) Fluorite due to its small size, highest electronegativity, low F—F bond dissociation enthalpy and non-availability of *d*-orbitals in valence shell differs from other halogens.

(ii) Most of the reactions of fluorine are exothermic (due to the small and strong bond formed by it with other elements).

(iii) It forms only one oxoacid (HOF, Hypoflourous acid) while other halogens form a number of oxoacids.

(iv) Hydrogen fluoride is liquid (b.p. 19°C) due to strong hydrogen bonding. Other hydrogen halides are gases.

(v) Fluorine when combines with sulphur, forms SF_6 while no other halogen forms the hexahalide with sulphur.

(vi) HF has a high tendency to form H-bond, thus, it is a liquid (b.p. 19°C) while HCl, HBr and HI due to lack of such a tendency, are gases under ordinary conditions.

(vii) Fluorides are more stable than corresponding chloride compounds.

(viii) Fluorine does not form polyhalides like F_3^- but other halogens do so, e.g. I_3^-, Br_3^- etc.

(ix) Hydrofluoric acid being a dibasic acid (H_2F_2), forms two series of salt such as $NaHF_2$ and Na_2F_2 while HCl, HBr and HI are monobasic in nature.

(x) Mostly fluorides are ionic and contain F^- ion while other halides have molecular lattices.

Study of Halogens

Fluorine

Let us study about occurrence, preparation and properties of fluorine.

Occurrence

Fluorine is extremely reactive and hence does not occur in free state. It is widely found in the combined state as fluorides. The important minerals are

- Calcium fluoride, CaF_2
- Cryolite, Na_3AlF_6
- Fluorapatite, $Ca_5(PO_4)_3F$

Preparation

In modern methods, fluorine is prepared by electrolysis of a fused fluoride (usually potassium hydrogen fluoride, KHF_2). The electrolytic cells are made of copper, nickel or monel metal. The anode is generally of graphite and the fluorine set free contains some carbon tetrafluoride.

Reactions in the Electrolytic Cell

$$KHF_2 \longrightarrow KF + HF$$

$$\Downarrow$$

$$\overset{\oplus}{K} + F^{\ominus}$$

Cathode	Anode
$K^+ + e^- \rightarrow K$	$F^- \rightarrow F + e^-$
$K + HF \rightarrow KF + H$	$2F \rightarrow F_2$
$2H \rightarrow H_2$	

Properties

- The gas is pale greenish yellow in colour. It can be condensed to yellow liquid at –188°C and pale yellow solid at –223°C.
- It has pungent odour resembling that of a mixture of ozone and chlorine.
- It is a poisonous gas but less poisonous than HF gas.
- It is the most reactive element.
- It can displace all the halogens from their halides.

$$F_2 + 2NaX \longrightarrow 2NaF + X_2$$

$$(X = Cl^-, Br^- \text{ or } I^-) \qquad (X_2 = Cl_2, Br_2 \text{ or } I_2)$$

- It combines with most of the metals and non-metals to form fluorides.

$$2Ag + F_2 \longrightarrow 2AgF$$

$$2Al + 3F_2 \longrightarrow 2AlF_3$$

$$Mg + F_2 \longrightarrow MgF_2$$

Hydrogen explodes violently in fluorine even in the dark.

$$H_2 + F_2 \longrightarrow H_2F_2$$

A mixture of oxygen and fluorine explodes in presence of silent electric discharge.

$$O_2 + F_2 \longrightarrow O_2F_2 \text{ (Dioxygen difluorides)}$$

It reacts with wood, charcoal, phosphorus, arsenic, antimony, boron and silicon producing a flame.

$$C + 2F_2 \longrightarrow CF_4 \text{ ; } Si + 2F_2 \longrightarrow SiF_4$$

$$2P + 3F_2 \longrightarrow 2PF_3 \text{ ; } 2As + F_2 \longrightarrow 2AsF_3$$

$$2B + 3F_2 \longrightarrow 2BF_3$$

However, fluorine does not react with oxygen, nitrogen and inert gases directly under ordinary conditions.

- Fluorine reacts with dilute alkalies to form oxygen difluorides (OF_2) and with conc. alkalies O_2 is formed.

$$2F_2 + \text{dil. NaOH} \longrightarrow OF_2 + 2NaF + H_2O$$

$$2F_3 + \text{conc. 4NaOH} \longrightarrow 4NaF + 2H_2O + O_2$$

- It acts as a strong oxidising agent. It oxidises chlorates to perchlorates, iodates to periodates and bisulphates to peroxysulphates.

$$KClO_3 + F_2 + H_2O \longrightarrow KClO_4 + H_2F_2$$

$$KIO_3 + F_2 + H_2O \longrightarrow KIO_4 + H_2F_2$$

$$2NaHSO_4 + F_2 \longrightarrow Na_2S_2O_8 + 2HF$$

- It attacks glass at about 100°C forming SiF_4. However, the attack of dry fluorine is slow. At low temperatures, dry fluorine can be stored in dry glass vessel.
- It reacts with hydrocarbons explosively and forms fluorinated hydrocarbons.

$$CH_4 \xrightarrow{F_2} CH_3F \xrightarrow{F_2} CH_2F_2 \xrightarrow{F_2} CHF_3 \xrightarrow{F_2} CF_4$$

Fluorine reacts with NH_3 to form nitrogen gas and H_2S with to form SF_6 (H_2S burns)

$$2NH_3 + 3F_2 \longrightarrow N_2 + 6HF$$

$$H_2S + 4F_2 \longrightarrow SF_6 + 2HF$$

- It combines with xenon to form XeF_2, XeF_4, XeF_6
- Fluorination of methanol

$$CH_3OH + 2F_2 \xrightarrow{AgF_2} CF_3OF + 4HF$$

- CF_3OF is very strong oxidising agent.

JEE Alert

- F_2 has the highest standard reduction potential (+2.87) and electronegativity (3.98), hence it is strongest oxidising agent and can oxidise Cl^-, Br^- and I^- respectively to Cl_2, Br_2 and I_2. F_2 can also oxidise H_2O to O_2

$$F_2 + H_2O \longrightarrow 2HF + \frac{1}{2}O_2$$

- Similarly Cl_2 will oxidise Br^- and I^- and Br_2 will oxidise I^-. In general any halogen (X_2) of lower atomic number will oxidise halide ions (X^-) of higher atomic number.

Chlorine

Let us study about occurrence, preparation and properties of chlorine.

Occurrence

Chlorine is widely distributed in nature in the combined state in the form of chlorides of various metals. Common salt (NaCl) is the most important chloride which occurs in seawater; lakes and in rocks. The other important chloride minerals are:

- Sylvine(potassium chloride), KCl
- Carnallite, KCl, $MgCl_2 \cdot 6H_2O$
- Chlorapatite, $Ca_5(PO_4)_3Cl$
- Horn silver, AgCl

Preparation

(i) By the oxidation of hydrochloric acid. The oxidising agents which can be used are MnO_2, PbO_2, Pb_3O_4 (red lead), $KMnO_4$ (Potassium permanganate), $K_2Cr_2O_7$ (Potassium dichromate), NaClO (Sodium hypochlorite), O_3, etc.

(a) $MnO_2 + 4HCl \longrightarrow MnCl_2 + 2H_2O + Cl_2$

(b) $PbO_2 + 4HCl \longrightarrow PbCl_2 + 2H_2O + Cl_2$

(c) $Pb_3O_4 + 8HCl \longrightarrow 3PbCl_2 + 4H_2O + Cl_2$

(d) $2KMnO_4 + 16HCl \longrightarrow 2KCl + 2MnCl_2 + 8H_2O + 5Cl_2$

(e) $K_2Cr_2O_7 + 14HCl \longrightarrow 2KCl + 2CrCl_3 + 7H_2O + 3Cl_2$

(f) $NaClO + 2HCl \longrightarrow NaCl + H_2O + Cl_2$

(ii) By the action of mineral acids or carbon dioxide on bleaching powder.

$$CaOCl_2 + H_2SO_4 \longrightarrow CaSO_4 + H_2O + Cl_2$$
$$CaOCl_2 + 2HCl \longrightarrow CaCl_2 + H_2O + Cl_2$$
$$CaOCl_2 + CO_2 \longrightarrow CaCO_3 + Cl_2$$

(iii) By heating any chloride with concentrated H_2SO_4 in presence of MnO_2.

$$2NaCl + MnO_2 + 3H_2SO_4 \longrightarrow 2NaHSO_4 + MnSO_4 + 2H_2O + Cl_2$$

(iv) **Pure Chlorine** It may be obtained by heating dry platinum tetrachloride ($PtCl_4$) or gold chloride ($AuCl_3$) in a hard glass tube.

$$PtCl_4 \xrightarrow{374°C} PtCl_2 + Cl_2 \xrightarrow{582°C} Pt + 2Cl_2$$
$$2AuCl_3 \xrightarrow{175°C} 2AuCl + Cl_2 \xrightarrow{185°C} 2Au + 3Cl_2$$

(v) **Nitrosyl Chloride Process** In this process, common salt (NaCl) is treated with concentrated nitric acid, a mixture of chlorine and nitrosyl chloride is evoled.

$$[NaCl + HNO_3 \longrightarrow NaNO_3 + HCl] \times 3$$
$$HNO_3 + 3HCl \longrightarrow NOCl + Cl_2 + 2H_2O$$
$$\overline{3NaCl + 4HNO_3 \longrightarrow 3NaNO_3 + NOCl + Cl_2 + 2H_2O}$$

The gaseous mixture is oxidised with oxygen.

$$2NOCl + O_2 \longrightarrow 2NO_2 + Cl_2$$

The gases are liquefied and chlorine distilled out. Nitrogen dioxide is absorbed in water in presence of oxygen to form nitric acid which can be used again.

$$4NO_2 + O_2 + 2H_2O \longrightarrow 4HNO_3$$

Properties of Chlorine

(i) Chlorine is a yellowish-green gas with a pungent suffocating smell.

(ii) It is 2.5 times heavier than air.

(iii) **Combustibility** Chlorine does not burn and also does not help in burning.

(iv) **Combination with Elements** It combines with all the non-metals except nitrogen, oxygen, carbon and inert gases.

It combines with hydrogen in light (but not in dark) with explosion to form HCl. However, in presence of charcoal as a catalyst, the reaction is safe.

$$H_2 + Cl_2 \longrightarrow 2HCl$$

Arsenic, boron, sulphur, phosphorus (red), etc., combine with chlorine when heated.

$$2As + 3Cl_2 \longrightarrow \underset{\text{Arsenic trichloride}}{2AsCl_3}$$

$$2B + 3Cl_2 \longrightarrow \underset{\text{Boron trichloride}}{2BCl_3}$$

$$2S + Cl_2 \longrightarrow \underset{\text{Disulphur dichloride}}{S_2Cl_2}$$

$$\underset{\text{(Red)}}{2P} + 3Cl_2 \longrightarrow \underset{\text{Phosphorus trichloride}}{2PCl_3}$$

Yellow phosphorus readily catches fire in chlorine.

$$2Na + Cl_2 \longrightarrow 2NaCl \; ; 2Fe + 3Cl_2 \longrightarrow 2FeCl_3$$
$$2Al + 3Cl_2 \longrightarrow \underset{(\text{or } Al_2Cl_6)}{2AlCl_3} \; ; Cu + Cl_2 \longrightarrow CuCl_2$$
$$Mg + Cl_2 \longrightarrow MgCl_2 \; ; Zn + Cl_2 \longrightarrow ZnCl_2$$

(v) **Affinity for Hydrogen** It has great affinity for hydrogen. It decomposes several hydrogen compounds forming HCl.

- Turpentine burns in chlorine forming HCl and carbon

$$C_{10}H_{16} + 8Cl_2 \longrightarrow 10C + 16HCl$$

- It reacts with water in the presence of sunlight and forms O_2.

$$2H_2O + 2Cl_2 \longrightarrow 4HCl + O_2$$

Chlorine water loses its yellow colour on exposure to sunlight. This is due to the formation of HCl.

JEE Alert

Chlorine (Cl_2) reacts with ammonia under two conditions :

1. **When ammonia in excess** The products are nitrogen and ammonium chloride.

$$8NH_3 + 3Cl_2 \longrightarrow N_2 + 6NH_4Cl$$

2. **When chlorine in excess** The products are nitrogen trichloride and HCl.

$$NH_3 + 3Cl_2 \longrightarrow NCl_3 + 3HCl$$

- It removes hydrogen from H_2S

$$H_2S + Cl_2 \longrightarrow 2HCl + S$$

(vi) **Oxidising and Bleaching Nature** In presence of moisture, chlorine acts as an oxidising and a bleaching agent. Chlorine reacts with water forming HCl and HClO (hypochlorous acid). HClO is not so stable and decomposes giving nascent oxygen which is responsible for oxidising and bleaching properties of chlorine.

$$Cl_2 + H_2O \longrightarrow HCl + HClO$$
$$HClO \longrightarrow HCl + O$$
$$\overline{Cl_2 + H_2O \longrightarrow 2HCl + O}$$

Coloured matter + Nascent oxygen ⟶ Colourless matter

The bleaching action is permanent. The delicate articles should not be bleached with chlorine.

- It displaces bromine and iodine from bromides and iodides respectively.

$$2KBr + Cl_2 \longrightarrow 2KCl + Br_2$$
$$2KI + Cl_2 \longrightarrow 2KCl + I_2$$

- Ferrous chloride/ferrous sulphate containing dilute H_2SO_4, is converted to ferric chloride/ferric sulphate.

$$2FeCl_2 + Cl_2 \longrightarrow 2FeCl_3$$
$$2FeSO_4 + H_2SO_4 + Cl_2 \longrightarrow Fe_2(SO_4)_3 + 2HCl$$

- Moist sulphur dioxide is oxidised to H_2SO_4.

$$SO_2 + 2H_2O + Cl_2 \longrightarrow H_2SO_4 + 2HCl$$

- Sulphites are oxidised to sulphates.

$$Na_2SO_3 + H_2O + Cl_2 \longrightarrow Na_2SO_4 + 2HCl$$

- Oxidises thiosulphates to bisulphates.

$$Na_2S_2O_3 + H_2O + Cl_2 \longrightarrow NaHSO_4 + 2HCl$$

(vii) **Action of Alkalies** When passed into cold dilute solution of alkalies, it forms chlorides and hypochlorites.

$$2NaOH + Cl_2 \longrightarrow NaCl + NaClO + H_2O$$
$$2KOH + Cl_2 \longrightarrow KCl + KClO + H_2O$$
$$\underset{\text{Cold and dilute}}{2Ca(OH)_2} + 2Cl_2 \longrightarrow CaCl_2 + Ca(ClO)_2 + 2H_2O$$

With hot concentrated alkali solutions, chlorates are formed.

$$6NaOH + 3Cl_2 \longrightarrow 5NaCl + NaClO_3 + 3H_2$$
$$2KOH + 3Cl_2 \longrightarrow KCl + KClO + H_2O$$
$$\underset{\text{Hot and conc.}}{6Ca(OH)_2} + 6Cl_2 \longrightarrow CaCl_2 + Ca(ClO_3)_2 + 6H_2O$$

However, when chlorine is passed over dry slaked lime, bleaching powder is obtained.

$$\underset{\text{Slaked lime}}{2Ca(OH)_2} + 2Cl_2 \longrightarrow \underset{\text{Bleaching powder}}{CaOCl_2 \cdot 2H_2O} + CaCl_2$$

(viii) **Addition Reactions** Chlorine forms addition compounds with SO_2, CO and unsaturated hydrocarbons.

$$SO_2 + Cl_2 \longrightarrow \underset{\text{Sulphuryl chloride}}{SO_2Cl_2}$$

$$CO + Cl_2 \longrightarrow \underset{\substack{\text{Carbonyl chloride}\\\text{(Phosgene)}}}{COCl_2}$$

Phosgene is highly poisonous gas.

$$C_2H_4 + Cl_2 \longrightarrow \underset{\text{Ethylene chloride}}{C_2H_4Cl_2}$$

Bromine

Let us study about, occurrence, preparation and properties of bromine.

Occurrence

It is never found in free state in nature. The chief sources of bromine are:

Sea water contains bromides such as NaBr, KBr, $MgBr_2$, $CaBr_2$, etc., in minute amounts.

Preparation

The following reactions can be used for its preparation.

(i) By passing chlorine through the solution of potassium or magnesium bromide.

$$2KBr + Cl_2 \longrightarrow 2KCl + Br_2$$
$$MgBr_2 + Cl_2 \longrightarrow MgCl_2 + Br_2$$

(ii) By adding hydrochloric acid to the mixture containing potassium bromide and potassium bromate.

$$5KBr + KBrO_3 + 6HCl \longrightarrow 6KCl + 3Br_2 + 3H_2O$$

(iii) By heating mixture of potassium bromide and manganese dioxide with conc. H_2SO_4.

$$MnO_2 + H_2SO_4 \longrightarrow MnSO_4 + H_2O + O$$
$$[KBr + H_2SO_4 \longrightarrow KHSO_4 + HBr] \times 2$$
$$2HBr + O \longrightarrow H_2O + Br_2$$

$$\overline{2KBr + MnO_2 + 3H_2SO_4 \longrightarrow 2KHSO_4 + MnSO_4 + Br_2 + 2H_2O}$$

This reaction is commonly used in the laboratory for the preparation of bromine.

Other Methods

(i) From carnallite mother-liquor
(ii) From sea water

Properties

- It is a reddish brown, heavy mobile liquid.
- In chemical behaviour, bromine closely resembles chlorine.

(i) **Combination with Elements**

- Bromine reacts directly with hydrogen, though less readily than chlorine. The reaction,

$$H_2 + Br_2 \rightleftharpoons 2HBr$$

is slightly reversible. It combines with hydrogen at 200°C or at room temperature in presence of platinum as catalyst.

- It combines with sulphur, phosphorus, arsenic, etc.

$$2As + 3Br_2 \longrightarrow 2AsBr_3$$

$$2B + 3Br_2 \xrightarrow{\text{Red heat}} 2BBr_3$$

- It combines directly with many metals.

$$2Na + Br_2 \longrightarrow 2NaBr \text{ (Slow reaction)}$$

$$2K + Br_2 \longrightarrow 2KBr \text{ (Fast reaction)}$$

$$2Al + 3Br_2 \longrightarrow 2AlBr_3 \text{ (Violent reaction)}$$

Zinc reacts in presence of moisture with bromine.

$$Zn + Br_2 \longrightarrow ZnBr_2$$

(ii) **Oxidising Action** Bromine is a good oxidising agent. It ordinarily does not react with water but in presence of an oxidisable substance it forms hydrogen bromide and oxygen with water.

$$Br_2 + H_2O \longrightarrow 2HBr + O$$

$$\underset{\text{Oxidisable substance}}{X} + O \longrightarrow XO$$

- It oxidises SO_2 into sulphuric acid.

$$SO_2 + Br_2 + 2H_2O \longrightarrow 2HBr + H_2SO_4$$

- It oxidises sulphites into sulphates.

$$Na_2SO_3 + Br_2 + H_2O \longrightarrow Na_2SO_4 + 2HBr$$

- It oxidises arsenites into arsenates.

$$Na_3AsO_3 + Br_2 + H_2O \longrightarrow Na_3AsO_4 + 2HBr$$

- It oxidises thiosulphate into sulphate.

$$Na_2S_2O_3 + Br_2 + H_2O \longrightarrow Na_2SO_4 + S + 2HBr$$

- Sulphur is formed by oxidation of hydrogen sulphide.

$$H_2S + Br_2 \longrightarrow 2HBr + S$$

- Iodine is liberated from iodides.

$$2KI + Br_2 \longrightarrow 2KBr + I_2$$

(iii) **Action with Alkalies** The action of bromine on alkalies is similar to that of chlorine, a hypobromite with a cold dilute solution and a bromate with a hot solution of alkali are formed.

$$\underset{\text{(Dil. and cold)}}{2KOH} + Br_2 \longrightarrow KBr + \underset{\text{Pot. hypobromite}}{KBrO} + H_2O$$

$$\underset{\text{(Conc. and hot)}}{6KOH} + 3Br_2 \longrightarrow 5KBr + \underset{\text{Pot. bromate}}{KBrO_3} + 3H_2O$$

$$\underset{\text{(Conc. and hot)}}{6Ba(OH)_2} + 6Br_2 \longrightarrow 5BaBr_2 + \underset{\text{Barium bromate}}{Ba(BrO_3)_2} + 6H_2O$$

$$\underset{\text{(conc. and hot)}}{3Na_2CO_3} + 3Br_2 \longrightarrow 5NaBr + NaBrO_3 + 3CO_2$$

However. with slaked lime (dry) it forms a compound similar to bleaching powder.

$$\underset{\text{Slaked lime (dry)}}{Ca(OH)_2} + Br_2 \longrightarrow CaOBr_2 + H_2O$$

(iv) **Action of Ammonia** It is similar to that of chlorine.

$$8NH_3 + 3Br_2 \longrightarrow 6NH_4Br + N_2$$

(v) **Action of Organic Compounds** It forms addition compounds with unsaturated compounds and substituted products with the saturated compounds.

$$C_2H_4 + Br_2 \longrightarrow C_2H_4Br_2\,;$$

$$CH_4 + Br_2 \longrightarrow CH_3Br + HBr$$

(vi) **Bleaching Action** The bleaching action of bromine is weaker than that of chlorine. The bleaching action is due to its oxidising property.

(vii) **Action of Mercuric Oxide** Bromine water reacts with mercuric oxide to form mercury oxybromide.

$$2HgO + 2Br_2 + H_2O \longrightarrow \underset{\text{Mercuryoxybromide}}{HgBr_2 \cdot HgO} + 2HBrO$$

However, on passing bromine vapours over dry HgO at 60°C, bromine monoxide is obtained.

$$HgO + 2Br_2 \longrightarrow Br_2O + HgBr_2$$

Iodine

Let us study about occurrence, preparation and properties of Iodine.

Occurrence **Caliche** or **crude chile saltpetre** which contains about 0.2% of $NaIO_3$ (sodium iodate).

Preparation

The following reactions can be applied for the preparation of iodine

(i) By passing chlorine through potassium iodide solution.

$$2KI + Cl_2 \longrightarrow 2KCl + I_2$$

(ii) By adding potassium iodide solution to copper sulphate solution.

$$CuSO_4 + 2KI \longrightarrow CuI_2 + K_2SO_4$$

$$\underset{\text{Cupric Iodide}}{2CuI_2} \longrightarrow \underset{\text{Cuprous iodide}}{Cu_2I_2} + I_2$$

(iii) By adding conc. sulphuric acid to a mixture of sodium potassium iodide and sodium/potassium iodate.

$$NaIO_3 + 5NaI + 6H_2SO_4 \longrightarrow 6NaHSO_4 + 3H_2O + 3I_2$$

(iv) By adding an oxidising agent such as hydrogen peroxide, ozone, acidified potassium permanganate or acidified potassium dichromate to potassium iodide.

$$2KI + H_2O_2 \longrightarrow 2KOH + I_2$$

(v) By reacting sodium iodate with sodium hydrogen sulphite.

$$2NaIO_3 + 5NaHSO_3 \longrightarrow 3NaHSO_4 + 2Na_2SO_4 + I_2 + H_2O$$

(vi) By heating mixture of potassium iodide and manganese dioxide with conc. H_2SO_4.

$$2KI + MnO_2 + 3H_2SO_4 \longrightarrow 2KHSO_4 + MnSO_4 + 2H_2O + I_2$$

Properties

- It is black shining solid.
- It sublime rapidly below melting point giving violet coloured vapours.
- Iodine is chemically less reactive in comparison to chlorine and bromine.

(i) **Combination with Elements** It combines directly with many elements.

$$2K + I_2 \longrightarrow 2KI$$

$$2Fe + 3I_2 \xrightarrow{\text{Heat}} 2FeI_3$$

(ii) **Oxidising Properties** It is a weak oxidising agent. The following reactions show its oxidising nature.

(i) $H_2S + I_2 \longrightarrow 2HI + S$

(ii) $SO_2 + I_2 + 2H_2O \longrightarrow H_2SO_4 + 2HI$

(iii) $Na_2SO_3 + I_2 + H_2O \longrightarrow Na_2SO_4 + 2HI$

(iv) $Na_3AsO_3 + I_2 + H_2O \longrightarrow Na_2AsO_4 + 2HI$

(v) $2FeSO_4 + H_2SO_4 + I_2 \longrightarrow Fe_2(SO_4)_3 + 2HI$

(iii) **Reaction with Alkalies** Iodine reacts with cold dilute solution of NaOH forming hypoiodite. The colour of the solution becomes faint yellow. However, hypoiodite undergoes hydrolysis forming HIO.

$$2NaOH + I_2 \longrightarrow NaIO + NaI + H_2O$$

$$NaIO + H_2O \longrightarrow NaOH + HIO$$

$$NaOH + I_2 \longrightarrow NaI + \underset{\text{Hypoiodous acid}}{HIO}$$

Iodine when heated with concentrated alkali solution, iodide and iodate are formed. The colour of iodine disappears.

$$6NaOH + 3I_2 \longrightarrow \underbrace{5NaI + NaIO_3}_{\text{colourless}} + 3H_2O$$

JEE Spotlite

- Iodine does not displace chlorine and bromine from chlorides and bromides respectively but it displaces them from their oxy salts.

$$2KClO_3 + I_2 \longrightarrow 2KIO_3 + Cl_2$$

$$2KBrO_3 + I_2 \longrightarrow 2KIO_3 + Br_2$$

- Strong oxidising agents convert iodine to iodic acid (HIO_3).

(i) with conc. HNO_3

$$I_2 + 10HNO_3 \longrightarrow 2HIO_3 + 10NO_2 + 4H_2O$$

(ii) with ozone

$$I_2 + H_2O + 5O_3 \longrightarrow 2HIO_3 + 5O_2$$

(iii) with chlorine water

$$I_2 + 5Cl_2 + 6H_2O \longrightarrow 2HIO_3 + 10HCl$$

(iv) **Reaction with Sodium Thiosulphate** Iodine solution is decolourised by sodium thiosulphate (hypo) as sodium tetrathionate and sodium iodide are formed. Both are colourless and soluble.

$$\underset{\text{Sodium thiosulphate}}{2Na_2S_2O_3} + I_2 \longrightarrow 2NaI + \underset{\text{Sodium tetrathionate}}{Na_2S_4O_6}$$

This reaction is involved in iodometric titrations in presence of starch indicator.

(v) **Action of NH_3** Iodine forms a mild explosive with ammonia.

$$2NH_3 + 3I_2 \longrightarrow \underset{\text{Explosive}}{NI_3 \cdot NH_3} + 3HI$$

$$8NI_3 \cdot NH_3 \longrightarrow 5N_2 + 9I_2 + 6NH_4I$$

(vi) **Reaction with Freshly Precipitated Mercuric Oxide** Iodine forms hypoiodous acid with mercuric oxide.

$$2HgO + 2I_2 + H_2O \longrightarrow HgI_2 \cdot HgO + 2HIO$$

(vii) Iodine when warmed with alcohol and alkali forms iodoform.

$$C_2H_5OH + 6KOH + 4I_2 \longrightarrow CHI_3 + HCOOK + 5KI + 5H_2O$$

viii) **Reaction with Chlorine** When chlorine is passed over iodine, at first iodine monochloride, ICl (dark liquid) and finally iodine trichloride, ICl_3 (yellow solid) is formed.

(ix) **Reaction with Starch** Iodine turns starch solution blue. This is one of the tests of iodine.

(x) **Action on Unsaturated Organic Compounds** Addition products are formed with unsaturated organic compounds.

$$C_2H_4 + I_2 \longrightarrow C_2H_4I_2$$

Uses of Halogens

Halogen	Uses	Remark
F_2	In the preparation of UF_6	UF_6 used in the gaseous diffusion process for separating isotopes of uranium (U-235 and U-238)
	In the preparation of teflon $\text{-(}CF_2\text{—}CF_2\text{)-}_n$	Teflon is used in electrical insulators, high temperature plastic and cooking utensils
Cl_2	Cl^- ion is the principal anion in intracellular and extracellular fluids	—
	Cl_2 as bleaching agent	Household laundry bleach contains the active ingredient NaOCl (sodium hypochlorite about 5% by mass)
	Cl_2 used to purify water (as disinfectant)	$Cl_2 + H_2O \longrightarrow HCl + HOCl$ ClO^- ions destroy bacteria by oxidising life-sustaining compounds within them
	As a chlorinating agent to prepare various organic compounds	$CHCl_3$, CCl_4, $CH_2{=}CHCl$, Benzene hexachloride, DDT

Halogen	Uses	Remark
Br_2	To prepare ethylene dibromide $BrCH_2CH_2Br$	$BrCH_2CH_2Br$ is used as an insecticide and as a scavenger for lead in gasoline to keep away lead deposits from clogging engines.
	To prepare AgBr	AgBr is used in photographic plate
I_2	To prepare **tincture of iodine** —an antiseptic	50% (by mass) alcohol solution of iodine is called **tincture of iodine**
	In iodised salt	Iodised salt contains 0.01 per cent KI or NaI which is more than sufficient to satisfy 1 mg iodine per week required for the formation of thyroxine in the human body.
	To prepare AgI	Used in cloud seeding—a process for inducing rainfall.

Compounds of Group 17 Elements

Following are the methods of preparation of compound of group 17

Methods of Preparation (HCl, HBr and HI)

(i) **By Direct combination of Elements** Hydrogen chloride (HCl) is formed by burning chlorine in excess of hydrogen.

$$H_2 + Cl_2 \longrightarrow 2HCl$$

HBr can be prepared by passing a mixture of H_2 and Br_2 over a platinum spiral heated to redness by an electric current.

$$H_2 + Br_2 \xrightarrow{Pt} 2HBr$$

HI can also be prepared in small quantities by passing hydrogen and iodine vapours over red hot fine platinum.

$$H_2 + I_2 \underset{450°C}{\overset{Pt}{\rightleftharpoons}} 2HI$$

(ii) **By Heating a Halide with Acid** Hydrogen chloride is prepared by heating sodium chloride with concentrated sulphuric acid.

$$NaCl + H_2SO_4 \longrightarrow NaHSO_4 + HCl$$

HBr and HI cannot be prepared by heating bromides and iodides with concentrated H_2SO_4 because HBr and HI are strong reducing agents and reduce H_2SO_4 to SO_2 and get themselves oxidised to bromine and iodine, respectively.

$$KBr + H_2SO_4 \longrightarrow KHSO_4 + HBr$$
$$KI + H_2SO_4 \longrightarrow KHSO_4 + HI$$
$$H_2SO_4 + 2HBr \longrightarrow SO_2 + Br_2 + 2H_2O$$
$$H_2SO_4 + 2HI \longrightarrow SO_2 + I_2 + H_2O$$

HBr and HI can also be prepared by heating bromides and iodides respectively with conc. orthophosphoric acid.

$$3KBr + H_3PO_4 \longrightarrow K_3PO_4 + 3HBr$$
$$KI + H_3PO_4 \longrightarrow K_3PO_4 + 3HI$$

(iii) HBr and HI can be prepared by hydrolysis of corresponding phosphorus trihalides.

$$2P + 3Br_2 \longrightarrow 2PBr_3$$
$$2P + 3I_2 \longrightarrow 2PI_3$$
$$PBr_3 + 3H_2O \longrightarrow H_3PO_3 + 3HBr$$
$$PI_3 + 3H_2O \longrightarrow H_3PO_3 + 3HI$$

Method of Preparation of Hydrogen Fluoride

It is an associated molecule and is represented by formula, H_2F_2.

Pure anhydrous hydrogen fluoride is obtained by heating potassium hydrogen fluoride (dry) in a platinum retort.

$$2KHF_2 \longrightarrow K_2F_2 + H_2F_2$$

The Vapours are condensed in a platinum condenser and collected in a platinum receiver.

The aqueous solution of H_2F_2 can be obtained by heating calcium fluoride with 90% conc. sulphuric acid in a lead retort. The vapours are condensed in a strongly called lead receiver. Aqueous acid of about 40% strength can be obtained by passing the vapours through water in a lead receiver.

$$CaF_2 + \text{conc.}\,H_2SO_4 \longrightarrow CaSO_4 + H_2F_2$$

The aqueous solution of H_2F_2 is kept in gutta-percha bottles when dilute and in wax bottles when concentrated. The anhydrous acid is stored in well cooled platinum, gold or silver vessels or steel cylinders.

Properties

(i) **Physical State** Except H_2F_2 other hydrogen halides are gases. They fume in air and have pungent odour. These are colourless liquids.

Their melting and boiling points increase with increase in atomic mass of the halogen. The low values are due to covalent nature.

Order of M.P. and B.P.

HI > HF > HBr > HCl (MP)

HF > HI > HBr > HCl (BP)

H_2F_2 is a liquid with boiling point 19.5°C. This behaviour is due to association of HF molecules through hydrogen bonding.

$$H—F—H \cdots F—H \cdots F—H \cdots F$$

JEE Spotlite

- **Use of HCl in detection of cation and anion**

For Cations

$$AgNO_3 + HCl \longrightarrow AgCl \downarrow (white) + HNO_3$$
$$(CH_3COO)_2Pb + 2HCl \longrightarrow PbCl_2 \downarrow (white) + 2CH_3COOH$$
$$Hg(NO_3)_2 + 2HCl \longrightarrow Hg_2Cl_2 \downarrow (white) + 2HNO_3 + Cl_2$$

For Anions

$$CO_3^{2-} \xrightarrow{\text{Dil. HCl}} CO_2$$
$$SO_3^{2-} \xrightarrow{\text{Dil. HCl}} SO_2$$
$$HCO_3^{-} \xrightarrow{\text{Dil. HCl}} CO_2$$

- HI reacts with $CuSO_4$ liberating iodine via the formation of cupric iodide (not by HCl or HBr).

$$2CuSO_4 + 4HI \longrightarrow 2CuI_2 + 2H_2SO_4 ;$$
$$2CuI_2 \longrightarrow Cu_2I_2 + I_2$$

HF attacks glass, while other halogen acids do not. Glass is silicates of sodium and calcium and are converted into complex fluorides :

$$Na_2SiO_3 + 6HF \longrightarrow Na_2SiF_6 + 3H_2O$$
$$CaSiO_3 + 6HF \longrightarrow CaSiF_6 + 3H_2O$$

- Hence, HF can't be stored in a glass vessel. Instead, it is stored in a wax-vessel which does not react with HF. This unique property of HF of attacking glass is used for making permanent marking on glass-wares.

(ii) **Stability** The bond strength of H—X decreases from HF to HI. Thus, HF is most stable while HI is least stable. The decrease in stability is due to decrease in electronegativity from F to I. This is also observed in the values of dissociation energy of H—X bond.

Order of dissociation energy

$$H—F > H—Cl > H—Br > H—I$$

HBr and HCl are stable upto 1200°C, HBr dissociates slightly while HI dissociated considerably (20%) at 440°C.

(iii) **Acid Strength** HF is only slightly ionised but HCl, HBr and HI are almost completely ionised, i.e., the relative acid strength increases from HF to HI. HF is the weakest acid and HI is the strongest acid. On the basis of electronegativity, this appears to rather surprising. [The electronegativity difference suggests that HF should be strongest and HI should be weakest acid.] The lower strength of HF is largely due to its high bond dissociation energy as the bond length is very small (1.01 Å).

(iv) **Reducing Nature** The reducing nature increases from HF to HI as the stability decreases from HF to HI. HF does not show reducing nature. It cannot be oxidised even by strong oxidising agents. HI is the strongest reducing agent. Its aqueous solution gets oxidised even by atmospheric oxygen.

$$4HI + O_2 \longrightarrow 2H_2O + 2I_2$$

The reducing action can also be explained on the basis of increasing size of the halide ions from F^- to I^-. The bigger ion can lose electron easily.

HCl can be oxidised by strong oxidising agents like MnO_2, $KMnO_4$, $K_2Cr_2O_7$, PbO_2, Pb_3O_4, etc.

HBr acts stronger reducing agent than HCl. It can be oxidised by H_2SO_4 and atmospheric oxygen.

$$H_2SO_4 + 2HBr \longrightarrow SO_2 + Br_2 + 2H_2O$$
$$4HBr + O_2 \longrightarrow 2H_2O + Br_2$$

HI is the strongest reducing agent.

It reduces H_2SO_4 to SO_2, S and H_2S, nitric acid to NO_2, nitrous acid to NO, $FeCl_3$ to $FeCl_2$ cupric salt to cuprous salt, etc.

$$H_2SO_4 + 2HI \longrightarrow SO_2 + I_2 + 2H_2O$$
$$H_2SO_4 + 6HI \longrightarrow S + 3I_2 + 4H_2O$$
$$H_2SO_4 + 8HI \longrightarrow H_2S + 4I_2 + 4H_2O$$
$$2HNO_3 + 2HI \longrightarrow 2NO_2 + 2H_2O + I_2$$
$$2HNO_2 + 2HI \longrightarrow 2NO + 2H_2O + I_2$$
$$2FeCl_3 + 2HI \longrightarrow 2FeCl_2 + I_2 + 2HCl$$
$$2CuSO_4 + 4HI \longrightarrow Cu_2I_2 + 2H_2SO_4 + I_2$$

(vi) **Precipitation Reactions** HCl forms insoluble chlorides with the soluble salts of Ag, Pb and Hg.

$$AgNO_3 + HCl \longrightarrow \underset{\text{(white)}}{AgCl} + HNO_3$$

AgCl is insoluble in HNO_3 but soluble in $NH_4OH \cdot PbCl_2$ is soluble in hot water while Hg_2Cl_2 is soluble in aqua-regia.

HBr reacts with soluble salts of Ag and Pb.

$$AgNO_3 + HBr \longrightarrow \underset{\text{(Pale yellow)}}{AgBr} + HNO_3$$

AgBr is insoluble in HNO_3 but sparingly soluble in $NH_4OH \cdot PbBr_2$ is soluble in hot water.

HI forms insoluble iodides with the salts of Ag, Pb and Hg.

$$AgNO_3 + HI \longrightarrow \underset{\text{(Yellow)}}{AgI} + HNO_3$$
$$Pb(CH_3COO)_2 + 2HI \longrightarrow \underset{\text{(Yellow)}}{PbI_2} + 2CH_3COOH$$

AgI is insoluble in HNO_3 and $NH_4OH \cdot PbI_2$ is soluble in hot water.

(vii) **Action of Halogens** F_2 can displace Cl_2, Br_2 and I_2 from HCl, HBr and HI.

$$2HCl + F_2 \longrightarrow 2HF + Cl_2$$
$$2HBr + F_2 \longrightarrow 2HF + Br_2$$
$$2HI + F_2 \longrightarrow 2HF + I_2$$

Cl_2 can displace Br_2 and I_2 from HBr and HI and Br_2 can displace only I_2 from HI. Iodine can displace none.

(viii) **Reaction with Ammonia** HCl, HBr and HI combine with ammonia giving white fumes of ammonium halides.

$$NH_3 + HCl \longrightarrow \underset{\text{(Ammonium chloride)}}{NH_4Cl}$$

$$NH_3 + HBr \longrightarrow NH_4Br$$
(Ammonium bromide)
$$NH_3 + HI \longrightarrow NH_4I$$
(Ammonium iodide)

(ix) **Acidic Properties** All the three (HCl, HBr and HI) react with certain metals, their oxides, carbonates, hydroxides. etc., and form salts.

$$Mg + 2HX \longrightarrow MgX_2 + H_2$$
$$MgO + 2HX \longrightarrow MgX_2 + H_2$$
$$CaCO_3 + 2HX \longrightarrow CaX_2 + H_2O + CO_2$$
$$NaHCO_3 + HX \longrightarrow NaX + H_2O + CO_2$$
$$NaOH + HX \longrightarrow NaX + H_2O$$
[HX = HCl, HBr or HI]

(x) **Action of Salts** HCl, HBr or HI decompose the salts of weaker acids.

$$Na_2S + 2HX \longrightarrow 2NaX + H_2S$$
$$Ca_3P_2 + 6HX \longrightarrow 3CaX_2 + 2PH_3$$
$$Na_2SO_3 + 2HX \longrightarrow 2NaX + H_2O + SO_2$$
$$2NaNO_2 + 2HX \longrightarrow 2NaX + NO + NO_2 + H_2O$$

Oxides of the Halogens

All the halogens forms oxides. Twelve such oxides are positively known. The oxides of fluorine are considered as oxygen fluorides since fluorine is more electronegative than oxygen.

Oxides of The Halogens

Fluorine	Chlorine	Bromine	Iodine
OF_2 (Pale yellow gas, b.p −145°C)	Cl_2O (orange liquid, b.p. 2°C)	Br_2O (dark-brown liquid, fr. p. −10°C)	
O_2F_2 (yellowish orange solid, stable below −95°C)	ClO_2 (yellowish-green liquid, b.p 11°C)	BrO_2 (yellow solid stable below − 40°C)	
O_3F_2 (blood-red viscous liquid, stable below −163°C)	Cl_2O_6 (dark red liquid, fr. p. 4°C)	BrO_3 (white crystalline solid, stable below −70°C)	I_2O_5 (white solid, m.p. 300°C) decomposes to I_2 and O_2 above 300°C
O_4F_2 (reddish-brown solid, stable below −183°C)	Cl_2O_7 (colourless oily liquid, stable)		

Most of these oxides are unstable and are liable to explode. All the oxides of halogens are powerful oxidising agents.

Important Oxoacids of the Halogens

Name of the acids and their salts	Oxidation state of the halogen in the acid	Oxoacids of : Cl	Br	I	Stability	Acid strength
Hypohalous	+1	HClO	HBrO	HIO	Stability decreases on moving down	Acidity increases on moving down
Hypohalites						
Halous						
Halites	+3	$HClO_2$				
Halic						
Halates	+5	$HClO_3$	$HBrO_3$	HIO_3		
Perhalic						
Perhalates	+7	$HClO_4$	$HBrO_4$	HIO_4		

Oxides of Chlorine

Chlorine forms a number of oxides such as Cl_2O, ClO_2, Cl_2O_6 and Cl_2O_7. All of them are unstable and highly reactive.

1. Dichloro Oxide (Cl_2O)

It is prepared by passing dry chlorine over freshly precipitated yellow mercuric oxide.

$$HgO + 2Cl_2(dry) \longrightarrow HgCl_2HgO + Cl_2O$$

It is a brownish-yellow gas which condenses to an orange coloured liquid in a freezing mixture (b.pt. = 2.2°C). It has characteristic penetrating odour. Liquid Cl_2O explodes readily on heating or sparking Cl_2 and O_2. It also undergoes photochemical decomposition.

$$2Cl_2O \longrightarrow 2Cl_2 + O_2$$

It dissolves in water giving golden yellow solution of hypochlorous acid, HClO. It is thus anhydride of hypochlorous acid.

$$Cl_2O + H_2O \rightleftharpoons 2HClO$$

Its gaseous mixture with ammonia explodes violently.

$$3Cl_2O + 10NH_3 \longrightarrow 2N_2 + 6NH_4Cl + 3H_2O$$

It is a strong oxidising agent. It oxidises HCl to Cl_2.

$$Cl_2O + 2HCl \longrightarrow 2Cl_2 + H_2O$$

Cl_2O has V-shaped structure. The oxygen atom undergoes sp^3 hybridisation. The Cl—O—Cl bond angle is 110°.

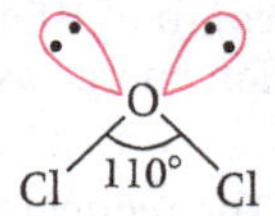

2. Chlorine Dioxide (ClO_2)

Pure ClO_2 is obtained by passing dry Cl_2 over $AgClO_3$ heated to 90°C.

$$2AgClO_3 + Cl_2(dry) \longrightarrow 2AgCl + 2ClO_2 + O_2$$

It can also be obtained by the action of Cl_2 on sodium chlorite.

$$2NaClO_2 + Cl_2 \longrightarrow 2NaCl + 2ClO_2$$

It can be condensed by cooling to a coloured liquid (b.pt. 11°C). The gas explodes and is decomposed to Cl_2 and O_2 by an electric spark. It dissolves in water giving a mixture of chlorous acid and chloric acid.

$$2ClO_2 + H_2O \longrightarrow \underset{\text{Chlorous acid}}{HClO_2} + \underset{\text{Chloric acid}}{HClO_3}$$

ClO_2 reacts with KOH forming $KClO_3$ and $KClO_2$.

$$2KOH + 2ClO_2 \longrightarrow KClO_2 + KClO_3 + H_2O$$

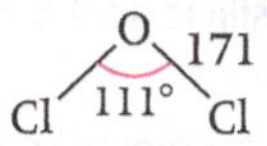

3. Dichlorine Hexoxide (Cl_2O_6)

It is obtained by mixing chlorine dioxide with ozonised air at 0°C.

$$2ClO_2 + 2O_3 \longrightarrow Cl_2O_6 + 2O_2$$

It is a dark red liquid. It is unstable and decomposed into ClO_2 and O_2. It is a strong oxidising agent. It reacts with water forming chloric and perchloric acids.

$$Cl_2O_6 + H_2O \longrightarrow HClO_3 + HClO_4$$

With HF, it gives $HClO_4$ and chloryl fluoride.

$$Cl_2O_6 + HF \longrightarrow HClO_4 + ClO_2F$$

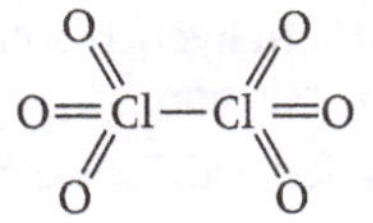

JEE Spotlite

- When Cl_2O_6 (or ClO_3) reacts with KOH, $KClO_3$ and $KClO_4$ are formed indicating that Cl_2O_6 is a mixed anhydride of perchloric acid and chloric acid
  $$2KOH + Cl_2O_6 \longrightarrow KClO_3 + KClO_4 + H_2O$$
- In the liquid state and in aqueous solution, there is paramagnetism indicating existence of ClO_3 formed due to dissociation of Cl_2O_6.
  $$Cl_2O_6 \rightleftharpoons 2ClO_3$$
- Paramagnetism is due to unpaired electrons in ClO_3, Cl_2O_6 is diamagnetic in solid state which is due to paired electrons.

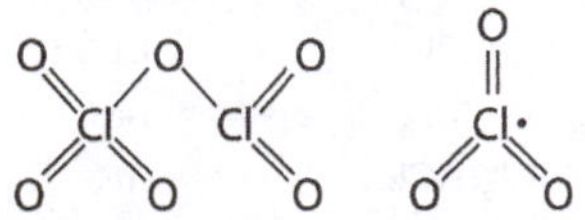

4. Chlorine Heptoxide (Cl_2O_7)

It is formed by dehydration of perchloric acid with P_2O_5 at –10°C.

$$2HClO_4 \xrightarrow{P_2O_5} Cl_2O_7 + H_2O$$

It is a colourless oily liquid which is explosive in nature. It slowly reacts with water forming perchloric acid. It is thus, anhydride of perchloric acid.

$$Cl_2O_7 + H_2O \longrightarrow 2HClO_4$$

It is less reactive in comparison to lower oxides of chlorine. Cl_2O_7 has the structure $O_3Cl—O—ClO_3$ in which two tetrahedral Cl share one O-atom.

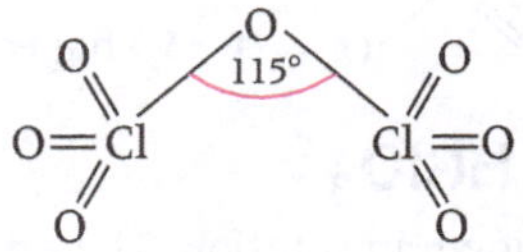

Oxo-Acids of Chlorine

Hypo-chlorous Acid, HClO

- The acid is known only in solution. It is obtained by shaking precipitated HgO with chlorine water.
  $$2HgO + 2Cl_2 + H_2O \longrightarrow \underset{\text{(Oxychloride of mercury)}}{Hg_2OCl_2} + 2HClO$$
- Commerically, it is obtained by passing CO_2 through suspension of bleaching powder and then distilling.
  $$2CaOCl_2 + H_2O + CO_2 \longrightarrow CaCl_2 + CaCO_3 + 2HClO$$
- It is a weak acid. It's concentrated solution is yellow in colour while dilute solution is colourless. It is unstable and decomposes.
  $$2HClO \longrightarrow 2HCl + O_2$$
- It dissolves magnesium with evolution of hydrogen.
  $$Mg + 2HClO \longrightarrow Mg(ClO)_2 + H_2$$
  With alkalies, it forms salts called hypochlorites.
  $$HClO(aq.) + NaOH(aq.) \longrightarrow \underset{\text{Sodium hypochlorite}}{NaClO(aq.)} + H_2O(l)$$
- It acts as a powerful oxidising and bleaching agent. This is due to release of nascent oxygen easily.
  $$HClO \longrightarrow HCl + O$$
  OCl^- disproportionates in hot solution

$$3OCl^- \xrightarrow{\text{Hot}} 2Cl^- + ClO_3^-$$

Oxidation number of Cl: $+1$ → -1 (red.), $+1$ → $+5$ (oxid.)

Structure

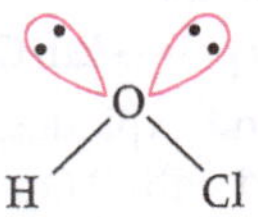

Chlorous Acid, $HClO_2$

It is obtained in aqueous solution when barium chlorite suspension in water is treated with H_2SO_4. The insoluble barium sulphate is filtered off.

$$Ba(ClO_2)_2 + H_2SO_4 \longrightarrow BaSO_4 + 2HClO_2$$

The freshly prepared solution is colourless but it soon decomposes into ClO_2 which makes the solution yellow.

$$5HClO_2 \longrightarrow 4ClO_2 + HCl + 2H_2O$$

The acid liberates iodine from KI.

$$4KI + NaClO_2 + 2H_2O \longrightarrow 4KOH + NaCl + 2I_2$$

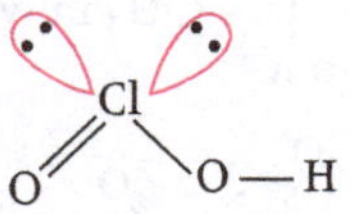

V shaped

Chloric Acid, $HClO_3$

This acid is only known in solution. The acid is prepared by the action of dilute H_2SO_4 on barium chlorate.

$$Ba(ClO_3)_2 + H_2SO_4 \longrightarrow BaSO_4 + 2HClO_3$$

$BaSO_4$ is filtered off.

Concentrated acid is colourless and pungent smelling liquid. It decomposes in light. However, it is stable in dark. It acts as a strong oxidising and bleaching agent in light. Organic substances like paper, cotton, wool, etc. catch fire in contact with the acid.

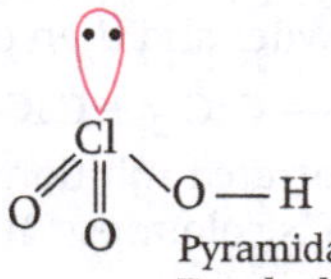

Pyramidal shape and Tetrahedral geometry.

Per-chloric Acid, $HClO_4$

It is the most stable oxyacid of chlorine. Anhydrous $HClO_4$ is obtained by doing distillation of $KClO_4$, potassium perchlorate, with 96-97.5% H_2SO_4 under low pressure at 90-160°C.

$$KClO_4 + H_2SO_4 \longrightarrow KHSO_4 + HClO_4$$

An aqueous solution of the acid is obtained by reaction $Ba(ClO_4)_2$, barium perchlorate with calculated quantity of dilute H_2SO_4. The insoluble barium sulphate is removed by filtration.

$$Ba(ClO_4)_2 + H_2SO_4 \longrightarrow BaSO_4 + 2HClO_4$$

Anhydrous $HClO_4$ is a colourless oily liquid which turns dark on keeping. It fumes in moist air. It is one of the strongest acid and ionises as follows:

$$HClO_4 \rightleftharpoons H^+ + ClO_4^-$$

It dissolves most of the metals.

$$Zn + 2HClO_4 \longrightarrow Zn(ClO_4)_2 + H_2$$

It is an oxidising agent and explodes in contact with organic matter. When dehydrated with P_2O_5, it yields, Cl_2O_7.

$$2HClO_4 + P_2O_5 \longrightarrow 2HPO_3 + Cl_2O_7$$

JEE MAPPER

Example Similar to PYQ Asked in JEE Advanced 2017

The correct statement(s) about the oxoacids $HClO_3$ and HIO_4 is(are)

(a) metaperiodic acid is obtained by heating para periodic acid.

(b) Iodic acid is obtained when iodine is evaporated with 25% $HClO_3$.

(c) metaperiodic acid and its salts are strong reducing agents in acidic medium.

(d) Action of hydrofluorosilicic acid on $KClO_3$ gives perchloric acid.

Sol. (a, b) Among the given statements only (a) and (b) are correct. The corrected form of incorrect statement(s) are as follows :

Metaperiodic acid and its salts are strong oxidising agents in acidic medium.

$$2IO_4^- + 16H^+ + 14e^- \longrightarrow I_2 + 8H_2O$$

Chloric acid is obtained by the action of hydrofluorosilicic acid on $KClO_3$.

$$2KClO_3 + H_2SiF_6 \longrightarrow K_2SiF_6(ppt.) + 2HClO_3$$

Competency Enhancer 3.1

The correct statement(s) about the oxyacids HClO and $HClO_4$ is(are)

(a) In the presence of light hypochlorous acid undergoes disproportionation reaction.

(b) $HClO_4$ on dehydration with P_2O_5 gives anhydride of chloric acid.

(c) Perchloric acid forms hydrates with 1, 2, 2.5, 3 and 3.5 molecules of water on crystallisation.

(d) The central atom in both $HClO_4$ and HClO is sp^3-hybridised.

Interhalogen Compounds

- The halogens react with each other to form **interhalogen compounds** of the type AX, AX_3, AX_5 and AX_7 of which A is of higher atomic number as shown :

AX	AX_3	AX_5	AX_7
ClF	ClF_3	ClF_5	
BrF	BrF_3	BrF_5	
ICl	$ICl_3(I_2Cl_6)$	IF_5	IF_7
IBr	IF_3		
BrCl			

- There are never more than two different halogens in a molecule. The bonds are covalent because of the small electronegativity difference. Ternary combinations occur in polyhalide ions (e.g., $IBrCl^-$)
  - Neutral interhalogen compounds are of the type AX_n where n is an odd number and X is always lighter halogen when $n > 1$. Because n is odd the compounds are diamagnetic, their valence electrons are present as bonding pairs or as unshared pairs.
  - Interhalogen ions can be either cations or anions. Halogen fluorides react with fluoride ion acceptors,

$$2ClF + AsF_5 \longrightarrow FCl_2^+AsF_6^-$$

or with fluoride ion donors,

$$IF_5 + CsF \longrightarrow Cs^+IF_6^-$$

  - The pale yellow triiodide ion (I_3^-) is formed by dissolving I_2 in aqueous KI.

$$I_2 + I^- \rightleftharpoons I_3^-$$

Other ions are not usually stable in aqueous solution although they can be obtained in CH_3OH or CH_3CN and as crystalline salts of large cations as Cs^+ or $R_4\overset{+}{N}$. Cl_3^- is formed only in concentrated solution

$$Cl_2 + Cl^- \rightleftharpoons Cl_3^-$$

  - The electrical conductance of molten I_2 is ascribed to self-ionisation

$$3I_2 \rightleftharpoons I_3^+ + I_3^-$$

  - The interhalogens are generally more reactive than the halogens (except F_2). This is because the *A*—*X* bond in interhalogens is weaker than the *X*—*X* bond in the halogens.
  - Hydrolysis of interhalogens gives halide and oxohalide. **Oxohalide is always formed from larger halogens present :**

$$BrF_5 \xrightarrow{H_2O} 5F^- + \underset{\text{Bromate ion}}{BrO_3^-}$$

$$ICl_3 \xrightarrow{H_2O} Cl^- + \underset{\text{Iodate ion}}{IO_3^-}$$

$$ICl \xrightarrow{H_2O} Cl^- + \underset{\text{Hypoiodite ion}}{IO^-}$$

  - Interhalogen compounds can fluorinate many metal oxides, metal halides and metals :

$$3UO_2 + 4BrF_3 \longrightarrow 3UF_4 + 2Br_2 + 3O_2$$

$$UF_4 + ClF_3 \longrightarrow UF_6 + ClF$$

Some interhalogen compounds are summarised below in Table.

Interhalogen Compounds and their Properties

Type of inter-halogen compound	Formulae and names of compounds	Physical state and colour at ordinary temperatures	Melting point (K)	Boiling point (K)
XY	ClF Chlorine fluoride	Gas, colourless	119	163
	BrF Bromine fluoride	Liquid below 293 K, Pale-brown gas above 293 K	240	293
	BrCl Bromine chloride	Liquid, reddish yellow	207	283
	ICl Iodine chloride	Solid, ruby red	—	310
	IBr Iodine bromide	Solid, black like iodine	232	
XY_3	ClF_3 Chlorine trifluoride	Liquid below 261 K, colourless gas above 261 K	197	261
	BrF_3 Bromine trifluoride	Liquid, Yellow green	282	400
	$BrCl_3$ Bromine trichloride	Solid, orange	374 (decomposes)	—
XY_5	ClF_5 Chlorine pentafluoride	Gas, colourless	170	259
	BrF_5 Bromine pentafluoride	Liquid colourless	213	314
	IF_5 Bromine pentafluoride	Liquid colourless	283	314
XY_7	IF_7 Iodine heptafluoride	Gas, colourless	279.5	

Structure of Interhalogen Compounds

The interhalogen compounds are generally covalent in nature in which the larger atom lies in the centre. Their shapes can be predicted by VSEPR theory.

Shapes of some of the interhalogen compounds are given below

Molecule	Total number of electron pairs around X	Bond pairs	Lone pairs	Shape
XY	4	1	3	Linear
XY_3	5	3	2	T-shaped
XY_5	6	5	1	Square pyramidal
XY_7	7	7	0	Pentagonal bipramidal

JEE Spotlite

- Thermal stability of AB type Interhalogen compounds decreases with the decrease in electronegativity difference between A and B atoms. IF > BrF > ClF > ICl> IBr > BrCl. More polar is the A—B bond more is the stability of interhalogen.
- Interhalogen compounds are more reactive than the parent halogens but less reactive than F_2.
$$ICl + 2Na \longrightarrow NaI + NaCl$$
- The order of reactivity of some interhalogens is as follows :
$$ClF_3 > BrF_3 > IF_7 > BrF_5 > BrF.$$
- These compounds can be used as non aqueous solvents.
- Interhalogen compounds are very useful fluorinating agents. ClF_3 and BrF_3 are used for the production of UF_6 in the enrichment of ^{235}U.
$$U(s) + 3ClF_3(l) \longrightarrow UF_6(g) + 3ClF(g)$$

Polyhalides and Polyhalonium Ions

Halide ions often associate with molecules of halogens or with interhalogen compounds to form polyhalide ions. For example, on addition of potassium iodide, the solubility of iodine in water is greatly enhanced due to the formation of the triiodide ion, I_3^- :

$$KI + I_2 \longrightarrow KI_3$$

- More complex ions of iodine, such as pentaiodide, I_5^-, heptaiodide, I_7^- and noniodide, I_9^- are also known.
- These are generally found in the form of salts of large metal ions, as $Rb^+I_9^- \cdot 2C_6H_6$ or large complex cations, as $NH_4^+I_5^-$, $(C_2H_5)_4N^+I_7^-$). A number of mixed polyhalide ions containing two or three different halogens are also known, as ICl_2^-, ICl_4^- and $IBrF^-$ and $IBrCl^-$.

All the polyhalides are hydrolysed to some extent in aqueous solution. The ease of hydrolysis increases with the introduction of the more electronegative halogen, into the ion. Thus, the triiodide being the most stable and Cl_3^- the least. In non-aqueous solutions, polyhalides behave as mild halogenating agents.

Polyhalonium cations, e.g., ICl_4^+ and BrF_2^+ are formed as a result of autoionisation of ICl_5 and BrF_3. Other cations like $Br_2^+, I_2^+, I_3^+, ClF_2^+, IF_2^+, IBr_2^+, IBrCl^+, ClF_4^+, BrF_4^+, IF_4^+, ClF_6^+, BrF_6^+$, IF_6^+, etc. are also known. These are stabilised by large anions like $BF_4^-, PF_6^-, AsF_6^-, AlCl_4^-, SbCl_6^-$, etc.

Pseudohalogens and Pseudohalides

- Some molecules like cyanogen, $(CN)_2$, thiocyanogen, $(SCN)_2$ and selenocyanogen, $(SeCN)_2$, have properties similar to those of the halogens. Therefore, these are called pseudohalogens.
- Pseudohalogens form hydro acids similar to the hydrohalic acids, e.g., H—CN. They also form anions such as cyanide, CN^-, cyanate, OCN^-, thiocyanate, SCN^-, selenocyanate, $SeCN^-$, tellurocyanate. $TeCN^-$ and azide, N_3^-, which resemble the halide ions to some extent.

The best known pseudohalide is the cyanide, CN^-, which resembles Cl^-, Br^- and I^- in the following respects :

(i) It can be oxidised to form a molecule, $(CN)_2$.

(ii) It forms an acid HCN similar to HCl, HBr, etc.

(iii) It forms insoluble salts with Ag^+, Pb^{2+} and Hg^{2+}.

(iv) Interpseudohalogen compounds ClCN, BrCN and ICN can also be formed.

(v) Like AgCl, AgCN is insoluble in water but soluble in liquor ammonia.

(vi) It forms a large number of complexes similar to the halide complexes, e.g., $[Cu(CN)_4]^{2-}$ is similar to $[CuCl_4]^{2-}$ and $[Co(CN)_6]^{3-}$ is similar to $[CoCl_6]^{3-}$.

Some Important Order		
(a)	$F < Cl < Br < I$	Atomic or ionic radius
(b)	$F > Cl > Br > I$	Ionisation enthalpy
(c)	$Cl > F > Br > I$	Electron affinity
(d)	$Cl_2 > Br_2 > F_2 > I_2$ BDE size ↑	*lp-lp* repulsion
(e)	$F_2 > Cl_2 > Br_2 > I_2$	oxidising nature, reactivity
(f)	$F^- < Cl^- < Br^- < I^-$	Reducing nature
(g)	$F^- > Cl^- > Br^- > I^-$	Hydration energy
(h)	$F_2 < Cl_2 < Br_2 < I_2$	Melting point/boiling point
(i)	$F_2 < Cl_2 < Br_2 < I_2$	Density
(j)	HF < HCl < HBr < HI	Acidic nature
(k)	HOF > HOCl > HOBr > HOI	Acidic nature
(l)	$HOCl < HClO_2 < HClO_3 < HClO_4$	Acidic nature
(m)	$HOCl < HClO_2 < HClO_3 < HClO_4$	Thermal stabilty
(n)	$HOCl > HClO_2 > HClO_3 > HClO_4$	Oxidising nature
(o)	$ClO^- > ClO_2^- > ClO_3^- > ClO_4^-$	Hydration energy
(p)	HF > HCl> HBr > HI	Thermal stability

• The important properties of halogen acids are summarised below in tabulated form.

Properties of Halogen Acids

Property	HF	HCl	HBr	HI
Monomeric or dimeric	Dimeric (H_2F_2)	Monomeric (HCl)	Monomeric (HBr)	Monomeric (HI)
Physical state at 15°C	Liquid	Gas	Gas	Gas
H—*X* bond length (Å)	0.92	1.27	1.41	1.61
	——— Increases ———			
Strength of H—*X* bond or thermal stability of H*X* molecule	Maximum	High	Not so high	Very little
	——— Decreases ———			
H—*X* bond dissociation energy or heat of dissociation (kJ mol^{-1})	+ 574.0	+ 428.1	+ 362.5	+ 294.6
	——— Decreases ———			
Dissociation temperature (°C)	Does not dissociate	1500	800	180
	——— Decreases ———			
Melting point (°C)	–83	–111	–86	–50.8
Boiling point (°C)	+ 19.4 (Maximum)	– 85 (Minimum)	– 67	–35.0
Hydrogen bonding	Maximum	Little	Very little	Very little
Solubility in water at 0°C (g/L)	85.3	42.0	49.0	57.1
Dipole moment values when H*X* molecules are assumed to be completely ionic [calculated values (C.m.)]	1.47×10^{-29}	2.03×10^{-29}	2.25×10^{-29}	2.57×10^{-29}
	——— Increases ———			
% of ionic character in the gaseous H*X* molecules				
(a) as calculated from their moment values	43.5	16.8	11.6	4.9
(b) as calculated from Henry-Smith's equation	40.14	19.5	15.04	8.87
Heat evolved (kJ mol^{-1}) in the reaction, $HX(g) + aq \longrightarrow HX(aq) \longrightarrow H^+(aq) + X^-(aq)$ or $HX(g) + H_2O \longrightarrow H_3O^+ + X^-(aq)$ (called heat of ionisation)	–9.0 Weakest acid	– 60.8 Very strong acid	– 64.6 Strong acid	– 58.4 Strongest acid
	——— Decreases ———			
Reducing property	Not a reducing agent	Mild reducing agent	Strong reducing agent	Strongest reducing agent
	——— Increases ———			
Heat of formation (kJ mol^{-1}) [$\frac{1}{2} X_2(s, l, g) + \frac{1}{2} H_2(g) \rightarrow HX(g)$ ΔH = heat required (+) or released (–)]	–271.1 (*g*)	– 92.3 (*g*)	–36.4 (*g*)	+25.4 (*g*)
Heat of dehydration (kJ mol^{-1}) [$HX(aq) + \text{heat} \longrightarrow HX(g)$]	+48.0	+18.0	+21.0	+23.0
Heat of neutralisation with NaOH (kJ mol^{-1})	+ 68.2	+57.3	+57.9	+57.6
Apparent degree of dissociation in 0.1 N solution at room temperature	0.08	0.93	0.94	0.95
Solubility of silver salt (*g* /100 g)	172	0.00154	0.000084	0.000028
	——— Increases ———			
Solubility of calcium salt (*g* /100 g)	0.0016	42.7	58.8	67.6
	——— Increases ———			

Elemental Practice 6.3

Type I MCQs with Only One Correct Option

1. Iodine is formed when potassium iodide reacts with a solution of
(a) $ZnSO_4$ (b) $CuSO_4$
(c) $(NH_4)_2SO_4$ (d) Na_2SO_4

2. Select the most volatile compound from the following.
(a) HCl (b) HI
(c) HBr (d) HF

3. Reduction potentials of some ions are given below. Arrange them in decreasing order of oxidising power.

Ion	ClO_4^-	IO_4^-	BrO_4^-
Reduction potential (E^V/V)	$E^V = 1.19$ V	$E^V = 1.65$ V	$E^V = 1.74$ V

(a) $ClO_4^- > IO_4^- > BrO_4^-$ (b) $IO_4^- > BrO_4^- > ClO_4^-$
(c) $BrO_4^- > IO_4^- > ClO_4^-$ (d) $BrO_4^- > ClO_4^- > IO_4^-$

4. Choose the anhydride of $HClO_4$ from the following
(a) ClO_2 (b) Cl_2O_7
(c) Cl_2O (d) Cl_2O_6

5. The correct decreasing order of acid strength of given oxoacids is
(a) $HOCl > HClO_2 > HClO_3 > HClO_4$
(b) $HClO_4 > HOCl > HClO_2 > HClO_3$
(c) $HClO_4 > HClO_3 > HClO_2 > HOCl$
(d) $HClO_2 > HClO_4 > HClO_3 > HOCl$

6. The products obtained when chlorine gas reacts with cold and dilute aqueous NaOH are
(a) ClO^- and ClO_3^- (b) ClO_2^- and ClO_3^-
(c) Cl^- and ClO^- (d) Cl^- and ClO_2^-

7. $HClO_4 + P_2O_5 \longrightarrow (A)$ and (B)
The product *A* and *B* are
(a) $HClO_3, H_3PO_4$ (b) Cl_2O_6, HPO_3
(c) ClO_2, H_3PO_4 (d) Cl_2O_7, HPO_3

8. Which species of I_2Cl_6 in solid state exist in sp^3 and sp^3d^2 hybridised state.
(a) ICl_2^+, ICl_2^- (b) ICl_2^-, ICl_4^-
(c) ICl_2^+, ICl_4^- (d) ICl_4^-, ICl_3^-

9. Choose the correct reaction that occurs between fluorine and hot NaOH (dil.).
(a) $3F_2 + 6NaOH \longrightarrow 5NaF + NaFO_3 + 3H_2O$
(b) $2F_2 + 4NaOH \longrightarrow 4NaF + 2H_2O + O_2$
(c) $2F_2 + 2NaOH \longrightarrow NaF + NaOF + H_2O$
(d) $F_2 + 2NaOH \longrightarrow NaF + HOF + H_2O$

10. Select the incorrect trend from the following.
(a) $Cl_2O < Cl_2O_6 < Cl_2O_7$ (oxidation state)
(b) $H_2O > NH_3 > HF$ (melting point)
(c) $Cl_2 < Br_2 < I_2$ (boiling point)
(d) $HClO_4 < HBrO_4 < HIO_4$ (acidity)

11. A reaction of $KClO_3$ with aqueous $H_2C_2O_4$ at 90°C gives a paramagnetic species, which upon reaction with ozone produces
(a) Cl_2O_7 (b) Cl_2O_6
(c) Cl_2O (d) ClO_2

12. For Cl_2O molecule, consider the following statements.
A. molecular geometry is linear.
B. oxidation state of Cl is +4.
C. number of lone pair on oxygen is 2.
D. molecule is bent or 'V'-shaped.
E. Cl—O—Cl angle is 110°.
Choose the correct statements from the option given below.
(a) A, B and D (b) B, E and A
(c) A, C and D (d) C, D and E

13. Concentrated and hot $Ba(OH)_2$ reacts with bromine to give
(a) $BaO, BaBr_2, HBr$ (b) $BaOBr_2, H_2O, HBr$
(c) $BaBr_2, Ba(BrO_3)_2, H_2O$ (d) $BaO, Ba(BrO_3)_2, H_2O$

14. Number of Cl=O bonds in hypochlorous, perchloric and chloric acid respectively are
(a) 1, 3, 2 (b) 1, 2, 3
(c) 0, 3, 2 (d) 3, 0, 2

15. The interhalogen compound formed from the reaction of chlorine with excess of fluorine at 250°C is
(a) difluorochlorate
(b) chlorine trifluoride
(c) chlorine pentafluoride
(d) chlorine monofluoride

Type II MCQs with One or More than One Correct Option

16. Fluorine is used in the manufacturing of
(a) freon, CCl_2F_2 used in refrigeration.
(b) cupric fluoride used in ceramic industry.
(c) uranium hexafluoride used in enrichment of ^{235}U
(d) sodium tetrafluoroacetate used as sweetener.

17. Bromine is soluble in which of the following solvents?
(a) Water (b) Benzene
(c) Chloroform (d) Carbon disulphide

18. Bromine undergoes disproportionation reaction with
(a) $Ca(OH)_2$ (b) Na_2SO_3
(c) Na_2CO_3 (d) $Na_2S_2O_3$

19. Coloured interhalogen is/are
(a) BrF_5 (b) BrF_3
(c) BrCl (d) BrF

20. Choose the correct order from the following.
(a) HOCl > HOBr > HOI $\rightarrow$ acidic strength
(b) $HBrO_4 > HIO_4 > HClO_4 \rightarrow$ oxidising power
(c) $HClO_4 < HClO_3 < HClO_2 \rightarrow$ oxidising power
(d) $IO^- < BrO^- < ClO^- \rightarrow$ ease of disproportionation

Type III 》 Numerical/IntegerAnswer Type Questions

21. Consider the following reactions :
I. $I_2 + SO_3^{2-} + H_2O \longrightarrow SO_4^{2-} + 2H^+ + 2I^-$
II. $HClO_4 + P_4O_{10} \longrightarrow Cl_2O_7 + HPO_3$
III. $ClO_2 + KOH \longrightarrow KClO_2 + KClO_3 + H_2O$
IV. $6KOH + 3Br_2 \longrightarrow 5KBr + KBrO_4 + 2H_2O_2$
V. $6Ba(OH)_2 + 6Br_2 \longrightarrow 5BaOBr + Ba(BrO_2)_3 + 4H_2O$
The number of reactions that are correctly shown are :

22. Consider the following statements
A. Iodine reacts with hypo to give NaI and $Na_2S_4O_6$.
B. In NO_2 and ClO_2, the central atom has an oxidation state +4.
C. Fluoride compounds are more stable than corresponding chlorine compounds.
D. Aqueous solution of $Na_2S_2O_3$ on reaction with Cl_2 gives $Na_2S_4O_6$ and NaOH.
E. Enthalpy of vaporisation and ionic radius of chlorine and iodine increases with increasing atomic number.
The total number of incorrect statement is/are :

23. A compound *X* is obtained by dehydration of perchloric acid with P_4O_{10} at 263 K, which may be distilled off under reduced pressure, with precaution against explosions. The oxidation state of chlorine in the compound '*X*' is

24. The sum of lone pair and bond pair electron present in BrF_3 and ClF_5 is ....

25. Among the following $OCN^{\ominus}$, $SCN^{\ominus}$, BrCN, ICl, ICN, IF_5, $TeCN^{\ominus}$, $I_3^{\ominus}$, $ICl_2^{\ominus}$, ClCN, $ONC^{\ominus}$ and $(CN)_2$. The total number of interpseudohalogens are

Elemental Practice 6.3 | Chapter 06

Connect with **Answers**

1. (b)	**2.** (a)	**3.** (c)	**4.** (b)	**5.** (c)	**6.** (c)
7. (d)	**8.** (c)	**9.** (a)	**10.** (d)	**11.** (b)	**12.** (d)
13. (c)	**14.** (c)	**15.** (b)	**16.** (a,b,c)	**17.** (a,b,c,d)	**18.** (a,c)
19. (b,c,d)	**20.** (a,b,c)	**21.** (3)	**22.** (1)	**23.** (7)	**24.** (11)
25. (3)					

Element 4

Group-18 : The Noble Gases and Their Compounds

Group 18 elements are collectively known as rare, inert, noble gases or group zero elements. These are monoatomic gases, helium (He), neon (Ne), argon (Ar), krypton (Kr), xenon (Xe), radon (Rn) and oganesson (Og).

Occurrence

All these gases occurs in the atmosphere. Except radon and oganesson.

The total abundance of He, Ne, Ar, Kr and Xe in dry air is about 1% by volume of which argon is the major constituent.

General and Physical Properties

Following are the general and physical properties of noble gases.

1. Electronic Configuration

The general electronic configuration is ns^2np^6 (except helium which has $1s^2$).

2. Atomic Radii

The atomic radii of the noble gases are the largest in their respective periods. In case of noble gases, covalent radii cannot be determined as they can be solidified at very low temperature only. Down the group i.e., from He to Rn, the atomic radii increases because at each successive step new shells are being added and the electron cloud is expanding.

The order of atomic radii is He < Ne < Ar < Kr < Xe

3. Ionisation Enthalpy

The ionisation enthalpies of noble gases are the highest as compared to ionisation enthalpies of other members in the same period due to presence of fully filled valence shell electronic configurations.

Down the group from the He to Rn, ionisation enthalpy decreases because of increase in atomic radii and screening effect of the inner electrons.

The order of ionisation enthalpy is

$$He > Ne > Ar > Kr > Xe > Rn$$

4. Electron Gain Enthalpy

The noble gases have large positive value of electron gain enthalpy due to presence of fully-filled valence shells

They have no tendency to add or lose electron thus, lack chemical reactivity as compared to other elements of periodic table.

5. Melting and Boiling Point

Generally noble gases have very low melting and boiling points. It is because there is no strong interatomic forces. Only weak van der waals forces operate which hold atoms together in liquid and solid state. Their value increases on moving down the group due to increase in the magnitude of van der waals' force of attraction.

Helium has the lowest boiling point among all the element, and its behaviour as a liquid is most unusual. It has no triple point that is there is no single combination of temperature and pressure at which the solid, the liquid and the gas all exist.

JEE Spotlite

- Noble gases have high solubility in water i.e., solubility of Ar in H_2O is greater than that of O_2 or N_2.
- Molecular weight (by vapour density method) of noble gases are same as atomic weight thus these are monoatomic gases.
- Liquifaction of noble gases is relatively difficult due to weak van der waals' force of attraction between the atoms. These forces and ease of liquifaction increases on moving down the group.

Physical Properties of Group 18 Element

Property	He	Ne	Ar	Kr	Xe	Rn
Atomic number	2	10	18	36	54	86
Electronic configuration	$1s^2$	[He] $2s^2 2p^6$	[Ne] $3s^2 3p^6$	[Ar] $3d^{10} 4s^2 4p^6$	[Kr] $4d^{10} 5s^2 5p^6$	[Xe] $4f^{14} 5d^{10} 6s^2 6p^6$
$(IE)_1$/kJ mol^{-1}	2372	2080	1520	1351	1170	1037
Melting point/K	—	24.6	83.8	115.9	161.3	202
Boiling point/K	4.2	27.1	87.2	119.7	165	211
Atomic radius/pm	120	160	190	200	220	—
Density at STP/ g/cm³	1.8×10^{-4}	9.0×10^{-4}	1.8×10^{-3}	3.7×10^{-3}	5.9×10^{-3}	9.7×10^{-3}
Atmospheric content/% by volume	5.24×10^{-4}	—	1.82×10^{-3}	0.934	1.14×10^{-3}	8.7×10^{-6}

JEE MAPPER

Example Similar to PYQ Asked in JEE Main 2021

A xenon compound '*B*' readily reacts with SiO_2 present in glass to give XeO_3 and SiF_4. The number of lone pair of electrons present in compound '*B*' is ....

Sol. (1) $\underset{(B)}{2XeF_6} + 3SiO_2 \longrightarrow 2XeO_3 + 3SiF_4$

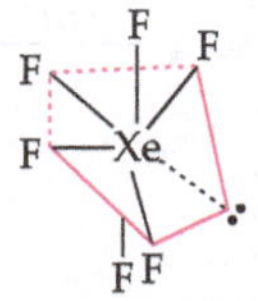

The number of lone pair of electron present in XeF_6 i.e compound *B* is 1.

Competency Enhancer 4.1

A compound '*P*' is formed by the reaction of conc. H_2SO_4 on barium xenate at room temperature. The total number of Xe—O double bonds containing $p\pi$ - $d\pi$ overlapping is ....

Study of Compounds of Group 18

- The noble gases were isolated and discovered because of their lack of reactivity. For a long time it was thought that they really were chemically inert. Before 1962, the only evidence for compound formation by the noble gases was some **molecular ions** formed in discharge tube and **clathrate** compounds.
- Several molecular ions such as He_2^+, HeH^+, HeH^{2+} and Ar^{2+} are formed under high energy conditions in discharge tubes.

Clathrate Compounds

- If an aqueous solution of quinol is crystallised under a pressure of 10–40 atm of Ar, Kr, or Xe, the gas becomes trapped in the cavities of about 4Å diameter in the β-quinol structure. These are called **clathrate compounds.** They do not form bonds in the cavities.
- When the clathrate is dissolved, the hydrogen bonded arrangement of β-quinol breaks down and the noble gas escapes. The smaller noble gases He and Ne do not form clathrate compounds because the gas atoms are small enough to escape from the cavities.
- Clathrate provides a convenient means of storing radioactive isotopes of Kr and Xe produced in nuclear reactors.

Xenon Fluorides

- Xenon reacts directly with fluorine when the gases are heated at 300–600°C in a sealed nickel vessel, and the products formed depend on the Xe / F_2 ratio.

$$\underset{\text{(xenon in excess)}}{Xe(g) + F_2(g)} \xrightarrow{673\text{ K, 1 bar}} XeF_2(s)$$

$$\underset{\text{(1.5 ratio)}}{Xe(g) + 2F_2(g)} \xrightarrow{873\text{ K, 7 bar}} XeF_4(s)$$

$$\underset{\text{(1 : 20 ratio)}}{Xe(g) + 3F_2(g)} \xrightarrow{573\text{ K, 60-70 bar}} XeF_6(s)$$

- These conversions are usually quantitative under the given conditions. XeF_6 may be completely separated from XeF_2 and XeF_4 by passing over dry NaF when XeF_6 alone is absorbed.

$$XeF_6 + 2NaF \longrightarrow Na_2XeF_8$$

The complex decomposes an heating to give XeF_6

- These are colourless (white) volatile solids. XeF_6 is yellow in the liquid and gaseous phases. The fluorides form large crystals on standing in closed vessels. XeF_2 and XeF_4 can be handled conveniently in glass vaccum system but XeF_6 attacks glass or quartz. They can be sublimed at room temperature, and can be stored indefinitely in nickel or monel (an alloy of nickel) containers.
- H_2 reduces xenon fluorides to Xe :

$$XeF_2 + H_2 \longrightarrow Xe + 2HF$$
$$XeF_4 + 2H_2 \longrightarrow Xe + 4HF$$
$$XeF_6 + 3H_2 \longrightarrow Xe + 6HF$$

(at room temperature)

- Xenon fluorides oxidise Cl^- to Cl_2 and I^- to I_2 :

Oxidising power increases in the order :

$$XeF_2 < XeF_4 < XeF_6$$
$$XeF_2 + 2HCl \longrightarrow 2HF + Xe + Cl_2$$
$$XeF_4 + 4KI \longrightarrow 4KF + Xe + 2I_2$$

This reaction is used to estimate XeF_4. I_2 formed is titrated using Hypo.

- They also oxidise Ce^{3+} salts to Ce^{4+} salts.
- They are also hydrolysed in alkaline solution rapidly

$$2XeF_2 + 4OH^- \xrightarrow{\text{Rapid}} 2Xe + 4F^- + 2H_2O + O_2$$

$$XeF_6 + 7OH^- \longrightarrow \underset{\text{Xenate ion}}{HXeO_4^-} + 3H_2O + 6F^-$$

$$HXeO_4^- + 2OH^- \xrightarrow{\text{Slow}} \underset{\text{Perxenate ion}}{XeO_6^{4-}} + Xe + 2H_2O + O_2$$

- They are also used as fluorinating agent

$$2SF_4 + XeF_4 \longrightarrow 2SF_6 + Xe$$
$$Pt + XeF_4 \longrightarrow PtF_4 + Xe$$
$$C_6H_6 + XeF_2 \longrightarrow C_6H_5F + Xe + HF$$

- XeF_2 is soluble in water but undergoes slow hydrolysis :

$$2XeF_2 + 2H_2O \longrightarrow 2Xe + 4HF + O_2$$

- XeF_4 and XeF_6 react violently with water to give XeO_3 :

$$3XeF_4 + 6H_2O \longrightarrow 2Xe + XeO_3 + 12HF + \frac{3}{2}O_2$$

$$XeF_6 + \underset{\text{(atmospheric moisture)}}{3H_2O} \longrightarrow XeO_3 + 6HF$$

- SiO_2 converts XeF_6 into $XeOF_4$:

$$2XeF_6 + SiO_2 \longrightarrow SiF_4 + 2XeOF_4$$
$$2XeOF_4 + SiO_2 \longrightarrow 2XeO_2F_2 + SiF_4$$
$$2XeO_2F_2 + SiO_2 \longrightarrow 2XeO_3 + SiF_4$$

SiO_2 is a part of glass or quartz. Hence, XeF_6 cannot be stored in glass or quartz vessel.

JEE Quicker

Oxidising power of fluorides of Xe in decreasing order is

$XeF_2 < XeF_4 < XeF_6$ *JEE Main 2020*

Greater the oxidation number of the central element, greater the tendency to be reduced to minimum state hence greater is the oxidising power.

- Xenon fluorides act as fluoride donor and forms complexes which are conducting due to formation of ions:

$$XeF_2 + MF_5 \longrightarrow [XeF]^+[MF_6]^-$$
$$(M = As^{3+}, Sb^{5+}, P^{5+}, \text{etc.})$$
$$XeF_6 + BF_3 \longrightarrow [XeF_5]^+[BF_4]^-$$
$$XeF_6 + HF \longrightarrow [XeF_5]^+[HF_2]^-$$

XeF_6 may also act as a fluoride acceptor:

$$XeF_6 + RbF \longrightarrow Rb^+ [XeF_7]^-$$
$$XeF_6 + CsF \longrightarrow Cs^+[XeF_7]^-$$
$$2Cs^+[XeF_7] \xrightarrow{\Delta} XeF_6 + Cs_2[XeF_8]$$

Reactions of xenon fluorides are summarised in flowchart below

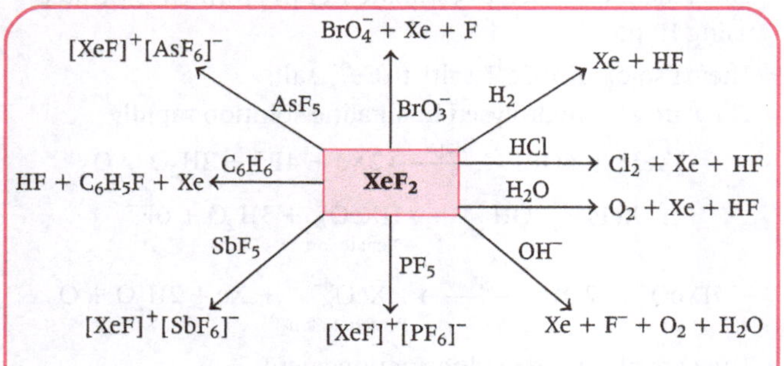

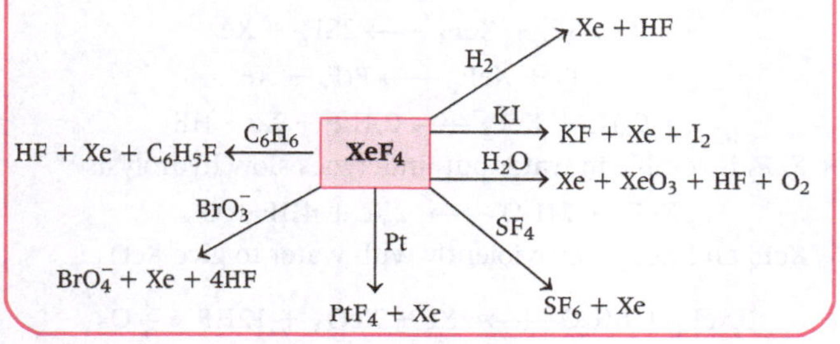

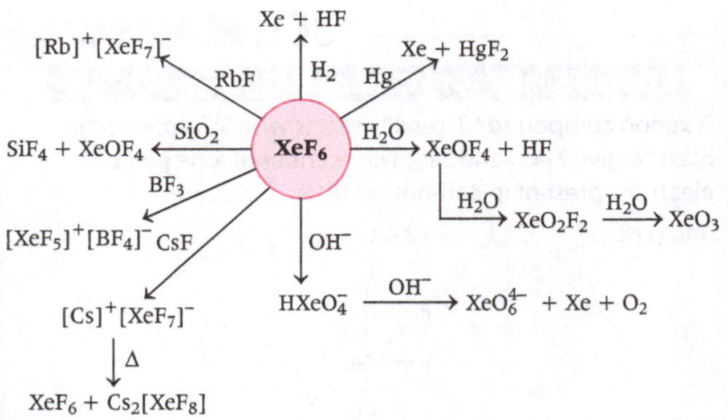

Structures

XeF_2 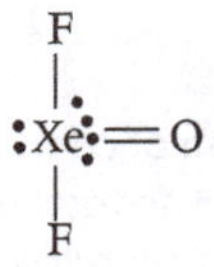 Linear structure

XeF_4  Square Planar structure

XeF_6 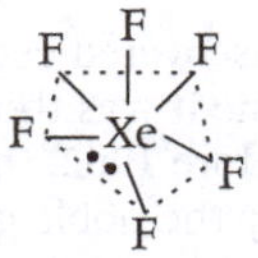 Distorted octahedral structure

Xenon Oxides

Two of its oxides are given below.

Xenon Trioxide, XeO_3

XeO_3 can be prepared by complete hydrolysis of XeF_4 and XeF_6 as,

$$6XeF_4 + 12H_2O \longrightarrow 2XeO_3 + 4Xe + 3O_2\uparrow + 24HF$$
$$XeF_6 + 3H_2O \longrightarrow XeO_3 + 6HF$$

It is a colourless solid, highly explosive and powerful oxidising agent. XeO_3 has sp^3-hybridisation trigonal pyramidal geometry because of the presence of one lone pair of electrons over Xe. The molecule has three Xe$=$O double bonds containing $p\pi$-$d\pi$ overlapping.

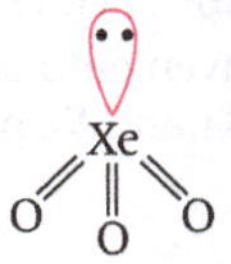

Xenon Tetraoxide, XeO_4

XeO_4 can be prepared by the action of conc H_2SO_4 on sodium or barium xenate (Na_4XeO_6; Ba_2XeO_6) at room temperature.

$$Na_4XeO_6 + 2H_2SO_4 \longrightarrow XeO_4 + 2Na_2SO_4 + 2H_2O$$
$$Ba_2XeO_6 + 2H_2SO_4 \longrightarrow XeO_4 + 2BaSO_4 + 2H_2O$$

XeO_4 is purified by vacuum sublimation at 195 K. It is quite unstable gas and decomposes to xenon and oxygen,

$$XeO_4 \longrightarrow Xe + 2O_2\uparrow$$

XeO_4 has tetrahedral structure due to sp^3-hybridisation of Xe. There are four Xe—O double bonds containing $p\pi$- $d\pi$ overlapping.

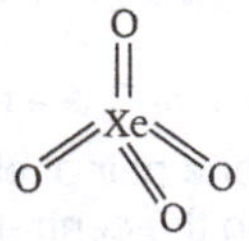

Xenon Oxyfluorides

Xenon forms number of oxyfluorides that are given below in the tabular form.

Molecule	Hybridi-sation	Geometry	Shape	Structure
$XeOF_2$	sp^3d	Trigonal bipyramidal	T - shaped	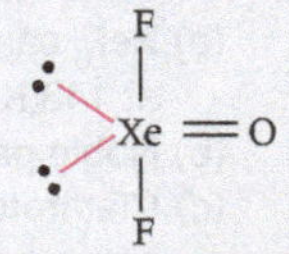
$XeOF_4$	sp^3d^2	Square pyramidal	Square pyramidal	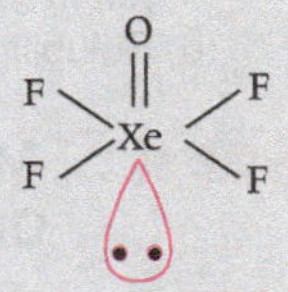
XeO_2F_2	sp^3d	Trigonal bipyramidal	Distorted trigonal	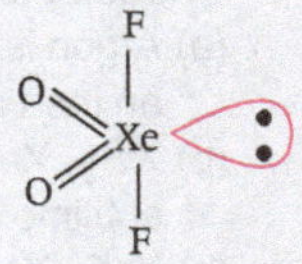
XeO_3F_2	sp^3d	Trigonal bipyramid	Trigonal bipyramidal	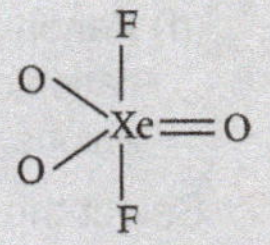
XeO_2F_4	sp^3d^2	Octahedral	Octahedral	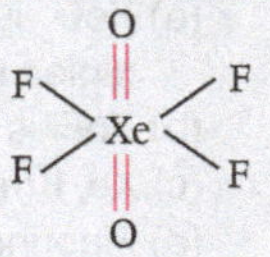

Xenon oxyfluorides can be prepared by the following reactions.

$$XeF_4 + H_2O \longrightarrow XeOF_2 + 2HF$$
$$XeF_6 + H_2O \longrightarrow XeOF_4 + 2HF$$
$$XeF_6 + 2\,H_2O \longrightarrow XeO_2F_2 + 4HF$$

Uses of the Noble Gases

Noble gas		Use	Reasons
Helium	1.	Filling of observation balloons and other lighter-than-air craft	Non-flammable; 93% lifting power as compared to flammable H_2
	2.	He/O_2 mixture for deep-sea breathing, instead of N_2/O_2 mixture	Low solubility in blood; prevents nitrogen narcosis and "bends"
	3.	Diluent for gaseous anaesthetics	Non-flammable, non-reactive
	4.	He/O_2 mixtures for respiratory patients	Low density flows easily through restricted passages
	5.	Heat transfer medium for nuclear reactions	Transfers heat readily; does not become radioactive; chemically inert
	6.	Liquid He maintains very low temperature in research (cryogenics)	Extremely low boiling point
Neon		Neon signs	Even at low Ne pressure, moderate electric current causes bright orange-red glow; can be modified by coloured glass or mixing with Ar or Hg vapour.
Argon	1.	Inert atmosphere for welding	Chemically inert
	2.	Filling incandescent light bulbs	Inert; prevents vaporisation of tungsten and blackening of bulbs
Krypton		Airport runway and approach lights	Gives longer life to incandescent lights than Ar, but more expensive
Xenon		Xe and Kr mixture in high-intensity, short-exposure photographic flash tubes	Both have fast response to electric current
Radon		Radiotherapy of cancerous-tissues	Radioactive

Elemental Practice 6.4

Type I MCQs with Only One Correct Option

1. Noble gases are sparingly soluble in water due to
(a) dipole-dipole interaction
(b) dipole-induced dipole interaction
(c) induced dipole-induced dipole interaction
(d) hydrogen bonding

2. The correct order of solubility in water for He, Ne, Ar, Kr, Xe is
(a) Xe > Kr > Ar > Ne > He (b) Ar > Ne > He > Kr > Xe
(c) He > Ne > Ar > Kr > Xe (d) Ne > Ar > Kr > He > Xe

3. Select from the following the life saving mixture for an asthma patient.
(a) Mixture of helium and oxygen
(b) Mixture of neon and oxygen
(c) Mixture of xenon and nitrogen
(d) Mixture of argon and oxygen

4. XeF_2 on hydrolysis gives
(a) XeO_3 (b) XeO
(c) Xe (d) XeO_2

5. Given below are few molecules.
(i) XeO_3 (ii) $XeOF_4$ (iii) $XeOF_2$
(iii) XeF_6 (iv) XeF_2
Select the molecule having same number of lone pairs on Xe are
(a) (i), (iii) and (iv) (b) (i), (ii), (iii) and (v)
(c) (ii), (iii) and (v) (d) (i), (ii) and (iii)

6. The pair of species having identical shape for molecules of both species is
(a) XeF_2, IF_2^- (b) BF_3, NH_3
(c) CF_4, SF_4 (d) PCl_5, ICl_5

7. Number of $p\pi$ - $d\pi$ bonds present in XeO_4 are
(a) four (b) two
(c) three (d) zero

8. The compounds that can not be stored in glass vessels is
(a) XeF_4 (b) XeF_6
(c) XeO_3 (d) XeF_2

9. The products formed when alkalies react with XeF_6 are :
(a) XeO_2F_2 and HF (b) $XeOF_4$ and HF
(c) Na_4XeO_6 and Xe (d) $XeOF_2$ and HF

10. The type of hybridisation and number of lone pair(s) of electrons of Xe in XeO_2F_2 is
(a) sp^3d and 2 (b) sp^3d^2 and 1
(c) sp^3d and 1 (d) sp^3d^2 and 2

11. Consider the following reaction sequence
$XeF_6 + 6H_2O \longrightarrow X \xrightarrow{XeOF_4} Y$
The sum of lone pair of electrons present on X and Y is
(a) 1 (b) 3
(c) 4 (d) 2

12. Select the incorrect statement from the following.
(a) XeF_6 is colourless crystalline solid and a powerful flourinating agents.
(b) XeF_4 and XeF_6 acts as both fluoride ion donor and acceptor.
(c) Partial hydrolysis of XeF_6 gives oxyfluorides, $XeOF_4$ and XeO_2F_2.
(d) Hydrolysis reaction of XeF_4 is a non-redox reaction.

13. The compound with lone pair of electron having only one $p\pi$-$d\pi$ multiple bond on the central atom is
(a) XeO_4 (b) XeO_3 (c) XeO_2F_2 (d) $XeOF_4$

14. The action of anhydrous H_2SO_4 on barium perxenate, produces a xenon compound Y. The total number of lone pair of electrons present on the whole number of (Y) is
(a) 3 (b) 2 (c) 4 (d) 0

15. Choose the incorrect statement from the following.
(a) XeF_6 can be prepared by the interaction of XeF_4 and O_2F_2 at 143 K.
(b) Noble gases have high boiling points.
(c) Clathrates play an important role in the separation of noble gases.
(d) Solubility of Ar in water is greater than of O_2 or N_2.

Type II MCQs with One or More than One Correct Option

16. Choose the correct statement from the following.
(a) Argon is used in welding of metals or alloys to provide an inert atmosphere.
(b) XeF_2, XeF_4 and XeF_6 are colourless crystalline solids and sublime readily at 298 K.
(c) XeF_2, XeF_4 and XeF_6 are readily hydrolysed.
(d) Xenon fluorides reacts with fluoride ion acceptor to form cationic species and fluoride ion donor to form fluoro anions.

17. Select the incorrect statement from the following.
(a) XeO_3 is colourless explosive solid and has a pyramidal molecular structure.
(b) XeF_2 is not a better oxidising agent.
(c) Xe, Kr and Ne all form clatherate compounds.
(d) Fluorine in dilute solution of sodium hydroxide disproportionate in fluoride and hypofluorite.

18. Select the correct reactions from the following.
(a) $XeF_2 + 2SO_3 \longrightarrow Xe\uparrow + S_2O_6F_2$
(b) $2NO + XeF_2 \longrightarrow 2NOF + Xe\uparrow$
(c) $IF + XeF_2 \xrightarrow{BF_3} IF_3 + Xe\uparrow$
(d) $I_2 + XeF_2 \longrightarrow XeI_2 + I_2$

19. Xe > Kr > Ar > Ne > He. This order represents
(a) solubility in water
(b) enthalpy of vapourisation
(c) ionisation enthalpy
(d) ease of vapourisation

20. Select the correct statements from the following.
    (a) Only type of interactions between particles of noble gases are due to weak dispersion forces.
    (b) Ionisation enthalpy of molecular oxygen is very close to that of xenon.
    (c) Hydrolysis of XeF_6 is a redox reaction.
    (d) Xenon fluorides are not reactive.

21. Which among the following statements is/are correct?
    (a) XeF_4 and SbF_5 combine to form salt.
    (b) He and Ne do not form clathrate.
    (c) He diffuses through rubber and polyvinyl chloride.
    (d) He has lowest boiling point in its group.

Type III 》 Numerical/Integer Answer Type Questions

22. The number of compounds in which Xe is having +8 oxidation state are :
    XeF_8, XeO_4, XeO_2F_4, $XeOF_4$, $XeOF_2$, XeO_3F_2

23. In the structure of $XeF_2 \cdot 2SbF_5$ in solid state.
    How many type of Xe—F bond lengths present are :

24. From the given compounds the number of hybrid orbital greater than or equal to 5 are :
    XeF_2, XeF_4, XeF_6, $XeOF_2$, XeO_2F_2, XeO_3

25. The number of hybrid orbitals present in the central atom in the cationic part of the compound formed by the reaction between antimony penta fluoride and xenon tetrafluoride is ....

26. If air is condensed to –180°C in the presence of coconut charcoal, then the number of different noble gases that can be obtained from the charcoal are :

27. A noble gas (Xe) reacts with excess of platinum hexafluoride to produce a orange yellow solid *X*. The oxidation state of metal in anionic part of the *X* is

Elemental Practice 6.4 | Chapter 06

Connect with **Answers**

1. (b)	**2.** (a)	**3.** (a)	**4.** (c)	**5.** (d)	**6.** (a)
7. (a)	**8.** (b)	**9.** (c)	**10.** (c)	**11.** (d)	**12.** (b)
13. (d)	**14.** (d)	**15.** (b)	**16.** (a,b,c,d)	**17.** (b,c,d)	**18.** (a,b,c)
19. (a,b,d)	**20.** (a,b)	**21.** (a,b,c,d)	**22.** (4)	**23.** (2)	**24.** (5)
25. (5)	**26.** (2)	**27.** (5)			

Advanced Exclusive Different Strokes

Some Important orders of Halogens are as follows

(a)	F < Cl < Br < I	Atomic or ionic radius
(b)	F > Cl > Br > I	$I.E._1$
(c)	Cl > F > Br > I	$E.A._1$
(d)	$Cl_2 > Br_2 > F_2 > I_2$	Bond dissociation energy
(e)	$F_2 > Cl_2 > Br_2 > I_2$	Oxidising nature or reactivity
(f)	F < Cl < Br < I	Reducing nature
(g)	F > Cl > Br > I	Hydration energy
(h)	$F_2 < Cl_2 < Br_2 < I_2$	Melting point/boiling point
(i)	$F_2 < Cl_2 < Br_2 < I_2$	Density (mass)
(j)	HF < HCl < HBr < HI	Acidic nature
(k)	HOF > HOCl > HOBr > HOI	Acidic nature
(l)	$HOCl < HClO_2 < HClO_3 < HClO_4$	Acidic nature
(m)	$HOCl < HClO_2 < HClO_3 < HClO_4$	Thermal stability
(n)	$HOCl < HClO_2 < HClO_3 < HClO_4$	Oxidising power
(o)	$ClO^- > ClO_2^- > ClO_3^- > ClO_4^-$	Hydration energy
(p)	HF > HCl > HBr > HI	Thermal stability

Thus with the help of above orders we can approach problems related to them in competitive exams.

PRACTICE ELEMENT 01

Target JEE Main

Objective Type Questions

1. Select the incorrect match of compounds with their uses.
   (a) $BaSO_4 + ZnS \longrightarrow$ Pigment
   (b) $NI_3 \longrightarrow$ explosive
   (c) $N_2O_4 \longrightarrow$ oxidiser in rocket propellants
   (d) $KO_2 \longrightarrow$ automobile exhaust gases

2. Choose the correct sequence in the following properties.
   (a) $SiF_4 < SiCl_4 < SiBr_4 \rightarrow$ Lewis acid order
   (b) $NH_3 > SbH_3 > AsH_3 \rightarrow$ Melting point
   (c) $NH_3 > SbH_3 > AsH_3 \rightarrow$ Bond dipole
   (d) N—H > P—H > As—H $\rightarrow$ Bond dissociation enthalpy

3. Which of the following reaction equation that is incorrectly written?
   (a) $P_4 + 20HNO_3 \longrightarrow 4H_3PO_4 + 20NO_2 + 4H_2O$
   (b) $S + 6HNO_3 \longrightarrow H_2SO_4 + 6NO_2 + 2H_2O$
   (c) $NH_3 + O_2 \xrightarrow[\Delta]{Pt} NO$
   (d) $PCl_3 + H_2O \longrightarrow POCl_3 + HCl$

4. Choose the incorrect statement from the following
   (a) $H_4P_2O_7$ and $H_4P_2O_6$ are tetrabasic in nature.
   (b) P_2O_5 has six P—O—P bond.
   (c) *Ortho*phosphate reacts with ammonium molybdate to give yellow precipitate and with $AgNO_3$ gives red precipitate.
   (d) OF_2 dissolves in water to give oxyacid.

5. Identify the incorrect statement from the following.
   (a) Hypophosphorous acid on heating gives orthophosphoric acid.
   (b) S_2 molecule is paramagnetic due to unpaired e^- in its M.O. configuration.
   (c) Copper produces NO gas when treated with dil. HNO_3.
   (d) In trisilylamine, only two sp^2-orbitals are used for σ-bonding.

6. Given below are few statements.
   I. Melting point of H_2O is greater than HF.
   II. Aqueous solution of I_2 is voilet in colour while organic solution of I_2 is brown in colour.
   III. NaBr and KBr are used as relative.
   IV. The correct stability order for the same halogen is $HOCl > HClO_2 > HClO_3 > HClO_4$.
   V. Fluorine reacts with water even in dark producing O_2 and O_3.

   Select the correct statements from the options given below.
   (a) I, II and III (b) I, III and V
   (c) III, IV and V (d) II, IV and V

7. The incorrect order for the properties given below.
   (a) $S_2O_4^{2-} > S_2O_5^{2-} > S_2O_6^{2-} \rightarrow$ S—S bond length
   (b) $PH_3 > AsH_3 > BiH_3 \rightarrow$ Basicity
   (c) $SbH_3 > AsH_3 > PH_3 \rightarrow$ Bond dipole
   (d) $SbH_3 > BiH_3 > AsH_3 \rightarrow$ Thermal stability

8. Choose the correct statement from the following :
   A. TeO_2 is an oxidising agent while SO_2 is reducing in nature.
   B. isoelectronic molecules or ions have identical bond order.
   C. bond length of O_2 is shorter than N_2.
   D. both rhombic and monoclinic sulphur exist as S_8 while oxygen exists as O_2.

   Choose the correct answer from the options given below.
   (a) A and B (b) B and C
   (c) A, B and D (d) A, C and D

9. Select the reaction of Xenon compounds that is not correct.
   (a) $XeF_6 + 2H_2O \longrightarrow XeO_2F_2 + 4HF$
   (b) $XeF_4 + O_2F_2 \longrightarrow XeF_6 + O_2$
   (c) $2XeF_2 + 2H_2O \longrightarrow 2Xe + 4HF + O_2$
   (d) $XeF_6 + RbF \longrightarrow [XeF^+] + [RbF_6]^-$

10. The number of P—O—P bonds in the structure of pyrophosphoric acid and P_2O_5 is
    (a) 1, 5 (b) 2, 3 (c) 1, 6 (d) 2, 4

11. Match list I with list II

	List I (Molecule)		List II (Method of preparation)
A.	H_3PO_2	I.	$P_4O_{10} + H_2O$
B.	$H_4P_2O_5$	II.	$P_2O_3 + H_2O$
C.	H_3PO_4	III.	$PCl_3 + H_3PO_3$
D.	H_3PO_3	IV.	White P_4 + alkali

Choose the correct answer from the options given below.

	A	B	C	D		A	B	C	D
(a)	II	IV	III	I	(b)	III	I	II	IV
(c)	IV	III	I	II	(d)	III	IV	II	I

12. Match list-I with list-II.

	List I (Compounds)		List II (Oxidation number)
A.	N_2O	I.	+5
B.	N_2O_3	II.	+3
C.	N_2O_4	III.	+1
D.	N_2O_5	IV.	+4

Choose the correct answer from the options given below.

	A	B	C	D
(a)	II	IV	I	III
(b)	III	II	IV	I
(c)	II	IV	III	I
(d)	IV	I	III	II

13. Select the incorrect statements from the following
(a) Welding of magnesium is done in the atmosphere of He.
(b) Boiling point of Xenon is greater than krypton.
(c) Argon gas can diffuse through rubber and glass easily.
(d) Clatherates are non-stoichiometric compounds.

14. The incorrect statement from the following is
(a) xenon hexafluorides can not be stored in glass vessels.
(b) number of $p\pi - d\pi$ bonds present in XeO_4 is 4.
(c) XeO_3 is obtained by hydrolysis of XeF_6.
(d) noble gases are not soluble in water.

15. If X is the number of moles of phosphine formed on thermal decomposition of hypophosphorus acid, then the value of $(x^2 - 0.4)$ is
(a) 0.6 (b) 0.5
(c) 0.3 (d) 0.2

16. In the preparation of HNO_3, NO gas is produced by catalytic oxidation of ammonia. The moles of NO produced by the oxidation of two moles of NH_3 will be
(a) 3 (b) 1
(c) 2 (d) 4

17. The oxo-acid of sulphur that contains S—S bond is
(a) Peroxodisulphuric acid (b) Pyrosulphuric acid
(c) Disulphurous acid (d) Sulphurous acid

18. Select the pair that contains two P—H bonds in each of the oxoacids is
(a) H_3PO_4, H_3PO_2 (b) H_3PO_2, $H_4P_2O_5$
(c) $H_4P_2O_7$, H_3PO_3 (d) $H_4P_2O_5$, H_3PO_4

19. Which of the following statements with respect to dinitrogen is incorrect?
(a) It can be used as an inert diluent for reactive chemicals.
(b) Pure nitrogen is obtained by thermal decomposition of barium azide.
(c) It is colourless, odourless and non-toxic gas.
(d) It combines with non-metals to form predominantly ionic hydride.

20. Choose the correct order of melting points of hydride.
(a) $H_2Se < H_2Te < H_2O$ (b) $H_2O < H_2Se < H_2Te$
(c) $H_2Te < H_2O < H_2Se$ (d) $H_2O < H_2Te < H_2Se$

Numerical Type Questions

21. Sodium nitrite upon reaction with ferrous sulphate in the presence of H_2SO_4 forms an oxide of nitrogen. The total number of resonating structures of the oxide of nitrogen formed will be ....

22. From the given oxoacids of phosphorus, orthophosphoric, pyrophosphoric, orthophosphorous and hypophosphorous acid the total number of tribasic compounds are ....

23. The sum of total number Cl═O bond present in chlorous acid and perchloric acid is

24. The total number of lone pair of electrons present on Xe in XeF_2 is ....

25. Consider the following oxoacids of sulphur.
Sulphurous acid, sulphuric acid, peroxodi sulphuric acid, pyrosulphuric acid and disulphurous acid from these oxo-acids, the number of acids with per oxo (O—O) bond is ....

26. Consider the following silicates :
Pyro silicate, double chain silicate, single chain silicate, cyclic silicate, sheet silicate, 3D silicate.
The number of silicates in which only two corners per tetrahedron are shared are

27. Consider the following pair of cations :
I. $Pb^{2+} > Pb^{4+}$, $Tl^{+} < Tl^{3+}$
II. $Tl^{3+} < In^{3+}$, $Sn^{2+} > Sn^{4+}$
III. $Sn^{2+} < Pb^{2+}$, $Sn^{4+} < Pb^{4+}$
IV. $Bi^{3+} < Sb^{3+}$, $Sn^{2+} < Sn^{4+}$
V. $Pb^{2+} > Pb^{4+}$, $Bi^{3+} > Bi^{5+}$
VI. $Sn^{2+} < Pb^{2+}$, $Sn^{4+} > Pb^{4+}$
The number of pairs having correct order for stability of oxidation state are

28. Consider the following reaction.
$$PCl_3 + H_3PO_3 \longrightarrow X$$
$$P_4O_{10} + H_2O \longrightarrow Y$$
The total number of O-atoms in X and Y is ....

29. The number of correct reactions from the following are :
(i) $2HNO_3 \rightleftharpoons NO_2^+ + NO_3^- + H_2O$
(ii) $Cu + 4HNO_3 \longrightarrow Cu(NO_3)_2 + 2H_2O + 2NO_2$
(iii) $4Zn + 10HNO_3 \longrightarrow 4Zn(NO_3)_2 + 3H_2O + 2NO_2$
(iv) $2HNO_3 \longrightarrow 2NO_2 + H_2O$
(v) $2HNO_3 \xrightarrow{h\nu} 2NO_2 + H_2O + \frac{1}{2}O_2$

30. In the following oxy anion(s);
$$H_2PO_3^-, H_2PO_2^-, H_2P_2O_6^{2-} \text{ and } H_2PO_4^-$$
P—O bond order is equal to P, X, Y and Z.
The sum of $P + X + Y + Z$ is ....

Check Through PYQs

Element 1 Group 15 : The Nitrogen Family and Their Compounds

1. Given below are two statements. *2024, 8 April Shift-I*

Statement I $N(CH_3)_3$ and $P(CH_3)_3$ can act as ligands to form transition metal complexes.

Statement II As N and P are from same group, the nature of bonding of $N(CH_3)_3$ and $P(CH_3)_3$ is always same with transition metals.

In the light of the above statements, choose the most appropriate answer from the options given below:

(a) Statement I is correct but Statement II is incorrect.
(b) Statement I is incorrect but Statement II is correct.
(c) Both Statement I and Statement II are incorrect.
(d) Both Statement I and Statement II are correct.

2. Identify the incorrect statements about group 15 elements:

(A) Dinitrogen is a diatomic gas which acts like an inert gas at room temperature.
(B) The common oxidation states of these elements are -3, $+3$ and $+5$.
(C) Nitrogen has unique ability to form $p\pi$-$p\pi$ multiple bonds.
(D) The stability of $+5$ oxidation states increases down the group.
(E) Nitrogen shows a maximum covalency of 6.

Choose the correct answer from the options given below: *2024, 8 April Shift-II*

(a) (A), (C) and (E) (b) (D) and (E)
(c) (B), (D) and (E) (d) (A), (B) and (D)

3. Given below are two statements : one is labelled as **Assertion (A)** and the other is labelled as **Reason (R).**

Assertion (A) PH_3 has lower boiling point than NH_3.

Reason (R) In liquid state NH_3 molecules are associated through van der Waals' forces, but PH_3 molecules are associated through hydrogen bonding. *2024, 1 Feb Shift-I*

In the light of the above statements, choose the **most appropriate** answer from the options given below

(a) A is false but R is true.
(b) Both A and R are true but R is not the correct explanation of A.
(c) Both A and R are true and R is the correct explanation of A.
(d) A is true but R is false.

4. Choose the correct statements about the hydrides of group 15 elements. *2024, 30 Jan Shift-II*

A. The stability of the hydrides decreases in the order $NH_3 > PH_3 > AsH_3 > SbH_3 > BiH_3$.
B. The reducing ability of the hydride increases in the order $NH_3 < PH_3 < AsH_3 < SbH_3 < BiH_3$.
C. Among the hydride, NH_3 is strong reducing agent while BiH_3 is mild reducing agent.
D. The basicity of the hydrides increases in the order $NH_3 < PH_3 < AsH_3 < SbH_3 < BiH_3$.

Choose the **most appropriate** from the options given below :

(a) A and D (b) B and C
(c) C and D (d) A and B

5. The number of P—O—P bonds in $H_4P_2O_7$, $(HPO_3)_3$ and P_4O_{10} are respectively *2023, 15 April Shift-II*

(a) 1, 2, 4 (b) 0, 3, 4
(c) 0, 3, 6 (d) 1, 3, 6

6. The ratio of sigma and π bonds present in pyrophosphoric acid is .... *2023, 8 April Shift-II*

7. Reaction of thionyl chloride with white phosphorus forms a compound [*A*], which on hydrolysis gives [*B*], a dibasic acid. [*A*] and [*B*] are respectively *2023, 25 Jan, Shift-I*

(a) PCl_3 and H_3PO_3 (b) PCl_5 and H_3PO_4
(c) $POCl_3$ and H_3PO_4 (d) P_4O_6 and H_3PO_3

8. Concentrated HNO_3 reacts with iodine to give *2022, 28 July Shift-II*

(a) HI, NO_2 and H_2O (b) HIO_2, N_2O and H_2O
(c) HIO_3, NO_2 and H_2O (d) HIO_4, N_2O and H_2O

9. Dinitrogen and dioxygen, the main constituents of air do not react with each other in atmosphere to form oxides of nitrogen because *2022, 28 July Shift-II*

(a) N_2 is unreactive in the condition of atmosphere
(b) oxides of nitrogen are unstable
(c) reaction between them can occur in the presence of a catalyst
(d) the reaction is endothermic and require very high temperature

10. White phosphorus reacts with thionyl chloride to give *2022, 28 July, Shift-II*

(a) PCl_5, SO_2 and S_2Cl_2 (b) PCl_3, SO_2 and S_2Cl_2
(c) PCl_3, SO_2 and Cl_2 (d) PCl_5, SO_2 and Cl_2

11. The number of non-ionisable protons present in the product *B* obtained from the following reaction is ....

$$C_2H_5OH + PCl_3 \longrightarrow C_2H_5Cl + A$$
$$A + PCl_3 \longrightarrow B$$ *2022, 26 July, Shift-II*

12. $A \xrightarrow{573\text{ K}} \text{Red phosphorus} \xrightarrow[\text{Under pressure}]{\text{Heat ; 803 K}} B$

Red phosphorus is obtained by heating "*A*" at 573 K, and can be converted to "*B*" by heating at 803 K under pressure. *A* and *B*, respectively, are *2022, 30 June, Shift-I*

(a) β-black phosphorus and white phosphorus
(b) White phosphorus and β-black phosphorus
(c) α-black phosphorus and white phosphorus
(d) White phosphorus and α-black phosphorus

13. The oxoacid of phosphorus that is easily obtained from a reaction of alkali and white phosphorus and has two P—H bonds, is *2022, 29 June Shift-I*

(a) phosphonic acid (b) phosphinic acid
(c) pyrophosphorus acid (d) hypophosphoric acid

14. Nitrogen gas is obtained by thermal decomposition of *2022, 28 June, Shift-I*
(a) $Ba(NO_3)_2$ (b) $Ba(N_3)_2$
(c) $NaNO_2$ (d) $NaNO_3$

15. Heating white phosphorus with conc. NaOH solution gives mainly *2022, 27 June Shift-I*
(a) Na_3P and H_2O
(b) H_3PO and NaH
(c) $P(OH)_3$ and NaH_2PO_4
(d) PH_3 and NaH_2PO_2

16. The gas produced by treating an aqueous solution of ammonium chloride with sodium nitrite is *2022, 27 June Shift-II*
(a) NH_3 (b) N_2
(c) N_2O (d) Cl_2

17. The oxide which contains an odd electron at the nitrogen atom is *2022, 26 June Shift-II*
(a) N_2O (b) NO_2
(c) N_2O_3 (d) N_2O_5

18. The most stable trihalide of nitrogen is *2022, 24 June Shift-I*
(a) NF_3 (b) NCl_3
(c) NBr_3 (d) NI_3

19. PCl_5 is well known but NCl_5 is not, because *2022, 24 June Shift-II*
(a) nitrogen is less reactive than phosphorus.
(b) nitrogen doesn't have *d*-orbitals in its valence shell.
(c) catenation tendency is weaker in nitrogen than phosphorus.
(d) size of phosphorus is larger than nitrogen.

20. Which one of the following group-15 hydride is the strongest reducing agent? *2021, 22 July Shift-II*
(a) AsH_3 (b) BiH_3
(c) PH_3 (d) SbH_3

21. Chemical nature of the nitrogen oxide compound obtained from a reaction of concentrated nitric acid and P_4O_{10} (in 4 : 1 ratio) is *2021, 20 July Shift-I*
(a) acidic (b) basic
(c) amphoteric (d) neutral

22. The oxidation states of nitrogen in NO, NO_2, N_2O and NO_3^- are in the order of *2021, 18 March Shift-II*
(a) $NO_3^- > NO_2 > NO > N_2O$
(b) $NO_2 > NO_3^- > NO > N_2O$
(c) $N_2O > NO_2 > NO > NO_3^-$
(d) $NO > NO_2 > N_2O > NO_3^-$

23. The set that represents the pair of neutral oxides of nitrogen is *2021, 17 March Shift-II*
(a) NO and N_2O (b) N_2O and N_2O_3
(c) N_2O and NO_2 (d) NO and NO_2

24. The reaction of white phosphorus on boiling with alkali in inert atmosphere resulted in the formation of product *A*. The reaction of 1 mol of *A* with excess of $AgNO_3$ in aqueous medium gives ...... moles of Ag (Round off to the nearest integer). *2021, 17 March Shift-I*

25. A group 15 element, which is a metal and forms a hydride with strongest reducing power among group 15 hydrides. The element is *2021, 16 March Shift-I*
(a) Sb (b) P
(c) As (d) Bi

Element 2 Group 16 : The Oxygen Family and Their Compounds

26. Incorrect statement among the following is *2025, 23 Jan Shift-I*
(a) SO_2 act as oxidising agent but not reducing agent
(b) NO_2 exists as dimer
(c) PF_5 exists but NF_5 does not
(d) PH_3 has lower proton affinity than NH_3

27. Given below are two statements : one is labelled as **Assertion (A)** and the other is labelled as Reason (R). *2024, 30 Jan Shift-II*
Assertion (A) H_2Te is more acidic than H_2S.
Reason (R) Bond dissociation enthalpy of H_2Te is lower than H_2S.
In the light of the above statements, choose the **most appropriate** answer from the options given below:
(a) A is false but R is true.
(b) Both A and R are true but R is not the correct explanation of A.
(c) A is true but R is not true.
(d) Both A and R are true and R is the correct explanation of A.

28. Anomalous behaviour of oxygen is due to its *2024, 29 Jan Shift-II*
(a) large size and high electronegativity
(b) small size and low electronegativity
(c) small size and high electronegativity
(d) large size and low electronegativity

29. Given below are two statements. *2024, 27 Jan Shift-I*
Statement I Oxygen being the first member of group 16 exhibits only – 2 oxidation state.
Statement II Down the group 16 stability of + 4 oxidation state decreases and + 6 oxidation state increases.
In the light of the above statements, choose the **most appropriate** answer from the options given below.
(a) Statement I is correct but Statement II is incorrect.
(b) Both Statement I and Statement II are incorrect.
(c) Statement I is incorrect but Statement II is correct.
(d) Both Statement I and Statement II are correct.

30. Consider the following sulphur based oxoacids.
H_2SO_3, H_2SO_4, $H_2S_2O_8$ and $H_2S_2O_7$.
Amongst these oxo-acids, the number of those with peroxo (O —O) bond is .... *2022, 29 July Shift-II*

31. Sulphur dioxide is one of the components of polluted air. SO_2 is also a major contributor to acid rain. The correct and complete reaction to represent acid rain caused by SO_2 is *2022, 29 June Shift-II*
(a) $2SO_2 + O_2 \longrightarrow 2SO_3$
(b) $SO_2 + O_3 \longrightarrow SO_3 + O_2$
(c) $SO_2 + H_2O_2 \longrightarrow H_2SO_4$
(d) $2SO_2 + O_2 + 2H_2O \longrightarrow 2H_2SO_4$

32. Consider the sulphides HgS, PbS, CuS, Sb_2S_3, As_2S_3 and CdS. Number of these sulphides soluble in 50% HNO_3 is *2021, 31 Aug Shift-I*

33. The depositions of *X* and *Y* on ground surfaces is referred to as wet and dry depositions, respectively. *X* and *Y* are *2021, 31 Aug Shift-II*
(a) *X* = Ammonium salts, *Y* = CO_2
(b) *X* = SO_2, *Y* = Ammonium salts
(c) *X* = Ammonium salts, *Y* = SO_2
(d) *X* = CO_2, *Y* = SO_2

34. The number of S=O bonds present in sulphurous acid, peroxodisulphuric acid and pyrosulphuric acid, respectively are *2021, 31 Aug Shift-II ; 2017*
(a) 2, 3 and 4 (b) 1, 4 and 3
(c) 2, 4 and 3 (d) 1, 4 and 4

35. The product obtained from the electrolytic oxidation of acidified sulphate solutions, is *2021, 27 July Shift-I*
(a) HSO_4^- (b) HO_3SOOSO_3H
(c) HO_2SOSO_2H (d) HO_3SOSO_3H

36. Match List -I with List II.

List-I (Industrial process)		List-II (Application)	
A.	Haber's process	(i)	HNO_3 synthesis
B.	Ostwald's process	(ii)	Aluminium extraction
C.	Contact process	(iii)	NH_3 synthesis
D.	Hall-Heroult process	(iv)	H_2SO_4 synthesis

Choose the correct answer from the options given below *2021, 16 March Shift-I*
(a) A-(ii), B-(iii), C-(iv), D-(i) (b) A-(iii), B-(iv), C-(i), D-(ii)
(c) A-(iii), B-(i), C-(iv), D-(ii) (d) A-(iv), B-(i), C-(ii), D-(iii)

37. Among the following allotropic forms of sulphur, the number of allotropic forms, which will show paramagnetism is .... *2021, 24 Feb Shift-II*
A. α-sulphur B. β-sulphur
C. S_2-form

38. If the boiling point of H_2O is 373 K, the boiling point of H_2S will be *2020, 03 Sep, Shift-I*
(a) less than 300 K
(b) equal to 373 K
(c) more than 373 K
(d) greater than 300 K but less than 373 K

39. Number of oxygen atoms present in chemical formula of fuming sulphuric acid is .... *2020, 9 April Shift-II*

40. Reaction of an inorganic sulphite *X* with dilute H_2SO_4 generates compound *Y*. Reaction of *Y* with NaOH gives *X*. Further, the reaction of *X* with *Y* and water affords compound *Y* and *Z*. respectively are *2020, 06 Sep, Shift-II*
(a) SO_2 and Na_2SO_3 (b) SO_3 and $NaHSO_3$
(c) SO_2 and $NaHSO_3$ (d) S and Na_2SO_3

Element 3 Group 17 : The Halogen Family and Their Compounds

41. Given below are two statements: *2024, 29 Jan Shift-II*
Statement I Fluorine has most negative electron gain enthalpy in its group.
Statement II Oxygen has least negative electron gain enthalpy in its group.
In the light of the above statements, choose the **most appropriate** from the options given below
(a) Statement I is false but Statement II is true.
(b) Both Statement I and Statement II are false.
(c) Statement I is true but Statement II is false.
(d) Both Statement I and Statement II are true.

42. Element not showing variable oxidation state is *2024, 27 Jan Shift-II*
(a) bromine (b) chlorine (c) fluorine (d) iodine

43. The correct group of halide ions which can be oxidised by oxygen in acidic medium is *2023, 13 April Shift-II*
(a) I^- only (b) Br^- only
(c) Cl^-, Br^- and I^- (d) Br^- and I^-

44. Which halogen is known to cause the reaction given below $2Cu^{2+} + 4X^- \longrightarrow Cu_2X_2(s) + X_2$ *2023, 8 April Shift-I*
(a) all halogens (b) only chlorine
(c) only iodine (d) only bromine

45. Element not present in Nessler's reagent is *2023, 6 April Shift-II*
(a) N (b) Hg (c) K (d) I

46. Which element is not present in Nessler's reagent? *2023, 1 Feb Shift-II*
(a) Oxygen (b) Iodine
(c) Potassium (d) Mercury

47. Formula for Nessler's reagent is *2023, 30 Jan Shift-II*
(a) $KHgI_3$ (b) HgI_2 (c) K_2HgI_4 (d) KHg_2I_2

48. Match List I with List II, match the gas evolved during each reaction.

List I	List II
(A) $(NH_4)_2Cr_2O_7 \xrightarrow{\Delta}$	(I) H_2
(B) $KMnO_4 + HCl \longrightarrow$	(II) N_2
(C) $Al + NaOH + H_2O \longrightarrow$	(III) O_2
(D) $NaNO_3 \longrightarrow$	(IV) Cl_2

Choose the correct answer from the options given below. *2022, 28 July Shift-I*
(a) (A) → (II), (B) → (III), (C) → (I), (D) → (IV)
(b) (A) → (III), (B) → (I), (C) → (IV), (D) → (II)
(c) (A) → (II), (B) → (IV), (C) → (I), (D) → (III)
(d) (A) → (III), (B) → (IV), (C) → (I), (D) → (II)

49. Given below are two statements. One is labelled as Assertion A and the other is labelled as Reason R.

Assertion (A) Fluorine forms one oxoacid.

Reason (R) Fluorine has smallest size amongst all halogens and is highly electronegative

In the light of the above statements, choose the most appropriate answer from the options given below. *2022, 27 June Shift-II*

(a) Both A and R are correct and R is the correct explanation of A.
(b) Both A and R are correct but R is not the correct explanation of A.
(c) A is correct but R is not correct
(d) A is not correct but R is correct

50. Which one of the following correctly represents the order of stability of oxides, X_2O (X = halogen) ? *2021, 31 Aug Shift-II*

(a) Br > Cl > I (b) Br > I > Cl
(c) Cl > I > Br (d) I > Cl > Br

51. Which one of the following is used to remove most of plutonium from spent nuclear fuel? *2021, 27 Aug Shift-II*

(a) ClF_3 (b) O_2F_2
(c) I_2O_5 (d) BrO_3

52. Choose the incorrect statement. *2021, 26 Aug Shift-I*

(a) Cl_2 is more reactive than ClF.
(b) F_2 is more reactive than ClF.
(c) On hydrolysis ClF forms HOCl and HF.
(d) F_2 is a stronger oxidising agent than Cl_2 in aqueous solution.

53. The absolute value of the electron gain enthalpy of halogens satisfies *2021, 17 March Shift-I*

(a) I > Br > Cl > F
(b) Cl > Br > F > I
(c) Cl > F > Br > I
(d) F > Cl > Br > I

54. Among the following, the number of halides which is/are inert to hydrolysis is .... *2021, 25 Feb Shift-I*

(i) BF_3 (ii) $SiCl_4$
(iii) PCl_5 (iv) SF_6

Element 4 Group 18 : The Noble Gases and Their Compounds

55. XeF_4 reacts with SbF_5 to form

$$[XeFm]^n\ [SbF_y]^{z-}$$

$m + n + y + z$ = ... *2023, 8 April Shift-I*

56. The difference between electron gain enthalpies will be maximum between *2023, 6 April Shift-I*

(a) Ar and Cl (b) Ar and F
(c) Ne and Cl (d) Ne and F

57. Match List I with List II.

	List I (Molecule)		List II (Hybridisation shape)
A.	XeO_3	I.	sp^3d; linear
B.	XeF_2	II.	sp^3 ; pyramidal
C.	$XeOF_4$	III.	sp^3d^3; distorted octahedral
D.	XeF_6	IV.	sp^3d^2; square pyramidal

Choose the correct answer from the options given below. *2022, 25 July Shift-II*

(a) A-II, B-I, C-IV, D-III
(b) A-II, B-IV, C-III, D-I
(c) A-IV, B-II, C-III, D-I
(d) A-IV, B-II, C-I, D-III

58. The sum of number of lone pairs of electrons present on the central atoms of XeO_3, $XeOF_4$ and XeF_6, is .... *2022, 25 July Shift-II*

59. A xenon compound '*A*' upon partial hydrolysis gives XeO_2F_2. The number of lone pair of electrons present in compound *A* is .... (Round off to the nearest integer). *2021, 18 March Shift-II*

60. The shape/structure of $[XeF_5]^-$ and XeO_3F_2, respectively, are *2020, 2 Sep Shift-II*

(a) pentagonal planar and trigonal bipyramidal
(b) octahedral and square pyramidal
(c) trigonal bipyramidal and pentagonal planar
(d) trigonal bipyramidal and trigonal bipyramidal

PRACTICE ELEMENT 02

Target JEE Advanced

Single Correct Option MCQs

1. A greenish yellow gas reacts with alkali metal hydroxide to form a halate which can be used in fireworks and safety matches. The gas and halate respectively are :
(a) Br_2, $KBrO_3$ (b) Cl_2, $KClO_3$
(c) I_2, $NaIO_3$ (d) Cl_2, $NaClO_3$

2. $Cl_2(g) + Ba(OH)_2 \longrightarrow X(aq) + BaCl_2 + H_2O$
$X + H_2SO_4 \longrightarrow Y + BaSO_4$
$Y \xrightarrow[\Delta > 365\,K]{\Delta} Z + H_2O + O_2$
Y and Z are respectively
(a) $HClO_4$, ClO_2 (b) $HClO_3$, ClO_2
(c) $HClO_3$, Cl_2O_6 (d) $HClO_4$, Cl_2O_7

3. Xe reacts with $F_2(g)$ in 1 : 5 ratio at 873 K and 7 bar to form a compound (A). (A) reacts with SbF_5 to form adduct. The shapes of cation and anion in the adduct respectively are :
(a) square planar, trigonal bipyramidal
(b) T-shaped, octahedral
(c) square pyramidal, octahedral
(d) square planar, octahedral

4. XeF_2 undergoes hydrolysis to form gas (A), gas (B) and a compound (C). The compound XeF_6 dissolves in anhydrous (C) to form conducting solution. The ions formed are :
(a) H^+ and XeF_7^- ions (b) HF_2^- and XeF_5^+ ions
(c) $HXeF_6^+$ and F^- ions (d) H_2F^+ and XeF_7^- ions

5. Given below are few statements.
I. $2Ca_3(PO_4)_2CaSiO_3$ is known thomas slag.
II. Acidic strength of pentaoxides follows the order : $N_2O_5 > P_4O_{10} > As_4O_{10} > Sb_4O_{10}$
III. H_2SO_4 acts as a dehydrating, oxidising and pitching agent.
IV. Reaction of As_2S_3 on reaction with NaOH gives sodium arsenite only.
V. Cl_2 is known as oxymuriatic acid gas.
Select the correct statements from the option given below.
(a) I, II and IV (b) II, III and V
(c) I, II, III and V (d) II and V

6. Compounds A and B are treated with dil. HCl. The gases liberated are Y and Z. Y turns acidified dichromate paper green while Z turns lead acetate paper black. So, compounds A and B respectively are
(a) Na_2SO_3, Na_2S (b) NaCl, Na_2CO_3
(c) Na_2S, Na_2SO_3 (d) Na_2SO_3, K_2SO_4

7. Nitrogen compound 'A' is produced by the oxidation of HCN by O_2 using silver catalyst.
The incorrect statement regarding compound A is
(a) It is a linear molecule
(b) It is a psuedohalogen
(c) It undergoes disproportionation in basic solution
(d) It can't be prepared by the action of Cu^{2+} and CN^-.

8. An element was burnt in limited supply of air to give an oxide 'A' which on treatment with water gives an acid 'B'. Acid 'B' on oxidation gives acid 'C', which gives a yellow precipitate with $AgNO_3$ solution. A is
(a) SO_2 (b) NO_2
(c) P_4O_6 (d) SO_3

One or More than One Correct MCQs

9. $KClO_3$ on heating with H_2SO_4 gives
(a) $HClO_4$ (b) ClO_2
(c) $KHSO_4$ (d) Cl_2

10. Select the correct reaction(s) from the following
(a) $2Cl_2 + 2HgO \longrightarrow Cl_2O + HgO \cdot HgCl_2$
(b) $Cl_2 + 2AgClO_3 \longrightarrow 2ClO_2 + O_2 + 2AgCl$
(c) $4HClO_4 \xrightarrow[\Delta]{P_4O_{10}} 2Cl_2O_7 + 4H_2PO_3$
(d) $3Ca(OH)_2 + 2Cl_2 \longrightarrow \underbrace{Ca(OCl)_2 \cdot CaCl_2 \cdot Ca(OH)_2 \cdot 2H_2O}_{\text{Bleaching powder}}$

11. The correct statement(s) among the following is/are :
(a) In analogy to $O_2^+PtF_6^-$, a compound $N_2^+PtF_6^-$ will not be formed because the ionisation enthalpy of N_2 gas is higher than O_2 gas.
(b) $Xe^+PtF_6^-$ is a red coloured compound formed by mixing PtF_6 and Xe.
(c) Partial hydrolysis of XeF_6 gives oxyfluorides, $XeOF_4$ and $XeOF_3$.
(d) XeO_3 is an explosive solid.

12. A square planar fluoride undergoes hydrolysis to give a noble gas (A), a pyramidal compound (B), a weak monobasic acid (C) and a gas (D) which supports combustion.
Based on the given reaction, select the correct answer from the options given below.
(a) The square planar fluoride is XeF_4
(b) $A = Xe$, $D = O_2$
(c) $(B) = XeOF_4$
(d) $(B) = XeO_3$

13. The correct statement(s) from the following option(s) is/are
(a) Marshall's acid on partial hydroysis gives caro's acid and sulphuric acid.
(b) Conc. H_2SO_4 on reaction with potassium chlorate gives chlorine dioxide.
(c) Iodine solution is decolourised by sodium thiosulphate solution.
(d) Phosphoric acid converts NaBr and NaI into HBr and HI respectively and H_2SO_4 oxidises both of them.

14. When an equimolar mixture of Na_2S and Na_2SO_3 is treated with excess iodine, the product(s) formed is/are
(a) $Na_2S_2O_3$ (b) $Na_2S_4O_6$
(c) NaI (d) HI

15. Select the correct statement(s) from the following
(a) In PF_3, the lone pair of F atom participate in $p\pi - d\pi$ bonds due to which double bond character arises.
(b) Bones glow in dark because it contains $Ca_3(PO_4)_2$, which undergoes slow oxidation in contact with air.
(c) $N(SiH_3)_3$ is triangular planar due to back bonding.
(d) $NH_3 \cdot NI_3$ when rubbed against hard surface forms ammonia.

16. Choose the correct statement(s) from the following
(a) NH_3 is oxidised to NO_2 by oxygen at 800°C in the presence of a catalyst platinum.
(b) Nitric acid on standing slowly turns yellowish brown.
(c) Colloidal sulphur is formed when H_2S gas is passed through nitric acid solution.
(d) N_2O_3 gas dissolves in water giving pole blue solution.

Numerical/Integer Type Questions

17. A dark violet solid (X) reacts with NH_3 to form mild explosive (Z), which decomposes to give a violet coloured gas. (X) also reacts with H_2 to give an acid (Y). (Y) can also be prepared by heating its salt with H_3PO_4.
The sum of iodine and nitrogen atoms in a molecule of (X), (Y) and (Z) are ....

18. 1.2 g sample of bleaching powder requires 34 mL of 0.2 M $Na_2S_2O_3$ to titrate the liberated iodine. The % of Cl in the sample is ....

19. Xe reacts with F_2 in 1:5 ratio of 873 K and 7 bar to form compound (A). Hydrolysis of compound (A) to form a compound (B), which explodes violently when dry (like TNT), along with other products. (B) reacts with NaOH and undergoes disproportionation to evolve Xe gas and the compound (C) can be recovered from the solution.
The number of Na atoms in compound (C) is ....

20. Barium perxenate reacts with anhydrous sulphuric acid to form a tetrahedral compound (A) along with other products. The compound (A) is not a stable compound and decomposes above –35.9°C to form (B) and (C).
The total number of oxygen atoms in a molecule of compound (A), (B) and (C) are ....

21. A colourless salt (X) on heating with NaOH give a gas 'Q' which can also be obtained when Mg_3N_2 is treated with H_2O. When the reaction of X with NaOH is complete the resultant solution on treatment with $FeSO_4$ and conc. H_2SO_4 gave a brown coloured ring (R) between the two layers. (X) on strong heating forms (S) and (T) which reacts together forming a diabasic acid (U) that can exist as *cis*- and *trans*- isomers. The number of oxygen atoms in X, Q, R and S (include both isomers) are ....

22. Consider the reaction scheme :

$$(X) \xrightarrow{KOH} (Y) \text{ (gas turns red litmus to blue)}$$
$$+ KNO_3 \xrightarrow{Zn + KOH} (Y)$$
$$(X) \xrightarrow[300°C]{} \text{gas (supports combustion)}$$

The number of N and O in the compounds (X) and (Y) are ....

23. Consider the reaction scheme below :

$$\text{Gas } A + Na_2CO_3 + H_2O \longrightarrow B + C \text{ (gas)}$$
$$B + Na_2CO_3 \longrightarrow D + C \text{ (gas)} + H_2O$$
$$D + S \xrightarrow{\Delta} E$$

The number of oxygen atoms in a molecule of A(gas), B, C(gas), D and E are ....

24. TeF_6 is completely hydrolysed by water to form compounds (X) and (Y). Compound (X) is a weak acid while compound (Y) has an octahedral structure. The sum of basicity of compound (X) and (Y) is ....

Matching Type Questions

25. Match the oxoacids in the column I with the preparation or characteristic bonds and their number in column II.

Column I	Column II
A. Hypophosphorous acid	I. Four P—OH One P—O—P
B. Hypophosphoric acid	II. White P_4 + alkali
C. An oxoacid of phosphorus which exists in polymeric form only	III. Red P_4 + NaOCl
D. Pyrophosphorous acid	IV. Phosphorus acid + Br_2, heat in a sealed tube.

Choose the correct answer from the options below.
(a) A-(II), B-(III), C-(IV), D-(I) (b) A-(I), B-(IV), C-(III), D-(II)
(c) A-(II), B-(IV), C-(III), D-(I) (d) A-(III), B-(II), C-(I), D-(IV)

26. Match the reaction in Column I with the properties of product in Column II

Column I	Column II
A. $KClO_3 \xrightarrow[MnO_2]{\Delta}$	I. a complex is formed
B. Al_2O_3 react with acid	II. a paramagnetic gas is the product.
C. Iodide ions reacts with ozone in water to form the solid product and other products	III. The shape of the gas is angular and has two canonical forms
D. This gas converts iron (III) ions to iron (II) ions and decolourises acidified $KMnO_4$ solution	IV. violet compound

Choose the correct answer from the options below.
(a) A-(II), B-(I), C-(IV), D-(III)
(b) A-(II), B-(IV), C-(I), D-(III)
(c) A-(III), B-(I), C-(IV), D-(II)
(d) A-(III), B-(IV), C-(II), D-(I)

27. Match the reactions in Column I and the property of products in Column II

Column I	Column II
A. $KMnO_4 + HCl \longrightarrow$	I. Colourless pungent smelling gas
B. $NaCl + H_2SO_4 \xrightarrow{420K}$	II. Pt
C. Noble metal which reacts with *aqua-regia* to form an octahedral complex	III. With dry slaked lime gives bleaching powder
D. Equal volumes of Cl_2 and F_2 at 437 K forms a colourless gas.	IV. ClF

Choose the correct answer from the options below.
(a) A-(IV), B-(I), C-(II), D-(III)
(b) A-(III), B-(II), C-(I), D-(IV)
(c) A-(III), B-(I), C-(II), D-(IV)
(d) A-(IV), B-(II), C-(I), D-(III)

28. Match the reactions in Column I and the physical state (colour) and the structure of the products in Column II.

Column I	Column II
A. $Cl_2 + \underset{\text{(Excess)}}{F_2} \xrightarrow{573\ K}$	I. Ruby red solid in α-form
B. $I_2 + Cl_2 \longrightarrow$	II. Colourless gas with bent T-shaped structure
C. $I_2 + \underset{\text{(Excess)}}{Cl_2} \longrightarrow$	III. Orange solid which dimerises
D. $Br_2 + \underset{\text{(Excess)}}{F_2} \longrightarrow$	IV. Colourless liquid with square pyramidal shape

Choose the correct answer from the options below.
(a) A-(II), B-(I), C-(IV), D-(III)
(b) A-(III), B-(II), C-(IV), D-(I)
(c) A-(III), B-(IV), C-(II), D-(I)
(d) A-(II), B-(I), C-(III), D-(IV)

29. Match the reactions in Column I and physical appearance, chemical nature or oxidation state of nitrogen in the oxide of nitrogen in Column II

Column I	Column II
A. $NaNO_2 + FeSO_4 + H_2SO_4 \longrightarrow$	I. Brown gas, acidic
B. $NO + N_2O_4 \xrightarrow{250\ K}$	II. Colourless, neutral gas
C. $Pb(NO_3)_2 \xrightarrow{673\ K}$	III. Blue solid, acidic
D. $HNO_3 + P_4O_{10} \longrightarrow$	IV. +5

Choose the correct answer from the options below.
(a) A-(III), B-(I), C-(IV), D-(II)
(b) A-(II), B-(I), C-(III), D-(IV)
(c) A-(IV), B-(III), C-(I), D-(II)
(d) A-(II), B-(III), C-(I), D-(IV)

30. Match the reactions in Column I and the shape of products or hybridisation of central atom in Column II.

Column I	Column II
A. $\underset{(1:5\ \text{ratio})}{Xe(g)} + 2F_2(g) \xrightarrow[7\ bar]{873\ K}$	I. Square pyramidal
B. $XeF_6 + H_2O \longrightarrow (Q) + HF$	II. sp^3d^2 hybridisation
C. $XeF_4 + H_2O \longrightarrow Xe + HF + O_2 + (R)$	III. *see-saw*
D. $XeF_6 + 2H_2O \longrightarrow (S) + HF$	IV. sp^3 hybridisation

Choose the correct answer from the options below.
(a) A-(II), B-(I), C-(IV), D-(III)
(b) A-(III), B-(I), C-(IV), D-(II)
(c) A-(II), B-(IV), C-(I), D-(III)
(d) A-(III), B-(II), C-(IV), D-(I)

Paragraph Based Questions

Paragraph 1

Nitrogen is fairly widely distributed in nature in free and combined both states. Coal containing compounds of nitrogen yield NH_3 on distillation which is an important compound. On commercial scale, nitrogen is invariably obtained by liquifying air and then carrying out its fractional evaporation.

31. Consider the following compounds :
I. NH_4NO_3
II. $(NH_4)_2Cr_2O_7$
III. Mg_3N_2
IV. $Ba(N_3)_2$
V. $(NH_4)_2SO_4$
Total number of compounds that generates N_2 gas upon thermal decomposition below 300°C is ....

32. Among N_2O, N_2O_3, N_2O_5 and N_2O_4, the nitrogen oxide that contain(s) N—N bond is ....

Paragraph 2

$FClO_2$ is a colourless gas which boils at −50°C and freezes at −115°C. It is thermally stable at room temperature but it is chemically more reactive than $FClO_3$.

33. The product formed when $FClO_2$ is treated with HNO_3 is
(a) ClO_3 (b) ClO_2 (c) F_3ClO (d) $FClO_3$

34. The oxidation number of the oxyen containing product formed when $FClO_2$ is treated with HCl is.

Paragraph 3

Xenon forms three binary fluorides i.e., XeF_2, XeF_4 and XeF_6 by the direct union of elements under appropriate experimental conditions. In these fluorides, Xe is in +2, +4 and +6 oxidation states respectively.

35. How many of the following compounds have one lone pair of electron at the central atom Xe?
$XeOF_2$, $XeOF_4$, XeO_2F_2, XeO_3F_2, XeO_2F_4

36. Xenon hexafluorides reacts with silica to form a xenon compound *X*. The oxidation state of xenon in *X* is ....

Species Selection Type (with 5 Species)

37. The number of reactions that yields $POCl_3$ are
(i) $PCl_3 + O_2 \longrightarrow$
(ii) $P_4O_{10} + NaCl \longrightarrow$
(iii) $PCl_5 + CH_3COOH \longrightarrow$
(iv) $PCl_5 + SO_2 \longrightarrow$
(v) $PCl_3 + H_3BO_3 \longrightarrow$
(a) 4 (b) 3 (c) 5 (d) 2

38. The number of reactions that will produce an oxide of nitrogen on heating are
$(NH_4)_2Cr_2O_7$, $(NH_4)_2HPO_4$, NH_4NO_2, NH_4NO_3, $Pb(NO_3)_2$
(a) 2 (b) 3 (c) 1 (d) 4

39. Select the number of compounds that can significantly react with sodium *meta*phosphate?
$CaCl_2$, Dry HCl, $MgSO_4$, CaO, Na_2CO_3
(a) 3 (b) 6
(c) 5 (d) 4

40. The number of possible products form when chlorine water is passed through hypo solution are
S, H_2S, Na_2S, Na_2SO_4, $Na_2S_4O_6$, HCl
(a) 4 (b) 2
(c) 3 (d) 5

Species Selection Type (with 7 Species)

41. Select the number compounds of having (*M*—*M*) bond (*M* may be P, C, S, N)?
Mg_2C_3, $H_2S_2O_3$, $H_2S_2O_5$, Ca_3P_2, CaC_2, S_3O_9, N_3H
(a) 5 (b) 6
(c) 3 (d) 4

42. The number of compounds having peroxide linkage in following given compounds are
$H_2S_2O_3$, H_2SO_5, $H_2S_2O_5$, $H_2S_2O_7$, $H_2S_2O_8$, S_3O_9, $H_2S_4O_6$
(a) 5 (b) 2
(c) 3 (d) 1

43. The number of compounds that generate nitrogen gas on thermal decomposition are
NH_4NO_3, $Ba(N_3)_2$, Mg_3N_2, $(NH_4)_2Cr_2O_7$, HNO_3, HNO_2, NH_2CONH_2
(a) 3 (b) 4
(c) 2 (d) 5

44. The number of species that turn blue litmus red as in aqueous solution are
SO_3, PCl_3, N_2O, NO_2Cl, SF_6, SO_2, $AsCl_3$
(a) 5 (b) 3
(c) 4 (d) 2

Check Through PYQs

Element 1 Group 15 : The Nitrogen Family and Their Compounds

1. At room temperature, disproportionation of an aqueous solution of *in situ* generated nitrous acid (HNO_2) gives the species *2024 Adv.*
(a) H_3O^+, NO_3^- and NO (b) H_3O^+, NO_3^- and NO_2
(c) H_3O^+, NO^- and NO_2 (d) H_3O^+, NO_3^- and N_2O

2. The species formed on fluorination of phosphorus pentachloride in a polar organic solvent are *2024 Adv.*
(a) $[PF_4]^+[PF_6]^-$ and $[PCl_4]^+[PF_6]^-$
(b) $[PCl_4]^+[PCl_4F_2]^-$ and $[PCl_4]^+[PF_6]^-$
(c) PF_3 and PCl_3
(d) PF_5 and PCl_3

3. The order of the oxidation state of the phosphorus atom in H_3PO_2, H_3PO_4, H_3PO_3 and $H_4P_2O_6$ is *2017 Adv.*
(a) $H_3PO_4 > H_3PO_2 > H_3PO_3 > H_4P_2O_6$
(b) $H_3PO_4 > H_4P_2O_6 > H_3PO_3 > H_3PO_2$
(c) $H_3PO_2 > H_3PO_3 > H_4P_2O_6 > H_3PO_4$
(d) $H_3PO_3 > H_3PO_2 > H_3PO_4 > H_4P_2O_6$

4. The nitrogen containing compound produced in the reaction of HNO_3 with P_4O_{10} *2016 Adv.*
(a) can also be prepared by reaction of P_4 and HNO_3
(b) is diamagnetic
(c) contains one N—N bond
(d) reacts with Na metal producing a brown gas

5. The treatment of galena with HNO_3 produces a gas that is *2022 Adv.*
(a) paramagnetic
(b) bent in geometry
(c) an acidic oxide
(d) colourless

6. The correct statement(s) related to oxoacids of phosphorous is(are) *2021 Adv.*
(a) upon heating, H_3PO_3 undergoes disproportionation reaction to produce H_3PO_4 and PH_3.
(b) while H_3PO_3 can act as reducing agent, H_3PO_4 cannot.
(c) H_3PO_3 is a monobasic acid.
(d) the H atom of P—H bond in H_3PO_3 is not ionisable in water.

7. The compound(s) which generate(s) N_2 gas upon thermal decomposition below 300°C is (are) *2018 Adv.*
(a) NH_4NO_3 (b) $(NH_4)_2Cr_2O_7$
(c) $Ba(N_3)_2$ (d) Mg_3N_2

8. Based on the compounds of group 15 elements, the correct statement(s) is (are) *2018 Adv.*
(a) Bi_2O_5 is more basic than N_2O_5
(b) NF_3 is more covalent than BiF_3
(c) PH_3 boils at lower temperature than NH_3
(d) The N—N single bond is stronger than the P—P single bond

9. Match the reaction (in the given stoichiometry of the reactants) in List-I with one of their products given in List-II and choose the correct option. *2023 Adv.*

List-I		List-II	
(P)	$P_2O_3 + 3H_2O \longrightarrow$	(1)	$P(O)(OCH_3)Cl_2$
(Q)	$P_4 + 3NaOH + 3H_2O \longrightarrow$	(2)	H_3PO_3
(R)	$PCl_5 + CH_3COOH \longrightarrow$	(3)	PH_3
(S)	$H_3PO_2 + 2H_2O + 4AgNO_3 \longrightarrow$	(4)	$POCl_3$
		(5)	H_3PO_4

(a) $P\rightarrow2$; $Q\rightarrow3$; $R\rightarrow1$; $S\rightarrow5$
(b) $P\rightarrow3$; $Q\rightarrow5$; $R\rightarrow4$; $S\rightarrow2$
(c) $P\rightarrow5$; $Q\rightarrow2$; $R\rightarrow1$; $S\rightarrow3$
(d) $P\rightarrow2$; $Q\rightarrow3$; $R\rightarrow4$; $S\rightarrow5$

Paragraph (Q. Nos. 10-11)

Upon heating $KClO_3$ in presence of catalytic amount of MnO_2, a gas *W* is formed. Excess amount of *W* reacts with white phosphorus to give *X*. The reaction of *X* with pure HNO_3 gives *Y* and *Z*. *2017 Adv.*

10. *W* and *X* are, respectively
(a) O_2 and P_4O_{10} (b) O_2 and P_4O_6
(c) O_3 and P_4O_6 (d) O_3 and P_4O_{10}

11. *Y* and *Z* are, respectively
(a) N_2O_4 and HPO_3 (b) N_2O_4 and H_3PO_3
(c) N_2O_3 and H_3PO_4 (d) N_2O_5 and HPO_3

Element 2 Group 16 : The Oxygen Family and Their Compounds

12. The compound(s) having peroxide linkage is(are) *2024 Adv.*
(a) $H_2S_2O_7$ (b) $H_2S_2O_8$
(c) $H_2S_2O_5$ (d) H_2SO_5

13. The total number of compounds having at least one bridging oxo group among the molecules given below is ....

N_2O_3, N_2O_5, P_4O_6, P_4O_7, $H_4P_2O_5$, $H_5P_3O_{10}$, $H_2S_2O_3$, $H_2S_2O_5$ *2018 Adv.*

Element 3 Group 17 : The Halogen Family and Their Compounds

14. The reaction of $HClO_3$ with HCl gives a paramagnetic gas, which upon reaction with O_3 produces *2022 Adv.*
(a) Cl_2O (b) ClO_2
(c) Cl_2O_6 (d) Cl_2O_7

15. With respect to hypochlorite, chlorate and perchlorate ions, choose the correct statement(s). *2020 Adv.*
(a) The hypochlorite ion is the strongest conjugate base.
(b) The molecular shape of only chlorate ion is influenced by the lone pair of electrons of Cl.
(c) The hypochlorite and chlorate ions disproportionate to give rise to identical set of ions.
(d) The hypochlorite ion oxidises the sulphite ion.

16. The colour of the X_2 molecules of group 17 elements changes gradually from yellow to violet down the group. This is due to *2017 Adv.*
(a) decrease in $\pi^* - \sigma^*$ gap down the group.
(b) decrease in ionisation energy down the group.
(c) the physical state of X_2 at room temperature changes from gas to solid down the group.
(d) decreases in HOMO-LUMO gap down the group.

17. The correct statement(s) about the oxoacids, $HClO_4$ and HClO, is (are) *2017 Adv.*
(a) The central atom in both $HClO_4$ and HClO is sp^3-hybridised.
(b) $HClO_4$ is formed in the reaction between Cl_2 and H_2O.
(c) The conjugate base of $HClO_4$ is weaker base than H_2O.
(d) $HClO_4$ is more acidic than HClO because of the resonance stabilisation of its anion.

18. The compound(s) with two lone pairs of electrons on the central atom is (are) *2016 Adv.*
(a) BrF_5 (b) ClF_3
(c) XeF_4 (d) SF_4

Element 4 Group 18 : The Noble Gases and Their Compounds

19. The reaction of Xe and O_2F_2 gives a Xe compound *P*. The number of moles of HF produced by the complete hydrolysis of 1 mole of *P* is .... *2022 Adv.*

20. At 143 K, the reaction of XeF_4 with O_2F_2 produces a xenon compound Y. The total number of lone pair(s) of electrons present on the whole molecule of Y is .... *2019 Adv.*

21. Among B_2H_6, $B_3N_3H_6$, N_2O, N_2O_4, $H_2S_2O_3$ and $H_2S_2O_8$, the total number of molecules containing covalent bond between two atoms of the same kind is .... *2019 Adv.*

HINTS & Solutions

Solutions : Competency Enhancer

1.1 ***(a,b)*** Among the given statements only a and b are correct, while c and d are incorrect. The corrected form of these two statements are as —

As_4O_6 and Sb_4O_6 both have tetrahedral structures.

Polyphosphoric acid have general formula $H_{n+2}P_nO_{3n+1}$.

2.1 ***(b)*** The formula of peroxodisulphuric acid is $H_2S_2O_8$. Its structure is follows

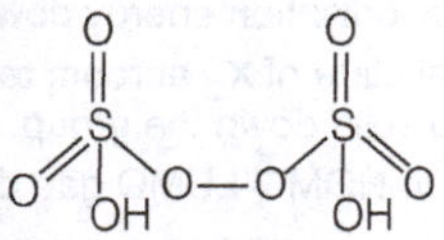

Thus, it contains one peroxy linkage.

2.2 ***(c)*** The structure of the given compounds are as follows

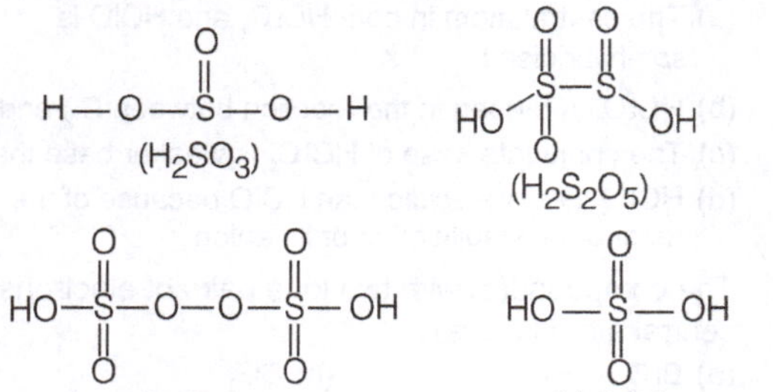

(H_2SO_3) ($H_2S_2O_5$)

($H_2S_2O_8$) (H_2SO_4)

3.1 ***(a,c,d)*** Among the given statements a, c and (d) are correct. The corrected form of incorrect statement 'b' is —

On dehydration with P_2O_5 at −10°C, it gives Cl_2O_7 which is the anhydride of perchloric acid.

$$2HClO_4 + P_2O_5 \xrightarrow{-10°C} Cl_2O_7 + 2HPO_3$$

4.1 ***(4)*** $Ba_2XeO_6 + 2H_2SO_4 \longrightarrow \underset{(P)}{XeO_4} + 2BaSO_4 \downarrow + 2H_2O$

XeO_4 has tetrahedral structure due to sp^3 hybridisation of Xe. It has four Xe—O double bonds containing $p\pi$-$d\pi$ overlapping.

Elemental Practice 6.1

1. ***(b)*** Due to very low ignition temperature (303 K) of phosphorus, it is always kept under water.

2. ***(b)*** Stability of +5 oxidation state decreases from top to bottom in group and +3 oxidation state increases from top to bottom because of inert pair effect. Due to this inert-pair effect bismuth only exhibit +3 oxidation state and form trihalides only. But because of small size and high electronegativity of fluorine bismuth forms BiF_5 only in which its oxidation state is +5.

3. ***(d)*** Statement given in option (d) is correct wrt dinitrogen while (a), (b) and (c) are incorrect. Their correct form are as follows. All electrons in N_2 are paired, thus it is diamagnetic, not paramagnetic.

(b) $N_2 + O_2 \underset{}{\overset{\text{Above } 2000°C}{\rightleftharpoons}} 2NO(g)$,

(c) Liquid N_2 gas is used to create extremely cold temperature to destroy diseased tissues located outside the body.

4. ***(a)*** On heating ammonium dichromate and barium azide separately we get N_2 gas in both cases.

$$(NH_4)_2Cr_2O_7(s) \longrightarrow N_2(g) + 4H_2O(g) + Cr_2O_3(s)$$

$$Ba(N_3)_2 \longrightarrow Ba + 3N_2$$

5. ***(a)*** In N_2O_5, the oxidation state of N is +5. Further, increase in oxidation state is not possible. That's why, its does not behave as reducing agent.

6. ***(d)*** A yellow explosive liquid nitrogen trichloride is formed as,

$$NH_3 + \underset{\text{(Excess)}}{3Cl_2} \longrightarrow 3HCl + \underset{\substack{\text{Nitrogen}\\\text{trichloride}}}{NCl_3}$$

Here, if ammonia is taken in excess then ammonium chloride is formed.

$$\underset{\text{(Excess)}}{8NH_3} + 3Cl_2 \longrightarrow 6NH_4Cl + N_2\uparrow$$

7. ***(c)*** The products of the reaction of copper with HNO_3 depends upon the concentration of HNO_3 used.

Copper metal reacts with dilute HNO_3 to form nitrogen (II) oxide (NO).

$$3Cu + 8HNO_3(\text{dilute}) \longrightarrow 3Cu(NO_3)_2 + 2NO\uparrow + 4H_2O$$

Copper metal reacts with conc. HNO_3 to form nitrogen (IV) oxide or nitrogen dioxide (NO_2).

$$Cu + 4HNO_3(\text{conc.}) \longrightarrow Cu(NO_3)_2 + 2NO_2\uparrow + 2H_2O$$

8. ***(c)*** White phosphorus combines with a concentrated solution of NaOH in inert atmosphere of CO_2, to yield a highly poisonous gas, phosphine. It has rotten fish like smell.

$$P_4 + 3NaOH + 3H_2O \longrightarrow 3NaH_2PO_2 + PH_3\uparrow$$

Its aqueous solution is neutral, so it is not more basic than NH_3.

9. ***(a)*** In Holmes signals of the ship, mixutre of CaC_2 and Ca_3P_2 is used.

10. ***(d)*** Solid PCl_5 shows ionic lattices. It has tetrahedral cations $[PCl_4]^+$ and octahedral anions $[PCl_6]^-$.

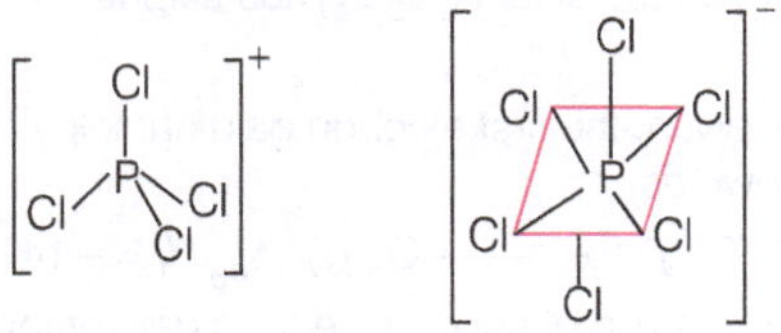

$[PCl]_4^+$ $[PCl]_6^-$

11. ***(a)*** Here, reactions are same as those with water (H_2O). PCl_5 shows following hydrolytic reactions with heavy water (D_2O).

Step I $PCl_5 + D_2O \longrightarrow POCl_3 + 2DCl$

Step II $POCl_3 + 3D_2O \longrightarrow D_3PO_4 + 3DCl$

Overall reaction

$$PCl_5 + 4D_2O \longrightarrow \underset{\text{Deuterio phosphoric acid}}{D_3PO_4} + \underset{\text{Deuterium chloride}}{5DCl}$$

12. ***(a)*** The structure of H_3PO_2 (hypophosphorous) acid is

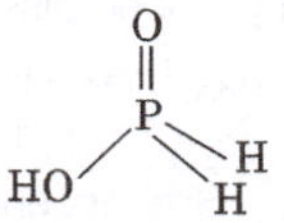

Due to the presence of two P—H bonds, H_3PO_2 acts as strong reducing agent.

13. ***(d)*** The correct decreasing order of the oxidation state of nitrogen is as follows

$$\underset{+5}{HNO_3} > \underset{+3}{HNO_2} > \underset{+2}{NO} > \underset{-3}{NH_4Cl}$$

14. ***(d)*** The incorrect order is written in option (d). Its corrected form is as —

$$PH_3 > AsH_3 > SbH_3$$

The bond strength between the central atom and hydrogen decreases down the group due to the increasing size of the central atom and decreasing overlap of orbitals.

15. ***(d)*** N_2O_3 has two proposed structures.

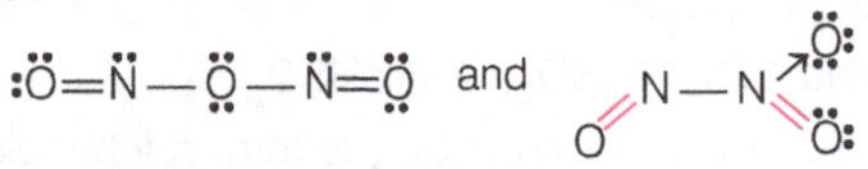

In both cases, number of lone pair of electrons is eight.

16. ***(a,c,d)*** Statement given in (a), (c) and (d) are correct while (b) is incorrect. This is because NH_3 is more stable than PH_3. As N is smaller and has a higher electronegativity than phosphorus, allowing it to more effectively share electrons and stabilise the molecule.

17. ***(b,c)*** $NH_3 + HOCl \longrightarrow NH_4Cl + H_2O$

$2NH_3 + OCl^- \longrightarrow N_2H_4 + Cl^- + H_2O$

18. ***(a,b,c)***

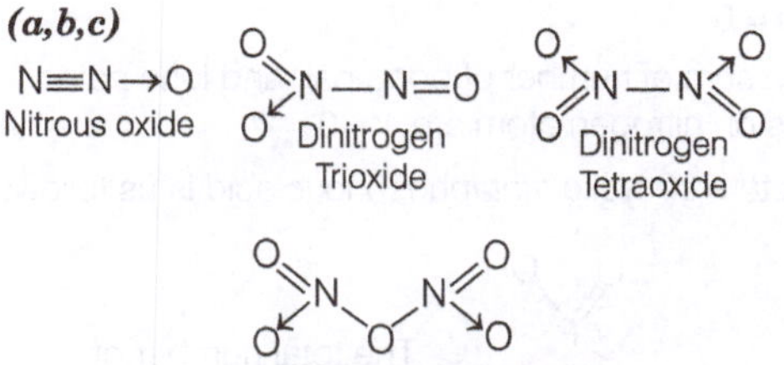

In among structure N_2O, N_2O_3 and N_2O_4 has N—N bond.

19. ***(a,c,d)*** Structure of P_4 molecules

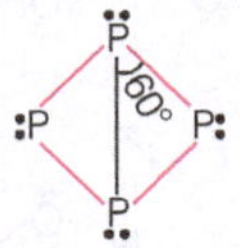

P_4 molecule has six P—P single bonds, four lone pairs of electron and P—P—P bond angle is 60°.

20. ***(a,c,d)*** Ammonium salts having non-oxidising anions on heating generally decompose to form ammonia. Ammonium nitrate on heating gives NO_2.

$$NH_4NO_3 \longrightarrow N_2O + 2H_2O$$

$$NH_4Cl \xrightarrow{\Delta} NH_3\uparrow + HCl\uparrow$$

$$(NH_4)_2SO_4 \xrightarrow{\Delta} 2NH_3\uparrow + H_2SO_4$$

$$(NH_4)_2PO_4 \xrightarrow{\Delta} 2NH_3\uparrow + H_3PO_4$$

21. ***(b,c)*** Among the given statements only (b) and (c) are correct. The corrected form of incorrect statement(s) are

$CrCl_3$ will give a green coloured precipitate with excess of NH_4OH, and ammonia gives a brown coloured compound on reacting with an alkaline solution of K_2HgI_4.

$$CrCl_3 + NH_4OH\text{ (excess)} \longrightarrow \underset{\text{(Green ppt)}}{Cr(OH)_3\downarrow}$$

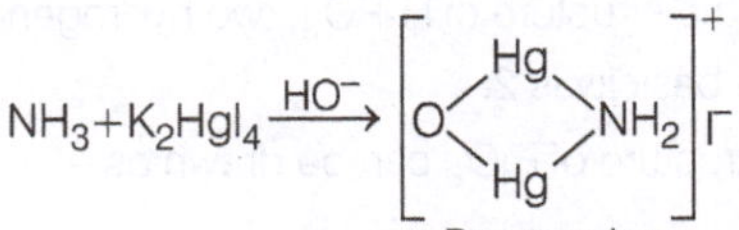

Brown colour
Iodide of Mllon's Base

$NiCl_2$ on reaction with excess NH_4OH forms an octahedral complex.

$$NiCl_2 + \underset{\text{Excess}}{NH_4OH} \rightarrow \underset{\text{Soluble}}{[Ni(NH_3)_6]Cl_2}$$

22. ***(4)*** Structure of NO_3^-

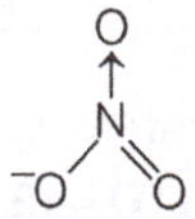

No. of bond pair on N = 4

No. of *lp* = 0

Thus, the sum of number of bond pair and lone pair of electrons on nitrogen atom are 4 + 0 = 4

23. ***(3)*** Structure of cyclic *meta*phosphoric acid is as follows

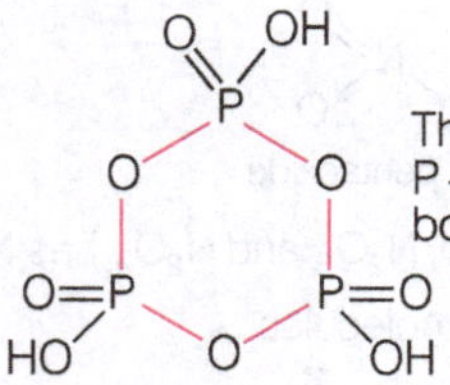

The total number of P—O—P bonds is 3

24. ***(12)***

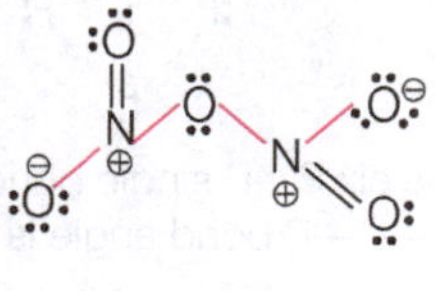

25. ***(9)***

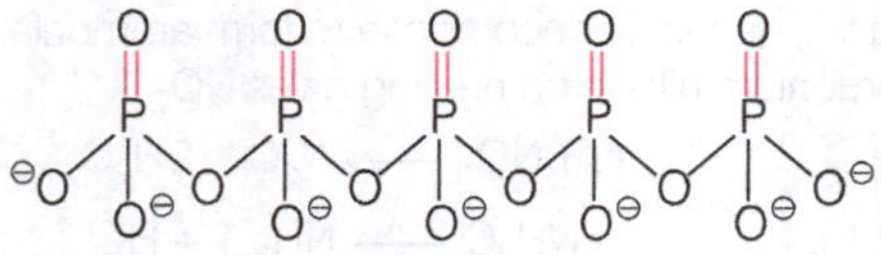

No. of P=O bonds = 5

No. of P—O—P bonds = 4

Total = 5 + 4 = 9

26. ***(2)*** $PCl_3 + 3H_2O \rightarrow H_3PO_3 + 3HCl$

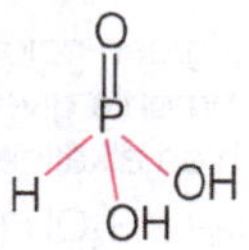

as per the structure of H_3PO_3, two hydrogen are replacable. So, the basicity is 2.

27. ***(28)*** Structure of P_4O_6 can be drawn as —

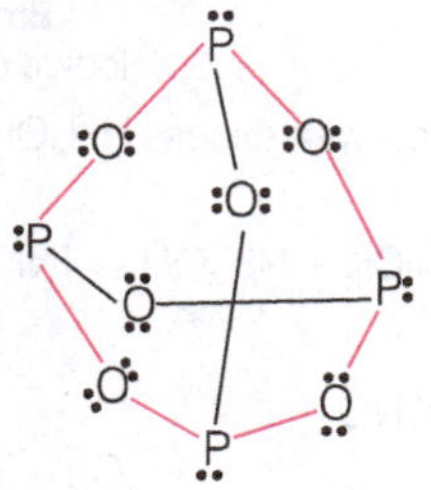

Total no. of lone pair at P = 4

No. of *lp* at O = 12

Total *lp* = 12 + 4 = 16

Total no. of P—O as per the given structure = 12

Thus, 12 + 16 = 28

Elemental Practice 6.2

1. ***(a)*** Dithionous acid ($H_2S_2O_4$) has sulphur in +3 oxidation state.

2. ***(a)*** As given, the first electron gain enthalpy of oxygen can be shown as,

$$O(g) + e^- \longrightarrow O^-(g),\ \Delta_{eg}H_1 = -141\ \text{kJ/mol}$$

The expression of second electron gain enthalpy of oxygen will be,

$$O^-(g) + e^- \longrightarrow O^{2-}(g),\ \Delta_{eg}H_2 = +\text{ve}$$

$\Delta_{eg}H_2$ of oxygen is positive, i.e. endothermic, because a strong electrostatic repulsion will be observed between highly negative O^- and the incoming electron (e^-).

A very high amount of energy will be consumed (endothermic) by the system to overcome the electrostatic repulsion.

3. ***(d)*** SO_2 acts as an oxidising agent particularly when treated with stronger reducing agents. SO_2 oxidises H_2S into S.

$$SO_2 + 2H_2S \longrightarrow 2H_2O + 3S$$

4. ***(c)*** Thermal stability ∝ bond dissociation energy,

$$\Delta_{diss}H(H—E)\ \text{kJ mol}^{-1} \propto \frac{1}{\text{Size of central atom}}$$

(where, *E* = 16 group elements)

On moving down the group, bond dissociation energy decreases because bond length increases.

Thus, the order of bond dissociation energy and thermal stability is :

$$H_2O > H_2S > H_2Se > H_2Te > H_2Po$$

5. ***(b)*** $3S + 6NaOH \xrightarrow{\text{Boiling}} Na_2S_2O_3 + 2Na_2S + 3H_2O$

6. ***(c)*** $\underset{(X)}{Na_2SO_3} \xrightarrow{\text{Dil.}H_2SO_4} \underset{(Y)}{SO_2} \xrightarrow{NaOH} \underset{(X)}{Na_2SO_3} \xrightarrow{SO_2+H_2O} \underset{(Z)}{NaHSO_3}$

Here, *X*, *Y*, *Z* are

$X = Na_2SO_3$, $Y = SO_2$, $Z = NaHSO_3$

Na_2SO_3 react with dil. H_2SO_4 to form sulphur dioxide (SO_2) gas. SO_2 on reaction with NaOH again form Na_2SO_3. By the reaction of SO_2 and H_2O with Na_2SO_3 it gives $NaHSO_3$.

7. ***(a)*** $P_4 + 6O_3 \xrightarrow{6H_2O} \underset{\substack{(X)\\ \textit{Ortho}\text{phosphoric acid}}}{4H_3PO_4} + 4O_2$

8. ***(c)*** $9O_3 + 2I_2 \longrightarrow I_4O_9 + 9O_2$

9. ***(d)*** $Cu(NO_3)_2 + H_2S \longrightarrow \underset{\text{(Black ppt.)}}{CuS} + 2HNO_3$

$$2AgNO_3 + H_2S \longrightarrow \underset{\text{(Black ppt.)}}{Ag_2S} + 2HNO_3$$

$$Hg(NO_3)_2 + H_2S \longrightarrow \underset{\text{(Black ppt.)}}{HgS} + 2HNO_3$$

10. ***(b)*** $6H_2SO_4 + P_4O_{10} \longrightarrow \underset{(A)}{4H_3PO_4} + \underset{(B)}{6SO_3}$

11. ***(d)*** SO_2 can act as a reducing agent as well as an oxidising agent, for example,

$$\underset{\text{Oxidising agent}}{SO_2} + 2CO \longrightarrow 2CO_2 + S$$

$$Ca(OH)_2 + SO_2 \longrightarrow \underset{\text{(Milkiness)}}{CaSO_3} + H_2O$$

$$CaSO_3 + H_2O + SO_2 \longrightarrow \underset{\text{(Soluble)}}{Ca(HSO_3)_2}$$

12. ***(b)*** $SO_2 + [O] \longrightarrow SO_3$

13. ***(a)*** Statement (b), (c) and (d) are correct whereas (a) is incorrect.

The correct form of (a) is :

Reducing property of dioxides decreases from SO_2 to TeO_2.

SO_2 undergoes oxidation to SO_4^{2-} and thus is reducing

$SO_2 \longrightarrow SO_4^{2-} + 2e^-$

More stable state.

TeO_2 undergoes reduction to TeO and thus is oxidising or less reducing. This is due to the inert pair effect lower 0.5 is more stable down the group.

$$2e^- + \overset{+4}{TeO_2} \longrightarrow \overset{+2}{TeO}$$

14. ***(d)*** The great affinity of H_2SO_4 for water is because it forms hydrates with water.

15. ***(a)*** In peroxoacids, —O—O— linkage is present H_2SO_5 and $H_2S_2O_8$ are peroxoacids of sulphur.

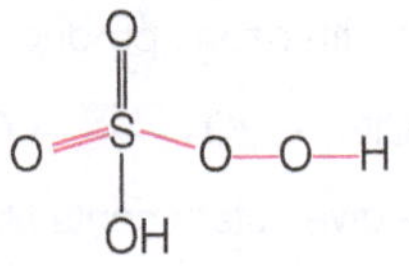

H_2SO_5
Peroxomonosulphuric acid or Caro's acid

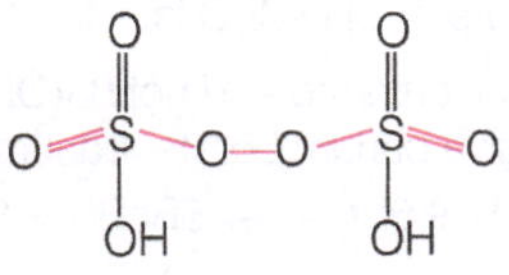

$H_2S_2O_8$

Peroxodisulphuric acid or Marshall's acid

16. ***(a,b)*** Among the given statements only a and b are correct. The corrected form of incorrect statement c and d are as

During preparation of ammonia, iron oxide with small amount of K_2O and Al_2O_3 is used as a catalyst to increase the rate of attainment of equilibrium.

Change in enthalpy is negative for the preparation of SO_3 by catalytic oxidation of SO_2.

17. ***(a,b,c)*** Among the given statements only a, b, c are correct. The corrected form of incorrect statement d is Ozone oxidises moist iodine to form iodic acid (HIO_3), not I_4O_9.

18. ***(a,d)*** $H_2S_2O_7$ and $H_2S_2O_8$ contains both 'S' in +6 oxidation states.

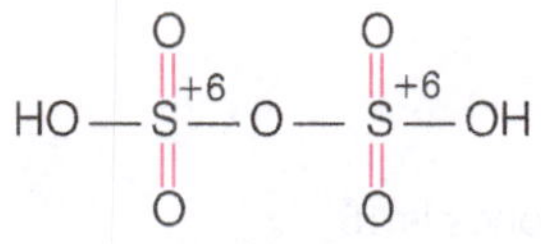

$(H_2S_2O_7)$

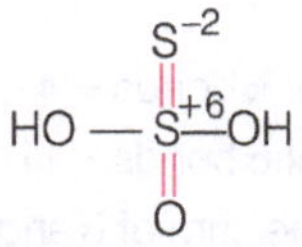

$(H_2S_2O_3)$

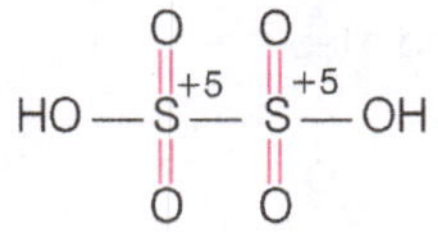

$(H_2S_2O_6)$

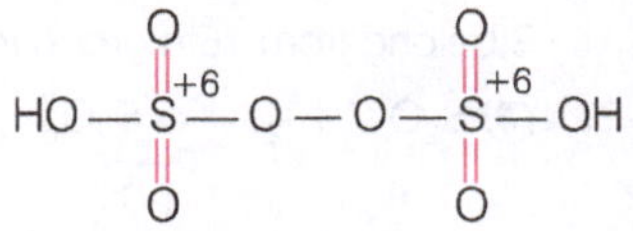

$(H_2S_2O_8)$

19. ***(b,c,d)*** PCl_5 produces $POCl_3$ with the following reagents.

$$PCl_5 + SO_2 \longrightarrow POCl_3 + SOCl_2$$

$$PCl_5 + P_4O_{10} \longrightarrow POCl_3$$

$$2PCl_5 + H_2SO_4 \longrightarrow SO_2Cl_2 + 2POCl_3 + 2HCl$$

20. ***(a,b,c)*** Among the given statements a, b and c are correct. The corrected form of statement d is — The oxidation state of sulphur ranges between –2 to +6 in different compound.

21. ***(b,c,d)***

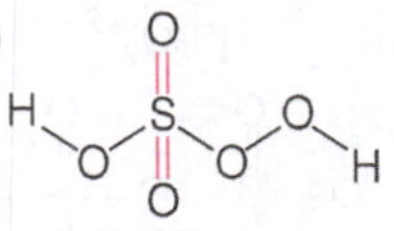

H_2SO_5

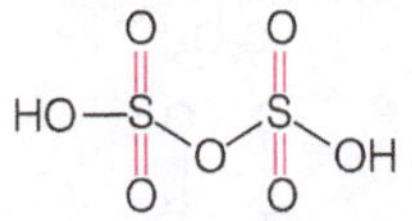

$H_2S_2O_7$

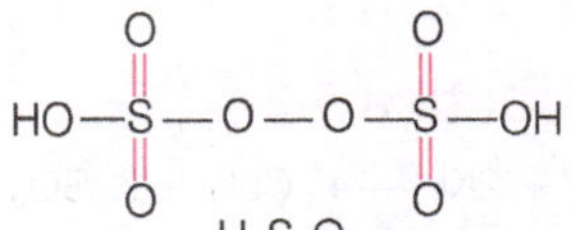

$H_2S_2O_8$

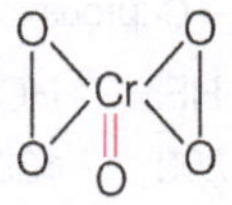

CrO_5

22. ***(b,c,d)*** $\overset{+4}{SO_2} + H_2O \longrightarrow H_2\overset{+4}{SO_3}$

$$SO_3 + H_2O \longrightarrow H_2\overset{+6}{SO_4}$$

$$H_2S_2O_7 + H_2O \longrightarrow 2H_2\overset{+6}{SO_4}$$

$$H_2S_2O_8 + H_2O \longrightarrow H_2\overset{+6}{SO_4} + H_2\overset{+5}{SO_5}$$

23. ***(3)*** Structure of S_3O_9 as

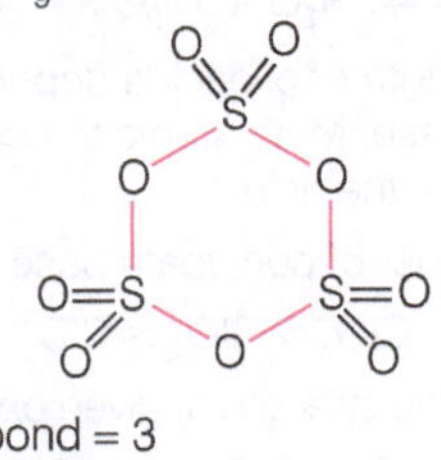

Total no. of SOS bond = 3

24. ***(15)*** Peroxydisulphuric acid ($H_2S_2O_8$) also known as marshall's acid. Structure is given below.

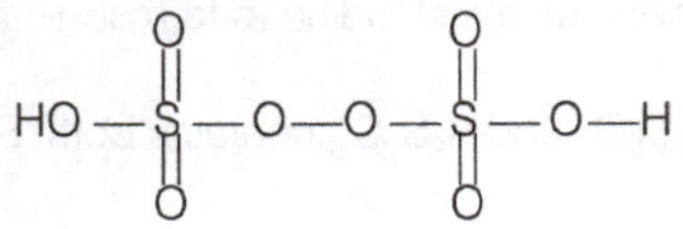

No. of π bonds = 4

No. of σ bonds = 11

So, the sum of σ and π bonds is 15.

25. ***(16)*** $SO_2 + H_2S \longrightarrow S + H_2O$

S belong from 16th group in periodic table.

26. ***(3)*** $S_2O_3^{2-} + I_2 \longrightarrow S_4O_6^{2-} + I^-$

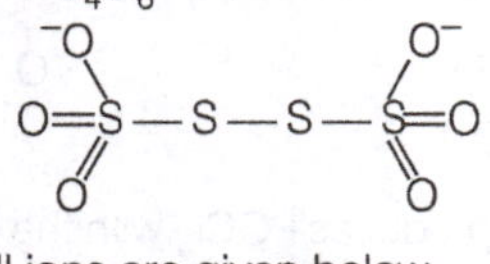

27. ***(4)*** Structure of all ions are given below.

$[S_2O_4]^{2-}$

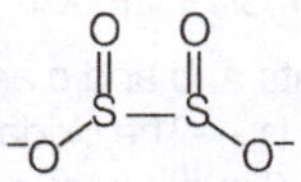

$[S_2O_6]^{2-}$

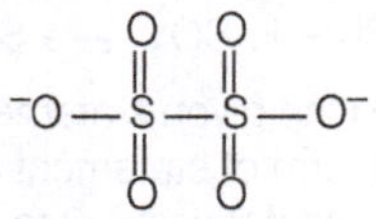

$[S_2O_3]^{2-}$

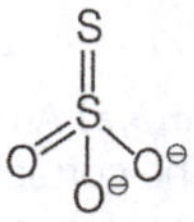

$[S_2O_5]^{2-}$

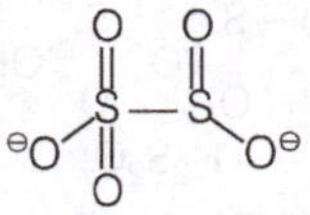

$[S_2O_7]^{2-}$

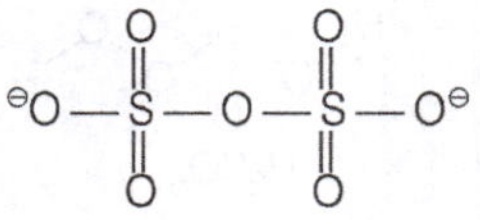

Elemental Practice 6.3

1. ***(b)*** $CuSO_4 + 2KI \longrightarrow CuI_2 + K_2SO_4$

$$2CuI_2 \longrightarrow \underset{\text{Cuprous iodide}}{2CuI} + I_2$$

2. ***(a)***

Hydride	HF	HCl	HBr	HI
B. pt. (in K)	293	189	206	238

Because of having low boiling point HCl is more volatile.

3. ***(c)*** Oxidising power of species is directly proportional to reduction potentials.

Therefore, order of oxidising power of given ions is as follows

Ion	BrO_4^-	>	IO_4^-	>	ClO_4^-
E_c (V)	1.74		1.65		1.19

4. ***(b)*** $2HClO_4 \longrightarrow H_2O + Cl_2O_7$

5. ***(c)*** Acidic strength of oxoacids depends upon the stability of conjugate base. More stable the conjugate base of an acid, stronger is the acid.

The stability order of conjugate base due to resonance is

$$ClO_4^- > ClO_3^- > ClO_2^- > ClO^-$$

Hence, the acidic strength of given oxoacids is as follows

$$HClO_4 > HClO_3 > HClO_2 > HClO$$

6. ***(c)*** Cl_2, Br_2 and I_2 form a mixture of halide and hypohalides when react with cold dilute alkalies while a mixture of halides and haloate when react with concentrated cold alkalies.

$$\underset{\text{(Cold and dilute)}}{Cl_2 + 2NaOH} \longrightarrow NaCl + NaClO + H_2O$$

$\therefore$ Cl^- and ClO^- are obtained as products when chlorine gas reacts with cold and dilute aqueous NaOH.

7. ***(d)*** The reaction takes place as

$$HClO_4 + P_2O_5 \longrightarrow \underset{(A)}{Cl_2O_7} + \underset{(B)}{HPO_3}$$

8. ***(c)*** In solid state I_2Cl_6 exist as :

$[ICl_2]^+$ sp^3 $[ICl_4]^-$ sp^3d^2

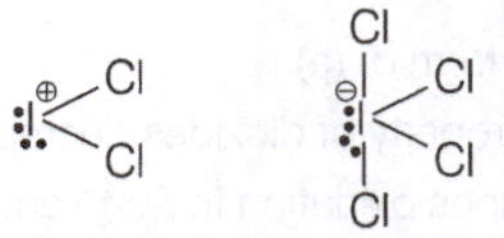

9. ***(a)*** The reaction takes place in option (a) represents the correct reaction between fluorine and hot NaOH.

$$3F_2 + 6NaOH \xrightarrow{\text{hot}} 5NaF + NaFO_3 + 3H_2O$$

10. ***(d)*** In any series, acidic character decreases as the electronegativity decreases.

$$HClO_4 > HBrO_4 > HIO_4$$

11. ***(b)*** $KClO_3$ reacts with $H_2C_2O_4$ to form metal chlorate.

$$2KClO_3 + 2H_2C_2O_4 \xrightarrow[90°C]{H_2O} 2ClO_2 + 2CO_2 + K_2C_2O_4 + 2H_2O$$

ClO_2 formed is paramagnetic. Since, it has one odd electron in a *p*-orbital.

It further reacts with ozone produces chlorine hexadioxide.

$$2ClO_2 + 2O_3 \xrightarrow{0°C} Cl_2O_6 + 2O_2$$

12. ***(d)*** Among the given statements about Cl_2O only C, D and E are correct.

The corrected form of incorrect statement A and B are as — molecular geometry is tetrahedral.

Oxidation state of Cl in Cl_2O is +1.

13. ***(c)*** When concentrated and hot $Ba(OH)_2$ reacts with bromine, it give barium borate, barium bromide and water.

$$6Ba(OH)_2 + 6Br_2 \longrightarrow 5BaBr_2 + Ba(BrO_3)_2 + 6H_2O$$

14. ***(c)***

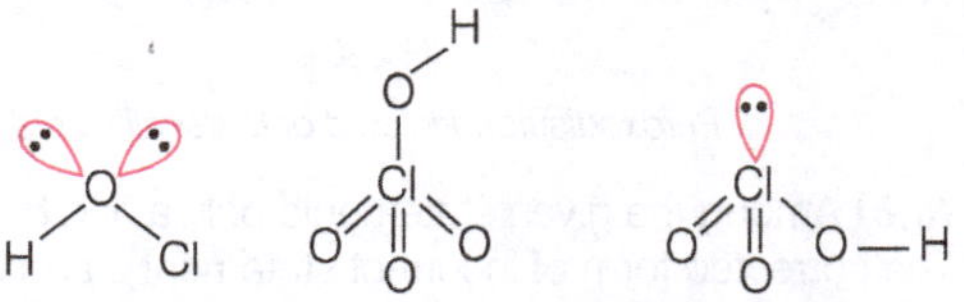

Hypochlorous Perchloric acid Chloric acid

Thus, the number of Cl=O bonds present in hypochlorous, perchloric and chloric acid respectively are 0, 3 and 2.

15. ***(b)*** When chlorine reacts with excess of fluorine at 250°C, it forms chlorine trifluoride.

$$Cl_2 + \underset{\text{(Excess)}}{3F_2} \xrightarrow{250°C} 2ClF_3$$

16. ***(a,b,c)*** Sodium tetrafluoroacetate is used as rat poison.
17. ***(a,b,c,d)*** Bromine is fairly soluble in water and more soluble in organic solvents.
18. ***(a,c)***

$$\overset{0}{Br_2} + Ca(OH)_2 \longrightarrow Ca(O\overset{+1}{Br}_3)_2 + Ca\overset{-1}{Br_2} + H_2O$$

$$\overset{0}{Br_2} + Na_2SO_3 \longrightarrow Na_2SO_4 + H\overset{-1}{Br}$$

$$\overset{0}{Br_2} + Na_2CO_3 \longrightarrow Na\overset{+5}{Br}O_3 + Na\overset{-1}{Br} + CO_2\uparrow$$

$$\overset{0}{Br_2} + Na_2S_2O_3 \xrightarrow{H_2O} Na_2SO_4 + S + H\overset{-1}{Br}$$

19. ***(b,c,d)*** All interhalogen compounds with bromine as central atom are colored except BrF_5.
20. ***(a,b,c)*** Among the given orders only a, b and c are correct. The corrected form of incorrect order d is —

$$IO^- > BrO^- > ClO^- \rightarrow \text{ease of disproportionation}$$

21. ***(3)*** Among the given reactions only I, II and III are correct. The corrected form of incorrect statement is —

$$6KOH + 3Br_2 \longrightarrow 5KBr + KBrO_3 + 3H_2O$$

$$6Ba(OH)_2 + 6Br_2 \longrightarrow 5BaBr_2 + Ba(BrO_3)_2 + 6H_2O$$

22. ***(1)*** Among the given statements only statement D is incorrect. Its corrected form is as—

Aqueous solution of $Na_2S_2O_3$ on reaction with Cl_2 gives $NaHSO_4$ and HCl.

23. ***(7)*** By dehydration of perchloric acid, with P_4O_{10} at 263 K.

$$4HClO_4 + P_4O_{10} \longrightarrow \underset{(X)}{2Cl_2O_7} + 4HPO_3$$

Cl_2O_7 may be distilled off under reduced pressure, with precaution against explosions.

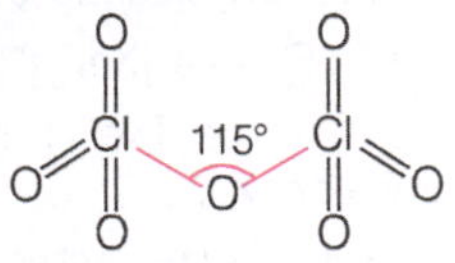

The oxidation state of chlorine is +7 in Cl_2O_7.

24. ***(11)*** The lone pair electron present in BrF_3 and ClF_5 is 2 and 1 respectively.

The bond pair electron present in BrF_3 and ClF_5 is 3 and 5 respectively.

Thus, their sum = 3 + 2 + 1 + 5 = 11

25. ***(3)*** An interpseudohalogen compound is a binary inorganic compound that has a structure similar to halogens, but contains at least one non-halogen radical such as cyanide. Thus, among the given compounds only ClCN, BrCN and ICN are interpseudohalogen compounds.

Elemental Practice 6.4

1. ***(b)*** Dipole of water $\overset{\delta-}{O}\langle^{H^{\delta+}}_{H^{\delta+}}$ induces dipole in noble gases which interact and causes solubility in water.
2. ***(a)*** The noble gases are only slightly soluble in water and their solubility increases with increasing molar mass

$$Xe > Kr > Ar > Ne > He$$

3. ***(a)*** Mixture of helium and oxygen is the life saving mixture for an asthma patient.
4. ***(c)*** $2XeF_2 + 2H_2O \longrightarrow 2Xe + 4HF + O_2\uparrow$
5. ***(d)***

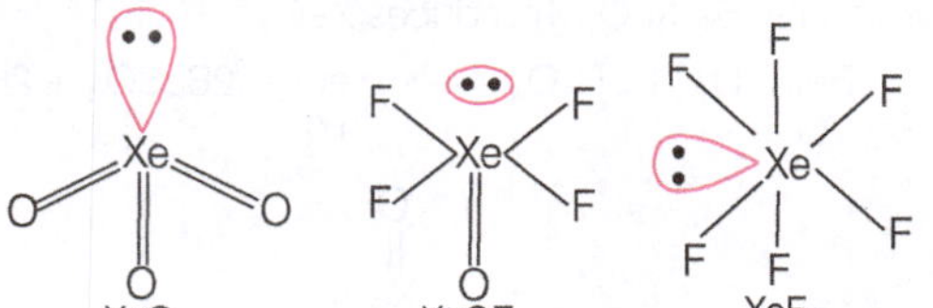

XeO_3 $XeOF_4$ XeF_6

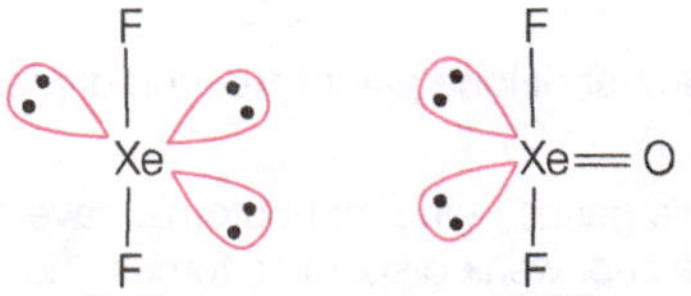

XeF_2 $XeOF_2$

6. ***(a)*** Both XeF_2 and IF_2^- are linear species but the central atoms Xe and I undergo sp^3d hybridisation with all the three equatorial positions occupied by the lone pairs of electrons.
7. ***(a)*** XeO_4 is formed by promoting one 5s and three 5*p*-electrons of Xe to higher energy 5*d* orbitals giving eight unpaired orbitals. It give sp^3 hybridisation in which form sigma bonds with four O atoms. The four unhybridised singly occupied 5*d* orbitals form four $p\pi$-$d\pi$ bonds with oxygen atoms.
8. ***(b)*** XeF_6 cannot be stored in glass vessels because it reacts with SiO_2 of the glass to give highly explosive XeO_3.

$$2XeF_6 + SiO_2 \longrightarrow 2XeOF_4 + SiF_4$$

$$2XeOF_4 + SiO_2 \longrightarrow 2XeO_2F_2 + SiF_4$$

$$2XeO_2F_2 + SiO_2 \longrightarrow \underset{\text{(explosive)}}{2XeO_3} + SiF_4$$

9. ***(c)*** $2XeF_6 + 16NaOH \longrightarrow Na_4XeO_6 + Xe + O_2 + 12NaF + 8H_2O$
10. ***(c)*** In XeO_2F_2, Xe is sp^3d-hybridised. Geometry of the molecule is distored trigonal bipyramidal.

Here, Xe contains one lone pair of electrons.

11. ***(d)*** $XeF_6 + 6H_2O \xrightarrow[-6HF]{} \underset{(X)}{XeO_3} \xrightarrow{XeOF_4} \underset{(Y)}{2XeO_2F_2}$

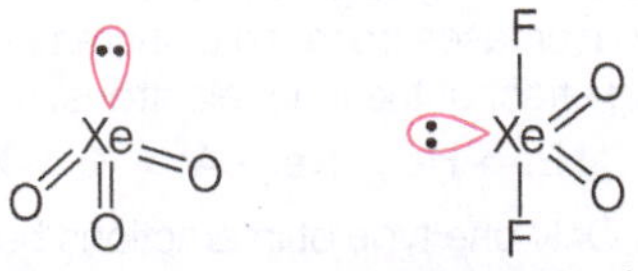

lone pair of e^- = 1 lone pair of electron = 1

Thus, $X + Y = 1 + 1 = 2$

12. ***(b)*** XeF_4 acts as only fluoride ion donor and forms complexes with lewis acids.

$$XeF_4 + SbF_5 \longrightarrow [XeF_3]^+ [SbF_6]^-$$

whereas XeF_6 acts both as fluoride ion donor and as fluoride ion acceptor.

$$XeF_6 + AsF_5 \longrightarrow XeF_6 \cdot AsF_5$$

$$XeF_6 + CsF \longrightarrow Cs^+[XeF_7]^-$$

13. ***(d)*** $XeOF_4$ has one lone pair of electron and have one $p\pi - d\pi$ multiple bond on the central atom.

14. ***(d)*** By the action of anhydrous or conc. H_2SO_4 on barium perxenate $[Ba(XeO_6)]$ produces XeO_3.

$$Ba[XeO_6] + 2H_5O_4 \longrightarrow \underset{(Y)}{XeO_4} + 2BaSO_4 + 2H_2O$$

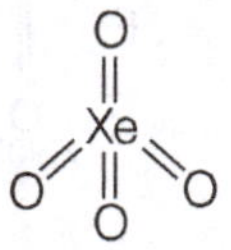

Total number of lone pair of electron present on XeO_4 is zero.

15. ***(b)*** Noble gases being monoatomic have no inter atomic forces except weak dispersion forces and therefore, they are liquified at very low temperature. Thus, they have very low boiling points.

16. ***(a,b,c,d)*** Argon act as shielded gas, protecting the molten metal from oxygen and preventing oxidation its has low thermal conductivity. All xenon fluoride are colourless solid. XeF_2, XeF_4 and XeF_6 hydrolysed as

$$2XeF_2 + 2H_2O \longrightarrow 2Xe + 4HF + O_2$$

$$2XeF_4 + 3H_2O \longrightarrow Xe + XeO_3 + 6HF + F_2$$

$$XeF_6 + 3H_2O \longrightarrow XeO_3 + 6HF$$

Xenon fluoride behave as both fluoride acceptors and fluoride donors, forming salts that contains such as XeF^+, $Xe_2F_3^+$ and anion such as XeF_5^-, XeF_7^- and XeF_8^{2-}.

17. ***(b,c,d)*** (a) XeO_3 is colourless explosive solid with sp^3 hybridisation.

(b) XeF_2 is good oxidising agent.

(c) Kr is rare gas in group 18 that does not form clatherate compound with water.

(d) Disproportionation reaction of fluorine —

$$4F_2 + 6NaOH \longrightarrow OF_2 + 6NaF + 3H_2O + O_2$$

18. ***(a,b,c)*** Reaction a,b,c are correct where d is incorrect.

The correct form of (d) is

$$I_2 + XeF_2 \longrightarrow 2IF + Xe\uparrow$$

19. ***(a,b,d)*** Down the group i.e., from He to Rn, ionisation enthalpy decreases because of increase in atomic radii and screening effect of the inner electrons.

$$\text{I.E.} \rightarrow He > Ne > Ar > Kr > Xe > Rn.$$

20. ***(a,b)*** (a) Only one type of interactions between particles of noble gases are due to weak dispersion forces.

(b) Ionisation enthalpy of molecular oxygen is very close to that of xenon. This is the reason for the formation of xenon oxides.

(c) Hydrolysis of XeF_6

$$(\overset{+6}{Xe}\overset{-1}{F_6} + 3\overset{+1}{H_2}\overset{-2}{O} \longrightarrow \overset{+6}{Xe}\overset{-2}{O_3} + 3\overset{+1}{H}\overset{-1}{F})$$ is not a redox reaction.

(d) Xenon fluorides are highly reactive they give hydrolysis readily even by traces of water.

21. ***(a,b,c,d)***

(a) $XeF_4 + SbF_5 \longrightarrow [XeF_3]^+[SbF_6]^-$

(b) He and Ne being smaller in size did not trap in the cavities formed by the water molecules and therefore, He and Ne escape from the cavities.

(c) He is a noble gas which can diffuse through rubber.

(d) He having lower atomic weight in group 18 and has small van der Waals force of attraction, so it has least boiling point.

22. ***(4)*** In XeF_8, XeO_4, XeO_2F_4 and XeO_3F_2, Xe is in +8 oxidation state whereas in $XeOF_4$Xe is in +6 oxidation state and in $XeOF_2$, Xe is in +4 oxidation state.

23. ***(2)***

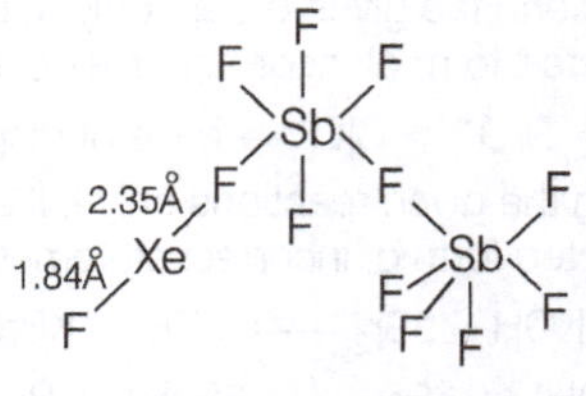

24. ***(5)*** sp^3d hybridisation has 5 hybrid orbitals.

$$XeF_2 \longrightarrow sp^3d \longrightarrow 5$$

$$XeF_4 \longrightarrow sp^3d^2 \longrightarrow 6$$

$$XeF_6 \longrightarrow sp^3d^3 \longrightarrow 7$$

$$XeOF_2 \longrightarrow sp^3d \longrightarrow 5$$

$$XeO_2F_2 \longrightarrow sp^3d \longrightarrow 5$$

$$XeO_3 \longrightarrow sp^3 \longrightarrow 4$$

25. ***(5)*** The compound formed by the reaction of xenon tetrafluoride and antimony fluoride is $[XeF_3]^+[SbF_6]^-$.

$$XeF_4 + SbF_5 \longrightarrow [XeF_3]^+[SbF_6]^-$$

Cationic part of product i.e., $[XeF_3]^+$ has 5 hybrid orbitals present at central atom Xe.

26. ***(2)*** When air is condensed to −180°C in the presence of coconut charcoal, then only two i.e., He and Ne noble gases are obtained.

27. ***(5)*** $$\underset{\text{(Deep red vapours)}}{PtF_6} + Xe \longrightarrow \overset{\oplus}{Xe}[PtF_6]^- \xrightarrow[25^\circ C]{PtF_6} \underset{\text{orange yellow solid}}{[XeF_5]^+[PtF_6]^-}$$

$[PtF_6]^-$

$$x + 6(-1) = -1$$

$$x = +5$$

Practice Element 1 : Target JEE Main

1. ***(d)*** I_2O_5 is used for estimation of carbon mono-oxide in automobile exhaust gases. KO_3 is used in oxygen cylinder in space and submarines.

2. ***(a)*** As the size of halogen atom increases crowding on Si-atom will increase. Hence, tendency of attack of lewis base decreases.

3. ***(d)*** Among the given reactions only (d) is incorrect. Its corrected form is as

$$PCl_3 + 3H_2O \longrightarrow H_3PO_3 + HCl$$

4. ***(d)*** Statement (d) is incorrect. Its corrected form is as —
OF_2 dissolves in water but does not give any oxyacid solution.

5. ***(d)*** In trisilylamine, three sp^2 orbitals are used for σ-bonding, giving a plane triangular structure.

6. ***(b)*** Statements (I), (III) and V are correct whereas statements (II) and (IV) are incorrect. Their corrected form is
Aqueous solution of I_2 is brown in colour while organic solution of I_2 is voilet in colour.
The correct stability order for the same halogen is
$HOCl < HClO_2 < HClO_3 < HClO_4$.

7. ***(d)*** The correct order of thermal stability of the given hydrides are as —
$$AsH_3 > SbH_3 > BiH_3$$

8. ***(c)*** Among the given statements all are correct except (c). Its correct form are as —
Bond length of N_2 is shorter than O_2 due to the presence of triple bond between N atoms.

9. ***(d)*** $XeF_6 + RbF \longrightarrow Rb^+[XeF_7]^-$

10. ***(c)*** The structure of pyrophosphoric acid and P_2O_5 are as :

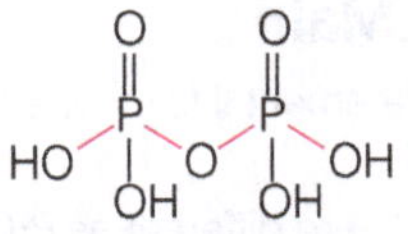

Pyrophosphoric acid
one → P—O—P bond

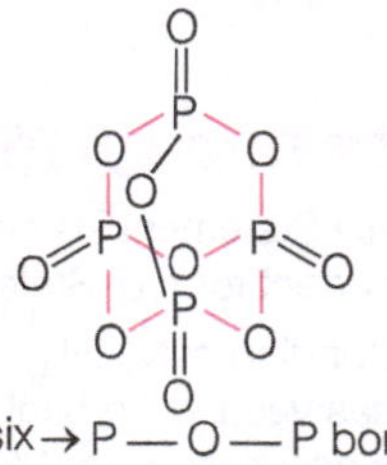

six → P—O—P bond

11. ***(c)*** The correct match is A-IV, B-III, C-I, D-II.

12. ***(b)*** The correct match is A-III, B-II, C-IV, D-I.

13. ***(c)*** He, because of its small size can diffuse through rubber, glass, PVC etc. easily.

14. ***(d)*** Noble gases are sparingly soluble in water. Dipole of water induces dipole in noble gases which interact and causes solubility in water.

15. ***(a)*** $2H_3PO_2 \xrightarrow{\Delta} H_3PO_4 + PH_3$
Here, $x = 1$
$$x^2 - 0.4 = 1^2 - 0.4 = 0.6$$

16. ***(c)*** In the preparation of HNO_3, NO gas is released by catalytic oxidation of ammonia. The chemical reaction is
$$4NH_3 + SO_2 \longrightarrow 4NO + 6H_2O$$
4 moles of NH_3 produced 4 moles of NO. So, moles of NO produced by the oxidation of moles of NH_3 will be 2 moles.

17. ***(c)*** Disulphurous acid contains S—S bond.

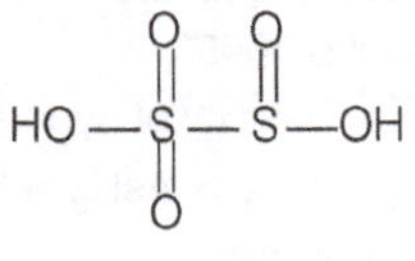

18. ***(b)*** The structure of the phosphorus oxoacids are

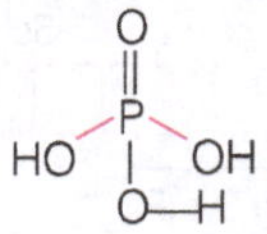

P—H bond = 0
H_3PO_4

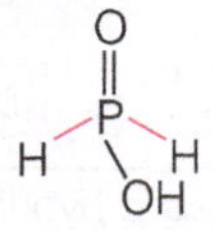

P—H bond = 2
H_3PO_2

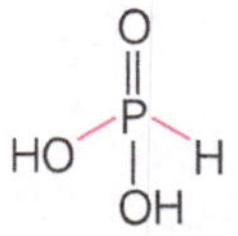

P—H bond = 1
H_3PO_3

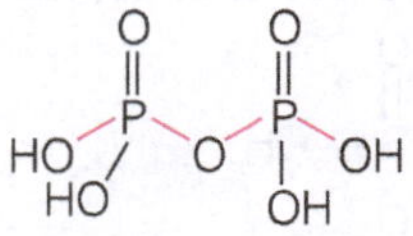

P—H bond = 0
$H_4P_2O_7$

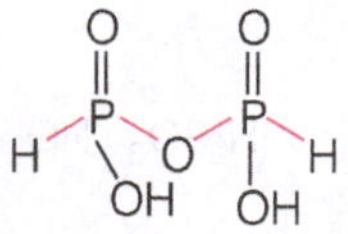

P—H bond = 2
$H_4P_2O_5$

19. ***(d)*** N_2 directly combines with non-metals to form covalent nitrides and with metal forms predominantly ionic nitrides.

20. ***(a)*** As we move down the group, molecular size and surface area increase and also vander waals' forces increase. Hence, the melting point down the group increases.
Thus, the correct order of melting points is
$$H_2Se < H_2Te < H_2O$$

21. ***(2)*** $2NaNO_2 + 2FeSO_4 + 3H_2SO_4 \longrightarrow$
$$Fe_2(SO_4)_3 + 2NaHSO_4 + 2H_2O + 2NO$$
The oxide of nitrogen formed is nitrogen monoxide. It has two resonating structure.

22. ***(1)*** The structure of given oxoacids of phosphorus are

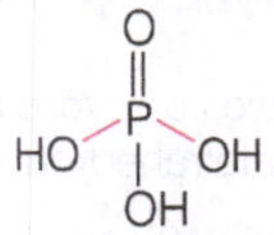

*Ortho*phosphoric acid

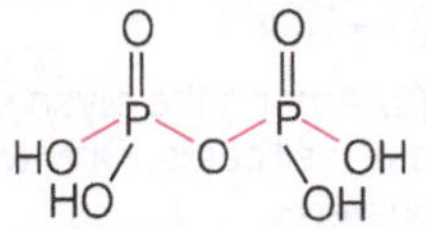

Pyrophosphoric acid

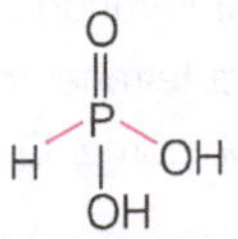

*Ortho*phosphorous acid

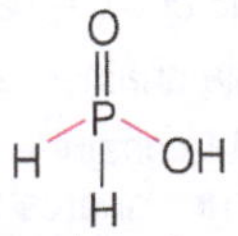

Hypophosphorous acid

Thus, there is only one oxoacid of phosphorus i.e., *ortho*phosphoric acid which is tribasic in nature.

23. ***(4)*** The structure of chlorous acid and perchloric acid are

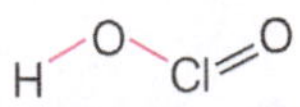

Chlorous acid

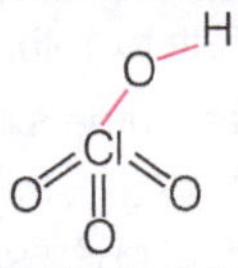

Perchloric acid

The total number of Cl=O bond is
$$1 + 3 = 4$$

24. ***(3)*** In XeF_2

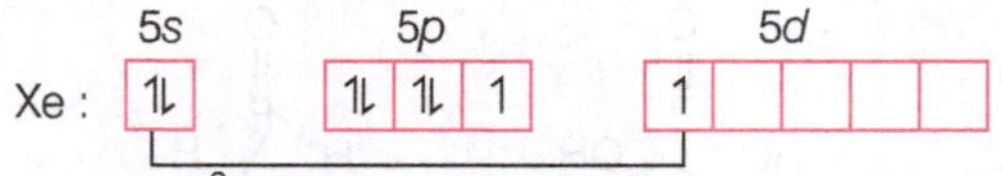

sp^3d hybridised with 3 L.P

Hence there are 3 L.P on Xe in XeF_2 is 2.

25. ***(1)*** Structure of oxoacids of sulphur are

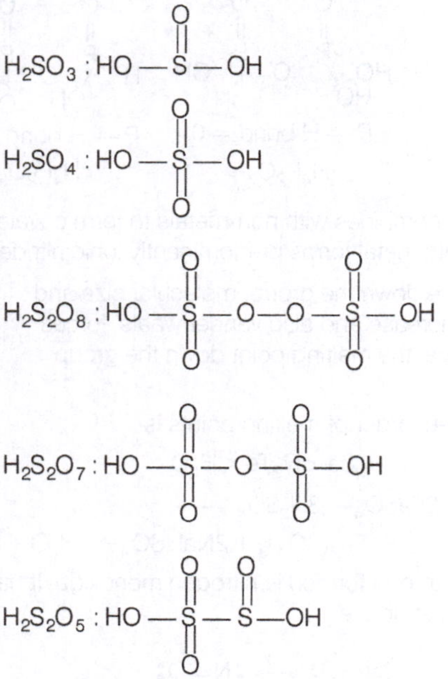

Therefore, number of oxoacids of sulphur with peroxo bond (O—O) is 1.

26. ***(2)*** Among the given silicates only two i.e., cyclic and single chain silicates. Only two corners per tetrahedron are shared.

pyro — one corner O-atom per tetrahedron

cyclic chain — 2 corner O-atom per tetrahedron

single chain — 2 corner O-atom per tetrahedron

double chain — one unit shares two corner O-atom while one unit shares 3-corner O-atom

sheet — 3-corner O-atom

3D — 4 corner O-atom

27. ***(2)*** Due to inert pair effect the stability of lower oxidation state gradually increases while stability of higher oxidation state gradually decreases down the group in elements of group 13th to 15th.

So, correct orders are

(v) $Pb^{2+} > Pb^{4+}$, $Bi^{3+} > Bi^{5+}$

(vi) $Sn^{2+} < Pb^{2+}$, $Sn^{4+} > Pb^{4+}$

28. ***(9)*** $PCl_3 + H_3PO_3 \longrightarrow H_4P_2O_5$

$P_4O_{10} + H_2O \longrightarrow H_2PO_4$

Thus, total oxygen atom is

$$X + Y = 5 + 4 = 9$$

29. ***(2)*** Reaction (ii) and (v) are correct. While (i), (iii) and (iv) are incorrect.

Their correct form are

$$2HNO_3 \longrightarrow 2NO_2 + H_2O + [O]$$

$$4Zn + 10HNO_3 \longrightarrow 4Zn(NO_3)_2 + N_2O + 5H_2O$$

30. ***(6)***

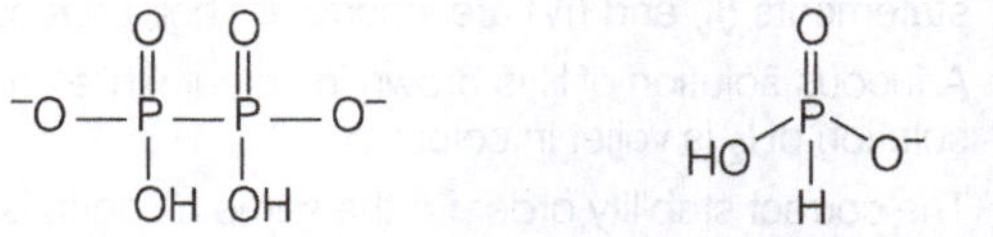

P—O bond order = 1.5   P—O bond order = 1.5

$H_2P_2O_6^-$ $H_2PO_3^-$

P—O bond order = 1.5   P—O bond order = 1.5

$H_2PO_4^-$ $H_2PO_2^-$

Thus, $P + X + Y + Z$

$= 1.5 + 1.5 + 1.5 + 1.5$

$= 6$

Check Through PYQs : JEE Main

1. ***(a)*** Statement I is correct but Statement II is incorrect. The correct form of Statement II is,

Bonding of $N(CH_3)_3$ and $P(CH_3)_3$ are different as $P(CH_3)_3$ has vacant *d*-orbital, hence acts as sigma donor as well as π-acceptor but $N(CH_3)_3$ can acts only as σ donor.

Thus, option (a) is correct.

2. ***(b)*** Statements given in *A*, *B* and *C* are correct, while in *D* and *E* are incorrect. The correct form of *D* and *E* are

The stability of + 5 oxidation states decreases down the group due to inert pair effect.

Nitrogen can show a maximum covalency of 4.

3. ***(d)*** A is true but R is false. The correct form of R is:

In liquid state, NH_3 molecules are associated through hydrogen bonding whereas PH_3 molecules are associated by van der Walls' forces only.

Thus, option (d) is correct.

4. ***(d)*** Among the given statements A and B are correct while statement C and D are incorrect.

The correct form of statements C and D are :

Statement C On moving down the group, bond strength of *M*—H bond decreases, which reduces the thermal stability but increases reducing nature of hydrides. Therefore, BiH_3 is a strong reducing agent.

Statement D The basicity of hydrides decreases in order

$$NH_3 > PH_3 > AsH_3 > SbH_3 > BiH_3$$

Thus, option (d) is correct.

5. ***(d)*** The structures of $H_4P_2O_7$, P_4O_{10} and $(HPO_3)_3$ are as follows:

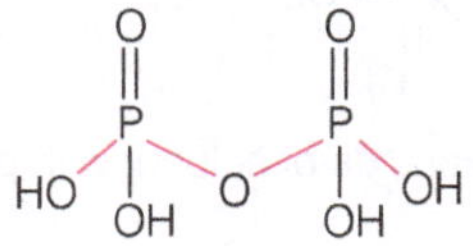

$H_4P_2O_7$
P—O—P bond = 1

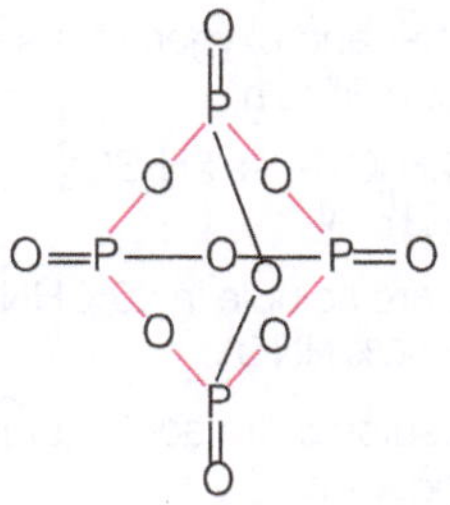

P_4O_{10}
P—O—P bonds = 6

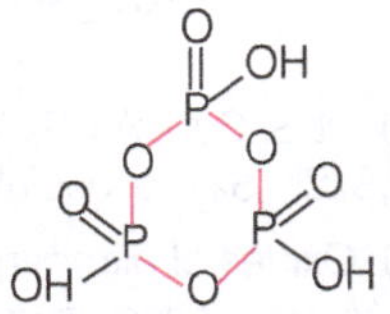

$(HPO_3)_3$
P—O—P bonds=3

6. ***(6)*** The structure of pyro-phosphoric acid is

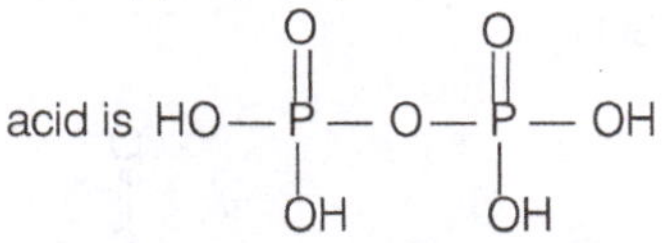

$$\frac{\text{Number of } \sigma\text{-bonds}}{\text{Number of } \pi\text{-bonds}} = \frac{12}{2} = 6$$

7. ***(a)*** The reactions will takes place as follows:

$$P_4 + 8SOCl_2 \longrightarrow \underset{(A)}{4PCl_3} + 4SO_2 + 2S_2Cl_2$$

$$\underset{(A)}{PCl_3} + 3H_2O \longrightarrow \underset{(B)}{H_3PO_3} + 3HCl$$

H_3PO_3 or $HPO(OH)_2$ is a dibasic acid.

Thus, option (a) is correct.

8. ***(c)*** HNO_3 is a strong oxidising agent. It oxidises I_2 to HIO_3.

$$I_2 + \underset{\text{(Conc.)}}{10\,HNO_3} \longrightarrow 2HIO_3 + 10NO_2 + 4H_2O$$

9. ***(d)*** The reaction of dinitrogen and dioxygen is highly endothermic. Thus, requires very high temperature.

10. ***(b)*** When white phosphorous reacts with thionyl chloride, it produces phosphorous trichloride and sulphur dioxide.

$$P_4 + 8SOCl_2 \longrightarrow 4PCl_3 + 4SO_2 + 2S_2Cl_2$$

11. ***(2)*** $C_2H_5OH + PCl_3 \longrightarrow C_2H_5Cl + \underset{(A)}{H_3PO_3}$

$$\underset{(A)}{H_3PO_3} + PCl_3 \longrightarrow \underset{(B)}{H_4P_2O_5} + HCl$$

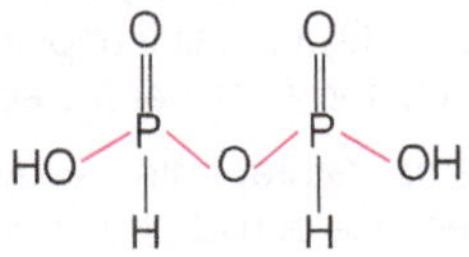

(*B*)

Number of non-ionisable protons in B = 2.

12. ***(d)*** Red phosphrous is produced by heating white phosphorous at 573 K in inert atmosphere. When red phosphorous is heated in a sealed tube at 803 K, α-black phosphorous is obtained.

13. ***(b)*** White phosphorus reacts with alkali in presence of CO_2 (inert atmosphere) as

$$\underset{\substack{\text{White}\\\text{phosphorus}}}{P_4} + NaOH \xrightarrow[CO_2]{\text{Inert atmosphere}} PH_3 + NaH_2PO_2 \xrightarrow{H^+} H_3PO_2$$

The structure of H_3PO_2 is

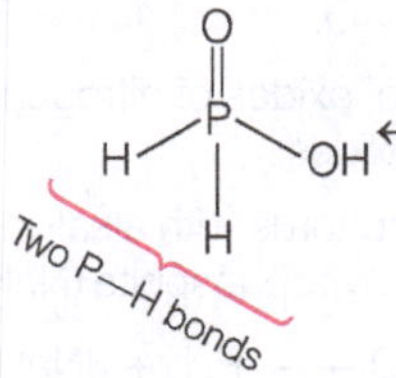

← Hypophosphorus or phosphinic acid

14. ***(b)***

$$Ba(N_3)_2 \xrightarrow{\Delta} Ba + 3N_2 \text{ (pure)}$$

$$2NaNO_2 \xrightarrow{>800°C} Na_2O + N_2 + \frac{3}{2}O_2$$

$$2NaNO_3 \xrightarrow{<800°C} Na_2O + N_2\uparrow + \frac{5}{2}O_2\uparrow$$

Note Thermal decomposition means, usually $T < 300°C$.

15. ***(d)*** White phosphorus is P_4. Its reaction with conc. NaOH produces sodium hypophosphite and phosphine.

$$P_4 + 3NaOH + 3H_2O \longrightarrow 3NaH_2PO_2 + PH_3$$

16. ***(b)*** The gas produced by treating an aqueous solution of ammonium chloride (NH_4Cl) with sodium nitrite ($NaNO_2$) is N_2.

$$NH_4Cl + NaNO_2 \xrightarrow{\Delta} NH_4NO_2 \downarrow N_2 + 2H_2O + NaCl$$

17. ***(b)*** Electronic configuration of $N = 1s^2\,2s^2\,2p^3$.

∴ N has 5 valence electrons.

NO_2 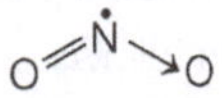 (odd electron species)

18. ***(a)*** NF_3 is the most stable trihalide of nitrogen because both nitrogen and fluorine have comparable sizes and electronegativity.

19. ***(b)*** PCl_5 forms five bonds using the vacant *d*-orbitals to expand the octet. NCl_5 has only *s* and *p*-orbitals and no *d*-orbitals in the second energy level. Therefore, NCl_5 does not exist.

20. ***(b)*** BiH_3 is a strongest reducing agent among group-15. It is because as we move down the group, the *M*—H bond can break more easily to evolve H_2 gas which acts as the reducing agent. Thus, BiH_3 is least stable and strongest reducing agent among the hydrides of group 15.

21. ***(a)*** Chemical nature of the nitrogen pentaoxide compound obtained from a reaction of concentrated nitric acid and P_4O_{10} (in 4 : 1 ratio) is acidic.

Chemical reaction is as follows

$$\underset{\substack{\text{Phosphorus}\\\text{pentaoxide}}}{P_4O_{10}} + \underset{\text{Nitric acid}}{4HNO_3} \longrightarrow \underset{\substack{\textit{Meta}\text{-phosphoric}\\\text{acid}}}{4HPO_3} + \underset{\substack{\text{Nitrogen}\\\text{pentaoxide}\\\text{(Acidic)}}}{2N_2O_5}$$

22. ***(a)*** Oxidation states of 'N' in the given compounds are as follows

$$NO \rightarrow x + 1(-2) = 0 \Rightarrow x = +2$$

$$NO_2 \rightarrow x + 2 \times (-2) = 0 \Rightarrow x = +4$$

$$N_2O \rightarrow 2x + (-2) = 0 \Rightarrow x = +1$$

$$NO_3^- \rightarrow x + 3(-2) = -1 \Rightarrow x = +5$$

Thus, $NO_3^- > NO_2 > NO > N_2O$.

23. ***(a)*** N_2O and NO are neutral oxides of nitrogen, whereas NO_2 and N_2O_3 are acidic oxides.

24. ***(4)*** Reaction of white phosphorus with alkali in inert atmosphere forms sodium hypophosphite (NaH_2PO_2).

$$P_4 + 3NaOH + 3H_2O \longrightarrow PH_3 + \underset{\substack{(A)\\ \text{Sodium}\\ \text{hypophosphite}}}{3NaH_2PO_2}$$

1 mole of NaH_2PO_2 reacts with excess of $AgNO_3$ in aqueous medium to give 4 moles of Ag.

$$NaH_2PO_2 + 4AgNO_3 + 2H_2O \longrightarrow 4Ag + H_3PO_4 + NaNO_3 + 3HNO_3$$

Hence, 1 mole A produces 4 moles of Ag.

25. ***(d)*** BiH_3 is the strongest reducing agent among group 15 hyrdrides. The reducing character of the group 15 element hydrides increases down the group.

So, correct answer is Bi (bismuth).

26. ***(a)*** SO_2 is oxidising as well as reducing agent as sulphur exists in +4 oxidation state.

27. ***(d)*** Both A and R are true and R is the correct explanation of A.

28. ***(c)*** Anomalous behaviour of oxygen is due to its small size and high electronegativity.

29. ***(b)*** Both Statement I and Statement II are incorrect.

Their correct forms are as follows.

Statement I Oxygen can have oxidation state from –2 to +2.

Statement II On moving down the group, stability of + 4 oxidation state increases whereas stability of + 6 oxidation state decreases due to inert pair effect.

30. ***(1)*** Structure of oxoacids of sulphur are

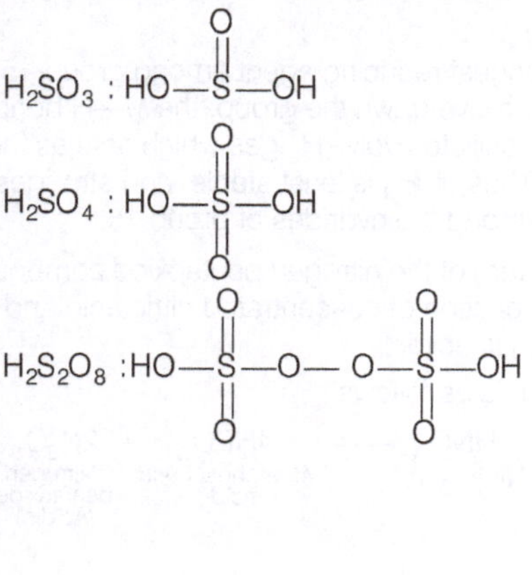

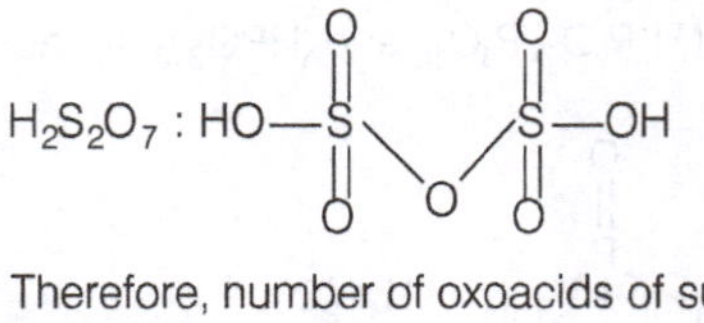

Therefore, number of oxoacids of sulphur with peroxo bond (O—O) is 1.

31. ***(d)*** SO_2 on reaction with water and oxygen forms sulphuric acid which is responsible for acid rain.

$$2SO_2 + O_2 + 2H_2O \longrightarrow \underset{\text{(Acid rain)}}{2H_2SO_4}$$

32. ***(4)*** PbS, CuS, As_2S_3, CdS, are soluble in 50% HNO_3 while HgS, Sb_2S_3 are insoluble in 50% HNO_3.

33. ***(c)*** Oxides of nitrogen and sulphur are acidic and settle down on ground as dry deposition.

Ammonium salts in rain drops result in wet deposition.

∴ X = Ammonium salts

$Y = SO_2$

34. ***(d)***

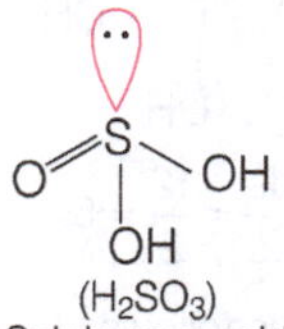

(H_2SO_3)
Sulphurous acid
No. of S ═ O bond = 1

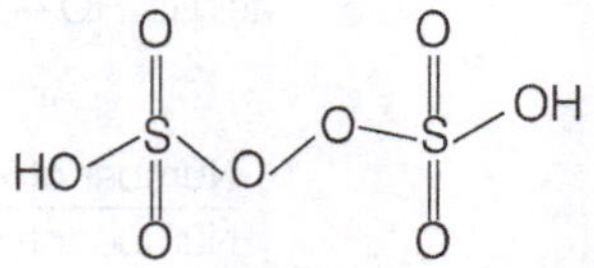

($H_2S_2O_8$)
Peroxidesulphuric acid
No. of S ═ O bonds = 4

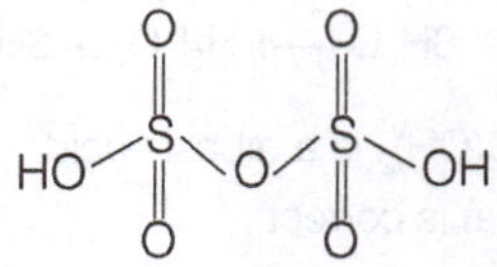

$H_2S_2O_7$
Pyrosulphuric acid
No. of S ═ O bonds = 4

35. ***(b)*** Electrolysis of concentrated solution of acidified sulphate solution yields peroxydisulphuric acid ($H_2S_2O_8$).

During electrolysis,

At cathode $2H_2O + 2e^- \longrightarrow 2OH^- + H_2 \uparrow$

At anode $2H_2SO_4 \longrightarrow H_2S_2O_8 + 2H^+ + 2e^-$

$$2H_2O \longrightarrow 4H^+ + O_2 + 2e^-$$

36. ***(c)*** The correct match is,

A→ (iii), B→ (i), C→ (iv), D→ (ii)

37. ***(1)*** Only S_2-form of sulphur is paramagnetic in nature. Because S_2 is like O_2 contains unpaired electrons and show paramagnetic character as per molecular orbital theory.

38. ***(a)*** At room temperature, water is liquid and has boiling point 373 K because of hydrogen bonding. But H_2S is a gas and it has no hydrogen bonding. So, boiling point of H_2S is less than 300 K (boiling point of H_2S is –60°C).

39. ***(7)*** Fuming sulphuric acids formula is $H_2S_2O_7$. So, total 7 oxygen atoms are present in it.

40. ***(c)*** $X = Na_2SO_3$

$$\underset{(X)}{SO_3^{2-}} + H_2SO_4 \longrightarrow [H_2SO_3] \longrightarrow H_2O + \underset{(Y)}{SO_2}$$

$$SO_2 + 2NaOH \longrightarrow \underset{(X)}{Na_2SO_3} + H_2O$$

$$\underset{(X)}{Na_2SO_3} + \underset{(Y)}{SO_2} + H_2O \longrightarrow \underset{(Z)}{2NaHSO_3}$$

Hence, $Y = SO_2$, $Z = NaHSO_3$

41. ***(a)*** Statement I is false and Statement II is true.

The correct form of Statement I is :

Chlorine instead of fluorine has most negative electron gain enthalpy in its group.

42. ***(c)*** Fluorine has no *d*-orbitals (3*d*-orbitals) and there is no scope for any electron excitation.

Therefore, flourine can show only oxidation state of –1 in its compounds.

Other members of family have vacant *d*-orbitals. Hence, they can show variable oxidation state.

43. ***(a)*** Among the given optios only I^- ions can be oxidised by oxygen in acidic medium.

$$4I^- + 4H^+ + O_2 \longrightarrow 2I_2 + 2H_2O$$

44. ***(c)*** Iodine is the only halogen which reacts with Cu^{2+} ion to give a salt of copper.

$$2Cu^{2+} + 4I^- \longrightarrow 2CuI + I_2$$

45. ***(a)*** Among the given options nitrogen is not present in Nessler's reagent. It is because Nessler's reagent is potassium tetraiodomercurate $[K_2(HgI_4)]$ with KOH solution. Hence, it contains K (potassium), Hg (mercury) and I (iodine).

46. ***(a)*** Nessler's reagent is potassium tetraiodomercurate II $[K_2(HgI_4)]$. Thus oxygen element is not present in it. It is prepared by combining potassium iodide (KI), mercuric chloride ($HgCl_2$) and KOH.

47. ***(c)*** Nessler's reagent = K_2HgI_4 +KOH
It is used for confirmation test of cation (NH_4^+).

Thus, option (c) is correct.

48. ***(c)*** The correct match is A-(II), B-(IV), C-(I), D-(III).

(A) $(NH_4)_2Cr_2O_7 \xrightarrow{\Delta} N_2 + 4H_2O + Cr_2O_3$

(B) $2\,KMnO_4 + 16HCl \longrightarrow 2KCl + 2MnCl_2 + 5Cl_2 + 8H_2O$

(C) $2\,Al + 2\,NaOH + 2\,H_2O \longrightarrow 2\,Na[Al(OH)_4] + 3\,H_2$

(D) $2NaNO_3(s) \xrightarrow{\Delta} 2NaNO_2(s) + O_2\,(g)$

49. ***(a)*** Fluorine forms only one oxoacid i.e., HOF due to its small size and high electronegativity.

Hence, both A and R are correct and R is the correct explanation of A.

50. ***(d)*** Iodine oxygen bond is stable due to greater polarity of bond. Stability of chlorine oxygen bond is due to multiple bond formation of oxygen with *d*-orbital of chlorine atom.

Bromine lacks both these characteristics. So, the stability order of oxide is

$$I > Cl > Br.$$

51. ***(b)*** Dioxygen difluoride is used to remove the plutonium from spent nuclear fuel.

$$3F—O—O—F + \underset{\text{(From nuclear fuel)}}{Pu} \longrightarrow PuF_6 + 3O_2\uparrow$$

52. ***(a)*** The Cl_2 is more reactive than ClF is incorrect statement as reactivity order can be written as follows

F_2 > ClF (interhalogen compounds) > Cl_2.

Interhalogen compounds are more reactive than pure halogen compounds as the bonds are polar and weaker than pure halogen compounds.

53. ***(c)*** Order of electron gain enthalpy (absolute value)

$$Cl > F > Br > I$$

Element	F	Cl	Br	I
ΔH_{eg} (kJ/mol)	328	349	325	295

Absolute value of electron gain enthalpy decreases down the group in a periodic table due to increase in size, with an exception in group 17 where, $|\Delta_{eg}H|$: Cl > F. It is because of smaller size than Cl and highest electronegativity of F.

54. ***(1)*** BF_3, $SiCl_4$ and PCl_5 are easily hydrolysed while SF_6 is inert to hydrolysis. In a polar covalent bond, the electrophilic centre (δ^+) able to expand covalency by the nucleophilic attack of $H_2\ddot{O}:$ undergoes hydrolysis. In SF_6, S is the electrophilic centre ($S^{\delta+}$——$F^{\delta-}$) but here S is being sp^3d^2 hybridised, it cannot expand covalency beyond 6. Hence, SF_6 is non-hydrolysable.

Thus, only 1 halide is inert to hydrolysis.

55. ***(11)*** When XeF_4 reacts with SbF_5

$$XeF_4 + SbF_5 \longrightarrow [XeF_3]^+ \; [SbF_6]^-$$

$\therefore$ $m = 3$; $n = 1$

$y = 6$; $z = 1$

$m + n + y + z = 3 + 1 + 6 + 1 = 11$

56. ***(c)*** Among the given options Cl has the most negative electron gain enthalpy while neon has the most positive electron gain enthalpy. Thus, Ne and Cl has the maximum difference of Δe_gH.

57. ***(a)*** (A) XeO_3

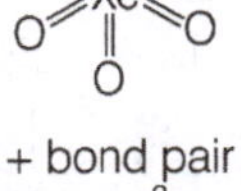

Hybridisation = lone pair + bond pair
$= 1 + 3 = 4 \Rightarrow sp^3$

Note Multiple bonds are treated as single bonds.
For AB_3E, shape = pyramidal
where, A = Xe; B = O and E = lone pair.

(B) XeF_2 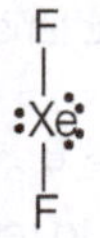

Hybridisation $= 3 + 2 = 5$; sp^3d

AB_2E_3, shape = linear

(C) $XeOF_4$ 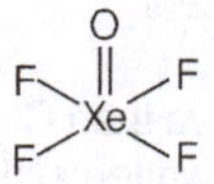

Hybridisation $= 5 + 1 = 6 \Rightarrow sp^3d^2$

For AB_5E, shape = square pyramidal ($\because B = F / O$)

(D) XeF_6 

Hybridisation $= 1 + 6 = 7 \Rightarrow sp^3d^3$

For AB_6E, shape = distorted octahedral ($\because$ B = F)

So, option (a) is correct.

58. ***(3)*** XeO_3 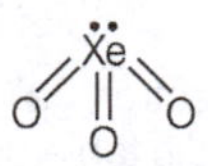

Xe is noble gas and therefore contain 8 electrons in valence shell. It gets bonded to oxygen by sharing its 2 electrons with each oxygen atom.

So, in this case the number of lone pair on Xe = 1

$XeOF_4$ 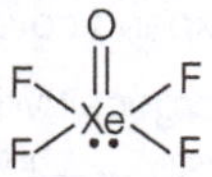

So, in this case the number of lone pair on Xe = 1

XeF_6 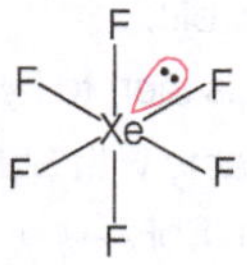

So, in this case the number of lone pair on Xe = 1

Thus the sum of lone pairs of electrons present on the Xe atoms of XeO_3, $XeOF_4$ and $XeF_6 = 1 + 1 + 1 = 3$.

59. ***(19)*** Xenon hexafluoride (*A*) on partial hydrolysis gives XeO_2F_2 as a product.

$$\underset{\substack{(A)\\ \text{Xenon}\\ \text{hexafluoride}}}{XeF_6} + \underset{\text{Partially}}{2H_2O} \longrightarrow XeO_2F_2 + 4HF$$

Structure of XeF_6 is given as

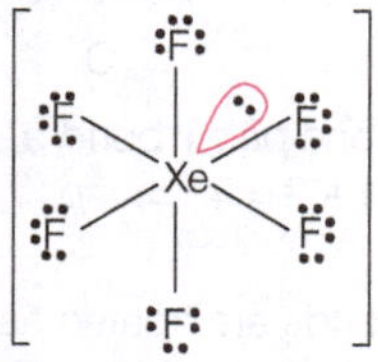

$\therefore$ Thus, total no. of lone pair

= lone pair on Xe + 6 × lone pair on F

$= 1 + 6 \times 3 = 19$.

60. ***(a)*** $[XeF_5]^-$

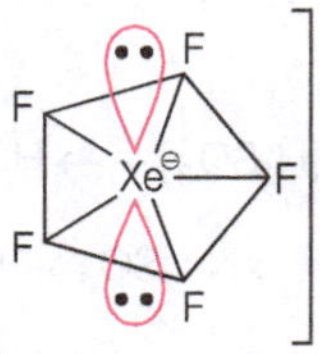

Xe : sp^3d^3-hybridised
Geometry = Pentagonal bipyramidal
Shape/Structure = Pentagonal planar

XeO_3F_2

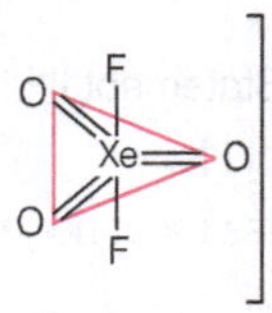

Xe: sp^3d-hybridised
Geometry = Shape/ structure = Trigonal bipyramidal
[because, Xe in XeO_3F_2 does not have lone pair of electrons]

Practice Element 02 : Target JEE Advanced

1. ***(b)*** $3Cl_2 + 6KOH \longrightarrow 5KCl + KClO_3 + 3H_2O$

$KClO_3$ is used in fire works and safety matches.

Cl_2 is a greenish yellow gas and the alkali metal hydroxide is KOH.

2. ***(b)*** $6Cl_2(g) + 6Ba(OH)_2 \longrightarrow \underset{(X)}{Ba(ClO_3)_2} + 5BaCl_2 + 6H_2O$

$$\underset{(X)}{Ba(ClO_3)_2} + H_2SO_4 \longrightarrow BaSO_4 + \underset{(Y)}{2HClO_3}$$

$$\underset{(Y)}{4HClO_3} \xrightarrow{\Delta} \underset{(Z)}{4ClO_2} + 2H_2O + O_2$$

3. ***(b)*** The reaction sequence is as under :

$$\underset{(1:5\text{ ratio})}{Xe(g) + 2F_2(g)} \xrightarrow[7\text{bar}]{873\text{ K}} XeF_4(s)$$

$$XeF_4 + SbF_5 \longrightarrow [XeF_3]^+[SbF_6]^-$$

XeF_3^+ is T shaped.

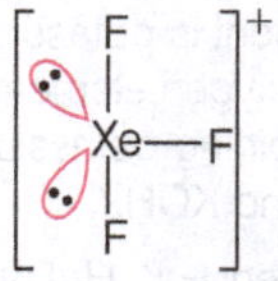

SbF_6^- is octahedral shaped.

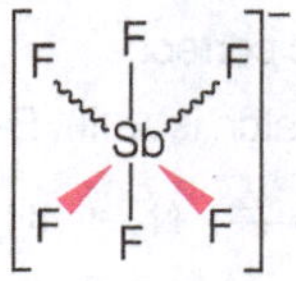

4. ***(b)*** $2XeF_2(s) + 2H_2O(l) \longrightarrow \underset{(A)}{2Xe(g)} + \underset{(C)}{4HF(aq)} + \underset{(B)}{O_2(g)}$

$$XeF_6(s) + HF(aq) \longrightarrow XeF_5^+(aq) + HF_2^-(aq)$$

So, the correct option is (b).

5. ***(c)*** Statements (I), (II), (III) and (V) are correct. The correct form of (IV) is

Reaction of Al_2S_3 on reaction with NaOH gives sodium thioaresenite as well as sodium arsenite.

$$N_2S_3 + 6NaOH \longrightarrow \underset{\substack{\text{Sodium}\\ \text{Thioaresenite}}}{Na_3AsS_3} + \underset{\substack{\text{Sodium}\\ \text{Arsenite}}}{Na_2AsO_3} + 3H_2O$$

6. ***(a)*** $\underset{(A)}{Na_2SO_3} + 2HCl \longrightarrow 2NaCl + H_2O + \underset{(Y)}{SO_2}$

$$\underset{(B)}{Na_2S} + 2HCl \longrightarrow 2NaCl + \underset{(Z)}{H_2S}$$

SO_2 and H_2S reduces acidified dichromate to green chromic sulphate. H_2S turns lead acetate to PbS but SO_2 has no effect.

7. ***(d)*** Oxidation of HCN with oxygen using silver as a catalyst produces cyanogen which can also be prepared by the action of CN^- with Cu^{2+}.

$$Cu^{2+} + 2CN^- \longrightarrow Cu(CN)_2$$

$$2Cu(CN)_2 \longrightarrow Cu_2(CN)_2 + (CN)_2$$

8. ***(c)*** $P_4 + 3O_2 \longrightarrow \underset{(A)}{P_4O_6}$

$$\underset{(A)}{P_4O_6} + 6H_2O \longrightarrow \underset{(B)}{4H_3PO_3}$$

$$\underset{(B)}{2H_3PO_3} + O_2 \longrightarrow \underset{(C)}{2H_3PO_4}$$

$$H_3PO_4 + 3AgNO_3 \longrightarrow \underset{\text{Yellow ppt.}}{Ag_3PO_4}\downarrow + 3HNO_3$$

9. ***(a,b,c)*** $3KClO_3 + H_2SO_4 \xrightarrow{330\,K}$

$$3KHSO_4 + HClO_4 + 2ClO_2 + H_2O$$

10. ***(a,b,c,d)*** All the reactions (a), (b), (c) and (d) are correct.

11. ***(a,b,d)*** Statements (a), (b) and (d) are correct. Statement (c) is incorrect. The correct form of statement (c) is :

Partial hydrolysis of XeF_6 gives oxyfluorides, $XeOF_4$ and XeO_2F_2.

$$XeF_6 + H_2O \longrightarrow XeOF_4 + 2HF$$

$$XeF_6 + 2H_2O \longrightarrow XeO_2F_2 + 4HF$$

12. ***(a,b,d)*** The reaction is as under :

$$6XeF_4 + 12H_2O \longrightarrow \underset{(A)}{4Xe} + \underset{(B)}{2XeO_3} + \underset{(C)}{24HF} + \underset{(D)}{3O_2}$$

The square planar complex is XeF_4.

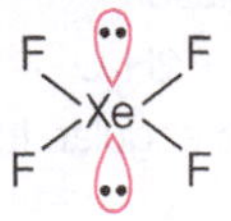

The pyramidal compound *B* is

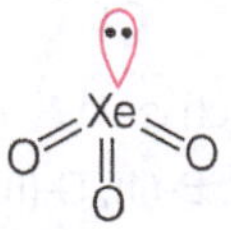

13. ***(a,b,c,d)*** All the statements (a), (b), (c) and (d) are correct.

The reactions are as under :

(a) $\underset{\text{Marshall's acid}}{H_2S_2O_8} + H_2O \longrightarrow H_2SO_4 + \underset{\text{Caro's acid}}{H_2SO_5}$

(b) $3KClO_3 + 3H_2SO_4 \longrightarrow$

$$3KHSO_4 + HClO_4 + 2ClO_2 + H_2O$$

(c) $2Na_2S_2O_3 + I_2 \longrightarrow H_2SO_4 + HI$

(d) $3NaBr + H_3PO_4 \longrightarrow HBr + Na_3PO_4$

$$3NaI + H_3PO_4 \longrightarrow HI + Na_3PO_4$$

$$2HBr + H_2SO_4 \longrightarrow Br_2 + SO_2 + 2H_2O$$

$$8HI + H_2SO_4 \longrightarrow 4I_2 + H_2S + 4H_2O$$

14. ***(b,c)*** The reaction is as under :

$$Na_2S + Na_2SO_3 + I_2 \longrightarrow \underset{\text{(Springs reaction)}}{Na_2S_2O_3} + 2NaI$$

$$Na_2S_2O_3 + \underset{\text{Excess}}{I_2} \longrightarrow Na_2S_4O_6 + 2NaI$$

So, the products of the reaction are $Na_2S_4O_6$ and NaI.

15. ***(a,b,c)*** Statements (a), (b) and (c) are correct. Statement (d) is incorrect. The correct form of statement (d) is :

$NH_3 \cdot NI_3$ when rubbed against hard surface forms N_2, I_2 and NH_4I.

$$8NH_3 \cdot NI_3 \longrightarrow 5N_2 + 9I_2 + 6NH_4I$$

16. ***(b,c,d)*** Statements (b), (c) and (d) are correct. Statement (a) is incorrect. The correct form of statement (a) is :

Ammonia is oxidised to nitric oxide (NO) and water (H_2O) by oxygen at 800°C, not nitrogen dioxide.

$$4NH_3 + 5O_2 \xrightarrow[800°C]{Pt} 4NO + 6H_2O + \text{Heat}$$

17. ***(8)*** $2NH_3 + \underset{(X)}{3I_2} \longrightarrow 3HI + \underset{\text{Mild explosive}}{\underset{(Z)}{NH_3 \cdot NI_3}}$

$$8NH_3 \cdot NI_3 \longrightarrow 5N_2 + 9I_2 + 6NH_4I$$

$$I_2 + H_2 \longrightarrow \underset{(Y)}{2HI}$$

$$3NaI + H_3PO_4 \longrightarrow Na_3PO_4 + 3HI$$

The sum of iodine and nitrogen atoms in a molecule of (*X*), (*Y*) and (*Z*) $= 2 + 1 + 5 = 8$

18. ***(20)*** Bleaching powder ($CaOCl_2$) reacts with iodide ion as :

$$ClO^- + 2I^- + 2H^+ \longrightarrow I_2 + Cl^- + H_2O$$

The liberated I_2 reacts with $Na_2S_2O_3$ according to the equation :

$$I_2 + 2Na_2S_2O_3 \longrightarrow 2NaI + Na_2S_4O_6$$

Moles of I_2 liberated $= \dfrac{0.2 \times 34}{2}$ m mol $= 3.4$ m mol

Moles of $ClO^- = 3.4$ m mol

Moles of Cl in bleaching powder = 6.8 m mol

Mass of Cl in bleaching powder ≈ 0.24

% Cl in bleaching powder $= \dfrac{0.24\text{ g}}{1.2\text{ g}} \times 100 = 20\%$

19. ***(4)*** The reaction sequence is as under :

$$\underset{(1:5\text{ ratio})}{Xe(g) + 2F_2(g)} \xrightarrow{873\,K,\ 7\,bar} \underset{(A)}{XeF_4(s)}$$

$$\underset{(A)}{XeF_4} + 12H_2O \longrightarrow 4Xe + \underset{(B)}{2XeO_3} + 24HF + 3O_2$$

$XeO_3(B)$ explodes violently when dry (like TNT).

$XeO_3(B)$ reacts with sodium hydroxide and undergoes disproportionation to form sodium perxenate, $Na_4XeO_6 \cdot 8H_2O$.

$$2XeO_3 + 4NaOH + 6H_2O \longrightarrow Xe + O_2 + \underset{(C)}{Na_4XeO_6 \cdot 8H_2O}$$

The number of Na atoms in compound (*C*) is 4.

20. ***(6)*** The reaction sequence is as under.

$$Ba_2XeO_6 + 2H_2SO_4 \longrightarrow \underset{(A)}{XeO_4} + 2BaSO_4 + 2H_2O$$

Xe in XeO_4 is sp^3 hybridised and the shape of XeO_4(*A*) is tetrahedral.

XeO_4 is not a stable compound and decomposes above –35.9°C to form Xe and O_2.

$$XeO_4 \longrightarrow \underset{(B)}{Xe} + \underset{(C)}{2O_2}$$

The total number of oxygen atoms in a molecule of compound (*A*), (*B*) and (*C*)

$$= 4 + 2 = 6$$

21. ***(17)*** The compound *X* is NH_4NO_3. The reactions are as follows :

$$\underset{(X)}{NH_4NO_3} + NaOH \longrightarrow NaNO_3 + H_2O + \underset{(Q)}{NH_3(g)}$$

$$Mg_3N_2 + 6H_2O \longrightarrow 3Mg(OH)_2 + \underset{(Q)}{2NH_3(g)}$$

$$NaNO_3 + H_2SO_4 \longrightarrow NaHSO_4 + HNO_3$$

$$2HNO_3 \longrightarrow H_2O + 2NO + 3[O]$$

$$6FeSO_4 + 3H_2SO_4 + 3[O] \longrightarrow 3Fe_2(SO_4)_3 + 3H_2O$$

$$FeSO_4 + 5H_2O + NO \longrightarrow \underset{(R)}{[Fe(H_2O)_5NO]SO_4}$$

$$NH_4NO_3 \xrightarrow{\Delta} \underset{(S)}{N_2O} + \underset{(T)}{2H_2O}$$

$$N_2O + H_2O \longrightarrow H_2N_2O_2$$

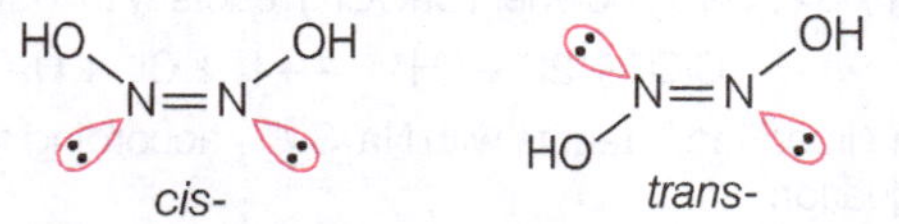

cis- *trans-*

Number of oxygen atoms in *X*, *Q*, *R* and *S*

$$= 3 + 0 + 10 + (2)2 = 17$$

22. ***(6)*** $\underset{(X)}{NH_4NO_3(aq.)} + KOH \longrightarrow KNO_3(aq.) + \underset{(Y)}{NH_3(g)} + H_2O(l)$

$NH_3(g)$ turns red litmus blue.

$$4Zn(s) + KNO_3(aq.) + 7KOH(aq.) \longrightarrow 4K_2ZnO_2(s) + \underset{(Y)}{NH_3(g)} + 2H_2O(l)$$

$$\underset{(X)}{NH_4NO_3(s)} \xrightarrow{300°C} N_2(g) + \underset{\text{(supports combustion)}}{\frac{1}{2}O_2(g)} + 2H_2O(g)$$

The number of N and O atoms in the compounds (*X*) and (*Y*) $= 5 + 1 = 6$

23. ***(13)*** $\underset{(A)}{2SO_2} + Na_2CO_3 + H_2O \longrightarrow \underset{(B)}{2NaHSO_3} + \underset{(C)}{CO_2}$

$$\underset{(B)}{2NaHSO_3} + Na_2CO_3 \longrightarrow \underset{(D)}{2Na_2SO_3} + \underset{(C)}{CO_2} + H_2O$$

$$\underset{(D)}{Na_2SO_3} + S \xrightarrow{\Delta} \underset{(E)}{Na_2S_2O_3}$$

The number of oxygen atoms in *A*(gas), *B*, *C*(gas), *D* and

$$E = 2 + 3 + 2 + 3 + 3 = 13$$

24. ***(3)*** $TeF_6 + 6H_2O \longrightarrow 6HF + H_6TeO_6$

HF is a weak monobasic acid while H_6TeO_6 is a weak dibasic acid and forms two series of salts $NaTeO(OH)_5$ and $Na_2TeO_2(OH)_4$.

25. ***(a)*** The correct match is

A-II, B-III, C-IV, D-I

$$P_4 + 3NaOH \longrightarrow 3NaH_2PO_2PH_3 + 3H_2O$$

$$2P\,(\text{red}) + 4NaOCl + 2H_2O \longrightarrow H_4P_2O_6 + 4NaCl$$

*Meta*phosphoric acid exists in polymeric form only and is formed from the reaction between phosphorous acid and Br_2 by heating in a sealed tube.

Pyrophosphorous acid has 4 P—OH and one P—O—P bond.

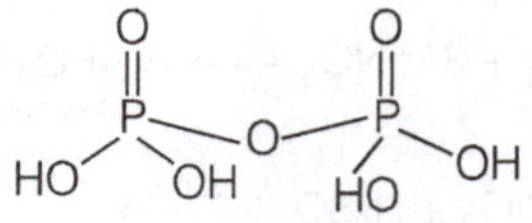

26. ***(a)*** The correct match is

A-II, B-I, C-IV, D-III

$$2KClO_3 \xrightarrow[MnO_2]{\Delta} 2KCl + 3O_2$$

Molecular oxygen is paramagnetic

$$Al_2O_3(s) + 6HCl(aq.) + 9H_2O(l) \longrightarrow 2[Al(H_2O)_6]^{3+}(aq.) + 6Cl^-(aq.)$$

Octahedral complex $[Al(H_2O)_6]^{3+}$ is formed.

Iodide ion reacts with ozone in water to form iodine, a violet compound.

$$2I^-(aq.) + H_2O(l) + O_3(g) \longrightarrow 2OH^-(aq.) + I_2(s) + O_2(g)$$

SO_2 converts iron (III) ions to iron (II) ions and decolourises acidified $KMnO_4$ solution.

$$5SO_2 + 2MnO_4^- + 2H_2O \longrightarrow 5SO_4^{2-} + 4H^+ + 2Mn^{2+}$$

The shape of SO_2 is angular. Its resonance hybrid has two canonical forms.

27. ***(c)*** The correct match is

A-(III), B-(II), C-(I), D-(IV)

$$2KMnO_4 + 16HCl \longrightarrow 2KCl + 2MnCl_2 + 8H_2O + 5Cl_2$$

Cl_2 reacts with dry slaked lime to form bleaching powder.

$$2Ca(OH)_2 + 2Cl_2 \longrightarrow Ca(OCl)_2 + CaCl_2 + 2H_2O$$

$$NaCl + H_2SO_4 \xrightarrow{420\text{ K}} NaHSO_4 + HCl$$

HCl is a colourless pungent smelling gas.

Pt is a noble metal which reacts with aqua regia to form octahedral complex.

$$3Pt + 16H^+ + 4HNO_3^- + 18Cl^- \longrightarrow 3PtCl_6^{2-} + 4NO + 8H_2O$$

$PtCl_6^{2-}$ is an octahedral complex.

Equal volumes of Cl_2 and F_2 at 437 K forms a colourless gas, ClF.

28. ***(d)*** The correct option is

A-(II), B-(I), C-(III), D-(IV)

$$Cl_2 + \underset{\text{(excess)}}{3F_2} \xrightarrow{573\text{ K}} 2ClF_3$$

ClF_3 is a colourless gas with bent T-shaped structure.

$$\underset{\text{(equimolar)}}{I_2 + Cl_2} \longrightarrow \underset{\text{(ruby red solid in }\alpha\text{-form)}}{2ICl}$$

$$I_2 + \underset{\text{(excess)}}{3Cl_2} \longrightarrow \underset{\text{(orange solid which dimerises to } I_2Cl_6)}{2ICl_3}$$

$$Br_2 + \underset{\text{(excess)}}{5F_2} \longrightarrow \underset{\text{(colourless liquid with square pyramidal shape)}}{2BrF_5}$$

29. ***(d)*** $2NaNO_2 + 2FeSO_4 + 3H_2SO_4 \longrightarrow Fe_2(SO_4)_3 + 2NaHSO_4 + 2H_2O + 2NO$

NO is a colourless neutral gas.

$$2NO + N_2O_4 \xrightarrow{250\text{ K}} 2N_2O_3$$

N_2O_3 is a blue solid which is acidic in nature.

$$2Pb(NO_3)_2 \xrightarrow{673\text{ K}} 4NO_2 + 2PbO + O_2$$

NO_2 is a brown gas which is acidic in nature.

$$4HNO_3 + P_4O_{10} \longrightarrow 4HPO_3 + 2N_2O_5$$

N is N_2O_5 is in +5 oxidation state.

Correct option is (d)

A-II, B-III, C-I, D-IV

30. ***(a)*** The correct option is

A-(II), B-(I), C-(IV), D-(III)

$$\underset{\text{(1 : 5 ratio)}}{Xe\,(g) + 2F_2(g)} \xrightarrow{873\text{ K, 7 bar}} XeF_4$$

XeF_4 is sp^3d^2 hybridised and square planar.

$$XeF_6 + H_2O \longrightarrow XeOF_4 + 2HF$$

$XeOF_4$ is square pyramidal in shape.

$$6XeF_4 + 12H_2O \longrightarrow 4Xe + \underset{sp^3\text{ hybridised}}{2XeO_3} + 24HF + 3O_2$$

$$XeF_6 + 2H_2O \longrightarrow \underset{\textit{see-saw}}{XeO_2F_2} + 2HF$$

31. **(2)** Among the given compounds only two i.e., $(NH_4)_2Cr_2O_7$ and $Ba(N_3)_2$ generates N_2 on thermal decomposition below 300°C.

32. **(3)** The structure of the given oxides are as

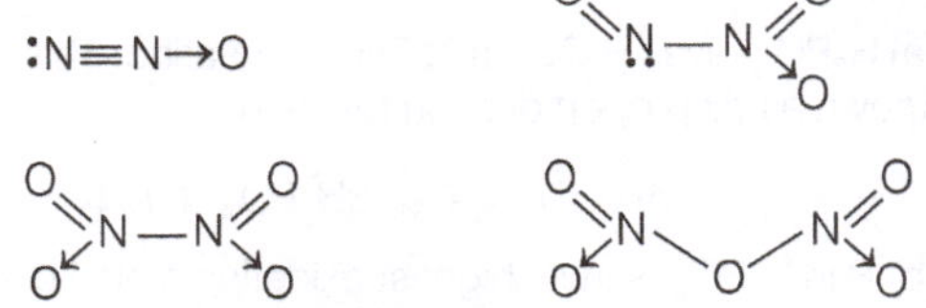

Thus, only three have N—N bonds.

33. ***(b)*** The reaction sequence involved is as follows

$$2FClO_2 + 2HONO_2 \longrightarrow 2HF + 2ClO_2 + N_2O_5 + \frac{1}{2}O_2$$

34. ***(+4)*** $FClO_2 + HCl \longrightarrow HF + ClO_2 + \frac{1}{2}Cl_2$

$ClO_2 : x + 2(-2) = 0$

$x - 4 = 0$

$x = +4$

35. ***(3)*** Among the given compounds only $XeOF_4$, XeO_2F_2 and XeO_3F_2 have one lone pair of electron at the central atom Xe while $XeOF_2$ have two and XeO_2F_4 have zero lone pair of electrons.

36. ***(6)*** $2XeF_6 + SiO_2 \longrightarrow 2XeOF_4 + SiF_4$

$\overset{x}{Xe}\overset{-2}{O}\overset{-1}{F_4}$

$$x + (-2) + 4(-1) = 0 \Rightarrow x = +6$$

37. ***(c)*** From the given reactions all 5 will produce $POCl_3$, balanced reactions are

$$PCl_3 + O_2 \longrightarrow POCl_3$$
$$P_4O_{10} + NaCl \longrightarrow POCl_3 + NaPO_3$$
$$PCl_5 + CH_3COOH \longrightarrow CH_3COCl + POCl_3$$
$$PCl_5 + SO_2 \longrightarrow SOCl_2 + POCl_3$$
$$PCl_3 + H_3BO_3 \longrightarrow POCl_3 + B_2O_3$$

38. ***(a)*** From the given compounds only 2 produce oxide of nitrogen, balanced chemical reactions are given below.

$$(NH_4)_2Cr_2O_7 \xrightarrow{\Delta} Cr_2O_3 + N_2 + 4H_2O$$
$$(NH_4)_2HPO_4 \xrightarrow{\Delta} 2NH_3 + H_3PO_4$$
$$NH_4NO_2 \xrightarrow{\Delta} N_2 + 2H_2O$$
$$NH_4NO_3 \xrightarrow{\Delta} N_2O + 2H_2O$$
$$Pb(NO_3)_2 \xrightarrow{\Delta} 2PbO + 4NO_2 + O_2$$

39. ***(d)*** From the given compounds only 4 compounds will react with $NaPO_3$. Chemical reactions are given below.

$$CaCl_2 + NaPO_3 \longrightarrow [Ca(P_3O_9)_2]^{4-} \text{ (forms chelate)}$$
$$\text{Dry } HCl + NaPO_3 \longrightarrow \text{No reaction}$$
$$MgSO_4 + NaPO_3 \longrightarrow [Mg(P_3O_9)_2]^{4-} \text{ (forms chelate)}$$
$$CaO + NaPO_3 \longrightarrow NaCaPO_4$$
$$Na_2CO_3 + NaPO_3 \longrightarrow Na_3PO_4 + CO_2$$

40. ***(c)*** Compounds which are possible to form are given in balanced chemical reaction

$$Cl_2 + H_2O + Na_2S_2O_3 \longrightarrow 2HCl + S + Na_2SO_4$$

41. ***(d)*** From the given compounds *M*—*M* bond is present in only 4, explanation is given below.

$$Mg_2C_3 \rightleftharpoons Mg^{2+} + 3C^{2-}$$

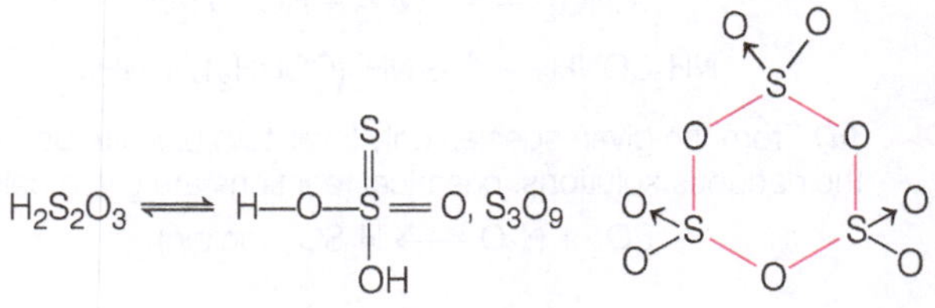

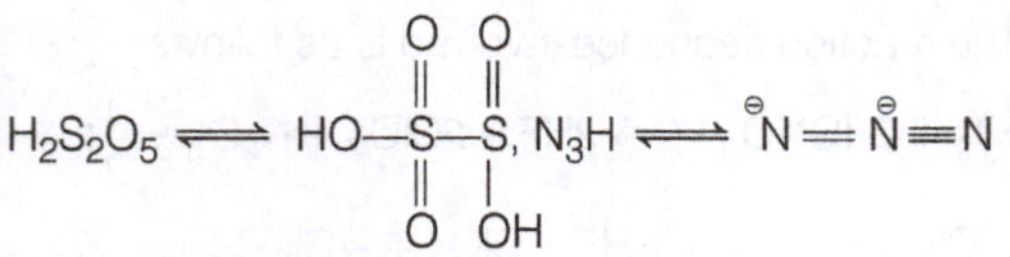

$Ca_3P_2 \rightleftharpoons 3Ca^{2+} + 2P^{3-}$, CaC_2

$$\rightleftharpoons Ca^{2+} + C^{2-}\ (^{-}C{\equiv}C^{-})$$

42. ***(b)*** From the given compounds only 2 have peroxy linkage in their structure, all structures are—

$H_2S_2O_3$

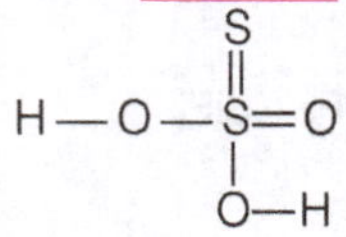

$H_2S_2O_5$

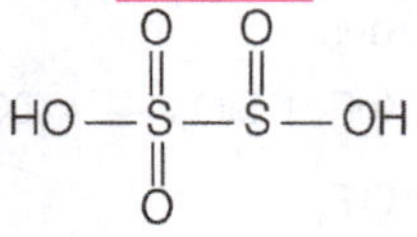

S_3O_9

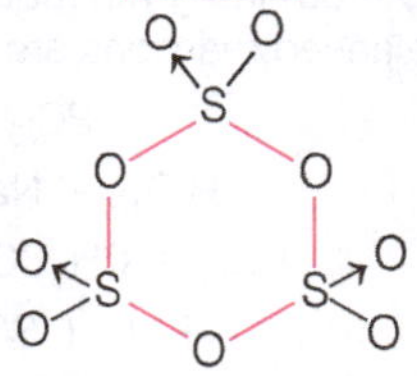

H_2SO_5

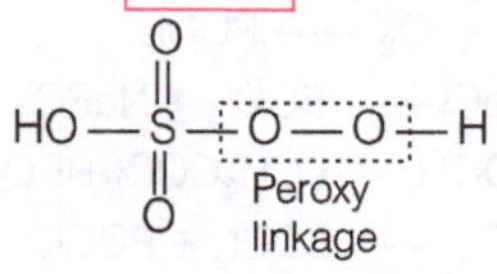

$H_2S_2O_7$

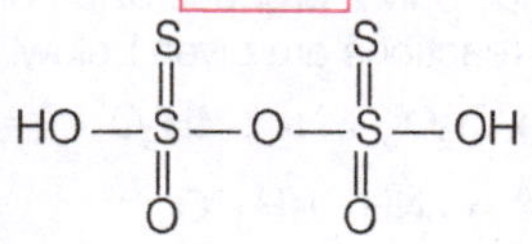

$H_2S_2O_8$

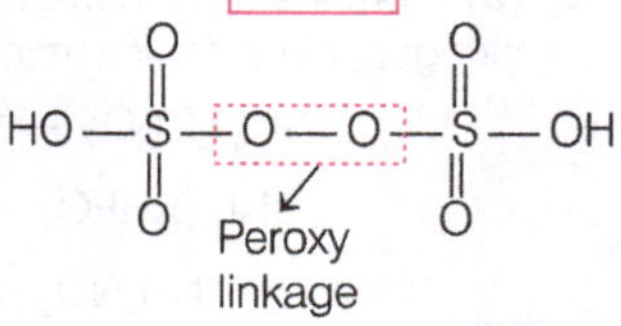

$H_2S_4O_6$

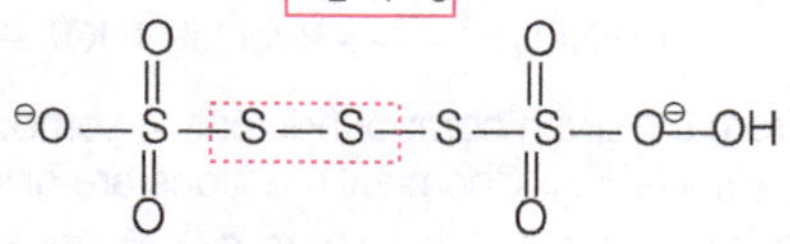

43. ***(a)*** From the given compounds, only 3 compounds will produce N_2 gas on heating, chemical reactions are given below

$$NH_4NO_3 \xrightarrow{\Delta} N_2O + 2H_2O$$

$$\xrightarrow{\text{Rapid heating}} 2NH_2 + O_2 + 4H_2O$$

$$Ba(N_3)_2 \xrightarrow{\Delta} Ba + 3N_2\uparrow$$

$$Mg_3N_2 \xrightarrow{\Delta} 3Mg + N_2\uparrow$$

$$(NH_4)_2Cr_2O_7 \xrightarrow{\Delta} N_2\uparrow + Cr_2O_3 + 4H_2O$$

$$4HNO_3 \xrightarrow{\Delta} 4NO_2 + O_2 + 2H_2O$$

$$HNO_2 \xrightarrow{\Delta} NO_2 + NO + H_2O$$

$$NH_2CONH_2 \xrightarrow{\Delta} NH_2(CONH_2)_2 + NH_3$$

44. ***(a)*** From the given species only 5 will turn blue litmus red in their aquous solutions, chemical reactions are given below

$$SO_3 + H_2O \longrightarrow H_2SO_4 \text{ (acidic)},$$

$N_2O \rightarrow$ neutral

$$PCl_3 + H_2O \longrightarrow H_3PO_3 \text{ (acidic)},$$

$SF_6 \rightarrow$ Inert with water

$$AsCl_3 + H_2O \longrightarrow H_3AsO_3 \text{ (acidic)}$$

$$SO_2 + H_2O \longrightarrow H_2SO_3 \text{ (acidic)}$$

$$NO_2Cl + H_2O \longrightarrow HNO_3 + HCl$$

Check Through PYQs : JEE Advanced

1. ***(a)*** The disproportionation reaction of an aqueous solution of in *situ* generated nitrous acid (HNO_2) is as follows

$$3HNO_2(aq.) \longrightarrow 2NO + NO_3^- + H_3O^+$$

Thus, the species generated are H_3O^+, NO_3^- and NO.

2. ***(b)*** Fluorination of phosphorus pentachloride in a polar organic solvent give ionic isomers which are as follows.

$[PCl_4]^+[PCl_4F_2]^- \Rightarrow$ Colourless crystal

$[PCl_4]^+[PF_6]^- \Rightarrow$ White crystal

3. ***(b)*** $H_3\overset{+5}{P}O_4 > H_4\overset{+4}{P_2}O_6 > H_3\overset{+3}{P}O_3 > H_3\overset{+1}{P}O_2$

4. ***(b,d)*** P_4O_{10} is a dehydrating agent and converts HNO_3 into N_2O_5

$$2HNO_3 \longrightarrow N_2O_5 + H_2O$$

$$P_4O_{10} + 6H_2O \longrightarrow 4H_3PO_4$$

(a) $P_4 + 20HNO_3 \longrightarrow 4H_3PO_4 + 20NO_2 + 4H_2O$

Thus, (a) is incorrect.

(b) N_2O_5 has no unpaired electron and thus, diamagnetic in nature.

(c)

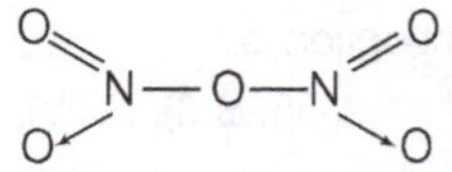

There is no N—N bond, thus, (c) is incorrect.

(d) $N_2O_5 + Na \longrightarrow NaNO_3 + NO_2$

NO_2 vapours are of brownish colour. Thus, (d) is correct.

5. ***(a,d)*** Galena is an ore of Pb. It reacts with HNO_3 to produce NO gas.

$$PbS(s) + \text{dil. } HNO_3(aq) \longrightarrow Pb(NO_3)_2(aq) + S(s) + NO(g) + H_2O(l)$$

NO contains 7 + 8 = 15 electrons. So, it is paramagnetic in nature as electrons are unpaired. NO is a colourless, neutral oxide of nitrogen. Also it is linear as it contains only 2 atoms.

Hence, (a) and (d) are correct.

6. ***(a,b,d)***

(a) H_3PO_3 gives H_3PO_4 and PH_3 on heating. This reaction is known as disproportionation reaction.

$$4H_3PO_3 \xrightarrow{\Delta} 3H_3PO_4 + PH_3$$

(b) P in H_3PO_4 is in its highest oxidation state i.e., + 5 hence, it cannot act as reducing agent. But P in H_3PO_3 is in oxidation state, +3 hence, it can act as reducing agent.

(c) H_3PO_3 contains two — OH groups, hence it is a dibasic acid.

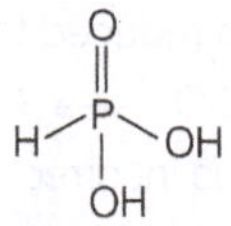

(d)Hydrogen attached to P in H_3PO_3, does not ionise in water. Therefore, options (a), (b) and (d) are correct.

7. ***(b, c)*** Among the given compounds, those which generate N_2 on thermal decomposition below 300°C are ammonium dichromate i.e., $(NH_4)_2Cr_2O_7$ and barium azide or nitride i.e., $Ba(N_3)_2$. Reactions of their thermal decomposition are given below

(i) $(NH_4)_2Cr_2O_7 \xrightarrow[\text{Below } 300°C]{\Delta} N_2\uparrow + Cr_2O_3 + 4H_2O$

(ii) $Ba(N_3)_2 \xrightarrow[\text{Around } 160° \text{ and above}]{\Delta} Ba + 3N_2\uparrow$

Ammonium nitrate (NH_4NO_3) on heating below 300°C gives N_2O

$$NH_4NO_3 \xrightarrow[\text{below } 300°C]{\Delta} N_2O + 2H_2O$$

However, on rapid heating or explosion (i.e. above 300°C) it gives off nitrogen as

$$2NH_4NO_3 \xrightarrow[\text{or explosion}]{\text{Rapid heating}} 2N_2 + O_2 + 4H_2O$$

Magnesium nitride (Mg_3N_2) does not decompose at lower temperatures being comparatively more stable. Its thermal decomposition requires a minimum temperature of 700°C and proceeds as

$$Mg_3N_2 \xrightarrow{700\text{–}1500°C} 3Mg + N_2\uparrow$$

8. ***(a,b,c)*** Statement wise explanation is

Statement (a) Bi_2O_5 is a metallic oxide while N_2O_5 is a non-metallic oxide.

Metallic oxides being **ionic** are **basic in nature** while non metallic oxides being **covalent** are **acidic in nature**. This confirms more basic nature of Bi_2O_5 in comparison to N_2O_5.

Hence, this is a correct statement.

Statement (b) The electronegativity difference between N(3) and F(4) is less as compared to the electronegativity difference between Bi (1.7) and F(4). More electronegativity difference leads to ionic compounds. Thus, NF_3 must be more covalent in nature as compared to BiF_3. Hence, this statement is also correct.

Statement (c) In NH_3 intermolecular hydrogen bonding is present, which is absent in PH_3. Thus, PH_3 boils at lower temperature than NH_3.Hence, this is also a correct statement.

Statement (d) Due to smaller size of N the lone pair-lone pair repulsion is more in N—N single bond as compared to P—P single bond. This results to weaker N—N single bond as compared to P—P single bond. Hence, this statement is incorrect.

9. ***(d)*** The correct match is

P-2; Q-3; R-4; S-5

(P) $P_2O_3 + 3H_2O \longrightarrow 2H_3PO_3$

(Q) $P_4 + 3NaOH + 3H_2O \longrightarrow PH_3 + 3NaH_2PO_2$

(R) $PCl_5 + CH_3COOH \longrightarrow CH_3COCl + POCl_3 + HCl$

(S) $H_3PO_2 + 2H_2O + 4AgNO_3 \longrightarrow H_3PO_4 + 4Ag\downarrow + 4HNO_3$

10. ***(a)*** $2KClO_3 \xrightarrow{MnO_2} 2KCl + 3O_2$

$P_4 + 5O_2 \longrightarrow P_4O_{10}$

11. ***(d)*** $P_4O_{10} + 4HNO_3 \longrightarrow 4HPO_3 + 2N_2O_5$

12. ***(b,d)*** The structures of given compounds are as follows:

$H_2S_2O_7$ 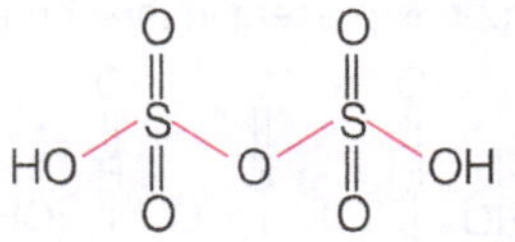

$H_2S_2O_8$ 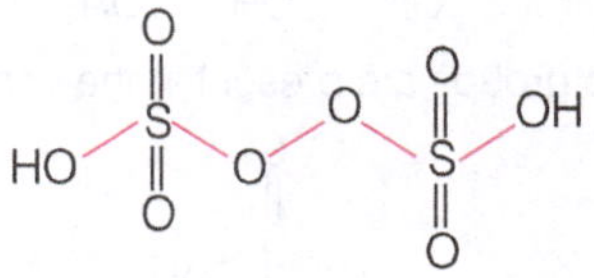

$H_2S_2O_5$ 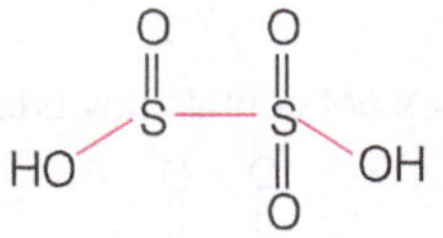

H_2SO_5 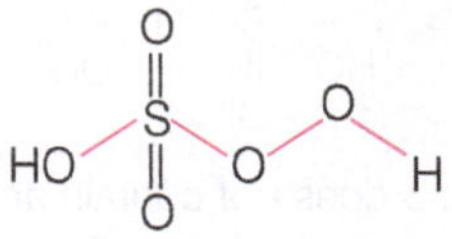

13. ***(6)*** The structures of various molecules given in problem are discussed below—

1. N_2O_3 It is the tautomeric mixture of following two structures—

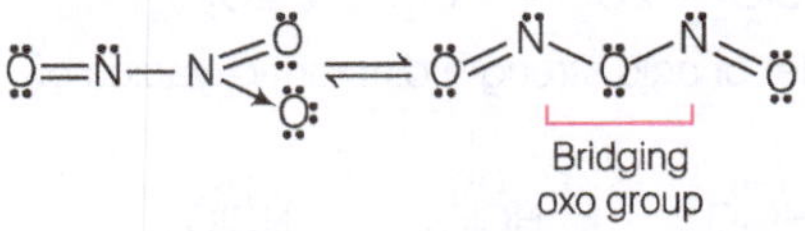

1 bridging oxo group is present in the compound.

2. N_2O_5 It has following structure.

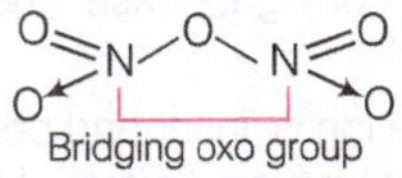

1 bridging oxo group is present in the compound.

3. P_4O_6

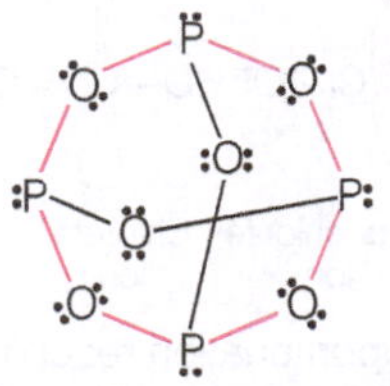

Conclusion 6 bridging oxo groups are present in the compound.

4. P_4O_7

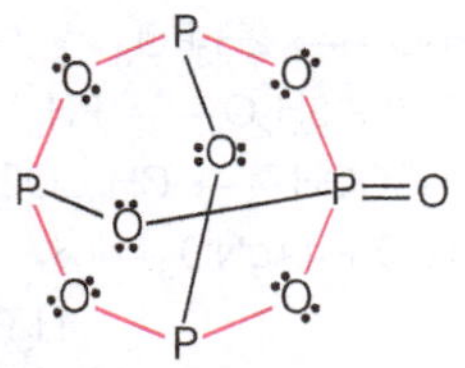

6 bridging oxo groups are present in the compound.

5. $H_4P_2O_5$

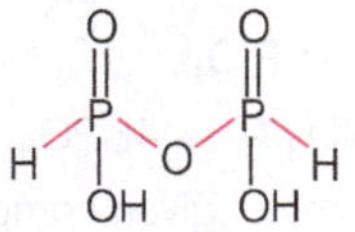

1 bridging oxo group is present in the compound.

6. $H_5P_3O_{10}$

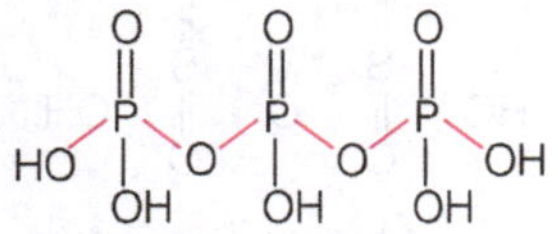

2 bridging oxo groups are present in the compound.

7. $H_2S_2O_3$

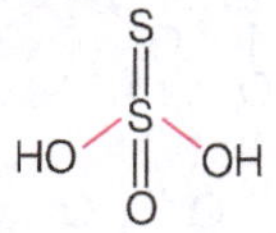

This compound does not contain any bridging oxo group.

8. $H_2S_2O_5$

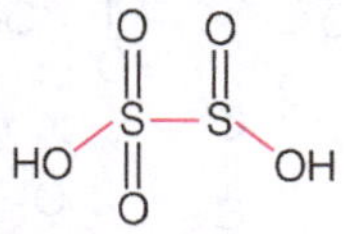

This compound also does not contain any bridging oxo group.

14. ***(c)*** The reaction is represented as

$$2HClO_3 + 2HCl \longrightarrow \underset{\text{(Paramagnetic)}}{2ClO_2} + Cl_2 + 2H_2O$$

$$2ClO_2 + 2O_3 \longrightarrow Cl_2O_6 + 2O_2$$

15. ***(a,b,d)*** (a) Order of acid strength different oxyacids of chlorine are :

$$\underset{\text{(Hypochlorous acid)}}{\overset{(+1)}{HClO}} < \underset{\text{(Chloric acid)}}{\overset{(+5)}{HClO_3}} < \underset{\text{(Perchloric acid)}}{\overset{(+7)}{HClO_4}}$$

Weak acid have strong conjugate base thus hypochlorite ion is strongest conjugate base. Therefore, statement (a) is correct.

(b) Hypochlorite ion is linear and perchlorate ion is tetrahedral and there is no effect of lone pair on hypochlorite ion. Thus statement (b) is correct.

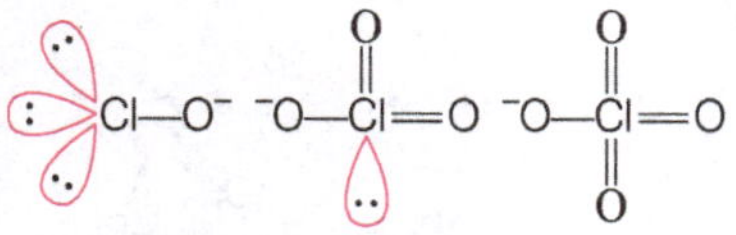

Hypochlorite ion | Chlorate ion | Perchlorate ion

(c) In the disproportionation reaction, chlorate ion Cl(+ 5) is oxidised to perchlorate, Cl(+ 7) and reduced to chloride, Cl (−1).

$$4ClO_3^- \longrightarrow 3\,ClO_4^- + Cl^-$$

While in hypochlorite ion, chlorite ion Cl (+ 1) is oxidised to chlorate, Cl (+ 5) and reduced to chloride, Cl(− 1) ion.

$$3ClO^- \longrightarrow ClO_3^- + 2\,Cl^-$$

Thus, statement (c) is incorrect.

(d)The hypochlorite ion oxidises the sulphite ion to sulphate ion, because HOCl is the strongest oxidising Cl oxoacid,

$$ClO^- + SO_3^{2-} \longrightarrow SO_4^{2-} + Cl^-$$

Thus, statement (d) is correct.

16. ***(a,d)*** Colour of halogen arises due to transition from HOMO to LUMO in the visible region. On moving down a group, the difference in energy between HOMO and LUMO decreases electronic transition occur more easily and colour intensity increases.

17. ***(a,c,d)*** The structure of HClO and $HClO_4$ are as follows.

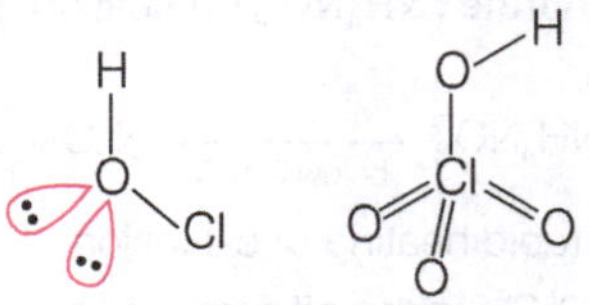

The central atom in both HClO and $HClO_4$ is sp^3.

Reaction of Cl_2 with H_2O gives HOCl which decomposes to give nascent oxygen.

$$Cl_2 + H_2O \longrightarrow [HCl + HOCl] \longrightarrow 2HCl + [O]$$

The conjugate base of $HClO_4$ is weaker base than H_2O.

$HClO_4$ is more acidic than HClO because of resonance stabilisation of its anion.

18. ***(b,c)***

Compounds	Hybridisation	Structures	Lone pair on central atom
BrF_5	sp^3d^2	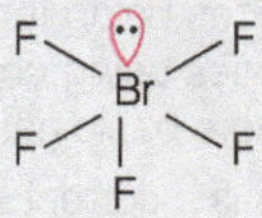	1
ClF_3	sp^3d	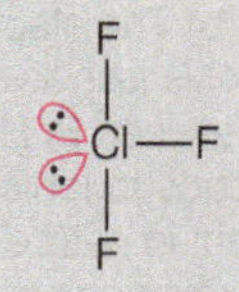	2
XeF_4	sp^3d^2	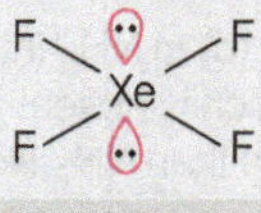	2
SF_4	sp^3d	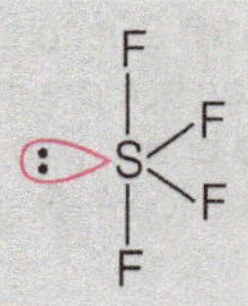	1

19. ***(4)*** The reaction of Xe with O_2F_2 gives XeF_4 as follows

$$Xe + 2\,O_2F_2 \longrightarrow \underset{(P)}{XeF_4} + 2\,O_2$$

Hydrolysis of XeF_4

$$\underset{(P)}{6XeF_4} + 12\,H_2O \longrightarrow 4\,Xe + 24HF + 2XeO_3 + 3O_2$$

6 moles of XeF_4 will give 24 moles of HF.

1 mole of XeF_4 will give $\frac{24}{6} = 4$ moles.

20. ***(19)*** XeF_4 reacts with O_2F_2 to form $XeF_6 \cdot O_2F_2$ is fluoronating reagent.

$$XeF_4 + O_2F_2 \xrightarrow{143\text{ K}} \underset{(Y)}{XeF_6} + O_2$$

The structore of XeF_6 is

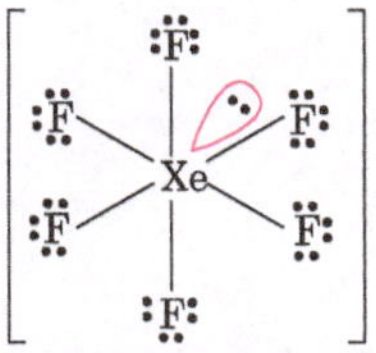

Y compound (XeF_6) has 3 lone pair in each fluorine and one lone pair in xenon.

Hence, total number of lone pairs electrons is 19.

21. ***(4)*** $N_2O, N_2O_4, H_2S_2O_3$ and $H_3S_2O_8$ molecules contains covalent bond of same kind between two atoms.

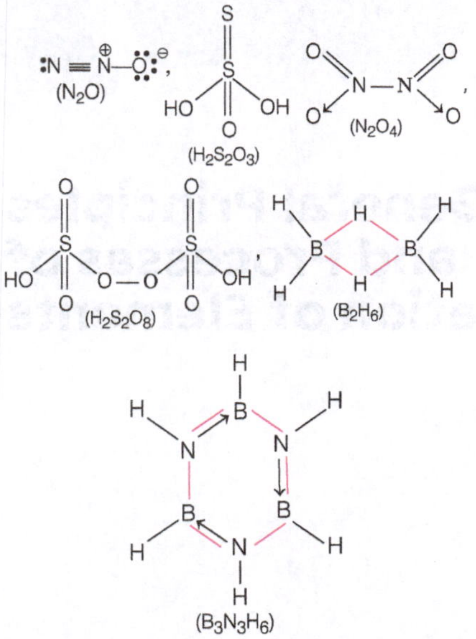

B_2H_6 and $B_3N_3H_6$ have polar bond, but do not have same kind of atom.

CHAPTER 7

General Principles and Processes of Isolation of Elements

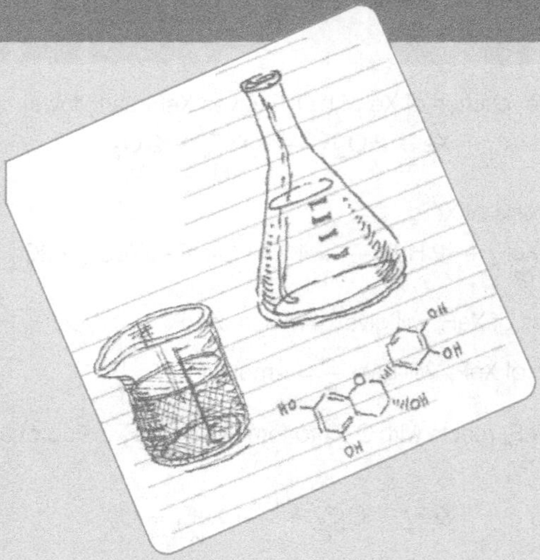

Learning Elements

Element 1 Metallurgy: General Principles
Modes of Occurence of Elements in Nature, Minerals, Ores and Matrix, Extraction of Metals-Metallurgy, Crushing and Grinding of the Ore, Principles Involved in the Extraction of Metals, Refining of Crude Metals.

Element 2 Thermodynamics of Metallurgy and Extraction of Metals
Thermodynamics of Metallurgy, Extraction of Aluminium, Extraction of Zinc, Extraction of Copper, Extraction of Iron, Extraction of Silver, Extraction of Mercury.

Practice Element

Practice Element Target JEE Advanced

Trend Insights

JEE Advanced

Typology	Years				
	2024	2023	2022	2021	2020
1. One option correct	–	–	–	–	–
2. One or More than one correct	–	1	3	1	1
3. Numerical/Integer Type	–	–	–	–	–
4. Matching Type	–	–	–	–	–
5. Paragraph Based	–	–	–	–	–

Current Dynamics
- This chapter is present only in the syllabus of JEE Advanced.
- Certain topics like name and formula of ores and minerals, Ellingham diagram, their applications, extraction and refining of metals were frequently asked in exam.

Insightful Advice
- Memorise the chemical reactions involved in roasting, smelting and leaching.
- Learn the composition, formula, properties and applications of ores, minerals and alloys like stainless steel, brass and bronze.
- Memorise the examples that are involved in various processes of extraction, refining and their flowcharts.

Element 1 Metallurgy : General Principles

Metals in their pure form are of great importance. These are utilised for the synthesis of several compounds, for making articles (as alloys) etc. However, most of the metals due to their high reactivity, are found in the combined form.
So, it is necessary to extract metal from its compound.
This module deals with the various principles and processes used during the extraction process.

Modes of Occurrence of Elements in Nature

Based on their reactivity, elements (metals) generally occur in nature in two forms, i.e.

(i) In native state
(ii) In combined state

Less reactive metals are found in **native state** (free state) in nature as nuggets, e.g. Ag, Au, Pt etc. Sometimes, Cu is also found in free state. Such metals are not attacked by O_2, H_2O, CO_2 etc.

Reactive metals are found in **combined state** in nature, e.g. of such metals include Na, Ca, Mg, Fe, Cu, Zn, Al etc. Such metals are attacked by O_2, H_2O, CO_2 etc.

Earth crust is a source of many elements. Oxygen is present in the most abundance in the earth crust. Among metals, Al is the most abundant metal of earth crust and Fe comes second. The percentage of different elements in the earth crust is O-49%; Si-26%; Al-7.5%; Fe-4.2%; Ca-3.2%; Na-2.4%; K-2.3%; Mg-.3%; H-1%; other elements-2%.

Besides earth crust, some soluble salts of metals, such as NaCl, $MgCl_2$, KBr, $MgBr_2$, KI etc., are also found in sea water. In earth crust metals are generally not found as their nitrates because of their high solubility in water.

Minerals, Ores and Matrix

The natural material in the form of which the metal is found in nature is called **mineral** and those minerals from which a metal can be extracted conveniently, economically and in large quantity are called **ores**.

All the ores are minerals but all the minerals are not ores.

Common ores/minerals of some important metals are given as follows

Metal	Ore/Mineral	Formula
Li	Spodumene	$LiAlSi_2O_6$
Na	Common salt	NaCl (rock salt)
	Chile salt petre	$NaNO_3$
	Glauberite	$Na_2SO_4 \cdot 10H_2O$ (Glauber's salt)
	Borax	$Na_2B_4O_7 \cdot 10H_2O$
	Trona	$Na_2CO_3 \cdot NaHCO_3 \cdot 2H_2O$
	Soda ash	Na_2CO_3
	Feldspar	$NaAlSi_3O_8$
K	Sylvine	KCl
	Nitre	KNO_3 (salt petre)
	Schonite	$K_2SO_4 \cdot MgSO_4 \cdot 6H_2O$
Mg	Magnesite	$MgCO_3$
	Dolomite	$MgCO_3 \cdot CaCO_3$
	Carnallite	$KCl \cdot MgCl_2 \cdot 6H_2O$
	Epsom salt	$MgSO_4 \cdot 7H_2O$
	Asbestos	$CaMg_3(SiO_3)_4$
	Talc	$Mg_2(Si_2O_5)_2Mg(OH)_2$
Ca	Gypsum	$CaSO_4 \cdot 2H_2O$
	Limestone	$CaCO_3$
	Phosphorite	$Ca_3(PO_4)_2$
	Fluorspar	CaF_2
Al	Bauxite	$Al_2O_3 \cdot 2H_2O$
	Diaspore	$Al_2O_3 \cdot H_2O$
	Corundum	Al_2O_3
	Cryolite	Na_3AlF_6
	Kaolinite	$Al_2O_3 \cdot 2SiO_2 \cdot 2H_2O$
	Mica	$K_2O \cdot 3Al_2O_3 \cdot 6SiO_2 \cdot 2H_2O$

JEE Quicker

01 Galena on treatment with HNO_3 produces nitric oxide gas which is paramagnetic in nature. *JEE Advanced 2022*

$3PbS + 8HNO_3 \longrightarrow 3Pb(NO_3)_2 + 3S\downarrow + 2NO\uparrow + 4H_2O$
Nitric oxide (NO) is a colourless, neutral and paramagnetic gas with linear geometry.

Metal	Ore/Mineral	Formula
Sn	Cassiterite	SnO_2 (tin stone)
Pb	Galena	PbS
	Cerussite	$PbCO_3$
	Anglesite	$PbSO_4$
	Lanarkite	$PbO \cdot PbSO_4$
Cu	Chalcopyrite	$CuFeS_2$ (copper pyrites)
	Chalcocite	Cu_2S (copper glance)
	Cuperite	Cu_2O (rubby copper)
	Azurite	$2CuCO_3 \cdot Cu(OH)_2$
	Malachite	$CuCO_3 \cdot Cu(OH)_2$
Ag	Argentite	Ag_2S (silver glance)
	Cerargyrite	AgCl (horn silver)
	Pyrargyrite	$Ag_2S \cdot Sb_2S_3$ (ruby silver)
Fe	Haematite	Fe_2O_3 (red haematite)
	Limonite	$Fe_2O_3 \cdot 3H_2O$ (brown haematite)
	Magnetite (lead stone)	Fe_3O_4 (magnetic oxide of iron)
	Siderite	$FeCO_3$
	Iron pyrite	FeS_2
Hg	Cinnabar	HgS
Zn	Zinc blende	ZnS (black zinc or sphalerite)
	Calamine	$ZnCO_3$
	Zincite	ZnO
	Willemite	Zn_2SiO_4
Mn	Pyrolusite	MnO_2
	Manganite	$Mn_2O_3 \cdot H_2O$
Cr	Chromite	$Cr_2O_3 \cdot FeO$

Metallic ores are often found to contain certain non-metallic rocky substances in them, e.g. sand, clay, quartz, feldspar, silicates, mica, etc. These unwanted impurities are called **gangue** or **matrix.** Thus, the waste material present in an ore is called **gangue.**

JEE MAPPER

Example Similar to PYQ Asked in JEE Advanced 2019

Epsom salt, fluorspar cryolite and cassiterite respectively are

(a) $MgCO_3 \cdot CaCO_3, CaSO_4 \cdot 2H_2O, Na_3AlF_6, Al_2O_3 \cdot H_2O$

(b) $KCl \cdot MgCl_2 \cdot 6H_2O, Ca_3(PO_4)_2, Al_2O_3, Na_3AlF_6$

(c) $MgSO_4 \cdot 7H_2O, CaF_2, Na_3AlF_6, SnO_2$

(d) $CaMg_3(SiO_3)_4 \cdot CaF_2, Al_2O_3 \cdot 2SiO_2 \cdot 2H_2O, SnO_2$

Sol. (c) $MgSO_4 \cdot 7H_2O$ — Epsom salt

CaF_2 — Fluorspar; Na_3AlF_6 — Cryolite

SnO_2 — Cassiterite

Thus, option (c) is correct.

Competency Enhancer 1.1

Cinnabar, pyrolusite, haematite and malachite, respectively are

(a) $FeS_2, ZnCO_3, Fe_2O_3 \cdot 3H_2O, C_4CO_3 \cdot Cu(OH)_2$

(b) HgS, $MnO_2, Fe_2O_3, CuCO_3 \cdot Cu(OH)_2$

(c) ZnS, $Mn_2O_3 \cdot H_2O, Fe_3O_4, Cu_2O$

(d) $Zn_2SiO_4, Cr_2O_3 \cdot FeO, Fe_2O_3, 2CuCO_3 \cdot Cu(OH)_2$

Extraction of Metals : Metallurgy

The process of extracting a metal in pure form from its ores is known as **metallurgy**. Metallurgical processes can be of following three types i.e. hydrometallurgy, pyrometallurgy and electrometallurgy.

(i) **Hydrometallurgy** The metal present in ore forms water soluble salt and comes in solution which is then recovered from the solution either by electrolysis or through precipitation by adding some suitable more electropositive metal in the solution. It is generally applicable for less reactive metals like AgBr or highly reactive metals like Al.

(ii) **Pyrometallurgy** Generally refers to the extraction through heat. Roasting, calcination, smelting etc., processes are included in it. Generally it is applicable for moderately active metals like Cu, Pb, Zn, Fe, etc.

(iii) **Electrometallurgy** Metal is generally extracted with the help of electrolysis. It is applicable for highly reactive metals like Na, K, Al, etc.

Steps Involved in Extraction of Metals

It is not possible to chalk out a universal scheme for the extraction of all metals since the extraction of each metal is an individual problem and the line of treatment depends upon the nature of the ore, impurities and the metal.

The various metallurgical operations used in the extraction of pure metals from their respective ores are given below

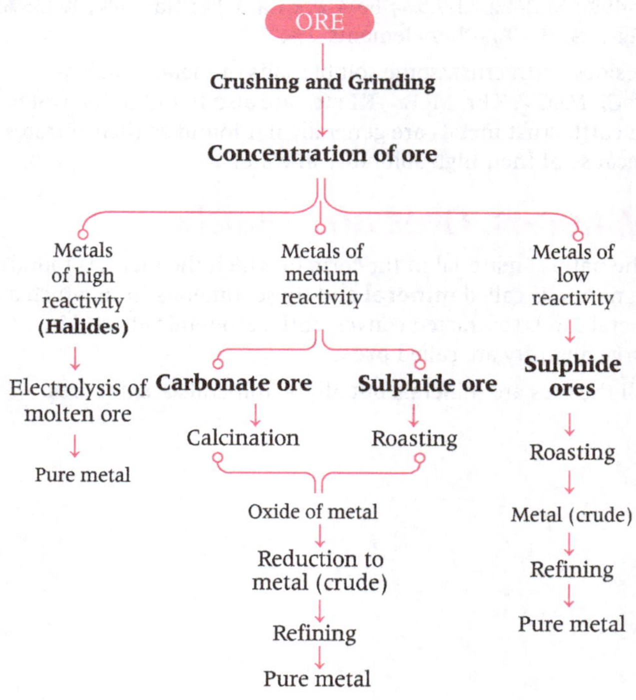

Crushing and Grinding of the Ore

Generally, ores occur in nature as huge lumps. They are crushed into small pieces in gyratory crushers. The crushed ore is then grinded with the help of rollers or in the stamp mill to powder form.

Concentration of the Ore

The process of gangue removal or increase in concentration of ore depends upon the nature of ore and the impurities present in it.

Some of the important methods involved in it are given below

1. Gravity Separation or Levigation

Principle This method is based on the difference in the specific gravity of the metallic ore and the impurity particles.

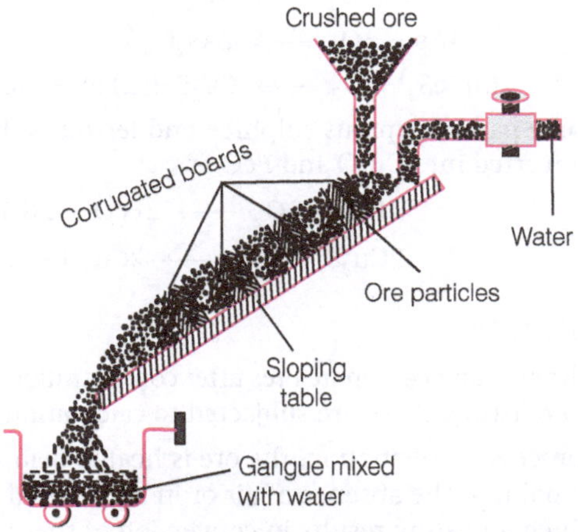

Concentration of ore by levigation

Process

In this method, the ore is powdered and then washed in a running stream of water. The lighter earthy material and gangue are washed away, while the heavy ore particles remain behind.

The oxide ores of iron i.e. Fe_2O_3 and Fe_3O_4 are concentrated by this method. This method is also called **levigation.**

2. Froth Floatation Process

Principle This method is based on the principle of difference in the wetting properties of the ore and gangue.

- Ore is preferentially wetted by oil.
- Gangue is preferentially wetted by water.

In this process, powdered ore is mixed with water containing collectors and froth stabilisers. The mineral particles become wet with oil while the gangue particles by water. A stream of hot compressed air is passed which agitates the mixture and produces froth.

Froth carries mineral particles. The froth is light and is skimmed off. It is then dried for recovery of ore particles.

Concept Visualizer

The details of various chemical substances which help in froth floatation process are given below

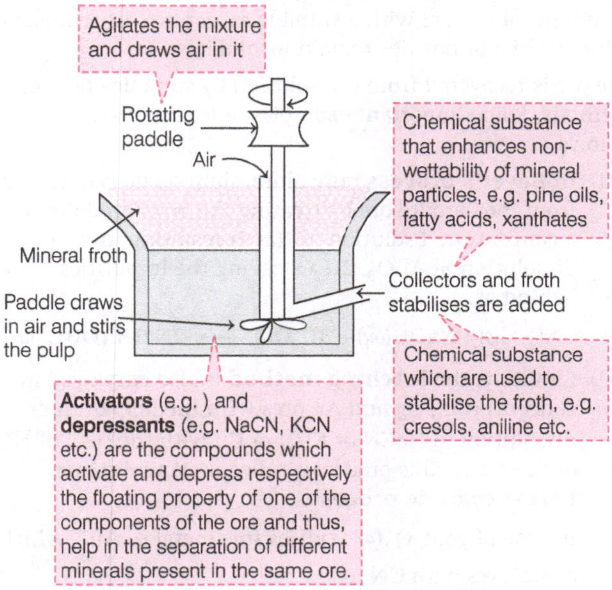

3. Magnetic Separation

Principle This process is based on the magnetic properties of the ore and the gangue. If the ore or the impurity is magnetic then this process is used to separate the magnetic substance from non-magnetic substance.

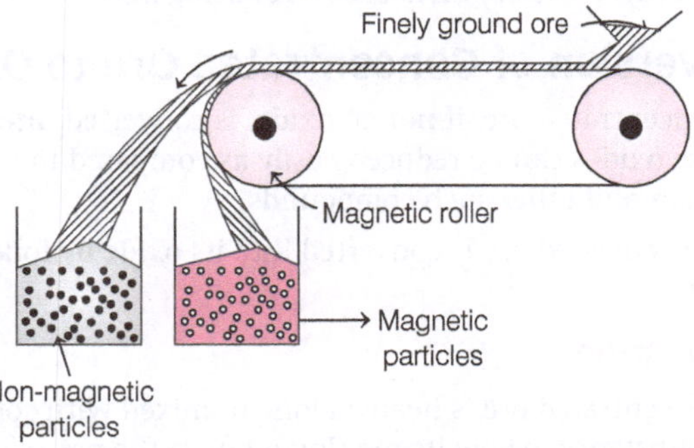

An electromagnetic separator, used to concentrate the ore

The ore is concentrated by a magnetic separator which consists of a leather belt moving over two rollers. One of the roller is magnetic. The method is useful for separating tungsten ore particles from cassiterite (SnO_2). The process may also be employed for separating other transition metal ores like magnetite (Fe_3O_4), chromite ($FeO \cdot Cr_2O_3$) and pyrolusite (MnO_2) from unwanted gangue.

4. Leaching

Principle This process is based on the difference in the chemical properties of ore and gangue. It involves the treatment of the ore with a suitable reagent, so as to make it soluble while impurities remain insoluble.

The ore is recovered from the solution by suitable chemical methods. Some important examples of leaching are as follows

(i) In **Bayer's process** pure aluminium oxide is obtained from the bauxite ore by treating the powdered ore with a concentrated solution of NaOH resulting in dissolution of $Al_2O_3 \cdot 2H_2O$ leaving the impurities behind as,

$$Al_2O_3(s) + NaOH(aq) + 3H_2O(l) \longrightarrow 2Na[Al(OH)_4](aq)$$

(ii) Similarly, the **leaching method** is also employed in concentrating Ag and Au ores with the help of their dissolution in NaCN or KCN or Cu with the help of H^+ or Fe scraps. This process is called as **Mac Arthur Forest cyanide process.**

In case of gold, $O_2(g)$ oxidises free metal to Au^+, which complexes with CN^-.

$$4Au(s) + 8CN^-(aq) + O_2(g) + 2H_2O(aq) \longrightarrow 4[Au(CN)_2]^-(aq) + 4OH^-(aq)$$

The pure metal is then displaced from the solution by active metal (as Zn).

$$2[Au(CN)_2]^-(aq) + Zn(s) \longrightarrow 2Au(s) + [Zn(CN)_4]^{2-}(aq)$$

In this reaction, Zn acts as a reducing agent.

Conversion of Concentrated Ore to Oxide

The concentrated ore, if not an oxide, is converted into oxide because oxides can be reduced easily as compared to sulphides and other such compounds.

The concentrated ore is converted into its oxide by following two ways

1. Roasting

The concentrated ore is heated alone or mixed with some other substance, below its melting point in the presence of air, resulting in oxidation of ore and impurities. This type of specialised heating of concentrated ore is called roasting. Usually the sulphide ores undergo roasting. In the process of roasting in general, normally the impurities like As and S are oxidised to volatile oxides like SO_2, As_2O_3 etc., and removed.

Some examples of roasting are

(i) In extraction of iron as

$$S + O_2 \longrightarrow SO_2\uparrow$$
$$4As + 3O_2 \longrightarrow 2As_2O_3\uparrow$$
$$4FeO + O_2 \longrightarrow 2Fe_2O_3$$

Here, sulphur and arsenic impurities are removed as volatile oxides due to roasting, while any ferrous oxide present is converted to ferric oxide.

(ii) Zinc blende (ZnS) is roasted to give ZnO in the extraction of Zn as

$$2ZnS + 3O_2 \longrightarrow 2ZnO + 2SO_2$$

(iii) On roasting, the copper ore chalcopyrite ($CuFeS_2$), the impurities S and As present in it are removed as volatile SO_2 and $As_2O_3 \cdot CuFeS_2$ is converted into cuprous sulphide and ferrous sulphide as

$$S + O_2 \longrightarrow SO_2\uparrow$$
$$4As + 3O_2 \longrightarrow 2As_2O_3\uparrow$$
$$2CuFeS_2 + O_2 \longrightarrow Cu_2S + 2FeS + SO_2$$

Some part of cuprous sulphide and ferrous sulphide is converted into Cu_2O and FeO as

$$2FeS + 3O_2 \longrightarrow 2FeO + 2SO_2\uparrow$$
$$2Cu_2S + 3O_2 \longrightarrow 2Cu_2O + 2SO_2\uparrow$$

2. Calcination

The hydroxide and carbonate ores after concentration does not undergo roasting, these are subjected to calcination instead.

In the process of calcination, the ore is heated below its melting point in the absence of air or in the limited supply of air. Such a heating results in conversion of these hydroxide and carbonate ores to metal oxides.

During calcination, the ore becomes porous, and volatile impurities are removed.

Some examples of calcination are given below

(i) Aluminium hydroxide is converted to alumina i.e.,

$$2Al(OH)_3 \xrightarrow{1500^\circ C} Al_2O_3 + 3H_2O$$

(ii) Limonite (iron ore) gives anhydrous ferric oxide i.e.,

$$Fe_2O_3 \cdot 3H_2O \xrightarrow{\Delta} Fe_2O_3 + 3H_2O$$

(iii) Siderite (iron ore) gives ferrous oxide i.e.,

$$FeCO_3 \xrightarrow{\Delta} FeO + CO_2$$

(iv) Calamine (zinc ore) gives zinc oxide i.e.,

$$ZnCO_3 \xrightarrow{\Delta} ZnO + CO_2$$

(v) $NaHCO_3$ gives Na_2CO_3 while $CaCO_3$ gives CaO i.e.,

$$2NaHCO_3 \xrightarrow{\Delta} Na_2CO_3 + CO_2 + H_2O$$
$$CaCO_3 \xrightarrow{\Delta} CaO + CO_2$$

- Calcination proceeds with the expulsion of some small molecules like H_2O, CO_2, SO_2, etc., without any other chemical change while during roasting definite chemical changes like oxidation, chlorination etc., takes place.
- Calcination and roasting also make the mass porous, so that it can easily be reduced to the metallic state in the next operation.
- Calcination and roasting are carried out in various types of furnaces, most important of which is **reverberatory furnace.** The furnaces used in calcination and roasting employ refractory materials which resist high temperature and do not become soft.
- Refractory material should not combine with the ore or the metal and must be able to protect the furnace from high temperature.

Principles Involved in the Extraction of Metals

Extraction of metal from its ore depends upon thermodynamic as well as electrochemical principles, which are as follows.

Electrochemical Principles Involved in Extraction/Reduction of Oxide to Metal

Once the ore has been concentrated, it is reduced to free metal. Selection of the method employed for extracting the metal from its ore depends on the nature of the metal and that of the ore and may be related to the position of the metal in the electrochemical series.

In general, metals with standard reduction potential $E° < -1.5$ V yield compounds which are very difficult to reduce. On the other hand, noble metals with $E° > +0.5$ V form easily reducible compounds.

JEE Spotlite

- The elements which lie below hydrogen in the electrochemical series are expected to occur in the nature in native state.
- A reaction is spontaneous if reducing agent is present above oxidising agent in ECS.
- Zn and Mg can reduce Fe^{2+} to Fe (to prevent rust) by cathodic protection since both are present above Fe in ECS.

In general, a metal higher up in the electrochemical series should be more difficult to reduce to metallic form. However, this general statement cannot be strictly applied because metals are rarely extracted from aqueous solution. Some of the important method for reduction of roasted/calcined oxide are given below

1. Smelting

It is a process of extracting metals like Fe, Zn, Sn, Pb, Cr etc. The reducing agent usually work on the oxide to extract the metal, for e.g. in the extraction of iron. The mixture of oxide with carbon is heated in the presence of air at high temperature and this heating is called **smelting.**

2. Flux and Slag

Sometime oxide ores contain some infusible earthy impurities even after concentration. The impurities may be **basic** (i.e. metallic oxides like CaO, FeO, MgO etc.) or **acidic** (i.e. non-metallic oxides like SiO_2, P_2O_5, etc.). In order to remove acidic or basic impurities, the concentrated ore is mixed with additional substance, called the **flux.**

The flux combines with acidic or basic impurities present in the oxide ore and forms a fusible mass, called **slag.** Thus, the impurity is removed in the form of fusible slag as

$$\text{Flux} + \text{Impurity} \longrightarrow \text{Fusible slag}$$

The slag floats over the molten metal and can be removed from upper exit. Smelting is carried out in blast furnaces or reverberatory furnace.

Fluxes are of two types, i.e.

(i) **Acidic fluxes** Basic impurities are mixed with acidic fluxes such as silica (SiO_2) and borax, hence removing them as fusible slag. e.g.

$$SiO_2 + FeO \longrightarrow FeSiO_3$$
$$SiO_2 + CaO \longrightarrow CaSiO_3$$

(ii) **Basic fluxes** (such as limestone, magnesite, haematite) are added to remove acidic impurities like silica as fusible slag, e.g.

$$MgCO_3 + SiO_2 \longrightarrow MgSiO_3 + CO_2\uparrow$$
$$CaCO_3 + SiO_2 \longrightarrow CaSiO_3 + CO_2\uparrow$$

Reducing Agents and Processes Used in Smelting

Various reducing agents and processes used in smelting are as follows

1. Reduction by Carbon and Carbon Monoxide

In case of tin, the concentrated ore is mixed with one-fifth of its weight of powdered anthracite (carbon) and a little limestone, $CaCO_3$ and heated in a reverberatory furnace at 1200-1300°C.

The ore is reduced to metallic state while silica (impurity) is removed as slag.

$$SnO_2 + 2C \longrightarrow Sn + 2CO\uparrow$$

$$CaCO_3 \xrightarrow[-CO_2]{\Delta} CaO \xrightarrow{SiO_2} \underset{\substack{\text{Calcium silicate}\\ \text{(slag)}}}{CaSiO_3}$$

Excess of lime must be avoided because it would otherwise react with tin to form calcium stannate.

The molten metal collects on the bottom of the furnace. It contains 99.5% of metallic tin, called the **black tin.**

Carbon (as coal, coke, charcoal, CO etc.,) reduces many metal oxides into respective metals, such as

$$\underset{\text{Cassiterite}}{SnO_2} + 2C \xrightarrow{1473-1573\text{ K}} Sn + 2CO$$

$$ZnO + CO \xrightarrow{1600\text{ K}} Zn + CO_2$$

$$Fe_2O_3 + CO \xrightarrow{823\text{ K}} 2FeO + CO_2$$

$$FeO + CO \xrightarrow{1123\text{ K}} Fe + CO_2$$

JEE Alert

- Some ores are self-fluxing because they contain some gangue (stony matrix accompanying the ore) which is self fusible and thus, no foreign flux is required.
- Blast furnace is used in the reduction of iron oxides while reverberatory furnace is used in the reduction of tin oxide.

2. Reduction with Hydrogen

Hydrogen being inflammable is used as a reducing agent in very few cases, e.g.

$$MO_3 + 3H_2 \longrightarrow M + 3H_2O \quad (M = \text{Mo or W})$$

This method is not widely used, because many metals react with H_2 at elevated temperatures forming hydrides. Also there are chances of explosion of H_2 with O_2.

3. Gold Schmidt Aluminothermic Process

Chromium and manganese oxides are reduced through aluminothermic reduction processes or Goldschmidt aluminothermic process, e.g.

$$Cr_2O_3 + 2Al \longrightarrow Al_2O_3 + 2Cr$$

$$3Mn_3O_4 + 8Al \longrightarrow 4Al_2O_3 + 9Mn$$

In this process, mixture of the metallic oxide and reducing agent (aluminium powder), commonly known as **thermite** is taken in a steel crucible placed in a bed of sand. A mixture of aluminium powder and barium peroxide (BaO_2) is placed over the charge in the form of a heap and magnesium wire is embedded in it.

The charge is covered by a thick layer of carbon followed by a thin layer of feldspar to avoid loss of heat and to protect the mass from oxidation.

The magnesium ribbon, which acts as a fuse is lighted. It starts burning and hence, mixture also starts burning.

Since, the reaction is highly exothermic, once it starts, it goes on till all the oxide is converted into metal.

4. Reduction by Water Gas

It is applied for nickel oxide.

$$2NiO + (CO + H_2) \longrightarrow 2Ni + CO_2 + H_2O$$

5. Reduction with Other Metals

Na and Mg metals are used in certain cases as reducing agents, e.g.

$$TiO_2 + 2Mg \longrightarrow Ti + 2MgO$$

$$TiO_2 + 4Na \longrightarrow Ti + 2Na_2O$$

Auto-Reduction or Self Reduction

This method is used when no external reducing agent is required. The sulphide ores of less electropositive metals like Hg, Pb, Cu etc., are heated in air to either convert the complete ore or part of the ore into oxide or sulphate which then reacts with the remaining sulphide ore to give the metal and sulphur dioxide, e.g.

(i) **Extraction of Cu from copper glance**

$$2Cu_2S + 3O_2 \longrightarrow 2Cu_2O + 2SO_2$$

$$Cu_2S + 2Cu_2O \longrightarrow 6Cu + SO_2$$

(ii) **Extraction of Hg from cinnabar**

$$2HgS + 3O_2 \longrightarrow 2HgO + 2SO_2$$

$$2HgO \xrightarrow{\Delta} 2Hg + O_2$$

(iii) **Extraction of Pb from galena**

$$2PbS + 3O_2 \longrightarrow 2PbO + 2SO_2$$

$$2PbO + PbS \longrightarrow 3Pb + SO_2$$

Displacement Method

If the temperature needed for carbon to reduce an oxide is too high for economic or practical purpose, the reduction may be affected by another highly electropositive metal. In this process, more electropositive metal displaces less electropositive metal from salt solution.

e.g. Ag and Au are obtained from their complex cyanides (cyanide process) when more reactive Zn metal displaces them as,

$$2M(CN)_2^- + Zn \longrightarrow [Zn(CN)]_4^{2-} + 2M \quad (M = \text{Ag, Au})$$

Electrolytic Method

The oxides of highly electropositive metals of group 1 and 2 cannot be reduced easily with carbon at moderate temperatures. These metals are thus, extracted by the electrolysis of their salts (generally, oxides, hydroxides or chlorides in fused state).

The metal is deposited at the cathode. e.g. Sodium is obtained by the electrolysis of fused NaCl or brine.

$$NaCl \rightleftharpoons Na^+ + Cl^-$$

$$Na^+ + e^- \longrightarrow Na \quad \text{(at cathode)}$$

$$Cl^- \longrightarrow Cl + e^- \quad \text{(at anode)}$$

$$Cl + Cl \longrightarrow Cl_2$$

In the case of NaCl (brine solution), Hg electrodes are used so that Na metal after deposition at cathode forms amalgam with Hg.

JEE Alert

- Metals other than those of *s*-block can also be extracted by electrolysis of fused compounds, e.g. fused Al_2O_3 mixed with Na_3AlF_6 is used for the production of Al.
- Electrolysis can be carried out in solvents other than water. F_2 reacts violently with H_2O hence, it is produced by electrolysis of KHF_2 in HF (anhydrous).

Some Specific Reduction Processes

Metal	Compound (ore)	Reduction process
Mercury	HgS (cinnabar)	Reduction by roasting-heating of ore in air $HgS + O_2 \xrightarrow{\Delta} Hg + SO_2$
Copper	Sulphides such as Cu_2S (chalcocite)	Blowing of oxygen through purified molten Cu_2S $Cu_2S + O_2 \xrightarrow{\Delta} 2Cu + SO_2$
Zinc	ZnS (sphalerite)	Conversion to oxide and reduction with carbon $2ZnS + 3O_2 \xrightarrow{\Delta} 2ZnO + 2SO_2$ $ZnO + C \xrightarrow{\Delta} Zn + CO$
Iron	Fe_2O_3 (haematite)	Reduction with carbon monoxide $2C\text{ (coke)} + O_2 \xrightarrow{\Delta} 2CO$ $Fe_2O_3 + 3CO \xrightarrow{\Delta} 2Fe + 3CO_2$
Titanium	TiO_2 (rutile)	Conversion of oxide to halide salt and reduction with an active metal $TiO_2 + 2Cl_2 + 2C \xrightarrow{\Delta} TiCl_4 + 2CO$ $TiCl_4 + 2Mg \xrightarrow{\Delta} Ti + 2MgCl_2$
Aluminium	$Al_2O_3 \cdot nH_2O$	Electrolytic reduction (electrolysis) in molten cryolite. $Na_3[AlF_6]$ at 1000°C. $2Al_2O_3 \xrightarrow{\Delta} 4Al + 3O_2$
Sodium	NaCl (sea water)	Electrolysis of molten chlorides $2NaCl \xrightarrow{\Delta} 2Na + Cl_2$

Refining of Crude Metals

Metals extracted through any of the methods described above usually contains some impurities which needs to be purified.

Following methods are used to purify the metals

1. Distillation Method

This process is used for those metals which are easily volatile. In this method, the impure metal is heated in a retort and its vapours are separately condensed in a receiver. The non-volatile impurities are left behind in the retort. This is used for the purification of Zn, Cd, Hg, etc.

2. Liquation Method

Low melting metals can be separated by this method. In this method, the impure metal is poured on the sloping hearth of a reverberatory furnance and heated gently to a temperature slightly above the melting point of the metal.

The pure molten metal runs out leaving behind the infusible matter (called dross) on the hearth. This is used for the purification of Bi, Sn, Pb, Hg, etc.

The process of liquation is shown below

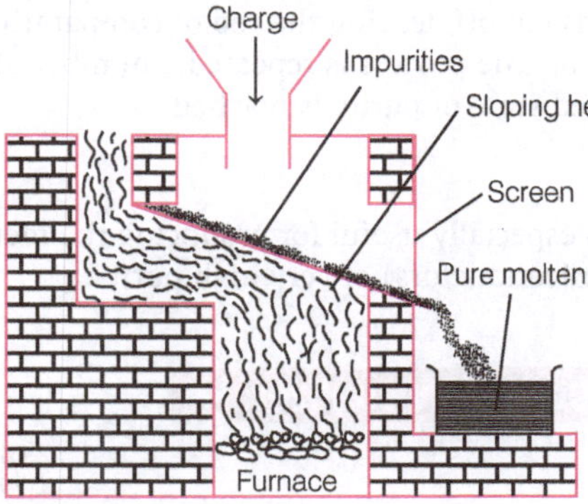

3. Electrolytic Method

Many metals such as Cu, Ag, Au, Al, Pb etc., are purified by this method. Here,

Anode $\longrightarrow$ impure metal
Cathode $\longrightarrow$ pure metal
Electrolyte $\longrightarrow$ salt of metal in aqueous solution

On passing electric current, pure metal deposits on cathode. The mass of anode dissolves in the form of salt and comes in the solution. The impurities either remain dissolved in solution or settled down as anode mud around anode.

The applied voltage here is such that more electropositive metals (impurity) remain as ions in the both whereas, the less electropositive metals (also impurities) remain unionised and fell down as anode mud.

(i) Electrorefining of Cu
Anode Blister copper (98%);
Cathode Pure copper
Electrolyte *Aq.* solution of $CuSO_4$ (15%) + 5% dil. H_2SO_4

(ii) Electrorefining of silver (Moebius process)
Anode Impure silver;
Cathode Pure silver
Electrolyte *Aq.* $AgNO_3$ + 1% dil. HNO_3.

(iii) Electrorefining of lead (Bett's process)
Anode Impure lead;
Cathode Pure lead
Electrolyte A mixture of $PbSiF_6$ and H_2SiF_6.

4. Zone-Refining Method

The method is based upon the principle that an impure molten metal on gradual cooling will deposit crystals of the pure metal while impurities will be left in remaining part of molten metal.

In this process, the impure metal is taken in the form of rod and a circular heater is fitted around this rod, which is slowly moved along the length of the rod. As the heater moved, the molten impurities also moved along with the heater while the pure metal recrystallises without leaving its position.

Lastly, the end of rod, where the impurities finally get concentrated is cut off, leaving the rod of comparatively more pure metal. The process is repeated a number of times until the desired state of purity is reached.

Uses

The method is especially useful for producing the metals especially (semiconductors) of very high purity.

5. Poling

The impure metal containing its oxides as impurity can be purified by this method. The molten impure metal is stirred with green poles of wood.

The green poles of wood release the hydrocarbon gases which reduces the oxide impurities. This method is especially used in the purification of copper (old method).

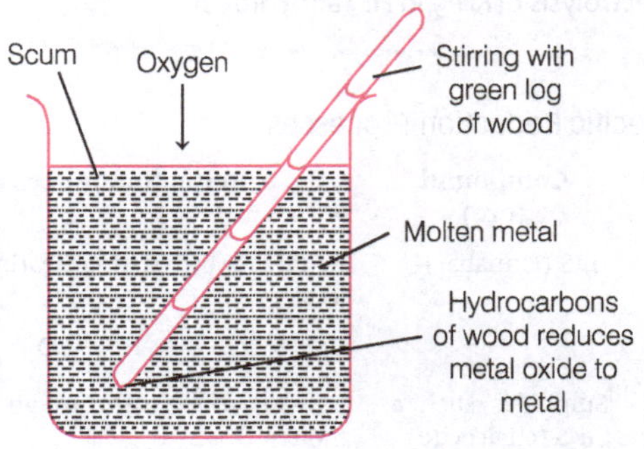

Refining of metal by poling

Concept Visualizer

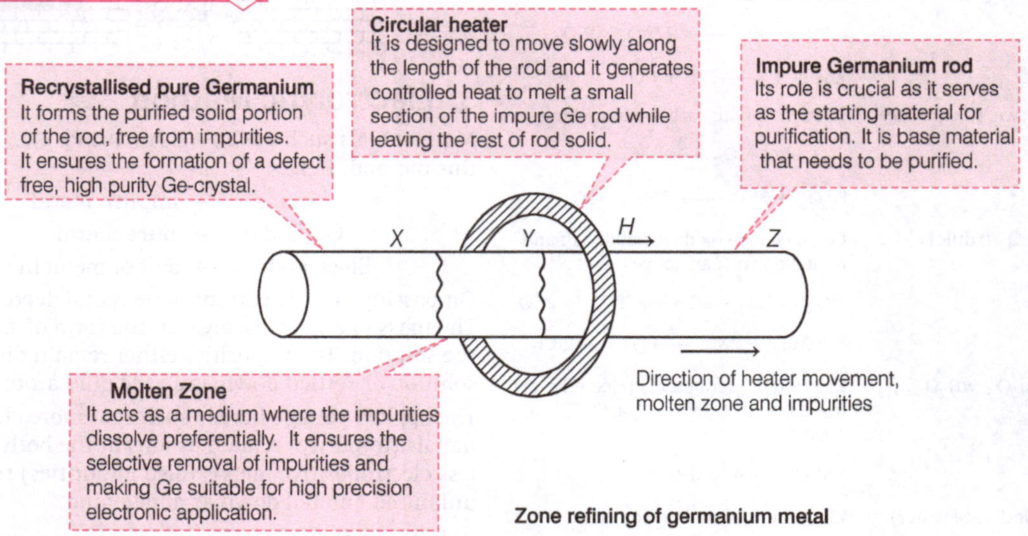

Zone refining of germanium metal

6. Vapour Phase Refining Method

Principle This method is based upon the principle that the impure metal is converted into suitable volatile compound which on being heated, gets decomposed to give pure metal.

Some important methods are as follows

(i) Mond process (also called carbonyl process)

(ii) van-Arkel method (also called iodine refining process)

The **Mond's process** is used for the purification of Ni. It is the most important process for getting 99.9% pure Ni metal from crude Ni.

In this process, the crude Ni is heated in the stream of CO to form volatile nickel carbonyl, $Ni(CO)_4$. This $Ni(CO)_4$ when heated at higher temperature, will decompose to give pure metal as

$$\underset{\text{Impure}}{Ni} + 4CO \xrightarrow{330\text{-}350\ K} Ni(CO)_4 \xrightarrow{450\text{ - }470\ K} \underset{\text{Pure}}{Ni} + 4CO$$

In the **van-Arkel method**, the impure metal is heated with iodine in a sealed vessel, so that the metal forms volatile metallic iodide and impurities do not react with iodine.

The metallic iodide is then decomposed when heated further at higher temperatures.

The metals purified through this way are Zr (zirconium), Ti (titanium), V (vanadium).

For example, purification of Ti through this method can be done as

$$\underset{\text{(Impure)}}{Ti} + 2I_2(g) \xrightarrow{150\text{-}250^\circ C} TiI_4(g) \xrightarrow[\text{Tungsten filament}]{1400^\circ C} \underset{\text{Pure}}{Ti(s)} + 2I_2(g)$$

7. Amalgamation Process

This method is used for the extraction of noble metals like Ag, Au etc., from the native ores. The finely powdered ore is brought in contact with Hg, which combines with the particles of the metal present in the ore and form amalgam.

The metal is recovered from the amalgam by subjecting it to distillation, where the Hg distills over, leaving behind the metal.

8. Cupellation

This method is used when impure metal contains impurities of other metals which form volatile oxides, e.g. traces of lead ore is removed from silver (as volatile PbO) by this process.

9. Chromatography

This method is used when the elements are available only in minute quantities and the impurities are not very much different in their chemical behaviour from the element to be purified.

Adsorption chromatography is generally used. In this, the impure metal is dissolved in a suitable solvent and the solution is allowed to run slowly into an adsorbent column packed with alumina (Al_2O_3).

The metal and the impurities present are adsorbed at different rates. These are then eluted with suitable eluent (solvent). In this method, weakly adsorbed component is eluted first and the strongly adsorbed component is eluted afterwards.

Elemental Practice 7.1

Type I » MCQs with Only One Correct Option

1. The process of isolation of metals by dissolving the ore in an aqueous solution of a suitable chemical reagent followed by precipitation of the metal by a more electropositive metal is called
   (a) electrometallurgy (b) hydrometallurgy
   (c) electro refining (d) zone refining

2. Identify the incorrect statement.
   (a) The scientific and technological process used for isolation of the pure metal from its ore is known as metallurgy.
   (b) Minerals are naturally occurring chemical substances in the earth's crust.
   (c) Ores are the minerals that contain a metal.
   (d) Gangue is an ore contaminated with undesired materials.

3. The correct formula for copper pyrite ore is
   (a) $MgCO_3$ (b) $FeCO_3$ (c) FeS_2 (d) $CuFeS_2$

4. Which among the following is an ore of sulphate?
   (a) Smithstone (b) Realgar (c) Pyrolusite (d) Anglesite

5. Sulphide ores of metals are usually concentrated by froth floatation process. Which one of the following sulphide ores offers an exception and is concentrated by chemical leaching?
   (a) Argentite (b) Galena
   (c) Tennantite (d) Sphalerite

6. Cassiterite is an ore of
   (a) Mn (b) Ni (c) Sb (d) Sn

7. Cinnabar is an ore of
   (a) Hg (b) Cu (c) Pb (d) Zn

8 Choose the method that is used to extract metals that are low in reactivity.
   (a) Roasting (b) Electrolysis
   (c) Reduction by carbon (d) Cyanide leaching

9. Complex formed in the following methods are
   I. Mond's process for purification of nickel
   II. removal of lead poisoning form the body
   III. Cyanide process for extraction of silver
   IV. Froth floatation process for separation of ZnS from galena ore by using depressant

	I	II	III	IV
(a)	$Ni(CO)_4$	$[Pb(EDTA)]^{2-}$	$[Ag(CN)_2]^{\ominus}$	$[Zn(CN)_2]$
(b)	$Ni(CO)_4$	$[Pb(EDTA)]^{2-}$	$[Ag(CN)_2]^{\ominus}$	$[Zn(CN)_4]^{2-}$
(c)	$Ni(CO)_4$	$[Pb(EDTA)]^{3-}$	$[Ag(CN)_2]^{2-}$	$[Zn(CN)_6]^{4-}$
(d)	$Ni(CO)_4$	$[Pb(EDTA)]^{3-}$	$[Ag(CN)_2]^{\ominus}$	$[Zn(CN)_2]^{2-}$

10. Match List-I with List-II.

	List-I (Ores)		**List-II** (Composition)
(A)	Haematite	(i)	$Al_2O_3 \cdot H_2O$
(B)	Diaspore	(ii)	Ag_3SbS_4
(C)	Stefinite	(iii)	Fe_2O_3
(D)	Kaolinite	(iv)	$[Al_2(OH)_4Si_2O_5]$

Choose the correct answer from the options given below
(a) (A) - (iii), (B) - (i), (C) - (ii), (D) - (iv)
(b) (A) - (iii), (B) - (i), (C) - (iv), (D) - (ii)
(c) (A) - (i), (B) - (iii), (C) - (ii), (D) - (iv)
(d) (A) - (i), (B) - (ii), (C) - (iii). (D) - (iv)

11. Select the correct statement from the following.
   (a) Copper matte consist of Cu_2S and $FeSiO_3$.
   (b) In the smelting step of Cu extraction, reduction of the ore takes place.
   (c) All minerals are ores while all ores are not minerals.
   (d) Bauxite is the ore of aluminium

12. Consider the following statements.

Roasting is carried out to

A. Convert sulphide to oxide and sulphate
B. Remove water of hydration
C. Melt the ore
D. Remove arsenic and sulphur impurities

Choose the correct answer from the options given below.

(a) A, B and C are correct (b) A and D are correct
(c) A, B and D are correct (d) B, C and D are correct

13. In the froth flotation process, ore particles float because

(a) they are lighter in weight
(b) surface is not easily wetted by water
(c) they bear electrostatic charge
(d) they are insoluble

14. From the following select the beneficiation processes used for extracting the metal from the $Al_2O_3 \cdot 2H_2O$

(a) froth flotation (b) leaching
(c) liquation (d) magnetic separation

15. Magnetic separation is used for increasing concentration of the

(a) horn silver (b) calcite
(c) haematite (d) magnesite

16. The basic refractories used in the furnaces of calcination and roasting is

(a) $SiO_2 + Al_2O_3$
(b) CaO and MgO
(c) Graphite
(d) Carborundum

17. The method used for the purification of Zr based on the given equation is

$$Zr + 2I_2 \longrightarrow ZrI_4$$
$$ZrI_4 \longrightarrow Zr + 2I_2$$

(a) cupellation (b) zone refining
(c) electrolytic refining (d) van Arkel method

Type II 》 MCQs with One or More than One Correct Options

18. Select the reactions that corresponds to calcination.

(a) $2PbS + 3O_2 \xrightarrow{\Delta} 2PbO + 2SO_2$

(b) $Fe_2O_3 \cdot xH_2O \xrightarrow{\Delta} Fe_2O_3 + xH_2O$

(c) $FeCO_3 \xrightarrow{\Delta} FeO + CO_2$

(d) $CaCO_3 \cdot MgCO_3 \xrightarrow{\Delta} CaO + MgO + 2CO_2$

19. Which of the following is/are ores of iron?

(a) Siderite (b) Cerargyrite
(c) Limonite (d) Willemite

20. The ore(s) that belong(s) to Li is/are

(a) spodumene (b) soda ash
(c) talc (d) lepidolite

21. Choose the reactions that shows slag formation processes?

(a) $SiO_2 + CaO \longrightarrow CaSiO_3$
(b) $CaO + P_2O_5 \longrightarrow Ca_3(PO_4)_2$
(c) $Cr_2O_3 + 2Al \longrightarrow Al_2O_3 + 2Cr$
(d) $MgCO_3 + SiO_2 \longrightarrow MgSiO_3 + CO_2$

22. Select the method(s) that is/are not involved in concentration of ore?

(a) Hydraulic washing (b) Liquation
(c) Electrolysis (d) Leaching

23. Choose the pair(s) that require(s) calcination.

(a) $ZnCO_3$ and CaO (b) ZnO and MgO
(c) ZnO and $Fe_2O_3 \cdot xH_2O$ (d) Fe_2O_3 and $CaCO_3 \cdot MgCO_3$

24. The compound(s) used as acidic flux is/are

(a) $CaCO_3$ (b) P_2O_5
(c) $MgSiO_3$ (d) $Na_2B_4O_7$

Type III 》 Numerical/Integer Answer Type Questions

25. The number of metallic ore(s) that is/are concentrated by magnetic separation method from the given ores is ....

cassiterite, pyrolusite, rutile, magnetite, galena, cinnabar.

26. Amongst the following, the number of ore(s) that can be concentrated by froth flotation process is ....

galena, sphalerite, cassiterite, calamine, chalcocite, haematite, argentite.

27. The number of ore(s) that is/are roasted to convert them into their corresponding metal oxide(s) is ....

alumina, zinc blende, iron pyrites, copper pyrites, galena.

28. The number of reaction(s) carried out by self reduction from the given reactions is ....

I. $Cu_2S + 2Cu_2O \longrightarrow 6Cu + SO_2$
II. $2HgS + 3O_2 \longrightarrow 2HgO + 2SO_2$
III. $TiO_2 + 2Mg \longrightarrow Ti + 2MgO$
IV. $2PbO + PbS \longrightarrow 3Pb + SO_2$
V. $Cr_2O_3 + 2Al \longrightarrow Al_2O_3 + 2Cr$

29. The number of metal(s) that is/are commercially reduced by Golds Schmidt's aluminothermic process from the given metals is ....

Na, Pb, Al, Mn, Sn, Cr

30. The number of metals which is/are purified by distillation processes from the given metals is ....

Fe, Al, Zn, Sn, Pb, Hg, Cd

Elemental Practice 7.1 | Chapter 07

Connect with **Answers**

1. (b)	2. (d)	3. (d)	4. (d)	5. (d)	6. (d)
7. (a)	8. (d)	9. (b)	10. (a)	11. (d)	12. (c)
13. (b)	14. (b)	15. (c)	16. (b)	17. (d)	18. (b,c,d)
19. (a,c)	20. (a,d)	21. (a,b,d)	22. (b,c)	23. (a,c,d)	24. (b,d)
25. (4)	26. (3)	27. (4)	28. (3)	29. (2)	30. (3)

Element 2 Thermodynamics of Metallurgy and Extraction of Metal

Thermodynamics of Metallurgy

- The free energy change (ΔG) occurring during the reduction processes help in deciding the suitable method for reduction.
- More the negative value of ΔG, the higher is the reducing power of an element. ΔG can be given as,

$$\Delta G = \Delta H - T\Delta S \quad \ldots(i)$$

or $$\Delta G = -RT \ln K$$

where, ΔH = enthalpy change; ΔG = Gibbs free energy
T = temperature; ΔS = entropy change

For the spontaneous reduction of an oxide, halide or sulphide by an element, the essential condition is that there is a decrease in the free energy of the system (–ve ΔG).

In Eq. (i), if ΔG is –ve then K should be +ve.

For the reduction of a metal oxide with a reducing agent, the plot of $\Delta G°$ against temperature is studied, which is called **Ellingham diagram.**

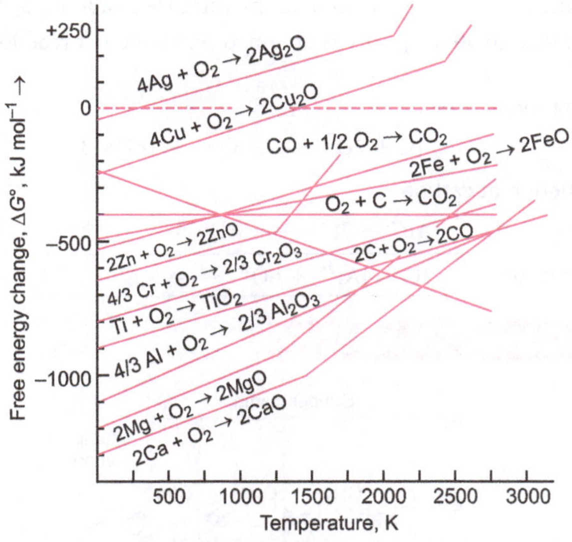

Combined Ellingham diagram for metals and carbon

For a general reaction,

$$2xM(s) + O_2(g) \longrightarrow M_xO(s)$$

In this reaction, O_2 is gas and M_xO is a solid. That means on increasing temperature, ΔS become negative due to which $T\Delta S$ becomes more negative.

In eq. (i), $T\Delta S$ is subtracted hence ΔG becomes less and less negative. That's why in ΔG *vs* T plot, most of the lines have positive slopes for most of the reactions involving the formation of metal oxides.

JEE Spotlite

- In Ellingham diagram all the plots slope upwards (except C) since $\Delta G°$ becomes more positive when temperature increases, i.e. stability of oxides decreases.
- Due to change in phase, some lines are not straight. The temperature at which such change occurs is indicated by an increase in the slope on the positive side.
- Ag_2O is unstable and decompose at high temperature that's why they have positive ΔG at high temperature.
- In the plot of CO, ΔG decreases as ΔS increases, this is indicated by downward trend.
- Any metal oxide with lower value of ΔG is more stable as compared to metal oxide with higher value of ΔG. Hence, a metal will reduce the oxide of other metals which lie above it in Ellingham diagram, i.e. the metals for which the free energy of formation ($\Delta_f G°$) of their oxides is more negative can reduce those metal oxides which has less negative $\Delta_f G°$.
- The decreasing order of the negative values of $\Delta_f G°$ of metal oxides is
  Ca > Mg (below 1773 K) > Al > Ti > Cr > C > Fe > Ag
  Thus, Al reduces FeO, CrO and NiO in thermite reduction but it will not reduce MgO at temperature below 1773 K.
  Mg can reduce Al_2O_3 below 162 K but above 1023 K, Al can reduce MgO.
- CO is more effective reducing agent below 1073 K and above 1073 K, coke is more effective reducing agent, e.g. CO reduces Fe_2O_3 below 1073 K but above it, coke reduces Fe_2O_3. Coke reduces ZnO above 1270 K.

Application

It is interesting to think of the reduction of ZnO with C as involving a competition between Zn and C for O atoms.

We consider following values at 1100°C for the oxidation of Zn and C.

(i) $2Zn + O_2 \longrightarrow 2ZnO; \Delta G° = -360 \text{ kJ mol}^{-1}$

(ii) $2C + O_2 \longrightarrow 2CO; \Delta G° = -460 \text{ kJ mol}^{-1}$

Eq. (i) and (ii) gives,

$2Zn + 2CO \longrightarrow 2ZnO + 2C; \Delta G° = +100 \text{ kJ mol}^{-1}$

(iii) $Zn + CO \longrightarrow ZnO + C; \Delta G° = +50 \text{ kJ mol}^{-1}$

(iv) $ZnO + C \longrightarrow Zn + CO; \Delta G° = -50 \text{ kJ mol}^{-1}$

For reaction (iii), in which Zn reduces CO, $\Delta G°$ is positive indicating that this reduction is non-spontaneous (in forward direction) but for the reaction (iv) with negative value of $\Delta G°$ in which C reduces ZnO is spontaneous (in forward direction).

The application of this diagram in pyrometallurgy can be illustrated by the extraction of iron, copper and zinc from their respective oxides.

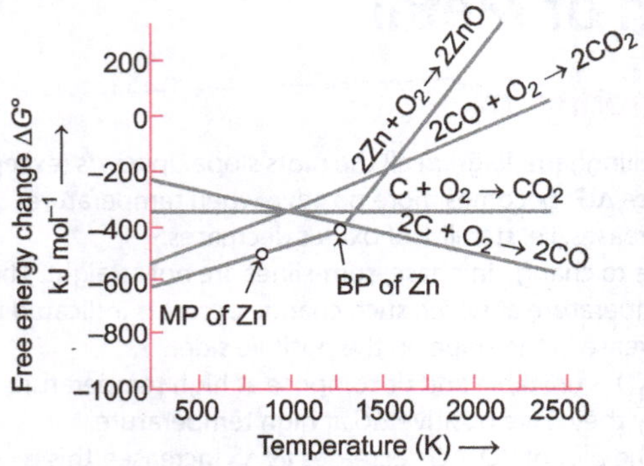

Ellingham diagram for carbon, carbon monoxide and zinc systems

Limitations

- It does not tell whether reduction reaction is slow or fast, i.e. kinetics of a reaction.
- For equation, $\Delta G° = RT \ln K$, the interpretation of value of $\Delta G°$ is based on the equilibrium constant K. That means, it is assumed that reactants and products are in equilibrium. But this assumptions is not always true for every case.

Extraction of Aluminium

Occurrence

Bauxite	:	$Al_2O_3 \cdot 2H_2O$
Feldspar	:	$K_2O \cdot Al_2O_3 \cdot 6SiO_2$
Orthoclase	:	$KAlSi_3O_8$
Beryl	:	$Be_3Al_2Si_6O_{18}$

Main source is bauxite.
Feldspar or orthoclase on weathering gives rise to porcelain-clay, China-clay or Kaolin.

Purification of Bauxite

Following methods are used for the purification of Bauxite.

1. Baeyer's Process

Step I Bauxite contains Fe_2O_3 and TiO_2 as impurities. Al_2O_3 is amphoteric and dissolves in NaOH. The other oxides are basic oxides and therefore, insoluble in NaOH.

$$Al_2O_3 + 2OH^- + 3H_2O \longrightarrow \underset{\text{soluble}}{2[Al(OH)_4]^-}$$

Insoluble oxides (as Fe_2O_3) are removed by filtration

Step II Soluble $[Al(OH)_4]^-$ is diluted and then acidified when $Al(OH)_3$ is precipitated which on ignition at 1250°C gives pure alumina :

$$Al(OH)_4^- + H_3O^+ \longrightarrow Al(OH)_3\downarrow + 2H_2O$$

$$2Al(OH)_3 \xrightarrow{1250°C} Al_2O_3 + 3H_2O$$

The complex is decomposed into $Al(OH)_3$ by passing CO_2 through it

$$2[Al(OH)_4]^- + CO_2 \longrightarrow 2Al(OH)_3 + CO_3^{2-} + H_2O$$

2. Serpeck's Process

$$Al_2O_3 + 3C + N_2 \xrightarrow{\Delta} 2AlN + 3CO\uparrow$$

$$AlN + 3H_2O \longrightarrow Al(OH)_3 + NH_3$$

$$2Al(OH)_3 \xrightarrow{\Delta} Al_2O_3 + 3H_2O$$

Electrolysis of Al_2O_3 (Hall-Heroult Process)

Al is usually extracted by this process. Al_2O_3 is melted with cryolite $Na_3[AlF_6]$, fluorspar, CaF_2 and then electrolysed in a graphite lined steel tank, which serves as cathode. The anodes are also made up of graphite. The cell runs continuously and at intervals molten Al (m.p. 660°C) is drained from the bottom of the cell and more bauxite is added. Cryolite improves the electrical conductivity of the cell as Al_2O_3 is poor conductor. This also serves as an added impurity and lowers the m.p. of the mixture to about 950°C.

Al of 99.6 to 99.8% purity is obtained. Probable net reactions are.

Oxidation at anode:

$$[C + 2O^{2-} \longrightarrow CO_2 + 4e^-] \times 3$$

Reduction at cathode:

$$[Al^{3+} + 3e^- \longrightarrow Al] \times 4$$

Net reaction $\quad 3C + 4Al^{3+} + 6O^{2-} \longrightarrow 4Al + 3CO_2$

Concept Visualizer

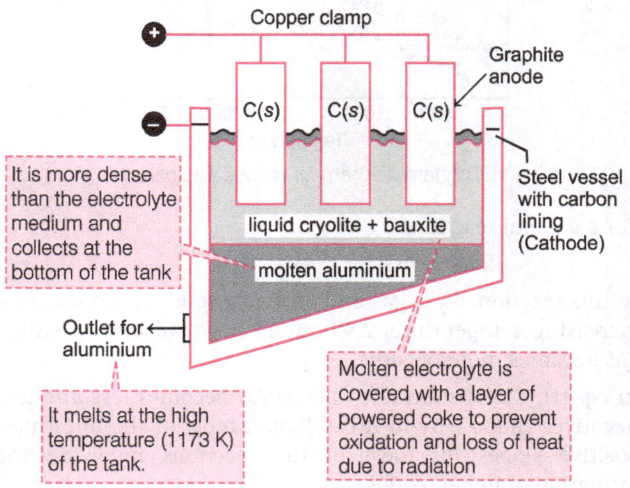

The flowchart for the extraction of Al from its ore is shown below.

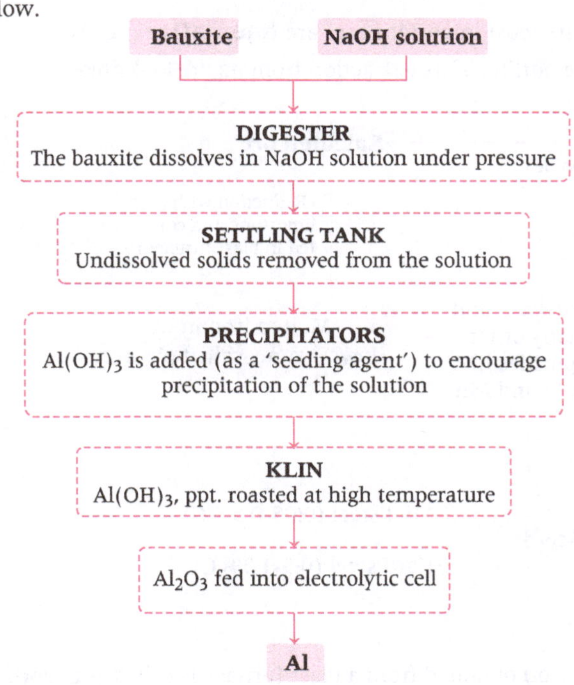

Extraction of Zinc

Its chief ore is zinc blende (ZnS) and other ores are calamine ($ZnCO_3$), zincite (ZnO), willemite (Zn_2SiO_4) etc.

The outline of its extraction is as follows

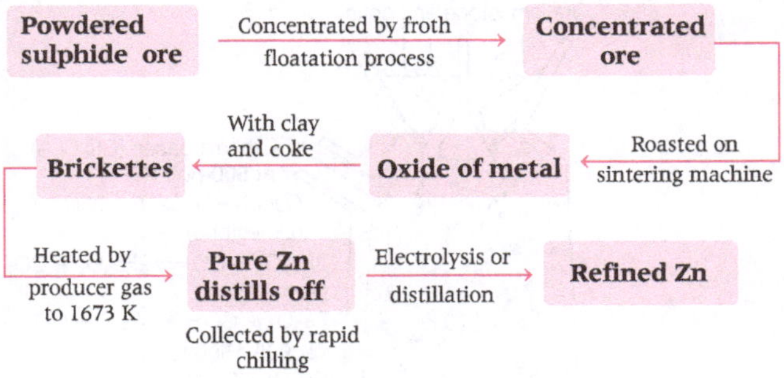

Roasting, $2ZnS + 3O_2 \longrightarrow 2ZnO + 2SO_2$

$$ZnS + 2O_2 \longrightarrow ZnSO_4$$

$$2ZnSO_4 \longrightarrow 2ZnO + 2SO_2 + O_2$$

When the ore is calamine, it shall decompose into oxide with evolution of CO_2 [calcination process is used. For roasting, a reverberatory furnace may be used].

Extraction of Copper

It does not occur abundantly in nature. Its chief ore are **copper pyrites** ($CuFeS_2$), **malachite** [$CuCO_3 \cdot Cu(OH)_2$], **cuperite** (Cu_2O), **copper glance** (Cu_2S).

The outline of copper extraction from its ore is as follows

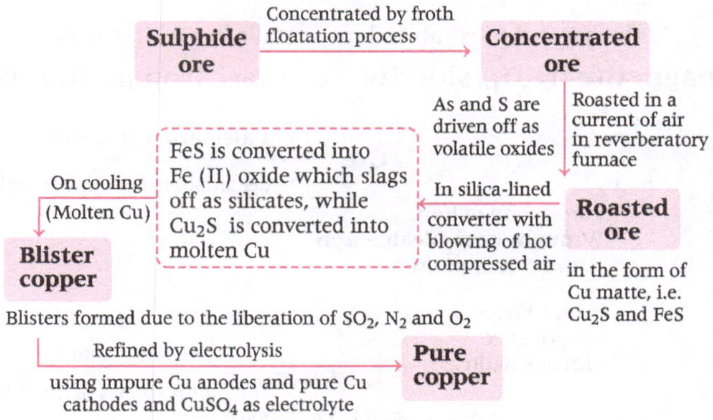

Low grade copper can be extracted by hydrometallurgical process (wet process) as

Step I Leaching with H_2SO_4 converts salts into sulphates

$$CuCO_3 + H_2SO_4 \xrightarrow{\Delta} CuSO_4 + H_2O + CO_2$$

$$Cu(OH)_2 + H_2SO_4 \xrightarrow{\Delta} CuSO_4 + 2H_2O$$

$$CuFeS_2 + 2H_2SO_4 \xrightarrow{\Delta} CuSO_4 + FeSO_4 + 2H_2S$$

Step II Electrochemical Displacement Fe is present above Cu in electrochemical series hence, if Fe scrap is added to $CuSO_4$ solution, Cu is displaced

$$CuSO_4 + Fe \longrightarrow FeSO_4 + Cu\downarrow$$

JEE MAPPER

Example Similar to PYQ Asked in JEE Advanced 2020

Which among the following statements is/are true for the extraction of copper from sulphide ore?

(a) Leaching with H_2SO_4 converts copper pyrites into copper sulphates.

(b) Low grade copper can be extracted by hydrometallurgical process.

(c) In silica-lined converter with blowing of hot compressed air, copper glance is converted into Cu(II) oxide.

(d) Blister copper is formed due to the liberation of carbon monoxide.

Sol. (*a*, *b*) Among the given statements (a) and (b) are correct statement while (c) and (d) are incorrect statements. Their corrected form are as follows.

In silica-lined converter with blowing of hot compressed air, the copper glance is converted into molten Cu. Blister copper is formed due to the liberation of SO_2, N_2 and O_2.

Competency Enhancer 2.1

Which among the following statements is/are true for the extraction of zinc from zinc blende?

(a) When concentrated ore of zinc sulphide is roasted on sintering machine, it forms zinc oxide.

(b) Calamine upon roasting decomposes into oxide with evolution of CO_2.

(c) For roasting, a reverberatory furnace is used.

(d) Zincite is obtained when brickettes is heated by producer gas upto 1673 K.

Extraction of Iron

Iron is the second most abundant metal after Al in the earth's crust. Its most important ores are **haematite** (Fe_2O_3), **magnetite** (Fe_3O_4), **siderite** ($FeCO_3$) and **iron pyrites** (FeS_2). The outline of its extraction from its ore looks like

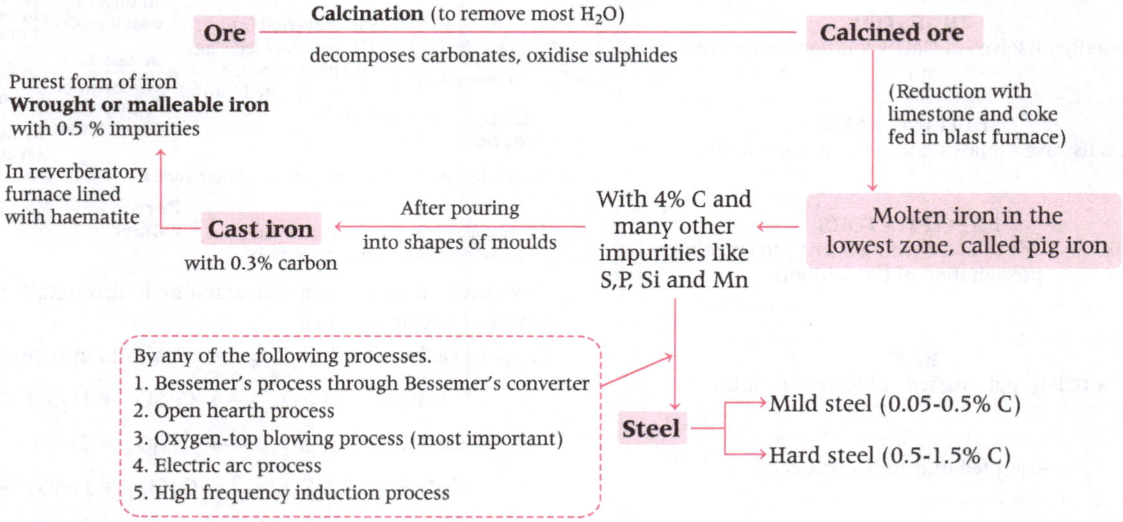

Reactions Occurring in Blast Furnace

The various zones and the reactions occurring in blast furnace are as follows

(i) **Reduction Zone** (uppermost part of the furnace) In this zone temperature is about 500-800K and metal oxide is reduced to metal.

$$3Fe_2O_3 + CO \xrightarrow{573-673\,K} 2Fe_3O_4 + CO_2\uparrow$$

$$Fe_3O_4 + 4CO \xrightarrow{773-883\,K} 3Fe + 4\,CO_2\uparrow$$

$$Fe_2O_3 + CO \xrightarrow{773-873\,K} 2FeO + CO_2\uparrow$$

(ii) **Combustion Zone** (middle part of furnace) At 900-1500 K coke burns to form CO_2.

$$C + O_2 \longrightarrow CO_2 + 97\text{ kcal}$$

CO_2 rises upward and gets reduced to carbon monoxide

$$CO_2 + C \longrightarrow 2CO(g)$$

$$FeO + CO \longrightarrow Fe + CO_2$$

Iron formed is called spongy iron.

$$CaCO_3 \longrightarrow CaO + CO_2$$

$$CaO + SiO_2 \longrightarrow \underset{\text{Slag}}{CaSiO_3}$$

CaO formed helps in slag formation of slag therefore, sometimes this zone is also called **slag formation zone**.

(iii) **Melting Zone** (lower part of furnace, 1500-2100 K) Spongy iron melts at 1600 K and collects at the bottom of the hearth. The slag being lighter, floats over the molten zone. The molten iron is called pig iron.

$$FeO + C \longrightarrow Fe + CO$$

Iron obtained from a blast furnace is called **pig iron**. It contains about 95% Fe, 4% C and varying quantities of other impurities. **Cast iron** can be obtained by pouring pig iron directly into molds of the desired shape.

Cast iron is very hard and brittle and can be used where it will not be subjected to mechanical or thermal shock.

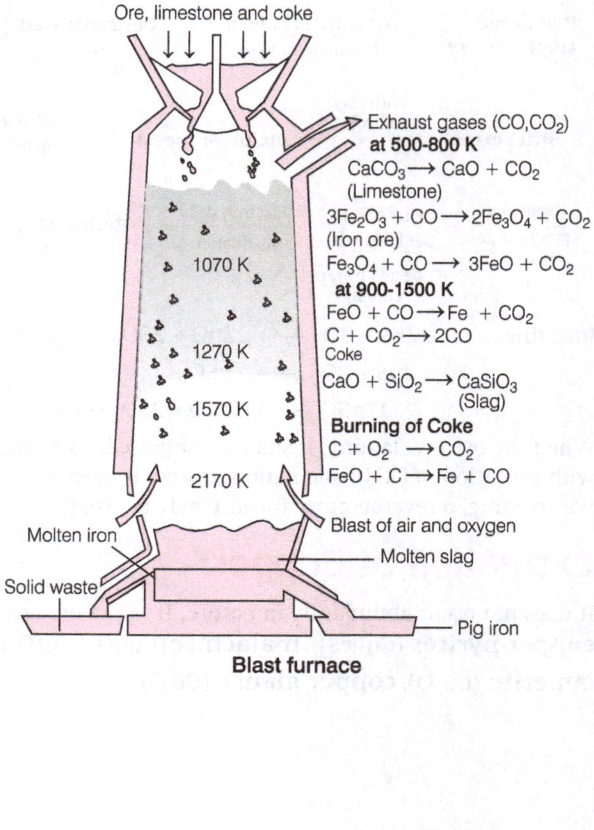

Blast furnace

Extraction of Silver

The extraction of silver involves leaching the metal with CN^-, which is also an oxidation reaction. The metal is later recovered by the displacement method using more electropositive zinc metal.

It occurs as argentite or silver glance (Ag_2S), pyrargyrite or ruby silver (Ag_3SbS_3), proustite (Ag_3AsS_3) and horn silver ($AgCl$). The outline of its extraction looks like.

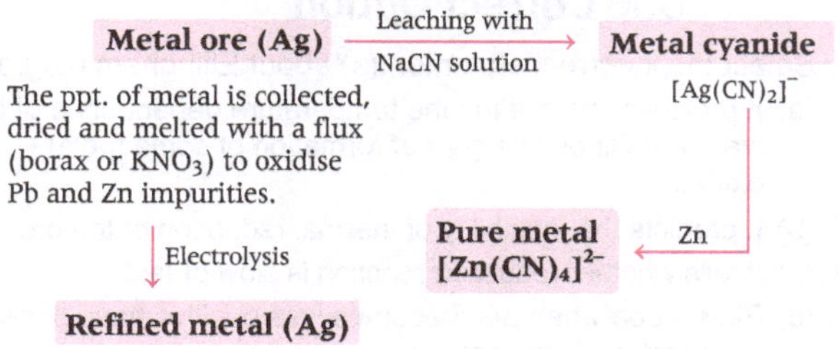

Extraction of Mercury

It is found as 1×10^{-5} % of earth crust and its most important ore is cinnabar (HgS).

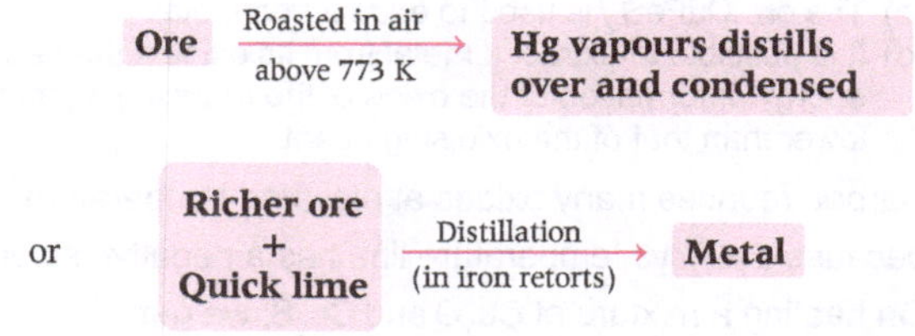

It can be purified by dropping slowly through dil. HNO_3. The metallic impurities displace Hg from nitrate and go into the solution.

Further purification is carried out by distillation under reduced pressure.

Elemental Practice 7.2

Type I 》 MCQs with Only One Correct Option

1. On the basis of the given Ellingham diagram, select the incorrect statement.

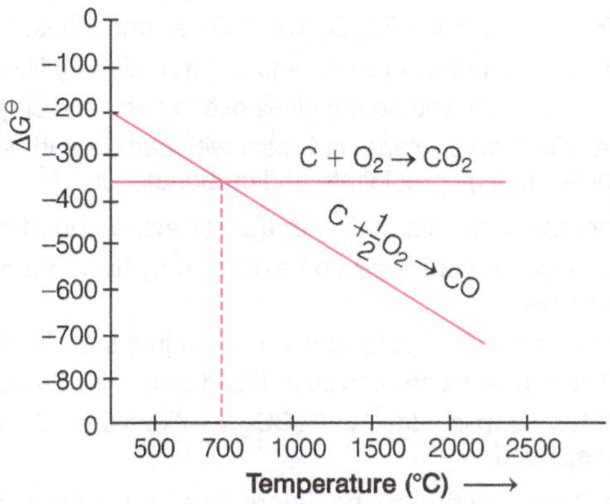

   (a) Carbon can be used to reduce any metal oxide at a high temperature.
   (b) Carbon reduces many oxides at elevated temperature because $\Delta_f G^\ominus$ of $CO(g)$ in temperature line has negative slope.
   (c) $\Delta S(C, CO) < \Delta S(C, CO_2)$
   (d) Upto 710°C, formation of CO_2 is more favourable energetically but above 710°C, the formation of CO is preferred.

2. Select the correct statements from the following.
   (a) In open hearth porcess, impurities present in cast iron are oxidised by adding iron ores.
   (b) Medium carbon or mild steel contains 0.5-1.5%
   (c) Li is extracted by electrolysis of fused LiCl with NaOH.
   (d) During the extraction of zinc, the concentrated ore is roasted at 900°-1000°C to convert Zn and $ZnSO_4$ to ZnS.

3. With respect to ore, Ellingham diagram helps to predict the feasibility of its
   (a) thermal reduction (b) electrolysis
   (c) zone refining (d) vapour phase refining

4. Bauxite ore is made up of $Al_2O_3 + SiO_2 + TiO_2 + Fe_2O_3$. This ore is treated with conc. NaOH solution at 500 K and 35 bar pressure for a few hours and filtered hot. In the filtrate, the species present is/are
   (a) $NaAl(OH)_4$ only
   (b) $Na_2Ti(OH)_6$ only
   (c) $NaAl(OH)_4$ and Na_2SiO_3 both
   (d) Na_2SiO_3 only

5. $\Delta_f G^\ominus$ vs T plot in the Ellingham diagram slopes downward for the reaction
   (a) $Mg + \frac{1}{2}O_2 \longrightarrow MgO$
   (b) $2Ag + \frac{1}{2}O_2 \longrightarrow Ag_2O$
   (c) $C + \frac{1}{2}O_2 \longrightarrow CO$
   (d) $CO + \frac{1}{2}O_2 \longrightarrow CO_2$

6. Select the reaction that does not occur in the combustion zone of blast furnace.
   (a) $C + O_2 \longrightarrow CO_2$
   (b) $CO_2 + C \longrightarrow 2CO(g)$
   (c) $FeO + CO \longrightarrow Fe + CO_2$
   (d) $FeO + C \longrightarrow Fe + CO$

7. During the process of electrorefining of copper some metals present as impurity settle down as anode mud. These are
   (a) Sn and Ag (b) Pb and Zn
   (c) Ag and Au (d) Fe and Ni

8. Select the incorrect statement.
   (a) Impurities are more soluble in the melt than in the solid state of the metal.
   (b) In Bessemerisation of sulphide ore of copper, there is self-reduction giving copper metal.
   (c) The ore $CuFeS_2$ is used to extract iron metal.
   (d) It is possible to extract a metal from its oxide if the free energy of formation of the oxide of the reducing agent is lower than that of the oxidising agent.

9. Carbon reduces many oxides at elevated temperature because $\Delta_f G^{\ominus}$ *vs* temperature line has a negative slope. On heating a mixture of Cu_2O and Cu_2S, we get
   (a) $Cu + SO_2$ (b) $Cu + SO_3$
   (c) $CuO + CuS$ (d) Cu_2SO_3

10. Considering Ellingham diagram, the metals that can be used to reduce alumina is
    (a) Mg (b) Zn
    (c) Fe (d) Cu

11. During the extraction of zinc, leaching is employed to dissolve ZnO in an alkaline medium. The primary reason for choosing an alkaline medium is
    (a) to avoid the precipitation of impurities
    (b) to prevent the hydrolysis of ZnO
    (c) to stabilise the tetrahydroxo complex of zinc
    (d) to reduce ZnO directly to metallic zinc

12. Identify the correct statement from the following.
    (a) Blister copper has blistered appearance due to evolution of CO_2.
    (b) The iron obtained from blast furnace contains only 4% carbon wih no impurities.
    (c) Pig iron can be moulded into a variety of shapes.
    (d) Wrought iron is impure iron with 4% carbon.

13. The elements that is present as the impurity to the maximum extent in the pig iron is
    (a) carbon (b) silicon
    (c) phosphorus (d) manganese

14. Select the incorrect statement from the following.
    (a) The extraction of Au by leaching with NaCN involves both oxidation and reduction.
    (b) $\Delta_f G$ of PbS is lowest which makes it formation more spontaneous.
    (c) In electrolytic reduction, pure alumina dissolved in molten cryolite containing more CaF_2 or NaF is electrolysed at 800-1500°C.
    (d) In Baeyer's process, finely grounded ore is roasted at a low temperature to convert FeO to Fe_2O_3.

15. Select the reaction that is not involved in Baeyer's process.
    (a) $2Al_2O_3 \longrightarrow 4Al + 3O_2$
    (b) $NaAlO_2 + 2H_2O \longrightarrow NaOH + Al(OH)_3\downarrow$
    (c) $2Al(OH)_3 \xrightarrow{\Delta} Al_2O_3 + 3H_2O$
    (d) $2NaAlO_2 + CO_2 + 3H_2O \longrightarrow 2Al(OH)_3 + Na_2CO_3$

Type II » MCQs with One or More than One Correct Option

16. Select the incorrect statement(s) about Ellingham diagram
    (a) It provides information the temperature dependence of the standard Gibbs energies of formation of some metal oxides.
    (b) It predicts the feasibility of thermal reduction of the ore.
    (c) It tells whether reduction reaction is slow or fast.
    (d) Plots slope when $\Delta G°$ becomes less positive have positive temperature increases.

17. Choose the reactions that occurs in reduction zone?
    (a) $Fe_2O_3 + CO \xrightarrow{773-873\,K} 2FeO + CO_2\uparrow$
    (b) $CaO + SiO_2 \longrightarrow CaSiO_3$
    (c) $FeO + CO \longrightarrow Fe + CO_2$
    (d) $Fe_3O_4 + 4CO \xrightarrow{773-883\,K} 3Fe + 4CO_2\uparrow$

18. Bauxite is purified by Serpeck's and Baeyer's process. The correct statement(s) about these process is/are
    (a) Bauxite contains Fe_2O_3 and TiO_2 as impurities.
    (b) Fe_2O_3 is insoluble oxide and are removed by filtration
    (c) Feldspar on weathering gives rise to porcelain-clay
    (d) Al_2O_3 is amphoteric and react with carbon and nitrogen to give $Al(OH)_3$ precipitate and carbonate ion.

19. Select the incorrect statement(s) for extraction of copper.
    (a) Low grade copper can be extracted by hydrometallurgical process.
    (b) Leaching with H_2SO_4 converts salts into sulphides.
    (c) The copper oxides can be reduced to metallic Cu using coke.
    (d) If Cu scrap is added to $FeSO_4$ solutions then Cu is displaced.

20. Select the reaction(s) that is/are involved in the extraction of Zn.
    (a) $2K[Au(CN)_2] + Zn \longrightarrow K_2[Zn(CN)_4] + 2Au\downarrow$
    (b) $2ZnS + 3O_2 \longrightarrow 2ZnO + 2SO_2$
    (c) $ZnS + 2O_2 \longrightarrow ZnSO_4$
    (d) $ZnSO_4 \longrightarrow ZnO + SO_2 + O_2$

Type III 》 Numerical/Integer Answer Type Questions

21. Select the number of processes that is/are involved in the extraction of gold.

Roasting, Calcination, Treatment with KCN, Crushing and grinding, Cupellation.

22. The number of correct statements regarding extraction of iron from haemetite is ....

I. Reduction of calcined ore with limestone and coke fed in blast furnace.

II. In combustion zone, iron formed is called as spongy iron.

III. CaO formed in combustion zone help in slag formation.

IV. Cast iron in the lowest zone is called pig iron.

V. Cast iron obtained by pouring pig iron that moulds into desired shape.

23. The number of reactions that is/are not involved in thermite process is ....

I. $3Mn_3O_4 + 8Al \longrightarrow 9Mn + 4Al_2O_3$

II. $Cr_2O_3 + 2Al \longrightarrow Al_2O_3 + 2Cr$

III. $2Al + Fe_2O_3 \longrightarrow 2Fe + Al_2O_3$

IV. $B_2O_3 + 2Al \longrightarrow 2B + Al_2O_3$

V. $2CuO + CuS \longrightarrow 3Cu + SO_2$

VI. $ZrI_4 \xrightarrow{\Delta} Zr + 2I_2$

VII. $TiCl_4 + Mg \xrightarrow{1000-1150°C} Ti + 2MgCl_2$

24. The number of reagents that is/are used in Hall Heroult process is ....

NaOH, CaO, Na_3AlF_6, AlF_3, Al_2O_3, $Al(OH)_3$

25. Consider the following steps

$$Cu_2S \xrightarrow{\text{Roast in air}} (A) \xrightarrow{\text{Roast without air}} (B)$$

The total number of correct statements are

I. It is self-reduction

II. It involves disproportionation

III. (*A*) is a mixture of Cu_2O and Cu_2S

IV. (*B*) is a mixture of Cu and SO_2

Elemental Practice 9.2 | **Chapter 07**

Connect with **Answers**

1. (c)	**2.** (a)	**3.** (a)	**4.** (c)	**5.** (c)	**6.** (d)
7. (c)	**8.** (c)	**9.** (a)	**10.** (a)	**11.** (c)	**12.** (c)
13. (a)	**14.** (c)	**15.** (a)	**16.** (c,d)	**17.** (a,d)	**18.** (a,b,c)
19. (b,d)	**20.** (b,c,d)	**21.** (3)	**22.** (4)	**23.** (4)	**24.** (2)
25. (3)					

Advanced Exclusive Different Strokes

Interpretation of Ellingham Diagram of Carbon

Elligham diagram representing reducing nature of carbon is shown below.

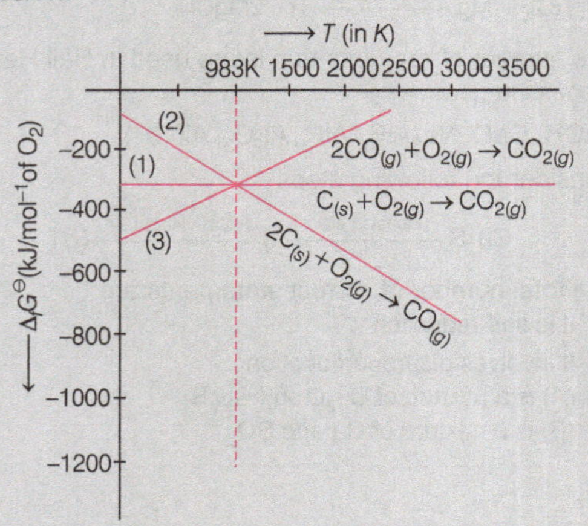

- From line (1), it can be inferred that C combines with O_2 at all temperatures to form of CO_2 with the increase in temperature. $\Delta_f G^\ominus$ value remains almost constant.
- From line (2), it can be inferred that as the temperature increases, $\Delta_f G^\ominus$ becomes more and more negative i.e. the thermodynamic feasibility of the reaction increases with the increase in temperature.
- From line (3) it can be concluded that with the increase in temperature. $\Delta_f G^\ominus$ becomes more and more positive i.e. CO becomes more stable than CO_2.
- **At 983 K,** i.e. the temperature at which the three lines intersect, $\Delta_f G^\ominus$ for the forward reaction is equal to $\Delta_f G^\ominus$ for the backward reaction or $\Delta_f G^\ominus$ for the reaction is zero.

$$\Delta_f G^\ominus = -2.303RT \log K = 0$$

where K = equilibrium constant

$$\log K = 0 \text{ or } K = 1$$

- **Below 983 K,** $\Delta_f G^\ominus(CO_2)$ is more negative than $\Delta_f G^\ominus(CO)$ and hence CO_2 will be formed predominantly. It is further concluded that below 983 K, CO acts as a better reducing agent than C.
- **Above 983 K,** $\Delta_f G^\ominus(CO)$ is more negative than $\Delta_f G^\ominus(CO_2)$ and hence CO will be formed predominantly.

Thus, the above points of Ellingham diagram helps to solve the problems related to reducing nature of carbon in JEE Main and Advanced exams.

PRACTICE ELEMENT

Target JEE Advanced

Single Correct Choice MCQs

1. In metallurgy, flux is a substance used to convert
   (a) soluble impurities to insoluble impurities
   (b) infusible impurities to fusible material
   (c) fusible impurities to infusible impurities
   (d) mineral into silicate

2. Choose the correct statement about the role of substances added in the froth floatation process.
   (a) Collectors enhance the wettability of the mineral particles.
   (b) Collectors enhance the wettability of gangue particles.
   (c) By using depressants in the process two sulphide ores can be separated.
   (d) Froth forms carrier the dust particles

3. Select the correct statement about electro-reduction of pure alumina.
   (a) Al^{3+} is oxidised to Al(*s*).
   (b) graphite anode is oxidised to carbon monoxide and carbon dioxide.
   (c) oxidation state of oxygen changes in the reaction at anode.
   (d) oxidation state of oxygen changes in the overall reaction involved in the process.

4. Electrolytic reduction of alumina to aluminium by Hall-Heroult process is carried out, not
   (a) in the presence of NaOH
   (b) in the presence of fluorite
   (c) in the presence of cryolite which forms a melt with lower melting point
   (d) in the presence of fused Al_2O_3

5. Select the incorrect statement from the following.
   (a) Silver glance mainly contains silver sulphide
   (b) Zinc blende mainly contains zinc chloride
   (c) Gold is found in native state
   (d) Copper pyrites also contains Fe_2S_3

6. The intersection point of the lines for ZnO and $C + O_2 \longrightarrow CO_2$ in the Ellingham diagram corresponds to
   (a) the melting point of zinc.
   (b) the temperature above which carbon can reduce zinc oxide.
   (c) the temperature above which zinc cannot be reduced by carbon.
   (d) the equilibrium temperature for the oxidation of carbon and zinc.

7. Of the following reduction processes
   I. $PbO + C \longrightarrow Pb$
   II. $ZnO + C \longrightarrow Zn$
   III. $Fe_2O_3 + C \longrightarrow FeO$
   IV. $Ca_3(PO_4)_2 + C \longrightarrow P$
   Correct processes are
   (a) I, II (b) I, II, IV
   (c) II, III (d) III and IV

8. Choose the incorrect match from the following.

(a)	Feldspar	$NaAlSi_3O_8$
(b)	Talc	$Mg_2(Si_2O_5)_2Mg(OH)_2$
(c)	Barytes	$BaSO_4$
(d)	Chalcopyrite	FeS_2

9. Select the ore that contains both silver and antimony?
   (a) Milarite (b) Ruby silver
   (c) Asbestus (d) Greenocite

10. Choose the incorrect match of metals and its extraction process

	List-I (Metals)		List-II (Extraction process)
(a)	Silver	p.	Amalgamation
(b)	Calcium	q.	Fused salt electrolysis
(c)	Zinc	s.	Carbon reduction
(d)	Copper	t.	mac-Arthur forest cyanide

One or More than One Correct MCQs

11. Self-reduction method is used in the extraction of
    (a) Hg (b) Pb (c) Ag (d) Ni

12. Vapour phase refining is used for the purification of
    (a) Ni (b) Ti
    (c) Zr (d) Au

13. Select the method of purification that used in refining of copper.
    (a) Bessemerisation (b) Poling
    (c) Electrorefining (d) Distillation

14. In Bayer's process the precipitation of gelatinous white insoluble compound, $Al(OH)_3$ is induced by
    (a) adding freshly precipitated $Al(OH)_3$
    (b) circulating CO_2 through the solution
    (c) dilution
    (d) adding calculated quantity of an acid

15. Choose the pairs which is/are incorrectly matched?
    (a) Mac-Arthur Forest process-refining of Ag
    (b) Electrolyte in Pb refining —$H_2SiF_6 + PbSiF_6$
    (c) Froth floatation process -preferential absorption
    (d) Chromate ore-Non-magnetic ore
16. Choose the correct statements regarding calcination.
    (a) Impurities are removed in the form of elemental vapours.
    (b) Carbonate ores are converted into their oxides.
    (c) Temperature of the process is maintained below the melting point of the metal.
    (d) Lower oxidation state oxides are oxidised further.
17. Select the correct match.
    (a) $ZnCO_3 \longrightarrow Zn$; Calcination followed by smelting
    (b) $FeCO_3 \longrightarrow Fe$; Calcination followed by carbon reduction
    (c) $HgS \longrightarrow Hg$; Partial roasting followed by self-reduction
    (d) $Al(OH)_3 \longrightarrow Al$; Roasting followed by carbon reduction
18. Select the metals that cannot be extracted through alkali leaching technique.
    (a) Sn (b) Cu
    (c) Au (d) Pb

Numerical/ Integer Type Questions

19. Rucklidgeite has the formula $Pb_3Bi_3Te_x$ and sylvanite has $Au_2Ag_2Te_y$. Then the value of $(x + y)$ is ....
20. Given below are calcination reaction.
    (A) $CaCO_3 \cdot MgCO_3 \xrightarrow{\Delta} CaO + MgO + xCO_2$
    (B) $CaCO_3 \cdot Cu(OH)_2 \xrightarrow{\Delta} yCuO + H_2O + xCO_2$
    The value of $x \times y$ will be ....
21. The number of elements is that occurs in the earth's crust in the native state is ....
    Au, Pt, Hg, Zn and Fe
22. The number of metals which can be commerically purified by zone refining methods is ....
    Si, Ge, Ga, Al, Ti and Zr
23. Consider the ores given below.
    Siderite, Calamine, Malachite, Cryolite, Magnetite.
    The number of ores in which Fe metal is present is ....
24. The metals that can be refined by vapour phase refining number of
    Zn, Zr, Hg, Cd, Ni, Ti, Co, Pt and Fe
25. The number of elements that is/are present as impurities in hard lead which are removed by cupellation is ....
    Zn, Fe, Cu, Ag, Au, Sn, As, Sb and Bi.
26. Select the number of correct statements from the following.
    I. In the purification of lead, $(H_2SiF_6 + PbSiF_6)$ is used as electrolyte since most of the salts of lead are insoluble.
    II. The impurities of FeS_2 and $FeCuS_2$ present in tin stone are removed by washing after roasting, when $FeSO_4$ and $CuSO_4$ are dissolved but SnO_2 is not.
    III. Magnesium oxide obtained from calcination of magnesite is thermally reduced by using reducing agents like carbon, silicon, aluminium or calcium carbide.
    IV. In Hoopes process the bottom layer consists of impure aluminium which acts as anode. Copper is added to it so that its specific gravity becomes highest and it occupies the bottom of the tank.
    V. During extraction of iron, in slag formation zone, various impurities of silicates, phosphates and manganates are reduced to Si, P and Mn respectively by carbon.

Paragraph Based Questions

Paragraph 1

Steel is a commerical variety of iron and is essentially an ore of iron with carbon. Different types of steel have different properties depending on the composition and the treatment given to it. Steel is manufactured by various procedures such as the puddling process or the Linz-Donawitz or the LD process.

27. The number of metals or non-metal that is/are involved to make stainless steel from the following is ....
    Fe, Cr, Cu, Ni, C, Cu
28. Select the correctly matched pairs.
    I. Percentage of carbon in steel-0.15-1.5%
    II. Spiegeleisen is an alloy of -Fe, Mn, Ni and C
    III. Stainless steel is an alloy of -Fe, Cr, Ni and small amount of C.
    IV. Quenching process-It is use to make steel hard and brittle
    V. Leaching process-To make steel soft
    VI. Reverberatory furnace- Use for smelting of sulphide ore

Paragraph 2

Dioxygen is used in the course of this reaction. Gases have a more random structure than liquid or solid. Free energy change increases with increase in temperature. The free energy changes that occur when one mole of common reactant is used may be plotted graphically against temperature for a number of reactions of metals to their oxides. Understanding of Ellingham diagram is extremely important for the efficient extraction of metals.

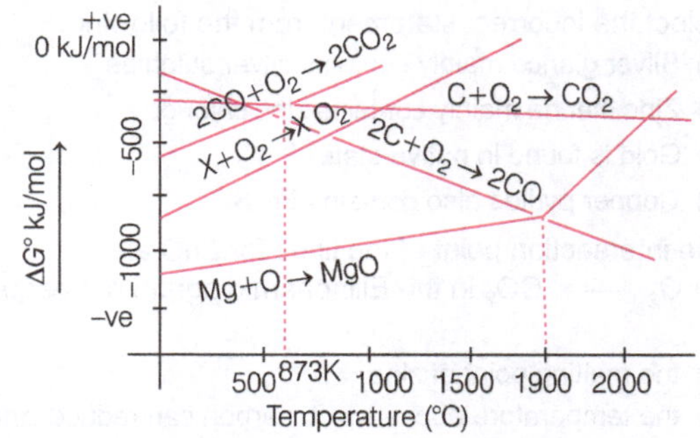

29. MgO can be reduced by carbon above ...... °C.
30. From the given diagram, the molar mass of the best reducing agent for the reduction of XO_2 at 1000°C, is .... g mol^{-1}.

Paragraph 3

The Ellingham diagram for zinc, magnesium and carbon converting into corresponding oxides is shown below

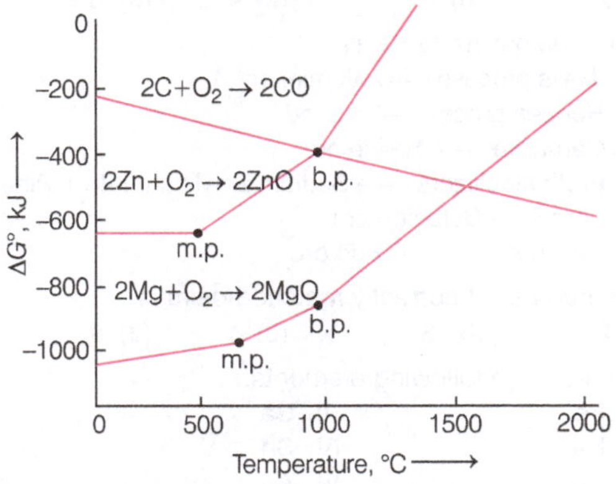

31. At 1100°C, the number of reactions that is/are non-spontaneous to a maximum extent is ....
(a) $MgO + C \longrightarrow Mg + CO$
(b) $ZnO + C \longrightarrow Zn + CO$
(c) $MgO + Zn \longrightarrow Mg + ZnO$
(d) $ZnO + Mg \longrightarrow MgO + Zn$

32. The temperature, at which carbon have equal affinity for oxygen is ...... °C.

Matching Type Questions

33. Match the type of ores given in Column I with different ores given in Column II.

Column-I		Column-II	
A.	Carbonate ore	I.	Mica
B.	Sulphide ore	II.	Cassiterite
C.	Silicate ore	III.	Sphalerite
D.	Oxide ore	IV.	Siderite

Choose the correct answer from the options given below.
(a) A-I, B-IV, C-II, D-III (b) A-III, B-I, C-IV, D-II
(c) A-IV, B-I, C-II, D-III (d) A-IV, B-III, C-I, D-II

34. Match the reactions given in Column I with suitable match given in Column II.

Column-I		Column-II	
A.	$Al_2O_3 + Na_2CO_3 \longrightarrow 2NaAlO_2 + CO_2$	I.	Calcination
B.	$PbS + PbSO_4 \longrightarrow 2Pb + 2SO_2$	II.	Slag formation
C.	$CaCO_3 \cdot MgCO_3 \longrightarrow CaO + MgO + 2CO_2$	III.	Self reduction
D.	$SiO_2 + FeO \longrightarrow FeSiO_3$	IV.	Halls process

Choose the correct answer from the options given below.
(a) A-I, B-IV, C-II, D-III (b) A-III, B-I, C-IV, D-II
(c) A-IV, B-I, C-II, D-III (d) A-IV, B-III, C-I, D-II

35. Match the elements given in Column I with appropriate methods used for their purification given in Column II.

Column-I		Column-II	
A.	Sn, Pb and Bi	I.	Zone refining
B.	Cu and Sn	II.	Liquation
C.	Si, Ge and Ga	III.	Fractional distillation
D.	Cd and Hg	IV.	Poling

Choose the correct answer from the options given below.
(a) A-I, B-IV, C-II, D-III (b) A-II, B-IV, C-I, D-III
(c) A-IV, B-I, C-II, D-III (d) A-IV, B-III, C-I, D-II

36. Match the Column I with Column II.

Column-I		Column-II	
A.	Poling	I.	Removes dissolved oxygen from molten copper using green logs.
B.	Cupellation	II.	Used to remove impurities like lead from silver.
C.	Distillation	III.	Used to purify metals based on volatility
D.	Electrolytic refining	IV.	Metals like copper and gold are refined

Choose the correct answer from the options given below.
(a) A-I, B-III, C-II, D-IV (b) A-IV, B-III, C-II, D-I
(c) A-II, B-IV, C-I, D-III (d) A-I, B-II, C-III, D-IV

37. Match the following.

Column-I		Column-II	
A.	Impure Lead → Pure Lead	I.	Dow's process
B.	Argentiferrous Lead → Crude Lead	II.	Hoopes process
C.	Impure Al → Pure Al	III.	Bett's electrolysis
D.	$MgCl_2 \cdot 6H_2O \rightarrow MgCl_2 + 6H_2O$	IV.	Parke and Pattinson process

Choose the correct answer from the options given below.
(a) A-I, B-IV, C-II, D-III (b) A-III, B-I, C-IV, D-II
(c) A-IV, B-I, C-II, D-III (d) A-III, B-IV, C-II, D-I

Species Selection (with 5 Species)

38. Given below are some ores.
(i) Bornite (ii) Horn silver
(iii) Zinc blende (iv) Cerussite
(v) Cryolite
The number of ores that are purified by froth floatation process
(a) 2 (b) 3
(c) 4 (d) 5

39. Given below are few statements.
I. In Serpeck's process silica is removed by heating the bauxite to 1800°C with coke in a current of N_2.

II. In extraction of lead from galena, roasting and self reduction takes place in the same furnaces, but under different conditions of temperature and supply of air.
III. The tin is obtained by the carbon reduction of blue tin.
IV. In Hall Heroult process, the graphite cathode is eaten away eventually and needs to be replaced eventually.
V. The slag is heavier and has higher melting point than the metal.

The number of incorrect statements are
(a) 2 (b) 3 (c) 4 (d) 5

40. Given below are few metals alongwith its purification method is
I. Sn refined from SnO_2 by poling method
II. Cu refined from Ag, Au by distillation
III. Si refinined by liquation
IV. Zn refined from Cd, Fe, Cu by distillation
V. Cu refined from Ag, Au by electrorefining

How many of the above statements are incorrect?
(a) 2 (b) 3 (c) 4 (d) 5

41. Given below are few ores with their formula.
I. Calamine-$ZnCO_3$
II. Galena-PbS
III. Carnallite-$KCl \cdot MgCl_2 \cdot 6H_2O$
IV. Fluorapatite-$3Ca_3(PO_4)_2CaF_2$
V. Limonite-$MgSO_4 \cdot 6H_2O$

How many of the above pairs are correctly matched?
(a) 2 (b) 3 (c) 4 (d) 5

Species Selection (with 7 Species)

42. Given below are few substances
I. CaO II. SiO_2
III. MgO IV. P_4O_{10}
V. $CaSiO_3$ VI. B_2O_3
VII. $Ca_3(PO_4)_2$

How many of the above substances can act as an acidic flux?
(a) 2 (b) 3 (c) 4 (d) 5

43. Consider the ores given below
I. Zinc blende II. Galena
III. Siderite IV. Amblygonite
V. Haematite VI. Calamine
VII. Bauxite

The number of sulphide ores from the given ores is
(a) 2 (b) 3 (c) 4 (d) 5

44. Given below are few pairs.
I. Halls process $\longrightarrow$ Aluminium
II. Hoopes process $\longrightarrow$ Lead
III. Carnallite $\longrightarrow$ Halide ore
IV. Froth stabilizers $\longrightarrow$ Sodium amyl xanthate + Pine oil
V. Mica $\longrightarrow$ Sulphide ore
VI. Calcination $\longrightarrow$ Oxide ore

The number of correctly matched pairs is
(a) 2 (b) 3 (c) 4 (d) 5

45. Consider the following elements.
I. Fe II. Ca
III. Na IV. Sn
V. Pb VI. Ag
VII. Au

The number of elements that are not used for pyrometallurgy is
(a) 2 (b) 4 (c) 5 (d) 6

46. Consider the metal oxides given below
I. CaO II. HgO
III. PbO IV. Cu_2O
V. Al_2O_3 VI. Cr_2O_3
VII. Fe_2O_3

The number of metal oxides that can be reduced by C is
(a) 2 (b) 4 (c) 5 (d) 6

47. Given below are methods of purification.
I. Mond's process and distillation
II. van-Arkel method and Mond's process
III. Distillation and van Arkel method
IV. Poling and Liquation
V. Zone refining
VI. Fractional crystallisation
VII. Selective adsorption

The number of process that are not included in vapour phase refining processes is
(a) 6 (b) 2 (c) 3 (d) 4

Check Through PYQs

Element 1 Metallurgy : General Principles

1. Calamine, malachite, magnetite and cryolite, respectively, are *2019 Adv.*
(a) $ZnCO_3$, $CuCO_3$, Fe_2O_3, Na_3AlF_6
(b) $ZnSO_4$, $CuCO_3$, Fe_2O_3, AlF_3
(c) $ZnSO_4$, $Cu(OH)_2$, Fe_3O_4, Na_3AlF_6
(d) $ZnCO_3$, $CuCO_3 \cdot Cu(OH)_2$, Fe_3O_4, Na_3AlF_6

2. The correct statement(s) related to processes involved in the extraction of metals is(are) *2023 Adv.*
(a) Roasting of malachite produces cuprite.
(b) Calcination of calamine produces zincite
(c) Copper pyrites is heated with silica in a reverberatory furnace to remove iron.
(d) Impure silver is treated with aqueous KCN in the presence of oxygen followed by reduction with zinc metal.

3. The treatment of galena with HNO_3 produces a gas that is *2022 Adv.*
(a) paramagnetic (b) bent in geometry
(c) an acidic oxide (d) colourless

4. The correct statement(s) related to the metal extraction processes is(are) *2021 Adv.*
(a) a mixture of PbS and PbO undergoes self-reduction to produce Pb and SO_2.
(b) in the extraction process of copper from copper pyrites, silica is added to produce copper silicate.
(c) partial oxidation of sulphide ore of copper by roasting, followed by self-reduction produces blister copper.
(d) in cyanide process, zinc powder is utilised to precipitate gold from $Na[Au(CN)_2]$

Element 2 Thermodynamics of Metallurgy and Extraction of Metals

5. The electrochemical extraction of aluminium from bauxite ore involves *2022 Adv.*
(a) the reaction of Al_2O_3 with coke (C) at a temperature > 2500°C.
(b) the neutralisation of aluminate solution by passing CO_2 gas to precipitate hydrated alumina ($Al_2O_3 \cdot 3H_2O$).
(c) the dissolution of Al_2O_3 in hot aqueous NaOH.
(d) the electrolysis of Al_2O_3 mixed with Na_3AlF_6 to give Al and CO_2.

6. The correct option(s) related to the extraction of iron from its ore in the blast furnace operating in the temperature range 900-1500 K is(are) *(2022 Adv.)*
(a) Limestone is used to remove silicate impurity.
(b) Pig iron obtained from blast furnace contains about 4% carbon.
(c) Coke (C) converts CO_2 to CO.
(d) Exhaust gases consist of NO_2 and CO.

7. Which among the following statement(s) is(are) true for the extraction of aluminium from bauxite? *2020 Adv.*
(a) Hydrated Al_2O_3 precipitates, when CO_2 is bubbled through a solution of sodium aluminate.
(b) Addition of Na_3AlF_6 lowers the melting point of alumina.
(c) CO_2 is evolved at the anode during electrolysis.
(d) The cathode is a steel vessel with a lining of carbon.

8. Extraction of copper from copper pyrite ($CuFeS_2$) involves *2016 Adv.*
(a) crushing followed by concentration of the ore by froth-floatation
(b) removal of iron as slag
(c) self reduction step to produce 'blister copper' following evolution of SO_2
(d) refining of 'blister copper' by carbon reduction

9. Copper is purified by electrolytic refining of blister copper. The correct statement(s) about this process is/are *(2015 Adv.)*
(a) impure Cu strip is used as cathode
(b) acidified aqueous $CuSO_4$ is used as electrolyte
(c) pure Cu deposits at cathode
(d) impurities settle as anode-mud

HINTS & Solutions

Solutions : Competency Enhancer

1.1 ***(b)*** Cinnabar—HgS

Pyrolusite—MnO_2

Haematite—Fe_2O_3

Malachite—$CuCO_3 \cdot Cu(OH)_2$

Thus, option (b) is correct answer.

2.1 ***(a,b,c)*** Among the given statements all are correct except statement d. Its corrected form is as

Pure Zn distills off when brickettes is heated by producer gas up to 1673 K.

Elemental Practice 7.1

1. ***(b)*** The process of isolating metals by dissolving the ore in an aqueous solution of a chemical reagent followed by precipitation of the metal by a more electropositive metal is called hydrometallurgy.
2. ***(d)*** The earthly impurities like sand, clay, mica, etc., associated with ores are called gangue or matrix. In other words, contaminated undesired materials present in an ore is called gangue. Thus, statement (d) is incorrect while other options contain correct statements.
3. ***(d)*** Copper pyrite is an ore of copper and its composition is $CuFeS_2$.

   $MgCO_3$ — Magnesite (ore of Mg)

   $FeCO_3$ — Siderite (ore of Fe)

   FeS_2 — Iron pyrite (ore of Fe)

   $CuFeS_2$ — Copper pyrite (ore of Fe)
4. ***(d)***

Mineral	Chemical composition
Smithstone	$ZnCO_3$
Realgar	As_4S_4
Pyrolusite	MnO_2
Anglesite	$PbSO_4$

   Thus, anglesite ($PbSO_4$) is a sulphate ore.

5. ***(d)*** Galena (PbS), tehnantite ($Cu_{12}As_4S_3$) and argentite (Ag_2S) are concentrated by froth floatation process but sphalerite [ZnS] or (Zn, Fe)S is concentrated by chemical leaching.
6. ***(d)*** Cassiterite is an ore of Sn, its chemical composition is SnO_2. It is also known as tin stone.
7. ***(a)*** Cinnabar is an ore of mercury which have formula HgS.
8. ***(d)*** Cyanide leaching process is used to extract metals that are low in reactivity such as gold.
9. ***(b)*** I. Mond's process

$$\underset{\text{Impure}}{Ni} + 4CO \xrightarrow{330-350K} \underset{\text{Volatile complex}}{[Ni(CO)_4]} \xrightarrow{450-470\,K} \underset{\text{Pure}}{Ni} + 4CO\uparrow$$

   II. Removal of lead poisoning

$$Pb^{2+} + EDTA^{4-} \rightleftharpoons [Pb(EDTA)]^{2-}$$

   III. Cyanide process for extraction of silver

$$4Ag + 8CN^- + 2H_2O + O_2 \longrightarrow [4Ag(CN)_2]^- + 4OH^-$$

   IV. Separation of ZnS from galena by using depressant (NaCN) in froth floatation process

$$ZnS + CN^{\ominus} \rightleftharpoons [Zn(CN)_4]^{2-}$$

10. ***(a)*** The correct match is A-(iii), B-(i), C-(ii), D-(iv)

    Haematite is an ore of iron. Its composition is Fe_2O_3.

    Diaspore is an ore of aluminium.

    Its composition is $Al_2O_3 \cdot H_2O$.

    Stefinite is an ore of silver antimony surfosalt. Its composition is Ag_3SbS_4.

    Kaolinite is a clay mineral with chemical formula $[Al_2(OH)_4Si_2O_5]$.
11. ***(d)*** Statement given in option (d) is correct. While (a), (b) and (c) incorrect. The corrected forms of incorrect statements are as follows.
    - Copper matte contains Cu_2S and FeS.
    - In the smelting step of Cu extraction, oxidation of the ore takes place.
    - All ores are minerals while all minerals are not ores.
12. ***(c)*** Among the given statements all are correct except statement (C). Its corrected form is roasting is the process in which concentrated ore is heated to high temperature in presence of excess of air but lower than melting point of the metal.
13. ***(b)*** In the froth flotation process, the ores particles float because their surface is not easily wetted by water.
14. ***(b)*** Leaching is the beneficiation process used for the extraction of metal (Al) from $Al_2O_3 \cdot 2H_2O$.
15. ***(c)*** Based on magnetic properties, haematite is the most suitable mineral for increasing concentration through magnetic separation.
16. ***(b)*** $SiO_2 + Al_2O_3$ — Acidic refractories

    CaO and MgO — Basic refractories graphite and carborundum are examples of neutral refractories.
17. ***(d)*** van Arkel method is used for the purification of Zr or Ti. Here, the crude metal is heated in an evacuated vessel with iodide. The metal iodide is decomposed on a tungsten filament, electrically heated to 1800 K. The pure metal deposits on the filament.

18. ***(b,c,d)*** Hydroxides, hydrated oxides and carbonate ores after concentration do not undergo roasting, these are subjected to calcination instead. Among the given processes only three i.e. b, c and d are examples of calcination processes.
19. ***(a,c)*** Among the given ores, only two i.e. siderite ($FeCO_3$) and limonite ($Fe_2O_3 \cdot 3H_2O$) are the ores of iron while cerargyrite (AgCl) and willemite (Zn_2SiO_4) are ores of Ag and Zn respectively.
20. ***(a,d)*** Spodumene ($LiAlSi_2O_6$) and Lepidolite $[K(Li, Al)_3 (Al, Si, Rb)_4O_{10}(F, OH)_2]$ are ores of Li whereas soda ash (Na_2CO_3) and Talc $[Mg_2(Si_2O_5)_2Mg(OH)_2]$ are ores of Na and Mg.
21. ***(a,b,d)*** Among the given reactions, except (c), all other show slag formation processes.
22. ***(b,c)*** Among the given techniques, liquation and electrolysis are not involved in concentration of ores. These processes are used for refining of crude metals.
23. ***(a,c,d)*** The hydroxide, hydrated oxides and carbonate ores, after concentration, are subjected to calcination. In this process, the ore is heated below its melting point in the limited supply or absence of air. As a result, these are converted into their oxides. So, among the given options, the options having either carbonates (e.g. $ZnCO_3$ and $CaCO_3 \cdot MgCO_3$) or hydrated oxide (e.g. $Fe_2O_3 \cdot xH_2O$), require calcination while the pair (ZnO and MgO) does not require calcination.
24. ***(b,d)*** Among the compounds only two i.e. b and d are acidic flux. $CaCO_3$ is a basic flux and $MgSiO_3$ is a slag.
25. ***(4)*** Cassiterite (SnO_2), rutile (TiO_2), magnetite (Fe_3O_4), cinnabar (PbS).
26. ***(3)*** Galena (PbS), sphalerite (ZnS), chalcocite (Cu_2S). Although argentite (Ag_2S) is a sulphide ore, it is not concentrated by froth floatation process since its silver content is low. It is better concentrated by leaching with NaCN.
27. ***(4)*** Zinc blende (ZnS), iron pyrites (FeS_2), copper pyrites ($CuFeS_2$), galena (PbS).
28. ***(3)*** Among the given reactions only three i.e. I, II and IV are carried out by self reduction while III and V are done by reduction with Mg and Al (Gold Schmidt aluminothermic process) respectively.
29. ***(2)*** Among the given metals, only two i.e. Mn and Cr are commercially reduced by Gold Schmidt's aluminothermic process.
30. ***(3)*** Among the given metals, only three i.e. Zn, Cd and Hg are purified by distillation processes.

Elemental Practice 7.2

1. ***(c)*** (i) $C(s) + \frac{1}{2}O_2(g) \longrightarrow CO(g)$

   (ii) $C(s) + O_2(g) \longrightarrow CO_2(g)$

   ΔS for reaction (i) is positive, since the number of moles of gases increases.

   ΔS for reaction (ii) is zero, since there is no change in the number of moles of gases.
2. ***(a)*** Statement (a) is correct whereas (b), (c) and (d) are incorrect. The corrected form of Statement (b), (c) and (d) are:

   Medium carbon or mild steel contains 0.05 – 0.5% C. Li is extracted by electrolysis of fused LiCl with KCl.

   During the extraction of Zn, the concentrated ore is roasted at 900°-1000°C to convert ZnS and $ZnSO_4$ to ZnO.
3. ***(a)*** Ellingham diagram helps us in predicting the feasibility of thermal reduction of an ore.
4. ***(c)*** Al_2O_3 and SiO_2 react with conc. NaOH to give $NaAl(OH)_4$ and Na_2SiO_3 respectively.
5. ***(c)*** $C(s) + \frac{1}{2}O_2(g) \longrightarrow CO(g)$; $\Delta S°$ increases.

   Hence, as the temperature increases, $T\Delta S°$ increases and hence $\Delta G(\Delta H - T\Delta S)$ decreases. In other words, the slope of the curve for formation of CO decreases. However, for all other oxides, it increases.
6. ***(d)*** Reaction (a), (b), (c) occurs in combustion zone whereas reaction (d) occurs in the melting zone.
7. ***(c)*** More electropositive metals associated with Cu pass in solution, whereas less electropositive metals (Au, Ag) get collected below the anode as anode mud.
8. ***(c)*** The incorrect statement is given in option (c). Its correct form is as $CuFeS_2$ ore is also known as chalcopyrite and is used to extract copper metal not iron.
9. ***(a)*** Auto-reduction occurs $Cu_2S + 2Cu_2O \longrightarrow 6Cu + SO_2$
10. ***(a)*** Gibbs energy $\Delta G°$ *vs* T plots (schematic) for formation of some oxides (Ellingham diagram).

    According to Ellingham diagram, the temperature at which two lines intersect shows that the metal will reduce the oxide of other metals which lie above it in Ellingham diagram.

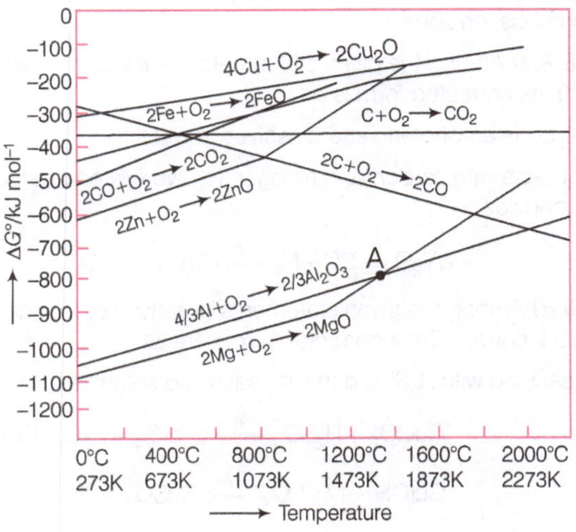

In other words, the metal oxide having more negative value of ΔG_f° can reduce the oxide having less negative ΔG_f°. As, MgO has more $-\Delta G^\circ$ value than alumina, so it will be in lower part of Ellingham diagram. Hence, Mg will be used to reduce alumina.

11. ***(c)*** $ZnO + 2NaOH + H_2O \longrightarrow Na_2[Zn(OH)_4]$

The alkaline medium ensures the formation and stability of this complex ion. Without the alkaline medium, ZnO might precipitate out as insoluble $Zn(OH)_2$ which hampens the leaching process.

12. ***(c)***

(a) Matte on auto-reduction produces blister copper which has blistered appearance due to evolution of SO_2 (not CO_2)

$$\underset{\text{Matte}}{Cu_2S} + 2Cu_2O \longrightarrow \underset{\text{Blister copper}}{6Cu} + SO_2 \uparrow$$

(b) The iron obtained from blast furnace contains 4% carbon and many impurities.

(c) Pig iron can be moulded into variety of shapes.

(d) Wrought iron the purest form of iron which contains 0.2 – 0.5% carbon (not 4%)

So, option (c) is correct.

13. ***(a)*** Pig iron contains about 4% carbon (major impurity) and other impurities (S, P, Si, Mn) in trace amounts.

14. ***(c)*** In electrolytic reduction, pure alumina dissolved in molten cryolite containing more CaF_2 or NaF is electrolysed at 800-1000°C.

15. ***(a)*** Among the given options, reaction given in option (a) is not involved in Baeyer's process.

16. ***(c,d)*** Among the given statements, only (c) and (d) are incorrect and their corrected forms are as,

It does not tell whether reduction reaction is slow or fast.

Plots will have positive slope when ΔG° becomes more positive as temperature increases.

17. ***(a,d)*** Reactions takes place in option (a) and (d) occur in reduction zone while reactions (b) and (c) occur in combustion zone.

18. ***(a,b,c)*** Among the given statements, all are correct except (d), its corrected form is as

Al_2O_3 is amphoteric and dissolves in NaOH.

It reacts with carbon and nitrogen to give AlN and carbon monoxide.

$$Al_2O_3 + 3C + N_2 \xrightarrow{\Delta} 2AlN + 3CO \uparrow$$

19. ***(b,d)*** Among the given statements only two i.e. (b) and (d) are incorrect. Their corrected forms are as,

Leaching with H_2SO_4 converts salts into sulphates

$$CuCO_3 + H_2SO_4 \xrightarrow{\Delta} CuSO_4 + H_2O + CO_2$$

$$Cu(OH)_2 + H_2SO_4 \xrightarrow{\Delta} CuSO_4 + 2H_2O$$

In electrochemical series Fe is above Cu. Thus, when Fe scrap is added to $CuSO_4$ solution, Cu is displaced.

20. ***(b,c,d)*** Reaction (b, c, d) are involved in the extraction of Zn whereas reaction (a) is used for the precipitation of gold.

21. ***(3)*** Crushing and grinding, then roasting and then treatment with KCN are involved in the extraction of gold.

22. ***(4)*** Among the given statements, all are correct except IV. Its corrected form is as follows

Molten iron in the lowest zone is called pig iron.

23. ***(4)*** Among the given reactions except I, II and III rest all are not involved in thermite process.

$B_2O_3 + 2Al \longrightarrow 2B + Al_2O_3$ (aluminothermic reduction)

$2CuO + CuS \longrightarrow 3Cu + SO_2$ (Self reduction)

$ZrI_4 \xrightarrow{\Delta} Zr + 2I_2$ (van Arkel-de-Boer process)

$TiCl_4 + Mg \xrightarrow{1000\text{–}1150°C} Ti + 2MgCl_2$ (Kroll process)

24. ***(2)*** Na_3AlF_6 and AlF_3 are the reagents that are used in Hall Heroult process whereas NaOH and CaO are used in Baeyer's process.

Al_2O_3 — Prime substrate in Hall Heroult process

$Al(OH)_3$ — Target species in Baeyer process.

25. ***(3)*** Among the given statements all are correct except II.

Practice Element : Target JEE Advanced

1. ***(b)*** Flux is mixed with concentrated ore which is not soluble in molten metal. It converts the infusible impurities to fusible material.

2. ***(c)*** In the froth floatation process, collectors enhance the non-wettability of the mineral particles. In this process, depressant helps in separating two different sulphide ores. Froth forms carries the mineral particles.

3. ***(b)*** In the metallurgy of aluminium (Al) graphite anode is oxidised to carbon monoxide (CO) and carbon dioxide (CO_2).

4. ***(a)*** In bauxite ore, only Al_2O_3 and SiO_2 react with conc. NaOH and forms sodium metal aluminate and silicate, respectively. Aluminate further dissolves in water (Baeyer's process).

$$Al_2O_3 + 2NaOH + 3H_2O \longrightarrow 2Na[Al(OH)_4]$$

5. ***(b)*** Zinc blende is ZnS, not $ZnCl_2$.

6. ***(b)*** The intersection point represents the temperature above which carbon can reduce zinc oxide (ZnO). Above this temperature the reduction reaction,
$ZnO + C \longrightarrow Zn + CO_2$ becomes thermodynamically favourable.

7. ***(b)*** Except III, all the reduction processes are correct.

Fe_2O_3 (haematite ore) is reduced into Fe, instead of FeO.

$$Fe_2O_3 + 4CO \longrightarrow 3Fe + 4CO_2$$

8. ***(d)*** Incorrect match is given in option (d)

The correct formula of chalcopyrite is $CuFeS_2$.

9. ***(b)*** Ruby silver ($Ag_2S \cdot Sb_2S_3$) contains both silver and antimony.

10. ***(d)***

(d) Incorrect match is given in option (d) Copper is extracted by self reduction method.

$$Cu_2S + O_2 \longrightarrow Cu_2O + SO_2$$

$$Cu_2O + Cu_2S \longrightarrow Cu + SO_2$$

11. ***(a,b)*** Self reduction method is used in case of sulphides of less electropositive metals e.g. Hg, Pb.

12. ***(a,b,c)*** Vapour phase refining includes Mond's process which is used for the purification of nickel and van Arkel process used for the purification of elements like Ti, Zr.

13. ***(b,c)*** Copper is refined from Cu_2O and CuO by poling and then further refined by electrorefining.

14. ***(a,b,c,d)*** $Al_2O_3 \cdot 2H_2O + 2NaOH \longrightarrow 2NaAlO_2 + 3H_2O$

$NaAlO_2 + 2H_2O \longrightarrow NaOH + Al(OH)_3 \downarrow$ (White gelatinous ppt.)

The precipitation of $Al(OH)_3$ is induced by addition of freshly prepared $Al(OH)_3$ or passing CO_2 or addition of small calculated amount of an acid. But if acid is used, care must be taken to avoid excess or else $Al(OH)_3$ formed will react with it to form Al^{3+} ions and aluminium will go back into solution in the form of ions.

$$Al(OH)_3 + 3H^+ \longrightarrow 3H_2O + Al^{3+}(aq)$$

15. ***(a,c,d)*** Mac-Arthur-Forest process is used for the purification of the ore of silver i.e. argentite not for the purification of silver metal itself. Froth floatation is based on the principle of preferential adsorption instead of absorption. Also, chromite ore is magnetic in nature.

16. ***(a,b,c)*** Since, calcination involves heating of the ore in absence or limited supply of air, the oxides in lower oxidation state are not oxidised to their higher oxidation states as in roasting which is done in the excess of oxygen.

17. ***(a,b,c)*** Aluminium is a highly electropositive metal and thus is electroreduced and carbon reduction is not used.

18. ***(a,b,d)*** Among the given options, only gold is extracted through alkali leaching technique. In this process, gold is leached with dilute solution of NaCN or KCN in the presence of air which supplies O_2.

19. ***(8)*** Rucklidgeite has formula $Pb_3Bi_3Te_4$ and sylvanite has formula $Au_2Ag_2Te_4$.

Thus, the value of $(x + y)$ is 8.

20. ***(2)*** (A) $CaCO_3 \cdot MgCO_3 \xrightarrow{\Delta} CaO + MgO + 1CO_2$

(B) $CaCO_3 \cdot Cu(OH)_2 \xrightarrow{\Delta} 2CuO + H_2O + 1CO_2$

Here, $x = 1, y = 2$

So, $x \times y$ will be 2.

21. ***(2)*** Au and Pt occur in the earth's crust in the native state.

22. ***(3)*** Metals that can be refined by zone refining are Si, Ge and Ga.

23. ***(2)*** Among the given ores only siderite and magnetite have Fe as central metal.

24. ***(3)*** Zr, Ni and Ti can be refined by vapour phase refining.

25. ***(7)*** The impurities of more electropositive elements are oxidised and are blown by hot air in the form of oxides from the surface. Less electropositive elements such as Ag and Au are removed by Parke and Pattinson process.

Here, the said impurities are

Zn, Cu, Ag, Sn, As, Sb and Bi

26. ***(5)*** Bett's electrolytic method is used for this purpose in which impure lead acts as anode, pure lead as cathode and lead hexafluorosilicate ($PbSiF_6$) containing 8-12% hexafluorosilicic acid (H_2SiF_6) and a little gelatin act as electrolyte as majority of common salts of lead are insoluble or are covalent and thus cannot be used as electrolyte.

27. ***(4)*** Stainless is the corrosion resistanst variety of steel and contains Cr and Ni along with the iron and some amount of carbon.

28. ***(5)*** Stainless steel is composition of Fe, Cr, Ni and some carbon. Quenching is a heat treatment that is used for steel in which the steel is heated to red hot and then suddenly cooled by immersing in cold oil. This will make steel hard and brittle, for sulphide ore reverberatory furnace is used. Carbon percentage in steel is around 0.15-1.5%. Leaching process is used for extracting a substance from a solid material that is dissolved in a liquid. So, only V is an incorrect match.

29. ***(1900)*** Above 1900°C the value of $\Delta G°$ becomes negative for the reaction $MgO + C \longrightarrow Mg + CO$.

The graph of carbon occupies lower position than the graph of Mg.

30. ***(24)*** Lower is the position of the metal (Mg) in the Ellingham diagram better is its reducing strength for any given metal oxide (Mg : 24 g/mol).

31. ***(3)*** At 1100°C, except (d), all are non-spontaneous.

32. ***(1000)*** At 1000°C, zinc and carbon have equal affinity for oxygen.

33. ***(d)*** (A→ IV; B→ III; C→ I; D→ II)

Mica ($K_2O \cdot 3Al_2O_3 \cdot 6SiO_2 \cdot 2H_2O$) and Willemite ($Zn_2SiO_4$) are silicate ores of aluminium and zinc respectively, Cassiterite (SnO_2) is an oxide ore of tin, Sphalerite or zinc blende (ZnS) is a sulphide ore of zinc and siderite ($FeCO_3$) is a carbonate ore of iron.

34. ***(d)*** (A→ IV; B→ III; C→ I; D→ II)

Calcination is the heating of the carbonate ore to obtain metal oxide with the evolution of CO_2. Slag formation represents the removal of oxide impurities by the addition of another oxide resulting in the formation of a fusible mass called slag ($FeSiO_3$). Self-reduction is the reduction of the oxide or sulphate of the metal by its own sulphide forming crude metal, for example in case of Pb, Cu and Hg. Halls process is the chemical leaching of the bauxite ore of aluminium using Na_2CO_3 and the formation of sodium metaluminate and evolution of CO_2.

35. ***(b)*** (A→ II; B→ IV; C→ I; D→ III)

Zone refining is used for the purification of the elements used for making semiconductors, for example, Si, Ge and Ga. Liquation method is used for the purification of the metals with low melting points such as Sn, Pb and Bi. Fractional distillation is used for the purification of the metals with low boiling points and poling is used to the oxide impurities form the impure copper or tin.

36. ***(d)*** The correct match is A→ I, B→ II, C→ III, D→ IV

Poling Green logs (wood) are used to remove dissolved oxygen from molten copper.

Cupellation Silver is purified by heating it in a furnace, removing Pb and other impurities

Distillation Metals like Zn and Hg are purified based on their volatility.

Electrolytic Refining Metals like Cu and Au are refined using electrolysis with an impure anode (crude metal) and pure cathode.

37. ***(d)*** (A→ III, B→ IV, C→ II, D→ I)

Impure lead is converted to pure lead using Bett's electrolysis in which $PbSiF_6+H_2SiF_6$ is used as the electrolyte. Argentiferous lead containing major impurity of Ag is converted to crude lead by Parke's and Pattinson's process using 1% zinc to form an alloy with silver. Impure aluminum is purified by Hoopes electrolysis and the extraction of magnesium from sea water is called Dow's process.

38. ***(a)*** All sulphide ore are purified by froth floatation process. Barnite (Cu_5FeS_4), zinc blende (ZnS), are sulphide ores. While cerussite ($PbCO_3$) is carbonate ore and horn silver (AgCl), cryolite (Na_3AlF_6) are halide ores.

39. ***(a)*** In Hall Heroult process, the reaction involved is

$$2C \text{ (Graphite anode)} + O_2 \longrightarrow 2CO$$

$$C \text{ (Graphite anode)} + O_2 \longrightarrow CO_2$$

The slag is lighter and has lower melting point than the metal.

Statements IV and V are incorrect.

40. ***(a)*** Silicon is refined by using zone refining and liquation is used for the purification of the metals having low melting point as Sn, Pb, Bi.

Statements II and III are incorrect.

41. ***(c)*** Limonite is $Fe_2O_3 \cdot 3H_2O$. Thus, option (V) is incorrect and rest all are correct

42. ***(b)*** Basic flux ⟶ CaO, MgO

Acidic flux ⟶ SiO_2, P_4O_{10}, B_2O_3

Slag ⟶ $Ca_3(PO_4)_2$, $CaSiO_3$

43. ***(a)*** Zinc blende (ZnS), galena (PbS), siderite ($FeCO_3$), amblygonite [(Li, Na)$AlPO_4$(F, OH)], haematite (Fe_2O_3), calamine ($ZnCO_3$), bauxite ($Al_2O_3 \cdot 2H_2O$).

44. ***(b)*** Hoope's process for aluminum, calcination is used for carbonate and sulphate ores. MiCa is silicate ore of Al.

45. ***(a)*** Pyrometallurgy is used for metals that are less electropositive. e.g. Fe, Cu, Pb, Sn, Ni, Hg, Cr, Zn etc. Ca and Na is highly electropositive so they are not use in pyrometallurgy.

46. ***(a)*** $CaO + C \longrightarrow$ ✗

$Al_2O_3 + C \longrightarrow$ ✗

$MgO + C \longrightarrow$ ✗

$Cr_2O_3 + C \longrightarrow$ ✗

$PbO + C \longrightarrow$ ✓

$Fe_2O_3 + C \longrightarrow$ ✗

$Cu_2O + C \longrightarrow$ ✓

47. ***(a)*** Mond's process and van Arkel methods the metal is converted to a volatile compound and is separated from the impurities in the form of vapours and thus both methods are collectively known as vapour phase refining.

Check Through PYQs : JEE Advanced

1. ***(d)*** $ZnCO_3$-Calamine (zinc ore)

$CuCO_3 \cdot Cu(OH)_2$-Malachite (copper ore)

Fe_3O_4-Magnetite (iron ore)

Na_3AlF_6-Cryolite (aluminium ore)

Thus, option (d) is correct.

2. ***(b, c, d)***

(a) Malachite is an impure ore of copper. The roasting of malachite produces copper (II) oxide, carbon dioxide and water.

$$\underset{\text{(Malachite)}}{CuCO_3 \cdot Cu(OH)_2} \xrightarrow{\Delta} 2CuO + H_2O + CO_2$$

(b) Calamine is an ore of zinc. The calcination of calamine produces zincite and carbon dioxide.

$$\underset{\text{(Calamine)}}{ZnCO_3} \xrightarrow{\Delta} \underset{\text{(Zincite)}}{ZnO} + CO_2$$

(c) Copper pyrite is a yellow copper ore made up of copper and iron sulphide. Its roasting gives copper oxide as a main product, ferrous oxide and sulphur dioxide. Ferrous oxide is then mixed with silica to form iron silicate (slag) which gets collected at the bottom of furnace.

$$2CuFeS_2 + O_2 \xrightarrow{\text{Roasting}} Cu_2S + 2FeS + SO_2$$

$$2FeS + 3O_2 \longrightarrow 2FeO + 2SO_2$$

$$FeO + SiO_2 \longrightarrow FeSiO_3$$

(d) During the extraction of silver, the finely powdered silver ore is treated with dilute KCN solution to form a cyano complex of silver.

$$4Ag + 8CN^- + H_2O + O_2 \longrightarrow 4[Ag(CN)_2]^- + 4OH^-$$

Then zinc is added to the solution formed. Being more reactive and electropositive, zinc displaces silver from the complex.

$$2[Ag(CN)_2]^- + Zn(s) \longrightarrow [Zn(CN)_4]^{2-} + 2Ag(s)\downarrow$$

Hence, except (a), remaining three statements (b, c, d) are correct with respect to processes involved in the extraction of metals.

3. ***(a, d)*** The treatment of galena with HNO_3 forms colourless nitric oxide gas which is paramagnetic.

4. ***(a, c, d)*** Statements (a), (c) and (d) are correct, whereas statement (b) is incorrect. All statements are explained as follows,

(a) A mixture PbO and PbS reacts as follows

$$2PbO + PbS \longrightarrow 3Pb + SO_2$$

This reaction is known as self-reduction.

(b) Silica is added to remove impurities of Fe in the form of slag, $FeSiO_3$.

(c) Partial oxidation (roasting) of $CuFeS_2$ produces copper matte which on self-reduction produces blister copper.

(d) Zn powder reacts with $Na[Au(CN)_2]$ to form gold. This process is called cyanide process.

$$2Zn + 4Na[Au(CN)_2] \longrightarrow 2Na_2[Zn(CN)_4] + 4Au$$

5. ***(b, d)***

(a) Al_2O_3 reacts with coke at temperature higher than 2500°C to form carbides. Thus, reduction of Al_2O_3 with coke (C) at a temperature greater than 2500°C is not carried out. Hence, option (a) is incorrect.

(b) Aluminate solution on passing CO_2 gas gives neutralisation reaction and forms precipitates of hydrated alumina ($Al_2O_3 \cdot 3H_2O$). So, it is a correct option.

(c) Dissolution of Al_2O_3 in hot aqueous NaOH takes place at 473 K - 523 K and 35-36 bar pressure. As no conditions are mentioned. So, option (c) is not completely correct.

(d) Electrolysis of Al_2O_3 is done by mixing it with Na_3AlF_6 to produce Al and CO_2. So, it is a correct statement.

6. ***(a, b, c)***

(a) Limestone provides flux CaO that removes SiO_2 impurity present in ore by forming fusible calcium silicate.

$$CaCO_3 \xrightarrow{\Delta} CaO + CO_2$$

$$\underset{\text{From limestone}}{CaO} + \underset{\text{From ore}}{SiO_2} \longrightarrow \underset{\text{Calcium silicate}}{CaSiO_3}$$

So, statement (a) is correct.

(b) Pig iron obtained from blast furnace contains 4% carbon and many other impurities.
So, statement (b) is also correct.

(c) Coke burns to give CO which reduces the oxide to metal.

$$C + O_2 \longrightarrow CO_2$$
$$CO_2 + C \longrightarrow 2CO$$

So, statement (c) is also correct.

(d) Exhaust gases are CO and CO_2.
So, statement (d) is incorrect.

7. ***(a, b, c, d)***

(a) $2Na[Al(OH)_4]\ (aq) + CO_2 \longrightarrow Na_2CO_3 + H_2O + 2Al(OH)_3 \downarrow$ or $Al_2O_3 \cdot 2H_2O$ (ppt.)

Hence, the statement (a) is true.

(b) The electrolysis of alumina by Hall-Heroult's process is carried by using a fused mixture of alumina and cryolite (Na_3AlF_6) along with minor quantities of aluminium fluoride and fluorspar. The addition of cryolite and fluorspar increases the electrical conductivity of alumina and lowers the fusion temperature. Hence, the statement (b) is true.

(c) At anode, alumina reacts with fluorine to liberate oxygen and evolved oxygen reacts with carbon anode to form carbon dioxide and hence, statement (c) is true.

(d) Steel cathode with carbon lining and graphite (anode) are used and hence,the statement (d) is true.

8. ***(a, b, c)*** $CuFeS_2$ (copper pyrite) is converted into copper into following steps:

Step I Crushing (grinding) followed by concentration by froth-floatation process.

Step II Roasting of ore in the presence of SiO_2 which removes iron as slag ($FeSiO_3$).

$$2CuFeS_2 + O_2 \longrightarrow Cu_2S + 2FeS + SO_2$$
$$2FeS + 3O_2 \longrightarrow 2SO_2 + 2FeO$$
$$FeO + SiO_2 \longrightarrow FeSiO_3(\text{Slag})$$

Step III Self-reduction in Bessemer converter

$$2Cu_2S + 3O_2 \longrightarrow 2Cu_2O + 2SO_2$$
$$2Cu_2O + Cu_2S \longrightarrow 6Cu + SO_2$$

Copper obtained is blister copper (98% pure).

Step IV Refining of blister copper is done by electrolysis.

Impure copper—Anode

Pure copper— Cathode

At anode , $Cu \longrightarrow Cu^{2+} + 2e^-$

At cathode , $Cu^{2+} + 2e^- \longrightarrow Cu$

Carbon-reduction method is not used. Thus, (d) is incorrect.

9. ***(b c, d)***

(a) is wrong statement. Impure copper (blistered) is set as anode where copper is oxidised to Cu^{2+} and goes into electrolytic solutions.

(b) $CuSO_4$ is used as an electrolyte in purification process.

(c) Pure copper is deposited at cathode as

$Cu^{2+} + 2e^- \longrightarrow Cu$: (At cathode)

(d) Less active metals like Ag, Au etc., settle down as anode mud.

CHAPTER 8

d- and *f*-Block Elements

Learning Elements

Element 1 Transition Elements and Their Properties

Atomic Radii, Ionic Radii, Metallic Character, Melting and Boiling Points, Enthalpy of Atomisation, Oxidation States, Ionisation Energies and Stability of Oxidation States, Electrode Potentials, Formation of Coloured Ions Magnetic Properties, Formation of Complex Ions, Formation of interstitial Compounds, Catalytic Properties, Alloy Formation, Chemical Reactivity, Nature of oxides, Hydroxides

Element 2 Some Important Compounds of *d*-Block Elements; *f*-Block Elements

Potassium Dichromate ($K_2Cr_2O_7$), Potassium Permanganate ($KMnO_4$), Silver Nitrate ($AgNO_3$), Inner-Transition Elements

Practice Elements

Practice Element 1 Target JEE Main

Practice Element 2 Target JEE Advanced

Trend Insights

JEE Main

	2024				2023				2022			
Topics	**E**	**M**	**T**	**O**	**E**	**M**	**T**	**O**	**E**	**M**	**T**	**O**
Transition Elements and their Properties	1	6	10	17	–	2	1	3	4	2	5	11
Some Important Compounds of *d*-Block Elements; *f*-Block Elements	3	3	1	7	3	2	4	9	3	5	13	21

E = Easy, **M** = Medium, **T** = Tough, **O** = Overall

Current Dynamics

- This chapter is more important from JEE Main aspect as more number of questions were asked from this chapter.
- In recent years most of the questions had been asked from electronic configuration and magnetic behaviour.
- Application based questions focusing on periodic trends and oxidation state had been asked in past years.
- Frequent number of questions focusing on colour due to *d*-*d* transition and charge transfer had been asked.

JEE Advanced

Typology	Years				
	2024	**2023**	**2022**	**2021**	**2020**
1. One option correct	–	1	–	–	–
2. One or More than one correct	–	–	–	–	–
3. Numerical/Integer Value	–	–	–	–	1
4. Matching Type	–	–	–	–	–
5. Paragraph Based	–	–	–	–	–

Current Dynamics

- At Advanced level few questions had been asked on mixed concepts of preparation and properties from this chapter.
- The frequency of direct or indirect question from this chapter is 0-1.

Insightful Advice

- Students are advised to grip the basis of stability in oxidation states.
- Practice on calculating magnetic moment related questions with a focus on concepts like spin pairing energy and electronic configurations.
- Focus on frequently asked topics like applications of $KMnO_4$ in redox titration, lanthanide contraction and its consequences.

Element 1 Transition Elements and Their Properties

Transition Elements may be defined as an element whose atom in the ground state or ion, in common oxidation state, has incomplete sub-shell i.e., has electron from 1 to 9. It is called transition element due to fact that it is in lying between **most electropositive** (s-block) and **most electronegative** (p-block) elements and represents a transition from them. The general electronic configuration of these elements is $(n-1)d^{1 \text{ to } 10} ns^{0 \text{ to } 2}$.

The definition of transition metal excludes Zn, Cd and Hg because they have completely filled d-orbitals. Their common oxidation state is +2. They also do not show the characteristics of transition elements. Zn, Cd and Hg are called **non-typical transition elements**.

Some exceptional outer electronic configuration of transition elements are :

$Cr = 3d^5 4s^1$, $Nb = 4d^4 5s^1$, $Pd = 4d^{10} 5s^0$, $Ag = 4d^{10} 5s^1$, $Cu = 3d^{10} 4s^1$, $Mo = 4d^5 5s^1$, $Ru = 4d^7 5s^1$, $Pt = 5d^9 6s^1$, $Au = 5d^{10} 6s^1$. These irregularities can be explained on the basis of half filled and full filled stability of d-orbitals.

Classification

Transition elements are classified in following series :

(i) First transition series ($3d$ series) = 21 to 30 i.e. Sc to Zn.

(ii) Second transition series ($4d$ series) = 39 to 48 i.e. Y to Cd.

(iii) Third transition series ($5d$ series) = 57, i.e., La and 72 to 80 i.e., Hf to Hg.

(iv) Fourth transition series ($6d$ series) = 89 i.e., Ac and 104 to 112 i.e., Rf to Cn.

Comparison of the First Row Transition Metals through the *d*-Orbital Electronic Configuration

(i) **The d^0 Configuration** Of the simple ions, only Sc^{3+} is known to have this configuration. This configuration occurs for those metals in which the formal oxidation states equal the total number of $3d$ and $4s$-electron.

This is true for Ti(IV), V(V), Cr(VI), and Mn(VII) but for Fe(VIII) is unknown.

(ii) **The d^1 Configuration** Except vanadium(IV), all other metals with this configuration are either reducing or undergo disproportionation reaction.

For example, disproportionation reaction occurs for Cr(V) and Mn(VI) are as follows :

$$3CrO_4^{3-} + 8H^+ \longrightarrow 2CrO_4^{2-} + Cr^{3+} + 4H_2O$$

$$3MnO_4^{2-} + 4H^+ \longrightarrow 2MnO_4^- + MnO_2 + 2H_2O$$

(iii) **The d^2 Configuration** This configuration ranges from Ti(II), which is very strongly reducing, to Fe(VI) which is very strongly oxidising. Vanadium (III) is also reducing.

(iv) **The d^3 Configuration** Chromium (III) is the important species with this configuration which is stable and well known for complex formation. In other cases, this configuration is relatively unimportant.

(v) **The d^4 Configuration** There are really no stable species with this configuration. The chromium (II) is strongly reducing and manganese(III) disproportionates.

(vi) **The d^5 Configuration** The two important species with this configuration are Mn^{2+} and Fe^{3+}, the latter may however be reduced to Fe^{2+}.

(vii) **The d^6 Configuration** Iron(II) and cobalt(III) are important species with this configuration. Iron(II) is quite stable although a mild reducing agent and cobalt(III) is stable in the presence of strong complexing reagents.

(viii) **The d^7 Configuration** The species with this configuration is cobalt(II) which is stable in aqueous solutions but gets oxidised to form Co(III) complexes in the presence of strong ligands.

(ix) **The d^8 Configuration** Nickel(II) is the most important species with this configuation.

(x) **The d^9 Configuration** The configuration is found in Cu^{2+} compounds and is by far the most important in the chemistry of copper. Otherwise, this configuration is of little importance.

(xi) **The d^{10} configuration** The two species Cu^+ and Zn^{2+} are important with this configuration. Whereas, copper(I) is easily oxidised to copper(II).

General Properties

Following are the general properties of transition elements.

1. Atomic Radii

The atomic radii and atomic volumes of d-block elements in any series decrease with increase in the atomic number. However the decrease, is not regular.

The atomic radii tend to reach minimum near at the middle of the series, and increase slightly towards the end of the series.

The atomic radii of 3*d*-series elements are compared with those of the neighbouring *s*- and *p*-block elements.

K	Ca	Sc	Ti	V	Cr	Mn	Fe	Co	Ni	Cu	Zn	Ga	Ge
227	174	162	147	134	127	136	126	125	124	128	138	135	122*

(* in pm units)

Explanation

- When we go in any transition series from left to right, the nuclear charge increases gradually by one unit with each element.
- The added electrons enter the same penultimate shell, (inner *d*-shell) these added electrons shield the outermost electron from the attraction of the nuclear charge.
- The increased nuclear charge tends to reduce the atomic radii, while the added electrons tend to increase the atomic radii.
- At the beginning of the series, due to smaller number of electrons in the d-orbitals, the effect of increased nuclear charge predominates, and the atomic radii decrease.
- Later in the series, when the number of *d*-electrons increases, the increased shielding effect and the increased repulsion between the electrons tend to increase the atomic radii.

2. Ionic Radii

For ions having identical charges, the ionic radii decrease slowly with the increase in the atomic number across a given series of the transition elements.

Elements (M)	Sc	Ti	V	Cr	Mn	Fe	Co	Ni	Cu	Zn
Ionic radius (M^{2+})/pm	—	—	79	82	82	77	74	70	73	75
(M^{3+})/pm	73	67	64	62	65	65	61	60	—	—

Explanation

The gradual decrease in the values of ionic radius across the series of transition elements is due to the increase in the effective nuclear charge.

JEE Alert

The ionic radii decreases with increase in oxidation state. Thus, the ionic size of M^{3+} cations are smaller than those of M^{2+} cations.

3. Ionisation Energies

The ionisation energies of the elements of first transition series are given below.

Elements Ionisation Energies	Sc	Ti	V	Cr	Mn	Fe	Co	Ni	Cu	Zn
I.E.$_1$	631	656	650	653	717	762	758	736	745	906
I.E.$_2$	1235	1309	1414	1592	1509	1561	1644	1752	1958	1734
I.E.$_3$	2393	2657	2833	2990	3260	2962	3243	3402	3556	3837

* in kJ mol^{-1}

The following generalisations can be obtained from the ionisation energy values given above.

(i) The ionisation energies of these elements are high, and in the most cases lie between those of *s*- and *p*-block elements. This indicates that the transition elements are less electropositive than *s*-block elements.

Explanation

Transition metals have smaller atomic radii and higher nuclear charge as compared to the alkali metals. Both these factors tend to increase the ionisation energy, as observed.

(ii) The ionisation energy in any transition series increases with atomic number. The increase however is not smooth and as sharp as seen in the case of *s*- and *p*-block elements.

Explanation

- The ionisation energy increases due to the increase in the nuclear charge with atomic number at the beginning of the series.
- Gradually, the shielding effect of the added electrons also increases.
- The shielding effect tends to decrease the attraction due to the nuclear charge.
- The two opposing factors lead to a rather gradual increase in the ionisation energies in any transition series.

(iii) The first ionisation energies of 5*d*-series elements are much higher than those of the 3*d*-and 4*d*-series elements.

Explanation

- In the 5*d*-series of transitions-elements, after lanthanum (La), the added electrons go to the next inner 4*f* orbitals.
- The 4*f* electrons have poor shielding effect. As a result, the outermost electrons experience greater nuclear attraction.
- This leads to higher ionisation energies for the 5*d*-series of transition elements.

4. Metallic Character

All the transition elements are metals. These are hard and good conductor of heat and electricity. All these metals are malleable, ductile and form alloys with other metals. These elements occur in three types e.g., face-centered cubic (fcc), hexagonal close-packed (hcp) and body-centered cubic (bcc), structures.

Explanation

- The ionisation energies of the transition elements are not very high.
- The outermost shell in their atoms have many vacant or partially filled orbitals. These characteristics make these elements metallic in character.
- Metallic bonding in these metals is indicated by the conducting nature of these metals.
- The hardness of these metals, suggests the presence of covalent bonding in these metals.
- The presence of unfilled *d*-orbitals favour covalent bonding. Therefore, it appears that there exists covalent and metallic bonding in transition elements.

5. Melting and Boiling Points

The melting and boiling points of transition elements, except Cd and Hg, are very high as compared to the *s*- and *p*-block elements. The melting and boiling points first increase, pass through maxima and then steadily decrease across any transition series. The maximum occurs around middle of the series.

Explanation

- Atoms of the transition elements are closely packed and held together by strong metallic bonds which have appreciable covalent character. This leads to high melting and boiling points of the transition elements.
- The strength of the metallic bonds depends upon the number of unpaired electrons in the outermost shell of the atom.

JEE Quicker

The melting point of iron is greater than that of manganese.
JEE Main 2025

Generally greater is the number of unpaired electrons stronger is the metallic bonding. Due to this melting and boiling point is high. But in case of Mn as they have exactly half-filled *d*-orbitals, thus they are stable. So, delocalisation is less. Thus, metallic bond is weaker. So, iron has greater melting point than manganese.

- Thus, the melting and boiling points first increase and then decrease, showing maxima around the middle of the series.
- The low melting points of Zn, Cd, and Hg may be due to the absence of unpaired *d*-electrons in their atoms.

6. Enthalpies of Atomisation

Transition metals exhibit high enthalpies of atomisation.

Explanation

- The atoms in these elements are closely packed and held together by strong metallic bonds.
- The metallic bond is formed as a result of the interaction of electrons in the outermost shell.
- Greater the number of valence electrons, stronger is the metallic bond higher is the enthalpies of atomisation.

7. Oxidation States

Most of the transition elements exhibit several oxidation states i.e., they show variable valency in their compounds. Some of common oxidation states of the first transition series elements are in bold types given below in table.

Outer electronic configurations and oxidation states for 3*d*-elements

Elements	Outer electronic configuration	Oxidation states
Sc	$3d^1 4s^2$	+3
Ti	$3d^2 4s^2$	+2, +3, **+4**
V	$3d^3 4s^2$	+2, +3, +4, +5
Cr	$3d^5 4s^1$	+2, **+3**, +4, +5, **+6**
Mn	$3d^5 4s^2$	**+2**, +3, +4, +5, +6, **+7**
Fe	$3d^6 4s^2$	**+2, +3**, +4, +6
Co	$3d^7 4s^2$	**+2, +3**, +4
Ni	$3d^8 4s^2$	**+2**, +3, +4
Cu	$3d^{10} 4s^1$	+1, **+2**
Zn	$3d^{10} 4s^2$	+2

Explanation

- The outermost electronic configuration of the transition elements is $(n-1)d^{1-10}ns^{0 \text{ to } 2}$. Since, the energy levels of $(n-1)d$ and *ns*-orbitals are quite close to each other, hence both the *ns* and $(n-1)$ *d*-electrons are available for bonding purposes.
- The number of oxidation states shown by these elements depends upon the number of *d*-electrons it has. For example, Sc having a configuration $3d^1 4s^2$ may show an oxidation state of +2 (only *s*- electrons are lost) and +3 (when *d*-electron is also lost).
- The highest oxidation state which an elements of this group might show is given by the total number of *ns*- and $(n-1)d$-electrons.
- The relative stability of the different oxidation states depends upon the factors such as, electronic configuration, nature of bonding, stoichiometry, lattice energies and solvation energies.

The common oxidation states of transition metals reveals the following conclusions.

(i) The variable oxidation states shown by the transition elements are due to the participation of outer *ns* and inner $(n-1)d$-electrons in bonding.

(ii) Except scandium, the most common oxidation state shown by the elements of first transition series is +2. This oxidation state arises from the loss of two 4*s* electrons. This means that after scandium, *d*-orditals become more stable than the *s*-orbital.

(iii) The highest oxidation states are observed in fluorides and oxides because fluorine and oxygen are the most electronegative elements. The highest oxidation state shown by any transition elements (by Ru and Os) is 8.

(iv) The transition elements in the +2 and +3 oxidation states mostly form ionic bonds. In compounds of the higher oxidation states (compound formed with fluorine or oxygen), the bonds are essentially covalent. For example, in permanganate ion MnO_4^-, all bonds formed between manganese and oxygen are covalent.

(v) Within a group, the maximum oxidation state increases with atomic number. For example, iron shows the common oxidation state of +2 and +3, but ruthenium and osmium in the same group form compound in the +4, +6 and +8 oxidation states.

(vi) Transition metals also form compounds in low oxidation states such as +1 and 0. For example, nickel in, nickel tetracarbonyl, $Ni(CO)_4$ has zero oxidation state.

(vii) Even though the ground state of the atom has a d^{10}-configuration, Pd and the coinage metals Cu, Ag and Au behave as typical transition elements. This is because of their most common oxidation states, Cu(II) has a d^9-configuration, and Pd (II) and Au (III) have d^8-configuration (incomplete *d* level). However, Zn (II), Cd (II) and Hg (II) have a d^{10} configuration. Because of this, these elements do not show the characteristic properties of transition elements.

(viii)

Reducing agent	Most stable	Oxidising agents
—	Sc^{3+}	—
Ti^{2+}, Ti^{3+}	Ti^{3+}	—
V^{2+}, V^{3+}	V^{4+}	V^{5+}
Cr^{2+}	Cr^{3+}	$Cr^{6+} (CrO_4^{2-})$
—	Mn^{2+}	$Mn^{3+}, Mn^{4+} (MnO_2)$ $Mn^{7+} (MnO_4^-)$
Fe^{2+}	Fe^{3+}	—
—	Co^{2+}	Co^{3+}
—	Ni^{2+}	—
Cu^+	Cu^{2+}	

JEE MAPPER

Example Similar to PYQ Asked in JEE Main 2024

The correct order of following 3*d*-metal oxides according to their oxidation state is

A. TiO_2 B. CoF_3 C. Mn_2O_7 D. CrO_3
E. FeO

(a) D > A > B > E > C (b) B > C > A > D > E
(c) A > C > B > D > E (d) C > D > A > B > E

Ans. (*d*) Oxidation state of the given 3*d*-series oxides are as follows

A. $TiO_2 \longrightarrow Ti \Rightarrow +4$
B. $CoF_3 \longrightarrow Co \Rightarrow +3$
C. $Mn_2O_7 \longrightarrow Mn \Rightarrow +7$
D. $CrO_3 \longrightarrow Cr \Rightarrow +6$
E. $FeO \longrightarrow Fe \Rightarrow +2$

So, oxidaion state order is C > D > A > B > E

Competency Enhancer 1.1

The correct order of following 3*d*-metal oxides according to their oxidation states is

A. V_2O_5 B. CrO_2 C. Cu_2O D. CoO
E. Mn_2O_3

(a) B > C > A > D > E (b) C > B > A > E > D
(c) A > B > E > D > C (d) A > C > D > E > B

8. Ionisation Energies and the Stability of Oxidation States

The values of the ionisation energies can be used in estimating the relative stability of various transition metal compounds (or ions). For example, Ni^{2+} compounds are found to be thermodynamically more stable than Pt^{2+}, whereas Pt^{4+} compounds are more stable than Ni^{4+} compounds. This can be explained in term of ionisation energy. Consider the following ionisation energies of Ni and Pt.

Metal	$(IE_1 + IE_2)$ kJ mol^{-1}	$(IE_3 + IE_4)$ kJ mol^{-1}	E_{total}, kJ mol^{-1} $(= IE_1 + IE_2 + IE_3 + IE_4)$
Ni	2490	8800	11290
Pt	2660	6700	9360

As you can see that, the ionisation of Ni to Ni^{2+} requires lesser energy (2490 kJ mol^{-1}) as compared to the energy required for the production of Pt^{2+} (2660 kJ mol^{-1}). Therefore, Ni^{2+} compounds are thermodynamically more stable than Pt^{2+} compounds.

On the other hand, formation of Pt^{4+} requires lesser energy (9360 kJ mol^{-1}) as compared to that required for the formation of Ni^{4+} (11290 kJ mol^{-1}). Therefore, Pt^{4+} compounds are more stable than Ni^{4+} compounds.

This is supported by the fact that $[PtCl_6]^{2-}$ complex ion is known, while the corresponding ion for nickel is not known. However, other factors which affect the stability of a compound are,

(a) enthalpy of sublimation of the metal.

(b) lattice and the solvation energies of the compound or ion.

9. Electrode Potentials ($E°$)

Standard electrode potentials of some half-cells involving 3*d*-series of transition elements and their ions in aqueous solution are given in table.

Elements	Ion	Electrode reaction	$E°$/volt
Sc	Sc^{3+}	$Sc^{3+} + 3e^- \rightarrow Sc$	−2.10
Ti	Ti^{2+}	$Ti^{2+} + 2e^- \rightarrow Ti$	−1.63
V	V^{2+}	$V^{2+} + 2e^- \rightarrow V$	−1.18
Cr	Cr^{3+}	$Cr^{3+} + 3e^- \rightarrow Cr$	−0.74
Mn	Mn^{2+}	$Mn^{2+} + 2e^- \rightarrow Mn$	−1.18
Fe	Fe^{2+}	$Fe^{2+} + 2e^- \rightarrow Fe$	−0.44
Co	Co^{2+}	$Co^{2+} + 2e^- \rightarrow Co$	−0.28
Ni	Ni^{2+}	$Ni^{2+} + 2e^- \rightarrow Ni$	−0.25
Cu	Cu^{2+}	$Cu^{2+} + 2e^- \rightarrow Cu$	+0.34
Zn	Zn^{2+}	$Zn^{2+} + 2e^- \rightarrow Zn$	−0.76

The negative values of $E°$ for the first series of transition elements (except for Cu^{2+}/Cu) indicate that,

(i) these metals should liberate hydrogen from dilute acids i.e., the reactions,

$$M + 2H^+ \longrightarrow M^{2+} + H_2(g)$$

$$2M + 6H^+ \longrightarrow 2M^{3+} + 3H_2(g)$$

are favourable in the forward direction. In actual practice however, most of these metals react with dilute acids very slowly. Some of these metals get coated with a thin protective layer of oxide. Such an oxide layer prevents the metal to react further.

(ii) these metals should act as good reducing agents. There is no regular trend in the $E°$ values. This is due to irregular variation in the ionisation and sublimation energies across the series.

Relative stabilities of transition metal ions in different oxidation states in aqueous medium can be predicted from the electrode potential data. To illustrate this, let us consider the following.

$$M(s) \longrightarrow M(g)$$

ΔH_1 = Enthalpy of sublimation, ΔH_{sub}

$$M(g) \longrightarrow M^+(g) + e^-$$

ΔH_2 = Ionisation energy, IE

$$M^+(g) \longrightarrow M^+(aq)$$

ΔH_3 = Enthalpy of hydration, ΔH_{hyd}

Adding these equations one gets,

$$M(s) \longrightarrow M^+(aq) + e^-,$$

$$\Delta H = \Delta H_1 + \Delta H_2 + \Delta H_3 = \Delta H_{sub} + IE + \Delta H_{hyd}$$

The ΔH represents the enthalpy change required to bring the solid metal M to the monovalent ion in aqueous medium, $M^+(aq)$.

The reaction, $M(s) \longrightarrow M^+(aq) + e^-$, will be favourable only if ΔH is negative. More negative is the value of ΔH, more favourable will be the formation of that cation from the metal. Thus, the oxidation state for which ΔH value is more negative will be stable in the solution.

Electrode potential for a M^{n+}/M half-cell is a measure of the tendency for the reaction, $M^{n+}(aq) + ne^- \longrightarrow M(s)$.

Thus, this reduction reaction will take place if the electrode potential M^{n+}/M half-cell is positive.

When an elements exists in more than one oxidation states, the standard electrode potential ($E°$) values can be used in the predicting the relative stabilities of different oxidation states in aqueous solutions. The oxidation state of a cation for which $\Delta H = (\Delta H_{sub} + IE + \Delta H_{hyb})$ or $E°$ is more negative (or less positive) will be more stable.

JEE Spotlite

- The transition metals are generally less electropositive (or more electronegative) than the alkali and alkaline-earth metals.
- In case of Cr, despite a negative standard reduction potential, it is quite inert chemically because of the formation of chromium (III) oxide, Cr_2O_3 on its surfaces. This fact finds application of Cr to use as a protective and non corrosive plating on other metals.
- Though the 4*s*-orbitals are occupied before 3*d*-orbitals, we cannot say that they are always more stable. In fact, the ionisation of transition elements takes place by the loss of *ns*-electrons first.

10. Formation of Coloured Ions

Most of the compound of the transition elements are coloured in the solid state and/or in the solution phase. The compounds of transition metals are coloured due to the presence of unpaired electrons in their *d*-orbitals.

Explanation

- In an isolated atom or ion of a transition elements, all the five *d*-orbitals are of the same energy (they are said to be degenerate).
- Under the influence of the combining anion(s) or electron-rich molecules, the five *d*-orbitals split into two (or sometimes more than two) levels of different energies.

- The difference between the two energy levels depends upon the nature of the combining ions, but corresponds to the energy associated with the radiation in the visible region, ($\lambda = 380 - 760$ nm).
- The transition metals in elemental form or in the ionic form have one or more unpaired electrons.
- When visible light falls on the sample, the electrons from the lower energy-level get promoted to a higher energy level due to the absorption of light of à characteristic wavelength (or colour).
- This wavelength (or colour) of the absorbed light depends upon the energy difference of the two levels. Rest of the light gets transmitted.
- The transmitted light has a colour complementary to the absorbed colour. Therefore, the compound or the solution appears to be of the complementary colour.
- For example, $[Cu(H_2O)_6]^{2+}$ ions absorb red radiation, and appear blue-green (blue-green is complementary colour to red). Hydrated Co^{2+} ions absorb radiation in the blue-green region, and therefore, appear red in sunlight.

Relationship between the colours of the absorbed and transmitted light: the complementary colours.

Colour of the		Colour of the	
Absorbed light	**Transmitted light**	**Absorbed light**	**Transmitted light**
IR	White	Blue-green	Red
Red	Blue-green	Blue	Orange
Orange	Blue	Indigo	Yellow
Yellow	Indigo	Violet	Yellow-green
Yellow-green	Violet	UV	White
Green	Purple		

- However, if radiations of all the wavelengths (or colours) except one are absorbed, then the colour of the substance will be the colour of the transmitted radiation. For example, if a substance absorbs all colours except green, then it would appear green to the eyes.
- The transition metal ions which have completely filled *d*-orbitals are colourless, as there are no vacant *d*-orbitals to permit promotion of the electrons. Therefore, Zn^{2+} ($3d^{10}$), Cd^{2+} ($4d^{10}$) and Hg^{2+} ($5d^{10}$) ions are colourless.

  In the 3*d* series, Sc (+3), Ti (+4), V (+5), Cr (+6) and Mn (+7) have empty *d*-orbitals, hence *d*- spectra are impossible and they should be colourless. However the following ions in aqueous solution are coloured:

  VO_2^{2+} (oxidation state +6) — pale yellow
  CrO_4^{2-} (oxidation state +6) — deep yellow
  MnO_4^- (oxidation state +7) — intense purple

  The **colours arise by charge transfer**, for example, in MnO_4^- an electron is momentarily transferred from oxygen to the metal and thus oxidation state of oxygen changes from O^{2-} to O^- and manganese from Mn(+7) to Mn(+6).
- Colours and the outer-electronic configurations of the some important ions of the first transition elements series are given below.

Ion	Outer configuration	Number of unpaired electrons	Colour of the ion
Sc^{3+}	$3d^0$	0	Colourless
Ti^{3+}	$3d^1$	1	Purple
Ti^{4+}	$3d^0$	0	Colourless
V^{3+}	$3d^2$	2	Green
Cr^{3+}	$3d^3$	3	Violet
Mn^{2+}	$3d^5$	5	Light pink
Mn^{3+}	$3d^4$	4	Violet
Fe^{2+}	$3d^6$	4	Green
Fe^{3+}	$3d^5$	5	Yellow
Co^{3+}	$3d^7$	3	Pink
Ni^{2+}	$3d^8$	2	Green
Cu^{2+}	$3d^9$	1	Blue
Cu^+	$3d^{10}$	0	Colourless
Zn^{2+}	$3d^{10}$	0	Colourless

JEE Quicker

The colour of $K_2Cr_2O_7$ and $KMnO_4$ is orange and purple respectively. It is due to charge transfer from ligand to metal.
JEE Main 2024

- Charge transfer from ligand to metal occurs when a ligand with a high tendency to oxidise is bound to a metal center with a high oxidation state.
- In $K_2Cr_2O_7$, the $Cr_2O_7^{2-}$ ion absorbs light to give the compound orange colour. While in $KMnO_4$ the oxygen donates electrons to the vacant orbitals of manganese. This leads to charge transfer spectra that gives the compound, a purple colour.

10. Magnetic Properties

Most of the transition elements and their compounds show paramagnetism. The paramagnetism first increases in any transition element series, and then decreases. The maximum paramagnetism is seen around the middle of the series. The paramagnetism is described in Bohr Magneton (BM) units.

Explanation

A substance which is attracted by magnetic field is called paramagnetic substance. The substances which are repelled by magnetic field are called diamagnetic substances. Paramagnetism is due to the presence of unpaired electrons in atoms, ions or molecules.

In *d*-orbitals belonging to a particular energy level, there can be maximum five unpaired electorns in d^5 cases. Therefore, paramagnetism in any transition series first increases, reaches a maximum value for d^5 cases and then decreases thereafter.

The magnetic moment of any transition element or its compound/ion is given by (assuming no contribution from the orbital magnetic moment).

$$\mu_S = \sqrt{4S(S+1)}$$
$$= \sqrt{n(n+2)} \text{ BM}$$

where, S is the total spin ($n \times s$), n is the number of unpaired electrons and s is equal to $\frac{1}{2}$ (representing the spin of an unpaired electron).

From the equation given above, the magnetic moment (μ_S) increases with an increase in the number of unpaired electrons.

Magnetic moments of some ions of the 3*d*-series elements

Ion	Outer configuration	No. of unpaired electrons	Magnetic moment (BM)	
			Calculated	Observed
Se^{3+}	$3d^0$	0	0	0
Ti^{3+}	$3d^1$	1	1.73	1.75
Ti^{2+}	$3d^2$	2	2.84	2.86
V^{2+}	$3d^3$	3	3.87	3.86
Cr^{2+}	$3d^4$	4	4.90	4.80
Mn^{2+}	$3d^5$	5	5.92	5.96
Fe^{2+}	$3d^6$	4	4.90	5.3-5.5
Co^{2+}	$3d^7$	3	3.87	4.4-5.2
Ni^{2+}	$3d^8$	2	2.84	2.9-3.4
Cu^{2+}	$3d^9$	1	1.73	1.8-2.2
Zn^{2+}	$3d^{10}$	0	0	0

JEE MAPPER

Example Similar to PYQ Asked in JEE Main 2024

Arrange the following ions in the increasing order of the magnetic moment.

A. V^{2+} B. Mn^{2+} C. Cr^{2+} D. Fe^{2+}
E. Ti^{2+}

Choose the correct answer from the options given below.

(a) C < E < B < A < D (b) B < D < E = A < C
(c) E < A < D = C < B (d) D < B < C < A < E

Sol. (*c*) The electronic configuration of given ions are as follows

	Ions	Electronic configuration	Number of unpaired electron
A.	V^{2+}	$[Ar]\,3d^3$	3
B.	Mn^{2+}	$[Ar]\,3d^5$	5
C.	Cr^{2+}	$[Ar]\,3d^4$	4
D.	Fe^{2+}	$[Ar]\,3d^6$	4
E.	Ti^{2+}	$[Ar]\,3d^2$	2

Greater is the number of unpaired electrons higher is the magnetic moment. Thus, the order is E < A < D = C < B.

Competency Enhancer 1.2

Arrange the following ions in the increasing order of magnetic moment.

A. V^{3+} B. Cr^{3+} C. Cu^{+} D. Mn^{2+} E. Fe^{2+}

Choose the correct answer from the options given below.

(a) B < C < A < E < D (b) B < A < C < E < D
(c) C < A < B < E < D (d) A < B < D < C < E

11. Formation of Complex Ions

Transition metals and their ions show strong tendency for complex formation. The cations of transition elements (*d*-block elements) form complex ions with certain molecules containing one or more lone-pairs of electrons, *viz*., CO, NO, NH_3, etc., or with anions such as, F^-, CN^- etc. This complex formation tendency is due to,

(i) small size and high nuclear charge of the transition metal cations.

(ii) the availability to vacant inner *d*-orbitals of suitable energy.

12. Formation of Interstitial Compounds

Transition elements form a few interstitial compounds with elements having small atomic radii, such as hydrogen, boron, carbon and nitrogen. The small atoms of these elements get entrapped in between the void spaces (called interstices) of the metal lattice. Some characteristics of the interstitial compound are as follows

(i) These are non-stoichiometric compounds and cannot be given definite formulae.

(ii) These compounds show essentially the same chemical properties as the parent metals, but differ in physical properties such as density and hardness. Steel and cast iron are hard due to the formation of interstitial compound with carbon. Some non-stoichiometric compounds are, VSe. (0.98%) (Vanadium selenide), $Fe_{0.94}O$, and titanium nitride.

Explanation Interstital compounds are hard and dense. This is because, the smaller atoms of lighter elements occupy the interstices in the lattice, leading to a more closely packed structure. Due to greater electronic interactions, the strength of the metallic bonds also increases.

13. Catalytic Properties

Most of the transition metals and their compounds, particularly oxides, have good catalytic properties. Platinum, iron, vanadium pentoxide, nickel, etc., are important catalysts. Platinum is a general catalyst. Nickel powder is a good catalyst for hydrogenation of unsaturated organic compound such as, hydrogenation of oils.

Explanation Most transition elements act as good catalyst because of,

(i) the presence of vacant *d*-orbitals.
(ii) the tendency to exhibit variable oxidation states.
(iii) the tendency to form reaction intermediates with reactants.
(iv) the presence of defects in their crystal lattices.

Some of the common catalysts used for important reactions are summarised as

Catalyst	Function
$TiCl_4$	Used as **Ziegler Natta catalyst** in the production of polythene
$FeSO_4 + H_2O_2$	known as **Fenton's reagent** which is used in the oxidation of alcohols to aldehydes.
Ni	**Raney nickel,** used in reduction processes like, — in manufacture of hexamethylenediamine, — in production of H_2 from NH_3, — in reducing anthraquinone to anthraquinol in the production of H_2O_2.
Ni complexes	**Reppe synthesis** (polymerisation of alkynes to give benzene, cyclooctatetraene).
Cu	Used in manufacturing of $(CH_3)_2SiCl_2$ (being used to make silicones).
Cu/V	Used in the oxidation of cyclohexanol/ cyclohexanone mixture to adipic acid which is used to prepare Nylon–6, 6.
$CuCl_2$	Used in **Deacon process** of making Cl_2 from HCl.
MnO_2	Used in the decomposition of $KClO_3$ into KCl and O_2.
V_2O_5	Used in **contact process** for manufacture of H_2SO_4.
Fe/Mo	Used in the **Haber-Bosch process** for manufacture of NH_3
$FeCl_3$	Used in the production of CCl_4 from CS_2 and Cl_2
$PdCl_2$	Used in **Wacker process** for converting C_2H_4 into CH_3CHO.
PtO_2	Used as **Adams catalyst** in reduction.
Pt	In three stage convertors for cleaning car exhaust fumes.
Pt/Rh	In **Ostwald process** for producing HNO_3 from NH_3
ZnO/CuO	In synthesis of CH_3OH from CO and H_2
Co/Fe	In synthesis of hydrocarbons by CO and H_2 in **Fischer-Tropsch process.**

14. Alloy Formation

An alloy is a homogeneous solid solution. Transition metals form alloys among themselves. The alloys of transition metals are hard and have high melting point as compared to that of host metal. Various steels are alloys of iron with metals such as chromium, vanadium, molybdenum, tungsten, manganese etc.

Explanation

The atomic radii of the transition elements in any series are not much different from each other. As a result, they can very easily replace each other in the lattice and form solid solutions (i.e., alloys) over an appreciable composition range.

15. Chemical Reactivity

The *d*-block elements (transition elements) have lesser tendency to react, i.e., these are less reactive, as compared to that of *s*-block elements.

Explanation

Low reactivity of transition elements is due to,

(i) their high ionisation energies.
(ii) low heats of hydration of their ions.
(iii) their high heats of sublimation.

Nature of Oxides/Hydroxides

While moving along a period from Sc to Zn the basic nature of the oxides of transition elements decreases and acidic nature increases. This behaviour differs when oxidation states are different

Sc_2O_3	TiO_2	V_2O_5	Cr_2O_3	MnO_2	Fe_2O_3	Co_2O_3	NiO	CuO	ZnO
A	A	A	A	A	A	A	B	B	A

A : Amphoteric, B : Basic

With increase in the oxidation state of a given transition metal, the covalent character of its compound increases and thus acidic character also increases.

	MnO	Mn_3O_4	Mn_2O_3	MnO_2	MnO_3	Mn_2O_7
Oxidation state of Mn	+2	+8/3	+3	+4	+6	+7
Nature of oxide	Basic	Amphoteric			Weakly acidic	Strongly acidic

	VO	V_2O_3	VO_2	V_2O_5
Oxidation state of V	+2	+3	+4	+5
Nature of oxide	Basic	Basic	Amphoteric	Amphoteric

	CrO $[Cr(OH)_2]$	Cr_2O_3 $[Cr(OH)_3]$	CrO_3 $[H_2Cr_2O_7]$
Oxidation state of Cr	+2	+3	+6
Nature of oxide	Basic	Amphoteric	Acidic

The basic and amphoteric oxides dissolve in non-oxidising acids and form hexaaquo ions $[M(H_2O)_6]^{n+}$. The acidic oxides like CrO_3 and Mn_2O_3 dissolve in water to form the oxyacids. These oxides also react with bases to form oxosalts.

$$CrO_3 + H_2O \longrightarrow \underset{\text{Chromic acid}}{H_2CrO_4}$$

$$CrO_3 + 2KOH \longrightarrow \underset{\text{Potassium chromate}}{K_2CrO_4} + H_2O$$

$$2CrO_3 + H_2O \longrightarrow \underset{\text{Dichromic acid}}{H_2Cr_2O_7}$$

$$2CrO_3 + 2KOH \longrightarrow \underset{\text{Potassium dichromate}}{K_2Cr_2O_7} + H_2O$$

$$Mn_2O_7 + H_2O \longrightarrow \underset{\text{Permanganic acid}}{2HMnO_4}$$

$$Mn_2O_7 + 2KOH \longrightarrow \underset{\text{Potassium permanganate}}{2KMnO_4} + H_2O$$

As we move along a given transition series, +2 oxidation state of the metals becomes more and more stable and hence the tendency of these metals to lose electrons increases hence, reducing nature of the metal oxide increases. e.g., VO and CrO are strong reducing agents.

Elemental Practice 8.1

Type I MCQs with Only One Correct Option

1. The stability of Cu^{2+} is more than Cu^{+} salts in aqueous solution due to
   (a) enthalpy of atomisation
   (b) hydration energy
   (c) second ionisation enthalpy
   (d) first ionisation enthalpy

2. The calculated spin only magnetic moment of Cr^{2+} ion is
   (a) 4.90 BM (b) 5.92 BM
   (c) 2.84 BM (d) 3.87 BM

3. Identify the incorrect statement.
   (a) The transition metals and their compounds are known for their catalytic activity due to their ability to adopt multiple oxidation states and to form complexes.
   (b) Interstitial compounds are those that are formed when small atoms like H, C or N are trapped inside the crystal lattice of metals.
   (c) The oxidation states of chromium in CrO_4^{2-} and $Cr_2O_7^{2-}$ are +3 and +6 respectively.
   (d) Cr^{2+} (d^4) is a stronger reducing agent than Fe^{2+} (d^6) in water.

4. Match the catalyst given in List-I with the process given in List-II.

List-I (Catalyst)		List-II (Process)	
A.	V_2O_5	I.	The oxidation of ethyne to ethanal
B.	$TiCl_4 + Al(CH_3)_3$	II.	Polymerisation of alkynes
C.	$PdCl_2$	III.	Oxidation of SO_2 in the manufacture of H_2SO_4
D.	Nickel complexes	IV.	Polymerisation of ethylene

   Choose correct answer from the option given below
   (a) A-III, B-IV. C-I, D-II
   (b) A-I, B-II, C-III, D-IV
   (c) A-I, B-III, C-II, D-IV
   (d) A-III, B-I, C-IV, D-II

5. Select the incorrect statement from the following.
   (a) The non-stoichiometric hydride form of V is $VH_{0.71}$
   (b) Copper can displace H^+ ions from acid solutions.
   (c) Most of the transition metals are coloured in solid or in solution form.
   (d) Anhydrous cobalt (II) compounds absorbs red light and appear as blue.

6. The correct stability order of given transition elements in +2 oxidation state is
(At. no. Cr = 24, Mn = 25, Fe = 26, Co = 27)
(a) Fe > Mn > Co > Cr (b) Co > Mn > Fe > Cr
(c) Cr > Mn > Co > Fe (d) Mn > Fe > Cr > Co

7. Arrange the following elements in the decreasing order of the number of unpaired electrons in it.
A. Mn B. Cr^{2+} C. Ni^{2+} D. Zn^{+}
E. V
Choose the correct answer from the options given below.
(a) A > B > D > C > E (b) A > B > E > C > D
(c) B > C > A > D > E (d) E > C > B > A > D

8. 'Spin only' magnetic moment is same for which of the following ions?
A. Ti^{3+} B. Cr^{2+} C. Mn^{2+} D. Fe^{2+} E. Sc^{3+}
Choose the most appropriate answer from the options given below.
(a) B and D only (b) A and E only
(c) B and C only (d) A and D only

9. Which of the following statements about the interstitial compounds is incorrect?
(a) They retain metallic conductivity
(b) They are chemically reactive
(c) They are much harder than the pure metal
(d) They have higher melting points than the pure metals

10. Match the following properties given in List-I with the respective element in List-II.

	List-I (Properties)		List-I (Elements)
A.	The metal that can show maximum number of oxidation states	I.	Scandium
B.	The metal although placed in 3*d* block is not considered as a transition element.	II.	Copper
C.	The metal which does not exhibit variable oxidation state	III.	Manganese
D.	The metal which in +1 oxidation state in aqueous solution undergoes disproportionation	IV.	Zinc

Choose the correct answer from the options given below
(a) A-I, B-IV, C-II, D-III (b) A-III, B-IV, C-I, D-II
(c) A-III, B-I, C-IV, D-II (d) A-II, B-IV, C-I, D-III

11. In which of the following pairs both the ions are coloured in aqueous solution?
(Atomic number Sc = 21, Ti = 22, Ni = 28, Cu = 29)
(a) Ni^{2+}, Ti^{3+} (b) Sc^{3+}, Ti^{3+} (c) Sc^{3+}, Cu^{2+} (d) Ni^{2+}, Cu^{+}

12. The interstitial alloy of iron and carbon has enhanced hardness due to
(a) formation of covalent bonds between iron and carbon.
(b) filling of interstitial voids by carbon atoms, preventing dislocation movement.
(c) reduction in the metallic bonding strength of iron.
(d) formation of ionic bonds between Fe and C.

13. Four successive members of the first row transition elements are listed below with their atomic numbers. Which one of them is expected to have the highest third ionisation enthalpy?
(a) Vanadium (Z = 23) (b) Chromium (Z = 24)
(c) Iron (Z = 26) (d) Manganese (Z = 25)

14. Match the metal ions given in Column I with the spin magnetic moments of the ions given in Column II and assign the correct code.

Column I	Column II
A. Co^{3+}	I. $\sqrt{8}$ BM
B. Cr^{3+}	II. $\sqrt{35}$ BM
C. Fe^{3+}	III. $\sqrt{3}$ BM
D. Ni^{2+}	IV. $\sqrt{24}$ BM
	V. $\sqrt{15}$ BM

Choose the correct answer from the options given below.
(a) A-IV, B-I, C-II, D-III (b) A-I, B-II, C-III, D-IV
(c) A-IV, B-V, C-II, D-I (d) A-III, B-V, C-I, D-II

15. Which one of the following ions has electronic configuration [Ar] $3d^6$?
(At. no. Mn = 25, Fe = 26, Co = 27, Ni = 28)
(a) Ni^{2+} (b) Mn^{3+}
(c) Fe^{3+} (d) Co^{3+}

16. Select the elements with the following outer orbital configurations may exhibit the largest number of oxidation states?
(a) $3d^5 4s^1$ (b) $3d^5 4s^2$
(c) $3d^2 4s^2$ (d) $3d^3 4s^2$

17. Choose the ions which is most stable in aqueous solution?
(At. no. Ti = 22, V = 23, Cr = 24, Mn = 25)
(a) Cr^{3+} (b) V^{3+}
(c) Ti^{3+} (d) Mn^{3+}

18. Which of the following option does not represent the correct order of the properties indicated?
(a) $Ni^{2+} > Cr^{2+} > Fe^{2+} > Mn^{2+}$ (Size)
(b) Mn > Ti > Cr > Sc (First ionisation energy)
(c) $Mn^{2+} > Fe^{2+} > Co^{2+} > Ni^{2+}$ (Spin only magnetic moment)
(d) $Fe^{2+} > Co^{2+} > Ni^{2+} > Cu^{2+}$ (Unpaired electron)

19. Select the correct statement about the colour of the complex $[Ti(H_2O)_6]^{3+}$
(a) The colour arises due to the absorption of light in the ultra-violet region.
(b) It is a yellow-coloured complex.
(c) The colour is due to *d-d* transition.
(d) The colour is due to charge transfer from the water molecule to Ti^{3+}.

20. The electronic configurations of four elements are given below. Among them which element does not belong to the same family as other?
(a) [Xe] $4f^{14} 5d^{10} 6s^2$ (b) [Kr] $4d^{10} 5s^2$
(c) [Ne] $3s^2 3p^5$ (d) [Ar] $3d^{10} 4s^2$

Type II 》 MCQs with One or More than One Correct Option

21. The incorrect order(s) of ionisation energy is
(a) Ti < V < Cr
(b) Zr < Nb < Mo
(c) Hf < Ta < W
(d) W < Hf < Ta

22. The metal oxide which decomposes on heating is/are
(a) ZnO (b) Al_2O_3
(c) Ag_2O (d) HgO

23. Transition elements have greater tendency to form complexes because they have
(a) vacant *d*-orbitals
(b) small size
(c) higher nuclear charge
(d) variable oxidation states

24. Which of the following ions give(s) coloured aqueous solution?
(a) Ni^{2+} (b) Fe^{2+}
(c) Cu^{2+} (d) Cu^{+}

25. What are the characteristics of products obtained when green vitriol is strongly heated?
(a) Basic oxide (b) Neutral oxide
(c) Acidic oxide (d) Reducing agent

Type III 》 Numerical/Integer Answer Type Questions

26. The total number of *d*-electrons in the penultimate, shell of platinum atom is *x*. Then the value of $\frac{x+1}{10}$ is

27. The number of elements having higher density than Ni is
Ti, Co, Pd, Ag, Fe, Au, Pt, Os

28. An octahedral complex of a *d*-block metal ion has a spin-only magnetic moment of 4.90 BM The number of unpaired electrons present in the complex is :

29. The number of transition metals among the following is
Fe, Ru, Hg, Cd, Ag, Pt, Zn, Au

30. If *x* is the number of *d*-electron present in the cation having highest ionisation energy among all the cations formed by manganese. Then the value of $\frac{x+4}{2}$ is

Elemental Practice 8.1 | Chapter 08

Connect with **Answers**

1. (b)	**2.** (a)	**3.** (c)	**4.** (a)	**5.** (b)	**6.** (d)
7. (b)	**8.** (a)	**9.** (b)	**10.** (b)	**11.** (a)	**12.** (b)
13. (d)	**14.** (c)	**15.** (d)	**16.** (b)	**17.** (a)	**18.** (a)
19. (c)	**20.** (c)	**21.** (a,c,d)	**22.** (c,d)	**23.** (a,b,c,d)	**24.** (a,b,c)
25. (a,b,c,d)	**26.** (1)	**27.** (5)	**28.** (4)	**29.** (5)	**30.** (2)

Element 2 Some Important Compounds of *d*-Block Elements; *f*-Block Elements

Potassium Dichromate ($K_2Cr_2O_7$)

It is one of the most important compound of chromium and also among dichromates. In this compound Cr is present in the hexavalent (+6) state.

Preparation

It can be prepared by any of the following methods,

1. From Potassium Chromate

Potassium dichromate can be obtained by adding a calculated amount of sulphuric acid to a saturated solution of potassium chromate.

$$\underset{\substack{\text{Potassium}\\\text{chromate}\\\text{(Yellow)}}}{2K_2CrO_4} + H_2SO_4 \longrightarrow \underset{\substack{\text{Potassium}\\\text{dichromate}\\\text{(Orange)}}}{K_2Cr_2O_7} + K_2SO_4 + H_2O$$

$K_2Cr_2O_7$ crystals can be obtained by concentrating the solution and crystallisation.

2. Manufacturing from Chromite Ore

$K_2Cr_2O_7$ is generally manufactured from chromite ore ($FeCr_2O_4$). The process involves the following steps.

(i) **Preparation of Sodium Chromate** Finely powdered chromite ore is mixed with soda ash and quicklime. The mixture is then roasted in a reverberatory furnace in the presence of air. Yellow mass, due to the formation of sodium chromate, is obtained.

$$4FeCr_2O_4 + O_2 \longrightarrow 2Fe_2O_3 + 4Cr_2O_3$$
$$4Cr_2O_3 + 8Na_2CO_3 + 6O_2 \longrightarrow 8Na_2CrO_4 + 8CO_2(g)$$
$$4FeCr_2O_4 + 8Na_2CO_3 + 7O_2 \longrightarrow 2Fe_2O_3 + 8CO_2(g) + \underset{\text{Sodium chromate}}{8Na_2CrO_4}$$

The yellow mass is extracted with water, and filtered. The filtrate contains sodium chromate.

The reaction may also be carried out by using NaOH instead of Na_2CO_3.

$$4FeCr_2O_4 + 16NaOH + 7O_2 \longrightarrow 8Na_2CrO_4 + 2Fe_2O_3 + 8H_2O$$

(ii) **Conversion of chromate into dichromate**. Sodium chromate solution obtained in step(i) is acidified with sulphuric acid to give sodium dichromate.

$$\underset{\substack{\text{Sodium}\\\text{chromate}}}{2Na_2CrO_4} + H_2SO_4 \longrightarrow \underset{\substack{\text{Sodium}\\\text{dichromate}}}{Na_2Cr_2O_7} + Na_2SO_4 + H_2O$$

On concentration, the less soluble sodium sulphate, $Na_2SO_4 \cdot 10H_2O$ crystallises out. This is filtered hot and allowed to cool when sodium dichromate, $Na_2Cr_2O_7 \cdot 2H_2O$, separate out on standing.

(iii) **Concentration of sodium dichromate to potassium dichromate**. Hot concentrated solution of sodium dichromate is treated wih a calculated amount of potassium chloride. As potassium dichromate being less soluble than sodium dichromate, thus crystallises out on cooling.

$$\underset{\substack{\text{Sodium}\\\text{dichromate (Hot)}}}{Na_2Cr_2O_7} + 2KCl \longrightarrow \underset{\substack{\text{Potassium}\\\text{dichromate}}}{K_2Cr_2O_7} + 2NaCl$$

Physical Properties

(i) Potassium dichromate forms orange-red coloured crystals.

(ii) It melts at 699 K.

(iii) It is very stable in air (near room temperature) and is generally, used as a primary standard in the volumetric analysis.

(iv) It is soluble in water though the solubility is limited.

Chemical Properties

1. Action of Heat

Potassium dichromate when heated strongly, decomposes to give potassium chromate and oxygen.

$$4K_2Cr_2O_7(s) \xrightarrow{\Delta} 4K_2CrO_4(s) + 2Cr_2O_3(s) + 3O_2\uparrow$$

2. Action of Acids

(i) In cold, with concentrated H_2SO_4, red crystals of chromium trioxide separate out.

$$K_2Cr_2O_7(aq) + 2H_2SO_4(\text{conc.}) \longrightarrow 2KHSO_4(aq) + 2CrO_3(s) + H_2O$$

On heating a dichromate-sulphuric acid mixture, oxygen gas is given out.

$$2K_2Cr_2O_7 + 8H_2SO_4 \xrightarrow{\Delta} 2K_2SO_4 + 2Cr_2(SO_4)_3 + 8H_2O + 3O_2\uparrow$$

(ii) With HCl, on heating chromic chloride is formed and Cl_2 is liberated.

$$K_2Cr_2O_7(aq) + 14HCl(aq) \xrightarrow{\Delta} 2CrCl_3(aq) + 2KCl(aq) + 7H_2O + 3Cl_2(g)$$

3. Action of Alkalies

With alkalies, it gives chromate which is yellow in colour.

$$\underset{\text{Orange}}{K_2Cr_2O_7} + 2KOH \longrightarrow \underset{\text{Yellow}}{2K_2CrO_4} + H_2O$$

On acidifying, the colour again changes to orange-red owing to the formation of dichromate.

$$2K_2CrO_4 + H_2SO_4 \longrightarrow K_2Cr_2O_7 + K_2SO_4 + H_2O$$

Actually, in the solution, the $Cr_2O_7^{2-}$ ions are in equilibrium with CrO_4^{2-} ions. Depending on the pH of the solution, equilibrium shifts in the forward and backward directions.

$$Cr_2O_7^{2-} + H_2O \rightleftharpoons 2CrO_4^{2-} + 2H^+$$

4. Oxidising Nature

In neutral or in acidic soluion, potassium dichromate acts as an excellent oxidising agent, i.e., $Cr_2O_7^{2-}$ gets reduced to Cr^{3+}. The standard electrode potential for the reaction, $Cr_2O_7^{2-} + 14H^+ + 6e^- \longrightarrow 2Cr^{3+} + 7H_2O$ is $+1.31$ V. Thus, it is widely used as an oxidising agent, for quantitative estimation of the reducing agents. It oxidises,

Ferrous Salts to Ferric Salts

$$K_2Cr_2O_7 + 4H_2SO_4 \longrightarrow K_2SO_4 + Cr_2(SO_4)_3 + 4H_2O + 3[O]$$
$$[2FeSO_4 + H_2SO_4 + [O] \longrightarrow Fe_2[SO_4]_3 + H_2O] \times 3$$
$$K_2Cr_2O_7 + 6FeSO_4 + 7H_2SO_4 \longrightarrow K_2SO_4 + Cr_2(SO_4)_3 + 3Fe_2(SO_4)_3 + 7H_2O$$

Ionic equation $Cr_2O_7^{2-} + 14H^+ + 6Fe^{2+} \longrightarrow 2Cr^{3+} + 6Fe^{3+} + 7H_2O$

Sulphites to Sulphates and Arsenites to Arsenates

$$K_2Cr_2O_7 + 4H_2SO_4 \longrightarrow K_2SO_4 + Cr_2(SO_4)_3 + 4H_2O + 3[O]$$
$$[Na_2SO_3 + [O] \longrightarrow Na_2SO_4] \times 3$$
$$K_2Cr_2O_7 + 4H_2SO_4 + 3Na_2SO_3 \longrightarrow K_2SO_4 + Cr_2(SO_4)_3 + 3Na_2SO_4 + 4H_2O$$

Ionic equation : $Cr_2O_7^{2-} + 8H^+ + 3SO_3^{2-} \longrightarrow 2Cr^{3+} + 3SO_4^{2-} + 4H_2O$

Similarly, arsenites are oxidised to arsenates.

$$Cr_2O_7^{2-} + 8H^+ + 3AsO_3^{3-} \longrightarrow 2Cr^{3+} + 3AsO_4^{3-} + 4H_2O$$

Hydrogen Halides to Halogens

$$K_2Cr_2O_7 + 4H_2SO_4 \longrightarrow K_2SO_4 + Cr_2(SO_4)_3 + 4H_2O + 3[O]$$
$$[2HX + O \longrightarrow H_2O + X_2] \times 3$$
$$K_2Cr_2O_7 + 4H_2SO_4 + 6HX \longrightarrow K_2SO_4 + Cr_2(SO_4)_3 + 7H_2O + 3X_2$$

where, X may be Cl, Br, I.

Ionic equation :

$$Cr_2O_7^{2-} + 8H^+ + 6HX \longrightarrow 2Cr^{3+} + 3X_2 + 7H_2O$$

Iodide to Iodine

$$K_2Cr_2O_7 + 4H_2SO_4 \longrightarrow K_2SO_4 + Cr_2(SO_4)_3 + 4H_2O + 3[O]$$
$$2KI + H_2O + [O] \longrightarrow 2KOH + I_2] \times 3$$
$$2KOH + H_2SO_4 \longrightarrow K_2SO_4 + 2H_2O] \times 3$$
$$K_2Cr_2O_7 + 7H_2SO_4 + 6KI \longrightarrow 4K_2SO_4 + Cr_2(SO_4)_3 + 3I_2 + 7H_2O$$

Ionic equation :

$$Cr_2O_7^{2-} + 14H^+ + 6I^- \longrightarrow 2Cr^{3+} + 7H_2O + 3I_2$$

Thus, when KI is added to an acidified solution of $K_2Cr_2O_7$ iodine gets liberated.

Hydrogen Sulphide to Sulphur

$$K_2Cr_2O_7 + 4H_2SO_4 \longrightarrow K_2SO_4 + Cr_2(SO_4)_3 + 4H_2O + 3[O]$$
$$H_2S + [O] \longrightarrow H_2O + S] \times 3$$
$$K_2Cr_2O_7 + 4H_2SO_4 + 3H_2S \longrightarrow K_2SO_4 + Cr_2(SO_4)_3 + 7H_2O + 3S$$

Ionic equation :

$$Cr_2O_7^{2-} + 8H^+ + 3H_2S \longrightarrow 2Cr^{3+} + 3S + 7H_2O$$

5. Formation of Insoluble Chromates

With soluble salts of lead, barium etc., potassium dichromate gives insoluble chromates. Lead chromate is an important yellow precipitate.

$$2Pb(NO_3)_2 + K_2Cr_2O_7 + H_2O \longrightarrow 2PbCrO_4 + 2KNO_3 + 2HNO_3$$

6. Chromyl Chloride Test

When potassium dichromate is heated with conc. H_2SO_4 in the presence of a soluble chloride salt, the orange-red vapours of chromyl chloride (CrO_2Cl_2) are formed.

$$K_2Cr_2O_7 + 4NaCl + \underset{\text{(Conc.)}}{6H_2SO_4} \xrightarrow{\text{Heat}} 2KHSO_4 + 4NaHSO_4 + 3H_2O + \underset{\substack{\text{Chromyl chloride} \\ \text{(Orange-red Vapour)}}}{2CrO_2Cl_2}$$

Chromyl chloride test can be used for the detection of chloride ion in any mixture.

> **JEE Alert**
> Always remember chlorides of Hg, Ag, Pb and Sn do not respond to chromyl chloride test.

Uses

Potassium dichromate is used as,

(i) an oxidising agent
(ii) in chrome tanning
(iii) the raw material for preparing large number of chromium compounds
(iv) primary standard in the volumetric analysis.

Structures of Chromate and Dichromate Ions

Chromates and dichromates are the salts of chromic acid (H_2CrO_4). In solution, these ions exist in equilibrium with each other. Chromate ion has four oxygen atoms arranged tetrahedrally around Cr atom. Dichromate ion involves a Cr—O—Cr bond. Their structure are as follows

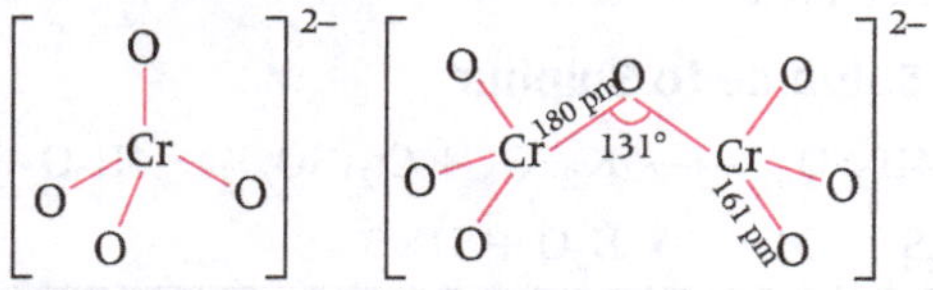

Chromate ion Dichromate ion

Structures of chromate $(CrO_4)^{2-}$ and dichromate $(Cr_2O_7)^{2-}$ ions.

Reaction of $K_2Cr_2O_7$

- In **less acidic solution,** $K_2Cr_2O_7$ and H_2O_2 give salts which are violet coloured and diamagnetic due to formation of $[CrO(O_2)(OH)]^-$.
- In **alkaline** solution with 30% H_2O_2, $K_2Cr_2O_7$ form a red-brown compound K_3CrO_8. It is tetraperoxo species $[Cr(O_2)_4]^{3-}$ and thus contains Cr(V) ion.
- In **ammoniacal solution,** $K_2Cr_2O_7$ forms $(NH_3)_3CrO_4$, a dark red-brown compound with Cr (IV) ion is formed.

$KCr(SO_4)_2 \cdot 12H_2O$ — Chrome alum

- It is obtained when acidified $K_2Cr_2O_7$ solution is saturated with SO_2:

$$K_2Cr_2O_7 + H_2SO_4 + 3SO_2 \xrightarrow{\Delta} \underbrace{K_2SO_4 + Cr_2(SO_4)_3}_{\text{Crystallises as}} \xrightarrow{+H_2O} KCr(SO_4)_2 \cdot 12H_2O$$

It is a deep purple compound used for leather tanning.

Estimation of Equivalent Weight $Cr_2O_7^{2-}$

$K_2Cr_2O_7$ can be estimated volumetrically by an iodometric titration. When acidified $K_2Cr_2O_7$ is treated with KI and iodine is liberate. The liberated I_2 is then titrated using hypo ($Na_2S_2O_3$) solution with starch indicator.

$$Cr_2O_7^{2-} + 14H^+ + 6e^- \longrightarrow 2Cr^{3+} + 7H_2O$$
$$6I^- \longrightarrow 3I_2 + 6e^-$$
$$\overline{Cr_2O_7^{2-} + 14H^+ + 6I^- \longrightarrow 2Cr^{3+} + 7H_2O + 3I_2}$$
$$I_2 + 2S_2O_3^{2-} \longrightarrow S_4O_6^{2-} + 2I^-$$

Thus, $$Cr_2O_7^{2-} \equiv 3I_2 \equiv 6I^- \equiv 6e^-$$

$\therefore$ $$1e^- \equiv 1I^- = \frac{Cr_2O_7^{2-}}{6}$$

$$\text{Equivalent weight of } K_2Cr_2O_7 = \frac{\text{molecular weight}}{6} = \frac{294}{6} = 49$$

$$2S_2O_3^{2-} \equiv I_2 \equiv 2I^- \equiv 2e^-$$

$\therefore$ $$S_2O_3^{2-} \equiv I^- = 1e^-$$

$$\text{Equivalent weight of } Na_2S_2O_3 \cdot 5H_2O = \frac{248}{1}$$

Concept Visualizer

The properties and preparation of $K_2Cr_2O_7$ can be visualised as

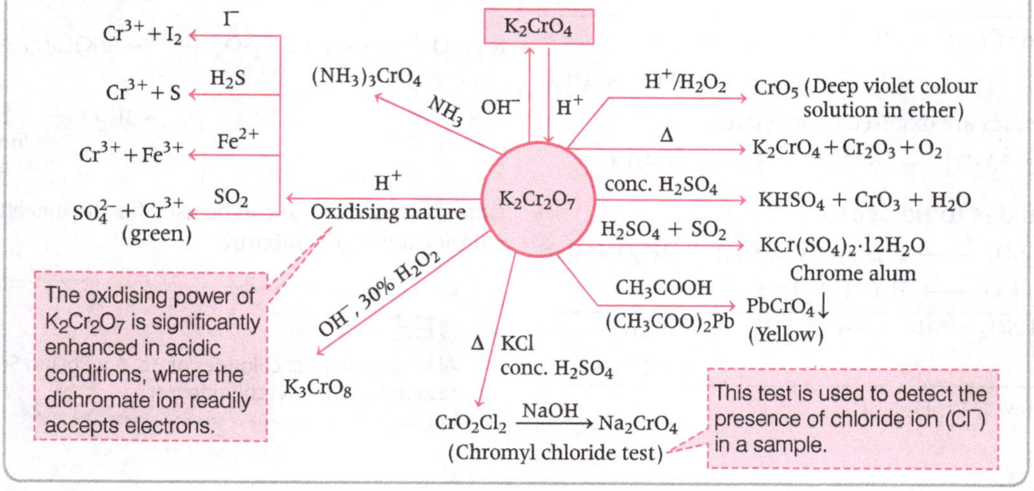

JEE MAPPER

Example Similar to PYQ Asked in JEE Advanced 2019

Fusion of $FeCr_2O_4$ with Na_2CO_3 in presence of O_2 produces a salt [*X*]. Acidic solution of [*X*] upon hydrolysis yields another salt [*Y*]. [*Y*] on further reaction with H_2O_2 / H_2SO_4 produces [*Z*].

Correct statement(s) is/are

(a) The yellow colour of [*X*] is due to the formation of Na_2CrO_4.

(b) The hybridisation state of metal in compounds [*X*] and [*Z*] is sp^3d.

(c) On reaction [*Y*] gives dark blue compound with H_2O_2 / H_2SO_4.

(d) In all the three compounds [*X*], [*Y*] and [*Z*] chromium is in +6 oxidation state.

Sol. *(a, c, d)* Among the given statements all are correct except statement (b). The correct form of statement (b) is, the hybridisation state of [X] and [Z] are sp^3 and sp^3d respectively.

$$4FeCr_2O_4 + 8Na_2CO_3 + 7O_2 \longrightarrow \underset{\text{(Yellow colour)}}{\underset{[X]}{8Na_2CrO_4}} + 2Fe_2O_3 + 8CO_2$$

$$\underset{[X]}{2Na_2CrO_4} + 2H^+ \xrightarrow{H_2O} \underset{[Y]}{Na_2Cr_2O_7} + 2Na^+ + H_2O$$

$$\underset{[Y]}{Na_2Cr_2O_7} \xrightarrow[H_2SO_4]{H_2O_2/H^+} \underset{\text{(Dark blue)}}{\underset{[Z]}{2CrO_5}} + Na_2SO_4 + 5H_2O$$

Competency Enhancer 2.1

Reaction of $BaCl_2$ with $Fe_2(SO_4)_3$ gives precipitate of *P* and coloured solution of *Q*. When KI is added to *Q* it forms *M* and its colour changes. At room temperature *M* dissociates to *N* and liberate I_2 gas. Correct statement(s) is/are

(a) Both *Q* and *N* are paramagnetic in nature.

(b) In aqueous solution of KI, *Q* undergoes disproportionation reaction.

(c) *Q* is paramagnetic and have trigonal planar shape.

(d) *N* is water soluble species.

Potassium Permanganate ($KMnO_4$)

It is a salt of an unstable acid $HMnO_4$ (permanganic acid). In this compound Mn is present in +7 oxidation state.

Preparation

Potassium permanganate is obtained from pyrolusite as follows.

Conversion of Pyrolusite to Potassium Manganate

When manganese dioxide is fused with potassium hydroxide in the presence of air or an oxidising agent such as potassium nitrate or chlorate, potassium manganate is formed, which disproportionates in a neutral or acidic solution to give permanganate.

$$\underset{\text{Pyrolusite}}{2MnO_2} + 4KOH + O_2 \xrightarrow{\text{Fused}} \underset{\text{[Dark-green mass]}}{\underset{\text{Potassium manganate}}{2K_2MnO_4}} + 2H_2O$$

$$3MnO_4^{2-} + 4H^+ \longrightarrow 2MnO_4^- + MnO_2 + 2H_2O$$

Oxidation of Potassium Manganate to Potassium Permanganate

The potassium manganate so obtained is oxidised to potassium permanganate by either of the following methods.

By Chemical Method

The fused dark-green mass is extracted with a small quantity of water. The filtrate is warmed and treated with a current of ozone, chlorine or carbon dioxide. Potassium manganate gets oxidised to potassium permanganate and the hydrated manganese dioxide precipitates out. The reactions taking place are,

When CO_2 is passed

$$\underset{\text{Potassium manganate}}{3K_2MnO_4} + 2H_2O \longrightarrow \underset{\text{Potassium permanganate}}{2KMnO_4} + MnO_2\downarrow + 4KOH$$

$$2CO_2 + 4KOH \longrightarrow 2K_2CO_3 + 2H_2O$$

When chlorine or ozone is passed

$$2K_2MnO_4 + Cl_2 \longrightarrow KMnO_4 + 2KCl$$

$$2K_2MnO_4 + O_3 + H_2O \longrightarrow 2KMnO_4 + 2KOH + O_2(g)$$

The purple solution so obtained is concentrated and dark purple, needle-like crystals having metallic lustre are obtained.

Electrolytic Method

Presently, potassium manganate (K_2MnO_4) is oxidised electrolytically. The electrode reactions are,

At anode $\underset{\text{Green}}{2MnO_4^{2-}} \longrightarrow \underset{\text{Purple}}{2MnO_4^-} + 2e^-$

At cathode $2H^+ + 2e^- \longrightarrow H_2(g)$

The purple solution containing $KMnO_4$ is evaporated under controlled condition to get crystalline sample of potassium permanganate.

Physical Properties

$KMnO_4$ crystallises as dark purple crystals with greenish luster (m.p. 523 K). It is soluble in water to an extent of 6.5 g per 100 g at room temperature. The aqueous solution of $KMnO_4$ has a purple colour.

Concept Visualizer

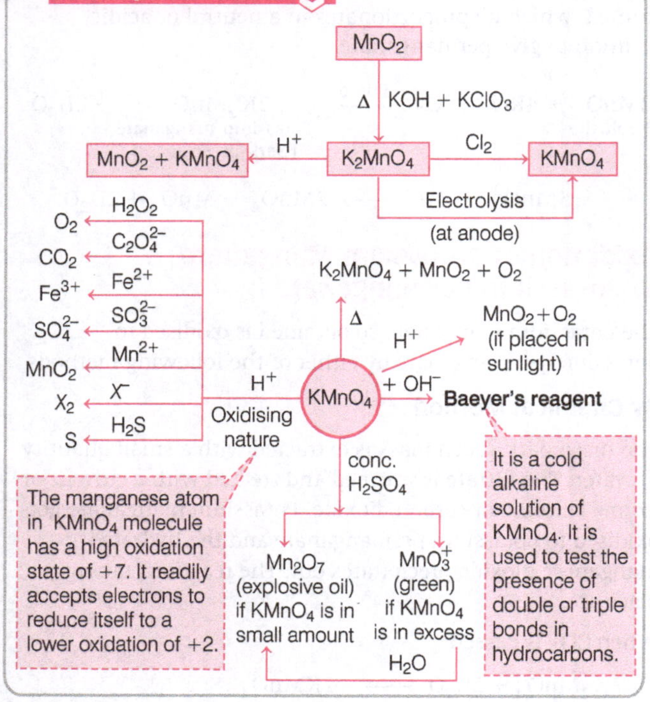

Chemical Properties

Some important chemical reactions of $KMnO_4$ are given below

1. Action of Heat

$KMnO_4$ is stable at room temperature, but decomposes to give oxygen potassium manganate and magnese oxide at higher temperatures.

$$2KMnO_4(s) \xrightarrow{\text{Heat}} K_2MnO_4(s) + MnO_2 + O_2(g)$$

2. Oxidising Actions

$KMnO_4$ is a powerful agent in neutral, acidic and alkaline media. The nature of reaction is different in each medium. The oxidising agent of $KMnO_4$ (to be more specific, of MnO_4^-) is indicated by high positive reduction potential for the followig reactions.

Acidic medium $MnO_4^- + 8H^+ + 5e^- \longrightarrow Mn^{2+} + 4H_2O$ $\quad E° = 1.51$ V

Neutral medium $MnO_4^- + 2H_2O + 3e^- \longrightarrow MnO_2 + 4OH^-$ $\quad E° = 1.23$ V

In strongly alkaline solutions and with excess of MnO_4^-, the reaction is

$$MnO_4^- + e^- \longrightarrow MnO_4^{2-} \qquad E° = 0.56 \text{ V}$$

There are a large number of oxidation-reduction reactions involved in the chemistry of manganese compounds. Some typical reactions are as follows

- In faintly acidic and neutral solutions, maganous ion is oxidised to manganese oxide by permanganate ion.

$$2MnO_4^- + 3Mn^{2+} + 2H_2O \longrightarrow 5MnO_2 + 4H^+$$

- In strongly basic solutions, permanganate oxidises manganese dioxide to manganate ion.

$$MnO_2 + 2MnO_4^- + 4OH^- \longrightarrow 3MnO_4^{2-} + 2H_2O$$

In acidic medium, $KMnO_4$ oxidises.

Ferrous Salts to Ferric Salts

$$2KMnO_4 + 3H_2SO_4 \longrightarrow K_2SO_4 + 2MnSO_4 + 3H_2O + 5[O]$$
$$[2FeSO_4 + H_2SO_4 + [O] \longrightarrow Fe_2(SO_4)_3 + H_2O] \times 5$$
$$2KMnO_4 + 8H_2SO_4 + 10FeSO_4 \longrightarrow K_2SO_4 + 2MnSO_4 + 5Fe_2(SO_4)_3 + 8H_2O$$

Ionic equation :

$$2MnO_4^- + 16H^+ + 10Fe^{2+} \longrightarrow 2Mn^{2+} + 10Fe^{3+} + 8H_2O$$

The reaction forms the basis of volumetric estimation of Fe^{2+} in any solution by $KMnO_4$.

Oxalic Acid to Carbon Dioxide

$$2KMnO_4 + 3H_2SO_4 \longrightarrow K_2SO_4 + 2MnSO_4 + 3H_2O + 5[O]$$
$$[(COOH)_2 + [O] \longrightarrow 2CO_2 + H_2O] \times 5$$
$$2KMnO_4 + 3H_2SO_4 + 5(COOH)_2 \longrightarrow K_2SO_4 + 2MnSO_4 + 10CO_2 + 8H_2O$$

Ionic equation

$$2MnO_4^- + 16H^+ + 5C_2O_4^{2-} \longrightarrow 2Mn^{2+} + 10CO_2 + 8H_2O$$

Sulphites to Sulphates

$$2KMnO_4 + 3H_2SO_4 \longrightarrow K_2SO_4 + 2MnSO_4 + 3H_2O + 5[O]$$
$$[Na_2SO_3 + [O] \longrightarrow Na_2SO_4] \times 5$$
$$2KMnO_4 + 3H_2SO_4 + 5Na_2SO_3 \longrightarrow K_2SO_4 + 2MnSO_4 + 5Na_2SO_4 + 3H_2O$$

Ionic equation

$$2MnO_4^- + 6H^+ + 5SO_3^{2-} \longrightarrow 2Mn^{2+} + 5SO_4^{2-} + 3H_2O$$

Iodides to Iodine in Acidic Medium

$$2KMnO_4 + 3H_2SO_4 \longrightarrow K_2SO_4 + 2MnSO_4 + 3H_2O + 5[O]$$
$$[2KI + H_2O + [O] \longrightarrow I_2 + 2KOH] \times 5$$
$$[2KOH + H_2SO_4 \longrightarrow K_2SO_4 + 2H_2O] \times 5$$
$$2KMnO_4 + 8H_2SO_4 + 10KI \longrightarrow 6K_2SO_4 + 2MnSO_4 + 5I_2 + 8H_2O$$

Ionic equation

$$2MnO_4^- + 16H^+ + 10I^- \longrightarrow 2Mn^{2+} + 5I_2 + 8H_2O$$

Hydrogen Peroxide to Oxygen

$$2KMnO_4 + 3H_2SO_4 \longrightarrow K_2SO_4 + 2MnSO_4 + 3H_2O + 5[O]$$
$$[H_2O_2 + [O] \longrightarrow H_2O + O_2\uparrow] \times 5$$
$$2KMnO_4 + 3H_2SO_4 + 5H_2O_2 \longrightarrow K_2SO_4 + 2MnSO_4 + 8H_2O + 5O_2$$

Ionic Equation

$$2MnO_4^- + 6H^+ + 5H_2O_2 \longrightarrow 2Mn^{2+} + 8H_2O + O_2\uparrow$$
$$2MnO_4^- + 3Mn^{2+} + 2H_2O \longrightarrow 5MnO_2 + 4H^+$$

Ammonia to Nitrogen

$$2KMnO_4 + H_2O \longrightarrow 2MnO_2 + 2KOH + 3[O]$$
$$2NH_3 + 3[O] \longrightarrow N_2(g) + 3H_2O$$
$$2KMnO_4 + 2NH_3 \longrightarrow 2MnO_2 + 2KOH + 2H_2O + N_2(g)$$

Uses

$KMnO_4$ is used,

(i) as an oxidising agent.
(ii) as a disinfectant against disease-causing germs.
(iii) for sterilising wells of drinking water.
(iv) in volumetric estimation of ferrous salts, oxalic acid etc.

Structure of Manganate and Permanganate

Both, manganate (MnO_4^{2-}) and permanganate, (MnO_4^-) are tetrahedral in shape i.e., exhibit sp^3 hybridisation. The green MnO_4^{2-} is paramagnetic with one unpaired electron while the purple MnO_4^- is diamagnetic.

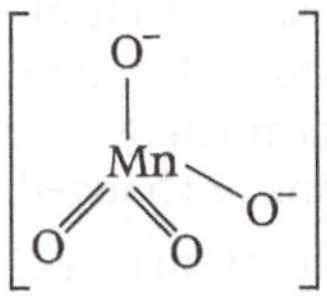

Tetrahedral Manganate ion (green)

Structure of MnO_4^{2-} ion

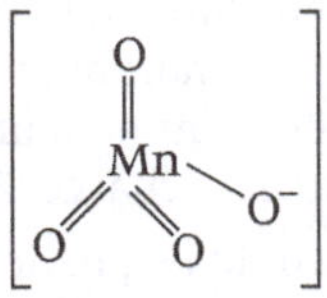

Tetrahedral Permanganate ion (Purple)

Structure of MnO_4^- ion

JEE MAPPER

Example Similar to PYQ Asked in JEE Main 2021

In the light of the given statements, choose the correct answer from the options given below:

(a) Both Statement I and Statement II are false.
(b) Statement I is true, but Statement II is false.
(c) Statement I is false but Statement II is true.
(d) Both Statement I and Statement II are true.

Statement I K_2MnO_4 does not undergo disproportionation in strong alkali medium.

Statement II MnO_2 is fused with KOH in the presence of air to form purple colour red $KMnO_4$.

Sol. *(b)* Statement I is true but Statement II is false. Its corrected form is

When MnO_2 is fused with KOH in the presence of air, the product formed is green colour red K_2MnO_4.

Competency Enhancer 2.2

Statement I Orange colour of solution turns blue when acidified CrO_4^{2-} ion reacts with H_2O_2 solution in presence of ether solvent.

Statement II Cr^{6+} ion in the form of dichromate in acidic medium is a strong oxidising agent.

Silver Nitrate ($AgNO_3$)

Its common name is Lunar caustic.

Preparation

When Ag is heated with dil. HNO_3, $AgNO_3$ is formed. Crystals separate out on cooling the concentrated solution of $AgNO_3$.

$$3Ag + 4HNO_3(\text{dil.}) \xrightarrow{\Delta} 3AgNO_3 + NO + 2H_2O$$

Properties

- Colourless crystalline compound which is soluble in H_2O and alcohol; m.p. 212°C
- When exposed to light, it decomposes hence, stored in a brown coloured bottle :

$$2Ag\downarrow + 2NO_2 + O_2 \xleftarrow{\Delta,\ \text{red hot}} 2AgNO_3 \xrightarrow{\Delta,\ T > 212^\circ C} 2AgNO_2 + O_2$$

- It is reduced to metallic Ag by more electropositive metals like Cu, Zn, Mg and also by PH_3.

$$2AgNO_3 + Cu \longrightarrow Cu(NO_3)_2 + 2Ag$$
$$6AgNO_3 + PH_3 + 3H_2O \longrightarrow 6Ag + 6HNO_3 + H_3PO_3$$

- It dissolves in excess of KCN :

$$AgNO_3 \xrightarrow{KCN} \underset{\text{White ppt.}}{AgCN} \xrightarrow{KCN} \underset{\substack{\text{(Soluble)} \\ \text{potassium argentocyanide}}}{K[Ag(CN)_2]}$$

- $AgNO_3$ gives white precipitate with $Na_2S_2O_3$, If this precipitate is heated with water, it turns black.

$$2AgNO_3 + Na_2S_2O_3 \longrightarrow \underset{\text{(White ppt.)}}{Ag_2S_2O_3} + 2NaNO_3$$

$$Ag_2S_2O_3 + H_2O \xrightarrow{\Delta} \underset{\text{(Black)}}{Ag_2S} + H_2SO_4$$

- It possesses powerful corrosive action on organic tissues, which it turns black especially in presence of light. The blackening is due to finely divided metallic silver, reduced by the organic matter.
- Ammoniacal $AgNO_3$ is called **Tollen's reagent** and is used to identify reducing sugars (including aldehydes) :

$$RCHO + 2Ag^+ + 3OH^- \xrightarrow{\Delta} RCOO^- + 2Ag\downarrow + 2H_2O$$

It is called **'silver mirror test'** of aldehydes and reducing sugar (like glucose, fructose).

Summary of Reactions of $AgNO_3$

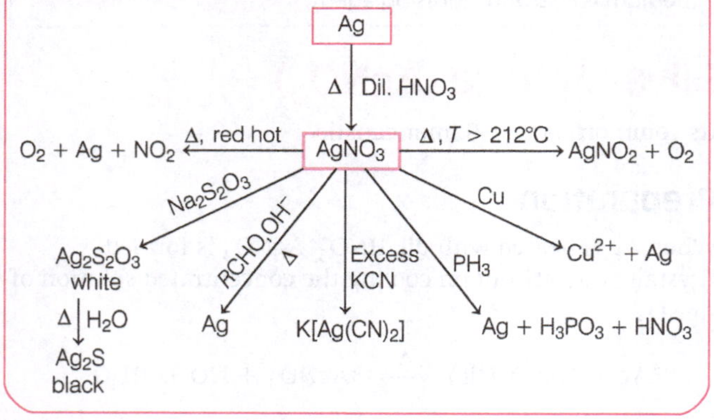

Inner-Transition Elements (or *f*-Block Elements)

As we have specified earlier, the elements with a partially filled *f*-subshell in common oxidation states are known as ***f*-block transition elements** or **inner-transition elements.** They are the **two rows** elements which are at the bottom of the Periodic Table. (i.e., $4f$ and $5f$-series).

- Fourteen elements of the first row ($4f$-series) from cerium ($Z = 58$) to lutetium ($Z = 71$) which follow lanthanum ($Z = 57$) in the Periodic Table are called **Lanthanides** or **Lanthanoids** or **Lanthanones.** These elements are characterised by successive filling of $4f$-orbitals in their atoms. Lanthanides along with yttrium ($Z = 39$) and lanthanum ($Z = 57$) were originally called as **rare earth elements** since their oxides (earths) were rare.
- Fourteen elements of the second row ($5f$-series) from thorium ($Z = 90$) to lawrencium ($Z = 103$) following actinium are known as **Actinides** or **Actinoids** or **Actinones.**
- These are characterised by successive filling of $5f$-orbital. Actinides from $Z = 93$ (after uranium $Z = 92$) have been produced artificially and are known as **transuranium elements.**

Lanthanoids

General and chemical properties of lanthanoids are as follows.

Electronic Configuration

- The general electronic configuration of lanthanoids are $6s^2 5d^{0-1} 4f^{1-14}$. In these elements n, $(n-1)$ and $(n-2)$ shells are incomplete and $(n-2)f$, *i.e.*, $4f$-orbital is being successively filled till Yb.
- Lanthanum ($Z = 57$) has electronic configuration $[Xe]\,5d^1 6s^2$.
- Only Ce ($Z = 58$), Gd ($Z = 64$) and Lu ($Z = 71$) have electrons in $5d$-orbitals as well. This occurs just to attain the extra stability of half-filled or completely filled $4f$-orbitals.
- Lanthanides mostly form ionic compounds in +3 oxidation state, the electronic configuration of M^{3+} ions from $Z = 58$ to $Z = 71$ varies in a regular manner from $[Xe]\,4f^1$ to $[Xe]4f^{14}$.

Atomic and Ionic Sizes : (The Lanthanide Contraction)

Like the ions of the transition elements, the ionic radii of lanthanoids ions (Ln^{3+}) show a progressive decrease with increase in atomic number. The decrease in size of Ln^{3+} ion in $4f$-series is known as **lanthanide contraction.** However, the decrease in atomic radii is not regular.

Explanation

In lanthanides, electrons in $4f$-orbitals are being filled progressively. Since addition of an extra electron in $4f$ (screening constant of $(n-2)f$ electron $= 1$) orbital exactly balances the additional unit of nuclear charge, and thus effective nuclear charge (Z_{eff}) remains unchanged.

Hence, it would be predicted that the atomic radii should also remain constant. Table given below shows that there is slight decrease in the value of atomic radius along the series, with exception that of Eu and Yb.

These two metals crystallise with cubic lattices and attain oxidation state of +2. It is to be noted that the $4f$-orbitals are half-filled ($4f^7$) and completely filled ($4f^{14}$).

When the trivalent ion Ln^{3+} is formed, then screening power of $4f$-electron is no longer equal to unity (but 0.85 since $4f$ is now [$(n-1)$, penultimate shell], and each time an electron is added to $4f$-orbitals, the effective nuclear charge (Z_{eff}) is increased by 0.15 and thus ionic size $\left(r_n \propto \frac{1}{Z_{eff}}\right)$ of Ln^{3+} decreases continuously from Ce^{3+} to Lu^{3+}.

JEE Spotlite

- As a result of lanthanide contraction, the normal increase in size from Sc→ Y→ La disappears after the lanthanide and the pairs of elements such as **Zr and Hf, Nb and Ta, Mo and W,** etc. have nearly same size. Thus, the properties of these elements are very similar.
- Due to lanthanide contraction, the elements of 5*d* and 4*d*-transition series resemble each other much more closely than that of the elements of 4*d* and 3*d* series.

Electronic Configuration and Other Physical Constants of Lanthanum and Lanthanides

Name	Atomic number	Symbol	Oxidation state	Electronic configuration outside [Xe] Core				Radius/pm		$E°/V$ M^{3+}/M	$I_1+I_2+I_3$ kJ mol^{-1}
				Ln	Ln^{2+}	Ln^{3+}	Ln^{4+}	Ln	Ln^{3+}		
Lanthanum	57	La	III	$5d^1 6s^2$	$5d^1$	$4f^0$		187	106	−2.52	3455
Cerium	**58**	**Ce**	**III, IV**	$4f^1 5d^1 6s^2$	$4f^2$	$4f^1$	$4f^0$	**183**	**103**	**−2.48**	**3524**
Praseodymium	59	Pr	III (IV)	$4f^3 6s^2$	$4f^3$	$4f^2$	$4f^1$	182	101	−2.46	3631
Neodymium	60	Nd	III	$4f^4 6s^2$	$4f^4$	$4f^3$	$4f^2$	181	100	−2.43	3692
Promethium	61	Pm	III	$4f^5 6s^2$	$4f^5$	$4f^4$		181	98	−2.42	3728
Samarium	62	Sm	III(II)	$4f^6 6s^2$	$4f^6$	$4f^5$		179	96	−2.41	3871
Europium	63	Eu	III(II)	$4f^7 6s^2$	$4f^7$	$4f^6$		199	95	−2.41	4057
Gadolinium	**64**	**Gd**	**III**	$4f^7 5d^1 6s^2$	$4f^7 5d^1$	$4f^7$		**180**	**94**	**−2.40**	**3763**
Terbium	65	Tb	III(IV)	$4f^9 6s^2$	$4f^9$	$4f^8$	$4f^7$	178	92	−2.39	3798
Dysprosium	66	Dy	III(IV)	$4f^{10} 6s^2$	$4f^{10}$	$4f^9$	$4f^8$	177	91	−2.35	3918
Holmium	67	Ho	III	$4f^{11} 6s^2$	$4f^{11}$	$4f^{10}$		176	89	−2.32	3920
Erbium	68	Er	III	$4f^{12} 6s^2$	$4f^{12}$	$4f^{11}$		175	88	−2.30	3930
Thulium	69	Tm	III(II)	$4f^{13} 6s^2$	$4f^{13}$	$4f^{12}$		174	87	−2.28	4044
Ytterbium	70	Yb	III(II)	$4f^{14} 6s^2$	$4f^{14}$	$4f^{13}$		194	86	−2.27	4193
Lutetium	**71**	**Lu**	**III**	$4f^{14} 5d^1 6s^2$	$4f^{14} 5d^1$	$4f^{14}$		**174**	**85**	**−2.26**	**3887**

Oxidation States

The sum of the first three ionisation energies of the lanthanides is comparatively low, so the elements are highly electropositive. They readily form Ln^{3+} ions by losing both the 6*s* and one 5*d*-electrons. In the absence of 5*d* electron, one of the electrons present in the $(n-2)f$ orbitals is lost. Besides the +3 state, some of the lanthanides show other oxidation states. For example,

$4f^0$ — La^{3+}

$4f^7$ — $Eu^{2+}, Gd^{3+}, Tb^{4+}$

$4f^{14}$ — Yb^{2+}, Lu^{3+}

Stability of these ions depend on, ionisation energy, sublimation energy and lattice energy.

Colour of Ions

Ions of lanthanides are coloured in the solid state as well as in aqueous solution (except $La^{3+}, Ce^{3+}, Gd^{3+}, Yb^{3+}$ and Lu^{3+}). Colour of these ions arise due to electronic transition in $4f$-orbitals ($f-f^*$).

Magnetic Properties

Paramagnetism is associated with the presence of unpaired electrons in a *f*-orbital. Ln^{3+} ions other than f^0 type (La^{3+} and Ce^{4+}) and the f^{14} type (Yb^{2+} and Lu^{3+}) are all paramagnetic.

The Colours and Magnetic Moment value of La^{3+} and Ln^{3+} Ions (Calculated and Observed)

Ion	Colour (aquo complex)	Electronic configuration	μ (unpaired electrons)	Magnetic moment (μ) of N unpaired electrons/μ BM	
				Calculated (only total spin $\sqrt{n(n+2)}$)	Observed
La^{3+}	colourless	$4f^0$	0	0.0	0
Ce^{3+}	colourless	$4f^1$	1	1.73	2.3–2.5
Pr^{3+}	green	$4f^2$	2	2.83	3.4–3.6
Nd^{3+}	lilac	$4f^3$	3	3.87	3.5–3.6
Pm^{3+}	yellow	$4f^4$	4	4.90	2.70
Sm^{3+}	yellow	$4f^5$	5	5.92	1.5–1.6
Eu^{3+}	pale pink	$4f^6$	6	6.93	3.4–3.6
Gd^{3+}	colourless	$4f^7$	7	7.94	7.8–8.0
Tb^{3+}	pale pink	$4f^8$	6	6.93	9.4–9.6
Dy^{3+}	yellow	$4f^9$	5	5.92	10.4–10.5
Ho^{3+}	pale yellow	$4f^{10}$	4	4.90	10.3–10.5
Er^{3+}	rose-red (pink)	$4f^{11}$	3	3.87	9.4–9.6
Tm^{3+}	pale-green	$4f^{12}$	2	2.83	7.1–7.4
Yb^{3+}	colourless	$4f^{13}$	1	1.73	4.4–4.9
Lu^{3+}	colourless	$4f^{14}$	0	0.00	0

JEE MAPPER

Example Similar to PYQ Asked in JEE Main 2021

Which one of the following inner transition elements exhibits +3 oxidation state with paramagnetic nature? (given Z for Lr = 103, Gd = 64, Lu = 71, La = 57)

(a) Lr (b) Gd (c) Lu (d) La

Sol. (*b*) Gadolinium shows + 3 oxidation state with paramagnetic nature because of stable configuration. (i.e., half-filled 4*f*-orbitals)

Competency Enhancer 2.3

Which of the following actinides exhibit +3 oxidation state with diamagnetic nature? (Given, Z for, Lu = 71, Pr = 59)

(a) Tm (b) Pr (c) Lu (d) Tb

Chemical Reactivity

- Most of the lanthanide elements (as well as La and Yb) are silvery white, soft and malleable with high electrical conductivity.
- They are highly electropositive and reactive. Most of them burn in air to form oxides Ln_2O_3 and nitrides LnN (cerium gives CeO_2). Powdered cerium is even pyrophoric. Yttrium usually forms a protective oxide coating on it and remains unattacked by air even at 1273 K.
- The hydride, form is in stable LnH_2, LnH_3 phases, usually **have a defect in lattice and are non-stoichiometric. They react with H_2O liberating H_2 gas.**

$$LnH_3 + 3H_2O \longrightarrow Ln(OH)_3 + 3H_2$$

The hydrides are remarkable stable to heat upto 1200 K

- They form trihalides with halogens but Ce and Tb give CeF_4 and TbF_4 respectively. Complex fluorides of Pr(IV), Nd(IV) and Dy(IV) are also formed.
- The hydroxides are ionic and basic. They are less basic than $Ca(OH)_2$ but more basic than amphoteric $Al(OH)_3$. **The base strength decreases from $Ce(OH)_3$ to $Lu(OH)_3$.**
- Non-availability of *d*-electrons for π-bonding does not favour the formation of carbonyls by most lanthanides.
- Since $E°$ for $Ln^{3+} + 3e^- \longrightarrow Ln$ is negative, they react directly with water, rapidly on heating, to liberate H_2 gas. Reactions with acids are more vigorous, but the metals do not dissolve in alkalies. They are also stable in HF and H_3PO_4 owing to the formation of a protective film of insoluble salts.

- Europium and ytterbium dissolve in liquid ammonia at 195 K forming blue solutions which give spectra characteristic of M^{2+} and ammoniated electrons. The solution decolourises slowly but the concentrated solution appears golden.
- An alloy of lanthanide metal is called **mischmetal.** It has lanthanide metal (95%) and iron about 5% with traces of S, C, Ca and Al. It is used in the production of bullets, shells and lighter flint.
- Mixed oxides of lanthanides are used as catalysts in petroleum cracking. Oxides are also used as **phosphors** in television screens. These phosphorus are essential for the generation of light in cathode ray tube displays.

Summary of chemical reactions of lanthanoids

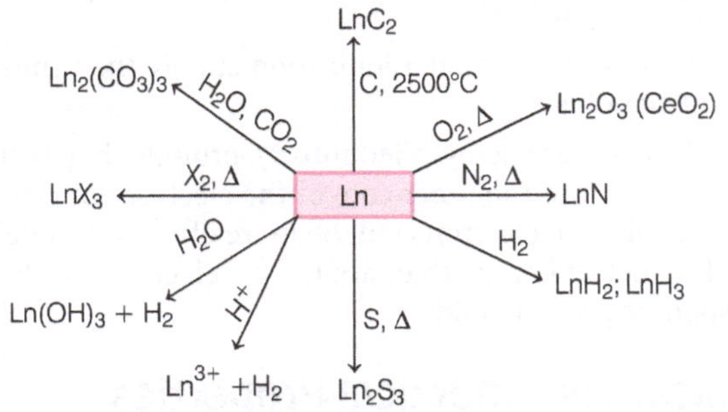

Actinoids

The actinoids are the fourteen elements from Th to Lr following actinium in the seventh period of the Periodic Table. They are radioactive, and therefore of the greatest importance in the study of nuclear chemistry and of the principles which underline the conversion of mass into energy.

General and Chemical properties actinodes ar as follows.

Electronic Configuration

Three shells $(n, (n-1)$ and $(n-2))$ are incompletely filled and differentiating electron enters into $5f$-orbital [i.e., $(n-2)f$]. The variation in the (EC) of the actinoids like those in lanthanoids is due to extra stabilities of f^0, f^7 and f^{14} EC of the $5f$-orbitals.

Some Properties of Actinium and Actinoides

Atomic number	Name	Symbol	Electronic configuration outside [Rn] core		
			An	An^{3+}	An^{4+}
89	Actinium	Ac	$6d^1 7s^2$	$5f^0$	—
90	Thorium	Th	$6d^2 7s^2$	$5f^1$	$5f^0$
91	Protactinium	Pa	$5f^2 6d^1 7s^2$	$5f^2$	$5f^1$
92	Uranium	U	$5f^3 6d^1 7s^2$	$5f^3$	$5f^2$
93	Neptunium	Np	$5f^4 6d^1 7s^2$	$5f^4$	$5f^3$
94	Plutonium	Pu	$5f^6 7s^2$	$5f^5$	$5f^4$
95	Americium	Am	$5f^7 7s^2$	$5f^6$	$5f^5$
96	Curium	Cm	$5f^7 6d^1 7s^2$	$5f^7$	$5f^6$
97	Berkelium	Bk	$5f^9 7s^2$	$5f^8$	$5f^7$
98	Californium	Cf	$5f^{10} 7s^2$	$5f^9$	$5f^8$
99	Einsteinium	Es	$5f^{11} 7s^2$	$5f^{10}$	$5f^9$
100	Fermium	Fm	$5f^{12} 7s^2$	$5f^{11}$	$5f^{10}$
101	Mendelevium	Md	$5f^{13} 7s^2$	$5f^{12}$	$5f^{11}$
102	Nobelium	No	$5f^{14} 7s^2$	$5f^{13}$	$5f^{12}$
103	Lawrencium	Lr	$5f^{14} 6d^1 7s^2$	$5f^{14}$	$5f^{13}$

JEE Alert

The allocation of electrons to the 5*f* or 6*d*-orbitals in the actinide atoms is more uncertain than the allocation to the 4*f* or 5*d*-orbitals in the lanthanide atoms. It is because the external shielding of the 5*f*-electrons is less than that of the 4*f*-electrons.

Atomic and Ionic Sizes

The ionic radii for the M^{3+} and M^{4+} ions contract slightly with increasing atomic number. There is thus an **actinide contraction** corresponding to the lanthanide contraction. There are two observed differences between the two series of ions. These are as follows :

(i) These are as follows although the actinide contraction initially parallels that of the lanthanides, the elements from curium onward are smaller than might be expected, probably resulting from poorer shielding by $5f$-electrons in these elements;

(ii) The lanthanide curve consists of two very shallow arcs with a discontinuity at the spherically symmetrical Gd^{3+} $(4f^7)$ ion. A similar discontinuity is not clearly seen at Cm^{3+}.

Oxidation States

The actinoids in general show +3 oxidation state. There is also a greater range of oxidation states due to comparable energies of $5f$, $6d$ and $7s$ levels. This have been shown in table.

- The maximum oxidation state increases from +4 in Th to +5 in Pa, +6 in U and +7 in Np and Pu, an then decreases in succeeding elements.
- The actinoids resemble the lanthanoids in having more compounds in +3 state than in +4 state but they tend to hydrolyse.
- U^{3+} in aqueous solution evolves hydrogen on standing; aqueous solutions of Np^{3+} and Pu^{3+} are stable, but are easily oxidised to Np^{4+} and Pu^{4+}. All the other trivalent ions up to No^{3+} are stable.
- U^{4+} and Np^{4+} are stable to water, but are slowly oxidised by air to UO_2^{2+} and NpO_2^{2+}.

- Pu^{4+} disproportionates to Pu^{3+} and PuO_2^{2+} when the solution is strongly acidic
- UO_2^{+} disproportionates to U^{4+} and UO_2^{2+}. Among which UO_2^{2+} is stable and difficult to reduce.

Oxidation States of Actinium and Actinoids

Ac	Th	Pa	U	Np	Pu	Am	Cm	Bk	Cf	Es	Fm	Md	No	Lr	Ds
+3		+3	+3	+3	+3	+3	+3	+3	+3	+3	+3	+3	+3	+3	+3
	+4	+4	+4	+4	+4	+4	+4	+4							
		+5	+5	+5	+5	+5									
			+6	+6	+6	+6									
				+7	+7										

Magnetic Properties

The magnetic properties of the actinoids is again dependent on unpaired electrons (N) and are given by

$$\mu \text{ (magnetic moment)} = \sqrt{n(n+2)} \text{ BM}$$

In this case observed values are more complex than those of lanthanoids and have been summarised in the table given below.

Magnetic Moment Value of Actinoids

Element	Z	N	$\mu = \sqrt{N(N+2)}$ BM (only total spin)
Th	90	2	2.83
Pa	91	3	3.87
U	92	4	4.90
Np	93	5	5.92
Pu	94	6	6.93
Am	95	7	7.94
Cm	96	8	8.94
Bk	97	5	5.92
Cf	98	4	4.90
Es	99	3	3.87
Fm	100	2	2.83
Md	101	1	1.73
No	102	0	0.00
Lr	103	1	1.73

Ionisation Energy

Early actinoids have smaller ionisation energy than those of early lanthanoids.

When electrons are being filled into $5f$-orbitals they will penetrate less into the inner core of the electrons and thus these occupied $5f$-electrons will be more effectively shielded from the nuclear charge than are the $4f$-electrons of the corresponding lanthanoids.

Physical and Chemical Properties

- Generally the actinoids metals are silvery in appearance with a variety of structure.
- The dominant feature of the actinoids is their nuclear instability as they have tendency to undergo spontaneous fission and decay becomes more pronounced with the heavier elements. The radioactivity of Th and U is probably responsible for much of the earth's internal heat.
- The actinoids metals are more electropositive and reactive then lanthanoids. The reactivity increase with increase in atomic number.
- They tarnish rapidly in air, forming an oxide coating which is protective in case of Th but less for the other elements.
- The metals react with most non-metals especially on heating, but resist alkali attack and are less reactive towards acids than might be expected. Concentrated HCl react rapidly but concentrated HNO_3 makes Th, U and Pu passive, which can be prevented in presence of F^-.
- With boiling water or steam, H_2 is obtained and metal is converted into oxide.
- Metals react rapidly with H_2 forming hydrides which are decomposed by H_2O.

Elemental Practice 8.2

Type I MCQs with Only One Correct Option

1. HCl is not used to make the medium acidic in oxidation reactions of $KMnO_4$ in acidic medium?
   (a) Both HCl and $KMnO_4$ act as oxidising agents
   (b) $KMnO_4$ oxidises HCl into Cl_2 which is also an oxidising agent
   (c) $KMnO_4$ is a weaker oxidising agent that HCl
   (d) $KMnO_4$ acts as a reducing agent in the presence of HCl

2. In dilute alkaline solution, MnO_4^- changes to
   (a) MnO_4^{2-} (b) MnO_2
   (c) Mn_2O_3 (d) MnO

3. Black coloured solid $(A) \xrightarrow[\Delta]{KNO_3 + KOH}$

   Green coloured solution $(B) \xrightarrow{2H_2O} \underset{\text{Pink}}{(C)} + (A)$

   Pink compound (C) is decolourised by Fe^{2+}.
   The compounds A, B and C are
   (a) MnO_2, K_2MnO_4, $KMnO_4$
   (b) MnO_2, $KMnO_4$, K_2MnO_4
   (c) $KMnO_4$, MnO_2, K_2MnO_4
   (d) K_2MnO_4, MnO_4, $KMnO_4$

4. Select the species that acts as an oxidising agent.
   (a) Np^{4+} (b) Sm^{2+}
   (c) Eu^{2+} (d) Yb^{2+}

5. Gadolinium belongs to 4*f* series, atomic number is 64. Which of the following is the correct electronic configuration of gadolinium?
   (a) $[Xe]4f^7 5d^1 6s^2$ (b) $[Xe]4f^6 5d^2 6s^2$
   (c) $[Xe]4f^8 6d^2$ (d) $[Xe]4f^9 5s^1$

6. Thermal decomposition of ammonium dichromate gives
   (a) N_2, H_2O and Cr_2O_3 (b) N_2, NH_3 and CrO
   (c) $(NH_4)_2CrO_4$ and H_2O (d) N_2, H_2O and CrO_3

7. Potassium permanganate ($KMnO_4$) reacts with oxalic acid in an acidic medium. Then choose the correct statement related to this reaction.
   (a) The oxidation state of Mn change from +7 to +3.
   (b) The reaction is autocatalytic because Mn^{2+} formed acts as a catalyst.
   (c) Oxalic acid is reduced to carbon monoxide.
   (d) Oxalic acid acts as an oxidising agent.

8. $K_2Cr_2O_7 \xrightarrow{\Delta} K_2CrO_4 + O_2 + X$. In the above reaction X is
   (a) CrO_3 (b) $Cr_2O_7^{2-}$
   (c) Cr_2O_3 (d) CrO_5

9. One of the product formed when $K_2Cr_2O_7$ reacts with conc. H_2SO_4 in cold is
   (a) CrO_3 (b) $Cr_2(SO_4)_3$
   (c) Cr_2O_3 (d) CrO_2Cl_2

10. The reaction of $K_2Cr_2O_7$ with NaCl and conc. H_2SO_4 gives
    (a) CrO_2Cl_2 (b) Cr_2O_3
    (c) $CrCl_3$ (d) $Cr_2(SO_4)_3$

11. $Cr_2O_7^{2-} \xrightarrow{pH = x} CrO_4^{2-} \xrightarrow{pH = y} Cr_2O_7^{2-}$ pH values x and y can be
    (a) 6, 6 (b) 7, 7 (c) 8, 6 (d) 6, 8

12. What are the species A and B in the following

    $$CrO_3 \xrightarrow{+H_2O} A$$
    $$CrO_3 \xrightarrow{+NaOH} B$$

    (a) H_2CrO_4, Na_2CrO_4
    (b) $H_2Cr_2O_7$, Cr_2O_3
    (c) CrO_4^{2-}, $Cr_2O_7^{2-}$
    (d) H_2CrO_4, $Na_2Cr_2O_7$

13. When acidified $K_2Cr_2O_7$ solution is added to Sn^{2+} salts, then Sn^{2+} changes to
    (a) Sn (b) Sn^{3+}
    (c) Sn^{4+} (d) Sn^+

14. CrO_3 dissolves in aqueous NaOH to give
    (a) $Cr_2O_7^{2-}$ (b) CrO_4^{2-}
    (c) $Cr(OH)_3$ (d) $Cr(OH)_2$

15. Which one of the following statements related to lanthanons is incorrect?
    (a) Europium shows +2 oxidation state.
    (b) The basicity decreases as the ionic radius decreases from Pr to Lu.
    (c) All the lanthanons are much more reactive than aluminium.
    (d) Ce(+4) solutions are widely used as oxidising agent in volumetric analysis.

16. Consider the following statements with respect of lanthanoids :
    Statement I The basic strength of hydroxides of lanthanoids increases from $La(OH)_3$ to $Lu(OH)_3$
    Statement II The lanthanoid ions Lu^{3+}, Yb^{2+} and Ce^{4+} are diamagnetic
    In the light of the statement given above, choose the correct answer from the options given below.
    (a) Both Statement I and Statement II are correct.
    (b) Both Statment I and Statement II are incorrect.
    (c) Statement I is correct but Statement II is incorrect
    (d) Statement I is incorrect but Statement II is correct.

17. Select the incorrect statement from the following.
    (a) The lanthanoid ions other than f^0, f^{14} type are all paramagnetic.

(b) The carbides Ln_3C, Ln_2C_3 and LnC_2 are formed when metals are heated with carbon.

(c) Configurations of Am and Cm are [Rn] $5f^6 7s^2$ and [Rn] $5f^7 6d^1 7s^2$.

(d) Magnetic properties of the actinoids are more complex than those of lanthanoids.

18. Due to lanthanoid contraction, which of the following pairs of elements have nearly same atomic radii? (Number in parenthesis are atomic numbers)
(a) Zr (40) and Hf (72) (b) Zr (40) and Ta (73)
(c) Ti (22) and Zr (40) (d) Zr (40) and Nb (41)

19. Lanthanide contraction occurs because
(a) *f*-orbitals are incompletely filled
(b) *f*-orbital electrons are easily lost
(c) *f*-orbitals do not come out on the surface of atom and are buried inside
(d) *f*-orbital electrons are poor shielders of nuclear charge

20. The colour of $_{62}Sm^{3+}$ is yellow. The expected colour of $_{66}Dy^{3+}$ is
(a) yellow (b) red (c) blue (d) green

Type II 》 MCQs with One or More than One Correct Option

21. Which of the following compounds are coloured due to charge transfer spectra?
(a) $K_2Cr_2O_7$ (b) $KMnO_4$
(c) $[Fe(H_2O)_5NO]SO_4$ (d) MnO_2

22. Select the correct statements from the following.
(a) $AgNO_3$ on reaction with phosphine produces, N_2 gas.
(b) $AgNO_3$ is used in Tollen's test for aldehydes.
(c) $AgNO_3$ on reaction with sodium thiosulphate gives white precipitates.
(d) On thermal decomposition $AgNO_3$ forms Ag metal.

23. Choose the correct statements about actinoids.
(a) Actinides exhibit more variable oxidation states compared to lanthanides.
(b) The 5*f*-orbitals in actinides are more shielded from the nucleus compared to the 4*f*-orbitals in lanthanides.
(c) The actinides shows a contraction similar to lanthanides.
(d) All actinides are radioactives.

24. Which of the given statements about *f*-block elements is correct?
(a) Actinides are affected more by spin-orbit coupling.
(b) Both follow Hund's rule.
(c) Lanthanides always have larger magnetic moments than actinides.
(d) Actinides are more reactive than lanthanides.

25. Consider the following reaction

$$\text{Chromite ore} + 8(X) + 7O_2 \longrightarrow 8(Y) + 2Fe_2O_3 + 8CO_2\uparrow$$

$$2(Y) \underset{2OH^-}{\overset{H^+}{\rightleftharpoons}} (Z) + 2Na^+ + H_2O$$

$$(Z) + 2KCl \longrightarrow W + 2NaCl$$

Choose the correct statements.
(a) *Y* is paramagnetic in nature.
(b) Oxidation number of transition metal ion is same in compound *Y* and *Z*.
(c) W is orange in colour.
(d) Compound *X* and *W* are Na_2O and K_2CrO_4 respectively.

Type III 》 Numerical/Integer Answer Type Questions

26. The number of electrons required to reduce chromium completely in $Cr_2O_7^{2-}$ to Cr^{3+} in acidic medium, is

27. The oxidation state of chromium in the final product formed by the reaction between KI and acidified potassium dichromate solution is

28. *x* moles of potassium dichromate oxidises 1 mole of ferrous oxalate, in acidic medium. Here, *x* is ....

29. How many of the following are yellow coloured insoluble compounds?
$AgI, PbI_2, Hg_2I_2, HgI_2, BiI_3, CuI_2, Cu_2I_2, PbCrO_4, BaCrO_4, CaCrO_4, Ag_2CrO_4, Hg_2CrO_4$.

30. The number of moles of $KMnO_4$ required to oxidise hydrogen sulphide are ....

Elemental Practice 8.2 | Chapter 08

Connect with **Answers**

1. (b)	2. (a)	3. (a)	4. (a)	5. (a)	6. (a)
7. (b)	8. (c)	9. (a)	10. (a)	11. (c)	12. (a)
13. (c)	14. (b)	15. (c)	16. (d)	17. (c)	18. (a)
19. (d)	20. (a)	21. (a,b,c)	22. (b,c,d)	23. (a,c,d)	24. (a,b,d)
25. (a,b,c)	26. (6)	27. (3)	28. (0.5)	29. (6)	30. (2)

Advanced Exclusive Different Strokes

- **Tips to solve problems related to proportion and properties of $FeCl_3$.**
  - When Fe is dissolved in *aqua-regia* or Fe_2O_3 is dissolved in HCl, hydrate $FeCl_3 \cdot 6H_2O$ is formed :

$$HNO_3 + 3HCl \longrightarrow NOCl + 2H_2O + 2Cl$$
$$Fe + 4HCl + 2Cl \longrightarrow 2FeCl_3 + 2H_2$$
$$Fe_2O_3 + 6HCl \longrightarrow FeCl_3 + 3H_2O$$

  - Anhydrous $FeCl_3$ is black but hydrate $FeCl_3 \cdot 6H_2O$ is yellowish brown, highly deliquescent crystalline solid.
  - It sublimes at 300°C giving a dimeric gas :

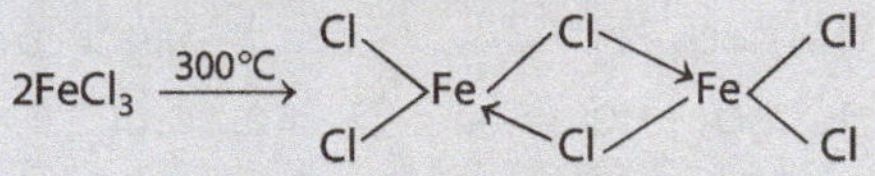

$(FeCl_3)_2$ gas dimer

  - $FeCl_3$ dissolves in both ether and water giving solvated monomeric species :

$$(C_2H_5)_2O \longrightarrow FeCl_3, \quad [Fe(H_2O)_4Cl_2]Cl \cdot 2H_2O$$

Solvated $FeCl_3$ Hydrate $FeCl_3$

  - It normally consists of *trans* $[Fe(H_2O)_4Cl_2]Cl \cdot 2H_2O$ but in strong HCl it forms tetrahedral $(FeCl_4)^-$ ions.

Detection of Fe^{3+} ion

- Fe^{3+} solution gives blood red colour with SCN^- ions :

$$Fe^{3+} + SCN^- \longrightarrow [Fe(SCN)]^{2+}$$

This red colour also contains $[Fe(SCN)(H_2O)_5]^{2+}$, $[Fe(SCN)_3]$ and $[Fe(SCN)_4]^-$. However, when F^- is added, colour fades due to formation of $[FeF_6]^{3-}$.

- Fe^{3+} solution also gives deep blue precipitate of **Prussian blue** with $K_4[Fe(CN)_6]$, potassium ferrocyanide :

$$4\overset{III}{Fe}Cl_3 + 3K_4[\overset{II}{Fe}(CN)_6] \longrightarrow \underset{\text{Prussian blue}}{\overset{III}{Fe}_4[\overset{II}{Fe}(CN)_6]_3} + 12KCl$$

$$\text{or } FeCl_3 + K_4[Fe(CN)_6] \longrightarrow \underset{\text{Prussian blue}}{K\overset{III}{Fe}[\overset{II}{Fe}(CN)_6]} + 3KCl$$

- A deep blue colour is also produced when Fe^{2+} reacts with $K_3[Fe(CN)_6]$, potassium ferricyanide :

$$\overset{II}{Fe}SO_4 + K_3[\overset{III}{Fe}(CN)_6] \longrightarrow \underset{\text{Turnbull's blue}}{K\overset{II}{Fe}[\overset{III}{Fe}(CN)_6]}$$

Let us apply the concept on the example problem:

If nitrogen is present in organic compound, then the sodium extract contains NaCN in Lassaigne's test.

$$Na + C + N \xrightarrow{\text{Fuse}} NaCN$$
$$FeSO_4 + 6NaCN \longrightarrow Na_4[Fe(CN)_6] + Na_2SO_4$$

The compound $Na_4[Fe(CN)_6]$ forms prussian blue colour on reaction with $FeCl_3$

$$4FeCl_3 + 3Na_4[Fe(CN)_6] \longrightarrow Fe_4[Fe(CN)_6]_3 + 12NaCl$$

The above scheme is used for detection of nitrogen (in an organic compound) while performing Lassaigne's test.

Thus, with the help of different tests and reactions, we can easily approach the questions related to proportions and properties of $FeCl_3$, that are important from competitive exam perspective.

PRACTICE
ELEMENT 01

Target JEE Main

Objective Type Questions

1. CeI_2 has metallic lustre. It is explained by formulating it as
(a) Ce (III), $2I^-$, e^- (b) Ce(II), $2I^-$
(c) Ce (IV), $2I^-$, $2e^-$ (d) Ce (I), $2I^-$, e^-

2. Select the element that shows maximum number of different oxidation states in its compounds.
(a) Eu (b) La
(c) Gd (d) Am

3. Which of the following lanthanoid ions is diamagnetic? (At. no. Ce = 58, Sm = 62, Eu = 63, Yb = 70)
(a) Ce^{2+} (b) Sm^{2+}
(c) Eu^{2+} (d) Yb^{2+}

4. Identify the incorrect statement among the following.
(a) Shielding power of 4*f*-electrons is quite weak.
(b) There is a decrease in the radii of the atoms or ions as one proceeds from La to Lu.
(c) Due to lanthanoid contraction, the properties of 4*d* series of the transition elements have no similarities with the 5*d* series of elements.
(d) The $E°$ value for Ce^{4+}/Ce^{3+} is 1.74 u which suggests that it can oxidise water.

5. The species which are diamagnetic in nature is
(a) Nd^{3+} (b) La^{3+}
(c) Tb^{3+} (d) Er^{3+}

6. There are 14 elements in actinoid series. The elements that does not belong to this series is
(a) U (b) Np
(c) Tm (d) Fm

7. Match List-I with List-II.

	List-I		List-II
A.	Catalyst used in the Haber process.	1.	Nd
B.	Elements that shows purple colour in +7 oxidation state.	2.	Fe
C.	Element used in smoke detectors.	3.	Mn
D.	Elements that forms powerful magnets.	4.	Cm

Choose the correct answer from the options given below.
(a) A-III, B-II, C-IV, D-I (b) A-IV, B-III, C-II, D-I
(c) A-II, B-III, C-IV, D-I (d) A-I, B-II, C-III, D-IV

8. Match List-I with List-II.

List I (Reaction)	List II (One of the product)
A. $2NaCrO_4 + H_2SO_4 \longrightarrow$	1. $Na_2Cr_2O_7$
B. $Na_2Cr_2O_7 + 3C \longrightarrow$	2. $Na_2Cr_2O_4$
C. $K_2Cr_2O_7 + HCl \longrightarrow$	3. $CrCl_3$
D. $K_2Cr_2O_7 + NaCl + H_2SO_4 \longrightarrow$	4. CrO_2Cl_2

Choose the correct answer from the options given below
(a) A-II, B-III, C-I, D-IV (b) A-IV, B-I, C-II, D-III
(c) A-I, B-II, C-III, D-IV (d) A-III, B-II, C-I, D-IV

9. Although, +3 is the characteristic oxidation state for lanthanoids yet cerium shows +4 oxidation state because
(a) it does not have variable ionisation enthalpy
(b) it does not have a tendency to attain noble gas configuration
(c) it has a tendency to attain f^0 configuration
(d) Ce^{4+} is a reducing agent

10. Choose the metallic ion that has zero spin only magnetic moment.
(a) Co^{2+} (b) Cr^{2+}
(c) Ni^{2+} (d) Zn^{2+}

11. In the form of dichromate, Cr (VI) is a strong oxidising agent in acidic medium but Mo (VI) in MoO_3 and W (VI) in WO_3 are not because
(a) Cr (VI) is more stable than Mo(VI) and W(VI).
(b) Mo(VI) and W(VI) are more stable than Cr(VI).
(c) Higher oxidation states of heavier members of group 6 of transition series are less stable.
(d) Mo is found in its pure metallic form.

12. In which case there is a change in oxidation number of Cr ?
(a) Aqueous solution of CrO_4^{2-} is acidified
(b) SO_2 gas is passed into $Cr_2O_7^{2-}/H^+$
(c) $Cr_2O_7^{2-}$ solution is made alkaline
(d) CrO_2Cl_2 is dissolved in NaOH

13. Arrange Ce^{3+}, La^{3+}, Pm^{3+} and Yb^{3+} in increasing order of their ionic radii.
(a) $Yb^{3+} < Pm^{3+} < Ce^{3+} < La^{3+}$
(b) $Ce^{3+} < Yb^{3+} < Pm^{3+} < La^{3+}$
(c) $Yb^{3+} < Pm^{3+} < La^{3+} < Ce^{3+}$
(d) $Pm^{3+} < La^{3+} < Ce^{3+} < Yb^{3+}$

14. The basic character of the transition metal monoxide follows the order
(At. no. of Ti = 22, V = 23, Cr = 24, Fe = 26)
(a) TiO > VO > CrO > FeO
(b) VO > CrO > TiO > FeO
(c) CrO > VO > FeO > TiO
(d) TiO > FeO > VO > CrO

15. The pair that will have equal effective magnetic moment is
(a) Ti^{2+} and V^{2+} (b) Cr^{2+} and Fe^{2+}
(c) Cr^{3+} and Mn^{2+} (d) V^{2+} and Sc^{3+}

16. Most basic hydroxide among the following is
(a) $Lu(OH)_3$ (b) $Eu(OH)_3$
(c) $Yb(OH)_3$ (d) $Ce(OH)_3$

17. When MnO_2 is fused with KOH, a coloured compound is formed. The product and its colour is
(a) K_2MnO_4, green (b) Mn_2O_3, brown
(c) Mn_2O_4, black (d) $KMnO_4$, purple

18. Select the compound that weigh less when weighted in magnetic field?
(a) $ScCl_3$ (b) $FeCl_3$
(c) $TiCl_3$ (d) VCl_3

19. An element is in M^{3+} form. Its electronic configuration is $[Ar]3d^1$. Here, *M* is
(a) Ca (b) Sc
(c) V (d) Tl

20. Transuranic elements begins with
(a) Np (b) Cm
(c) Pu (d) U

21. If *M* is element of actinoids series, the degree of complex formation decreases in the order
(a) $M^{4+} > M^{3+} > MO_2^{2+} > MO_2^{+}$
(b) $MO_2^{+} > MO_2^{2+} > M^{3+} > M^{4+}$
(c) $M^{4+} > MO_2^{2+} > M^{3+} > MO_2^{+}$
(d) $MO_2^{2+} > MO_2^{+} > M^{4+} > M^{3+}$

22. The electronic configuration of actinoids cannot be assigned with degree of certainty because of
(a) overlapping of inner orbitals
(b) free movement of electrons over all the orbitals
(c) small energy difference between 5*f* and 6*d* levels
(d) Large atomic radii

23. Select the arrangements which does not represent the correct order of the property stated against it
(a) $V^{2+} < Cr^{2+} < Mn^{2+} < Fe^{2+}$: paramagnetic behaviour
(b) $Ni^{2+} < Co^{2+} < Fe^{2+} < Mn^{2+}$: ionic size
(c) $Co^{3+} < Fe^{3+} < Cr^{3+} < Sc^{3+}$: stability in aqueous solution
(d) Sc < Ti < Cr < Mn : number of oxidation states

24. Which series of reactions correctly represents chemical relations related to iron and its compound ?
(a) $Fe \xrightarrow{\text{Dil. } H_2SO_4} FeSO_4 \xrightarrow{H_2SO_4, O_2} Fe_2(SO_4)_3 \xrightarrow{\text{Heat}} Fe$
(b) $Fe \xrightarrow{O_2, \text{ Heat}} FeO \xrightarrow{\text{Dil. } H_2SO_4} FeSO_4 \xrightarrow{\text{Heat}} Fe$
(c) $Fe \xrightarrow{Cl_2, \text{ Heat}} FeCl_3 \xrightarrow{\text{Heat, air}} FeCl_2 \xrightarrow{Zn} Fe$
(d) $Fe \xrightarrow{O_2, \text{ Heat}} Fe_3O_4 \xrightarrow{CO, 600°C} FeO \xrightarrow{CO, 700°C} Fe$

Numerical Type Questions

25. The oxidation state of Cr in butterfly structure is ....

26. Out of the following
$TiO, Sc_2O_3, Ti_2O_3, VO, V_2O_5, Cr_2O_3, CuO, TiO_2$
The number of basic oxides will be ....

27. When the same amount of zinc is treated separately with excess of sulphuric acid and excess of sodium hydroxide the ratio of volumes of hydrogen evolved is $x : y$. The value of $x + y$ will be ....

28. The magnetic moment of a metal ion of first transition series is 2.83 BM. Therefore, it will have unpaired electrons ....

29. In the reduction of dichromate by Fe(II), the number of electrons involved per chromium atom is ....

30. Consider the following oxides.
$Mn_2O_7, CrO_3, Cr_2O_3, CrO, V_2O_5, V_2O_4$.
Among them the number of amphoteric oxides are ....

31. On complete reaction of $FeCl_3$ with oxalic acid in aqueous solution containing KOH, resulted in the formation of product *A*. The oxidation number of Fe in product (*A*) is ....

32. Consider the following reaction
$$aCrO_4^{2-} + bH^+ + cH_2O_2 \longrightarrow dCrO(O_2)_2 + eH_2O$$
The value of $a + b + c + d + e$ will be ....

33. Number of moles of iodine are liberated when 1 mole of potassium dichromate reacts with potassium iodide.

Check Through PYQs

Element 1 Transition Elements & Their Properties

1. Consider the following oxides, V_2O_3, V_2O_4 and V_2O_5. Oxidation state of vanadium in amphoteric oxide is *2025, 28 Jan Shift-II*
(a) +3 (b) +4
(c) +5 (d) +6

2. Match Column-I with the Column-II and select the correct option. *2025, 24 Jan Shift-II*

Column-I (Ionic species)		Column-II (Spin only magnetic moment (BM))	
A.	Sc^{3+}	(P)	2.84
B.	Ti^{2+}	(Q)	0
C.	V^{2+}	(R)	5.92
D.	Mn^{2+}	(S)	3.87

(a) A → (P), B → (Q), C → (R), D → (S)
(b) A → (R), B → (S), C → (P), D → (Q)
(c) A → (Q), B → (P), C → (S), D → (R)
(d) A → (Q), B → (P), C → (R), D → (S)

3. The correct order of melting point of d-block elements is *2025, 22 Jan Shift-II*
(a) Fe > Mn (b) Tc > Ru (c) Os > Re (d) Ta > W

4. Given below are two statements. *2024, 9 April Shift-II*
Statement I The higher oxidation states are more stable down the group among transition elements unlike p-block elements.
Statement II Copper cannot liberate hydrogen from weak acids.
In the light of the above statements, choose the correct answer from the options given below.
(a) Both Statement I and Statement II are false.
(b) Statement I is true but Statement II is false.
(c) Statement I is false but Statement II is true.
(d) Both Statement I and Statement II are true.

5. The 'spin only' magnetic moment value of MO_4^{2-} is .... BM. (Where M is a metal having least metallic radii among Sc, Ti, V, Cr, Mn and Zn).
(Given atomic number : Sc = 21, Ti = 22, V = 23, Cr = 24, Mn = 25 and Zn = 30) *2024, 8 April Shift-II*

6. Among CrO, Cr_2O_3 and CrO_3 the sum of spin-only magnetic moment values of basic and amphoteric oxides is .... 10^{-2} BM (Nearest integer).
(Given, atomic number of Cr is 24) *2024, 6 April Shift-I*

7. The spin-only magnetic moment value of the ion among Ti^{2+}, V^{2+}, Co^{3+} and Cr^{2+}, that acts as strong oxidising agent in aqueous solution is .... BM (Nearest integer).
(Given, atomic numbers : Ti : 22, V : 23, Cr : 24, Co : 27) *2024, 5 April Shift-I*

8. The metal that shows highest and maximum number of oxidation state is *2024, 5 April Shift-I*
(a) Ti (b) Fe
(c) Co (d) Mn

9. A first row transition metal with highest enthalpy of atomisation, upon reaction with oxygen at high temperature forms oxides of formula M_2O_n (where $n = 3,4,5$). The 'spin-only' magnetic moment value of the amphoteric oxide from the above oxides is...... BM. (Nearest integer)
(given, atomic number: Sc : 21, Ti : 22, V : 23, Cr : 24, Mn : 25, Fe : 26, Co : 27, Ni : 28, Cu : 29, Zn : 30) *2024, 4 April Shift-II*

10. The element which shows only one oxidation state other than its elemental form is *2024, 4 April Shift-I*
(a) Nickel (b) Cobalt
(c) Titanium (d) Scandium

11. Choose the correct option having all the elements with d^{10} electronic configuration from the following. *2024, 27 Jan Shift-II*
(a) ^{27}Co, ^{28}Ni, ^{26}Fe, ^{24}Cr (b) ^{28}Ni, ^{24}Cr, ^{26}Fe, ^{29}Cu
(c) ^{46}Pd, ^{28}Ni, ^{26}Fe, ^{24}Cr (d) ^{29}Cu, ^{30}Zn, ^{48}Cd, ^{47}Ag

12. A first row transition metal in its +2 oxidation state has a spin-only magnetic moment value of 3.86 BM. The atomic number of the metal is *2024, 4 April Shift-II*
(a) 25 (b) 26 (c) 22 (d) 23

13. Identify the incorrect pair from the following: *2024, 27 Jan Shift-II*
(a) Haber process—Iron
(b) Polythene preparation—$TiCl_4 \cdot Al(CH_3)_3$
(c) Wacker process—$PtCl_2$
(d) Photography—AgBr

14. Which of the following electronic configuration would be associated with the highest magnetic moment? *2024, 27 Jan Shift-I*
(a) [Ar] $3d^7$ (b) [Ar] $3d^3$
(c) [Ar] $3d^6$ (d) [Ar] $3d^8$

15. Given below are two statements: one is labelled as "Assertion A" and the other is labelled as "Reason R"
Assertion (A) In the complex $Ni(CO)_4$ and $Fe(CO)_5$ the metals have zero oxidation state.
Reason (R) Low oxidation states are found when a complex has ligands capable of π-donor character in addition to the σ-bonding.
In the light of the above statements, choose the most appropriate answer from the options given below *2023, 6 April Shift-II*
(a) Both A and R are correct but R is not the correct explanation of A
(b) Both A and R are correct and R is the correct explanation of A
(c) A is correct but R is not correct
(d) A is not correct but R is correct

16. Given below are two statements.
One is labelled as Assertion (A) and the other is labelled as Reason (R).
Assertion (A) The first ionisation enthalpy of 3*d* series elements is more than that of group 2 metals.
Reason (R) In 3*d* series of elements successive filling of *d*-orbitals takes place.
In the light of the above statements, choose the correct answer from the options given below.
2023, 31 Jan Shift-II
(a) (A) is true but (R) is false.
(b) (A) is false but (R) is true.
(c) Both (A) and (R) are true and (R) is the correct explanation of (A).
(d) Both (A) and (R) are true but (R) is not the correct explanation of (A).

17. Which of the following 3*d*-metal ion will give the lowest enthalpy of hydration ($\Delta_{hyd}H$), when dissolved in water ? *2022, 29 July Shift-II*
(a) Cr^{2+} (b) Mn^{2+}
(c) Fe^{2+} (d) Co^{2+}

18. The electronic configuration of Pt (atomic number 78) is *2022, 29 June Shift-I*
(a) $[Xe]\ 4f^{14}5d^{9}6s^{1}$ (b) $[Kr]4f^{14}5d^{10}$
(c) $[Xe]\ 4f^{14}5d^{10}$ (d) $[Xe]\ 4f^{14}5d^{8}6s^{2}$

19. Which of the following has least tendency to liberate H_2 from mineral acids? *2022, 28 July Shift-I*
(a) Cu (b) Mn (c) Ni (d) Zn

20. In 3*d*-series, the metal having the highest M^{2+}/M standard electrode potential is *2022, 27 June Shift-II*
(a) Cr (b) Fe (c) Cu (d) Zn

21. Metals generally melt at very high temperature. Amongst the following, the metal with highest melting point will be *2022, 24 June Shift-II*
(a) Hg (b) Ag
(c) Ga (d) Cs

22. Among the following, which is the strongest oxidising agent? *2022, 25 June Shift-I*
(a) Mn^{3+} (b) Fe^{3+}
(c) Ti^{3+} (d) Cr^{3+}

23. Identify the elements for which electronic configuration in +3 oxidation state is $[Ar]\ 3d^5$. *2021, 1 Sep Shift-II*
(a) Ru (b) Mn
(c) Co (d) Fe

24. Which one of the following when dissolved in water gives coloured solution in nitrogen atmosphere? *2021, 26 Aug Shift-I*
(a) $CuCl_2$ (b) AgCl
(c) $ZnCl_2$ (d) Cu_2Cl_2

25. The spin only magnetic moments (in BM) for free Ti^{3+}, V^{2+} and Sc^{3+} ions respectively are (Atomic number Sc : 21, Ti : 22, V : 23) *021, 25 July Shift-II*
(a) 1.73, 0, 3.87 (b) 3.87, 1.73, 0
(c) 0, 3.87, 1.73 (d) 1.73, 3.87, 0

26. Match List-I and List-II.

	List-I		List-II
(A)	Chlorophyll	(i)	Ruthenium
(B)	Vitamin-B_{12}	(ii)	Platinum
(C)	Anticancer drug	(iii)	Cobalt
(D)	Grubbs catalyst	(iv)	Magnesium

Choose the most appropriate answer from the options given below. *2021, 18 March Shift-I*
(a) (A)-(iv), (B)-(ii), (C)-(iii), (D)-(i)
(b) (A)-(iv), (B)-(iii) (C)-(i), (D)-(ii)
(c) (A)-(iii), (B)-(ii), (C)-(iv), (D)-(i)
(d) (A)-(iv), (B)-(iii), (C)-(ii), (D)-(i)

27. The common positive oxidation states for an element with atomic number 24, are *2021, 17 March Shift-II*
(a) + 2 to + 6 (b) + 1 and + 3 to + 6
(c) + 1 and + 3 (d) + 1 to + 6

28. What is the spin only magnetic moment value (BM) of a divalent metal ion with atomic number 25, in its aqueous solution? *2021, 17 March Shift-I*
(a) 5.26 (b) 5.0
(c) 5.92 (d) Zero

29. In which of the following pairs, the outermost electronic configuration will be the same? *2021, 25 Feb Shift-I*
(a) Ni^{2+} and Cu^{+} (b) Fe^{2+} and Co^{+}
(c) Cr^{+} and Mn^{2+} (d) V^{2+} and Cr^{+}

30. What is the correct order of the following elements with respect to their density ? *2021, 24 Feb Shift-II*
(a) Cr < Zn < Co < Cu < Fe (b) Zn < Cu < Co < Fe < Cr
(c) Zn < Cr < Fe < Co < Cu (d) Cr < Fe < Co < Cu < Zn

31. The major components in Gun metal are *2021, 24 Feb Shift-I*
(a) Cu, Sn and Zn (b) Cu, Zn and Ni
(c) Cu, Ni and Fe (d) Al, Cu, Mg and Mn

32. The electrode potential of M^{2+}/M of 3*d*-series elements shows positive value for *2021, 24 Feb Shift-I*
(a) Fe (b) Co
(c) Zn (d) Cu

Element 2 Some Important Compounds of *d*-Block Elements; *f*-Block Elements

33. The electronic configuration of Einsteinium is (Given atomic number of Einsteinium = 99) *2024, 9 April Shift-II*
(a) $[Rn]\ 5f^{12}\ 6d^{0}\ 7s^{2}$ (b) $[Rn]\ 5f^{11}6d^{0}7s^{2}$
(c) $[Rn]\ 5f^{13}6d^{0}7s^{2}$ (d) $[Rn]\ 5f^{10}6d^{0}7s^{2}$

34. Number of colourless lanthanoid ions among the following is ....
Eu^{3+}, Lu^{3+}, Nd^{3+}, La^{3+}, Sm^{3+} *2024, 9 April Shift-I*

35. The number of elements from the following that do not belong to lanthanoids is
Eu, Cm, Er, Tb, Yb and Lu *2024, 6 April Shift-I*
(a) 5 (b) 4
(c) 3 (d) 1

36. The orange colour of $K_2Cr_2O_7$ and purple colour of $KMnO_4$ is due to *2024, 30 Jan Shift-II*
(a) $d \rightarrow d$ transitions in $KMnO_4$ and charge transfer transitions in $K_2Cr_2O_7$
(b) $d \rightarrow d$ transitions in $K_2Cr_2O_7$ and charge transfer transitions in $KMnO_4$
(c) Charge transfer transition in both
(d) $d \rightarrow d$ transitions in both

37. Alkaline oxidative fusion of MnO_2 gives "*A*" which on electrolytic oxidation in alkaline solution produces *B*. *A* and *B* respectively are *2024, 30 Jan Shift-II*
(a) MnO_4^{2-} and MnO_4^- (b) Mn_2O_3 and MnO_4^{2-}
(c) Mn_2O_7 and MnO_4^- (d) MnO_4^{2-} and Mn_2O_7

38. Given below are two statements. *2024, 27 Jan Shift-II*
Statement I In the lanthanoids, the formation of Ce^{4+} is favoured by its noble gas configuration.
Statement II Ce^{4+} is a strong oxidant reverting to the common + 3 state.
In the light of the above statements, choose the **most appropriate** answer from the options given below.
(a) Statement I is false but Statement II is true.
(b) Statement I is true but Statement II is false.
(c) Both Statement I and Statement II are true.
(d) Both Statement I and Statement II are false.

39. The electronic configuration for Neodymium is [Atomic number for Neodymium 60] *2024, 27 Jan Shift-I*
(a) $[Xe]\ 5f^7 7s^2$ (b) $[Xe]\ 4f^4 6s^2$
(c) $[Xe]\ 4f^1 5d^1 6s^2$ (d) $[Xe]\ 4f^6 6s^2$

40. Given below are two statements, one is labelled as Assertion (A) and the other is labelled as Reason (R).
Assertion (A) 5*f* electrons can participate in bonding to a far greater extent than 4*f* electrons.
Reason (R) 5*f* orbitals are not as buried as 4*f* orbitals.
In the light of the above statements, choose the correct answer from the options given below. *2023, 12 April Shift-I*
(a) A is true but R is false
(b) Both A and R are true and R is the correct explanation of A
(c) Both A and R are true but R is not the correct explanation of A
(d) A is false but R is true

41. Nd^{2+} = ... *2023, 31 Jan Shift-I*
(a) $4f^3$ (b) $4f^4$
(c) $4f^4 6s^2$ (d) $4f^2 6s^2$

42. Which one amongst the following are good oxidising agents?
A. Sm^{2+} B. Ce^{2+} C. Ce^{4+} D. Tb^{4+}
Choose the most appropriate answer from the options given below. *2023, 24 Jan Shift-II*
(a) C and D (b) A and B
(c) Only C (d) Only D

43. Highest oxidation state of Mn is exhibited in Mn_2O_7. The correct statements about Mn_2O_7 are
A. Mn is tetrahedrally surrounded by oxygen atoms.
B. Mn is octahedrally surrounded by oxygen atoms.
C. contains Mn—O—Mn bridge.
D. contains Mn—Mn bond.
Choose the correct answer from the options given below. *2023, 1 Feb Shift-I*
(a) B and D only (b) B and C only
(c) A and C only (d) A and D only

44. When Cu^{2+} ion is treated with KI, a white precipitate, *X* appears in solution. The solution is titrated with sodium thiosulphate, the compound *Y* is formed. *X* and *Y* respectively are *2023, 31 Jan Shift-I 2023*
(a) $X = Cu_2I_2$ $Y = Na_2S_4O_5$
(b) $X = CuI_2$ $Y = Na_2S_2O_3$
(c) $X = CuI_2$ $Y = Na_2S_4O_6$
(d) $X = Cu_2I_2$ $Y = Na_2S_4O_6$

45. The total number of Mn=O bonds in Mn_2O_7 is *2022, 27 July Shift-I*
(a) 4 (b) 5
(c) 6 (d) 3

46. The products obtained from a reaction of hydrogen peroxide and acidified potassium permanganate are *2022, 26 July Shift-II*
(a) Mn^{4+}, H_2O only (b) Mn^{2+}, H_2O only
(c) Mn^{4+}, H_2O, O_2 only (d) Mn^{2+}, H_2O, O_2 only

47. The '*f*' orbitals are half and completely filled, respectively in lanthanide ions
(Given, atomic number : Eu 63; Sm 62; Tm 69; Tb 65; Yb 70; Dy 66] *2022, 27 June Shift-II*
(a) Eu^{2+} and Tm^{2+}
(b) Sm^{2+} and Tm^{3+}
(c) Tb^{4+} and Yb^{2+}
(d) Dy^{3+} and Yb^{3+}

48. The oxidation states of transition metal atoms in $K_2Cr_2O_7$, $KMnO_4$ and K_2FeO_4, respectively, are *x*, *y* and *z*. The sum of *x*, *y* and *z* is .... *2022, 2 Sept Shift-II*

49. The disproportionation of MnO_4^{2-} in acidic medium resulted in the formation of two manganese compounds *A* and *B*. If the oxidation state of Mn in *B* is smaller than that of *A*, then the spin-only magnetic moment (μ) value of *B* in BM is .... (Nearest integer) *2022, 28 July Shift-I*

50. The number of terminal oxygen atoms present in the product *B* obtained from the following reaction is .... *2022, 29 June Shift-I*
$$FeCr_2O_4 + Na_2CO_3 + O_2 \longrightarrow A + Fe_2O_3 + CO_2$$
$$A + H^+ \longrightarrow B + H_2O + Na^+$$

51. An acidified manganate solution undergoes disproportionation reaction. The spin-only magnetic moment value of the product having manganese in higher oxidation state is ...... BM. (Nearest integer) *2022, 29 June Shift-I*

52. The Eu^{2+} ion is a strong reducing agent inspite of its ground state electronic configuration (outermost) [Atomic number of Eu = 63] *2021, 31 Aug Shift-II*

(a) $4f^7 6s^2$ (b) $4f^6$

(c) $4f^7$ (d) $4f^6 6s^2$

53. The nature of oxides V_2O_3 and CrO is indexed as '*X*' and '*Y*' type respectively. The correct set of *X* and *Y* is *2021, 27 Aug Shift-I*

(a) X = acidic Y = acidic
(b) X = basic Y = amphoteric
(c) X = basic Y = basic
(d) X = amphoteric Y = basic

54. The correct order of following 3*d*-metal oxides, according to their oxidation numbers is

(A) CrO_3 (B) Fe_2O_3
(C) MnO_2 (D) V_2O_5
(E) Cu_2O *2021, 25 July Shift-I*

(a) (D) > (A) > (B) > (C) > (E)
(b) (A) > (C) > (D) > (B) > (E)
(c) (A) > (D) > (C) > (B) > (E)
(d) (C) > (A) > (D) > (E) > (B)

55. Given below are two statements

Statement I Potassium permanganate, on heating at 573 K forms potassium manganate.

Statement II Both potassium permanganate and potassium manganate are tetrahedral and paramagnetic in nature.

In the light of the above statements, choose the most appropriate answer from the options given below *2021, 17 March Shift-I*

(a) Both statement I and statement II are true.
(b) Both statement I and statement II are false.
(c) Statement I is false but statement II is true.
(d) Statement I is true but statement II is false.

56. Given below are two statements.

Statement I The $E°$ value of Ce^{4+}/Ce^{3+} is +1.74 V.

Statement II Ce is more stable in Ce^{4+} state than Ce^{3+} state.

In the light of the above statements, choose the most appropriate answer from the options given below. *2021, 16 March Shift-I*

(a) Both statement I and statement II are correct.
(b) Statement I is incorrect but statement II is correct.
(c) Both statement I and statement II are incorrect.
(d) Statement I is correct but statement II is incorrect.

57. Mischmetal is an alloy consisting mainly of

(a) lanthanoid metals *2020, 6 Sep Shift-II*
(b) actinoid and transition metals
(c) lanthanoid and actinoid metals
(d) actinoid metals

58. The lanthanoid that does not show +4 oxidation state is *2020, 6 Sep Shift-I*

(a) Dy (b) Ce
(c) Eu (d) Tb

59. The correct electronic configuration and spin-only magnetic moment (BM) of Gd^{3+} ($Z = 64$), respectively, are *2020, 5 Sep Shift-I*

(a) [Xe] $4f^7$ and 8.9
(b) [Xe] $4f^7$ and 7.9
(c) [Xe] $5f^7$ and 8.9
(d) [Xe] $5f^7$ and 7.9

60. The elements with atomic numbers 101 and 104 belong to, respectively, *2020, 4 Sep Shift-I*

(a) actinoids and group 4
(b) actinoids and group 6
(c) group 6 and actinoids
(d) group 11 and group 4

61. The sum of the total number of bonds between chromium and oxygen atoms in chromate and dichromate ions is .... *2020, 9 Jan Shift-II*

PRACTICE ELEMENT 02

Target JEE Advanced

Single Correct Choice MCQs

1. Which of the statements is not true?
(a) On passing H_2S through acidified $K_2Cr_2O_7$ solution, a milky colour is observed.
(b) $Na_2Cr_2O_7$ is preferred over $K_2Cr_2O_7$ in volumetric analysis.
(c) $K_2Cr_2O_7$ solution in acidic medium is orange.
(d) $K_2Cr_2O_7$ solution becomes yellow on increasing the pH beyond 7.

2. $CuSO_4$ when reacts with KCN forms CuCN which is insoluble in water. It is soluble in excess of KCN due to the formation of the complex
(a) $K_2[Cu(CN)_4]$
(b) $K_3[Cu(CN)_4]$
(c) $Cu(CN)_2$
(d) $Cu[KCu(CN)_4]$

3 The reaction of potassium permanganate with thiosulphate in the presence of water gives
(a) MnO_2 (b) Mn_2O_7 (c) MnO_4^- (d) Mn^{2+}

4. Cuprous compounds such as CuCl, CuCN and CuSCN are the only salts stable in H_2O due to
(a) high hydration energy of Cu^+ ions
(b) their inherent tendency not to disproportionate
(c) diamagnetic nature (d) insolubility in water

5. The incorrect statement among the following is
(a) actinoid contraction is greater for element to element than lanthanoid contraction.
(b) most of the trivalent lanthanoid ions are colourless in the solid state.
(c) lanthanoids are good conductors of heat and electricity.
(d) actinoids are highly reactive metals, especially when finely divided.

6. The correct order of ionisation energy (IE) for actinides is
(a) Th < U < Pu < Np (b) Th < Pu < U < Np
(c) Th < Np < U < Pu (d) Th < U < Np < Pu

7. The correct order of ionic radii of Y^{3+}, La^{3+}, Eu^{3+} and Lu^{3+} is
(At. no. Y = 39, La = 57, Eu = 63, Lu = 71)
(a) $Lu^{3+} < Eu^{3+} < La^{3+} < Y^{3+}$
(b) $La^{3+} < Eu^{3+} < Lu^{3+} < Y^{3+}$
(c) $Y^{3+} < La^{3+} < Eu^{3+} < Lu^{3+}$
(d) $Y^{3+} < Lu^{3+} < Eu^{3+} < La^{3+}$

8. Given below are two statements.
Assertion (A) Actinides tend to form compounds with ligands like EDTA that involve chelation.
Reason (R) Actinides have high charge densities and a strong affinity for donor atoms such as oxygen and nitrogen.
In the light of the above statements, choose the most appropriate answer from the options given below.
(a) Both A and R are correct but R is not the correct explanation of A.
(b) Both A and R are correct and R is the correct explanation of A.
(c) A is correct but R is not correct.
(d) A is not correct but R is correct.

One or More than One Correct MCQs

9. Which statements are correct regarding copper sulphate?
(a) It reacts with NaOH and glucose to give Cu_2O.
(b) It reacts with KCl to give Cu_2O.
(c) It gives CuO on strong heating in air.
(d) It reacts with KI to give brown colouration.

10. Pick out the correct statements (s):
(a) MnO_2 dissolves in conc. HCl, and releases Cl_2 gas.
(b) Decomposition of acidic $KMnO_4$ is not catalysed by sunlight.
(c) MnO_4^{2-} is strongly oxidising and stable only in very strong alkali. In dilute alkali, water or acidic solutions, it disproportionates.
(d) $KMnO_4$ does not act as oxidising agent in alkaline medium.

11. Mercuric chloride is converted into mercury by
(a) Placing copper metal in aqueous solution of $HgCl_2$.
(b) Treating aqueous solution of $HgCl_2$ with excess of stannous chloride.
(c) Treating aqueous solution of $HgCl_2$ with $PbCl_4$ solution.
(d) With the exposure of UV light.

12. Choose correct statement(s) regarding the following reaction:
$$Cr_2O_7^{2-}(aq) + 3SO_3^{2-}(aq) + 8H^+ \longrightarrow 2Cr^{3+}(aq) + 3SO_4^{2-}(aq) + 4H_2O$$
(a) $Cr_2O_7^{2-}$ is an oxidising agent.
(b) SO_3^{2-} is a reducing agent.
(c) The oxidation number of per S-atom in SO_3^{2-} is increased by two.
(d) The oxidation number of per Cr-atom in $Cr_2O_7^{2-}(aq)$ is decreased by three.

13. Select the correct statements about actinoids and lanthanoids.
(a) Uranium is used as fuel in nuclear reactors.
(b) The binding energies of 5*f*-electrons in actinoids are higher than 4*f*-electrons in the lanthanoids.
(c) The +3 oxidation state is the most stable oxidation state for all actinoids.
(d) Lanthanoids exhibit sharp absorption bands due to *f*-*f* transitions.

14. Which of the following statements are correct when a mixture of NaCl and $K_2Cr_2O_7$ is gently warmed with conc. H_2SO_4?
(a) Deep red vapours are liberated
(b) Deep red vapours dissolve in NaOH forming a yellow solution.
(c) Greenish yellow gas is liberated
(d) Deep red vapours dissolve in water forming yellow solution

15. Choose the correct statements.
(a) Mixed lanthanide oxides are used in optical glass to reduce chromatic aberration.
(b) Gd^{3+} complexes are used as MRI contrast agents due to their high magnetic moment.
(c) CeO_2 is widely used as UV absorber in sunscreens.
(d) Pr^{6+} compounds are commonly used as oxidising agents in organic synthesis.

16. Which of the following acids attack(s) on copper and silver?
(a) dilute HNO_3 (b) dilute HCl
(c) conc. H_2SO_4 (d) aqua regia

Numerical/Integer Type Questions

17. Sum of highest stable oxidation states of following elements is:
Sc, Zn, Ti, Mn, Cr

18. The number of Mn containing products formed when manganate ions changes into permanganate in the absence of CO_2 is ....

19. $FeC_2O_4 \longrightarrow$ Products
Number of diamagnetic product(s) = x
Number of unpaired electrons in paramagnetic product(s) = y
then $(x + y)$ is ....

20. $KMnO_4 \xrightarrow[\text{R.A.}]{H^+} Mn^x$

$KMnO_4 \xrightarrow[\text{R.A.}]{OH^-} Mn^y$

$K_2Cr_2O_7 \xrightarrow{OH^-} Cr^z$

$x + y + z$ is:
(here x, y and z are oxidation states, R.A = Reducing agent)

21. A bright blue compound is formed on the reaction of potassium permanganate with potassium sulphite. The number of transition metals present in the product(s) is/are

22. In basic medium CrO_4^{2-} oxidises $S_2O_3^{2-}$ to form SO_4^{2-} and itself changes into $Cr(OH)_4^-$. The volume of 0.154 M CrO_4^{2-} required to react with 40 mL of 0.246 M $S_2O_3^{2-}$ is .... mL. (Rounded-off to the nearest integer)

23. The number of species that are used as catalysts in various chemical reactions are
$CeO_2, La_2O_3, Sm_2O_3, Eu_2O_3, Yb_2O_3$

24. The spin-only magnetic moment value of the most basic oxide of vanadium among V_2O_3, V_2O_4 and V_2O_5 is .... BM. (Nearest integer)

Matching Type Questions

25. Match the List-I with List-II

List-I	List-II
A. Nd	I. Used in gas mantles
B. Ce	II. Used as a contrast agent in MRI
C. Gd	III. Used in glass polishing
D. Th	IV. Used in making powerful magnets

Choose the correct answer from the options given below.
(a) A-IV, B-III, C-II, D-I (b) A-III, B-IV, C-II, D-I
(c) A-I, B-II, C-III, D-IV (d) A-III, B-I, C-II, D-IV

26. Match List I with List II match the gas evolved during each reaction.

List I	List II
A. $(NH_4)_2Cr_2O_7 \xrightarrow{\Delta}$	I. H_2
B. $KMnO_4 + HCl \longrightarrow$	II. N_2
C. $K_2MnO_4 + H_2O \longrightarrow$	III. O_2
D. $2MnO_2 + 2H_2SO_4 \xrightarrow{\Delta}$	IV. Cl_2

Choose the correct answer from the options given below.
(a) A-IV, B-I, C-III, D-II (b) A-II, B-IV, C-I, D-III
(c) A-I, B-IV, C-II, D-III (d) A-III, B-II, C-IV, D-I

27. Match the catalysts to the correct processes.

Catalyst	Processes
A. $TiCl_4$	I. Wacker process
B. $PdCl_2$	II. Ziegler-Natta polymerisation
C. $CuCl_2$	III. Contact process
D. V_2O_5	IV. Deacon's process

Choose the correct answer from the options given below.
(a) A-IV, B-III, C-II, D-I (b) A-II, B-I, C-III, D-IV
(c) A-III, B-II, C-I, D-IV (d) A-II, B-I, C-IV, D-III

28. Match the List-I with List-II

	Column I		Column II
A.	Pt	I.	used in stainless steel
B.	Ca	II.	used in aerospace applications
C.	Cu	III.	used as a catalyst in the hydrogenation of alkenes
D.	Ti	IV.	used in electrical wiring.

Choose the correct answer from the options given below.
(a) A-III, B-I, C-IV, D-II (b) A-I, B-II, C-III, D-IV
(c) A-II, B-IV, C-III, D-I (d) A-IV, B-II, C-III, D-I

29. Match the List-I with List-II

	Column I		Column II
A.	$MnO_4^{2-} + H^+ \longrightarrow$	I.	$2MnO_4^- + MnO_2 + 2H_2O$
B.	$MnO_4^- + 4H^+ \longrightarrow$	II.	$MnO_2 + H_2O$
C.	$MnO_4^- + 8H^+ \longrightarrow$	III.	$Mn^{2+} + H_2O$
D.	$MnO_4^- + Mn^{2+} + H_2O \longrightarrow$	IV.	$MnO_2 + H^+$

Choose the correct answer from the options given below.
(a) A-III, B-II, C-I, D-IV (b) A-II, B-I, C-III, D-IV
(c) A-I, B-II, C-III, D-IV (d) A-IV, B-III, C-II, D-I

Species Selection (with 5 Species)

30. Among the following
(i) MnO_2 is an acidic oxide whereas Mn_3O_4 is basic oxide.
(ii) Alloys are generally hard and have high melting point but lower than parent metal.
(iii) VF_2 and Cu_2F_2 do not exist but CuI_2 does.
(iv) On moving left to right in the 3*d*-series the number of unpaired electron increases.
(v) Mn_2O_3 is amphoteric oxide
How many of the following are incorrect statements?
(a) 2 (b) 3 (c) 4 (d) 5

31. Among the following,
(i) Aqueous solution of B_2O_3, V_2O_5 have pH < 7 and both react with conc. HCl.
(ii) Aqueous solutions of B_2O_3, V_2O_5 have pH < 7 and both react with NaOH
(iii) Aqueous solutions of V_2O_5 has pH < 7 whereas that of B_2O_3 has pH > 7.
(iv) B_2O_3, V_2O_5 will react with NaOH as well as conc. HCl.
(v) Al_2O_3 and Ti_2O_3 both will react with conc. HCl
How many of the following statements are correct.
(a) 2 (b) 3 (c) 4 (d) 5

Species Selection (with 7 Species)

32. Consider the elements given below.
(i) Fe (ii) Co
(iii) Ru (iv) Rh
(v) V (vi) Sc
(vii) Mn
The number of elements that forms interstitial hydrides are
(a) 3 (b) 4 (c) 5 (d) 6

33. Consider the oxides given below.
(i) CoO (ii) Fe_2O_3
(iii) FeO (iv) Cr_2O_3
(v) Mn_2O_3 (vi) TiO_2
(vii) Sc_2O_3
The number of compounds that contains a cation corresponding to a magnetic moment of $\sqrt{15}$ BM are
(a) 2 (b) 3 (c) 4 (d) 5

34. Consider the compounds given below.
(i) $VOSO_4$ (ii) VF_2
(iii) Cu_2F_2 (iv) MnO_2
(v) Mn_2O_3 (vi) Fe_2O_3
(vii) $ZnCl_2$
The number of coloured species among the given compounds is
(a) 4 (b) 5 (c) 6 (d) 7

35. Consider the elements given below.
(i) Ti (ii) V
(iii) Cr (iv) Mn
(v) Co (vi) Zn
(vii) Fe
The number of metals that exhibit their highest oxidation state with fluorine are
(a) 4 (b) 5 (c) 6 (d) 7

36. Consider the oxides given below.
(i) CoO (ii) Co_2O_3
(iii) Co_3O_4 (iv) CrO_3
(v) V_2O_4 (vi) V_2O_5
(vii) Fe_3O_4
Among the given oxides the total number of oxygen atoms in the acidic oxide is
(a) 2 (b) 3 (c) 4 (d) 5

Paragraph Based Questions

Paragraph 1

An emerald green crystals of compound (*A*) form a blue coloured aqueous solution, due to the formation of a complex (*B*). On adding conc. HCl or KCl to the blue coloured dilute solution, the colour changes to yellow results to the formation of another complex (*C*). Also, the concentrated aqueous solution of a compound (*D*) is green in color due to presence of complex (*B*) and (*C*) in equilibrium.

37. The number of water molecules present per molecule of the emerald green crystalline compound (*A*) is ....
38. Co-ordination number of complex (*B*) ....

Paragraph 2

Pyrolusite ore on oxidation with $KClO_3/KNO_3$ in basic medium produces dark green coloured compounds (*A*), which on electrolysis produces a purple coloured compound (*B*). The purple coloured compound can be crystallised to deep purple rhombic prisms. It shows different reactions in different mediums. Excess of compound (*B*) on heating with concentrated H_2SO_4 gives an explosive oil (*C*), which on heating decomposes to give another compound (*D*) along with oxygen.

39. Number of oxygen atom in compound *C* is ....
40. Number of O atom in compound *D* is ....

Paragraph 3

MnO_2 is the most important oxide of manganese. It occurs naturally as the black coloured mineral pyrolusite. It is an oxidising agent, and decomposes to Mn_2O_3 on heating to 530°C. It is used in the preparation of potassium permanganate and in the production of Cl_2 gas. Over half a million tonnes per year of MnO_2 is used in dry batteries.

41. When MnO_2 is fused with KOH in the presence of air, the product formed as
(a) purple colour $KMnO_4$ (b) green colour K_2MnO_4
(c) colourless MnO_4^- (d) purple colour K_2MnO_4

42. In which of the following species, the colour is due to charge transfer.
(i) $[Mn(OH)_4]^{2-}$ (ii) MnO_4^{2-}
(iii) MnO_2 (iv) $KMnO_4$
(a) I, II, III (b) II, IV
(c) I, II (d) Only IV

Check Through PYQs

Element 1 Transition Elements and Their Properties

1. Which of the following combination will produce H_2 gas? *2017 Adv.*
(a) Fe metal and conc. HNO_3
(b) Cu metal and conc. HNO_3
(c) Au metal and NaCN (*aq*) in the presence of air
(d) Zn metal and NaOH (*aq*)

2. The correct statement(s) about Cr^{2+} and Mn^{3+} is/are [atomic number of Cr = 24 and Mn = 25] *2015 Adv.*
(a) Cr^{2+} is a reducing agent.
(b) Mn^{3+} is an oxidising agent.
(c) Both Cr^{2+} and Mn^{3+} exhibit d^4 electronic configuration.
(d) when Cr^{2+} is used as a reducing agent, the chromium ion attains d^5 electronic configuration.

3. In the scheme given below, *X* and *Y*, respectively, are

$$\text{Metal halide} \xrightarrow{\text{aq. NaOH}} \text{White precipitate } (P) + \text{Filtrate } (Q)$$

$$P \xrightarrow[\text{Heat}]{\text{aq. } H_2SO_4,\ PbO_2 \text{ (excess)}} X \text{ (a coloured species in solution)}$$

$$Q \xrightarrow[\text{Warm}]{MnO(OH)_2,\ \text{conc. } H_2SO_4} Y \text{ (gives blue-colouration with KI-starch paper)}$$

2023 Adv.
(a) CrO_4^{2-} and Br_2 (b) MnO_4^{2-} and Cl_2
(c) MnO_4^- and Cl_2 (d) $MnSO_4$ and HOCl

4. Consider the following reactions (unbalanced).
$Zn + \text{Hot conc. } H_2SO_4 \longrightarrow G + R + X$
$Zn + \text{conc. NaOH} \longrightarrow T + Q$
$G + H_2S + NH_4OH \longrightarrow Z \text{ (a precipitate)} + X + Y$
Choose the correct option(s). *2019 Adv.*
(a) The oxidation state of Zn in *T* is +1
(b) *R* is a V-shaped molecule
(c) Bond order of *Q* is 1 in its ground state
(d) *Z* is dirty white in colour

5. Fe^{3+} is reduced to Fe^{2+} by using *2015 Adv.*
(a) H_2O_2 in presence of NaOH
(b) Na_2O_2 in water
(c) H_2O_2 in presence of H_2SO_4
(d) Na_2O_2 in presence of H_2SO_4

Element 2 Some Important Compounds of *d*-Block Elements, *f*-Block Elements

6. Fusion of MnO_2 with KOH in presence of O_2 produces a salt *W*. Alkaline solution of *W* upon electrolytic oxidation yields another salt *X*. The manganese containing ions present in *W* and *X*, respectively, are *Y* and *Z*. Correct statement(s) is (are) *2019 Adv.*
(a) Both *Y* and *Z* are coloured and have tetrahedral shape
(b) *Y* is diamagnetic in nature while *Z* is paramagnetic
(c) In both *Y* and *Z*, π-bonding occurs between *p*-orbitals of oxygen and *d*-orbitals of manganese
(d) In aqueous acidic solution, *Y* undergoes disproportionation reaction to give *Z* and MnO_2

7. An acidified solution of potassium chromate was layered with an equal volume of amyl alcohol. When it was shaken after the addition of 1 mL of 3% H_2O_2, a blue alcohol layer was obtained. The blue colour is due to the formation of a chromium (VI) compound '*X*'. What is the number of oxygen atoms bonded to chromium through only single bond in a molecule of *X*? *2020 Adv.*

8. In dilute aqueous H_2SO_4 the complex diaquadioxalatoferrate (II) is oxidised by MnO_4^-. For this reaction, the ratio of the rate of change of $[H^+]$ to the rate of change of $[MnO_4^-]$ is .... *2015 Adv.*

HINTS & Solutions

Solutions : Competency Enhancer

1.1. **(c)** Oxidation number of given 3*d*-series oxides are as follows

A. $V_2O_5 \longrightarrow V \longrightarrow +5$
B. $CrO_2 \longrightarrow Cr \longrightarrow +4$
C. $Cu_2O \longrightarrow Cu \longrightarrow +1$
D. $CoO \longrightarrow Co \longrightarrow +2$
E. $Mn_2O_3 \longrightarrow Mn \longrightarrow +3$

So, the correct order is A > B > E > D > C.

1.2. **(c)** The electronic configuration of given ions

S.No.	Ions	Electronic Configuration	Unpaired electron
A.	V^{3+}	$[Ar]\ 3d^2$	2
B.	Cr^{3+}	$[Ar]\ 3d^3$	3
C.	Cu^+	$[Ar]\ 3d^{10}$	0
D.	Mn^{2+}	$[Ar]\ 3d^5$	5
E.	Fe^{2+}	$[Ar]\ 3d^6$	4

Greater is the number of unpaired electrons higher will be the magnetic moment. Thus, the correct order is
$C < A < B < E < D$

2.1. **(a, c, d)** Among the given statements all are correct except (b)

$$\underset{}{Fe_2(SO_4)_3} + 3BaCl_2 \longrightarrow \underset{\substack{\text{(White ppt.)}\\ P}}{3BaSO_4\downarrow} + \underset{\substack{\text{(Coloured solution)}\\ Q}}{2FeCl_3}$$

$$\underset{\substack{\text{(Yellow)}\\ Q}}{FeCl_3} + 3KI \longrightarrow \underset{(M)}{FeI_3} \xrightarrow{\text{R.T.}} \underset{\substack{\text{(Water soluble)}\\ (N)}}{FeI_2} + \frac{1}{2}I_2$$

In aqueous solution of KI, *Q* undergoes redox reaction.

2.2. **(d)** Both Statement I and Statement II are true.

2.3. **(c)** Lutetium shows + 3 oxidation state with diamagnetic nature because of stable configuration.

Elemental Practice 8.1

1. **(b)** In aqueous solution, copper (I) undergoes disproportionation reaction,

$$2Cu^+(aq) \longrightarrow Cu^{2+}(aq) + Cu(s)$$

The highest stability of Cu^{2+} ion in aqueous solution is due to negative enthalpy of hydration.

2. **(a)** Electronic configuration of Cr^{2+} ion is

$\underset{(22e^-)}{Cr^{2+}}$: $[Ar]\ 3d^4$ or [Ar] | 1 | 1 | 1 | 1 | | ($3d^4$)

It has four unpaired electrons ($n = 4$).
∴ Spin only magnetic moment

$$(\mu) = \sqrt{n(n+2)}\ \text{BM}$$
$$= \sqrt{4(4+2)}\ \text{BM} = 4.90\ \text{BM}$$

3. **(c)** Statements in options (a), (b) and (d) are correct.
Statement in option (c) is incorrect, Its correct form is; Oxidation states of Cr in CrO_4^{2-} (chromate) and $Cr_2O_7^{2-}$ (dichromate) are same and it is +6.

i.e., $CrO_4^{2-} \Rightarrow x + 4(-2) = -2 \Rightarrow x = +6$
$Cr_2O_7^{2-} \Rightarrow 2y + 7(-2) = -2 \Rightarrow y = +6$

4. **(a)**
A. V_2O_5 – (III) oxidation of SO_2 in the manufacture of H_2SO_4 by contact process.
B. $TiCl_4 + Al(CH_3)_3$ – (*Ziegler-Natta* catalyst) – (IV) Polymerisation of ethylene.
C. $PdCl_2$ – (I) Oxidation of ethyne to ethanal.
D. Nickel complexes – (II) Polymerisation of alkynes.

Thus, the correct match is
(A) → (III), (B) → (IV), (C) → (I), (D) → (II)

5. **(b)** Copper has a positive electrode potential. This means that copper is not able to displace H^+ ions from acid solution.

6. **(d)** $_{24}Cr = [Ar]\ 3d^5\ 4s^1$, $Cr^{2+} = [Ar]\ 3d^4$
$_{26}Fe = [Ar]\ 3d^6\ 4s^2$ $Fe^{2+} = [Ar]3d^6$
$_{25}Mn = [Ar]\ 3d^5\ 4s^2$ $Mn^{2+} = [Ar]3d^5$
$_{27}Co = [Ar]\ 3d^7\ 4s^2$, $Co^{2+} = [Ar]\ 3d^7$

Stability order can be determined on the basis of half-filled and fully-filled orbitals.
And half-filled orbitals are more stable than partially filled.
So, here Mn has higher stability.
In Fe^{2+} (d^6), the placing of 1 extra electron in a subshell makes it less stable. Placing 2 electrons in Co^{2+} (d^7) destabilises it more Cr^{2+} (d^4) has 1 vacant subshell.
But here, Fe^{2+} gets stabilisation compared to Cr^{2+} due to exchange energy.
Thus, the correct order is

$$Mn > Fe > Cr > Co$$

7. **(b)** The electronic configuration of given ions are

	Elements	Electronic Configuration	Unpaired electron(s)
A.	Mn	$[Ar]\ 3d^5 4s^2$	5
B.	Cr^{2+}	$[Ar]\ 3d^4$	4
C.	Ni^{2+}	$[Ar]\ 3d^8$	2
D.	Zn^+	$[Ar]\ 3d^{10} 4s^1$	1
E.	V	$[Ar]\ 3d^3 4s^2$	3

8. **(a)** Spin only magnetic moment is given by,

$$\mu_s = \sqrt{n(n+2)}\ \text{BM}$$

where, n = number of unpaired electrons

A. $Ti^{3+} \longrightarrow 3d^1, n = 1, \mu_s = \sqrt{1(1+2)} = \sqrt{3}$ BM

B. $Cr^{2+} \longrightarrow 3d^4, n = 4, \mu_s = \sqrt{4(4+2)} = \sqrt{24}$ BM

C. $Mn^{2+} \longrightarrow 3d^5, n = 5, \mu_s = \sqrt{5(5+2)} = \sqrt{35}$ BM

D. $Fe^{2+} \longrightarrow 3d^6, n = 4, \mu_s = \sqrt{4(4+2)} = \sqrt{24}$ BM

E. $Sc^{3+} \longrightarrow 3d^0, n = 0, \mu_s = 0$

Hence, B and D have same value of magnetic moment.

9. ***(b)*** Interstitial compounds are obtained when small atoms like H, B, C, N, etc., fit into the interstitial space of lattice metals. These retain metallic conductivity. These resemble with (parent metal in chemical properties). But differ in physical properties like hardness, melting point, etc.

10. ***(b)***

(A) Mn shows six oxidation states in its compounds, i.e. +2, +3, +4, +5, +6 and +7 ⇒ (III)

(B) Zn is a pseudo transition element like Cd and Hg of groups 12 (d^{10} configuration) ⇒ (IV)

(C) Sc does not exhibit variable oxidation states. Only +3 oxidation state is shown by Sc in its compounds ⇒ (I)

(D) Cu^+ disproportionates in aqueous solution as,

$$2Cu^+ \longrightarrow Cu^0 + Cu^{2+} \Rightarrow \text{(II)}$$

11. ***(a)*** $_{28}Ni = 1s^2, 2s^2 2p^6, 3s^2 3p^6 3d^8, 4s^2$

$Ni^{2+} = 1s^2, 2s^2 2p^6, 3s^2 3p^6 3d^8$ (2 unpaired electrons)

$_{22}Ti = 1s^2, 2s^2 2p^6, 3s^2 3p^6 3d^2, 4s^2$

$Ti^{3+} = 1s^2, 2s^2 2p^6, 3s^2 3p^6 3d^1$ (1 unpaired electron)

$_{21}Sc = 1s^2, 2s^2, 2p^6, 3s^2 3p^6 3d^1, 4s^2$

$Sc^{3+} = 1s^2, 2s^2 2p^6, 3s^2 3p^6$ (no unpaired electron)

$_{29}Cu = 1s^2, 2s^2 2p^6, 3s^2 3p^6 3d^{10}, 4s^1$

$Cu^+ = 1s^2, 2s^2 2p^6, 3s^2 3p^6 3d^{10}$ (no unpaired electron)

$Cu^{2+} = 1s^2, 2s^2 2p^6, 3s^2 3p^6 3d^9$ (1 unpaired electron)

Hence, in the above ions, Ni^{2+} and Ti^{3+} are coloured in aqueous solution due to the presence of unpaired electrons in d-subshell.

12. ***(b)*** When carbon atoms occupy the interstitial spaces in the iron lattice, they create distortions that impede dislocation movement, thereby increasing the material's hardness.

13. ***(d)*** In $_{23}V = 1s^2, 2s^2 2p^6, 3s^2 3p^6 3d^3, 4s^2$

Third electron is removed to give third ionisation potential which belongs to $3d^3$ subshell.

$$_{24}Cr = 1s^2, 2s^2 2p^6, 3s^2 3p^6 3d^5, 4s^1$$

Third electron which is removed to give third ionisation potential, belongs to $3d^5$ subshell.

$$_{26}Fe = 1s^2, 2s^2 2p^6, 3s^2 3p^6 3d^6, 4s^2$$

Third electron which is removed to give third ionisation potential, belongs to $3d^6$ subshell.

$$_{25}Mn = 1s^2, 2s^2 2p^6, 3s^2 3p^6 3d^5, 4s^2$$

Third electron which is removed to give third ionisation potential, belongs to $3d^5$ subshell.

In above all elements, orbitals involved are same. Required amount of energy (enthalpy) is based upon the stability of d-subshell.

The $3d^5$-subshell has highest stability in all because it is half-filled subshell. So, Mn shows highest third, ionisation potential.

14. ***(c)*** The electronic configuration of Co^{3+} is [Ar] $3d^6$.

Here, $n = 4$

$$\mu = \sqrt{4(4+2)} = \sqrt{24} \text{ BM.}$$

The electronic configuration of Cr^{3+} is [Ar] $3d^3$.

Here, $n = 3$

$$\mu = \sqrt{3(3+2)} = \sqrt{15} \text{ BM.}$$

The electronic configuration of Fe^{3+} is [Ar] $3d^5$.

Here, $n = 5$

$$\mu = \sqrt{5(5+2)} = \sqrt{35} \text{ BM}$$

The electronic configuration of Ni^{2+} is [Ar] $3d^8$.

Here, $n = 2 \Rightarrow \mu = \sqrt{2(2+2)} = \sqrt{8}$ BM

So, the correct option is (c).

15. ***(d)***

$$Ni^{2+}(28) = [Ar]\,3d^8$$
$$Mn^{3+}(25) = [Ar]\,3d^4$$
$$Fe^{3+}(26) = [Ar]\,3d^5$$
$$Co^{3+}(27) = [Ar]\,3d^6$$

Hence, Co^{3+} has $3d^6$ electronic configuration correct answer is (d).

16. ***(b)*** The outer electronic configuration of element that exhibits largest number of oxidation state i.e. manganese is : $3d^5 4s^2$

3d						4s
↿	↿	↿	↿	↿		⥮

The number of various oxidation states possible are +2, +3, +4, +5, +6, +7

17. ***(a)*** $Cr^{3+} = [Ar]\,3d^3 4s^0 \Rightarrow t_{2g}^3\, e_g^0$

$V^{3+} = [Ar]\,3d^2 4s^0 \Rightarrow t_{2g}^2\, e_g^0$

$Ti^{3+} = [Ar]\,3d^1 4s^0 \Rightarrow t_{2g}^1 e_g^0$

$Mn^{3+} = [Ar]\,3d^4 4s^0 \Rightarrow t_{2g}^3 e_g^1$

Half-filled and fully filled orbital are more stable than partially filled orbitals.

Among the given ions Cr^{3+} has half-filled t_{2g} orbital and is more stable in aqueous solution.

Although Mn^{3+} ion has half-filled t_{2g} orbital but there is one electron filled in e_g orbital which reduces the stability.

18. ***(a)*** In a period on moving from left to right ionic radius decreases. So, the order of cationic radii for option (a) is incorrect.

$$Ni^{2+} > Cr^{2+} > Fe^{2+} > Mn^{2+}$$

The correct order is $Cr^{2+} > Mn^{2+} > Fe^{2+} > Ni^{2+}$

19. ***(c)*** The colour of $[Ti(H_2O)_6]^{3+}$ arises due to d-d transitions of the Ti^{3+} ion which has a $3d^1$ electronic configuration.

20. ***(c)*** [Ne] $3s^2 3p^5$ is the electronic configuration of p-block elements whereas all other configurations are of d-block elements.

21. ***(a, c, d)*** In second transition series, IE increases regularly from Y to Cd except Ag. Whereas in the first and third transition series V and Ta have low IE values than their corresponding previous elements.

22. ***(c, d)*** $2Ag_2O \xrightarrow{\Delta} 4Ag + O_2$

$2HgO \xrightarrow{\Delta} 2Hg + O_2$

23. ***(a, b, c, d)*** Conditions required to form complexes are:
(a) Metal ion must have vacant orbitals.
(b) Metal ion must have small size or high charge density or higher nuclear charge.
(d) They shows variable oxidation state.

24. ***(a, b, c)*** $Ni^{2+} = [Ar]\,3d^8 4s^0$
$Fe^{2+} = [Ar]\,3d^6 4s^0$
$Cu^{2+} = [Ar]\,3d^9 4s^0$
$Cu^{+} = [Ar]\,3d^{10} 4s^0$

The transition metals are coloured due to the presence of unpaired electrons in their d-orbitals (i.e., from d^1 to d^9 configuration). Hence, aqueous solution of Cu^+ is colourless.

25. ***(a, b, c, d)***

$$\underset{\text{(Green vitriol)}}{FeSO_4 \cdot 7H_2O} \xrightarrow{\text{Strongly heated}} Fe_2O_3 + SO_2 + SO_3 + H_2O$$

Fe_2O_3 is basic oxide.
H_2O is neutral oxide.
SO_2 and SO_3 are acidic oxide.
SO_2 is a reducing agent.

26. ***(1)*** Electronic configuration Pt = $[Xe]\,4f^{14}\,5d^9 6s^2$
Thus, it has $9e^-$ in its d-orbitals.
Thus,

$$\frac{x+1}{10} = \frac{9+1}{10} = 1$$

27. ***(5)*** In d-block elements, density increases from left to right but zinc has lower density than Ni due to larger metallic radius So, Pd, Ag, Au, Pt and Os have higher density than Ni.

28. ***(4)*** $\mu = \sqrt{n(n+2)}$
$4.90 = \sqrt{n(n+2)}$
$24.01 = n(n+2) \Rightarrow n = 4$

29. ***(5)*** Zn, Cd and Hg are d-block elements, but they are not regarded as transition element due to fully-filled d-orbitals.

30. ***(2)*** Among all the cations formed by Mn; Mn^{7+} ($3d^0$) will have highest ionisation energy due to highest positive charge.

$$\therefore \quad x = 0, \quad \frac{4}{2} = 2$$

Elemental Practice 8.2

1. ***(b)*** As hydrochloric acid is oxidised to chlorine which itself is an oxidising agent. Thus, HCl is not used to make the medium acidic in oxidation of $KMnO_4$ in acidic medium.

2. ***(a)*** $MnO_4^- + OH^- \longrightarrow MnO_4^{2-}$

3. ***(a)*** Black coloured compound is MnO_2 (A).
When it is fused with KOH and KNO_3, potassium manganate (K_2MnO_4) is formed. It is indicated by its green colour.

In acidic medium, K_2MnO_4 is unstable and disproportionates

$$\underset{(A)}{MnO_2} + KOH + (KNO_3) \xrightarrow{\Delta} \underset{\text{Green colour } (B)}{K_2MnO_4}$$

$$2K_2MnO_4 + H_2O \xrightarrow[\text{reduction}]{\text{Electrolytic}} \underset{(C)}{2KMnO_4} + 2KOH + H_2$$

(disproportionation reaction)

4. ***(a)*** All those inner-transition elements having +2 oxidation state, changes to +3, and act as reducing agents. While those having +4 oxidation state tend to change to +3 oxidation state and act as oxidising agents. Therefore, Np^{4+} acts as an oxidising agent.

5. ***(a)*** Gadolinium, Gd = $[Xe]4f^7\,5d^1\,6s^2$

6. ***(a)*** $(NH_4)_2Cr_2O_7 \xrightarrow{\Delta} N_2\uparrow + Cr_2O_3 + 4H_2O$

7. ***(b)*** The reaction between $KMnO_4$ and $H_2C_2O_4$ in acidic medium is

$$2MnO_4^- + 5C_2O_4^{2-} + 16H^+ \longrightarrow 2Mn^{2+} + 10CO_2 + 8H_2O$$

(a) The oxidation state of Mn changes from +7 to +2.
(b) Mn^{2+} ions produced during the reaction acts as a catalyst, accelerating the decomposition of $KMnO_4$.
(c) Oxalic acid is oxidised to CO_2.
(d) Oxalic acid acts a reducing agent and is itself oxidised to CO_2 while $KMnO_4$ is reduced to Mn^{2+}.

8. ***(c)*** Potassium dichromate on heating gives oxygen and chromic oxide (Cr_2O_3).

$$4K_2Cr_2O_7 \xrightarrow{\Delta} 4K_2CrO_4 + 3O_2 + 2Cr_2O_3$$

9. ***(a)*** $K_2Cr_2O_7 + 2H_2SO_4 \xrightarrow{\text{Cold}} 2CrO_3 + 2KHSO_4 + H_2O$

CrO_3 is highly acidic and oxidising. It is called chromic acid.

10. ***(a)*** $4NaCl + \underset{\text{(Conc.)}}{6H_2SO_4} + K_2Cr_2O_7 \longrightarrow \underset{\text{Chromyl chloride}}{2CrO_2Cl_2} + 2KHSO_4 + 4NaHSO_4 + 3H_2O$

11. ***(c)*** $Cr_2O_7^{2-} + 2OH^- \longrightarrow 2CrO_4^{2-} + H_2O \qquad pH > 7\,(x > 7)$
$2CrO_4^{2-} + 2H^+ \longrightarrow Cr_2O_7^{2-} + H_2O \qquad pH < 7\,(y < 7)$

12. ***(a)*** $CrO_3 + H_2O \longrightarrow \underset{(A)}{H_2CrO_4}$

$CrO_3 + 2NaOH \longrightarrow \underset{(B)}{Na_2CrO_4} + H_2O$

13. ***(c)*** $Cr_2O_7^{2-} + 14H^+ + 3Sn^{2+} \longrightarrow 2Cr^{3+} + 3Sn^{4+} + 7H_2O$

14. ***(b)*** $CrO_3 + 2NaOH \longrightarrow Na_2CrO_4 + H_2O$

15. ***(c)*** The first few members of the lanthanons are quite reactive like calcium. However, with increasing atomic number, their behaviour becomes similar to that of aluminium.

16. ***(d)*** Statement I is incorrect but Statement II is correct. The correct form of Statement I is :

The basicity of hydroxides of lanthanoids decreases with increase in atomic number due to lanthanide contraction.

Ce = [Xe] $4f^1 5d^1 6s^2$; Ce^{4+} = [Xe], Yb= [Xe] $4f^{14} 6s^2$;

Yb^{2+} = [Xe] $4f^{14}$, Lu= [Xe] $4f^{14} 5d^1 6s^2$; Lu^{3+} = [Xe] $4f^{14}$.

The given ions contain no unpaired electrons and therefore, all are diamagnetic.

17. ***(c)*** The configuration of Am and Cm are [Rn] $5f^7 7s^2$ and [Rn] $5f^7 6d^1 7s^2$.

18. ***(a)*** Zr and Hf have nearly same atomic radii due to lanthanoid contraction.

19. ***(d)*** The size of lanthanides are smaller than expected. This is associated with the filling up of 4*f*-orbitals which must be filled before the 5*d*-orbitals.

The electrons in *f*-orbitals are not effective in screening other electrons from the nuclear charge.

20. ***(a)*** The electronic configuration of $_{62}Sm^{3+}$ is $4f^5$ and that of $_{66}Dy^{3+}$ is $4f^9$. The colour of f^n and f^{14-n} are often identical.

21. ***(a, b, c)*** Charge transfer spectra is due to instant charge transfer from metal to ligand, $K_2Cr_2O_7$, $KMnO_4$ and $[Fe(H_2O)_5NO]SO_4$ are coloured due to charge transfer spectra.

22. ***(b, c, d)*** Statements (b), (c) and (d) are correct whereas (a) is incorrect.

(a) $AgNO_3 + PH_3 \longrightarrow Ag + H_3PO_3 + HNO_3$

(b) $RCHO + 2Ag^+ + 3OH^- \longrightarrow RCOO^- + 2Ag\downarrow + 2H_2O$

(c) $2AgNO_3 + Na_2S_2O_3 \longrightarrow \underset{\text{White ppt.}}{Ag_2S_2O_3} + 2NaNO_3$

(d) $AgNO_3 \xrightarrow{\Delta} Ag + O_2 + NO_2$

23. ***(a, c, d)*** Statements (a), (c) and (d) are correct whereas Statement (b) is incorrect.

The correct form of (b) is:

The 5*f* orbitals in actinides are less shielded from the nucleus compared to 4*f* orbitals in lanthanides, resulting in greater overlap with 6*d* and 7*s* orbitals.

24. ***(a, b, d)*** Statements (a), (b), (d) are correct whereas Statement (c) is incorrect.

The correct form of (c) is

The magnetic moments of lanthanides are not necessarily larger than those of actinides because of differences in orbital contributions and spin-orbit coupling.

25. ***(a, b, c)*** Among the given statements (a) and (c) are correct while (b) and (d) are incorrect. Their corrected form are as

$$\underset{(X)}{4Fe(CrO_2)_2 + 8Na_2CO_3} + 7O_2 \longrightarrow 2Fe_2O_3 + \underset{(Y)}{8Na_2CrO_4} + 8CO_2\uparrow$$

$$\underset{(Y)}{2Na_2CrO_4} \underset{OH^-}{\overset{H^+}{\rightleftharpoons}} \underset{(Z)}{Na_2Cr_2O_7} + Na_2SO_4 + H_2O$$

$$\underset{(Z)}{Na_2Cr_2O_7} + 2KCl \longrightarrow \underset{(\text{Orange } W)}{K_2Cr_2O_7} + 2NaCl$$

- Oxidation number of transition metal ion in compound *Y* and *Z* is 6.
- Compound *X* and *W* is Na_2CO_3 and $K_2Cr_2O_7$ respectively.

26. ***(6)*** $Cr_2O_7^{2-}(aq) + 14H^+(aq) + 6e^- \longrightarrow 2Cr^{3+}(aq) + 7H_2O$

Thus, Cr(VI) in $Cr_2O_7^{2-}$ requires 6 e^- to undergo reduction completely to Cr^{3+} in acidic medium.

27. ***(3)*** $Cr_2O_7^{2-} + 14H^+ + 6I^- \longrightarrow 2Cr^{3+} + 7H_2O + 3I_2$

Thus, final oxidation state of Cr is + 3.

28. ***(0.5)*** Potassium dichromate oxidises ferrous oxalate in acidic medium in following way

$$2FeC_2O_4 + Cr_2O_7^{2-} + 14H^+ \longrightarrow 2Fe^{3+} + 2Cr^{3+} + 4CO_2 + 7H_2O$$

Since, 2 moles of FeC_2O_4 are oxidised by 1 mole of $Cr_2O_7^{2-}$ therefore, 1 mole of FeC_2O_4 will be oxidised by 0.5 mole of $Cr_2O_7^{2-}$.

29. ***(6)*** AgI, PbI_2, Hg_2I_2, CuI_2, $PbCrO_4$ and $BaCrO_4$ are insoluble yellow compounds whereas $CaCrO_4$ is a soluble yellow compounds. All other have following colours: HgI_2—red colour, Hg_2CrO_4 — Orange-red colour, BiI_3 — Grey black, Ag_2CrO_4 — Brick red colour, Cu_2I_2 — White.

30. ***(2)*** $H_2S \longrightarrow 2H^+ + S^{2-}$

$5S^{2-} + 2MnO_4^- + 16H^+ \longrightarrow 2Mn^{2+} + 8H_2O + 5S$

Practice Element 01 : Target JEE Main

1. ***(c)*** CeI_2 is supposed to have metal excess defect due to anion vacancies and the electrons associated with anions left behind are trapped in the vacancies. Thus, CeI_2 is formulated as Ce (IV), $2I^-$, $2e^-$. Due to the presence of these trapped electrons, the compound shows metallic lustre.
2. ***(d)*** Oxidation states of Americium are + 3, + 4, + 5 and + 6.
3. ***(d)*** Yb^{2+} has an electronic configuration of [Xe] $4f^{14}$. Thus, all the electrons are paired up and hence, it is diamagnetic in nature.
4. ***(c)*** Due to lanthanoid contraction, the sizes of elements of 4*d* transition series are almost similar to those of 5*d* transition series. Hence, they show similarities in properties.
5. ***(b)*** Paramagnetism is shown by the positive ions of lanthanides except $La^{3+}(4f^0)$ and $Lu^{3+}(4f^{14})$. These ions are diamagnetic.
6. ***(c)*** Tm(thulium) does not belong to actinoides.

7. ***(c)*** The correct match is A-II, B-III, C-IV, D-I.
Fe is the catalyst used in Haber's process for the synthesis of ammonia.
$KMnO_4$ forms a deep purple solution due to Mn in the +7 oxidaiton state.
Cm is used in smoke detectors due to its radioactive properties.
Nd, a lanthanide, is used in Nd-Fe-B magnets.
8. ***(c)*** The correct match is A-I, B-II, C-III, D-IV
9. ***(c)*** $Ce = [Xe]\,4f^1\,5d^1\,6s^2$
$Ce^{4+} = [Xe]\,4f^0$
Ce also shows + 4 oxidation state because it has the tendency to attain noble gas configuration and $4f^0$ configuration.
10. ***(d)*** $Co^{2+} = [Ar]\,3d^7$, $Cr^{2+} = [Ar]\,3d^4$ and $Ni^{2+} = [Ar]\,3d^8$, $Zn^{2+} = [Ar]\,3d^{10}$
Zn^{2+} ion does not have any unpaired electrons. So, it has zero spin only magnetic moment.
11. ***(b)*** In the form of dichromate, Cr (VI) is a strong oxidising agent in acidic medium. But Mo (VI) in MoO_3 and W (VI) in WO_3 are not because Mo (VI) and W (VI) are more stable than Cr (VI).
Further more, in heavier members of group 6 higher oxidation states are more stable.
Mo is found in the form of ores like MoS_2.
12. ***(b)***
(a) $2\overset{+6}{Cr}O_4^{2-} + 2H^+ \longrightarrow \overset{+6}{Cr_2}O_7^{2-} + H_2O$
(No change in oxidation state of Cr.)
(b) $\overset{+6}{Cr_2}O_7^{2-} + 2H^+ + 3SO_2 \longrightarrow 2Cr^{3+} + H_2O + 3SO_4^{2-}$
(Oxidation state of Cr changes from + 6 to + 3 in this reaction.)
(c) $\overset{+6}{Cr_2}O_7^{2-} + 2OH^- \longrightarrow 2\overset{+6}{Cr}O_4^{2-} + H_2O$
(No change in oxidation state of Cr)
(d) $\overset{+6}{Cr}O_2Cl_2 + 2NaOH \longrightarrow Na_2\overset{+6}{Cr}O_4 + 2HCl$
(No change in oxidation state of Cr)
13. ***(a)*** Due to lanthanoid contraction order will be
$$Yb^{3+} < Pm^{3+} < Ce^{3+} < La^{3+}$$
14. ***(a)*** Basic character of oxides decreases from left to right in a period of periodic table.
15. ***(b)*** Cr^{2+} and Fe^{2+}

$Cr^{2+} - 3d^4$ | 1 | 1 | 1 | 1 | | (4 unpaired electrons)

$Fe^{2+} - 3d^6$ | 1l | 1 | 1 | 1 | 1 | (4 unpaired electrons)

16. ***(d)*** Due to lanthanide contraction, the size of M^{3+} ions (i.e. Lu^{3+}, Eu^{3+}, Yb^{3+} and Ce^{3+}) decreases and thus, the basic strength of their hydroxides decreases.
The order of size of given M^{3+} ions is
$$Ce^{3+} > Eu^{3+} > Yb^{3+} > Lu^{3+}$$
∴ The order of basic strength of their hydroxides is
$$\underset{\text{(Most basic)}}{Ce(OH)_3} > Eu(OH)_3 > Yb(OH)_3 > Lu(OH)_3$$
17. ***(a)*** $2MnO_2 + 4KOH + O_2 \longrightarrow \underset{\text{Green}}{2K_2MnO_4} + 2H_2O$
18. ***(a)*** $ScCl_3 \longrightarrow Sc^{3+} + 3Cl^-$

Sc^{3+}: $3s^2$ [1l] $3p^6$ [1l][1l][1l] $3d^0$ [ ][ ][ ][ ][ ]

No unpaired electron, so will show diamagnetic character so, will weigh less in magnetic field.
Other have unpaired electron thus, they are paramagnetic, so they weigh more in magnetic field Fe^{3+} have 5, Ti^{3+} have 1, V^{3+} have 2 unpaired electrons.
19. ***(d)*** Electronic configuration of M^{3+} is $[Ar]3d^1$. It is Ti which have this electronic configuration in its ionic form (Ti^{3+}).
20. ***(a)*** Transuranic elements start after uranium that means begin with Np (Neptunium).
21. ***(c)*** The higher the charge on the metal ion, smaller is the ionic size and more is the complex forming ability. Thus, the degree of complex formation decreases in the order $M^{4+} > MO_2^{2+} > M^{3+} > MO_2^{+}$.
The higher tendency of complex formation of MO_2^{2+} as compared to M^{3+} is due to high concentration of charge on metal atom M in MO_2^{2+}.
22. ***(c)*** There is very small difference in energies of 5f and 6d orbitals of actinoids, therefore their electronic configuration cannot assigned with a degree of certainty.
23. ***(a)*** V^{2+} = 3 unpaired electrons
Cr^{2+} = 4 unpaired electrons
Mn^{2+} = 5 unpaired electrons
Fe^{2+} = 4 unpaired electrons
Hence, the order of paramagnetic behaviour should be
$$V^{2+} < Cr^{2+} = Fe^{2+} < Mn^{2+}$$
(b) Ionic size decreases from left to right in the same period.
(c) $Co^{3+}/Co^{2+} = 1.97$; $Fe^{3+}/Fe^{2+} = 0.77$;
$Cr^{3+}/Cr^{2+} = -0.41$
Sc^{3+} is highly stable (It does not show + 2).
(d) The oxidation states increases as we go from group 3 to group 7 in the same period.
24. ***(d)*** The correct reactions are as follows
(a) $Fe + Dil.H_2SO_4 \longrightarrow FeSO_4 + H_2\uparrow$
$$H_2SO_4 + 2FeSO_4 + \frac{1}{2}O_2 \longrightarrow Fe_2(SO_4)_3 + H_2O$$
$$Fe_2(SO_4)_3 \xrightarrow{\Delta} Fe_2O_3(s) + 3SO_3\uparrow$$
The given reaction is incorrect in question.

(b) $Fe \xrightarrow{O_2} FeO$ (It could also be Fe_2O_3 or Fe_3O_4)

$$FeO + H_2SO_4 \xrightarrow{\Delta} FeSO_4 + H_2O$$

$$2FeSO_4 \xrightarrow{\Delta} Fe_2O_3 + SO_2 + SO_3$$

This is also an incorrect reaction.

(c) $Fe \xrightarrow[Cl_2]{\Delta} FeCl_3 \xrightarrow[Air]{\Delta}$ No reaction

(It cannot give $FeCl_2$)

(d) $Fe \xrightarrow[\Delta]{O_2} Fe_3O_4 \xrightarrow[600°C]{CO} FeO \xrightarrow[700°C]{CO} Fe$

This is correct reaction.

25. ***(6)*** Butterfly structure is shown by CrO_5.

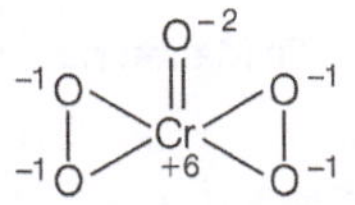

26. ***(5)*** TiO, Sc_2O_3, Ti_2O_3, CuO and VO are basic oxides. V_2O_5, Cr_2O_3 are amphoteric and TiO_2 is acidic oxide.

27. ***(2)*** $Zn + H_2SO_4 \longrightarrow ZnSO_4 + H_2 \uparrow$
$Zn + 2NaOH \longrightarrow Na_2ZnO_2 + H_2 \uparrow$
Therefore, the value of x and y is 1 and value of $x + y = 2$.

28. ***(2)*** Magnetic moment $= \sqrt{n(n+2)}$

$$2.83 = \sqrt{n(n+2)}$$
$$(2.83)^2 = n(n+2)$$
$$8 = n^2 + 2n$$
$$n^2 + 2n - 8 = 0 \Rightarrow n^2 + 4n - 2n - 8 = 0$$
$$n(n+4) - 2(n+4) = 0$$
$$(n-2)(n+4) = 0$$
$$n = 2 \text{ or } -4.$$

But, −4 cannot be possible. Thus, number of unpaired electrons are 2.

29. ***(3)*** $Cr_2O_7^{2-} + 2Fe^{2+} + 14H^+ \longrightarrow 2Cr^{3+} + 7H_2O + 2Fe^{3+}$
Electron per Cr-atom = 3.

30. ***(2)*** V_2O_5 and Cr_2O_3 are amphoteric oxides because both reacts with alkalies as well as acids. (In lower oxides, the basic character is predominant while in higher oxides, the acidic character is predominant). Here, Mn_2O_7 and CrO_3 are acidic white CrO and V_2O_4 are basic in nature.

31. ***(3)*** $Fe^{3+} + 3K^+ + 3C_2O_4^{2-} \longrightarrow \underset{(A)}{K_3[Fe(C_2O_4)_3]}$
Fe is in +3 oxidation state.

32. ***(9)*** $CrO_4^{2-} + 2H^+ + 2H_2O_2 \longrightarrow \underset{\substack{\text{Chromic peroxide} \\ \text{(deep blue-violet)}}}{CrO(O_2)_2} + 3H_2O$

The value of $a + b + c + d + e = 1 + 2 + 2 + 1 + 3 = 9$

33. ***(3)*** $K_2Cr_2O_7 + 4H_2SO_4 \longrightarrow$
$$K_2SO_4 + Cr_2(SO_4)_3 + 4H_2O + 3(O)$$
$$[2KI + H_2SO_4 + (O) \longrightarrow K_2SO_4 + I_2 + H_2O] \times 3$$
$$K_2Cr_2O_7 + 7H_2SO_4 + 6KI \longrightarrow 4K_2SO_4 + Cr_2(SO_4)_3 + 7H_2O + 3I_2$$

Thus, 1 mole of $K_2Cr_2O_7$ reacts with KI to give 3 moles of I_2.

Check Through PYQs : JEE Main

1. ***(c)*** Among the given oxides, V_2O_5 is amphoteric in nature. In this, vanadium is in +5 oxidation state.

2. ***(c)*** The correct match is
$$A \to Q, B \to P, C \to S, D \to R$$

3. ***(a)*** Melting point order is
Fe > Mn, Ru > Tc, Re > Os, W > Ta
Thus, the correct order is given in option (a).

4. ***(d)*** Both Statement I and Statement II are true.

5. ***(0)*** Metal having least metallic radii among given transition metals is Cr.
Spin only magnetic moment of $CrO_4^{2-} = \sqrt{n(n+2)}$ B.M.
Here Cr^{6+} is in d^0 configuration, means $n = 0$
Thus, spin only magnetic moment is 0.

6. ***(877)*** Among the given compound,
CrO is basic oxide.
In CrO, Cr exists as Cr^{2+} and have 4 unpaired electrons.
Spin only magnetic moment
$$\mu = \sqrt{n(n+2)} \text{ B.M.}$$
$$\mu = \sqrt{4(4+2)} = 4.90 \text{ B.M.}$$
Cr_2O_3 is amphoteric oxide.
Cr^{3+} has 3 unpaired electrons.
Spin only magnetic moment $\mu = \sqrt{3(3+2)} = 3.87$ B.M.
$$\text{Sum} = 4.90 + 3.87 = 8.77$$
$$\mu_{total} = 877 \times 10^{-2}$$
Comparing with given equation, X will be 877.

7. ***(5)*** Among the given ions, Co^{3+} is strong oxidising agent.
Number of unpaired electrons in $Co^{3+} = [Ar]\,3d^6$ is 4
Spin only magnetic moment $= \mu = \sqrt{n(n+2)}$ B.M
$$\mu = \sqrt{4(4+2)} \text{ B.M} = \sqrt{24} \approx 5 \text{ B.M}$$
Hence, nearest integer value is 5.

8. ***(d)*** The metal which shows highest and maximum number of oxidation states is Mn.
Oxidation number (Highest) = +7

9. ***(0)*** In first transition series elements, vanadium, 'V' has highest enthalpy of atomisation (515 kJ/mol). Its oxide i.e. V_2O_5 has V in +5 oxidation state.
So the configuration of V^{5+} is $1s^2 2s^2 2p^6 3s^2 3p^6$. Hence it has no unpaired electrons. Thus, its spin only magnetic moment value is also zero.

10. ***(d)*** Among the given elements, scandium shows only one oxidation state in its compound i.e. +3 while cobalt, titanium and nickel can show +2, +3 and +4 oxidation state.

11. ***(d)*** All the elements of option (d) have d^{10} electronic configuration in its outermost shell. The elecronic configuration of given elements in option (d) are
$[Cd] = [Kr]\,4d^{10}5s^2$ $\qquad$ $[Cu] = [Ar]\,3d^{10}4s^1$
$[Ag] = [Kr]\,4d^{10}5s^1$ $\qquad$ $[Zn] = [Ar]\,3d^{10}4s^2$

12. ***(d)*** Given $\mu = 3.86$ B.M.

So, using $\mu = \sqrt{n(n+2)}$

we get $n = 3$

Thus, electronic configuration of ion can be [Ar] $3d^3$.

So, the electronic configuration of atom will be [Ar] $3d^3 4s^2$.

Hence, atomic number is 23.

13. ***(c)*** The pairs given in option (a), (b) and (d) are correctly match, while option (c) is incorrectly matched.

The correct form is :

The catalyst used in Wacker's process is $PdCl_2$.

Hence, option (c) is the final answer.

14. ***(c)*** Magnetic moment is given by

$$\mu = \sqrt{n(n+2)} \text{ BM}$$

where, n is number of unpaired electron.

[Ar] $3d^7$ has 3 unpaired electrons.

$$\mu = \sqrt{3(3+2)} = \sqrt{15} \text{ BM}$$

[Ar] $3d^3$ has 3 unpaired electrons.

$$\mu = \sqrt{3(3+2)} = \sqrt{15} \text{ BM}$$

[Ar] $3d^6$ has 4 unpaired electrons.

$$\mu = \sqrt{4(4+2)} = \sqrt{24} \text{ BM}$$

[Ar] $3d^8$ has 2 unpaired electrons.

$$\mu = \sqrt{2(2+2)} = \sqrt{8} \text{ BM}$$

Hence, [Ar] $3d^6$ has highest value of magnetic moment.

15. ***(c)*** A is correct but R is incorrect. In $Ni(CO)_4$, let oxidation state of Ni be x.

So, $x + (0) \times 4 = 0$

$\Rightarrow$ $x = 0$

Similarly, let oxidation state of Fe in $Fe(CO)_5$ be y

$\therefore$ $y + (0) \times 5 = 0$

$\Rightarrow$ $y = 0$

The oxidation states of both Ni and Fe are zero in their respective complexes.

Hence, Assertion (A) is correct.

Low oxidation state of metals can be stabilised by synergic bonding. So, ligand has to be π-acceptor. Hence, Reason (R) is incorrect.

16. ***(c)*** Correct option is (c).

Since, in d-block elements the successive filling of d-orbital takes place due to which the outer shell is poorly shielded as compared to group 2 elements. Thus d -block elements have more ionisation enthalpy than group 2 elements.

17. ***(b)*** In $3d$ metal ions, the enthalpy of hydration generally increases as the charge density of the ion increases. Also the charge density is inversly proportional to the ionic radius. Thus, among the given options metal ion (Mn^{2+}) with largest ionic radius should have the lowest charge density and weakest ion-water interactions (i.e. hydration enthalpy)

18. ***(a)*** The atomic number of Pt is 78. Its exceptional electronic configuration can be written as [Xe] $4f^{14} 5d^9 6s^1$.

According to Aufbau's principle of filling electrons, the electronic configuration of Pt should be [Xe] $4f^{14} 5d^8 6s^2$. But as the number of electrons increases, interelectronic repulsion also increases. In higher atomic number elements energy difference between shells decreases. Hence, $6s$ and $5d$ come closer due to which electronic transition from $6s$ to $5d$ is easily done. Therefore, we have the electronic configuration as [Xe] $4f^{14} 5d^9 6s^1$.

19. ***(a)*** The metal atom whose oxidation potential is greater than that of hydrogen can release H_2 from mineral acid. ($E^\circ_{H/H^+} = 0$)

Metal	**Oxidation potential** (in Volt)
$E^\circ_{Zn/Zn^{2+}}$	0.76
$E^\circ_{Ni/Ni^{2+}}$	0.25
$E^\circ_{Mn/Mn^{2+}}$	1.18
$E^\circ_{Cu/Cu^{2+}}$	− 0.34

Therefore, Cu has least tendency to liberate hydrogen from mineral acids.

20. ***(c)*** The standard electrode potential of given elements are

$$Cr^{2+}/Cr \longrightarrow -0.90 \text{ V}$$
$$Fe^{2+}/Fe \longrightarrow -0.44 \text{ V}$$
$$Cu^{2+}/Cu \longrightarrow +0.34 \text{ V}$$
$$Zn^{2+}/Zn \longrightarrow -0.76 \text{ V}$$

So, it is clearly seen from above values that copper (Cu) has highest M^{2+}/M standard electrode potential.

21. ***(b)***

Metal	Melting point (°C)
Hg	− 38.83
Ag	961.8
Ga	29.76
Cs	28.44

The metal with highest melting point is Ag.

22. ***(a)*** The electronic configuration of ions are

$$Mn^{3+} = 1s^2 2s^2 2p^6 3s^2 3p^6 3d^4 4s^0$$
$$Fe^{3+} = 1s^2 2s^2 2p^6 3s^2 3p^6 3d^5 4s^0$$
$$Ti^{3+} = 1s^2 2s^2 2p^6 3s^2 3p^6 3d^1 4s^0$$
$$Cr^{3+} = 1s^2 2s^2 2p^6 3s^2 3p^6 3d^3 4s^0$$

Strongest oxidising ion is that which has a strong tendency to gain the electrons. Among the given option Mn^{3+} is strongest oxidising agent as it needs just 1 electron to attain half-filled $3d^5$ subshell which is comparatively more stable.

23. ***(d)***

Metal (atomic number)	E.C.	+3 (Oxidation state)
Ru(44)	[Kr] $4d^7 5s^1$	[Kr] $4d^5$
Mn(25)	[Ar] $4s^2 3d^5$	[Ar] $3d^4$
Co(27)	[Ar] $4s^2 3d^7$	[Ar] $3d^6$
Fe(26)	[Ar] $4s^2 3d^6$	[Ar] $3d^5$

Thus, Fe has electronic configuration of $3d^5$ in +3 O.S.

24. ***(a)*** $CuCl_2$ dissolves in water to give blue coloured Cu^{2+} ions. The colour is due to the presence of unpaired e^- ($3d^9$) in Cu^{2+} ions.

$$CuCl_2 + nH_2O \longrightarrow \underset{\text{(Blue colour)}}{Cu^{2+}(aq)}$$

AgCl and Cu_2Cl_2 are insoluble in water while $ZnCl_2$ on dissolving in water forms colourless solution due to formation of Zn^{2+} ions, which has no unpaired e^- ($3d^{10}$).

25. ***(d)*** Ti^{3+} : [Ar] $3d^1$

(Unpaired electron = 1)

$$\mu = \sqrt{1(1+2)} = 1.73 \text{ B.M.}$$

V^{2+} : [Ar] $3d^3$

(Unpaired electrons = 3)

$$\mu = \sqrt{3(3+2)} = \sqrt{15} = 3.87 \text{ B.M.}$$

Sc^{3+} : [Ar] $3d^0$

$$\mu = 0 \text{ B.M.}$$

26. ***(d)*** A → (iv), B → (iii), C → (ii), D → (i)

So, correct option is (d).

27. ***(a)*** Common positive oxidation states for an element with atomic number 24 (Cr), are + 2 to + 6.

28. ***(c)*** The element with atomic number 25 is Mn. Mn^{2+} is divalent ion and has the outer electronic configuration $3d^5$ giving 5 unpaired electrons.

So, $$\mu = \sqrt{5(5+2)} = \sqrt{35} = 5.916 \approx 5.92 \text{ BM}$$

29. ***(c)*** $Cr^+ - 4s^0 3d^5$

$Mn^{2+} - 4s^0 3d^5$

So, the outermost electronic configuration will be same in case of Cr^+ and Mn^{2+} metal ions.

30. ***(c)***

Metal	Density (g/cm^3)
Zn	7.14
Cr	7.19
Fe	7.8
Co	8.9
Cu	8.96

Correct order is

Cu > Co > Fe > Cr > Zn.

31. ***(a)*** 'Gun metal' also called as red brass (in USA). It is greyish in colour and originally used for making guns. The major components of 'Gun metal' are

Cu = 87%

Zn = 3%

Sn = 10%

32. ***(d)*** In the electrode potential series, only copper have positive value for electrode potential because copper has lower tendency than hydrogen to form ions.

∴ Electrode potential of Cu i.e. $E^\circ_{Cu^{2+}/Cu}$ show positive value.

33. ***(b)*** Given, atomic number of Es = 99

So, its electronic configuration = [Rn] $5f^{11} 6d^0 7s^2$

34. ***(2)*** Colours of lanthanoid ions are due to presence of unpaired electron.

The electronic configurations of given lanthanoid ions are

La^{3+} — [Xe] $4f^0$

Nd^{3+} — [Xe] $4f^3$

Sm^{3+} — [Xe] $4f^5$

Eu^{3+} — [Xe] $4f^6$

Lu^{3+} — [Xe] $4f^{14}$

La^{3+} and Lu^{3+} do not show any colour due to absence of unpaired electrons.

35. ***(d)*** Lanthanoids = Eu, Er, Tb, Yb and Lu

Actinoides = Cm

Hence, Cm does not belong to lanthanoid.

36. ***(c)*** Potassium dichromate ($K_2Cr_2O_7$) and $KMnO_4$ both are coloured due to ligand to metal charge transfer in both.

37. ***(a)*** Alkaline oxidative fusion of MnO_2 gives, MnO_4^{2-}

$$2MnO_2 + 4OH^- + O_2 \longrightarrow \underset{(A)}{2MnO_4^{2-}} + 2H_2O$$

On electrolysis of MnO_4^{2-} in alkaline medium, the reaction is

$$MnO_4^{2-} \longrightarrow \underset{(B)}{MnO_4^-} + e^-$$

Hence, option (a) is correct.

38. ***(c)*** Both Statements I and II are true. Ce^{4+} has noble gas electronic configuration.

Also due to high reduction potential of Ce^{4+}/Ce^{3+} and stability of Ce^{3+} is greater than Ce^{4+}, thus Ce^{4+} acts as strong oxidising agent.

39. ***(b)*** Atomic number for Nd = 60

Electronic configuration is

$1s^2 2s^2 2p^6 3s^2 3p^6 3d^{10} 4s^2 4p^6 4d^{10} 4f^4 5s^2 5p^6 6s^2$

= [Xe] $4f^4 6s^2$

40. ***(b)*** Both (A) and (R) are true and (R) is the correct explanation of (A).

Since, 5*f* orbitals are not buried as 4*f* orbitals. Hence electron present in 5*f* orbitals experiences less nuclear attraction as compared to the electron of 4*f* orbitals. Hence, 5*f* electrons can participate in bonding to a far extent.

41. ***(b)*** Neodymium (atomic number 60) is an inner transition element (lanthanoid) with electronic configuration as
$1s^2 2s^2 2p^6 3s^2 3p^6 3d^{10} 4s^2 4p^6 4d^{10} 5s^2 5p^6 4f^4 5d^0 6s^2$
Electronic configuration of Nd^{2+} is $[Xe]\ 4f^4 5d^0 6s^0$.

42. ***(a)*** Ce^{4+} and Tb^{4+} are good oxidising agents.

Ce is most stable in + 3 state. In + 4 state it is most oxidising because in + 4 state it can take an electron to become more stable at + 3 state.

Tb^{4+} can be easily converted into stable Tb^{3+} by gain of an electron. Due to this reason, Tb^{4+} is also a good oxidising agent.

43. ***(c)*** The correct statements regarding Mn_2O_7, are A and C only. In the structure of Mn_2O_7, each Mn atom is tetrahedrally surrounded by four oxygen atoms. Also there is a bridging of one coordinated oxygen atom between two tetrahedral units.

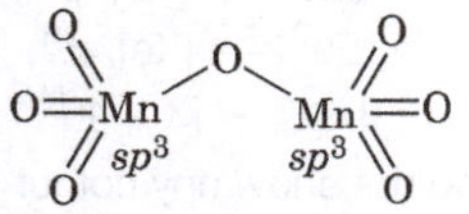

44. ***(d)*** $X = Cu_2I_2$, $Y = Na_2S_4O_6$

$$2CuSO_4 + 4KI \longrightarrow \underset{\text{White ppt.}}{Cu_2I_2} + \underset{\text{Violet}}{2I_2} + 2K_2SO_4$$

$$\xrightarrow{2Na_2S_2O_3} 2NaI + Na_2S_4O_6$$

I^- being strong reducing agent reduces Cu^{2+} to Cu^+.

45. ***(c)*** Structure of Mn_2O_7 is as follows :

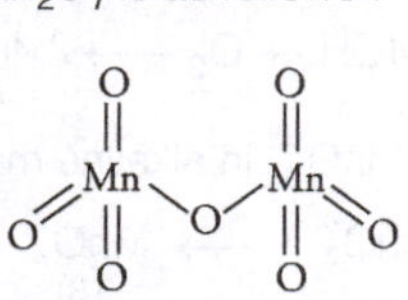

∴ Total 6 Mn =O bonds are present in Mn_2O_7 compound.

46. ***(d)*** In acidic medium,

$$2KMnO_4 + 3H_2SO_4 + 5H_2O_2 \longrightarrow K_2SO_4 + 2MnSO_4 + 8H_2O + 5O_2$$

47. ***(c)*** $Tb \longrightarrow [Xe]4f^9, 6s^2$

$Tb^{4+} \longrightarrow [Xe], 4f^7$ (Half-filled configuration)

$Yb \longrightarrow [Xe]\ 4f^{14}, 6s^2$

$Yb^{2+} \longrightarrow [Xe]\ 4f^{14}$ (Completely filled configuration)

According to the above given configurations, Tb^{4+} and Yb^{2+} have half-filled and completely filled *f*-orbitals respectively.

48. ***(19)*** $K_2Cr_2O_7 : +2 + 2x + 7(-2) = 0$

$2x = 14 - 2 = 12,\ x = +6$

$KMnO_4 : +1 + y + 4(-2) = 0$

$+1 + y - 8 = 0 \Rightarrow y = +7$

$K_2FeO_4 : 2(+1) + z + 4(-2) = 0$

$+2 + z - 8 = 0 \Rightarrow z = +6$

Thus, sum of oxidation states = + 6 + 7 + 6 = 19.

49. ***(4)*** The disproportionation reaction of MnO_4^{2-} in acidic medium is as follows

$$3MnO_4^{2-} + 4H^+ \longrightarrow \underset{(B)}{MnO_2} + \underset{(A)}{2MnO_4^-} + 2H_2O$$

Oxidation state of Mn in MnO_2 is + 4
Oxidation state of Mn in MnO_4^- is + 7
Hence, $A = MnO_4^-$ and $B = MnO_2$

$Mn = [Ar]3d^5\ 4s^2$

$Mn^{4+} = [Ar], 3d^3$

$Mn^{4+} = [Ar]$ | 1 | 1 | 1 | | | ($3d^3$)

Total number of unpaired electrons $(n) = 3$

Spin only magnetic moment (μ) spin only of B =

$$\therefore \quad \mu = \sqrt{n(n+2)}\ \text{BM}$$

$$= \sqrt{3(3+2)} = \sqrt{15} = 3.87\ \text{BM} \approx 4\ \text{BM}$$

50. ***(6)*** The balanced equation will be

$$4FeCr_2O_4 + 7O_2 + 8Na_2CO_3 \longrightarrow \underset{(A)}{8Na_2CrO_4} + 2Fe_2O_3 + 8CO_2$$

$$2Na_2CrO_4 + 2H^+ \longrightarrow \underset{(B)}{Na_2Cr_2O_7} + 2Na^+ + H_2O$$

$Na_2Cr_2O_7$

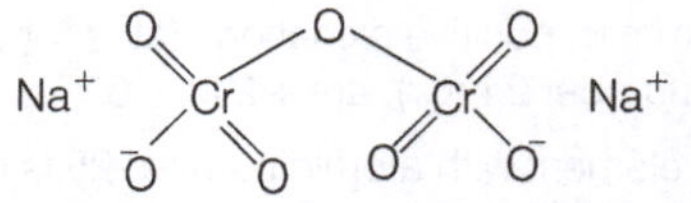

Number of terminal oxygen atoms is 6.

51. ***(0)*** Disproportionation reaction of acidified manganate solution is

$$3MnO_4^{2-} + 4H^+ \longrightarrow 2\overset{+7}{Mn}O_4^- + \overset{+4}{Mn}O_2 + 2H_2O$$

Higher oxidation state of manganese is +7 (in MnO_4^-).

Electronic configuration of Mn in + 7 oxidation state will be

$Mn\ (25) : [Ar]\ 3d^5 4s^2$

$Mn^{(+7)} : [Ar]$

i.e. It does not have any unpaired electron.

∴ Magnetic moment $(\mu) = 0$ as $n = 0$.

52. ***(c)*** The electronic configuration of Eu and Eu^{2+} ion is as follows

$Eu\ (Z = 63) = [Xe]\ 4f^7 6s^2$

$Eu^{2+} (Z = 63) = [Xe]\ 4f^7$

53. ***(c)*** V_2O_3 is a basic oxide as on dissolving in acids, give solution of vanadium (III) complexes. In case of transition metal oxide, the metal with lower oxidation states are basic. So, CrO is also basic as oxidation state of Cr is +2.

54. ***(c)*** Oxidation number of 3*d*-metal oxides are

A. $CrO_3 \rightarrow Cr \Rightarrow +6$

B. $Fe_2O_3 \rightarrow Fe \Rightarrow +3$

C. $MnO_2 \rightarrow Mn \Rightarrow +4$

D. $V_2O_5 \rightarrow V \Rightarrow +5$

E. $Cu_2O \rightarrow Cu \Rightarrow +1$

So, oxidation state order is

$$CrO_3 > V_2O_5 > MnO_2 > Fe_2O_3 > Cu_2O$$

or $$A > D > C > B > E.$$

55. ***(d)*** $2KMnO_4 \xrightarrow{\Delta} \underset{\text{Potassium manganate}}{K_2MnO_4} + MnO_2 + O_2$

Potassium permanganate is diamagnetic while potassium manganate is paramagnetic. Both of these are tetrahedral in structure.

56. ***(d)*** $E^{\circ}_{Ce^{4+}/Ce^{3+}} = 1.74$ (data given)

Ce^{4+} can be reduced to Ce^{3+} and can oxidise water.

$$Ce^{4+} + e^- \longrightarrow Ce^{3+}$$

Ce^{4+} is having noble gas configuration [Xe] $4f^0$ but it is strong oxidant and gets converted to Ce^{3+}.

Statement I is correct but statement II is incorrect.

57. ***(a)*** A well known alloy is mischmetal which has the following composition.

Mischmetal – lanthanoid metals = 95%

(About 25% La, 50% Ce and the rest are other lanthanoids) with traces of iron S, C, Ca and Al = 5%

58. ***(c)*** Europium (Eu = atomic number 63)

Electronic configuration of Eu = [Xe] $4f^7$, $6s^2$

It can show +2 and +3 oxidation states, in +2 oxidation:

$$Eu^{2+} = [Xe]\,4f^7, 6s^0$$

in +3 oxidation :

$$Eu^{3+} = [Xe]\,4f^6, 6s^0$$

Being a typical member of the lanthanide, Eu usually assumes the oxidation states +3 and +2 but it doesn't show +4 oxidation state due to very high ionisation energy (4140 kJ/mol).

Hence, the correct option is (c).

59. ***(b)*** Electronic configuration of Gd^{3+}: [Xe] $4f^7$

$\therefore$ Number of unpaired electrons = 7

Spin only magnetic moment, $\mu = \sqrt{n(n+2)}$ B.M.

$= \sqrt{7(7+2)}$ B.M.

$= 7.93$ B.M.

So, option (b) is correct.

60. ***(a)*** Actinoid series have atomic number from 90 to 103 (5*f*-block element).

So, element with atomic number (*Z*) 101 belongs to actinoid series and elements with atomic number (*Z*) 104 belongs to 4th group ($6d^2$).

61. ***(12)*** Chromate (CrO_4^{2-}) Dichromate ($Cr_2O_7^{2-}$)

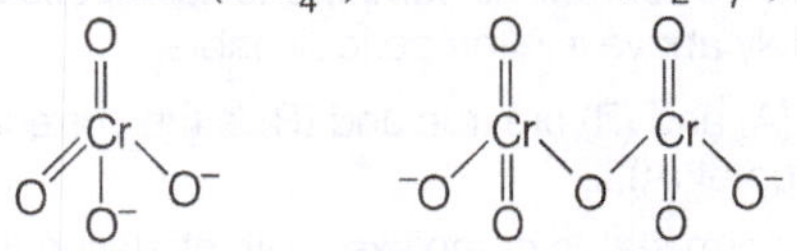

4 Cr—O or 8Cr—O

Total number of bonds between chromium and oxygen atoms in chromate and dichromate ions = 4 + 8 = 12.

Practice Element 02 : Target JEE Advanced

1. ***(b)*** $K_2Cr_2O_7$ is preferred over $Na_2Cr_2O_7$ in volumetric analysis, primarily because $Na_2Cr_2O_7$ is hygroscopic in nature and therefore, accurate weighing is not possible in normal atmosphere.

2. ***(b)*** $CuSO_4$ when react with KCN to give precipitate of cupric cyanide and cyanogen gas. The cuprous cyanide dissolves in excess of KCN forming $K_3[Cu(CN)_4]$.

$$2Cu^{2+} + 2CN^- \longrightarrow 2Cu^+ + C_2N_2$$

$$2Cu^+ + 2CN^- \longrightarrow \underset{\text{ppt.}}{2CuCN}$$

$$CuCN + 3KCN \longrightarrow \underset{\text{Soluble}}{K_3[Cu(CN)_4]}$$

3. ***(a)*** $2MnO_4^- + 3S_2O_3^{2-} + H_2O \longrightarrow 2MnO_2 + 3SO_4^{2-} + 3S + 2OH^-$

4. ***(a)*** Cuprous compounds contains Cu^+ ion which has small size, so the hydration is maximum and hence, the system has lower energy which results in stability of the compounds.

5. ***(b)*** The shielding effect of 5*f*-orbitals in actinoids is poor than the shielding effect of 4*f*-orbitals. So, the effective nuclear charge on valence electrons is more in actinoids. Hence, actinoid contraction is greater than lanthanoid contraction.

$\therefore$ Statement (a) is correct.

Trivalent lanthanoid ions are coloured in the solid state due to presence of *f*-electrons.

$\therefore$ Statement (b) is incorrect.

Lanthanoids are inner transition metals. So, they are good conductors of heat and electricity.

$\therefore$ Statement (c) is correct.

The surface area increases when actinoids are finely divided which results in exposure of more reactant molecules to react. Hence, rate increases and so, actinoids are highly reactive metals when finely divided.

$\therefore$ Statement (d) is correct.

6. ***(d)*** The gradual decrease in atomic and ionic radii across the series leads to an increase in ionisation energy. Thus, the correct order is

$$Th < U < Np < Pu$$

7. ***(d)*** The correct order of ionic radii is $Y^{3+} < Lu^{3+} < Eu^{3+} < La^{3+}$ because Eu and Lu are the members of lanthanide series (so they show lanthanide contraction) and La is the representative element of all elements of such series and Y^{3+} ion has lower radii as compare to La^{3+} because it lies immediately above it in the periodic table.

8. ***(b)*** Both (A) and (R) are true and (R) is the correct explanation of (A).

   Actinides form stable complexes with chelating ligands like EDTA due to their high charge to radius ratio, which enhances their interaction with donor atoms such as oxygen and nitrogen.

9. ***(a, c, d)*** $\underset{\text{Oxidising agent}}{\overset{+2}{CuSO_4}} + 2NaOH + \underset{\text{reducing agent}}{\text{Glucose}} \longrightarrow \underset{(a)}{\overset{+1}{Cu_2O}} + Na_2SO_4 + C_6H_{12}O_7 + H_2O$

$$2KCl + CuSO_4 \longrightarrow K_2SO_4 + CuCl_2$$
$$CuSO_4 + O_2 \longrightarrow CuO + SO_2$$
$$CuSO_4 + KI \longrightarrow \underset{\text{Brown colour}}{CuI} + I_2 + K_2SO_4$$

10. ***(a,c)*** $MnO_2 + 4HCl \longrightarrow MnCl_2 + Cl_2 + 2H_2O$

    Decomposition of acidic $KMnO_4$ is catalysed by sunlight.

$$4MnO_4^- + 4H^+ \longrightarrow 4MnO_2 + 2H_2O + 3O_2$$
$$3K_2MnO_4 + 2H_2O \longrightarrow 2KMnO_4 + H_2 + 4KOH$$
$$MnO_4^- + 2H_2O + 3e^- \longrightarrow MnO_2 + 4OH^-$$

    ($KMnO_4$ also acts as oxidising agent in alkaline medium).

11. ***(a,b,d)*** $Cu + HgCl_2 \longrightarrow CuCl_2 + Hg$

$$SnCl_2 + 2HgCl_2 \longrightarrow Hg_2Cl_2 + SnCl_4$$
$$Hg_2Cl_2 + SnCl_2 \longrightarrow 2Hg + SnCl_4$$
$$Hg_2Cl_2 \xrightarrow{h\nu} HgCl_2 + Hg$$

12. ***(a,b,c,d)***

$$\underset{\text{Oxidising agent}}{\overset{+6}{Cr_2O_7^{2-}}} + \underset{\text{Reducing agent}}{3\overset{+4}{SO_3^{2-}}} + 8H^+ \longrightarrow 2Cr^{3+} + 3\overset{+6}{SO_4^{2-}} + 4H_2O$$

13. ***(a,d)*** Statements (a), (d) are correct whereas (b), (c) is incorrect. The correct form of (b), (c) is : 5*f* electrons in actinoids have lower binding energies (less shielded). +3 is common oxidation state not the stable oxidation state for all actinoids.

14. ***(a,b, d)*** $NaCl + K_2Cr_2O_7 + H_2SO_4 \text{ (conc.)} \longrightarrow \underset{\text{(Deep red)}}{CrO_2Cl_2} + NaHSO_4 + H_2O$

$$CrO_2Cl_2 + 4NaOH \longrightarrow \underset{\text{Yellow}}{Na_2CrO_4} + 2NaCl + 2H_2O$$
$$CrO_2Cl_2 + H_2O \longrightarrow \underset{\text{Yellow}}{H_2CrO_4} + HCl$$

15. ***(a, b)*** Statements (a), (b) are correct whereas (c), (d) are incorrect. The correct form of (c), (d) is

    CeO_2 is used as a polishing agent and in catalytic convertors but it is not typically used in sunscreens.

    Pr^{6+} compounds are rare and unstable, and they are not commonly used as oxidising agents is organic synthesis.

16. ***(a, c, d)*** $3Cu + 8HNO_3 \text{ (dil.)} \longrightarrow 3Cu(NO_3)_2 + 2NO + 4H_2O$

$$Cu + 2H_2SO_4\text{(conc.)} \longrightarrow CuSO_4 + SO_2 + 2H_2O$$
$$Cu + \textit{aqua-regia}\ (3HCl + HNO_3) \longrightarrow CuCl_2$$

17. ***(22)***

Element	Higher stable oxidation state
Sc	+3
Zn	+2
Ti	+4
Mn	+7
Cr	+6

18. ***(2)*** $3MnO_4^{2-} + 2H_2O + 4CO_2 \longrightarrow MnO_2 + 2MnO_4^- + 4HCO_3^-$

19. ***(6)*** $FeC_2O_4 \longrightarrow \underset{\text{(Paramagnetic)}}{FeO} + \underbrace{CO + CO_2}_{\text{Diamagnetic}}$

    Number of diamagnetic products $(x) = 2$

    Number of unpaired e^- in FeO $(y) = 4$

$$x + y = 6$$

20. ***(12)*** $KMnO_4 \xrightarrow[\text{R.A.}]{H^+} Mn^{2+}$

$$KMnO_4 \xrightarrow[\text{R.A.}]{OH^-} Mn^{4+}$$
$$K_2Cr_2O_7 \xrightarrow{OH^-} Cr^{6+}$$
$$x + y + z = 12$$

21. ***(1)*** Mn(V) is unstable state of Mn only one compound of this state is known i.e., K_3MnO_4.

$$KMnO_4 + K_2SO_3 + H_2O \longrightarrow K_3MnO_4 + H_2SO_4$$

22. ***(170)*** $8CrO_4^{2-} + 3S_2O_3^{2-} \longrightarrow 6SO_4^{2-} + 8Cr(OH)_4^-$

    Normality of 0.246 M $S_2O_3^{2-}$ is 0.246×8 N

$$N_1V_1 = N_2V_2$$
$$V \times 0.154 \times 3 = 0.246 \times 8 \times 40$$
$$V = 170.3 \approx 170 \text{ mL}$$

23. ***(2)*** CeO_2, La_2O_3 are commonly used as catalysts in oxidation reduction reactions and catalytic converters.

    Sm_2O_3, Eu_2O_3 and Yb_2O_3 are not widely used as catalysts in industrial processes.

24. ***(3)*** Most basic oxide of vanadium is V_2O_3.
(An oxide with less positive charge and less number of oxygen atom will be more basic.)

$$V = [Ar]\,3d^3\,4s^2$$
$$V^{3+} = [Ar]\,3d^2$$
$$\mu = \sqrt{n(n+2)}$$

(n = number of unpaired electrons)

$$= \sqrt{2(2+2)} = 2.84\text{ BM} \approx 3\text{ BM}$$

25. ***(a)*** A → IV; B → III; C → II; D → I
26. ***(b)*** A → II; B → IV; C → I; D → III
27. ***(d)*** A → II; B → I; C → IV; D → III
28. ***(a)*** A → III; B → I; C → IV; D → II
29. ***(c)*** A → I; B → II; C → III; D → IV

$$3MnO_4^{-} + 4H^+ \longrightarrow 2MnO_4^{-} + MnO_2 + 2H_2O$$
$$MnO_4^{-} + 4H^+ + 3e^- \longrightarrow MnO_2 + 2H_2O$$
$$MnO_4^{-} + 8H^+ + 5e^- \longrightarrow Mn^{2+} + 4H_2O$$
$$2MnO_4^{-} + 3Mn^{2+} + 2H_2O \longrightarrow 5MnO_2 + 4H^+$$

30. ***(c)*** Mn_3O_4 and MnO_2 both are amphoteric oxide, CuI_2 is unstable and undergoes redox reaction to form Cu_2I_2.

$$2CuI_2 \longrightarrow Cu_2I_2 + I_2$$

On moving left to right in the 3*d*, the number of unpaired electron decrease.
Mn_2O_3 is a basic oxide.

31. ***(b)*** B_2O_3 and V_2O_5 both are amphoteric thus they will react with NaOH as well as HCl. Also aqueous solution of both of them is acidic in nature (pH < 7).

32. ***(c)*** Transition metals such as Fe, Co, V, Mn, Sc etc. which belongs to 3*d* series forms interstitial compound.

33. ***(a)*** Species having 3 unpaired electron in *d*-orbital will have magnetic moment $\sqrt{15}$ BM

$$\mu = \sqrt{n(n+2)}$$

$CoO \Rightarrow Co^{2+} = [Ar]\,3d^7$ = 3 unpaired electrons
$Fe_2O_3 \Rightarrow Fe^{3+} = [Ar]\,3d^5$ = 5 unpaired electrons
$FeO \Rightarrow Fe^{2+} = [Ar]\,3d^6$ = 4 unpaired electrons
$Cr_2O_3 \Rightarrow Cr^{3+} = [Ar]\,3d^3$ = 3 unpaired electrons
$Mn_2O_3 \Rightarrow Mn^{3+} = [Ar]\,3d^4$ = 4 unpaired electrons
$TiO_2 \Rightarrow Ti^{4+} = [Ar]$ = 0 unpaired electrons
$Sc_2O_3 \Rightarrow Sc^{3+} = [Ar]$ = 0 unpaired electrons.

34. ***(b)*** Species which contains unpaired electrons in *d*-orbital are coloured.

$VOSO_4 = V^{4+} = [Ar]\,3d^1$ = 1 unpaired electron
$VF_2 = V^{2+} = [Ar]\,3d^3$ = 3 unpaired electrons
$Cu_2F_2 = Cu^+ = [Ar]\,3d^{10}$ = 0 unpaired electrons
$MnO_2 = Mn^{4+} = [Ar]\,3d^3$ = 3 unpaired electrons
$Mn_2O_3 = Mn^{3+} = [Ar]\,3d^4$ = 4 unpaired electrons
$Fe_2O_3 = Fe^{3+} = [Ar]\,3d^5$ = 5 unpaired electrons
$ZnCl_2 = Zn^{2+} = [Ar]\,3d^{10}$ = 0 unpaired electron

35. ***(c)*** Mn does not show its highest oxidation state. i.e., +7 with fluorine as MnF_7 does not exist.

36. ***(b)*** Among the following compound only CrO_3 is an acidic oxide so the number of oxygen is 3.

37. ***(6)*** $$\underset{\substack{(A)\\ \text{Emegold green crystal}}}{NiSO_4\cdot 6H_2O} \xrightarrow{H_2O} \underset{(B)}{[Ni(H_2O)_6]^{2+}} \xrightarrow{HCl} \underset{\substack{(C)\\ \text{Yellow colour}}}{[NiCl_4]^{2-}}$$

38. ***(6)*** $[Ni(H_2O)_6]^{2+}$ is complex *B*.
So, co-ordiantion number becomes 6.

39. ***(7)*** $$\underset{\text{Pyrolusite}}{MnO_2} + 2KOH + KClO_3 \xrightarrow{\Delta} \underset{(A)}{K_2MnO_4} + H_2O$$

$$\underset{(A)}{MnO_4^{2-}} \xrightarrow{\text{Electrolysis}} \underset{(B)}{MnO_4^{-}}$$

$$\underset{(B)}{MnO_4^{-}} + H_2SO_4(\text{conc.}) \longrightarrow \underset{(C)}{Mn_2O_7}$$

Mn_2O_7 is an acidic oxide.

$$Mn_2O_7 \longrightarrow \underset{(D)}{MnO_2} + O_2\uparrow$$

40. ***(2)***

41. ***(b)*** $MnO_2 + KOH + O_2 \longrightarrow \underset{\text{Green}}{K_2MnO_4} + H_2O$

42. ***(b)*** Cause of colour in MnO_4^{2-} and $KMnO_4$ is $L \longrightarrow M$ charge transfer.

Check Through PYQs : JEE Advanced

1. ***(d)*** $Zn + 2NaOH \longrightarrow Na_2ZnO_2 + H_2$

2. ***(a, b, c)***
(a) In aqueous solution $Cr^{2+}(3d^4)$ acts as a reducing agent, oxidising itself to $Cr^{3+}(3d^3)$ that gives a completely half-filled t_{2g} level in octahedral ligand field of H_2O.
(b) $Mn^{3+}(3d^4)$ is an oxidising agent as it is reduced to $Mn^{2+}(3d^5)$, a completely half-filled stable configuration.
(c) Both Cr^{2+} and Mn^{3+} have d^4 configuration.
(d) $Cr^{2+}(3d^4)(aq) \xrightarrow{\text{R.A}} Cr^{3+}(3d^3)(aq) + e^-$
Hence, (*d*) is wrong statement.

3. ***(c)*** $$MnCl_2 \xrightarrow{\text{aq. NaOH}} \underset{\substack{\text{White ppt}\\(P)}}{Mn(OH)_2}\downarrow + \underset{\substack{\text{Filtrate}\\(Q)}}{NaCl}$$

$$Mn(OH)_2 \xrightarrow[\substack{PbO_2(\text{excess})\\ \text{Heat}}]{\text{aq. }H_2SO_4,} \underset{\substack{\text{Purple}\\(X)}}{MnO_4^{-}}$$

$$NaCl \xrightarrow[\text{Warm}]{MnO(OH)_2,\ \text{conc. }H_2SO_4} \underset{(Y)}{Cl_2} \xrightarrow{\text{KI-starch}} \text{Blue colouration}$$

So, $X = MnO_4^{-}$ and $Y = Cl_2$.

4. ***(b, c, d)*** When Zn react with hot conc. H_2SO_4 then SO_2 is released and $ZnSO_4$ is obtained.

$$\underset{(\text{Hot + Conc.})}{Zn + 2H_2SO_4} \longrightarrow \underset{(G)}{ZnSO_4} + \underset{(R)}{SO_2}\uparrow + \underset{(X)}{2H_2O}$$

$R(SO_2)$ molecule is V-Shaped

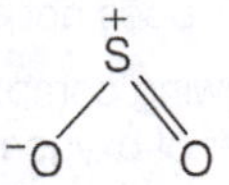

Thus, option (b) is correct.

When Zn is react with conc. NaOH then H_2 gas is evolved and Na_2ZnO_2 is obtained.

$$\underset{}{Zn} + 2\,NaOH\,(conc.) \longrightarrow \underset{(T)}{Na_2ZnO_2} + \underset{(Q)}{H_2\uparrow}$$

In ground state, H—H (Q) (bond order = 1)

Thus, option (c) is correct.

The oxidation state of Zn in $T(Na_2ZnO_2)$ is +2

Thus, option (a) is incorrect.

$$\underset{(G)}{ZnSO_4} + H_2S + NH_4OH \longrightarrow \underset{(Z)}{ZnS\downarrow} + \underset{(X)}{2H_2O} + \underset{(Y)}{(NH_4)_2SO_4}$$

ZnS (Z) compound is dirty white coloured.

Thus, option (d) is correct.

5. ***(a, b)*** H_2O_2 in alkaline medium and Na_2O_2 in water acts as reducing agent, reduces Fe^{3+} to Fe^{2+}. In acidic medium, the same H_2O_2 oxidises Fe^{2+} to Fe^{3+}.

6. ***(a, c, d)*** $MnO_2 + 2KOH + \frac{1}{2}O_2 \xrightarrow{\Delta} \underset{\text{(W) potassium manganate}}{K_2MnO_4} + H_2O$

$$\underset{(W)}{K_2MnO_4\,(aq)} \rightleftharpoons 2K^+(aq) + \underset{(Y)}{MnO_4^{2-}(aq)}$$

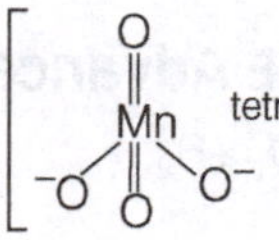

sp^3-hybridisation, tetrahedral (manganate ion) Green coloured complex

MnO_4^{2-} ion has one unpaired electrons, therefore it gives *d-d* transition to form green colour. *Y* complex has paramagnetic nature due to presence of one unpaired electron.

In aqueous solution,

$$\underset{(W)}{K_2MnO_4} + H_2O \xrightarrow{\text{Electrolytic oxidation}} H_2 + KOH + \underset{(X)}{KMnO_4}$$

$$\underset{(X)}{KMnO_4(aq)} \xrightarrow{\Delta} K^+ + \underset{(Z)}{MnO_4^-}$$

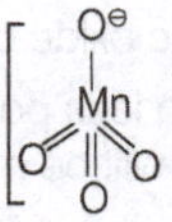

sp^3, tetrahedral (purple coloured complex ion)

MnO_4^- ions gives charge transfer spectrum in which a fraction of electronic charge is transferred between the molecular entities.

$$\because \quad \underset{(Y)}{MnO_4^{2-}} \xrightarrow[\text{oxidation}]{\text{Electrolytic}} \underset{(Z)}{MnO_4^-} + e^-$$

In acidic medium, *Y* undergoes disproportionation reaction.

$$\underset{(Y)}{3MnO_4^{2-}(aq)} + 4H^+ \longrightarrow \underset{(Z)}{2MnO_4^-} + MnO_2 + 2H_2O$$

$\underset{(Y)}{MnO_4^{2-}}$ and $\underset{(Z)}{MnO_4^-}$ both ions form π-bonding between *p*-orbitals of oxygen and *d*-orbitals of manganese.

In (MnO_4^-), Mn(VII) has no unpaired $e^-(3d^0)$ and hence it is diamagnetic.

Thus, options (a, c, d) are correct.

7. ***(4)*** When a solution of K_2CrO_4 is treated with amyl alcohol and acidified H_2O_2, the layer of amyl alcohol turns blue because acidified H_2O_2 converts K_2CrO_4 to CrO_5 to give the blue colouration,

$$CrO_4^{2-} + 2H + 2H_2O_2 \longrightarrow \underset{\text{(Blue coloured compound)}}{CrO_5} + 3H_2O$$

$CrO_5 \Rightarrow$ 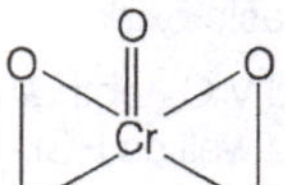

Number of oxygen atom bonded with chromium with single bond is 4.

8. ***(8)*** The balanced redox reaction is

$$MnO_4^- + [Fe(H_2O)_2\,(C_2O_4)_2]^{2-} + 8H^+ \longrightarrow Mn^{2+} + Fe^{3+} + 4CO_2 + 6H_2O$$

$$\Rightarrow \quad \frac{r\,[H^+]}{r\,[MnO_4^-]} = \frac{8}{1} = 8$$

CHAPTER 9

Coordination Compounds

Learning Elements

Element 1 Basic Terms Used in Coordination Compounds and IUPAC Nomenclature

Molecular or Addition Compounds, Terminology Related to Coordination Compounds, Coordination Number, IUPAC Nomenclature of Coordination Compounds

Element 2 Isomerism in Coordination Compounds

Structural Isomerism, Stereoisomerism, Geometrical Isomerism, Optical Isomerism

Element 3 Bonding in Coordination Compounds

Werner's Theory of Coordination Compounds, Valence Bond Theory (VBT), Crystal Field Theory (CFT), Colour and the Spectrochemical Series, Stability Constants and Stability of Coordination Compounds, Importance and Applications of Coordination compounds

Practice Elements

Practice Element 1 Target JEE Main

Practice Element 2 Target JEE Advanced

Trend Insights

JEE Main

	2024				2023				2022			
Topics	**E**	**M**	**T**	**O**	**E**	**M**	**T**	**O**	**E**	**M**	**T**	**O**
Basic Terms Used in Coordination Compounds and IUPAC Nomenclature	2	4	2	8	1	6	2	9	–	1	5	6
Isomerism in Coordination Compounds	–	9	7	16	1	7	8	16	2	2	2	6
Bonding in Coordination Compounds	–	–	5	5	–	5	1	6	–	–	4	4

E = Easy, **M** = Medium, **T** = Tough, **O** = Overall

Current Dynamics

- Overall weightage and difficulty level of questions were increased in 2024.
- The trend is changing now-a-days, less number of questions involving applications of coordination compounds and organometallic compounds were asked.
- Easy questions were asked from valence bond theory and CFT.

JEE Advanced

Typology	**Years**				
	2024	**2023**	**2022**	**2021**	**2020**
1. Simple MCQs	1	1	1	2	1
2. One or more than one correct	–	–	–	–	–
3. Numerical Value/Integer	2	–	–	1	–
4. Matching Type	–	1	1	–	–
5. Paragraph Based	–	–	–	–	–

Current Dynamics

- Mostly moderate to difficult level of questions had been asked in previous years.
- In present scenario weightage of one option correct type questions is almost constant.

Insightful Advice

- Students must focus on understanding the concepts of ligands type, coordination number, isomerism, IUPAC nomenclature and applications of VBT and CFT.
- Practice consistently with past year JEE question paper and revise key topics regularly.

Element 1 Basic Terms Used in Coordination Compounds and IUPAC Nomenclature

- The concept of coordination compounds arises from the complex formation tendency of transition elements.
- One of the earliest known coordination compound is deep blue pigment called **prussian blue** i.e, $[KFe_2(CN)_6]$ which was accidently prepared by a Berlin color maker, Diebach in 1704.
- These compounds play a vital role in our lives, as chlorophyll of plants and haemoglobin of animal blood are also coordination compounds of Mg(II) and Fe(II) respectively.
- The field of such compounds is expanding due to their utilisation in **metallurgy, analytical** chemistry and **polymerisation**.

Molecular or Addition Compounds

When solutions containing two or more simple stable compounds in molecular proportions are allowed to evaporate, crystals of new substances are obtained. These substances are termed as molecular or addition compounds.

Some common examples are as follows.

$$CuSO_4 + 4NH_3 \longrightarrow CuSO_4 \cdot 4NH_3$$

$$\underset{\text{Simple stable compounds (Reactants)}}{AgCN + KCN} \longrightarrow \underset{\text{Addition or molecular compounds (Product)}}{KCN \cdot AgCN}$$

$$4KCN + Fe(CN)_2 \longrightarrow Fe(CN)_2 \cdot 4KCN$$

$$\underset{\text{(Reactants)}}{K_2SO_4 + Al_2(SO_4)_3 + 24H_2O} \longrightarrow \underset{\text{(Product)}}{K_2SO_4 \cdot Al_2(SO_4)_3 \cdot 24H_2O}$$

The molecular or addition compounds are of two types double salts or lattice compounds and coordination or complex compounds.

Double Salts or Lattice Compounds

The addition compounds which are stable in solid state only however, down into individual constituents when dissolved in water are called double salts or lattice compounds.

For example when carnallite $(KCl \cdot MgCl_2 \cdot 6H_2O)$ is dissolved in water it exhibits the properties of KCl and $MgCl_2$

Coordination or Complex Compounds

The addition compounds in which some of the constituents ions or molecules lose their identity and when dissolved in water they do not break up completely into individual ions are called coordination compounds.

The properties of their solutions are different than those of their constituents.

In such compounds, there is a complex ion in which a central metal ion with Lewis bases is attached to it through coordinate covalent bonds.

On the basis of stability, complex ions are further divided as follows

(i) **Perfect Complexes** Those complexes in which complex ion is fairly stable and is either not dissociated or feebly dissociated in solution state, e.g.

$$K_4[Fe(CN)_6] \longrightarrow 4K^+ + [Fe(CN)_6]^{4-}$$
$$\downarrow$$
$$Fe^{2+} + 6CN^-$$
(Feebly dissociated)

The ferrocyanide ion, $[Fe(CN)_6]^{4-}$ is so insignificantly dissociated that it can be considered as practically undissociated and does not give the test of Fe^{2+} and CN^- ions.

(ii) **Imperfect Complexes** Those complexes in which complex ion is less stable and is reversibly dissociated to give enough simple ions and thus imparts their tests, e.g $K_2[Cd(CN)_4] \longrightarrow 2K^+ + [Cd(CN)_4]^{2-}$

$$\downarrow$$
$$Cd^{2+} + 4CN^-$$

Terminology Related to Coordination Compounds

To understand the concepts related to coordination compounds and their nature, it is essential to discuss some important terms. These are as follows.

Central Ion

The cation to which one or more neutral molecules or anions are attached is called as central ion.

Since the central ion acts as an acceptor and thus has to accommodate electron pairs donated by the donor atom of the ligands, it must have empty orbitals.

This explains why the transition metals having empty *p*-orbitals form coordination compounds very readily.

In the complexes, $[Ni(NH_3)_6]^{2+}$ and $[Fe(CN)_6]^{3-}$, Ni^{2+} and Fe^{3+} respectively are the central ions

Ligands

The neutral molecules, anions or cations which are directly linked with the central metal atom or ion in a complex ion are called ligands.

- Ligand donate a pair of electrons to the central atom.

- They are attached to the central metal ion or atom through coordinate bonds or dative linkage.
- Ligands are normally polar molecules like $\ddot{N}H_3$; $H_2\ddot{O}$: or anions such as Cl^-, OH^-, CN^- etc. which contain at least one unshared pair of valence electrons.

Types of Ligands

Following are the basis of classification of ligands on the basis of number of donor atoms present

1. Mono or Unidentate Ligands

They have one donor atom, i.e. they supply only one atom. They can be positive or negative or neutral. For example

Anionic Monodentate Ligands

F^-	Fluorido/fluoro
Cl^-	Chlorido/chloro
Br^-	Bromido/bromo
I^-	Iodido/iodo
O^{2-}	Oxido/oxo
S^{2-}	Sulphido/sulpho
OH^-	Hydroxido/hydroxo
CH_3-O^-	Methoxido/Methoxo
O_2^-	Superoxido/Superoxo
O_2^{2-}	Peroxido/Peroxo
N^{3-}	Nitrido
N_3^-	Azido
$(NH_4)^-$	Amido

JEE Alert

The 2004 IUPAC draft recommends that anionic ligands will end with-ido, i-to or -ato e.g. chloro would become chlorido, etc.

Neutral Monodentate Ligands

NH_3	Ammine
H_2O	Aqua
NO	Nitrosyl
PH_3	Phosphine
PPh_3	Triphenyl phosphine
O_2	Dioxygen
N_2	Dinitrogen
$CH_3—OH$	Methyl alcohol
$CH_3—NH_2$	Methyl amine
NH_2CONH_2	Urea
NH_2NH_2	Hydrazine
$CH_3—O—CH_3$	Dimethyl ether

Cationic Monodentate Ligands

O_2^+	Oxygenium
NO^+	Nitrosylium or Nitrosonium
NO_2^+	Nitronium
$H_2N—\overset{+}{N}H_3$	Hydrazinium

2. Bidentate Ligands

Ligands which have two donor atoms and have the ability to link with central metal ion at two positions are called bidentate ligands. Some examples are

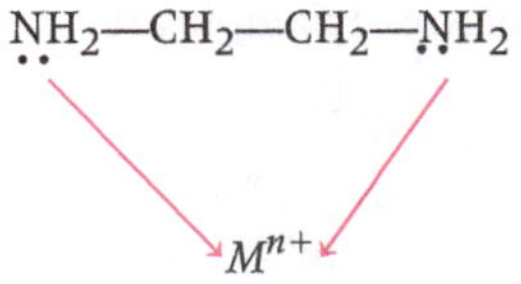

Ethylene diamine
(en) (5-membered chelate ring)

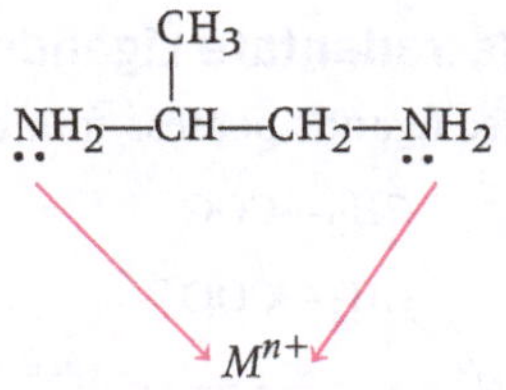

Propylenediamine (pn)
(5 membered chelate ring)

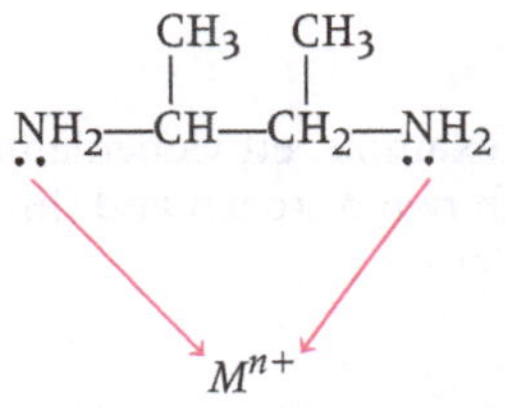

Butylenediamine(bn)
(5 membered chelate ring)

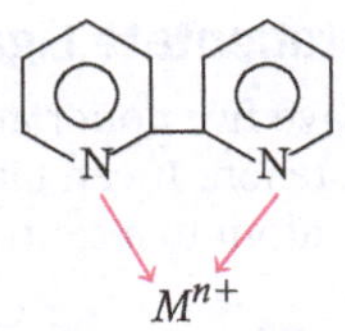

Dipyridyl(dipy)
(5 membered chelate ring)

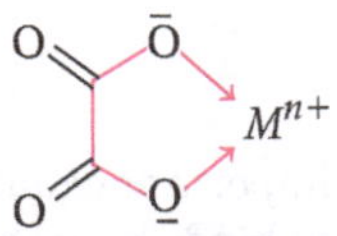

Oxalato(ox)$^{2-}$ or $C_2O_4^{2-}$
(5 membered chelate ring)

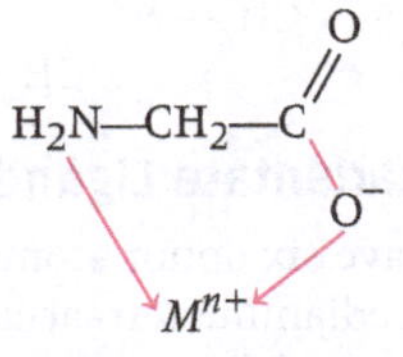

Glycinato(gly)$^-$
(Unsymmetrical)
(5 membered chelate ring)

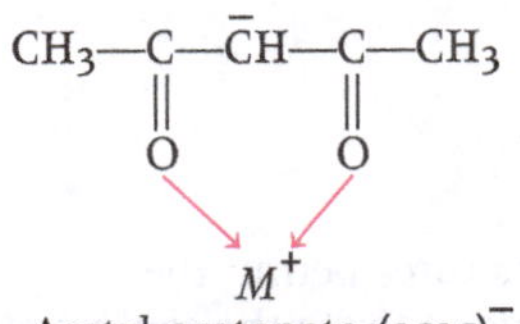

Acetyl acetonato (acac)$^-$
(6 membered chelate ring)

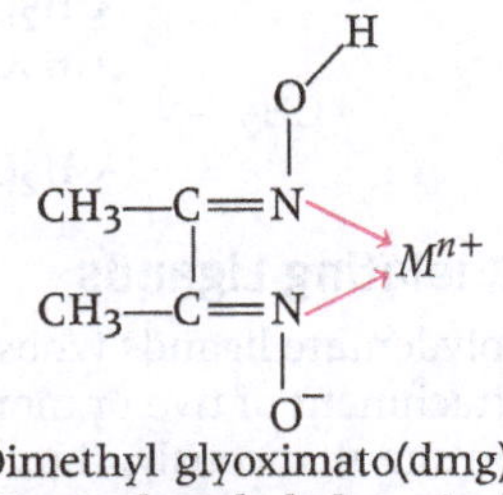

Dimethyl glyoximato(dmg)$^-$
(5 membered chelate ring)

3. Tridentate Ligands

The ligands having three donor atoms are called tridentate ligands.

Examples are:

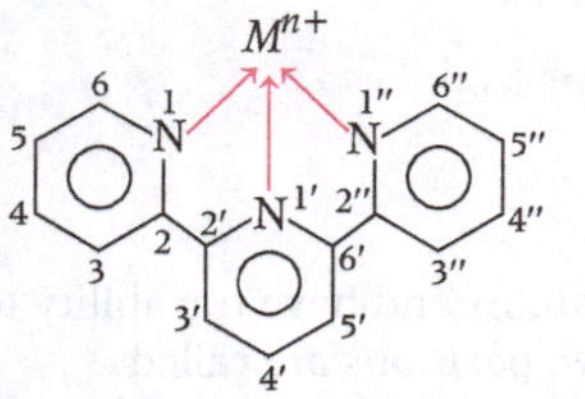

2,2′,6′,2″-terpyridine (terpy)

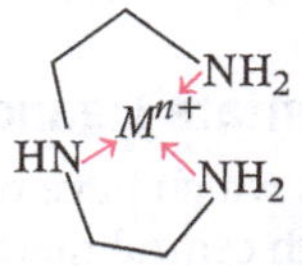

Diethylene triamine (dien)

4. Tetradentate Ligands

These ligands possess four donor atoms. Example are

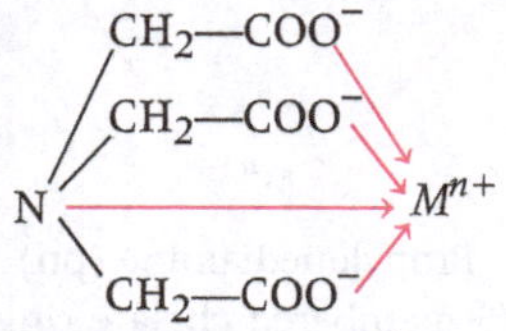

(Nitriloacetato)$^{3-}$

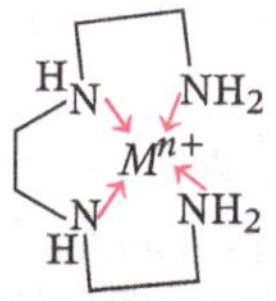

Triethylene tetramine (trien)

5. Pentadentate Ligands

They have five donor atoms. For example, ethylenediamine triacetate ion. It can bind through two nitrogen and three oxygen atom to a central metal ion.

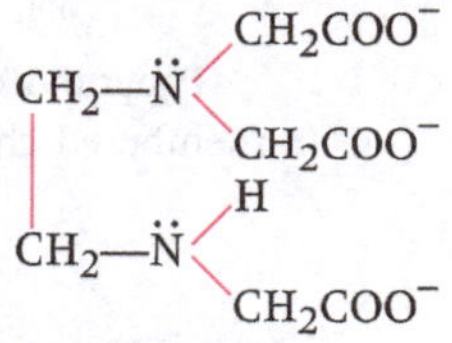

or EDTA^{3-}

6. Hexadentate Ligands

They have six donor atoms. The most important example is ethylenediamine tetraacetate ion. It can bind through two nitrogen and four oxygen atom to a central metal ion.

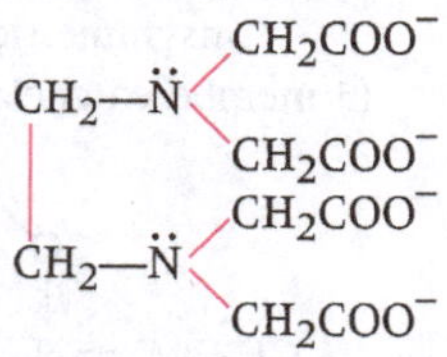

or EDTA^{4-}

7. Chelating Ligands

- Polydentate ligands whose structures permit the attachment of two or more donor sites to the same metal ion simultaneously, thus closing one or more rings are called chelating ligands and the compounds formed are known as chelate compounds.
- A chelate may be defined as a ring structure formed by the combination of a polydentate ligand having two or more donor atoms with a metal ion forming part of the ring. The process of formation of chelates is called chelation.
- In the complex ion given below, 5 membered rings are formed. So this is a chelate complexe.

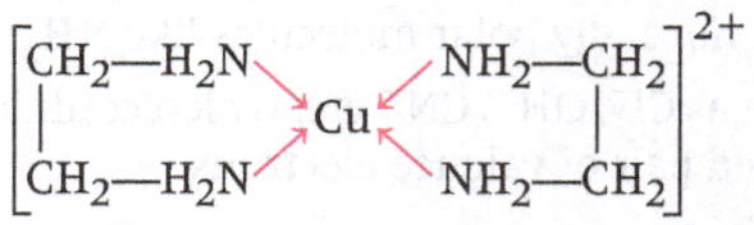

JEE Spotlite

- Chelate complexes are more stable than ordinary complexes in which the ligand is a not a chelating ligand.
- The increased stability of the compound due to chelation is called the chelate effect.
- Generally the chelate complexes with 5 or 6 membered rings are more stable.
- 5-membered rings are very stable when they involve saturated ligand.
- 6-membered ring structures acquire maximum stability when they involved unsaturated ligands containing conjugated double bonds. This is due to the resonance effects involving metal *d*-orbitals and ligand *p*-orbital electrons.

8. Flexidentate Ligands

Ligands which can change their denticity are called flexidentate ligands.

SO_4^{-2}, $S_2O_3^{-2}$ CO_3^{-2}, NO_3^-, CH_3COO^- etc., generally act as monodentate ligands, but in some compounds they can also act as bidentate ligand, e.g.

- $[Co(NH_3)_5(SO_4)]Cl$, in this complex SO_4^{-2} acts as a monodentate ligand.
- $[Co(en)_2(SO_4)]Cl$, in this complex SO_4^{-2} acts as a bidentate ligand.

9. Ambidentate Ligands

Ligands which have two different donor atoms but at the time of coordination they can donate electron pair from any one donor atom are called ambidentate ligands.

(i) $M \leftarrow \overset{\ominus}{C}\equiv N$ — Cyanido (CN)

$M \leftarrow N\equiv \overset{\ominus}{C}$ — Isocyanido (NC)

(ii) $M \leftarrow \overset{\ominus}{O}—C\equiv N$ — Cyanato/cyanato-O

$M \leftarrow N\equiv C—\overset{\ominus}{O}$ — Isocyanato/cyanato-N

(iii) $M \leftarrow \overset{\ominus}{S}—C\equiv N$ — Thiocyanato/Thiocyanato-S

$M \leftarrow N\equiv C—\overset{\ominus}{S}$ — Isothiocyanato/thiocyanato-N

(iv) $M \leftarrow \overset{\ominus}{O}—N=O$ — Nitro/Nitrito-O

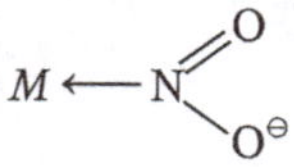

Nitro/Nitrito-N

On the Basis of Nature of Bonding between Central Metal Atom and Ligand

- **Normal or Classical Ligands** They only donate electron pair to central metal ion and form coordinate (σ) bonds. e.g. $OH^-, NH_2^-, Cl^-, N^{-3}, O^{-2}$ etc.
- **Non-Classical or π-acid or π-acceptor Ligands** They donate electron pair to central metal ion and form coordinate σ bond but simultaneously they accept electron pair from central metal ion through back-bonding or synergic bonding. e.g., CO, NO^+, CN^-, R_3P, R_3As etc.

The CO molecule has lone pair of electrons on carbon and oxygen atom each. Carbon atom can donate its electron pair to a transition metal atom (M), forming $OC \rightarrow M$ coordinate bond.

Since the metal atom in metal carbonyl is in zero oxidation state, the formation of $M \leftarrow CO$ σ-bond accumulates a negative charge on the metal atom. The accumulation of negative charge on the metal atom can be counter balanced by transferring some negative charge from the metal atom to CO molecule (ligand). This transfer can be done by making a $M \rightarrow CO'$ π bond by the overlap between an appropriate filled orbital on the metal atom and empty π_y^* or π_z^* molecular orbital on C of CO molecule. This type of bonding between M and CO is called **synergic bonding**.

(i) 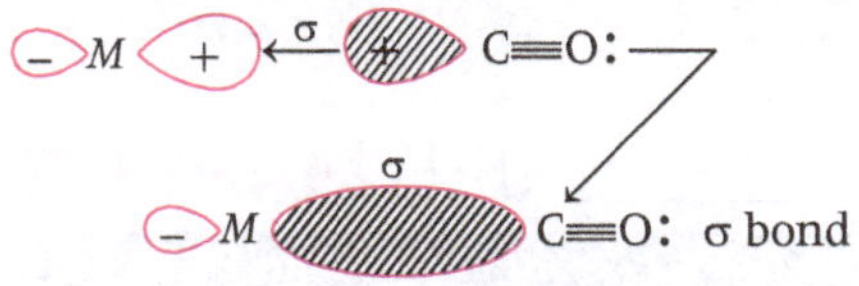

(ii) 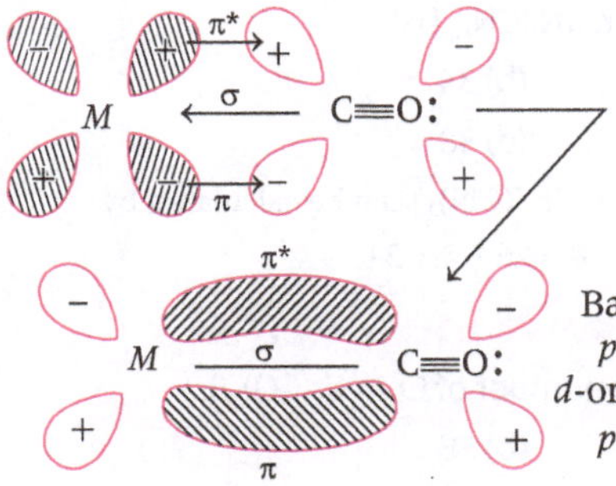

Back bonding dative p-bond from filled d-orbital on M to empty p-orbital (π*) on C

Conclusion of Synergic Bonding: due to Synergic Bonding,

- M—C bond strength increases; M—C bond length decreases; because double bond character increases
- C—O bond strength decreases; C—O bond length increases; because bond order of C—O decreases, electron density in *ABMO* of CO increases.

π-donor and π-acceptor Ligands

They can donate π-electrons to central metal ion and also accept electron density from central metal ion through synergic bonding.

(i) $H_2C = CH_2$ (η^2-ethylene): it is a 2π electron donor

(ii)  (η^6-benzene): it is a 6π electron donor.

- $[Cr(\eta^6—C_6H_6)_2]$ 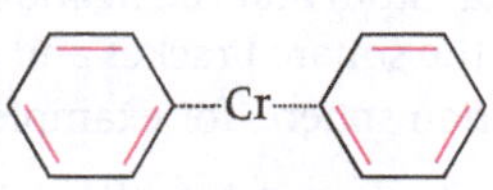

Sandwich compound

- $[Fe(\eta^5—C_5H_5)_2]$ Ferrocene (sandwich compound)
- $K[PtCl_3(\eta^2—C_2H_4)]$ (Zeise's salt)

JEE Spotlite

The bonding of alkenes to a transition metal to form complexes has two components. First, the π-electron density of the alkene overlaps with a σ-type vacant orbital of the metal atom. Second is the back bonding formed by the flow of electron density from a filled d-orbital on the metal into the vacant π^*-antibonding molecular orbital of the carbon atom as shown below.

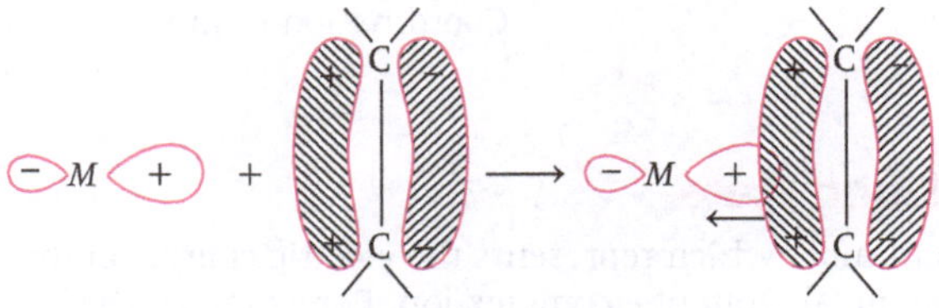

σ-overlap

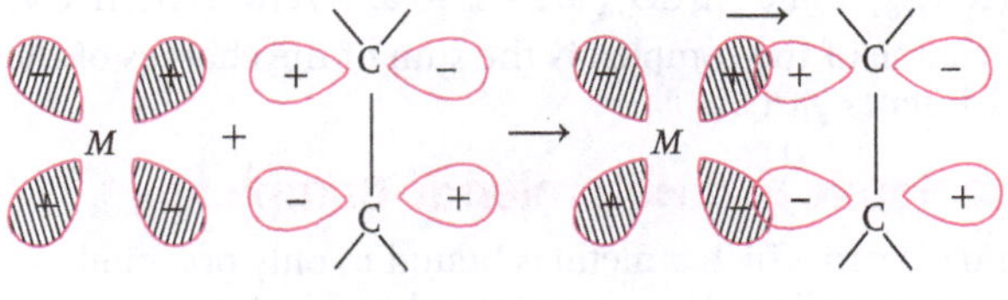

Back-bonding

Coordination Number

The number of atoms of the ligands that are directly bonded to the central metal atom or ion by coordinate bonds is known as the coordination number of the metal atom or ion. It is actually the number of coordinate covalent bonds which the ligands form with the central metal atom or ion.

Examples of complexes of various C.N.

Complex	C.N.
$[Ag(NH_3)_2]^+$	2
$[HgI_3]^-$	3
$PtCl_4^{2-}$, $Ni(CO)_4$	4
$Fe(CO)_5$, $[Co(CN)_5]^{3-}$	5
$[Co(NH_3)_6]^{3+}$, $W(CO)_6$	6
$[Mo(CN)_7]^{3-}$	7
$[W(CN)_8]^{4-}$	8

Coordination Sphere

The central metal atom and the ligands directly attached to it are enclosed in the square bracket and are collectively termed as the coordination sphere, for example $[Co(NH_3)_6]^{3+}$.

The central metal atom and the ligands inside the square bracket behave as a single entity. The part outside the bracket is called ionisation sphere or counter ions. The species present in the ionisation sphere are ionisable while the species present in the coordination sphere are non-ionisable.

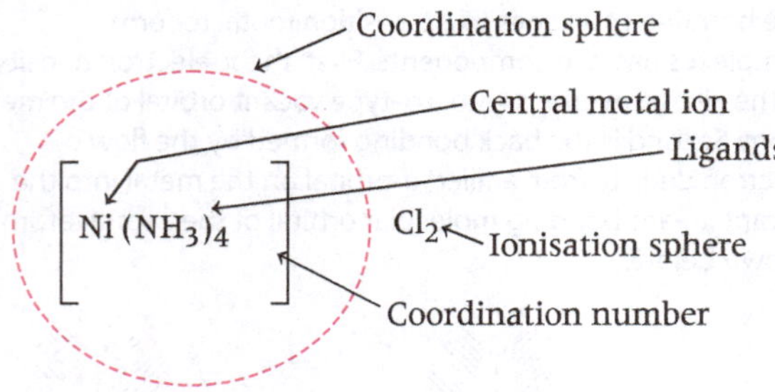

Oxidation State

It is a number which represents the electric charge on the central metal atom of a complex ion. For example, the oxidation numbers of Fe, Co and Ni in $[Fe(CN)_6]^{4-}$, $[Co(NH_3)_6]^{3+}$ and $Ni(CO)_4$ are +2, +3 and zero respectively. The charge of the complex is the sum of the charges of the constituents parts.

Homoleptic and Heteroleptic Complexes

Complexes in which a metal is bound to only one kind of donor group (ligand) are known as homoleptic. e.g. $[Co(NH_3)_6]^{3+}$ whereas complexes in which a metal is bound to more than one kind of donor groups (ligands) are known as heteroleptic. e.g. $[Co(NH_3)_4Cl_2]^+$.

Effective Atomic Number (EAN)

In order to explain the stability of a complex, Sidgwick proposed effective atomic number (EAN). It can be defined as the resultant number of electrons with the metal atom or ion after gaining electrons from the donor atoms of the ligands.

The EAN generally coincides, with the atomic number of next noble gas in some cases. It can be calculated by the following relation.

EAN = Atomic number of the central metal/ion – Number of electrons lost in ion formation + Number of electrons gained from the donor atoms of the ligands.

Complex	Metal (Oxid. state)	Atomic No. of metal	Coordination number	Effective atomic number
$K_4[Fe(CN)_6]$	+2	26	6	$(26-2)+(6\times2)$ = 36 [Kr]
$[Cu(NH_3)_4]SO_4$	+2	29	4	$(29-2)+(4\times2)$ = 35
$[Co(CH_3)_6]Cl_3$	+3	27	6	$(27-3)+(6\times2)$ = 36 [Kr]
$Ni(CO)_4$	0	28	4	$(28-0)+(4\times2)$ = 36 [Kr]
$K_2[PtCl_6]$	+4	78	6	$(78-4)+(6\times2)$ = 86 [Rn]
$K_3[Cr(C_2O_4)_3]$	+3	24	6	$(24-3)+(6\times2)$ = 33
$K_3[Fe(CN)_6]$	+3	26	6	$(26-3)+(6\times2)$ = 35
$K_2[HgI_4]$	+2	80	4	$(80-2)+(4\times2)$ = 86 [Rn]
$[Ag(NH_3)_2]Cl$	+1	47	2	$(47-1)+(2\times2)$ = 50
$K_2[PdCl_4]$	+2	46	4	$(46-2)+(4\times2)$ = 52

JEE MAPPER

Example Similar to PYQ Asked in JEE Main 2020

The EAN of nickel in $K_2[Ni(CN)_4]$ is

(a) 35 (b) 34
(c) 36 (d) 38

Sol. (b) EAN of Ni in $K_2[Ni(CN)_4]$ can be calculated by

EAN of Ni = $(28-2)+8=26+8=34$

Competency Enhancer 1.1

The effective atomic number of Cr in $Cr(CO)_6$ is

(a) 36 (b) 38
(c) 28 (d) 54

IUPAC Nomenclature of Coordination Compounds

Nomenclature is important in coordination chemistry. The formulas and names adopted for coordination entities are based on the recommendation of International Union of Pure and Applied chemistry (IUPAC).

Following rules are adopted for naming a complex ion:

(i) Coordination compounds contain two parts: Cation and anion. Cations are named before anions.

(ii) Oxidation state (O.S.) of the central metal ion is denoted by Roman numeral.

	Cation (O.S.)	**Anion**
CuCl	Copper (I)	Chloride
$CuCl_2$	Copper (II)	Chloride
$FeCl_2$	Iron (II)	Chloride
$FeCl_3$	Iron (III)	Chloride

(iii) If more than one type of ligands are present then they are written in alphabetical order.

(iv) Anionic ligands ending with 'ide' are named by replacing 'ide' by suffix 'ido'. e.g.

Symbol	Name as ligand
N^{3-}	Nitrido
Cl^-	Chlorido
O_2^{2-}	Peroxido
Br^-	Bromido
O_2H^-	Perhydroxido
CN^-	Cyanido
S^{2-}	Sulphido
O^{2-}	Oxido
NH^{2-}	Imido
OH^-	Hydroxido

(v) Ligands whose names end in 'ite' or 'ate' become 'ito' or ato i.e. by replacing the ending 'e' with 'o' as follows. e.g.

Symbol	Name as ligand
CO_3^{2-}	Carbonato
$C_2O_4^{2-}$	Oxalato
SO_4^{2-}	Sulphato
NO_3^-	Nitrato
SO_3^{2-}	Sulphito
CH_3COO^-	Acetato
NO_2^-	Nitrito

(vi) Neutral ligands are given the same names as the neutral molecules. for example. Ethylene diamine as a ligand is named ethylene diamine [(en), i.e., ethane 1,2-diamine] in the complex. However some exceptions to this rule are

H_2O	Aqua
NH_3	Ammine
CO	Carbonyl
NO	Nitrosyl
CS	thiocarbonyl

(vii) Names of positive ligands ends in 'ium' e.g.

NH_4^+	Ammonium
NO^+	Nitrosylium
$NH_2NH_3^+$	Hydrazinium

JEE Alert

- When there are several ligands of the same kind, we normally use the prefixes **di, tri, tetra, penta** and **hexa** to show the number of ligands of that type.
- An exception occurs when the name of the ligands includes a number, for example as in ethylenediamine (en). To avoid confusion in such cases, **bis, tris** and **tetrakis** are used.

(viii) **If the complex is an anion then metal ends with 'ate'**

e.g. $[Ni(CN)_4]^{2-}$ tetracyanidonickelate(II) ion.

(ix) If the complex contains two or more metal atoms, it is termed polynuclear. The bridging ligands which link the two metal atoms together are indicated by the prefix μ—.

(x) Ambidentate ligands may be attached through different atoms

e.g. $M—NO_2$ (NO_2 joined to metal M through N; it is **nitro**)

M—ONO (NO_2 joined to metal M through O; it is **nitrito**)

Similarly, the SCN group may bond M—SCN (thiocyanato) or M—NCS (isothiocyanato). They may be named thiocyanato–S [to indicate S coordinated to metal M] thiocyanato–N [to indicate N coordinated to metal M]

(i) In the following examples, **complex ion** exists as **cation**

- $[Fe(NH_3)_6]Cl_3$
  Hexaammineiron(III) chloride
- $[CoCl(NH_3)_5]^{2+}$
  Pentaamminechloridocobalt(III) ion
- $[CoSO_4(NH_3)_4]NO_3$
  Tetraamminesulphatocobalt(III) nitrate
- $[Co(Cl)(NO_2)(NH_3)_4]^+$
  Tetraamminechloridonitrito-N-cobalt(III) ion
- $K_2[Cr(CN)(O)_2(O_2)NH_3]$
  Potassium ammine cyanidodioxidoperoxido chromate(VI)
- $[Zn(NCS)_4]^{2-}$
  Tetrathiocyanato-N-zincate(II) ion
  (N indicates that ligand joined to metal ion through N-side)

(ii) **In the following examples, complex ion** exists as **anion**

- $[ZnCl_4]^{2-}$
Tetrachloridozincate(II) ion
- $[AlH_4]^-$
Tetrahydridoaluminate(III) ion
- $K_4[Fe(CN)_6]$
Potassium hexacyanidoferrate(II)
- $Na_3[Ag(S_2O_3)_2]$
Sodium dithiosulphatoargentate(I)
- $Na_2[OsCl_5N]$
Sodium pentachloridonitridoosmate(VI)
- $K_2[PtCl_6]$
Potassium hexachloridoplatinate(IV)

(iii) In the following examples, **organic ligands** have been used :

- $[Pt(Py)_4][PtCl_4]$
Tetrapyridineplatinum(II) tetrachloroplatinate(II)
- $[Cr(en)_3]Cl_3$
tris(ethane-1,2-diamine) chromium(III) chloride
- $[Pt(en)_2]^{2+}$
bis(ethane-1,2-diamine)platinum(II) ion
- $[Cr\eta^6\text{-}(C_6H_6)_2]$
bis(benzene)chromium(0)
- $[Fe(\eta^5\text{-}C_5H_5)_2]$
bis(cyclopentadienyl)iron(II)

4. In the following examples, **bridging groups** have been used:

- 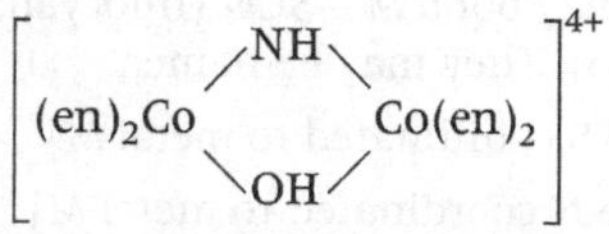

Tetrakis(ethane-1,2-diamine)–μ– hydroxido–μ–imidodicobalt(III) ion.
- 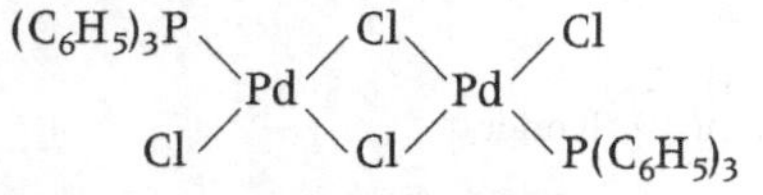

trans-bis(chloridotriphenylphosphine-μ-chloridopalladium(II))
or
Chloridotriphenylphosphinepalladium(II)-μ-dichloridochloridotriphenylphosphinepalladium(II)

The following Examples Illustrates the Nomenclature of Complexes

$[Cr(H_2O)_4Cl_2]Cl$	–	Tetraaquadichloridochromium (III) chloride
$[Co(NH_3)_5CO_3]Cl$	–	Pentaamminecarbonatocobalt (III) chloride
$[Ag(NH_3)_2]Cl$	–	Diamminesilver (I) chloride
$[Co(en)_2Cl_2]SO_4$	–	Dichloridobis (ethane1,2-diamine) cobalt (III) sulphate
$[Co(NH_3)_4(NO_2)Cl]NO_3$	–	Tetraamminechloridonitro-N-cobalt (III) nitrate
$[Co(NH_3)_3(NO_2)_3]$	–	Triamminetrinitro-N-cobalt (III)
$[Pt(NH_3)_6]Cl_4$	–	Hexaammineplatinum (IV) chloride
$[Cr(H_2O)_3(NH_3)_3]Cl_3$	–	Triamminetriaquachromium (III) chloride
$[CoF_2(en)_2]ClO_4$	–	*Bis* (ethane-1,2-diamine) difluoridocobalt (III) perchlorate
$Na_2[SiF_6]$	–	Sodium hexafluoridosilicate (IV)
$Fe_4[Fe(CN)_6]_3$	–	Iron (III) hexacyanidoferrate(II) or ferric hexacyanidoferrate (II)
$Na_2[CrF_4O]$	–	Sodium tetrafluoridooxidochromate (IV)
$K_2[OsCl_5N]$	–	Potassium pentachloridonitridoosmate (VI)
$K_4[Ni(CN)_4]$	–	Potassium tetracyanidonickelate (0)
$[Ni(dmg)_2]$	–	*Bis* (dimethylglyoximato) nickel (II)
$[Pt(NH_3)_2Cl_2]$	–	Diamminedichloridoplatinum (II)
$[Cr(PPh_3)(CO)_5]$	–	Pentacarbonyltriphenylphosphinechromium (0)
$[Co(NH_3)_4Cl_2]_3[Cr(CN)_6]$	–	Tetraamminedichloridocobalt (III) hexacyanidochromate (III)
$[Pt(NH_3)_4Cl_2][PtCl_4]$	–	Tetraammine dichloridoplatinum (IV) tetrachloridoplatinate (II)
$[(NH_3)_5Cr—OH—Cr(NH_3)_5]Cl_5$	–	Pentaamminechromium (III)-μ-hydroxidopentaammine chromium (III) chloride
$[(NH_3)_5CoNH_2Co(NH_3)_5](NO_3)_5$	–	Decammine-μ-amidodicobalt (III) nitrate
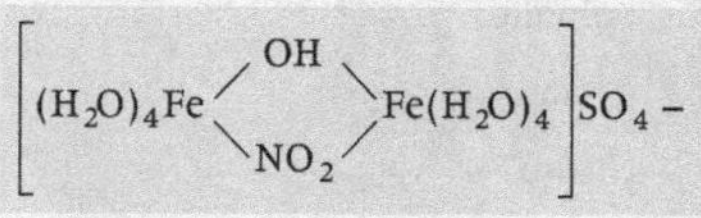	–	Octaaqua-μ-hydroxo-μ-nitrodiiron (III) sulphate
$[Mn_3(CO)_{12}]$	–	Dodecacarbonyltrimanganese (0)
$[Fe(C_5H_5)_2]$	–	*Bis*(cyclopentadienyl)iron (II) or ferrocene
$[PtBrClI(NO_2)(NH_3)(Py)]$	–	Amminebromidochloridoiodidonitro-N-pyridineplatinum (IV)
$Na_3[Ag(S_2O_3)_2]$	–	Sodium *bis*(thiosulphato) argentate (I)
$Na_2[Ni(EDTA)]$	–	Disodium ethylenediaminetetraacetatonickel (II)
$Hg[Co(SCN)_4]$	–	Mercuric tetrathiocyanato-S-cobaltate (II)

JEE MAPPER

Example Similar to PYQ Asked in JEE Main 2024

The correct IUPAC name of $[Co(H_2O)_4(NH_3)_2]Br_3$ is
(a) diamminetetraaquacobalt (III) bromide
(b) tetraaquadiamminecobalt (III) bromide
(c) diaminetetraaquacobalt (II) bromide
(d) diaminetetraaquacobalt (IV) bromide

Sol. (*a*) IUPAC name of the given complex is diamminetetra aquacobalt (III) bromide.

Compentency Enhancer 1.2

The correct IUPAC name of $K[Cr(NH_3)_2Cl_4]$ is
(a) potassium diamine tetrachlorochromate (IV)
(b) potassium diammine tetrachloridochromate (III)
(c) potassium diammine tetrachlorochromium (III)
(d) potassium diammine tetrachloridochromate (II)

Solved Booster 1.1

The correct IUPAC name of $K_3[Cr(C_2O_4)_3]$ is
(a) potassium trioxalatochromium(II)
(b) potassium trioxalatochromate(III)
(c) potassium tris(oxalato)chromate(II)
(d) potassium trioxalatocobalt(III)

Solution (*b*)
IUPAC name of the given complex is potassium trioxalatochromate (III).

Rules for writing the Formula of Coordination Complexes

Rules given below are followed for writing the formula of coordination complex.

- Cation whether simple or complex is written first followed by the anion.
- The order of formulating a complex ion is reverse to that adopted in naming, i.e. the central metal atom is written first followed by the ligand.
- When there are more than one type of ligands present these are named, alphabetically according to the first symbol of their formulae.
- Whole of the complex ion is enclosed in a square bracket.
- The charge on the complex species is equal to the charge on the central metal atom, i.e. its oxidation state plus the total charge carried by all the ligands coordinated to the metal ion or atom for example the formula of tetraamminecopper (II) chloride is $[Cu(NH_3)_4]Cl_2$.
- When writing the formula of the complex : ligands are placed after metal in the alphabetical order but first negative ligands, then neutral, then positive.

$[Pt(H_2O)_4(NH_3)_2]^{4+}$ — wrong
(Aqua) (Ammine)

$[Pt(NH_3)_2(H_2O)_4]^{4+}$ — right

$[Cr(CN)_4(NH_3)_2]^-$ — right
(Negative) (Neutral)

Solved Booster 1.2

Which among the following will be named as dibromidobis-(ethylenediamine) chromium (III) bromide?
(a) $[Cr(en)_3Br]Br_2$
(b) $[Cr(en)_2Br_2]Br$
(c) $[Cr(en)Br_4]^-$
(d) $[Cr(en)Br_2]Br$

Solution (*b*)
Two Br, two (en) and one Cr are parts of complex.

$$\text{Charge on the complex is } \left\{\begin{matrix} 2(Br) = -2 \\ 2(en) = 0 \\ 1(Cr) = +3 \end{matrix}\right\} = +1$$

Thus, the correct complex ion is $[Cr(en)_2Br_2]^+$.
Since, anion is bromide thus, complex is $[Cr(en)_2Br_2]Br$.

Elemental Practice 9.1

Type I MCQs with Only One Correct Option

1. Incorrect statement for addition compound is
(a) simple salts do not lose their identity in double salt.
(b) complex compounds retain their identity in aqueous solution.
(c) simple salts lose their identity in complex compound.
(d) double salts retain their identity in aqueous solution.

2. Choose the option containing incorrect order of stability.
(a) $[Cu(NH_3)_4]^{2+} < [Cu(en)_2]^{2+} < [Cu(trien)]^{2+}$
(b) $[Fe(H_2O)_6]^{3+} < [Fe(NH_3)_6]^{3+} < [Fe(NO_2)_6]^{3+}$
(c) $[Co(H_2O)_6]^{3+} < [Rh(H_2O)_6]^{3+} < [Ir(H_2O)_6]^{3+}$
(d) $[Cr(NH_3)_6]^{+} > [Cr(NH_3)_6]^{2+} > [Cr(NH_3)_6]^{3+}$

3. Select the pair containing complex salt and double salt respectively.
(a) $FeSO_4$, $K_4[Fe(CN)_6]$
(b) $[Cu(NH_3)_4]SO_4$, $FeSO_4.7H_2O$
(c) $[Cu(NH_3)_4]SO_4$, $K_2SO_4Al_2(SO_4)_3 \cdot 24H_2O$
(d) $MgSO_4.7H_2O$, $CuSO_4 \cdot 5H_2O$

4. Which of the following complexes are heteroleptic?
(a) $[Cr(NH_3)_6]^{3+}$
(b) $[Fe(NH_3)_4Cl_2]^{+}$
(c) $[Mn(CN)_6]^{4-}$
(d) $[Co(NH_3)_6]^{+2}$

5. Choose the pair containing only ambidenate ligand
(a) CN^-, NH_3
(b) NO_2^-, SCN^-
(c) H_2O, en
(d) en, dien

6. Which of the following option can not act as ligand?
(a) $H_2N—CH_2—COO^-$
(b) $H_2N—NH_2$
(c) $[H_3N—CH_2—CH_2—NH_3]^{2+}$
(d) $H_2N—CH_3$

7. The correct order of C—O bond length is
(a) $[V(CO)_6]^- > [V(CO)_6] > [V(CO)_6]^+$
(b) $[V(CO)_6]^+ > [V(CO)_6] > [V(CO)_6]^-$
(c) $[V(CO)_6]^- > [V(CO)_6]^+ > [V(CO)_6]$
(d) $[V(CO)_6]^- = [V(CO)_6]^+ > [V(CO)_6]$

8. The ligand incapable to form synergic bonding is
(a) $(CH_3)_3—P$
(b) $H_2C—CH_2$
(c) NO^+
(d) $CH_3—O^-$

9. The effective atomic number for the complex ion $[Co(NH_3)_6]^{3+}$ is
(a) 35
(b) 33
(c) 34
(d) 36

10. Which of the following can act as π-acid ligand?
(a) CO
(b) $P(CH_3)_3$
(c) NO^+
(d) All of these

11. The number of electrons donated by $\sigma-C_5H_5^-$ and $\pi-C_5H_5^-$ respectively are
(a) 3 and 4
(b) 2 and 6
(c) 6 and 2
(d) 4 and 6

12. The correct IUPAC name for the compound $[Co(NH_3)_4ClONO]Cl$
(a) Tetraammine chloronitro cobalt (III) chloride
(b) Chloronitritotetraammine cobalt (II) chloride
(c) Dichloronitritotetraammine cobalt (III)
(d) Tetraammine chloridonitrito N-cobalt (III) chloride

13. Which of the following is the correct IUPAC name of $[Pt(NH_3)_3(Br)(NO_2)Cl)]Cl$
(a) triamminechlorobromonitroplatinum (IV) chloride
(b) triamminebromochloronitroplatinum (IV) chloride
(c) triamminechlorobromoplatinum (IV) chloride
(d) triamminechloronitrobromoplatinum (IV) chloride

14. Select the bidentate ligands from the following.
(a) Diethylene triamine, oxalate anion
(b) Iminodiacetate anion, 2, 2′, 2′′ terpyridine
(c) 2, 2′-dipyridyl, 1, 10 phenanthroline.
(d) Ethylenediamine triacetate anion, acetylacetonate anion.

15. In sodium nitroprusside the oxidation number, coordination number and effective atomic number of iron are respectively
(a) +3, 6, 35
(b) +3, 6, 36
(c) +2, 3, 36
(d) +2, 6, 36

16. Coordination number of Cr is six. A complex with $C_2O_4^{2-}$, en and superoxide O_2^- will be in the ratio to make complex $[Cr(C_2O_4)_x(en)_y(O_2)_z]^{\ominus}$

x y z
(a) 1, 1, 1
(b) 1, 1, 2
(c) 1, 2, 2
(d) 2, 1, 1

17. The IUPAC name for $K_2[Cr(CN)_2O_2(O)_2NH_3]$ is
(a) potassium amminedicyanotetraoxo chromium (III)
(b) potassium amminedicyanodioxygendioxo chromate (IV)
(c) potassium amminedicyanosuperoxoperoxo chromate (III)
(d) potassium amminedicyanodioxoperoxo chromate (VI)

18. While acting as a chelating ligand forming an octahedral complex, the maximum number of rings will be formed by
(a) $EDTA^{3-}$
(b) $EDTA^{4-}$
(c) ethylene diammine
(d) oxalate

19. The correct order of the C—O bond order is
(a) $[Fe(CO)_5]^- > [Fe(CO)_5] > [Fe(CO)_5]^{3+} > [Fe(CO)_5]^{2+}$
(b) $[Fe(CO)_5]^- > [Fe(CO)_5] > [Fe(CO)_5]^{2+} > [Fe(CO)_5]^{3+}$
(c) $[Fe(CO)_5]^- < [Fe(CO)_5] < [Fe(CO)_5]^{3+} < [Fe(CO)_5]^{2+}$
(d) $[Fe(CO)_5]^- < [Fe(CO)_5] < [Fe(CO)_5]^{2+} < [Fe(CO)_5]^{3+}$

20. The correct IUPAC name of coordination compound $Mn_3(CO)_{12}$ is
(a) dodecacarbonylmanganate (III)
(b) dodecacarbonylmanganate
(c) dodecacarbonyltrimanganese (0)
(d) dodecacarbonyltrimanganese (II)

Type II 》 MCQs with One or More than One Correct Option

21. Select the correct statements from the following.
(a) The coordination number of Co^{3+} ion in $[CoCl_3(NH_3)_3]$ is 6.
(b) Iminodiacetate anion is an example of tridentate ligand.
(c) The IUPAC name of $[Co(NH_3)_6]Cl_3$ is hexammine cobalt (III) chloride.
(d) Carnallite is an example of double salt.

22. Which of the following statements is/are correct for imperfect complexes?
(a) These are less stable.
(b) It is reversibly dissociated.
(c) It will give simple ions and imparts test for their individual ions.
(d) For the complex $K_2[Cd(CN)_4]$ it gives tests for K^+, Cd^{+2}, CN^- ions.

23. Given below are statements regarding chelating ligands. Choose the option(s) containing correct statement.
(a) They form stable complexes than monodentate ligands.
(b) They form stable rings with large group due to steric effect.
(c) These are used in softening hard water and in the separation of lanthanoids and actinoids.
(d) They will form strain free rings with the metal ion.

24. Choose the incorrect IUPAC name of complex compound.
(a) Tetrachloronickel (II) tetraamminenickel (II)
(b) *Bis* (trimethylphosphine) dibromoplatinum (II)
(c) Pentaamminecyanidochrominum (III) hexanitrito-N-irridate (III)
(d) Diamminetetraaquacobalt (III) chloride
(e) Potassium tetra-chloridopalladate (II).

25. Which of the following is/are incorrect statements?
(a) $[Co(NH_3)_6]Cl_3$ is an example of homoleptic complex.
(b) $CuSO_4 \cdot 4NH_3 \cdot H_2O$, $K_2SO_4 \cdot Al_2(SO_4)_3 \cdot 24H_2O$ and $Fe(CN)_2 \cdot 4KCN$ are the example of double salt.
(c) The coordination number of central metal atom in a complex is equal to number of ligands around the central metal ion bonded by coordinate bonds.
(d) NO_2^-, SCN^-, $C_2O_4^{2-}$ and SO_4^{2-} are ambidentate ligand.

26. Choose the correct statements from the following.
(a) $EDTA^{4-}$ forms five membered rings in its coordination complex with a metal ion.
(b) Three of 5 rings formed by $EDTA^{4-}$ are in the same plane, while the remaining two are in a plane perpendicular to the three.
(c) $EDTA^{4-}$ forms 5 membered chelate rings that include coordination bonds from both oxygen and nitrogen donor atoms.
(d) The five rings formed by $EDTA^{4-}$ all lie in the same plane.

Type III 》 Numerical/Integer Type Questions

27. How many of the following species will form chelate complex.
$C_2O_4^{-2}$, NH_2NH_2, en, dien, trien, $[EDTA]^{4-}$, $(acac)^{-1}$, $(gly_4)^{1-}$

28. The number of σ-donor and π-acceptor species from the following are
RNC, phen, AsR_3, NCO^-, NCS^-, C_6H_6, $RC\equiv CR$

29. The number of ring formed in the complex $[Ni(DMG)_2]$ is

30. The effective atomic number (EAN) of the central metal in the complex $[Cr(NH_3)_4(Cl_2)]^+$ is ....

31. Sum of the ON and co-ordination in Prussian blue complex is ....

32. In the ferrocene molecule $[Fe(\eta^5-C_5H_5)_2]$, the total number of electrons donated to the central atom by the two cyclopentadienyl (C_5H_5) ligands is ....

33. In the complex $Cr(CO)_x^{2+}$, the value of x is ....

Elemental Practice 9.1 | Chapter 09

Connect with **Answers**

1. (d)	2. (d)	3. (c)	4. (b)	5. (b)	6. (c)
7. (a)	8. (d)	9. (d)	10. (d)	11. (b)	12. (d)
13. (b)	14. (c)	15. (d)	16. (b)	17. (d)	18. (b)
19. (d)	20. (c)	21. (a,b,c,d)	22. (a,b,c,d)	23. (a,b,c,d)	24. (a,b)
25. (b,d)	26. (a,b,c)	27. (7)	28. (3)	29. (4)	30. (33)
31. (8)	32. (12)	33. (6)			

Element 2 Isomerism in Coordination Compounds

The compounds having same molecular formula but different physical and chemical properties on account of different structures are called isomers and the phenomenon is called as isomerism.

Classification

- Structural isomerism
  - Ionisation
  - Hydrate
  - Polymerisation
  - Coordination
  - Linkage
  - Coordination position
- Stereo isomerism
  - Geometrical
  - Optical

Structural Isomerism

These isomers differ in, how the atoms are joined together—that is, in the order in which the atoms are bonded to one another.

These are of the following types:

1. Ionisation Isomerism

- This type of isomerism arises due to exchange of groups or ions between the coordinating sphere and the ionisation sphere.
- It gives different ions in solution because only the ion from ionisation sphere is released in solution.

e.g. $[Co(NH_3)_5(SO_4)]Br$ red

pentaamminesulphatocobalt (III) bromide

- SO_4^{2-} inside coordination sphere and Br^- outside it

thus, gives yellow ppt. with Ag^+ ionisation being as

$$[(Co(NH_3)_5(SO_4)]Br \rightleftharpoons [Co(NH_3)_5SO_4]^+ + Br^-$$

$[Co(NH_3)_5Br]SO_4$ violet

pentaamminebromidocobalt (III) sulphate

- Br^- inside coordination sphere and SO_4^{2-} outside it thus,
- gives white ppt. with Ba^{2+} ionisation being as

$$[Co(NH_3)_5Br]SO_4 \rightleftharpoons [Co(NH_3)_5Br]^{2+} + SO_4^{2-}$$

Other examples are:

$[Pt(NH_3)_4Cl_2]Br_2$ and $[Pt(NH_3)_4(Br_2)]Cl_2$

$[Co(NH_3)_5NO_2]SO_4$ and $[Co(NH_3)_5SO_4]NO_2$

$[Cr(NH_3)_5SO_4]Br$ and $[Cr(NH_3)_5Br]SO_4$

2. Coordination Isomerism

When both the positive and negative ions are complex ions, isomerism may be caused by the interchange of ligands between the anion and cation.

This arises only if cationic and anionic metals have same C.N. and charge. Examples are

(i) $[Co(NH_3)_6]^{3+}$ $[Cr(CN)_6]^{3-}$

Hexaamminecobalt(III) hexacyanidochromate(III)

$[Cr(NH_3)_6]^{3+}$ $[Co(CN)_6]^{3-}$

Hexamminechromium(III) hexacyanocobaltate(III)

(ii) $[Co(en)_3][Cr(CN)_6]$

$[Cr(en)_3][Co(CN)_6]$

(iii) $[Pt(NH_3)_4Cl_2][PtCl_4]$

$[Pt(NH_3)_4][PtCl_6]$

3. Position Isomerism

In polynuclear complexes an interchange of ligands between the different metal nuclei gives rise to position isomerism.

Example are

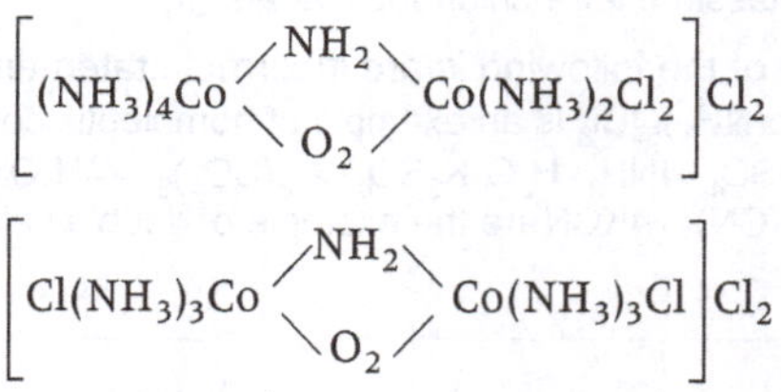

4. Hydrate (Solvate) Isomerism

This type of isomerism arises where water is involved as solvent.

Hydrate isomers are isomers of a complex that differ in the placement of water molecules in the complex.

$CrCl_3 \cdot 6H_2O$ have following hydrate isomers:

$[Cr(H_2O)_6]Cl_3$ — violet (anhydrous)

$[Cr(H_2O)_5Cl]Cl_2 \cdot H_2O$ — light green (monohydrate)

$[Cr(H_2O)_4Cl_2]Cl \cdot 2H_2O$ — dark green (dihydrate)

5. Polymerisation Isomerism

This term is used to describe compounds having same empirical formula but different molecular compositions. The difference from normal polymerisation is that here we have differences in arrangements of group as multiplication of molecular weight. Thus, value of n in the empirical formula $[ML_m]_n$ varies.

$[Pt(NH_3)_2Cl_2]_n$ gives

(A) $[Pt(NH_3)_2Cl_2]$ if $n = 1$ and (B) $[Pt(NH_3)_4]$ $[PtCl_4]$ if $n = 2$ and thus (A) and (B) are polymerisation isomers,

$[Co(NH_3)_3(NO_2)_3]_n$ gives following isomers

Formula	Molecular weight
$[Co(NH_3)_6][Co(NO_2)_6]$	Double ($n = 2$)
$[Co(NH_3)_4(NO_2)_2][Co(NH_3)_2(NO_2)_4]$	Double ($n = 2$)
$[Co(NH_3)_5(NO_2)][Co(NH_3)_2(NO_2)_4]_2$	Triple ($n = 3$)
$[Co(NH_3)_6][Co(NH_3)_2(NO_2)_4]_3$	Quadruple ($n = 4$)
$[Co(NH_3)_4(NO_2)_2]_3[Co(NO_2)_6]$	Quadruple ($n = 4$)
$[Co(NH_3)_5(NO_2)]_3[Co(NO_2)_6]_2$	Quintuple ($n = 5$)

6. Linkage Isomerism

This type of isomerism arises when the ligand may attach to the central metal ion of a complex in different ways. (Such ligands are called **ambidentate ligands**), e.g. Nitrite ion has electron pairs available for coordination both on N and O atoms. Similarly SCN can bind to metal through N and S.

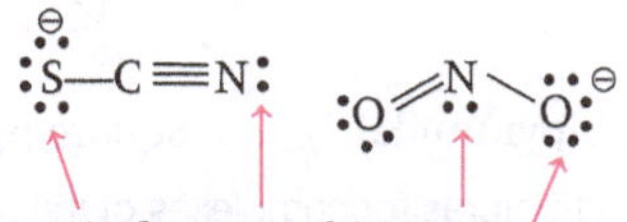

Bind to metal ion using either of these lone pair of electrons

e.g.

(i) $[Co(NH_3)_5ONO]Cl_2$ Pentaamminenitritoocobalt(III) chloride (red), decomposes in acids and $[Co(NH_3)_5NO_2]Cl_2$ Pentaamminenitrito-N-cobalt(III) chloride (yellow), stable in acids

(ii) $[Mn(CO)_5(SCN)]^+$ Pentacarbonylthiocyanato–S–manganese(II) ion and $[Mn(CO)_5(NCS)]^+$ Pentacarbonylthiocyanato–N-manganese(II) ion

This type of isomerism also occurs with other ligands such as SCN^-, OCN^-, $S_2O_3^{2-}$, CN^-, NOS^-, NO and $C_2O_2S_2^{2-}$ (dithiooxalate ion).

JEE MAPPER

Example Similar to PYQ Asked in JEE Main 2024

Match List-I with List-II.

List-I (Complex)		List-II (Type of isomerism)	
A.	$[Co(NO_2)(NH_3)_5]Cl_2$	1.	Linkage isomerism.
B.	$[Cr(NH_3)_6]$ $[Co(CN)_6]$	2.	Ionisation isomerism
C.	$[PtCl_2(en)_2]$ Br_2	3.	Solvate isomerism
D.	$[Fe(H_2O)_5]Cl_3$	4.	Coordination isomerism

Choose the correct answer from the options given below.

	A	B	C	D		A	B	C	D
(a)	2	4	3	1	(b)	1	4	2	3
(c)	3	1	4	2	(d)	2	4	1	3

Sol. (*b*) The correct match is A-1, B-4, C-2, D-3.

A. $[Co(NH_3)_5(NO_2)]Cl_2$ is an example of linkage isomerism, it arises in a compound containing ambidentate ligand (here it is NO_2).

B. $[Cr(NH_3)_6]$ $[Co(CN)_6]$ is an example of coordination isomerism. it arises from interchange of ligands between cationic and anionic entities of different metal ions present in a complex.

C. $[PtCl_2(en)_2]Br_2$ is an example of ionisation isomerism. This form of isomerism arises when the counter ion in a complex salt is itself a potential ligand and can displace a ligand which can become counter ion and here, they are Br and Cl.

D. $[Fe(H_2O)_5]Cl_3$ is an example of hydrate (solvate) isomerism, in this isomerism water is involved as a solvent.

Competency Enhancer 2.1

Match List-I with List-II.

List-I (Complex)		List-II (Type of isomerism)	
A.	$[Cr(SCN)(NH_3)_5]Br$	1.	Coordination isomerism
B.	$[Cu(NH_3)_4]$ $[PdCl_4]$	2.	Ionisation isomerism
C.	$[CoCl(NH_3)_5]SO_4$	3.	Solvate isomerism
D.	$[Co(ox)_2(H_2O)Cl]Cl_2$	4.	Linkage isomerism

Choose the correct answer from the options given below.

	A	B	C	D		A	B	C	D
(a)	2	4	1	3	(b)	2	1	4	3
(c)	4	1	2	3	(d)	3	1	2	4

Stereoisomers

These are the isomers in which the atoms are bonded to each other in the same order but that differ in the precise arrangement of these atoms in space. These are of the following types:

1. Geometrical Isomerism

- This type of isomerisms arises due to ligands occupying different positions around the central ion.
- The ligands occupy positions either adjacent to one another or opposite to one another. These are referred to as *cis* form and *trans* form respectively.

Geometrical Isomerism of Metals with C.N. of 4

The complexes with coordination number four (e.g. Ma_4) can have two possible geometries i.e. tetrahedral or square planar.

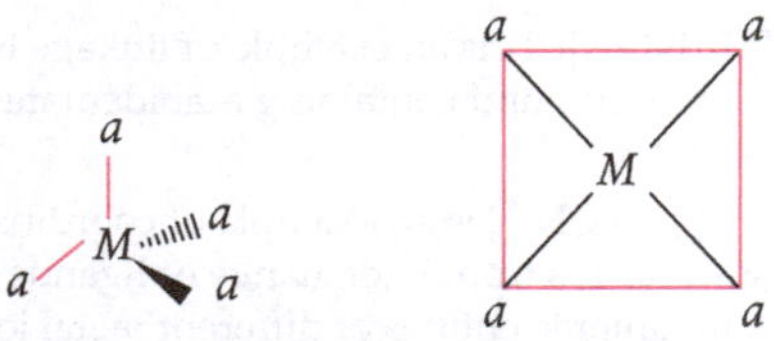

Tetrahedral Square planar

Possible structures for complexes with coordination number four.

- **For Tetrahedral Geometry** No geometrical isomerism is observed in tetrahedral geometry.
- **For Square Planar Geometry** For square planar complexes Ma_4, Ma_3b or Mab_3, $M(aa)_2$ where *a* and *b* etc., are monodenate ligands, geometrical isomerism is not possible. However, square planar complexes of the type Ma_2b_2, Ma_2bc, *Mabcd* gives geometrical isomers.

These type of arrangements are discussed below

(i) Complexes with general formula, Ma_2b_2 (where both *a* and *b* are monodentate) can have *cis*-and *trans*-isomers.

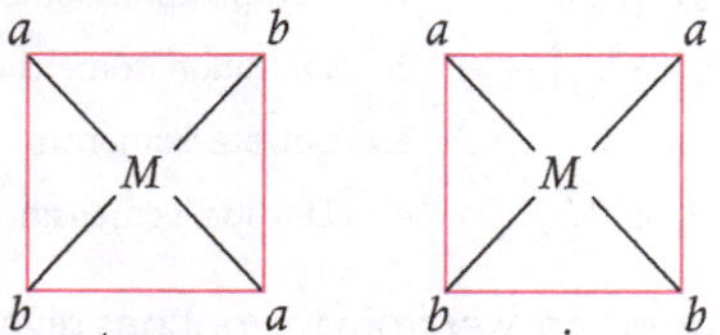

trans *cis*

e.g. : $Pt(NH_3)_2Cl_2$

(ii) Complexes with general formula Ma_2bc can have *cis*-and *trans*-isomers.

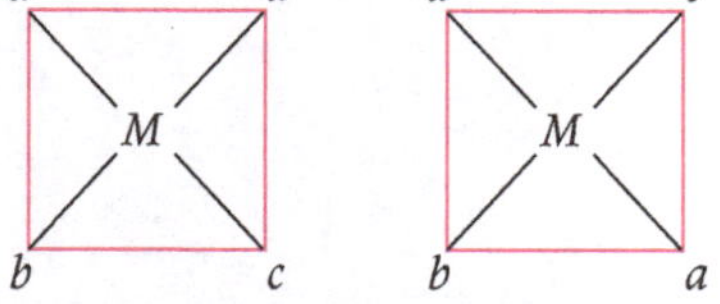

cis *trans*

$[Ma_2bc]$

e.g. : $[Pt(NH_3)_2ClNO_2]$

(iii) Complexes with general formula, *Mabcd*, can have three isomers.

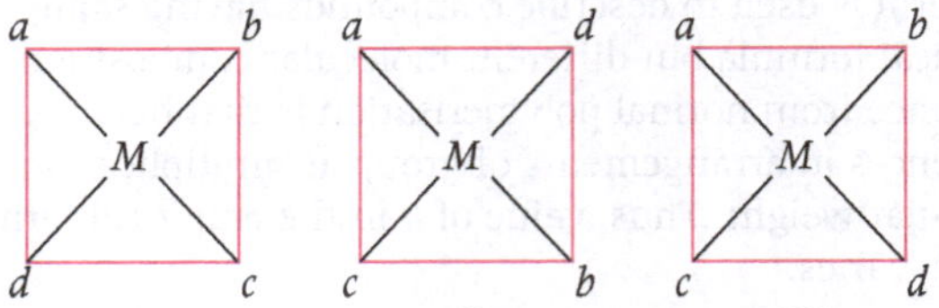

(i) (ii) (iii)

e.g. : $[Pt(py)(NH_3)ClBr]$

(iv) For complex with the type $[M(AB)_2]$, two geometrical isomers are possible

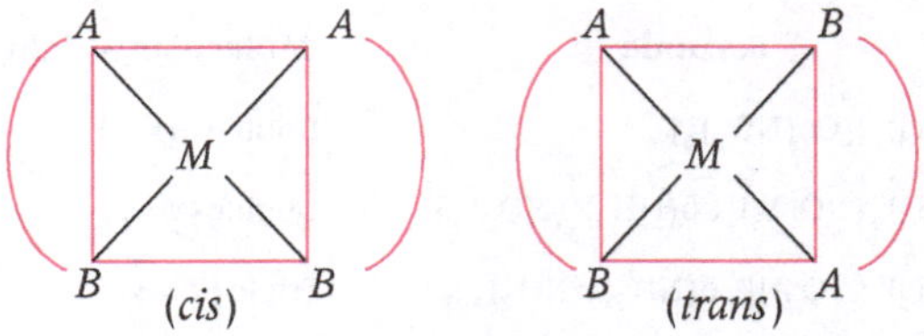

(*cis*) (*trans*)

e.g. : $[Pt(gly)_2]$

For Coordination Number 5

(i) The formula Ma_5 can exist in two possible geometries, i.e. trigonal bipyramidal and square pyramidal. These two are also called allogon isomers

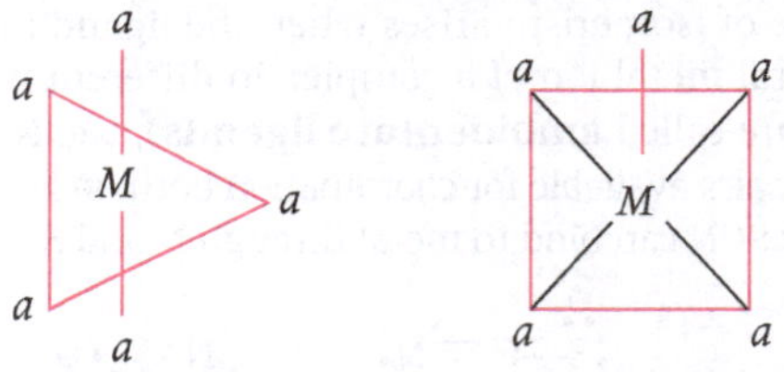

Trigonal bipyramidal Square pyramidal

Possible structures for complexes of the type Ma_5.

(ii) The formula Ma_2b_3 can exist in six possible geometries as shown in Figure

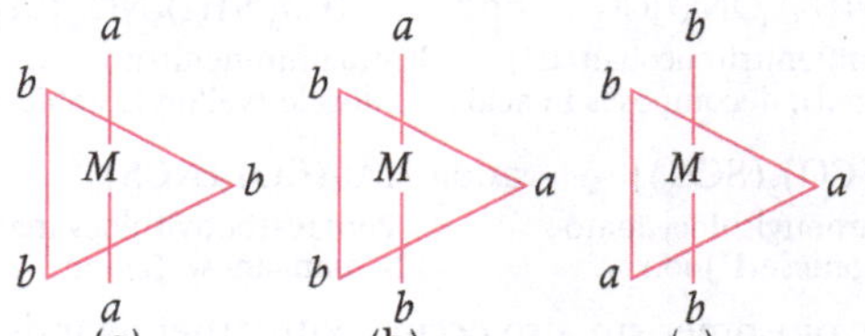

(a) (b) (c)

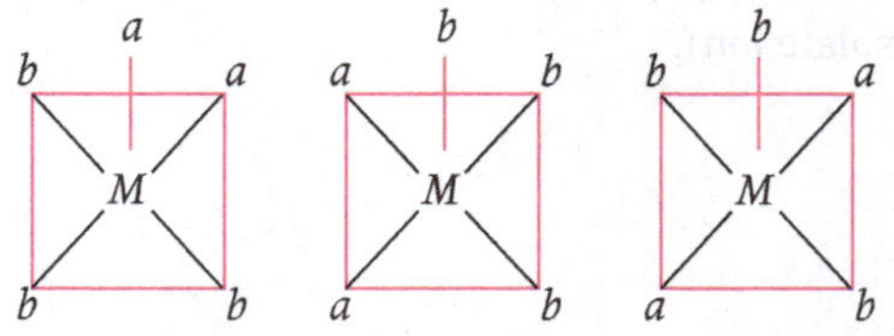

(d) (e) (f)

Here (a), (b), (c) are geometrical isomers.

Geometrical Isomerism of Metals with C.N. of 6

The complexes with coordination number 6 can exist in octahedral geometry. The following cases may arise in complexes with octahedral geometry.

(i) **All Ligands are Monodentate** The various structures possible are listed below. Here M is the metal ion and a,b,c,d,e and f represent monodentate ligands.

Formula	Possible number of geometrical isomers
Ma_6	0
Ma_5b	0
Ma_4b_2	2
Ma_4bc	2
Ma_3b_3	2 (*fac*- and *mer*-)
Ma_3b_2c	3
Ma_3bcd	4
$Ma_2b_2c_2$	5
Ma_2b_2cd	6
Ma_2bcde	9
$Mabcdef$	15

Concept Visualizer

Different geometrical isomers of $MA_2B_2C_2$ can be visualised as

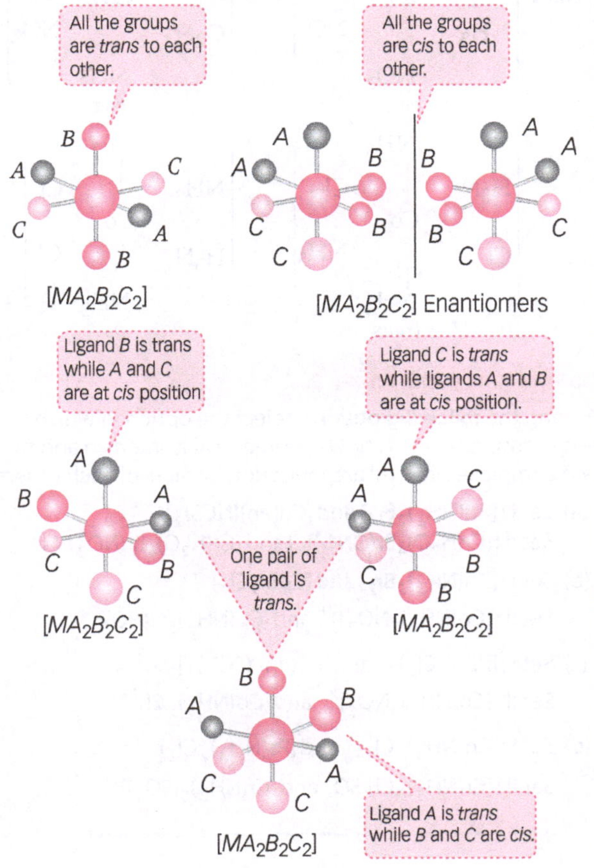

(ii) **When Ligands are Bidentate Symmetrical and Monodentate Type** Structures possible are listed below. Here M is the metal ion, AA is a bidentate symmetrical ligand and a, b, c and d represent monodentate ligands.

Formula	Possible number of geometrical isomers
$[M(AA)_3]$	0
$[M(AA)_2a_2]$	2
$[M(AA)_2ab]$	2
$[M(AA)a_4]$	0
$[M(AA)a_3b]$	2
$[M(AA)a_2b_2]$	3
$[M(AA)a_2bc]$	4
$[M(AA)abcd]$	6

(iii) **When Ligands are Bidentate Unsymmetrical and Monodentate Type** The various possible structures are listed below. Here M is the metal ion, AB is a bidentate unsymmetrical ligand and a, b, c and d represent monodentate ligands.

Formula	Possible number of geometrical isomers
$[M(AB)_3]$	2
$[M(AB)_2a_2]$	5
$[M(AB)_2ab]$	6
$[M(AB)a_4]$	0
$[M(AB)a_3b]$	3
$[M(AB)a_2b_2]$	4
$[M(AB)a_2bc]$	7
$[M(AB)abcd]$	12

Some examples of few kind are illustrated as follows:

(i) **For $[Ma_2b_2c_2]$** The various structures possible are shown in Figures

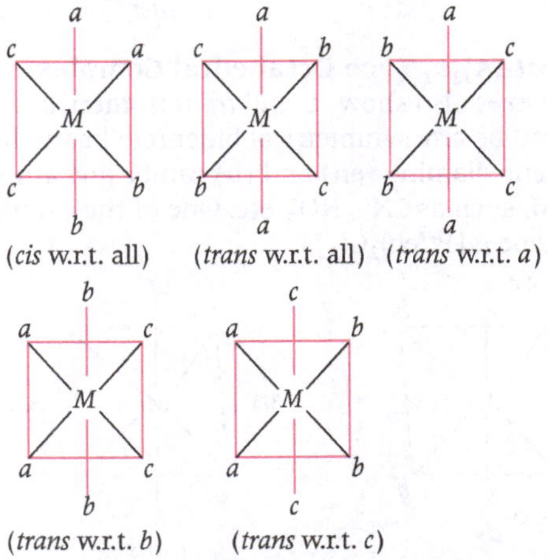

One of the example of this type is $[Pt(py)_2(NH_3)_2Cl_2]^{2+}$.

(ii) **For [$M(AA)a_2bc$]** The various structures possible are shown in Figures.

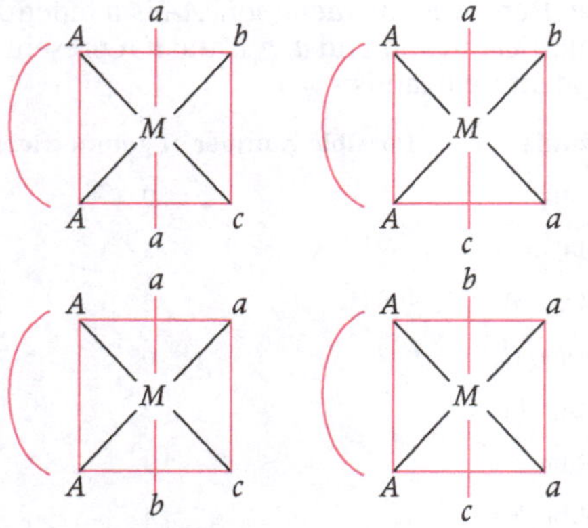

One of the example of this type is $[Cr(NH_3)_2Cl_2(en)]^+$.

(iii) **For [$M(AB)a_2b_2$]** The various structures possible are shown in figure.

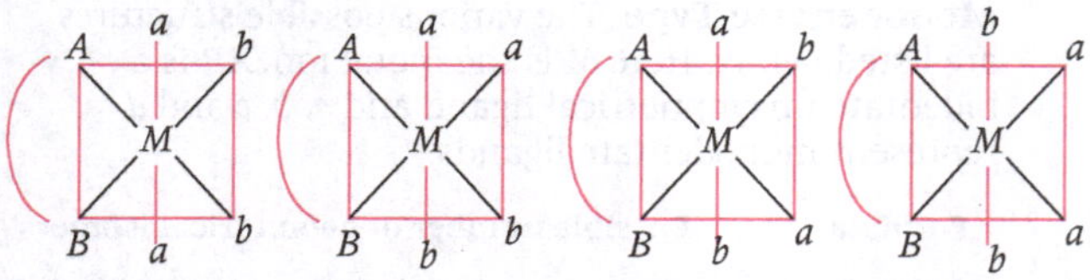

(iv) **For Ma_3b_3** Another type of geometrical isomerism occurs in octahedral coordination entities of the type $[Ma_3b_3]$ like $[Co(NO_2)_3(NH_3)_3]$. If each trio of donor atoms occupy adjacent positions at the corners of an octahedral face, it is called facial (*fac*) isomer. When the positions are around the meridian of the octahedron the isomer is called meridional (*mer*) isomer.

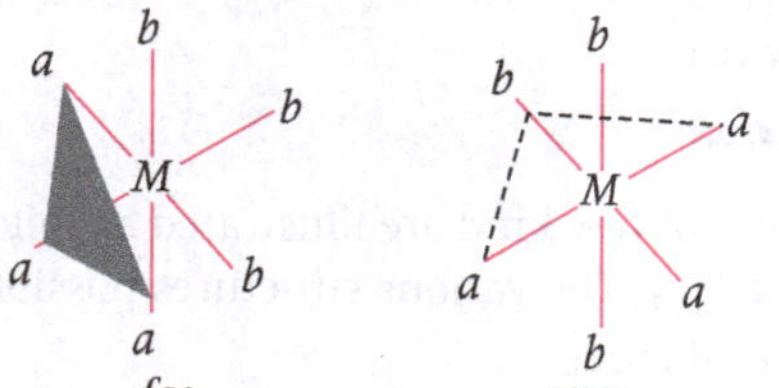

fac *mer*

(v) **For $M(AA)_2b_2$ Type Octahedral Complexes** These complexes also show *cis* and *trans* isomerism where, *A-A* can be any symmetrical bidentate ligand like ethylene diamine (en) and (b) can be any anionic ligand, such as CN^-, NO_2^- etc. One of the example of this type is $[Pt(en)_2Cl_2]$.

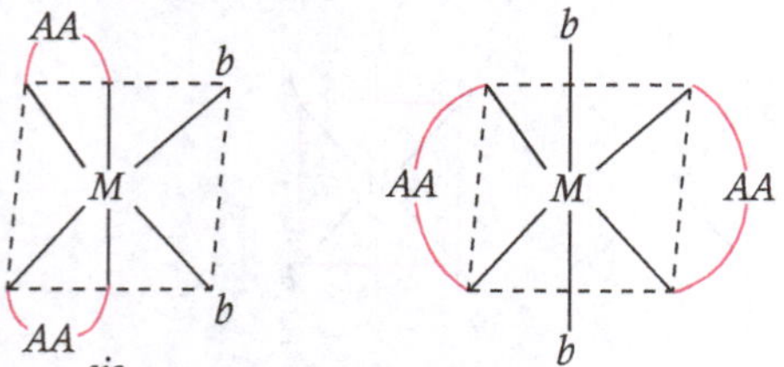

cis *trans*

JEE MAPPER

Example Similar to PYQ Asked in JEE Advanced 2024

Among the following options, select the option in which each complex in set-I shows geometrical isomerism and the complexes in set-II are ionisation isomers of each other.

(a) Set I : $[Co(NH_3)_3(NO_2)_3]$ and $[Co(NH_3)_4Cl_2]^+$
Set II : $[Cr(H_2O)_4Cl(NO_2)]Cl$ and $[Cr(H_2O)_4Cl_2](NO_2)$

(b) Set I : $[Ni(CO)_4]$ and $[PdBr_2(PPh_3)_2]$
Set II : $[Co(NH_3)_5Br]SO_4$ and $[Co(NH_3)_5(SO_4)]Br$

(c) Set I : $[Cr(en)(NH_3)_2Br_2]$ and $[Co\ Br_2(PPh_3)_2]$
Set II : $[Co(NH_3)_6][Cr(CN)_6]$ and $[Cr(NH_3)_6][Co(CN)_6]$

(d) Set I : $[Co(NH_3)_5Br]Br_2$ and $[Cr(en)(NH_3)_2Br_2]$
Set II : $[Co(H_2O)_6]Br_3$ and $[Co(H_2O)_5Br]Br_2 \cdot H_2O$

Sol. (*a*) Geometrical isomerism arises in heteroleptic complexes due to different possible geometric arrangements of the ligands. While ionisation isomerism arises when the counter ion in a complex salt is itself a potential ligand and can displace a ligand which then becomes the counter ion.

The complexes given in option (a) shows geometrical (Set I) and ionisation isomerism (Set II) respectively.

Set I

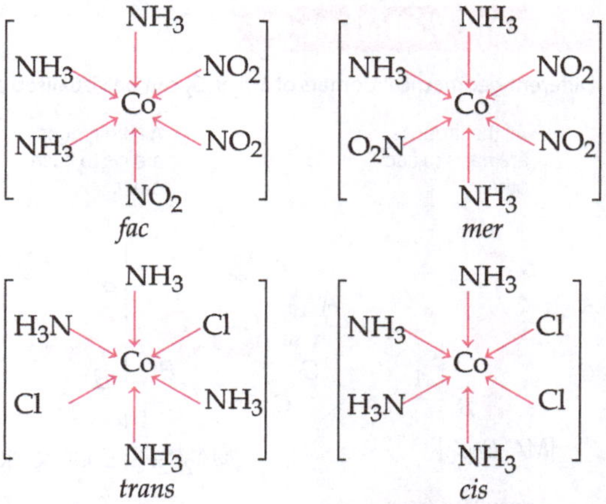

Competency Enhancer 2.2

Among the following options, select the option in which each complex in set-I shows geometrical isomerism and the two complexes in set-II are ionisation isomers of each others.

(a) Set I : $[Pd(NH_3)_2Br_4]$ and $[Co(en)(NCS)_2]$
Set II : $[Cr(H_2O)_4Br(ONO)]Cl$ and $[Cr(H_2O)_4Br(NO_2)]Cl$

(b) Set I : $[Zn(NH_3)_2Br_2]$ and $[CoBr_2Cl_2]^{2+}$
Set II : $[Co(NH_3)_5NO_2]^{2+}$ and $[Co(NH_3)_5(ONO)]^{2+}$

(c) Set I : $[Pt\ Br_2Cl_2]^{2-}$ and $[Pt\ (en)\ (SCN)_2]$
Set II : $[Co(NH_3)_5NO_2]^{2+}$ and $[Co(NH_3)_5\ Cl]^{2+}$

(d) Set I : $[Co(NH_3)_4Cl_2]^+$ and $[Pt(NH_3)_2Cl_2]$
Set II : $[Cr(NH_3)_5Cl]\ SO_4$ and $[Cr(NH_3)_5(SO_4)]Cl$

Optical Isomerism

When the coordination compounds have same formula but differ in their ability to rotate directions of the plane of polarised light are said to exhibit optical isomerism and the molecules are optical isomers. The optical isomers are pair of molecules which are non-superimposable mirror images of each other.

The molecules or ions that cannot be superimposed are called **chiral**.

The optically active complex which rotates plane polarised light to right is dextrorotatory (*d* or +) and which rotates to left is laevorotatory (*l* or −). These '*d*' and '*l*' isomers of a complex are called **enantiomers**.

Optical Isomerism in Octahedral Complex

Optical isomerism is very common in octahedral complexes.

(i) $[Ma_2b_2c_2]^{n+}$: e.g. $[Pt(py)_2(NH_3)_2Cl_2]^{2+}$

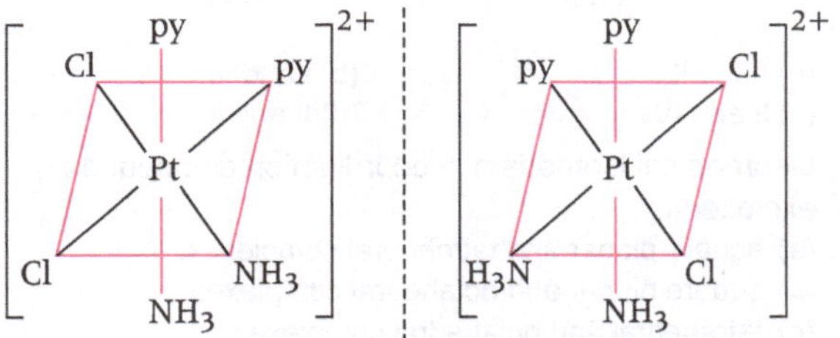

cis-d-isomer Mirror *cis-l*-isomer

(ii) [*Mabcdef*] : e.g. $[Pt(py)NH_3NO_2ClBrI]$

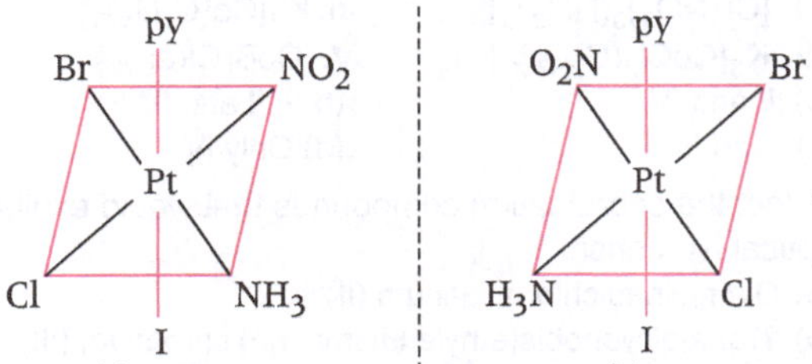

d-isomer Mirror *l*-isomer

(iii) $[M[AA)_3]^{n+}$: e.g. $[Co(en)_3]^{3+}$

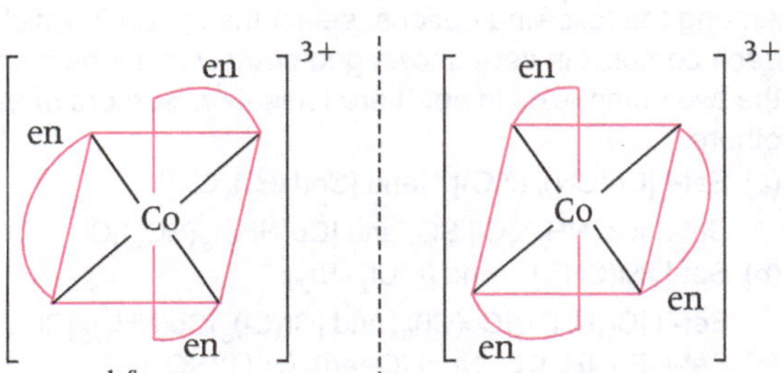

d-form Mirror *l*-form

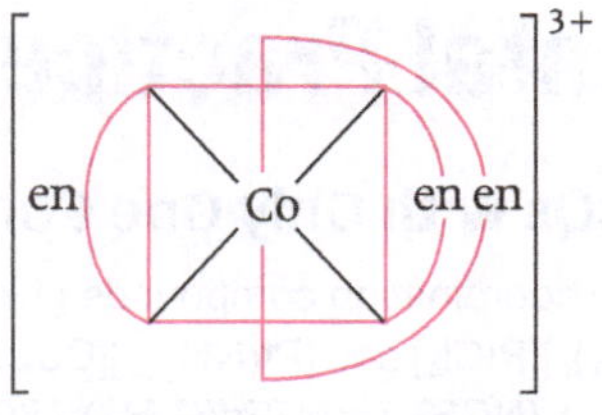

'*meso*' or optical inactive form

(iv) $[M[AA)_2a_2]^{n\pm}$ $[Co(en)_2Cl_2]^+$

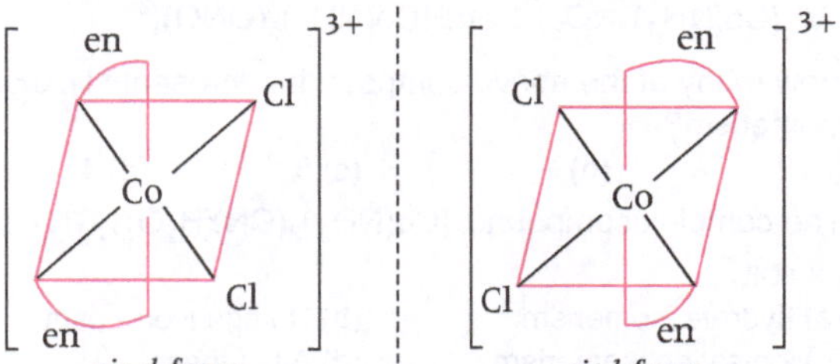

cis-d-form Mirror *cis-l*-form

trans form $[M(AA)_2a_2]^{n\pm}$ does not show optical isomerism.

(v) $[M(AA)_2ab]^{n\pm}$: e.g. $(Co(en)_2NH_3Cl]^{2+}$

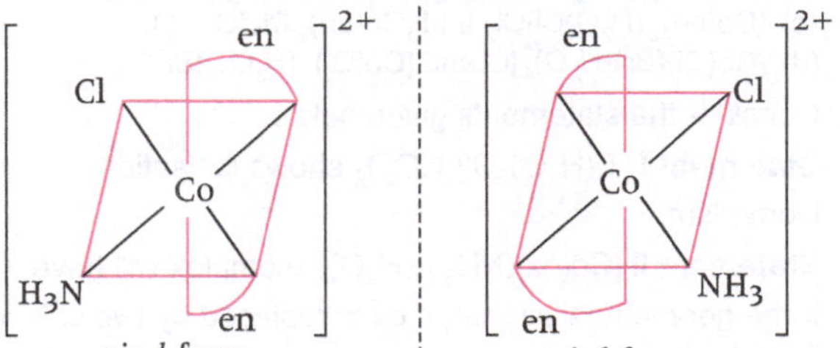

cis-d-form Mirror *cis-l*-form

(vi) $[M(AB)_3]$: e.g. $[Cr(gly)_3]$

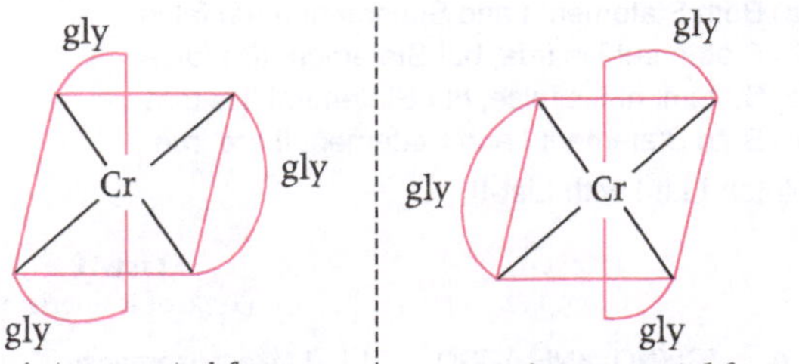

cis (or *trans*)-*d*-form Mirror *cis* (or *trans*)-*l*-form

Some more example are :

$[Cr(ox)_3]^{3-}$; $[Fe(dipy)_3]^{2+}$; $[Cr(ox)_2(H_2O)_2]^-$; $[Pt(en)_3]^{4+}$

JEE Alert

- Optical isomerism is not possible in square planar complexes except by using chiral ligand or a specially chosen bidentate ligand on account of the presence of axis of symmetry.
- Only *M* (*ABCD*) type of tetrahedral complex gives optical isomerism.

Elemental Practice 9.2

Type I » MCQs with Only One Correct Option

1. Consider the coordination compounds given below.
   I. $[Cu(NH_3)_4][PtCl_4]$ and $[Pt(NH_3)_4][CuCl_4]$
   II. $[Pd(C_6H_5)_2(NCS)_2]$ and $[Pd(C_6H_5)_2(SCN)_2]$
   III. $[Co(NH_3)_5NO_3]SO_4$ and $[Co(NH_3)_5SO_4]NO_3$
   IV. $[PtCl_2(NH_3)_4]Br$ and $[PtBr_2(NH_3)_4]Cl$
   V. $[Co(NH_3)_5NO_2]^{2+}$ and $[Co(NH_3)_5(ONO)]^{2+}$

   How many of the above compounds represents linkage isomerism?
   (a) 2 (b) 1 (c) 5 (d) 4

2. The complex compound, $[Co(NH_3)_3(CN)(H_2O)_2]Cl_2$ can exhibit
   (a) hydrate isomerism (b) linkage isomerism
   (c) ionisation isomerism (d) All of these

3. Which of the following pairs of complex compounds does not represent hydrate isomers?
   (a) $[Mn(py)(H_2O)_3Cl_2]Cl_2$ and $[Mn(py)(H_2O)_2Cl_3]Cl\cdot H_2O$
   (b) $[Co(NH_3)_5(H_2O)](NO_3)_2$ and $[Co(NH_3)_5(NO_3)](NO_3)\cdot H_2O$
   (c) $[Co(en)_2(H_2O)Cl]Cl_2$ and $[Co(en)_2Cl_2]Cl\cdot H_2O$
   (d) $[Co(Cl)(Br)(H_2O)_4]Cl$ and $[Co(Cl)_2(H_2O)_4]Br$

4. Consider the statements given below.
   Statement I $[Ti(H_2O)_5Cl](NO_3)_2$ shows ionisation isomerism.
   Statement II $[Co(ox)(NH_3)_3(H_2O)]^+$ complex will have three geometrical isomer, if ox is replaced by two chloride ligand.
   In the light of the above statements, choose the correct answer from the options given below.
   (a) Both Statement I and Statement II are false.
   (b) Statement I is true, but Statement II is false.
   (c) Statement I is false, but Statement II is true.
   (d) Both Statement I and Statement II are true.

5. Match List-I with List-II.

List-I (Complex)		List-II (Type of isomerism)	
A.	$[Co(NO_2)(NH_3)_5]SO_4$	1.	Linkage isomerism
B.	$[Fe(NO_2)(NH_3)_5]Br_2$	2.	Ionisation isomerism
C.	$[CoCl(en)_2(H_2O)]Cl_2$	3.	Optical isomerism
D.	*cis*$[CrBr_2(en)_2]^{3-}$	4.	Hydrate isomerism

   Choose the correct answer from the options given below.
   (a) A-1, B-2, C-4, D-3 (b) A-2, B-1, C-3, D-4
   (c) A-4, B-1, C-2, D-3 (d) A-1, B-4, C-2, D-3

6. Choose the incorrect statement about the complex ion $[CrCl_2(en)_2]^+$.
   (a) It has two geometrical isomers, i.e., *cis* and *trans*.
   (b) Both the -*cis* and -*trans* isomers shows optical activity.
   (c) Only the *cis* isomer shows optical activity.
   (d) Only the -*cis* isomer has non-superimposable mirror image

7. Which of the following are optical isomers?

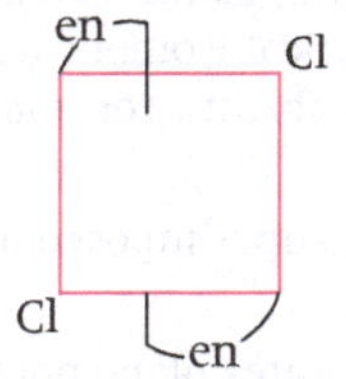

(I)

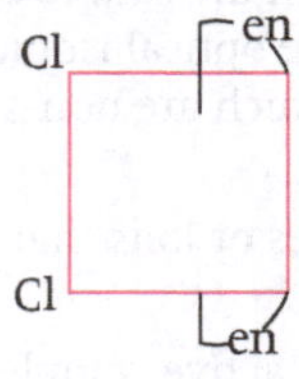

(II)

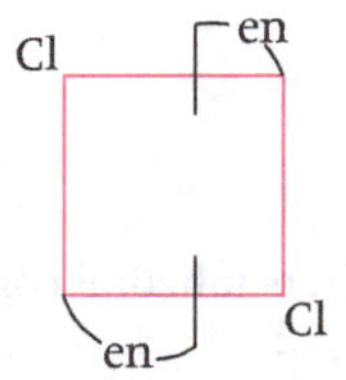

(III)

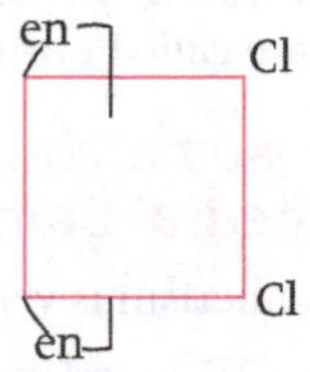

(IV)

   (a) I and II (b) I and III
   (c) II and IV (d) II and III

8. Geometrical isomerism in coordination compounds is exhibited by
   (a) square planar and tetrahedral complexes.
   (b) square planar and octahedral complexes.
   (c) tetrahedral and octahedral complexes.
   (d) square planar, tetrahedral and octahedral complexes.

9. Which of the following will have three stereoisomeric forms?
   I. $[Cr(NO_3)_3(NH_3)_3]$ II. $K_3[Co(C_2O_4)_3]$
   III. $K_3[CoCl_2(C_2O_4)_2]$ IV. $[CoBrCl(en)_2]$
   (a) III and IV (b) I, II and IV
   (c) I and III (d) Only IV

10. Select the coordination compounds that would exhibit optical isomerism.
   (a) Diamminedichloroplatinum (II)
   (b) *Trans*-dicyanobis(ethylendiammine) chromium (III) chloride
   (c) Tris-(ethylenediammine) cobalt (III) bromide
   (d) Pentaamminenitrocobalt (III) iodide.

11. Among the following options, select the option in which each complex in set-I shows geometrical isomerism and the two complexes in set-II are ionisation isomers of each others.
   (a) Set-I $[Co(CN)_5(NC)]^{3-}$ and $[Co(NH_3)_4Cl_2]^+$
   Set-II $[Co(NH_3)_5Cl]SO_4$ and $[Co(NH_3)_5(SO_4)]Cl$
   (b) Set-I $[Ni(CN)_4]^{2-}$ and $[NiCl_2\cdot Br_2]^{2-}$
   Set-II $[Cr(NH_3)_6[Co(Cl)_6]$ and $[Cr(Cl)_6[Co(NH_3)_5]Cl$
   (c) Set-I $[Pt(NH_3)_2Cl_4]$ and $[Cr(en)_2(H_2O)(SO_4)]^+$
   Set-II $[Pt(NH_3)_3(NO_3)]Br$ and $[Pt(NH_3)_3Br]NO_3$
   (d) Set-I $[Pt(en)(SCN)_2]$ and $[Zn(NH_3)_2Cl_2]$
   Set-II $[Co(H_2O)_4Cl(NO_2)]Cl$ and $[Co(H_2O)_4Cl(ONO)]Cl$

12. Which of the following will have only two stereoisomeric forms?

I. $[Cr(NO_3)_3(NH_3)_3]$ II. $K_3[Fe(C_2O_4)_3]$
III. $[CoCl_2(en)_2]^+$ IV. $[CoBrCl(ox)_2]^{3-}$

(a) I only (b) I and II (c) III and IV (d) II and IV

13. The complexes given below show

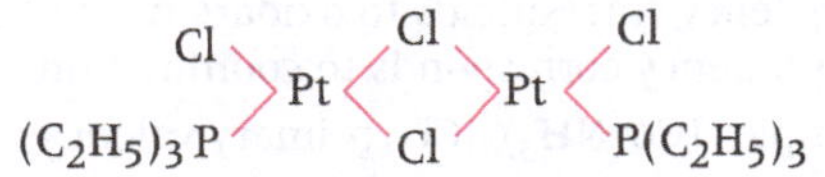

and

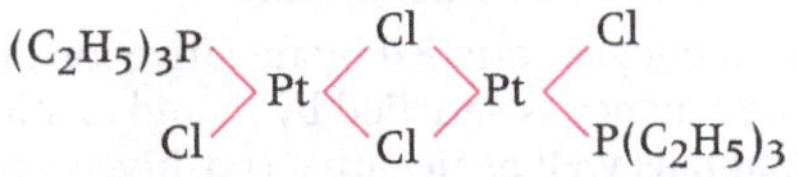

(a) optical isomerism (b) coordination isomerism
(c) geometrical isomerism (d) bridged isomerism

14. Which of the following give maximum number of isomers?

(a) $[Co(NH_3)_4Cl_2]$ (b) $[Ni(en)(NH_3)_4]^{2+}$
(c) $[Ni(Cl)(Br)(en)_2]$ (d) $[Cr(SCN)_2(NH_3)_4]^+$

15. The compounds that will exhibit optical isomerism are:

(i) $[Co(en)_3]^+$
(ii) $[CoCl_2(en)(NH_3)_2]^+$
(iii) *Bis* (benzoylacetonato) beryllium (II)
(iv) $[CoCl_3(NH_3)_3]$

Choose the correct answer from the options given below.

(a) (i), (iii) (b) (ii), (iv) and (i)
(c) (iv) and (iii) (d) (i), (ii) and (iii)

16. The coordination complex which shows two geometrical isomers and is also a non-ionisable complex is:

(a) $PtCl_4 \cdot 2NH_3$ (b) $PtCl_4 \cdot 3NH_3$
(c) $PtCl_4 \cdot 4NH_3$ (d) $PtCl_4 \cdot 5NH_3$

Type II 》 MCQs with One or More than One Correct Option

17. Choose the correct statement(s).

(a) $[Co(en)_3][Cr(CN)_6]$ will shows coordination isomerism.
(b) $[Mn(CO)_5(SCN)]$ will shows linkage isomerism.
(c) $[Co(H_2O)(NO_2)_5]SO_4$ will shows ionisation and linkage isomerism both.
(d) Tris-(ethylene diamine) cobalt (III) chloride shows optical isomerism.

18. Which of the following statements is/are incorrect?

(a) $[Pt(NO_3)_2(en)_2]^{2+}$ complex ion can show linkage isomerism .
(b) $[Cr(CO_3)(NH_3)_4]Br$ can show ionisation isomerism.
(c) $FeCl_2 \cdot 6H_2O$ can show hydrate isomerism.
(d) $[FeCl_3(NH_3)_3]$ can exhibit structural isomerism.

19. Choose the option containing correct statement(s)

(a) $[Co(NH_3)_5SO_4]Br$ will give a pale yellow colored precipitate with $AgNO_3$.
(b) The ionisation isomer of $[Co(NH_3)_5Br]SO_4$ will give a white precipitate with $AgNO_3$ solutions.
(c) The molar conductance of $[Co(NH_3)_5SO_4]Br$ is higher than that of its ionisation isomer.
(d) $[Co(NH_3)_5SO_4]Br$ will cause a lesser depression in the freezing point than its ionisation isomer.

20. Choose the correct statement about the isomerism in coordination compounds.

(a) $[CoCl_2(NH_3)_4]NO_2$ and $[Co(Cl)(NO_2)(NH_3)_4]Cl$ shows ionisation isomerism
(b) $[Co(NH_3)_6][Cr(CN)_6]$ and $[Cr(NH_3)_6][Co(CN)_6]$ shwos coordination isomerism.
(c) $[CrCl(H_2O)_5]Cl_2 \cdot H_2O$ and $[CrCl_2(H_2O)_4]Cl \cdot 2H_2O$ shows hydrate isomerism.
(d) $[Co(NO_2)(NH_3)_5]Cl_2$ and $[Co(ONO)(NH_3)_5]Cl_2$ shows ionisation isomerism.

21. Which one of the following complexes will not have four different isomers?

(a) $[Co(en)_2Cl_2]Cl$ (b) $[Co(en)(NH_3)_2Cl_2]Cl$
(c) $[Co(PPh_3)_2(NH_3)Cl_2]Cl$ (d) $[Co(en)_3]Cl_3$

22. Select the compound that can shows coordination isomerism.

(a) $[Cu(NH_3)_4][PtCl_4]$
(b) $[Fe(NH_3)_6]_2[Pt(CN)_6]_3$
(c) $[Co(NH_3)_6][Cr(C_2O_4)_3]$
(d) $[Pt(en)_3](SO_4)_2$

Type III 》 Numerical/Integer Answer Type Questions

23. The total number of different ionisation isomers of the complex compound, $[Mn(H_2O)_3(NH_3)(CN)(Br)]Cl_2$ is ....

24. The total number of structural isomers of $[Mn(CN)_2(NO_2)_2(en)]$ are ....

25. The number of geometrical isomers of $[Co(NH_3)_3(NO_3)_3]$ are ....

26. The octahedral complex $[Rh(NO_2)(SCN)(en)_2]^+$ can exist in a total number of isomeric forms including stereoisomers.

27. The mononuclear complex salt having the molecular composition $[Co(en)_2(SCN)(NO_2)]Br$ can exist in a number of isomeric forms. The total number of possible isomers of all type is ....

28. The total number of structural isomers for the molecular formula. $[Cr(SCN)_2(H_2O)_2(NO_2)_2]Cl_2$ will be ....

1. (a)	2. (d)	3. (d)	4. (d)	5. (a)	6. (b)
7. (c)	8. (b)	9. (a)	10. (c)	11. (c)	12. (b)
13. (c)	14. (d)	15. (d)	16. (a)	17. (a,b,c)	18. (a,b,d)
19. (a,b,d)	20. (a,b,c)	21. (a,c,d)	22. (a,c)	23. (3)	24. (6)
25. (2)	26. (12)	27. (9)	28. (7)		

Elemental Practice 9.2 | Chapter 09

Connect with **Answers**

Element 3 Bonding in Coordination Compounds

Several theories have been proposed to explain the bonding pattern in coordination compounds. These theories are discussed below

Werner Theory of Coordination Compounds

- Beginning of the coordination chemistry is not based on the first formation of $CoCl_3 \cdot 6NH_3$ by Tassaqert but is actually based on the outstanding work of the Alsatian-Swiss chemist, Alfred Werner in 1892.
- Werner prepared and isolated many different coordination compounds from $CoCl_3$ and NH_3 like,

(a)	$CoCl_3 \cdot 6NH_3$	$[Co(NH_3)_6]Cl_3$	orange-yellow
(b)	$CoCl_3 \cdot 5NH_3$	$[Co(NH_3)_5Cl]Cl_2$	violet (purple)
(c)	$CoCl_3 \cdot 4NH_3$	$[Co(NH_3)_4Cl_2]Cl$	violet
(d)	$CoCl_3 \cdot 3NH_3$	$[Co(NH_3)_3Cl_3]$	green

Treatment of these compounds with aqueous hydrochloric acid did not remove the ammonia, which suggested that the ammonia was somehow closely bound with the cobalt ions. Treatment with aqueous silver nitrate at 273 K, however gave interesting results. One mole each of the complexes (a), (b) and (c) gave respectively three, two and one mole of white precipitates of AgCl, with excess of $AgNO_3$. Complex (d) did not give the precipitate at all.

Postulates

- There are two types of valencies shown by central metal/metal ion in a compound :
  (i) primary (ii) secondary

Primary valency corresponds to oxidation number and secondary valency corresponds to coordination number.

- In the complex $[Co(NH_3)_6]Cl_3$, primary valency of Co is **three** and secondary valency **six.**
- Primary valency is satisfied by negative ions (anions) while secondary valency is satisfied by ligands which can be neutral, and as well as negative (positive in rare cases)
  e.g., In $[Co^{III}(NH_3)_6]Cl_3$, six NH_3 ligands satisfy secondary valencies while three Cl^- satisfy primary valencies.
  – In $[Co^{II}(NH_3)_4(H_2O)_2]SO_4$, four NH_3 and two H_2O (ligands) satisfy secondary and one SO_4^{2-} satisfies primary valencies.
- Ligands/ions attached by secondary valency do not ionise while ions attached by primary valency ionise.
  e.g., $K_4[Fe(CN)_6] \rightleftharpoons 4K^+ + [Fe(CN)_6]^{4-}$
  $[Pt(NH_3)_6]Cl_4 \rightleftharpoons [Pt(NH_3)_6]^{4+} + 4Cl^-$
- The secondary valencies are directional and are responsible for the isomerism in complexes.
- Primary valency in the complex is represented by ...... while secondary valency is by ______ .
- In all cases, metal or metal ion should satisfy primary and secondary valencies both. Some negative ions may satisfy primary as well as secondary valencies **(dual nature).** In those complexes, they are represented as ....

JEE Quicker

The primary and secondary valencies of cobalt in $[Co(NH_3)_5Cl]Cl_2$ are 3 and 6 respectively. *JEE Main 2023*

↘ Primary valency is equal to oxidation number of the metal atom. While secondary valency corresponds to the coordination number of Co(III).

Werner's Representation

Consider the case of $CoCl_3 \cdot xNH_3$; where, maximum value of x = C.N. of Co(III) = 6 and minimum value of x = C.N. – O.N. = 3

Various possible possible structures are summarised as

Werner's Coordination Compounds

	Werner complex	Modern notation	Ionisation	Secondary valency satisfied by	Primary valency satisfied by
(A)	$CoCl_3 \cdot 6NH_3$	$[Co(NH_3)_6]Cl_3$	$[Co(NH_3)_6]^{3+} + 3Cl^-$	six (NH_3)	three (Cl^-)
(B)	$CoCl_3 \cdot 5NH_3$	$[Co(NH_3)_5Cl]Cl_2$	$[Co(NH_3)_5Cl]^{2+} + 2Cl^-$	five (NH_3) and one (Cl^-)	three (Cl^-) including one (Cl^-) with **dual nature**
(C)	$CoCl_3 \cdot 4NH_3$	$[Co(NH_3)_4Cl_2]Cl$	$[Co(NH_3)_4Cl_2]^+ + Cl^-$	four (NH_3) and two (Cl^-)	three (Cl^-) including two (Cl^-) with **dual nature**
(D)	$CoCl_3 \cdot 3NH_3$	$[Co(NH_3)_3Cl_3]$	$[Co(NH_3)_3Cl_3]$ (single species)	three (NH_3) and three (Cl^-)	three (Cl^-) all with **dual nature**

- From the above table, it is clear that electrical conductance of the complexes which depends on the number of ions will be in order:

$$D < C < B < A$$

- They are represented as :

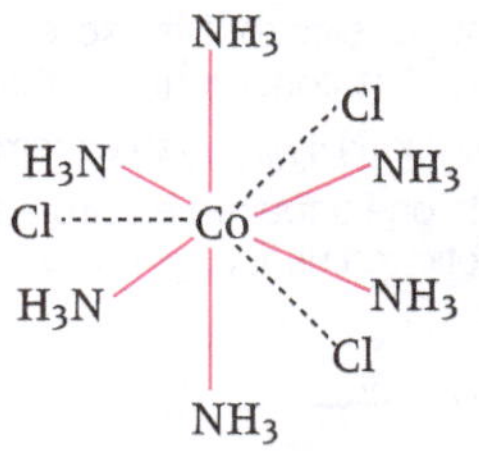

(A)

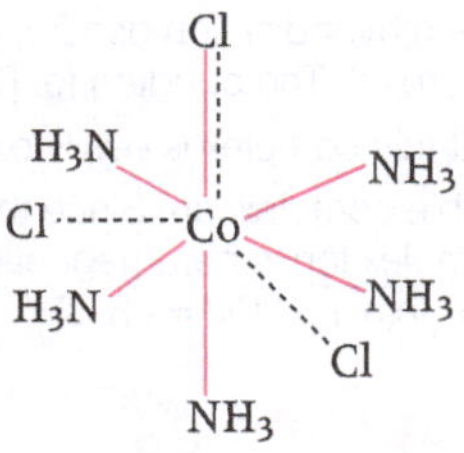

(B)

[only Cl^- ions joined by (........) will ionise].

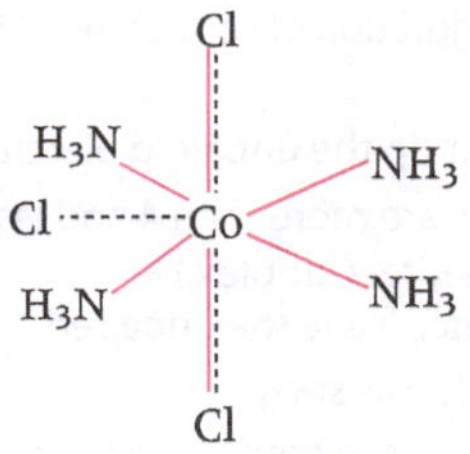

(C)

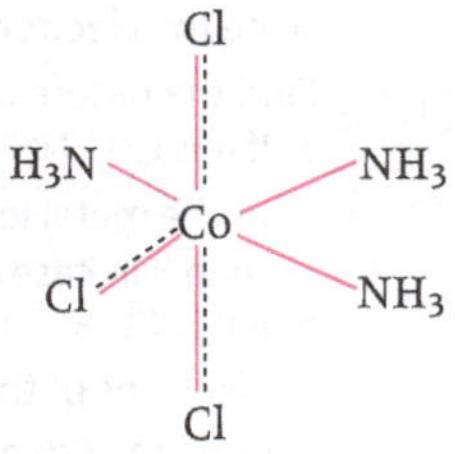

(D)

Limitations

Werner's theory did not adequately explain the following aspects.

- The distinct geometry of coordination compounds.
- The magnetic and optical properties of coordination compounds.

To address these shortcomings, alternative theories like valence bond theories and crystal field theory were proposed.

Valence Bond Theory (VBT)

This theory was proposed by L. Pauling in 1930. The main assumptions of this theory, are given below.

- The central metal ion in the complex makes available a number of empty orbitals for the formation of coordination bonds with suitable ligands. The number of empty orbitals made available for this reason is equal to coordination number of metal ion.
- Ligands donate its lone pairs of electrons, to form bond with metal ion. It describes the geometric structure of complex ion.
- The empty atomic orbitals of the metal hybridised to give a set of equivalent orbitals of definite geometry such as square planar, tetrahedral, octahedral and so on.

Number of Orbitals and Types of Hybridisations

Coordination number	Hybridisation	Geometry
4	sp^3	Tetrahedral
4	dsp^2	Square planar
5	sp^3d or dsp^3	Trigonal bipyramidal
6	sp^3d^2 or d^2sp^3	Octahedral

- If $(n-1)d$-orbitals are involved in hybridisation, then inner orbital or low spin or spin paired complex are formed while involvement of nd-orbitals results in outer orbital or high spin or spin free complexes.

JEE Alert

The hybrid orbitals do not actually exist. In fact, hybridisation is a mathematical manipulation of wave equation for the atomic orbitals involved.

Application of VBT

Some applications of this theory are given below:

Formation of Complex which have Coordination Number 6 These complexes are inner orbital complexes (d^2sp^3 hybridisation) or outer orbital complexes (sp^3d^2 hybridisation). These complexes have octahedral geometry. Let us study some complexes to see how the valence bond theory explains their properties.

(i) $[Fe(H_2O)_6]^{3+}$. The complex is known to be paramagnetic, with a magnetic moment corresponding to five unpaired electrons.

This can be described if we follow:

		3d					4s
Electronic configuration of Fe_{26}	[Ar]	↑↓	↑	↑	↑	↑	↑↓
Electronic configuration of Fe^{3+} (it is formed by loss of the two 4s-electrons and one of the 3d-electrons)	[Ar]	↑	↑	↑	↑	↑	

- To account for the experimentally observed fact that $[Fe(H_2O)_6]^{3+}$ has five unpaired electrons, each 3*d*-orbital is assumed to have one unpaired electron in the complex. The vacant $4d_{x^2-y^2}$ and $4d_{z^2}$ orbitals are hybridised with the vacant 4*s*-and 4*p*-orbitals.
- Each of the six H_2O ligands donates one electron pair into one of the six sp^3d^2-orbitals, forming six coordinate-covalent bonds.

  These donated electrons (from O of H_2O ligands) have been represented as "x" rather than "↑". These are the only bonding electrons, none of the 3*d*-electron of iron is involved in bonding.

  A set of outer *d* orbitals is used in hybridisation, and hence $[Fe(H_2O)_6]^{3+}$ is called an **outer orbital complex.**

$[Fe(H_2O)_6]^{3+}$:

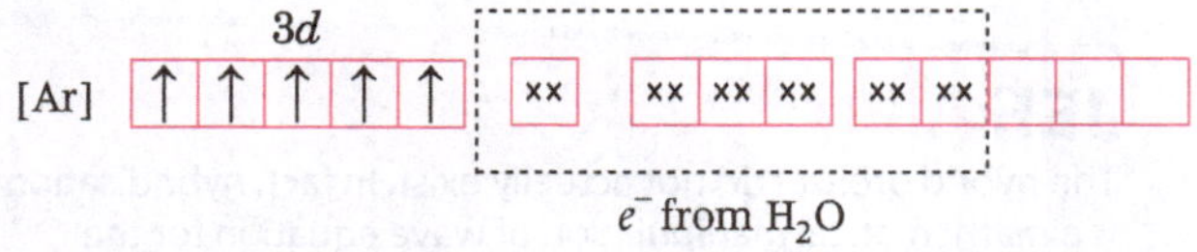

(ii) In $[Fe(CN)_6]^{3-}$, Fe^{3+} is involved (d^5 ion). But magnetic measurements indicate. The presence of only one unpaired electron per iron atom. The $3d_{x^2-y^2}$ and $3d_{z^2}$ orbitals (rather than those in 4*d*-shell) are involved in d^2sp^3 hybridisation. All but two of the non-bonding 3*d*-electrons of Fe^{3+} are paired in this complex.

$[Fe(CN)_6]^{3-}$: [Ar]

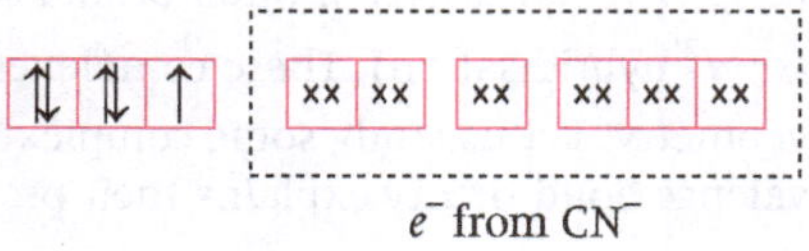

Only inner *d*-orbitals are used in hybridisation, hence $[Fe(CN)_6]^{3-}$ is called **an inner orbital complex.**

Solved Booster 3.1

Explain the paramagnetic behaviour of $[Co(NH_3)_6]^{2+}$.

Solution

Oxidation state of Co = + 2

When hybridisation occurs, one of the 3*d*-electrons is excited to 5*s*-orbital. The bonding for $[Co(NH_3)_6]^{2+}$ is consistent with the fact that this complex is easily oxidised to $[Co(NH_3)_6]^{3+}$, an extremely stable complex ion. Since there exists one unpaired electron, this complex ion is paramagnetic. Magnetic moment is given by:

$\mu = \sqrt{n(n+2)}$ BM $= \sqrt{3}$ BM

JEE Spotlite

In order to find the geometry, hybridisation and magnetic character, follow the steps given below.

Step I Find the oxidation number of central metal atom and write the electronic configuration of central metal ion.

Step II Find the nature of ligand,
- If it is CN^-, NH_3^-, CO, pair up the unpaired electrons of the metal ion (if they are more than 4 and less than 8 in case of octahedral complex.)
- If it is Cl^-, Br^-, I^-, H_2O, etc., leave the unpaired electrons of the metal ion as such.

Step III Now fill the ligand's electrons in empty available orbitals. The orbitals occupied by ligands give an idea about the hybridisation.

Step IV From the hybridisation, geometry can be predicted.

Step V Also see whether unpaired electrons are present, or not. If they are present, species is paramagnetic, otherwise diamagnetic.

Step VI
- If inner [(*n* – 1)*d*]-orbital takes part in hybridisation, the complex is inner orbital, if a set of outer *d*-orbitals is used then it is outer orbital complex.
- In inner orbital complex, the principle quantum number of *d*-orbitals is one less than the principle quantum number of the *s* and *p*-orbital. While in outer complex, all the hybrids, i.e, *s*, *p* and *d* have same value of principle quantum number.

Complexes with Coordination Number-4

Coordination compounds which have coordination number of 4 can have tetrahedral or square planar geometry. It depends upon the orbitals available for hybridisation.

1. In Tetrahedral Complexes

Complexes which involve one *s* and three *p*-orbitals of the central metal ion/atom for bonding, i.e. sp^3, are said to be tetrahedral complexes.

e.g. $[NiCl_4]^{2-}$, $[Ni(CO)_4]$, $[CuCl_4]^{2-}$, $[Zn(NH_3)_4]^{2+}$ etc.

$[Ni(CO)_4]$

Since, CO is neutral ligand thus, Ni has zero oxidation state.

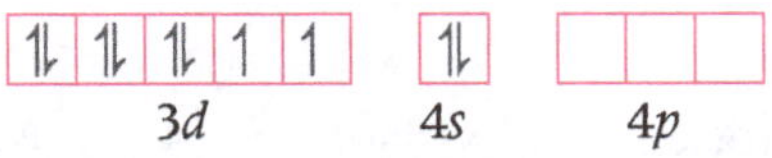

CO is a strong field ligand, it can pair up the unpaired electrons of Ni.

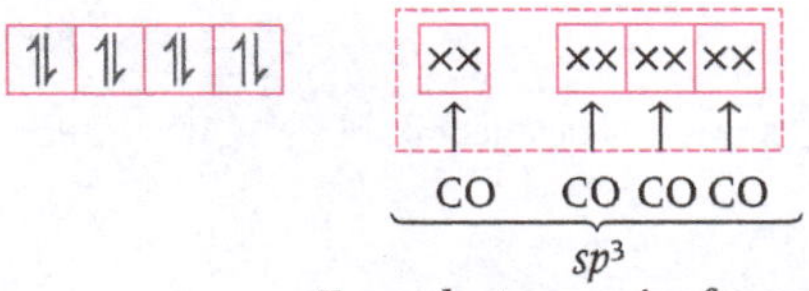

Four electron pairs from 4CO

There is no unpaired electron, hence, $[Ni(CO)_4]$ is diamagnetic in nature.

2. In Square Planar Complexes

Complexes whose central metal ion/atom involves one *s*, two *p* and one *d* orbitals for bonding, i.e. dsp^2 are said to be square planar complexes. e.g. $[Ni(CN)_4]^{2-}$, $[Pt(CN)_4]^{2-}$, $[Cu(NH_3)_4]^{2+}$ etc.

$[Ni(CN)_4]^{2-}$

Ni is present in +2 oxidation state due to four CN^- ligands.

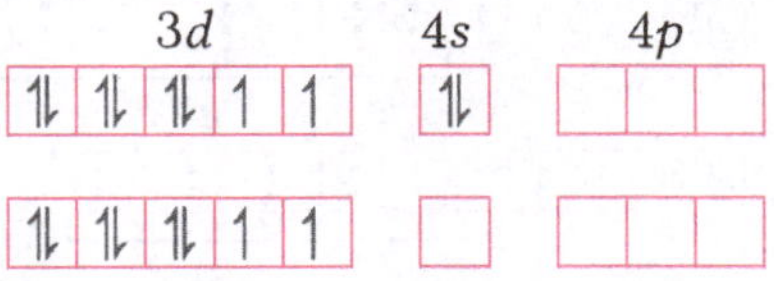

Since, CN^- is a strong field ligand, it pair-up the electrons of Ni^{2+} ion. Thus, one $(n-1)d$ orbital is vacant.

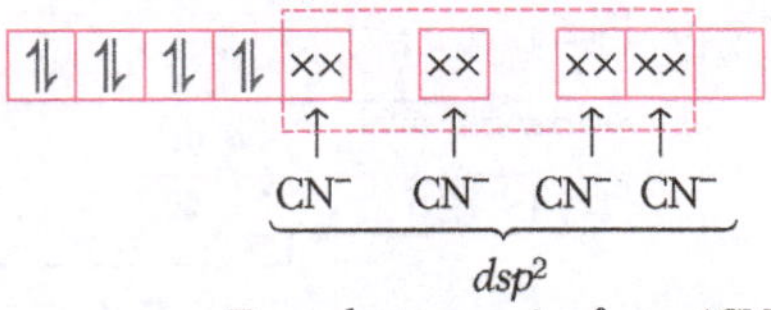

Four electron pairs from $4CN^-$

All the electrons in $[Ni(CN)_4]^{2-}$ complex are paired. Therefore, it is diamagnetic in natrue.

> **JEE Quicker**
>
> $NiCl_4^{2-}$ is a tetrahedral complex with a +2 charge on central metal nickel. *JEE Main 2025*
>
> ↘ $NiCl_4^{2-}$ has a weak field ligand i.e. Cl, due to which pairing of electron does not takes place. So, Ni^{2+} with $[Ar]3d^8$ configuration has sp^3 hybridisation and tetrahedral shape.

Geometry and Hybridisation of Some Other Complexes on the Basis of VBT

Atom/Ion complex	Configuration	Oxidation state of metal	Type of hybridisation	Geometry (Shape)	No. of unpaired electrons	Magnetic nature
$[Mn^{2+}(d^5)]$	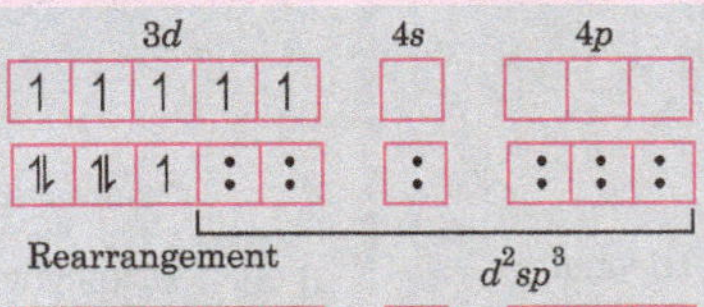	+2			5	Paramagnetic
$[Mn(CN)_6]^{4-}$	Rearrangement, d^2sp^3	+2	d^2sp^3 (Inner)	Octahedral	1	Paramagnetic
$[MnCl_4]^{2-}$	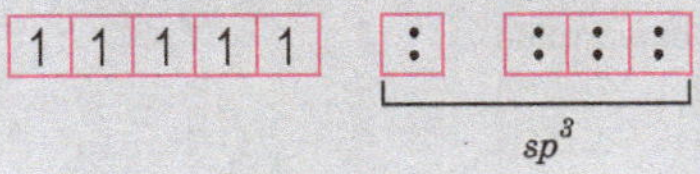 sp^3	+2	sp^3	Tetrahedral	5	Paramagnetic
$Cu^{2+}(d^9)$	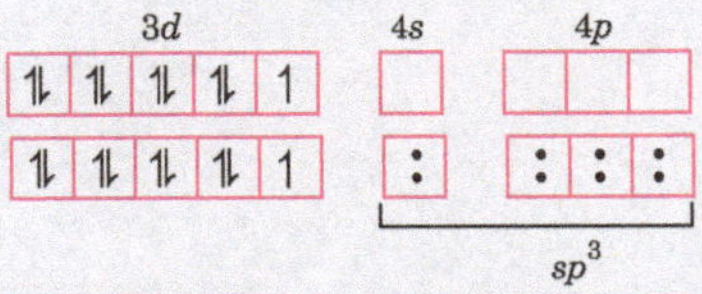	+2			1	Paramagnetic
$[CuCl_4]^{2-}$	sp^3	+2	sp^3	Tetrahedral	1	Paramagnetic
$[Cu(NH_3)_4]^{2+}$	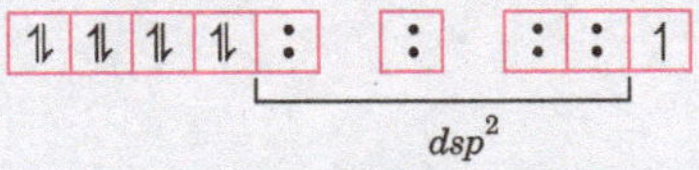 dsp^2 One electron is shifted from 3*d* to 4*p*-orbital	+2	dsp^2 (inner)	Square planar	1	Paramagnetic

Atom/Ion complex	Configuration	Oxidation state of metal	Type of hybridisation	Geometry (Shape)	No. of unpaired electrons	Magnetic nature
Cr^{3+} (d^3)	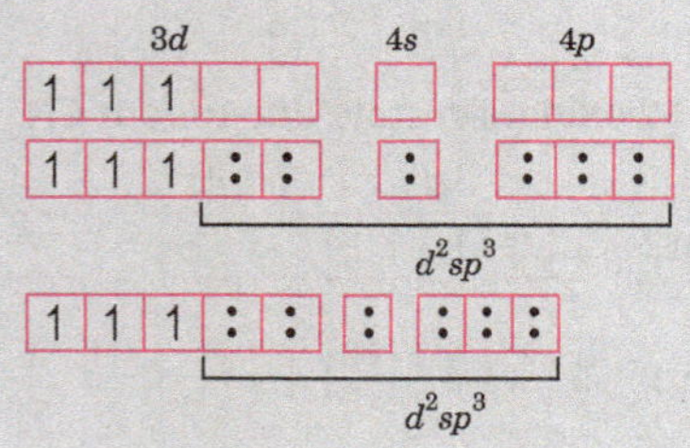	+3			3	Paramagnetic
$[Cr(NH_3)_6]^{3+}$		+3	d^2sp^3(Inner)	Octahedral	3	Paramagnetic
$[Cr(H_2O)_6]^{3+}$		+3	d^2sp^3(Inner)	Octahedral	3	Paramagnetic
Co^{3+} (d^6)	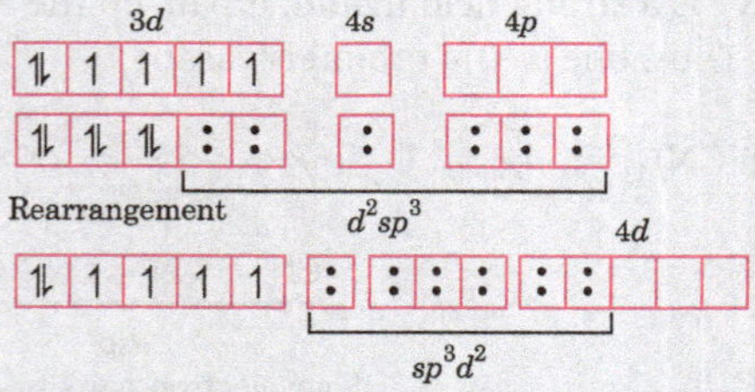	+3			4	Paramagnetic
$[Co(NH_3)_6]^{3+}$		+3	d^2sp^3(Inner)	Octahedral	0	Diamagnetic
$[CoF_6]^{3-}$		+3	sp^3d^2 (Outer)	Octahedral	4	Paramagnetic
Co^{2+} (d^7)	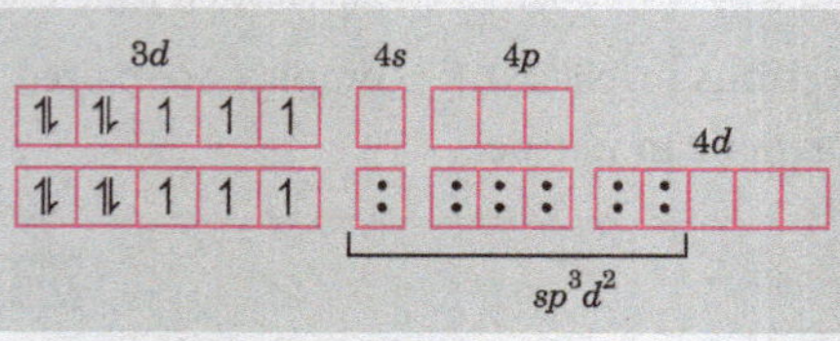	+2			3	Paramagnetic
$[Co(H_2O)_6]^{2+}$		+2	sp^3d^2(Outer)	Octahedral	3	Paramagnetic
Fe^{2+} (d^6)	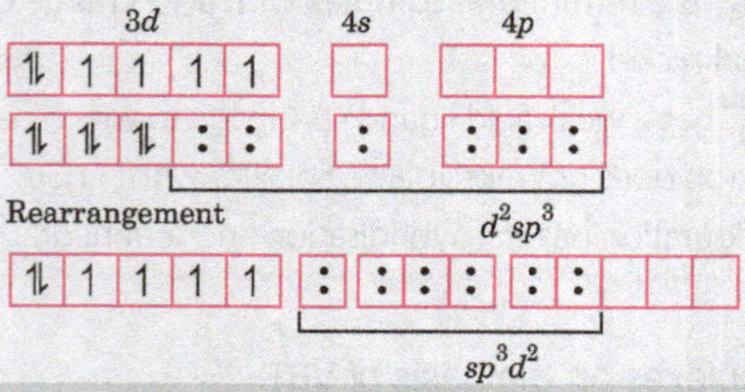	+2			4	Paramagnetic
$[Fe(CN)_6]^{4-}$		+2	d^2sp^3(Inner)	Octahedral	0	Diamagnteic
$[Fe(H_2O)_6]^{2+}$						
$[Fe(NH_3)_6]^{2+}$		+2	sp^3d^2(Outer)	Octahedral	4	Paramagnetic
Fe^{3+} (d^5)	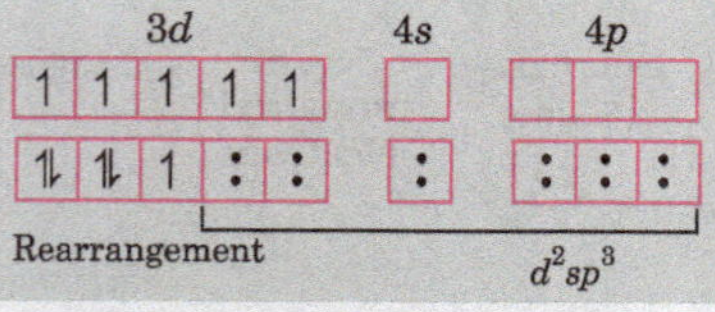	+3			5	Paramagnetic
$[Fe(CN)_6]^{3-}$		+3	d^2sp^3 (Inner)	Octahedral	1	Paramagnetic
$Fe(d^6s^2)$	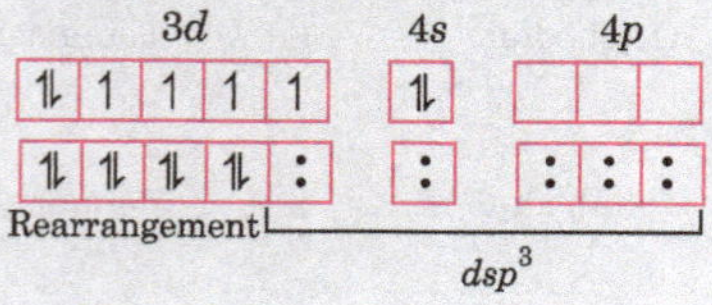	0			4	Paramagnetic
$[Fe(CO)_5]$		0	dsp^3 (Inner)	Trigonal bipyramidal	0	Diamagnetic

Limitations

The valence bond theory has some shortcomings. These are as follows

- It does not provide insight into the origin of characteristic colour of the complex ions.
- It does not distinguish between weak and strong ligands.
- It does not give quantitative interpretation of the thermodynamic or kinetic stabilities of coordination compounds.
- There is no quantitative interpretation of magnetic data.
- It does not explain why some complexes are inner orbital complexes and some complexes are outer orbital.
- It fails to give a satisfactory explanation for the formation of some complexes like $[Cu(NH_3)_4]^{2+}$. As it does not give any explanation for exciting an electron from 3*d* to 4*p*-orbital which is not energetically favoured.

JEE **MAPPER**

Example Similar to PYQ Asked in JEE Main 2024

Select the option with correct property.

(a) $[Ni(CN)_4]^{2-}$ and $[NiCl_4]^{2-}$ both are paramagnetic.

(b) $[Ni(CN)_4]^{2-}$ is paramagnetic and $[NiCl_4]^{2-}$ is diamagnetic.

(c) $[Ni(CN)_4]^{2-}$ is diamagnetic and $[NiCl_4]^{2-}$ is paramagnetic.

(d) $[Ni(CN)_4]^{2-}$ and $[NiCl_4]^{2-}$ both are diamagnetic.

Sol. (c) In $[Ni(CN)_4]^{2-}$, Ni^{2+} has $3d^8$ configuration but due to the presence of strong field ligand, all the *d*-electrons are paired giving dsp^2 hybridisation, diamagnetic nature. In $[NiCl_4]^{2-}$, Ni has $3d^8$ configuration and there are two unpaired electrons in *d*-orbital of central metal, hence paramagnetic (Ni^{2+} : sp^3).

Competency Enhancer 3.1

Select the option with correct property.

(a) $[Cr(H_2O)_6]^{3+}$ and $[Cu(py)_4]^+$ both are paramagnetic.

(b) $[Cr(H_2O)_6]^{3+}$ is diamagnetic and $[Cu(py)_4]^+$ is paramagnetic.

(c) $[Cr(H_2O)_6]^{3+}$ is paramagnetic and $[Cu(py)_4]^+$ is diamagnetic.

(d) $[Cr(H_2O)_6]^{3+}$ and $[Cu(py)_4]^+$ both are diamagnetic.

Crystal Field Theory

Most of the short comings of VBT of coordination compounds were removed in crystal field theory (CFT). It attributes partial covalent character and partial ionic character to bonds.

Some assumptions of crystal field theory are as follows

- Ligands are considered as point charges in case of anions or point dipoles in case of neutral molecules.
- The interaction between metal ion and ligand is purely electrostatic. Therefore, metal ion and ligands do not mix their orbitals, i.e. no overlap of orbitals occur.
- The *d*-orbitals present in metal ion are degenerate. This degeneracy is lost in presence of ligands as the field produced by ligands is not symmetrical.
- Due to this loss in degeneracy, in octahedral field, *d*-orbitals are splitted into t_{2g} and e_g sets of orbitals.
- t_{2g} orbitals (d_{xy}, d_{yz}, d_{zx}) are triply degenerate while e_g orbitals ($d_{x^2-y^2}$ and d_{z^2}) are doubly degenerate.

Calculation of Crystal Field Stabilising Energy (CFSE)

(i) For octahedral CFSE $= [-0.4(nt_{2g}) + 0.6(ne_g)]\Delta_O +$ Pairing energy (P.E)

where, nt_{2g} = number of electron in t_{2g} orbitals

ne_g = number of electron in e_g orbitals

Δ_0 = crystal field splitting energy

(ii) For tetrahedral CFSE $= [-0.6(n_e) + 0.4(n_{t_2})]\Delta_t +$ Pairing energy (P.E.)

where, n_{t_2} = number of electron in t_2 orbitals

n_e = number of electron in *e* orbitals

Δ_t = crystal field splitting energy

Factors Affecting the Magnitude of Δ_o and Δ_t

The magnitude of Δ_o or Δ_t, the orbitals splitting energy is decided by

- **Nature of the Ligand** Spectrochemical series, which have been arranged in increasing field strength as:
  $I^- < Br^- < SCN^- < Cl^- < S^{2-} < F^- > OH^- < C_2O_4^{2-} < H_2O < NCS^- < edta^{4-} < NH_3 < en < CN^- < CO$
- **Geometry of the Complex** Δ_t value (of tetrahedral complex) is about 50% compared to Δ_o value (of octahedral complexes)
- **Nature of the Metal Ion** Going from Cr to W (through Mo), Δ_o increases 50% in each series change (i.e., 3*d* to 4*d* to 5*d*). Thus, there is greater tendency of the second (4*d*) and third (5*d*) transition series to be low spin as compared to first (3*d*) transition series.
- **Oxidation State of the Metal Ion**
  eg. $\Delta(Fe^{3+}) > \Delta(Fe^{2+})$; $\Delta(Cu^{2+}) > \Delta(Cu^+)$

Greater the ionic charge on the central metal ion, the greater the value of Δ.

Complexes with C.N. 6 (Octahedral Crystal Field)

Formation of an Octahedral Complex

Let us consider the case of six ligands forming an octahedral complex. For convenience, we may regard the ligands as being symmetrically positioned along the axes of a Cartesian co- ordinate system with the metal ion at the origin. To simplify the situation, we can consider an octahedral complex as a cube, having the metal ion at the centre of the body and the 6 ligands at the face centres

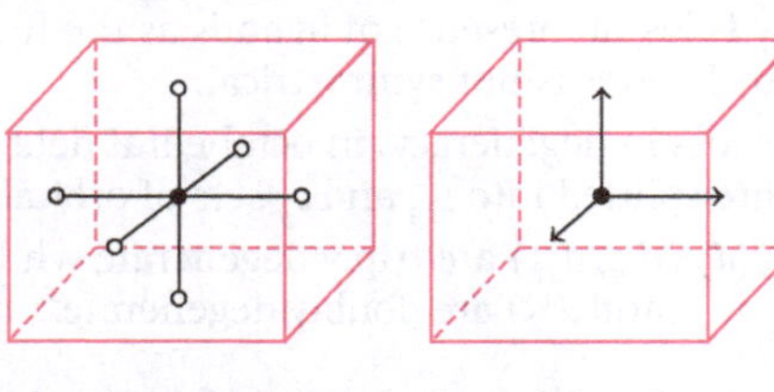

and if we take the metal ion as the origin of a Cartesian co-ordinate, the ligands will be along the axes. As in the case of a spherical field, all of the *d*-orbitals will be raised in energy relative to the free ion because of negative charge repulsions. However it should be pictorially obvious that not all of the orbitals will be affected to the same extent. The orbitals lying along the axes, (d_{z^2} and $d_{x^2-y^2}$) will be more strongly repelled than the orbitals with lobes directed between the axes (d_{xy} d_{zx}, d_{yz}). The *d*-orbitals are thus split into two sets with the d_{z^2} and $d_{x^2-y^2}$ at a higher energy than the other three (d_{xy}, d_{zx}, d_{yz}). The splitting is known as crystal field splitting.

The energy separation between the two sets is called $\Delta_{octahedral}$ or Δ_{oct}. It is proportional to the crystal field of the strength of the ligands.

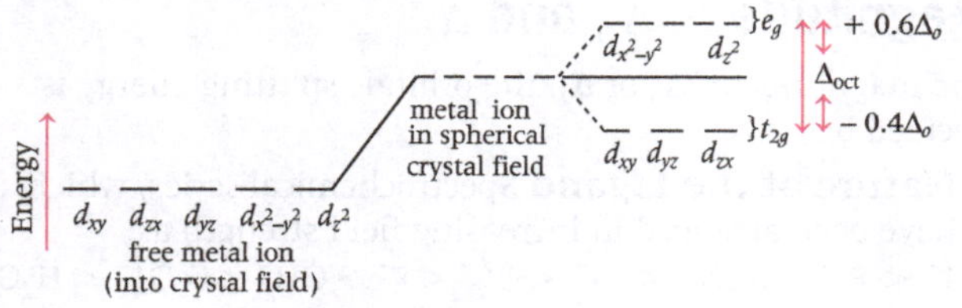

JEE Spotlite

- The $d_{x^2-y^2}$ and d_{z^2} orbitals are directed along a set of mutually perpendicular *x*, *y* and *z*-axes. As a group, these orbitals are called e_g orbitals.
- The d_{xy}, d_{yz} and d_{zx} orbitals, lie between the axes and are collectively called t_{2g} orbitals.

- The *d*-electrons on a metal ion occupy the t_{2g} set in preference to the higher energy, e_g set. Electrons that occupy the e_g orbitals are strongly repelled by the relatively close approach of ligands. Electrons in e_g set tends to destabilise octahedral complexes.

- Based on valence bond theory, $[CoF_6]^{3-}$ is a paramagnetic outer orbital complex while $[Co(NH_3)_6]^{3+}$ is a diamagnetic inner orbital complex. Both contain d^6 Co^{3+} ions (four unpaired electrons) in its 3*d*-orbitals.

Magnetic measurements indicate that $[CoF_6]^{3-}$ also has four unpaired electrons per ion. Thus, there must be four electrons in t_{2g} orbitals and two in e_g orbitals.

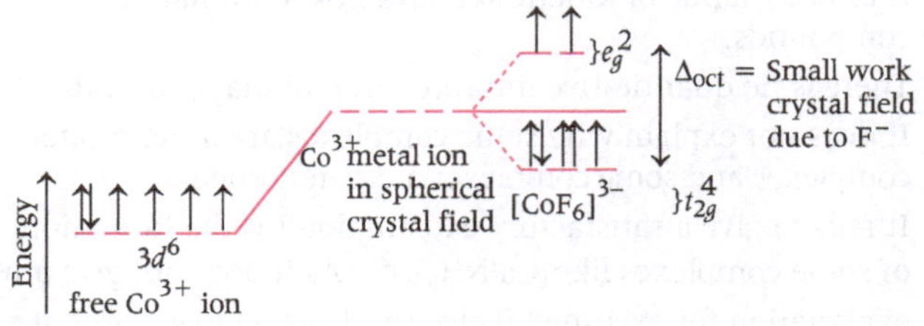

On the other hand, $[Co(NH_3)_6]^{2+}$ is diamagnetic, thus, all the six *d*-electrons must be paired in the t_{2g} orbitals.

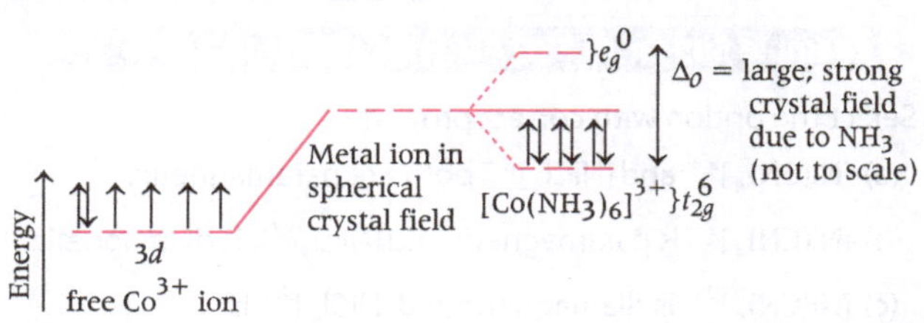

- The difference in configuration between $[CoF_6]^{3-}$ and $[Co(NH_3)_6]^{3+}$ is due to the relative magnitude of the crystal field splitting, Δ_{oct}, caused by the different crystal field strengths of F^- and NH_3. The NH_3 molecule interacts with vacant metal orbitals more strongly than the F^- ion does.

$$\Delta_{oct} \text{ for } [Co(NH_3)_6]^{3+} > \Delta_{oct} \text{ for } [CoF_6]^{3-}$$

For $[CoF_6]^{3-}$: F^- is a weak field ligand, so $\Delta_o < P$ (electron pairing energy), thus it is a **high spin complex.** ($t_{2g}^4 e_g^2$)

A high spin complex in crystal field terminology corresponds to an outer orbital complex in VBT.

For $[Co(NH_3)_6]^{3+}$: NH_3 is a strong field ligand so $\Delta_o > P$, thus it is a **low spin complex** ($t_{2g}^6 e_g^0$).

A low spin complex corresponds to an inner orbital complex.

- Low spin configurations exist only for octahedral complexes having metal ions with d^4, d^5, d^6 and d^7 configurations. For $d^1 - d^3$ and $d^8 - d^{10}$ ions, configuration is designated as high spin.

Electronic Configurations and Crystal Field Stabilisation Energies (CFSE) for High and Low Spin Octahedral Complexes

	Configuration	d^1	d^2	d^3	d^4	d^5	d^6	d^7	d^8	d^9	d^{10}
	Examples	Ti^{3+}	Ti^{2+}, V^{3+}	V^{2+}, Cr^{3+}	Mn^{3+}, Re^{3+}	Mn^{2+}, Fe^{3+}	Fe^{2+}, Pd^{4+}	Co^{2+}, Rh^{2+}	Ni^{2+}, Pt^{2+}	Cu^{2+}	Zn^{2+}, Ag^{+}
High spin	e_g	— —	— —	— —	↑ —	↑ ↑	↑ ↑	↑ ↑	↑ ↑	⇅ ↑	⇅ ⇅
	t_{2g}	↑ — —	↑ ↑ —	↑ ↑ ↑	↑ ↑ ↑	↑ ↑ ↑	⇅ ↑ ↑	⇅ ⇅ ↑	⇅ ⇅ ⇅	⇅ ⇅ ⇅	⇅ ⇅ ⇅
	CFSE	$-\frac{2}{5}\Delta_o$	$-\frac{4}{5}\Delta_o$	$-\frac{6}{5}\Delta_o$	$-\frac{3}{5}\Delta_o$	0	$-\frac{2}{5}\Delta_o$	$-\frac{4}{5}\Delta_o$	$-\frac{6}{5}\Delta_o$	$-\frac{3}{5}\Delta_o$	0
Low spin	e_g				— —	— —	— —	↑ —			
	t_{2g}				⇅ ↑ ↑	⇅ ⇅ ↑	⇅ ⇅ ⇅	⇅ ⇅ ⇅			
	CFSE	Same as high spin			$-\frac{8}{5}\Delta_o$	$-\frac{10}{5}\Delta_o$	$-\frac{12}{5}\Delta_o$	$-\frac{9}{5}\Delta_o$	Same as high spin		

Splitting in a Tetrahedral Complex

The co-ordination number for tetrahedral complexes is 4. The tetrahedral arrangement of four ligands surrounding a metal ion may be visualized by placing ligands at the alternate corners of a cube, as shown In figure.

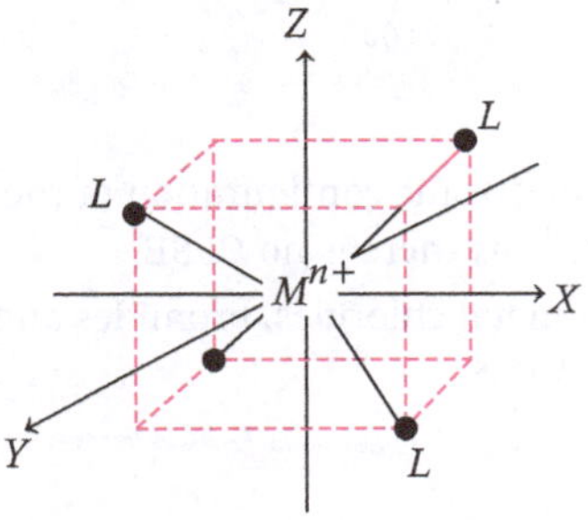

Tetrahedral arrangement of four ligands in $[ML_4]^{n+}$

It can be shown that in a tetrahedral structure, none of the d-orbitals points exactly towards the ligands. When ligand approaches it is more close d_{xy}, d_{yz}, d_{zx} in comparision of $d_{x^2-y^2}$ and d_{z^2}. This is because d_{xy}, d_{yz}, d_{zx} are between the axis and d_{z^2} and $d_{x^2-y^2}$ are along the axes. So, d_{xy}, d_{yz}, d_{zx} orbitals feel more repulsion as compared to d_{z^2} and $d_{x^2-y^2}$ orbitals.

Thus, the d orbitals are also splitted into two groups but in a reverse order of octahedral field. The three orbitals, d_{xy}, d_{yz} and d_{zx}, are designated as t_2 orbitals, now have higher energy than the two orbitals $d_{x^2-y^2}$ and d_z designated as e-orbitals.

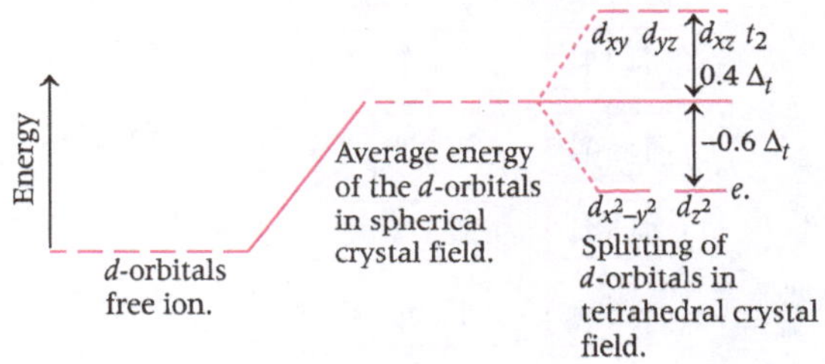

The magnitude of the crystal field splitting Δ_t in tetrahedral complexes is considerably less than in octahedral fields. There are two reasons for this:

(i) There are only four ligands instead of six, so the ligand field is only two thirds the size and hence the ligand field splitting is also two thirds the size.

(ii) The direction of the d-orbitals of the metal ion/atom does not coincide with the direction of the ligands. This reduces the crystal field splitting by roughly a further two thirds.

Thus, the tetrahedral crystal field splitting, Δ_t roughly $\frac{2}{3} \times \frac{2}{3} = \frac{4}{9}$ of the octahedral crystal field splitting Δ_o i.e. $\left(\Delta_t = \frac{4}{9}\Delta_o\right)$. Strong field ligands cause a bigger energy difference between, t_{2g} and e_g (or t_2 and e), than weak field ligands. However, the tetrahedral splitting Δ_t is always much smaller than the octahedral splitting, Δ_o. Thus, it is never energetically favourable to pair electrons and tetrahedral complexes are mostly high-spin in nature.

CFSE and electronic arrangements in tetrahedral complexes

Number of *d* electrons	Arrangement of electrons		Spin only magnetic moment	Tetrahedral CFSE	Tetrahedral CFSE scaled for comparison with octahedral values, assuming	Octahedral CFSE (Δ_o)	
	e	t_2	μ (BM)	Δ_t	$\Delta_t = \frac{4}{9}\Delta_o$	Weak field	Strong field
d^1	↑		1.73	− 0.6	− 0.27	− 0.4	− 0.4
d^2	↑ ↑		2.83	− 1.2	− 0.53	− 0.8	− 0.8
d^3	↑ ↑	↑	3.87	− 1.2 + 0.4 = − 0.8	− 0.36	− 1.2	− 1.2
d^4	↑ ↑	↑ ↑	4.90	− 1.2 + 0.8 = − 0.4	− 0.18	− 0.6	− 1.6
d^5	↑ ↑	↑ ↑ ↑	5.92	− 1.2 + 1.2 = 0.0	0.00	0.0	− 2.0
d^6	↑↓ ↑	↑ ↑ ↑	4.90	− 1.8 + 1.2 = − 0.6	− 0.27	− 0.4	− 2.4
d^7	↑↓ ↑↓	↑ ↑ ↑	3.87	− 2.4 + 1.2 = − 1.2	− 0.53	− 0.8	− 1.8
d^8	↑↓ ↑↓	↑↓ ↑ ↑	2.83	− 2.4 + 1.6 = − 0.8	− 0.36	− 1.2	− 1.2
d^9	↑↓ ↑↓	↑↓ ↑↓ ↑	1.73	− 2.4 + 2.0 = − 0.4	− 0.18	− 0.6	− 0.6
d^{10}	↑↓ ↑↓	↑↓ ↑↓ ↑↓	0.00	− 2.4 + 2.4 = 0.0	0.00	0.0	0.0

The CFSE in both octahedral and tetrahedral environments is given in above Table. This shows that for d^0, d^5 and d^{10} arrangements the CFSE is zero in both octahedral and tetrahedral complexes. For all other electronic arrangements there is some CFSE, and the octahedral CFSE is greater than the tetrahedral CFSE.

It follows that octahedral complexes are generally more stable and more common than tetrahedral complexes. This is partly because there are six bond energy terms rather than four, and partly because there is a larger CFSE term. Despite this some tetrahedral complexes are formed, and are stable.

Tetrahedral complexes are favoured,

(i) where the ligands are large and bulky and could cause crowding in an octahedral complex.

(ii) where attainment of a regular shape is important. For tetrahedral structures d^0, d^2, d^5, d^7 and d^{10} configurations are regular. Some tetrahedral complexes which are regular are: $Ti^{IV}Cl_4(e_g^0, t_{2g}^0)$, $[Mn^{VII}O_4]^-$ (e_g^0, t_{2g}^0), $[Fe^{VI}O_4]^{2-}(e_g^2, t_{2g}^0)$, $[Fe^{III}Cl_4]^-$ (e_g^2, t_{2g}^3), $[Co^{II}Cl_4]^{2-}$ (e_g^4, t_{2g}^3) and $[Zn^{II}Cl_4]^{2-}$ (e_g^4, t_{2g}^6).

(iii) when the ligands are weak field, and the loss in CFSE is thus less important.

(iv) where the central metal has a low oxidation state. This reduces the magnitude of Δ.

(v) where the electronic configuration of the central metal is d^0, d^5 or d^{10} as there is no CFSE.

Many transition metal chlorides, bromides and iodides form tetrahedral structures.

JEE Alert

The crystal field splitting energy for square planar (Δ_{sp}) complexes is greater than the octahedral splitting energy $\Delta_{sp} = \frac{4}{3}\Delta_O$ and the order of splitting energy is $\Delta_{sq} > \Delta_O > \Delta_t$.

Limitations of CFT

- The crystal field theory can explain the spectra of the metal ions and complexes on the assumption that these arise from the transition of electrons from lower energy d-orbitals to higher energy *d*-orbitals. However, the position and intensities of spectral bands calculated on the basis of crystal field theory do not always coincide with those determined experimentally.
- Apart from this, a pure electrostatic interaction between central metal ion and ligand fails to explain the relative positions of ligands in spectrochemical series. Along with this there is clear evidence that covalent bonding too makes a significant contribution towards the metal ligand bonding.

- As ligands are considered as point charges the anionic ligands should exert greater splitting effect. But in actual practice anionic ligands are present at low end of spectrochemical series.
- The above written facts about the crystal field theory was modified so as to include the contribution of covalent bonding in the metal ligand bond and is called ligand field theory, (LFT) and molecular orbital theory (MOT).

JEE MAPPER

Example Similar to PYQ Asked in JEE Advanced 2021

Match the electronic configuration in List-I with appropriate metal complex ions in List-II and choose the correct option.
[Atomic number : Fe = 26, Mn = 25, Co = 27]

	List-I		List-II
P.	$t_{2g}^4e_g^2$	1.	$[Fe(H_2O)_6]^{2+}$
Q.	$t_{2g}^3e_g^2$	2.	$[Mn(NH_3)_6]^{2+}$
R.	$t^4t_2^3$	3.	$[Co(H_2O)_6]^{3+}$
S.	$e^4t_2^6$	4.	$[Ni(CO)_4]$
		5.	$[CoCl_4]^{2-}$

Codes

(a) P-(1), Q-(2), R-(5), S-(4) (b) P-(2), Q-(3), R-(1), S-(4)
(c) P-(3), Q-(1), R-(4), S-(2) (d) P-(3), Q-(5), R-(2), S-(4)

Sol. (*a*) The correct match is P-(1), Q-(2), R-(5), S-(4).

Competency Enhancer 3.2

Match the electronic configuration in List-I with appropriate metal complex ions in List-II and choose the correct options.
[Atomic number: Ti = 22, Fe = 26, Cu = 29, Ni = 28]

	List-I		List-II
P.	$e^4t_2^5$	1.	$[TiCl_4]$
Q.	$e^2t_2^0$	2.	$[FeO_4]^{2-}$
R.	$e^4t_2^6$	3.	$[Cu(NH_3)_4]^{2+}$
S.	$e^2t_2^3$	4.	$[FeF_4]^-$
		5.	$[Ni(CO)_4]$

Codes

(a) P-(2), Q-(1), R-(3), S-(4) (b) P-(2), Q-(3), R-(4), S-(5)
(c) P-(3), Q-(2), R-(5), S-(4) (d) P-(1), Q-(5), R-(2), S-(3)

Colour and the Spectrochemical Series

A substance appears coloured because it absorbs light that corresponds to one or more of the wavelengths in the visible region of the electromagnetic spectrum (4000 to 7000Å) and transmits or reflects the other wavelengths. A combination of all wavelengths in the visible region is called **"white light"**, sunlight is an example. The absence of all wavelengths in the visible region is blackness.

Most transition metal compounds are coloured. In transition metal compounds, the *d*-orbitals in any one energy level of the metal are not degenerate. They are often split into two sets of orbitals separated by energies, Δ_o, that correspond to wavelength of light in the visible region. The absorption of visible light causes electronic transition between orbitals in these sets. This transition is called *d-d* transition.

Colour of some transition metal nitrates in aqueous solutions are given below:

Transition metal ion	Colour of aqueous solution
Cr^{3+}	Deep blue
Mn^{2+}	Pale pink
Fe^{2+}	Pale green
Fe^{3+}	Orchid
Co^{2+}	Pink
Ni^{2+}	Green
Cu^{2+}	Blue

One transition of a high spin octahedral Co(III) complex is represented below :

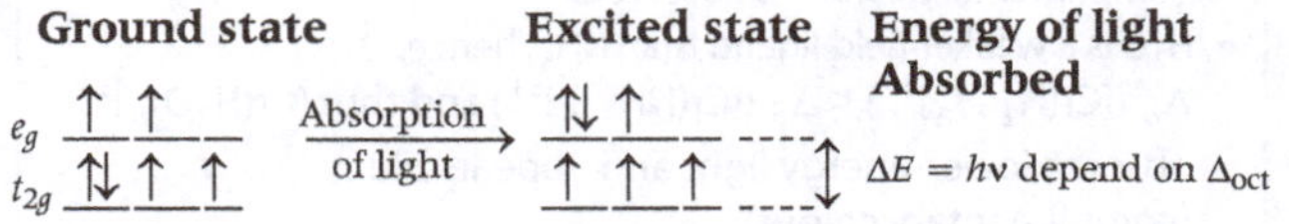

The frequency (ν), and thus the wavelength and colour, of the light absorbed are related to Δ_o. This, in turn, depends on the crystal-field strength of the ligands. Hence, the colour and the visible absorption spectra of transition metal complexes, as well as their magnetic properties, provide information about the strengths of the ligand-metal interactions.

The **spectral colour** is the colour associated with the wavelengths of the light absorbed by the sample.
The **complimentary colour** is the colour associated with the wavelengths that are not absorbed by the sample, and is seen when the spectral colour is removed from white light. Complimentary colour of orange is spectral colour blue and *vice-versa* and is represented in the form of a wheel.

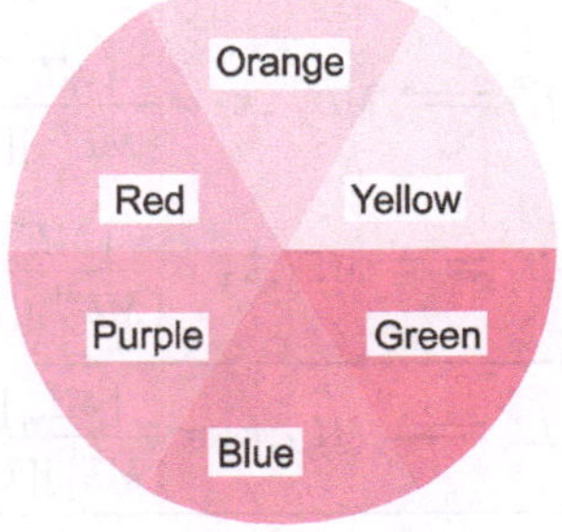

Spectral colour and complimentary colour are opposite to each other

Relationship Between Colours Absorbed and Colours Transmitted or Reflected in the Visible Region

Wavelength absorbed (Å)	Spectral colour (colour absorbed)	Complimentary colour (colour observed)
4100	violet	lemon yellow
4300	indigo	yellow
4800	blue	orange
5000	blue-green	red
5300	green	purple
5600	lemon yellow	violet
5800	yellow	indigo
6100	orange	blue
6800	red	blue-green

JEE Spotlite

- Low spin complexes usually absorb higher-energy (shorter-wavelength) light than that of high spin complexes.
- In $[Cr(NH_3)_6]^{3+}$, the Cr(III) is bonded to six NH_3 ligands, which produce a relatively high value of Δ_o. This absorbs light in the blue and violet regions of visible light and thus orange-yellow complimentary colour is observed.
- H_2O is a weaker field ligand than NH_3, hence, Δ_o $([Cr(H_2O)_6]^{3+}) < \Delta_o$ $([Cr(NH_3)_6]^{3+})$ and thus $[Cr(H_2O)_6]^{3+}$ absorbs lower-energy light and appears blue (complimentary colour)
- Some complex like CrO_4^{2-}, $Cr_2O_7^{2-}$, MnO_4^- etc. have d^0-configuration of metal ion but have intense colour. This is due to charge transfer spectra and not due to *d-d* transition.

Stability Constants and Stability of Coordination Compounds

Consider the stepwise formation of the complex, ML_4 from the metal ion M^{4+} (Lewis acid) and ligand L^- (Lewis base). Let k_1, k_2, k_3 and k_4 be stepwise formation constants and $\beta_4 (= k_f)$ be the overall formation constant. Thus,

$$M^{4+} + L^- \rightleftharpoons ML^{3+}, \quad k_1 = \frac{[ML^{3+}]}{[M^{4+}][L^-]}$$

$$ML^{3+} + L^- \rightleftharpoons ML_2^{2+}, k_2 = \frac{[ML_2^{2+}]}{[ML^{3+}][L^-]}$$

$$ML_2^{2+} + L^- \rightleftharpoons ML_3^{+}, k_3 = \frac{[ML_3^{+}]}{[ML_2^{2+}][L^-]}$$

$$ML_3^{+} + L^- \rightleftharpoons ML_4, k_4 = \frac{[ML_4]}{[ML_3^{+}][L^-]}$$

$$\therefore \quad M^{4+} + 4L^- \rightleftharpoons ML_4, \beta_4 = \frac{[ML_4]}{[M^{4+}][L^-]^4}$$

$$\therefore \quad \beta_4 = k_1 k_2 k_3 k_4$$

$$\therefore \quad \log \beta_4 = \log k_1 + \log k_2 + \log k_3 + \log k_4$$

If the complex is ML_n, and β_n the overall formation constant, then

$$M + nL \rightleftharpoons ML_n \quad \text{(charges omitted)}$$

$$\beta_n = \frac{[ML_n]}{[M][L]^n} = k_1 k_2 k_3 k_4 \ldots k_n$$

$$\log \beta_n = \log k_1 + \log k_2 + \log k_3 + \ldots + \log k_n$$

β_n, the stability constant, is related to thermodynamic stability when the system has reached equilibrium. Most of the measurements have been made from aqueous solutions, which means that when complex is formed, stronger ligand (L) (say CN^-, en) displaces weaker ligand like H_2O of the aqua complex of the metal ion.

$$M(H_2O)_n + nL \rightleftharpoons ML_n + nH_2O$$

Importance and Applications of Coordination Compounds

Coordination compounds have great importance and widely used in various fields. Some important applications of transition metal complexes are given below

1. In Quantitative and Qualitative Analysis

- Traces of Ni^{2+} salt can be detected by dimethyl glyoxime when cherry red precipitate of nickel-dimethyl glyoximate (chelate) is formed.

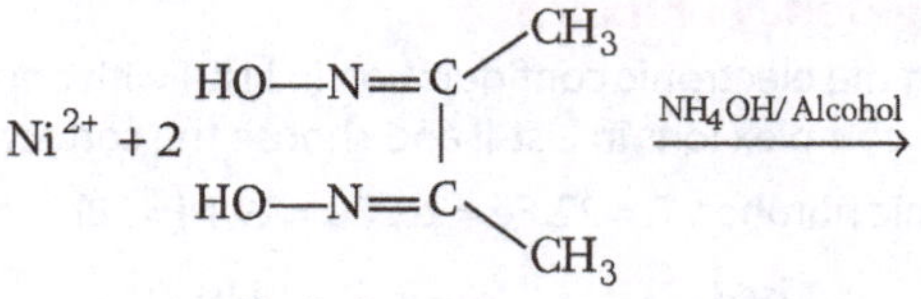

Dimethyl glyoxime

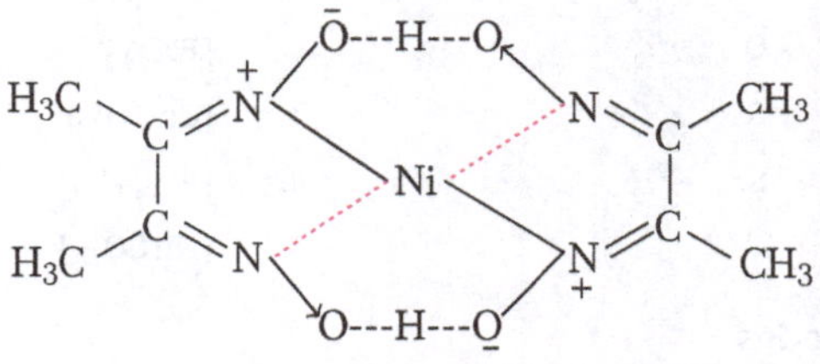

Nickel-dimethyl glyoximate (chelate) (red ppt.)

- In qualitative analysis of group I, there is formation of white precipitate of AgCl, Hg_2Cl_2, and $PbCl_2$. $PbCl_2$ is soluble in hot water.

  AgCl can be removed as soluble $[Ag(NH_3)_2]Cl$ on adding $NH_3(aq)$.

$$AgCl(s) + 2NH_3(aq) \rightleftharpoons \underset{\text{Soluble}}{Ag[(NH_3)_2]Cl}$$

- In group II, Cd^{2+} can be precipitated as CdS in presence of Cu^{2+}.

- By treating the solution of Cu^{2+} and Cd^{2+} with an excess of CN^-, Cu^{2+} forms a stable complex in a redox reaction.

$$2Cu^{2+} + 10CN^- \longrightarrow \underset{\text{Stable}}{2[Cu(CN)_4]^{3-}} + (CN)_2\uparrow$$

while Cd^{2+} forms less stable complex

$$Cd^{2+} + 4CN^- \rightleftharpoons \underset{\text{Unstable}}{[Cd(CN)_4]^{2-}}$$

When H_2S gas is passed, $[Cd(CN)_4]^{2-}$ is precipitated as CdS without affecting $[Cu(CN)_4]^{3-}$ complex.

2. In Medicinal Chemistry

- The platinum complex *cis*-$[Pt(NH_3)_2Cl_2]$ commonly known as ***cis*-platin** is used in the treatment of cancer. It has ability to block the uncontrolled division of cancerous cells that results in growth of tumours.
- EDTA complex of calcium, $[Ca(EDTA)]^{2-}$ is used to treat a person suffering from lead poisoning.

$$Pb^{2+} + [Ca(EDTA)]^{2-} \longrightarrow [Pb(EDTA)]^{2-} + Ca^{2+}$$

EDTA complex of lead is more stable than $[Ca(EDTA)]^{2-}$ complex. Thus, lead complex is excreted from the body and Ca^{2+} remains as the body nutrient.

3. In Extraction of Metals

It can be achieved through formation and subsequent decomposition of their coordination compounds.

e.g. Nickel can be extracted by Mond's process which involves formation of carbonyl complex of nickel.

$$Ni(s) + 4CO(g) \longrightarrow Ni(CO)_4(g)$$

Silver (Ag) and gold (Au) can be extracted by formation of cyanide complex.

For silver, reactions are,

$$4Au(s) + 8CN^-(aq) + O_2(g) + 2H_2O(l) \longrightarrow 4OH^-(aq) + 4[Au(CN)_2]^-(aq)$$

$$2[Au(CN)_2]^-(aq) + Zn(s) \longrightarrow [Zn(CN)_4]^{2-}(aq) + 2Au(s)$$

4. In Purification of Water

Purification of water can be done through complex formation. It involves chelation with sodium salt of EDTA.

The formation constant of $[Ca(EDTA)]^{2-}$ and $[Mg(EDTA)]^{2-}$ are very large.

Hence, on treating water with sodium salt of EDTA, concentration of Ca^{2+} and Mg^{2+} can be reduced to the point that these ions will not precipitate with soap or detergent.

$$Ca^{2+} + (EDTA)^{4-} \rightleftharpoons [Ca(EDTA)]^{2-}$$

$$Mg^{2+} + (EDTA)^{4-} \rightleftharpoons [Mg(EDTA)]^{2-}$$

5. In Photography

The photographic "fixing" process removes unreacted AgBr which forms soluble complex with sodium thiosulphate.

$$AgBr(s) + 2S_2O_3^{2-} \longrightarrow \underset{\text{Soluble}}{[Ag(S_2O_3)_2]^{3-}} + Br^-$$

6. In Industries as Catalysts

They are used as catalysts for many industrial processes. e.g. Rh complex, $[(Ph_3P)_3RhCl]$ (Wilkinson catalyst) is used for hydrogenation of alkenes.

7. In Electroplating

Articles can be electroplated with Ag and Au much more smoothly and evenly from solutions of the complexes, $[Ag(CN)_2]^-$ and $[Au(CN)_2]^-$ than from a solution of simple metal ions.

8. In Biological Processes

Many important biological substances are coordination compounds, e.g.

- Haemoglobin is a protein that carries O_2 in blood. It contains iron (II) ions bound to large porphyrin rings.
- Chlorophyll is necessary for photosynthesis in plants. It contains magnesium ions bound to porphyrin rings.
- Vitamin B_{12} is a large complex of cobalt (II).

Elemental Practice 9.3

Type I MCQs with Only One Correct Option

1. A white precipitate will be formed by adding excess of $AgNO_3$ to the aqueous solution of
   (a) $[Co(NH_3)_4ClBr]I$ (b) $[Co(NH_3)_4ICl]Br$
   (c) $[Co(NH_3)_4BrI]Cl$ (d) $[Co(NH_3)_3IBrCl]$
2. 1 molar aqueous solution of which of the following will show highest conductance?
   (a) $K_3[Fe(CN)_6]$ (b) $K_4[Fe(CN)_6]$
   (c) $Fe_4[Fe(CN)_6]_3$ (d) $Fe_3[Fe(CN)_6]_2$
3. In aqueous solution, $CuSO_4 \cdot 4NH_3 \cdot 2H_2O$ will show the properties of
   (a) Cu^{2+} (b) NH_3
   (c) SO_4^{2-} (d) Cu^+
4. Consider the statements given below
   (I) The presence of primary valencies gives rise to stereo isomerism in complex.
   (II) Secondary valencies have directional properties.
   (III) Secondary valencies are non-ionisable.
   Choose the correct statment. According to Werner's theory.
   (a) (I), (II) and (III) are correct. (b) (II) and (III) are correct.
   (c) (I) and (III) are correct. (d) (I) and (II) are correct.

5. Which of the following is most likely the formula of platinum complex, if $\frac{1}{4}$ of total chlorine of the compound is precipitated by adding $AgNO_3$ to its aqueous solution?
(a) $PtCl_4 \cdot 5H_2O$ (b) $PtCl_4 \cdot 4H_2O$
(c) $PtCl_4 \cdot 6H_2O$ (d) $PtCl_4 \cdot 3H_2O$

6. Choose the option containing correct statement
(a) $[Co(C_2O_4)_3]^{3-}$ and $[Ni(en)_3]^{2+}$ both paramagnetic.
(b) $[Co(C_2O_4)_3]^{3-}$ is paramagnetic and $[Ni(en)_3]^{2+}$ is diamagnetic.
(c) $[Co(C_2O_4)_3]^{3-}$ is diamagnetic and $[Ni(en)_3]^{2+}$ is paramagnetic.
(d) $[Co(C_2O_4)_3]^{3-}$ and $[Ni(en)_3]^{2+}$ both diamagnetic.

7. Inner orbital complex which is paramagnetic in nature?
(a) $[Ni(CN)_5]^{3-}$ (b) $[Fe(CN)_6]^{4-}$
(c) $[Fe(H_2O)_5(NO)]SO_4$ (d) $[Fe(CN)_6]^{3-}$

8. The complex ion $[Fe(CN)_6]^{4-}$ contains
(a) total of 36 electrons on Fe^{2+} cation
(b) sp^3d^2 hybrid orbitals with octahedral structure
(c) Twelve coordinate bonds
(d) six sigma bonds

9. $[NiCl_4]^{-2}$ and $[Ni(CN)_4]^{-2}$ show similarity in:
(a) geometry
(b) magnetic nature
(c) hybridisation state of Ni
(d) primary valency of Ni

10. VBT cannot explain the geometry of
(a) $[Cr(NH_3)_6]^{+3}$ (b) $[Co(NH_3)_6]^{+3}$
(c) $[Cu(NH_3)_4]^{+2}$ (d) $[Zn(NH_3)_4]^{+2}$

11. In the following complex ions, order of paramagnetism is
P : $[V(H_2O)_6]^{3+}$ Q : $[CoF_6]^{3-}$
R : $[FeF_6]^{3-}$ S : $[Ti(H_2O)_6]^{3+}$
(a) R > Q > P > S (b) Q > R > P > S
(c) P = Q = R = S (d) R > Q > S > P

12. The hybridisation, shape and magnetic moment of the complex, $K_4[Ni(CN)_6]$ is
(a) d^2sp^3, octahedral and 0 BM
(b) sp^3d^2, octahedral and 3.87 BM
(c) d^2sp^3, octahedral and 3.87 BM
(d) sp^3d^2, octahedral and 0 BM

13. Consider the compounds given below.
(I) $Ni(CO)_4$ (II) $Fe(CO)_5$
(III) $V(CO)_6$ (IV) $Cr(CO)_6$
Which amongst the following metal carbonyls are inner orbital complex with diamagnetic property?
(a) (I) and (II) (b) (II), (III) and (IV)
(c) (II) and (IV) (d) (I), (II) and (IV)

14. The complex compound having square planar geometry is
(a) $[Ni(CO)_4]$ (b) $[Zn(CN)_4]^{2-}$
(c) $[Cu(NH_3)_4]Cl_2$ (d) $[Cu(NH_3)_4]Cl_3$

15. In which of the following complexes the crystal field splitting energy in octahedral field (Δ_O), will be maximum?
(a) $[Co(CN)_6]^{3-}$ (b) $[Co(C_2O_4)_3]^{3-}$
(c) $[Co(H_2O)_6]^{3+}$ (d) $[Co(NH_3)_6]^{3+}$

16. Among the following pairs of complexes, in which case the Δ_o value is higher for the first one?
(a) $[Mn(NH_3)_6]^{3+}$ and $[Mn(CN)_6]^{3-}$
(b) $[MnF_6]^{3-}$ and $[Mn(NH_3)_6]^{3+}$
(c) $[Mn(H_2O)_6]^{2+}$ and $[Mn(H_2O)_6]^{3+}$
(d) $[Tc(H_2O)_6]^{3+}$ and $[Mn(H_2O)_6]^{3+}$

17. Electronic configuration of a system if $\Delta_O < P$ and the magnetic nature will be
(a) t_{2g}^4, e_g^0 and diamagnetic.
(b) t_{2g}^3, e_g^1 and paramagnetic.
(c) t_{2g}^4, e_g and paramagnetic.
(d) t_{2g}^3, e_g^3 and diamagnetic.

18. Given below are two statements:
Statement I *cis*-$[Pt(Cl_2)(NH_3)_2]$ is used as an anti-cancer drug to inhibit the growth of tumor.
Statement II Desferrioxamine-B is used in the treatment of lead poisoning.
In the light of the above statements. Choose the correct answer from the options given below:
(a) Both Statement I and Statement II are correct.
(b) Statement I is correct but Statement II is incorrect.
(c) Both Statement I and Statement II are incorrect.
(d) Statement I is incorrect but Statement II is correct.

19. Which of the following is the strongest ligand based on the value of the given stability constants?
(a) $Cu^{2+} + 4NH_3 \longrightarrow [Cu(NH_3)_4]^{2+}, K = 4.5 \times 10^{11}$
(b) $Cu^{2+} + 4CN^- \longrightarrow [Cu(CN)_4]^{2-}, K = 2.0 \times 10^{27}$
(c) $Cu^{2+} + 2en \longrightarrow [Cu(en)_2]^{2+}, K = 3.0 \times 10^{15}$
(d) $Cu^{2+} + 4H_2O \longrightarrow [Cu(H_2O)_4]^{2+}, K = 9.5 \times 10^8$

20. Match List-I with List-II.

	List-I (Complex ion)		List-II (Electronic configuration)
A.	$FeCl_4^-$	I.	t_{2g}^6, e_g^2
B.	$[Ni(H_2O)_6]^{2+}$	II.	t_{2g}^2, e_g^0
C.	$[V(H_2O)_6]^{3+}$	III.	e^2, t_2^3
D.	$[FeO_4]^{2-}$	IV.	e^2, t_2^3

Choose the correct answer from the options given below:
(a) A-IV, B-I, C-II, D-III
(b) A-IV, B-III, C-I, D-II
(c) A-II, B-IV, C-I, D-III
(d) A-III, B-II, C-I, D-IV

Type II 》 MCQs with One or More than One Correct Option

21. Select the correct statement:
(a) The strength of anionic ligands can not be explained by crystal field theory.
(b) Greater the charge on the central metal cation, greater the value of Δ (CFSE).
(c) In complex ion $[CoF_6]^{3-}$, F^- is a weak field ligand, so that $\Delta_{oct} < P$ (Pairing energy) and it is low spin complex.
(d) $[CoCl_2(NH_3)_2(en)]^{\oplus}$ complex ion will have four different isomers.

22. In test of NO_3^- ion, the dark brown ring complex is formed, which is true of this complex?
(a) The colour is due to charge transfer spectra
(b) Iron and NO both have + 1 charge
(c) The complex species can be represented as $[Fe^{I}(H_2O)_5NO]^{2+}$
(d) Iron has + 2 oxidation state and NO is neutral

23. The d-orbitals involved in sp^3d^2 or d^2sp^3 hybridisation of the central metal ion are:
(a) $d_{x^2-y^2}$ (b) d_{xy} (c) d_{yz} (d) d_{z^2}

24. Which of the following is the correct statement(s)?
(a) $[Ag(NH_3)_2]^+$ is linear with sp hybridised Ag^+ ions
(b) $NiCl_4^{2-}$, CrO_4^{2-} and MnO_4^-, have tetrahedral geometry
(c) $[Cu(NH_3)_4]^{2+}$, $[Pt(NH_3)_4]^{2+}$ and $[Ni(CN)_4]^{2-}$ have with dsp^2 hybridisation of the metal ion.
(d) $Fe(CO)_5$ has trigonal bipyramidal structure with dsp^3 hybridised ion.

25. $K_2[Ni(CN)_4] \xrightarrow[NH_3]{\text{K in liq.}}$ 'X'
Regarding this reaction correct statement is/are:
(a) 'X' is $K_4[Ni(CN)_4]$
(b) The oxidation state of Ni changed +2 to zero
(c) The structure of 'X' is tetrahedral
(d) $[Ni(CN)_4]^{2-}$ is square planar complex

26. Select correct statement(s) regarding given complexes:
(a) $[Fe(CO)_5]$, the orbitals used for hybridisation in Fe atom are $s, p_x, p_y, p_z, d_{z^2}$ and it is low spin complex.
(b) $[Pt(NH_3)_2Cl_2]$, the orbitals used for hybridisation on Pt atom are $s, p_x, p_y, d_{x^2-y^2}$ and it is low spin complex.
(c) $[Cr(H_2O)_6]^{3+}$, the orbitals used for hybridisation in Cr atom are $s, p_x, p_y, p_z, p_{z^2}, d_{x^2-y^2}$ and it is high spin complex.
(d) $Ni(CO)_4$, the orbitals used for hybridisation in Ni atom are, s, p_x, p_y, p_z and it is low spin complex.

27. A d-block element forms octahedral complex but its magnetic moment remains same either in strong field or in weak field ligand. Which of the following is/are correct?
(a) Element always forms colourless compound
(b) Number of electrons in t_{2g} orbitals are higher than in e_g orbitals
(c) It can have either d^3 or d^8 configuration
(d) It can have either d^7 or d^8 configuration

Type III 》 Numerical/Integer Type Questions

28. The most likely formula of platinum complex is $PtCl_4 \cdot 3H_2O$. If x chlorine atom get precipitated by adding $AgNO_3$ to its aqueous solution. Then the value of x ....

29. The number of unpaired electron in $[ZnCl_4]^{2-}$ is x and number of unpaired e^- in $[Zn(NH_3)_4]^{2+}$ is y. Then $\frac{x}{y}$ will be.

30. The sum of inner d-orbitals used for bonding by the complex below is
$[Ti(H_2O)_6]Cl_2$, $K_2[Ni(CN)_6]$, $(NH_4)_2[Ni(CN)_4]$ and $K_2[NiCl_4]$

31. How many of the following complexes are low spin and diamagnetic $(NH_4)_4[Fe(CN)_6]$, $[Mo(CO)_6]$, $[Mn(NH_3)_6]^{2+}$, $[Fe(CN)_6]^{3-}$, $[Co(NO_2)_6]^{3-}$, $[FeF_6]^{3-}$, $[Ni(NH_3)_6]^{2+}$.

32. The total number of unpaired electrons in t_{2g} orbital of $[Ni(en)_3]^{2-}$ is

33. In the complex ions, MX_6 and MY_6, the metal cation Mn^{+n} has five d electrons where X is weak ligand and Y is strong field ligand. According to CFT, the ratio of unpaired e^- of MX_6^{n+} and MY_6^{n+} is ....

34. Consider the following reactions.
$AgBr(s) + 2S_2O_3^{2-} \longrightarrow A$
$Au + CN^- + O_2 + 2H_2O \longrightarrow B$
The total number of correct statements regarding the product A and B is ....
I. Articles can be electroplated with Au from solution of B.
II. The complex formed in A is water insoluble.
III. Gold can be extracted by the complex B.
IV. Oxidation state of metal in complex B is 2.
V. The IUPAC name of complex formed in A is dithiosulphate argentate (I).

Elemental Practice 9.3 | Chapter 09

Connect with **Answers**

1. (c)	2. (c)	3. (c)	4. (b)	5. (d)	6. (d)
7. (d)	8. (a)	9. (d)	10. (c)	11. (a)	12. (d)
13. (c)	14. (c)	15. (a)	16. (d)	17. (b)	18. (b)
19. (b)	20. (a)	21. (a,b,d)	22. (a,b,c)	23. (a,d)	24. (a,b,c,d)
25. (a,b,c,d)	26. (a,b,c,d)	27. (b,c)	28. (1)	29. (0)	30. (3)
31. (3)	32. (0)	33. (5)	34. (3)		

Advanced Exclusive Different Strokes

Tips to Identify the Labile and Inert Complexes

- Complexes which permit quick exchange of one or more ligands from their coordination sphere by other ligands are called labile complexes. On the other hand, complexes which either do not permit exchange of ligands or in which the exchange of ligands is slow are known as inert complexes.
- In general, complex ions of the first transition series except for those of Cr(III) and Co(III) are kinetically labile, those of the second and third transition series are generally kinetically inert.
- The inertness of a complex has nothing to do with its thermodynamic stability.

Let us understand this with the help of example

- The complex $[Ni(CN)_4]^{2-}$ is thermodynamically stable but kinetically it is labile.

$$[Ni(CN)_4]^{2-} + (^{13}CN)^- \xrightarrow[\text{in aqueous solution}]{\text{Very fast}} [Ni(CN)_3(^{13}CN)]^{2-} + (CN)^-$$

- In the substitution reaction

$$[Co(NH_3)_6]^{3+}(aq) + 6H_3O^+(aq) \rightleftharpoons [Co(H_2O)_6]^{3+}(aq) + 6NH_4^+(aq)$$

- The products are favoured by an enormous amount, yet the inert $[Co(NH_3)_6]^{3+}$ complex ion last for weeks in acidic solution because there is no low-energy pathway for the reaction. The cobalt (III) ion, $[Co(NH_3)_6]^{3+}$, is thermodynamically unstable relative to $[Co(H_2O)_6]^{3+}$ but kinetically stable (inert). The closely related cobalt (II) complex, $[Co(NH_3)_6]^{2+}$, reacts with water in a matter of seconds.

$$[Co(NH_3)_6]^{2+}(aq) + 6H_3O^+(aq) \longrightarrow [Co(H_2O)_6]^{2+}(aq) + 6NH_4^+(aq)$$

The complex $[Co(NH_3)_6]^{2+}$ is thermodynamically unstable and also kinetically labile.

d^x ion	Labile or inert
d^0	Fast to react (Labile)
d^1	Fast to react
d^2	Fast to react
d^3	Slow to react (Inert)
d^4 (HS)	Fast to react
d^4 (LS)	Slow to react
d^5 (HS)	Fast to react
d^5 (LS)	Slow to react
d^6 (HS)	Fast to react
d^6 (LS)	Slow to react
d^7 (HS)	Fast to react
d^7 (LS)	Fast to react
d^8	Slow to react
d^9	Fast to react
d^{10}	Fast to react

- For a given ion and ligand, greater the charge on the metal ion, greater will be the stability. Thus, stability of $[Fe^{III}(CN)_6]^{3-} > [Fe^{II}(CN)_6]^{4-}$
- For the divalent ions of the first row transition elements (3*d*-series), the stabilities vary in the **Irving-Williams order :** $Mn^{II} < Fe^{II} < Co^{II} < Ni^{II} < Cu^{II} < Zn^{II}$
- Ligands containing N, O or F donor atoms form most stable coordination compounds when metal ions are:
  - groups 1 and 2 elements, the inner transition elements and transition elements of groups 3 to 6 (Sc, T, V, Cr) called **'class a' acceptors.**
  - Transition elements —Rh, Pd, Ag, Ir, Au and Hg having relatively completely filled *d*-orbitals called **'class b' acceptors.**
- If a multidentate ligand happens to be cyclic and there are no unfavourable steric effects, a further increase in stability occurs. This is termed the **macrocyclic effect.**
- **Thus, with the help of concept discussed, students can easily approach the problem related to inert and labile complexes that are visible in JEE Advanced Exam.**

PRACTICE

ELEMENT 01

Target JEE Main

Objective Type Questions

1. Aqueous solution of Mohr's salt gives a positive test for
   (a) ferrous ions only
   (b) sulphate ions only
   (c) ammonium and sulphate ions only
   (d) ferrous, ammonium and sulphate ions

2. Select the incorrect statement:
   (a) Hydrazine can act as bidentate ligand.
   (b) Oxalate is a chelating ligand.
   (c) All bidentate ligands are chelating ligands.
   (d) Number of chelate rings = (denticity – 1).

3. On the basis of Sidgwick EAN rule, which of the following statement is not correct?
   (a) $[Mn(CO)_6]$ can act as reducing agent.
   (b) $[V(CO)_6]$ can act as oxidising agent.
   (c) $[Fe(CO)_5]$ can act as both oxidising agent and reducing agent.
   (d) $[Mn(CO)_5]$ shows dimerisation to gain stability.

4. $[Fe(CO)_5]$ and $[Ni(CO)_4]$ do not show similarity in:
   (a) participation of *d*-orbital in hybridisation.
   (b) polarity and magnetic nature.
   (c) presence of synergic bonding.
   (d) shifting of *ns* electron into $(n-1)d$ subshell.

5. Which of the following pairs of name and formula complexes is not correct?
   (a) Tetraamminecopper (II) sulphate $[Cu(NH_3)_4]SO_4$
   (b) Diamminesilver (I) chloride $[Ag(NH_3)_2]Cl$
   (c) Potassium hexacyanidoferrate (III) $K_4[Fe(CN)_6]$
   (d) Potassium amminepentachloridoplatinate (IV) $K[Pt(NH_3)Cl_5]$

6. The complex that exhibits lowest energy absorption band is
   (a) $[NiCl_4]^{2-}$ (b) $[Ni(CO)_4]$
   (c) $[Ni(CN)_4]^{2-}$ (d) $[Ni(H_2O)_6]^{2+}$

7. For which one of the following ion the colour is not due to a *d-d* transition?
   (a) CrO_4^{2-} Lemon yellow
   (b) $[Cu(NH_3)_4]^{2+}$ Deep blue
   (c) $[Fe(H_2O)_6]SO_4$ Green
   (d) $[Ti(H_2O)_6]^{3+}$ Purple

8. Choose the incorrect match from the following.
   (a) $FeCl_3 + KCNS \longrightarrow$ Red colour
   (b) $KI + PbCl_2 \longrightarrow$ Yellow ppt.
   (c) NH_4Cl + Nesseler's reagent $\rightarrow$ Blue colour
   (d) $DMG + Ni^{2+} + NH_4OH \longrightarrow$ Scarlet red ppt.

9. Each of the compounds $Pt(NH_3)_6Cl_4$, $Cr(NH_3)_6Cl_3$, $(Co(NH_3)_4Cl_3$ and K_2PtCl_6 were dissolved in water to make its 0.001 M solution. The correct order of their increasing conductivity in solution is
   (a) $K_2PtCl_6 < Co(NH_3)_4Cl_3 < Cr(NH_3)_6Cl_3 < Pt(NH_3)_6Cl_4$
   (b) $Cr(NH_3)_6Cl_3 < Co(NH_3)_4Cl_3 < K_2PtCl_6 < Pt(NH_3)_6Cl_4$
   (c) $Co(NH_3)_4Cl_3 < K_2PtCl_6 < Cr(NH_3)_6Cl_3 < Pt(NH_3)_6Cl_4$
   (d) $Pt(NH_3)_6Cl_4 < Co(NH_3)_4Cl_3 < Cr(NH_3)_6Cl_3 < K_2PtCl_6$

10. Incorrect order of splitting energy is
    (a) $[NiF_6]^{4-} < [NiF_6]^{2-}$
    (b) $[Fe(H_2O)_6]^{3+} < [Ru(H_2O)_6]^{3+}$
    (c) $[Co(NH_3)_6]^{3+} < [Co(en)_3]^{3+}$
    (d) $[Ni(CN)_4]^{2-} < [Ni(CN)_6]^{4-}$

11. In which of the following complex ion, the metal ion will have $t_{2g}^6 e_g^0$ configuration according to CFT?
    (a) $[FeF_6]^{3-}$ (b) $[Fe(CN)_6]^{3-}$
    (c) $[Fe(CN)_6]^{4-}$ (d) $[Fe(H_2O)_6]^{+2}$

12. The Δ_0 (CFSE) for $[CoCl_6]^{4-}$ is 18000 cm^{-1}. The splitting energy for $[CoCl_4]^{2-}$ will be
    (a) 18000 cm^{-1} (b) 16000 cm^{-1}
    (c) 8000 cm^{-1} (d) 2000 cm^{-1}

13. Which of the following is correct order of stability?
    (a) $[NiCl_4]^{2-} < [PdCl_4]^{-2} < [PtCl_4]^{-2}$
    (b) $[Co(H_2O)_6]^{+3} < [Co(NH_3)_6]^{+3} < [Co(CN)_6]^{-3}$
    (c) $[Co(H_2O)_6]^{+3} < [Rh(H_2O)_6]^{+3} < [Ir(H_2O)_6]^{+3}$
    (d) All of these

14. The incorrect statement is
    (a) Fe^{+2} salt gives blue colloidal solution with $K_3[Fe(CN)_6]$
    (b) $FeCl_3$ gives red colour with KSCN
    (c) Cu^{+2} salt gives blue colloidal solution with $K_4[Fe(CN)_6]$
    (d) Light blue solution of $CuSO_4$ turn into dark blue in presence of ammonia.

15. Mixture X = 0.02 mole $[Co(NH_3)_5SO_4]$ Br and 0.02 mole of $[Co(NH_3)_5Br]SO_4$ prepared in 2 L of solution
    1 L of mixture X + excess $AgNO_3 \rightarrow Y$
    1 L of mixture X + excess $BaCl_2 \rightarrow Z$
    Number of moles of Y and Z are
    (a) 0.01 , 0.01
    (b) 0.01, 0.02
    (c) 0.02, 0.01
    (d) 0.02, 0.02

16. Which of the following statements Is correct?
(a) Zinc (II) ion has a zero CFSE for any geometry
(b) A solution of $[Fe(CN)_6]^{4-}$ and $[Fe(H_2O)_6]^{2+}$ appear colourless in dilute soluitons
(c) $[Ni(H_2O)_6]^{3+}$ is an octahedral complex, where the single electron in the metal *d*-orbital is in the t_{2g} level in the ground state of the complex.
(d) CFSE is always greater for high spin complexes than for low spin complexes.

17. The calculated spin only magnetic moments of $[Cr(H_2O)_6]^{3+}$ and $[CuF_6]^{3-}$ in BM, respectively, are (Atomic numbers of Cr and Cu are 24 and 29 respectively).
(a) 2.83, 3.87 (b) 3.87, 2.83
(c) 0, 0 (d) 1.67, 3.87

18. One mole of the complex compound $Co(NH_3)_5Cl_3$, gives 3 moles of ions on dissolution in water. One mole of the same complex reacts with two moles of $AgNO_3$, solution to yield two moles of AgCl(s). The structure of the complex is
(a) $[Co(NH_3)_5Cl]Cl_2$ (b) $[Co(NH_3)_3Cl_3]\cdot 2NH_3$
(c) $[Co(NH_3)_4Cl_2]Cl\cdot NH_3$ (d) $[Co(NH_3)_4Cl]Cl_2\cdot NH_3$

19. Among $[TiF_6]^{2-}$, $[CoF_6]^{3-}$, Cu_2Cl_2 and $[Ni(Cl_4)]^{2-}$, the colourless species are:
(a) $[CoF_6]^{3-}$ and $[NiCl_4]^{2-}$ (b) $[TiF_6]^{2-}$ and $[CoF_6]^{3-}$
(c) $[NiCl_4]^{2-}$ and Cu_2Cl_2 (d) $[TiF_6]^{2-}$ and Cu_2Cl_2

20. Select the incorrect statement.
(a) EDTA shows flexidentate character.
(b) All the lone pairs are not necessarily used in coordinate bonding.
(c) EDTA does not alter the oxidation states of metal ions, it only chelates them.
(d) Ambidentate ligands are those in which only one donor atom is attached to metal atom.

Numerical Type Questions

21. The magnetic moment (spin only) of $[NiCl_4]^{2-}$ is ...... (nearest integer)

22. The sum of coordination number and the oxidation state of the element '*E*' in the complex $[E(en)_2(C_2O_4)]NO_2$ (where (en) is ethylenediamine) is ....

23. The sum of values of *m* and *n* in the anionic species $[V(CO)_m]^{n-}$, if it is following Sidgwick EAN rule and having octahedral shape is

24. Consider the following carbonyl complex compounds (I) $H_xCr(CO)_5$ (II) $Co(CO)_y$, (III) $Mo(CO)_z$ then the value of $\left(\frac{x+y+z}{5}\right)$ is .... (nearest integer)

25. Brown colour of the complex $[Fe(H_2O)_5(NO)]SO_4$ is due to charge transfer spectrum which causes momentary change in oxidation state. Find out oxidation state of Fe in this complex.

26. Sum of denticity of following ligands are Glycinate ion, Oxalate ion, *o*-phenanhroline, 2, 2′-bipyridyl, diethylenetriamine, ethylenediamine

27. The sum of number of geometrical isomers for following complexes is
(1) $[CoCl_2Br_2]^{2-}$ (2) $[Rh(en)_3]^{3+}$
(3) $[Cr(en)_2Br_2]^+$ (4) $[Pt(en)Cl_2]$
(5) $[Co(NH_3)_3(NO_2)_3]$

28. In the complex $Fe(CO)_x$, the value of *x* is

29. Count the number of ions which can form both low spin and high spin complexes when co-ordination number is Co^{+3}, Ni^{+2}, Cr^{+3}, Fe^{+2}, Fe^{+3}, Cu^{+2}, Ti^{+3}, Co^{+2}

30. The number of unpaired electrons present in $[NiF_6]^{2-}$ is ....

Check Through PYQs

Element 1 Basic Terms Used in Coordination Compounds and IUPAC Nomenclature

1. The F^- ions make the enamel on teeth much harder by converting hydroxyapatite (the enamel on the surface of teeth) into much harder fluoroapatite having the formula. *2024, 9 April Shift-I*
(a) $[3(Ca_3(PO_4)_2\cdot CaF_2]$ (b) $[3(Ca_3(PO_4)_2)\cdot Ca(OH)_2]$
(c) $[3(Ca_2(PO_4)_2)\cdot Ca(OH)_2]$ (d) $[3(Ca_3)(PO_4)_3)\cdot CaF_2]$

2. An octahedral complex with the formula $CoCl_3.nNH_3$ upon reaction with excess of $AgNO_3$ solution gives 2 moles of AgCl. Consider the oxidation state of Co in the complex '*x*'. The value of "*x* + *n*" is .... *2024, 8 April Shift-I*
(a) 3 (b) 6 (c) 5 (d) 8

3. The IUPAC name of $K_3[Co(C_2O_4)_3]$ is *2023, 6 April Shift-II*
(a) potassium trioxalatocobaltate (III)
(b) potassium tris(oxalato)cobalt (III)
(c) potassium tris(oxalato)cobaltate (III)
(d) potassium trioxalatocobalt (III)

4. Which of the following are the example of double salt? *2023, 1 Feb Shift-I*
A. $FeSO_4\cdot(NH_4)_2SO_4\cdot 6H_2O$
B. $CuSO_4\cdot 4NH_3\cdot H_2O$
C. $K_2SO_4.Al_2(SO_4)_3.24H_2O$
D. $Fe(CN)_2.4KCN$
Choose the correct answer given below.
(a) A and B (b) A, B and D
(c) A and C (d) B and D

5. Sum of oxidation state (magnitude) and coordination number of cobalt in $Na[Co(bpy)Cl_4]$ is ....

(Given, bpy = 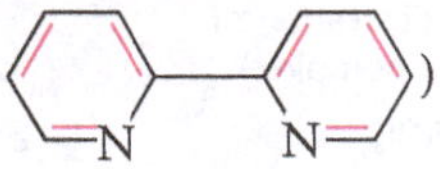)

2022, 29 July Shift-II

6. Number of complexes which will exhibit synergic bonding amongst, $[Cr(CO)_6]$, $[Mn(CO)_5]$ and $[Mn_2(CO)_{10}]$ is .... **2022, 28 June Shift-I**

7. In the cobalt-carbonyl complex $[Co_2(CO)_8]$, number of Co — Co bonds is "X" and terminal CO ligands is "Y". $X + Y =$ .... **2022, 24 June Shift-I**

8. 1 mol of an octahedral metal complex with formula $MCl_3 \cdot 2L$ on reaction with excess of $AgNO_3$ gives 1 mol of AgCl. The denticity of ligand L is .... (Integer answer) **2021, 27 Aug Shift-I**

9. Given below are two statements.

Statement I The identification of Ni^{2+} is carried out by dimethyl glyoxime in the presence of NH_4OH.

Statement II The dimethyl glyoxime is a bidentate neutral ligand.

In the light of the above statements, choose the correct answer from the options given below. **2021, 25 Feb Shift-II**

(a) Both statements I and II are true.
(b) Both statements I and II are false.
(c) Statement I is true but statement II is false.
(d) Statement I is false but statement II is true.

10. Complex (A) has a composition of $H_{12}O_6Cl_3Cr$. If the complex on treatment with conc. H_2SO_4 loses 13.5% of its original mass, the correct molecular formula of (A) is[Given : atomic mass of Cr = 52 amu and Cl = 35 amu] **2020, 3 Sep Shift-II**

(a) $[Cr(H_2O)_4Cl_2]Cl \cdot 2H_2O$
(b) $[Cr(H_2O)_6]Cl_3$
(c) $[Cr(H_2O)_5Cl]Cl_2 \cdot H_2O$
(d) $[Cr(H_2O)_3Cl_3] \cdot 3H_2O$

Element 2 Isomerism in Coordination Compounds

11. Which of the following compound can show fac mer isomerism? **2025, 23 Jan Shift-I**

(a) $[Co(NH_3)_6]Cl_3$
(b) $[Co(NH_3)_3Cl_3]$
(c) $[Co(en)_2(NH_3)_2]Cl_3$
(d) $[Co(H_2O)_6]Cl_3$

12. Number of complexes which show optical isomerism among the following is ....

cis-$[Cr(ox)_2Cl_2]^{3-}$, $[Co(en)_3]^{3+}$, *cis*-$[Pt(en)_2Cl_2]^{2+}$, *cis*-$[Co(en)_2Cl_2]^+$, *trans*-$[Pt(en)_2Cl_2]^{2+}$, *trans*-$[Cr(ox)_2Cl_2]^{3-}$

2024, 30 Jan Shift-II

13. The total number of stereoisomers for the complex $[Cr(ox)_2ClBr]^{3-}$ (where ox = oxalate) is **2023, 13 April Shift-II**

(a) 1 (b) 3
(c) 2 (d) 4

14. (i) $CoCl_3 \cdot 4NH_3$, (ii) $CoCl_3 \cdot 5NH_3$, (iii) $CoCl_3 \cdot 6NH_3$ and (iv) $CoCl(NO_3)_2 \cdot 5NH_3$

Number of complex(es) which will exist in *cis-trans* form is/are .... **2022, 28 June Shift-II**

15. Given below are two statements.

Statement I In $CuSO_4 \cdot 5H_2O$, Cu—O bonds are present.

Statement II In $CuSO_4 \cdot 5H_2O$, ligands coordinating with Cu(II) ion are O-and S-based ligands.

In the light of the above statements, choose the correct answer from the options given below **2022, 29 June Shift-II**

(a) Both Statement I and Statement II are correct.
(b) Both Statement I and Statement II are incorrect.
(c) Statement I is correct but Statement II is incorrect.
(d) Statement I is incorrect but Statement II is correct.

16. Match List-I and List-II.

List-I	List-II
A. $[Co(NH_3)_6][Cr(CN)_6]$	1. Linkage isomerism
B. $[Co(NH_3)_3(NO_2)_3]$	2. Solvate isomerism
C. $[Cr(H_2O)_6]Cl_3$	3. Co-ordination isomerism
D. *cis*-$[CrCl_2(ox)_2]^{3-}$	4. Optical isomerism

Choose the correct answer from the options given below. **2021, 17 March Shift-II**

	A	B	C	D
(a)	3	1	2	4
(b)	4	2	3	1
(c)	2	1	3	4
(d)	1	2	3	4

17. The number of geometrical isomers found in the metal complexes $[PtCl_2(NH_3)_2]$, $[Ni(CO)_4]$, $[Ru(H_2O)_3Cl_3]$ and $[CoCl_2(NH_3)_4]^+$ respectively, are **2021, 27 July Shift-I**

(a) 1, 1, 1, 1 (b) 2, 1, 2, 2
(c) 2, 0, 2, 2 (d) 2, 1, 2, 1

18. Indicate the complex/complex ion which did not show any geometrical isomerism. **2021, 26 Aug Shift-II**

(a) $[CoCl_2(en)_2]$ (b) $[Co(CN)_5(NC)]^{3-}$
(c) $[Co(NH_3)_3(NO_2)_3]$ (d) $[Co(NH_3)_4Cl_2]^+$

19. The number of possible optical isomers for the complexes MA_2B_2 with sp^3 and dsp^2 hybridised metal atom, respectively, is

Note : *A* and *B* are unidentate neutral and unidentate monoanionic ligands, respectively. **2020, 7 Jan Shift-II**

(a) 0 and 0 (b) 0 and 1
(c) 2 and 2 (d) 0 and 2

20. Among (A) - (D), the complexes that can display geometrical isomerism are
(A) $[Pt(NH_3)_3Cl]^+$
(B) $[Pt(NH_3)Cl_5]^-$
(C) $[Pt(NH_3)_2Cl(NO_2)]$
(D) $[Pt(NH_3)_4ClBr]^{2+}$
2020, 8 Jan Shift-II
(a) (D) and (A) (b) (C) and (D)
(c) (A) and (B) (d) (B) and (C)

Element 3 Bonding in Coordination Compounds

21. For complex ion $[NiCl_4]^{2-}$ what is the charge on metal and shape of complex respectively? *2025, 22 Jan Shift-I*
(a) +2, Tetrahedral (b) +2, Square planar
(c) +4, Tetrahedral (d) +4, Square planar

22. Which of the following complex is paramagnetic *2025, 28 Jan Shift-II*
(a) $[NiCl_4]^{2-}$ (b) $[Ni(CO)_4]$
(c) $[Ni(CN)_4]^{2-}$ (d) $[Fe(CO)_5]$

23. Match List I with List II

List-I	List-II
A. $K_2[Ni(CN)_4]$	I. sp^3
B. $[Ni(CO)_4]$	II. sp^3d^2
C. $[Co(NH_3)_6]Cl_3$	III. dsp^2
D. $Na_3[CoF_6]$	IV. d^2sp^3

Choose the correct answer from the options given below : *2024, 9 April Shift-II*
(a) A-III, B-I, C-II, D-IV
(b) A-III, B-I, C-IV, D-II
(c) A-I, B-III, C-II, D-IV
(d) A-III, B-II, C-IV, D-I

24. Match List-I with List-II.

List-I (Complex ion)	List-II (Spin only magnetic moment in B.M.)
A. $[Cr(NH_3)_6]^{3+}$	I. 4.90
B. $[NiCl_4]^{2-}$	II. 3.87
C. $[CoF_6]^{3-}$	III. 0.0
D. $[Ni(CN_4)]^{2-}$	IV. 2.83

Choose the correct answer from the options given below: *2024, 8 April Shift-II*
(a) A-I, B-IV, C-II, D-III (b) A-II, B-III, C-I, D-IV
(c) A-II, B-IV, C-I, D-III (d) A-IV, B-III, C-I, D-II

25. Match List-I with List-II *2024, 6 April Shift-II*

List-I (Tetrahedral complex)	List-II (Electronic configuration)
A. $TiCl_4$	I. e^2,t_2^0
B. $[FeO_4]^{2-}$	II. e^4,t_2^3
C. $[FeCl_4]^-$	III. e^0,t_2^0
D. $[CoCl_4]^{2-}$	IV. e^2,t_2^3

Choose the correct answer from the options given below.

	A	B	C	D
(a)	I	III	IV	II
(b)	III	IV	II	I
(c)	III	I	IV	II
(d)	IV	III	I	II

26. Consider the following complexes. *2024, 6 April Shift-I*
$[CoCl(NH_3)_5]^{2+}$, $[Co(CN)_6]^{3-}$,
(A) (B)
$[Co(NH_3)_5(H_2O)]^{3+}$, $[Cu(H_2O)_4]^{2+}$
(C) (D)
The correct order of *A*, *B*, *C* and *D* in terms of wave number of light absorbed is :
(a) $B < C < A < D$ (b) $D < A < C < B$
(c) $C < D < A < B$ (d) $A < C < B < D$

27. Given below are two statements. *2024, 1 Feb Shift-I*
Statement I A solution of $[Ni(H_2O)_6]^{2+}$ is green in colour.
Statement II A solution of $[Ni(CN)_4]^{2-}$ is colourless.
In the light of the above statements, choose the **most appropriate** answer from the options given below.
(a) Statement I is correct but Statement II is incorrect.
(b) Both Statement I and Statement II are incorrect.
(c) Both Statement I and Statement II are correct.
(d) Statement I is incorrect but Statement II is correct.

28. The correct statements from following are: *2024, 31 Jan Shift-I*
A. The strength of anionic ligands can be explained by crystal field theory.
B. Valence bond theory does not give a quantitative interpretation of kinetic stability of coordination compounds.
C. The hybridisation involved in formation of $[Ni(CN)_4]^{2-}$ complex is dsp^2.
D. The number of possible isomer(s) of *cis*-$[PtCl_2(en)_2]^{2+}$ is one

Choose the correct answer from the options given below:
(a) B and D (b) B and C
(c) A and D (d) A and C

29. Choose the correct statements from the following. *2024, 30 Jan Shift-I*

(A) Ethane-1, 2-diamine is a chelating ligand.
(B) Metallic aluminium is produced by electrolysis of aluminium oxide in presence of cryolite.
(C) Cyanide ion is used as ligand for leaching of silver.
(D) Phosphine act as a ligand in Wilkinson catalyst.
(E) The stability constants of Ca^{2+} and Mg^{2+} are similar with EDTA complexes.

Choose the correct answer from the options given below.

(a) (A), (B) and (C) (b) (B), (C) and (E)
(c) (C), (D) and (E) (d) (A), (D) and (E)

30. The mismatched combinations are

A. chlorophyll - Co
B. water hardness - EDTA
C. photography - $[Ag(CN)_2]^-$
D. Wilkinson catalyst - $[(Ph_3P)_3RhCl]$
E. chelating ligand -D-penicillamine

Choose the correct answer from the options given below *2023, 13 April Shift-I*

(a) A and C (b) D and E
(c) A, C, and E (d) A and E

31. Match List-I with List-II.

List-I (Complex)		List-II (Colour)	
A.	$Mg(NH_4)PO_4$	I.	Brown
B.	$K_3[Co(NO_2)_6]$	II.	White
C.	$MnO(OH)_2$	III.	Yellow
D.	$Fe_4[Fe(CN)_6]_3$	IV.	Blue

Choose the correct answer from the options given below. *[2023, 11 April Shift-II]*

(a) A-III, B-IV, C-II, D-I (b) A-II, B-III, C-IV, D-I
(c) A-II, B-IV, C-I, D-III (d) A-II, B-III, C-I, D-IV

32. If Ni^{2+} is replaced by Pt^{2+} in the complex $[NiCl_2Br_2]^{2-}$, which of the following properties are expected to get changed?

A. Geometry
B. Geometrical isomerism
C. Optical isomerism
D. Magnetic properties *2023, 11 April Shift-II*

(a) A, B and D (b) A and D
(c) A, B and C (d) B and C

33. The correct order of the number of unpaired electrons in the given complexes is

A. $[Fe(CN)_6]^{3-}$ B. $[FeF_6]^{3-}$
C. $[CoF_6]^{3-}$ D. $[Cr(oxalate)_3]^{3-}$
E. $[Ni(CO)_4]$

Choose the correct answer from the options given below : *[2023, 10 April Shift-II]*

(a) E < A < B < D < C (b) A < E < C < B < D
(c) A < E < D < C < B (d) E < A < D < C < B

34. The correct order of spin only magnetic moments for the following complex ions is *2023, 8 April Shift-I*

(a) $[Fe(CN)_6]^{3-} < [CoF_6]^{3-} < [MnBr_4]^{2-} < [Mn(CN)_6]^{3-}$
(b) $[Fe(CN)_6]^{3-} < [Mn(CN)_6]^{3-} < [CoF_6]^{3-} < [MnBr_4]^{2-}$
(c) $[MnBr_4]^{2-} < [CoF_6]^{3-} < [Fe(CN)_6]^{3-} < [Mn(CN)_6]^{3-}$
(d) $[CoF_6]^{3-} < [MnBr_4]^{2-} < [Fe(CN)_6]^{3-} < [Mn(CN)_6]^{3-}$

35. If the CFSE of $[Ti(H_2O)_6]^{3+}$ is – 96.0 kJ/mol, this complex will absorb maximum at wavelength .... nm. (Nearest integer) *2023, 31 Jan Shift-II*

[Assume Planck's constant $(h) = 6.4 \times 10^{-34}$ Js, speed of light $(c) = 3.0 \times 10^8$ m/s and Avogadro's constant $(N_A) = 6 \times 10^{23}$/mol]

36. Which of the following is correct order of ligand field strength? *2023, 31 Jan Shift-I*

(a) $NH_3 < en < CO < S^{2-} < C_2O_4^{2-}$
(b) $CO < en < NH_3 < C_2O_4^{2-} < S^{2-}$
(c) $S^{2-} < C_2O_4^{2-} < NH_3 < en < CO$
(d) $S^{2-} < NH_3 < en < CO < C_2O_4^{2-}$

37. Octahedral complexes of copper (II) undergo structural distortion (Jahn-Teller). Which one of the given copper (II) complexes will show the maximum structural distortion? (en–ethylenediamine; $H_2N—CH_2—CH_2—NH_2$) *2022, 29 July Shift-II*

(a) $[Cu(H_2O)_6]SO_4$ (b) $[Cu(en)(H_2O)_4]SO_4$
(c) *cis* - $[Cu(en)_2Cl_2]$ (d) *trans*-$[Cu(en)_2Cl_2]$

38. The spin only magnetic moment of the complex present in Fehling's reagent is .... BM. (nearest integer). *2022, 27 July Shift-II*

39. Correct formula of the compound which gives a white precipitate with $BaCl_2$ solution, but not with $AgNO_3$ solution is *2022, 30 June Shift-I*

(a) $[Co(NH_3)_5Br]SO_4$ (b) $[Co(NH_3)_5SO_4]Br$
(c) $[Pt(NH_3)_4Cl_2]Br_2$ (d) $[Pt(NH_3)_4Br_2]Cl_2$

40. Arrange the following coordination compounds in the increasing order of magnetic moments. (Atomic numbers : Mn = 25 ; Fe = 26)

(A) $[FeF_6]^{3-}$ (B) $[Fe(CN)_6]^{3-}$
(C) $[MnCl_6]^{3-}$ (high spin) (D) $[Mn(CN)_6]^{3-}$

Choose the correct answer from the options given below : *2022, 27 June Shift-II*

(a) A < B < D < C (b) B < D < C < A
(c) A < C < D < B (d) B < D < A < C

41. Transition metal complex with highest value of crystal field splitting (Δ_o) will be *2022, 24 June Shift-II*

(a) $[Cr(H_2O)_6]^{3+}$ (b) $[Mo(H_2O)_6]^{3+}$
(c) $[Fe(H_2O)_6]^{3+}$ (d) $[Os(H_2O)_6]^{3+}$

42. Arrange the following cobalt complexes in the order of increasing crystal field stabilisation energy (CFSE) value.

$\underset{(A)}{[CoF_6]^{3-}}$, $\underset{(B)}{[Co(H_2O)_6]^{3+}}$, $\underset{(C)}{[Co(NH_3)_6]^{3+}}$ and $\underset{(D)}{[Co(en)_3]^{3+}}$

Choose the correct option. **2021, 26 Aug Shift-II**

(a) $A < B < C < D$ (b) $B < A < C < D$
(c) $B < C < D < A$ (d) $C < D < B < A$

43. An aqueous solution of $NiCl_2$ was heated with excess sodium cyanide in presence of strong oxidising agent to form $[Ni(CN)_6]^{2-}$. The total change in number of unpaired electrons on metal centre is .... **2021, 20 July Shift-II**

44. The correct order of intensity of colors of the compound is **2021, 20 July 20 Shift-I**

(a) $[Ni(CN)_4]^{2-} > [NiCl_4]^{2-} > [Ni(H_2O)_6]^{2+}$
(b) $[Ni(H_2O)_6]^{2+} > [NiCl_4]^{2-} > [Ni(CN)_4]^{2-}$
(c) $[NiCl_4]^{2-} > [Ni(H_2O)_6]^{2+} > [Ni(CN)_4]^{2-}$
(d) $[NiCl_4]^{2-} > [Ni(CN)_4]^{2-} > [Ni(H_2O)_6]^{2+}$

45. $[Ti(H_2O)_6]^{3+}$ absorbs light of wavelength 498 nm during a *d-d* transition. The octahedral splitting energy for the above complex is .... $\times 10^{-19}$ J (Round off to the nearest intger).
$[h = 6.626 \times 10^{-34}$ Js, $c = 3 \times 10^8 ms^{-1}]$ **2021, 16 March Shift-II**

46. The hybridisation and magnetic nature of $[Mn(CN)_6]^{4-}$ and $[Fe(CN)_6]^{3-}$, respectively are **2021, 25 Feb Shift-I**

(a) d^2sp^3 and paramagnetic (b) sp^3d^2 and diamagnetic
(c) d^2sp^3 and diamagnetic (d) sp^3d^2 and paramagnetic

47. The stepwise formation of $[Cu(NH_3)_4]^{2+}$ is given below

$$Cu^{2+} + NH_3 \overset{K_1}{\rightleftharpoons} [Cu(NH_3)]^{2+}$$

$$[Cu(NH_3)]^{2+} + NH_3 \overset{K_2}{\rightleftharpoons} [Cu(NH_3)_2]^{2+}$$

$$[Cu(NH_3)_2]^{2+} + NH_3 \overset{K_3}{\rightleftharpoons} [Cu(NH_3)_3]^{3+}$$

$$[Cu(NH_3)_3]^{2+} + NH_3 \overset{K_4}{\rightleftharpoons} [Cu(NH_3)_4]^{2+}$$

The value of stability constants K_1, K_2, K_3 and K_4 are 10^4, 1.58×10^3, 5×10^2 and 10^2 respectively. The overall equilibrium constants for dissociation of $[Cu(NH_3)_4]^{2+}$ is $x \times 10^{-12}$. The value of x is .... (Rounded off to the nearest integer) **2021, 24 Feb Shift-I**

48. For a d^4 metal ion in an octahedral field, the correct electronic configuration is **2020, 6 Sep Shift-II**

(a) $t_{2g}^3 e_g^1$ when $\Delta_0 < P$
(b) $t_{2g}^3 e_g^1$ when $\Delta_0 > P$
(c) $t_{2g}^4 e_g^0$ when $\Delta_0 < P$
(d) $t_g^2 e_{2g}^2$ when $\Delta_0 < P$

49. The crystal field stabilisation energy (CFSE) of $[CoF_3(H_2O)_3] (\Delta_0 < P)$ is **2020, 4 Sep Shift-II**

(a) $-0.8\,\Delta_o$ (b) $-0.8\Delta_o + 2P$
(c) $-0.4\Delta_o$ (d) $-0.4\Delta_o + P$

50. The *d*-electron configuration of $[Ru(en)_3]Cl_2$ and $[Fe(H_2O)_6]Cl_2$, respectively are **2020, 3 Sep Shift-II**

(a) $t_{2g}^6 e_g^0$ and $t_{2g}^6 e_g^0$ (b) $t_{2g}^4 e_g^2$ and $t_{2g}^6 e_g^0$
(c) $t_{2g}^6 e_g^0$ and $t_{2g}^4 e_g^2$ (d) $t_{2g}^4 e_g^2$ and $t_{2g}^4 e_g^2$

51. Simplified absorption spectra of three complexes [(i), (ii) and (iii)] of M^{n+} ion are provided below; their λ_{max} values are marked as *A*, *B* and *C* respectively. The correct match between the complexes and their λ_{max} values is

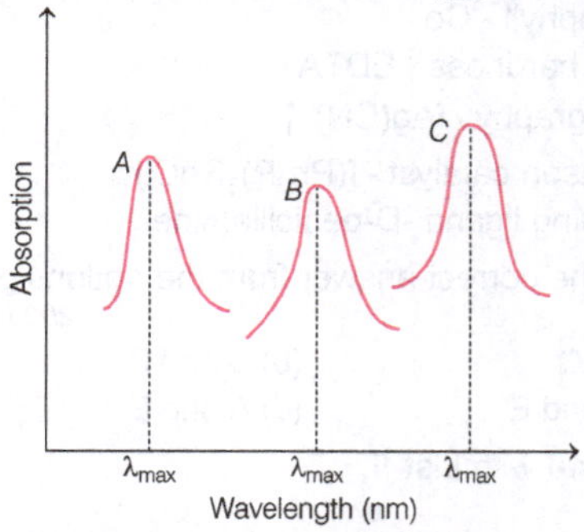

(i) $[M(NCS)_6]^{(-6+n)}$ (ii) $[MF_6]^{(-6+n)}$
(iii) $[M(NH_3)_6]^{n+}$ **2020, 2 Sep Shift-II**

(a) *A*-(iii), *B*-(i), *C*-(ii) (b) *A*-(ii), *B*-(i), *C*-(iii)
(c) *A*-(ii), *B*-(iii), *C*-(i) (d) *A*-(i), *B*-(ii), *C*-(iii)

52. The correct order of the calculated spin only magnetic moments of complexes (A) to (D) is **2020, 8 Jan Shift-II**

(A) $Ni(CO)_4$ (B) $[Ni(H_2O)_6]Cl_2$
(C) $Na_2[Ni(CN)_4]$ (D) $PdCl_2(PPh_3)_2$

(a) (A) ≈ (C) < (B) ≈ (D)
(b) (C) ≈ (D) < (B) < (A)
(c) (C) < (D) < (B) < (A)
(d) (A) ≈ (C) ≈ (D) < (B)

53. The correct statements among I to III are:

(I) Valence bond theory cannot explain the color exhibited by transition metal complexes.
(II) Valence bond theory can predict quantitatively the magnetic properties of transition metal complexes.
(III) Valence bond theory cannot distinguish ligands as weak and strong field one. **2019, 9 April Shift-II**

(a) (II) and (III) only
(b) (I), (II) and (III)
(c) (I) and (III)
(d) (I) and (II)

PRACTICE ELEMENT 02

Target JEE Advanced

Single Correct Choice MCQs

1. In the following complex ions order of paramagnetism is

P : $[Fe(CN)_6]^{3-}$ Q : $[CoF_6]^{3-}$

R : $[Fe(H_2O)_6]^{3+}$ S : $[Ni(CN)_4]^{2-}$

(a) S < P < Q = R (b) Q > P > R > S

(c) P = Q = R = S (d) P > R > Q > S

2. Select the correct match from the following.

	Complex	d-orbitals having highest energy
(a)	$[Ni(CN)_4]^{2-}$	d_{xy}, d_{yz}
(b)	$[NiCl_4]^{2-}$	$d_{x^2-y^2}, d_{z^2}$
(c)	$[Cr(en)_3]Cl_3$	$d_{x^2-y^2}, d_{z^2}$
(d)	$[PtCl_4]^{2-}$	d_{xy}, d_{yz}, d_{xz}

3. Which of the following can show both geometrical and optical isomerism?

(a) $[Co(ox)_3]^{3-}$

(b) $[Fe(NH_3)_4Cl_2]^+$

(c) $[Fe(NH_3)(H_2O)(Py)(Br)(Cl)(OH)]$

(d) $[Co(NH_3)_3(NO_2)_3]$

4. One mole of the complex compound $Co(NH_3)_5Cl_3$, gives 3 moles of ions on dissolution in water. One mole of the same complex reacts with two moles of $AgNO_3$ solution to yield two moles of AgCl(*s*). The IUPAC nomenclature of complex formed is

(a) pentaammine chloridocobalt (III) dichloride.

(b) Triammine trichloridocobalt (III) ammonia.

(c) Tetraammine dichloridocobalt (III) monochlorine ammonia.

(d) Tetraammine chloridocobalt (III) dichlorine ammonia.

5. The incorrect statement is:

(a) The stability constant of $[Co(NH_3)_6]^{3+}$ is larger than $[Co(NH_3)_6]^{2+}$

(b) The cyano complexes are far more stable than those formed by halide ions

(c) The stability of halide complexes follows the order $I^- < Br < Cl^-$

(d) The stability constant of $[Cu(NH_3)_4]^{2+}$ is lesser than $[Cu(H_2O)_4]^{2+}$ ion

6. The value of 'spin only" magnetic moment for one of the following configuration is 2.84 BM. The correct one is

(a) d^4 (in strong field ligand)

(b) d^2 (in weak field ligand)

(c) d^3 (in weak as well as in strong field ligand)

(d) d^5 (in strong field ligand)

7. Which of the following is incorrect statement?

(a) Octahedral complexes of coordination no. of '6' showing geometrical isomerism

(b) Tetrahedral complex of coordination no. of '4' show geometrical isomerism

(c) Square planar complexes of coordination no. of '4' shows geometrical isomerism

(d) Geometrical isomerism is not noticed in complex coordination no. 2 and 3.

8. On adding excess of HCl to a light pink coloured aqueous solution of cobalt (II) chloride, a deep blue coloured solution is formed. This is due to

(a) Transformation of octahedral $[Co(H_2O)_6]^{2+}$ into octahedral $[CoCl_4]^{2-}$

(b) Transformation of octahedral $[Co(H_2O)_6]^{2+}$ into tetrahedral $[CoCl_4]^{2-}$

(c) formation of undissociated $[CoCl_4]^{2-}$

(d) formation of a complex of Co(III) in the redox reaction

$$[Co(H_2O_6)]^{2+} + H^+ + Cl^- \longrightarrow [Co(H_2O)_5]^{2+} + H_2O + \frac{1}{2}H_2$$

9. Which one of the following has highest number of isomers?

(a) $[Co(NH_3)_5Cl]^{2+}$ (b) $[Co(en)_2Cl_2]^+$

(c) $[Ru(NH_3)_4]Cl_2$ (d) $[Ir(PR_3)_2H(CO)]^{2+}$

10. On treatment of 100 mL of 0.1 M solution of $CrCl_3 \cdot 6H_2O$ with excess of $AgNO_3$; 1.2×10^{22} ions are precipitated. The complex is

(a) $[Cr(H_2O)_4Cl_2]Cl \cdot 2H_2O$ (b) $[Cr(H_2O)_3Cl_3] \cdot 3H_2O$

(c) $[Cr(H_2O)_6]Cl_3$ (d) $[Cr(H_2O)_5Cl]Cl_2 \cdot H_2O$

One or More than One Correct MCQs

11. Choose the complexes that shows optical isomerism.

(a) $[Co(NH_3)_3Cl_3]$ (b) *cis*$[Co(en)_2Cl_2]Cl$

(c) $[Co(en)_3]^{3+}$ (d) $[Co(en)_2Cl_2]^+$

12. If Co^{3+} is replaced by Cr^{3+} in the complex $[Co(NH_3)_6]^{3+}$, which property would not show the most significant change?
(a) Colour of the complex
(b) Crystal field splitting energy
(c) Geometry of the complex
(d) Total number of ligands

13. Select the correct statements.
(a) Octahedral complexes are more stable than tetrahedral complexes.
(b) In case of strong field ligand, CFSE for 5 unpaired electrons is 2.0 Δ_o.
(c) Magnitude of Δ_o decreases an moving down the group of transition metals.
(d) Valence bond theory explains about the thermodynamic properties of the complexes.

14. Which of the following complex ion show(s) *cis-trans* isomerism?
(a) $[CrCl_2(C_2O_4)_2]^{3-}$ (b) $[Fe(NH_3)_2(CN)_4]^-$
(c) $[Co(NH_3)_4(H_2O)Cl]^{2+}$ (d) $[Fe(H_2O)_4(OH)_2]^+$

15. The complex that have even number of electrons in t_{2g} orbital are
(a) $[Fe(H_2O)_6]^{2+}$ (b) $[Co(H_2O)_6]^{2+}$
(c) $[Cu(H_2O)_6]^{2+}$ (d) $[Cr(H_2O)_6]^{2+}$

16. Which of the column is correctly matched?
(a) $[CuCl_4]^{2-}$ — removal of Cl from drinking water
(b) $[Ag(CN)_2]^-$ — Electroplating of metals
(c) $[PtCl_2(NH_3)_2]$ — used in cancer treatment
(d) EDTA — Chelating agent to remove heavy metals

17. Which of the following complexes does not exhibit square planar geometry?
(a) $[Fe(CO)_4]^{2-}$ (b) $[Co(CO)_4]^-$
(c) $[Cu(py)_4]^+$ (d) $[Ni(CN)_4]^{2-}$

18. Select the compounds that have same magnetic moment.
(a) $[Cr(H_2O)_6]^{2+}$ (b) $[Fe(H_2O)_6]^{2+}$
(c) $[CoCl_4]^{2-}$ (d) $[Mn(H_2O)_6]^{2+}$

Numerical/Integer Type Questions

19. The total number of complexes with odd number of electrons in t_{2g} orbitals is $[Fe(H_2O)_6]^{2+}$, $[Co(H_2O)_6]^{2+}$, $[Co(H_2O)_6]^{3+}$, $[Cu(H_2O)_6]^{2+}$ and $[Cr(H_2O)_6]^{2+}$.

20. Among $[Zn(H_2O)_6]^{2+}$, $[Fe(NH_3)_6]^{2+}$, $[Mn(H_2O)_6]^{2+}$, $[Mn(CN)_6]^{4-}$ and $[Mn(CN)_6]^{3-}$, the complexes that are examples of outer orbital octahedral complexes is/are

21. If the CFSE of $[Ti(H_2O)_6]^{3+}$ is – 86.0 kJ/mol, this complex will absorb maximum at wavelength ..... nm (nearest integer) [Assume Planck's constant $(h) = 6.4 \times 10^{-34}$ J-s, speed of light $(c) = 3 \times 10^8$ m/s and Avogadro's constant $N_A = 6 \times 10^{23}$/mol]

22. Among $[Ni(CO)_4]$, Na_2O_2, CsO_2, $Na_3[CoF_6]$, $[Co(NH_3)_4Cl_2]Cl$, $[NiCl_4]^{2-}$ and $[Ni(CN)_4]^{2-}$, the total number of diamagnetic species will be

23. In the complex acetylbromidodicarbonyl bis (triethyl phosphine) iron (II), the sum of Fe—C and Fe—P bond is ....

24. Consider the following statements.
I. Geometrical and ionisation isomerism is shown by $Co(NH_3)_4Br_2Cl$.
II. Metal ions that are hard acids form less stable complexes with ligands containing, N, O, F.
III. Electronegativity decreases the stability of the complexes.
IV. $[Co(NH_3)_5NO_2]^{2+}$ cation has two isomers.
V. The set $C_2O_4^{2-}$, ethylenediammine and H_2O does not have ambidentate ligand.

The total number of incorrect statement is/are

25. The sum of oxidation state of Cr in $[Cr(H_2O)_6]Cl_3$, $[Cr(C_6H_6)_2]$ and $K_2[Cr(CN)_2(O)_2(O_2)(NH_3)]$ will be

26. The sum of calculated spin only magnetic moments of $[Cr(NH_3)_6]^{3+}$ and $[CuF_6]^{3-}$ in BM will be .... (nearest integer)

27. Among the following complexes, the total number of paramagnetic species is ....
$[Mn(NH_3)_6]^{3+}$, $[Co(en)_3]^{3+}$, $[FeF_6]^{3-}$, $[Cu(NH_3)_4]^{2+}$, $[Ni(CN)_4]^{2-}$, $[Fe(H_2O)_6]^{2+}$, $[Ni(CO)_4]$

28. Consider the following complex ions
$[FeF_6]^{3-}$, $[V(H_2O)_6]^{2+}$ and $[Fe(H_2O)_6]^{2+}$

The total number of complex ions, that have spin-only magnetic moment value greater than 2 BM.

Matching Type Questions

29. Match List-I with List-II.

	List-I (Complex ion)		List-II (Spin only magnetic moment in (BM))
A.	$[Cr(NH_3)_6]^{3+}$	I.	4.90
B.	$[Ni(CO)_4]$	II.	3.87
C.	$[CoF_6]^{3-}$	III.	0.00
D.	$[Mn(NCS)_6]^{4-}$	IV.	2.83
		V.	5.41

Choose the correct answer from the options given below:
(a) A-III, B-I, C-II, D-V
(b) A-II, B-III, C-I, D-V
(c) A-II, B-III, C-IV, D-I
(d) A-IV, B-II, C-I, D-III

30. Match List-I with List-II.

	List-I (Metal complex)		List-II (EAN)
A.	$[Co(NO_2)_6]^{3-}$	I.	36
B.	$[Cr(CO)_6]$	II.	36
C.	$K_2[HgI_4]$	III.	86
D.	$K_3[Cr(C_2O_4)_3]$	IV.	34

Choose the correct answer from the options given below:
(a) A-II, B-I, C-III, D-IV (b) A-I, B-II, C-III, D-IV
(c) A-III, B-IV, C-I, D-II (d) A-II, B-I, C-IV, D-III

31. Match List-I with List-II.

	List-I (Complex)		List-II (EAN)
A.	$[Pt(NH_3)_4]^{2+}$	I.	84
B.	$[Ni(NH_3)_6]^{2+}$	II.	38
C.	$[Fe(CN)_6]^{3-}$	III.	35
D.	$[Cr(NH_3)_6]^{3+}$	IV.	33

Choose the correct answer from the options given below:
(a) A-I, B-II, C-III, D-IV
(b) A-II, B-III, C-I, D-IV
(c) A-III, B-II, C-IV, D-I
(d) A-IV, B-III, C-II, D-I

32. Match List-I with List-II.

	List-I (Coordination complex)		List-II (Number of unpaired electrons)
A.	$[Cr(CN)_6]^{3-}$	I.	2
B.	$[Fe(H_2O)_6]^{2+}$	II.	0
C.	$[NiCl_4]^{2-}$	III.	4
D.	$[Co(NH_3)_6]^{3+}$	IV.	3

Choose the correct answer from the options given below:
(a) A-III, B-I, C-IV, D-II (b) A-IV, B-III, C-I, D-II
(c) A-IV, B-I, C-III, D-II (d) A-III, B-IV, C-II, D-I

33. Match Column-I with Column-II.

	Column-I (Coordination complex)		Column-II (Characteristics)
A.	$[Ti(H_2O)_5Cl](NO_3)_2$	I.	Paramagnetic and exhibits optical isomerism
B.	$[Co(NH_3)_4(NO_3)_2]NO_3$	II.	Paramagnetic and exhibits ionisation isomerism
C.	$[Ni(H_2O)_6]Cl_2$	III.	Diamagnetic and exhibits geometrical isomerism
D.	$[Pt(NH_3)_2Cl_2]$	IV.	Diamagnetic and exhibits ionisation isomerism

Choose the correct answer from the options given below:
(a) A-IV, B-I, C-II, D-III (b) A-II, B-IV, C-I, D-III
(c) A-III, B-I, C-IV, D-II (d) A-III, B-II, C-IV, D-I

34. Match List-I with List-II.

	List-I (Complex)		List-II (CFSE)
A.	$[Fe(CN)_6]^{3-}$	I.	1.2
B.	$[Ti(H_2O)_6]^{3+}$	II.	− 2.0
C.	$[CoCl_4]^{2-}$	III.	− 0.4
D.	$[FeCl_4]^{2-}$	IV.	0

Choose the correct answer from the options given below:
(a) A-II, B-III, C-I, D-IV (b) A-IV, B-I, C-II, D-III
(c) A-II, B-I, C-IV, D-III (d) A-III, B-II, C-I, D-III

35. Match List-I with List-II.

	List-I (Metal complex)		List-II (Electronic configuration)
A.	$[FeO_4]^{2-}$	I.	$t_{2g}^6\, e_g^0$
B.	$[TiCl_4]$	II.	$e^0 t_2^0$
C.	$[CoCl_4]^{2-}$	III.	$e^2 t_2^0$
D.	$[Fe(H_2O)_6]^{2+}$	IV.	$e^2 t_2^3$

Choose the correct answer from the options given below:
(a) A-IV, B-III, C-II, D-I
(b) A-III, B-II, C-IV, D-I
(c) A-II, B-III, C-IV, D-I
(d) A-II, B-I, C-III, D-IV

Paragraph Based Questions

Paragraph 1

An isomer of the complex $CoBrCl_2(en)_2(H_2O)$, on reaction with concentrated H_2SO_4 (dehydrating agent), suffers no loss in weight and on reaction with $AgNO_3$ solution it gives only white precipitate, which is soluble in NH_3 solution.

36. The total number of stereoisomer for the complex formed is ....

37. The sum of oxidation state (x) and coordination number (n) of the complex formed will be ......

Paragraph 2

According to CFT, attraction between the central metal ion and ligands in a complex is purely electrostatic. The transition metal which forms the central atom cation in the complex is regarded as positive ion. It is surrounded by negative ligands or neutral molecules which have a lone pair of electrons, if the ligand is a neutral molecule such as NH_3, the negative end of the dipole in the molecule is directed towards the metal cation. The electrons on the central metal ion are under repulsive forces from those on the ligands. Thus the electrons occupy the *d*-orbitals remain away from the direction of approach of ligands.

38. The crystal field stabilisation energy for the complex $[Ti(H_2O)_6]^{3+}$ is ....

39. For a d^4 metal ion in an octahedral field, ($\Delta_0 < P$) the sum of electron present in t_{2g} and e_g-orbital will be......

Paragraph 3

The crystal field theory (CFT) is now much more widely accepted than the valence bond theory. It assumes that the attraction between the central metal and the ligands in a complex is purely electrostatic. According to CFT, ligands are treated as a point charge and crystal field splitting energy (CFSE) increases the thermodynamic stability of the complexes. Value of CFSE depends upon nature of ligand and a spectrochemical series has been made experimentally. For tetrahedral complexes, Δ is about 4/9 times to Δ_0 (CFSE for octahedral complexes). This energy lies in visible region and that is why electronic transitions are responsible for color.

40. Consider the following statement about CFT.
   (a) Diamagnetic metal ions cannot have an odd number of electrons.
   (b) In an octahedral crystal field, the d-electrons of a metal ion occupy the e_g set of orbitals before they occupy the t_{2g} set of orbitals.
   (c) Low spin complex may be paramagnetic only.
   (d) In high spin octahedral complex, Δ_0 is less than the electron pairing energy and is relatively very small.

   The total number of incorrect statement is...

41. Crystal Field stabilisation energy for $[CoF_6]^{3-}$ is
   (a) $0.6\Delta_0 + P$ (b) $-0.4\Delta_0$
   (c) $1.2\Delta_0 + 2P$ (d) $0.4\Delta_0$
   [P is pairing energy]

Species Selection (with 5 Species)

42. Consider the following pair of complexes.
   I. $[FeCl_4]^-$ and $[Fe(CO)_4]^{2-}$
   II. $[Co(CO)_4]^-$ and $[CoCl_4]^{2-}$
   III. $[Ni(CO)_4]$ and $[Ni(CN)_4]^{2-}$
   IV. $[Cu(py)_4]^+$ and $[Cu(CN)_4]^{3-}$
   V. $[NiCl_4]^{2-}$ and $[MnCl_4]^{2-}$

   The total number of pair(s) of complexes where in both exhibit tetrahedral geometry is
   (a) 3 (b) 2 (c) 4 (d) 1

43. Consider the following pair of complexes.
   I. $[Cr(H_2O)_6]^{2+}$ and $[Fe(H_2O)_6]^{2+}$
   II. $[Mn(H_2O)_6]^{2+}$ and $[Cr(H_2O)_6]^{2+}$
   III. $[FeF_6]^{3-}$ and $[Mn(H_2O)_6]^{2+}$
   IV. $[CoCl_4]^{2-}$ and $[Fe(H_2O)_6]^{2+}$
   V. $[Cr(H_2O)_6]^{2+}$ and $[CoCl_4]^{2-}$

   The pair of complexes having the same magnetic moment is
   (a) 1 (b) 2 (c) 3 (d) 4

44. Consider the following pair of coordination complexes:
   I. $[CoBr_2Cl_2]^{2-}$ and $[PtBr_2Cl_2]^{2-}$
   II. $[Co(NH_3)_4Cl_2]^+$ and $[Pt(NH_3)_2(H_2O)Cl]^+$
   III. $[Cr(NH_3)_5Cl_2$ and $[Cr(NH_3)_4Cl_2]Cl$
   IV. $[Pt(NH_3)_3(NO_3)Cl]$ and $[Pt(NH_3)_3Cl]Br$
   V. *cis*-$[Co(en)_2Cl_2]^+$ and $[Co(en)_3]^{3+}$

   The total number of complexes that exhibits optical isomerism is
   (a) 2 (b) 3 (c) 4 (d) 1

45. Consider the following complexes:
   I. $[Pt(en)_2Cl_2]$ II. $[Cr(en)_2(ox)]^+$
   III. $[Zn(en)_2Cl_2]$ IV. $[Pt(en)_2Cl_2]^{2+}$
   V. $[Co(NH_3)_4Cl_2]^+$

   The total number of species that have trans isomer is
   (a) 1 (b) 4 (c) 3 (d) 2

46. Consider the following coordination complexes with their IUPAC names:
   A. $[Co(H_2O)_4(NH_3)_2]Cl_3$—diamminetetraaquacobalt (III) chloride
   B. $[Ni(NH_3)_4][NiCl_4]$—tetraamminenickel (II)-tetrachloronickelate (II)
   C. $[Pt(Br_2)(PMe_3)_2]$—bis [bromo (trimethylphosphine)] platinum (IV)
   D. $K_3[Co(C_2O_4)_3]$—potassium tris(oxalato) cobalt (III)
   E. K_2MnO_4—potassium tetraoxidomanganate (VI)

   The total number of complexes with incorrect IUPAC name is
   (a) 3 (b) 2 (c) 4 (d) 1

Species Selection (with 7 Species)

47. Consider the following complexes:
   I. $[Co(H_2O)_6]^{2+}$ II. $[Co(en)_3]^{3+}$
   III. $[Ni(H_2O)_6]^{2+}$ IV. $[Zn(H_2O)_6]^{2+}$
   V. $[Cr(H_2O)_6]^{3+}$ VI. $[V(H_2O)_6]^{2+}$
   VII. $[FeO_4]^{2-}$

   The total number of complex that will exhibit maximum attraction to an applied magnetic field?
   (a) 2 (b) 3 (c) 1 (d) 4

48. Consider the following complexes.
   I. $[Fe(CN)_6]^{4-}$ II. $[Fe(CN)_6]^{3-}$
   III. $[Ti(H_2O)_6]^{3-}$ IV. $[Ni(CN)_4]^{2-}$
   V. $[Co(CN)_6]^{3-}$ VI. $[Cu(NH_3)_4]^{2+}$
   VII. $[Fe(H_2O)_6]^{2+}$

   The total number of paramagnetic complex is
   (a) 3 (b) 4 (c) 5 (d) 2

49. Consider the following complexes.
   (i) *cis* $[Co(en)_2Cl_2]Cl$ (ii) *cis*-$[Cr(ox)_2Cl_2]^{3-}$
   (iii) *trans* $[Co(en)_2Cl_2]Cl$ (iv) $[Co(en)_3]^{3+}$
   (v) $[Co(NH_3)_4Cl_2]Cl$ (vi) *cis* $[Pt(en)_2Cl_2]^{2+}$
   (vii) $[Co(NH_3)_3Cl_3]$

   The total number of complexes that will exhibit optical isomerism.
   (a) 3 (b) 4 (c) 5 (d) 2

50. Consider the following complexes:

(i) $[Pt(en)(SCN)_2]$ (ii) $[Zn(NH_3)_2Cl_2]$
(iii) $[Pt(NH_3)_2Cl_4]$ (iv) $[Cr(en)_2(H_2O)SO_4]^+$
(v) $[Co(en)_2Cl_2]$ (vi) $[Co(en)_3]^{3+}$
(vii) $[Co(NH_3)_3Cl_3]$

The total number of complexes that can exhibit the type of isomerism shown by $[Pt(NH_3)_2Br_2]$ is

(a) 3 (b) 4
(c) 5 (d) 2

51. Consider the following complexes.

I. $[Cu(NH_3)_6]^{2+}$ II. $[Ti(H_2O)_6]^{3+}$
III. $[Fe(CN)_6]^{3-}$ IV. $[NiF_6]^{4-}$
V. $[V(H_2O)_6]^{2+}$ VI. $[Fe(H_2O)_6]^{3+}$
VII. $[Mn(H_2O)_6]^{3+}$

The total number of complexes that have crystal field splitting energy is $-1.2\,\Delta_0$.

(a) 3 (b) 2 (c) 4 (d) 5

Check Through PYQs

Element 1 Basic Terms Used in Coordination Compounds and IUPAC Nomenclature

1. The reaction of $Pb(NO_3)_2$ and NaCl in water produces a precipitate that dissolves upon the addition of HCl of appropriate concentration. The dissolution of the precipitate is due to the formation of *2022 Adv.*

(a) $PbCl_2$ (b) $PbCl_4$
(c) $[PbCl_4]^{2-}$ (d) $[PbCl_6]^{2-}$

Element 2 Isomerism in Coordination Compounds

2. Among the following options, select the option in which each complex in Set-I shows geometrical isomerism and the two complexes in Set-II are ionisation isomers of each other. [en = $H_2NCH_2CH_2NH_2$] *2024 Adv.*

(a) Set-I. $[Ni(CO)_4]$ and $[PdCl_2(PPh_3)_2]$
Set-II $[Co(NH_3)_5Cl]SO_4$ and $[Co(NH_3)_5(SO_4)]Cl$

(b) Set-I. $[Co(en)(NH_3)_2Cl_2]$ and $[PdCl_2(PPh_3)_2]$
Set-II $[Co(NH_3)_6][Cr(CN)_6]$ and $[Cr(NH_3)_6][Co(CN)_6]$

(c) Set-I. $[Co(NH_3)_3(NO_2)_3]$ and $[Co(en)_2Cl_2]$
Set-II $[Co(NH_3)_5Cl]SO_4$ and $[Co(NH_3)_5(SO_4)]Cl$

(d) Set-I. $[Cr(NH_3)_5Cl]Cl_2$ and $[Co(en)(NH_3)_2Cl_2]$
Set-II $[Cr(H_2O)_6]Cl_3$ and $[Cr(H_2O)_5Cl]Cl_2 \cdot H_2O$

3. The complex(es), which can exhibit the type of isomerism shown by $[Pt(NH_3)_2Br_2]$, is (are) [en = $H_2NCH_2CH_2NH_2$] *2023 Adv.*

(a) $[Pt(en)(SCN)_2]$ (b) $[Zn(NH_3)_2Cl_2]$
(c) $[Pt(NH_3)_2Cl_4]$ (d) $[Cr(en)_2(H_2O)(SO_4)]^+$

4. Among the complex ions,
$[Co(NH_2CH_2CH_2NH_2)_2Cl_2]^+$, $[CrCl_2(C_2O_4)_2]^{3-}$, $[Fe(H_2O)_4(OH)_2]^+$, $[Fe(NH_3)_2(CN)_4]^-$, $[Co(NH_2—CH_2—CH_2—NH_2)_2(NH_3)Cl]^{2+}$ and $[Co(NH_3)_4(H_2O)Cl]^{2+}$ the number of complex ion(s) that show(s) *cis-trans* isomerism is .... *2015 Adv.*

Element 3 Bonding in Coordination Compounds

5. The total number of possible isomers for $[Pt(NH_3)_4Cl_2]Br_2$ is .... *2021 Adv.*

6. The possible number of geometrical isomers for the complex $[CoL_2Cl_2]^-$ ($L = H_2NCH_2CH_2O^-$) is (are) .... *2016 Adv.*

7. Choose the correct statement(s) among the following *2020 Adv.*

(a) $[FeCl_4]^-$ has tetrahedral geometry.
(b) $[Co(en)(NH_3)_2Cl_2]^+$ has 2 geometrical isomers.
(c) $[FeCl_4]^-$ has higher spin-only magnetic moment than $[Co(en)(NH_3)_2Cl_2]^+$.
(d) The cobalt ion in $[Co(en)(NH_3)_2Cl_2]^+$ has sp^3d^2 hybridisation.

8. A tin chloride Q undergoes the following reactions (not balanced)

$$Q + Cl^- \longrightarrow X$$
$$Q + Me_3N \longrightarrow Y$$
$$Q + CuCl_2 \longrightarrow Z + CuCl$$

X is a monoanion having pyramidal geometry. Both *Y* and *Z* are neutral compounds. *2019 Adv.*

Choose the correct option(s).

(a) There is a coordinate bond in *Y*
(b) The central atom in *Z* has one lone pair of electrons
(c) The oxidation state of the central atom in *Z* is + 2
(d) The central atom in *X* is sp^3 hybridised

9. The correct option(s) regarding the complex $[Co(en)(NH_3)_3(H_2O)]^{3+}$ (en = $H_2NCH_2CH_2NH_2$) is (are) *2018 Adv.*

(a) It has two geometrical isomers
(b) It will have three geometrical isomers, if bidentate 'en' is replaced by two cyanide ligands
(c) It is paramagnetic
(d) It absorbs light at longer wavelength as compared to $[Co(en)(NH_3)_4]^{3+}$

10. The correct statement(s) regarding the binary transition metal carbonyl compounds is (are)
(Atomic numbers : Fe = 26, Ni = 28) *2018 Adv.*
(a) Total number of valence shell electrons at metal centre in $Fe(CO)_5$ or $Ni(CO)_4$ is 16
(b) These are predominantly low spin in nature
(c) Metal-carbon bond strengthens when the oxidation state of the metal is lowered
(d) The carbonyl C—O bond weakens when the oxidation state of the metal is increased

11. Addition of excess aqueous ammonia to a pink coloured aqueous solution of $MCl_2 \cdot 6H_2O(X)$ and NH_4Cl gives an octahedral complex Y in the presence of air. In aqueous solution, complex Y behaves as 1 : 3 electrolyte. The reaction of X with excess HCl at room temperature results in the formation of a blue coloured complex Z. The calculated spin only magnetic moment of X and Z is 3.87 B.M., whereas it is zero for complex Y.
Among the following options, which statement(s) is (are) correct? *2017 Adv.*
(a) The hybridisation of the central metal ion in Y is d^2sp^3
(b) Addition of silver nitrate to Y gives only two equivalents of silver chloride
(c) When X and Y are in equilibrium at 0°C, the colour of the solution is pink
(d) Z is a tetrahedral complex

12. Among $V(CO)_6$, $Cr(CO)_5$, $Cu(CO)_3$, $Mn(CO)_5$, $Fe(CO)_5$, $[Co(CO)_3]^{3-}$, $[Cr(CO)_4]^{4-}$ and $Ir(CO)_3$, the total number of species isoelectronic with $Ni(CO)_4$ is ....
[Given, atomic number : V = 23, Cr = 24, Mn = 25, Fe = 26, Co = 27, Ni = 28, Cu = 29, Ir = 77] *2024 Adv.*

13. Among the following complexes, the total number of diamagnetic species is ....
$[Mn(NH_3)_6]^{3+}$, $[MnCl_6]^{3-}$, $[FeF_6]^{3-}$, $[CoF_6]^{3-}$, $[Fe(NH_3)_6]^{3+}$ and $[Co(en)_3]^{3+}$
[Given, atomic number : Mn = 25, Fe = 26, Co = 27 ; en = $H_2NCH_2CH_2NH_2$] *2024 Adv.*

14. The calculated spin only magnetic moments of $[Cr(NH_3)_6]^{3+}$ and $[CuF_6]^{3-}$ in BM, respectively, are (Atomic numbers of Cr and Cu are 24 and 29, respectively) *2021 Adv.*
(a) 3.87 and 2.84 (b) 4.90 and 1.73
(c) 3.87 and 1.73 (d) 4.90 and 2.84

15. Total number of *cis* N—Mn—Cl bond angles (that is Mn—N and Mn—Cl bonds in *cis* positions) present in a molecule of *cis* $[Mn(en)_2Cl_2]$ complex is ....
(en = $NH_2CH_2CH_2NH_2$) *2019 Adv.*

16. Among $[Ni(CO)_4]$, $[NiCl_4]^{2-}$, $[Co(NH_3)_4Cl_2]Cl$, $Na_3[CoF_6]$, Na_2O_2 and CsO_2, the total number of paramagnetic compounds is *2016 Adv.*
(a) 2 (b) 3
(c) 4 (d) 5

17. For the octahedral complexes of Fe^{3+} in SCN^- (thiocyanato-S) and in CN^- ligand environments, the difference between the spin only magnetic moments in Bohr magnetons (when approximated to the nearest integer) is [atomic number of Fe = 26] *2015 Adv.*

18. Match the electronic configurations in List-I with appropriate metal complex ions in List-II and choose the correct option.
[Atomic number : Fe = 26, Mn = 25, Co = 27] *2023 Adv.*

List-I		List-II	
(P)	$t_{2g}^6 e_g^0$	(1)	$[Fe(H_2O)_6]^{2+}$
(Q)	$t_{2g}^3 e_g^2$	(2)	$[Mn(H_2O)_6]^{2+}$
(R)	$e^2 t_2^3$	(3)	$[Co(NH_3)_6]^{3+}$
(S)	$t_{2g}^4 e_g^2$	(4)	$[FeCl_4]^-$
		(5)	$[CoCl_4]^{2-}$

(a) P → 1; Q → 4; R → 2; S → 3
(b) P → 1; Q → 2; R → 4; S → 5
(c) P → 3; Q → 2; R → 5; S → 1
(d) P → 3; Q → 2; R → 4; S → 1

HINTS & Solutions

Solutions : Competency Enhancer

1.1 ***(a)*** EAN of Cr in $Cr(CO)_6$ is

$24 + 12 = 36$

1.2 ***(b)*** IUPAC name of the given compound is potassium diammine tetrachloridochromate (III).

2.1 ***(c)*** The correct match is A-4, B-1, C-2, D-3.

2.2 ***(d)*** $[Co(NH_3)_4Cl_2]^+$ is a octahedral complex and hence can show geometrical isomerism.

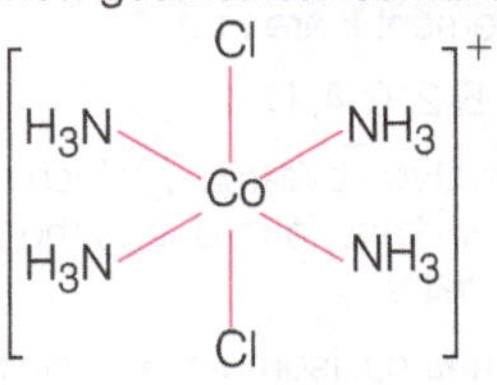

trans w.r.t.Cl

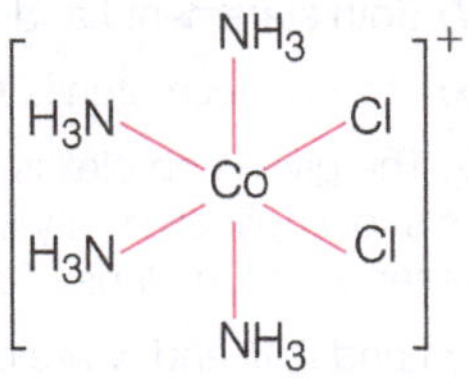

cis w.r.t.Cl

$[Pt(NH_3)_2Cl_2]$ is a square planar complex and hence can show geometrical isomerism.

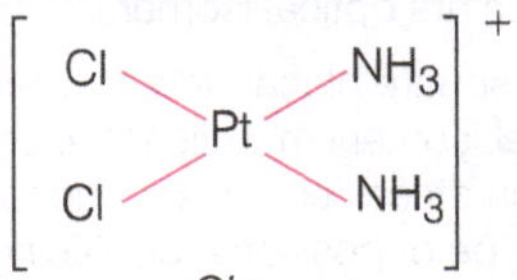

Cis

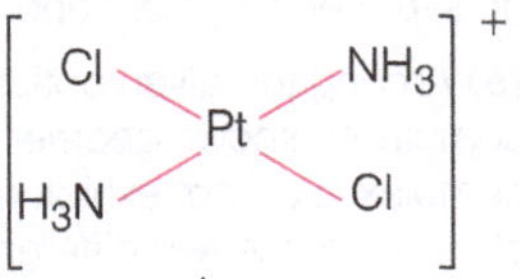

trans

$[Cr(NH_3)_5Cl]SO_4$ and $[Cr(NH_3)_5(SO_4)]Cl$ are ionisation isomers.

3.1 ***(c)*** In $[Cr(H_2O)_6]^{3+}$, Cr has $3d^3$ configuration but due to weak field ligand, all the *d* electrons spin are paramagnetic.

In $[Cu(Py)_4]^+$, Cu has $3d^{10}$ configuration and there are no unpaired electrons in *d*-orbitals, hence diamagnetic.

3.2 ***(c)*** The correct match is P-(3), Q-(2), R-(5), S-(4).

Elemental Practice 9.1

1. ***(d)*** Incorrect statement for addition compound is given in option (d). It is because double salts completely ionise in aqueous solution. So, it does not retain its identity.
2. ***(d)*** Oxidation state of chromium atom increases from +1 to +3. Hence, stability increases. Thus, the correct order of stability is

   $[Cr(NH_3)_6]^{3+} > [Cr(NH_3)_6]^{2+} > [Cr(NH_3)_6]^{+}$

   Thus, the order given in option (d) is incorrect.
3. ***(c)*** $[Cu(NH_3)_4]SO_4$ is a complex salt

   $K_2SO_4Al_2(SO_4)_3 \cdot 24H_2O$ (potash alum) is a double salt.
4. ***(b)*** $[Fe(NH_3)_4Cl_2]^+$ is a heteroleptic complex because it has more than one type of ligands.
5. ***(b)*** Among the given options NO_2^- and SCN^- are ambidentate ligand.
6. ***(c)*** In the structure, $[H_3N—CH_2—CH_2—NH_3]^{2+}$, no atom has any lone pair.
7. ***(a)*** Greater is the electron density on the central atom, stronger will be metal carbonyl back bonding and lower will be the C—O bond order resulting in a longer C—O bond length.
8. ***(d)*** To act as non-classical ligand, i.e., exhibit synergic bonding a ligand must have vacant orbital. Among the given ligands $CH_3—O^{\ominus}$ does not have any vacant orbital. Thus, it is incapable to form synergic bonding.
9. ***(d)*** The atomic number of cobalt is 27.

   Co : $[Ar]3d^7 4s^2$

   Co^{3+} $[Ar]3d^6$

   $EAN = 24 + 2 \times 6$

   $= 36$
10. ***(d)*** Any ligand having a vacant orbital (atomic or molecular) may act as π-acid ligand.
11. ***(b)*** $\sigma - C_5H_5^-$: donates $2e^-$ and $\pi - C_5H_5^-$: donates $6e^-$.
12. ***(d)*** The correct IUPAC name of the given compound is tetraamminechloridonitrito-Ncobalt (III) chloride.
13. ***(b)*** The IUPAC name of given complex is triamminebromo chloronitroplatinum (IV) chloride.
14. ***(c)*** 2, 2′-dipyridyl, 1, 10-phenanthroline, acetylacetonate anion, oxalate anion, ethylene diamine are bidentate ligands.

    Diethylene triamine is a tetradentate ligand, imino diacetate anion, 2, 2′, 2′′-terpyridine is a tridentate ligand.

    Ethylenediamine triacetate is a pentadentate ligand.
15. ***(d)*** Sodium nitroprusside is

    $Na_2[\overset{+2}{Fe}(CN)_5\overset{+1}{NO}]$

    EAN of $Fe = 26 - 2 + 12 = 36$
16. ***(b)*** If $x = 1$, $y = 1$; $z = 2$

    $[Cr(C_2O_4)(en)(O_2)_2]^-$ then co-ordination number of Cr is 6.
17. ***(d)*** $K_2[Cr(CN)_2O_2(O)_2NH_3]$

    ↑ ↑

    oxo peroxo

    Potassium amminedicyano-dioxoperoxochromate (VI)
18. ***(b)*** Among the given options, maximum number of rings will be formed by $EDTA^{4-}$. It will form five rings.
19. ***(d)*** Higher is the electron density on the central metal atom, stronger will be the metal carbonyl back bonding and thus lower will be the C—O bond order.
20. ***(c)*** The IUPAC name of the given compound is dodecacarbonyltrimanganese (0).

21. ***(a,b,c,d)*** All the given statements are correct.
22. ***(a,b,c,d)*** All the given statements are correct.
23. ***(a,b,c,d)*** All the given statements are correct.
24. ***(a, b)*** Tetraamminenickel (II). tetrachloronickelate (II) $[Ni(NH_3)_4][NiCl_4]$
Dibromobis (trimethylphosphine) platinum (II) $[Pt Br_2(PMe_3)_2]$
25. ***(b, d)*** $CuSO_4 \cdot 4NH_3 \cdot H_2O$ and $Fe(CN)_2 \cdot 4KCN$ are not the examples of double salt.
Only potash alum $[K_2SO_4 \cdot Al_2(SO_4)_3 \cdot 24H_2O]$ is an example of double salt.
(d) Ligands which have two different sites but at a time connect with only one donor site to central metal are called ambidentate ligands.
Only NO_2^-, and SCN^- are examples of ambidentate ligands.
26. ***(a,b,c)*** Not all five rings formed by $EDTA^{4-}$ lie in the same plane. Only 3 of them are in the same plane, the other two are in a plane perpendicular to that plane.
27. ***(7)*** Hydrazine cannot form a chelate complex due to formation of unstable three membered ring. Rest of all gives polydentate ligand form chelate complex due to formation of stable 5 or 6 member ring.
28. ***(3)*** RNC, phen, AsR_3 are σ-donor and π acceptor species.
NCO^-, NCS^- are σ-donor and π donor species.
C_6H_6, $RC\equiv CR$ are π donor and π acceptor species.
29. ***(4)***

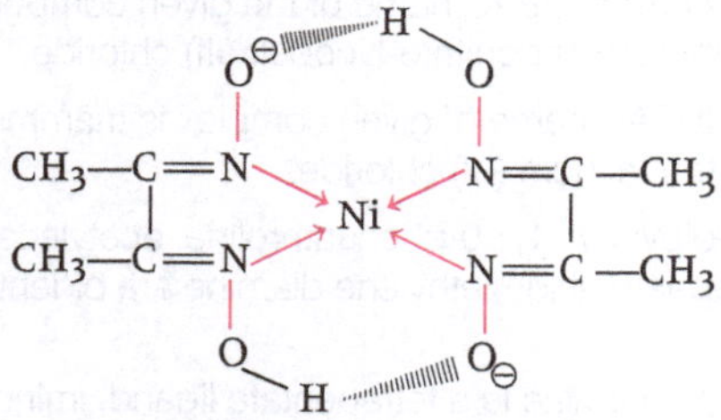

In $[Ni(DMG)_2]$, a total no. of 4 rings are formed as shown.
30. ***(33)*** Oxidation state of Cr

$$x + (4 \times 0) + 2 \times (-1) = +1 \Rightarrow x = +3$$

$$\text{EAN} = Z - \text{Oxidation state} + 2 \times \text{(number of ligands)}$$

$$= 24 - 3 + 2 \times 6 = 33$$

31. ***(8)*** Prussian blue is $Fe_4[Fe(CN)_6]_3$
Oxidation no of central metal is (+2)
Co-ordination No = 6
Sum of O.N & CN = 8
32. ***(12)*** Each $C_5H_5^-$ ligand is aromatic with 6π electrons and each C_p ligand is negatively cahrged (−1).
Total electrons = 2 rings × 6 electrons per ring = 12 electrons
33. ***(6)*** The complex formed is supposed to follow sidgwick rule and thus will have an EAN value of 36
$\text{EAN} = 24 + x \times 2 = 36$
$x = 6$

Elemental Practice 9.2

1. ***(a)*** Linkage isomerism arises in a coordination compound containing ambidentate ligand. So, compounds given in II and V shows linkage isomerism.
2. ***(d)*** The given complex will show the following isomerism:
Linkage isomerism: $[Co(NH_3)_3(NC)(H_2O)_2]Cl_2$
Hydrate isomerism: $[Co(NH_3)_3(CN)(H_2O)(Cl)]Cl \cdot H_2O$
Ionisation isomerism: $[Co(NH_3)_3(Cl)(H_2O)_2]Cl \cdot CN$
3. ***(d)*** $[Co(Cl)(Br)(H_2O)_4]Cl$ and $[Co(Cl)_2(H_2O)_4]Br$ are ionisation isomers since they will produce different ions in their aqueous solutions. They are not hydrate isomers as they do not have different number of molecules of water of hydration.
4. ***(d)*** Both statement I and statement II are true.
5. ***(a)*** The correct match is A-1, B-2, C-4, D-3.
6. ***(b)*** The given complex is of the type $[Ma_2(bb)_2]$ which does not show optical activity in their *-trans* form due to the presence of the plane of symmetry.
7. ***(c)*** I and II, III and IV are geometrical isomers i.e., *-cis* and *-trans*. I and III are both same compounds i.e., *-trans* form with a plane of symmetry and II and IV are non-superimposable mirror images of the *-cis* form having no symmetry element and thus are optical isomers.
8. ***(b)*** Among the given options square planar and octahedral complexes shows geometrical isomerism while tetrahedral complexes do not exhibit geometrical isomerism due to the absence of the two different type of positions for placing the various ligands as all the bond angles are equal.
9. ***(a)*** The given complexes represent the general type:
(I) $[Cr(NO_3)_3(NH_3)_3]$: Ma_3b_3: Two stereoisomers (geometrical isomers: 1 facial and 1 mer)
(II) $K_3[Co(C_2O_4)_3]$: $M(aa)_3$: Two steroisomers (d and l)
(III) $K_3[CoCl_2(C_2O_4)_2]$: $M(aa)_2b_2$: Three stereoisomers (geometrical isomers: *-cis* and *-trans* among them the -cis form is optically active so a total of three stereoisomers).
(IV) $[CoBrCl(en)_2]$: $M(aa)_2bc$: Three stereoisomers (geometrical isomers: *-cis* and *-trans* among them the *-cis* form is optically active so a total of three stereoisomers).
10. ***(c)*** The given complexes are:
Diamminedichloroplatinum(II): $[Pt(NH_3)_2(Cl_2)]$: Ma_2b_2: Square planar: No optical isomers.
Trans dicyanobis (ethylenediamine) chromium (III) chloride *trans* $[Cr(en)_2(CN)_2]Cl$: No optical isomers.
tris-(ethylenediamine)cobalt(III) bromide: $[Co(en)_3]Br_3$: $M(aa)_3$: Two optical isomers.
Pentaamminenitrocobalt (III) iodide: $[Co(NH_3)_5(NO_2)]I_2$: Ma_5b: No optical isomerism.

11. ***(c)*** $[Pt(NH_3)_2Cl_4]$ is an octahedral complex and hence, can show geometrical isomerism.

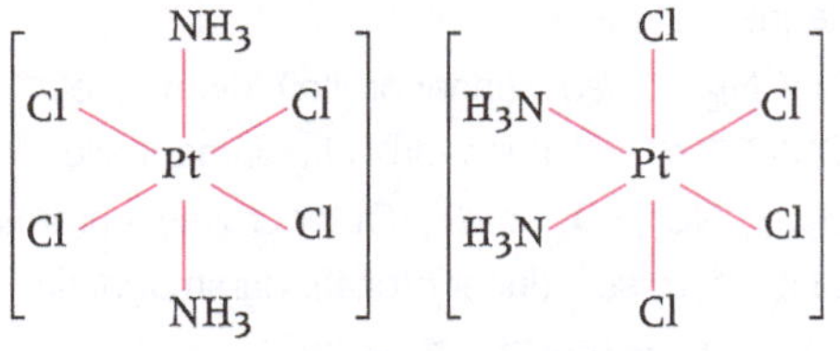

trans *cis*

$[Cr(en)_2(H_2O)(SO_4)]^+$ is an octahedral complex and is of type $[M(aa)_2bc]$ can show geometrical isomerism.

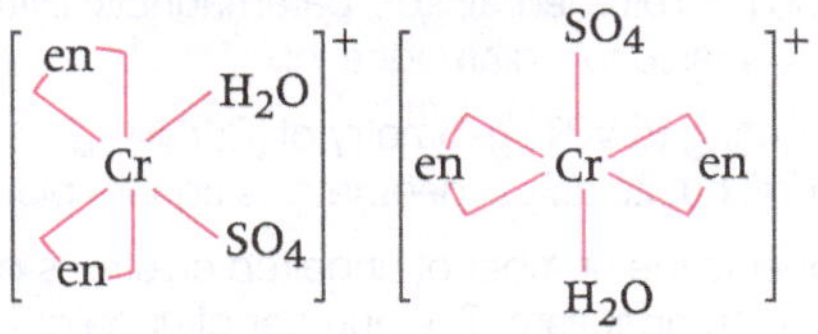

$[Pt(NH_3)_3(NO_3)]Br$ and $[Pt(NH_3)_3Br]NO_3$ show ionisation isomerism.

12. ***(b)*** The given complexes represent:

$[Cr(NO_3)_3(NH_3)_3]$: Ma_3b_3: Two geometrical isomers; facial and meridional.

$K_3[Fe(C_2O_4)_3]$: $M(aa)_3$: Two optical isomers

$[CoCl_2(en)_2]^+$: $M(aa)_2b_2$: 1-*cis* and 1-*trans*: since the -cis is optically active, thus, three stereoisomers.

$[CoBrCl(ox)_2]^{3-}$: $M(aa)_2bc$: 1-*cis* and 1-*trans*: Since the -*cis* is optically active, thus, three streoisomers.

13. ***(c)*** In the given complexes, the position of the triethylphosphine group is opposite in one of the complexes whereas it is adjacent in the other. So, these are -*cis* and -*trans* isomers.

14. ***(d)*** The total number of isomers in the complex $[Cr(SCN)_2(NH_3)_4]^+$ will be four. The given complex has three linkage isomers i.e., $[Cr(SCN)_2(NH_3)_4]^+$, $[Cr(SCN)(NCS)(NH_3)_4]^+$, $[Cr(NCS)_2(NH_3)_4]^+$. Also, the given complex represents Ma_4b_2 type having two geometrical isomers. Thus, a total of four isomers.

15. ***(d)*** Compounds (i), (ii) and (iii) shows optical isomerism whereas (iv) does not due to presence of plane of symmetry.

16. ***(a)*** The given complexes contain Pt^{4+}, thus an expected coordination number is six.

17. ***(a, b, c)*** $[Co(en)_3][Cr(CN)_6]$ is a mixed complex and thus can show coordination isomerism, $[Mn(CO)_5(SCN)]$ and $[Co(H_2O)(NO_2)_5]SO_4$ have ambidentate ligands thus linkage isomerism is possible and $[Co(H_2O)(NO_2)_5]SO_4$ will have an ionisation isomer i.e., $[Co(H_2O)(NO_2)_4(SO_4)](NO_2)$.

18. ***(a, b, d)*** Option (a), Incorrect. $[Pt(NO_3)_2(en)_2]^{2+}$ does not have any ambidentate ligands and thus it cannot show linkage isomerism.

Option (b) Incorrect $[Cr(CO_3)(NH_3)_4]Br$ cannot show ionisation isomerism since Br^- cannot replace the bidentate CO_3^{2-} ligand.

Option (c) Correct. The hydrate isomers of $FeCl_2 \cdot 6H_2O$ are as follows.

$$[Fe(H_2O)_6]Cl_2$$

and $$[Fe(H_2O)_5Cl]Cl \cdot H_2O$$

Option (d) incorrect. In $[FeCl_3(NH_3)_3]$ all three ammonia ligands are identical and there is only one way to arrange them around metal central. Hence, this complex cannot exhibit structural isomerism.

19. ***(a, b, d)***

$$[Co(NH_3)_5Br]SO_4 \xrightarrow{AgNO_3} \underset{\text{(White)}}{Ag_2SO_4}$$

$$[Co(NH_3)_5SO_4]Br \xrightarrow{AgNO_3} \underset{\text{(Pale yellow)}}{AgBr}$$

The ionisation isomer of $[Co(NH_3)_5SO_4]Br$ i.e., $[Co(NH_3)_5Br]SO_4$ will have a higher molar conductance due to greater amount of charge present on the ions formed by it in the aqueous solution. Also, the presence of higher charge on the ions produced by the ionisation isomer of $[Co(NH_3)_5SO_4]Br$ i.e., $[Co(NH_3)_5Br]SO_4$ will cause a greater depression in the freezing point of water.

20. ***(a, b, c)*** $[Co(NO_2)(NH_3)_5]Cl_2$ and $[Co(ONO)(NH_3)_5]Cl_2$ shows linkage isomerism.

21. ***(a, c, d)*** Among the given complexes a, c and d have no four different isomers.

22. ***(a, c)*** The compounds in which cation and anion both are complex and metals have same coordination number, exhibit coordination isomerism. Only a and c can show coordination isomerism.

23. ***(3)*** The different ionisation isomers will be three

$[Mn(H_2O)_3(NH_3)(Cl)(Br)]Cl(CN)$

$[Mn(H_2O)_3(NH_3)(CN)(Cl)]Cl(Br)$

$[Mn(H_2O)_3(NH_3)(Cl)_2]Br(CN)$

24. ***(6)*** $[Mn(CN)_2(NO_2)_2en]$ will show linkage isomerism due to the presence of ambidentate ligands i.e. (CN^- and NO_2^-, the various linkage isomers are

$[Mn(CN)(NC)(NO_2)_2(en)]$,

$[Mn(NC)_2(NO_2)_2(en)]$

$[Mn(CN)_2(ONO)(NO_2)(en)]$

$[Mn(CN)_2(ONO)_2(en)]$

$[Mn(CN)(NC)(NO_2)(ONO)(en)]$ and

$[Mn(NC)_2(ONO)_2(en)]$

25. ***(2)*** The given complex represents Ma_3b_3 type complex having two geometrical isomer i.e. *fac* and *mer*.

26. ***(12)*** The various different isomeric forms of the given complex is $[Rh(NO_2)(SCN)(en)_2]^+$, $[Rh(ONO)(SCN)(en)_2]^+$, $[Rh(ONO)(NCS)(en)_2]^+$.

Thus a total of four structural isomers each representing the type $M(aa)_2bc$ having three stereoisomers each (1*cis* and 1 *trans*) so total of $4 \times 3 = 12$ isomer.

27. ***(9)*** The given complex will exhibit different types of isomerism as follows

Ionisation isomerism:

$[Co(en)_2(SCN)(NO_2)]Br$, $[Co(en)_2(Br)(NO_2)](SCN)$ and $[Co(en)_2(SCN)(Br)]NO_2$.

Linkage isomerism:

$[Co(en)_2(NCS)(NO_2)]Br$, $[Co(en)_2(SCN)(ONO)]Br$ and $[Co(en)_2(NCS)(ONO)]Br$

Stereoisomers: The given complex represents $M(aa)_2bc$ having one *cis* and 1-*trans*. The *cis* form is optically active thus a total of three stereoisomers.

28. ***(7)*** The given complex will exhibit linkage isomerism and hydrate isomerism and the different isomers will be as

Hydrate isomer:

$[Cr(SCN)_2(H_2O)(Cl)(NO_2)_2]Cl \cdot H_2O$

Linkage isomerism:

$[Cr(SCN)(NCS)(H_2O)_2(NO_2)_2]Cl_2$

$[Cr(NCS)_2(H_2O)_2(NO_2)_2]Cl_2$,

$[Cr(SCN)_2(H_2O)_2(NO_2)(ONO)]Cl_2$

$[Cr(SCN)_2(H_2O)_2(ONO)_2]Cl_2$

$[Cr(SCN)(NCS)(H_2O)_2(NO_2)(ONO)]Cl_2$ and

$[Cr(NCS)_2(H_2O)_2(ONO)_2]Cl_2$

Elemental Practice 9.3

1. ***(c)*** The complex having chloride ions outside the coordination sphere will produce a white precipitate of AgCl with excess of $AgNO_3$ solution.

2. ***(c)*** The complex compound producing maximum number of ions will show highest conductance in 1 molar aqueous solution.

3. ***(c)*** $CuSO_4 \cdot 4NH_3 \cdot 2H_2O$ is a complex compound and will exist as $[Cu(NH_3)_4(H_2O)_2]SO_4$, and in aqueous solution it will dissociate as

$$[Cu(NH_3)_4(H_2O)_2]SO_4 \longrightarrow [Cu(NH_3)_4(H_2O)_2]^{2+} + SO_4^{2-}$$

and thus will exhibit the properties of sulphate ions only.

4. ***(b)*** The presence of 2° valencies gives rise to stereo isomerism in complex.

5. ***(d)*** Since, platinum is present in + 4 oxidation state, the coordination number of Pt (IV) in the given complexes will be 6. Thus, six monodentate ligands must be present inside the coordination sphere and the structural formulae of the given complexes can be deduced as:

$PtCl_4 \cdot 6H_2O$ — $[Pt(H_2O)_6]Cl_4$

$PtCl_4 \cdot 5H_2O$ — $[Pt(H_2O)_5Cl]Cl_3$

$PtCl_4 \cdot 4H_2O$ — $[Pt(H_2O)_4Cl_2]Cl_2$

$PtCl_4 \cdot 3H_2O$ — $[Pt(H_2O)_3Cl_3]Cl$

6. ***(d)*** In $[Co(C_2O_4)_3]^{3-}$, Co^{3+} has $3d^6$ configuration but due to strong field ligand, all the *d* electrons spin are paired hence diamagnetic in nature.

In $[Ni(en)_3]^{2+}$, Ni has $3d^8$ configuration but due to strong field ligand, all the *d* electrons spin are paired, hence diamagnetic in nature.

7. ***(d)*** $[Ni(CN)_5]^{-3}$, dsp^3, (Inner orbital), diamagnetic

$[Fe(CN)_6]^{-4}$, d^2sp^3, (Inner orbital), diamagnetic

$[Fe(H_2O)_5(NO)]SO_4$ sp^3d^2, (Outer orbital), paramagnetic

$[Fe(CN)_6]^{-3}$, d^2sp^3, (Inner orbital), paramagnetic

8. ***(a)*** EAN of Fe in $[Fe(CN)_6]^{4-} = 36$

Hybridisation of Fe is d^2sp^3. It has 6 co-ordinate bonds and 12 sigma bonds.

9. ***(d)*** $[NiCl_4]^{-2}$ Tetrahedral, sp^3, paramagnetic $[Ni(CN)_4]^{-2}$ Square planar, dsp^2, diamagnetic.

10. ***(c)*** According to VBT, geometry of $[Cu(NH_3)_4]^{+2}$ is tetrahedral but its actual geometry is square planar.

11. ***(a)*** Higher is the number of unpaired electrons greater will be the paramagnetism. The number of unpaired electrons in the given complexes is as under:

$[FeF_6]^{3-}$: d^5 system with weak ligands, thus five unpaired electrons, $[CoF_6]^{3-}$: d^6 system with weak ligands, thus 4 unpaired $[V(H_2O)_6]^{3+}$ d^2; system with weak ligands, thus two unpaired electrons and $[Ti(H_2O_6)]^{3+}$: d^1 system thus one unpaired electron.

12. ***(d)*** The given complex has Ni^{2+} ion having a configuration of d^8 and is attached to six strong field ligands. In d^8 system, the hybridisation is always sp^3d^2 when coordination number is 6 and 0 unpaired electrons.

13. ***(c)*** $Ni(CO)_4$ due to force pairing will have d^{10} system, so outer orbital complex with no unpaired electron and $[V(CO)_6]$ will have $3d^5$ system due to force pairing, so it is an inner orbital complex having one unpaired electron and thus paramagnetic in nature.

$[Fe(CO)_5]$ has $3d^6 4s^2$ configuration which due to forced pairing will convert to system having dsp^3 hybridisation. Also, $[Cr(CO)_6]$ due to forced pairing will form d^2sp^3 hybrid complex having $3d^6$ configuration.

14. ***(c)*** Transference will be observed in the complex, $[Cu(NH_3)_4]Cl_2$ due to the presence of a strong field ligand (SFL) and the possibility of the formation of inner orbital complex after shifting of one electron from 3*d* to 4*p*-orbital. Thus shows dsp^2 hybridisation i.e. square planar geometry.

15. ***(a)*** On the basis of the spectrochemical series, CN^- is the second strongest ligand and thus will give high spilting energy as compared to all other ligands given.

16. ***(d)*** The CFSE of the complexes of the second and the third transition series is higher than those of the first transition series e.g. $[Tc(H_2O)_6]^{3+} > [Mn(H_2O)_6]^{3+}$. Stronger is the ligand, higher will be the CFSE, so CFSE is $[Mn(NH_3)_6]^{3+} <$ $[Mn(CN)_6]^{3-}$ and $[MnF_6]^{3-} < [Mn(NH_3)_6]^{3+}$. Also, higher is the oxidation state of the central atom higher is the CFSE e.g, $[Mn(H_2O_6]^{2+} < [Mn(H_2O)_6]^{3+}$.

17. ***(b)*** When $\Delta_0 < P$, then a higher energy is required to pair up the electrons. Due to this the electrons prefer to occupy the e_g instead of pairing up in t_{2g} set.

18. ***(b)*** Statement I is correct but statement II is incorrect. Their corrected form are as—

EDTA is used in the treatment of lead posioning.

19. ***(b)*** Higher is the value of the stability constant, greater will the crystal field splitting energy and thus higher will be the strength of the ligand.

20. ***(a)*** The correct match is A-IV, B-I, C-II, D-III.

21. ***(a, b, d)*** $[CoF_6]^{3-}$: $\Delta_0 < P$ and high spin complex

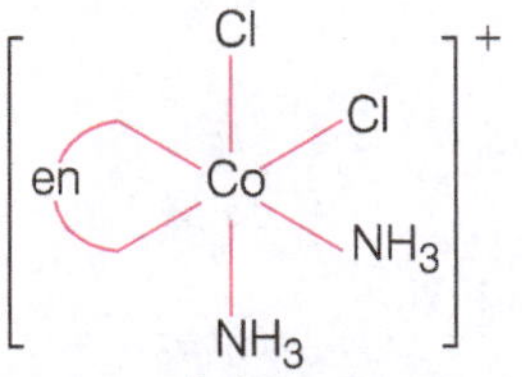

cis-form

⇒ Asymmetric configuration hence exist in *d* and *l* forms

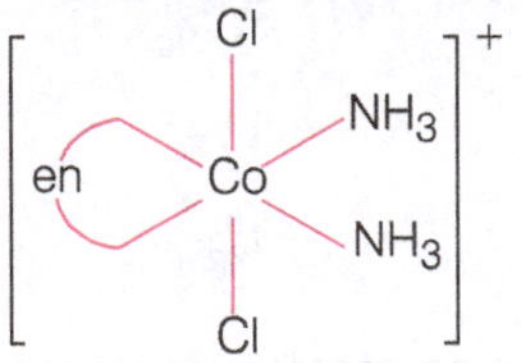

trans-form

⇒ Optically inactive

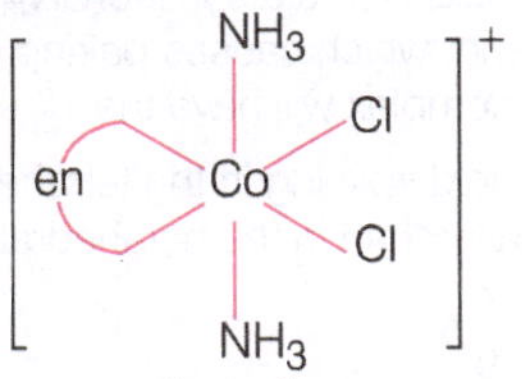

trans-form

⇒ Optically inactive

Total isomers = 4

22. ***(a, b, c)*** Nitrate ion gives a brown ring when reacts with conc. H_2SO_4 in presence of $FeSO_4$ due to formation of $[Fe(H_2O)_5NO]SO_4$ complex compound, Brown colour is just due to charge transfer spectra.

23. ***(a, d)*** The *d*-orbitals involved in sp^3d^2 or d^2sp^3 hybridisation of the central metal ion are $d_{x^2-y^2}$ and d_{z^2}.

24. ***(a, b, c, d)*** All the given statements are correct.

25. ***(a, b, c, d)*** All the given statements are correct.

26. ***(a, b, c, d)*** All the given statements are correct.

27. ***(b,c)*** Irrespective of nature of ligand field, magnetic moment of octahedral complexes having metal ions in d^1, d^2, d^3, d^8, d^9 configuration, remains same.

Element may or may not form colourless complex.

28. ***(1)*** Since Pt in present in (+ 4) oxidation state in given complex. The co-ordination number of Pt(IV) in the given complex will be 6. Thus six monodentate ligands must be present inside the co-ordination sphere and the structural formula of given complex is $[Pt(H_2O)_3Cl_3]Cl$.

29. ***(0)*** Zn^{+2} has d^{10} configuration thus the number of unpaired electron will always be zero regardless of the strength of ligand.

30. ***(3)*** $[Ti(H_2O)_6]Cl_2$ is d^2 system having d^2sp^3 hybridisation, $K_2[Ni(CN)_6]$ is d^8 system having sp^3d^2 hybridisation, $(NH_4)_2[Ni(CN)_4]$ is d^8 system with strong field ligands having dsp^2 hybridisation and $K_2[NiCl_4]$ is d^8 system with weak field ligands having sp^3 hybridisation.

31. ***(3)*** $(NH_4)_4[FeC(N)_6] \rightarrow d^6$ with strong field ligand thus low spin and diamagnetic

$[Mo(CO)_6] \rightarrow d^4s^2$ configuration with strong field system thus it is low spin diamagnetic complex.

$[Co(NO_2)_6]^{3-} \rightarrow d^6$ with strong field ligand thus low spin and diamagnetic complex.

32. ***(0)*** The electronic configuration for Ni^{+2} is $[Ar]3d^8$ and en is strong field ligand.

For a d^8 system, irrespective of nature of ligand the no of e^- in e_g and t_{2g} set will remain same. Hence, there are zero unpaired e^- in t_{2g} orbitals.

33. ***(5)*** For a d^5 system, in presence of weak field ligand the configuration will be t_{2g}^3, e_g^2. Thus there will be 5 unpaired electrons whereas in presence of strong field ligand the configuration will be t_{2g}^5, e_g^0. Thus one unpaired e^-, so the ratio become 5.

34. ***(3)*** Among the given statements regarding product *A* and *B* only three i.e. I, III and V are correct, while II and IV are incorrect.

The photographic "fixing" process removes unreacted AgBr which forms water soluble complex with thiosulphate.

$$AgBr(s) + 2S_2O_3^{2-} \longrightarrow \underset{\text{(Soluble)}}{[Ag(S_2O_3)_2]^{3-}} + Br^-$$

Oxidation state of metal in complex *B* i.e. $[Au(CN)_2]^-$ is + 1.

$$4Au(s) + 8CN^-(aq) + O_2(g) + 2H_2O(l) \longrightarrow 4OH^-(aq) + 4[Au(CN)_2]^-(aq)$$

Let oxidation state of Au is x.

Then, $x + 2(-1) = +1 \Rightarrow x = 1$

Practice Element 01 : Target JEE Main

1. ***(d)*** Mohr's salt ($FeSO_4 \cdot (NH_4)_2SO_4 \cdot 6H_2O$) is a double salt. Aqueous solution of a double salt gives a positive test of all constituent ions.
2. ***(a)*** Hydrazine ($H_2N—NH_2$) is a monodentate ligand. All bidentate ligands are chelating ligands, oxalate is a bidentate ligand.
3. ***(c)*** $[Mn(CO)_6]$

   EAN of Mn = 25 − 0 + 12 = 37

   To gain stability it has to lose an e^- hence, it can act as reducing agent.

   $[V(CO)_6]$

   EAN of V = 23 − 0 + 12 = 35

   To gain stability it has to gain an e^- hence, it can act as oxidising agent.

   $[Fe(CO)_5]$

   EAN of Fe = 26 − 0 + 10 = 36

   It follows EAN rule. It does not behave as oxidising agent and reducing agent.

   $[Mn(CO)_5]$ can dimerise $[Mn_2(CO)_{10}]$ to gain stability.
4. ***(a)*** Hybridisation of Fe in $[Fe(CO)_5]$ is dsp^3 while hybridisation of Ni in $[Ni(CO)_4]$ is sp^3.

   $[Fe(CO)_5]$ and $[Ni(CO)_4]$ both are diamagnetic.
5. ***(c)*** Among the given options, formula and name of the complex is incorrectly matched in option (c). The correct formula of potassium hexacyanido ferrate (III) is $K_3[Fe(CN)_6]$
6. ***(a)*** Order of CFSE (Δ) is

   $$\underset{\text{(Tetrahedral)}}{\Delta_t} < \underset{\text{(Octahedral)}}{\Delta_o} < \underset{\text{(Square planar)}}{\Delta_{sp}}$$

   Absorb energy = Δ

   $[NiCl_4]^{2-}$ and $[Ni(CO)_4]$ have tetrahedral geometry. So, they have low absorption energy. Cl^- is a weaker ligand than CO hence, $[NiCl_4]^{2-}$ exhibits lower energy absorption band.
7. ***(a)*** Cause of colour in chromate ion (CrO_4^{2-}) is ligand to metal charge transfer. In all other complexes, unpaired e^- is present and cause of colour is d-d transition.
8. ***(c)*** $FeCl_3 + 3KCNS \longrightarrow \underset{\text{Red colour}}{Fe(SCN)_3} + 3KCl$

   $$KI + PbCl_2 \longrightarrow \underset{\text{Yellow}}{PbI_2 \downarrow}$$

   $$NH_4Cl + K_2HgI_4 + OH^- \longrightarrow \underset{\text{Reddish-brown}}{NH_2—HgO—HgI}$$

   $$DMG + Ni^{2+} + NH_4OH \longrightarrow \underset{\text{Scarlet red}}{[Ni(DMG)_2]}$$
9. ***(c)*** In aqueous solution (0.001 M), the complexes will dissociate to give the ions:

   $Pt(NH_3)_6Cl_4 \rightleftharpoons [Pt(NH_3)_6]^{4+} + 4Cl^-$; 5 ion.

   $Cr(NH_3)_6Cl_3 \rightleftharpoons [Cr(NH_3)_6]^{3+} + 3Cl^-$; 4 ions.

   $Co(NH_3)_4Cl_3 \rightleftharpoons [Co(NH_3)_4Cl_2]^+ + Cl^-$; 2 ions.

   $K_2PtCl_6 \rightleftharpoons [PtCl_6]^{2-} + 2K^+$; 3 ions.
10. ***(d)*** CFSE represents the stabilisation energy gained by a complex ion due to the splitting of its d-orbitals in a crystal field. Generally, a complex ion with a higher CFSE tends to be more stable.

Complex	Electronic configuration	CFSE
$[NiF_6]^{4-}$	$t_{2g}^6e_g^2$	− 1.2
$[NiF_6]^{2-}$	$t_{2g}^4e_g^2$	− 0.4
$[Fe(H_2O)_6]^{3+}$	$t_{2g}^3e_g^2$	0
$[Ru(H_2O)_6]^{3+}$	$t_{2g}^3\ e_g^3$	0
$[Co(NH_3)_6]^{3+}$	$t_{2g}^6\ e_g^0$	− 2.4
$[Co(en)_3]^{3+}$	$t_{2g}^6\ e_g^0$	− 2.4
$[Ni(CN)_4]^{2-}$	$t_g^4\ e_2^4$	− 0.6
$[Ni(CN)_6]^{4-}$	$t_{2g}^6e_g^2$	− 1.2

   Thus incorrect order of splitting energy is (d).

   Its correct form is $[Ni(CN)_4]^{2-} > [Ni(CN)_6]^{4-}$
11. ***(c)*** Fe is in + 2 oxidation state in $[Fe(CN)_6]^{4-}$. Cyanide is a strong field ligand, which causes pairing of electrons. Therefore, this complex will have the $t_{2g}^6e_g^0$ configuration.
12. ***(c)*** The crystal field splitting in the tetrahedral field is intrinsically smaller than in the octahedral field.

   $$\Delta_t = \frac{4}{9}\Delta_0$$

   $$= \frac{4}{9} \times 18000 = 8000\ cm^{-1}$$
13. ***(d)*** On moving down the group stability of complex increases. Hence, all the given order are correct.

   $$3d < 4d < 5d$$

   According to spectrochemical series as field strength increases, stability increases ligand.
14. ***(c)*** Cu^{2+} salt gives reddish brown ppt with $K_4[Fe(CN)_6]$.

   $$2Cu^{2+} + K_4[Fe(CN)_6] \longrightarrow Cu_2[Fe(CN)_6]$$
15. ***(a)*** In 1L solution, there will be 0.01 mole of each $[Co(NH_3)_5SO_4]Br$ and $[Co(NH_3)_5Br]SO_4$. Addition of excess of $AgNO_3$ will give 0.01 mole of AgBr. Addition of excess of $BaCl_2$ will give 0.01 mole of $BaSO_4$.
16. ***(a)*** Zinc (II) ion has a zero CFSE for any geometry.

   (b) Both $[Fe(CN)_6]^{4-}$ and $[Fe(H_2O)_6]^{2+}$ are coloured due to $d-d$ electronic transitions in visible light.

   (c) In $[Ni(H_2O)_6]^{2+}$, Δ_o is not two large but falls within the visible spectrum, which results in the absorption of light and gives the complex its green colour.

(d) CFSE is not always greater for high spin complexes than for low spin complexes as low spin complexes can have higher CFSE due to greater electron pairing.

17. ***(b)*** $[Cr(H_2O)_6]^{3+}$, oxidation number of Cr = + 3

Electronic configuration of $Cr^{3+} = 1s^2\ 2s^2\ 2p^6\ 3s^2\ 3p^6\ 3d^3$

H_2O is a weak field ligand,

	$3d^3$					$4s$	$4p$		
$[Cr(H_2O)_6]^{3+} =$	1	1	1	××	××	××	××	××	××

d^2sp^3 hybridised

3 unpaired electrons

$$\mu = \sqrt{3(3+2)} = \sqrt{15} = 3.87$$

$[CuF_6]^{3-}$, oxidation number of Cu = + 3

Electronic configuration of $Cu = 1s^2 2s^2 2p^6 3s^2 3p^6 3d^8$

	$3d^8$					$4s$	$4p$			$4d$	
$[CuF_6]^{3-} =$	1L	1L	1L	1	1	××	××	××	××	××	××

sp^3d^2

2 unpaired electrons

$$\mu = \sqrt{2(2+2)} = \sqrt{8} = 2.83$$

18. ***(a)*** $[Co(NH_3)_5Cl]Cl_2 \longrightarrow [Co(NH_3)_5Cl]^{2+} + 2Cl^-$ (3 ions)

$\downarrow AgNO_3$ (2 moles)

$[Co(NH_3)_5Cl]^{2+} + 2AgCl$

19. ***(d)*** $[TiF_6]^{2-}$ and Cu_2Cl_2 are colourless species due to absence of unpaired electron.

20. ***(d)*** An ambidentate ligand is a molecule or ion that can attach to a central metal atom through two different atoms.

21. ***(3)*** The spin only magnetic moment of $[NiCl_4]^{2-}$ is

$[NiCl_4]^{2-}$, $Ni^{2+} = [Ar]\ 3d^8$

1L	1L	1L	1	1

Cl is weak field ligand. Hence, pairing will not take place.

No. of unpaired electron = 2

$$\mu = \sqrt{n(n+2)}$$
$$= \sqrt{2(2+2)} = 2.82 \simeq 3$$

22. ***(9)*** In the given complex $[E(en)_2(C_2O_4)]NO_2$, ethylenediamine and $[C_2O_4]^{2-}$ are bidentate ligands. Therefore coordination number of complex is 6.

Oxidation number $\Rightarrow x + 2 \times 0 + 1 \times (-2) = 1 \Rightarrow x = +3$

Thus, the sum of coordination number and oxidation state $= 6 + 3 = 9$

23. ***(8)*** $[V(CO)_m]^{n-}$

$_{23}V = [Ar]3d^3 4s^2$

For octahedral complex, $m = 6$

EAN of $V = Z +$ (negative charge (n)) $+ 2 \times 6 = 36$

$36 = 22 + n + 12$

$n = 2$

So, $m + n = 6 + 2 = 8$

24. ***(2)*** $H_xCr(CO)_5$

EAN of chromium = 36

$24 + 2 \times 5 + x = 36$

$x = 2$

$Co(CO)_y$

EAN of cobalt = 35

$27 + 2y = 35$

$2y = 8$

$y = 4$

$Mo(CO)_z$

EAN of Mo = 54

$42 + 2z = 54$

$z = 6$

Thus, $\dfrac{x+y+z}{5} = \dfrac{2+4+6}{5}$

$= \dfrac{12}{5}$

$= 2.4 \approx 2$

25. ***(1)*** The brown colour complex formed in $[Fe(H_2O)_5NO]SO_4$. Let the oxidation state of iron is x.

$$x + (+1) + 5 \times 0 = 2$$
$$x = +1$$

26. ***(13)*** Denticity of the given ligand are as

glycinate ion = 2

oxalate ion = 2

o-phenanthroline = 2

2-2-Bipyridyl = 2

Diethylenetriamine = 3

ethylenediamine = 2

Thus, sum of denticity of ligands

$2 + 2 + 2 + 2 + 3 + 2 = 13$

27. ***(4)*** Total number of complexes that will show geometrical isomers is 2 compounds i.e. 3 and 5 shows geometrical isomerism. So, their sum will be

$$= 0 + 0 + 2 + 0 + 2 = 4$$

28. ***(5)*** Number of electrons form Fe = 26

x ligands contribute electrons = $2x$

$$26 + 2x = 36 \Rightarrow x = 5$$

Thus, the value of $x = 5$.

29. ***(5)*** The number of ions that can form both low spin high spin complex is 5 i.e. Co^{3+}, Cr^{3+}, Fe^{2+}, Fe^{3+}, Ti^{3+}.

30. ***(4)*** The number of unpaired electron present in $[NiF_6]^{2-}$ are four.

$Ni^{4+} = [Ar]\ 3d^6$

F^- is a weak field ligand so pairing does not occur.

1	1	1	1	1

$\therefore$ Unpaired electrons = 4.

Check Through PYQs : JEE Main

1. **(a)** The formula of fluoroapatite is $[3(Ca_3(PO_4)_2 \cdot CaF_2)]$.

2. **(d)** $CoCl_3 \cdot nNH_3 \xrightarrow[\text{Excess}]{AgNO_3} 2$ mol of AgCl

   It means $2Cl^-$ ions will be present in ionisation sphere. So coordination compound should be $[Co(NH_3)_5Cl]\,Cl_2$.

   Oxidation state of cobalt is +3

   $x = 3, n = 5 \Rightarrow x + n = 8$

3. **(a)** $C_2O_4^{2-}$ is an oxalato ion which is bidentate ligand. In this complex, let the oxidation state of cobalt is $\begin{bmatrix} +1\times 3 + x + (-2)\times 3 = 0 \\ x = +3 \end{bmatrix}$. So, the IUPAC name of $K_3[Co(C_2O_4)_3]$ is potassium trioxalatocobaltate (III).

4. **(c)** The examples of double salt are given in A and C only.

   $FeSO_4 \cdot (NH_4)_2SO_4 \cdot 6H_2O$ is hydrated ferrous ammonium sulphate known as Mohr's salt.

   $K_2SO_4 \cdot Al_2(SO_4)_3 \cdot 24H_2O$, potash alum is a double salt of K_2SO_4 and $Al_2(SO_4)_3$.

5. **(9)** Here, bpy is bidentate ligand. So, coordination number of cobalt is 6.

   Let the oxidation state of Co in $[Co(bpy)Cl_4]^-$ be x.

   $\therefore \quad x + 0 + 4(-1) = -1 \Rightarrow x = 3$

   $\therefore$ Oxidation state of Co = 3

   Sum of oxidation state and coordination number of cobalt is 6 + 3 i.e., 9.

6. **(3)** The $(M-C)\pi$-bond is formed by the donation of a pair of electrons from a filled *d*-orbital of metal to the vacant antibonding $\overset{*}{\pi}$-orbital of carbon of carbonyl ligand. Thus, CO acts as a σ- donor ($CO \longrightarrow M$) and a π-acceptor ($M \longrightarrow CO$), with the two interaction creating a synergic effect which strengthens the bond between CO and the metal.

   So, all the given three complexes have CO ligands and all will exhibit synergic bonding.

7. **(7)** The structure of $[Co_2(CO)_8]$ is

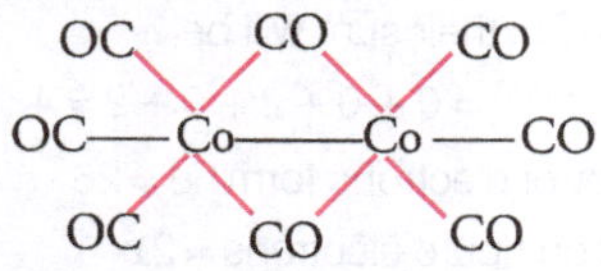

   Number of Co—Co bond (*X*) = 1

   Number of terminal CO ligands (*Y*) = 6

   $\therefore X + Y = 1 + 6 = 7$

8. **(2)** Since, the compound is octahedral, the central metal *M* will form 6 bonds. On reaction with excess of $AgNO_3$, only 1 mol of AgCl is precipitated that means only 1 Cl^- is present as counter ion and $2Cl^-$ ions are present in coordinate sphere.

   So '*L*' should be bidentate to form an octahedral complex alongwith $2Cl^-$ ions.

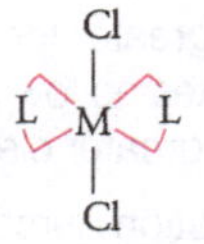

$[MCl_2L_2]Cl$

9. **(a)** The identification of Ni^{2+} is carried out by dimethyl glyoxime in the presence of NH_4OH

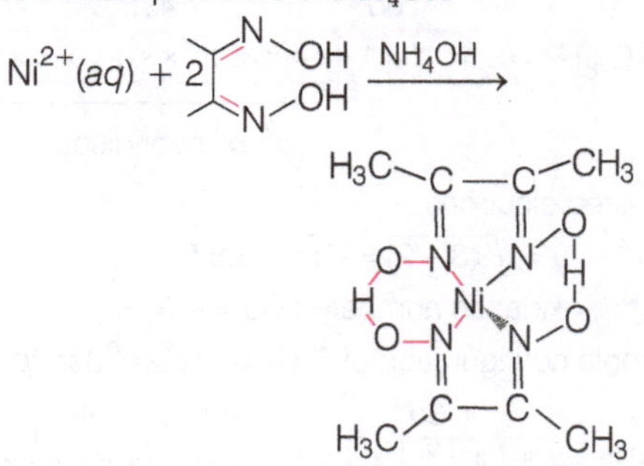

   Both statements are true. Dimethyl glyoxime (DMG) is a neutral bidentate ligand.

10. **(a)** Complex

    $(A) = [Cr(H_2O)_4Cl_2]Cl \cdot 2H_2O$

    Molar mass of complex = 266.5 g/mol

    On reaction with conc. H_2SO_4 the mass last by complex $= \frac{13.5}{100} \times 266.5 = 35.9775 \approx 36$ g

    It means that 2 moles of H_2O are present in outside of coordination sphere. [$\because$ Molar mass of H_2O = 18 g/mol]

    Then, formula of complex is

    $[Cr(H_2O)_4Cl_2]Cl \cdot 2H_2O$

11. **(b)** $[Ma_3b_3]$ type complex compound can show fac-mer isomerism. Where *a*, *b* are monodentate ligands.

    Among the given compounds $[Co(NH_3)_3Cl_3]$ is $[Ma_3b_3]$ type complex and will show fac-mer isomerism.

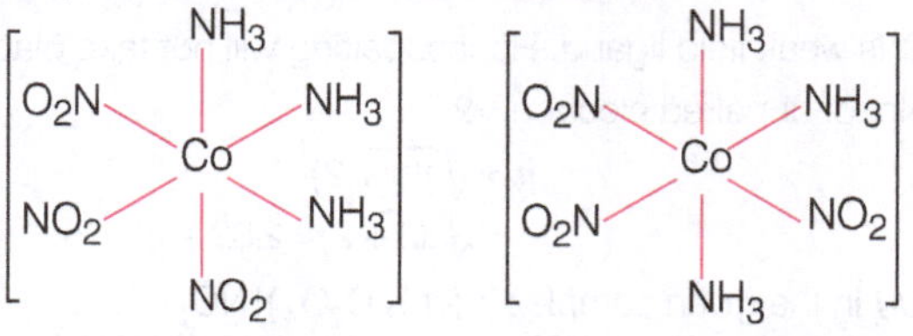

fac-isomer   *mer*-isomer

12. **(4)**

    cis-$[Cr(ox)_2Cl_2]^{3-}$
    $[Co(en)_3]^{3+}$
    cis-$[Pt(en)_2Cl_2]^{2+}$
    cis-$[Co(en)_2Cl_2]^+$
    → Can show optical isomerism (no plane of symmetry and no centre of symmetry)

    Hence, total 4 complex shows optical isomerism.

13. **(b)** $[Cr(ox_2ClBr)]^{3-} = [M(aa)_2bc]$ type gives 2-Geometrical isomers - *cis* and *trans* where is the *cis*- form is optically active.

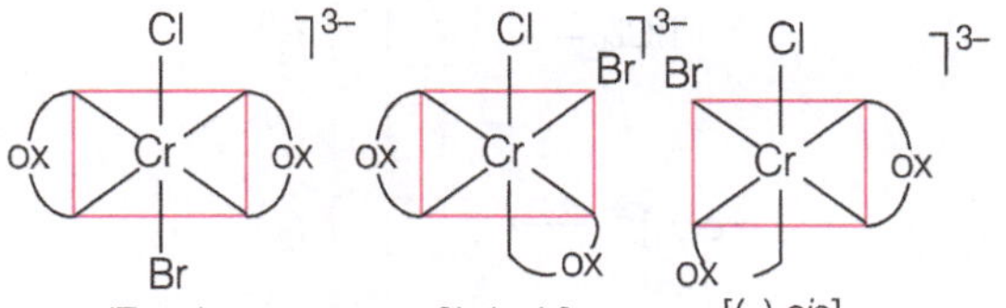

(*Trans*) [(+) *cis*] [(–) *cis*]

Thus, the total three stereoisomers for the $[Cr(ox)_2ClBr]^{3-}$.

14. ***(1)*** The structure of complex
$CoCl_3 \cdot 4NH_3$ is $[Co(NH_3)_4Cl_2]Cl$
Geometrical isomers i.e., *cis* and *trans* are possible

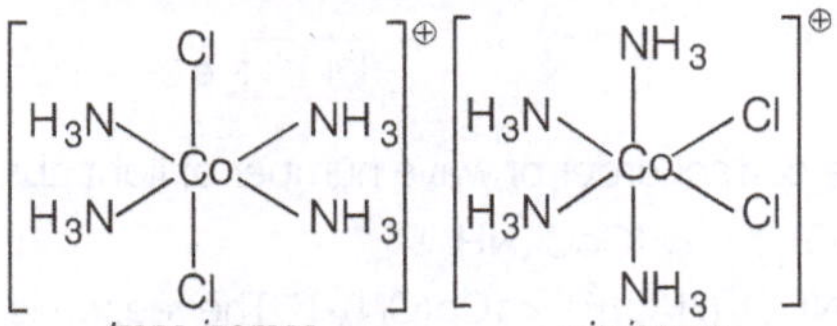

trans-isomer *cis-isomer*

15. ***(c)***

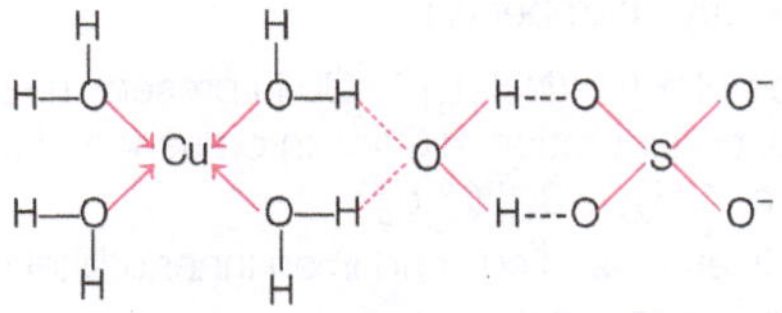

In $CuSO_4 \cdot 5H_2O$, Cu—O bonds are present. It is a correct statement.

In $CuSO_4 \cdot 5H_2O$, ligands coordinating with Cu(II) ion are O - and S-based ligands. The statement is incorrect. The ligands coordinating with Cu(II) ion is O-based and not S-based. It is a incorrect statement.

16. ***(a)*** The correct match is (A)-3, (B)-1, (C)-2, (D)-4.

17. ***(c)*** Number of geometrical isomers of $[PtCl_2(NH_3)_2]$ = two geometrical isomers.

In $[Ni(CO)_4]$ complex all ligands are same. Therefore, it does not show geometrical isomerism.

$[Ru(H_2O)_3Cl_3]$: two geometrical isomers.

$[CoCl_2(NH_3)_4]^+$: two geometrical isomerism.

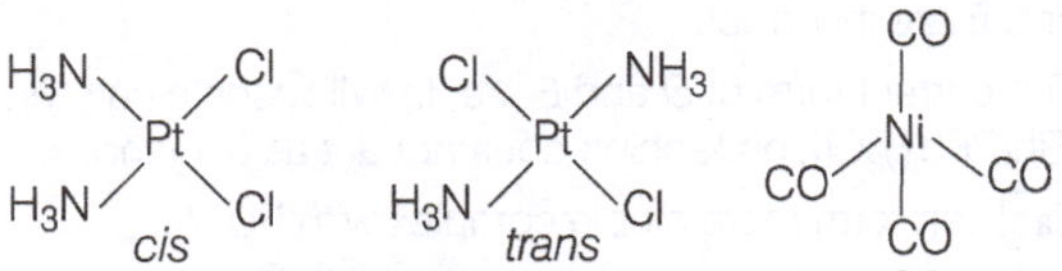

cis *trans* $[PtCl_2(NH_3)_2]$ $[Ni(CO)_4]$ (no isomerism)

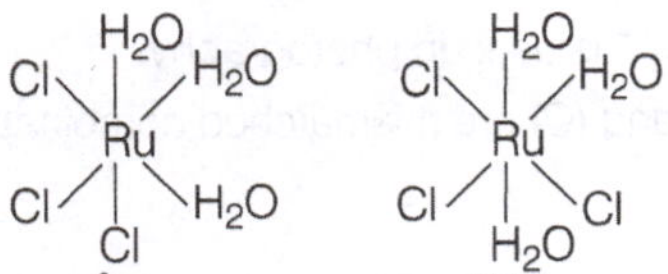

fac *mer*

$[Ru(H_2O)_3Cl_3]$

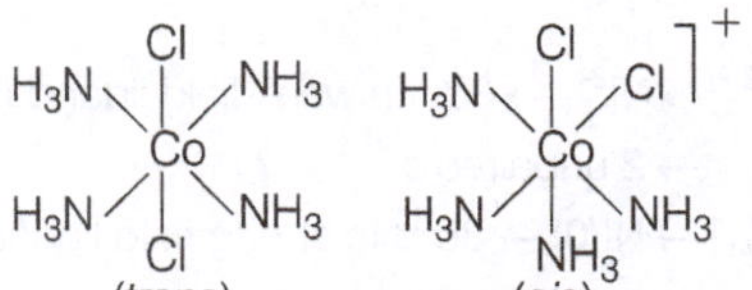

(*trans*) (*cis*)

$[CoCl_2(NH_3)_4]^+$

18. ***(b)*** $[Co(CN)_5(NC)]^{3-}$ is of MA_5B type complex, which will not show any isomerism and the rest complexes will show geometrical isomerism.

∴ Option (b) is correct.

19. ***(a)*** There are clearly many planes of symmetry in the tetrahedral (M is sp^3 in MA_2B_2) structure and the structure is superimposable on its mirror image.

∴ It has no optical isomers.

MA_2B_2 complex of dsp^2-hybridised metal (M) has square planar geometry.

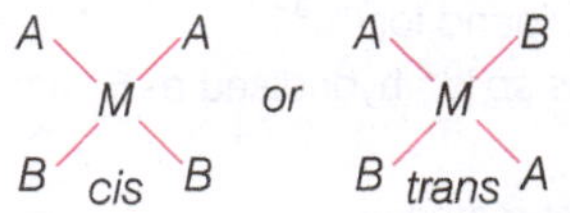

There are two geometrical isomers *cis* and *trans*.

But, since they are planar and therefore they always have a plane of symmetry.

∴ No optical isomerism.

20. ***(b)*** Pt^{2+} complexes with coordination number equals to 4 are square planar. In $[Pt(NH_3)_2Cl(NO_2)]$ two NH_3 ligands could arrange in *cis* or *trans* positions.

∴ There are two geometrical isomers.

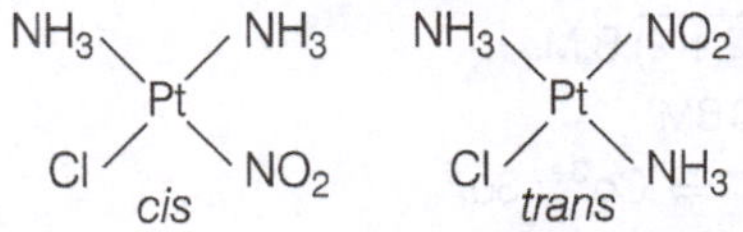

cis *trans*

$[Pt(NH_3)_4ClBr]^{2+}$: Two geometrical isomers are possible coordination number = 6 and Octahedral geometry

Cl and Br can be arranged *cis* or *trans*

∴ 2 geometrical isomers

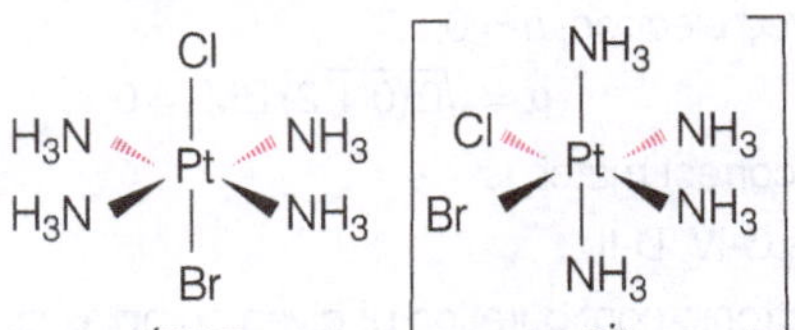

trans *cis*

Hence, (C) and (D) will show geometrical isomerism.

21. ***(a)*** $[NiCl_4]^{2-}$

$\Rightarrow Ni^{2+} \rightarrow 3d^8$

Cl^- ligand is weak field ligand and hybridisation is sp^3. Shape of complex is tetrahedral.

22. ***(a)***

- $[NiCl_4]^{2-} \rightarrow Ni^{2+} \rightarrow 3d^8$ in weak field ligand (WFL)
  (sp^3) $\rightarrow 2$ unpaired e^-
- $[Ni(CO)_4] \rightarrow Ni(0) \rightarrow 3d^{10}$ in strong field ligand (SFL)
  (sp^3) $\rightarrow 0$ unpaired e^-
- $[Ni(CN)_4]^{2-} \rightarrow Ni^{2+} \rightarrow 3d^8$ in SFL
  (dsp^2) $\rightarrow 0$ unpaired e^-
- $[Fe(CO)_5] \rightarrow Fe(0) \rightarrow 3d^8$ in SFL
  (dsp^2) $\rightarrow 0$ unpaired e^-

22. ***(b)*** The correct match is

A-III, B-I, C-IV, D-II

- $K_2[Ni(CN)_4]$ is dsp^2 hybridised as Ni is present in + 2 oxidation state and CN^- is a strong field ligand.
- $[Ni(CO)_4]$ is sp^3 hybridised as Ni is present in zero oxidation state.
- $[Co(NH_3)_6]Cl_3$, Co is d^2sp^3 hybridised as NH_3 acts as strong field ligand for Co^{3+}.
- $Na_3[CoF_6]$ is sp^3d^2 hybridised as F^- act as weak field ligand.

23. ***(c)*** The correct match is

A-II, B-IV, C-I, D-III

A. $[Cr(NH_3)_6]^{3+} \Rightarrow Cr^{3+}; 3d^3$

unpaired electron, $n = 3$

Using the formula, spin only magnetic moment

$$= \sqrt{n(n+2)} \text{ B.M.}$$

$$\mu = 3.87 \text{ B.M.}$$

B. $[NiCl_4]^{2-} \Rightarrow Ni^{2+} = 3d^8$

unpaired electron, $n = 2$,

$\mu = \sqrt{2(2+2)}$ B.M.

$\mu = 2.83$ BM

C. $[CoF_6]^{3-} \Rightarrow Co^{3+}; 3d^6$

unpaired electron,

$n = 4, \mu = \sqrt{4(4+2)}$ B.M.

$\mu = 4.90$ BM

D. $[Ni(CN)_4]^{2-} \Rightarrow Ni^{2+}; 3d^8$

unpaired electron, $n = 0$,

$$\mu = \sqrt{0(0+2)} \text{ BM } = 0$$

24. ***(c)*** The correct match is,

A-III, B-I, C-IV, D-II

The electronic configuration of given complex is,

$TiCl_4 \longrightarrow$ [ ][ ][ ] t_2^0
[ ][ ] e^0

$[FeO_4]^{2-} \longrightarrow$ [ ][ ][ ] t_2^0
[1][1] e^2

$[FeCl_4]^- \longrightarrow$ [1][1][1] t_2^3
[1][1] e^2

$[CoCl_4]^{2-} \longrightarrow$ [1][1][1] t_2^3
[⇅][⇅] e^4

25. ***(b)*** The correct order of wave number of light absorbed is
$[Cu(H_2O)_4]^{2+} < [CoCl(NH_3)_5]^{2+}$
$< [Co(NH_3)_5(H_2O)]^{3+} < [Co(CN)_6]^{3-}$ The reason is, as ligand field increases, light of more energy is absorbed.

Energy $\propto$ wave number $(\bar{\nu})$

26. ***(a)*** In complex $[Co(NH_3)_6]^{3+}$, Co is present in +3 oxidation state. So, configuration of Co^{3+} in presence of strong field ligand (i.e., NH_3) is $3d^6(t_{2g}^6e_g^0)$.
Its hybridisation is d^2sp^3 and is an inner orbital complex *i.e.*, (spin paired complex).
In $[CoF_6]^{3-}$, Co is present in +3 oxidation state. So, configuration of Co^{3+} in presence of weak field ligand (i.e. F^-) is $3d^6(t_{2g}^4e_g^2)$.
Its hybridisation is sp^3d^2 and is an outer orbital complex *i.e.*, (spin free complex).

27. ***(c)*** Both Statement I and Statement II are correct.

28. ***(b)*** Statement given in *B* and *C* are correct while statements *A* and *D* are incorrect. Their correct form are as follows
- The strength of anionic ligands cannot be explained by crystal field theory.
- The number of possible isomers of *cis* $[PtCl_2(en)_2]^{2+}$ is more than one.

29. ***(a)*** Statement given in *A, B* and *C* are correct, while in *D* and E are incorrect.
The correct form of *D* and *E* are: In Wilkinson's catalyst. $[Rh(PPh_3)_3Cl]$, phosphine does not act as a ligand.
Ca^{2+} ion form more stable complex with EDTA.

30. ***(a)*** Chlorophyll is a coordination compound of magnesium (Mg).
$[Ag(S_2O_3)_2]^{3-}$ is used in photography.
Hence (A) and (C) are mismatched combinations.

31. ***(d)*** The correct match is A-II, B-III, C-I, D-IV.

	Complex		Colour
(A)	$Mg(NH_4)PO_4$	II.	White
(B)	$K_3[Co(NO_2)_6]$	III.	Yellow
(C)	$MnO(OH)_2$	I.	Brown
(D)	$Fe_4[Fe(CN)_6]_3$	IV.	Blue

32. ***(a)*** In the complex $[NiCl_2Br_2]^{2-}$, the geometry is tetrahedral due to presence of weak field ligands and do not show geometrical isomerism.
- However for complex $[PtCl_2Br_2]^{2-}$ the geometry is square planar and it shows two geometrical isomers.
- Both the complex species are optically inactive.
- Also they contain different number of unpaired electron. Hence, their magnetic properties varies.

33. ***(d)*** The correct order of the number of unpaired electrons in the given complexes is $E < A < D < C < B$.

(A) $[Fe(CN)_6]^{3-}$ $n = 1$
(B) $[FeF_6]^{3-}$ $n = 5$
(C) $[CoF_6]^{3-}$ $n = 4$
(D) $[Cr(oxalate)_3]^{3-}$ $n = 3$
(E) $[Ni(CO)_4]$ $n = 0$

34. ***(b)***

Complex	Configuration of *d* –orbital	Unpaired electron	Spin moment, $\mu = \sqrt{n(n+2)}$
$[Fe(CN)_6]^{3-}$	$Fe^{3+} \Rightarrow t_{2g}^5 e_g^0$	1	1.732
$[Mn(CN)_6]^{3-}$	$Mn^{3+} \Rightarrow t_{2g}^4 e_g^0$	2	2.828
$[CoF_6]^{3-}$	$Co^{3+} \Rightarrow t_{2g}^4 e_g^2$	4	4.899
$[MnBr_4]^{2-}$	$Mn^{2+} \Rightarrow e^2 t_2^3$	5	5.916

Hence, correct order of spin only magnetic moment is

$$[Fe(CN)_6]^{3-} < [Mn(CN)_6]^{3-} < [CoF_6]^{3-} < [MnBr_4]^{2-}.$$

35. ***(480)*** In $[Ti(H_2O)_6]^{3+}$, Ti^{3+} has outer electronic configuration $3d^1$

$$\text{CFSE for } [Ti^{3+}] = -0.4 \times \Delta_o = -\frac{96 \times 10^3}{N_A} \text{ J}$$

$$\Rightarrow \Delta_o = \frac{96 \times 10^3}{0.4 \times 6 \times 10^{23}} = \frac{hc}{\lambda}$$

$$\therefore \lambda = \frac{0.4 \times 6 \times 10^{23} \times 6.4 \times 10^{-34} \times 3 \times 10^8}{96 \times 10^3}$$

$$= 0.48 \times 10^{-6} \text{ m} = 480 \times 10^{-9} = 480 \text{ nm}$$

36. ***(c)*** In general, ligands can be ordered in the following sequence in terms of increasing field strength and in accordance with the spectrochemical series.

$$I^- < Br^- < SCN^- < Cl^- < S^{2-} < F^- < OH^- < C_2O_4^{2-} < H_2O < NCS^- < EDTA^{4-} < NH_3 < en < CN^- < CO.$$

37. ***(a)*** Jahn-Teller distortion is shown in those octahedral complexes which have unsymmetrically filled t_{2g} or e_g orbital.

In case of $[Cu(H_2O)_6]SO_4$, uneven filling of electron in e_g orbital ($t_{2g}^6 e_g^3$) leads to structural distortion of octahedral geometry.

38. ***(2)*** Fehling's solution contains $Cu^{2+} \rightarrow d^9$ configuration | ⥮ | ⥮ | ⥮ | ⥮ | 1 |

$\therefore$ Number of unpaired $e^-(n) = 1$

So, spin magnetic moment (μ).

$$= \sqrt{n(n+2)} \text{ BM}$$
$$= \sqrt{1(3)} = 1.73 \text{ BM} \approx 2 \text{ BM}$$

39. ***(a)*** The counter ions are exchanged by other reagents only.

$$[Co(NH_3)_5Br]SO_4 + BaCl_2 \longrightarrow [Co(NH_3)_5Br]Cl_2 + \underset{\text{White ppt.}}{BaSO_4 \downarrow}$$

It does not have chloride ion as counter ion so it will not give white ppt with $AgNO_3$.

40. ***(b)*** As the number of unpaired electrons (n) increases magnetic moment of complex also increases.

(A) $[FeF_6]^{3-}$ is a high-spin complex. So, pairing of electrons will not occur.

$$Fe^{3+} \Rightarrow t_{2g}^3 e_g^2 \ (n = 5)$$

(B) $[Fe(CN)_6]^{3-}$ is a low-spin complex. So, pairing of electrons occur in *d*-orbital.

$$Fe^{3+} \Rightarrow t_{2g}^5 e_g^0 \ (n = 1)$$

(C) $[MnCl_6]^{3-}$ is a high spin complex. So, pairing of electrons will not occur.

$$Mn^{3+} \Rightarrow t_{2g}^3 e_g^1 \ (n = 4)$$

(D) $[Mn(CN)_6]^{3-}$ is a low-spin complex. So, pairing of electrons take place.

Where n = number of unpaired electrons

$$Mn^{2+} \rightleftharpoons t_{2g}^3 e_g \ (n = 2)$$

So, increasing order of magnetic moment : B< D< C< A.

41. ***(d)*** All the transition metals have same oxidation states.

$[Cr(H_2O)_6]^{3+} \longrightarrow 3d$ series
$[Mo(H_2O)_6]^{3+} \longrightarrow 4d$ series
$[Fe(H_2O)_6]^{3+} \longrightarrow 3d$ series
$[Os(H_2O)_6]^{3+} \longrightarrow 5d$ series

For the same oxidation state, CFSE increasing order will be $3d < 4d < 5d$.

So, $[Os(H_2O)_6]^{3+}$ has maximum CFSE (Δ_o).

42. ***(a)*** For the same central metal ion, the CFSE increases with increase in strength of the ligand. The order of strength of ligand is given by the spectrochemical series :

$$I^- < Br^- < SCN^- < Cl^- < S^{2-} < F^- < OH^- < C_2O_4^{2-}$$
$$< H_2O < NCS^- < EDTA^{4-} < NH_3 < en < CN^- < CO$$

Thus, the order of CFSE of given complexes will be :

$$\underset{(A)}{[CoF_6]^{3-}} < \underset{(B)}{[Co(H_2O)_6]^{3+}} < \underset{(C)}{[Co(NH_3)_6]^{3+}} < \underset{(D)}{[Co(en)_3]^{3+}}$$

43. ***(2)*** In $[Ni(CN)_6]^{2-}$, Ni is in +4 oxidation state.

$Ni^{+4} \rightarrow 3d^6 = t_{2g}^6, e_g^0$

(Presence of strong field)

Unpaired electron = 0

Similarly, $NiCl_2 \longrightarrow Ni^{2+}$

d^8 = ⇅ ⇅ ⇅ 1 1

(Two unpaired electrons)

Number of unpaired electron in $NiCl_2$ and $[Ni(CN)_6]^{2-}$ are two and zero respectively.

Change in number of unpaired electrons ⇒ 2 to 0.

Change = 2

44. ***(c)*** The CFSE order of different geometries are

$$\Delta_t < \Delta_0 < \Delta_{sq.}$$

$$[NiCl_4]^{2-} < [Ni(H_2O)_6]^{2+} < [Ni(CN)_4]^{2-}$$

$$\text{CFSE} \propto \frac{1}{\text{Intensity of colour}}$$

⇒ Intensity of (complementary) colour of compounds will be

$$[NiCl_4]^{2-} > [Ni(H_2O)_6]^{2+} > [Ni(CN)_4]^{2-}$$

45. ***(4)*** $[Ti(H_2O)_6]^{3+}$ is an octahedral complex.

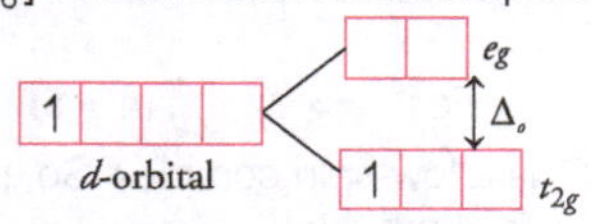

For transition of electron from t_{2g} to e_g orbital, Δ_o amount of energy is required.

Given, $\lambda = 498\text{ nm} = 498 \times 10^{-9}$ m

$$\Delta_o = hc/\lambda$$

where, h = Planck's constant

c = speed of light

λ = wavelength of radiation

$$\text{So, } \Delta_o = \frac{6.626 \times 10^{-34} \times 3 \times 10^8}{498 \times 10^{-9}}$$

$$= 3.99 \times 10^{-19}\text{ J} \approx 4 \times 10^{-19}\text{ J}$$

46. ***(a)*** $[Mn(CN)_6]^{4-}$ In this complex, oxidation state of Mn is +2.

$Mn^{2+} = [Ar]\,3d^5$

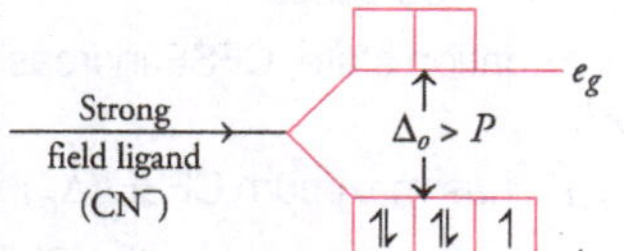

Hybridisation- d^2sp^3

Magnetic nature-Paramagnetic

$[Fe(CN)_6]^{-3}$

$Fe^{3+} = [Ar]\,3d^5$

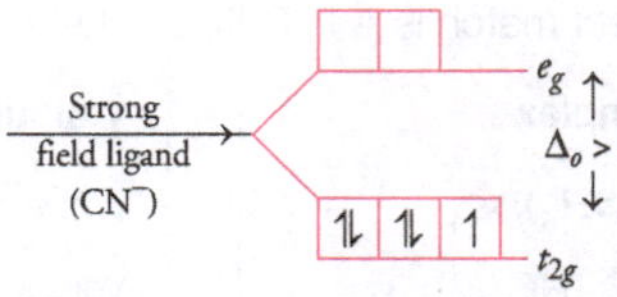

Hybridisation- d^2sp^3

Magnetic nature-Paramagnetic

47. ***(1)*** Given, stability constant value, $k_1 = 10^4$; $k_2 = 1.58 \times 10^3$

$$k_3 = 5 \times 10^2,\ k_4 = 10^2$$

On adding all equations,

$$Cu^{2+} + 4NH_3 \overset{k}{\rightleftharpoons} [Cu(NH_3)_4]^{2+}$$

∴ The overall reaction constant (k) or equilibrium constant for formation of $[Cu(NH_3)_4]^{2+}$ is

$$k = k_1 \times k_2 \times k_3 \times k_4$$

$$k = 10^4 \times 1.58 \times 10^3 \times 5 \times 10^2 \times 10^2$$

$$k = 7.9 \times 10^{11}$$

where, k = equilibrium constant for formation of $[Cu(NH_3)_4]^{2+}$

So, equilibrium constant k' for dissociation of $[Cu(NH_3)_4]^{2+}$ is $\frac{1}{k}$.

$$k' = \frac{1}{k} = \frac{1}{7.9 \times 10^{11}} = 1.26 \times 10^{-12}$$

Hence, $k' = x \times 10^{-12} \Rightarrow x = 1.26 = 1 \times 10^{-12}$

48. ***(a)*** In octahedral complexes

If $\Delta_0 < P$ (weak field, high spin situation).

The fourth electron enters one of the e_g orbitals giving the configuration $t_{2g}^3 e_g^1$ (metal ion : sp^3d^2).

49. ***(c)*** So the electronic configuration of Co (III) will be $t_{2g}^4 e_g^2$, i.e. it has four unpaired electrons.

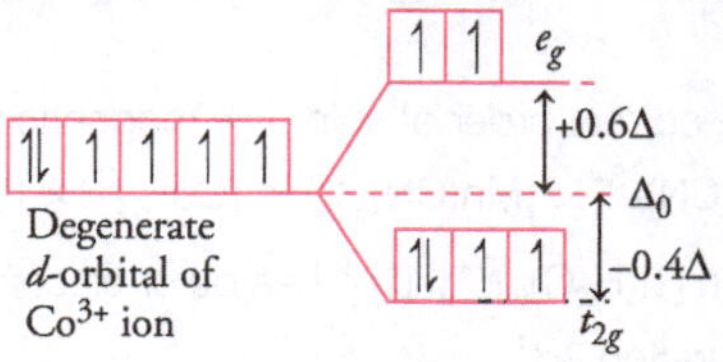

Here, CFSE can be calculated as

$$\text{CFSE} = [-0.4x + 0.6y]\,\Delta_0 = [-0.4 \times 4 + 0.6 \times 2]\,\Delta_0$$

$$= [-1.6 + 1.2]\,\Delta_0 = [-0.4\,\Delta_0]$$

Hence, the crystal field stabilisation energy (CFSE) of $[CoF_3(H_2O)_3]$ will be $-0.4\,\Delta_0$.

50. ***(c)*** The electronic configuration is

$[Ru(en)_3]^{2+} \Rightarrow Ru^{2+} = 4d^6 = t_{2g}^6, e_g^0$

$[Fe(H_2O)_6]^{2+} \Rightarrow Fe^{2+} = 3d^6 = t_{2g}^4, e_g^2$

So, correct answer is (c).

51. ***(a)*** We have to compare their CFSE (Δ_0) as well as wavelength (λ) values, where

$$\Delta E(\text{CFSE}) = \frac{hc}{\lambda} \text{ or, } \Delta_0 \propto \frac{1}{\lambda}$$

Power of ligand $\propto \Delta_0 \propto \frac{1}{\lambda}$, ligand field strength order

$$F^- < NCS^- < NH_3$$

So, for the given complexes, it is evidented from the plot (Absorption vs. λ)

$$\underset{\substack{(C)\\ [F^-]}}{\lambda_{max}^{(ii)}} > \underset{\substack{(B)\\ [NCS^-]}}{\lambda_{max}^{(i)}} > \underset{\substack{(A)\\ [NH_3]}}{\lambda_{max}^{(iii)}}$$

52. ***(d)*** (A) : $Ni(CO)_4$

Ni has $3d^{10}4s^2$ configuration (sp^3) and tetrahedral (strong field ligand).

$\therefore$ Unpaired electrons = 0, μ = 0 BM

(B) : $[Ni(H_2O)_6]Cl_2$

Ni^{2+} has $(3d^8)$ configuration (sp^3d^2) and has two unpaired electrons.

$[Ni(H_2O)_6]^{2+}$ = 

$$\mu = \sqrt{n(n+2)} = \sqrt{2 \times 4}$$
$$= \sqrt{8}\text{ B.M} = 2.82 \text{ BM}$$

(C) : $Na_2[Ni(CN)_4]$

Ni^{2+} has (d^8) configuration and square planar (strong field ligand).

$\therefore$ dsp^2 hybridisation and no unpaired electron

$\therefore$ μ = 0 BM

(D) : $PdCl_2(PPh_3)_2$

Pd^{2+} has $(3d^8)$ configuration. All coordination number = 4

Complexes of Pd^{2+} are square planar.

$\therefore$ dsp^2 hybridised.

No unpaired electron, μ = 0 BM

The correct order of the calculated spin only magnetic moments of complexes is

$$(A) \approx (C) \approx (D) < (B)$$

53. ***(c)*** Valence bond theory cannot distinguish between weak field ligands and strong field ligands. It can't explain the color exhibits by transition metal complex.

Practice Element 02 : Target JEE Advanced

1. ***(a)*** $[Fe(CN)_6]^{3-}$

Fe^{3+} = [Ar] $4s^0 3d^5$

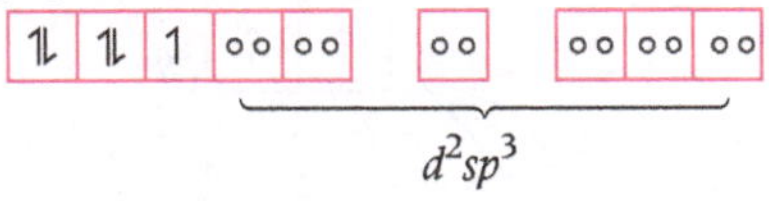

Number of unpaired e^- = 1

$[CoF_6]^{3-}$

Co^{3+} = [Ar] $4s^0$ $3d^6$

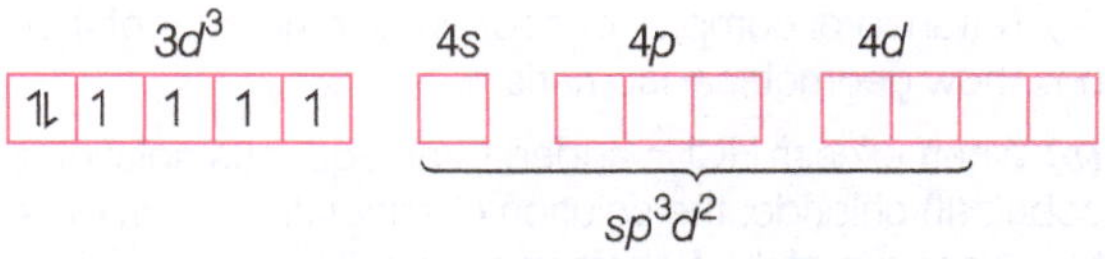

Number of unpaired e^- = 4

$[Fe(H_2O)_6]^{2+}$

Fe^{2+} = [Ar] $3d^6$

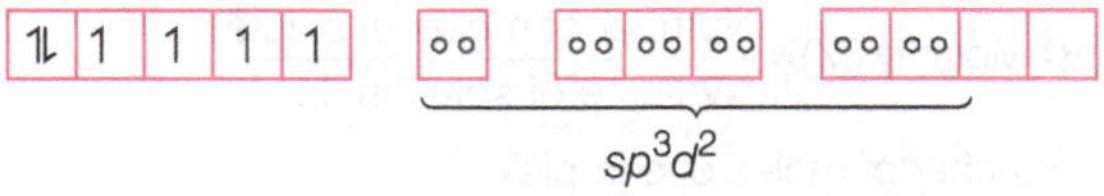

Number of unpaired e^- = 4

$[Ni(CN)_4]^{2-}$

Ni^{2+} = [Ar] $3d^8$

Ni^{2+} = [Ar]$4s^0 3d^8$

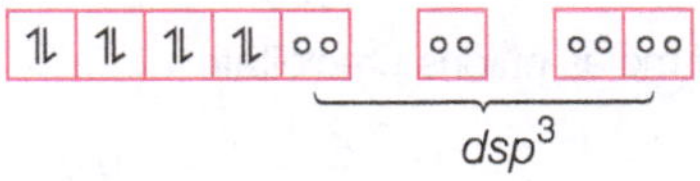

Number of unpaired e^- = 0

2. ***(c)***

	Complex	Hybridisation	*d*-orbitals having highest energy
(a)	$[Ni(CN)_4]^{2-}$	dsp^2	$d_{x^2-y^2}$
(b)	$[NiCl_4]^{2-}$	sp^3	d_{xy}, d_{yz}, d_{xz}
(c)	$[Cr(en)_3]Cl_3$	d^2sp^3	$d_{x^2-y^2}, d_{z^2}$
(d)	$[PtCl_4]^{2-}$	dsp^2	$d_{x^2-y^2}$

3. ***(c)***

(a)	$[Co(ox)_3]^{-3}$	$M(aa)_3$ complex does not show geometrical isomerism
(b)	$[Fe(NH_3)_4Cl_2]^+$	Ma_4b_2 complex does not show optical isomerism.
(c)	$[Fe(NH_3)(H_2O)(Py)(Br)(Cl)(OH)]$	*Mabcdef* complex can show both geometrical and optical
(d)	$[Co(NH_3)_3(NO_2)_3]$	Ma_3b_3 complex does not show optical isomerism.

4. ***(a)*** The IUPAC nomenclature of the complex is pentaammine chloridocobalt (III) dichloride.

$Co(NH_3)_5Cl_3 + H_2O \longrightarrow$ 3 moles of ions $[Co(NH_3)_5Cl]Cl_2$

$[Co(NH_3)_5Cl]Cl_2 + 2AgNO_3 \longrightarrow [Co(NH_3)_5Cl] + 2AgCl$

5. ***(d)*** The stability constant of $[Cu(NH_3)_4]^{2+}$ is larger than that of $[Cu(H_2O)_4]^{2+}$ due to more ligand field strength.

6. ***(b)*** Only d^2 in weak field ligand can have two unpaired electrons.

$$\mu = \sqrt{n(n+2)} = \sqrt{2(2+2)} = 2.84$$

7. ***(b)*** Tetrahedral complex of coordination number of 4 does not show geometrical isomerism.

8. ***(b)*** When excess HCl is added to an aqueous solution of cobalt (II) chloride, the solution changes from pink to deep blue because of the transformation of $[Co(H_2O)_6]^{2+}$ into $[CoCl_4]^{2-}$.

9. ***(b)*** $[Co(en)_2Cl_2]^+$ has highest number of isomers including both geometrical as well as optical.

10. ***(d)*** Molarity $(M) = \dfrac{\text{Number of moles of solute}}{\text{Volume of solution (in L)}}$

$\therefore$ Number of moles of complex

$$= \frac{\text{Molarity} \times \text{Volume (in mL)}}{1000}$$

$$= \frac{0.1 \times 100}{1000} = 0.01 \text{ mol}$$

Number of moles of ions precipitate

$$= \frac{1.2 \times 10^{22}}{6.02 \times 10^{23}} = 0.02 \text{ mol}$$

$\therefore$ Number of Cl^- present in ionisation sphere

$$= \frac{\text{Number of moles of ions precipitated}}{\text{Number of moles of complex}}$$

$$= \frac{0.02}{0.01} = 2$$

$\therefore 2Cl^-$ are present outside the square brackets, i.e. in ionisation sphere. Thus, the formula of complex is $[Cr(H_2O)_5Cl] \cdot Cl_2 \cdot H_2O$.

11. ***(b, c, d)*** Optical isomerism is exhibited by only those complexes which lacks elements of symmetry. Among the given complexes b, c and d exhibits optical isomerism.

12. ***(b, c, d)*** Co^{3+} is d^6 while Cr^{3+} is d^3 different d-electron configurations means different $d-d$ transitions which results in the change of colour of complex.

Both maintain octahedral geometry with 6 ligands.

Both are M^{3+} ions with NH_3 ligands, so Δ changes only slightly.

13. ***(a, b)*** Statements (a, b) are correct whereas (c, d) are incorrect. The correct form of (c and d) is :

Magnitude of Δ_o increases on moving down the group of transition metals. Valence bond theory does not explains about the thermodynamic properties of the complexes.

14. ***(a, b, c, d)*** All the given complexes shows *cis-trans* isomerism.

15. ***(a, c)*** Among the given complexes only a, c, have even number of electron in t_{2g} orbital.

$$Fe(H_2O)_6^{2+} \longrightarrow t_{2g}^4 e_g^2$$
$$[Co(H_2O)_6]^{2+} \longrightarrow t_{2g}^5 e_g^2$$
$$[Cu(H_2O)_6]^{2+} \longrightarrow t_{2g}^6 e_g^3$$
$$[Cr(H_2O)_6]^{2+} \longrightarrow t_{2g}^3 e_g^1$$

16. ***(a, b, c, d)*** All are the correctly matched.

17. ***(a, b, c)*** Among the given complexes a, b, and c does not exhibit square planar geometry.

$$[Fe(CO_4)]^{2-} \longrightarrow sp^3, \text{ tetrahedral}$$
$$[Co(CO)_4]^- \longrightarrow sp^3, \text{ tetrahedral}$$
$$[Cu(py)_4]^+ \longrightarrow sp^3, \text{ tetrahedral}$$
$$[Ni(CN)_4]^{2-} \longrightarrow dsp^2, \text{ square planar}$$

18. ***(a, b)*** Complex have same number of unpaired electron have same magnetic moment. Thus, $[Cr(H_2O)_6]^{2+}$ and $[Fe(H_2O)_6]^{2+}$ have same magnetic moment.

19. ***(2)*** $[Fe(H_2O)_6]^{2+}$

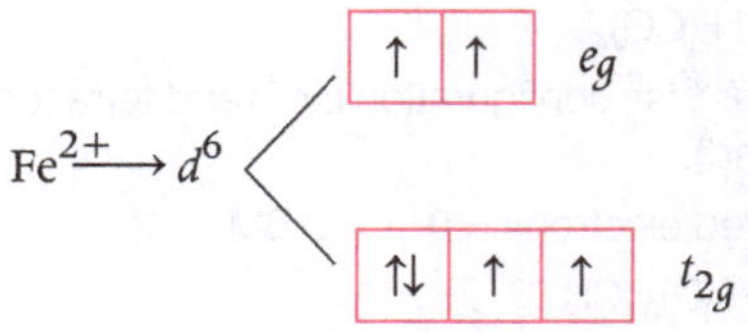

electron in $t_{2g} = 4$ (even)

$[Co(H_2O)_6]^{2+}$

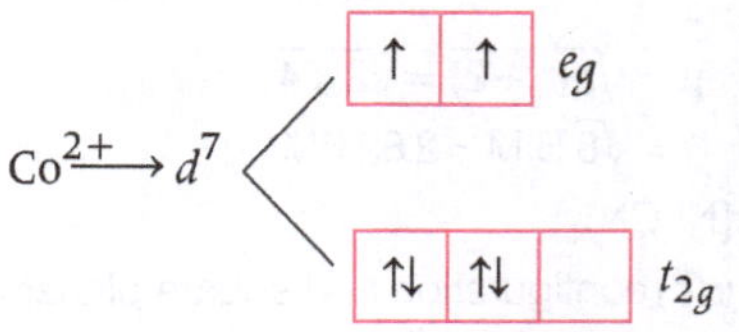

electron in $t_{2g} = 1$ (odd)

$[Cu(H_2O)_6]^{2+}$

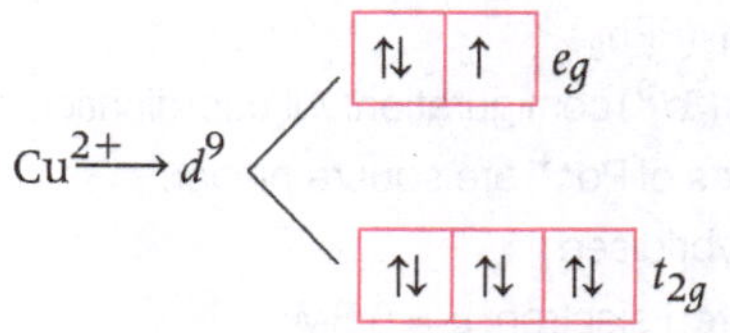

electron in $t_{2g} = 6$ (even)

$[Cr(H_2O)_6]^{2+}$

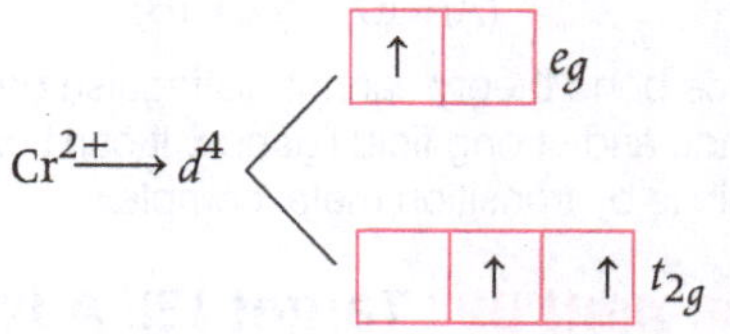

Electron in $t_{2g} = 3$ (odd)

$[Co(H_2O)_6]^{3+}$

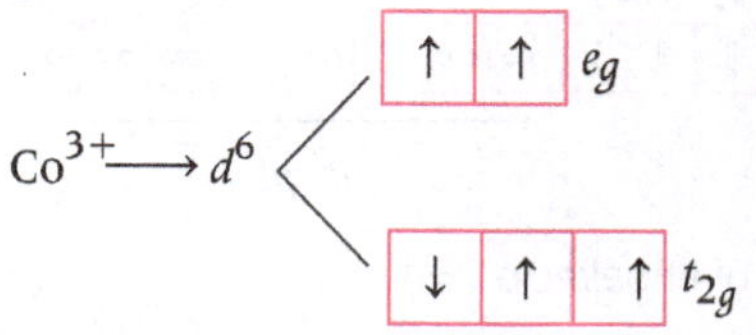

Electrons in $t_{2g} = 2$ (even)

Hence, total two complex have odd number of electrons.

20. ***(3)*** $[Zn(H_2O)_6]^{2+}$, $[Fe(NH_3)_6]^{2+}$, $[Mn(H_2O)_6]^{2+}$ forms sp^3d^2 hybridisation and forms outer orbital octahedral complexes $[Mn(CN)_6]^{4-}$ and $[Mn(CN)_6]^{3-}$ forms d^2sp^3 hybridisation and forms inner orbital octahedral complexes.

21. ***(535)*** In $[Ti(H_2O)_6]^{3+}$, Ti^{3+} has outer electronic configuration $3d^1$.

$$\text{CFSE or } [Ti^{3+}] = -0.4 \times \Delta_0 = \frac{-86 \times 10^3}{N_A} \text{ J}$$

$$\Delta_0 = \frac{0.4 \times 6 \times 10^{23} \times 6.4 \times 10^{-34} \times 3 \times 10^8}{86 \times 10^3} = \frac{hc}{\lambda}$$

$$\lambda = \frac{46.08 \times 10^{-3}}{86 \times 10^3} = 0.535 \times 10^{-6}$$

$$= 535 \times 10^{-9} = 535 \text{ nm}$$

22. ***(4)***

Compounds	Hybridisation	Unpaired e^-	Mangetic Property
$Ni(CO)_4$	sp^3	No	Diamagnetic
$[NiCl_4]^{2-}$	sp^3	Two	Paramagnetic
CsO_2	—	One	Paramagnetic (superoxide ion is paramagnetic)
Na_2O_2	—	No	Diamagnetic (O_2^{2-})
$Na_3[CoF_6]$	sp^3d^2	Four	Paramagnetic
$[Co(NH_3)_4Cl_2]Cl$	d^2sp^3	No	Diamagnetic
$[Ni(CN)_4]^{2-}$	dsp^2	No	Diamagnetic

Thus, the total number of diamagnetic species will be 4.

23. ***(5)***

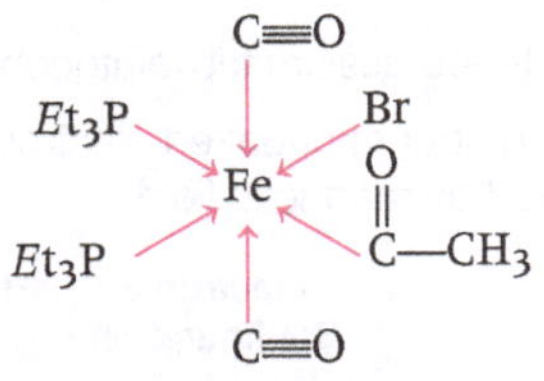

acetylbromidodicarbonylbis (triethyl phosphine) iron (II)

Fe—C bond ⟶ 3

Fe—P bond ⟶ 2

Thus, the sum of Fe—C and Fe—P bond will be, 3 + 2 = 5

24. **(2)** Among the given statement only two statements are incorrect. Their corrected form are as;

II. Metal ions that are hard acids forms more stable complexes with ligands containing N, O, F.

III. Electronegativity increases the stability of the complexes.

25. **(9)** Let the oxidation states of Cr in all cases is 'x'.

(i) Oxidation state of Cr in $[Cr(H_2O)_6]Cl_3$

$$x + 0 \times 6 + (-1 \times 3) = 0$$

$$x + 0 - 3 = 0$$

$$x = 3$$

(ii) Oxidation state of Cr in $[Cr(C_6H_6)_2]$

$$x + 2 \times 0 = 0$$

$$x = 0$$

(iii) Oxidation state of Cr in $K_2[Cr(CN)_2(O)_2(O_2)(NH_3)]$

$$1 \times 2 + x + (-1 \times 2) + (-2 \times 2) + (-2) + 0 = 0$$

$$x = 6$$

Thus, the sum of oxidation state of chromium in all cases—

$$3 + 0 + 6 = 9$$

26. ***(7)*** In $[Cr(NH_3)_6]^{3+}$,

$$Cr^{3+} = 1s^2 2s^2 2p^6 3s^2 3p^6 3d^3$$

| ↑ | ↑ | ↑ | | |

NH$_3$ is weak field ligand, so pairing will not takes place.

$$\text{magnetic moment } (\mu) = \sqrt{n(n+2)}$$

$$= \sqrt{3(3+2)} = 3.87 \text{ BM}$$

In $[CuF_6]^{3-}$,

$$Cu^{3+} = 1s^2 2s^2 2p^6 3s^2 3p^6 4s^2 3d^8$$

| ⇅ | ⇅ | ⇅ | ↑ | ↑ |

F^- is weak field ligand, so pairing will not takes place.

$$\text{Magnetic moment } (\mu) = \sqrt{n(n+2)}$$

$$= \sqrt{2(2+2)} = 2.84 \text{ B.M.}$$

Thus, the sum of their spin only magnetic moment will be 3.87 + 2.84

$$= 6.71 \approx 7$$

27. ***(4)***

Species	Number of unpaired electrons	Magnetic nature
$[Mn(NH_3)_6]^{3+}$	4	Paramagnetic
$[Co(en)_3]^{3+}$	0	Diamagnetic
$[FeF_6]^{3-}$	5	Paramagnetic
$[Ni(CN)_4]^{2-}$	0	Diamagnetic
$[Cu(NH_3)_4]^{2+}$	1	Paramagnetic
$[Ni(CO)_4]$	0	Diamagnetic
$[Fe(H_2O)_6]^{2+}$	4	Paramagnetic

28. ***(3)***

Complex	Oxidation number	Electronic configuration	Unpaired electron	Magnetic moment
$[FeF_6]^{3-}$	+ 3	$[Ar]3d^5$	5	$\sqrt{35}$ BM
$[V(H_2O)_6]^{2+}$	+2	$[Ar]3d^3$	3	$\sqrt{15}$ BM
$[Fe(H_2O)_6]^{2+}$	+ 2	$[Ar]3d^6$	4	$\sqrt{24}$ BM

29. ***(b)*** The correct match is A-II, B-III, C-I, D-V

Complex	No. of unpaired e^-	Magnetic moment
$[Cr(NH_3)_6]^{3+}$	3	3.87
$[Ni(CO)_4]$	0	0
$[CoF_6]^{3-}$	4	4.90
$[Mn(NCS)_6]^{4-}$	5	5.91

30. ***(b)*** The correct match is A-I, B-II, C-III, D-IV
31. ***(a)*** The correct match is A-I, B-II, C-III, D-IV

$[Pt(NH_3)_4]^{2+}$: EAN $= 76 + 2 \times 4 = 84$

$[Ni(NH_3)_6]^{2+}$: EAN $= 26 + 2 \times 6 = 38$

$[Fe(CN)_6]^{3-}$: EAN $= 23 + 2 \times 6 = 35$

$[Cr(NH_3)_6]^{3+}$: EAN $= 21 + 2 \times 6 = 33$

32. ***(b)*** The correct match is A-IV, B-III, C-I, D-II
33. ***(b)*** The correct match is A-II, B-IV, C-I, D-III
34. ***(a)*** The correct match is A-II, B-III, C-I, D-IV
35. ***(b)*** The correct match is A-III, B-II, C-IV, D-I
36. ***(2)*** The formula of the complex formed is $[CoBr(H_2O)(en)_2]Cl_2$. This complex is a type of $[M(AA)_2BC]$ and give 2-geometrical isomers *cis* and *trans*.
37. ***(9)*** The complex formed is $[CoBr(H_2O)(en)_2]Cl_2$

Co-ordination number = 6

Oxidation state $\Rightarrow x + (-1) + 0 + 0 = 2 \Rightarrow x = 3$

Thus, $x + n = 3 + 6 = 9$

38. ***(– 0.4)*** The electronic configuration of Ti^{3+} in complex $[Ti(H_2O)_6]^{3+}$ is $t_{2g}^1 e_g^0$.

C.F.S.E $= [-0.4 \times 1 + 0.6 \times 0]\Delta_0 = -0.4\Delta_0$

39. ***(4)*** If $\Delta_0 < P$ (weak field, high spin situation)

Thus, the electronic configuration will be $t_{2g}^3\, e_g^1$ (metal ion: sp^3d^2)

Therefore, the sum of electron present in t_{2g} and e_g-orbital is $3 + 1 = 4$.

40. ***(2)*** Diamagnetic metals ions cannot have an odd number of electrons as their magnetic moment is zero. Low spin complex may be paramagnetic if they have unpaired electrons. In an octahedral crystal field, the *d*-electrons of metal ion occupy the t_{2g} set of orbital before they occupy the e_g set of orbitals.
41. ***(6)*** $[CoF_6]^{3-}$; $Co^{3+} = t_{2g}^4 e_g^2$

$CFSE = 4 \times (-0.4)\Delta_o + 2 \times (0.6)\Delta_o = -1.6\Delta_o + 1.2\Delta_o = -0.4\Delta_o$

42. ***(c)*** Among the given pair of complexes only four i.e. I, II and IV, V, both complex exhibits tetrahedral geometry.

Complex	Hybridisation	Geometry
$[FeCl_4]^-$	sp^3	tetrahedral
$[Fe(CO)_4]^{2-}$	sp^3	tetrahedral
$[Co(CO)_4]^{2-}$	sp^3	tetrahedral
$[CoCl_4]^{2-}$	sp^3	tetrahedral
$[Ni(CO)_4]$	sp^3	tetrahedral
$[Ni(CN)_4]^{2-}$	dsp^2	square planar
$[Cu(py)_4]^+$	sp^3	tetrahedral
$[Cu(CN)_4]^{3-}$	sp^3	tetrahedral
$[NiCl_4]^{2-}$	sp^3	tetrahedral
$[MnCl_4]^{2-}$	sp^3	tetrahedral

43. ***(b)*** Among the given pair of complexes only two i.e. I and III have the same magnetic moment.

Complex ions	Electronic configuration of metal ion	Number of unpaired e^-
$Cr(H_2O)_6^{2+}$	Cr^{2+} : [Ar] $3d^4$	4
$Fe(H_2O)_6^{2+}$	Fe^{2+} : [Ar] $3d^6$	4
$Mn(H_2O)_6^{2+}$	Mn^{2+} : [Ar] $3d^5$	5
$[CoCl_4]^{2-}$	Co^{2+} : [Ar]$3d^7$	3
$[FeF_6]^{3-}$	Fe^{3+} : [Ar]$3d^5$	5

44. ***(d)*** Among the given pair of complexes only three i.e. II, IV and V can exhibits same kind of isomerism.

II. $[Co(NH_3)_4Cl_2]^+$ and $[Pt(NH_3)_2H_2OCl]^+ \Rightarrow$ geometrical

IV. $[Pt(NH_3)_3NO_3]Cl$ and $[Pt(NH_3)_3Cl]Br \Rightarrow$ ionisation

V. *Cis*- $[Co(en)_2Cl_2]^+$ and $[Co(en)_3]^{3+} \Rightarrow$ optical

45. ***(d)*** Octahedral complex of general formula $[M(AA)_2B_2]$ can show geometrical (*cis-trans*) isomerism. Among the given species only IV and V have *trans* isomers.
46. ***(b)*** Among the given co-ordination complexes with their IUPAC names only two are incorrect. Their corrected form are as follows.

$[Pt(Br_2)(PMe_3)_2$ —dibromobis (trimethyl phosphine) platinum (II)

$K_3[Co(C_2O_4)_3]$—potassium trioxalatocobaltate (III)

47. ***(a)*** More the number of unpaired electron in *d*-orbital, more it will be affected by magnetic field.

Complex	Electronic Configuration	Unpaired Electron
$[Co(H_2O)_6]^{2+}$	$t_{2g}^5\, e_g^2$	3
$[Ni(H_2O)_6]^{2+}$	$t_{2g}^6\, e_g^2$	2
$[Zn(H_2O)_6]^{2+}$	$t_{2g}^6\, e_g^4$	0
$[Co(en)_3]^{3+}$	$t_{2g}^6\, e_g^0$	0
$[Cr(H_2O)_6]^{3+}$	$t_{2g}^3\, e_g^0$	3
$[V(H_2O)_6]^{2+}$	$t_{2g}^2 e_g^0$	2
$[FeO_4]^{2-}$	$t_2^0 e^2$	2

48. ***(b)*** Among the given complexes only four i.e. II, III, VI and VII are paramagnetic complex.

Complex	Hybridisation	Magnetic property
$[Fe(CN)_6]^{4-}$	$d^2sp^3 (3d^6)$	Diamagnetic
$[Fe(CN)_6]^{3-}$	$d^2sp^3 (3d^5)$	Paramagnetic
$[Ti(H_2O)_6]^{3+}$	$d^2sp^3 (3d^1)$	Paramagnetic
$[Ni(CN)_4]^{2-}$	$sp^3 (3d^8)$	Diamagnetic
$[Co(CN)_6]^{3-}$	$d^2sp^3 (3d^6)$	Diamagnetic
$[Fe(H_2O)_6]^{2+}$	$sp^3d^2 (3d^6)$	Paramagnetic
$[Cu(NH_3)_4]^{2+}$	$d^2sp^3 (3d^5)$	Paramagnetic

49. ***(b)*** Among the given complexes only four i.e (i), (ii), (iv) and (vi) will exhibit optical isomerism.

Optical isomerism is exhibited by the compounds that have no plane of symmetry and no centre of symmetry.

50. ***(b)*** The given complex $[Pt(NH_3)_2Br_2]$ is a square planar complex and shows geometrical isomerism. Among the given complexes only four i.e. (iii), (iv), (v) and (vii) can exhibit geometrical isomerism like the given compound $[Pt(NH_3)_2Br_2]$.

51. ***(b)*** Among the given complexes only two i.e, IV and V have CFSE value – 1.2.

Complex	Configuration	CFSE Value
$[Cu(NH_3)_6]^{2+}$	$t_{2g}^6 e_g^3$	$-0.6\Delta_0$
$[Ti(H_2O)_6]^{3+}$	$t_{2g}^1 e_g^0$	$-0.4\Delta_0$
$[Fe(CN)_6]^{3-}$	$t_{2g}^5 e_g^0$	$-2\Delta_0$
$[NiF_6]^{4-}$	$t_{2g}^6 e_g^2$	$-1.2\Delta_0$
$[V(H_2O)_6]^{2+}$	$t_{2g}^3 e_g^0$	$-1.2\Delta_0$
$[Fe(H_2O)_6]^{3+}$	$t_{2g}^3 e_g^2$	$0\Delta_0$
$[Mn(H_2O)_6]^{3+}$	$t_{2g}^3 e_g^1$	$-0.6\Delta_0$

Check Through PYQs : JEE Advanced

1. ***(c)*** $Pb(NO_3)_2 + 2NaCl \longrightarrow PbCl_2\downarrow + 2NaNO_3$

$PbCl_2 + 2Cl^-$ (excess) $\longrightarrow$ $[PbCl_4]^{2-}$ Tetrachloridoplatinate (II) ion

Thus, $[PbCl_4]^{2-}$ is formed.

2. ***(c)***
   - Geometrical isomerism arises in heteroleptic complexes due to different possible geometric arrangements of the ligands.
   - In square planar complexes *cis*-and *trans*-geometrical isomers are there while in octahedral complexes facial and meridional isomers are there.
   - While ionisation isomerism arises when the counter ion in a complex salt is itself a potential ligand and can displace a ligand which can then becomes the counter ion.

Thus, the complexes given in option (c) shows geometrical and ionisation isomerism respectively.

Set I

$[Co(NH_3)_3(NO_2)_3]$ (Geometrical isomers)

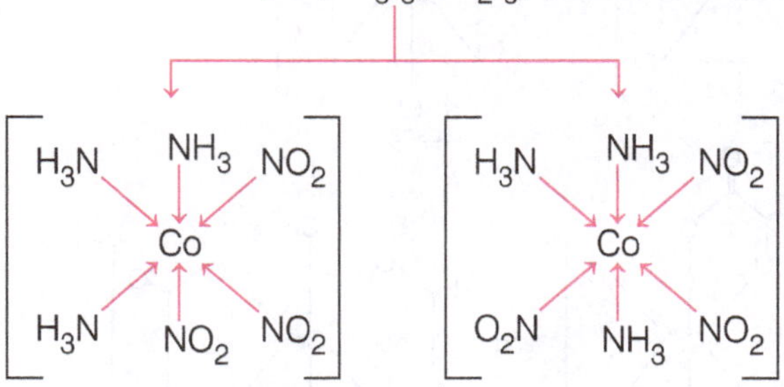

fac *mer*

$[Co(en)_2Cl_2]$

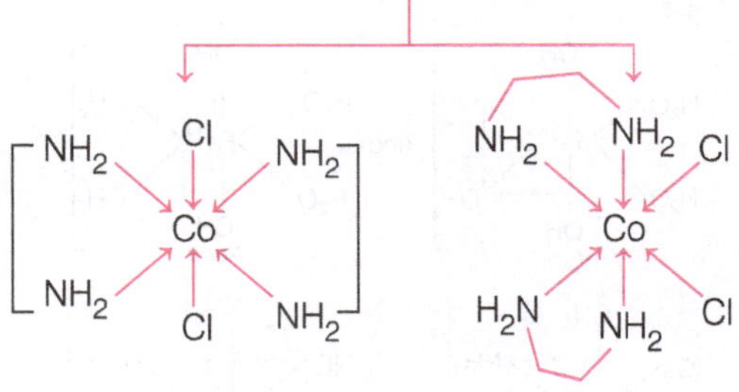

trans *cis*

Set II $[Co(NH_3)_5Cl]SO_4$ and $[Co(NH_3)_5(SO_4)]Cl$ are ionisation isomers.

3. ***(c, d)*** The given complex $[Pt(NH_3)_2Br_2]$ is a square planar complex and shows geometrical isomerism i.e. (*cis* and *trans*)

(a) $[Pt(en)(SCN)_2]$ cannot show geometrical isomerism.

(b) $[Zn(NH_3)_2Cl_2]$ is a tetrahedral complex and hence, cannot show geometrical isomerism.

(c) $[Pt(NH_3)_2Cl_4]$ is a octahedral complex and hence, can show geometrical isomerism.

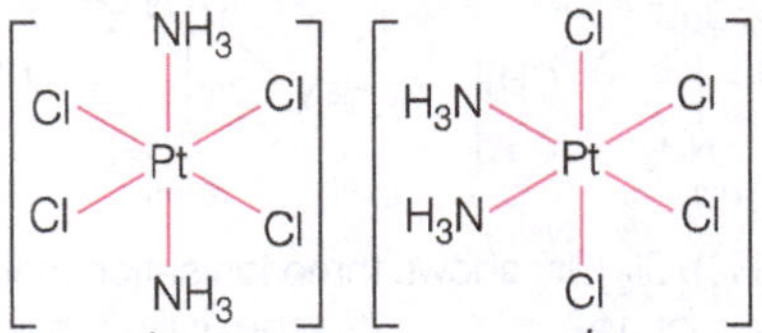

trans *cis*

(d) $[Cr(en)_2(H_2O)(SO_4)]^+$ is octahedral complex and is of type $[M(AA)_2bc]$ can show geometrical isomerism.

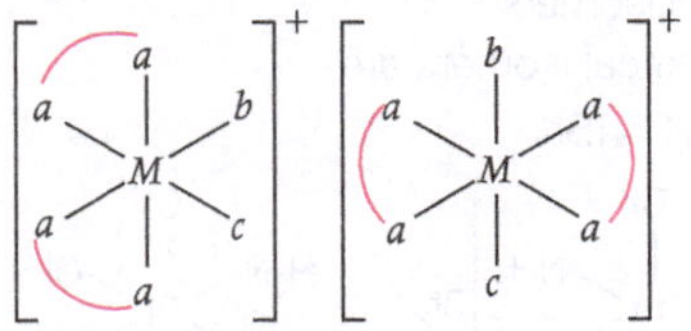

Where, M = Cr, (aa) = (en),

$b = H_2O$ and $c = SO_4$

4. ***(6)*** All six complex will show *cis-trans* isomerism

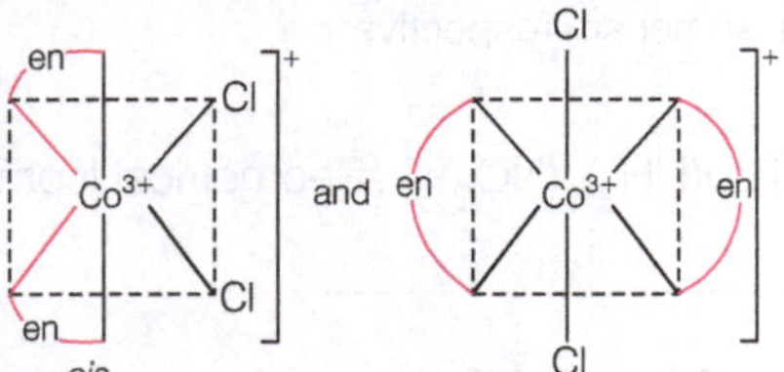

cis and *trans*

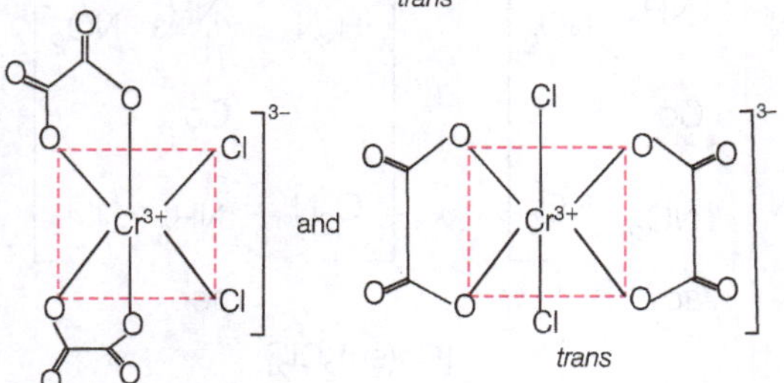

cis and *trans*

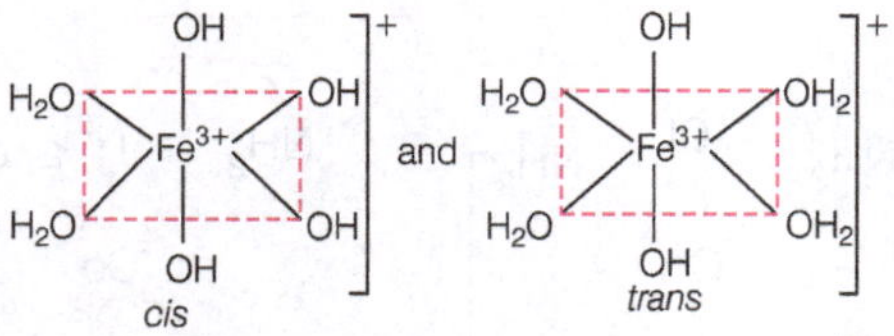

cis and *trans*

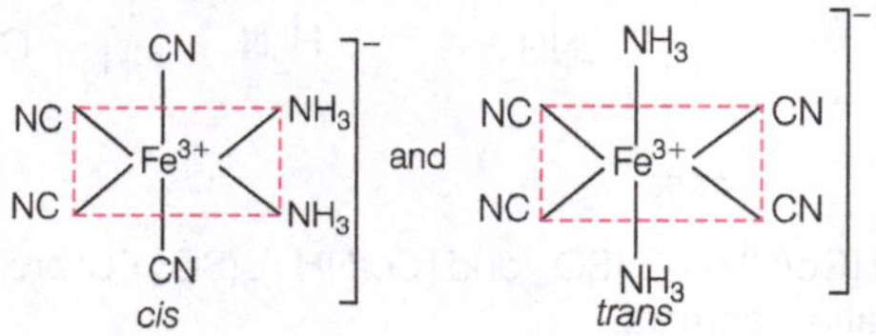

cis and *trans*

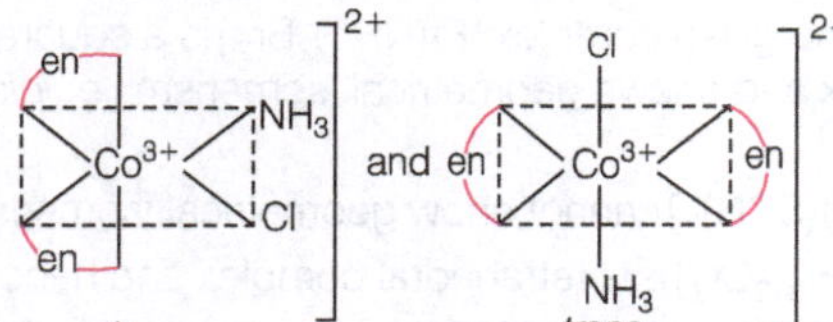

cis and *trans*

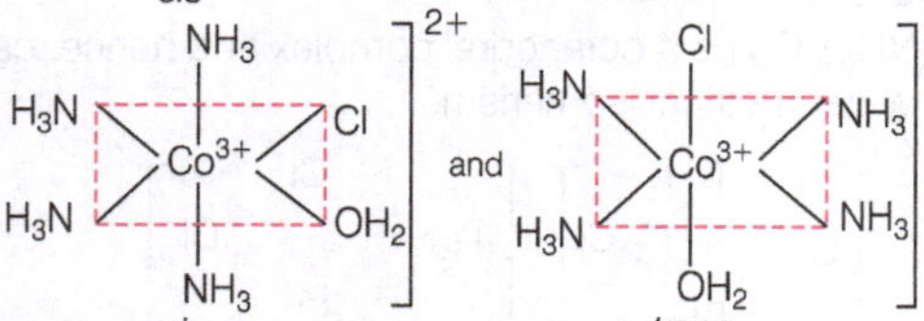

cis and *trans*

5. ***(6)*** $[Pt(NH_3)_4Cl_2]Br_2$ shows three ionisation isomers.

(i) $[Pt(NH_3)_4Cl_2]Br_2$ (ii) $[Pt(NH_3)_4ClBr]BrCl$

(iii) $[Pt(NH_3)_4Br_2]Cl_2$

Each isomer shown above also possess two more geometrical isomers.

The geometrical isomers are :

(i) $[Pt(NH_3)_4Cl_2]Br_2$

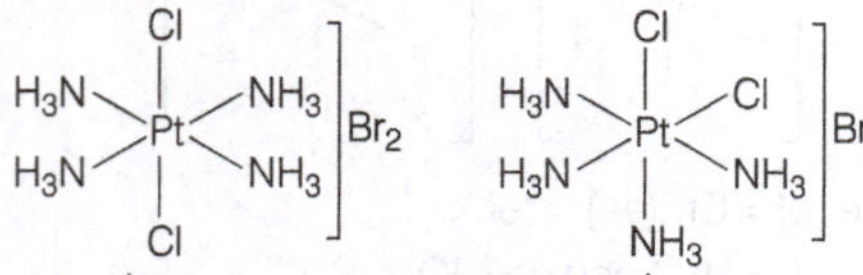

trans *cis*

(ii) $[Pt(NH_3)_4ClBr]ClBr$

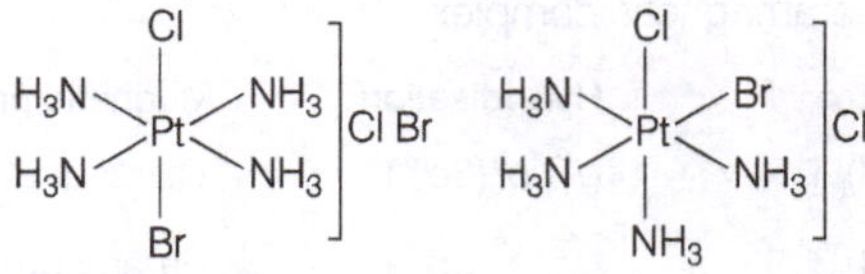

trans *cis*

(iii) $[Pt(NH_3)_4Br_2]Cl_2$

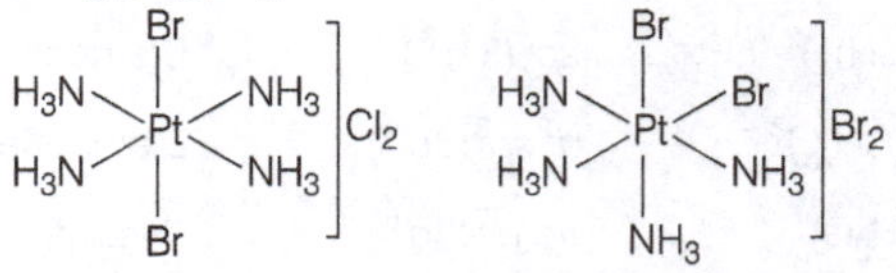

trans *cis*

Thus, total number of possible isomers is 6.

6. ***(5)*** Ligand is $CH_2—NH_2$ (glycinato)
$|$
CH_2O^-

Geometrical isomers are

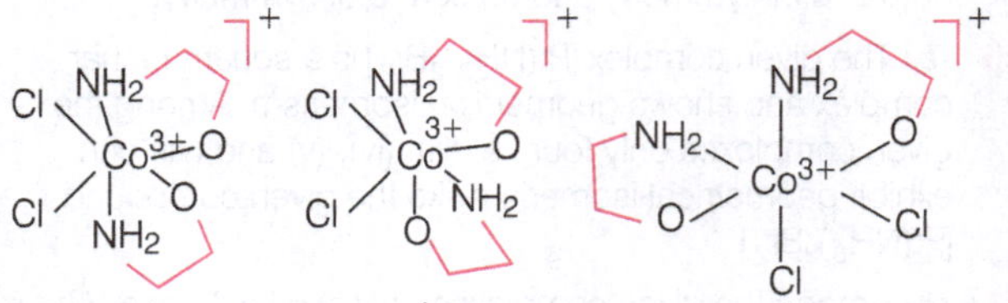

cis *trans* *cis*

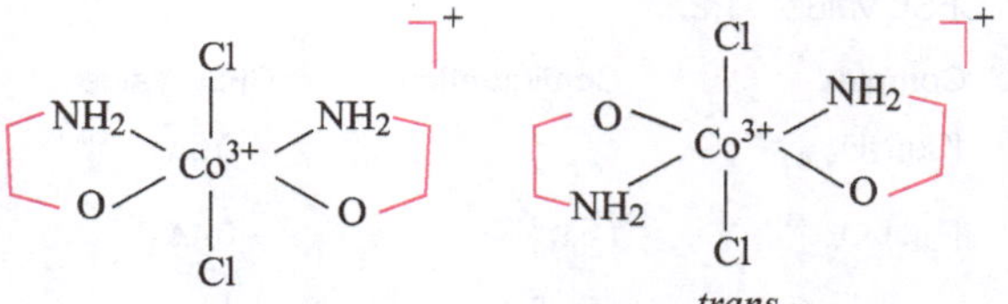

cis *trans*

7. ***(a,c)***

(a) In $[FeCl_4]^-$, oxidation number of Fe atom = + 3

Electronic configuration of Fe in ground state = $3d^6 4s^2$

Electronic configuration of Fe^{3+} = $3d^5 4s^0$

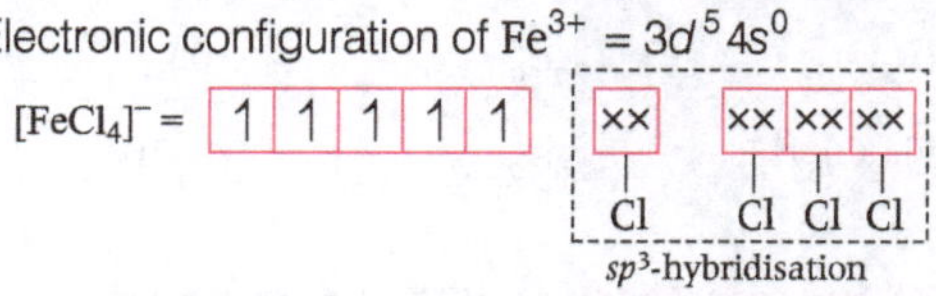

Thus, $[FeCl_4]^-$ has tetrahedral geometry.

(b) $[Co(en)(NH_3)_2Cl_2]^+$ have three geometrical isomers. Thus, statement (b) is incorrect.

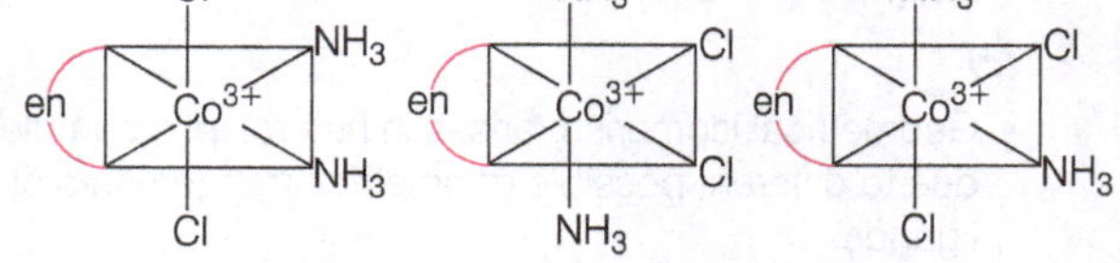

(c) Fe^{3+} in $[FeCl_4]^-$ is sp^3-hybridised with 5 unpaired electrons. (higher spin-only magnetic moment $= \sqrt{n(n+2)} = 5.92$ BM). While Co^{3+} in $[Co(en)(NH_3)_2Cl_2]^+$ is d^2sp^3-hybridised with zero unpaired electrons (low spin-only magnetic moment $= \sqrt{n(n+2)} = 0$ BM).

Thus, the statement (c) is correct.

(d) In $[Co(en)(NH_3)_2Cl_2]^+$, oxidation state of Co is +3.
Electronic configuration of Co in ground state = [Ar] $3d^7 4s^2$
E.C. of Co^{3+} = [Ar] $3d^6 4s^0$.
Due to the presence of strong field ligand thus pairing of electron will take place.

$\therefore [Co(en)(NH_3)_2Cl_2]^+ =$ 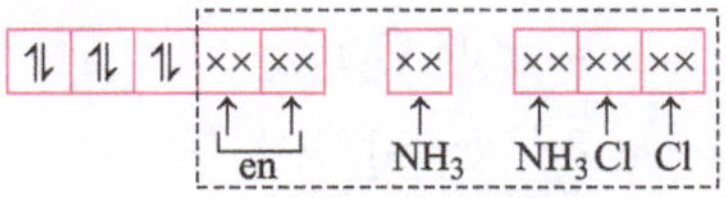

d^2sp^3 hybridised

$\therefore Co^{3+}$ in $[Co(en)(NH_3)_2Cl_2]^+$ is d^2sp^3-hybridised and has octahedral geometry with 0 unpaired electron. Thus, statement (d) is incorrect.

8. ***(a,d)*** $SnCl_2 + Cl^- \longrightarrow SnCl_3^-$
Tin chloride (*Q*) (*X*)

⇒ Structure of $SnCl_3^-$ is as follows.

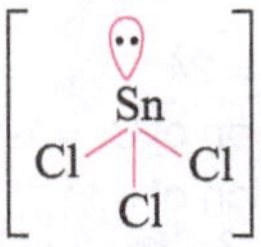

sp^3 (pyramidal)

⇒ $SnCl_3^-$ has (3σ + 1*lp*) and exist in pyramidal structure.

$SnCl_2 + Me_3N \longrightarrow SnCl_2 \times NMe_3$ or 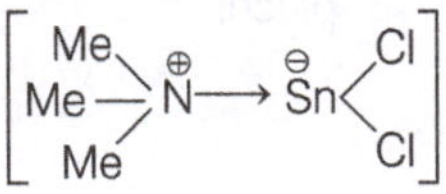

(3°amine) (*Q*) (*Y*)

Y complex has coordinate bond in between nitrogen and Sn metal.

Reduction

$\overset{+2}{SnCl_2} + 2\overset{+2}{Cu}Cl_2 \longrightarrow \overset{+4}{Sn}Cl_4 + 2\overset{+1}{Cu}Cl$
(*Q*) (*Z*)

Oxidation

Z is oxidised product of $SnCl_2$ and oxidation state of Sn is +4 in *Z* compound. Structure of $SnCl_4$(*Z*) is

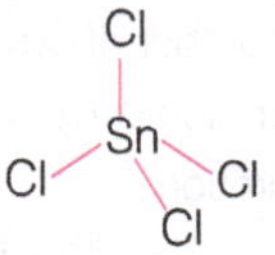

Thus, options (a, d) are correct.

9. ***(a,b,d)*** Statement wise explanation is

Statement (a) $[Co(en)(NH_3)_3H_2O]^{3+}$ have following 2 geometrical isomers.

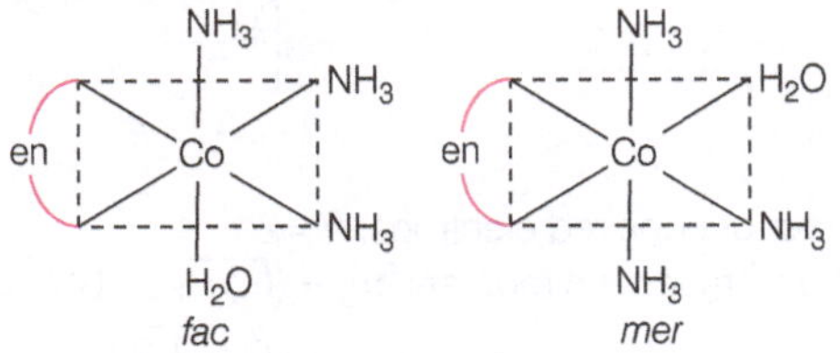

[*M*(*AA*)*B*$_3$*C*] type complex

Hence, this is correct statement.

Statement (b) If bidentate ligand 'en' is replaced by two cyanide ligands then $[Co(NH_3)_3(H_2O)(CN)_2]^+$ is formed.
It is [MA_3B_2C] type complex which has following 3 geometrical isomers.

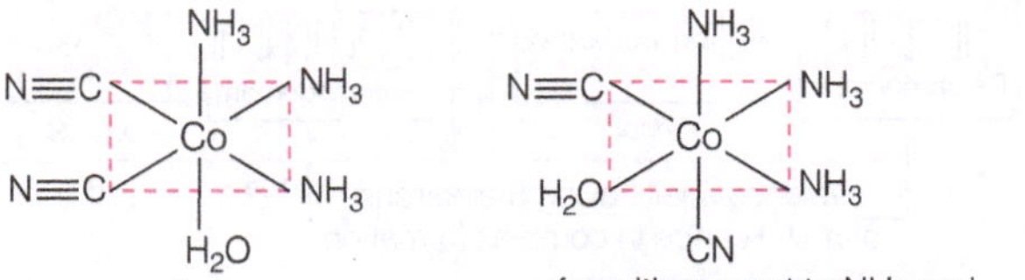

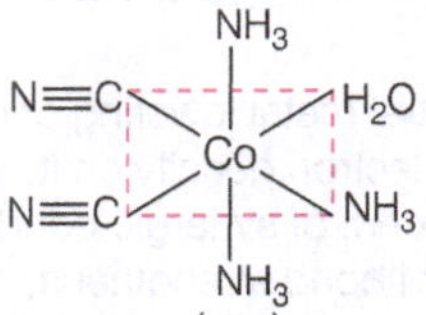

Hence, this statement is also correct.

Statement (c) Co metal has [Ar]$3d^7 4s^2$ configuration while in $[Co(en)(NH_3)_3(H_2O)]^{3+}$ it is in +3 oxidation state. Thus, Co^{3+} has [Ar]$3d^6$ configuration.

$Co^{3+} =$ 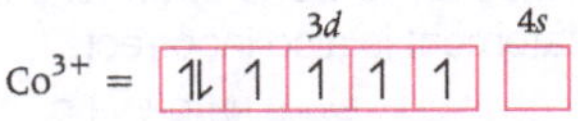

As *en* is a strong ligand, so pairing will occur

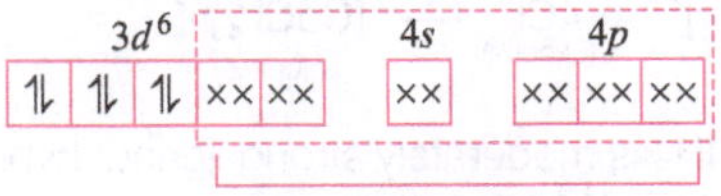

d^2sp^3 hybridised

Due to the presence of all paired electrons it show diamagnetic behaviour rather than paramagnetic.
Hence, this statement is incorrect.

Statement (d) According to CFT, absorption of light by coordination complexes depends upon CFSE i.e., crystal field splitting energy (Δ_o) as $\Delta_o \propto \frac{1}{\lambda}$

Among the complexes given $[Co(en)(NH_3)_4]^{3+}$ has more Δ_o value as compared to complex $[Co(en)(NH_3)_3(H_2O)]^{3+}$. Thus, $[Co(en)(NH_3)_3(H_2O)]^{3+}$ absorbs the light at longer wavelength for *d-d* transition. Hence, this statement is also correct.

Note : For any complex, the value of Δ_o can be calculated via the difference or gap between e_g and t_{2g} values.

10. ***(b,c)*** Statement wise explanation is

Statement (a) The total number of valence shell electrons at metal centre in $Fe(CO)_5$ and $Ni(CO)_4$ are 8 and 10 respectively.

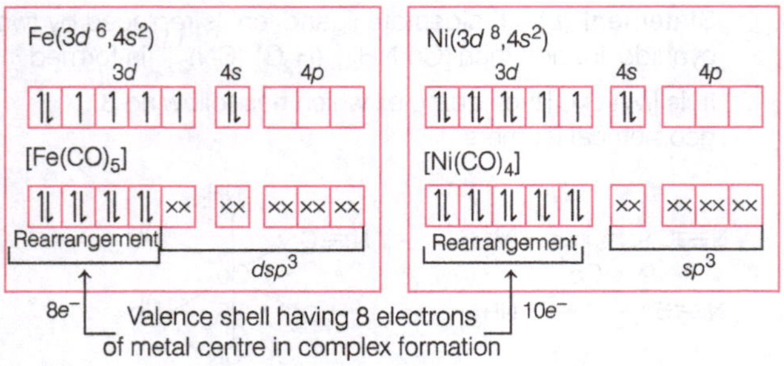

Hence, this statement is incorrect.

Statement (b) Carbonyl complexes are predominantly low spin complexes due to strong ligand fields. Hence, this statement is correct.

Statement (c) For central metal lowering of oxidation state results to increase in electron density on it. This in turn results to increase in extent of synergic bonding. Thus, we can say "metal carbonyl bond strengthens, when oxidation state of metal is lowered".

Hence, it is a correct statement.

Statement (d) Increase in positive charge on metal (i.e., increase in oxidation state) results to decrease in synergic bonding strength.

This in turn makes C—O bond stronger instead of weaker. Hence, this statement is also incorrect.

11. ***(a,c,d)*** $\underset{\text{Pink }(X)}{[Co(H_2O)_6]Cl_2} \xrightarrow[O_2(\text{Air})]{\text{Excess } NH_4OH/NH_4Cl} \underset{Y}{[Co(NH_3)_6]Cl_3}$

$\underset{X}{[Co(H_2O)_6]^{2+}} + \underset{(\text{Excess})}{4Cl^-} \longrightarrow \underset{\text{blue }(Z)}{[CoCl_4]^{2-}}$

(a) Since, NH_3 is moderately strong ligand, hybridisation of cobalt in Y is d^2sp^3.

(b) $\underset{Y}{[Co(NH_3)_6]Cl_3} + 3AgNO_3(aq) \longrightarrow 3AgCl\downarrow$

(c) $\underset{\text{Blue}}{[CoCl_4]^{2-}} + 6H_2O \rightleftharpoons \underset{\text{Pink}}{[Co(H_2O)_6]^{2+}} + 4Cl^-;\ \Delta H < 0$

(d) Cobalt is sp^3-hybridised in $[CoCl_4]^{2-}$ (tetrahedral).

12. ***(3)***

- For the complexes to be isoelectronic with $Ni(CO)_4$, they should have same value of effective atomic number (EAN).
- Values of EAN for all the given species are as follows:

$Ni(CO)_4 = 28 + 4(2) = 36$

(i) $V(CO)_6 = 23 + 2(6) = 35$

(ii) $Cr(CO)_5 = 24 + 2(5) = 34$

(iii) $Cu(CO)_3 = 29 + 2(3) = 35$

(iv) $Mn(CO)_5 = 25 + 2(5) = 35$

(v) $Fe(CO)_5 = 26 + 2(5) = 36$

(vi) $[Co(CO)_3]^{3-} = 27 + 3 + 2(3) = 36$

(vii) $[Cr(CO)_4]^{4-} = 24 + 4 + 2(4) = 36$

(viii) $[Ir(CO)_3] = 77 + 2(3) = 83$

Thus, there are three compounds, that are isoelectronic with $Ni(CO)_4$.

13. ***(1)***

	Species	No. of unpaired electrons	Magnetic nature
1.	$[Mn(NH_3)_6]^{3+}$	2	Paramagnetic
2.	$[MnCl_6]^{3-}$	4	Paramagnetic
3.	$[FeF_6]^{3-}$	5	Paramagnetic
4.	$[CoF_6]^{3-}$	4	Paramagnetic
5.	$[Fe(NH_3)_6]^{3+}$	1	Paramagnetic
6.	$[Co(en)_3]^{3+}$	0	Diamagnetic

Thus, among the given species only 1, i.e. $[Co(en)_3]^{3+}$ is a diamagnetic species.

14. ***(a)* $[Cr(NH_3)_6]^{3+}$**

Atomic number of Cr = 24

Electronic configuration of Cr = $1s^2\ 2s^2\ 2p^6\ 3s^2\ 3p^6\ 3d^5\ 4s^1$

Electronic configuration of

$$Cr^{3+} = 1s^2 2s^2 2p^6\ 3s^2 3p^6 3d^3\ 4s^0$$

NH_3 is a weak field ligand. Pairing of electron will not takes place.

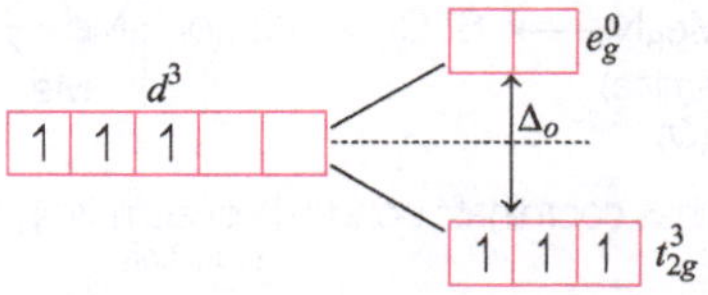

Number of unpaired electrons, $n = 3$

Magnetic moment (spin only), $\mu_s = \sqrt{n(n+2)}$ BM

$= \sqrt{3(3+2)}$

$= \sqrt{3 \times 5} = \sqrt{15}$

$= 3.87$ BM

$[CuF_6]^{3-}$ Atomic number of Cu = 29.

Electronic configuration of Cu = $1s^2 2s^2 2p^6\ 3s^2 3p^6 3d^{10}\ 4s^1$

Electronic configuration of

$$Cu^{3+} = 1s^2 2s^2 2p^6\ 3s^2 3p^6\ 3d^8\ 4s^0$$

F^- is a weak field ligand, so pairing of electron will not occur and splitting of d-orbitals occur as follows

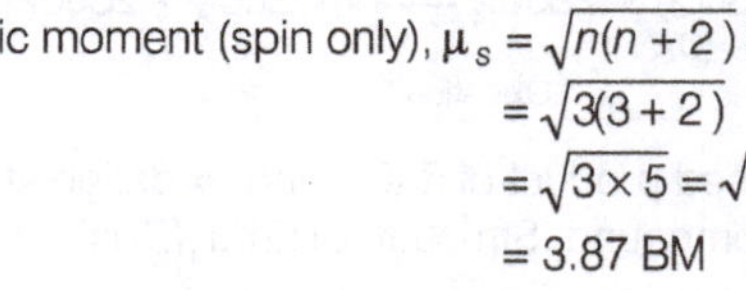

Number of unpaired electrons, $n = 2$

Spin only magnetic moment, $\mu_s = \sqrt{n(n+2)}$ BM

$= \sqrt{2(2+2)}$

$= \sqrt{2 \times 4} = 2\sqrt{2}$

$= 2.84$ BM

15. ***(6)*** The structure of *cis*-$[Mn(en)_2Cl_2]$ complex is

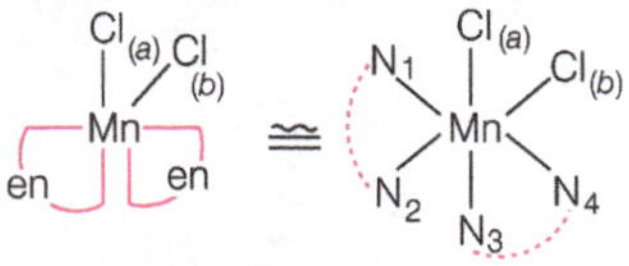

Bond angles (Mn—N and Mn—Cl bond in *cis* positions)

Cl (*a*) —— Mn —— N_1
Cl (*a*) —— Mn —— N_2
Cl (a) —— Mn —— N_4
Cl (*b*) —— Mn —— N_1
Cl (*b*) —— Mn —— N_3
Cl (*b*) —— Mn —— N_4

Number of *cis* Cl—Mn—N = 6

16. ***(b)***

Compounds	Hybridisation	Unpaired electron(s)	Magnetic character
$Ni(CO)_4$	sp^3	No	Diamagnetic
$[NiCl_4]^{2-}$	sp^3	two	Paramagnetic
$[Co(NH_3)_4Cl_2]Cl$	d^2sp^3	No	Diamagnetic
$Na_3[CoF_6]$	sp^3d^2	four	Paramagnetic
Na_2O_2	—	No	Diamagnetic (O_2^{2-})
CsO_2	—	One	Paramagnetic O_2^- (superoxide ion is paramagnetic)

17. ***(4)*** When S is donor atom of SCN^-, it produces weak field ligand and forms high spin complex as

$[Fe(SCN)_6]^{3-}$ = [1|1|1|1|1] 4s [××] 4p [××|××|××] 4d [××|××| | |]
$3d^5 (n=5)$ ← sp^3d^2 →

Spin only magnetic moment $(\mu_s) = \sqrt{5(5+2)}$ BM $= \sqrt{35}$ BM

⇒ In case of CN^- ligand, carbon is the donor atom , it produces strong field ligand and forms low spin complex as

$[Fe(CN)_6]^{3-}$ = 3d [⇅|⇅|1|××|××] 4s [××] 4p [××|××|××]
$(n = 1)$ ← d^2sp^3 →

Spin only magnetic moment $(\mu_s) = \sqrt{1(1+2)}$ BM $= \sqrt{3}$ BM

Hence, difference in spin only magnetic moment

$$= \sqrt{35} - \sqrt{3} \approx 4 \text{ BM}$$

18. ***(d)*** The correct match is

P-3; Q-2; R-4; S-1

(1) $[Fe(H_2O)_6]^{2+}$

$Fe^{2+} \rightarrow [Ar]\ 3d^6$ 3d [⇅|1|1|1|1] 4s [ ] 4p [| |]

As H_2O is a weak field ligand, thus it cannot pair electrons in orbitals,

∴ Electronic configuration = $3d^6$

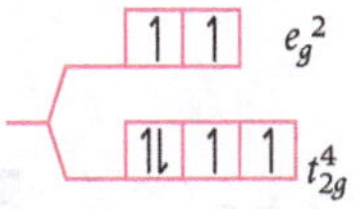

(2) $[Mn(H_2O)_6]^{2+}$

$Mn^{2+} \rightarrow [Ar]\ 3d^5$: 3d [1|1|1|1|1] 4s [ ] 4p [| |]

As H_2O is a weak field ligand, it cannot pair electrons in orbitals,

∴ Electronic configuration = $3d^5$

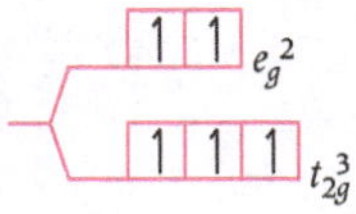

(3) $[Co(NH_3)_6]^{3+}$

$Co^{3+} \rightarrow [Ar]\ 3d^6$: 3d [⇅|1|1|1|1] 4s [ ] 4p [| |]

As NH_3 is a strong field ligand, pairing of e^-'s will takes place.

∴ Electronic configuration = $3d^6$

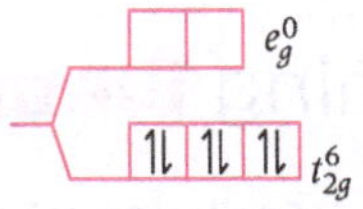

(4) $[FeCl_4]^-$

$Fe^{3+} \rightarrow [Ar]\ 3d^5$ 3d [1|1|1|1|1] 4s [ ] 4p [| |]

As Cl^- is a weak field ligand, pairing cannot take place.

∴ Electronic configuration

$= 3d^5$

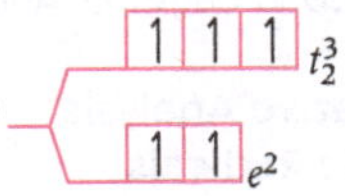

(5) $[CoCl_4]^{2-}$

$Co^{2+} \rightarrow [Ar]\ 3d^7$: 3d [⇅|⇅|1|1|1] 4s [ ] 4p [| |]

As Cl^- is a weak field ligand, it cannot pair electrons.

∴ Electronic configuration= $3d^7$

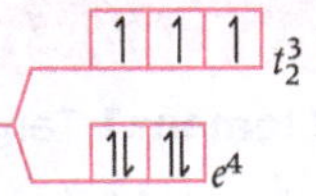

CHAPTER 10

Salt Analysis

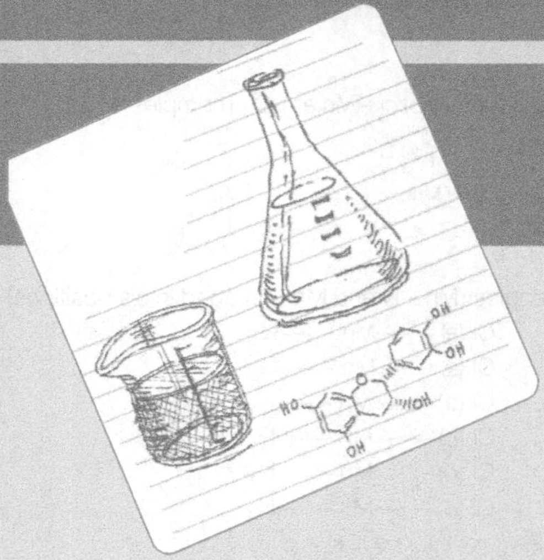

Learning Elements

Element 1 Preliminary Tests and Qualitative Analysis of Acidic Radicals

Preliminary Test : Physical Examination of Unknown Salt, Dry Heating Test, Solubility of Salts, Borax-Bead Test, Microcosmic Salt Test, Sodium Carbonate Bead Test, Flame Test, Analysis of Acidic Radicals-Group A & B, Analysis of Second Category Anions

Element 2 Qualitative Analysis of Basic Radicals

Analysis of Cation Mixtures, Analysis of Group zero, Group I, Group II, Group III, Group IV, Group V and Group VI radicals

Practice Elements

Practice Element 1 Target JEE Main

Practice Element 2 Target JEE Advanced

Trend Insights

JEE Main

	2024				2023				2022			
Topics	**E**	**M**	**T**	**O**	**E**	**M**	**T**	**O**	**E**	**M**	**T**	**O**
Preliminary Tests and Qualitative analysis of acidic radicals	1	1	–	2	1	1	2	4	1	1	1	3
Qualitative analysis of Basic Radicals	1	2	3	6	2	2	2	6	2	2	1	5

E = Easy, **M** = Medium, **T** = Tough, **O** = Overall

Current Dynamics

- Most of the questions Focussing on systematic process of separating cations and anions into analytical group had been asked in previous years
- Confirmatory tests for ions had been asked in past years.
- A frequent number of questions have been asked from the colour of the compound, evolved gases and their identification through specific tests.

JEE Advanced

Typology		Years			
	2024	**2023**	**2022**	**2021**	**2020**
1. Simple MCQs	–	–	1	–	1
2. One or More than one Correct	–	–	–	1	–
3. Numerical/Integer Type	–	–	–	–	–
4. Matching Type	–	–	–	–	–
5. Paragraph Based	1	–	–	1	–

Current Dynamics

- The weightage of this chapter is less in JEE Advanced
- 0-1 question is visible in recent years.
- Application based concepts have been asked in questions.

Insightful Advice

- Students are advised to focus on identifying anions and cations through confirmatory test.
- Memorise the keen observations like colour change, precipitate formation, evolved gases, colour of residue etc. to deduce the composition of the salt.

Element 1 Preliminary Tests and Qualitative Analysis of Acidic Radicals

Qualitative salt analysis is a method of analytical chemistry that aims to find the chemical composition of (cations/anions present in a salt or mixture) inorganic compounds.
The qualitative salt analysis can be broadly studied under two categories.

- Preliminary or dry test
- Wet test

In this module, we will study about analysis of anions.

Preliminary Tests

Some preliminary tests are done before going to the anion analysis.

1. Physical Examination of Unknown Salt

It involves the study of colour, odour and density.

	Observation	Inference
A. Colour of the Substance		
(i)	**Blue**, whose aqueous solution is also blue	Hydrated salts of Cu^{2+}
(ii)	**Colourless** substance	Transition metal ions absent (except some salts of Mn^{2+})
(iii)	**Dark green**, whose aqueous solution is also dark green, but becomes light on dilution.	Salts of Cr^{3+}
(iv)	**Yellow-green**, aqueous solution is light green or almost colourless.	Salts of Fe^{2+}
(v)	**Yellow-brown**, aqueous solution is yellow.	Salts of Fe^{3+}
(vi)	**Violet-pink**, whose aqueous solution is pink.	Salts of cobalt.
(vii)	**Black** substance	CuO, NiO_2, SnO, FeS, CuS, HgS, PbS, NiS, CoS, $CuBr_2$, Ag_2S, Cu_2S, MnO_2, Fe_3O_4, FeO, Co_3O_4, Ni_2O_3 etc.
(viii)	**Red** substance	Cu_2O, HgO, Pb_3O_4, HgI_2 etc.
B. Odour of the substance		
(i)	Ammonical smell	NH_4^+ salts
(ii)	Vinegar like smell	Acetates
(iii)	Smell like rotten eggs.	S^{2-} salts
C. Density		
(i)	Mixture of salts is heavy	Salts of Hg and Pb
(ii)	Mixture of salts is light	Salts of Zn, Al, Bi, Ca, Ba, Sr, Mg etc. (Chiefly carbonates)

JEE MAPPER

Example Similar to PYQ Asked in JEE Main 2025, JEE Adv. 2014

Among $(NH_4)_2SO_4$, As_2S_3, $Bi(OH)_3$, AsI_3 anhy. $CrCl_3$, Cu_2I_2, CdS, ZnS, $PbCl_2$, Cr_2O_3 and $BaSO_4$ the total number of white coloured salt is

Sol. (6) Among the given salts only six i.e., $(NH_4)_2SO_4$, $Bi(OH)_3$, Cu_2I_2, ZnS, $PbCl_2$ and $BaSO_4$ are white coloured. While remaining salts are of different colours which are as follows

$$AsI_3 \rightarrow \text{red}$$
$$As_2S_3 \rightarrow \text{yellow}$$
$$\text{anhy. } CrCl_3 \rightarrow \text{green}$$
$$CdS \rightarrow \text{yellow}$$
$$Cr_2O_3 \rightarrow \text{green}$$

Competency Enhancer 1.1

Among CdS, Cu_2I_2, CuS, $Cu(CN)_2$, As_2S_3, SbI_3, $BaCl_2$ and PbI_2 the total number of yellow coloured salt is/are

2. Dry Heating Test

This test is performed by heating a small amount of salt in a dry test tube. On heating, some salts undergo decomposition thus evolving the gases.

Effect of Heating

Take the given substance in a clear, dry test tube and heat it first gently and then strongly. Observe the changes takes place upon heating.

S.No.	Observation	Inference
(i)	**Colour of residue obtained after heating**	
	Hot Cold	Salts
	Yellow White	Zn salts
	Brown Yellow	Salts of Pb, Bi or Sn
	Red or black Brown	Cd salts
	White Blue	Cupric salts ($CuSO_4$)
	Blue Blue-red	$CoCl_2$

S.No.	Observation	Inference
	Green Dark-red	$CoBr_2$
	Violet Dark-red	CoI_2
	Yellow Green	Ni salts
	Green Violet	Cr salts
	Black (non-fusible) Black	CuO, MnO_2, NiO
	Dark red brown or Light brown(non-fusible)	Fe_2O_3
	Dark orange, red or light orange	HgO
(ii)	**Substance sublimes on heating and colour of sublimate is**	
	White	$HgCl_2$, Hg_2Cl_2, As_2O_3, $AlCl_3$, Sb_2O_3, halides of NH_4^+
	Yellow	S, As_2S_3 and HgI_2 etc.
	Greyish black	Sulphides of Hg, Sb, As
	Yellow, blue or violet vapours	I_2
	Grey (having garlic odour)	As
(iii)	**Observation of gases evolved**	
	A. Colourless and odourless gas	
	They supports the combustion of burning match stick (O_2)	Nitrates of Na and K
	Which turns the lime water milky (CO_2).	CO_3^{2-} or $C_2O_4^{2-}$ salts
	B. Colourless, odorous gas	
	Smell of ammonia (NH_3)	Ammonium salts
	Smell of burning sulphur (SO_2)	Sulphite salts or $FeSO_4$
	Smell of rotten eggs (H_2S)	Sulphide salts.
	Pungent smelling gas and forms white fumes with NH_4OH.	Hydrated chloride salts
	C. Coloured, odourless gas	
	Brown gas which turns starch iodide paper blue, (NO_2)	Bromide salts.
	Violet gas which turns starch paper blue.	Iodide salts
	Yellow-green gas which decolourised the litmus paper.	Chloride salts
	Red-brown gas which turns starch paper yellow	Bromide salts

3. Solubility of Salts

- **Nitrates and Nitrites** All metal salts are soluble in water.
- **Acetates** All metal acetates are soluble in water.
- **Chlorides** All common chlorides are soluble in water except AgCl, Hg_2Cl_2 and $PbCl_2$.
- **Bromides** All common bromides are soluble in water except AgBr, Hg_2Br_2,$PbBr_2$ and $HgBr_2$.
- **Iodides** All common iodides are soluble in water except AgI, Hg_2I_2, HgI_2 and PbI_2.
- **Sulphides** All common sulphides are insoluble in water except sulphides of group I and group II metals and $(NH_4)_2S$.
- **Carbonates** All common carbonates are insoluble in water except carbonates of group I and $(NH_4)_2CO_3$.
- **Sulphates** All common sulphates are soluble in water except $PbSO_4$, Hg_2SO_4, $BaSO_4$, $CaSO_4$ and Ag_2SO_4 which are sparingly soluble.
- **Phosphates** All common phosphates are insoluble in water except phosphates of group I and $(NH_4)_3PO_4$.
- **Hydroxides** All common metal hydroxides are insoluble in water except group I hydroxides and $Ba(OH)_2$, $Sr(OH)_2$ and some group II hydroxides such as $Ca(OH)_2$.
- **Perchlorates** All perchlorates are soluble in water.

4. Borax-Bead Test

If borax, $Na_2B_4O_7 \cdot 10H_2O$ is heated on the platinum loop, a transparent colourless glass like bead of sodium metaborate ($NaBO_2$) and boric anhydride (B_2O_3) is formed.

$$Na_2B_4O_7 \xrightarrow{\Delta} 2NaBO_2 + B_2O_3$$

Characteristics coloured beads are produced with salts of copper, iron, chromium, manganese, cobalt and nickel.

$$CuO + B_2O_3 \xrightarrow{\Delta} \underset{\text{Copper (II) metaborate}}{Cu(BO_2)_2}$$

Results have been summarised in table below.

Oxidising flame		Reducing flame		Metal
Hot	Cold	Hot	Cold	
Green	Blue	Colourless	Opaque red-brown	Copper
Yellowish -brown	Yellow	Green	Green	Iron
Green	Green	Green	Green	Chromium
Pale purple	Pale purple	Colourless	Colourless	Manganese
Blue	Blue	Blue	Blue	Cobalt
Brown	Reddish-brown	Grey	Grey	Nickel
Yellow	Colourless	Brown	Brown	Molybdenum

5. Microcosmic Salt Test

A test similar to borax bead test is used for identification of coloured cations if microcosmic salt, $Na(NH_4)HPO_4 \cdot 4H_2O$, is used.

$$\underset{\text{Sodium ammonium hydrogen phosphate}}{Na(NH_4)HPO_4 \cdot 4H_2O} \xrightarrow{\Delta} \underset{\text{Transparent bead}}{NaPO_3} + H_2O\uparrow + NH_3\uparrow$$

$$NaPO_3 + CoO \longrightarrow \underset{\text{Brown bead}}{NaCoPO_4}$$

Results have been summarised in table.

Oxidising flame	Reducing flame	Metal
Green when hot, blue when cold	Colourless when hot, red when cold	Copper
Yellowish-or reddish-brown when hot, yellow when cold	Yellow when hot, colourless to green when cold	Iron
Green when, hot and cold	Green, hot and cold	Chromium
Violet when, hot and cold	Colourless, hot and cold	Manganese
Blue when, hot and cold	Blue, hot and cold	Cobalt
Brown when, hot and cold	Green when cold	Nickel
Yellow when, hot and cold	Grey when cold	Vanadium
Yellow when hot, yellow-green when cold	Green, hot and cold	Uranium
Pale yellow when hot, colourless when cold	Green when hot, blue when cold	Tungsten
Colourless, when hot and cold	Yellow when hot, violet when cold	Titanium

6. Sodium Carbonate Bead Test

The sodium carbonate bead is prepared by fusing a small quantity of sodium carbonate on a platinum wire loop in the Bunsen flame, a white, opaque bead is produced. If this is moistened, dipped into a little KNO_3 and then into a small quantity of a manganese (for example) and the whole mixture heated in the oxidising flame, a green bead of sodium manganate (Na_2MnO_4) is formed.

$$MnO + Na_2CO_3 + O_2 \xrightarrow{\Delta} \underset{\substack{\text{(Sodium manganate)} \\ \text{Green bead}}}{Na_2MnO_4} + CO_2\uparrow$$

A yellow bead is obtained with chromium compounds, due to formation of sodium chromate (Na_2CrO_4).

$$2Cr_2O_3 + 4Na_2CO_3 + 3O_2 \xrightarrow{\Delta} \underset{\substack{\text{(Sodium manganate)} \\ \text{Yellow bead}}}{4Na_2CrO_4} + 4CO_2\uparrow$$

7. Flame Test

Paste of the salt and conc. HCl is taken into the lower oxidising zone and colour imparted to the flame by salts is observed; salts, particularly of group V (Ba^{2+}, Ca^{2+}, Sr^{2+}), are identified by colours of the flame and summarised in table.

Flame Test

Colour	Cation
Golden yellow	Na^+
Violet	K^+
Carmine-red	Li^+
Brick red	Ca^{2+}
Apple-green	Ba^{2+}, Mo^{2+}
Green	Cu^{2+}, (BO_3^{3-}), Tl^{3+}
Crimson red	Sr^{2+}

The yellow colouration due to sodium masks that of potassium. In such cases view the flame through cobalt glass, the yellow sodium colour is absorbed and the potassium flame appears crimson.

Beryllium and magnesium do not impart colour to flame due to high ionisation energy.

JEE Quicker

In the flame test of a mixture of salts, a green flame with blue centre is observed in Cu^{2+} cation. *JEE Main 2022*

The colour of the flame in the flame test depends upon the metal ion present in the substance. When a salt is brought in contact of oxidising flame, it dissociates into ions. The electrons of ions are excited to higher energy level and when they get de-excited to ground state, they emit flame in visible region. Thus, a green flame with blue centre is observed in Cu^{2+} cation.

Analysis of Anions (Acidic Radicals)

Analysis of anions can be divided into two groups

Group 'A' Radicals

Group 'A' contains anions, which are characterised by volatile products obtained on treatment with acids. It is further divided into two sub groups.

(i) **Gases liberated with dilute HCl/dilute H_2SO_4**
Carbonate (CO_3^{2-}), bicarbonate (HCO_3^-), sulphide (S^{2-}), sulphite (SO_3^{2-}) nitrite (NO_2^-) and acetate (CH_3COO^-).

(ii) **Gases or acid vapours evolved with concentrated H_2SO_4** Fluoride (F^-), chloride (Cl^-), bromide (Br^-), iodide (I^-), nitrate (NO_3^-), oxalate ($C_2O_4^{2-}$), permanganate (MnO_4^-) and all anions of (1).

Group 'B' Radicals

Group 'B' includes anions that are characterised by their specific reactions in solutions.

These reactions may be

- **Precipitation reactions** SO_4^{2-}, PO_4^{3-}, AsO_3^{3-}, AsO_4^{3-}, BO_3^{3-} etc.
- **Oxidation and Reduction in Solution** CrO_4^{2-}, $Cr_2O_7^{2-}$, MnO_4^-, MnO_4^{2-}, CrO_4^{2-}, $Cr_2O_7^{2-}$ etc.

Analysis of Group 'A' Radicals

Salt or mixture is treated with dil. H_2SO_4 and also with conc. H_2SO_4 separately and by observing the types of gases evolved, confirmatory tests of anions are performed.

Observation with Dilute H_2SO_4

S.No.	Observation	Acid radical	Confirmatory test*
1.	Brisk effervescence with evolution of colourless and odourless gas	CO_3^{2-} (carbonate)	Gas turns lime water (or baryta water) milky but milkyness disappears on passing gas in excess C.
2.	Brown fumes	NO_2^- (nitrite)	Add KI and starch solution forms blue colour compounds.
3.	Smell of rotten eggs (H_2S smell) on heating	S^{2-} (sulphide)	Gas turns lead acetate paper black. Sodium carbonate extract (SE) + sodium nitroprusside solution → purple colour this purple colour confirms the presence of sulphur in SE
4.	Colourless gas with pungent smell of burning sulphur	SO_3^{2-} (sulphite)	Gas turns acidified $K_2Cr_2O_7$ solution green [different from CO_3^{2-}] since gas also turns lime water milky
5.	Solution gives smell of vinegar	CH_3COO^- (acetate)	Aqueous solution + neutral $FeCl_3$ → blood red colour changing to brownish red ppt on boiling
6.	White or yellowish white turbidity on warming due to colloidal sulphur	$S_2O_3^{2-}$ (thiosulphate)	Aqueous solution + $AgNO_3$ → white ppt changing to black PbS on warming

Test for Carbonate (CO_3^{2-})

All carbonates except those of alkali metals and ammonium are insouble in H_2O.

(i) **Dilute HCl** With dilute HCl, it decomposes with effervescences due to the evolution of carbon dioxide.

$$CO_3^{2-} + 2H^+ \longrightarrow CO_2\uparrow + H_2O$$

The gas produces white turbidity with lime water, $Ca(OH)_2$ or baryta water, $Ba(OH)_2$.

$$CO_2\uparrow + Ca^{2+} + 2OH^- \longrightarrow \underset{\text{White turbidity}}{CaCO_3\downarrow} + H_2O$$

$$CO_2\uparrow + Ba^{2+} + 2OH^- \longrightarrow \underset{\text{White turbidity}}{BaCO_3\downarrow} + H_2O$$

JEE Alert

It must be remembered that with prolonged passage of carbon dioxide in calcium carbonate will lead to disappearance of turbidity slowly, due to the formation of soluble bicarbonate.

$$CaCO_3 + CO_2 + H_2O \longrightarrow \underset{\text{Soluble}}{Ca(HCO_3)_2}$$

(ii) **Barium Chloride or Calcium Chloride Solution**

Carbonates on treatment with $BaCl_2$ or $CaCl_2$ gives white precipitate of barium or calcium carbonate, which is soluble in mineral acids and carbonic acid.

$$CO_3^{2-} + Ba^{2+} \longrightarrow \underset{\text{White ppt.}}{BaCO_3\downarrow}$$

$$CO_3^{2-} + Ca^{2+} \longrightarrow \underset{\text{White ppt.}}{CaCO_3\downarrow}$$

(ii) **Silver Nitrate Solution**

- Carbonates give a white precipitation of silver carbonate with $AgNO_3$ solution.

$$CO_3^{2-} + 2Ag^+ \longrightarrow \underset{\text{White ppt.}}{Ag_2CO_3\downarrow}$$

The precipitate is soluble in nitric acid and in ammonia. The precipitate becomes yellow brown on addition of excess reagent results in the formation of silver oxide. The same happens if the mixture is boiled.

$$Ag_2CO_3\downarrow \longrightarrow \underset{\text{Yellow ppt.}}{Ag_2O\downarrow} + CO_2\uparrow$$

- Aqueous carbonate solution is alkaline due to hydrolysis (with H_2O)

$$CO_3^{2-} + 2H_2O \longrightarrow H_2CO_3 + 2OH^-$$

- Alkaline solution turns pink when a drop of phenolphthalein is added to it. If CO_2 (liberated from the reaction of given carbonate with dilute H_2SO_4) is passed into above pink-coloured solution, it is decolourised by HCO_3^- formed with CO_2.

$$CO_2 + CO_3^{2-} + H_2O \longrightarrow 2HCO_3^-$$

Test for Nitrite (NO_2^-)

The analysis of nitrite ions is carried out as follows

(i) **Dilute HCl** On adding dilute HCl to solid nitrite in cold produces a pale blue liquid first (due to the presence of free nitrous acid, HNO_2 or its anhydride N_2O_3) and then evolution of reddish-brown fumes of nitrogen dioxide (NO_2) takes place. The NO_2 is produced by the combination of nitric oxide (NO) with oxygen of the air.

$$NO_2^- + H^+ \longrightarrow HNO_2$$

$$2HNO_2 \longrightarrow H_2O + N_2O_3$$

$$3HNO_2 \longrightarrow HNO_3 + 2NO\uparrow + H_2O$$

$$2NO\uparrow + O_2\uparrow \longrightarrow \underset{\text{Reddish - brown}}{2NO_2\uparrow}$$

(ii) **Silver Nitrate Solution** With silver nitrate solution, a white crystalline precipitate of $AgNO_2$ is obtained.

$$NO_2^- + Ag^+ \longrightarrow \underset{\text{White ppt.}}{AgNO_2\downarrow}$$

All other nitrites except $AgNO_2$ are soluble in H_2O.

(iii) **Potassium Iodide Solution** Addition of a nitrite solution to that of KI followed by acidification with CH_3COOH or dilute H_2SO_4 produces iodine, which turns starch-iodine complex blue.

$$2NO_2^- + 3I^- + 4CH_3COOH \longrightarrow I_2 + 2NO\uparrow + 4CH_3CO_2^- + 2H_2O$$

$$I_2 + \text{Starch} \longrightarrow \text{Deep blue colour}$$

$$I_2 + \text{Excess KI} \longrightarrow K^+I_3^- \text{ (Dark brown)}$$

(iv) **Brown Ring Test** When the nitrite solution is added carefully to a concentrated solution of iron(II) sulphate acidified with dilute acetic or dilute sulphuric acid, a brown ring appears due to the formation of $[Fe(H_2O)_5NO]SO_4$ at the junction of the two liquids. If the addition has not been made slowly and caustiously, a brown colouration results.

$$NO_2^- + CH_3COOH \longrightarrow HNO_2 + CH_3COO^-$$

$$3HNO_2 \longrightarrow H_2O + HNO_3 + 2NO\uparrow$$

$$FeSO_4 + 6H_2O \longrightarrow [Fe(H_2O)_6]SO_4$$

$$[Fe(H_2O)_6]SO_4 + NO \longrightarrow \underset{\text{Brown ring}}{[Fe(H_2O)_5NO]SO_4} + H_2O$$

(v) **Sulphamic Acid ($HO—SO_2—NH_2$) Test** When a solution of a nitrite is treated with solid sulphamic acid, it is completely decomposed.

$$HO—SO_2—NH_3 + NO_2^- \longrightarrow N_2 + H^+ + SO_4^{2-} + H_2O$$

Since, no nitrate is formed in this reaction, this is an excellent method for the complete removal of nitrite.

Test for Sulphide (S^{2-})

(i) **Dilute HCl or Dilute H_2SO_4** Sulphide on treatment with dilute HCl or dilute H_2SO_4 gives a pungent smelling gas, H_2S (smell of rotten eggs).

$$S^{2-} + 2H^+ \longrightarrow H_2S\uparrow$$

The blackening of filter paper moistened with lead acetate solution may identify the gas.

$$(CH_3COO)_2Pb + H_2S\uparrow \longrightarrow \underset{\text{(Shining black)}}{PbS\downarrow} + 2CH_3COOH$$

Alternatively, a filter paper moistened with cadmium acetate solution turns yellow.

$$H_2S\uparrow + Cd^{2+} \longrightarrow \underset{\text{Yellow ppt}}{CdS\downarrow} + 2H^+$$

(ii) **Silver Nitrate Solution** With $AgNO_3$ solution, sulphide gives a black precipitate of silver silphide which is insoluble in cold but soluble in hot dilute nitric acid.

$$S^{2-} + 2Ag^+ \longrightarrow \underset{\text{Black ppt}}{Ag_2S\downarrow}$$

JEE Spotlite

- **Sodium Nitroprusside Solution Test**
  With sodium nitroprusside solution, ionic sulphide gives a purple colour in alkaline medium.

$$Na_2S + Na_2[Fe(CN)_5NO] \longrightarrow \underset{\text{Purple colour}}{Na_4[Fe(CN)_5NOS]}$$

No reaction occurs with solutions of hydrogen sulphide or free gas. If however, filter paper moistened with a solution of the reagent is made alkaline with sodium hydroxide or ammonia solution, a purple colouration is produced with free hydrogen sulphide also.

- **Catalysis of Iodine-Azide Reaction Test**
  Solution of sodium azide, NaN_3 and iodine as I_3^- do not react, but on addition of traces of sulphide, (which acts as a catalyst) nitrogen gas is evolved immediately.

$$\underset{\text{Colourless}}{2N_3^-} + \underset{\text{Dark brown}}{I_3^-} \xrightarrow{\text{In presence of } S^{2-}} 3I^- + \underset{\text{Colourless gas}}{3N_2\uparrow}$$

Thiosulphate and thiocyanate behave similarly and hence must be absent for this test.

Test for Sulphite (SO_3^{2-})

Only the sulphites of alkali metals and ammonium are soluble in water.

(i) **Dilute HCl or Dilute H_2SO_4** These acids decomposes sulphites with the evolution of sulphur dioxide.

$$SO_3^{2-} + 2H^+ \longrightarrow SO_2\uparrow + H_2O$$

The gas can be identified.

- By suffocating odour of burning sulphur.
- By green colour formation, when passed through acidified $K_2Cr_2O_7$ solution.

$$3SO_2 + \underset{\text{Orange}}{Cr_2O_7^{2-}} + 2H^+ \longrightarrow 3SO_4^{2-} + \underset{\text{Green colour}}{2Cr^{3+}} + H_2O$$

- **Lime Water Test**
  On passing SO_2 gas through lime water, a milky precipitate of calcium sulphite is formed.

$$SO_2\uparrow + Ca(OH)_2 \longrightarrow \underset{\text{Milky ppt}}{CaSO_3\downarrow} + H_2O$$

Precipitate dissolves on prolonged passage of the gas, due to the formation of calcium bisulphite.

$$CaSO_3\downarrow + SO_2\uparrow + H_2O \longrightarrow \underset{\text{Soluble}}{Ca(HSO_3)_2}$$

- **Potassium Iodate-Starch Paper**
  When the evolved gas (SO_2) comes in contact with filter paper moistened with KIO_3 and starch solution, the paper turns blue due to iodine-starch complex.

$$KIO_3 + 5SO_2\uparrow + 4H_2O \longrightarrow 2KHSO_4 + I_2 + 3H_2SO_4$$

The iodine produced reacts with the starch to create a blue colured iodine starch complex.

(ii) **Barium Chloride or Strontium Chloride Solution** With $BaCl_2$ or $SrCl_2$ solution, sulphites gives a white precipitate of barium sulphite or strontium sulphite.

$$SO_3^{2-} + Ba^{2+} \longrightarrow \underset{\text{White ppt.}}{BaSO_4\downarrow}$$

$$SO_3^{2-} + Sr^{2+} \longrightarrow \underset{\text{White ppt.}}{SrSO_3\downarrow}$$

The precipitate dissolves in dilute hydrochloric acid, and sulphur dioxide is liberated.

$$BaSO_3\downarrow + 2H^+ \longrightarrow Ba^{2+} + SO_2\uparrow + H_2O$$

On standing, the precipitate is slowly oxidised to sulphate and then insoluble in dilute mineral acids.

Test for Acetate (CH_3COO^-)

(i) **Dilute Sulphuric Acid** On adding a small quantity of dilute H_2SO_4 to the acetate salt, acetic acid is produced, which can be easily recognized by its vinegar-like odour.

$$CH_3COO^- + H^+ \longrightarrow \underset{\text{Vinegar like odour}}{CH_3COOH}$$

(ii) **Iron (III) Chloride Solution** With $FeCl_3$ solution, acetates give a deep red colour due to the formation of ferric acetate.

$$3CH_3COONa + FeCl_3 \xrightarrow{\text{On boiling}} \underset{\text{Ferric acetate (red colour)}}{(CH_3COO)_3Fe + 3NaCl}$$

$$(CH_3COO)_3Fe + 2H_2O \xrightarrow{\Delta} \underset{\text{Raddish brown ppt.}}{[Fe(OH)_2(CH_3COO)]}$$

(iii) **Silver Nitrate Solution** Acetates on treatment with $AgNO_3$ solution give a white crystalline precipitate of silver acetate.

$$CH_3COO^- + Ag^+ \rightarrow \underset{\text{(White ppt.)}}{CH_3COOAg\downarrow} \xrightarrow{\Delta} \text{Clear solution}$$

(iv) **Cacodyl Oxide Reaction** Acetate salt on heating with solid As_2O_3 gives cacodyl oxide, which have an extremely nauseating odour. The cacodyl oxide is poisonous also.

$$4CH_3CO_2K + As_2O_3 \longrightarrow$$

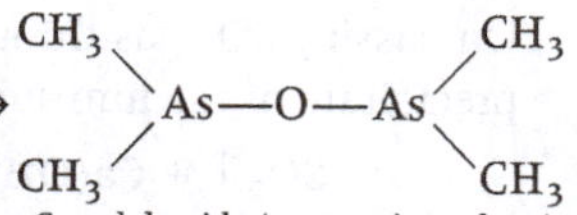

Cacodyl oxide (nauseating odour)

$$+ 2K_2CO_3 + 2CO_2\uparrow$$

Test for Thiosulphate ($S_2O_3^{2-}$)

(i) **Dilute HCl or Dilute H_2SO_4** These acids decomposes thiosulphate with formation of white precipitate of sulphur and evolution of SO_2 gas.

$$S_2O_3^{2-} + 2H^+ \longrightarrow S\downarrow + SO_2\uparrow + H_2O$$

SO_2 gas turns $Cr_2O_7^{2-}/H^+$ solution green.

(ii) **Silver nitrate Solution** When sodium thiosulphate is treated with silver nitrate a white precipitate of silver thiosulphate is formed. This precipitate change colour over the time from white to black.

$$Na_2S_2O_3 + 2AgNO_3 \longrightarrow \underset{\text{White}}{Ag_2S_2O_3\downarrow} + 2NaNO_3$$

$$Ag_2S_2O_3 + H_2O \xrightarrow{\text{Warm}} \underset{\text{Black}}{Ag_2S\downarrow} + H_2SO_4$$

(iii) **Iodine Solution** I_2 solution (in KI) is decolourised by thiosulphate solution

$$I_2 + 2S_2O_3^{2-} \longrightarrow S_4O_6^{2-} + 2I^-$$

(iv) **Lead Nitrate or Lead Acetate Solution** $S_2O_3^{2-}$ gives white precipitate with $Pb(NO_3)_2$ or $(CH_3COO)_2Pb$; white precipitate changes to black on boiling :

$$S_2O_3^{2-} + Pb^{2+} \longrightarrow \underset{\text{White}}{PbS_2O_3\downarrow}$$

$$PbS_2O_3 + H_2O \longrightarrow \underset{\text{Black}}{PbS\downarrow} + 2H^+ + SO_4^{2-}$$

(v) **Chloride Solution** When $FeCl_3$ solution is added to $S_2O_3^{2-}$ solution, a dark-violet colour appears due to formation of the complex

$$2S_2O_3^{2-} + Fe^{3+} \longrightarrow \underset{\substack{\text{Dark-violet} \\ \text{(dithiosulphatoiron (III) complex)}}}{[Fe(S_2O_3)_2^-]}$$

But on standing, colour disappears rapidly due to the following change

$$[Fe(S_2O_3)_2]^- + Fe^{3+} \longrightarrow \underset{\text{Colourless}}{2Fe^{2+}} + \underset{\text{Tetrathionate ion}}{S_4O_6^{2-}}$$

Observation with Concentrated H_2SO_4

S. No.	Observation	Acid radical	Confirmatory test
1.	Colourless pungent gas giving white fumes with *aq* NH_4OH	Cl^- (chloride)	Add MnO_2 in the same test tube and heat — pale green Cl_2 gas, SE + HNO_3 + $AgNO_3$ solution ⟶ white ppt soluble in *aq* NH_3 **Chromyl chloride test**
2.	Reddish brown fumes	Br^- (bromide)	Add MnO_2 and heat — yellowish brown Br_2 gas. SE + HNO_3 + $AgNO_3$ solution — pale yellow ppt partially soluble *aq* NH_3. **Layer test**
3.	Violet pungent vapours turning starch paper blue	I^- (iodide)	SE + HNO_3 + $AgNO_3$ ⟶ yellow ppt insoluble in *aq* NH_3 **Layer test** (*H*)
4.	Brown pungent fumes intensified by the addition of Cu-turnings	NO_3^- (nitrate)	**Ring test**
5.	Colourless gases turning lime water milky and burning with blue flame	$C_2O_4^{2-}$ (oxalate)	Acidified $KMnO_4$ solution is decolorised SE + CH_3COOH + $CaCl_2$ solution → white ppt decolorising acidified $KMnO_4$ solution

Analysis of Second Category Anions

Following are the tests for analysis of second category anions.

1. Test for Chloride (Cl^-)

Most chlorides are soluble in water except Hg_2Cl_2, CuCl, (Slightly soluble in hot water) AgCl, $PbCl_2$, soluble in hot water BiOCl and SbOCl are insoluble in hot water.

(i) **Concentrated H_2SO_4** With concentrated H_2SO_4, chlorides gives vapours of HCl.

$$Cl^- + H_2SO_4 \longrightarrow HCl + HSO_4^-$$

Vapour evolved

(a) Turns blue litmus paper red

(b) Gives white fumes of NH_4Cl when a glass rod moistened with aqueous ammonia solution is brought close to the mouth of test tube.

(ii) **Silver Nitrate Solution** Chlorides on treatment with $AgNO_3$ solution gives a white curdy precipitate of AgCl insoluble in water and in dilute nitric acid but soluble in dilute ammonia solution due to the formation of soluble complex.

$$Cl^- + Ag^+ \longrightarrow \underset{\text{White curdy ppt}}{AgCl\downarrow}$$

$$AgCl + 2NH_3 \longrightarrow \underset{\text{Soluble}}{[Ag(NH_3)_2]Cl}$$

(iii) **Lead Acetate Solution** With $(CH_3CO_2)_2Pb$ solution, chlorides gives a white precipitate of lead chloride.

$$2Cl^- + Pb^{2+} \longrightarrow \underset{\text{White ppt}}{PbCl_2\downarrow}$$

(iv) **Chromyl Chloride Test** When a mixture containing chloride ion is heated with $K_2Cr_2O_7$ and concentrated H_2SO_4, deep orange-red fumes of chromyl chloride (CrO_2Cl_2) are formed.

$$K_2Cr_2O_7 + 4NaCl + 6H_2SO_4 \longrightarrow 2KHSO_4 + 4NaHSO_4 + \underset{\text{Orange-Red fumes}}{2CrO_2Cl_2\uparrow} + 3H_2O$$

When chromyl chloride vapours are passed into sodium hydroxide solution, a yellow solution of sodium chromate is formed, which when treated with lead acetate, gives yellow precipitate of lead chromate.

$$CrO_2Cl_2 + 2NaOH \longrightarrow \underset{\text{Yellow solution}}{Na_2CrO_4} + H_2O + 2NaCl$$

$$Na_2CrO_4 + (CH_3COO)_2Pb \longrightarrow 2CH_3COONa + \underset{\text{Yellow ppt}}{PbCrO_4\downarrow}$$

JEE Alert

Chromyl chloride test is given by ionic chlorides only. Chlorides of Hg^{2+}, Pb^{2+}, Ag^+, Sn^{2+} and Sb^{3+} do not respond to chromyl chloride test due to their covalent character, which allows them to ionise only slightly.

2. Test for Bromide (Br^-)

All bromides are soluble in water except AgBr, Hg_2Br_2, CuBr and $PbBr_2$ (Slightly soluble in boiling warer)

(i) **Concentrated H_2SO_4** If concentrated sulphuric acid is poured in a bromide solution, first a reddish-brown solution is formed, later reddish-brown vapours of bromine accompany the hydrogen bromide.

$$2KBr + H_2SO_4 \longrightarrow KHSO_4 + 2HBr\uparrow$$

$$2HBr + H_2SO_4 \longrightarrow 2H_2O + SO_2\uparrow + \underset{\text{Reddish-brown}}{Br_2\uparrow}$$

If concentrated H_3PO_4 is used instead of H_2SO_4 and the mixture is warmed, only hydrogen bromide is formed.

$$KBr + H_3PO_4 \longrightarrow HBr\uparrow + KH_2PO_4$$

(ii) **Manganese dioxide and Concentrated Sulphuric Acid** When a mixture of solid bromide, MnO_2 and concentrated H_2SO_4 is heated, reddish-brown vapour of bromine are evolved.

$$2KBr + MnO_2 + 2H_2SO_4 \longrightarrow \underset{\text{Reddish-brown}}{Br_2\uparrow} + KHSO_4 + MnSO_4 + 2H_2O$$

(iii) **Silver Nitrate Solution** With $AgNO_3$ solution, bromide gives a curdy pale yellow precipitate of silver bromide. This precipitate is sparingly soluble in dilute ammonia but readily soluble in concentrated ammonia solution and insoluble in dilute HNO_3.

$$Br^- + Ag^+ \longrightarrow \underset{\text{Pale yellow ppt}}{AgBr\downarrow}$$

(iv) **Lead Acetate Solution** Bromides on treatment with lead acetate solution, gives a white crystalline precipitate of lead bromide, which is soluble in boiling water.

$$2Br^- + Pb^{2+} \longrightarrow \underset{\text{White ppt}}{PbBr_2\downarrow} \xrightarrow{\text{on boiling}} \text{Clear solution} \xrightarrow{\text{cooled}} \text{White ppt.}$$

(v) **Chlorine Water** When chlorine water is added to a solution of bromide, free bromine is liberated which colours the solution orange-red.

If CS_2, $CHCl_3$ or CCl_4 is added to the solution and the liquid is shaken. the bromine dissolves in the organic solvent and after allowing to stand forms a reddish-brown solution below the colourless aqueous layer.

$$2KBr + Cl_2\,(\text{Water}) \longrightarrow 2KCl + Br_2$$

$$Br_2 + \text{Chloroform} \longrightarrow \text{Reddish-brown solution}$$

With excess of chlorine water, the bromine is converted into yellow bromine monochloride and a pale yellow solution results.

$$Br_2\uparrow + Cl_2\uparrow \longrightarrow \underset{\text{Pale yellow solution}}{2BrCl}$$

(vi) **Potassium Dichromate and Concentrated H_2SO_4**

When a mixture of solid bromide, $K_2Cr_2O_7$ and concentrated H_2SO_4 is heated and passing the evolved vapours into water, a orange-red solution is obtained.

$$6KBr + K_2Cr_2O_7 + 7H_2SO_4 \longrightarrow \underset{\text{Orange-red solution}}{3Br_2} + Cr_2(SO_4)_3 + 4K_2SO_4 + 7H_2O$$

3. Test for Iodide (I^-)

Iodides are generally soluble in water except AgI, Hg_2I_2, HgI_2, CuI and PbI_2.

(i) **Concentrated H_2SO_4** With concentrated H_2SO_4 iodides gives violet vapours of iodine on warming.

$$2I^- + \underset{\text{Oxidising agent}}{2H_2SO_4} \longrightarrow \underset{\text{Violet vapours}}{I_2} + 2H_2O + SO_2\uparrow$$

(ii) **Silver Nitrate Solution** With $AgNO_3$ solution, iodides form a yellow curdy precipitate of silver iodide, which is very slightly soluble in concentrated ammonia solution, but is completely insoluble in dilute HNO_3.

$$I^- + Ag^+ \longrightarrow \underset{\text{Yellow curdy ppt}}{AgI\downarrow}$$

(iii) **Lead Acetate Solution** With $(CH_3CO_2)_2Pb$ solution, a yellow precipitate of lead iodides (PbI_2) is formed, which is soluble in hot water forming a colourless solution and yielding golden-yellow precipitate on cooling.

$$2I^- + Pb^{2+} \longrightarrow \underset{\text{Yellow ppt}}{PbI_2\downarrow}$$

(iv) **Potassium Dichromate and Concentrated Sulphuric Acid** When iodides are warmed with $K_2Cr_2O_7$ and concentrated H_2SO_4, iodine is liberated.

$$6I^- + Cr_2O_7^{2-} + 7H_2SO_4 \longrightarrow \underset{\text{Violet vapours}}{3I_2\uparrow} + 2Cr^{2+} + 7SO_4^{2-} + 7H_2O$$

(v) **Chlorine Water** When this reagent is added dropwise to a solution of an iodine, free iodine is liberated, which colours the solution brown and on shaking with CS_2, $CHCl_3$ or CCl_4 it dissolves in organic layer forming a violet solution, which settles below the aqueous layer.

$$2KI + Cl_2 \longrightarrow I_2 + 2KCl$$

$$I_2 + \text{Chloroform} \longrightarrow \text{Violet solution}$$

(vi) **Copper Sulphate Solution** With $CuSO_4$ solution, iodide produces a brown precipitate consisting of a mixture of copper (I) iodide and iodine. On addition of hypo ($Na_2S_2O_3$) to the solution, brown precipitate changes to white (colourless).

$$4I^- + 2Cu^{2+} \longrightarrow \underset{\text{Brown ppt}}{Cu_2I_2\downarrow + I_2}$$

$$I_2 + 2S_2O_3^{2-} \longrightarrow 2I^- + S_4O_6^{2-}$$

(vii) **Mercury (II) Chloride Solution** With $HgCl_2$ solution, iodide gives a scarlet precipitate of HgI_2.

$$2I^- + HgCl_2 \longrightarrow \underset{\text{Scarlet ppt}}{HgI_2\downarrow} + 2Cl^-$$

The precipitate dissolves in excess of KI, forming tetraiodomercurate (II) complex.

$$HgI_2 + 2I^- \longrightarrow \underset{\text{Soluble}}{[HgI_4]^{2-}}$$

4. Test for Nitrate (NO_3^-)

All nitrates are soluble in water. The nitrates of mercury and bismuth give basic salts on treatment with H_2O but are soluble in dilute nitric acid.

(i) **Concentrated H_2SO_4** Nitrates produces reddish-brown vapours of nitrogen dioxide on treatment with concentrated H_2SO_4.

$$4NO_3^- + 2H_2SO_4 \longrightarrow \underset{\text{Reddish-brown vapours}}{4NO_2^-} + 2SO_4^{2-} + 2H_2O + O_2\uparrow$$

(ii) **Brown Ring Test** When a freshly prepared saturated solution of iron (II) sulphate is added to nitrate solution and then concentrated H_2SO_4 is added slowly from the side of the test tube, a brown ring is obtained at the junction of two layers.

$$2NO_3^- + 4H_2SO_4 + 6Fe^{2+} \longrightarrow 6Fe^{3+} + 2NO + 4SO_4^{2-} + 4H_2O$$

$$FeSO_4 + 6H_2O \longrightarrow [Fe(H_2O)_6]SO_4$$

$$[Fe(H_2O)_6]SO_4 + NO \longrightarrow \underset{\text{Brown ring}}{[Fe(H_2O)_5NO]SO_4} + H_2O$$

5. Test for Oxalate ($C_2O_4^{2-}$)

Alkali metal oxalates are soluble in water.

(i) **Silver Nitrate Solution** With silver nitrate solution, a white curdy precipitate of silver oxalate is obtained which is sparingly soluble in water, soluble in ammonia solution and in dilute nitric acid.

$$(C_2O_4)^{2-} + 2Ag^+ \longrightarrow \underset{\text{White curdy ppt}}{Ag_2C_2O_4} \xrightarrow{\Delta} \text{No change}$$

$$Ag_2C_2O_4 + 4NH_3 \longrightarrow 2[Ag(NH_3)_2]^+ + (C_2O_4)^{2-}$$

$$Ag_2C_2O_4 \xrightarrow{\Delta} 2Ag^+ + C_2O_4^{2-}$$

(ii) **Calcium Chloride Solution** With calcium chloride solution, a white crystalline precipitate of calcium oxalate from neutral solutions is obtained, which is insoluble in dilute acetic acid and oxalic acid but soluble in dilute hydrochloric acid and in dilute nitric acid.

$$(C_2O_4)^{2-} + Ca^{2+} \longrightarrow \underset{\text{White ppt}}{CaC_2O_4}$$

(iii) **Potassium Permanganate Solution**

Potassium permanganate solution gets decolourised when warmed in acid solution with an oxalate salt to

60°C. Many other organic compounds also effect the bleaching of permanganate but if the evolved carbon dioxide is tested by the lime water reaction, the test becomes specific for oxalates.

$$\underset{\text{(Purple)}}{5C_2O_4^{2-} + 2MnO_4^-} + 16H^+ \longrightarrow \underset{\text{(Colourless)}}{10CO_2\uparrow + 2Mn^{2+}} + 8H_2O$$

Group 'B' Radicals

Let us study about the ions involved in group radicals.

1. Test for Sulphate (SO_4^{2-})

Sulphates of barium, strontium and lead are practically insoluble in water, those of calcium and mercury (II) are slightly soluble and most of the remaining metallic sulphates are soluble.

(i) **Barium Chloride Solution** On adding $BaCl_2$ solution to a sulphate salt solution, a white precipitate of barium sulphate ($BaSO_4$) insoluble in warm dilute hydrochloric acid and in dilute nitric acid but moderately soluble in boiling concentrated hydrochloric acid is formed.

$$SO_4^{2-} + Ba^{2+} \longrightarrow \underset{\text{White ppt}}{BaSO_4\downarrow}$$

(ii) **Mercury (II) Nitrate Solution** With $Hg(NO_3)_2$ solution, sulphates form a yellow precipitate of basic mercury (II) sulphate.

$$SO_4^{2-} + 3Hg^{2+} + 2H_2O \longrightarrow \underset{\text{Yellow ppt}}{HgSO_4 \cdot 2HgO\downarrow} + 4H^+$$

2. Test for Phosphate (PO_4^{3-})

(i) **Barium Chloride Solution** With barium chloride solution, white amorphous precipitate of barium phosphate, $Ba_3(PO_4)_2$ is formed from neutral solutions, soluble in dilute mineral acids and in acetic acid.

$$2PO_4^{3-} + 3Ba^{2+} \longrightarrow \underset{\text{White ppt}}{Ba_3(PO_4)_2\downarrow}$$

(ii) **Silver Nitrate Solution** With silver nitrate solution, a yellow precipitate of silver orthophosphate, Ag_3PO_4 is formed which is soluble in dilute ammonia solution and in dilute nitric acid.

$$PO_4^{3-} + 3Ag^+ \longrightarrow \underset{\text{Yellow ppt}}{Ag_3PO_4\downarrow}$$

$$Ag_3PO_4\downarrow + 6NH_3 \longrightarrow 3[Ag(NH_3)_2]^+ + PO_4^{3-}$$

(iii) **Ammonium Molybdate Reagent** When ammonium molybdate is treated with a solution containing phosphate a canary yellow crystalline precipitate of ammonium phosphomolybdate (ammonium dodecamolybdatophosphate), $[NH_4]_3[PMo_{12}O_{40}]$ or $(NH_4)_3[P(Mo_3O_{10})_4]$ is formed. In the formed compound the Mo_3O_{10} group replaces each oxygen atom form phosphate.

$$PO_4^{3-} + 3NH_4^+ + 12MoO_4^{2-} + 24H^+ \longrightarrow \underset{\text{Canary-Yellow ppt}}{(NH_4)_3[P(Mo_3O_{10})_4]\downarrow} + 12H_2O$$

Elemental Practice 10.1

Type I MCQs with Only One Correct Option

1. The acidic solution of a salt produced a deep blue colour with starch iodide solution. The salt may be
(a) chloride (b) nitrite
(c) acetate (d) bromide

2. When a mixture of solid NaCl, solid $K_2Cr_2O_7$ is heated with conc. H_2SO_4, orange red vapours are obtained. These are of the compound.
(a) Chromous chloride
(b) Chromyl chloride
(c) Chromic chloride
(d) Chromic sulphate

3. Nitrate is confirmed by the ring test. The brown colour of the ring is due to the formation of
(a) ferrous nitrite
(b) nitroso ferrous sulphate
(c) ferrous nitrate
(d) $FeSO_4NO_2$

4. A mixture, on heating with conc. H_2SO_4 and MnO_2, liberates brown vapour of
(a) Br_2 (b) NO_2
(c) HBr (d) I_2

5. Which of the following combines with Fe(II) ions to form a brown complex
(a) N_2O (b) NO
(c) N_2O_3 (d) N_2O_4

6. A substance on treatment with dil. H_2SO_4 liberates a colourless gas which produces turbidity with baryta water and turns acidified dichromate solution green. The reaction indicates the presence of
(a) CO_3^{2-} (b) S^{2-}
(c) SO_3^{2-} (d) NO_2^-

7. A white solid is first heated with dil. H_2SO_4 and then with conc. H_2SO_4. No action was observed in either case. The solid salt contains
(a) sulphide (b) sulphite
(c) thiosulphate (d) sulphate

8. Sodium borate on reaction with conc. H_2SO_4 and C_2H_5OH gives a compound *A* which burns with a green edged flame. The compound *A* is
(a) $H_2B_4O_7$ (b) $(C_2H_5)_2B_4O_7$
(c) H_3BO_3 (d) $(C_2H_5)_3BO_3$

9. A white sodium salt dissolves readily in water to give a solution which is neutral to litmus. When silver nitrate solution is added to the solution, a white precipitate is obtained which does not dissolve in dil. HNO_3. The anion could be
(a) CO_3^{2-} (b) Cl^- (c) SO_4^{2-} (d) S^{2-}

10. When I_2 is passed through KCl, KF, KBr
(a) Cl_2 and Br_2 are evolved
(b) Cl_2 is evolved
(c) Cl_2, F_2 and Br_2 are evolved
(d) No reaction occurs

11. The pairs that will produce $Cl_2(g)$ are
(a) NaCl + conc. H_2SO_4
(b) NaCl + conc. H_3PO_4
(c) NaCl + MnO_2 + conc. H_2SO_4
(d) NaCl + H_2O_2

12. HBr will be obtained by the action of
(a) conc. HNO_3 on NaBr
(b) conc. H_2SO_4 on NaBr
(c) conc. H_3PO_4 on NaBr
(d) MnO_2 on NaBr in the presence of H_2SO_4

13. SO_2 and CO_2 can be distinguished by using
(a) acidified $KMnO_4$ (b) acidified $K_2Cr_2O_7$
(c) $FeCl_3$ + dil. HCl (d) all of these

14. Sulphur dioxide gas responds to the starch iodide test due to
(a) oxidising property of SO_2 (b) acidic nature of SO_2
(c) reducing nature of SO_2 (d) bleaching action of SO_2

15. Sulphide ions can be identified by
(a) sodium pentacyanonitrosylferrate (III)
(b) sodium pentacyanonitrosoniumferrate (II)
(c) sodium pentacyanonitrosylferrate (II)
(d) sodium pentacyanonitrosoniumferrate (III)

16. Given below are few statements.
(I) Nitrate ions can be tested in presence of nitrite ions using conc. H_2SO_4.
(II) Brown ring complex will be formed by adding conc. H_2SO_4 followed by freshly prepared $FeSO_4$ solution to a mixture of nitrate and nitrite ions.
(III) Brown ring complex will be formed by adding dil. H_2SO_4 followed by freshly prepared $FeSO_4$ solution to a mixture of nitrate and nitrite ions.
(IV) Brown ring complex will be formed by adding dil. CH_3COOH followed by freshly prepared $FeSO_4$ solution to aqueous solution of nitrite ions.
Choose the correct statements from the options given below.
(a) (I), (II) and (IV) (b) (I), (II) and (III)
(c) (II), (III) and (IV) (d) (I), (II), (III) and (IV)

17. A compound (*P*) on reaction with NaOH gives a gas (*Q*) which gives white fumes with ammonia. The compound (*P*) does not respond to chromyl chloride test. Then, the compound (*P*) is
(a) NaCl (b) $SnCl_4$
(c) $CrCl_3$ (d) $FeCl_2$

Type II 》 MCQs with One or More than One Correct Option

18. Choose the compounds that are insoluble in water is/are
(a) $(NH_4)_2C_2O_4$ (b) $BaCl_2$
(c) $SrSO_4$ (d) CaC_2O_4

19. $NaNO_2 + H_2SO_4 \xrightarrow{\Delta} A + B, B \longrightarrow H_2O + HNO_3 + C$
and $C + O_2 \longrightarrow D$
Identify *B*, *C* and *D* in the given reaction
(a) $B = 2HNO_2, C = 2NO$ (b) $B = 2NO, C = 2HNO_2$
(c) $B = Na_2SO_4, D = 2NO$ (d) $B = HNO_2, D = 2NO_2$

20. Which of the following compounds liberate NH_3 on heating?
(a) $(NH_4)_2SO_4$ (b) NH_4Cl
(c) $(NH_4)_2CO_3$ (d) NH_4NO_3

21. In how many of the following reactions, the products is obtained as a yellow precipitate?
(a) $Ag^+ + CrO_4^{2-} \longrightarrow$ Product
(b) $Ba^{2+} + CrO_4^{2-} \longrightarrow$ Product
(c) $NH_4^+ + [Co(NO_2)_6]^{3-} \longrightarrow$ Product
(d) $Hg^{2+} + Co^{2+} + 4SCN^{\ominus} \longrightarrow$ Product

22. The compounds that gives white precipitate when treated with $AgNO_3$ solution is/are
(a) Na_2SO_3 (b) Na_2HPO_4
(c) $Na_2C_2O_4$ (d) Na_2CrO_4

23. Which of the following combination in an aqueous medium will give a white precipitate?
(a) $SO_4^{2-} + Ba^{2+}$
(b) $Na_2 + PO_4 + Mg(NO)_2 + NH_3$
(c) $CaCl_2 + NaF$
(d) $HgI_2 + 2KI$

Type III 》 Numerical/Integer Answer Type Questions

24. Consider the following metal carbonates
$CuCO_3, K_2CO_3, Na_2CO_3, MgCO_3, CaCO_3, Ag_2CO_3$
The total number of carbonates that give metal oxide on heating is ....

25. In how many of the following reaction one of the products is obtained as a black precipitate?
(a) $Hg_2Cl_2 + SnCl_2 \longrightarrow$ Product
(b) $Pb(NO_3)_2 + K_2CrO_4 \longrightarrow$ Product
(c) $Cu(NO_3)_2 + 2KI \longrightarrow$ Product
(d) $2BiCl_3 + 2Na_2SnO_2 + 6NaOH \longrightarrow$ Product
(e) $Bi(OH)_3 \downarrow + [Sn(OH)_4]^{2-}(aq) \longrightarrow$ Product

26. The number of white coloured salts, among the following is ....
I. $PbCrO_4$ II. CaC_2O_4
III. $PbSO_4$ IV. $Bi(OH)_3$
V. $BaCl_2$ VI. $CuSO_4$
VII. $Cu(CN)_2$ VIII. $CdCO_3$
IX. Cu_2O X. $CrCl_3 \cdot 6H_2O$

27. Total number of metal oxides which is yellow in colour in cold medium are
$ZnO, SnO_2, Bi_2O_3, Fe_2O_3, PbO$

28. Total number of pair of acid radicals that can be distinguished by using dil. H_2SO_4 is
I. $C_2O_4^{2-}$ and NO_3^-
II. NO_3^- and NO_2^-
III. HCO_3^- and CO_3^{2-}
IV. Cl^- and Br^-
V. CH_3COO^- and $S_2O_3^{2-}$

Elemental Practice 10.1 | Chapter 10
Connect with **Answers**

1. (b)	2. (b)	3. (b)	4. (a)	5. (b)	6. (c)
7. (d)	8. (d)	9. (b)	10. (d)	11. (c)	12. (c)
13. (d)	14. (c)	15. (b)	16. (c)	17. (b)	18. (c,d)
19. (a,d)	20. (a,b,c)	21. (b,c)	22. (a,c)	23. (a,b,c)	24. (5)
25. (3)	26. (6)	27. (3)	28. (2)		

Element 2 Qualitative Analysis of Basic Radicals

Analysis of Cation Mixtures

The identification of individual species of cations present in an unknown mixture of electrolytes involves a preliminary segregation of the cations into selected classifiable groups. A simple system devised for the purpose is based on the selective precipitation of sparingly soluble compounds of the cations from an original solution (O.S.) of the electrolyte mixture.

In its most simplified form, for the more common cations only, these compounds fall into five groups. Within each group the anion is the same for the different cations and the solubility products are small and do not differ too greatly from one another.

Group	Group reagent	Basic radical	Composition and colour of precipitate
Zero	NaOH or $Ca(OH)_2$, heat if required	NH_4^+	Ammonia gas is evolved
1.	Dil. HCl	Ag^+	AgCl ; White
		Hg_2^{2+}	Hg_2Cl_2 ; White
		Pb^{2+}	$PbCl_2$; White
2.(A)	H_2S in presence of dil. HCl (Insoluble in YAS)	Hg^{2+}	HgS ; Black
		Pb^{2+}	PbS ; Black
		Bi^{3+}	Bi_2S_3 ; Black
		Cu^{2+}	CuS ; Black
		Cd^{2+}	CdS ; Yellow
2.(B)	H_2S in presence of dil. HCl (Soluble in YAS)	As^{3+}	As_2S_3 ; Yellow
		Sb^{3+}	Sb_2S_3 ; Orange
		Sn^{2+}	SnS ; Brown
		Sn^{4+}	SnS_2 ; Yellow
3.	NH_4OH in presence of NH_4Cl	Fe^{3+}	$Fe(OH)_3$; Reddish brown
		Cr^{3+}	$Cr(OH)_3$; Green
		Al^{3+}	$Al(OH)_3$; Gelatinous white
4.	H_2S in presence of NH_4OH and NH_4Cl	Zn^{2+}	ZnS ; Dirty white
		Mn^{2+}	MnS ; Buff (or light pink)
		Co^{2+}	CoS ; Black
		Ni^{2+}	NiS ; Black
5.	$(NH_4)_2CO_3$ in presence of NH_4OH	Ba^{2+}	$BaCO_3$; White
		Sr^{2+}	$SrCO_3$; White
		Ca^{2+}	$CaCO_3$; White
6.	Na_2HPO_4 in presence of NH_4OH	Mg^{2+}	$Mg(NH_4)PO_4$: White

[YAS = Yellow ammonium sulphide, $(NH_4)_2S_x$]

- **Group I** The sparingly soluble chlorides derived from Pb^{2+}, Hg_2^{2+} and Ag^+ ions are precipitated by the addition of dilute HCl. Other cations do not get precipitated as chloride because their K_{sp} is quite high.
- **Group II** The sparingly soluble sulphides derived from Hg^{2+}, Pb^{2+}, Cu^{2+}, Cd^{2+} and Bi^{3+} ions (and in addition the sparingly soluble covalent sulphides As_2S_3, Sb_2S_3 and SnS) are precipitated by the passage of hydrogen sulphide (H_2S) through an acidic solution in which concentration of hydrogen ions is small.

  The K_{sp} value of group II sulphide is quite low in comparison to K_{sp} values of group IV sulphides, hence they do not get precipitated in acidic medium, where S^{2-} ion concentration is quite low.
- **Group III** The sparingly soluble hydroxides derived from Fe^{3+}, Cr^{3+} and Al^{3+} ions are precipitated by the addition of ammonium hydroxide, (NH_4OH) solution in the presence of excess ammonium chloride, NH_4Cl and NH_4OH helps in maintaining the pH, that does not allow dissolving of amphoteric hydroxide Al_2O_3 and Cr_2O_3.
- **Group IV** A further group of sparingly soluble sulphides, those derived from Co^{2+}, Ni^{2+}, Mn^{2+} and Zn^{2+} ions, are precipitated by the passage of H_2S through a basic solution. In basic solution H_2S is fully ionised to give sufficient sulphide ion concentrations to precipitate group IV sulphides.
- **Group V** The sparingly soluble carbonates derived from Ca^{2+}, Sr^{2+} and Ba^{2+} ions are precipitated by the addition of ammonium carbonate, $(NH_4)_2CO_3$, solution in the presence of NH_4OH and NH_4Cl.

  The most common cations remaining in solution after the precipitation of group V are Na^+, K^+ (all the simple salts of the alkali metals are water-soluble) and Mg^{2+} ions. Role of NH_4Cl is protonation of CO_3^{2-} ions produced by dissociation of $(NH_4)_2CO_3$ to give limited concentration of CO_3^{2-}, so that Mg^{2+} do not get precipitated. Also, buffer solution ($NH_4Cl + NH_4OH$) help in maintaining pH to go too high that avoids precipitation of cations including Mg^{2+} as hydroxides.

Preparation of Original Solution

Transparent, aqueous solution of salt is known as original solution and it is prepared by dissolving salt/mixture in suitable solvent. To prepare original solution, following solvents are used strictly in the order given below:

(i) Cold water (ii) Hot water
(iii) Dilute HCl (iv) Conc. HCl

To prepare original solution small quantity of substance is shaken with cold, distilled water.

- If substance dissolves, whole substance is dissolved in water to prepare original solution.
- If substance remains insoluble then, mixture is heated and solubility is tested.
- If substance is insoluble in hot water also then a few drops of dil HCl are added.
- If substance remains insoluble in dil. HCl also, then we try to dissolve in dil. HNO_3.
- If substance does not dissolve in the solvents used in above steps, then it is dissolved in conc. HCl. If it remains insoluble even in concentrated HCl, then a paste of substance and concentrated HCl is made in a porcelein dish and this mixture is heated till it becomes semi-solid. Again concentrate HCl is added to make paste and is heated again to get a semi-solid.
- The procedure is repeated twice or thrice and semi-solid thus obtained is dissolved in distilled water. The solution is filtered and filtrate is called original solution. If some insoluble part is obtained then neglect it and do not use. The filtrate obtained as original solution is necessarily diluted with water.

JEE Alert

HCl is the preferred acid over dil. HNO_3 and H_2SO_4 for the preparation of original solution. As dilute HNO_3 and H_2SO_4 may interfere with the analysis due to oxidation and precipitation effects, respectively.

Analysis of Group Zero

Ammonium (NH_4^+)

Ammonium salts are decomposed by alkali and NH_3 is liberated which can be identified by the following methods.

(i) **Sodium Hydroxide Solution** All ammonium salts on heating with alkali (NaOH) gives smell of NH_3.

$$NH_4^+ + OH^- \longrightarrow NH_3\uparrow + H_2O$$

- The gas evolved can be detected by its smell.
- Gas evolved gives white fumes of NH_4Cl with HCl.

$$NH_3 + HCl \longrightarrow \underset{\text{White fumes}}{NH_4Cl\uparrow}$$

- Paper soaked in $CuSO_4$ solution, becomes deep-blue by NH_3 due to the complex formation.

$$CuSO_4 + 4NH_3 \longrightarrow \underset{\text{Deep-blue colouration}}{[Cu(NH_3)_4]SO_4}$$

- Gas can be identified by its ability to turn filter paper moistened with mercury (I) nitrate solution black.

$$2NH_3 + Hg_2^{2+}\ NO_3^- \longrightarrow \underset{\substack{\text{Mercury (II) amidonitrate}\\ \text{white ppt.}}}{Hg(NH_2)NO_3\downarrow} + \underset{\text{Black}}{Hg\downarrow} + NH_4^+NO_3^-$$

(ii) **Nessler's Reagent** With Nessler's reagent and an alkaline solution of potassium tetraiodomercurate (II), ammonium salts forms a brown precipitate or brown or yellow colouration is produced depending on the amount of NH_4^+ ions present in the solution. The precipitate is a basic mercury (II) amido-iodine.

$$NH_4Cl + 2K_2HgI_4 + 4KOH \longrightarrow$$

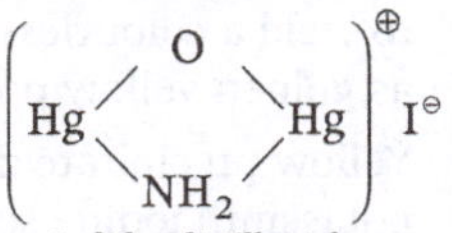

Iodide of Millon's base
Brown ppt.

$$+ 7KI + 3H_2O + KCl$$

This test can detect even traces of NH_3 present in a sample.

Analysis of Group I (Pb^{2+}, Ag^+, Hg_2^{2+}) Radicals

On adding dilute HCl to the salt solution if white precipitate is obtained, it indicates the presence of Pb^{2+}, Ag^+ or Hg_2^{2+} ion in the solution.

$$Ag^+ \xrightarrow{\text{Dil. HCl}} \underset{\text{White ppt.}}{AgCl\downarrow}$$

$$Pb^{2+} \xrightarrow{\text{Dil. HCl}} \underset{\text{White ppt.}}{PbCl_2\downarrow}$$

$$Hg_2^{2+} \xrightarrow{\text{Dil. HCl}} \underset{\text{White ppt.}}{Hg_2Cl_2\downarrow}$$

Test for Lead (II)

(i) **Sodium Hydroxide Solution** With NaOH, Pb^{2+} forms a white precipitate of lead hydroxide. The precipitate dissolves in excess of the reagent (NaOH) and tetrahydroxyplumbate(II) ions are formed.

$$Pb^+ + 2OH^- \longrightarrow \underset{\text{White ppt.}}{Pb(OH)_2\downarrow}$$

$$Pb(OH)_2\downarrow + 2OH^- \longrightarrow \underset{\text{Soluble}}{[Pb(OH)_4]^{2-}}$$

(ii) **Ammonia Solution** With ammonia solution, Pb^{2+} gives a white precipitate of lead hydroxide.

$$Pb^{+2} + 2NH_4OH \longrightarrow \underset{\text{White ppt.}}{Pb(OH)_2} + 2NH_4^+$$

The precipitate is insoluble in excess reagent (NH_4OH).

(iii) **Potassium Chromate Solution** $PbCl_2$ is soluble in hot water and gives a yellow precipitate with K_2CrO_4. The precipitate obtained is insoluble in acetic acid but soluble in NaOH and nitric acid.

$$PbCl_2 + K_2CrO_4 \longrightarrow \underset{\text{Yellow ppt.}}{PbCrO_4\downarrow} + 2KCl$$

$$PbCrO_4\downarrow + 4NaOH \longrightarrow Na_2PbO_2 + Na_2CrO_4 + 2H_2O$$

$$2PbCrO_4\downarrow + 2H^+ \longrightarrow 2Pb^{2+} + Cr_2O_7^{2-} + H_2O$$

(iv) **Potassium Iodide Solution** $PbCl_2$ on addition of KI solution gives bright yellow precipitate of PbI_2.

$$PbCl_2 + 2KI \longrightarrow \underset{\text{Yellow ppt}}{PbI_2\downarrow} + 2KCl$$

The precipitate is moderately soluble in boiling water to yield a colourless solution, from which it separates as golden yellow precipitate on cooling.
Yellow precipitate dissolves on adding excess of potassium iodide solution.

$$PbI_2 + 2KI\,(\text{excess}) \rightleftharpoons \underset{\text{Colourless soluble complex}}{K_2[PbI_4]}$$

The reaction is reversible and on diluting with H_2O, the precipitate reappears.

(v) **Reaction with KCN**

$$Pb^{+2} + KCN \longrightarrow \underset{\text{White}}{Pb(CN)_2\downarrow} \xrightarrow{\text{Excess KCN}} \text{Insoluble}$$

JEE Alert

Pb^{2+} is not completely precipitated in group I because $PbCl_2$ is partially soluble in water. It is completely precipitated in group II.

Test for Silver (I)

(i) **Dilute Hydrochloric Acid** With dilute hydrochloric acid (or soluble chlorides), a white precipitate of silver chloride is formed.

$$Ag^+ + Cl \longrightarrow \underset{\text{White ppt.}}{AgCl\downarrow}$$

With concentrated hydrochloric acid precipitation does not occur after decanting the liquid form over the precipitate. It can be dissolved in concentrated hydrochloric acid, when a dichloroargentate complex is formed.

$$AgCl + Cl^- \rightleftharpoons \underset{\text{Soluble}}{[AgCl_2]^-}$$

On dilution with water, the equilibrium shifts back to the left and the precipitate reappears. Dilute ammonia solution dissolves the precipitate to form the diammineargentate(I) ion, (complex ion).

$$AgCl\downarrow + 2NH_3 \rightleftharpoons \underset{\text{Soluble}}{[Ag(NH_3)_2]^+} + Cl^-$$

Dilute nitric acid or hydrochloric acid neutralises the excess ammonia and the precipitate reappears because the equilibrium is shifted backwards.

(ii) **Ammonia Solution** Ag^+ gives brown precipitate of silver oxide with NH_3 solution.

$$2Ag^+ + 2NH_3 + H_2O \rightleftharpoons \underset{\text{Brown ppt.}}{Ag_2O\downarrow} + 2NH_4^+$$

The reaction reaches equilibrium, thus the precipitation is incomplete at any stage. The precipitate dissolves in excess of the reagent forming diammineargentate(I) ion.

$$Ag_2O\downarrow + 4NH_3 + H_2O \longrightarrow \underset{\text{Soluble}}{2[Ag(NH_3)_2]^+} + 2OH^-$$

(iii) **Potassium Iodide Solution** Ag^+ gives yellow precipitate of silver iodide on reaction with KI solution.

$$Ag^+ + I^- \longrightarrow \underset{\text{Yellow ppt.}}{AgI\downarrow} \xrightarrow{\text{excess KI}} \text{No change}$$

The precipitate is insoluble in dilute or concentrated ammonia but dissolves in KCN and in sodium thiosulphate.

$$AgI\downarrow + 2CN^- \longrightarrow [Ag(CN)_2]^- + I^-$$

$$AgI\downarrow + 2S_2O_3^{2-} \longrightarrow [Ag(S_2O_3)_2]^{3-} + I^-$$

(iv) **Disodium Hydrogen Phosphate Solution** With disodium hydrogen phosphate in neutral solution, a yellow precipitate of silver phosphate is obtained.

$$3Ag^+ + HPO_4^{2-} \longrightarrow \underset{\text{Yellow ppt.}}{Ag_3PO_4\downarrow} + H^+$$

$$\xrightarrow[\text{Solution}]{NH_3} \underset{\text{Soluble complex}}{[Ag(NH_3)_2]^+}$$

Nitric acid and ammonia solution dissolves the precipitate.

(v) **Hydrazine Sulphate (Saturated)** When hydrazine sulphate is added to a solution of diammineargentate ions, it forms finely divided silver metal and gaseous nitrogen is evolved.

$$4[Ag(NH_3)_2]^+ + H_2N{-}NH_2 + H_2SO_4 \longrightarrow$$

$$\underset{\text{Silver mirror}}{4Ag\downarrow} + N_2\uparrow + 6NH_4^+ + 2NH_3 + SO_4^{2-}$$

If the vessel in which the reaction is carried out is clean, silver adheres to the glass walls forming an attractive mirror.

(vi) **Reaction with NaOH**

$$Ag^+ + NaOH \longrightarrow \underset{\text{Brownish black}}{Ag_2O\downarrow} \xrightarrow[\text{NaOH}]{\text{Excess}} \text{Insoluble}$$

Test for Mercury (I)

(i) **Sodium Hydroxide Solution** With NaOH, Hg_2^{2+} forms a black precipitate of mercury (I) oxide.

$$Hg_2^{2+} + 2OH^- \longrightarrow \underset{\text{Black ppt.}}{Hg_2O\downarrow} + H_2O \xrightarrow[\text{NaOH}]{\text{Excess}} \text{Insoluble}$$

The precipitate is insoluble in excess reagent but dissolves in dilute nitric acid. When the solution is boiled, the colour of precipitate changes to grey owing to the disproportionation, when mercury(II) oxide and mercury metal are formed.

$$Hg_2O\downarrow \longrightarrow HgO\downarrow + Hg\downarrow$$

(ii) **Ammonia Solution** Hg_2Cl_2 on treatment with NH_4OH results in giving black precipitate, which is a mixture of mercury metal and basic mercury aminochloride (black precipitate)

$$2Hg_2Cl_2 + 4NH_4OH \longrightarrow$$

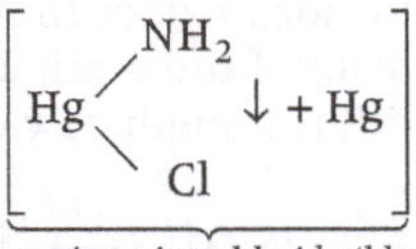

$+ NH_4Cl + 2H_2O$

Mercuric amino chloride (black)

(iii) **Potassium Iodide Solution** Hg_2^{2+} gives a green precipitate of mercury(I) iodide on reaction with KI solution.

$$Hg_2^{2+} + 2I^- \longrightarrow \underset{\text{Green ppt.}}{Hg_2I_2}$$

If excess reagent is added, a disproportionation reaction takes place and a soluble tetraiodomercurate(II) ions and black precipitate of mercury is formed.

$$Hg_2I_2\downarrow + 2I^- \longrightarrow \underset{\text{Soluble complex}}{[HgI_4]^{2-}} + \underset{\text{Black ppt.}}{Hg\downarrow}$$

Boiling the mercury(I) iodide precipitate with water, disproportionation again takes place and a mixture of red mercury(II) iodide precipitate and black mercury precipitate is formed.

$$Hg_2I_2\downarrow \longrightarrow \underset{\text{Scarlet red ppt.}}{HgI_2\downarrow} + \underset{\text{Black ppt.}}{Hg\downarrow}$$

(iv) **Potassium Chromate Solution** Hg_2^+ gives a red crystalline precipitate of mercury(I) chromate with potassium chromate solution in hot.

$$Hg_2^{2+} + CrO_4^{2-} \longrightarrow \underset{\text{Brick red ppt.}}{Hg_2CrO_4\downarrow}$$

$$\xrightarrow[\text{solution}]{NH_3} \underbrace{Hg\downarrow + Hg(NH_2)X\downarrow}_{\text{Over all black ppt.}}$$

X = Anion

Addition of sodium hydroxide turns the precipitate into black mercury(I) oxide.

$$Hg_2CrO_4\downarrow + 2OH^- \longrightarrow \underset{\text{Black ppt}}{Hg_2O\downarrow} + CrO_4^{2-} + H_2O$$

Solved Booster 2.1

The correct option(s) to distinguish nitrate salts of Hg_2^{2+} and Ca^{2+} taken separately is(are)

(a) Ca^{2+} shows the characteristic violet colour in the flame test.

(b) Calcium nitrate shows the formation of white precipitate by reaction with ammonium hydroxide.

(c) Only mercury (I) nitrate reacts with dilute HCl to form precipitate.

(d) Mercury does not impart any characteristic colour to the flame.

Solution *(c, d)*

Among the given statements only (c) and (d) are correct. The corrected form of incorrect statements are

- Ca^{2+} shows brick-red colour in the flame test.
- Calcium nitrate does not react with NH_4OH to form any precipitate as calcium salts are soluble in water.

Analysis of Group II A (Pb^{2+}, Hg^{2+}, Cu^{2+}, Bi^{3+}, Cd^{2+}) Radicals

Filtrate of group I + dil. HCl + H_2O. Pass H_2S gas $\rightarrow$

- yellow ppt - CdS
- black ppt - PbS, HgS, Bi_2S_3, CuS (salt is blue)
- bright yellow ppt - As_2S_3
- dark brown ppt - SnS
- orange ppt - Sb_2S_3
- As_2S_3, SnS_2, Sb_2S_3, SnS (II B-Arsenic group) are soluble in yellow ammonium sulphide (YAS) or NaOH.

$$As_2S_3 + \underset{\text{YAS}}{2(NH_4)_2S_2} \longrightarrow As_2S_5 + 2(NH_4)_2S$$

$$Sb_2S_3 + \underset{\text{YAS}}{2(NH_4)_2S_2} \longrightarrow Sb_2S_5 + 2(NH_4)_2S$$

$$SnS_2 + \underset{\text{YAS}}{(NH_4)_2S_2} \longrightarrow \underset{\text{Ammonium tetra thiostannate}}{(NH_4)_2SnS_3}$$

$$As_2S_3 + 6NaOH \longrightarrow Na_3AsO_3 + Na_3AsS_3 + 3H_2O$$

- PbS, CdS, HgS, Bi_2S_3, CuS (II A-Copper group) are insoluble in YAS.
- If on dilution with H_2O (before passing H_2S), there is white turbidity — Bi^{3+} confirmed, or orange turbidity — Sb^{3+} confirmed. Turbidity disappears on adding dil. HCl.

$$BiCl_3 + H_2O \longrightarrow \underset{\text{White turbidity}}{BiOCl} + 2HCl$$

$$SbCl_3 + H_2O \longrightarrow \underset{\text{Orange turbidity}}{SbOCl} + 2HCl$$

$$BiOCl + 2HCl \longrightarrow \underset{\text{Soluble}}{BiCl_3} + 2H_2O$$

$$SbOCl + 2HCl \longrightarrow \underset{\text{Soluble}}{SbCl_3} + H_2O$$

- PbS, CdS, CuS, Bi_2S_3 are soluble in HNO_3 (1 : 1) while HgS is insoluble; HgS, however, is soluble in *aqua-regia*.

1. Test for Mercury (II)

HgS precipitated dissolves in aqua regia (3HCl : HNO_3) forming undissociated $HgCl_2$.

$$3HgS\downarrow + 6HCl + 2HNO_3 \longrightarrow 3HgCl_2 + 3S\downarrow + 2NO\uparrow + 4H_2O$$

(i) **Potassium Iodide Solution** Potassium iodide when added slowly to the solution of Hg^{2+}, a scarlet red precipitate mercury (II) iodide is formed.

$$Hg^{2+} + 2I^- \longrightarrow \underset{\text{Scarlet red ppt.}}{HgI_2\downarrow}$$

The precipitate dissolves in excess reagent, when colourless tetraiodomercurate(II) ions are formed.

$$HgI_2 + 2I^- \longrightarrow \underset{\text{Soluble}}{[HgI_4]^{2-}} \text{ or } HgI_2 + 2KI \longrightarrow K_2[HgI_4]$$

An alkaline solution of potassium tetraiodomercurate(II) serves as a selective and sensitive reagent for ammonium ions (Nessler's reagent)

(ii) **Tin(II) Chloride Solution** When $SnCl_2$ solution is added to a solution of Hg^{2+}, a white silky precipitate of mercury(I) chloride (calomel) is obtained.

$$2Hg^{2+} + SnCl_2 \longrightarrow \underset{\text{White Silky ppt.}}{Hg_2Cl_2\downarrow} + Sn^{4+}$$

If more reagent is added, mercury(I) chloride is further reduced and black precipitate of mercury is formed.

$$Hg_2Cl_2\downarrow + SnCl_2 \longrightarrow \underset{\text{Black ppt.}}{2Hg\downarrow} + SnCl_4$$

(iii) **Cobalt(II) Thiocyanate Test** When $[Co(SCN)_4]^{2-}$ is added to the solution of Hg^{2+} and walls of the vessel are stirred with a glass rod, a deep-blue crystalline precipitate of cobalt tetrathiocyanatomercurate(II) is formed.

$$Hg^{2+} + Co^{2+} + 4SCN^- \longrightarrow \underset{\text{Deep-blue ppt.}}{Co[Hg(SCN)_4]\downarrow}$$

2. Test for Copper (II)

Hot, concentrated nitric acid dissolves copper(II) sulphide, leaving behind sulphur as a white precipitate.

$$3CuS + 8HNO_3 \longrightarrow 3Cu^{2+} + 6NO_3^- + \underset{\text{White ppt.}}{3S\downarrow} + 2NO\uparrow + 4H_2O$$

When boiled for long sulphur is oxidised to H_2SO_4 and a clear blue solution is obtained.

$$S\downarrow + 2HNO_3 \longrightarrow 2H^+ + SO_4^{2-} + 2NO\uparrow$$

(i) **Ammonia Solution** When ammonia solution is added to solution of Cu^{2+}, a blue precipitate of a basic copper sulphate is obtained, which is soluble in excess reagent giving deep-blue colouration of tetraamminecopper(II) sulphate.

$$2Cu^{2+} + SO_4^{2-} + 2NH_3 + 2H_2O \longrightarrow \underset{\text{Blue ppt.}}{Cu(OH)_2\cdot CuSO_4\downarrow} + 2NH_4^+$$

$$Cu(OH)_2\cdot CuSO_4\downarrow + 8NH_3 \longrightarrow \underset{\text{Deep-blue colouration}}{2[Cu(NH_3)_4]^{2+}} + SO_4^{2-} + 2OH^-$$

(ii) **Potassium Iodide** Potassium iodide with Cu^{2+} gives a white precipitate of copper(I) iodide but the solution is intensely brown because of the formation of tri-iodide ions (or iodine).

$$2Cu^{2+} + 5I^- \longrightarrow \underset{\text{White ppt.}}{Cu_2I_2\downarrow} + I_3^-$$

Adding an excess of sodium thiosulphate (hypo) to the solution, tri-iodide ions reduce to colourless iodide ions and the white colour of the precipitate becomes visible. The reduction with thiosulphate yields tetrathionate ions.

$$I_3^- + 2S_2O_3^{2-} \longrightarrow \underbrace{3I^- + S_4O_6^{2-}}_{\text{Overall colourless}}$$

These reactions are used in quantitative analysis for the iodometric determination of copper.

(iii) **Potassium Hexacyanoferrate(II) Solution** Cu^{2+} ions give chocolate-brown precipitate with $K_4[Fe(CN)_6]$ solution.

$$2Cu^{2+} + K_4[Fe(CN)_6] \longrightarrow \underset{\text{Chocolate-brown ppt.}}{Cu_2[Fe(CN)_6]\downarrow} + 4K^+$$

(iv) **Potassium Thiocyanate Solution** With potassium thiocyanate, a black precipitate of copper(II) thiocyanate is obtained.

$$Cu^{2+} + 2SCN^- \longrightarrow \underset{\text{Black ppt.}}{Cu(SCN)_2\downarrow}$$

The precipitate decomposes slowly to form white copper(I) thiocyanate and thiocyanogen are formed.

$$2Cu(SCN)_2\downarrow \longrightarrow \underset{\text{White ppt.}}{2CuSCN\downarrow} + (SCN)_2\uparrow$$

Cyanogen decomposes rapidly in aqueous solutions. Copper(II) thiocyanate can be transformmed to copper(I) thiocyanate immediately by adding a suitable reducing agent like saturated solution of sulphur dioxide.

$$2Cu(SCN)_2\downarrow + SO_2 + 2H_2O \longrightarrow \underset{\text{White ppt.}}{2CuSCN\downarrow} + 2SCN^- + SO_4^{2-} + 4H^+$$

(v) **Test by NaCN and KCN** Addition of KCN to $CuSO_4$ solution first causes reduction and then precipitates CuCN (cuprous cyanide). This reacts with excess CN^-, forming a soluble four co-ordinated complex $[Cu(CN)_4]^{3-}$ which is tetrahedral in shape :

$$2Cu^{2+} + 4CN^- \longrightarrow 2Cu^ICN + \underset{\text{Cyanogen}}{(CN)_2}$$

$$CuCN + 3CN^- \longrightarrow \underset{\text{Colourless Complex}}{[Cu(CN)_4]^{3-}}$$

Note $[Cu(CN)_4]^{3-}$ is a stable complex. Cd^{2+} also forms complex $[Cd(CN)_4]^{2-}$ but unstable, which ionises to form Cd^{2+} and CN^-. Thus if Cd^{2+} and Cu^{2+} both are present, Cu^{2+} and Cd^{2+} both are complexed by CN^-. If H_2S gas is passed, Cd^{2+} (in unstable $[Cd(CN)_4^{2-}]$) gives yellow precipitate of CdS.

3. Test for Bismuth (III)

Black precipitate of Bi_2S_3 is obtained which dissolves in hot dilute nitric acid, leaving behind sulphur in the form of a white precipitate.

$$Bi_2S_3\downarrow + 8H^+ + 2NO_3^- \longrightarrow 2Bi^{3+} + \underset{\text{White ppt.}}{3S\downarrow} + 2NO\uparrow + 4H_2O$$

(i) **Sodium Hydroxide** With NaOH solution, Bi^{3+} gives a white precipitate of bismuth(III) hydroxide.

$$Bi^{3+} + 3OH^- \longrightarrow \underset{\text{White ppt.}}{Bi(OH)_3\downarrow}$$

The precipitate is soluble in acids.

$$Bi(OH)_3\downarrow + 3H^+ \longrightarrow Bi^{3+} + 3H_2O$$

When boiled, the precipitate loses water and turns yellowish-white.

$$Bi(OH)_3\downarrow \longrightarrow \underset{\text{Yellowish-white ppt.}}{BiO\cdot OH\downarrow} + H_2O$$

$Bi(OH)_3$ when reduced by tetrahydroxostannate(II) ions gives black precipitate of bismuth metal.

$$2Bi(OH)_3 + 3[Sn(OH)_4]^{2-} \longrightarrow 2Bi\downarrow + 3[Sn(OH)_6]^{2-}$$

(ii) **Potassium Iodide** When KI solution is added dropwise to Bi^{3+} solution, a brownish black precipitate of bismuth(III) iodide is obtained.

$$Bi^{3+} + 3I^- \longrightarrow \underset{\text{Brownish black ppt.}}{BiI_3\downarrow}$$

The precipitate dissolves readiy in excess reagent and orange-coloured tetraiodobismuthate ions are formed.

$$BiI_3 + I^- \rightleftharpoons [BiI_4]^-$$

Heating the precipitate of BiI_3, with water, it turns orange due to the formation of bismuthyl oxide.

$$BiI_3\downarrow + H_2O \longrightarrow \underset{\text{Orange ppt.}}{BiO\downarrow} + 2H^+ + 2I^-$$

(iii) **Water** When a solution of a bismuth salt is poured into a large volume of water, a white precipitate of the corresponding basic salt is produced. This precipitate is soluble in dilute mineral acids but is insoluble in alkali hydroxides.

$$Bi^{3+} + NO_3^- + H_2O \longrightarrow \underset{\text{White ppt.}}{BiO(NO_2)\downarrow} + 2H^+$$

$$Bi^{3+} + Cl^- + H_2O \longrightarrow \underset{\text{White ppt.}}{BiOCl\downarrow} + 2H^+$$

4. Test for Cadmium (II)

Yellow precipitate of CdS dissolves in hot dilute nitric acid giving Cd^{+2} ions.

(i) **Ammonium Hydroxide** With NH_4OH solution, Cd^{2+} give a white precipitate of cadmium hydroxide.

$$Cd^{2+} + 2NH_4OH \rightleftharpoons \underset{\text{White ppt.}}{Cd(OH)_2\downarrow} + 2NH_4^+$$

The precipitate dissolves in acid when the equilibrium shifts towards the left.

An excess of reagent dissolves the precipitate, when tetraamminecadmiate(II) ions are formed.

$$Cd(OH)_2 + 4NH_3 \longrightarrow [Cd(NH_3)_4]^{2+} + 2OH^-$$

(ii) **Potassium Cyanide** With KCN solution, Cd^{2+} forms a white precipitate of cadmium cyanide.

$$Cd^{2+} + 2CN^- \longrightarrow \underset{\text{White ppt.}}{Cd(CN)_2\downarrow}$$

An excess of reagent dissolves the precipitate due to the formation of tetracyanocadmiate(II) ions.

$$Cd(CN)_2\downarrow + 2CN^- \longrightarrow [Cd(CN)_4]^{2-}$$

The colourless complex is not too stable. Thus, when hydrogen sulphide gas is passed, cadmium sulphide is precipitated.

$$[Cd(CN)_4]^{2-} + H_2S \longrightarrow CdS + 2H^+ + 4CN^-$$

The marked difference in the stabilities of the copper and cadmium tetracyanato complexes serves as the basis for the separation of Cu^{2+} and Cd^{2+} ions.

(iii) **Potassium Iodide** With KI solution, no precipitate is formed (distinction from copper).

Analysis of Group III (Fe^{3+}, Al^{3+}, Cr^{3+})

1. Test for Iron (III)

(i) **Ammonium Sulphide Solution** With ammonium sulphide solution, Fe^{3+} gives a black precipitate of iron(II) sulphide and sulphur.

$$2Fe^{3+} + 3S^{2-} \longrightarrow \underset{\text{Black ppt.}}{2FeS\downarrow} + S\downarrow$$

In hydrochloric acid, the black iron(II) sulphide precipitate dissolves and a white colour precipitate of sulphur precipitate becomes visible.

$$FeS\downarrow + 2H^+ \longrightarrow \underset{\text{White ppt.}}{S\downarrow} + Fe^{2+}$$

The damp iron(II) sulphide precipitate, when exposed to air, is slowly oxidised to brown iron(III) hydroxide.

$$4FeS\downarrow + 6H_2O + 3O_2 \longrightarrow 4Fe(OH)_3\downarrow + 4S\downarrow$$

From alkaline solutions of ammonium sulphide, black iron(III) sulphide is obtained.

$$2Fe^{3+} + 3S^{2-} \longrightarrow Fe_2S_3\downarrow$$

On acidification with hydrochloric acid, iron(III) ions are reduced to iron(II) ions and sulphur is formed.

$$Fe_2S_3\downarrow + 4H^+ \longrightarrow 2Fe^{2+} + 2H_2S\uparrow + S\downarrow$$

(ii) **Sodium Hydroxide Solution** With sodium hydroxide solution, a reddish-brown precipitate of iron(III) hydroxide, insoluble in excess of the reagent (distinc from aluminium and chromium) is obtained.

$$Fe^{3+} + 3OH^- \longrightarrow \underset{\text{Reddish-brown ppt.}}{Fe(OH)_3\downarrow}$$

(iii) **Potassium Hexacyanoferrate(II)** With potassium hexacyanoferrate(II) solution, Fe^{3+} gives intense blue precipitate of iron (III) hexacyanoferrate (Prussian blue).

$$4Fe^{3+} + 3[Fe(CN)_6]^{4-} \longrightarrow \underset{\text{Prussian blue}}{Fe_4[Fe(CN)_6]_3\downarrow}$$

The precipitate is insoluble in dilute acids but decomposes in concentrated hydrochloric acid. A large excess of the reagent dissolves it partly or entirely, when an intense blue solution is obtained. Sodium hydroxide turns the precipitate red as iron (III) oxide and hexacyanoferrate(II) ions are formed.

$$Fe_4[Fe(CN)_6]_3 + 12OH^- \longrightarrow \underset{\text{Reddish-brown ppt.}}{4Fe(OH)_3\downarrow} + 3[Fe(CN)_6]^{4-}$$

Oxalic acid also dissolves Prussian blue precipitate forming a blue solution. This process was once used to manufacture blue writing inks. If iron(III) chloride is added to an excess of potassium hexacyanoferrate(II), a product with the composition $KFe[Fe(CN)_6]$ is formed. This tends to form colloidal solutions (Soluble Prussian Blue) and cannot be filtered.

(iv) **Potassium Hexacyanoferrate(III)** With potassium hexacyanoferrate(III), a brown colouration is produced, due to the formation of an undissociated complex, iron(III) hexacyanoferrate(III).

$$Fe^{3+} + [Fe(CN)_6]^{3-} \longrightarrow \underset{\text{Brown colouration}}{Fe[Fe(CN)_6]}$$

$$\xrightarrow[\text{or } SnCl_2 \text{ solution}]{H_2O_2 \text{ solution}} \underset{\text{Prussian blue}}{Fe_4[Fe(CN)_6]_3}$$

Upon adding hydrogen peroxide or some tin(II) chloride solution, the hexacyanoferrate(III) part of the compound is reduced and Prussian blue coloured precipitate is obtained.

(v) **Disodium Hydrogen Phosphate Solution** With disodium hydrogen phosphate solution a yellowish-white precipitate of iron(III) phosphate is formed.

$$Fe^{3+} + HPO_4^{2-} \longrightarrow \underset{\text{Yellowish-white ppt.}}{FePO_4\downarrow} + H^+$$

This reaction is reversible, because a strong acid is formed which dissolves the precipitate. It is advisable to add small amounts of sodium acetate, which acts as a buffer.

(vi) **Sodium Acetate Solution** With sodium acetate solution, a reddish-brown colouration is obtained, attributed to the formation of a complex ion with the composition $[Fe_3(OH)_2(CH_3COO)_6]^+$. The reaction

$$[Fe_3(OH)_2(CH_3COO)_6]^+ + 4H_2O \longrightarrow$$

$$\underset{\text{Reddish-brown ppt.}}{3Fe(OH)_2CH_3COO\downarrow} + 3CH_3COOH + H^+$$

The excess of acetate ion acts as a buffer and the reaction goes to completion.

(vii) **Ammonium Thiocyanate Solution** With ammonium thiocyanate solution in slightly acidic medium, a deep-red colouration is produced (difference from iron(II) ions), due to the formation of a non-dissociated iron (III) thiocyanate complex.

$$Fe^{3+} + 3SCN^- \longrightarrow \underset{\text{Deep-red colouration}}{Fe(SCN)_3}$$

$$\xrightarrow[\text{or } HgCl_2]{NaF} \text{colour becomes faded}$$

This neutral molecule can be extracted by ether or amyl alcohol.

2. Test for Aluminium (III)

Halides, nitrates, sulphates of Al are water soluble and the aqueous solutions display acidic character owing to hydrolysis.

(i) **Sodium Hydroxide Solution** With sodium hydroxide solution, Al^{3+} gives a white precipitate of aluminum hydroxide.

$$Al^{3+} + 3OH^- \longrightarrow \underset{\text{White ppt.}}{Al(OH)_3\downarrow}$$

The precipitate dissolves in excess reagent, forming tetrahydroxoaluminate ions.

$$Al(OH)_3 + OH^- \rightleftharpoons \underset{\text{Soluble}}{[Al(OH)_4]^-}$$

The reaction is reversible and any reagent, which will reduce the hydroxyl ion concentration sufficiently should cause the reaction to proceed from right to left with the consequent precipitation of aluminium hydroxide. This may be effected with a solution of ammonium chloride (the hydroxyl ion concentration is reduced owing to the formation of the weak base ammonia, which can be readily removed as ammonia gas by heating) or by the addition of acid; in the latter case, a large excess of acid causes the precipitated hydroxide to redissolve.

$$[Al(OH)_4]^- + NH_4^+ \longrightarrow Al(OH)_3\downarrow + NH_3\uparrow + H_2O$$

$$[Al(OH)_4]^- + H^+ \rightleftharpoons Al(OH)_3\downarrow + H_2O$$

$$Al(OH)_3 + 3H^+ \rightleftharpoons Al^{3+} + 3H_2O$$

(ii) **Disodium Hydrogen Phosphate Solution** With disodium hydrogen phosphate solution, a white gelatinous precipitate of aluminium phosphate is obtained.

$$Al^{3+} + HPO_4^{2-} \rightleftharpoons \underset{\text{White ppt.}}{AlPO_4\downarrow} + H^+$$

The reaction is reversible; strong acids dissolve the precipitate. However, the precipitate is insoluble in acetic acid (different from phosphates of alkaline earth, which are soluble). The precipitate can also be dissolved in sodium hydroxide.

(iii) **Cobalt Nitrate Solution** Aluminium compounds, when heated with sodium carbonate upon charcoal gives a white infusible solid, which glows when hot. If the residue is moistened with a little cobalt nitrate solution and again heated, a blue infusible mass is obtained.

$$2Al_2O_3 + 2Co^{2+} + 4NO_3^- \longrightarrow 2CoAl_2O_4 + 4NO_2\uparrow + O_2\uparrow$$

Use of excess cobalt nitrate solution should be avoided since this will produce black cobalt oxide (Co_3O_4) upon ignition, which will mask the blue colour.

3. Test for Chromium (III)

(i) **Sodium Hydroxide Solution** With sodium hydroxide solution, a green precipitate of chromium(III) hydroxide is formed.

$$Cr^{3+} + 3OH^- \longrightarrow \underset{\text{Green ppt.}}{Cr(OH)_3\downarrow}$$

The reaction is reversible; on the addition of acids the precipitate dissolves. In excess reagent, the precipitate dissolves readily, tetrahydroxochromate(III) ions (or chromite ions) are formed.

$$Cr(OH)_3 + OH^- \longrightarrow \underset{\text{Soluble}}{[Cr(OH)_4]^-}$$

The solution is green. The reaction is reversible; on (slight) acidification and also on boiling with chromium(III) hydroxide precipitates again.

(ii) **Ammonia Solution** Bluish-green gelatinous precipitate of $Cr(OH)_3$ is obtained when treated with ammonia solution but dissolves in excess of ammonia due to the formation of a soluble complex.

$$CrCl_3 + 3NH_4OH \longrightarrow \underset{\text{Bluish-Green ppt.}}{Cr(OH)_3\downarrow} + 3NH_4Cl$$

$$Cr(OH)_3\downarrow + \underset{\text{Excess}}{6NH_3} \longrightarrow \underset{\text{Pink colouration}}{[Cr(NH_3)_6]^{3+}} + 3OH^-$$

(iii) **Chromium Pentoxide (Chromium Peroxide, Peroxochromic Acid) Test** On acidifying the solution with dilute sulphuric acid, adding few drops of ether or amyl alcohol to the mixture and finally adding some hydrogen peroxide, blue colouration is formed, which can be extracted into the organic phase by gently shaking. During the reaction, chromium pentoxide is formed.

$$CrO_4^{2-} + 2H^+ + 2H_2O_2 \longrightarrow \underset{\substack{\text{Blue colouration}\\ \text{in ethane layer}}}{CrO_5} + 3H_2O$$

Chromium pentoxide has the following

structure : 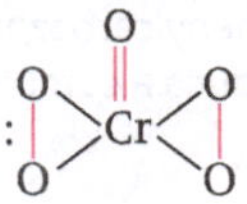

Because of the two peroxide groups, the compound is often called chromium peroxide. The name peroxochromic acid is less appropriate, because the compound does not contain hydrogen at all. In aqueous solution, the blue colour fades rapidly, because chromium pentoxide decomposes to chromium(III) and oxygen.

$$4CrO_5 + 12H^+ \longrightarrow 4Cr^{3+} + 7O_2\uparrow + 6H_2O$$

JEE MAPPER

Example Similar to PYQ Asked in JEE Advanced 2016

In the following reaction sequence the species X, Y and Z, respectively, are

$$Cr_2O_7^{2-} \xrightarrow[NH_4Cl]{H_2SO_4} X \xrightarrow[AgNO_3]{NaOH} \underset{\text{(red ppt)}}{Y} \xrightarrow[\text{dil. HCl}]{NH_3} \underset{\text{(white ppt)}}{Z}$$

(a) $CrCl_3, Ag_2O, AgCl$ (b) $CrO_2Cl_2, Cr_2O_7, Ag_2O$

(c) $Cr_2(SO_4)_3, NaNO_3, AgCl$ (d) $CrO_2Cl_2, Ag_2CrO_4, AgCl$

Sol. (*d*)

$$Cr_2O_7^{2-} + 6H^+ + NH_4Cl \xrightarrow[-3H_2O]{-4NH_4^+} \underset{(X)}{2CrO_2Cl_2}$$

$$\underset{(X)}{2CrO_2Cl_2} \xrightarrow[-2HCl,\ -2NaNO_3]{2NaOH,\ 2AgNO_3} \underset{\substack{\text{(Red ppt.)}\\(Y)}}{Ag_2CrO_4}$$

$$\underset{\substack{(Y)}}{Ag_2CrO_4} \xrightarrow[2HCl,\ -CrO_4^{2-}]{4NH_3} \underset{\substack{(Z)\\ \text{(White ppt.)}}}{2AgCl^-} + 2H^+$$

Competency Enhancer 2.1

In the following reaction sequence, the species X, Y, P and Z respectively are

$$K_3[Fe(CN)_3] + \text{excess (KI)} \xrightarrow{\text{dil. } H_2SO_4} X \xrightarrow{ZnSO_4} \underset{\text{(white ppt.)}}{Y} \xrightarrow{NaOH} P + \underset{\text{(Zinc complex)}}{Z}$$

(a) $K_2[Fe(CN)_6], K_2Zn_3[Fe(CN)_6]_2, NH_4NO_2, NaOH$

(b) $K_4[Fe(CN)_6], K_2Zn[Fe(CN)_6], [Zn(OH)_4]^{2-}(aq.)$, $[Fe(CN)_6]^{4-}(aq.)$

(c) $K_4[Fe(CN)_6], Zn_2[Fe(CN)_6], [Fe(CN)_3(OH)]^{4-}, NH_4NO_2$

(d) $K_2[Fe(CN)_6], K_2Zn_3[Fe(CN)_6]_2, Zn_2[Fe(CN)_6], [Zn(OH)_4]^{2-}$

JEE Spotlite

1,5-Diphenylcarbazide Test In dilute mineral acid solution, diphenylcarbazide produces a soluble violet colour, which is a characteristic test for chromium. During the reaction, chromate is reduced to chromium(III) and diphenylcarbazone is formed. These reaction products in turn produce a complex with the characteristic colour.

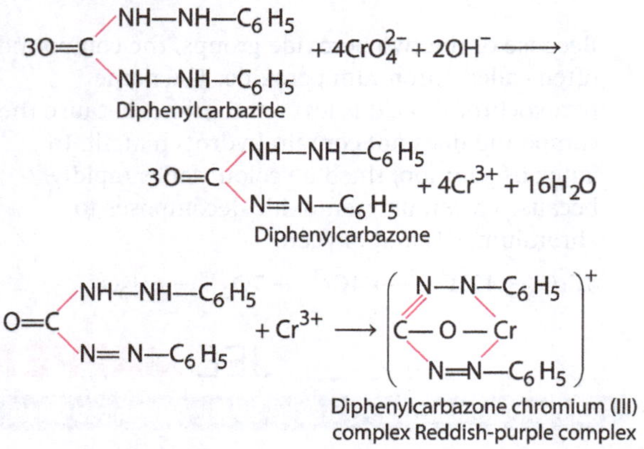

Analysis of Group IV

(Zn^{2+}, Mn^{2+}, Co^{2+}, Ni^{2+})

1. Test for Zinc (II)

(i) **Sodium Hydroxide Solution** With sodium hydroxide solution, a white gelatinous precipitate of zinc hydroxide is formed.

$$Zn^{2+} + 2OH^- \longrightarrow \underset{\text{White gelatinous ppt.}}{Zn(OH)_2\downarrow}$$

The precipitate is soluble in acids.

$$Zn(OH)_2\downarrow + 2H^+ \longrightarrow Zn^{2+} + 2H_2O$$

and also in the excess of the reagent

$$Zn(OH)_2\downarrow + 2OH^- \longrightarrow [Zn(OH)_4]^{2-}$$

Zinc hydroxide is thus an amphoteric compound.

(ii) **Ammonia Solution** With ammonia solution, Zn^{2+} forms a white gelatinous precipitate of $Zn(OH)_2$, which is readily soluble in excess reagent.

$$Zn^{2+} + 2NH_3 + 2H_2O \longrightarrow \underset{\text{White gelatinous ppt.}}{Zn(OH)_2\downarrow} + 2NH_4^+$$

$$Zn(OH)_2\downarrow + 4NH_3 \longrightarrow [Zn(NH_3)_4]^{2+} + 2OH^-$$

(iii) **Disodium Hydrogen Phosphate Solution** With disodium hydrogen phosphate solution, a white precipitate of zinc phosphate is formed.

$$3Zn^{2+} + 2HPO_4^{2-} \rightleftharpoons \underset{\text{White ppt.}}{Zn_3(PO_4)_2\downarrow} + 2H^+$$

In the presence of ammonia ions, zinc ammonium phosphate is formed.

$$Zn^{2+} + NH_4^+ + HPO_4^{2-} \rightleftharpoons Zn(NH_4)PO_4\downarrow + H^+$$

Both precipitates are soluble in dilute acids, when the reactions are reversed. Also, both precipitates are soluble in ammonia.

$$Zn_3(PO_4)_2 + 12NH_3 \longrightarrow 3[Zn(NH_3)_4]^{2+} + 2PO_4^{3-}$$

$$Zn(NH_4)PO_4 + 3NH_3 \longrightarrow [Zn(NH_3)_4]^{2+} + HPO_4^{2-}$$

(iv) **Potassium Hexacyanoferrate(II)** With potassium hexacyanoferrate(II) solution, a white precipitate of variable composition is obtained. If the reagent is added in some excess, the composition of the precipitate is $K_2Zn_3[Fe(CN)_6]_2$.

$$3Zn^{2+} + 2K^+ + 2[Fe(CN)_6]^{4-} \longrightarrow \underset{\text{White ppt.}}{K_2Zn_3[Fe(CN)_6]_2\downarrow}$$

The precipitate is insoluble in dilute acids but dissolves readily in sodium hydroxide.

$$K_2Zn_3[Fe(CN)_6]_2 + 12OH^- \longrightarrow 2[Fe(CN)_6]^{4-} + 3[Zn(OH)_4]^{2-} + 2K^+$$

This reaction can be used to distinguish zinc from aluminium.

(v) **Ammonium tetrathiocyanatomercurate(II)** Copper salts alone do not form a precipitate with the ammonium tetrathiocyanatomercurate(II) reagent while zinc ions, if present alone form a white precipitate.

$$Zn^{2+} + [Hg(SCN)_4]^{2-} \longrightarrow \underset{\text{White ppt.}}{Zn[Hg(SCN)_4]\downarrow}$$

In the presence of copper ions, the copper complex coprecipitates with that of zinc and the violet (or blackish-purple) precipitate consisting of mixed crystals of $Zn[Hg(SCN)_4] + Cu[Hg(SCN)_4]$ is obtained.

(vi) **Diphenylthiocarbazone (dithizone) test** Dithizone forms complexes with a number of metal ions, which can be extracted with chloroform. The zinc complex, formed in neutral, alkaline or acetic acid solutions, is red in colour.

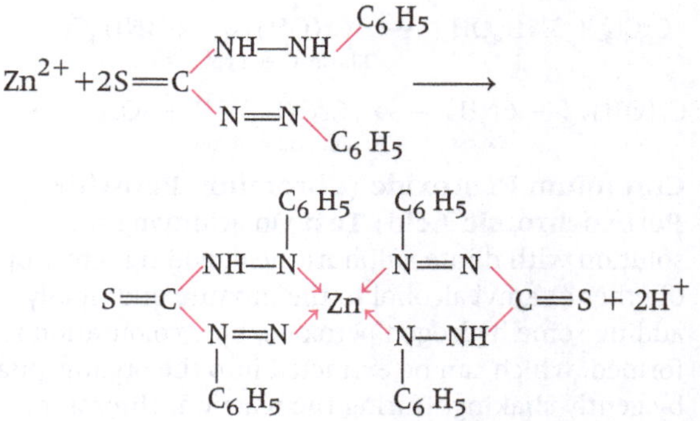

Red ppt

2. Test for Manganese (II)

(i) **Sodium Hydroxide Solution** With sodium hydroxide solution, an initially white precipitate of manganese(II) hydroxide is obtained.

$$Mn^{2+} + 2OH^- \longrightarrow \underset{\text{White ppt.}}{Mn(OH)_3 \downarrow}$$

The precipitate is insoluble in excess reagent. It rapidly oxidises on exposure to air, becoming brown, and hydrated manganese dioxide, $MnO(OH)_2$, is formed.

$$2Mn(OH)_2 \downarrow + O_2 \longrightarrow \underset{\text{Brown ppt.}}{2MnO(OH)_2 \downarrow}$$

(ii) **Ammonia Solution** With NH_3 solution, Mn^{2+} gives a white precipitate of manganese(II) hydroxide.

$$Mn^{2+} + 2NH_3 + 2H_2O \rightleftharpoons \underset{\text{Pinkish White ppt.}}{Mn(OH)_2 \downarrow} + 2NH_4^+$$

The precipitate is soluble in ammonium salts, when the reaction proceeds towards the left.

(iii) **Disodium Hydrogen Phosphate Solution** With disodium hydrogen phosphate solution, a pink precipitate of manganese ammonium phosphate $Mn(NH_4)PO_4 \cdot 7H_2O$, in the presence of ammonia (or ammonium ions) is obtained.

$$Mn^{2+} + NH_3 + HPO_4^{2-} \longrightarrow \underset{\text{Pink ppt.}}{Mn(NH)_4PO_4 \downarrow}$$

If ammonium salts are absent, pink precipitate of manganese(II) phosphate is formed.

$$3Mn^{2+} + 2HPO_4^{2-} \longrightarrow \underset{\text{Pink ppt.}}{Mn_3(PO_4)_2 \downarrow} + 2H^+$$

Both precipitates are soluble in acids.

(iv) **Lead dioxide and Concentrated Nitric Acid** On boiling a dilute solution of manganese(II) ions with lead dioxide and a little concentrated nitric acid and allowing the suspended solid containing unattacked lead dioxide to settle, the supernatant liquid acquires a violet-red (or purple) colour due to permanganate acid.

$$5PbO_2 + 2Mn^{2+} + 4H^+ \longrightarrow \underset{\text{Purple colour}}{2MnO_4^-} + 5Pb^{2+} + 2H_2O$$

(v) **Sodium Bismuthate ($NaBiO_3$) Solution** When sodium bismuthate ($NaBiO_3$)) is added to a cold solution of manganese(II) ions in dilute nitric acid or in dilute sulphuric acid, the mixture stirred and excess reagent filtered off, a violet red (or purple) solution of permanganate is produced.

$$2Mn^{2+} + 5NaBiO_3 + 14H^+ \longrightarrow \underset{\text{Purple colour}}{2MnO_4^-} + 5Bi^{3+} + 5Na^+ + 7H_2O$$

3. Test for Nickel (II)

The black precipitate of NiS(II) is insoluble in cold dilute HCl and in acetic acid but dissolves in hot concentrated nitric acid and in *aqua-regia* with the separation of sulphur.

$$NiS\downarrow + 2HNO_3 + 6H^+ \longrightarrow 3Ni^{2+} + 3S\downarrow + 2NO\uparrow + 4H_2O$$

$$NiS\downarrow + HNO_3 + 3HCl \longrightarrow Ni^{2+} + S\downarrow + NOCl\uparrow + 2Cl^- + 2H_2O$$

(i) **Sodium Hydroxide Solution** With Ni^{2+}, NaOH gives a green precipitate of $Ni(OH)_2$.

$$Ni^{2+} + 2OH^- \longrightarrow \underset{\text{Green ppt.}}{Ni(OH)_2 \downarrow}$$

The precipitate is insoluble in excess reagent. The precipitate dissolves in ammonia and excess alkali hydroxide.

$$Ni(OH)_2 \downarrow + 6NH_3 \longrightarrow \underset{\text{Deep-blue colouration}}{[Ni(NH_3)_6]^{2+}} + 2OH^-$$

$$Ni(OH)_2 \downarrow + 6NH_4^+ + 4OH^- \longrightarrow \underset{\text{Deep-blue colouration}}{[Ni(NH_3)_6]^{2+}} + 6H_2O$$

(ii) **Ammonia Solution** With ammonia solution, Ni^{2+} gives a green precipitate of nickel(II) hydroxide.

$$Ni^{2+} + 2NH_3 + 2H_2O \longrightarrow \underset{\text{Green ppt.}}{Ni(OH)_2 \downarrow} + 2NH_4^+$$

The precipitate dissolves in excess reagent and the solution turns deep blue.

$$Ni(OH)_2 \downarrow + 6NH_3 \longrightarrow \underset{\text{Deep-blue colouration}}{[Ni(NH_3)_6]^{2+}} + 2OH^-$$

If ammonium salts are present, no precipitation occurs, but the complex is formed immediately.

(iii) **Potassium Nitrite Solution** No precipitate is produced in the presence of acetic acid (difference from cobalt)

(iv) **Dimethylglyoxime Reagent ($C_4H_8O_2N_2$)** Ni^{2+} in presence of ammonia gives a rosy red precipitate of *bis*(dimethylglyoximato) nickel(II).

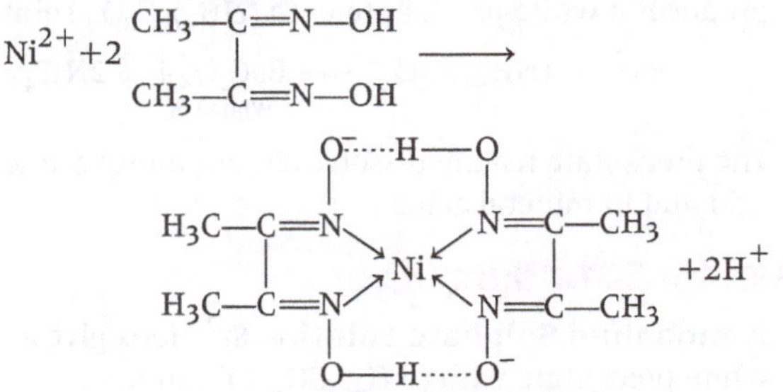

Bis (dimethylglyoximato) nickel (II)
Rosy red ppt.

Iron(II) (red colouration), bismuth (yellow precipitate) and larger amounts of cobalt (brown colouration) interfere in ammoniacal solution.

(v) **KHCO$_3$, NaOH and Br$_2$ Water** On addition of $KHCO_3$, NaOH and Br_2 water to solution of Ni^{2+}, a black precipitate of Ni_2O_3 is formed.

$$NiCl_2 + 2KHCO_3 \longrightarrow NiCO_3 + 2KCl + H_2O + CO_2\uparrow$$

$$2NiCO_3 + 4NaOH + [O] \longrightarrow \underset{\text{Black ppt.}}{Ni_2O_3\downarrow} + 2Na_2CO_3 + 2H_2O$$

Analysis of Group V
(Ba^{2+}, Sr^{2+}, Ca^{2+})

1. Test for Barium (II)

(i) **Potassium Chromate Solution** Ba^{2+} ion in solution produces a yellow precipitate with K_2CrO_4 solution.

$$Ba^{2+} + K_2CrO_4 \longrightarrow \underset{\text{Yellow ppt.}}{BaCrO_4\downarrow} + 2K^+$$

The precipitate is insoluble in dilute acetic acid but readily soluble in mineral acids. Addition of acid to K_2CrO_4 solution causes the yellow colour of the solution which changes to reddish-orange due to formation of $Cr_2O_7^{2-}$.

$$\underset{\text{Yellow}}{2CrO_4^{2-}} + 2H^+ \rightleftharpoons \underset{\text{Orange}}{Cr_2O_7^{2-}} + H_2O$$

(ii) **Ammonium Sulphate Solution** Ba^{2+} ions in solution produces a white precipitate with $(NH_4)_2SO_4$ solution.

$$Ba^{2+} + (NH_4)_2SO_4 \longrightarrow \underset{\text{White ppt.}}{BaSO_4\downarrow} + 2NH_4^+$$

The precipitate is insoluble in dilute acids and in ammonium sulphate solution but appreciably soluble in boiling concentrated H_2SO_4.

$$BaSO_4 + H_2SO_4(\text{conc.}) \longrightarrow Ba^{2+} + 2HSO_4^-$$

(iii) **Ammonium Oxalate Solution** Ba^{2+} ions in solution produces a white precipitate with $(NH_4)_2C_2O_4$ solution.

$$Ba^{2+} + (NH_4)_2C_2O_4 \longrightarrow \underset{\text{White ppt.}}{BaC_2O_4\downarrow} + 2NH_4^+$$

The precipitate readily dissolves in hot dilute acetic acid and in mineral acids.

2. Test for Strontium (II)

(i) **Ammonium Sulphate Solution** Sr^{2+} ions give a white precipitate with $(NH_4)_2SO_4$ solution.

$$Sr^{2+} + (NH_4)_2SO_4 \longrightarrow \underset{\text{White ppt.}}{SrSO_4\downarrow} + 2NH_4^+$$

The precipitate is slightly soluble in boiling hydrochloric acid.

(ii) **Ammonium Oxalate Solution** Sr^{2+} ions give a white precipitate with $(NH_4)_2C_2O_4$ solution.

$$Sr^{2+} + (NH_4)_2C_2O_4 \longrightarrow \underset{\text{White ppt.}}{SrC_2O_4\downarrow} + 2NH_4^+$$

The precipitate is insoluble in acetic acid but soluble in mineral acids.

JEE MAPPER

Example Similar to PYQ Asked in JEE Advanced 2015

The pair(s) of ions where both the ions mixed with sodium hydroxide solutions give white precipitate is/are

(a) Zn^{2+}, Mn^{2+} (b) Ba^{2+}, Zn^{2+}

(c) Ni^{2+}, Co^{2+} (d) Hg^{2+}, Bi^{3+}

Sol. (*a, b, d*) Among the given pair(s) of ions only Zn^{2+}, Mn^{2+}, Ba^{2+}, Zn^{2+}, Hg^{2+} and Bi^{3+} when mixed with sodium hydroxide gives white precipitate.

$$Zn^{2+} + 2OH^- \longrightarrow \underset{\text{(White gelatinous ppt,)}}{Zn(OH)_2\downarrow}$$

$$Mn^{2+} + 2OH^- \longrightarrow \underset{\text{(White ppt,)}}{Mn(OH)_2\downarrow}$$

$$Ni^{2+} + 2OH^- \longrightarrow \underset{\text{Green ppt,}}{Ni(OH)_2\downarrow}$$

$$Co^{2+} + 2OH^- \longrightarrow \underset{\text{(Blue ppt,)}}{Co(OH)_2\downarrow}$$

$$Ba^{2+} + 2OH^- \longrightarrow \underset{\text{(White ppt,)}}{Ba(OH)_2\downarrow}$$

$$Hg^{2+} + 2OH^- \longrightarrow \underset{\text{(White ppt,)}}{Hg(OH)_2\downarrow}$$

$$Bi^{3+} + 3OH^- \longrightarrow \underset{\text{(White ppt,)}}{Bi(OH)_3}$$

Competency Enhancer 2.2

The pair(s) of ions where both the ions reacts with ammonia solution to give white precipitate.

(a) Pb^{2+}, Cd^{2+} (b) Ag^+, Hg^+

(c) Cu^{2+}, Cr^{3+} (d) Zn^{2+}, Mg^{2+}

3. Test for Calcium (II)

(i) **Ammonium Oxalate Solution** Ca^{2+} ions give a white precipitate with concentrated $(NH_4)_2C_2O_4$ solution immediately.

$$Ca^{2+} + (NH_4)_2C_2O_4 \longrightarrow \underset{\text{White ppt.}}{CaC_2O_4\downarrow} + 2NH_4^+$$

The precipitate is insoluble in acetic acid but soluble in mineral acids.

(ii) **Potassium Hexacyanoferrate(II) Solution** With potassium hexacyanoferrate(II) solution, Ca^{2+} ions give a white precipitate of a mixed salt.

$$Ca^{2+} + K_2[Fe(CN)_6] \longrightarrow K_2Ca[Fe(CN)_6]\downarrow + 2K^+$$

The test can be used to distinguish calcium ion from strontium and barium ions.

Analysis of Group VI (Na^+, K^+, Mg^{2+})

1. Test for Magnesium (II)

(i) **Ammonia Solution** Mg^{2+} gives white gelationous precipitate of magnesium hydroxide on reaction with ammonium hydroxide.

$$Mg^{2+} + 2NH_4OH \longrightarrow \underset{\text{White ppt.}}{Mg(OH)_2 \downarrow} + 2NH_4^+$$

The precipitate obtained is sparingly soluble in water but readily soluble in ammonium salts.

(ii) **Ammonium Carbonate Solution** Mg^{2+} reacts with ammonium carbonate solution in the absence of NH_4^+ salts to give a white precipitate of basic magnesium carbonate.

$$5Mg^{2+} + 6CO_3^{2-} + 7H_2O \longrightarrow \underset{\text{White ppt.}}{4MgCO_3 \cdot Mg(OH)_2 \cdot 5H_2O \downarrow} + 2HCO_3^-$$

In the presence of NH_4^+ salts no precipitation occurs, because the equilibrium

$$NH_4^+ + CO_3^{2-} \rightleftharpoons NH_3 + HCOO_3^-$$

is shifted towards the formation of HCO_3^- ions.

(iii) **Disodium hydrogen phosphate Solution** With disodium hydrogen phosphate solution, Mg^{2+} gives a white crystalline precipitate of magnesium ammonium phosphate in the absence of NH_4Cl and ammonia solution.

$$Mn^{2+} + NH_3 + HPO_4^{2-} \longrightarrow \underset{\text{White ppt.}}{Mg(NH_4)PO_4 \downarrow}$$

A white flocculent precipitate of magnesium hydrogen phosphate ($MgHPO_4$) is obtained in neutral solutions.

$$Mg^{2+} + HPO_4^{2-} \longrightarrow \underset{\text{White ppt.}}{MgHPO_4 \downarrow}$$

Elemental Practice 10.2

Type I MCQs with Only One Correct Option

1. Select the correct statement from the following?
(a) Fe^{2+} gives brown colour with ammonium thiocyanate.
(b) Fe^{2+} gives blue precipitate with potassium ferricyanide.
(c) Fe^{3+} gives brown colour with potassium ferricyanide.
(d) Fe^{3+} gives red colour with potassium ferrocyanide.

2. An aqueous solution of colourless metal sulphate *M* gives a white precipitate with NH_4OH. This was soluble in excess of NH_4OH. On passing H_2S through this solution a white ppt. is formed. The metal *M* in the salt is
(a) Ca (b) Ba
(c) Al (d) Zn

3. A laboratory reagent imparts green colour to the flame. On heating with solid $K_2Cr_2O_7$ and conc. H_2SO_4, it evolves a orange red gas. Identify the reagent.
(a) $CaCl_2$ (b) $BaCl_2$
(c) $CuCl_2$ (d) NaCl

4. The reagent that can be used to identify nickel ion is
(a) Resorcinol (b) Dimethyl glyoxime
(c) Diphenyl benzidine (d) Potassium ferrocyanide

5. Which of the following reagents can be used to distinguish between sodium carbonate and sodium sulphite?
(a) Lime water (b) Baryta water
(c) Acidified $K_2Cr_2O_7$ solution (d) H_2SO_4 solution

6. In Nessler's reagent for the detection of ammonia the active species is
(a) Hg_2Cl_2 (b) Mg^{2+}
(c) Hg_2I_2 (d) HgI_4^{2-}

7. Select the reaction that occurs in the confirmatory test for NH_4^+.
(a) $NH_4^+ + OH^- \longrightarrow NH_3 + H_2O$
(b) $NH_4^+ + Cl^- \longrightarrow NH_4Cl$
(c) $NH_4^+ + H_2O \longrightarrow NH_3 + HO^-$
(d) $NH_4^+ + H_2SO_4 \longrightarrow NH_4^+HSO_4^-$

8. The correct reason for using $(NH_4)_2CO_3$ in group analysis is
(a) It selectively precipitates alkali metals.
(b) It prevents precipitation of alkali earth metals.
(c) It precpitates carbonates of alkali metals in a basic medium.
(d) It precipitates hydroxides of transition metals.

9. $K_4[Fe(CN)_6]$ cannot be used to test
(a) Fe^{3+} (b) Zn^{2+}
(c) Cd^{2+} (d) Cr^{3+}

10. For the given aqueous reaction which of the following statement(s) is false?

$$KI + K_3[Fe(CN)_6] \xrightarrow{\text{Dil. } H_2SO_4} \text{brownish yellow solution.}$$
$$\downarrow ZnSO_4$$
$$\text{Colourless solution} \longleftarrow \text{(White ppt. + brownish yellow filtrate)}$$

(a) The first reaction is redox reaction
(b) White ppt. is $Zn_3[Fe(CN)_6]_2$
(c) Addition of filtrate to starch solution gives blue colour
(d) White ppt. is soluble in NaOH solution

11. In qualitative analysis, when H_2S is passed through an aqueous solution of salt acidified with dilute HCl, a black ppt. is obtained. On boiling the precipitate with dil. HNO_3, it forms a solution of blue colour. Addition of excess of aqueous solution of NH_3 to this solution gives
(a) deep blue ppt. of $Cu(OH)_2$
(b) deep blue solution of $[Cu(NH_3)_4]^{2+}$
(c) deep blue solution of $Cu(NO_3)_2$
(d) deep blue solution of $Cu(OH)_2 \cdot Cu(NO_3)_2$

12. If Fe^{3+} and Cr^{3+} both are present in group III of qualitative analysis, then distinction can be made by
(a) addition of NH_4OH in the presence of NH_4Cl when only $Fe(OH)_3$ is precipitated
(b) addition of NH_4OH in the presence of NH_4Cl when $Cr(OH)_3$ and $Fe(OH)_3$ both are precipitated and on adding Br_2 water and NaOH, $Cr(OH)_3$ dissolves
(c) precipitate of $Cr(OH)_3$ and $Fe(OH)_3$ as obtained in (b) are treated with conc. HCl when only $Fe(OH)_3$ dissolves
(d) Addition of NH_4OH in the presence of NaCl when only $Fe(OH)_3$ is precipitated.

13. $CuSO_4$ decolourises on addition of KCN, the product is
(a) $[Cu(CN)_4]^{2-}$ (b) $[Cu(CN)_4]^{3-}$
(c) $Cu(CN)_2$ (d) CuCN

14. $Fe(OH)_3$ can be separated from $Al(OH)_3$ by addition of
(a) $BaCl_2$
(b) Dil. HCl
(c) NaOH solution
(d) NH_4Cl and NH_4OH

15. An aqueous solution of a substance, on treatment with dilute HCl, gives a white precipitate soluble in hot water. When H_2S is passed through the hot acidic solution, a black precipitate is formed. The substance is
(a) Hg_2^{2+} salt (b) Cu^{2+} salt
(c) Ag^+ salt (d) Pb^{2+} salt

16. Which of the following pairs of cations can be separated by adding NH_4Cl and NH_4OH to the mixture and then passing H_2S through it?
(a) Fe^{3+}, Al^{3+} (b) Cr^{3+}, Ni^{2+}
(c) Al^{3+}, Cr^{3+} (d) Fe^{3+}, Cr^{3+}

17. In the precipitation of the radicals of iron group in qualitative analysis, NH_4Cl is added before adding NH_4OH. This causes
(a) decrease in the concentration of OH^- ions
(b) removal of PO_4^{3-} ions
(c) increase in the concentration of Cl^- ions
(d) increase in the concentration of NH_4^+ ions

18. The aqueous solution of which of the following reagent will give Prussian blue coloured ppt. with an aqueous solution containing iron (III) ions?
(a) Potassium thiocyanate
(b) Potassium hexacyanoferrate (II)
(c) Potassium pyroantimonate
(d) Potassium tetracyanoferrate (III)

19. Aqueous solution of salt *A* gives yellow precipitate with aqueous solution of K_2CrO_4, which of the following series of cation may be present in *A*?
(a) Pb^{2+}, Ag^+ (b) Pb^{2+}, Ba^{2+}
(c) Ag^+, Cu^{2+} (d) Hg^{2+}, Ag^+

Type II 》 MCQ with One or More than One Correct Option

20. Select the correct statements with respect to bromide ions?
(a) KBr on heating with MnO_2 and concentrated H_2SO_4 liberates Br_2 and SO_2 gases.
(b) KBr on heating with concentrated H_2SO_4 liberates Br_2 and SO_2 gases.
(c) KBr forms HBr with concentrated H_3PO_4.
(d) KBr(s) liberates Br_2 on gentile warming with concentrated H_2SO_4 and $K_2Cr_2O_7(s)$.

21. Choose the correct statement from the following.
(a) Nickel salts give rosy red precipitate with dimethyl glyoxime in excess of NH_4OH
(b) Fe(III) salts give red colour with potassium sulphocyanide.
(c) In nitroprusside, the iron and NO exist as Fe(III) and NO.
(d) Mn(II) salts give white precipitate with NaOH which turns brown on adding Br_2 water.

22. Select the correct statements from the following.
(a) Ag^+ gives brown precipitate of silver oxide with NH_3 solution.
(b) Ag^+ gives yellow precipitate of silver iodide on reaction with KI solution.
(c) With NaOH, Hg_2^+ forms a black precipitate of mercury (I) oxide.
(d) Hg_2^{2+} given a red precipitate of mercury (I) iodide on reaction with KI solution.

23. Select the sulphates which are soluble in water.
(a) $CuSO_4$ (b) $PbSO_4$
(c) Ag_2SO_4 (d) $BaSO_4$

24. Which of the following substances on being heated will give a gas that turns lime water milky?
(a) Na_2CO_3
(b) $ZnCO_3$
(c) $ZnSO_3$
(d) $MgCO_3$

25. A yellow precipitate is obtained when
(a) lead acetate solution is treated with K_2CrO_4
(b) $Pb(NO_3)_2$ solution is treated with K_2CrO_4
(c) $AgNO_3$ solution treated with KI
(d) H_2S is passed through a solution of $CdSO_4$

26. Select the species that will be decomposed on acidification
(a) $[Ag(NH_3)_2]^+$ (b) $[Cu(NH_3)_4]^{2+}$
(c) $[Zn(OH)_4]^{2-}$ (d) $[Pb(OH)_4]^{2-}$

Type III 》 Numerical/Integer Answer Type Questions

27. How many of the following reactions gives yellow ppt?
(a) $NaBr + AgNO_3 \longrightarrow$
(b) $NaI + AgNO_3 \longrightarrow$
(c) $NaBr + Pb(NO_3)_2 \longrightarrow$
(d) $NaI + Pb(NO_3)_2 \longrightarrow$
(e) $Na_2S + Cd(CH_3COO)_2 \longrightarrow$
(f) $K_2CrO_4 + Pb(CH_3COO)_2 \longrightarrow$
(g) $K_2CrO_4 + (CH_3COO)_2Ba \longrightarrow$
(h) $K_2CrO_4 + AgNO_3 \longrightarrow$
(i) $NaBr + Cl_2$ water (excess) $\longrightarrow$

28. An aqueous solution contains Hg_2^{2+}, Hg^{2+}, Pb^{2+}, Ag^+, Ba^{2+} and Cd^{2+}. The number of ions that will produce white precipitate with dilute HCl are

29. Aq. $CuSO_4$ decolourises on addition of KCN due to formation of complex (A). In complex "A".
(i) Number of d-orbital in hybridisation is/are "a"
(ii) Geometry of complex (b)
(iii) Coordination number of Cu is "c", then find $8a + 7b + 5c$.

30. The number of pairs of ions that can be separated by H_2S in dilute HCl is
(a) Bi^{3+} and Sn^{4+}
(b) Al^{3+} and Hg^{2+}
(c) Cd^{2+} and Zn^{2+}
(d) Fe^{3+} and Cu^{2+}
(e) As^{3+} and Sb^{3+}

31. $\underset{\text{Black}}{X(s)} \xrightarrow{\text{dil. HCl}} Y\uparrow \xrightarrow[\text{NaOH}]{Na_2[Fe(CN)_5(NO)]}$ Purple solution

Gas Y has been allowed to react with following species in neutral/acidic medium :
(a) $FeCl_3$
(b) $CuSO_4$
(c) $BaCl_2$
(d) SO_2
(e) $Cr_2O_7^{2-}$
(f) CH_3COONa
(g) Hg^{2+}

Then calculate value of $(P + Q - R)$

P : Number of species which undergoes redox reaction with gas Y.

Q : Number of species with which gas Y undergoes precipitation.

R : Number of species with which gas Y produce no observable change.

Elemental Practice 10.2 | Chapter 10 — Connect with Answers

1. (b)	2. (d)	3. (b)	4. (b)	5. (c)	6. (d)
7. (a)	8. (d)	9. (d)	10. (b)	11. (b)	12. (b)
13. (d)	14. (c)	15. (d)	16. (b)	17. (a)	18. (b)
19. (b)	20. (b,c,d)	21. (a,b,d)	22. (a,b,c)	23. (a,c)	24. (b,c,d)
25. (a,b,c,d)	26. (a,b,c,d)	27. (7)	28. (3)	29. (34)	30. (3)
31. (3)					

Advanced Exclusive Different Strokes

Tips to solve problems related to identify mixtures containing multiple components of salts

In the systematic analysis of salts, complex mixtures of multiple ions often leads to overlapping reaction, making it difficult to identify individual ions. This challenge is addressed through selective precipitation technique.

It is a technique used to isolate a specific ion from a mixture by adding reagents that react with only one ion, forming a precipitate while leaving other in solution.

Let us understand this with the help of an example.

- Barium sulphate ($BaSO_4$) forms a precipitate when barium ions (Ba^{2+}) react with sulphate ions (SO_4^{2-}) but does not react with other common cations like Sodium (Na^+).
- Silver chloride (AgCl) precipitates when silver ions (Ag^+) react with chloride ions (Cl^-), but it won't precipitate with other anions like sulphate (SO_4^{2-}).
- Additionally, **masking agent** are used to block the reactivity of certain ions, allowing for the identification of others. For e.g. in the presence of excess chloride ions, silver ions (Ag^+) can be masked by adding a complexing agent like ammonia (NH_3), preventing the formation of AgCl, which would otherwise interfere with the analysis of other ion in the sample.

Thus, the above key points helps to identify mixtures with multiple components of salts. That are usually asked in JEE Main and Advanced Exams.

PRACTICE
ELEMENT 01

Target JEE Main

Objective Type Questions

1. During qualitative test of nitrate radical, a brown ring is formed. The ring formed is due to the formation of
(a) $FeSO_4NO$ (b) $(FeSO_4)_2NO$
(c) $FeSO_4(NO)_2$ (d) $[Fe(H_2O)_5NO]SO_4$

2. Acidified $K_2Cr_2O_7$ changes to green on reaction with
(a) SO_2 (b) $FeSO_4$
(c) KI and then adding hypo (d) All of these

3. An inorganic compound gives a white ppt. with a solution of $AgNO_3$, a white ppt. with dil. H_2SO_4 and impart green colour to flame. The probable compound is
(a) $CuCl_2$ (b) $BaCl_2$
(c) $Cu(NO_3)_2$ (d) $PbCl_2$

4. Excess of NaOH added will separate
(a) $Al(OH)_3$, $Zn(OH)_2$ (b) $AlCl_3$, $ZnCl_2$
(c) $Fe(OH)_3$, $Mg(OH)_2$ (d) $Fe(OH)_3$, $Al(OH)_3$

5. An inorganic salt in its aq. solution produced a white ppt. with NaOH which dissolves in excess of NaOH, Also its aq. solution produced light yellow ppt. with $AgNO_3$, sparingly soluble in NH_4OH. The probable salt is
(a) $AlBr_3$ (b) AlI_3 (c) $AlCl_3$ (d) $ZnCl_2$

6. A compound produced blue mass in cobalt nitrate test and formed a brown ring with $FeSO_4$ and conc. H_2SO_4, The probable compound is
(a) $Al(NO_3)_3$ (b) $Zn(NO_3)_2$
(c) $Cu(NO_3)_2$ (d) $MgCl_2$

7. CrO_4^{2-} (yellow) changes to $Cr_2O_7^{2-}$ (orange) at pH = x and *vice versa* at pH = y. x and y can be
(a) 6,5 (b) 6,8 (c) 8,9 (d) 7,7

8. $A \longrightarrow B_2O_3 + H_2O$
$CaF_2 + H_2SO_4 \longrightarrow B + C$
$B_2O_3 + C \longrightarrow D + H_2O$
The compound D that burns with green flame is
(a) HF (b) BF_3
(c) H_3BO_3 (d) Na_2BO_3

9. Sometimes yellow turbidity appears on passing H_2S gas even in absence of second group basic radicals. This happens because
(a) sulphur is present in the mixture
(b) fourth group radicals are precipitated
(c) H_2S is oxidised by some acid radicals
(d) third group radicals are precipitated

10. The sulphide not soluble in hot dilute nitric acid is
(a) CuS (b) ZnS
(c) CdS (d) HgS

11. A yellow fuming liquid (A) undergoes partial decomposition to produce Cl_2 gas and another product whose acidic solution produced an orange ppt. with H_2S. The liq. (A) is
(a) $SbCl_3$ (b) $SbCl_5$
(c) $AsCl_3$ (d) $AsCl_5$

12. Which of the following give(s) canary yellow ppt. with ammonium molybdate?
(a) PO_4^{3-} (b) As^{3+}
(c) Both (a) and (b) (d) Cu^{2+}

13. H_2S will precipitate the sulphides of all the metals from the solution of chlorides of Cu, Zn and Cd if
(a) the solution is aqueous
(b) the solution is acidic
(c) the solution is dilute acidic
(d) the solution is basic

14. In third group of qualitative analysis, the precipitate employed is a mixture of NH_4Cl and NH_4OH. If NH_4Cl is not available in the laboratory and the mixture does not contain Mn^{2+}, we can use
(a) $(NH_4)_2SO_4$ (b) $(NH_4)_2CO_3$
(c) NH_4NO_3 (d) $(NH_4)_2C_2O_4$

15. Which of the following pairs of ions cannot be separated by H_2S in dil. HCl?
(a) Bi^{3+}, Sn^{4+}
(b) Al^{3+}, Hg^{2+}
(c) Zn^{2+}, Cu^{2+}
(d) Ni^{2+}, Cu^{2+}

16. Na_2CO_3 cannot be used in place of $(NH_4)_2CO_3$ for the precipitation of fifth group radicals, since:
(a) magnesium will be precipitated
(b) concentration of carbonate ions is very low
(c) sodium ions will react with acidic radicals
(d) Na^+ ions interfere with the detection of fifth group

17. To a solution of a substance, gradual addition of ammonium hydroxide results in a black precipitate which does not dissolve in excess of NH_4OH. However, when HCl is added to the original solution, a white precipitate is formed. The solution contained.
(a) Lead salt (b) Silver salt
(c) Mercurous salt (d) Copper salt

18. A solution of $(NH_4)_2C_2O_4$, when added to a solution containing Ba^{2+}, Sr^{2+} and Ca^{2+} ions, will precipitate
(a) Ca^{2+} ions only (b) Ca^{2+} and Sr^{2+} ions
(c) Ba^{2+}, Sr^{2+} and Ca^{2+} ions (d) Ba^{2+} ions only

19. A compound is soluble in water. If ammonia is added to aqueous solution of the compounds a brown precipitate appears which is soluble in dil. HCl. The compound has
(a) Aluminium (b) Zinc
(c) Iron (d) Cadmium

20. A compound (A) forms a unstable pale blue colour solution in water. The solution decolourised Br_3 water and an acidified solution of $KMnO_4$. The possible compound (A) is
(a) HNO_2 (b) HNO_3 (c) N_2O_5 (d) NO_2

Numerical Type Questions

21. The number of compounds that are soluble in excess of NaOH are
Ag_2O, Hg_2O, HgO, $Cu(OH)_2$, $Cr(OH)_3$, $Al(OH)_3$, $Fe(OH)_3$ and $AsCl_3$.

22. The total number of species among the following that will produce a white precipitate with NaOH are
Pb^{2+}, Sn^{2+}, Sn^{4+}, Cu^{2+}, Sb^{3+}, Ni^{2+}, Zn^{2+}, Fe^{3+}, Co^{2+}, Bi^{3+} and Cd^{2+}.

23. The ratio of the sum of Fe^{2+} and Fe^{3+} ions in prussian blue to turnbull's blue is

24. The number of radicals among the following that can be tested both by potassium ferrocyanide and potassium ferricyanide are
Ag^+, Zn^{2+}, Fe^{3+}, Al^{3+}, Fe^{2+}, Cu^{2+}, Co^{2+} and Cr^{3+}.

25. The number of species that will give a colored precipitate with disodium hydrogen phosphate are
$AgNO_3$, $BaCl_2$, $\{Mg(NO_2)_3 + NH_4NO_3 + NH_3\}$, $(NH_4)_6Mo_7O_{24}\cdot 4H_2O$ and $FeCl_3$.

26. If the number of reagents that can be used to detect sulphide radical among the following given below is x, then the value of $x/3$ is
$AgNO_3$, $FeCl_3$, $Pb(CH_3COO)_2$, $ZnCl_2$, $CuCl_2$, $AsCl_3$, $SnCl_2$, $SnCl_4$, Sodium nitroprusside, $K_2Cr_2O_7$, O_3, Methylene blue and $(NaN_3 + I_2)$.

27. The number of yellow coloured insoluble compounds are
AgI, PbI_2, Hg_2I_2, BiI_3, CuI_2, Cu_2I_2, $PbCrO_4$, $BaCrO_4$, $CaCrO_4$, Ag_2CrO_4, Hg_2CrO_4.

28. $NaHSO_4$ will not co-exist with how many of the following?
$Ca(OH)_2$, $Mg(OH)_2$, ZnO, $Al(OH)_3$, Na_2CO_3, $NaHCO_3$, $NaHPO_4$, $NaHPO_3$.

29. How many of the following ions does not give flame test?
Mg^{2+}, Ba^{2+}, Ca^{2+}, Be^{2+}, Co^{2+}, Cu^{2+}, Sr^{2+}, K^+

Check Through PYQs

Element 1 Preliminary Tests and Qualitative Analysis of Acidic Radicals

1. Which of the following compound(s) are yellow in colour? *JEE Main 2025*
(A) Cds, (B) PbS, (C) CuS, (D) ZnS(cold), (E) $PbCrO_4$
Choose the correct answer from the options given below.
(a) (A), (C) and (E) only (b) (A) and (E) only
(c) (B) and (D) only (d) (A), (B) and (E) only

2. Match List I with List II. *2024, 8 April Shift-I*

List I (Name of the test)		List II (Reaction sequence involved) [M is metal]
A. Borax bead test	I.	$MCO_3 \rightarrow MO \xrightarrow[+\Delta]{Co(NO_3)_2} CoO\cdot MO$
B. Charcoal cavity test	II.	$MCO_3 \rightarrow MCl_2 \rightarrow M^{2+}$
C. Cobalt nitrate test	III.	$MSO_4 \xrightarrow[\Delta]{Na_2B_4O_7} M(BO_2)_2 \rightarrow MBO_2 \rightarrow M$
D. Flame test	IV.	$MSO_4 \xrightarrow[\Delta]{Na_2CO_3} MCO_3 \rightarrow MO \rightarrow M$

Choose the correct answer from the options given below
(a) A-III, B-II, C-IV, D-I (b) A-III, B-IV, C-I, D-II
(c) A-III, B-I, C-II, D-IV (d) A-III, B-I, C-IV, D-II

3. During the detection of acidic radical present in a salt, a student gets a pale yellow precipitate soluble with difficulty in NH_4OH solution when sodium carbonate extract was first acidified with dil. HNO_3 and then $AgNO_3$ solution was added. This indicates presence of *2024, 6 April Shift-II*
(a) Cl^- (b) CO_3^{2-}
(c) I^- (d) Br^-

4. The compound that is white in colour is *2024, 31 Jan Shift-I*
(a) lead sulphate
(b) ammonium arsinomolybdate
(c) ammonium sulphide (d) lead iodide

5. Given below are two statements. *2024, 30 Jan Shift-I*
Statement I The gas liberated on warming a salt with dil. H_2SO_4, turns a piece of paper dipped in lead acetate into black, it is a confirmatory test for sulphide ion.
Statement II In statement-I the colour of paper turns black because of formation of lead sulphite.
In the light of the above statements, choose the **most appropriate** answer from the options given below
(a) Statement I is true but Statement II is false.
(b) Both Statement I and Statement II are true.
(c) Both Statement I and Statement II are false.
(d) Statement I is false but Statement II is true.

6. When a solution of mixture having two inorganic salts was treated with freshly prepared ferrous sulphate in acidic medium, a dark brown ring was formed whereas on treatment with neutral $FeCl_3$, it gave deep red colour which disapeared on boiling and a brown red ppt was formed. The mixture contains *2023, 11 April Shift-I*
(a) CH_3COO^- and NO_3^- (b) $C_2O_4^{2-}$ and NO_3^-
(c) SO_3^{2-} and $C_2O_4^{2-}$ (d) SO_3^{2-} and CH_3COO^-

7. Match List-I with List-II.

List-I (Element)		List-II (Colour imparted to the flame)	
A.	K	I.	Brick red
B.	Ca	II.	Violet
C.	Sr	III.	Apple green
D.	Ba	IV.	Crimson red

Choose the correct answer from the options given below *2023, 25 Jan Shift-I*
(a) A-II, B-I, C-IV, D-III (b) A-II, B-IV, C-I, D-III
(c) A-IV, B-III, C-II, D-I (d) A-II, B-I, C-III, D-IV

Element 2 Qualitative Analysis of Basic Radicals

8. Match List I with List II.

List I (Precipitating reagent and conditions)		List II (Cation)	
A.	$NH_4Cl + NH_4OH$	I.	Mn^{2+}
B.	$NH_4OH + Na_2CO_3$	II.	Pb^{2+}
C.	$NH_4OH + NH_4Cl + H_2S$ gas	III.	Al^{3+}
D.	Dilute HCl	IV.	Sr^{2+}

Choose the correct answer from the options given below *2024, 6 April Shift-I*
(a) A-III, B-IV, C-I, D-II (b) A-III, B-IV, C-II, D-I
(c) A-IV, B-III, C-I, D-II (d) A-IV, B-III, C-II, D-I

9. A reagent which gives brilliant red precipitate with nickel ions in basic medium is *2024, 29 Jan Shift-II*
(a) *meta*-dinitrobenzene (b) dimethyl glyoxime
(c) sodium nitroprusside (d) neutral $FeCl_3$

10. In the wet tests for detection of various cations by precipitation, Ba^{2+} cations are detected by obtaining precipitate of *2023, 13 April Shift-II*
(a) Ba(*ox*) : Barium oxalate (b) $BaSO_4$
(c) $Ba(OAc)_2$ (d) $BaCO_3$

11. Formation of which complex, among the following, is not a confirmatory test of Pb^{2+} ions *[2023, 6 April Shift-II]*
(a) lead chromate (b) lead nitrate
(c) lead sulphate (d) lead iodide

12. In the wet tests for identification of various cations by precipitation which transition element cation doesn't belong to group IV in qualitative inorganic analysis? *2023, 30 Jan Shift-I*
(a) Ni^{2+} (b) Co^{2+} (c) Fe^{3+} (d) Zn^{2+}

13. Match List-I with List-II.

List-I (Cations)		List-II (Group reagents)	
A.	Pb^{2+}, Cu^{2+}	I.	H_2S gas in presence of dilute HCl
B.	Al^{3+}, Fe^{3+}	II.	$(NH_4)_2CO_3$ in presence of NH_4OH
C.	Co^{2+}, Ni^{2+}	III.	NH_4OH in presence of NH_4Cl
D.	Ba^{2+}, Ca^{2+}	IV.	H_2S in presence of NH_4OH

Correct match is *2023, 25 Jan Shift-I*
(a) A-III, B-I, C-IV, D-II (b) A-I, B-III, C-IV, D-II
(c) A -I, B-III, C-II, D-IV (d) A-IV, B-II, C-III, D-I

14. Fe^{3+} cation gives a prussian blue precipitate on addition of potassium ferrocyanide solution due to the formation of *2022, 27 July Shift-II*
(a) $[Fe(H_2O)_6]_2[Fe(CN)_6]$ (b) $Fe_2[Fe(CN)_6]_2$
(c) $Fe_3[Fe(OH)_2(CN)_4]_2$ (d) $Fe_4[Fe(CN)_6]_3$

15. Which statement is not true with respect to nitrate ion test? *2022, 26 June Shift-I*
(a) A dark brown ring is formed at the junction of two solutions.
(b) Ring is formed due to nitroferrous sulphate complex.
(c) The brown complex is $[Fe(H_2O)_5(NO)]SO_4$.
(d) Heating the nitrate salt with conc. H_2SO_4, light brown fumes are evolved.

16. During the qualitative analysis of salt with cation Y^{2+}, addition of a reagent (X) to alkaline solution of the salt gives a bright red precipitate. The reagent (X) and the cation (Y^{2+}) present respectively are *2022, 24 June Shift-I*
(a) dimethylglyoxime and Ni^{2+}
(b) dimethylglyoxime and Co^{2+}
(c) Nessler's reagent and Hg^{2+}
(d) Nessler's reagent and Ni^{2+}

17. Which one of the following when dissolved in water gives coloured solution in nitrogen atmosphere? *2021,26 Aug Shift-I*
(a) Cu_2Cl_2 (b) $ZnCl_2$ (c) $CuCl_2$ (d) AgCl

18. To an aqueous solution containing ions such as Al^{3+}, Zn^{2+}, Ca^{2+}, Fe^{3+}, Ni^{2+}, Ba^{2+} and Cu^{2+} conc. HCl, was added followed by H_2S. The total number of cations precipitated during this reaction is/are *2021, 27 July Shift-II*
(a) 1 (b) 3 (b) 4 (d) 2

19. Reagent 1-napthylamine and sulphanilic acid in acetic acid is used for the detection of *[2021, 18 March Shift-I]*
(a) N_2O (b) NO_2^- (c) NO_3^- (d) NO

PRACTICE ELEMENT 02

Target JEE Advanced

Single Correct Choice MCQs

1. $[X] + H_2SO_4 \longrightarrow [Y]$ a colourless gas with irritating smell;
$[Y] + K_2Cr_2O_7 + H_2SO_4 \longrightarrow$ green solution. $[X]$ and $[Y]$ is
(a) SO_3^{2-}, SO_2 (b) Cl^-, HCl
(c) S^{2-}, H_2S (d) CO_3^{2-}, CO_2

2. A dilute aqueous solution of a sodium salt forms white precipitate with $MgCl_2$, only after boiling. The anion of the sodium salt is
(a) HCO_3^- (b) CO_3^{2-}
(c) NO_3^- (d) SO_4^{2-}

3. The species present in solution when CO_2 is dissolved in water are
(a) CO_2, H_2CO_3, HCO_3^-, CO_3^{2-}
(b) HCO_3^-, CO_3^{2-}
(c) CO_3^{2-}, HCO_3^-
(d) CO_2, H_2CO_3

4. A white precipitate is obtained when a solution is diluted with H_2O and boiled. On addition of excess NH_4Cl/NH_4OH, the volume of precipitate decreases leaving behind a white gelatinous precipitate. Identify the precipitate which dissolves in ammonia solution or NH_4Cl.
(a) $Al(OH)_3$ (b) $Zn(OH)_2$
(c) $Mg(OH)_2$ (d) $Ca(OH)_2$

5. In blue solution of copper sulphate excess of KCN is added then solution becomes colourless due to the formation of
(a) $[Cu(CN)_4]^{2-}$
(b) Cu^{2+} get reduced to form $[Cu(CN)_4]^{3-}$
(c) $Cu(CN)_2$
(d) CuCN

6. $MgSO_4 + NH_4OH + Na_2HPO_4 \longrightarrow$ white crystalline precipitate. The formula of crystalline precipitate is
(a) $MgCl_2 \cdot MgSO_4$ (b) $MgSO_4$
(c) $Mg(NH_4)PO_4$ (d) $Mg(PO_4)_2$

7. A solution of a metal ion when treated with KI gives a red precipitate which dissolves in excess KI to give a colourless solution. Moreover, the solution of metal ion on treatment with a solution of cobalt(II) thiocyanate gives rise to a deep blue crystalline precipitate. The metal ion is
(a) Pb^{2+} (b) Hg^{2+}
(c) Cu^{2+} (d) Co^{2+}

8. Formation of which complex, among the following is not a confirmatory test of Cd^{2+} ions.
(a) $CdCrO_4$ (b) CdS
(c) $Cd(OH)_2$ (d) $K_3[Cd(CN)_4]$

One or More than One Correct MCQs

9. A solution of colourless salt of ammonia on boiling with excess NaOH produces a non-flammable gas. The gas evolution ceases after some time. Upon addition of Zn dust to the same solution, the gas evolution restarts. The colourless salts(s) H is (are)
(a) NH_4NO_3 (b) NH_4NO_2
(c) NH_4Cl (d) $(NH_4)_2SO_4$

10. $Cu(NO_3)_2 + 2NaOH \longrightarrow$ Blue coloured Compound $(A) \xrightarrow{\Delta}$ Black colured compound $(B) \xrightarrow{\text{Glucose}}$ Red coloured compound (C). The compound C formed is
(a) CuO (b) Cu_2O
(c) $Cu(OH)_2$ (d) Cu_2O_2

11. In the flame test of a mixture of salts, a bluish-green flame colour through blue glass was observed. Which one of the following cations may be present?
(a) K^+ (b) Ba^{2+}
(c) Cu^{2+} (d) Sr^{2+}

12. The reagent(s) that can selectively precipitate Cl^- from a mixture of Cl^- and CH_3COO^- in aqueous solution is/are
(a) KI (b) $SnCl_2$
(c) Na_2CrO_4 (d) NH_4OH

13. Which of the following statement is correct with respect to rint test of nitrate ion?
(a) Brown ring is formed at the junction of the two liquid.
(b) Heating the nitrate salt with few drops of conc. H_2SO_4, reddish brown with pungent odour fumes are evolved.
(c) Brown ring is formed due to the formation of complex $[Fe(H_2O)_5(NO)]SO_4$.
(d) The brown complex contains 4 paired electron and is diamagnetic.

14. Select the combinations in an aqueous medium that will give a red colour or precipitate?
(a) $Fe^{2+} + [Fe(CN)_6]^{3-}$
(b) $Fe^{2+} + [Fe(CN)_6]^{3+}$
(c) $Fe^{3+} + SCN^-$
(d) $Hg^{2+} + SCN^- + Co^{2+}$

15. Choose the correct statements regarding chromyl chloride test?
(a) Deep orange red vapours of chromyl chloride is evolved.
(b) Colour of NaOH solution changes to red when the vapours of mixture is passed from 5% NaOH solution.
(c) Bromides and iodides do not interfere with the chromyl chloride test.
(d) Hg_2Cl_2 and $HgCl_2$ do not respond to the chromyl chloride test.

16. Choose the correct reaction
(a) $BaCl_2 + CH_3COOH + K_2CrO_4 \longrightarrow$ Yellow precipitate
(b) $2Cu(NO_3)_2 + K_4[Fe(CN)_6] \longrightarrow$ Chocolate brown precipitate
(c) $SrCO_3 + K_2CrO_4 + CH_3COOH \longrightarrow$ No precipitate
(d) $Cu(NO_3)_2 + 2KI \xrightarrow{\Delta}$ Black precipitate

Numerical/Integer Type Questions

17. An aqueous solution contains Hg_2^{2+}, Hg^{2+}, Pb^{2+}, Ag^+, Bi^{3+} and Cd^{2+}. Out of these. The number of ions that will produce white precipitate with dilute HCl are

18. Na_2SO_3, NaCl, $Na_2C_2O_4$, Na_2HPO_4, Na_2CrO_4, $NaNO_2$, CH_3CO_2Na are separately treated with $AgNO_3$ solution. In how many cases is/are white ppt. obtained?

19. The number of species that will not be reduced in the charcoal cavity test on heating in the reducing flame?
Al_2O_3, CaO, As_2O_3, SrO, Ag_2O, CdO, Cu_2O, CuO and MgO.

20. Find the number of compounds which have yellow colour ppt. from the given compounds.
Ag_2CrO_4, $PbCrO_4$, Hg_2CrO_4, $BaCrO_4$

21. Na_2SO_3, $Na_2S_2O_3$, Na_2CO_3, Na_2CrO_4 are separately treated with $AgNO_3$ solution. The number of cases in which red ppt. obtained are

22. In how many of the following reactions, one of the products obtained as a yellow precipitate?
$Ba^{2+} + CrO_4^{2-} \longrightarrow$ Product
$Hg^{2+} + Co^{2+} + SCN^{\ominus} \longrightarrow$ Product
$NH_4^{\oplus} + [PtCl_6]^{2-} \longrightarrow$ Product
$Ag^{\oplus} + CrO_4^{2-} \longrightarrow$ Product

23. A solution of Hg^{2+} ion on treatment with a solution of cobalt (II) thiocyanate gives rise to a deep blue crystalline precipitate. Then the coordination number of mercury in the deep blue coloured compound is

24. $Fe^{2+}(aq) + NO_3^-(aq) + H_2SO_4(\text{conc.}) \longrightarrow$ Brown ring
The oxidation number of iron in brown ring complex is

Matching Type Questions

25. Match List-I with List-II

	List-I (Reaction)		List-II (Colour of underlined compound in List I)
(A)	$NH_2CSNH_2 + NO_2 \xrightarrow{FeH_3} Fe(SCN)_3$	I.	Black
(B)	$Ag_2S_2O_3 + H_2O \longrightarrow Ag_2S + H_2SO_4$	II.	White
(C)	$S_2O_3^{2-} + 2Ag^+ \longrightarrow Ag_2S_2O_3 \downarrow$	III.	Purple
(D)	$Na_2[Fe(CN)_5NO] + Na_2S \longrightarrow Na_4[Fe(CN)_5NOS]$	IV.	Blood red

Choose the correct answer from the options given below.
(a) A-IV, B-I, C-II, D-III (b) A-III, B-I, C-II, D-IV
(c) A-IV, B-II, C-I, D-III (d) A-III, B-II, C-I, D-IV

26. Match the following.

	Column I		Column II
(A)	HgS	I.	Raddish brown
(B)	AgCl	II.	Green
(C)	$Cr(OH)_3$	III.	White
(D)	$Fe(OH)_3$	IV.	Black

Choose the correct answer from the options given below.
(a) A-III, B-IV, C-II, D-I (b) A-IV, B-III, C-II, D-I
(c) A-II, B-I, C-IV, D-III (d) A-IV, B-I, C-II, D-III

27. Match the following.

	Column I		Column II
(A)	White turbidity	I.	$IO_3^- + SO_2 + \text{starch} \rightarrow$
(B)	Rotten egg smell	II.	$SO_2 + MnO_4^- \rightarrow$
(C)	Colourless solution	III.	$Zn + NaOH + SO_2 \rightarrow$
(D)	Blue colour	IV.	$CO_2 + Ca(OH)_2 \rightarrow$

Choose the correct answer from the options given below.
(a) A-IV, B-III, C-II, D-I (b) A-III, B-IV, C-I, D-II
(c) A-IV, B-II, C-III, D-I (d) A-III, B-I, C-IV, D-II

28. Match List-I with List-II.

	List-I		List-II
(A)	AgCl	I.	Yellow precipitate with KI
(B)	$BaSO_4$	II.	White Precipitate soluble in NH_3
(C)	PbI_2	III.	White precipitate in soluble in olilute HCl
(D)	Cu^{2+}	IV.	Blue precipitate with NH_4OH

Choose the correct answer from the options given below.
(a) A-II, B-III, C-I, D-IV
(b) A-I, B-II, C-III, D-IV
(c) A-IV, B-III, C-I, D-II
(d) A-II, B-IV, C-III, D-I

29. Match List-I with List-II.

List-I		List-II	
(A)	Fe^{3+}	I.	Blood red coluration with thiocyanate
(B)	Al^{3+}	II.	White gelatinous precipitate dissolves in excess NaOH
(C)	Zn^{2+}	III.	Green precipitate soluble in excess NH_4OH
(D)	Ni^{2+}	IV.	Pale green precipitate soluble in excess HCl

Choose the correct answer from the options given below.
(a) A-IV, B-III, C-II, D-I
(b) A-I, B-II, C-III, D-IV
(c) A-III, B-II, C-IV, D-I
(d) A-II, B-IV, C-I, D-III

30. Match List-I with List-II.

List-I		List-II	
(A)	Hg^{2+}	I.	Effervercence with HCl
(B)	Sn^{2+}	II.	Decolourisation with SO_3^{2-}
(C)	MnO_4^-	III.	White precipitate turning grey with $HgCl_2$
(D)	CO_3^{2-}	IV.	Black ppt with NaOH

Choose the correct answer from the options given below.
(a) A-IV, B-II, C-I, D-III
(b) A-III, B-II, C-IV, D-I
(c) A-I, B-II, C-III, D-IV
(d) A-IV, B-III, C-II, D-I

Paragraph Based Questions

Paragraph 1

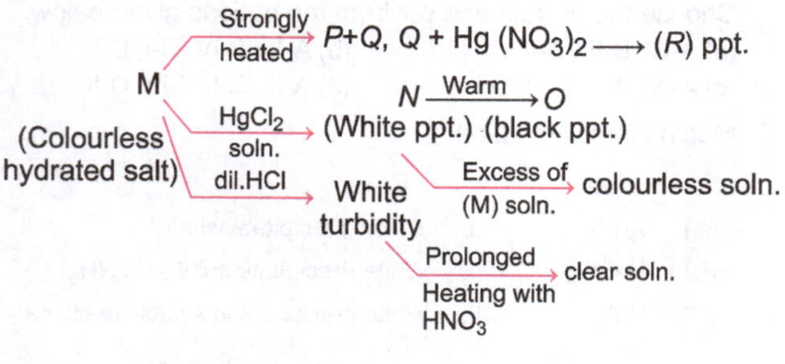

31. How many statement is correct for compound *M*.
I. It is used in photography.
II. It is used in analytical chemistry.
III. It is used as dehydrating agent.
IV. It is used as oxidising as well as reducing agent.
V. It is colourless crystalline and efforescent substance.
VI. It is soluble in water.

32. Number of anionic atom in compound is

Paragraph 2

p-amino-*N*, *N*-dimethylaniline is added to a strongly acidic solution of *X*. The resulting solution is treated with a few drops of aqueous solution of *Y* to yield blue colouration due to the formation of methylene blue. Treatment of the aqueous solution of *Y* with the reagent potassium hexacyanoferrate(II) leads to the formation of an intense blue precipitate. The precipitate dissolves on excess additon of the reagent. Similarly, treatment of the solution of *Y* with the solution of potassium hexacyanoferrate(III) leads to a brown colouration due to the formation of *Z*.

33. The sum of cationic and anionic species present in *X* is ....

34. Number of unpaired electron of cation in compound *Y* is

Paragraph 3

An aqueous solution of a mixture of two inorganic salts, when treated with dilute HCl, gave a precipitate (*P*) and a filtrate (*Q*). The precipitate *P* was found to dissolve in hot water. The filtrate (*Q*) remained unchanged, when treated with H_2S in a dilute mineral acid medium. However, it gave a precipitate (*R*) with H_2S in an ammonical medium. The precipitate (*R*) gave a coloured solution(s), when treated with H_2O_2 in an aqueous NaOH medium.

35. Among PbS, CuS, HgS, MnS, Ag_2S, NiS, CoS, SnS_2. Total number of black coloured sulphide is

36. No. of ions which get precipitated upon passing H_2S gas in presence of dil. HCl is
Bi^{+3}, Fe^{+3}, Hg^{2+}, Cu^{+2}, Pb^{+2}, Ba^{+2}, Zn^{+2}

Species Selection (with 5 Species)

37. Consider the following mixture of ions in solution.
I. Fe^{3+} and Pb^{2+}
II. Pb^{2+} and Sn^{2+}
III. Zn^{2+} and Sn^{2+}
IV. Al^{3+} and Cu^{2+}
V. Mn^{2+} and Cu^{2+}

The total number of ions that can be separated by using NaOH solution?
(a) 4 (b) 2 (c) 3 (d) 1

38. Consider the following reactions.
A. $(CH_3COO)_2Pb + K_2CrO_4 \longrightarrow$
B. $Pb(NO_3)_2 + K_2CrO_4 \longrightarrow$
C. $AgNO_3 + KI \longrightarrow$
D. $H_2S + CdSO_4 \longrightarrow$
E. $Cu(NO_3)_2 + KI \xrightarrow{\Delta}$

The total number of reaction produces white precipitate?
(a) 1 (b) 5
(c) 3 (d) 4

39. Consider the following cations
A. Fe^{2+}
B. Mn^{2+}
C. Cr^{3+}
D. Cu^{2+}
E. Co^{2+}

The total number of cations that will turn a borax bead green in an oxidising flame is ......
(a) 1 (b) 5
(c) 3 (d) 2

Species Selection (with 7 Species)

40. Consider the following compounds
(a) $(NH_4)_2SO_4$ (b) $(NH_4)_2CO_3$
(c) NH_4Cl (d) NH_4NO_3
(e) $(NH_4)_2Cr_2O_7$ (f) NH_4NO_2
(g) NH_4ClO_4
How many compounds liberate NH_3 on heating from the following?
(a) 1 (b) 2 (c) 3 (d) 4

41. Consider the following reactions
(a) $NaBr + AgNO_3 \longrightarrow$ (b) $NaI + AgNO_3 \longrightarrow$
(c) $NaBr + Pb(NO_3)_2 \longrightarrow$
(d) $Na_2S + Cd(CH_3COO)_2 \longrightarrow$
(e) $NaI + Pb(NO_3)_2 \longrightarrow$
(f) $K_2CrO_4 + Pb(CH_3COO)_2 \longrightarrow$
(g) $K_2CrO_4 + (CH_3COO)_2Ba \longrightarrow$
The number of reactions that will give yellow ppt. is
(a) 2 (b) 3 (c) 5 (d) 6

42. Consider the following pair of species
(a) Bi^{3+} and Sn^{4+} (b) Al^{3+} and Hg^{2+}
(c) Cd^{2+} and Zn^{2+} (d) Fe^{3+} and Cu^{2+}
(e) As^{3+} and Sb^{3+} (f) Mg^{2+} and NH_4^+
(g) Al^{3+} and Fe^{3+}
How many of the above pair of ions can be separated by H_2S in dilute HCl?
(a) 1 (b) 2
(c) 3 (d) 4

43. Consider the following combinations is an aqueous medium.
I. $Fe^{2+} + [Fe(CN)_6]^{3-}$
II. $Fe^{3+} + [Fe(CN)_6]^{4-}$
III. $Hg^{2+} + SCN^- + Co^{2+}$
IV. $Fe^{3+} + SCN^-$
V. $Co^{2+} + SCN^-$
VI. Ni^{2+} + dimnethylglyoxime + NH_3
VII. $AgNO_3 + KI$
The total number of combinations that will give a red colour or precipitate?
(a) 4 (b) 2
(c) 5 (d) 3

Check Through PYQs

Element 1 Preliminary Tests and Qualitative Analysis of Acidic Radicals

1. The reaction of $Pb(NO_3)_2$ and NaCl in water produces a precipitate that dissolves upon the addition of HCl of appropriate concentration. The dissolution of the precipitate is due to the formation of *2022 Adv.*
(a) $PbCl_2$ (b) $PbCl_4$
(c) $[PbCl_4]^{2-}$ (d) $[PbCl_6]^{2-}$

2. In the following reaction sequence in aqueous solution, the species *X*, *Y* and *Z*, respectively, are *2016 Adv.*

$$S_2O_3^{2-} \xrightarrow{Ag^+} \underset{\text{(Clear solution)}}{X} \xrightarrow{Ag^+} \underset{\text{(White ppt.)}}{Y} \xrightarrow{\text{With time}} \underset{\text{(Black ppt.)}}{Z}$$

(a) $[Ag(S_2O_3)_2]^{3-}$, $Ag_2S_2O_3$, Ag_2S
(b) $[Ag(S_2O_3)_3]^{5-}$, Ag_2SO_3, Ag_2S
(c) $[Ag(SO_3)_2]^{3-}$, $Ag_2S_2O_3$, Ag
(d) $[Ag(SO_3)_3]^{3-}$, Ag_2SO_4, Ag

3. The reagent(s) that can selectively precipitate S^{2-} from a mixture of S^{2-} and SO_4^{2-} in aqueous solution is (are) *2016 Adv.*
(a) $CuCl_2$
(b) $BaCl_2$
(c) $Pb(OOCCH_3)_2$
(d) $Na_2[Fe(CN)_5NO]$

Element 2 Qualitative Analysis of Basic Radicals

4. A colourless aqueous solution contains nitrates of two metals, *X* and *Y*. When it was added to an aqueous solution of NaCl, a white precipitate was formed. This precipitate was found to be partly soluble in hot water to give a residue *P* and a solution *Q*. The residue *P* was soluble in aqueous NH_3 and also in excess sodium thiosulphate. The hot solution *Q* gave a yellow precipitate with KI. The metals *X* and *Y*, respectively, are *2020 Adv.*
(a) Ag and Pb (b) Ag and Cd
(c) Cd and Pb (d) Cd and Zn

5. A mixture of two salts is used to prepare a solution *S*, which gives the following results

$$\text{White precipitates } (s) \text{ only} \xleftarrow[\text{Room temperature}]{\text{Dilute NaOH}(aq)} \underset{(aq \text{ solution of the salts})}{S} \xrightarrow[\text{Room temperature}]{\text{Dilute HCl}(aq)} \text{White precipitate(s) only}$$

The correct option(s) for the salt mixture is (are) *2021 Adv.*
(a) $Pb(NO_3)_2$ and $Zn(NO_3)_2$
(b) $Pb(NO_3)_2$ and $Bi(NO_3)_3$
(c) $AgNO_3$ and $Bi(NO_3)_3$
(d) $Pb(NO_3)_2$ and $Hg(NO_3)_2$

6. The correct option(s) to distinguish nitrate salts to Mn^{2+} and Cu^{2+} taken separately is (are) *2018 Adv.*
(a) Mn^{2+} shows the characteristic green colour in the flame test
(b) Only Cu^{2+} shows the formation of precipitate by passing H_2S in acidic medium
(c) Only Mn^{2+} shows the formation of precipitate by passing H_2S in faintly basic medium
(d) Cu^{2+}/Cu has higher reduction potential than Mn^{2+}/Mn (measured under similar conditions)

7. The pair(s) of ions where both the ions are precipitated upon passing H_2S gas in presence of dilute HCl, is (are) *2015 Adv.*
(a) Ba^{2+}, Zn^{2+} (b) Bi^{3+}, Fe^{3+}
(c) Cu^{2+}, Pb^{2+} (d) Hg^{2+}, Bi^{3+}

Paragraph Based Questions

Paragraph (Q. Nos. 8-9)

When potassium iodide is added to an aqueous solution of potassium ferricyanide, a reversible reaction is observed in which a complex *P* is formed. In a strong acidic medium, the equilibrium shifts completely towards *P*. Addition of zinc chloride to *P* in a slightly acidic medium results in a sparingly soluble complex *Q*. *2024 Adv.*

8. The number of moles of potassium iodide required to produce two moles of *P* is ....

9. The number of zinc ions present in the molecular formula of *Q* is ....

Paragraph (Q. Nos. 10-11)

The reaction of $K_3[Fe(CN)_6]$ with freshly prepared $FeSO_4$ solution produces a dark blue precipitate called Turnbull's blue. Reaction of $K_4[Fe(CN)_6]$ with the $FeSO_4$ solution in complete absence of air produces a white precipitate *X*, which turns blue in air. Mixing the $FeSO_4$ solution with $NaNO_3$, followed by a slow addition of concentrated H_2SO_4 through the side of the test tube produces a brown ring. *2021 Adv*

10. Precipitate *X* is
(a) $Fe_4[Fe(CN)_6]_3$ (b) $Fe[Fe(CN)_6]$
(c) $K_2Fe[Fe(CN)_6]$ (d) $KFe[Fe(CN)_6]$

11. Among the following, the brown ring is due to the formation of
(a) $[Fe(NO)_2(SO_4)_2]^{2-}$ (b) $[Fe(NO)_2(H_2O)_4]^{3+}$
(c) $[Fe(NO)_4(SO_4)_2]$ (d) $[Fe(NO)(H_2O)_5]^{2+}$

HINTS & Solutions

Solutions : Competency Enhancer

1.1 ***(4)*** Among the given salt only four i.e.,

CdS, $Cu(CN)_2$, As_2S_3 and PbI_2 are yellow coloured.

$Cu_2I_2 \rightarrow$ white

$CuS \rightarrow$ black

$SbI_3 \rightarrow$ red-yellow

$BaCl_2 \rightarrow$ white

2.1 ***(b)***

$$K_3[Fe(CN)_6] + \text{Excess (KI)} \longrightarrow \underset{(X)}{K_4[Fe(CN)_6]} + KI_3$$

$$\underset{(X)}{K_4[Fe(CN)_6]} \xrightarrow{ZnSO_4} \underset{\substack{\text{(white ppt.)}\\(Y)}}{K_2Zn[Fe(CN)_6]}$$

$$\underset{(P)}{[Zn(OH)_4]^{2-}_{(aq.)}} + \underset{(Z)}{[Fe(CN)_6]^{4-}_{(aq.)}} \xleftarrow{NaOH} \underset{\substack{\text{(white ppt.)}\\(Y)}}{K_2Zn[Fe(CN)_6]}$$

2.2 ***(a, d)*** Among the given pair of ions only Pb^{2+}, Cd^{2+}, Zn^{2+} and Mg^{2+} reacts with ammonia solution to give white precipitate.

$$Pb^{2+} + 2NH_4OH \longrightarrow \underset{\text{(White ppt.)}}{Pb(OH)_2\downarrow} + 2NH_4^+$$

$$2Ag^+ + 2NH_3 + H_2O \rightleftharpoons \underset{\text{(Brown ppt.)}}{Ag_2O\downarrow} + 2NH_4^+$$

$$Hg_2Cl_2 + 4NH_4OH \longrightarrow \left[\underset{\text{Black ppt.}}{Hg\begin{smallmatrix}NH_2\\ Cl\end{smallmatrix}\downarrow + Hg\downarrow}\right] + NH_4Cl + 2H_2O$$

$$2Cu^{2+} + SO_4^{2-} + 2NH_3 + H_2O \longrightarrow \underset{\text{(Blue ppt.)}}{Cu(OH)_2 \cdot CuSO_4\downarrow} + 2NH_4^+$$

$$Cd^{2+} + 2NH_4OH \rightleftharpoons \underset{\text{(White ppt.)}}{Cd(OH)_2\downarrow} + 2NH_4^+$$

$$CrCl_3 + 3NH_4OH \longrightarrow \underset{\text{(Bluish-green ppt.)}}{Cr(OH)_3\downarrow} + 3NH_4Cl$$

$$2Zn^{2+} + 2NH_4OH \longrightarrow \underset{\text{(White ppt.)}}{2Zn(OH)_2\downarrow} + 2NH_3$$

$$Mg^{2+} + 2NH_4OH \longrightarrow \underset{\text{(White ppt.)}}{Mg(OH)_2\downarrow} + 2NH_4^+$$

Elemental Practice 10.1

1. ***(b)*** Acidic solution of a nitrite salt produce when deep blue colour with starch and iodide solution.

2. ***(b)*** Due to the formation of chromyl chloride, when a mixture of solid NaCl and solid $K_2Cr_2O_7$ is heated with conc. H_2SO_4, deep red vapours are obtained.

$$4NaCl + K_2Cr_2O_7 + 3H_2SO_4 \longrightarrow 2CrO_2Cl_2 + 2Na_2SO_4 + K_2SO_4 + 3H_2O$$

3. ***(b)*** The brown colour of the ring is due to formation of $\underset{\text{(Brown ring complex)}}{[Fe(H_2O)_5(NO)]SO_4}$ i.e., nitroso ferrous sulphate

4. ***(a)*** On heating bromide salt with conc. H_2SO_4, reddish brown colour fumes evolve. This indicates the presence of Br^- ions.

$$2NaBr + 3H_2SO_4 + MnO_2 \longrightarrow Br_2 + MnSO_2 + 2NaHSO_4 + 2H_2O$$

5. ***(b)*** Fe(II) ions combines with NO (nitric acid) to form a brown ring. It is used as a test to identify the presence of nitrate ions in a solution.

6. ***(c)*** $SO_3^{2-} + H^+ \longrightarrow SO_2\uparrow$

$$SO_2 + Ba(OH)_2 \longrightarrow BaSO_3\downarrow \text{ (White ppt)}$$

$$Cr_2O_7^{2-} + 2H^+ + 3SO_2 \longrightarrow \underset{\text{(Green ppt.)}}{2Cr^{3+}} + 3SO_4^{2-} + H_2O$$

7. ***(d)*** SO_4^{2-} show no effect with dil. or conc. acid. It gives test with ppt reaction only.

8. ***(d)*** $2Na_2BO_3 + 3H_2SO_4(\text{Conc.}) \longrightarrow 2H_3BO_3 + 2Na_2SO_4$

$$H_3BO_3 + 3C_2H_5OH \xrightarrow{\Delta} \underset{\substack{\text{Burns with green}\\ \text{edged flame}}}{(C_2H_5O)_3B\uparrow} + 3H_2O$$

9. ***(b)*** $\underset{(pH = 7)}{NaCl + AgNO_3} \longrightarrow AgCl \text{ (white)}$

$$AgCl \xrightarrow{\text{dil. } HNO_3} \text{not soluble}$$

10. ***(d)*** I_2 is less reactive and weak oxidising agent. It cannot displace any of the halogen.

11. ***(c)*** Only a strong oxidising agent like MnO_2 can oxidise the chloride ion.

$$2NaCl + 3H_2SO_4 + MnO_2 \longrightarrow 2NaHSO_4 + MnSO_4 + Cl_2\uparrow + 2H_2O$$

12. ***(c)*** Conc. HNO_3, conc. H_2SO_4 and MnO_2 are strong oxidising agents and thus will oxidise Br^- ion to free Br_2 whereas conc. H_3PO_4 is not an oxidising agent and thus will form HBr by ion exchange reaction.

$$6NaBr + 2H_3PO_4 \longrightarrow 6HBr\uparrow + 2Na_3PO_4$$

13. ***(d)*** SO_2 has reducing properties whereas CO_2 doesn't. Therefore, only SO_2 will react with the given oxidising agents and show color change whereas CO_2 will not

$$SO_2 + MnO_4^- \xrightarrow{H^+} \underset{\text{Colorless/light pink}}{Mn^{2+}} + SO_4^{2-} + H_2O$$

$$SO_2 + Cr_2O_7^{2-} \xrightarrow{H^+} \underset{\text{Green}}{Cr^{3+}} + SO_4^{2-} + H_2O$$

$$\underset{\substack{\text{Yellow}\\ \text{solution}}}{FeCl_3} + SO_2 + H_2O \longrightarrow \underset{\substack{\text{Colorless}\\ \text{light green}}}{FeCl_2} + SO_4^{2-} + H^+ + Cl^-$$

14. ***(c)*** Sulphur dioxide oxidises iodate to iodine which gives a blue colour in presence of starch.

$$\underbrace{IO_3^- + \text{Starch}}_{\substack{\text{Starch iodate}\\ \text{colorless}}} + SO_2 \xrightarrow{H^+} \underset{\substack{\text{Deep blue}\\ \text{Solution}}}{(I_2 + \text{Starch})} + SO_4^{2-}$$

15. ***(b)*** Purple colouration is observed when sodium nitroprusside is added to solution of sulphide ions,e.g., Na_2S.

$$Na_2S + Na_2[Fe(CN)_5NO] \longrightarrow Na_4[Fe(CN)_5NOS]$$

16. ***(c)*** Nitrite ions will form brown ring complex with dil. H_2SO_4, conc. H_2SO_4 and even dil. CH_3COOH so (II), (III) and (IV) are correct. Though nitrate ions will form brown ring complex with conc. H_2SO_4 and so does nitrite, thus we cannot know for sure it nitrate was even present if nitrite is already there.

17. ***(b)*** HCl gas gives white fumes with ammonia thus the anion is chloride, but the compound (*P*) doesn't respond to chromyl chloride test then (*P*) must be a covalent chloride because ionic chlorides respond to chromyl chloride test.

18. ***(c, d)*** Strontium sulphate and calcium oxalate both are insoluble in water as they have low hydration enthalpy.

19. ***(a, d)*** Complete reaction inolved is as follows

$$2NaNO_2 + H_2SO_4 \xrightarrow{\Delta} \underset{A}{Na_2SO_4} + \underset{B}{2HNO_2}$$

$$3HNO_2 \longrightarrow H_2O + HNO_3 + \underset{C}{2NO}$$

$$2NO + O_2 \longrightarrow \underset{D}{2NO_2}$$

Thus, *A*, *B*, *C* and *D* respectively are

Na_2SO_4, HNO_2, NO, NO_2

20. ***(a, b, c)*** $(NH_4)_2SO_4 \xrightarrow{\Delta} NH_4HSO_4 + NH_3$

$$NH_4Cl \xrightarrow{\Delta} NH_3 + HCl$$

$$(NH_4)_2CO_3 \xrightarrow{\Delta} CO_2 + H_2O + 2NH_3$$

$$NH_4NO_3 \xrightarrow{\Delta} N_2O + 2H_2O$$

21. ***(b, c)*** There are only two reaction in which product obtained is as yellow precipitate.

$$Ag^+ + CrO_4^{2-} \longrightarrow \underset{\text{(Red ppt.)}}{Ag_2CrO_4}$$

$$Ba^{2+} + CrO_4^{2-} \longrightarrow \underset{\text{(Yellow)}}{BaCrO_4}$$

$$NH_4^+ + [Co(NO_2)_6]^{3-} \longrightarrow \underset{\text{(Yellow)}}{(NH_4)_3[Co(NO_2)_6]}$$

$$Hg^{2+} + Co^{2+} + 4SCN^- \longrightarrow \underset{\text{(Deep blue ppt.)}}{Co[Hg(SCN)_4]}$$

22. ***(a, c)*** Among the given compounds Na_2SO_3 and $Na_2C_2O_4$ give white precipitate of Ag_2SO_3 and $Ag_2C_2O_4$ with $AgNO_3$ while Na_2HPO_4 and Na_2CrO_4 gives yellow precipitate of Ag_3PO_4 and Ag_2CrO_4 respectively.

23. ***(a, b, c)*** Among the given combinations only (a), (b) and (c) can give white precipitate.

$$SO_4^{2-} + Ba^{2+} \longrightarrow \underset{\text{(White ppt.)}}{BaSO_4 \downarrow}$$

$$Na_2HPO_4 + Mg(NO_3)_2 + NH_3 \longrightarrow \underset{\text{White ppt.}}{Mg(NH_4)PO_4 \downarrow}$$

$$CaCl_2 + NaF \longrightarrow \underset{\text{(White ppt.)}}{CaF_2} + 2NaCl$$

$$HgI_2 + 2KI \longrightarrow \underset{\text{(Grey ppt.)}}{K_2[HgI_4]}$$

24. ***(5)*** Among the given carbonates except Ag_2CO_3 all give metal oxide on heating.

$$Ag_2CO_3 \xrightarrow{\Delta} 2Ag + \frac{1}{2}O_2 + CO_2$$

$$Na_2CO_3 \xrightarrow{\Delta} Na_2O + CO_2 \text{ (at high temperature)}$$

$$K_2CO_3 \xrightarrow{\Delta} K_2O + CO_2 \text{ (at high temperature)}$$

$$MgCO_3 \xrightarrow{\Delta} MgO + CO_2$$

$$CuCO_3 \xrightarrow{\Delta} CuO + CO_2$$

$$CaCO_3 \xrightarrow{\Delta} CaO + CO_2$$

25. ***(3)*** Among the given reactions only three i.e., (a), (d) and (e) only give black ppt.

$$Hg_2Cl_2 + SnCl_2 \longrightarrow \underset{\text{(Black ppt.)}}{2Hg} + SnCl_4$$

$$Pb(NO_3)_2 + K_2CrO_4 \longrightarrow \underset{\text{(Yellow ppt.)}}{PbCrO_4} + 2KNO_3$$

$$Cu(NO_3)_2 + 2KI \longrightarrow \underset{\text{(Brown)}}{CuI_2} + 2KNO_3$$

$$2BiCl_3 + 2Na_2SnO_2 + 6NaOH \longrightarrow \underset{\text{(Black ppt.)}}{2Bi \downarrow} + 3Na_2SnO_3 + 6NaCl + 3H_2O$$

$$Bi(OH)_3 \downarrow + [Sn(OH)_4]^{2-}(aq) \longrightarrow \underset{\text{(Black ppt.)}}{Bi} + [Sn^{4+}(OH)_6]^{2-}$$

26. ***(6)***

$$\left.\begin{array}{l} CaC_2O_4 \\ PbSO_4 \\ Bi(OH)_3 \\ BaCl_2 \\ CuSO_4 \\ CdCO_3 \end{array}\right\} \text{White coloured salt}$$

$PbCrO_4 \rightarrow$ yellow
$Cu(CN)_2 \rightarrow$ yellow
$Cu_2O \rightarrow$ red
$CrCl_3 \cdot 6H_2O \rightarrow$ violet

27. ***(3)*** Among the given metal oxides only three i.e., SnO_2, Bi_2O_3 and PbO are yellow coloured in cold medium.

28. ***(2)*** Among the given pair of acid radicals only two i.e., NO_3^- and NO_2^- and CH_3COO^- and $S_2O_3^{2-}$ are distinguished by using dil. H_2SO_4

NO_3^- : no reaction with dil. H_2SO_4

NO_2^- : $NO_2^- + H^+ \longrightarrow HNO_2$

$$\xrightarrow{\text{Disproportionation}} + HNO_3 + NO_2 \uparrow \xrightarrow{\text{atm. air}} \underset{\text{Light brown}}{NO_2 \uparrow}$$

CH_3COO^- : Smell of vinegar

$S_2O_3^{2-}$: White turbidity on warming

Elemental Practice 10.2

1. **(b)** The blue precipitate of Fe^{2+} ions with potassium ferricyanide is due to the formation of Turnbull's blue $K\overset{II}{Fe}[\overset{III}{Fe}(CN)_6]$ product.

$$Fe^{2+} + \underset{\text{Potassium ferricyanide}}{K_3[Fe(CN)_6]} \longrightarrow \underset{\text{Turnbull's blue}}{K\overset{II}{Fe}[\overset{III}{Fe}(CN)_6]} + 2K^+$$

2. **(d)** All the given metals form white precipitate with NH_4OH but only precipitate of zinc is soluble in excess of NH_4OH and on passing H_2S it gives white precipitate of ZnS.

3. **(b)** Ba^{2+} ion imparts green colour to the flame and Cl^- ion forms chromyl chloride (which is orange red in colour) when treated with $K_2Cr_2O_7$ and conc. H_2SO_4. Thus, the reagent is

$$Ba^{2+} + 2Cl^- \longrightarrow BaCl_2$$

$$2BaCl_2 + K_2Cr_2O_7 + 3H_2SO_4 \longrightarrow K_2SO_4 + 2BaSO_4 + \underset{\substack{\text{Chromyl chloride}\\\text{(orange red gas)}}}{2CrO_2Cl_2} + 3H_2O$$

4. **(b)** The reagent dimethyl glyoxime is used to identify nickel ions.

5. **(c)** Acidifid $K_2Cr_2O_7$ solution is used to distinguish between sodium carbonate and sodium sulphite. On treatment with dil. HCl, both Na_2CO_3 and Na_2SO_3 produce CO_2 and SO_2 respectively. SO_2 turns an acidified $K_2Cr_2O_7$ solution green whereas CO_2 does not change the colour of the solution.

6. **(d)** $[HgI_4]^{2-} + NH_4Cl + 4OH^- \longrightarrow NH_2HgOHgI$

7. **(a)** During this test, the NH_4^+ ions react with OH^- from the strong base and produces NH_3 and gas. The NH_3 gas can be detect by its characteristic smell or using red limtus paper which turns blue.

8. **(d)** $(NH_4)_2CO_3$ provides both CO_3^{2-} ions and a basic medium CO_3^{2-} ions form insoluble carbonates with alkali earth metals. The basic medium helps in complete precipitation.

The reaction is $M^{2+} + CO_3^{2-} \longrightarrow MCO_3 \downarrow$

$(NH_4)_2CO_3$ is used to precipitate the hydroxide of transition metals in group analysis.

9. **(d)** $4FeCl_3 + 3K_4[Fe(CN)_6] \longrightarrow \underset{\text{Prussian blue}}{Fe_4[Fe(CN)_6]_3} + 12KCl$

For option (b) and (c), reaction is given below

$$M^{2+} + [Fe(CN)_6]^{4-} \xrightarrow[\text{of } CH_3COOH]{\text{In presence}} \underset{\text{Bluish white ppt.}}{M_2[Fe(CN)_6]\downarrow}$$

$M = Zn^{2+}, Cd^{2+}$

10. **(b)** $K_3[\overset{+3}{Fe}(CN)_6] + \overset{-1}{KI}\text{ (excess)} \xrightarrow{\text{Dil. } H_2SO_4} K_4[\overset{+2}{Fe}(CN_6] + \underset{\text{Brownish yellow solution}}{\overset{+3\ 0}{KI_3}}$

$$K_4[Fe(CN)_6] + ZnSO_4 \longrightarrow \underset{\text{White ppt.}}{K_2Zn[Fe(CN)_6]}$$

$$\underset{\text{Brownish yellow filtrate}}{I_3^-} + 2Na_2S_2O_3 \longrightarrow \underset{\text{Clear solution}}{Na_2S_4O_6} + 2NaI + \underset{\text{Turns starch solution blue}}{I_2}$$

$K_2Zn[Fe(CN)_6]$ reacts with NaOH as

$$K_2Zn[Fe(CN)_6] + 4NaOH \longrightarrow [Zn(OH)_4]^{2-} + [Fe(CN)_6]^{4-}$$

11. **(b)** On passing H_2S gas in the aqueous solution of salt in the presence of dilute. HCl, black ppt. of CuS is formed.

$$CuS + 4HNO_3 \longrightarrow Cu(NO_3)_2 + 2NO_2 + 2H_2O$$

$$Cu^{2+} + 4NH_4OH \longrightarrow \underset{\text{Deep blue complex}}{[Cu(NH_3)_4]^{2+}} + 4H_2O$$

12. **(b)** $2NaOH + Br_2 \longrightarrow NaOBr + NaBr + H_2O$

$$NaOBr \longrightarrow NaBr + [O]$$

$$2Cr(OH)_3 + 4NaOH + 3[O] \longrightarrow \underset{\text{Yellow solution}}{2Na_2CrO_4} + 5H_2O$$

Solution is acidified and treated with lead acetate solution.

$$Na_2CrO_4 + Pb(CH_3COO)_2 \longrightarrow PbCrO_4 + 2CH_3COONa$$

13. **(d)** $CuSO_4$ decolourises on addition of KCN. The product is CuCN along with $(CN)_2$ but in excess of KCN, colourless potassium tetracyanocuperate (I) is obtained.

$$CuSO_4 + 2KCN \longrightarrow Cu(CN)_2 + [K_2SO_4] \times 2$$

$$\underset{\text{Unstable}}{2Cu(CN)_2} \rightleftharpoons 2CuCN + \underset{\text{Cyanogen}}{(CN)_2}$$

$$CuCN + 3KCN \rightleftharpoons \underset{\text{Colourless}}{K_3[Cu(CN)_4]}$$

14. **(c)** $Al(OH)_3$ dissolves in excess NaOH while $Fe(OH)_3$ does not dissolves in NaOH.

15. **(d)** $Pb^{2+} + HCl\text{ (dil.)} \longrightarrow \underset{\text{white}}{PbCl_2\downarrow}$ (soluble in hot water)

$$Pb^{2+} + H_2S \longrightarrow \underset{\text{(Black ppt.)}}{PbS\downarrow}$$

16. **(b)** Fe^{+3}, Al^{+3} and Cr^{+3} are III group basic radicals while Ni^{+2} is IV group basic radical.

17. **(a)** $NH_4Cl \longrightarrow NH_4^+ + Cl^-$

$$NH_4OH \rightleftharpoons NH_4^+ + OH^-$$

NH_4Cl controls the concentration of OH^- ions by suppressing the ionisation of NH_4OH due to common ion effect.

18. **(b)** $Fe^{+3} + K_4[Fe(CN)_6] \longrightarrow \underset{\text{(Prussian blue)}}{Fe_4[Fe(CN)_6]_3} + K^+$

19. **(b)** Both Pb^{2+} and Ba^{2+} gives yellow precipitate with aqueous solution of K_2CrO_4.

20. **(b, c, d)**

$$MnO_2 + H_2SO_4\text{(conc.)} + KBr \xrightarrow{\Delta} KHSO_4 + MnSO_4 + H_2O + Br_2$$

$$KBr + H_2SO_4\text{(conc.)} \xrightarrow{\Delta} SO_2 + Br_2 + K_2SO_4 + H_2O$$

$$KBr + H_3PO_4\text{(conc.)} \xrightarrow{\Delta} KH_2PO_4 + HBr$$

$$K_2Cr_2O_7 + H_2SO_4\text{(conc.)} + KBr \longrightarrow Cr_2(SO_4)_3 + Br_2 + H_2O + K_2SO_4$$

21. **(a, b, d)** In nitroprusside, the iron and NO exist as Fe(II) and NO^+.

22. **(a, b, c)** The reaction involved is each statement are as follows

(a) $2Ag^+ + 2NH_3 + H_2O \rightleftharpoons \underset{\text{Brown ppt.}}{Ag_2O \downarrow} + 2NH_4^+$

(b) $Ag^+ + I^- \longrightarrow \underset{\text{Yellow ppt.}}{AgI}$

(c) $Hg_2^{2+} + 2OH^- \longrightarrow \underset{\text{Black ppt.}}{Hg_2O \downarrow} + H_2O$

(d) $Hg_2^{2+} + 2I^- \longrightarrow \underset{\text{Green ppt.}}{Hg_2I_2}$

Thus, statement a, b and c are correct.

23. ***(a, c)*** $CuSO_4$ and Ag_2SO_4 are water soluble.

24. ***(b, c, d)*** CO_2 and SO_2 both gas can turn lime water milky.

$$ZnCO_3 \xrightarrow{\Delta} ZnO + CO_2 \uparrow$$

$$ZnSO_3 \xrightarrow{\Delta} ZnO + SO_2 \uparrow$$

$$MgCO_3 \xrightarrow{\Delta} MgO + CO_2 \uparrow$$

25. ***(a, b, c, d)*** $PbCrO_4$, AgI, CdS are yellow precipitate.

26. ***(a, b, c, d)*** All complex will decompose on acidification.

27. ***(7)***

$NaBr + AgNO_3 \longrightarrow AgBr$ (yellow)

$NaI + AgNO_3 \longrightarrow AgI$ (yellow)

$NaI + Pb(NO_3)_2 \longrightarrow PbI_2$ (yellow)

$Na_2S + Cd(CH_3COO)_2 \longrightarrow CdS$ (yellow)

$K_2CrO_4 + Pb(CH_3COO)_2 \longrightarrow PbCrO_4$ (yellow)

$K_2CrO_4 + (CH_3COO)_2Ba \longrightarrow BaCrO_4$ (yellow)

$NaBr + Cl_2$ water (excess) $\longrightarrow BrCl$ (yellow)

28. ***(3)*** Hg_2Cl_2, $PbCl_2$, AgCl (all are white precipitate)

29. ***(34)*** $CuSO_4(aq.) + \underset{\text{(Excess)}}{KCN} \longrightarrow \underset{\text{(Tetrahedral)}}{\overset{sp^3}{K_3[Cu(CN)_4]}}$

$a = 0 ; b = 2 ; c = 4$

$8a + 7b + 5c = 34$

30. ***(3)***

$\underset{\text{(group III)}}{Al^{3+}}$ and $\underset{\text{(group II)}}{Hg^{2+}}$ $\qquad$ $\underset{\text{(group II)}}{Cd^{2+}}$ and $\underset{\text{(group IV)}}{Zn^{2+}}$

$\underset{\text{(group III)}}{Fe^{3+}}$ and $\underset{\text{(group II)}}{Cu^{2+}}$ $\qquad$ $\underset{\text{(group II)}}{Bi^{3+}}$ and $\underset{\text{(group II)}}{Sn^{4+}}$

$\underset{\text{(group II)}}{As^{3+}}$ and $\underset{\text{(group II)}}{Sb^{3+}}$

31. ***(3)*** $\underset{(X)}{FeS(s)} \xrightarrow{\text{dil. HCl}} \underset{(Y)}{H_2S \uparrow} \xrightarrow[\text{NaOH}]{Na_2[Fe(CN)_5(NO)]} \underset{\text{Purple solution}}{Na_4[Fe(CN_5)(NO)]}$

(a) $2FeCl_3 + 2H_2S \uparrow \xrightarrow[\text{Neutral}]{\text{Acidic/}} 2Fe^{2+} + S \downarrow + 4H^+ + 6Cl^-$

(b) $CuSO_4 + H_2S \uparrow \xrightarrow[\text{Neutral}]{\text{Acidic/}} \underset{\text{Black}}{CuS \downarrow} + 2H^+ + SO_4^{2-}$

(c) $BaCl_2 + H_2S \uparrow \xrightarrow[\text{Neutral}]{\text{Acidic/}} Ba^{2+} + 2Cl^- + 2H^+ + S^{2-}$
No observable change

(d) $SO_2 \uparrow + 2H_2S \uparrow \longrightarrow 2S \downarrow + H_2O$

or $SO_2 \uparrow + H_2O \longrightarrow H_2SO_3 \xrightarrow{H_2S} S \downarrow + H_2O$

(e) $Cr_2O_7^{2-} + 8H^+ + 3H_2S \uparrow \xrightarrow[\text{Neutral}]{\text{Acidic/}} 2Cr^{3+} + S \downarrow + 7H_2O$

(f) $2CH_3COONa + H_2S \uparrow \xrightarrow[\text{Neutral}]{\text{Acidic/}}$

$2CH_3COOH + 2Na^+ + S^{2-}$
No observable change

(g) $Hg^{2+} + H_2S \uparrow \xrightarrow[\text{Neutral}]{\text{Acidic/}} HgS \downarrow + 2H^+$

$\therefore \; P = 3 ; Q = 2 ; R = 2$

Hence value of $(P + Q - R) = 3 + 2 - 2 = 3$

Practice Element 01 : Target JEE Main

1. ***(d)*** $NaNO_3 + H_2SO_4 \longrightarrow NaHSO_4 + HNO_3$

$6FeSO_4 + 2HNO_3 + 2H_2SO_4 \longrightarrow$

$2Fe_2[SO_4]_3 + 2NO + 4H_2O$

$FeSO_4 + NO + 5H_2O \longrightarrow \underset{\text{Nitrosyl ferrous sulphate}}{[Fe(H_2O)_5NO]SO_4}$

2. ***(d)***

$SO_2 \longrightarrow SO_4^{2-}$

$Fe^{2+} \longrightarrow Fe^{3+}$

$I^- \longrightarrow I_2$

$I_2 + Na_2S_2O_3 \longrightarrow NaI + Na_2S_4O_6$

all these oxidised hence $Cr_2O_7^{2-}$ is reduced to Cr^{3+} (green)

3. ***(b)*** $2AgNO_3 + BaCl_2 \rightarrow 2AgCl + Ba(NO_3)_2$

$BaCl_2 + H_2SO_4 \longrightarrow \underset{\text{White ppt.}}{BaSO_4} + 2HCl$

Barium imparts green colour to flame.

4. ***(d)***

$AlCl_3 \xrightarrow{NaOH} Al(OH)_3 \xrightarrow{NaOH} NaAlO_2$ (soluble)

$ZnCl_2 \xrightarrow{NaOH} Zn(OH)_2 \xrightarrow{NaOH} Na_2ZnO_2$ (soluble)

$Fe(OH)_3 \xrightarrow{NaOH} Fe(OH)_3$ (insoluble)

$Mg(OH)_2 \xrightarrow{NaOH} Mg(OH)_2$ (insoluble)

5. ***(a)*** $AlBr_3 + 3NaOH \longrightarrow \underset{\text{White ppt.}}{Al(OH)_3} + 3NaBr$

$Al(OH)_3 + NaOH \longrightarrow \underset{\text{Soluble}}{NaAlO_2} + 2H_2O$

$3AgNO_3 + AlBr_3 \longrightarrow 3AgBr + Al(NO_3)_3$
White yellow under AgBr

6. ***(a)*** $Al(NO_3)_3$ decomposes to Al_2O_3 which forms a blue mass (Thenard blue) with cobalt oxide obtained from decomposition of $Co(AlO_2)_3$ Blue mass

$Al_2O_3 + CoO = CoO \cdot Al_2O_3$ or $\underset{\text{Blue mass}}{Co(AlO_2)_2}$

7. ***(b)*** $\underset{\text{Orange}}{Cr_2O_7^{2-}} + 2OH^- \longrightarrow \underset{\text{Yellow}}{2Cr_2O_4^{2-}} + H_2O$

$2Cr_2O_4^{2-} + 2H^+ \longrightarrow 2CrO_7^{2-} + H_2O$

8. ***(b)*** $H_3BO_3 \longrightarrow B_2O_3 + H_2O$

$CaF_2 + H_2SO_4 \longrightarrow CaSO_4 + 2HF$

$B_2O_3 + 6HF \longrightarrow \underset{\text{Burns with green flame(volatile)}}{2BF_3 \uparrow} + 3H_2O$

9. ***(c)*** This is due to oxidation of H_2S into S by NO_2^-, SO_3^{2-} or ferric salt.

e.g. $2FeCl_3 + H_2S \longrightarrow 2FeCl_2 + 2HCl + S$

10. ***(d)*** HgS is insoluble in conc. HNO_3. It is soluble in aqua regia.

11. ***(b)*** $SbCl_5 \rightleftharpoons SbCl_3 + Cl_2$

$2SbCl_3 + 3H_2S \longrightarrow Sb_2S_3 + 6HCl$

12. ***(c)*** $Na_3PO_4 + 12(NH_4)_2MoO_4$

$+ 24HNO_3 \longrightarrow \underset{\text{Canary yellow ppt.}}{(NH_4)_3PO_4 \cdot 12MoO_3}$

$+ 3NaNO_3 + 12H_2O + 21NH_4NO_3$

$H_3AsO_4 + 21HNO_3 + 12(NH_4)_2MoO_4$

$\longrightarrow \underset{\text{Canary yellow ppt.}}{(NH_4)_3AsO_4 \cdot 12MoO_3} + 12H_2O + 21NH_4NO_3$

Thus both PO_4^{3-} and As^{3+} give canary yellow ppt.

13. ***(a)*** H_2S in neutral medium provides sufficient S^{2-} to precipitate Cu, Cd, Zn and Mn as sulphide.

14. ***(c)*** $(NH_4)_2SO_4$ will give white ppt. in presence of Ba^{2+} and Sr^{2+}. $(NH_4)_2CO_3$ will give white ppt., in presence of Ba^{2+}, Sr^{2+} and Ca^{2+}. To produce common ion (NH_4^+) and to suppress the ionisation of NH_4OH, NH_4NO_3 can be used in absence of Mn^{2+}.

15. ***(a)*** Bi^{3+} and Sn^{4+} both will form ppt., with H_2S.

$Bi^{3+} + S^{2-} \longrightarrow Bi_2S_3$ (brown black ppt.)

$Sn^{4+} + S^{2-} \longrightarrow SnS_2$ (dirty yellow ppt.)

Al^{3+}, Zn^{2+} and Ni^{2+} will not form ppt. with H_2S in acidic medium.

16. ***(a)*** Na_2CO_3 will yield large concentration of CO_3^{2-} ions to exceed the solubility product of $MgCO_3$ and it will be precipitated along with carbonates of Ca^{2+}, Sr^{2+} and Ba^{2+} in fifth group. Further, in absence of common ion NH_4OH will ionise more to give sufficient $[OH^-]$ to exceed the solubility product of $Mg(OH)_2$ and its ppt.

17. ***(c)*** Hg_2Cl_2 is white insoluble salt.

$Hg_2Cl_2 + 2NH_4OH \longrightarrow \underbrace{Hg + HgOHg(NH_2)Cl}_{\text{Black}} + NH_4Cl + 2H_2O$

18. ***(c)*** $Ba(CH_3COO)_2 + (NH_4)_2C_2O_4 \longrightarrow$

$\underset{\text{White ppt.}}{BaC_2O_4} + 2CH_3COONH_4$

$Sr(CH_3COO)_2 + (NH_4)_2C_2O_4 \longrightarrow$

$\underset{\text{White ppt.}}{SrC_2O_4} + 2CH_3COONH_4$

$Ca(CH_3COO)_2 + (NH_4)_2C_2O_4 \longrightarrow$

$\underset{\text{White ppt.}}{CaC_2O_4} + 2CH_3COONH_4$

19. ***(c)*** $Fe(OH)_3$ is brown.

20. ***(a)*** HNO_2 is pale blue in colour due to dissolution of N_2O_3. In concentrated solution it decomposes as :

$2HNO_2 \longrightarrow NO + NO_2 + H_2O$

and in dilute solution is

$3HNO_2 \longrightarrow HNO_3 + H_2O + 2NO$

Reaction with :

(a) Br_2 water

$HNO_2 + H_2O + Br_2 \longrightarrow HNO_3 + 2HBr$

(b) $KMnO_4$

$2KMnO_4 + 3H_2SO_4 + 5HNO_2 \longrightarrow$

$K_2SO_4 + 2MnSO_4 + 3H_2O + 5HNO_3$

21. ***(3)*** $Cr(OH)_3$, $Al(OH)_3$ and $AsCl_3$ are soluble in excess of NaOH due to the formation of soluble $[Cr(OH)_4]^-$, $[Al(OH)_4]^-$ and AsO_3^{3-} respectively.

22. ***(7)*** Pb^{2+}, Sn^{2+}, Sn^{4+}, Sb^{3+}, Zn^{2+}, Bi^{3+} and Cd^{2+} will produce white precipitates with NaOH solution.

23. ***(1)*** Turnbulls blue and Prussian blue are same compounds with molecular formula $Fe_4[Fe(CN)_6]_3$, so both have four ferric ions and three ferrous ions.

24. ***(4)*** Ag^+, Fe^{3+}, Fe^{2+} and Cu^{2+} will form precipitate with both potassium ferrocyanide as well as potassium ferricyanide.

25. ***(3)*** Phosphate ions give yellow colored precipitate of Ag_3PO_4, $FePO_4$, $(NH_4)_3[P(Mo_3O_{10})_4]$ with $AgNO_3$, $FeCl_3$ and $(NH_4)_6MoO_7O_{24} \cdot 4H_2O$ respectively.

26. ***(4)*** All the reagents except O_3 can be used to detect sulphide radical either by precipitation reaction (colored precipitate formed) or by redox reaction with oxidising agent showing some color change.

27. ***(5)*** AgI, PbI_2, CuI_2, $PbCrO_4$ and $BaCrO_4$ are insoluble yellow compounds whereas $CaCrO_4$ is a soluble yellow compound. All others are not yellow in color.

28. ***(4)*** $NaHSO_4$ has an acidic hydrogen atom thus it will react with all basic and amphoteric oxides and hydroxides.

29. ***(2)*** Among the given ions only two i.e. Be^{2+} and Mg^{2+} that does not show any colour on flame test.

Check Through PYQs : JEE Main

1. ***(b)*** CdS, $PbCrO_4 \Rightarrow$ yellow coloured

PbS, CuS $\Rightarrow$ black coloured

ZnS $\Rightarrow$ white coloured (when cold)

2. ***(b)*** The correct match is A-III, B-IV, C-I, D-II.

3. ***(d)*** The reaction involves in the given experiments are

$Ag^+ + I^- \longrightarrow AgI$ (Yellow ppt.)

$Ag^+ + Cl^- \longrightarrow AgCl$ (White ppt.)

$Ag^+ + Br^- \longrightarrow AgBr$ (Pale yellow ppt.)

Thus pale yellow precipitate indicates the presence of Br^-.

4. ***(a)*** $PbSO_4$ (lead sulphate) is white in colour. PbI_2 (lead iodide) is a yellow ppt. $(NH_4)_2S$ (ammonium sulphide) is soluble. $(NH_4)_3AsO_4 \cdot 12MoO_3$ (ammonium arsinomolybdate) is yellow.

5. ***(a)*** Statement I is true but Statement II is false.

The correct form of Statement II is : The colour of paper turns black because of formation of lead sulphide.

The reaction involved is as follows

$$Na_2S + H_2SO_4 \longrightarrow Na_2SO_4 + H_2S$$

$$\underset{\text{Lead acetate}}{(CH_3COO)_2Pb} + H_2S \longrightarrow \underset{\substack{\text{(Black)}\\\text{Lead sulphide}}}{PbS} + 2CH_3COOH$$

6. ***(a)*** According to question,

$$CH_3COO^- + 3FeCl_3 + H_2O \longrightarrow \underset{\text{Blood red colour}}{[Fe_3(OH)_2(CH_3COO)_6]^+}$$

$$\downarrow \Delta$$

$$\underset{\text{Red-brown ppt.}}{Fe(OH)_2(CH_3COO)\downarrow}$$

$$2NO_3^- + 4H_2SO_4 + 6Fe^{2+} \longrightarrow 6Fe^{3+} + 2NO\uparrow + 4SO_4^{2-} + 4H_2O$$

$$[Fe(H_2O)_6]^{2+} + NO \longrightarrow \underset{\text{Brown}}{[Fe(H_2O)_5(NO)]^{2+}} + H_2O$$

Thus, the mixture contains CH_3COO^- and NO_3^-.

7. ***(a)*** The correct match is A-II, B-I, C-IV, D-III.
8. ***(a)*** The correct match is A-III, B-IV, C-I, D-II.
9. ***(b)*** Dimethyl glyoxime when reacts with nickel ions in basic medium gives pink precipitate. The complete reaction is as follows

$$Ni^{2+} + 2DMG \xrightarrow{\text{Base}} \underset{\text{Pink}}{[Ni(DMG)_2]}$$

10. ***(d)*** In group V, barium ions are precipitated as their carbonates by adding ammonium carbonate to their solution.
11. ***(b)*** $Pb[NO_3]_2$ lead nitrate is a soluble colourless compound. Hence, formation of lead nitrate complex is not used as a confirmatory test. While other complexes given in options gives different precipitates i.e.

$PbCrO_4$ — yellow ppt

$Pb(NO_3)_2$ — soluble

$PbSO_4$ — white ppt

PbI_2 — yellow ppt

12. ***(c)*** Among the given options, Fe^{3+} cation does not belongs to group IV in qualitative inorganic analysis. Instead it belongs to group III.
13. ***(b)*** The correct match is A-I, B-III, C-IV, D-II.
14. ***(d)*** $4Fe^{3+} + 3[Fe(CN)_6]^{4-} \longrightarrow \underset{\text{(Prussian blue in colour)}}{Fe_4[Fe(CN)_6]_3}$
15. ***(b)*** Ring is formed due to $Fe[H_2O)_5(NO)]SO_4$ i.e., complex nitrosoferrous sulphate.
16. ***(a)*** On addition of dimethylglyoxime to alkaline solution of Ni^{2+}, a bright red ppt is obtained

$$Ni^{2+} + 2DMG \longrightarrow [Ni(DMG)_2]^{2+}$$

17. ***(c)*** AgCl and Cu_2Cl_2 are not dissolved in H_2O. $ZnCl_2$ and $CuCl_2$ are dissolved in water but $ZnCl_2$ is colourless and $CuCl_2$ is coloured.
18. ***(a)*** Only Cu^{2+} get precipitated when HCl followed by H_2S was added.

Al^{3+} and Fe^{3+} sulphides hydrolyse in water. Ni^{2+} and Zn^{2+} require basic medium with H_2S to form ppt. Ca^{2+} and Ba^{2+} sulphides are soluble.

Hence, we will recieve ppt. of only CuS.

19. ***(b)*** 1-naphthyl amine and sulphanilic acid is used for the detection of NO_2^- with the help of acetic acid.

Practice Element 02 : Target JEE Advanced

1. ***(a)*** $\underset{[X]}{SO_3^{2-}} + H_2SO_4 \longrightarrow \underset{[Y]}{SO_2}$

$$SO_2 + K_2Cr_2O_7 + H_2SO_4 \longrightarrow \underset{\text{(Green)}}{Cr_2(SO_4)_2} + K_2SO_4 + H_2O$$

2. ***(a)*** $NaHCO_3 + MgCl_2 \xrightarrow{\Delta} \underset{\text{(White)}}{MgCO_3\downarrow}$
3. ***(a)*** $CO_2 + H_2O \longrightarrow H_2CO_3\ (H^+, HCO_3^-, CO_3^{2-})$
4. ***(b)*** $Zn(OH)_2 + NH_3(\text{Solution}) \longrightarrow \underset{\text{Soluble complex}}{[Zn(NH_3)_4]^{2+}}$
5. ***(b)*** $\overset{+2}{Cu}SO_4 + KCN(\text{Excess}) \longrightarrow K_3[\overset{+1}{Cu}(CN)_4]$
6. ***(c)*** $MgSO_4 + NH_4OH + Na_2HPO_4 \longrightarrow \underset{\text{White}}{Mg(NH_4)PO_4}$
7. ***(b)*** $Hg^{2+} + KI \longrightarrow \underset{\text{Red}}{HgI_2\downarrow}$

$$HgI_2 + KI(\text{Excess}) \longrightarrow \underset{\text{Soluble}}{K_2[HgI_4]}$$

8. ***(d)*** $K_3[Cd(CN)_4]$ is soluble complex. Hence, formation of potassium tetracyanido cadmium(I), is not used as confirmatory test of Cd^{2+}.
9. ***(a, b)***

$$NH_4NO_3 + NaOH \longrightarrow NH_3 + NaNO_3 + H_2O$$

$$NaOH + NaNO_3 + Zn\text{ dust} \longrightarrow NH_3 + Na_2ZnO_2$$

$$NH_4NO_2 + NaOH \longrightarrow NH_3 + NaNO_2 + H_2O$$

$$NaOH + NaNO_2 + Zn\text{ dust} \longrightarrow NH_3 + Na_2ZnO_2$$

10. ***(b)*** $Cu(NO_3)_2 + 2NaOH \longrightarrow \underset{\text{Blue}}{Cu(OH)_2} + 2NaNO_3$

$$\xrightarrow{\Delta} \underset{\text{Black}}{CuO} + H_2O \xrightarrow{C_6H_{12}O_6} C_6H_{12}O_7 + \underset{\text{Red}}{Cu_2O}$$

11. ***(a, b)*** Cations K^+ and Ba^{2+} give bluish-green flame colour through blue-glass.
12. ***(a, b, c)*** $HgCl_2 + 2KI \longrightarrow \underset{\substack{\text{Scarlet}\\\text{red ppt.}}}{Hg_2I_2} + 2KCl$

$$(CH_3COO)_2Hg + 2KI \longrightarrow \underset{\text{Yellow solid}}{HgI_2} + (CH_3COO)_2K$$

$$2HgCl_2 + SnCl_2 \longrightarrow \underset{\text{White ppt.}}{Hg_2Cl_2} + SnCl_4$$

$$(CH_3COO)_2Hg + SnCl_2 \longrightarrow Hg + \underset{\substack{\text{White}\\\text{crystalline}\\\text{solid}}}{SnCl_4} + 2CH_3COOH$$

$$(CH_3COO)_2Pb + Na_2CrO_4 \longrightarrow \underset{\text{Yellow ppt.}}{PbCrO_4\downarrow}$$

$$PbCl_2 + Na_2CrO_4 \longrightarrow \underset{\text{Yellow ppt.}}{PbCrO_4} + 2NaCl$$

$$AgCl + NH_4OH \longrightarrow \underset{\text{(Soluble)}}{[Ag(NH_3)_2]Cl} + H_2O$$

$$(CH_3COO)_2Ag + NH_4OH \longrightarrow \underset{\text{(White ppt.)}}{AgOH} + (CH_3COO)_2NH_4$$

13. ***(a, b, c)*** Among the given statements all are correct except statement (d). Its corrected form is

The brown complex $[Fe(H_2O)_5(NO)]SO_4$ contains 3 unpaired electrons and is paramagnetic with $\mu = \sqrt{3(3+2)} = \sqrt{15}$ B.M.

14. ***(a, c)*** Among the given combinations only (a) and (c) give a red colour or precipitate in aqueous medium.

15. ***(a, c, d)*** Among the given statements all are correct except 'b' regarding chromyl chloride test. Its corrected form is as

When the vapours obtained from mixing $K_2Cr_2O_7$ solid with conc. H_2SO_4, is passed in 5% NaOH solution in a test tube, then colour of NaOH solution changes to yellow.

16. ***(a, b, c)***

$$Cu(NO_3)_2 \xrightarrow[\Delta]{2KI} \underset{\text{Brown}}{CuI_2} + 2KNO_3$$

$$CuI_2 \xrightarrow{\Delta} \underset{\text{(Yellow ppt.)}}{\frac{1}{2}Cu_2I_2}$$

17. ***(3)*** Hg_2Cl_2, $PbCl_2$, AgCl (all are white precipitate)

18. ***(5)*** Na_2SO_3, NaCl, $Na_2C_2O_4$, $NaNO_3$ and CH_3CO_2Na gives white ppt. with $AgNO_3$ of Ag_2SO_3, AgCl, $Ag_2C_2O_4$, $AgNO_3$ and CH_3COOAg respectively.

But Na_2HPO_4 and Na_2CrO_4 gives yellow ppt. of Ag_3PO_4 and Ag_2CrO_4 respectively.

19. ***(4)*** Al_2O_3, CaO, SrO and MgO are reduced by charcoal.

20. ***(2)*** $PbCrO_4$ and $BaCrO_4$ are of yellow colour but Ag_2CrO_4 and Hg_2CrO_4 are of red colour ppt.

21. ***(1)*** Na_2CrO_4 with $AgNO_3$ gives red ppt. of Ag_2CrO_4 but other gives white ppt. of Ag_2SO_3, $Ag_2S_2O_3$ and Ag_2CO_3.

22. ***(3)***

I. $Ba^{2+} + CrO_4^{2-} \longrightarrow BaCrO_4$ (yellow ppt.)

II. $Hg^{2+} + Co^{2+} + 4SCN^{\ominus} \longrightarrow \underset{\text{Deep blue ppt.}}{Co[Hg(SCN)_4]}$

III. $NH_4^{\oplus} + [PtCl_6]^{2} \longrightarrow \underset{\text{Yellow ppt.}}{NH_4[PtCl_6]}$

IV. $Ag^{\oplus} + CrO_4^{2-} \longrightarrow \underset{\text{Yellow}}{Ag_2CrO_4}$

23. ***(4)*** $Hg^{3+} + Co^{2+} + 4SCN^{\ominus} \longrightarrow \underset{\text{Deep blue ppt.}}{Co[Hg(SCN)_4]}$

24. ***(1)*** $\underset{\text{Brown ring}}{(Fe(H_2O)_5NO)SO_4}$

Here, NO^+ is nitrosonium ion.

$$x + 5(0) + (+1) = +2$$

$$x = +1$$

25. ***(a)*** A—IV; B—I; C—II; D—III

26. ***(b)*** The correct match is : A—IV; B—III; C—II; D—I

27. ***(a)*** A—IV; B—III; C—II; D—I

28. ***(a)*** The correct match is : A—II; B—III; C—I; D—IV

AgCl : When AgCl is treated with NH_3, it forms a soluble complex $[Ag(NH_3)_2]Cl$. This is a characteristic test for silver salt.

$BaSO_4$: $BaSO_4$ remains insoluble in dilute HCl. This property distinguishes it from other white precipipates.

PbI_2 : Lead salts form a characteristic yellow precipitate of PbI_2 with KI. This is a specific test for lead ions.

Cu^{2+} : Cu^{2+} forms a blue precipitate of $Cu(OH)_2$ with NH_4OH, it forms deep blue $[Cu(NH_3)_4]^{2+}$ complex.

29. ***(b)*** The correct match is

A—I; B—II; C—III; D—IV

Fe^{3+} reacts with KSCN to form blood-red $Fe(CN)^{2+}$.

Al^{3+} gives a white gelationus precipitate of $Al(OH)_3$ which dissolve in excess NaOH due to amphoteric nature of $Al(OH)_3$. Zn^{2+} forms $Zn(OH)_2$, which is amphoteric and dissolves in excess NH_4OH.

Ni^{2+} forms a pale green precipitate $Ni(OH)_2$ which are soluble in acids like HCl.

30. ***(d)*** The correct match is

A—IV; B—III; C—II; D—I

Hg^{2+} : Reacts with alkalis to form insoluble HgO, appearing black.

Sn^{2+} : Reduces $HgCl_2$ to Hg_2Cl_2 white and Hg(grey)

MnO_4^- : Purple MnO_4^- is reduced to colurless Mn^{2+} by SO_3^{2-}

CO_3^{2-} : Effervescence due to CO_2 gas when treated with HCl.

31. ***(4)*** $\underset{(M)}{4Na_2S_2O_3 \cdot 5H_2O} \xrightarrow[-20\,H_2O]{>220°C} \underset{(P)}{Na_2S_5} + \underset{(Q)}{3Na_2SO_4}$

$$\underset{(Q)}{Na_2SO_4} + Hg(NO_3)_2 \longrightarrow \underset{\substack{(R)\\ \text{Yellow}}}{HgSO_4\downarrow} + 2Na^+ + 2NO_3^-$$

$$\underset{(M)}{Na_2S_2O_3} + HgCl_2 \longrightarrow \underset{\substack{(N)\\ \text{White}}}{HgS_2O_3\downarrow} + 2NaCl$$

$$\underset{(N)}{HgS_2O_3\downarrow} + H_2O \longrightarrow \underset{\substack{(O)\\ \text{Black}}}{HgS\downarrow} + 2H^+ + SO_4^{2-}$$

$$\underset{(N)}{HgS_2O_3\downarrow} + \underset{(M)}{Na_2S_2O_3} \longrightarrow 2Na^+ + \underset{\text{Soluble}}{[Hg(S_2O_3)_2]^{2-}}$$

$$Na_2S_2O_3 + 2HCl \longrightarrow 2NaCl + SO_2 + \underset{\substack{\text{White/yellow}\\ \text{Turbidity}}}{S\downarrow} + H_2O$$

$$S\downarrow + 2HNO_3 \longrightarrow \underset{\text{Clear sol.}}{H_2SO_4} + 2NO\uparrow$$

32. ***(5)***

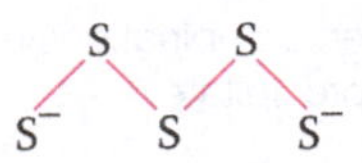

S^{2-}(chain structure)

33. ***(2)*** Here, the compound *X* is Na_2S. It contains 1 Na^+ and 1 S^{2-} ion. So, the sum of cationic and anionic species is 2.

34. ***(5)*** Compound *Y* is $FeCl_3$.

Cation in *Y* is Fe^{+3}

$$Fe \rightarrow 1s^2, 2s^2, 2p^6, 3s^2, 3p^6, 4s^2, 3d^6$$
$$Fe^{+3} \rightarrow 3d^5$$

So, no. of unpaired e^- is 5.

35. ***(6)*** PbS, CuS, HgS, Ag_2S, NiS, CoS (Black) MnS (buff or pink)

SnS_2 (yellow coloured)

36. ***(4)*** Cu^{2+}, Pb^{2+}, Hg^{2+} and Bi^{3+} all are group II radicals.

37. ***(c)*** Among the given pair of ions only three i.e., I, IV and V can be separated by using NaOH solution.

38. ***(d)*** Among the given reactions except *E* all produces white precipitate.

$$Cu(NO_3)_2 + 2KI \longrightarrow CuI_2 + 2KNO_3$$
$$\downarrow \Delta$$
$$\frac{1}{2}Cu_2I_2 + I_2$$
(Yellow ppt.)

39. ***(a)*** Among the given ions only Cr^{3+} will turn a borax bead green in an oxidising flame.

40. ***(c)*** $(NH_4)_2SO_2 \xrightarrow{\Delta} NH_3 + H_2SO_4$

$$(NH_4)_2CO_3 \xrightarrow{\Delta} NH_3 + CO_2 + H_2O$$
$$NH_4Cl \xrightarrow{\Delta} NH_3 + HCl$$
$$(NH_4)_2Cr_2O_4^7 \xrightarrow{\Delta} N_2 + Cr_2O_3 + H_2O$$
$$NH_4NO_3 \xrightarrow{\Delta} N_2O + H_2O$$
$$NH_4NO_2 \xrightarrow{\Delta} N_2 + H_2O$$
$$NH_4ClO_4 \xrightarrow{\Delta} N_2 + HCl + H_2O$$

41. ***(d)*** $NaBr + AgNO_3 \longrightarrow AgBr$ (yellow)

$NaI + AgNO_3 \longrightarrow AgI$ (yellow)

$NaI + Pb(NO_3)_2 \longrightarrow PbI_2$ (yellow)

$Na_2S + Cd(CH_2COO)_2 \longrightarrow CdS$ (yellow)

$K_2CrO_4 + Pb(CH_3COO)_2 \longrightarrow PbCrO_4$ (yellow)

$K_2CrO_4 + (CH_3COO)_2Ba \longrightarrow BaCrO_4$ (yellow)

42. ***(b)*** Al^{3+} (Group III) and Hg^{2+} (group II) Cd^{2+} (Group II) and Zn^{2+} (group IV)

Fe^{3+} (Group III) and Cu^{2+} (Group II) Bi^{3+} (Group II) and Sn^{4+} (Group II)

As^{3+} (Group II) and Sb^{3+} (Group II)

43. ***(b)*** Among the given combinations only two i.e., I and IV will give red colour or precipitate.

Check Through PYQs : JEE Advanced

1. ***(c)*** $Pb(NO_3)_2 + 2NaCl \longrightarrow PbCl_2 + 2NaNO_3$

$$\Rightarrow \underset{\text{Solid}}{PbCl_2} + \underset{\text{From HCl}}{2Cl^-} \longrightarrow [PbCl_4]^{2-}$$

Solid $PbCl_2$ reacts with chloride ion to form ion $[PbCl_4]^{2-}$ which is soluble. So, option (c) is correct.

2. ***(a)*** $2S_2O_3^{2-} + Ag^+ \longrightarrow \underset{\text{Clear solution}}{[Ag(S_2O_3)_2]^{3-}}$

$$[Ag(S_2O_3)_2]^{3-} + 3Ag^+ \longrightarrow \underset{\text{White ppt.}}{2Ag_2S_2O_3}$$
$$Ag_2S_2O_3 + H_2O \longrightarrow \underset{\text{Black ppt.}}{Ag_2S} + H_2SO_4$$

3. ***(a.c)***

(a) $S^{2-} + CuCl_2 \longrightarrow \underset{\text{Black ppt.}}{CuS\downarrow} + 2Cl^-$

$SO_4^{2-} + CuCl_2 \longrightarrow$ Soluble $(CuSO_4 + 2Cl^-)$

Thus,

$CuCl_2$ selectively precipitates S^{2-}.

(b) $S^{2-} + BaCl_2 \longrightarrow BaS\downarrow$ (soluble) $+ 2Cl^-$

$SO_4^{2-} + BaCl_2 \longrightarrow \underset{\text{White ppt.}}{BaSO_4\downarrow} + 2Cl^-$

Thus, $BaCl_2$ precipitates SO_4^{2-} and not S^{2-}.

(c) $S^{2-} + Pb^{2+} \longrightarrow PbS\downarrow$ (black ppt.)

$SO_4^{2-} + Pb^{2+} \longrightarrow \underset{\text{White ppt.}}{PbSO_4\downarrow}$

$\Rightarrow S^{2-}$ and SO_4^{2-}, both are precipitated.

(d) $S^{2-} + \underset{\text{Sodium nitroprusside}}{Na_2[Fe(CN)]_5NO} \longrightarrow \underset{\text{(Purple colour) (not a ppt.)}}{Na_4[Fe(CN)]_5NOS}$

But no colour or ppt. with SO_4^{2-}.

4. ***(a)*** *X* : Ag ; *Y* : Pb ; *P* : AgCl ; *Q* : $PbCl_2$

$$AgNO_3 + Pb(NO_3)_2 \xrightarrow{NaCl} \underset{(P)}{AgCl(\downarrow)} + \underset{(Q)}{PbCl_2}$$

Heated and filtered

AgCl (*P*) (White ppt.) $PbCl_2$ (*Q*) (Hot solution) $\xrightarrow{KI} PbI_2$ (Yellow ppt.)

$$\underset{(P)}{AgCl(s)} + \underset{\text{(Excess)}}{2NH_3} \longrightarrow [Ag(NH_3)_2]^+Cl^-$$

$AgCl(s) \xrightarrow{2Na_2S_2O_3} Na_3[Ag(S_2O_3)_2] + NaCl$
Soluble complex salt

Hence, the correct option is (a).

5. ***(a, b)*** $Pb(NO_3)_2$, $Zn(NO_3)_2$ and $Bi(NO_3)_3$ give white precipitate with dil. NaOH and dil. HCl. Complete reactions are as follows

- $\underset{\text{White ppt.}}{PbCl_2} \xleftarrow[\text{Room temperature}]{\text{Dil. HCl}} \underset{\text{Lead nitrate (S)}}{Pb(NO_3)_2} \xrightarrow[\text{Room temperature}]{\text{Dil. NaOH}} \underset{\text{White ppt.}}{Pb(OH)_2}$

- $\underset{\text{White ppt.}}{ZnCl_2} \xleftarrow[\text{Room temperature}]{\text{Dil. HCl}} \underset{\substack{\text{Zinc nitrate}\\(S)}}{Zn(NO_3)_2} \xrightarrow[\text{Room temperature}]{\text{Dil. NaOH}} \underset{\text{White ppt.}}{Zn(OH)_2}$

- $\underset{\text{White ppt.}}{BiCl_3} \xleftarrow[\text{Room temperature}]{\text{Dil. HCl}} \underset{\substack{\text{Bismuth nitrate}\\(S)}}{Bi(NO_3)_3} \xrightarrow[\text{Room temperature}]{\text{Dil. NaOH}} \underset{\text{White ppt.}}{Bi(OH)_3}$

Whereas, $AgNO_3$ and $Hg(NO_3)_3$ give ppt. of different colours.

- $\underset{\text{White ppt.}}{AgCl} \xleftarrow[\text{Room temperature}]{\text{Dil. HCl}} \underset{\text{Silver nitrate}}{AgNO_3} \xrightarrow[\text{Room temperature}]{\text{Dil. NaOH}} \underset{\text{Brown ppt.}}{Ag_2O}$

$\underset{\text{White ppt.}}{HgCl_2} \xleftarrow[\text{Room temperature}]{\text{Dil. HCl}} \underset{\text{Mercury}}{Hg(NO_3)_2} \xrightarrow[\text{Room temperature}]{\text{Dil. NaOH}} \underset{\text{Yellow ppt.}}{HgO}$

6. ***(b, d)*** Statement wise explanation is

Statement (a) Mn^{2+} produces yellow- green colour in flame test while Cu^{2+} produces bluish-green colour in flame test. Thus, due to the presence of green colour in both the cases, flame test is not the suitable method to distinguish between nitrate salts of Cu^{2+} and Mn^{2+}. Hence this statement is incorrect.

Statement (b) Cu^{2+} belong to group II of cationic or basic radicals. It gives black ppt. of CuS if H_2S is passed, through it in the presence of acid (e.g HCl). Mn^{2+} does not show this property hence this can be considered as a suitable method to distinguish between Mn^{2+} and Cu^{2+}.

Hence, this statement is correct.

Statement (c) In faintly basic medium when H_2S is passed, both Cu^{2+} and Mn^{2+} form precipitates. Thus, it is not suitable method to distinguish between them.

Hence, this statement is incorrect

Statement (d) The standard reduction potential of Cu^{2+}/Cu is +0.34 V while that of Mn^{2+}/Mn is –1.18V. This can be used to distinguish between Cu^{2+} and Mn^{2+}. In general, less electropositive metals have higher SRP.

Hence, this statement is correct.

7. ***(c, d)*** Only radicals of I and II group of qualitative analysis get precipitated with H_2S in the presence of dilute HCl.

(c) $Cu^{2+} + H_2S \xrightarrow{H^+} \underset{\text{Black}}{CuS} \downarrow$

$Pb^{2+} + H_2S \xrightarrow{H^+} \underset{\text{Black}}{PbS} \downarrow$

(d) $Hg^{2+} + H_2S \xrightarrow{H^+} \underset{\text{Black}}{HgS} \downarrow$

$Bi^{3+} + H_2S \xrightarrow{H^+} \underset{\text{Brown ppt}}{Bi_2S_3} \downarrow$

Ba^{2+}, Zn^{2+} and Fe^{3+} are not precipitated as sulphide in acid medium.

8. ***(2)*** The reaction involved is as follows

$3KI + 2K_3[Fe(CN)_6] \longrightarrow \underset{(P)}{2K_4[Fe(CN)_6]} + KI_3$

Thus, to produce two moles of *P*, 3 moles of KI is required.

9. ***(2 or 3)***

$\underset{\text{Excess}}{3ZnCl_2} + 2K_4[Fe(CN)_6] \longrightarrow \underset{\substack{\text{White ppt.}\\(Q)}}{K_2Zn_3[Fe(CN)_6]_2}$

or $2ZnCl_2 + K_4[Fe(CN)_6] \longrightarrow \underset{\substack{\text{white ppt.}\\(Q)}}{Zn_2[Fe(CN)_6]} + 4KCl$

Thus, the number of zinc ions in the molecular formula of *Q* is 2 or 3.

10. ***(c)*** Precipitate *X* is $K_2Fe[Fe(CN)_6]$.

$K_4[\overset{II}{Fe}(CN)_6] \xrightarrow[\text{Absence of air}]{\overset{II}{Fe}SO_4} \underset{\text{White precipitate 'X'}}{K_2\overset{II}{Fe}[\overset{II}{Fe}(CN)_6]}$

11. ***(d)*** Brown ring is due to the formation of $[Fe(NO)(H_2O)_5]^{2+}$.

$FeSO_4 \xrightarrow[\text{Slow addition of Conc. } H_2SO_4]{NaNO_3} \underset{\text{Brown ring complex}}{[Fe(NO)(H_2O)_5]^{2+}}$